EVERY MANAGER'S DESK REFERENCE

ALPHA

A MEMBER OF PENGUIN GROUP (USA) INC.

International Standard Book Number: 978-0-02-864268-0
Library of Congress Catalog Card Number: 2001098464

10 09 08   12 11 10

Interpretation of the printing code: The rightmost number of the first series of numbers is the year of the book's printing; the rightmost number of the second series of numbers is the number of the book's printing. For example, a printing code of 02-1 shows that the first printing occurred in 2002.

Printed in the United States of America

Most Alpha books are available at special quantity discounts for bulk purchases for sales promotions, premiums, fund-raising, or educational use. Special books, or book excerpts, can also be created to fit specific needs.

For details, write: Special Markets, Alpha Books, 375 Hudson Street, New York, NY 10014.

Publisher: *Marie Butler-Knight*
Product Manager: *Phil Kitchel*
Managing Editor: *Jennifer Chisholm*
Senior Acquisitions Editor: *Renee Wilmeth*
Senior Production Editor: *Christy Wagner*
Cover Designer: *Doug Wilkins*
Book Designer: *Trina Wurst*
Creative Director: *Robin Lasek*
Indexer: *Lisa Wilson*
Layout/Proofreading: *Angela Calvert, Svetlana Dominguez, Mary Hunt, Gloria Shurick*

Contents

Leadership   299

Organizational Management Basics   383

Hiring Employees   407

Problem-Solving and Decision-Making   921

Project Management   949

Customer Service   1069

Appendixes

Introduction

Welcome to *Every Manager's Desk Reference*, an easy to use, complete reference covering everything today's modern manager needs to know. From performance appraisals to PowerPoint presentations, this reference is the cornerstone of a complete business library.

In this book you will find the following:

PLAIN ENGLISH

A concise definition of a word or concept.

TIP

A handy piece of information or shortcut for success.

CAUTION

A warning showing what not to do.

ABOUT THE CONTRIBUTORS

Carol R. Anderson is Director of Career Development and Placement for the Robert J. Milano Graduate School of Management and Urban Policy at the New School University in New York and a career management consultant in private practice (www.careercc.org). She is an advisor to the Wharton Alumni Club of New York, an "Ask the Experts" panelist for CollegeRecruiter.com, and a frequent speaker to professional associations and job search groups.

Janet Bigham Bernstel is a financial journalist with a nationally syndicated column, *Janet Talks Money*. She is the Managing Editor of the Women's Financial Network, www.wfn.com, and the co-author of *Alpha Teach Yourself Personal Finance in 24 Hours*.

Patricia Buhler is a professor at Goldey-Beacom College and a consultant specializing in management issues. She is a contributing editor to *Supervision* magazine, where she writes a bi-monthly column, "Managing in the New Millennium."

Jeff Davidson is an international speaker and trainer specializing in stress, time, and information management. He works with several major national trainers, including SkillPath, to educate professionals on how to improve their worklives. He is the author of numerous books and courses including *The Complete Idiot's Guide to Managing Your Time* and *The Complete Idiot's Guide to Managing Stress.*

Steve Dennis is President of Dennis-McCain Consulting, a marketing strategy consulting firm specializing in paradigm transformations. He has worked as a consultant for the Brown Shoe Co., Charles Schwab & Co., The PGA Tour, The Proctor & Gamble Company, and *The Washington Post.*

Dale Furtwengler is the president of Furtwengler & Associates, P.C., a business-consulting firm that specializes in improving organizational and individual performance.

Paula Garrett is a former partner is The Maxxwell Group, an interactive marketing consulting firm specializing in health care. She has worked or consulted for The Coca-Cola Co, Johnston & Murphy, Macmillan Publishing, The PGA Tour, and The Procter and Gamble Company.

George Kops has been helping large companies, such as MCI, Ford, and IBM, to learn effective business presentation skills for almost 20 years. In 1985, he founded Focus Communications (www.focuscommunications.com), a company that helps business professionals communicate in a more effective manner through lectures, courses, and one-on-one timing.

William W. Larson, Ph.D., has more than 20 years' experience training people in the area of human resource management. He is founder and president of Selection Dynamics Institute of Tacoma, where he offers personalized training to supervisors and managers who make critical hiring decisions for their companies.

Elizabeth O'Leary learned her leadership skills from the best—her father, a U.S. Army Lieutenant General. She served as Senior Editor for America Online's newsroom, managing a staff of journalists through some of the late twentieth century's most important news stories.

Nancy Stevenson is the author of more than a dozen books on topics ranging from the Internet to project management and reading comprehension. Prior to her writing career, Ms Stevenson ran a division of a major software company, producing books, videos, and courseware, and learned firsthand how to motivate a staff.

Stephen Windhaus is the principal of Windhaus Associates, a marketing and business planning firm. Additionally, he writes for the Experts Panel at Palo Alto Software and is the online SmallBiz Q&A columnist for the financial Web site www.bankrate.com.

Nancy D. Warner is a freelance editor specializing in business, computing, and real estate books. In addition to the hundreds of books she has edited, she has also written or contributed to dozens of books, including *Easy Office 2000, StarOffice Writer Handbook,* and *The Complete Idiot's Guide to Buying and Selling a Home, Third Edition.*

Stress Management

The Toxic Workplace

In this section, you learn why much of the stress you experience in the workplace may be organizationally induced, and you get tips as a manager or staff worker for carving a saner path.

IT'S A JUNGLE IN THERE

New projects, new tasks, a new e-mail about that old project—the tasks add up and threaten to choke you with an ever-deepening sensation of stress. With rising deadline pressure, the frustrations of constantly evolving technology, and the increasing challenges in management, the modern workplace has many employees feeling constantly stressed. Every day feels like a fight to survive in a jungle-like environment.

THE NUMBER-ONE HEALTH RISK

Increasing numbers of career professionals report that job stress is the leading cause of personal stress. Only recently have studies directly assessed the effects of *job stress* on personal health. According to Princeton Survey Research Associates, "Three-fourths of employees believe the worker has more on-the-job stress than a generation ago." In a study by Northwestern National Life, 40 percent of workers report that their job is "very or extremely stressful."

PLAIN ENGLISH

Job stress   The physical and emotional response to harmful working conditions, including circumstances in which the job requirements exceed the capabilities, resources, or needs of the worker.

The Encyclopedia of Occupational Safety and Health reports that disease, musculoskeletal disorders, and psychological disorders are all linked to job stress. Researchers are still exploring the probable connections between job stress and increased risk for workplace injury, suicide, cancer, ulcers, and impaired immune function.

CAUTION

All of these findings and inquiries attest to the long-term detrimental effects of job stress on the working individual.

THE PRICE WE PAY

According to a study by the National Institute for Occupational Safety and Health (NIOSH), job stress accounts for a high volume of health problems reported in the United States. A statistic taken from the *Journal of Occupational and Environmental Medicine* shows that "Health care expenditures are nearly 50 percent greater for workers who report high levels of stress."

In simpler terms, people who work in stressful jobs cost the healthcare economy *1.5 times that of the average unstressed worker.* And this is without consideration of the other economic costs directly resulting from stressed workers, such as decreased productivity. Essentially, the economic costs of job stress are not limited to healthcare costs; they affect the overall economy.

AN ORGANIZATIONAL CULTURE OF STRESS

If you're a manager or supervisor, this section may alter your view of your workplace and how to foster a more nurturing environment. If you have responsibility at work solely for yourself, you nevertheless will gain insights about the degree to which stress in the workplace is endemic to early twenty-first century organizations.

For years, much attention has been given to the concept of job stress as an individual problem. The symptoms of job stress have been limited to recognizable characteristics in individual workers. The results of job stress have been understood primarily on the same level—that of the individual worker.

CAUTION

Job stress is an American workplace phenomenon, and job stress pervades the entire fabric of many work environments, affecting the performance of entire organizations and the overall economy in general!

NIOSH reports that either the individual manages the working stress conditions and decreases the risk of injury or illness, or the individual succumbs to the pressures of the situation and falls prey to the job stress, thus resulting in risk of injury or illness.

Job stress no longer only affects the individual worker, who may lose a job due to an inability to perform all the required tasks. Job stress also affects the organization as a whole—its performance in the market may be jeopardized by internal problems with job stress.

CULPRITS FOR JOB STRESS

Many job conditions within an organization can lead to job stress. Here are some particular culprits that tend to induce job stress:

- **The design of tasks.** Heavy workload; infrequent rest breaks; long work hours and shiftwork; and hectic and routine tasks that have little inherent meaning, do not use workers' skills, and provide little sense of control.

- **Management style.** Lack of participation by workers in decision-making, poor communication in the organization, and lack of family-friendly policies.

- **Interpersonal relationships.** Poor social environment and lack of support or help from co-workers and supervisors.

- **Work roles.** Conflicting or uncertain job expectations, too much responsibility, too many "hats to wear."

- **Career concerns.** Job insecurity and lack of opportunity for growth, advancement, or promotion; rapid changes for which workers are unprepared.

- **Environmental conditions.** Unpleasant or dangerous physical conditions, such as crowding, noise, air pollution, or ergonomics problems.

PRODUCTIVITY PLUS

Understandably, a key goal in any organization is to operate effectively and efficiently and to compete successfully in the market. Because companies with healthy workplace policies consistently perform better than others, most organizations and the managers who can effect change need to reconsider their own policies and work to establish a healthier working environment.

Here are several key characteristics for reduced job stress, a healthier workplace, and more motivated workers:

- Recognition of employees' work performance
- Career development opportunities
- An organizational structure and culture that value the individual worker
- Management actions consistent with organizational values

STRESS IN THE STARTUP COMPANY

The growth in Internet startup companies has spawned a whole new job market for employees with computer skills. It also has developed into one of the most stressful fields—one in which companies face the "make it or break it" strains of establishing themselves almost every day.

Let's look at the situation of one worker.

Casey worked for many years as a computer network administrator with a small corporation. Months ago, headhunters approached him and offered him a new position with a Web startup company, which he accepted.

While his salary has nearly doubled, Casey's new job brings him a load of stress. After years in an established office, working regular 40- to 45-hour weeks, his new work schedule is grueling—often 10- to 12-hour days, 5 or 6 days a week.

The office environment is different, too. In his old job, Casey and the other employees frequently interacted. Things are stiff and hectic in his new office. Some co-workers would rather send him an e-mail than walk 30 or 40 paces to his office.

CASEY AT THE BAT

Casey knows he is capable of performing his new job, and he is continually learning more. Nevertheless, every day leaves him feeling overworked and burned out. He doesn't feel motivated by the office environment, and increasingly he feels that his new job is at risk.

The young company is facing a rough period. So far the company has done well; however, a new product release is coming up, and the company is behind schedule. Casey feels pressure from all sides. Not only is he dealing with his own job stress, trying to handle an increased workload and a different atmosphere, but now he is faced with the stressful atmosphere of the entire company. If this new product doesn't get released on time and perform successfully in the market, the company may fold.

ALL TOO COMMON

What Casey is experiencing is an increasingly common situation. While he faces challenges of adjusting to his new job, he also faces the difficulties of workplace-related job stress. His new company is too concerned with survival to address the needs of the employees. This might backfire on the company in the near future, though.

CAUTION

Without adequate stress management and some efforts to modify the workplace stress, all of the workers—from upper-level management down to the very lowest spot on the totem pole—will be headed down the road to burnout.

Casey's situation reflects the intricate nature of the job stress experienced by workers today. There are his own situational factors—being new on the job and unaccustomed to the faster pace of a newly forming company—that influence his ability to handle the job. It is the stressful job conditions, however, that truly threaten his performance. Casey is capable of handling his own situation, but he is handling it in a stressful environment. With these overall job conditions, anyone in his company is bound to experience job stress.

Taming the Beast

Many companies and organizations have made efforts to help their employees deal with job stress. Unfortunately, in their efforts to reduce stress among workers, most organizations fail to inspect their role in developing a stressful working environment. Only a comprehensive approach, including a combination of individual stress management and organizational changes, effectively eliminates job stress.

The first component in this process is stress management. This involves educating individuals on ways to manage their stress. Many organizations offer in-house seminars or design stress management counseling programs. These are very effective on the individual level, but for overall improvement, it is necessary to evaluate the structure of the organization and its effects on working conditions.

TIP

If you work in an inherently stressful environment, investigate all programs your organization offers to assist employees in maintaining balance. In addition to seminars and courses, ask about day care, flex time, mental health days, telecommuting, counseling, and any other support programs.

Different companies and organizations use different methods to evaluate and restructure for job-stress reduction. If you're in management and have the opportunity to effect change, your first step is to identify the problem. Have each worker evaluate the workplace to identify stressful conditions and areas for restructuring or policy change.

TIP

The smaller the group, the easier it is to make the evaluation totally inclusive. Sometimes a group meeting to discuss the situation will even suffice. In a larger organization, it might be necessary to establish a task force.

Using the results of your findings, push for new initiatives to change policies or procedures within the workplace—for example, to allow for more family leave or to require that each job position periodically be reevaluated and a reasonable job description developed.

WHEN YOUR BOSS ENCOURAGES WORKAHOLISM

A closing point: What about when your stress, in large part, can be traced directly back to a boss or bosses who encourage workaholism? Get prepared! With great tact and professionalism, say something along the lines of, "I'm really overcommitted right now, and if I take that on, I can't do it justice."

Here are some other helpful responses:

- "I appreciate your confidence in me. I wouldn't want to take this on, knowing my other tasks and responsibilities right now would prohibit me from doing an excellent job."

- "I'd be happy to handle this assignment for you, but realistically I can't do it without forgoing some other things I'm working on. Of tasks *a* and *b*, which would you like me to do? Which can I put aside?"

- "I can do that for you. Will it be okay if I get back to you in the middle of next week? I currently have ____, ____, and ____ in the queue."

- "The number of tasks and complexity of assignments I'm handling are mounting. Perhaps we could look at a two- or four-week scenario of what's most important to you and when the assignments need to be completed, versus what I can realistically handle over that time period."

Dealing with job stress is today's never-ending story. As organizations vie for position or survival, as technology develops and the world around us brings continuous change, the workplace and career professionals who want to remain in balance must change along with it all, particularly if the work environment itself is inherently stressful.

THE 30-SECOND RECAP

- Each worker in a stressful job costs the healthcare economy 1.5 times that of the average unstressed worker.

- Job stress plagues the modern workplace, resulting not only in health risks for individual workers, but in overall poor performance by companies and organizations.

- In most cases, job stress involves stressful working conditions as well as the individual worker's characteristics and circumstances. Thus, effectively managing job stress requires addressing both personal stress management and overall organizational issues.

Managing Office Stress

In this section, you learn about the impact of deadline pressure, the importance of keeping your stress level in check, and simple ways to maintain balance.

INCREASING DEADLINE PRESSURE IS INEVITABLE

Everything in society has sped up as a result of technology and information. This is especially true for life in the office. As societies and work environments rev at a faster pace, so do the individuals within them. With the constant advent of faster computers and more efficient machines, however, the expectations on workers are higher than ever. Communication has become instantaneous. Less time is spent waiting for a reply, because information can travel as fast as an e-mail or a fax.

CAUTION

While once we might have imagined a future full of machines taking over for humans, the present reality is that with greater interconnectivity and more machines populating our offices, we are expected to do even more.

People are always connected to the office somehow, which has resulted in a lack of escape time. Long gone are the days when you were only reachable when you were physically in the office. Thanks to pagers, cellular phones, voicemail, and fax machines, you can no longer hide from the deadlines at work. They ride home with you.

Communication the Average U.S. Household (3.6 People) Receives Each Week

Type	Number
Phone calls	54
Mail	35
E-mail	16
Voicemail	4
Cell phone calls	3
Pages	2
Faxes	1

Note: The numbers are even larger for a high-volume household.

Deadline pressure is as inevitable as the advent of a computer that is faster than the last, or a cellular phone that has better reception than the current model. Deadline pressure filters down through the hierarchy at the office.

If extra pressure is being put on your boss, chances are that *his* boss is being pressured. Chances are even greater that *you'll* be pressured. Pressure can also come from within. People constantly raise their expectations of their own performance.

As the speed of office communication and correspondence increases, so does the speed at which deadlines must be met! Everyone is expected to move at a faster pace, while still working with the constant resources of time and money.

CAUTION

People constantly put undue pressure on themselves by worrying about whether they are meeting other people's expectations.

THE IMPORTANCE OF KEEPING STRESS LEVELS IN CHECK

Increases in deadline pressure often bring about increases in stress levels. The more you have to get done, the more stress your mind and body experience. Each new task or deadline adds to your stress, resulting in an accumulation throughout the day. Stress levels can rise as suddenly as spotting your boss over the tops of the cubicles, hearing a phone ringing, or having an e-mail arrive.

Deadline pressure, fueled by organization climates and individual working styles (see "The Toxic Workplace" on page 2), result in many people working longer hours. As you've undoubtedly witnessed, it's not unusual for people to work straight through their lunch breaks and on into the late evening to try to meet deadlines (all the while snacking at their desks). If the workplace is your main source of stress, the more time you find yourself in the office, the greater your need to minimize potential office stressors.

THE GOOD AND THE BAD

Stress can be both motivating and detrimental.

PLAIN ENGLISH

Motivating stress   Stress that stimulates and challenges you, as opposed to preventing you from accomplishing tasks.

Stress is necessary to your working energy level. Negative stress, however, often results from increased work pressure and may make you anxious and irritable. Stress in the workplace can come from many sources:

- A difficult boss or co-worker
- Lack of recognition
- Long hours
- Unclear expectations
- Lack of job security
- Multiple, complex tasks with deadlines
- Fluctuating expectations

TIP

Dozens of other factors or combinations of factors may also prove stressful to you. A single cause of an individual's stress is hard to pinpoint. No matter what the source, it's important to work toward finding ways to keep the stress in balance.

STRESS AT YOUR DESK

At work or at home, stress is unhealthy for the body. It can cause a tightening of muscles, leading to muscle soreness. Affected muscles include those in the face, shoulders, and neck. This causes headaches in the back of the head, which spread from there. Working at a desk in front of PC tends to exacerbate the situation. As everyone who has ever had a headache knows, this makes it difficult to concentrate and focus on the task at hand.

TIP

Time away from work should be just that—time away.

WHEN STRESS THREATENS YOUR PROFESSIONAL RELATIONSHIPS

It is vital to keep stress levels in check, because they can lead to job *burnout*. With burnout, you end up "down on yourself," detached from your work, and low on energy. A vicious cycle ensues: Becoming removed from your work and from the people you work with makes your working habits less productive.

PLAIN ENGLISH

Burnout   A specific type of stress that involves diminished personal accomplishment, depersonalization, and emotional exhaustion.

If you fail to keep your stress levels in check, your relationships at the office will be affected. Your co-workers will notice changes in your attitude, your anxiety, and your emotions. These changes will serve to isolate you from people. No one wants to spend time with someone who is volatile.

CAUTION

Lashing out or blowing up at someone in the office because of stress should be avoided at all costs. Even one such incident can leave you with a reputation as an unfriendly and dangerous person. Co-workers could have a hard time approaching you, and you could end up being isolated or outcast.

SIMPLE WAYS TO MAINTAIN BALANCE

You can do many simple things to maintain balance—many of which require simple adjustments to what you already do:

- While at work, *move* more! You can relieve tension and soreness in muscles due to stress by flexing and relaxing your muscles periodically.

- Spend more time walking. If you tend to spend hours at your desk, stand up and walk around the room or just stretch in place at least every 20 minutes.

- If you consistently use an elevator, take the stairs every now and then.

TIP

Keeping stress levels in check creates a healthier personal working environment. If your stress levels are controlled, you have a better ability to focus, concentrate, and relax.

ELIMINATE UNNEEDED TASKS

In his book, *The Effective Executive*, management sage Dr. Peter Drucker tells us that 80 percent of what we do at work is dictated by habit and not by need. That means much of what you do during the workday is done because you always do things that way. Is it the best way, though? And does performing unnecessary tasks add to your workload and hence your stress level?

TIP

Ask yourself this question: "Does this need to be done at all?" This question often leads to greater focus, less time wasted on nonessential tasks, and less stress.

What kinds of tasks may not need to be done at all anymore? Try these on for size:

- Checking for e-mail messages three times a day when once a day is sufficient.
- Making a backup hard copy of documents on your disk.
- Sending a fax and then sending a follow-up letter containing the same information as the fax.
- Reviewing previous policies and procedures that have been replaced by newer ones.
- Reviewing training manuals and guides that have been replaced by newer ones.

ORDER CAN BRING RELIEF

When stress affects your concentration at work, a simple solution is to make a schedule. Scheduling not only allows you to plan and control your use of time, but also forces you to consider your priorities and goals.

Along with scheduling, set goals. Jotting down long-term and short-term goals in your weekly planner will keep you focused on your priorities rather than someone else's. Well-structured time and feelings of accomplishment when a goal is met will come as a direct result.

TIP

You will use your time more effectively if you not only write down goals, but also write down the steps and activities required to meet those goals.

Taking time for yourself each week can also make time spent in the office more productive. Find a way to relax so that you can keep your perspective. Spend your lunch break outside, go for a massage, listen to a favorite CD all the way through, or engage in whatever it takes to clear your mind. Including a special break will leave you feeling more calm and focused at your work.

Face Your Space

Along with organizing your time, organizing your space in a manner conducive to your work style is important. Don't let your desk become a mess of papers, mail, and sticky notes. In such cases, reminders are hard to find and can easily be overlooked, time is wasted looking for documents, and you have less space to work.

TIP

Stay organized. The organization of your physical environment is as important as the organization of goals in your weekly planner. Filing cabinets, folders, and labeling systems can be wonderful tools—use them.

Envisioning Calm

If you absolutely can't get out of the office for a break, take a few minutes for some visualization. This technique focuses on creating a mental picture of something that cultivates a feeling of calm or simply makes you happy. If you need to, you can close your eyes to do this.

You can also use visualization to calm your fears of future events. If you fear a meeting with a certain person, for example, you can visualize the encounter going well before it happens.

Breathe and Recoup

Another helpful strategy is to take a 5- to 10-minute break to breathe. Find a *quiet* place. Close your eyes and focus all of your attention on taking deep, steady breaths. Like visualization, this technique allows you to pause and recenter yourself in the midst of your work. You will be surprised at what a calming effect this has.

When you return to your desk, you will find yourself with a better ability to concentrate.

THE QUEST FOR BALANCE

To maintain balance at work among otherwise stress-inducing events, remind yourself of the positive side of all situations. When a situation arises that you view as negative, pause momentarily to find the positive side of it.

TIP

Stressful situations often are a matter of interpretation. If you have a hard time finding any positive attributes for a given situation at work, say to yourself, "It could be worse," and proceed from there. You will be surprised what a difference perception makes.

A simple source of balance for some people is keeping a plant in their office. Many small plants require minimal care and can flourish in an office setting.

TIP

Adding something living to your office to mingle among the abundance of inanimate objects can help liven up the atmosphere and lift your spirits.

It is also important to exercise your creativity. If the nature of your job does not lend itself to creative expression, find your own ways to express yourself. Even if it is something as simple as color-coding your daily planner, the use of colors is a good release and will contribute to relaxation.

MAKE YOUR TIME AWAY COUNT

Outside the office, prepare your mind and body for the time you spend in the office:

- **Eat a balanced diet.** Avoid heavy, carbohydrate-laden lunches/snacks. Eat more fruit and vegetable snacks. You'll have more energy and less internal discomfort.
- **Exercise.** If you work out a little every day or just a few days a week, you will notice a decrease in muscle tension, which will make your office chair much more comfortable. This time is important for you, so schedule it if necessary.
- **Build relationships.** Never underestimate the importance of time spent with friends. Your good friends have a way of calming you,

whether you need someone to talk to, laugh with, or take a break with. Who else would listen to you vent about work?

- **Get enough sleep.** As well-rested body and mind are your best tools for higher performance. There is little at work that you can do well when you are groggy and tired.

Fortunately you have a variety of stress-management options in and out of the office, before work, after work, and during breaks. Using these options will increase your balance, allowing you to be more productive and making you an easier co-worker to be around.

THE 30-SECOND RECAP

- With an increase in the speed of communication and the continually changing marketplace, time pressure within the modern office environment equals increased stress.

- Although some stress might be motivating, over time, negative stress can harm individuals' working relationships and decrease their overall ability to work productively.

- With an awareness of stress's harmful effects, individuals can practice lifestyle changes and simple techniques to manage stress and maintain more balance in the workplace.

Stress at Home

In this section, you learn about sources of household stress, tips for conflict management, and suggestions for dealing with specific household stresses.

SOURCES OF HOUSEHOLD STRESS

For many people, stress in the workplace is the least of their worries. In fact, studies conducted by the American Medical Association (AMA) show that family-related stress often has a stronger impact on people's health and well-being than other types of stress that get more press. Stress in the home comes from more than just family. There is also household management stress, or financial stress. Certain times of the year are also infamous for inducing stress, especially holidays.

CAUTION

AMA studies show that people with high levels of family stress spend more time in doctors' offices, are referred to specialists more often, and are hospitalized more often.

Keeping domestic stresses in check is not only a key to improving quality of life, but also an important means of staying healthy.

COUPLEHOOD AND BLENDED FAMILIES

Some of the most prevalent household stressors are family relationships. Couples constantly face stress, and the most obvious source is when the relationship is in trouble. Household stress can wear on a marriage or partnership. When things don't work out and families experience separation and divorce, the result is even more stress for parents and children. As the following table indicates, a high divorce rate in society is a continuing fact.

Marriages and Divorces in the United States

Year	Marriages (in Millions)	Rate/1,000 Pop. (Percent)	Divorces (in Millions)	Rate/1,000 Pop. (Percent)
1990	2.443	9.8	1.182	4.7
1991	2.371	9.4	1.187	4.7
1992	2.362	9.3	1.215	4.8
1993	2.334	9.0	1.187	4.6
1994	2.362	9.1	1.191	4.6

Source: U.S. National Center for Health Statistics

Blended families often endure more household stresses than other families. More than one third of all children in the United States become part of a stepfamily before the age of 18. These children have a higher risk of both behavioral and emotional problems, which can cause stress for the whole family.

CAUTION

Blended families can be a source of stress for all family members.

To reduce some of the stress, adults should discuss, *before* they marry, where they will live and how they will share their money. Sometimes buying a house together is better for everyone because it feels like a new beginning.

TIP

If you are remarrying, you should also discuss the role the stepparent will play in raising any children from previous relationships. This will eliminate confusion and possible stepping on toes that could put stress on the marriage.

Children are especially vulnerable to the stress created by blended families. Children are expected to adjust to a new environment and a new stepparent, while combating feelings of abandonment by the noncustodial parent. Children also will experience stress if they are put in the position of defending a parent if one speaks badly about the other. Therefore, it is important to keep their emotional needs in mind when you make decisions.

The following are pointers for parents to keep in mind:

- Stepparents should not rush a close relationship with their stepchildren.
- Avoid speaking against your ex-spouse in front of the children so they won't get defensive.
- Avoid putting the children in the middle by questioning whether your spouse is more loyal to you or them.

CAUTION

When parents remarry, often they don't maintain as much contact with their children, which can be damaging to the child's self-esteem.

MANAGING FINANCES

Keeping finances under control helps reduce stress in the home. Balance checkbooks regularly, and file receipts and bills away in an accessible place. Being in debt, whether it is credit cards or loans, causes stress for too many people. It is important to live within your means to avoid owing money you don't have (see the section "The Time/Money/Stress Connection" on page 52).

To deal with debt, you should eliminate nonessential spending. This can be done without cutting back in crucial areas like food and insurance. For example, you can dine at home, rather than eat out, or watch a video at home, instead of going out to the movies. Do this until you can pay off all your debts. When that is taken care of, start saving money.

TURKEY AND YULETIDE

The holiday season is another huge precipitator of stress in the household. It seems like holiday stress affects us all at some point. Most holiday stress happens when we put unrealistic expectations on ourselves and others because of an image we have of how the holiday season should be.

CAUTION

Many people expect to have the perfect holiday season, as portrayed in movies and on television. Be true to your own feelings and limits, and try to ignore the hype that focuses on what a "real" home should be like during the holidays.

People also feel obligated to buy too many gifts, or gifts that are too expensive for their budget. You will be less stressed if you can accept that it is better to stay within your spending limit.

TIP

Watch your spending at holiday time and resist the urge to use credit cards too much. This can lead to year-round financial stress, because the bills linger on until fully paid.

CAUTION

Holidays tend to magnify other existing stressors, such as family illnesses, tragic losses, and relatives who you don't get along with. The key to keeping stress levels in check is, again, being true to yourself. Do not expect the holidays to be a magical time when problems disappear. The idea is not to turn into a scrooge but to simply be realistic. Know what you can do with the resources you have.

TIPS FOR CONFLICT MANAGEMENT

Much of the domestic stress that people experience comes from arguments among family members. So let's focus on *conflict management*.

PLAIN ENGLISH

Conflict management   Strategies for resolving sharp disagreements, of interests or ideas, or emotional disturbances.

Arguments can be highly disruptive, not only to the individuals involved, but also to other members of the family who might feel obligated to choose sides or play mediator. Whether the conflict is a minor difference or a full-blown argument, methods of conflict resolution can reduce the stress it causes.

All relationships have conflict. Its existence is actually a healthy sign. The part that can be unhealthy is how you handle the conflict.

Unhealthy management styles include the following:

- Denying that there is a problem
- Giving in just to avoid a conflict
- Blaming others
- Using power to get one's way

Many of these approaches only prolong the problem, because they never solve it entirely. As a result, the problem festers and generally resurfaces in another form.

WIN-WIN SOLUTIONS

It is important to enter any conflict with the right frame of mind. Never lose sight of the relationship you have with that person. If you feel like you might say something you'll regret, take the time to cool off. When you approach any conflict with a negative attitude, you can expect trouble.

Healthy solutions to conflicts means everybody wins. This is possible when a conflict has more than two alternatives, which it often does. You might have one solution in mind while your adversary has another. If you don't like each other's choices, there might be an alternative solution that you can mutually devise to suit both parties.

COMPROMISES

Another healthy solution, instead of everyone winning, is having no one lose. When you arrive at a point where neither person likes the other person's choice, you again try to come up with an alternate solution, but there might not be one that you both like. You might have to put up with some things that you don't like, but so will the other person.

PLAIN ENGLISH

Compromise   A settlement in which both sides make concessions, or a solution that is midway between two alternatives.

TIP

In this case, try to find a solution that you can both at least live with. In other words, a solution that is more of a compromise.

TAKING TURNS

When neither of the two earlier approaches works, or when a problem has only two, polar solutions and you can't bridge the gap, take turns. In this situation, only one person gets his way, for now. Next time, the other person gets *his* way. This win-lose, lose-win approach diminishes the impact of the losses, because the losing party knows that, next time, he will win.

Both parties should try to be respectful and have the other person's interests in mind. Other people want to have their chance to be heard as much as you do. Don't always feel like you have to win. A disagreement should not turn into a competition, and if it feels that way, you and the other person are more likely to get defensive.

CAUTION

Sometimes it is hard to see any other side but yours, but you have to try to understand the other person's side.

CARING COUNTS

When the person you are in conflict with is someone you care about, you must be willing to give and receive apologies. Inevitably, there will be times when you or someone else involved gets hurt or upset. Apologies can help speed up the healing process, and so can declarations of love.

TIP

Even during disagreements, it is helpful to be able to say "I love you" or "I care for you."

BECOMING MORE AWARE

Practicing basic conflict management skills will reduce some household stress. However, other techniques can help, too. Become aware of what stressors affect you, and notice your reactions to those stressors.

TIP

Don't ignore your domestic stress. Determine specifically what causes you stress in the home and how your body responds to the stress. Notice if you become nervous or physically upset. Then examine what you're telling yourself about the meaning of these things. Are they worth anguish?

GRANT ME THE SERENITY

Be aware of what you can and cannot change. Perhaps you can work on avoiding your stressors, eliminating them completely, or reducing the intensity of their influence.

TIP

Shorten your exposure to stressors by taking a break or getting away, using the time to relax and gain new perspective.

Learn to reduce the intensity of your emotional reactions to potential stress. Stress reactions are triggered by your body's perception of danger. By keeping your perspective in check, you can avoid viewing your stressors in an exaggerated way.

TIP

You can't always please everyone, and most issues are not urgent.

If you can put each situation in perspective, you will be able to recognize your excess emotions and understand the stressor as something you can deal with.

PHYSICAL RESERVES

You can also learn to moderate your physical reactions to stress. Taking slow, deep breaths will bring your heart rate down and your respiration back to normal. A variety of relaxation techniques can reduce muscle tension.

CAUTION

Numerous medications can assist you, but learning to moderate these stress reactions in natural ways is a more effective long-term solution.

Building up your physical reserves will better prepare you to face everyday household stresses. Moderate exercise and a well-balanced diet are extremely important. Getting enough sleep and being consistent with your sleep schedule are also important. Avoid nicotine, excessive caffeine, and other stimulants.

TIP

If you maintain a healthy, conditioned body, potentially stressful situations won't hit you as hard.

EMOTIONAL RESERVES

Emotional reserves are as important as physical reserves for handling potential household stressors. Maintain healthy friendships and relationships.

TIP

A good support network can help you put things in perspective when you can't do it alone or when you need an outside opinion.

Most important, be a friend to yourself. Expect some frustrations, failures, and sorrows—and take them gracefully. Don't be hard on yourself. You have to be willing to be human.

THE 30-SECOND RECAP

- Stress in the home results from many factors, including family relationships, finances, and how one approaches the holidays.
- Healthy conflict resolution solves family disagreements and arguments, helping relieve household stress.
- Keeping a level head and being aware of your limits can help you deal with stress in the home.
- Strive to be a friend to yourself, recognizing that frustrations, failures, and sorrows are part of every life. Take them with as much grace as you can muster.

Getting Sleep, Staying in Balance

In this section, you learn the importance of keeping your life in balance by getting proper sleep, avoiding overwork, and recognizing when you could be overcontrolling.

THERE IS NO SUBSTITUTE FOR GOOD SLEEP

Keeping your life stress-free and in balance is highly desirable, yet as we've seen, there are forces throughout society conspiring to ensure that you remain in any state other than balanced. With each passing month, more things compete for your time and attention. Take the time now to carve out a pattern that fits the way you work and the way you want to live. The lessons you've completed so far will aid you greatly, but the need for sleep cannot be denied.

NAME THAT EVENT

A momentous event occurred in 1878. Can you guess what it is? Before telling you the answer, here are some clues. Prior to that time, the typical person slept anywhere from nine to eleven hours a night. People usually retired within an hour or two of the sun going down and rose at sunrise.

After 1878, within a few short years, the average amount of sleep per adult fell from around 10 hours per night to 8. Since then it has fallen even more, hovering just above seven hours.

What happened in 1878? Give up? Thomas Edison invented the light bulb.

TIP

It is an anthropological phenomenon to fall asleep when it is dark and wake up when it is light.

Artificial light via the light bulb, as well as all the other inventions that followed, dramatically shifted our sleeping patterns. Yet for tens of thousands of years, humans slept an average of 10 hours a night and more. Is it possible that human physiology could change in the course of 10 or 12 decades? Not likely. If you're getting eight hours of very good sleep a night, you still may not get all the rest your body requires.

TIP

Be generous with yourself when it comes to sleep. Give yourself rest when your body feels the need for it. Proper sleep is one of the best stress inhibitors available.

HARD-FOUGHT GAINS

Your quest for more sleep will not come without its battles. In the United States, people have added 158 hours to their annual work and commuting time since three decades ago. The rest of the world is beginning to catch up!

CAUTION

Without adequate sleep, you cannot possibly perform your best work—no matter how well you have lulled yourself into believing otherwise.

Studies of Japanese workers who put in inordinately long days reveal that instead of increasing overall productivity, after a given number of hours, productivity actually declined. After a few more hours, these workers actually became counterproductive—they started to make errors that undid the previous good work they had done.

TIP

The amount of sleep you need on a regular basis is something only you can determine. Everyone differs in this category, and there is no point in comparing yourself to others.

Don't believe the reports of others. With great bravado, people routinely announce in offices that they got by with three or four hours of sleep last night, that they average five hours a night, that they routinely get to bed at 2 A.M., or that "I was up the entire night." Such statements only further the propagation of myths around sleep.

CAUTION

Everyone needs good sleep on a regular basis. In tests of those who claimed to be able to get by on less sleep, very few exhibited the ability to do so.

The Signs Are Highly Visible

Inadequate sleep leads to a variety of undesirable results:

- You become less aware.
- You constantly feel worn out.
- Your immune system is weakened.

On top of this, combined with too little sleep, any illness you do contract will be more severe.

If you feel tired day after day, that is indication enough that you need more sleep. If any of the following are evident, you need to get to bed immediately, because you are taking chances with your health, and potentially the well-being of others:

- **Lack of appetite or indigestion.** You may be a chow hound from way back, but if you have trouble when it comes to mealtimes, particularly trouble swallowing, sleep deprivation may be at the root.

- **Fatigue in the morning even after a full night's sleep.** Sleep experts agree that, if people are otherwise healthy, there is little reason for them to be less than chipper following a full night of sleep. If you find yourself wanting to nod off at 10 or 11 in the morning, it is time to pay attention to your body's signal.

- **Loss of libido.** If you are not as interested in sex as you used to be, it is probably not your age that is the cause, but rather your lack of sleep. This generally occurs gradually enough as to be unnoticeable by you but is entirely of concern to your partner.

- **Prolonged fatigue.** If you feel out of sorts following several nights of full sleep, chances are that you have gone too long getting far too little sleep prior to those recent nights. Embark on a course right now of getting at least eight hours of uninterrupted sleep and taking some extra time on the weekends.

- **Annoyance with minor tasks.** If you have trouble adding up numbers, don't want to field phone calls, and find yourself avoiding tasks that previously represented no real challenge, chances are you may not have the rest you need and hence the mental clarity to proceed with these tasks.

- **Red eyes.** If your eyes are red, and you didn't just arrive from the West coast on a late-night flight, you've had too little sleep. The condition of your eyes is one of the clearest indications of too little sleep.

Having too little sleep can contribute to diminished joy in life. Everything seems so blasé. Stress is predictable. On top of that, you can be a danger to others.

CAUTION

If you suffer from sleeplessness and work in a situation where you operate equipment, your health and safety, as well as that of those around you, can be in jeopardy. If you operate a motor vehicle, you may be gambling with your life, the lives of fellow passengers, and the lives of others on the road.

THE MICROSLEEP PHENOMENA

Martin Ede, Ph.D., in his book *The Twenty-Four Hour Society,* observes that too many people unknowingly engage in *microsleep.* Occurrences of microsleep are 10- to 15-second bouts of sleep that occur in the middle of the day while the person otherwise appears to be fully functional. For example, the following all represent times at which microsleep occurs:

- Office professionals engage in microsleep right at their desks, which is not particularly harmful to the people around them.
- Parents engage in microsleep while driving their children to and from lessons.
- Vanpool drivers engage in microsleep while transporting six or eight people.

PLAIN ENGLISH

Microsleep   Very brief, nondiscernable sleep episodes in the middle of the day.

The danger is obvious. Think about your own sleep pattern over the last week, month, and year. Have you been chronically depriving yourself of sleep? Could you be among those who engage in microsleep? The possibility is more distinct than you might have thought.

UNFAIR TO YOURSELF AND TO YOUR EMPLOYER

If you arrive at work exhausted, you can't possibly be as efficient as you would be otherwise. In many respects, you are gypping your employer. Presumably your organization hired the full and complete you, which you are not able to offer if you continually arrive in less than your best condition.

To ensure that you get proper sleep, you need to be comfortable in your bedroom. The climate and atmosphere should be right for you and your mate. If possible, once you get to sleep, you need to stay asleep until you have to get up. If you're not comfortable, you won't sleep well.

The following are suggestions for making your bedroom more comfortable:

- Keeping your bedroom slightly cool will help you and your mate sleep better. It seems like one person is always hot while the other person is always cold. Bring out the extra blankets for the cold one so both of you can be happy.

- Don't be jostled out of a deep sleep by the telephone ringing. Whether it's an important call, misdial, or a prank, once your sleeping pattern has been disrupted for the night, you may not have the same benefits of a full night's sleep. Turn the ringer off before you go to bed, or have the calls rerouted to an answering machine or service. This tip goes for pagers, also!

- Eliminate distractions in the bedroom. You may be more comfortable falling asleep with the television on, especially if you live by yourself, but most likely the television will wake you up in the middle of the night with the volume seemingly a lot louder than it was when you went to sleep.

- Keep pets from jumping up and down on your bed and running around your house all night.

CAUTION

Even if you have a TV that turns off automatically, the extra time you spend in bed watching it until it goes off will have an accumulated de-energizing effect.

- If you need the alarm clock to wake up in the morning, make sure you get up the first time it goes off. If you hit the snooze button and fall back to sleep, you're doing yourself more harm than good. You won't fully get back to sleep before the alarm clock goes off again, which disrupts your sleeping and makes you feel worse than if you had just gotten up to begin with.

- Allow yourself enough room to move while sleeping. Make sure you have a bed sufficiently large enough to allow you and your partner freedom of movement. Fear of bumping into one another will restrict your movements and unknowingly diminish the quality of your sleep.

■ Avoid caffeine for at least six hours before retiring, and avoid alcohol altogether if you're interested in having a good sleep that night. Alcohol disrupts the sleep. You'll fall asleep quickly, but you'll wake up too early. Then you're likely to have trouble getting back to sleep.

Finally, go to sleep when you're tired, not because the clock happens to say a particular time. When you ignore the message your body is giving you, you pay a price.

Is Lack of Sleep Diminishing Your Staff's Effectiveness?

What if one of your key stressors is the lack of alertness or productivity you observe in your staff? If you supervise others (see the section "The Toxic Workplace" on page 2), how often have you looked out across your office or plant floor and seen employees dragging their tails, even at midmorning?

Here is data that may prompt you to explore innovative ways to tackle one of the most pervasive problems in society: an *exhausted* workforce. In a survey conducted by the National Sleep Foundation, 51 percent of the American workforce reports that sleepiness on the job interferes with the amount of work they get done. Forty percent of employees admit that the quality of their work suffers when they are sleepy, and nearly 1 out of 5 (19 percent) report making occasional or frequent work errors due to sleepiness.

CAUTION

While sleep experts recommend at least eight hours of sleep a night in order to function properly, one third of American adults (33 percent) sleep only 6½ hours or less nightly during the work week.

PLAIN ENGLISH

Exhaustion   The state of being used up, tired out, or completely emptied or drained. Many adults experience exhaustion because of a lack of adequate sleep.

Is it any wonder that some of the people you supervise are consistently less productive than they could be? One out of four adults has difficulty getting up for work two or more days per week, and 27 percent of adults say they are sleepy at work two or more days a week. At least two thirds of adults report that sleepiness makes concentrating (68 percent) and *handling stress* (66 percent) on the job more difficult.

As if this data weren't bad enough, 58 percent say that making decisions and solving problems are more difficult when they are sleepy. Listening to co-workers is more difficult when sleepy, according to 57 percent of respondents. Overall, employees estimate that the quality and quantity of their work is diminished by about 30 percent when they are sleepy.

CAUTION

Sleep deprivation is a serious issue for supervisors and entrepreneurs running their own ventures. At risk is productivity and safety, as well as employment longevity.

INNOVATIONS NEEDED!

To retain and get the best of your staff calls for innovative measures. Here are some possibilities:

- Encourage employees to take quick naps at their desks.
- Send employees home early (without reprimand) when their need for sleep is apparent.
- Encourage employees to maintain sleep logs.
- Establish nap rooms.

It's far better to encourage naps than to have employees pretend to be alert.

We've got a lot to do in this world, and we each have the greatest chance of being at our best when we're well rested!

THE 30-SECOND RECAP

- Getting good sleep night after night is the primary prerequisite for being productive in your job and keeping your stress levels in check.
- The amount of sleep you need on a regular and continual basis is unique and highly personal.
- It is easy to determine how much sleep you require—if you pay attention, your body will tell you.
- Devise a strategy to ensure that you get the amount of sleep you need to feel rested, awake, and alert in the morning.

Curbing Procrastination

In this section, you learn ways to prevent procrastination and its associated stress so that you'll be better able to accomplish overwhelming and unpleasant tasks with relative ease.

PROCRASTINATION AND STRESS

Whenever you let low-priority tasks get in the way of higher priority tasks, you are *procrastinating*.

PLAIN ENGLISH

Procrastination   To put off doing a task, to delay an activity or task, or to ignore something that demands your attention.

Putting things off inevitably leads to a pile-up—too much to do and not enough time to do it. Whether you procrastinate at home or in the office, the demands it puts on your time cause stress.

CAUTION

Your stress level increases as minor tasks pile up and begin to seem larger than they really are.

PLEASANT TASKS ARE NOT THE PROBLEM

Things that are enjoyable to you are usually not the problem. You get those tasks done with relative ease. The problem comes when you perceive a task as difficult, inconvenient, or scary. This is when you are likely to shift into procrastination mode.

People often fool themselves by saying things like, "I work better under pressure, so I don't need to do this now," or "I'll wait until I'm in the mood to do it." Statements like these help us convince ourselves to procrastinate, which causes unnecessary stress.

SMALL TASKS MOUNT UP

Suppose you have several tasks before you, each of which would take only 5 to 10 minutes to complete. Any one of these tasks would be no big deal to tackle. The thought of handling all of them, however, becomes daunting.

As the list of things you need to take care of grows, and you feel yourself getting somewhat behind, all those tasks start to loom even larger! There are many ways to break through procrastination and reduce the stress that it causes.

FIRST, GET ORGANIZED

When you "divide and conquer," you have a good chance of overcoming procrastination. Regard each task before you as a distinct entity. If you have a large job, break it down into individual tasks, each regarded as separate. When you tackle a five-minute job and gain the satisfaction of having completed it, you have more energy, focus, and direction for another five-minute job.

Likewise, if you do five five-minute jobs, with each job you feel a sense of victory—however minor—and you're spurred on to the next job, and the next. In this manner, five 5-minute jobs can actually be easier to complete than one 25-minute job.

TIP

On my way to writing 27 books, I saw each chapter as a distinct task in and of itself, completely apart from the book.

When completing this chapter, for example, I got up, stretched, walked around, took a big drink of water, and forgot all about what's next. Then as I approached the section "The Stress of Information Overload," on page 37, I gave it my full energy and attention. By approaching each of the sections in this book as individual tasks, the daunting project of writing a book in a very short time didn't seem so bad.

TIP

If I had to write an entire manuscript with no individual sections in it (in other words, if the book were one huge section), it would be a far more difficult task. Why? No ability to divide and conquer.

CLEAR YOUR DESK

Simply having too much in your visual field can be an impediment to getting started. When you have one project or one task at hand, your odds of maintaining clarity and focus increase dramatically. This works even better if you're not in your own office but at a conference table or at some other post where you have only the project materials at hand.

Identify the Real Issue

Sometimes you can't get started on something because you haven't identified some lingering issues that are affecting your feelings:

- Perhaps you're ambivalent about the task.
- Perhaps you think it's unnecessary or unworthy of you.
- Perhaps you resent doing it—for example, you weren't able to say no in the first place, and now you have to make good on your earlier promise.

Whatever the reason, when you identify some of the causes behind procrastination, you have a much better chance of getting past those barricades and getting started.

Eliminate Distractions

Sometimes the reason you procrastinate on a project is because you fear you will be interrupted. To eliminate this possibility, eliminate distraction. Tell your receptionist to hold all calls. Turn off the ringer on your phone. Don't check your e-mail. Do whatever it takes to give yourself an uninterrupted span of time.

TIP

If you think the task will take an hour, make sure that you don't have distractions for at least 90 minutes. Then, if you finish some time between 30 and 90 minutes later, you can always reenter "the world" when you choose.

Proceeding Without Pain

Look for an "easy win." For whatever you're trying to tackle, find some element of it that you can complete quickly and easily and get an easy win. That's a far better method of getting started than tackling some difficult portion of it first.

TIP

Suppose you're facing a difficult project. How could you get an easy win right off the bat? Open the file folder, scan the contents, and look for an easy entry point, some aspect of the project you can tackle now.

Sometimes simply organizing materials, putting them into smaller file folders, stapling items, or rearranging the order of things represents a good, easy win. Now at least you have a better handle on the project, the supporting items are arranged according to importance, and the probability of your continuing is reasonably assured.

CAUTION

Be careful. Too much rearrangement and organizing is a classic procrastination technique. Do not dwell on smaller, lower priority tasks. Use them as stepping stones.

Reframe the Task

When novelist Tom Wolfe was working for *Esquire* magazine and was already past the deadline on an article, his editor gave him a wonderful suggestion. Wolfe was to start writing a letter to the editor, describing how he would approach the article and what he would put in it.

So Wolfe submitted a draft that started off like a letter. Sure enough, by eliminating the first paragraph or two and retaining the body of what Wolfe had written, the editor had the requisite material. The editor had simply *reframed* the task so that Wolfe could get started.

PLAIN ENGLISH

Reframe   To restructure so as to allow a different perspective.

TIP

Wolfe didn't have trouble writing the article; he simply had trouble getting started. By converting the notion of the assignment to a letter, the block was gone.

Give It Five Minutes

Suppose you don't want to tackle something now but know eventually you're going to have to start it. One way to get yourself immersed in it, kind of like dabbling your feet in a wading pool, is to devote five minutes of your attention to the task. At the end of five minutes, you may stop.

TIP

Most people who use this five-minute approach don't want to stop after the fifth minute. A body, or a mind for that matter, tends to keep progressing in the same direction. If you've been on a project for five minutes, there is no reason why the sixth or seventh minute should be any more trying.

JUMP-STARTING

Sometimes the mere gesture of turning on your computer, popping a video into the VCR, or flipping on your pocket dictator is enough to get started on a task that you have been putting off. In essence, flipping on the switch to your PC, having it boot up, and perhaps taking it to the appropriate folder and file is analogous to jump-starting your car.

Suppose your car conks out on the side of the road, and your battery gets a jump-start. All of a sudden, the engine is revving—this is certainly not the time to turn off the car. You want to keep it on for a good 20 minutes. Likewise, once that PC boots up and your hard drive is humming, you may experience a jump-start in your ability to dive into the project.

USE TRADEOFFS

If you face many things competing for your attention (and who doesn't?), trade one project off against another.

Here's how it works: Suppose you have to do project A, and you've been putting it off. Along comes project B, which is more difficult, more involved, much scarier. Suddenly project A doesn't look so bad. Now tackle A headlong. You'll still have B to deal with, and that may keep you humming along on A!

GO COLD TURKEY

This is not recommended for everyone, and certainly not every time. Sometimes the only way to get started on a task is to dive into it headlong, cold turkey, not allowing yourself the opportunity to stray. Surprisingly, when you practice the cold-turkey approach to procrastination, it's not nearly as upsetting as it sounds. In fact, it can be a great relief.

My friend Jim Cathcart, a fellow professional speaker, made the decision a few years back to chuck all of his hard-copy slides *en masse,* so that he would be forced to learn presentation software and convert his audiovisuals to the newer, more powerful media.

SEEKING HELP FROM OTHERS

Suppose that no matter what you try, you still can't get started on the task you've been putting off, and the associated stress is mounting. In that case, get a little help from your friends.

HAVE SOMEONE HOLD RANSOM MONEY

Suppose you want to accomplish something and you've been putting it off for weeks on end. You give a friend $500 and tell him or her, "If I don't finish this task by next Thursday, you get to keep the $500." (This approach is not for the meek or the broke.)

TIP
If $500 isn't enough to do the trick, make it $1,000 or $2,000. When you find the right sum, I guarantee you'll finish the task on time.

AFFILIATE

Some tasks are too challenging—you can't face them alone. Is somebody else trying to accomplish the same task you've been putting off? If so, you have a perfect partner or *affiliate* with whom to join forces.

PLAIN ENGLISH
Affiliate   An associate who has the same interests or goals that you have.

Whenever you can find someone who's up against the same challenges you are, you have the increased potential to achieve your goal.

REPORT TO SOMEBODY

One of the reasons you don't procrastinate at work as often as you might at home is that at work you generally report to a boss who is waiting for the results of your efforts and who pays you based on your efforts. If you don't complete your work, identifiable penalties will ensue.

TIP
If you have somebody waiting for your results, or waiting to hear about your progress, you significantly increase your ability to get started and to stay with the task at hand.

Although you don't necessarily want to treat personal tasks like assigned tasks, having to report your progress to someone increases your odds of starting and finishing in a timely manner. Even though this person isn't paying you, you're completing the task based on personal pride.

DELEGATE

Is there a portion of the task you can delegate? Particularly the part you don't like to do or are not good at doing?

Let's face it: There are some tasks that no matter how hard you try, how many lessons you take, and how long you practice, you're not going to be good at. But someone else will be good at them. Delegate the tasks to that person.

If you don't have the luxury of being able to delegate, maybe you can swap tasks. In return, take over what the other person doesn't want to do or isn't good at.

TIP

Some people will never be good at playing the piano, some will never be good at programming, and some will never be good at creative writing. This is simply human nature. If you want to "nurture your nature," as Jim Cathcart says in his book, *The Acorn Principle,* capitalize on your strengths and shore up your weaknesses by getting help.

FIND A GUIDE

Is there someone in your office or the organization who can talk to you for 5 or 10 minutes to get you started when procrastination is holding you back?

Particularly for tasks that seem overwhelming, if you can find someone knowledgeable about the situation who can give you a running start, ask that person to do so. After that person leaves, keep going on that task.

WAYS TO HELP YOURSELF

If you're facing an unpleasant task, it makes sense to follow it up with something you enjoy doing. In other words, you don't get to do what you enjoy until you do the unpleasant task.

TIP

In his book *Bringing Out the Best in People,* Dr. Aubrey Daniels calls arranging an award following a good performance the "grandma principle." As Grandma would say, you don't get to eat your ice cream until you eat your spinach.

Got Rest?

Half the time you can't get started on something because you are fatigued (see "Getting Sleep, Staying in Balance" on page 23). When you're well rested and well nourished, you have the greatest chance of doing your best work. Conversely, when you don't have enough sleep and haven't eaten well, even the simplest of tasks can loom larger than it really is.

Barricade Yourself

Sometimes it makes sense to simply hole up somewhere so you can give your full attention to the task at hand.

Instead of going in to work, maybe you can work at home one day. Maybe you need to go to a hotel room. The point is to get yourself totally away from others so that no one can reach or find you, so that you have the opportunity to give your full attention to what you want to accomplish. When you're done, you'll find that your stress about it is vanquished!

The 30-Second Recap

- Identifying in vivid terms the consequences of not getting started and not accomplishing what you want to accomplish may be a sufficient incentive for you to get started.

- At any time, for any task, if you have trouble getting started, you have a variety of techniques to draw on to get you over the hurdle.

- Not all techniques work for all people, and no technique will necessarily work for any individual all the time. Try as many as necessary until you successfully get rolling.

The Stress of Information Overload

In this section, you learn techniques for more effectively managing the information that overloads you on a daily basis.

I'm Overwhelmed by Information, Therefore I Am

The amount of information that you ingest to further your career can be staggering when you add it all up. In the course of a week, you may find yourself reading anywhere from 10 to 20 hours. In the information-packed society we all face today, information intake, largely in the form of reading, has undoubtedly become a major issue for you.

BASIC READING TECHNIQUES

Fortunately you can employ a variety of techniques to help get through your reading in record time, retaining what information you need to retain, and still feeling as if you have a life.

By *skimming,* you quickly find out whether you should read the article or chapter in greater depth. Often, skimming the first sentence or two is all you need to gain the essence of the information being provided.

PLAIN ENGLISH

Skimming   Reading only the first few sentences of each paragraph in an article in a magazine, on the Web, or in a chapter in a book.

Scanning allows you to review a greater amount of material. If you encounter a large book or report, it is not often practical to skim. Using the scanning technique, you can learn enough about the book or document to determine whether it merits greater attention.

PLAIN ENGLISH

Scanning   Reviewing lists, charts, or exhibits in a book, an index, a table of contents, some of the chapter leads, and an occasional paragraph.

TIP

Often, through scanning, you can identify the handful of relevant passages or pages worth photocopying, and then just recycle the book or report. (If you are concerned about the legality of photocopying, remember that if it is for limited personal use, you are not violating any copyright laws.)

EVALUATING THE SOURCE

Rather than plow through dozens of industry journals or Web sites, pick the best two or three, extracting or downloading articles of importance. Then you've cut down on the total volume you are exposed to, while relatively assuring that you're being exposed to the best and latest of what's going on in your industry or profession.

TIP

The best sources are "the best" because they routinely provide the best information.

ASSEMBLING YOUR TOOLS

If you use a stick-em pad, paper clips, felt-tip pens, magic markers, scissors, and the like when you read hardcopy items, be sure to have them nearby.

When you extract or highlight information, you reduce your reading burden. Organize your information by maintaining a lean, mean file consisting of the material you're most likely to act upon.

CUTTING BOOKS DOWN TO SIZE

Many professionals lament the lack of opportunity to tackle some of the current longer, nonfiction books available. Amazon.com and BarnesandNoble. com make it abundantly clear just how many new books are out there. An article or slim report is one thing, but a 280- or 300-page book is a whole 'nother story.

TIP

As the Internet economy advances, much of what we know about management, product distribution, marketing, and customer service will change dramatically as a result of e-business opportunities.

Unquestionably there will be longer books you will want to read. Here are some ideas for getting through them in a highly productive manner:

- First, read the back jacket in detail. Here you will see what others have said about the book. This may prompt you to make a more concerted effort once you actually get inside.

- Also read the inside flaps. This material is usually written by the author but is presented as if written by the publisher. This is what the author wants you to know about the book and about him- or herself.

- Read the foreword to the book, if there is one. A friend of the author who is saying things about the author and the book that the author wanted to have said usually writes the foreword. A well-written foreword often serves as an "executive summary" to the entire book. It also often gives some insights as to the author's slant or bias.

- Read the table of contents. There may be some chapters that you decide to read immediately. Likewise, there may be other chapters that you determine you can safely skip.

■ Read the introduction, usually written by the author and also providing an executive summary of sorts.

TIP

As you proceed to the chapters you have decided are most worth your attention, read at least the first two paragraphs. This will often tell you if you want to read the rest of the chapter. For those chapters where you don't want to continue, the first two paragraphs will usually at least give you a reasonable idea of what was covered.

■ Go to the last page of each chapter and read either the last paragraph, any summary, or highlights list that is presented. These can be invaluable and, in some cases, serve as a substitute for reading the entire book.

■ Review any resource lists, reference lists, charts, or graphs that strike your fancy as you flip through the book. When you are trying to save time, such features can be worthwhile.

■ Go to the last chapter and read the last two or three pages. The author's major conclusions and observations are usually presented here. This will save you from reading at least the last chapter, possibly the last section of the book, and possibly the entire book.

■ Always, always, always photocopy the handful of key pages you believe will have future value for you.

READING ON THE RUN

A two- or three-page article can easily be folded and kept in your pocket. The next time you're stuck in any kind of line, pull out the article and read for a couple of minutes. You won't feel much stress or anxiety for having to wait in line, because you're being productive. Sometimes you'll finish the whole article. Sometimes you'll hardly get started, when you find yourself at the head of the line. No problem—put the article back in your pocket for the next line.

TIP

Pull out your article on the bus, train, plane, or taxi ride.

Don't take a ton of reading material with you when you're traveling for business, because you inevitably end up creating more stress and more tasks for yourself that you can't fully act upon when you are on the road.

TIP

Do take the thin files representing the few key articles and few key pages you want to get to. This is easy to handle and will only get lighter as you chuck the pages you no longer need.

If you have a lot of reading to do, sometimes it is more effective and easier mentally to mix some of the longer, involved articles with the shorter, easier ones. By alternating back and forth between the complex and the simple, you continue to mow down the pile without taxing your intellect too much.

GET THEE TO A QUIET PLACE

Obviously, the quieter the place where you read, the faster and easier you will be able to get through the pile. Yet, if you have some familiarity with what you are reading, even a somewhat noisy place can be a sufficient environment. Find a quiet sanctuary whenever you are reading the following:

- Highly technical issues
- Items with which you have little familiarity
- Heavily philosophical or think pieces
- Anything that requires you to pause and reflect before proceeding.

It is just too difficult to do this kind of reading when surrounded by distractions. In any case, make it part of your reading task to find the place where you personally find it most conducive to tackle the subject matter at hand.

TIP

Undoubtedly you know the value of reading early in the morning before others come into your office, or before you have left your house. The same holds true for the evening, after everyone has left the office, or at home, after everyone else has retired.

Anytime you find yourself unable to sleep, particularly for more than a 30-minute stretch, fill in the time with reading. Sleep specialists say that reading is a worthwhile technique to engage in until you feel drowsy again and can nod off.

LESSENING YOUR TASK

When you suspect that a subscription is perhaps still worth the money but not worth your time, let it go with the last issue. If you don't miss it, you are ahead of the game. If you do miss it, the publication will take you back, often at a reduced rate. Perhaps you can gain the same information online, or visit the library periodically and peruse three or four issues of the same publication at high speed.

TIP

Anytime you come across a review of a book, an excerpt, a critique, or anything else that gives you the essence of what the book says, you are ahead of the game.

You can safely listen to a cassette as you drive (an entirely different activity than talking on a cell phone, which actively competes for the attention crucial to safe driving). This is a relatively easy way to gain information, avoid eye-strain, and still arrive on time.

TIP

Many libraries stock books and lectures on tape—and, in most cases, abridged versions.

NEWSLETTERS HELP ENORMOUSLY

By scanning a couple of newsletter directories in the reference section of your library, you can determine the key newsletters in your industry or profession. The *Oxbridge Directory of Newsletters, The Newsletter Yearbook,* and *National Trade and Professional Organization* each gives information about key newsletters that are available for a fee or for free.

TIP

Newsletters cut down on your overall reading time. Their implied mission is to supply you with succinct, well-crafted, critical infor-mation so that you don't have to round it up yourself.

With the plethora of online 'zines, you can achieve the same results without leaving your desk. Be wary of surfing the Web aimlessly because the infinite labyrinth of information out there will consume your life if you let it!

TIP

BarCharts at www.barcharts.com and Permachart Quick Refer-ence Guides at www.cram.com offer well-constructed, full-color, information-laden, laminated charts on a variety of computer, acad-emic, health, and business topics. The charts are illustrated, light-weight, durable, and a marvel to behold.

THE 30-SECOND RECAP

■ Skimming the first sentence or two of each paragraph of an article, and scanning a book's table of contents for selected chapters, are two highly effective ways to get through massive amounts of reading material.

■ Don't take too much reading material with you when you're traveling for business.

■ Do take the thin files representing the few key articles and pages you want to read.

■ Invest in any online service, newsletter, or briefing service that succinctly captures the essence of important issues in your industry.

Taking the Stress Out of Travel

In this section, you learn ways to manage stress while traveling, including organizational tips and ideas for relieving stress on the road.

ATTITUDE ADJUSTMENT

If you've traveled anywhere lately, particularly by air, you don't need a lecture on how hectic travel has become. More people are traveling to more places than ever before. The travel industry hasn't caught up, or apparently woken up, to the fact that yesterday's level of service is no longer sufficient. Often your challenge as an individual traveler is making the journey from point A to point B with the least amount of stress.

A key to reducing travel stress is simply maintaining a positive attitude. Much of the stress of travel results from encountering new things and experiencing situations beyond our control. Most people are accustomed to having a large degree of control over situations in their daily life. Frustrating as it may be, even with perfect planning, traveling is one of the activities we often cannot control.

TIP

If you can step back and evaluate your attitude, you likely can curb many of the emotional responses that lead to travel stress. It is your option to control the way you experience a situation. Relax and focus on maintaining your perspective and a positive attitude.

GETTING ORGANIZED IS THE KEY

Getting organized and establishing systems (much as you do in the work-place) is fundamental to traveling with less stress. For example, long before your next trip, make yourself a packing list and keep it in a file on your computer. Print it every time you pack for a trip, and you save yourself a lot of time and energy.

TIP

For some trips, not all items on your list need to be printed because you won't be taking them. So print a modified, *shorter* list.

Personal organization expert Barbara Hemphill advises making a box next to each item and checking it off as it is packed. Here are her suggestions, clothing and personal items excluded:

Basics:

- Tickets, itinerary
- Passport and necessary visas
- One or more business outfits
- Address book
- Car/hotel confirmation numbers
- Maps and directions
- Daily calendar, appointment information
- Calculator
- Notepad
- Business cards
- Medications
- Basic toiletries and makeup
- Reading glasses/contact lenses
- Cash and credit cards
- Small bills for tipping

Electronics:

- Portable phone
- Notebook or palm-size computer
- Power adapters and cables

- Floppy disk drive, zip disks, CD-ROM
- Drive and blank disks
- Modem and connector cable
- Phone cord with connectors
- AC extension cord or power strip
- Electrical and phone adapters
- Pocket dictator and tapes

Presentation tools:

- Overhead transparencies or slides
- Laser pointer
- Handouts (or master copy)
- Company brochures
- Product samples

Office supplies:

- Notepaper or letterhead, envelopes
- Blank overnight courier forms
- Return address labels
- Mini-stapler and staples
- File folders, sticky notes

Miscellaneous:

- Money belt or pouch
- Portable alarm clock
- Neck/back pillow
- Earplugs and eye mask
- Luggage tags

Travel has become the largest international industry. Large numbers of retailers offer items geared toward the needs of travelers. Not all travel gadgets are worth your attention; however, you should consider any product that you feel will help you manage your travel hassles.

PREPARATION GOES A LONG WAY

The more you travel, the more important preparation becomes. Make lists of all the travel resources—airlines, hotels, car rental agencies—you frequently use. Categorize these services and include their contact numbers and any important details about their service.

TIP

Always keep a copy of this list with you when you travel. That way, if something happens or your plans change, you have the numbers to contact.

For safety purposes, it helps to carry one copy of everything on your person and another copy in your luggage. One traveler uses business-card-size information cards that include his name, address, insurance numbers, and contact numbers for credit card companies and banks. He then keeps several of these cards stashed away throughout his luggage and on his person, thereby guaranteeing that this information will be at hand whenever necessary.

PACKING ONLY WHAT YOU NEED—AND NO MORE

As a general rule, most travelers overpack. *Overpacking* is unnecessary and causes extra hassle.

PLAIN ENGLISH

Overpacking   Taking more items than is necessary while traveling. This extra baggage generally overburdens travelers, taking up their time and energy.

At most destinations in the developed world, one can purchase nearly anything. As for those extremely necessary and hard-to-find items (prescription drugs, contact lenses, your favorite kind of herbal tea), you won't forget them if they're included on your detailed packing list.

TIP

If you tend to overpack, lay out everything you think you need and then cut this by half.

Consider keeping a bag already packed with your essentials. How much time would you save by keeping your travel toiletries prepacked in your luggage? Organize your arsenal of travel essentials (your headphones, that little pillow, those great earplugs), and don't bother unpacking them each time you return home.

TIP

Learning to minimize your packing makes traveling less of a hassle.

Your Wardrobe

Particularly for business travel, it's necessary to keep your wardrobe looking coordinated and sharp. Create a basic travel wardrobe filled with some essentials that you can coordinate with many items. Invest in a basic suit and several coordinating shirts and accessories. Also consider reserving several pieces of clothing just for travel. By creating a designated travel wardrobe, you eliminate the hassle of having to make endless choices when you pack.

When packing, the primary objectives are to keep items organized and wrinkle-free. Putting different items in plastic bags—one for socks, one for underwear, and so on—can keep your wardrobe organized. Also keep shoes wrapped so they won't dirty other clothing.

TIP

When packing clothing in a suitcase, rolling items will minimize the space necessary for each item and also reduce the amount of wrinkling and creasing. For nicer garments, especially dresses and suits, hanging bags greatly reduce wrinkling.

Scout Your Destination and Check the Weather

Even if you weren't in the Boy Scouts, "Be prepared" is the lesson to be learned here. One of the best ways to reduce stress when traveling is to be prepared and know what to expect at your destination(s). Travel guides are a great resource for any traveler, business or recreational.

Besides providing information on restaurants, hotels, and sightseeing, travel books usually explore history and culture, as well as provide information on public transport and prices for everyday items. Guidebooks also include information on language, especially regional slang.

TIP

Knowing ahead of time what to expect when you are traveling in a new city or country will help you stay calm and in control.

When planning a trip, try to be aware of any travel-related news regarding your destination. Also pay attention to news that might be affecting the city and its business community. Needless to say, checking the weather is a must.

TIP

The Web is a great tool for travel preparation. At www.weather.com, among many other sites, you can get up-to-the-minute weather reports. Also use any popular search engine to find Web sites about the cities and areas where you will be traveling.

MAINTAIN A ROUTINE

Perhaps the most stressful element of travel is the strain it puts on your body. Crossing time zones, eating airplane food, sleeping in unfamiliar beds, and maneuvering in unfamiliar places all disrupt your normal routine. The most effective way to reduce travel stress is to be aware of the routines that you *can* maintain and to make every effort to do so.

Many people exercise to manage stress in their daily lives, and there is no reason they shouldn't continue to do so while traveling.

CAUTION

The stress of travel, both physical and emotional, means that exercise is probably all the more necessary during travel if you are accustomed to a daily workout.

GET THEE TO THE FITNESS CENTER

In response to the complaints of overstressed travelers, many hotels and airports now have fitness centers. Most of these centers have weight machines and cardiovascular machines.

Outdoor exercise, such as walking or jogging, is a great way to enjoy a new city. If schedule or circumstance won't allow for a full workout, a routine of floor exercises and stretches can significantly reduce tension and muscle tightness.

PERSONAL RITUALS

Maintaining small routines and rituals also helps you adjust to a new place. Do you usually listen to music while you get ready in the morning? If so, you might want to consider purchasing a small travel radio or set of headphones in case your accommodations don't provide such.

Do you read a little before you go to bed? Then don't forget that book you've been working on.

TIP

Keeping such essentials prepacked or included on a detailed packing list ensures that traveling won't disrupt your small routines.

FUEL FOR THE ROAD

Perhaps the biggest challenge of all while traveling is maintaining a healthy diet. This becomes even more difficult if you are sensitive to certain foods or maintain a vegetarian or otherwise specific diet. When eating out, look for restaurants with large menus offering a variety of options. These allow you the most room to tailor your meal to suit your needs.

CAUTION

Travel can pose a serious threat to your digestive tract. Not only does your body suffer stress from the changes in dietary habits, but the stress that often accompanies travel can also affect the way you digest food.

To build up a good resistance before traveling, eat yogurt for several days before a long trip. The good bacteria in active yogurt cultures help your digestive system do its job well. Think of it as getting a tune-up before a long car trip.

FAST FOOD, CRASS MOOD

Beware of fast food. While it may be convenient, fast food contains gluttonous amounts of fat and unhealthy carbohydrates. Your body doesn't appreciate this food on a normal day, much less when you're enduring hours in an uncomfortable car or airline seat.

TIP

For emergency travel rations, carry packets of soup mix or dried fruits and nuts. Focus on foods that pack a lot of energy, without heavy grease or carbohydrates.

If you must resort to fast food (and there's no logical reason why you should), avoid the condiments (worse than the food), the highly sugared drinks (water is still free), and the calorie-laced deserts (the last thing you need while in motion).

The Evils of Airline "Food"

Airplane food is an evil deserving of its own circle in Dante's *Inferno*. No matter what the flight time, an airline usually schedules at least one meal or snack. Unless you are genuinely hungry, graciously decline the food. Also avoid alcohol when flying.

CAUTION

Although it can be relaxing at first, alcohol will later dehydrate your system.

To compensate for the dry air, try drinking water or juices, avoiding soft drinks, which will dehydrate your system. I suggest bringing a bottle of water with you.

TIP

Avoiding unnecessary food relieves your body from having to work overtime on digestion.

Travel breeds bad food habits. Succumbing to bad food and unhealthy meal-times puts undue stress on your body in the long run. By watching your diet while you travel, not only will you help your digestive system, but you also help maintain the routine of your daily life, making travel less stressful on your body.

CAUTION

Be aware of your body and its needs. Travel-related overexertion or stress on your body can cause illness. Often people return from a vacation or business trip and get sick. Days of bad sleep and unhealthy food eventually catch up with us—hence the frequency of the post-travel bug.

Sleepless in Seattle?

Like dietary habits, sleep is easily disrupted by travel, partly because of the stress placed on your body. Also like food habits, disrupting your sleep pattern can significantly add to the stress you experience while on the road.

Some people are lucky enough to be habitually deep sleepers. Nothing can stop them from getting a good night's sleep. Unfortunately, most of us need our own bed, our room, and our comfy pajamas to get a good night's rest. We're the ones who have trouble sleeping while we travel.

If you have trouble sleeping, pack some of your sleeping accessories. Bring your favorite pajamas and go through all the normal motions of going to bed. If you are accustomed to sleeping with earplugs or an eye mask, don't forget to bring them when you travel.

TIP

Why worry about making yourself adjust to a new environment when you can adjust the environment to your needs?

When you find yourself under a lot of stress and unable to sleep, consider relaxation techniques. Take a few moments to practice deep breathing. Do some exercises or stretches to work out the tension of the day. Or try taking a bath or indulging in some hot herbal tea.

INTERNATIONAL TRAVEL

Besides the obvious difficulties of long flights and jet lag, international travel poses the problems of navigating through a radically different everyday world. Being prepared is even more crucial to handling your stress in international travel.

TIP

International travel requires attention to language and cultural differences. This is when reading guidebooks can help you prepare. Most guides help you address what amenities you can expect to find in another country and what extras you might want to bring along.

The most stressful priority of international travel is keeping track of all your important documents and information. The earlier tips on getting organized are particularly helpful if you travel abroad.

Guidebooks address problems such as getting or changing money and what to expect when going through customs or immigration upon entry. Be sure to bring along any books or other information that might help you while traveling, or simply copy the necessary pages and leave the rest of the book behind.

TIP

Contact Kemal Cagri at Briggs Passport and Visa Expeditors when you need able assistance with paperwork and documents often required by foreign governments. Call 202-347-2240 or visit www.abriggs.com.

THE 30-SECOND RECAP

- Simple steps to organize your plans and your packing can significantly reduce your travel stress.

- Maintaining daily routines, such as diet, exercise, and sleep habits, also decreases the effects of travel stress.

- Days of bad sleep and unhealthy food eventually catch up with us—hence the frequency of the post-travel bug.

- By being aware of your body and attitude, you can maintain balanced habits and a positive frame of mind.

The Time/Money/Stress Connection

In this section, you learn the relationship between debt and the stress of having to work longer to pay for it, and you learn ways to keep your expenditures to a minimum.

THE MORE YOU SPEND, THE MORE YOU MUST EARN

Suppose you woke up one morning and found yourself in a society in which the typical person continually overspends. Suppose that the average person were in debt by several thousand dollars, as reflected by national credit card statistics. The people, furthermore, literally count on their next paycheck to meet monthly expenses (stressful!) and pay down credit card debt. In spending more than they earn, the people in this society work longer hours so as not to fall further behind. Hence, they have less discretionary time.

If you found yourself in such a place, where do you think you would be? If you guessed the United States, you are correct. Personal savings in the last few years have continued to dip while personal debt continues to rise. The typical person in a debt situation, in terms of liquid assets, has greater debt than savings. This may seem astounding to you, or you may understand it completely if you fall into this category.

CAUTION

When you continually spend more than you take in, you set yourself up for a life—at least in the short run—of working more and enjoying it less. And you may end up squeezing out moments of leisure time because of the obligation that you have incurred.

Living within your means is one of the best techniques you can employ for effective stress management, although it is curious that this observation is rarely cited.

TIP

In *The Millionaire Next Door,* authors Dr. Thomas Stanley and William Danko reveal how the typical millionaire in America today long ago developed a habit of living below his or her means. Most millionaires found a way to spend less than they earned week after week, month after month, year after year. They invested the savings and benefited from the compound interest that accrued.

Optimism Is Fine, Up to a Point

The U.S. Social Security Administration figures indicate that 80 percent of Americans who retire have less than $10,000 a year to support themselves. What is worse, 50 percent have less than $5,000 per year to support themselves. The typical person between the ages of 45 and 54 has only $2,300 in assets, and by retirement, those assets have grown to only $19,500. "Not so bad: People will be covered by pension plans," you say?

CAUTION

Less than half of all Americans are able to participate in any kind of company pension plan. Among those who can participate, average annual payments are less than $5,000, and this sum has been decreasing for many years.

Concurrently, optimism among baby boomers regarding their retirement years is substantial, if not unwarranted. In a Gallup Poll of successful baby boomers from Rocky Mountain states, 43 percent said that they are not contributing to any kind of retirement plan. Twenty-five percent said that they have not done any financial planning. At the same time, 92 percent of respondents felt that Social Security would not provide the level of financial support they will need for retirement.

CAUTION

The combination of insufficient savings and insufficient support in later years can only spell one thing: great masses of people working well past what would normally be considered retirement.

TAKE A WALK WITHOUT YOUR WALLET

When was the last time you went for a walk without bringing any cash, checks, or credit cards with you? All around us, household goods, professional goods, electronic gadgets, leisure items, gourmet foods, and sleek transportation vehicles abound. Too easily, we are caught up in consumerism, in what is proving to be a highly materialistic society.

One way to get in some good exercise without spending is to leave home some evening without your wallet. Walk around your neighborhood, or if you are in the vicinity of a shopping center, walk to it. As I pointed out in my book *The Joy of Simple Living,* it's a revealing test of character to walk past a row of stores without stopping in or buying something.

TIP

Taking a walk without your wallet enables you to discover the simple pleasure of walking!

Taking a walk without your wallet diminishes impulse buys. Often, when contemplating whether to buy that item you saw on your stroll, the notion subsides and you conclude that you can do without it. If you happen to see something that makes good sense to acquire, you always have the option of returning at another time.

What if you encounter something on a walk that will save you time or hassle? So much of what is offered today is couched in terms of being a time-saver. Consult with the most successful people in your profession. Have they retained such devices? How do they use them? Whether or not such assessment is available, use a simple rule of thumb: If you value your time at $20 an hour, and in a year you can save at least 50 hours, that accounts for the $1,000 purchase. If you can save more than an hour and the device will last longer than a year, the answer is abundantly clear.

TIP

If a device will save you an hour or two a week for at least a year, you make $40,000 or more, and the device costs $1,000 or less, buy it.

MAKING FRUGALITY PAY OFF

Consider the situation in which you are thinking of buying a new car. The old one still runs well but is starting to look a bit worn. If you use your car extensively as part of a job, and clients need to perceive you as highly successful in order to do a lot of business with you, this may be a no-brainer issue: Go buy a new car.

Short of being a salesperson or in a situation in which your car is a fundamental part of your interaction with clients or customers, there is a host of issues to consider. For most people, $1,500 to $2,000 for auto-body repairs and a paint job would be more than sufficient to restore that new-car look to their vehicles. The payoff for such a maneuver is many-fold:

■ The job can be done in as little as three or four days, so whatever disruption ensues, it is less than if you purchased a new car, which would either be delivered from the factory or require all kinds of dealer "prep" before you could actually drive it.

■ Because of technological improvements in automobile repainting, you can easily choose among hundreds of high-quality, highly durable colors.

■ Because you are retaining the same car, your annual vehicle taxes and insurance premiums do not go up.

■ If you already own your car, you have no new car payments. If you are still making payments on your car, chances are that the monthly outlay is less than a new car payment.

TIP

When you clean the interior of your car thoroughly and give it a new paint job, the combined feeling you experience closely rivals that of actually buying a new car.

This is just one example of how recycling, refurbishing, and upgrading what you already own enables you to reduce stress, save money, and ultimately continue to live within your means. Hence, you do not fall prey to the syndrome of working harder and longer to cover the debts you have incurred.

INVESTING FOR THE LONG TERM

Suppose you have two children, ages three and seven, and you intend for them to go to college. What a wonderful situation. You have a clear indication that roughly 11 years and 15 years from now, you'll need a certain sum per year for 4 years so that your child can attend a private or public university.

TIP

If you begin saving for such an eventuality now, in 11 years, you will be able to live a relatively normal life and work a relatively normal day while your children go to college.

Contrast this with what happens in far too many families: Too little is put away, even though the date the children will enter college is easily computed. Then with a few years to go, parents work harder and longer. Because they are working longer, they miss the time they could have spent with their children at ages 16, 17, and 18.

Unfortunately, by the time one of the children is ready to enter college, there still isn't enough money for the remaining college years, so the parents keep working while the child is in college. The child needs to get a job as well, which intensifies time pressure when it comes to studying. Ultimately, both parents and child experience time pressure for several years, because the parents didn't develop the discipline of saving regularly 15 years ago.

"Wait!" you say, this is a 10-minute guide on stress management. Why do I want to read about establishing a long-term savings plan? Because whether it is living within your means; saving for your child's future education; or saving for that special vacation, new home, or retirement, unless you start now, you will find yourself experiencing increasing pressure as you proceed in your career—particularly during those years you would prefer not to be working so hard.

CAUTION

Look around your office. Do you see people in their 50s and 60s who, by now, could have been well-off but still appear to be scrambling? Chances are they have not sufficiently developed the habit of investing for the future.

Assessing Yourself

If it is clear that you are heading down the same path, here are some ideas to ensure that you put aside some of your earnings today for the things that you want to do tomorrow:

- Practice the time-honored principle of paying yourself first. Every time you are paid, allocate a small amount—be it 5, 10, or 15 percent—from your paycheck and invest it immediately. There are many safe ways of investing, and any financial planner can advise you accordingly:

Savings accounts

Stock funds

Mutual funds

IRAs

SEPs

Keogh plans

401(k)s

TIP

If it helps, have your employer automatically withdraw a portion of your paycheck so that the investment becomes automatic and you don't have to think about it.

■ Continue to pay off loans after you have retired them, except now, pay yourself. For example, if you are about to pay off your car loan, the month after the loan is completely paid, redirect the usual amount paid on the car loan into your savings. Each month, continue to put the same amount into savings.

TIP

After paying off a debt, redirecting the payment to savings shouldn't be a burden, because you are already accustomed to not having that sum of money. You are not doing anything differently, except that you now contribute to a more prosperous future.

■ Do the same with pay raises. If you get a pay increase, instead of going out and immediately spending your money, invest the extra amount in some type of savings account. Again, since you are already getting by on the previous amount you were earning, it is well within your capability to invest the amount of your increase in a regular savings plan.

CAUTION

Don't fall prey to the trap of already "spending the money" in your head before you get to a new level of pay. This will only ensure that there is never enough, and well into your 50s and 60s, you will face recurrent income pressures because your debts exceed your earnings.

■ Get in control of your credit cards. If, when you sum up all the debt on all your credit cards, you find that it exceeds 15 percent of your monthly take-home income, you need to limit your spending right now. Pay down your credit card balances to zero if you can, or however far down you can go.

TIP

The goal in any given month is to have credit card balances that do not exceed 10 percent of your monthly take-home income. Also, you should try to pay the whole amount so that you incur no finance charges, which tend to be exorbitant.

Forewarned Can Lead to Forearmed

Remember that in terms of liquid assets, the typical income-earner today has greater debt than savings. In the short term, being in a cash-deficit position can be frustrating and routinely yield feelings of pressure. In the long term, it can diminish the quality of your life.

Develop the habit now of investing a portion of your earnings every month. You can do this through automatic withdrawals from your paycheck, "paying yourself" after completing loans, investing the difference each month after you receive a pay raise, or any other method that works for you.

The 30-Second Recap

■ The link between time, money, and stress is inextricable.

■ When you continually spend more than you take in, you set yourself up for working more and enjoying it less.

■ If you live within your means and invest wisely, financial security may be within reach.

Time Management

Understanding Time Management

In this section, you will learn the nature of time, explore the common myths surrounding time management, and develop a strategy that will allow you to systematically increase your personal productivity.

GRASP THE NATURE OF TIME

You know that there are 24 hours in a day and 168 hours in a week. You also know that sometimes these periods of time seem to race by without warning, offering you far less than the actual number of hours.

You don't have to study theoretical physics to understand that, for all practical purposes, time is relative. When you're facing a deadline, the minutes seem to click off the clock at a faster pace than when you're attending a lecture that bores you senseless. In the daily rush of contemporary society, too many hours seem to go by in far less than 60 minutes. When you get to spend an hour with a long lost friend or someone you genuinely look forward to seeing, for example, it seems as if you cover so much ground within that hour; compare this to how quickly an hour passes when you watch two television sit-coms.

CAUTION

The more tasks and activities you attempt to cram into a fixed time period, the faster that time period seems to go by—and the less you're likely to enjoy the time at all.

Why do we feel uncomfortable when our time races along? Human physiology has been in formation for tens of thousands of years; it took us a long time to develop into the type of species that we are today. Meanwhile, contemporary society is moving faster and faster. At work, more phone calls, more faxes, more e-mail, and more people knocking at our office doors all but ensure that each hour races by, at least from a perceptual standpoint. At home, more TV stations, more movies, more magazines, more books, and a greater variety of consumer goods all conspire to make it seem as if each hour and each day is flying by.

LESS CAN BE MORE ENJOYABLE

All around us society says, "Take on more; click me; sign on." However, we can only cram so much into a week, a day, or an hour. And we can only focus on so much. These days, it's rare to encounter advice that says …

- Take on less.
- Limit the field.
- Be more selective.

TIP

To maintain control of your time, it's wise not to have too many things competing for your time and attention.

Although there may be exponential growth in the number of items that compete for our time and attention, our lives are quite finite. You will die, I will die, everyone will die. Hopefully, each of us will die after a long and happy life. When we get to the end of our lives, will we be able to look back and say that we had time for reflection, time for quiet moments, and long stretches when things did not race by?

RIGHT NOW IS EVERYTHING

One of the keys to effective use of time involves recognizing a fundamental principle put forth by Robert Fritz, author of *The Path of Least Resistance*. He writes, "Right now is the most important moment in your life." How does Fritz know that right now, this moment, is the most important moment in each of our lives? What does he mean by this bold statement? Fritz is saying that at any given moment in your life, particularly right now, you should recognize that you can only take action in the present. For example, you can only enjoy your meal right now, or your workout, or that challenging assignment you're tackling.

TIP

If you know that right now is the most important moment, and then the next moment is the most important moment, and then the next and so on, you are far more inclined to be judicious with the use of your time.

Picture this: You're supposed to work on a project, but instead you're dawdling, or engaged in trivia, or diverting your attention in five other directions. Are you truly acknowledging that right now is the most important moment in your life? Probably not. When you can acknowledge that right now is the most important time of your life, it is far easier for you to concentrate on the task at hand. Plan to do this hour's job this hour, this day's work today, and so on.

More than 100 years ago, Bruce Barton wrote, "The most important thing about getting somewhere is starting right where we are." Less than a score later, Theodore Roosevelt said, "Do what you can, with what you have, where you are."

How can you ever get some place if you don't start with where you are?

Right now, you're starting by reading this section of the book, and delving into the nature of time. Good for you. It's worth your while, so stay with it. Don't turn on the TV; don't have music playing in the background; don't run to the refrigerator. Instead, stay right here and recognize that right now is the most important moment in your life.

Cut Through the Myths Surrounding Time Management

Managing your time is a worthwhile pursuit; beware, though—the myths surrounding the effective management of time can all but quash your efforts.

Time management, as we know it, essentially started with the work of Frederick Taylor and Frank Gilbreth.

One hundred years ago, they astounded the industrial world by establishing *time and motion* procedures that enabled employers to get higher productivity from their workers. In doing so, Taylor and Gilbreth established the basis of modern-day time management techniques, which were widely adopted by executives.

PLAIN ENGLISH

Time and motion studies   The attempt to elicit greater productivity from workers by closely examining their workstations, movements, and available resources.

In recent years, the backlash against Taylor, in particular, has been mighty. Some authors contend that his ceaseless quest for "the one best way" changed the very texture of twentieth-century life. Others contend that Taylor taught us not to stop and smell the roses, and that his compulsions eerily foreshadowed that time-pressure that everyone feels today.

CAUTION

More information is generated on Earth every hour than you could partake of in the rest of your life.

In any case, the industrial age has given over to the dawn of the information age. As I see it, the current difficulty is that we all face too much information, and that today many myths still abound as to what constitutes effective time management. Time management is subjective, varying from one situation to another. For example, time management advocates often advise handling each piece of paper that comes across your desk once. This sounds like reasonable advice; however, the number of times you handle a piece of paper should always depend on the contents or significance of the piece of paper.

Some pieces of paper are worth handling 25 times or more. Most pieces of paper, though, are best handled zero times—in short, never. You'll want to set up systems where much of what used to come across your desk never even comes into your field of vision. I will discuss this more in subsequent sections.

CAUTION

Every time you're exposed to paper, articles, or documents that are not related to what you are working on in your career or your life, you potentially add to the glut of all the things that compete for your time and attention, and perceptually make the hours slide by faster.

The Limits All Around Us

Suppose I start stacking bricks on a table, and that I can go as high as I want. What will eventually happen? The table will fall over—there are structural limits as to how much weight the table can bear. Or suppose I start stuffing college students into a Volkswagen Beetle. How many will fit? Who knows? If they are all slender, more will fit than if they are not. Whether it's 6, 8, or 10 students, at some point, I can't get another student into the car—there are spatial limitations.

Bearing this in mind, why, in allowing all manner of paper to cross our desks and all other things to compete for our time and attention, do we pretend that we can take on more and more and more, not paying attention to the temporal (time) limits that each of us face? An hour will remain 60 minutes, a week will remain 168 hours, and so forth.

TIP

The myth of "handling each piece of paper once" must give way to the reality that most pieces of paper should never cross your desk at all.

WHEN SPEED IS NOT DESIRABLE

Another myth of time management is that of the need to complete things faster. You see ads in magazines for speed-reading, speed-listening, speed-learning, and so on. The anthropological reality, however, is that we walk, talk, eat, and read—as well as listen and learn—at a certain pace for a reason.

When you attempt to undertake any bodily function, such as eating or talking, at a speed that is faster than is comfortable for you, you actually do harm to yourself. In the short run, you can get by with this kind of behavior. In the long run, though, you'll be prone to stress, anxiety, ulcers, and reduced immunity.

TIP

You need to operate at a pace that is comfortable for you.

If you feel time-pressured because of the responsibilities and tasks facing you, you must learn to marshal the resources necessary to meet the challenges (which I'll discuss in subsequent sections). However, don't walk faster, talk faster, eat faster, and sleep less in an attempt to be more productive.

PLANNING AND SCHEDULING TOOLS ARE NOT OMNISCIENT

Another time management myth, particularly common in recent years, is that you must rely on sophisticated *scheduling tools* as if they are the be all and end all. It only makes sense to use palmtop organizers, electronic calendars, time management software, day planners, and so on if they ...

- Support the way you live and work.
- Are convenient and easy for you to use.
- Are always up-to-date.

PLAIN ENGLISH

Scheduling tools   Palmtop organizers, electronic calendars, time management software, day planners, and any other device that supports one's use of time and productivity.

CAUTION

I bet you can't name a time management tool in the entire world that won't let you down the minute you cease to maintain it.

Even with forthcoming voice recognition time management scheduling tools, you will still have to "feed" the system. I will cover how to select and use a planner effectively in the section "Scheduling for Results" on page 81. For now, recognize that all tools you use to schedule your time—from simple to-do lists to complicated scheduling software—require your continual input and updating; otherwise, they quickly fail to reflect your current reality—including the tasks and responsibilities you face.

Moreover, until sophisticated time management tools come packed with a mechanical arm that literally moves the items that have been placed on your desk, logs them in, and then ranks them based on the workload you already face, you will forever be out of sync.

CAUTION

Until time management tools check your e-mail, fax machine, or voice mail, and similarly assess and rank what each of those messages represents in terms of what you now have to accomplish, you will continue to be out of sync.

Put simply, your brain is the most important tool in managing your schedule, your time, and your life.

Work Smarter According to Whom?

Another time management myth involves the notion that you must work smarter, not harder. If you had perfect information, a team of advisors, and an abundance of relevant resources, I suppose you'd have the opportunity to work smarter rather than harder. But what does "work smarter" really mean? Was Thomas Edison smarter after making more than 8,000 attempts to identify the proper filament in making the light bulb? After he finally found the right filament, did his IQ suddenly rise?

Working longer and being open to new ideas can help you to work smarter. To simply say to someone, "Work smarter, not harder," is out of context. Keep in mind that "work smarter, not harder" really means that you should take a little time to think about what you want to accomplish so that you start off in the right direction and assemble the necessary resources. This, in turn, increases the odds that you'll be able to complete the job more quickly and easily.

TIP

Sometimes the only way to work smarter is to work harder so that the insights that enable you to work smarter finally emerge!

INCREASE YOUR PERSONAL PRODUCTIVITY

Drawing upon Robert Fritz's observation that "right now is the most important moment of your life," you will find that you have the opportunity to systematically increase your personal productivity at any moment of the day. Similarly, Alan Lakein, author of *How to Get Control of Your Time and Your Life,* advised his readers to constantly ask themselves the following question: "What's the highest and best use of my time?" Fritz's observation, coupled with Lakein's question, produces a powerful combination.

On the one hand, you acknowledge that this moment is the most important moment of your life—the only moment when you can take action. At the same time, you ask yourself, "What would be the highest and best use of my time at this important moment?"

When you ask yourself this question, strange and wonderful answers often emerge:

- Sometimes the highest and best use of your time is to simply take a walk. For example, this is true when you're facing a tough problem and are not thinking clearly. A walk can help to clear out your mind. Sometimes, when you come back, the correct path simply emerges.

- Sometimes the highest and best use of your time is to look out the window and reflect; to make a key telephone call; or to lock your door, turn off the ringer on your phone, and barricade yourself in until you finish a particular task.

The highest and best use of your time often involves marshaling the resources you need to complete the project or task on time and within budget. Too many career professionals today throw their time and life at a problem, deplete their physical resources, and incur all kinds of stress and anxiety. They might finish by the deadline, but at what cost personally?

CAUTION

It's okay occasionally to maintain a deadline orientation. You will get things done; there is no real harm if you do this now and again. But if a deadline mentality ensues, meaning that's the way you do things all the time, you're either going to shorten your life or diminish your quality of life.

Determining the highest and best use of your time may necessitate clearing your desk, assembling material you need to tackle the project at hand, and delving into it headlong. Furthermore, determining the highest and best use of your time in the most important moment of your life, which is always the present moment, may require that you ask your boss for additional resources in the form of staff help, technology, or lesser burden in other areas.

Rely on Your Inner Wisdom

You already have a strong idea as to how to best proceed with most any situation that you face—even highly challenging situations. Too often, the problem is that you don't follow your own inner wisdom. Instead, you let yourself be buffed by external sources that in reality offer little contribution.

Rely on your instincts more often. Recent discoveries have demonstrated that there is far more to instinct, intuition, and gut feelings than was previously imagined. All the cellular intelligence throughout your body is called upon when you make a decision based on instinct. It is not random, it is not whimsical, and it is not foolish. Decisions based on instinct and intuition rapidly and automatically encompass all your life experiences and acquired knowledge.

The 30-Second Recap

- Recognize that the more items there are competing for your time and attention, the more time seems to speed by. Your quest should be to have fewer stimuli, to increase your powers of concentration on the task at hand, and to maintain your focus.

- Right now is the most important moment in your life, as is the next, and then the next. The realization that here and now is the only place in which you can take action is simple yet profound.

- Walk, talk, eat, read, and live in a manner that is comfortable for you. Don't fall prey to the false economy of speeding up bodily functions in the hope that this will somehow make you more efficient in the long run. Marshall the resources you need to handle a task, instead of continually throwing your time and life at tasks.

- Keep asking yourself the following question: "What is the highest and best use of my time right now?"

- Trust your instincts; they represent your accumulated experiences and acquired knowledge.

Shaping Your Future

In this section, you will learn how to identify priorities, set goals, and achieve the important things in life, in spite of the many demands on your time.

THE IMPORTANCE OF ESTABLISHING PRIORITIES

Why should you bother establishing priorities? When you identify what's important in your life, you are in a better position to meet the challenges and demands you face on a daily basis that can otherwise fritter away your time.

PLAIN ENGLISH

Your life's priorities   Those things that are most important to you.

Some people say that seeing their good friends on a regular basis is important, yet they make the cross-town trip only once a month. Some people say that maintaining their health and level of fitness is important, yet they never seem to find the time to exercise. Establishing and paying homage to the choices in your life that are important to you and how you prefer to dispense your time in pursuit of those priorities is essential to your having a more fulfilling life and managing your time more effectively.

TIP

Identify your priorities in some quiet place, away from distraction. At your desk, in your office, or in other familiar places, you're too likely to be interrupted by co-workers or friends.

THE BROAD CATEGORIES OF LIFE

Your life's priorities are uniquely yours. However, most people's priorities fall into a few basic categories. To help you get started with creating a list of priorities, take a look at the seven broad categories identified by Dr. Tony Alessandra:

1. **Mental.** Mental priorities might include improving your intellect, improving your memory, increasing your concentration, being a better learner, and being more creative.

2. **Physical.** Physical priorities could include achieving and maintaining overall fitness; acquiring skills in particular sports; improving agility, stamina, and endurance; and having a good level of well-being.

3. **Family.** Priorities related to family might include having a better relationship with your spouse, children, parents, siblings, or other loved ones. This category also encompasses the special people you consider to be part of your extended family.

4. **Social.** Social priorities might include being part of your community and having relationships with people in your neighborhood and outside of the family, as well as relationships with people in your business and industry. In short, priorities in this category ensure that your friends have an important part in your life.

5. **Spiritual.** Spiritual priorities might include having religion play a large part in your life, strengthening your relationship between you and your creator, becoming a humanitarian, and developing a personal philosophy.

6. **Career.** Career priorities might include rising to a certain level in your profession, gaining recognition, and achieving particular milestones. Priorities in this category can also encompass having a positive influence on others or developing yourself in unique ways.

7. **Financial.** Financial priorities could include securing your nest egg, putting your children through college, buying that dream house, and otherwise establishing a financial safety net for you and your loved ones.

This list is general; you may have major priority areas that aren't listed here. Perhaps one or more of the categories on the previous list aren't priority areas for you at all. The key notion is that you need to identify your priorities so that you can establish goals that will support those priorities. I can't give you an exact number, but you want to have only a few priorities in life. Eighteen is probably too much, and three might be too few. The number varies from person to person. In general, though, you should have just a handful of priorities. After all, a priority is a part of your life that you have identified as important. If you have too many priorities, then, paradoxically, they can't all be priorities!

CAUTION

If you have too many priorities, you are not likely to give each the required respect.

THE NITTY-GRITTY OF IDENTIFYING PRIORITIES

The procedure that follows is simple and direct and will help you establish priorities. Be careful! Priorities are broad elements of life. They are so basic that you can often misplace them somewhere in your go-go schedule. To stay on top of your priorities, follow these steps:

1. Write down everything that is important to you or that you seek to achieve. Feel free to make this list long and involved.

2. Revisit your list several hours later or even the next day. Cross out everything that, on second reading, no longer appears crucial. Combine any items that appear similar to each other. Your goal is to dramatically pare down your list.

CAUTION

If you have too many priorities, you are likely to feel anxious and frustrated, which is how most people these days feel most of the time.

3. Restructure, redefine, and rewrite your list if necessary. Keep looking to streamline it. If you are not sure if an item belongs on the list, the chances are that it does not.

4. Put your list away and take it out the next day or the day after that. Now review it as if you are seeing it for the first time. Can any items be combined? Can anything be dropped? Should anything be reworded? As always, if something seems as if it is not that important, it probably isn't, so feel free to drop it. Go ahead and create a working list of what you feel are your priorities at this time. Yes, things will shift and change as time marches on. After all, your priorities are based on what you identify as important in your life at a particular point in time, and because the details of your life are constantly changing, it makes sense that your priorities will change as well.

For now, however, concentrate on the few key important areas in your life and make them part of your list. For each of the items on your list, consider using an active, positive verb phrase, as in the following examples:

- "Achieve financial independence"
- "Strengthen my relationship with my spouse"
- "Provide for the education of my children"

By wording your priorities in this way, you are more inclined to take action than if you simply say "happy marriage" or "children's education."

You might find it particularly helpful if you make a *priority list.* Print your priorities on a small card that you can keep in your scheduler, purse, appointment book, or wallet. Carrying your list with you affords you the opportunity to review your priorities periodically throughout the day, particularly when you are stuck in a line somewhere. Losing sight of the things we have deemed as important is all too easy in our rush-rush world. Simply reading your list of priorities on a regular basis is powerful and reinforcing. As Dr. Tony Alessandra put it, reading your priority list often contributes to "your sensation of owning your life."

PLAIN ENGLISH

Priority list   A simple roster, preferably easy to access, that names a handful of things in life that are important to you.

GOALS TO SUPPORT YOUR PRIORITIES

You can establish a variety of goals in support of each of the priority areas you have chosen. Suppose that health and fitness are a priority for you; you can establish several goals to support this priority. For example, your stated goal could be: "I will join a health club this week and visit the gym at least three times a week for a 45-minute workout."

TIP

It is essential when establishing a goal to be as precise as possible.

Notice that this goal is very specific; it provides precise timelines and numbers. If you were to simply say, "I'll join a health club and work out a lot," you're not likely to get the same results as using a more precise statement. When will you join the health club? How often will you go? How long will you work out? Numbers and specific timelines give you something to strive for. Visiting the gym at least three times a week for a 45-minute workout is much different than simply being in the health club, gabbing with someone else, heading over to the juice machine, leaving early, and pretending that you got a good workout. By contrast, if rising in your career is one of your priorities, you might want to add these specific goals to your list:

■ To achieve a salary of \$___,000 by December 31 of this year.

■ To finish the three courses at the local community college this semester, so I'll have the requisite skills to move into x position.

■ To add two more people to my staff by the end of the month so that I will have the opportunity in the next quarter to experience supervising a staff of six.

■ To be transferred to the London office for two years by the end of the next quarter.

When setting your goals, follow these guidelines:

1. **Be sure the goal you set is something that you want to do as opposed to something that you have to do.** As I discuss in *The Complete Idiot's Guide to Reaching Your Goals,* your goals do not initially have to be set by you. If you are in sales, your sales manager may set your monthly or quarterly sales quota. Yet you can make a goal your own even if it is initially imposed upon you. There could be many very good reasons why you personally want to achieve that goal, such as an increase in income, competitive spirit, pride, or a job promotion.

2. **Establish your goals in positive terms, using positive terminology.** If one of your priority areas is health and fitness, and you have been chain-smoking for 10 years, it won't help to set a goal such as, "I will not smoke for one week." What happens during that week? You begin to dwell on smoking day after day, hour after hour, until you get to the point where you can barely stand it. A more effective goal statement would be "I will maintain clear, clean lungs this week."

3. **Write down your goals.** Writing down your goals helps solidify your efforts. Having your goals in a place where you can review them makes them more real. At the least, written goals serve as a visual reminder and confirmation of their importance. At the most, they are the guiding formula that will lead to a highly desirable end result.

WAYS TO REINFORCE YOUR GOALS

Anybody can establish goals. Unfortunately, most people's goals are all but forgotten days or weeks after they first establish them. Reinforcing the goals that you set so that you will achieve them is much tougher. Fortunately, there are many techniques you can employ to see that you stick to the goals that you set for yourself. For example, you could try the following:

■ Join a group of like-minded individuals

■ Harness the power of deadlines

- Visualize the completion of your goals
- Create backup systems

PLAIN ENGLISH

Reinforcement   Reward directly following a particular behavior.

Let's look at these options in more detail. Joining up with those who have common goals with you is a time-honored tradition in accomplishing goals. This might involve joining an organized group of people who have common goals (for example, many people who want to stay sober have joined Alcoholics Anonymous) or simply finding a friend who wants to achieve the same thing you do at around the same time you do.

Being accountable and reporting your progress to one or more others helps to ensure that your progress will continue. For example, if you tell me that you are going to accomplish something by next week, then next week when we meet, I will ask you about your goal. You'll either tell me that you accomplished it, or you will tell me something different. Simply knowing that we will be meeting and discussing the accomplishment of your goal may be the driving force that you need to be successful in achieving it.

TIP

When you have no one to report to, it is easy to slide. Having someone who is waiting to hear about your progress will increase the odds of your success.

Harnessing the power of deadlines also works well for many people. Up to now, you may have dreaded deadlines, seeing them as something imposed upon you that routinely fosters stress and anxiety. Yet deadlines can serve as powerful motivators toward the accomplishment of your goals.

For example, my contract for this book stated that I would turn in a certain portion of my manuscript by a certain date. If I had tried to write the entire book at once, I would have never finished it. Instead, my goal in approaching this book was to write one chapter at a time. In fact, because the chapters are made of subsections, I simply aimed to finish one subsection at a time, until I had finished a chapter. By the time I was finished with a chapter, I felt so good about my work for that day that the rest of the day seemed like a vacation.

The next day, I went back and started another chapter, approaching it one subsection at a time and always keeping the deadlines in mind. Without a contract that clearly stated the milestone dates by which I had to deliver portions of my manuscript, the likelihood of my delivering the work on time (if at all) would have dramatically decreased.

TIP

Always consider what deadlines you face that you can turn around and use to your advantage. What deadlines can you impose upon yourself to increase the probability of you achieving your goals?

Visualizing the completion of your goals is another powerful technique for increasing your probability of success. Most sports heroes today visualize successfully completing the foul shot, catching the touchdown pass, hitting the home run, completing the triple axle jump, or clearing the hurdle before engaging in the sport. By visualizing their performance, these pros increase their odds of success. Likewise, virtuoso pianists, ballet dancers, and even professional speakers visualize successfully engaging in the task at hand before they perform.

TIP

Visualizing yourself successfully completing the steps that lead to a goal you have established will increase your chances of success.

You probably visualize all the time by thinking about being with a loved one, having dinner that evening, or skiing during your next vacation in Colorado. You can use the same process to see yourself completing your goals.

Any goal, large or small, lends itself to the visualization process. Find a quiet place where you won't be disturbed, close your eyes, and let your imagination take hold. See yourself accomplishing exactly what you want to accomplish, in the way you want to accomplish it. If your goal is to achieve your ideal weight, visualize yourself working out and enjoying it and then stepping on the scale and seeing the pounds go down. Visualize yourself in front of the mirror without your love handles or without saddlebag thighs. See yourself as the trimmed, toned you that you know you can be.

Creating *backup systems* is another powerful technique that can help you reinforce your goals. Surround yourself with goal reminders; use Post-it notes that list your goal-reinforcing statements and post them on a mirror, in your appointment book, on the dashboard of your car, on or near your nightstand, on the refrigerator, by your front door, and wherever you are likely to pass during the course of a day.

PLAIN ENGLISH

Backup system   An established procedure whereby you help to reinforce established goals.

Write something that is uplifting and supportive of your efforts such as, "Today is going to be a great day for accomplishing my goals of ...." Vary the statements so that you don't start to ignore them. Put them in creative places where you know you will encounter them and where they will have the most impact.

I like to leave a note to myself in my appointment book at the end of each day. When I open up the appointment book to start the upcoming day, I see the uplifting note, smile broadly, and get to work.

THE 30-SECOND RECAP

- Priorities are the most important things in your life, so you can only have so many of them. If you have too many priorities, then, paradoxically, they can't all be priorities.

- For many people, priorities fall into seven broad categories including mental, physical, family, social, career, and financial priorities.

- Establishing written, specific goals with timelines is an effective way to support your priorities. Using a variety of goal-reinforcing techniques increases the probability that you will accomplish the goal.

Avoiding the Tyranny of the Urgent

In this section, you will learn to differentiate between the urgent and the important and to be able to use the Pareto Principle to identify your areas of focus.

KNOW WHAT'S IMPORTANT

If I could construct a simple grid into which all items that compete for your time and attention might fall, it would look like this:

	Urgent	Not Urgent
Important	1	2
Not important	3	4

Quadrant 1 holds those items that are important and *urgent.* Quadrant 2 collects those items that are important and not urgent. Quadrant 3 has those items that are not important but urgent, and Quadrant 4 holds those items that are not important and not urgent.

All too often in the workaday world, we find ourselves engaging in tasks that are urgent but, in retrospect, not important. If you could manage your time in an ideal way, then as often as possible you would focus on those tasks that are important and urgent. Assuming that urgency announces itself, like the rent coming due, the real question is knowing what's important.

In his lectures, author Dr. Stephen Covey contends that if you do pay homage to the most important things in your life, as you've identified them, you begin to find ways to fit everything. He uses the analogy of filling a glass jar with rocks, pebbles, and sand. If you begin to fill the jar with the pebbles and sand, you run the risk of not being able to get all the rocks into the jar. Now suppose you put the rocks in first, followed by some of the smaller pebbles, and then sprinkle in the sand. Voilà! Everything fits into the jar.

PLAIN ENGLISH

Urgent   That which cries out for attention independent of its importance, typically announcing itself much like a microwave beeping when it's time to take the food out of it.

In this analogy, the rocks represent important tasks that support your priority. The pebbles represent secondary tasks that are perhaps urgent but not important, and the grains of sand represent tasks that are neither important nor urgent. When you deal with the rocks first, a magical thing happens: You still find room for the secondary and tertiary items. They fit in and around the spaces available. If you attempt to do it the other way around, too often you end up giving short shrift to what is truly important in your life and dissipating your energy and efforts on the minutiae of life.

TIP

Stop doing what's unimportant and without urgency. Where the important and the urgent intersect (Quadrant 1) is where you need to expend most of your energies.

APPLY PARETO'S PRINCIPLE

Curiously, the relationship between urgency and importance was illuminated more than 100 years ago by the Italian economist Vilfredo Pareto (1848–1923). In 1897, Pareto discovered a relationship between inputs and outputs that has come to be known as the 80/20 rule, or the *Pareto Principle*. He found that 80 percent of what a person achieves is derived from 20 percent of the time the person expends. The key to effectiveness, then, is to continually identify the 20 percent of activities that are most important (that is, yield the greatest results).

PLAIN ENGLISH

Pareto's Principle   An observation about the relationship between inputs and outputs, essentially that 80 percent of one's effectiveness is derived from 20 percent of one's activities.

CAUTION

On any given day, only about $1/5$ of what you do accounts for $4/5$ of what you achieve.

When the Pareto Principle was applied in business and industry, startling observations followed. Within an insurance agency, for example, 20 percent of the agents generally produced 80 percent of the sales. In a hardware store, 20 percent of the floor space accounted for 80 percent of the profits. In an accounting firm, 20 percent of the clients generated 80 percent of the revenues. It made sense for such firms to focus their energy on finding and keeping long-term, profitable clients.

DOUBLE YOUR PLEASURE

In his book, *The Secret to Achieving More with Less,* Richard Koch observes that you can identify where your company is getting back more than it is putting in, and then focus on that area and become highly profitable. Conversely, if you can figure out where your company is getting back much less than it is investing, you can reduce expenses or diminish losses considerably. Your mission becomes one of continuing to identify the important activities—those that yield the greatest desirable results.

TIP

Koch advises that when something is working well, double or redouble your efforts. If something isn't working so well, change course often and early rather than infrequently and late.

Even among successful people, most individuals don't sufficiently engage in the activities that would make them successful, even when they know what those activities are. Either by habit or by decree, they maintain a schedule that pretty much allocates the same time and effort to the same kinds of tasks, even though not all tasks provide the same contribution to desirable ends.

Think about the times in the last month or quarter when you were highly successful on the job. What elements were present? Could you map it all out? What 20 percent of those elements were crucial to your success?

THE FEW KEY FACTORS

Of the hundreds and hundreds of factors that could influence the impact of my presentation when I make keynote speeches to groups, a handful are of paramount importance. For example, the lighting must be excellent, the sound system must be working well, and the temperature of the room has to be comfortable. If I take care of the handful of things that I know have the greatest impact on my success for that presentation, the odds are that everything will go well.

Sure, a host of other little things can crop up, but I could spend an inordinate amount of time trying to take care of everything. Instead, I focus on the handful of key factors that have proven themselves to be prominent. Likewise, in your own career, in big, long-duration goals as well as daily ones, you need to identify the handful of elements that need to be in place in order to dramatically increase your probability of success.

CAUTION

Too few career professionals spend enough time and thought on the handful of important factors that make a pronounced difference in what they are trying to achieve.

SYSTEMIZE, SYSTEMIZE, SYSTEMIZE

To make maximum use of your time, create simple but effective systems that accomplish what you want to accomplish without stressing your resources. The most ideal management system is that which works automatically with little or no input on your part.

TIP

Never manage what you can eliminate altogether.

A dramatic example of this occurred years ago when steel magnate Andrew Carnegie hired a high-priced consultant to increase the productivity of workers in Carnegie's factory. The consultant came in, studied the factory workers, and studied their daily output. Then one Sunday evening, he took a piece of chalk and wrote a huge number six on the floor. As the day shift assembled on Monday, they saw the number and assumed that it was related to how many units the evening shift was able to produce. That day, they produced seven units, and before leaving, they crossed out the six and near it wrote the number seven.

That evening, the night shift saw the number seven, heard that that was how many units the day shift was able to produce, and set about to produce eight. Over the course of the next two weeks, the number of units produced increased markedly, leveled off a bit, and then became the new standard.

The consultant had done his job with a piece of chalk and an understanding of the factory and its workers. He had prompted a friendly competition between the day and night shifts that resulted in a higher level of output thereafter.

BEYOND PARETO'S PRINCIPLE

Out of all the possibilities within your organization, what are the few key projects, the task forces, and the special teams you need to be on to propel your career? If you identify these and strive to be a part of them, you will benefit from the 80/20 rule!

You need to have friends in your field and nurture them on a regular basis. Without such allies, you're going to continually be reinventing the wheel and skating over thin ice. With such allies on your side, you catapult your career, transform your life, and accomplish so much more than you thought before you knew them.

 CAUTION

The larger your organization, the harder it is to be successful entirely on your own.

Who are the few key players with whom you need to ally within your organization? Yes, it pays to be on cordial terms with as many people as you can, but who are the few key people with whom it is crucial? A couple of co-workers? A mentor? A few people in another department? Protégés? Some of the higher-ups in the organization?

The best relationships are those that are what author Robert Ringer calls *value-for-value relationships*. Perhaps you give each other vital information, have high respect for each other, or have a shared experience. Long-standing and winning relationships are based on trust, reciprocity, and mutual enjoyment of each other's company. These relationships develop over time; it's hard to take shortcuts.

PLAIN ENGLISH

Value-for-value relationship   The parties both offer equally valuable or worthwhile contributions to one another.

If you are new in your career, choose mentors who can open doors for you, point you in the right direction, and save you bundles of time that you may have otherwise expended heading down wrong paths. What value do mentors get associating with you? Prudent mentors know that protégés help to keep them in touch with the times and alert to new opportunities and new trends on the horizon. If you doubt this, think of the last time you learned something from your kids that you wouldn't ever have learned on your own.

WELCOME PARETO'S PRINCIPLE IN SMALL FIRMS

If you work in a service organization, what are the key ways you can most effectively serve clients or customers that would cause them to perceive a dramatic increase in value-added services? You can't be all things to all customers. If you attempt this, you are like the man who jumped on his horse and rode off in all directions.

These questions will help you focus on the subject and goals at hand:

- What can you offer faster and easier than anyone else?
- How can you carve out a niche for yourself?
- How can you position yourself in the minds of those you want to serve and serve them in a way such that they remain loyal to you?

To answer these questions, you have to study what the best in your industry do and improvise. Don't necessarily do exactly what they do; do something a little different, a little more innovative, a little better. The key is recognizing the few important things that you need to do and having the mental and emotional strength to let go of the rest.

CAUTION

If you try to do it all, you end up frustrated, anxious, and sometimes burned out.

Are you willing to use your time to concentrate on those elements of your career or your business that add the most value to your constituents? To do this, you need to know where the companies or organizations in your industries make healthy or even gargantuan profits. Constantly be on the lookout to uncover the 80/20 principles at play in your own industry. If you are already very good at something, and it is in demand, work harder to be even better at it.

Do you already have a focus area where you are more knowledgeable than anyone else? Then study it even further and become the leader. Identify all the ways to benefit from the Pareto Principle, capitalizing on your service or knowledge advantage so that you induce strong demand for your services, engender loyal clients or customers, or even have people seeking you out rather than vice versa.

THE 30-SECOND RECAP

- After you have identified what is important and urgent, you are better able to allocate your time more effectively.

- To consistently stay productive, focus on what is important and urgent and have the mental and emotional strength to stick with it.

- The Pareto Principle or 80/20 rule applies to many aspects of life, and in particular, it applies to your career. Identify the handful of activities in your career that produce the greatest results and watch your career soar.

- Identify the handful of key allies you need to have in your organization or within your career and have them help you achieve your best.

- Identify the handful of key service elements you can offer to clients or customers that will encourage them to remain loyal and prompt others to seek you out.

Scheduling for Results

In this section, you will learn how to plan effectively so that important and urgent projects are accomplished on time.

THE FUNDAMENTALS REMAIN THE SAME

The ever-accelerating onslaught of new technology is constantly providing more and more tools to help you manage your time effectively. Today's planning software enables you to accomplish the following tasks:

- Manage your daily, weekly, and monthly schedules
- Align your daily activities with important and urgent tasks you face
- Plan projects
- Share files via downloads
- Electronically link your plans and schedules with others

With a palmtop computer, you can easily take your plans with you when you travel, maintain your database of contacts, send faxes, send and receive e-mail, and log onto the Internet (for more details see "Taming Technology" on page 113).

Despite the proliferation of these electronic and digital aids, however, the underlying components of effectively scheduling your time and making progress on selected tasks and projects remain the same. Any goal that you intend to achieve needs to be written down and quantified and has to have specific timeframes (as discussed in the section "Avoiding the Tyranny of the Urgent" on page 75). If you don't have a timeline attached to a task or project, it probably will never get done.

Whether you use traditional, nontechnical types of tools, such as hand-drawn charts or grids, or more sophisticated project management and scheduling software (on your desktop computer, notebook computer, or palmtop), you still need to plan. Carefully plotting the steps that lead to the desired result ...

- Greatly increases your probability of accomplishment.
- Can contribute to greater productivity.
- Is a fundamental concept in effective time management.

The basic three forms of project management and/or scheduling include milestone charts, flowcharts, and calendars.

The Milestone Chart Method

If you've ever been involved in any type of project management, you're probably already familiar with milestone charts, also known as *Gantt charts*. Milestone charts offer you an at-a-glance view of your progress on a variety of tasks and projects in relation to time, as shown in the following example.

PLAIN ENGLISH

Gantt chart   A linear, visual tool for measuring progress made in pursuit of various activities over the course of time.

	Month 1	Month 2	Month 3	Month 4	Month 5
Project 1	>>>>>>	>>>>>>>>>>	>>>		
Project 2	>	>>>>>>	>>>>>>	>>>>>	
Project 3			>>>>>	>>>>>>>	
Project 4				>>>>>>>>>>	>>

Milestone (Gantt) Chart.

Here is how these charts work: Suppose one of your priorities is to continue to advance in your career. One of your goals in support of that priority is to get a raise of $6,000 at the next quarterly performance and appraisal session scheduled in 11 weeks. To support that goal, you've identified five projects that will greatly enhance the value of your services to your boss and the higher-ups in your division:

- Rewriting the orientation manual for new hires
- Getting an article published in one of the top three magazines in your industry
- Starting an online monthly newsletter for your firm's top clients and prospects
- Completing the DEF report three weeks earlier than it is due
- Participating at the key trade show, where you make important contacts and gather critical information for your boss

Adding these five accomplishments to your performance record over the next 11 weeks beyond what you already do in the normal course of the day and week will be challenging, but you feel up to it.

How can you allocate your time and resources so as to complete each of these projects with a flourish and thus position yourself for the salary increase that you are after? One way is to plot each of the activities on a weekly milestone chart so that you have a clear indication of the timeline and sequencing of each of these activities and support of your overall goal.

Item	1	2	3	4	5	6	7	8	9	10	11
Rewrite manual	>>	>>>>>	>>>>>	>>							
Publish article		>>>	>>			>>>>		>>>			
Online zine				>>>	>>>>>	>>>>>	>>>>>	>>>>>	>>>>>		
DEF report					>>	>>>	>>>				
Trade show							>>>	>			

Milestone Chart (in weeks).

To begin, you plot the most basic information for each project. Then, extending the process a bit further, you can even have subtasks under each task area. For example, in getting an article published, you may first have to interview some people or conduct some research. Then you might have to organize your notes, create an outline, and then write a first draft. Next, you would write your second draft, have peer review, go for a final draft, and then submit the article to the leading industry publications. Finally, you have to follow up to ensure that the publishers are paying attention to what you have written. A milestone chart with subtasks may look something like the following example.

Item	1	2	3	4	5	6	7	8	9	10	11
Rewrite manual	>>	>>>>>	>>>>>	>>							
Publish article											
Interviews		>>									
Research		>	>								
Organize			>								
Outline				>>							
First draft						>>					
Peer Review						>>					
Second draft								>>			
Submit									>		
Follow up											>
Online zine				>>>	>>>>>	>>>>>	>>>>>	>>>>>	>>>>>		
DEF report					>>	>>>	>>>				
Trade show							>>>	>			

Milestone Chart with Subtasks.

You may have anywhere from 6 to 10 subtasks in pursuit of this task of getting an article published. The amount of detail is your choice. The important thing is that what you record is of value to you; it helps you to continue your progress toward your chosen goals. Likewise, with the other tasks, you may find yourself plotting anywhere from two or three subtasks to 15 or more.

CAUTION

List the level of detail that will serve you and no more. If you unnecessarily complicate the chart, it will be counterproductive to your purposes.

You can enhance the chart by adding symbols such as a broken line that denotes the beginning of the project, numbers that refer to footnotes at the bottom of the chart, left and right arrows that indicate periods of activity, and so on. If the chart is on the wall, on a single piece of paper on a file folder, or on your hard drive, you can use colors to help guide you along as well. Green, for example, could mark the start of tasks. Yellow could indicate some critical function. Blue could represent completion.

TIP

Write people's initials next to particular subtasks to represent the people whose cooperation is needed or perhaps to whom you will delegate the entire subtask.

Depending on the level of detail you are comfortable with, you could devise separate milestone charts for each task and carefully plot out all of the subtasks, assign start and stop times, use symbols to add detail, and use colors to denote progress. If you're working with different people on each task, then a separate milestone chart might make it easier for them. Similarly, when you consider the priority areas of your life and the goals you have selected in support of them, multiple milestone charts may suit you. However, you want to keep things as simple as possible.

The Flowchart Method

Most people have had experience with flowcharts at one time or another. Perhaps your grade-school teachers used circles and squares connected by lines to depict the relationship between numbers, explain the migration of nomadic peoples, or illuminate the interaction of chemical compounds.

Although flowcharts are widely used to convey the essence of a process, they also can be used to do the following:

- Track project progress
- Help you stay on target
- Help you accomplish your goals

Flowcharts are particularly useful in plotting activities related to one task or project area where many different people or resources are required and contingencies come into play.

Flowcharts also allow for feedback loops. If the answer to a question is *yes,* the flowchart proceeds along one path; if the answer is *no,* it proceeds along another. For example, if an article is submitted to a publication and the editor wants specific changes, the feedback loop could encompass where you go next, such as back to your desk for rewrite, before resubmitting the article and continuing along the line you have already traversed, but this time having made improvements.

Flowcharts can extend downward or to the right. In business, they usually extend to the right so that a timeline can be added to the top or bottom of the chart, as shown in the following example.

As with milestone charts, you can use colors and symbols to convey different types of information at a glance. For example, a triangle conveys a yes/no decision, a circle can be a connecting point, and squares offer information. A straight line represents a direct connection, a broken line is a partial or one-way connection, and a squiggly line indicates an interrupted or intermittent connection. You can draw symbols and lines in specific colors to convey another level of at-a-glance information. As always, remember to keep things simple.

TIP

Add a key at the bottom of the flowchart that shows exactly what each symbol and color represents.

THE CALENDAR METHOD

Using a calendar to ensure progress toward chosen goals is a time-honored method. Suppose one of your projects is to prepare a completely new orientation manual for new hires. This project must be completed by March 31, so you write "Complete manual" on the March 31 box on your calendar, as the following figure shows.

TIP

To make this system work, use calendar pages from the current year for however many months are relevant to the project you are managing.

Working from that end date of March 31 back to the present, you need to figure out what has to take place just before delivering the new orientation manual. For example, you need to meet with several department heads to offer your executive briefing and obtain their vital input at least a week before you turn in the manual. So you schedule a conference for March 22. Then you need to determine what has to happen before the conference.

In each case, plot the dates on the calendar, and then connect them with arrows that show the relationships of the dates. As in the case of milestone charts and flowcharts, you may use colors and symbols to give you a quick visual review of your progress.

Interestingly, with this calendar "block-back" method, you can quickly see that if you miss any interim date on the calendar, you will jeopardize the completion of the subtasks at the following interim dates. In essence, each interim date represents a mini-deadline. Hence, you have a nearly built-in system for ensuring that your project will continue according to plan.

TIP

For goals that stretch on for years or decades, starting with the end in mind is the only practical way to proceed.

The concept of starting with the end in mind and working backward also works well in other goal areas you may have selected. Suppose that you want to retire by age 65 with $850,000, and you are currently 32 years old. By making basic assumptions about interest rates and inflation and taking taxes into account, you can numerically determine how much you would have to save per year or per month to achieve your desired end.

TIP

Milestone charts, flowcharts, and large wall calendars are available at office supply stores or office supply Web sites. You can also buy erasable charts to make course corrections easier.

Scheduling Tools Fit for the Pros

More powerful, feature-laden scheduling software, calendar systems, and other project organizers become available with each passing month. All these scheduling aids offer some highly convenient common tools, including the following:

- A calendar system for tracking appointments, identifying schedule conflicts, and flagging areas and times of critical activity

- A variety of chart forms to choose from, including milestone charts, flowcharts, and calendars

- Drop-down menus, a drag-and-drop feature, and convenient icons

- The flexibility to add or subtract subtasks and activities in any desired sequence

- Colors, symbols, and other tools that offer at-a-glance information
- Alarms, bells, and buzzers that can be toggled on and off easily and set at certain times and intervals
- The ability to fax, e-mail, or download onto a Web site any chart file
- Multiple options for printing any chart

CAUTION

No matter how sophisticated the project manager or scheduling software you use is, it will be of little use if the information you are adding to it is not current or is inaccurate.

As with any planning or scheduling tool, someone has to be in the driver's seat. If you are not keeping up with the timelines you have established, particularly if you are sharing a scheduler with others, the schedule will quickly become ineffectual. Likewise, if you bite off more than you can chew, scheduling and planning tools may alert you to what you have done, but it is up to you to get back on track. In that respect, the most critical factor in planning and scheduling at all times is you!

THE 30-SECOND RECAP

- Milestone charts, flowcharts, and calendars are three of the most common types of scheduling tools. They offer a quick visual review of the sequence and interim progress toward completing tasks and projects in pursuit of a goal.
- Planning tools as part of a software program can easily be shared with others, making them ideal for team or group efforts.
- Any tool, whether manual or software-based, will break down the minute you don't keep it up-to-date.

Getting Organized

In this section, you will learn the principles of personal organization that will enable you to accomplish more in less time with less stress.

ENTROPY IN YOUR OFFICE

Some people seem to be born organized. When you look at their desks, offices, cars, and homes, everything seems to be in its place. The way they schedule and complete projects or even make time for leisure seems to say "I'm organized." Conversely, others seem to have a knack for disorganization. All the spaces in their lives seem to be cluttered. They never know where anything is.

However, being organized is not a matter of being born under a lucky star. Being personally organized involves learning a simple set of techniques and mastering a few basic skills.

Everything in the universe is subject to *entropy*. If you leave a field alone and come back several years later, the grass will be higher, weeds will abound, new plants will spring up. Indeed the natural state of planet Earth is abundance.

PLAIN ENGLISH

Entropy   That physical phenomena whereby everything, even the entire universe itself keeps expanding, keeps going forward.

Likewise, if you leave a house empty and abandoned for 10 years, the house will be subject to entropy. The yard will be overgrown. Cracks will start to show up in the foundation or elsewhere. The paint would begin to chip. The roof might leak, and bricks in the chimney might come loose. However, when people live in the house and a little thing goes wrong, they fix it; they continually restore the house to operable condition.

CAUTION

Like an untreated cavity can lead to a root canal, a little clutter can become a big problem if you ignore it.

Entropy is alive and well on your hard drive, on your desk, on your shelf, and in all the spaces of your life. In this day and age, when we are all subject to so much information coming at us, piles can accumulate quickly. These piles might include documents, reports, newspapers, bills, magazines, certificates, you name it.

CAUTION

Piles by their very nature represent disorganization.

It is hard to manage stuff stacked up in a pile. Many organizational experts contend that accumulations represent a basic lack of decision-making capability. In other words, you have piles of stuff because you haven't decided what to do with the stuff in the first place.

Identifying your priorities and establishing goals in support of those priorities can help you to better use your time and to stay more focused and more directed. Likewise, priorities and goals also help you to have a clear handle on what to do when stuff comes your way.

Those individuals with the most highly refined set of priorities and most well-developed goals are more likely to have fewer piles and less clutter confronting them. Why? Because they know where things go as soon as they encounter them. Better still, as you learned from the section "Understanding Time Management," on page 60, they eliminate the possibility of most pieces of paper coming to their desks to begin with.

Piled High but Not Hopeless

If you find yourself continually confronted with clutter, take heart. The situation is not hopeless. First, gather all the tools and accoutrements you will need to break down those piles or disband that clutter. These tools may include file folders, rubber bands, paper clips, staplers, boxes, and so on. In the next section, "Managing Your Desk and Office," I will get into the details of managing your workspace so you will be able to find things easily. For now, recognize that piles and clutter don't magically go away, just as they didn't magically accumulate.

Allow yourself 30 minutes or, if that's too much, 15 minutes to go through each item in the pile and assess what to do with it. In essence, you can only do one of four things with the stuff that confronts you:

- Act on it.
- Delegate it.
- File it.
- Recycle it.

Of any given pile of stuff on your desk, chances are most of it can be recycled. You don't need to hang on to it. A lesser portion can probably be filed, and a slightly lesser portion of that can probably be delegated. That leaves you with a thin file of things to act on.

TIP

By categorizing the various items in your pile, you stand a better chance of whittling out the unnecessary items, and dealing with the rest becomes a more manageable task.

Don't spend too much time thinking about which group to place each item in; make a quick assessment and go on to the next item. After you have placed everything into its group, you will notice undoubtedly that the recycle group is the largest. The file group, hopefully, is much smaller. The group of stuff to delegate to other people is smaller still, and the group of things you need to act on should be the smallest of all.

Go through the items you need to act on and rank them according to what is most important. If an item is both urgent and important (see "Avoiding the Tyranny of the Urgent" on page 75), put it on top of the group. If an item is important but not urgent, place it next. If it is simply urgent, place it after that, and if it is neither urgent nor important, recycle it, file it, or delegate it.

After you have determined which items or tasks are urgent and important, rank those items as well. Research has confirmed that when you have multiple items competing for your time and attention, ranking them according to their importance and working on each item in order until it is completed is the fastest and most efficient way to tackle the tasks or projects facing you.

SUPPORTING PRINCIPLES

Anytime you face a pile or *clutter* in general or feel disorganized, keep in mind the following principles:

PLAIN ENGLISH

Clutter   An unorganized accumulation of items, the collective value of which is suspect.

- ■ **Recycling.** Identifying items for recycling (chucking) is usually easiest. You want to get your pile to a lean and mean state; by chucking things at high speed, you have the best chance.
- ■ **Order of importance or urgency.** Frequently downgrade the status of items as you see fit. If you have too many items in your important file, you are stuck with the same problem you had before you dealt with the pile. Everything seems to be competing for your time and attention with equal fervor. If you can successfully downgrade the status of an item (for example, from important and urgent to simply

important or simply urgent or to something that someone else can handle), then you have reduced the immediate burden that you face.

- **Classification.** Continue to look for what can be combined, automated, systemized, delegated, delayed, ignored, or used for fireplace kindling.

- **Organization.** When you have pared down piles to the least possible volume, use whatever tools you have available (rubber bands, paper clips, file folders, and so on) to keep them neat and orderly.

TIP

The more like things that you can group together, the easier it will be to deal with them. Also, the easier it will be to see duplicates that you can recycle or discard.

Make a game of staying organized: Continually look for backsides of pieces of paper that are reusable for rough drafts and copies and keep an eye out for items that someone else might appreciate but that you don't really need to retain.

TIP

If something you are holding on to can truly help another person, it will be far easier for you to give it away.

TACKLING THE IMPORTANT PILE

When you're ready to begin working on the items in your important group, list them all and make an estimate of how long it will take to complete each item. Then add all the estimates together and multiply that number by 1.5. This amount compensates for your underestimation. Let's face it: Things often take longer than we think they will. We don't know how long a project will take until we do it, at which point all kinds of other issues sometimes arise.

If the number of task hours facing you to complete the important tasks grows to an astronomical figure, don't get overly concerned. At least you now have more accurate information regarding the challenge facing you.

Now, marshal your resources. Realistically, what will it take to accomplish all that you have laid out before you as important and urgent, important, and so on? You may need additional staff help, a bigger budget, or, in the short run, a longer workday.

TIP

Sometimes you can't complete a task because certain steps are dependent on others. Take it as far as you can go, and then consult with others. During the interim, start on the next project.

Now and then, no matter how methodical your approach or well-organized your desk and office are, new items will compete for your time and attention and conspire to upset your perfectly arranged kingdom. This is going to happen on a daily, if not hourly, basis. In the next section, I will explain how to arrange your office, desk, and files so as to be able to accommodate the influx of new materials.

MIX IT UP

As time passes, you'll find that you need a break from working on the important tasks that you have so carefully arranged. You can give your rapt attention and earnest efforts to the primo projects for only so long, and then your mind starts to wander. You need a mental break.

At this point, feel free to turn to items far lower down on the pile that still require your attention, but don't require so much mental effort. Give yourself a 10-, 15-, or 20-minute run on lower-level items that are less mentally taxing. When you feel ready, turn back to the most important items.

KEEPING IT IN PERSPECTIVE

You already know that smaller piles are easier to manage than larger ones. Hence, your goal should be to continue to keep your piles as slim and trim as possible, although there are exceptions that I will discuss shortly. Reduce the weight and volume of each pile by retaining only the highly relevant information and nothing more. For example, rather than retaining a 10-page report, hang on to only the single page that you need.

Taking that principle further, if you only need one paragraph, phone number, address, or Web site on a page, then clip that portion and recycle the rest of the page. Attach the small clipping that you have retained to a sheet that contains other small, relevant tidbits, and then photocopy the page. You now have a dossier page that fully supports what you are working on, but doesn't take up much space physically or psychologically.

Sometimes it does pay to let piles or accumulations mount up. When you receive a plethora of like items, it is okay to let the pile grow temporarily. Perhaps a stack of everything related to the competitor's product is accumulating in the corner of that table in your office. That's okay, because the pile is temporary and you intend to handle it completely in short order.

When that sacred time arrives, delve into the pile like a buzz saw. Immediately discard duplicate information. Combine like items, and then consider which of those items can be recycled as well. Pare down so that you have the slimmest, most potent pile possible.

When the pile is reasonably thin, look at it once more and ask yourself what else can be thrown away. What items represent something that you already know quite well, but you are holding on to as an information crutch? Don't be surprised to find that you can reduce the pile by yet another 33 percent.

TIP

If you have several slimmed-down piles, arrange them in a stair-step fashion down one side of your desk. This arrangement allows you to quickly withdraw any particular pile in the arrangement while keeping the others in order.

A PSYCHIC REWARD

I've discussed the issue of *being organized* with top achievers in many different professions. Each agrees that when his or her desk or office and personal surroundings are in order, he or she feels far more energized at the start of the day. Conversely, when these top achievers come into their offices at the start of the day and see a huge mess, they feel somewhat defeated.

From the standpoint of managing your time and staying organized, as well as feeling energized, clear your desk and surroundings each evening as you end work for the day so that the next day you can be at your best. When you leave with a clear desk, you give yourself a sense of closure or completion to your day. This sense of completion gives you a greater chance to enjoy the rest of your evening.

PLAIN ENGLISH

Being organized   Arranging one's possessions, time, or life to remain comfortably in control.

When you arrive in the morning and are greeted by a clear, clean surrounding, you gain a psychological boost much as the high achievers did. What's more, you are automatically drawn to the most important issue, or you get to make a fresh decision about what materials to extract from your desk, filing cabinet, or shelves based on what you want to accomplish that morning. This situation is far different than merely dealing with what you left on the desk the night before.

TIP

Some projects span several days, and in that sense, it can be prudent on occasion to simply leave a file folder open on your desk so that it will greet you the next morning. However you don't want to fall into the habit where you are always being greeted by stuff you left on the desk the night before.

When you begin each morning with a clear, clean desk and clear, clean office and focus on tasks that you deem most important and urgent at that time, you work with more energy, more focus, and more direction. You tend to get things done in less time overall, because you begin working right away on the thing that you deem is most important. You also experience less stress.

EXTENDING THE NOTION

Getting organized in your personal life supports your efforts in your professional life. The more organized you are at home, in your car, and in the other places in your life, the greater the probability that you will have more focus, energy, and direction when you head to work. You will certainly be more efficient and perhaps have greater piece of mind.

At home, if your closets are jammed with stuff you have been stowing since you moved into the house, it's time to engage in spring cleaning, whether spring is here or not. If you can't bear to part with all the stuff you crammed in there, at least separate it by the seasons.

TIP

As spring approaches, box up all the winter items and put them in the attic, basement, or some infrequently used room. It should take you 60 minutes or less for each closet.

As you go through your house reclaiming spaces, you will find the pay-off spills over into your career. Twenty-first century men and women are inundated with too many items competing for their time and attention at work, at home, and in between. Just as cramming too many activities into a given unit of time tends to make that time speed by perceptually, cramming too many items into a physical space tends to make one feel somewhat out of control. By reclaiming spaces, you can find things faster and easier, which saves time and makes it easier to get out of the house in the morning and stow things at the end of the day.

FROM HOME TO OFFICE AND BACK AGAIN

The fastest and easiest way to maintain order in your home and have that principle spread to your office is to defend your borders. That means you must semi-fanatically guard your home and your life so that no extraneous items enter to begin with. Similar to limiting the number of the pieces of paper that cross your desk at work, you want to limit the number of items that come into your home and make their way onto your shelves. At work, you want to keep your flat surfaces relatively clear and leave ample room in your filing cabinets, on your shelves, and in other spaces around your office (more on this in the next section).

THE 30-SECOND RECAP

- Though personal organizational skills aren't handed out at birth, people who are organized and stay organized practice some specific behaviors that people who are disorganized don't do.

- Any pile that you face, particularly on your desk, can be pared down in 30 minutes or less. Most of what you face can be recycled, a lesser amount can be filed, many items can be delegated, and generally, a few items will need to be worked on.

- Getting organized takes some time, but the payoff is worth it! To get organized in the office requires assembling the tools that will help you keep like items together.

- Getting organized at home ultimately supports your career organization efforts. Cleaning up your closets, drawers, and shelf space pays off in all aspects of your life.

Managing Your Desk and Office

In this section, you will learn how to arrange your office, desk, working materials, and files so that you can find things quickly and easily.

STARTING AT THE TOP

When you arrange your office for high productivity, start with your desk, specifically with your desktop. You have to treat your desktop as sacred space.

Everything on your desktop has to be there for a reason and must be positioned precisely to support the way you work.

No one is going to help you manage your desk or desktop. If you have a mentor or co-worker who is a pro at organization, then consider yourself among the fortunate few. If not, you have to roll up your sleeves and learn by trial and error. You already know from the previous section that if you have one project, one file folder, or one of whatever you're working on in front of you and the rest of your desk is clutter free, you are going to have more:

- More energy
- More focus
- More direction

What precisely do you need to have on your desktop? A quick answer is anything that you use on a recurring and daily basis. This could include a pen, a roll of tape, a stapler, a staple remover, Post-it pads, a ruler, and paper clips. Anything that you can't use on a daily or recurring basis does not belong on your desktop. Such items are best stored in a drawer within your desk or possibly a table or credenza in your office.

Why bother to make the distinction between what you use on a daily or recurring basis versus what you don't? Because your goal at all times is to have as few things on your desk as possible so that you will have as much open space as possible. You need open space and clear, clean, flat surfaces because more information will be coming onto your desk each day, each week, and each year of your career.

TIP

Establish a disembarking area where you can open packages, break down mail, or otherwise diminish piles of stuff.

IT'S WHAT'S INSIDE THAT COUNTS

Inside your desk you want to retain items that you use at least on a weekly basis, although items used daily can be stored there as well if they are particularly large or bulky. Recognize, however, that your desk drawers are not for storing supplies per se. You may store a pad of paper, but not pads of paper. You need only one pad at a time, and the general principle is to have the minimum amount of an item that you need, but then have no more.

TIP

Keep pads of paper and other supplies in a file folder, a storage locker, or further away from the epicenter of your creative and productive post.

When you have only those things on your desktop that ought to be on your desktop and only those things in your desk that ought to be there, proceed to the other storage compartments around your office. If you choose to use one of your desk drawers to contain file folders, then these file folders should contain only current projects. Also, they should be arranged in the fashion discussed in the section "Getting Organized," that begins on page 88. The important and urgent materials come first, and the least important and least urgent materials are last. These files should be as thin and potent as you can make them.

TIP

Routinely discard extraneous information and be on the lookout for reducing, shrinking, and paring down where you can. Retain only the materials that are essential to retain.

WHAT TO SHELVE

Undoubtedly, you have some kind of shelves in your office. The question of what should be housed on your shelves versus what is best contained in a filing cabinet is relatively easy to answer. Shelves are best used to …

- Temporarily store items you will use within 10 to 15 days.
- Store items that are too large to go in a filing cabinet.
- Hold a collection of like items, such as 12 issues of the same magazine in an upright magazine storage box.
- Contain current projects, the total contents of which you don't necessarily have to have on your desk.
- Store books, directories, supply catalogs, and other items with spine labels.

CAUTION

Make sure you allocate items you are temporarily storing on shelves in 10 to 15 days. When a temporary pile becomes a permanent pile, you begin to lose control of what you're retaining.

Be careful when you store elements of a project in progress on your shelves. It's fine to temporarily park the brunt of materials you are working with so that you can have just a few materials in front of you at any given time. However, if you're maintaining complete control of your desk, your shelves, and the project at hand, then ideally the materials should rotate from the desk to the shelf and back to your desk, become thinner in the process, and eventually *not* appear on your shelves at all.

LIGHTEN THE LOAD

As more and more material comes into your office, you'll find it's easy to fill up your shelves in record time. With all the office supply catalogs, annual directories, software instruction guides, and company policy and procedure manuals, what was once an open space can quickly turn into a "no vacancy" situation.

To maximize shelf space, keep supplies in a supply cabinet. Ideally your supply cabinet is farther away from your desk than your shelves. Supply cabinets are designed to house items in bulk. The goal in using supply cabinets is to be able to readily find what you need when you open them. Keeping like items together makes items easier to find. These items might be stacked on top of one another, horizontally, or end-to-end. Although you arrange items on your shelves with precision, supply cabinets allow for a lot more leeway.

 TIP
Extreme neatness is not necessary in a supply cabinet. However, the bigger the office staff sharing the supply cabinet is, the more important neatness becomes.

EVERYTHING IS CONNECTED

Highly organized individuals know that the relationship between one's desk, shelves, and supply cabinet is not static. What is housed in one location at one point in time ultimately may be housed somewhere else depending on the following factors:

- The tasks at hand
- The available resources to meet those tasks
- The time frame for completing the tasks

At all times, you want to be on the prowl for items that can be tossed or recycled. If you don't need it, it's not worth filing or storing.

Too many people feel fearful about tossing items because they just know they will need them someday. But the truth is that tossing something out and then discovering you need it later may not be the major problem you imagine. Almost any list, report, or document that you can name can be replaced. Somebody else has a copy, it's on the Internet, or it's on somebody's hard drive. Not being able to think of a good reason to hang on to something is a good reason to toss it.

Professional organizers claim that as much as 80 percent of what executives retain at work never again sees the light of day. Even if they are off by 25 percent to 50 percent in their estimates, it still means that much of what you are hanging on to is dead wood! The more you have cleared out of your office, the easier it is to find what you've retained.

PAPER IS STILL KING

Despite the long-standing promise that we'll all be working in "paperless offices," most career professionals today are plagued by even more paper than their predecessors of a generation ago. If you analyze your most repetitive tasks, chances are that handling paper would be on the top of the list on most given days. In many respects, time management is synonymous with paper handling. Your mission is to whittle out all those pages of catalogs, magazines, and other voluminous work that come your way so that you deal only with what you need and nothing more.

TIP

Reduce the potential for disorganization by dealing with paper right away when you get the mail, when somebody hands you something, or when you see something in your in basket after returning from being away.

Here are some paper-reducing ideas:

- Use your copy machine as often as possible to capture the few pages you need from a book or large document. Get rid of the part you don't need.

- Use a scanner to put key paragraphs and pages on your hard drive, where they are searchable and retrievable via your word processing program. This method is superior to filing something and then trying to find it on your own.

CAUTION

Don't make the mistake of scanning indiscriminately, or you'll fill up your hard drive as quickly as you filled up your filing cabinets. Electronic disorganization is as anxiety-provoking as the manual kind.

■ Use a junk drawer as a holding bin when stuff comes in too fast or when you're in the middle of an important project. Later, when the dust dies down, go to your junk drawer and whittle out as much as you can. Use the four-step process in assessing and allocating where the items should go: Act on it, delegate it, file it, or recycle or toss it.

TIP

The act-on-it pile should always be the smallest. Rank the items in that pile according to what is important and urgent heading down to what is unimportant and not urgent.

Asking yourself the following series of questions can help you quickly determine what to do with the next item that crosses your desk:

■ What does this document represent?

■ Do I have to retain this at all?

■ Who else should know about this?

■ What if I don't do anything?

If an item you receive merits your attention and requires that you get in touch with someone, use the path of least resistance to resolve the issue. Determine whether you can ...

■ Fax instead of mail.

■ E-mail instead of fax.

■ Pay by credit card instead of by check.

■ Call instead of visit.

CONTINUALLY BE ON THE LOOKOUT

Throughout the day, when the spirit moves you, examine your desktop, desk drawers, shelves, filing cabinet, and any storage cabinet to determine what, if anything, no longer needs to be retained. Outdated directories, instruction manuals, flyers, annual reports, brochures, public relations materials, announcements, catalogs, and invitations can all be tossed. Chuck the excess vendor supply catalogs that you may have on hand, duplicate items, annual reports that you don't look at, software you received in the mail that you are never going to explore, and take-out menus from restaurants you no longer frequent. Feel free to throw out old editions of books that you won't open again, back issues of magazines you haven't touched for more than a year, and bottles of correction fluid that have dried solid.

TIP

Get rid of scraps, rough drafts, memos, correspondence, reports, and any other documents that do not have to be retained.

The Nuts and Bolts of Filing

Filing is the ultimate organizational tool. When you file items effectively, you enable yourself to efficiently withdraw what you need when you need it. As author Jim Cathcart says, "Filing is not about storing; it is about retrieval." You file things either because they will help you to be prosperous in the future (for example, the information you retain has power) or because there are penalties for not filing them (for example, you won't be able to complete your taxes). The items that you file, therefore, should have potential future value.

CAUTION

If it has been a long time since you have reorganized your files, you are probably facing a gargantuan task. Nevertheless, this task is one that is well worth undertaking.

Rather than try to redo your entire filing cabinet, tackle one half of one drawer every week. This pace is safe and sane. Assemble the tools you'll need to be effective, such as several blank file folders, file folder labels, magic markers, color-coded dots, paper clips, fasteners, and such.

Rather than using two- or three-cut manila folders, splurge and buy black, green, pink, orange, or blue folders. Color-coded files help you to find things more quickly and easily. Think of the last time you were in your doctor's or dentist's office. If their patient files were exposed and in view, chances are you saw some kind of color-coded filing system. This system enables the people in the office to go right to the appropriate area, which cuts down the time searching for any particular file. You could use green file folders for anything that has to do with, say, money, blue for anything that has to do with your career progression, yellow for anything related to taxes, and so on.

Grab the first file in the first drawer you have chosen to tackle. Examine its contents:

- What can be chucked?
- What can be combined?
- What needs to be reallocated?
- What color folder or what color label will you use to house the remaining materials, knowing what you now know?

Everything in the file is subject to being combined, deleted, or moved around. Your goal at all times is to ensure that the things that you have chosen to file are housed in their best possible location.

Go to the second file in the drawer and allocate its contents as you will. If you're not sure that something is worth retaining, chances are it's not worth retaining. Management expert Edwin Bliss says, "When in doubt, throw it out."

TIP

Because most of us keep more than is necessary, chances are you can pare down your files significantly and not suffer any negative consequences. And the less you have, the easier it is to find what you need.

When you have gone through the half-drawer for this particular session, relax, give yourself a break, and go do something else. You don't have to tackle the second half of the drawer until a week or so from now.

FEWER FILES, MORE IN THEM

At all times, you want to have fewer large files of like items as opposed to a number of smaller files. Why? You'll find it far easier to extract what you are looking for if you have to deal with only a few large files to begin with. Any search you do begins with the right file. It will then take you time to go through that file to find the particular document, but your odds of success will be high.

Conversely, if you have dozens and dozens of small files, you might not extract the correct file in three or four tries. If you are lucky and you do extract the correct file, the time required to extract the desired page within the file won't be that much quicker than extracting the desired page from a larger file.

Some organizational experts swear by *date stamping*. Every time something goes into your file you stamp the corner of it indicating on what day it was placed in the file. If you're comfortable with doing this, go ahead. Keep in mind that an item's importance is not necessarily related to the date in which you filed it, although the longer an item has sat in your files without ever being used, the higher the probability is that you can safely chuck it.

PLAIN ENGLISH

Date stamping   The process of fixing a date to items as they arrive, and preferably before they are filed.

FILE HEADINGS ARE THE KEY

What you file and how you file is largely governed by your file headings, which are the labels you place on the tab section of each file folder. It is easy enough to label one file folder Office Supplies, and another Insurance, and another New Technology. However, you probably want to be more creative than that to accommodate the variety of stuff that comes your way. Some of it appears worth retaining, at least in the short run, but it doesn't seemingly have a proper home. You could label your file folders with the following headings:

- Review After the First of the Year
- Hold Until After the Merger
- Check in a Month
- Check Next Spring
- Don't Know Where to File

By having a file labeled Don't Know Where to File, you automatically create a home for the handful of things that your instincts tell you to retain but that don't fit with anything else you're doing. Now at least you have a fair chance of getting your hands back on such items when, lo and behold, the time might be right to reread the items closely.

TIP

If you're worried that a file labeled Don't Know Where to File may grow too large too quickly, remember that you can easily review its contents at any time and decide what to do with them.

LOCATING TICKLER FILES

As is described at length in the book, *The Complete Idiot's Guide to Managing Your Time* (Alpha Books, 1999), setting up a daily and monthly rotating tickler (reminder) file provides big benefits. Suppose something crosses your desk in March that looks interesting, but you don't have to act on it until April 25. If you have one file folder for each month of the year, you can park the item in the April folder.

Going further, you set up an additional 31 file folders marked 1, 2, and so on all the way up to 31 for the days in the month. Now, when April approaches, you open up the April file folder, take out all the contents, and allocate them to file folders 1 through 31 as appropriate. Stick the now-empty April file folder at the end of the pack so that the month of May is now in front, preceded by file folders 1 through 31.

TIP

These 43 file folders (1 through 31 and January through December) enable you to park anything in the appropriate place when the item doesn't have to be dealt with too soon.

If you receive something on the third day of the month but don't have to deal with it until the eighteenth, put it in the folder marked 18, or better yet, give yourself some slack and put it in a folder two or three days before the eighteenth.

The tickler file provides a home for much of the clutter and stuff on your desk and around your office, because you've determined a date when you're going to review the materials. They are off your desk, off your counters, and off your mind. Yet you haven't lost them, you have just parked them in a location where you'll be able to retrieve them when you need to.

TIP

You can use a tickler file to write out your checks and pay your bills, and then store the envelopes in the folder that's prior to their due dates.

Many people who use tickler files find it convenient to review them at the start of each week and perhaps one or two more times during that week. One of the benefits of this process is that when you review the item days, weeks, or a month after first putting it in the tickler file, you often have a greater sense of objectivity. Choosing to act on the item, delegate it, file it again, or toss it becomes easier. Happily, much of what you review will be tossed. Having less clutter means you have greater organization and greater focus and direction on the pressing tasks that you face.

CREATING FILES IN ADVANCE OF THE NEED

A variation of the theme of employing both file labels and using tickler files is to create files in advance of when you need to store anything in them. Suppose you've decided that you absolutely want to work in the London office of your company by the end of next year. Perhaps you haven't even announced your intentions to anyone. Nevertheless, place a file in your filing cabinet labeled London.

Hereafter, every time you see something about London, you now have a home for it. Maybe you encounter documents from the London office. Maybe you find something related to travel in London. Later, perhaps you come across something related to housing in England.

Creating a file folder in advance of having anything to put into the folder is an affirmation of the goals you have chosen. At the least, it helps to keep you organized. If you don't have such a folder, where the heck are you going to put items relating to this goal? On top of something else where it will get buried by yet something else?

By extending the principle, you can create several file folders in advance of having anything to put into them, based on what priorities you have identified and what goals you have established in support of those priorities. Here are some ideas for file folders for this category:

- Retirement Villages
- Vacation to Bali
- Daycare Centers
- Palmtop Computers
- Vision Correction
- Scholarships

ORGANIZE YOUR HARD DRIVE

The concept of filing is no less valid when it comes to your hard drive. There may be six or so file folders you don't need to create, but would be most appropriate for you to create based on where you are heading in your career and your life.

TIP

When you create an empty file folder on your hard drive, especially off of another folder that you visit often, you are frequently reminded that you have a home to park files as they emerge for this new topic area.

If you supervise a staff, electronic filing can work particularly well. Create a file folder for each staff person, using his or her name. Thereafter, when you come across anything that needs to go into Erika's folder, drag it over and park it there. As time passes, and it's time for Erika to tackle another assignment, you flip open the directory, see what's in the hopper, and delegate accordingly.

You can even create a file folder for yourself on your hard drive called In Progress that you open at the start of each day, or a shortcut to such a folder on your desktop. The possibilities are endless! The point is for you to create space to house that which is worth housing so that you can quickly and easily retrieve what you need.

THE 30-SECOND RECAP

- Look upon managing your desk, shelves, filing cabinet, and storage cabinet as the means to an end, the end being that you are far more efficient in the use of your time.

- Your continual quest is to whittle out that which you do not need to retain and continually revisit your files and holdings to further pare down. You want to stay lean and mean. You want your files to be thin and potent.

- Rather than seeing filing as drudgery, consider it an effective tool for storing items that contribute to your future prosperity or at least help you avoid penalties.

Surviving Information Overload

In this section, you will learn how to limit the amount of information that confronts you while ensuring that you are exposed to issues critical to your job and personal well-being.

HOW BAD IS IT?

You have only to log onto the Internet, switch on the television, walk into a magazine store, or open your e-mail file to be deluged by information. The aggregate volume of information generated on Earth in a single minute exceeds what you could absorb in the next 80 years of your life, should you live that long. The next minute, the process repeats itself. No one can possibly keep up with the volume of information confronting humankind.

To effectively manage your time, set up filters in all aspects in your life so that you have access to information that you want or need to be exposed to but are not subject to the floodgate levels of information plaguing so many others. When you make active choices regarding the information you want to receive versus allowing yourself to be simply inundated, you set yourself up for success. You have charted a course unlike so many others who have never stopped and decided what information they want to be exposed to versus what information they simply are exposed to. This key distinction will sustain your career for decades to come.

CAUTION

Even the industry or profession in which you have chosen to excel, however narrow a niche that may be, generates so much information that you cannot keep up with it all.

You can't subscribe to all the top magazines, read all the latest books, and attend all the big symposiums. Thus, you have to draw upon the Pareto Principle (see "Avoiding the Tyranny of the Urgent" on page 75), recognizing that about 20 percent of the information to which you are exposed yields 80 percent or more of the insights, key facts, and essential knowledge that will propel you in your efforts.

So you ask, "How do I identify that important 20 percent?" It is easier than you might think. If there are several magazines, journals, and newsletters within your profession, choose the two or three that represent the leading sources and have the most in-depth coverage, the largest research staff, and the best writing.

TIP

Find out what the top professionals in your industry read. These are the magazines that you'll probably want to subscribe to as well.

Keep Pace with Your Clients

Beyond reading what your top peers read, you also want to discover the top industry journals read by your clients, customers, or constituents. After all, the organization that employs you serves some type of constituent, whether they are called customers, clients, patients, or consumers. Find out what these people read, identify the few key publications, and subscribe to those as well.

By receiving the same information that the top people whom you are trying to serve receive, you begin to understand the issues that confront them, the terminology, the players, and all facets of their world. You are homing in on the key bits of information that will help you to understand what it takes to serve your constituency. What could be more efficient?

CAUTION

Far too many career professionals are steeped in the information of their own industry but forget to take the vital step of reading what their clients read.

As you read articles and news briefs related to your constituents, fill your file folders and hard-drive space with information you can draw upon, massage, combine, and use to even better serve your clients and customers. When you're in face-to-face meetings, on the phone, or delivering correspondence to your constituents, the quality of your message will be higher because you have taken the time and effort to delve into the information that defines their world.

GETTING OTHERS TO SIFT FOR YOU

What if someone could sift through information for you and act as a filter so that you receive only the essence of voluminous amounts of information that you might otherwise be tempted to weed through yourself? Although not many people use this technique, you can have somebody else serve as your information scout.

Look around your office and around your home. If you are the type of person who routinely amasses piles of reading materials, then you could use a *prereader*. Rather than continually feeling swamped by too much information, delegate somebody, hire somebody, or enlist one of your children to read through materials for you.

PLAIN ENGLISH

Prereader   Someone who serves as an information scout for another, paring down voluminous reading materials to their essence.

How does this work? Although I will explore multiplying your time through delegation in the following section, "Multiplying Your Time Through

Delegation" on page 128, or now, consider that if you can offer clear instructions on what type of information you're seeking and how you want it to be presented, someone else can wade through those key chapters in the latest book, that stack of magazines you have been accumulating, and those reports piling up on the corner of your desk. The key is to draw up a roster of essential terms and phrases, key themes, and key issues that you want the prereader to flag. Perhaps you want the prereader to copy any page where a key issue appears or underline key paragraphs.

TIP

By properly conveying what you want when you delegate your reading material and choosing the right person to be your prereader, you can dramatically cut down on the amount of information you are exposed to and increase the speed with which you can take action on information.

Begin by giving your prereader some light assignments. For example, after he or she has followed your instructions in reviewing a particular magazine, scan the entire magazine as you normally would have done without a prereader. This will help you assess how close your prereader was to identifying the few key sections that are important to you.

Be sure to give your prereader detailed feedback following the first several assignments. As he or she begins to exhibit increasing capability for highlighting and underscoring precisely those articles and passages that you would have selected yourself, increase the scope of your assignments.

Regardless of what you assign, having a prereader doesn't prevent you from reading things on your own that you choose not to delegate. However, as you learn to trust the judgment of your prereader, increasingly you'll find that it is far more efficient to have him or her sift through more and more of what you would have spent hours going through. Suppose your prereader is finished going through a magazine for you. He or she is now a veteran of selecting what you want. You still can quickly read over other things that the prereader may not have highlighted, yet you find yourself being able to delve into the preselected materials that the prereader found for you at record speeds.

Remember, you can absorb and, more important, apply only so much of the information that you are exposed to. When a prereader whittles down large volumes of information so that what is left is fertile, you've not only saved a great deal of time and storage space, but you have also set up an environment where you are more easily able to act on the few things highlighted for your attention.

You're Not Done Yet

Continue to look for other easy ways to handle all the information that competes for your time and attention. Instead of reading voluminous amounts of materials that someone else in your office has already read, have him or her brief you.

TIP

If you discuss information with a co-worker or friend who has read what you want to read, you may not have to read the original subject matter yourself.

You may have heard the story about Franklin D. Roosevelt. One of his advisors brought him a 100-page report on some current, crucial topic. Roosevelt looked at it and said, "This is far too much for me to go through. Can you boil it down?" The advisor came back in a day or two with a 10-page executive summary. Roosevelt looked at it for a few seconds and said, "Still too much. Boil it down." The advisor, very miffed, came back after a couple hours with one page of key notes. Roosevelt looked at the page and said, "Come on, man, I'm busy; boil it down." The advisor came back in a half-hour with a single paragraph. Roosevelt's eyes darted over it for a moment. Then he looked up at the advisor and said, "Can you give it to me in a sentence?"

Continue to Prune Your Files

The time and effort that you spend whittling out what you no longer need pays off in many ways. For one, you physically have the space both within your desk and file cabinets and on your hard drive to accommodate new information, which, as we know by now, is on its way. Chucking what you don't need to hang on to also gives you the opportunity to review that which you have filed and choose to retain. Sometimes the information that you filed months ago combined with something you just learned adds up to new knowledge on which you can capitalize.

CAUTION

The tendency to hang on to too much information is endemic to early twenty-first-century man and woman. Keep asking yourself, "Do I really need to retain this?"

Here are some good places to look for material you no longer need:

- Clean out your database. There are contacts in your database who have left the area or perhaps passed away or who you know you will never call on again. Delete them without remorse from your database.

- Review your files. Toss out every piece of paper in your files that represents issues that are neither important, urgent, or, for that matter, even interesting. Keep the others in the aforementioned holding bins (see "Managing Your Desk and Office" on page 96).

- Eliminate files on your hard drive that were once able to capture your attention, but now, after months or perhaps years, have overstayed their welcome.

- Examine your office at large. Have you collected business cards of people you know whom you will never call back? Are there gifts and mementos you have received that hold little meaning for you or take up more space than they are worth? Are there book reports and documents that are no longer (or have yet to be) useful? If so, throw them out!

CHART YOUR PROGRESS

The following chart, adapted from my book, *The Joy of Simple Living,* offers a quick and easy guide for what to retain versus what to toss:

Items	Toss or Recycle If ...	Retain If ...
Business cards	You have many cards and never call anyone, or you can't recall the person or his goods or services.	You already have a cardholder, can scan it, know you'll use it, or feel you will.
Notes, files, and documents	They're old, outdated, and uninformative; they've been transferred to disk; or they no longer cover your derriere.	It's your duty to retain them, you refer to them often, or they have future value.
Reports and magazines	They're old, outdated, stacking up; you think you need them to keep up; or you fear a quiz on them.	They're vital to your career or well-being, you choose to retain them, or there will be a quiz on them.
Books, guides, and directories	You've copied, scanned, or made notes on the key pages; they're obsolete; or there is an updated version.	They're part of a life collection, you refer to them monthly, they have sentimental value, or you want them.

Items	Toss or Recycle If ...	Retain If ...
CDs, cassettes, and videos	You never play them, and if you do, they don't evoke any feelings or memories. They play poorly.	You play them, you like them, and you couldn't bear to part with them. They're keepsakes.
Outdated office equipment	You know who would like it as a donation, you can sell it, it's collecting dust, or it's in the way.	It serves a specific purpose, it adds to the décor, or it can be overhauled or revitalized.
Mementos and memorabilia	They no longer hold meaning, you have many similar items, you do not have room, or you've changed.	They still evoke strong memories, you will hand them down someday, or they look good on display.
Gifts, cards, and presents	They're never in use and are unwanted, and the giver won't know or be concerned that you tossed them.	You use them often, are glad you have them, or are saving them for some special reason.

THE 30-SECOND RECAP

- Every minute, more information is generated on Earth than you can possibly absorb in the rest of your life. There is no chance of keeping up with all the information. Fortunately, you can make choices about what to give your time and attention.

- Use prereaders to help you dramatically reduce the volume of information/reading that you face.

- Whittle out that which you do not need to retain both in your physical spaces and on your computer.

- For each item that you are retaining, use the chart at the end of the previous section to make a simple determination about whether the item is worth retaining or can easily be tossed.

Taming Technology

In this section, you will learn how to manage voice mail, e-mail, facsimiles, and other high-tech equipment so that they will save you time rather than consume it.

You've Got the Whole World in Your Palm

For the foreseeable future, Moore's Law, which says that microchip capacity will double every 18 months, will continue unabated. That means that desktop computers will have awesome power, notebook computers will get thinner and be more versatile than ever, and palmtop computers are likely to become as universal as carrying a wallet. As of this writing, handheld computing devices or palmtops are already providing wireless links to the Internet, e-mail, and fax capabilities to users around the globe. Palmtops can store thousands of addresses, years' and years' worth of appointments, thousands of memos, and thousands of to-do items, all uniquely arranged based on user preferences.

PLAIN ENGLISH

Personal digital assistants (PDA)   Another name for handheld computing devices or palmtops.

What else do these miniature wonders provide? They have the following capabilities:

- Support for a variety of software applications
- Automatic linking to a variety of hardware devices, peripherals, and accessories
- Quick access to information
- Battery life exceeding five hours
- Ultraconvenient, ultrapowerful address books, to-do lists, memo pads, calendars, trip logs, and expense calculators
- Enhanced, full-color, high-clarity screens

When choosing a palmtop device, you have various options:

- **Power.** Some palmtops use AA cells, AAA cells, or rechargeable lithium ion batteries.
- **Memory.** Anything from 2 megabits to 16 megabits is currently available, but this amount will change in a hurry. Some devices enable you to upgrade memory so that you can store more information.
- **Displays.** Palmtops are available in monochrome, four-level gray scale, 256 color, or 65,536 colors!
- **Screens.** Flip-up screens, back lighting, and high-color screens are some of the available options.

■ **Other options.** Voice recognition, stereo headphones, bundled software, built-in modems, and flip-up screen covers are also available.

Even if you are not currently using a handheld computing device, the odds are astronomical that within a few short years you will be. Soon enough, the computing power on your wrist will exceed what was possible on a desktop in the 1990s. Regardless of the device you ultimately use, there are a variety of techniques that you can quickly and easily employ to ensure that you maximize your use of time when engaging in such functions as voice mail, e-mail, surfing the Internet, and faxing.

VOICE MAIL

You call another party, and you are subjected to the usual voice mail runaround: Press one for this; press two for that. After you finally find your way through the system, how do you leave a message that is succinct, has impact, and generates results? Unlike the old answering machines where you had to finish your message in one or two minutes, most systems today have no time limit. Yet it is to your benefit to finish in 45 seconds or less. Why? Attention spans are becoming shorter all the time, and people often become frustrated when they retrieve a two- or three-minute message.

TIP

The party you are trying to reach may have dozens of messages, so yours needs to be brief and elicit the type of response you want. (The following "Keeping Interruptions to a Minimum" section on page 120 gives hints for leaving messages.)

The biggest bugaboo of most people retrieving their voice mail is the speed at which people leave their telephone numbers. Because you know your number quite well, it's easy to say it so fast that the recipient must replay the part of the message with your phone number four or five times to get the whole number. A good rule of thumb is to say your number at the speed at which you can write it yourself, either on paper or with a finger in the air.

E-MAIL

With popular programs such as Outlook and Outlook Express, Netscape Communicator, Eudora Pro, and Claris, you have more than enough choices for e-mail software. Each program offers an impressive array of benefits and features.

Because all are downloadable, at least on a trial basis, and none is too diffi-cult to learn, you could spend three or four days working with each one to gain a better understanding of what each provides. A faster and easier way would be to have co-workers or friends who already use one of the various programs as their e-mail mainstay walk you through the basic functions and let them allow you to do some test-driving.

In terms of deftly handling e-mail, management trainer Laura Stack advocates a "6-D" system to handle e-mail regardless of what package you use:

1. **Discard it.** Delete the e-mail as soon as you receive it.

2. **Delegate it.** Forward it to someone else who can take care of it.

3. **Do it.** Respond to the e-mail, and then delete it.

4. **Dungeon it.** File it so that you can retrieve it again if you need to.

5. **Don't see it again.** Call the sender and get off the routing list.

6. **Decide.** When are you going to deal with it?

Notice that the 6-D system is related to the four-part system for handling paper files: Act on it, delegate it, file it, or recycle it.

CAUTION

Some people print each e-mail that they can't handle immediately. Stack says that this will probably add to your office clutter, but if you have an organized way of handling these messages, go ahead and print them.

Unless you're waiting for some crucial message, it's best to check your mail about twice a day, and perhaps a third time if you're feeling ahead of the game. Some people become obsessed with checking their e-mail at every spare moment. These people usually spend too much time at work sending off letters to friends, passing on unsubstantiated virus warnings, and sending and receiving the latest jokes.

THE VERSATILE FAX MACHINE

With the advent of e-mail, the fax machine seems to have declined in status. Yet creative use of the fax machine in both sending and receiving can yield tremendous productivity and time-saving benefits. For example, instead of spelling out a five-line message to a distracted receptionist or having to slowly and carefully speak to a voice mail system, fax your information or request to others. Because all of your identifying information undoubtedly is already included on the fax form, you've saved a heap of time.

TIP

The best way of figuring out what combination of fax features is right for you is to find others who will walk you through the software they use and let you get a feel for the different systems.

Suppose you're trying to reach someone by phone, and despite using automatic redial, you're having trouble. Send a quick message by fax saying that you're having trouble getting through or listing the hours when you will be available to talk. Such a transmission accomplishes several objectives. You get your message through to the party you have been trying to reach, your phone line remains open to make or receive other calls, and the option is always available to include additional information on your fax transmission.

Depending on the type of phone service you have, long-distance phone and fax rates may be lower after 5 P.M. and before 8 A.M. Many commercial offices and home-based entrepreneurs have dedicated fax lines or fax lines that share limited online time. Because in many offices a gatekeeper (receptionist) or office early birds often arrive before 8 A.M., you can inexpensively submit a fax message to be forwarded to your target. The same holds true even if the office is closed.

As with e-mail, a variety of high-powered fax software programs are available with such features as multiple mailboxes, broadcast faxing, delayed transmission, enormous storage, speed-dialing, alternative headers, custom cover pages, and extravagant reports. As the typical personal computer becomes more powerful, with more hard-drive space, faster transmission speeds, more memory, and so on, the paper-handling aspects of faxing will noticeably diminish. More and more people will be able to receive your faxes and store them directly on their hard drives.

THE INTERNET PREVAILS

With 62 million Web sites now accessible and user-friendly applications becoming available all the time, the Internet is poised to take over as the dominant entertainment, communication, and information vehicle in society. It also can become a major time drain. Searching for the precise information you seek can tie up as much as five hours a week.

Fortunately, on the heels of each problem related to using the Internet comes application software and service-oriented sites that provide an antidote. Because the specifics of the Internet change so quickly, I'll just describe broad-based categories of this type of help:

■ *Bots.* The most popular bot is used for shopping. You can unload one of these little buggers, and it will search the Internet all day long, giving you the best possible prices and best deals for the products and services you're seeking. Bots can also be used to ferret out information on health, travel, and on other bots!

PLAIN ENGLISH

Bots   Software enabling you to automatically extract and receive information gathered from the Web based on your parameters or specifications.

- **Push software.** This software visits sites and topic areas that you preprogram to provide you with regular updated information from destinations on the Web that you deem important.

- **Mega search engines.** These search engines enable you to type a keyword or key phrase and automatically have an intelligent search of the top search engines. For example, www.google.com provides rosters of Web sites based on the number of links to particular sites as opposed to what the sites' meta words and meta tags happen to say.

CAUTION

Meta words and meta tags can be artificially loaded with terms that have nothing to do with the site or that don't accurately reflect the information provided at the site.

- **Electronic clipping services.** Sites such as www.luceonline.com and www.cyberclipping.com offer you highly customized topic searches for a fee. For any single day, such sites can generate nearly everything that appears on the entire Web about a given company or topic.

Beyond employing application software and intelligent search engines to help you make better use of the Web, you can discover key sites that you might not otherwise have found by asking peers, clients, customers, or Web specialists which sites they have found helpful.

In general, good Web sites have these common features:

- **They keep visitors from getting lost.** A good Web site includes multiple links that take you back to the home page, to the previous page, or to another value-packed page of your choice. This type of navigation system ensures that you can quickly return to something familiar and comfortable or move forward to something else.

- **They go easy on the graphics.** Many Web sites are truly works of art by master graphic artists. However, smaller graphics and text-only hyperlinks enable you to navigate much faster.

■ **They include multiple contact links.** Good sites contain clear links that point you to contact information such as e-mail, fax, mail address, and phone numbers.

■ **They are visitor-focused.** A good site focuses on your needs, ensuring that the most valuable information has the most direct access with the fewest graphics.

Sites that offer most of what is discussed here help you to optimize your time online.

GO FOR A WALK IN THE WOODS

As the world in general and your life in particular becomes ever more dependent upon communication technology supplying you with just in time information, education, and entertainment, it becomes that much more important to get away from this technology periodically. No virtual reality device, at least in the foreseeable future, will provide a quick substitute for all the sensations, physical exercise, and effect on your psyche of taking a walk in the woods, doing the backstroke in a tranquil lake, or skating through the park.

If the late twentieth century taught us anything, it was that although technology may increase the frequency of communication between parties at a distance, it doesn't necessarily promote or encourage in-depth relationships:

■ It has not brought families closer together.

■ It has not helped to decrease the rate of divorce in society.

■ It has not conclusively resulted in increased scores on standardized tests among schoolchildren.

Use voice mail, e-mail, fax machines, the Internet, palmtops, and all manner of gadgetry to enhance your career, broaden your perspectives, and enrich your life. But withdraw from technology on a daily and regular basis in order to keep things in perspective. Remember that technology is a tool to help you accomplish goals that support your chosen priorities. Do not become a slave to technology, and do not allow the time you invest in technology to rob you of other vital aspects and experiences of a well-rounded life.

THE 30-SECOND RECAP

■ When leaving a message on someone's voice mail, aim for 45 seconds or so and be clear, concise, and memorable. Leave your phone number at a speed at which it can easily be retrieved. Be upbeat and positive and end succinctly.

- To gain a fuller understanding of the options available via e-mail and fax software, enlist others to give you a friend-to-friend demonstration. Get them to let you test-drive the software yourself so you can gain a firsthand experience as to what suits you and what does not.

- Use technology to enhance your career or life. Withdraw from it regularly to maintain perspective and to engage in activities that lead to a more balanced life.

Keeping Interruptions to a Minimum

In this section, you'll learn how to reduce distractions, interruptions from others, and self-interruptions so that you can increase your concentration and improve your productivity.

HAVE YOU BEEN DISTRACTED TODAY?

It's far too easy to be distracted today: There is more competing for your time and attention now than at any time in history. By some estimates, world information is doubling every 68 days. More than 2,000 books are published worldwide every 24 hours, and more than 2,000 Web sites go online in the same period of time.

A study by the Reuters Group found that 33 percent of managers in industrialized nations are suffering ill health as a direct result of information overload. Nearly two thirds of these managers reported that they felt tension with colleagues and reduced job satisfaction and felt that it was directly related to the stress of information overload. Almost an equal number responded that their social and personal relationships have suffered as a result of the stress of having to cope with too much information. Chances are your responses would be much the same.

Staying in control of your time requires greater effort and vigilance than ever before. Fortunately, once you put a few simple practices into motion and stick to them, you'll find that it's entirely possible to carve out blocks of time for yourself.

GET SERIOUS ABOUT QUIET TIME

The ease with which you can visit any one of 62 million Web sites is the all-time potential distraction within the workplace. As recently as the early

1990s, surfing the Web at work wasn't a possibility for most people. Now, with a click of the mouse, you can go on the Internet and be exposed to more information than you could possibly digest.

PLAIN ENGLISH

Quiet time   An interval during the day in which you are not sub-jected to noise.

With a simple effort, you can gain access to almost any information, organiza-tion, or person. And almost anyone can get in touch with you. People knock at your door, buzz you over the intercom, leave you voice mail, send you e-mail, page you, fax you, hand you memos, and mail things to you. Because distractions come in more forms than ever before, you need to be vigilant about barring yourself from them.

CAUTION

Don't fall into the trap of incessantly checking for e-mail or free-wheeling on the Internet when you need to be working on another task. Establish specific times to check e-mail and surf the Web for information.

Although there might be more potential items competing for your time and attention at any given moment than any career professional of any previous generation could possibly have conceived of, the elements of maintaining focus and concentration remain the same:

■ **Shut out all noise.** Forget what you read about having background music playing while you're engaging in challenging tasks. Yes, back-ground music has been proven to be effective for certain types of workers engaging in certain types of tasks, but engaging in any type of breakthrough or conceptual thinking requires your utmost concen-tration. Any competing noise in your environment potentially dis-rupts your ability to concentrate.

CAUTION

Most workplaces are not completely free of noise, but don't let machine noises and HVAC sounds serve as an excuse as to why you can't offer your full attention to the task at hand.

■ **Assemble the resources you need in advance.** This will diminish your need to get up and walk around to collect things. At the outset, the more prepared you are to tackle a project, the greater your chance of sticking with it.

- **Enlist the support of others.** If you're in an office environment, hang a sign on your door, circulate a memo, or broadcast an e-mail message that says essentially, "I need quiet from 9 to 11 this morning," or whatever timeframe suits you. Your co-workers may surprise you as to the level of support they offer you (that is, not bugging you during this time). After all, many of them seek the same thing you do.

- **Commit to the task at hand.** Unfortunately, many of us have been trained since an early age to divert our attention all over creation. We watch television shows where the typical camera angle changes every three to five seconds. We watch rock music videos where scenes shift in a second or less. All around us contemporary society seems to be telling us to give our attention everywhere all at once. Yet some of the tasks you face require several minutes of focused concentration, and some of them require several hours.

CAUTION

Unless you commit your mind and emotions to the task at hand, you're likely to find your concentration foundering.

- **Clear your desk and office** (see "Managing Your Desk and Office" on page 96). Remove from view everything except what you need to work on the task at hand. The more items that visually compete for your time and attention, the more potential there is for you to be distracted. This is why it's often highly effective to work in the conference room, at a library table, or wherever else you have few items or materials to distract you.

KNOW THY TURF

The longer you've been working within an environment, the better able you are to pinpoint potential distractions at the outset. If you've been with your present organization for several years, then you're familiar with the office and building noises, when deliveries are made, when service professionals make their calls, and so forth. When you need to tackle that big, important project and you need as few distractions as possible, devote some effort at the outset to head off distractions.

Schedule your work to coincide with those times of least distractions. Also, flip off the ringer on your phone, tell your receptionist to hold all your calls until such and such a time, and announce at a group meeting that you'll be requiring quiet time on Thursday morning. In other words, pull out the stops to ensure that anticipated distractions are eliminated or at least diminished. Then, you'll have merely to deal with the unanticipated distractions, the likes of which I can't even begin to address in one short chapter.

INTERRUPTIONS FROM OTHERS

The larger the company or organization is, the greater the potential is for being interrupted by others. However, that doesn't mean that if you work in a small organization or business with a staff of only three, interruptions from others won't be a problem with you.

CAUTION

If you're working on something important, even one other person interrupting you at the wrong time or one too many times can throw you off course.

A study conducted by *Industrial Engineer,* a professional magazine, indicated that the average interruption sustained by a manager was only six to nine minutes. Amazingly, the study also revealed that the average time it took such managers to recover from such interruptions was anywhere from 3 to 23 minutes.

So if the average interruption is 6 to 9 minutes with a midpoint of 7.5 minutes, and the average recovery time is 3 to 23 minutes, with a midpoint of 13 minutes, that means that the typical interruption results in 20.5 minutes of lost work. That being the case, it takes only one or two interruptions to consume nearly an entire hour. It takes only a few more interruptions a day to throw your entire schedule out of whack!

It's no surprise that interruptions prove to be the most stressful aspects of many people's jobs. A survey by the American Management Society reveals that 65 percent of the managers surveyed regard their jobs as more stressful than the average job. When asked to rank 15 workplace stressors, including workload, firing someone, working within budgets, balancing work and personal life, reprimanding or disciplining someone, and interruptions, the managers ranked interruptions as the most stressful of all!

CAUTION

If you don't try to minimize interruptions, you run the risk of getting far less done in a day than you had hoped for, feeling highly stressed, and having to face the same problem again and again.

Here are some ideas for keeping interruptions from others to the bare minimum:

- Devise a system where only a fraction of the questions your staff has for you have to be asked of you. How can this be done? Any question that can be answered by asking a fellow staff member instead of you should be asked of that fellow staff member. Likewise, any question that could be answered by consulting the policies and procedures manual or department, division, or team memos should be consulted so that you don't need to field the question and incur the interruption.

- Any question you need to answer that requires only a short answer should be asked of you in the least intrusive way. If the staff person can ask it by e-mail, have it asked by e-mail; if it can't wait, have them buzz you on the intercom, leave a voice mail message, or page you. Every time the question can be delayed, have it be delayed until you're finished with the task at hand that demands your full concentration. When can a staff person interrupt you without trepidation? When the issue absolutely needs to be answered by you because it's big, it's important, and you wouldn't have it any other way.

TIP

Stratifying the types of interruptions that staff members make will cause the number of interruptions per person per week to fall dramatically, perhaps by as much as 75 percent.

- Prepare your staff as well as you can so that the answers to what they need to know can be readily found. Perhaps you can produce your own orientation kit, dossier, or briefing guide. Perhaps there's a set of Frequently Asked Questions (FAQs) worth preparing. Perhaps you can steer them toward your organization's intranet where such answers are provided. Perhaps there is a forum within the intranet where staff members exchange ideas.

- Tap one of your more senior staff members to be the surrogate manager during the time when you need quiet. As you'll see in the section, "Multiplying Your Time Through Delegation" on page 128, the more often you can delegate tasks and responsibilities to others, the more your time is freed up. A good senior staffer should be able to deflect many of the questions and concerns that would otherwise come your way. The byproduct of handling this responsibility is that he or she one day will be able to handle the reins of manager. By that time, you'll have moved up as well.

- Give your good staff members multiple assignments (see "Interruptions in the Age of Beepers") so that if they run into a road block on one, they can turn to something else instead of interrupting you during this time.

- Give staff members who have a propensity to ask many questions assignments that are relatively straightforward or routine for them. Then, for at least the duration of when you need a quiet, uninterrupted stretch, you'll know that they're tackling assignments that pretty much don't require your input.

INTERRUPTIONS IN THE AGE OF BEEPERS

Are you among the legions of professionals who have to wear a beeper as part of their overall responsibilities? If so, establish some simple protocols so that you can minimize the interruptions as a result of having to be on call.

Negotiate for some days during the week and some hours during specific days for which you will not have to be on call. In other words, you can turn off the beeper. As professionally and succinctly as possible, let your boss know that having to maintain constant responsiveness in the form of having to wear a pager greatly diminishes your ability to handle tasks and projects that call for deep concentration or highly creative thinking. A wise boss knows that this is true and is likely to grant you some beeper-free periods during the week as you request.

CAUTION

When you can't work, go to lunch, take a nap, or even go to the restroom free of a pager or a cell phone, you're not really free to work and to live.

If you manage your own business or are otherwise in charge of when you wear a pager, recognize that you need stretches throughout the day and week when you won't be interrupted. If you're convinced of the need to be connected at all times, then chances are you're micromanaging, or overmanaging, all aspects of your business or your department, division, or staff. Micromanaging isn't pretty. In the short run, in a specific campaign, and during crunch time, it's okay. In the long run, it will keep you from rising to greater heights within your organization or within your own business.

Not All Messages Are Created Equal

Another essential strategy, which is laid out in the book *The Complete Idiot's Guide to Managing Your Time,* is to create a message hierarchy. Suppose that many of your cell phone calls and pages originate from a main source, such as an executive assistant. Work with that person and let him or her know when it is okay to interrupt you versus when it's best to hold messages until later, based on the following four-level system for deflecting pages:

Level A: Contact me now. This level includes messages that you want to receive, the sooner the better.

Level B: Contact me within *x* number of hours. This level includes messages about items that are important but not necessarily urgent (see "Avoiding the Tyranny of the Urgent" on page 75).

Level C: Contact me sometime later today. This level includes messages that you could receive at any time during the day because they're not time-related in the least. Fortunately, most messages fall into this category. When your assistant recognizes this, you'll gain more uninterrupted time, more often.

Level D: No need to contact me at all. This level includes messages or questions that your assistant might have felt were worth sending you in the past. Now, however, based on a clearer and mutual understanding of what needs to be transmitted and what doesn't, these messages no longer come to you because the assistant has the resources to find the answers to most questions and knows which messages you need to receive.

To make this system work, lavishly praise your assistant anytime he or she sends you a Level A message. Admonish the assistant anytime he or she sends a Level D message, because you never needed to be interrupted with that in the first place. Point out that, "That was a Level D message," if you happen to receive one.

Within a week, possibly even days, your assistant will be on the same wavelength as you and begin to understand what needs to be transmitted and when. This meeting of the minds will enable you to have uninterrupted stretches when you can do the things that you need to do.

Extending the Principle

To avoid being interrupted by nonurgent phone calls, leave instructive messages on your voice mail and other answering devices that tell callers how their issues can be resolved. Announce in your messages that such and such person can take care of particular issues, or that you'll be available by phone Wednesday morning at 11:30, or that the best way to handle a particular problem is to e-mail the production department. In essence, deflect and win. If you have various voice mail boxes available, let callers know that they can gain the answer to questions about XYZ by pressing 1, pressing 2 will divert them to Sandra who can help them, and so on.

TIP

The more you're able to deflect and reroute messages to a person who can answer questions for you, the more uninterrupted time you'll have.

INTERRUPTIONS ARE MY BUSINESS

Suppose where you work constant interruptions are the norm, and you've been hired to take care of them. How can you remain effective, practice good time management, and still keep your sanity?

TIP

However deftly you dart from task to task, you'll do your best work if you concentrate on the task at hand, even if it's just for a brief time.

Think about when you're about to board a flight and then you hear an announcement that the flight has been canceled. Passengers in the airport lobby are up in arms. They rush to the gate agent and demand to be rebooked on the next flight immediately.

Does the gate agent handle 5 or 10 customers at a time? No. He or she focuses intently on the passenger who is first in line, eyeing the computer monitor to determine what alternatives are possible. The attendant works on that customer's new itinerary until it is complete. The process may take 3 minutes or 10 minutes. The skilled gate agent knows that there's no faster way to handle this mini-crisis than to stay calm and remain in control of the situation and to give full attention to the customer at hand.

Likewise, for every demand you face, eliminating distractions, reducing interruptions, and giving your full and undivided attention to the current task so that you can concentrate and do your best work is the best way to proceed.

The 30-Second Recap

- We live in an age that offers more distractions than anyone has ever faced previously. Thus, we must make a concerted effort to keep distractions to a minimum.

- The typical interruption at work is only 6 to 9 minutes. Recovery from the interruption, averaging 13 minutes, is what spells trouble. It only takes one interruption an hour to throw off your whole day.

- If you wear a pager, you have some special challenges to face because you're on call every minute of every hour of every day, theoretically. Strive to safeguard stretches of your time by working with others who are most likely to interrupt you. Also work with your boss so that you have some pager-free time throughout the week.

Multiplying Your Time Through Delegation

In this section, you'll learn the do's, don'ts, principles, and techniques for delegation, as well as how to handle delegated responsibility.

Making It Work

It is said that management is the art of getting things done through other people. The most effective managers are skilled at delegating tasks and assignments to others and assuring that those assignments are successfully completed. Delegating is important to your career because the amount of time you can save by delegating is enormous.

TIP

Nothing you do on your own can rival what you can do when you successfully harness the skills and ideas of others.

Before you delegate a task to somebody else, you have to know a little about that person:

- What is his or her workload?
- What are his or her skills?

- What kind of supervision is needed?
- How often do you need to follow up with this person?

You may be thinking, "This is a lot of information to have prior to delegating to somebody. If I have an assignment, can't I just hand it off?" You can, but the results are likely to be less than desirable. By understanding as much as you can about those to whom you delegate, you have the best chance of delegating effectively and accomplishing your objectives.

Take the case of someone who reports to two bosses or more. If you're trying to delegate to such a person, you need to understand this person's workload. Perhaps he or she can share his or her assignment list or scheduling calendar with you. The more heavily burdened the worker is, the more important it is for you to schedule your task so as to fit the other person's schedule.

TIP

It's best to assign tasks that fit the interests, skills, and experiences of the worker. After all, you don't want somebody translating Greek if they don't know one word of the language.

If you've worked with a person before, then you might have a reasonably good understanding of his or her working habits. Does this person need to check in with you regularly to ask several questions or receive your feedback and praise? Or is this person a self-starter who wants to receive primary instructions and then be allowed free rein in getting the job done?

TIP

The longer and more involved the task, the more often you'll need to check in with the worker. However, if it's something he or she has done before, oodles of instruction and follow-up may not be necessary.

THE DO'S OF DELEGATING

This list of quick do's will help make your delegating efforts more successful:

- **Do plan your delegations carefully before making them.** You want to parcel out doable assignments that are a reasonable match for the worker handling them.

- **Do offer clear instructions.** These instructions could be typed up, sent by e-mail, or perhaps recorded on cassette tape or videotape.

Don't underestimate the value of taping your conversation when you make the assignment. Particularly if the assignment is something the worker has not done before or if the assignment is long and involved with many subparts, taping the session can be extremely beneficial because the worker can play the tape and capture your exact words on an as-needed basis.

- **Do be flexible regarding the due date.** At times, you may have no alternative but to offer a fixed deadline. For many tasks, however, it may not make a difference to you exactly when the worker finishes the task.

TIP

When time is not critical, offer a due date to the worker and then be generous when he or she misses by a day or two.

- **Do ensure that the worker has sufficient resources to get the job done.** There is nothing worse than assigning people to your project and then watching them fail because they don't have the right equipment, staff, or other resources at their disposal. In your role as delegator, work with staff to ensure that they know sufficient support is available.

- **Do monitor progress as is practical.** Be available for questions and guidance. Ideally, the worker takes the project, doesn't bug you for a single second, and returns with everything done correctly and on time. Realistically, the worker is going to need to get back in touch with you on occasion for questions, concerns, and sometimes just to have a sounding board. If you recognize this in advance, you have a better chance of being effective.

- **Do be both firm and flexible.** Convey an accurate picture of what needs to be done, but allow leeway in how it's accomplished. Sometimes the worker will approach a problem in an entirely different way than you would. That's okay if it gets the job done, if it doesn't tie up an inordinate amount of resources, and if the work is delivered on time.

TIP

Pay attention to how workers complete projects. Often, you'll get wind of some new procedure that's faster and more effective than how you would have done the job yourself.

- **Do acknowledge the worker's contributions.** Everyone likes recognition for his or her efforts. You, of course, are more interested in results. Because sufficient efforts lead to results, you increase the probability of having the end result being what you want by acknowledging efforts throughout the process. Offer constructive feedback when you sense or see that the project is heading somewhat off course.

- **Do keep records of how the project was completed.** When the job is completed, make notes as to what the worker completed, the skills and ingenuity he exhibited, and other observations about accomplishment of the task. Later, you can draw upon these notes in devising more assignments to be delegated.

DELEGATION TAKES TIME

Undoubtedly you have heard the expression, "If you want to get something done, do it yourself." This expression was probably coined by someone who was not an effective delegator.

Yes, there are some tasks you could finish yourself in the time it takes you to explain what needs to be done to someone else. If the task is not recurring, go ahead and do it yourself. However, for any other type of task, it pays for you to explain to someone what you want done. Taking the time to explain a task helps establish a system in which this particular task or others like it no longer need to stay on your plate; you're training somebody else how to relieve your burden.

CAUTION

If it's taking longer to explain how to do something than it would take to do it on your own, keep in mind that your efforts will bear fruit the next time the task is delegated.

Anytime two or more parties are working together, however, the probability for unsuccessful results is present. Much of what is delegated is not handled properly or is not turned in on time. Why? Sometimes the task was not delegated to the right person. More often than not, however, the way in which the task was delegated was insufficient.

THE DON'TS OF DELEGATION

Avoid these pitfalls when delegating a task to another person:

- **Don't rush.** Don't be in such a rush to hand the assignment over to someone else that you do not fully explain all the steps involved to successfully complete the project.

- **Don't pass on incomplete instructions.** If you give the worker a list of instructions, make sure the instructions are complete. Leaving out one little thing that seems obvious to you may spell the worker's downfall.

- **Don't ignore the worker's concerns.** Delegating involves a lot of explaining, but it also involves a lot of listening. Be prepared to listen to the questions and concerns of the worker. Listen between the lines for the worker's fears.

TIP

Receiving a new task can be a little scary for a worker. Also, depending on how much else competes for his time and attention, the worker may feel stressed or anxious.

- **Don't give the wrong image of yourself.** Don't profess to be open to questions and concerns and then make yourself unavailable. A little frustration for the workers can turn into a major one if you're not around to handle the 10-second question that would get them back on the right path. (Think about how you feel when you're trying to learn a new software package. Would you rather spend a half-hour trying to find the right keystroke combination to proceed or ask somebody who can show you in 10 seconds?)

- **Don't arbitrarily delegate to anyone.** Pick a person for the job who can schedule the task, handle it effectively, and turn it in on time.

- **Don't think your way is the only way.** Don't be so concerned if the worker proceeds differently than you would, as long as the worker is progressing toward the desired result. Offer sufficient slack for the worker to get the job done in the way he or she sees fit, as long as he or she is not unnecessarily expending resources and taking inordinate amounts of time.

WHAT TO DELEGATE

Often, otherwise effective career professionals don't make the progress in their careers that they otherwise could because they are not delegating enough to others. The more competent one is, the more often one is likely to keep too many tasks on one's own to-do list. Therefore, examine all the tasks and projects on your plate with an eye as to where you can get help.

CAUTION

As a manager, you want to cultivate your ability to work with and through other people, as opposed to continuing to take on more and more on your own.

Suppose you're a sales manager who is working later and later into the evening and enjoying it less. Even the most junior staff person within your office can give you enormous help, if you expand your view of what can be delegated. For example, with a little time and effort, this junior person could be put in charge of handling customer requests for information by directing people to the Web site, mailing out literature, and referring people to the appropriate party within your department.

What other kinds of tasks could be delegated to even the most junior person on your staff? Here are some ideas:

- Sending out mailings of any sort. If you have a flyer or a brochure that needs to go out to targeted recipients, initiating this campaign and handing it over to a junior staff person makes good sense.

- Routing and sorting incoming mail.

- Serving routine customer needs. This person could establish a list of FAQs (frequently asked questions).

- Producing a department or division directory of key staff and how to reach them and offering customers contact information, product announcements, and service literature.

- Picking up and delivering things.

- Researching or surveying customers to learn more about their needs and potential opportunities for additional sales. Research could be as simple as gathering articles on the customer base or visiting some customer sites and making notes. Surveys could be as brief as five questions asked over the phone, via e-mail, via fax, or simple mail campaign.

- Keeping track of trade publications. This person could set up a small library that also houses key directories and industry newsletters.

- Logging names into the customer database. Whether you use Access, ACT!, GoldMine, or any of the other popular databases, virtually anyone who has worked with a PC can be instructed how to enter names in as little as five minutes.

- Studying competitors' literature, products and services, Web sites, and publications. What better way to keep on top of what others are doing than by having the most junior staff person of your office assemble dossier packets for each of the sales professionals?

- Doing searches on the Web. If you want to find a particular product or service, company, or organization, make a list and hand it over. Your time will be freed up, you'll get the answers you'll need, and you'll feel more in control of your day.

- Tracking or arranging inventory or displays, setting up materials at trade shows, or shipping materials to and from trade shows.

- Proofreading or double-checking copy for marketing literature, memos, sales letters, follow-up letters, and boilerplate materials.

- Doing many other things that you don't need to be doing, because with a little instruction and a little guidance, this worker can handle your delegated assignments.

After this worker has gained some experience as a result of all you have delegated, you can then delegate even more important tasks and free up more of your time. Here are some of the higher-order tasks that you can delegate to workers as they prove their *mettle:*

- **Call customers after a sale to see whether they feel satisfied, what else they may need, and how they feel about the purchase.** This kind of follow-up is an excellent way to learn about your product or service performance, and you often gain critical feedback from customers that you ordinarily wouldn't have time to collect. Many companies are able to make quick follow-up sales as a result of these calls that they wouldn't ordinarily be able to make.

- **Seek out new sources of supply.** Depending on what you offer, the price of supplies and raw materials that you use may differ widely. A junior staff person can get on the Web and start making comparisons or go to industrial directories, such as Thomas's register or even the Yellow Pages of your phonebook, and make inquiries. Having someone periodically assess new sources of supply and delivery can make the difference between having a profitable quarter and having a highly profitable quarter.

PLAIN ENGLISH

Mettle   Value or worthiness, particularly when tested by challenging conditions.

DELEGATING TO HIGHLY EFFECTIVE WORKERS

If you're blessed to be working with a highly effective staff, you're likely to have rewarding experiences when it comes to delegation. You may have the opportunity to delegate often and even delegate several assignments at once. Effective workers understand their productive peaks and valleys throughout the course of a day and a normal week.

When you delegate several tasks to a good worker, he or she instinctively knows how to maintain high productivity by handling assignments on those days and at those hours that achieve a relatively constant effort-to-task ratio. Good workers know how to harness their varying energy levels throughout the workweek so that they know what can best be tackled when.

If you give such an employee several assignments and can be flexible as to when they're due, you'll receive each of the completed assignments in a manner that probably exceeds what you would have expected. Productive employees have their own internal time grid. Allowed to pace themselves, they can accomplish more and remain energetic.

TIP

Continually meeting with someone who offers arbitrary deadlines is draining. So when you give good employees assignments, let them work out the schedule.

Here are some additional tips to delegating to highly effective employees:

- Provide enough and varied assignments so that the worker knows what to undertake and when.

- Be as flexible as you can regarding when assignments are due. Good employees tend to finish the important jobs on time. They finish the less important assignments as soon as possible thereafter.

- Avoid late afternoon assignments and surprise assignments throughout the week. Sometimes this isn't possible because you've been hit with a surprise and have no choice but to pass it on. However, try not to upset the personal productivity cycle the good workers have already established for themselves in accordance to the assignments you have already delegated to them.

- Always seek to provide enough advance notice of assignments so that productive employees have sufficient time to integrate the new assignment into their current schedule of assignments.

Delegating to Veterans

When working with more senior workers, you have the opportunity to delegate large tasks and projects. In this case, it makes sense to build follow-up into the overall assignment period. Perhaps you meet every Thursday at 10 A.M., or perhaps you exchange e-mails at the end of each day. Or perhaps you have a Monday morning chalk talk, where you chart the progress of the project, make course corrections, see what additional resources are required, and so on.

TIP

For larger, ongoing projects that you have delegated, your regular input becomes a vital resource in the overall success of the project.

Suppose you've delegated several large projects to several different veteran workers. You may end up having several meetings about these projects throughout the week. In each case, you are ensuring that the entrusted staff person stays on course in the critical projects you have delegated. That's just fine, and that's what a good manager does.

Ideally, everything on your plate would be handed off to others, and you would work in a supervisory capacity, guiding here, cajoling there, extending resources there, and so on. This is not to be confused with having people interrupt you all day and all week long (see "Keeping Interruptions to a Minimum" on page 120) for questions and concerns that you don't need to be exposed to.

As you rise within your organization, you may find that regular meetings with key staff or entire teams to whom you've delegated assignments becomes the norm. That's fine; you're doing your job.

One day you may find yourself as CEO, where you're literally handing off everything, keeping your eye focused on the big picture of the organization, making critical decisions, and offering crucial observations and advice. Consider the president of the United States. He doesn't do anything, but rather relies on a bevy of top advisors, top administrators, and top White House staff to ensure that the wheels of the nation stay well oiled.

The 30-Second Recap

- Effective managers are effective delegators. The higher you want to rise in your organization, the more important it will be for you to delegate.

- You have considerable leeway when it comes to delegating tasks to good workers. You can give them several assignments, and if you're flexible with your due dates, they'll perform in a manner that meets or exceeds your expectations.

- Even the most junior person on your staff can handle a wide variety of assignments with a minimum of direction and support. The more often people handle tasks that are appropriate for them, the less guidance and fewer resources they require in order to be successful.

Avoiding the Time Traps

In this section, you will learn how to say no without fear, defeat perfectionism, manage your anger, and avoid other time traps such as television and idle time.

THE FEAR OF SAYING NO

You are requested to do something at work, and your automatic response is "Sure." You are asked to attend something that you would rather not attend, but you agree to go. Many career professionals who have little problem saying no in their home life find that saying no in the workplace is difficult. And this difficulty causes time management problems.

CAUTION

Simply uttering the word *no* is difficult for many people.

Suppose a co-worker asks you to participate in some extra-curricular activity after work. Suppose, too, that it is an activity you enjoy, but it is not something that you care to engage in right now. Your plate is already full. It makes far more sense for you to get home early at night than to hang around for yet another activity that consumes your precious leisure time.

Nevertheless, you want to be one of the pack, part of the in-crowd. So what do you do? You say "Sure, why not?" Thereafter, every Tuesday you find yourself lingering at work for another hour, getting home later than you prefer, and resenting the fact that you agreed to be part of the group. Maybe it's the kind of a group where each meeting draws you in further. Perhaps you have some crucial responsibility. Everyone is counting on you. Now you can't withdraw, even though the time investment is upsetting you.

Let's look at a second scenario. You're invited to attend a one-time event. Perhaps it is a retirement party for Bob up on the third floor, or maybe you have been invited to attend a baby shower for Jessica in production. Maybe you have been asked to volunteer one Saturday two months from now, and it appears that your schedule is open. So you say yes to the retirement party, the baby shower, and the Saturday volunteer job.

When you stop and think about each activity, however, what you wanted to say was no. You've never liked Bob; you simply said hello to him a few times in the hall and tolerated his corny jokes. If you go, it would be for reasons of office politics, which have some value. As for Jessica, what is this, her third or fourth child? Didn't you attend a shower of hers two and a half years ago where you were utterly bored?

When you looked at your calendar two months in advance and saw that the time for the Saturday volunteer effort was wide open, it was relatively easy for you to say yes. When you have no competing responsibilities or scheduled items, why not be generous with your time? Yet a curious phenomenon occurs as you approach that date for which you said that you would volunteer. Your schedule starts to fill in, and when the date of your volunteering finally arrives, you barely have enough time to honor your commitment. Again you become resentful and wish you had said no two months before.

PLAIN ENGLISH

Volunteering   Willingly giving of one's time or effort.

DECLINE WITH TACT AND EMPATHY

The common denominator in these situations is the inability to politely and tactfully decline an invitation. It's one thing if your boss asks you to take on extra work or your team is staying late one evening to tackle some tough problem that hasn't gone away after considerable effort. It is quite another issue to participate in all manner of quasi-office activities presented to you, largely as a function of your working in that environment.

Take the case of Bob's retirement party. Have you ever had lunch with Bob? Have you and he ever had a meaningful conversation of longer than five minutes? Has Bob helped you in some specific way, or have you helped Bob in some specific way? Do you share any kind of bond? If the answers to these questions are no, no, no, and no, why would you want to attend Bob's retirement party? For appearances? Perhaps. Out of respect? Possibly. Because you feel it is your duty? No way.

What could you say when presented with the invitation? Try these statements:

- "I wish Bob well, but I'm already committed for that time."
- "Please express my congratulations. Unfortunately, I'll be unable to attend."
- "I promised my son that we would XYZ, but give Bob my best."
- "I can't attend, but I would like to offer a small gift, what do you suggest?"
- "Sounds like it will be a great event, but that evening I'll be at XYZ."

In the case of the baby shower, similar responses will work, as well as the following: "Oh my, this will be my fourth shower in about four months. I'll have to pass on this one," or "I appreciate the invitation, but I'm already scheduled."

Finally, in the case of someone asking you to commit your time at some distant point, be on guard! As is relayed in *The Complete Idiot's Guide to Managing Your Time,* we all tend to fall into the trap of believing that two to three months from now our calendar or our schedule will somehow work itself out and the time pressure that we feel today will subside. The first step in helping your cause is to not say yes when you prefer to say no.

Here are some appropriate and tactful ways to decline requests for your time at some distant future date:

- "That's going to be too close to the time when our family is going to be traveling."
- "I can't make a commitment right now; I'll know better in a couple of weeks."
- "I appreciate the invitation, but Saturday afternoon is the time when I do XYZ."
- "It sounds worthwhile, but count me as doubtful. I need that time to XYZ."

TIP

When declining an offer, acknowledge the invitation and respect the fact that the event has importance to the inviter. Also, convey your good wishes even if you can't attend.

You cannot give someone a flat-out no without explanation. They will be offended, have hurt feelings, or feel somehow that they have let you down or wronged you in the past and now you are retaliating. Therefore, the no's that you offer need to be respectful and firm while being gracious and compassionate.

DEFEAT PERFECTIONISM

At times, the drive for perfectionism is appropriate. A doctor performing a complex operation, a pilot landing a jumbo jet plane, and a police detective investigating a murder all need to strive to do the best possible job. Yet even these professions have times and situations where perfectionism is unnecessary, unwarranted, and overly time-consuming. For the doctor, a bandaging job that is 95 percent toward perfect is just fine. For the airline pilot, a landing where one wheel touches down a half-second after the other does not diminish the quality of the flight. For the police detective, not interviewing an eleventh witness after interviewing 10 witnesses who independently corroborate each other's observations is probably okay.

In your own work, there are countless times throughout the day when not being perfect makes more sense from the standpoint of practicality and saving time than striving for perfection. When you're assembling data to make a decision, the opportunity before you may have passed if you wait to decide until you have reams of information. If you collect too much data, then you get to a point where you are more confused than informed. Assemble only the body of information necessary to help you feel comfortable with your decision, but no more than that. Let go of the tendency to overcollect.

TIP

Many decisions made based on instinct and intuition turn out just fine. This is because all the data to which you have ever been exposed is brought to bear when you're making a decision.

Look for opportunities throughout the workday where a 90 or 95 percent effort is just fine. If you're turning in a report, and your department is structured so that the production team does copyediting, it doesn't pay for you to turn in a 100 percent grammatically correct report. Studies show that the additional time you spend to take a project from the 95 percent mark to the 100 percent mark is not worth it in most cases. Striving for perfection (that is, ensuring that the final 5 percent is done correctly) often takes as much time as the initial 95 percent effort required!

When giving instructions to your staff, if you give them 9 or 10 suggestions on how to effectively do a job, but forget one or two suggestions, your staff will still have plenty to work with. If you strive to give them every great suggestion you can come up with, the time and effort that you expend may be inordinate, and the marginal value of the extra suggestions for your staff may not be nearly worth the effort.

AVOID CREATING THE PERFECT ENVIRONMENT

Some people waste oodles of time trying to create the perfect *environment* before starting tasks. They adjust the blinds just so. They sharpen three pencils. They refill their coffee cup. They wait until the top of the hour. They stack up the papers on their desk neatly.

PLAIN ENGLISH

Environment   One's surroundings; in the context of the workaday world, one's office and surrounding offices and, in general, one's workplace.

To be sure, there is nothing wrong with arranging your immediate environment to accommodate the way you work. Having your office and work setting the way you want it is conducive to your productivity. The problem starts when you find yourself continually in need of having a perfect environment before getting anything done. Delaying the start of a project until everything is just right is just a form of procrastination.

MANAGE YOUR ANGER

What does managing your anger have to do with a lesson on avoiding time traps? Isn't it natural to get upset on occasion? Yes, it is. The problem with anger from a time standpoint is how long it takes you to overcome its effects so that you can get back to rational, clear-headed thinking.

Some people go into a tizzy over the smallest of things and spend half the morning stewing about it. If your anger has arisen, how can you mute its effects so as to not waste time and be rather ineffectual while you are in a state of anger? Here are some suggestions:

■ Decide how much time you are going to allow yourself to be angry. A reasonable timeframe is five minutes. Then hold yourself to it. When the appointed time comes, get back to the job at hand.

■ Pull out a motivation-inspiring poem, passage from a book, or a saying, particularly those passages that you have already earmarked as effective for getting you back on track during times when you are otherwise out of sorts.

■ Talk to a co-worker or call a friend who is good at listening, can help you work things out, and can help you get back on track in near-record time.

■ Take that walk, count to 10, throw cold water on your face, or engage in any other activity rationally used to ward off anger.

The following suggestions can work just as well, after you have blown your top:

■ **Fight for objectivity.** Try to look at the big picture. Take whatever incident occurred and keep it in context.

■ **Write down how you are feeling and why.** Sometimes the mere act of expressing your thoughts on paper helps to release some of the pent-up emotion. Afterward, chuck the piece of paper.

■ **Break your routine.** If your anger arose while you were sitting, then stand. If you were standing, then sit. If you were in motion, then stop. If you were inside, then go outside. If you were outside, then go inside. For many people, a change of venue improves their mood greatly.

■ **Change your physiology.** If you throw your shoulders back, stand erect, and force a small smile, your psychology begins to follow. Studies have shown that people who hold their heads up high, smile, and walk proudly, feel more confident than people who mope along, stare at the ground, and let their shoulders droop. Likewise, it is hard to feel angry if your *physiology* emulates something other than the closed, clenched, restricted posture that is characteristic of anger.

■ **Get physical.** I don't mean punch somebody. Rather, stretch, practice isometrics, or if no one is around, do jumping jacks. By getting physical, you divert your energy and focus from anger.

PLAIN ENGLISH

Physiology   The science that deals with processes and functions of living organisms.

Turn Off the Boob Tube

Do you arrive at work exhausted some mornings? If so, there are probably identifiable behaviors you engage in that lead to such a situation. You stay up a little late, watch an extra television show or two, and find yourself getting to bed a little later than your body needs. The simple truth in Western society, and increasingly throughout the world, is that too many of us watch too much television too often.

CAUTION

Sitting and watching television zaps your creativity. Television's words, sounds, graphics, and images tend to drown out your imagination.

It's time to recognize television for what it is: a plug-in drug. Sure, there are dozens of worthwhile programs in the course of a week, including movies worth seeing, educational shows, and history programs. Sometimes the show is good: The themes are compelling, and you actually learn something. However, how often do you focus on these highly worthwhile programs? And even if you limited your focus to these programs, do you watch in measured amounts, maintaining a balance of other activities? Watching even the best television show pales by comparison with what you could learn by reading great literature, participating in your community, or being a parent, a spouse, or a friend to a live person.

CAUTION

The average person spends nine solid years of his life watching how other people supposedly live on television.

Japan and other Southeast Asian cultures that now find themselves thoroughly ensconced in television programming have experienced the following marked, undesirable changes in their societies in the last decade:

- The attitude of workers has changed.
- Materialism runs rampant.
- People are awash in gadgets and electronic goods.

DISCOVER AUDITORY MEDICATION

Radio can instill the same languor as television. When you drive to work in the morning, do you turn on the radio to listen to some shock jock dispense his brand of socially contemptible humor? These shock jocks are paid megadollars to medicate you for 15 or 20 minutes while you make your way through roads jam-packed with cars.

What is the harm, you say, in listening to some witty, if not deviant, shock jock while making your way in to work? After all, you have to be in the car anyway, so how can this be a drain on your time? The problem lies in the opportunity cost of what else you could be doing with your time in the car:

- Listening to classical music would filter into your being and prepare you from a physiological standpoint to have a more pleasant morning.

- Listening to a book on tape or motivational tape could provide you with new insights while entertaining you and stimulating your imagination.

- If you share a ride on the way in to work, conversing with a friend can yield many benefits.

If you find yourself automatically flipping on the television as soon as you get home or flipping on the radio as soon as you get in the car, and think that you are not hooked on these devices, then try this simple test. For one week, every time you get into your car, drive for at least five minutes before turning on the radio. If you're like most people, you'll probably find that you can't do it.

At home, go a whole evening without turning on the television. If you are able to do that (and you will be among the few), go a whole weekend without doing it. Likewise, rather than wantonly surfing the Web, engage in something else for a weekday evening or weekend.

These activities are not simply exercises in abstinence, but rather they are telling indicators of just how much we have allowed the electronic connection to infiltrate our lives and, in many respects, dominate our lives.

CAUTION

There are certainly good things to hear on the radio and many Web sites worth exploring. The problem arises when you allow such media to overstep its bounds and facilitate the ease with which you idle away your hours, your days, your weeks, and your life.

The 30-Second Recap

- Until you learn how to say no with grace and ease, you are likely to find yourself saying yes to all manner of activities that you prefer not to be involved in.

- Depending on your profession, there are situations in which it pays to do a perfect job. For most people, however, perfectionism is a huge time trap.

- Turning off your television may be the single most effective step you can make to reclaim your time.

Managing Time on the Road

In this section, you will learn how to increase personal effectiveness by being productive while traveling by car, public transportation, or airplane.

BE PRODUCTIVE WHILE DRIVING

As each month passes, a variety of new electronic gadgets becomes available with increasing capabilities over those of their predecessors. Using plug-in or wireless equipment, you can connect with phones, faxes, e-mail accounts, the Web, and everything in between. Regardless of the type of equipment you employ, the fundamentals of being productive while on the road stay relatively the same.

Make no mistake, when you're driving, your principal activity is driving. Studies show that driving while speaking on a cell phone quadruples the risk of an accident and increases the risk of dying in an accident by 11 times. You can give your sharp attention in only one basic direction.

CAUTION

If you are pulled up to a traffic light or sitting in slow-moving traffic, it is still dangerous to talk on a cell phone, even a hands-free cell phone. Don't do it. Pull off to the side of the road if you must make a call.

Listening to music or speaking with someone in the passenger seat does not pose the same risk. The reason is that your sharp attention can continue to be on the road, and as practical, you can give some attention to the radio, CD, or the passenger in the seat next to you. However, at any given moment, your driving takes precedence. This is not the case with the use of the cell phone; concentrating on the conversation with someone at a distance and driving compete with one another.

If you ride with people on the way to work because you are part of a car pool or van pool, try to commute with those with whom you enjoy conversing. Surprisingly, you may have more lively conversations with someone who does not work with you and benefit from the cross-fertilization of ideas.

TIP

Keep your car windows closed and the heat or air conditioner on. Studies show that you will obtain the same miles per gallon as you do with the windows open and the heater or air conditioner off, and the ride will be much quieter.

If you decide to listen to something, play a CD or cassette that is invigorating or inspiring. Visit your library and find lectures, plays, and essays on cassettes or CDs. Or play classical music whose rhythms and composition have been shown to promote healing and well-being as opposed to other forms of music, which can have a disconcerting effect.

MAKE THE MOST OF YOUR COMMUTE

A daily commute can be drudgery. You crawl along bumper to bumper, inhaling the fumes of the thousands of cars before you, on a superhighway that effectively operates like a slow-moving parking lot. Whether the traffic is moving fast or slow, use commuting time to contemplate your day. Consider what is on your agenda for the morning, who you will be meeting, what you will be doing, and then see yourself successfully handling it all.

TIP

A major key to personal effectiveness while commuting is to use that time for reflection, instead of automatically flipping on the radio or engaging in some other activity that essentially represents filling the time.

One way to avoid the masses in the morning and afternoon is to depart when everyone else isn't. If you can leave an hour or an hour and a half earlier or later than everyone else, you're likely to have smoother sailing. Consider getting up at your normal time, working for an hour and a half at home, and then departing for the office. Perhaps you can do the same at the end of the day by leaving early in the afternoon, getting home without fighting a lot of traffic, and then working for another hour or hour and a half. Or perhaps you prefer to leave after everyone else does at the end of the day.

Once a week, try telecommuting instead of going into the office. These days almost everyone is wired to their offices by fax, modem, and telephone. If you can stay home even one Wednesday every other week, you'll find that you're far more productive in handling the kinds of tasks that are hard to tackle in a hectic office.

For variety, one time a week take a different route home. Even if you end up spending an extra five or eight minutes driving home, it's worth it to see another section of town, to pass other stores and neighborhoods, and to stimulate your thinking.

CAUTION

Commuting back and forth on exactly the same path day after day, week after week, can put you in a rut. Varying your routine a little can be beneficial in many ways.

PREPARE FOR CONTINGENCIES

Keeping your car in absolutely the best running condition is the first prerequisite to success on the road. You only have to break down once in a strange location to experience how unproductive a day can be. Take your car in for a tune-up on a regular basis, as the manufacturer recommends. It doesn't hurt to take the car in anytime you even suspect that something is not operating as it should be.

If you're not a member of one of the national auto clubs, it pays for you to become one. If you have to have your car jump-started or towed only once per year, the annual cost of membership has already paid for itself. Having this kind of security is priceless. By dialing an 800 number, you can have a top-flight garage with a qualified towing specialist on the scene almost wherever you are, usually in 45 minutes or less.

Keep an extra set of car keys someplace under the bumper in one of those hide-a-key compartments. Also, have spare house keys hidden in your car, just as you would have spare car keys somewhere in your house. Getting locked out is not productive. Having to call somebody to open your car is a waste of time and money.

Hide a roll of dimes and a roll of quarters in your car to use for parking meters, pay phones, and vending machines. Keep a backup briefcase or folder in your trunk with stamps, envelopes, pen, paper, calculator, and perhaps important phone numbers. What else is worth storing in the car? A gym bag with socks, extra underwear, a toothbrush, tissues, flashlight, sunglasses, less frequently used credit cards, library cards, first-aid kit, umbrella, raincoat, hat, and some gloves among other things.

If you ride with a notebook or palmtop computer, undoubtedly you have key addresses and key phone numbers with you. If not, hide important phone numbers, PIN numbers, and access numbers someplace in your car where they will never be found, but where you can draw upon them in a hurry if you need to.

ORGANIZE YOUR ERRANDS

Instead of letting all your errands stack up for the weekends, designate one night per week as errand night. For example, make Monday, Tuesday, or Wednesday night the night when you handle errands on the way back from work. Prepare for multiple stops by making a brief list and affixing it to your dashboard.

Keep a file folder, envelope, or pouch handy for assembling the various tickets, sales slips, and so forth that you will be dispensing and collecting. If you can, keep the passenger side of your car clear so that it serves as your command center on wheels.

TIP

Buy in bulk so you don't have to return to various stores as often, or have the stores come to you by finding vendors on the Internet who can pick up and deliver.

While running your errands, listen to books on tape or uplifting music as discussed previously. Whenever you control your environment, particularly in your car, you have a better chance of staying energetic and alert. If you incur traffic backups, long lines, or other delays, fold up the tent and head home. It's no use trying to force your way through the crowds. You can handle errands another night, preserve your weekends, and get it all done in less time and with less bother.

As more and more of what you need to do can be done via catalogs and the Internet, you may find that a couple of hours a week is more than enough to take care of errands. Rather than pick up stamps at the post office, order them by mail. Rather than dropping off deposits at the bank, mail them in. Every time that you don't have to get into your car to accomplish something, you save time, preserve your vehicle, and keep your sanity.

BE PRODUCTIVE ON PUBLIC TRANSPORTATION

If you are one of the less than 10 percent of the working population who gets to work via public transportation, my hat is off to you. Though cities have designed vast subway and bus systems, the majority of commuters still get to work by automobile. There are many ways to be productive while on a bus, subway, train, or van.

To tune out surrounding noise, use a portable cassette or CD player. Choose what you want to listen to, but make sure that it's uplifting, informative, and generally supports how you want to be and feel in life.

If you travel with a palmtop or notebook computer, you may wish to sit on the nonsunny side of the vehicle, depending on the brightness of your screen. Also, be sure to have plenty of recharged batteries available for the ride. *Murphy's Law* says that your batteries will fail you about five minutes after you get started. Quash that possibility by always traveling with fresh batteries, and having a backup pair ready to draw upon.

PLAIN ENGLISH

Murphy's Law   The age-old axiom stating that if something can go wrong, it will go wrong.

CAUTION

Do not house your expensive computer in a traditional carrying case, because these are targets for thieves. Instead, carry expensive equipment in a satchel or worn briefcase.

The lighter you travel, the more adept you will be at getting on and off the bus, subway, train, or other vehicle. If you have been commuting for any length of time, you know how long the ride will take, so you can plan your work accordingly. I've seen many adept professionals practice what I call vest-pocket management. They are able to pull out a pad or pen, business cards, Post-it notes, a palmtop computer, a handheld calendar, a pocket dictator, or a variety of other work-related tools from their vest pocket, get to work at the drop of a hat, and pack up just as quickly. If you continually have to fumble through a large briefcase to find a pen or key folder, you're not going to be highly efficient while working on public transportation.

If you read a lot during your time on public transportation, bring materials you can quickly pare down. For example, if you are plowing through several magazines, quickly detach the articles that appear to be of interest and recycle the rest of the magazine. You may want to purchase a small *slasher* (available in any office supply store), which enables you to deftly remove articles from a newspaper or magazine by making a light incision around what you have selected. Your goal while traveling is to always have less to carry at the end of your trip.

TIP

Always retain the smallest volume of paper that serves your purposes. For example, save the one page from an article that contains key information instead of saving the whole thing.

With the availability of handheld scanners, you can now travel with a pocket scanner, scan in one line of a document at a time, and end up carrying little paper. Likewise, if you travel with a pocket dictator, simply dictate the key phrases, phone numbers, and other tidbits of information you want to retain. Later you can transcribe your own tape or have someone else transcribe it and have the information on hard disk.

If you travel with a cell phone, be respectful of other passengers. Turn away from the open area, modulate your voice, and keep your conversations as short as practical. You may think that you're taking care of all kinds of business and that you're so efficient, but to everyone else around you, you are a crashing bore.

Checking for voice mail messages, e-mail, and other correspondence can now, of course, all be easily handled while in transit. However, don't whip yourself into a frenzy over the gathering of these messages. They will all still be there when you arrive at your destination. Too many career professionals, in the erroneous belief that they have to stay connected, wired, and available every nanosecond of the day, heap far more stress and anxiety upon themselves than the previous generation of career professionals ever had to contend with.

 CAUTION

Incessantly checking voice mail and e-mail is usually not the hallmark of a highly efficient person; it's the hallmark of someone who is obsessed.

FLY THE FRIENDLY SKIES

With increasing passenger loads and more restrictive airline configurations, airline travel has become increasingly stressful in the last few years. The key to being productive while traveling by air is to stay light and take care of as many things as you can beforehand:

- Pack the night before and pack as light as you can.
- Use the smallest possible size of various toiletries.
- Use rolling luggage so that you don't have to lift your bag. Most airlines will accept carry-on luggage of 22 inches by 14 inches by 9 inches. Thus, you can roll your luggage onto the plane and never have to check your bag, which saves a good 15 to 20 minutes at the end of each flight.
- Don't pack anything that you know your hotel or host destination already supplies. You can always call in advance to get a list of what

is offered. You'll have a lot more room in your suitcase if you don't have to pack a bathrobe, an alarm clock, a hairdryer, and so on.

The airlines will let you take two bags onboard. If you have to pack a second bag, use something that fits on the top of your rolling cart luggage so that you can roll them both instead of lifting either bag. If the second bag is your briefcase, pack it lightly and efficiently. If you have to have more than two bags, you might as well check them all, because waiting for one bag is going to be roughly equal to the time you have to wait for all of your bags.

If you have a lengthy trip with many stops, rather than bringing enough clothes for each day, bring enough clothing for half the trip plus one day. In other words, if you are traveling for nine days, bring five days' worth of clothing. If you are traveling for 10 days, bring 6 days' worth of clothing. Then, as you approach the halfway point of your trip, get everything cleaned while on the road. Taking advantage of laundry and valet services costs a little money, but you're far better off dispensing a few dollars here and there than toting an incredible burden of heavy clothing.

Bring U.S. Priority Mail packages with you so that as you collect paper information during your travels you can mail them back to yourself rather than continuing to carry them. At a little more than $3, a U.S. Priority Mail pack is relatively inexpensive, is made of tyvek material so that it can't rip, and has a self-adhesive closing flap. You can stuff the package full, and the post office hardly ever loses them. Bring address labels for both your destination and your home base to save you from having to write out your name and address.

PLAIN ENGLISH

Valet   Traditionally, a personal attendant; hotel/business services that pick up and drop off of garments and other personal items.

BOOK YOUR FLIGHT AND GET IT RIGHT

Never, ever buy tickets at the airline counters the day of your departure. If you do, you're likely to get the worst seats at the highest price. You want to buy your tickets in advance so that you can get the bulkhead, the wing row, or an aisle, each of which offers more room than being in the middle or in a window location. If you prefer the window, fine. Most business travelers want the flexibility of an aisle seat. On an aisle seat, you can get to the bathroom more easily, you can stretch, and you can get to the magazine rack if you so choose.

Always bring a water bottle with you so that you don't have to wait for flight attendants to come around to quench your thirst. A few sips here and there can make all the difference between maintaining high energy and high productivity, and being sluggish and dehydrated and not getting the quality of work done that you had hoped to. Always bring your own snacks. Pack carrots, cucumbers, apples, bananas, sunflower seeds, peanuts, and anything else that is healthful and will give you an energy boost.

CAUTION

Avoid bringing heavily sugared or salted snacks that offer nothing more than empty carbohydrates. These snacks will drain you of energy, leave your body starved for nutrients, and make you far less efficient.

If you're meeting a client after you touch down, you may have to wear your full business suit; otherwise, wear loose and comfortable clothing. You want to be able to move around freely. Sitting in an airplane seat for hours can be confining. Of late, with smaller seats and heavier passengers, it can be an ordeal. Avoid heavy clothing, tight shoes, restrictive belts, and anything else that reduces respiration, ventilation, and circulation.

If you're flying in the middle of the day and the sun's ultraviolet rays are more pronounced, especially if you're flying above the clouds, don some sunglasses. Also use the airline overhead lighting and lower your window cover. Your eyes won't get nearly as fatigued.

TIP

If you need to sleep on the plane, put on a baseball cap with a message on the rim saying something like "Sleeping, do not disturb." If you need to work, consider wearing a cap that says, "On deadline, please do not disturb." You'd be surprised how well people obey these messages.

Avoid alcohol at any time during your flight, even if it's at the end of the day, you are heading home, and there is no more work to be done. You might think that it is relaxing to finish off the day with a beer, wine, or other alcoholic beverage, but you'll end up dehydrated and more tired than you would otherwise feel. If you need a nightcap, wait until you are home.

THE 30-SECOND RECAP

- In a highly mobile society, the chances are increasing that you will be spending some time in a moving vehicle. By making adequate preparations beforehand, you maximize your potential for being at your best while in motion and afterward.

■ Assemble in advance the equipment, reporting items, snack items, and other creature comforts that enhance the way you work and rest. This will give you the highest probability of being productive while on the road.

■ Check for voice and e-mail messages periodically throughout the day, but don't become obsessed about it. You don't need to check every few minutes.

Getting Organized

Easy Organizing Basics

In this section, you will learn how to become a task master by identifying organizational problems and acting on them accordingly.

GETTING STARTED

Every day of our lives is filled with tasks. Some are daily, such as brushing your teeth, taking a bath, and putting on your clothes. Others happen weekly, monthly, or less often. Examples include paying the bills, going to church, collecting a paycheck, or getting that annual checkup.

Finally those tasks for which, generally, we are not prepared. No one wants to think of going to the hospital. And, whether we anticipate it or not, there are those words from the mouths of our children, "Mom, Dad, I'm going to get married."

TIP

We need to be prepared for what the world hands us. Living an organized life helps prepare you not only for planned events, but also for the unexpected.

Where do we begin to get organized? Ground zero. Get out two of the most common instruments of organization—a pencil and paper. You are going to begin learning the basics of becoming a taskmaster. You can start with the essential formula for becoming organized:

Organization = Planning + Routine + Refinement

This may seem simple, but it does work.

TIP

Close the door and let the machine take your calls. Getting organized requires the time and space to concentrate.

PLANNING THE DAY AHEAD

The best place to begin is at the office, whether at home or work. Get out that pencil and paper, and begin developing a task matrix like the following:

#	Task	Time	Due
1	Open and respond to postal mail	30 minutes	2 P.M.
2	Open and respond to e-mail	30 minutes	10 A.M.
3	Give work assignments to staff	30 minutes	9 A.M.
4	Review daily work in progress	1 hour	4 P.M.
5	Plan staff assignments for next day	1 hour	4:30 P.M.
6	Plan monthly calendar	1 hour	1 P.M.

Fill in a list of all the tasks you are expected to start and complete every day on the job.

TIP

Determine the time that it usually takes you to start and complete the task. Then list the time of day by which the task must be finished; realign those tasks in order, beginning with the earliest time of day.

You have successfully developed a basic plan. Make sure to leave enough time between each task to allow you to finish in the order they are due. Also, leave time for the unexpected, as follows:

#	Task	Start	Finish
1	Give work assignments to staff 30 minutes	8:30 A.M.	9 A.M.
2	Open and respond to all mail 30 to 45 minutes	9 A.M.	10 A.M.
3	Plan monthly calendar 1 hour	10 A.M.	11 A.M.
	OPEN 2.5 hours	11 A.M.	1:30 P.M.
4	Return phone calls 1 hour	1:30 P.M.	2:30 P.M.
	OPEN 1 hour	2:30 P.M.	3:30 P.M.
5	Review daily work in progress 30 minutes	3:30 P.M.	4 P.M.

continues

continued

#	Task	Start	Finish
6	Plan staff assignments for next day 1 hour	4 P.M.	5 P.M.
7	Update your to-do list 15 minutes	5 P.M.	5:15 P.M.

Now you have created time modules to complete known tasks, as well as those that occur on a less frequent or emergency basis.

CAUTION

You may be required to submit a weekly report to your supervisor every Friday. Don't wait until Friday to write, edit, and submit it. Make time *every day* to begin developing that report.

That "last-minute" routine only defeats the purpose of everything you are trying to do—get organized, become more productive, and gain more time to do other things.

CREATING A "TO-DO" TEMPLATE

Take your task matrix to your computer, and design a personalized "to-do" list template form. Print out a few blank sheets at the start of each week. Make a *habit* of filling it out every afternoon before you leave.

When you arrive at work the next day, you're geared up. You don't have to spend time visualizing the day ahead because you're already in motion.

PLAIN ENGLISH

Habit   A pattern of behavior acquired by repetition. Psychologists and behavior experts say that it takes about 20 to 70 days to form a new habit.

REFINE YOUR LIST

Begin refining your "to-do" list every morning. Practice using it. Keep the list with you throughout the day. You'll want to determine whether tasks are being started and completed as scheduled.

Problems may arise. You may have two or more tasks that must be completed by the same time every day. Soon, learning to prioritize will become a habit.

TIP

Try giving your tasks a priority level, such as A, B, and C. If you have two A priorities, choose A1 and A2, and so on. You obviously can't do them all at once, so this will add order to what may seem like chaos.

Repetition of your routine will allow for refinement. Trust your abilities to prioritize and schedule your obligations. Your boss wouldn't have put you in that position if she didn't believe that you could accomplish the tasks.

Still Have Problems?

If you still can't complete the tasks in a timely fashion, don't panic. It will take some time, especially if you're not a naturally organized person. There are ways to solve the problem:

- *Delegate.* If you have subordinates, do they appear to have more free time than you? You might be able to assign some of your tasks to them.

PLAIN ENGLISH

Delegate   To assign authority or responsibility to another.

- **Get proper training.** Do you rely on others to help you finish certain tasks? Ask for or get additional training in weak areas, such as computers.
- **Turn off the noise.** It's easy to get distracted by the problems of others, telephone calls, and even impromptu meetings. Set your schedule (with flexibility built in) and make it clear to colleagues.
- **Put in quality time.** Are you getting to work on time? Are you putting in the number of hours expected of your position? Make the most of it by being organized.

An asset of good organizational skills is the ability to identify problems and act on them accordingly.

Put Technology to Work

The beginning of this section was devoted to incorporating simple organizing habits into your daily life. Technology has done a lot for us in terms of providing tools for organization. These tools are not that difficult to implement, either, once you decide what you need.

COMPUTER FILING SYSTEMS

Most of what you read and write for your business is stored somewhere, in a physical, paper version (or hard copy). It should also be stored on your computer. Try to label both using the same protocol—for example, client files can be arranged alphabetically in your paper system, Alvarez, Brown, and so on. Try to do the same on the computer:

- Name your main computer folder Clients. In your physical office, Clients would be the label on the file drawer.

- Name the subfolders under Clients in your computer with client names. Let's use Brown, Alice as an example. Under Clients, you could name a folder Brown, Alice. In your filing drawer, Brown, Alice would be a hanging file of its own.

Each new document for Brown would be labeled with a date system—for example, Brown, Alice 72800 for a July 28, 2000, document. You could create a new subfolder by month or by topic, depending on the nature of the work.

As an example, the file Brown, Alice would look something like this in your computer:

Drive: C

Folder: My Documents

    Folder: Clients

        Folder: Brown, Alice

           Folder: July

               Document: Brown, A 72800

The July 28th document is about five levels down, or five clicks down, in your computer files from your C drive. Now you can easily put your hand on both the hard copy and the electronic file.

BACKING UP

The best filing system can be quickly destroyed by a computer virus or a power strike. Protect your files by backing them up. A backup is a copy of your computer files stored on either a disc, a tape, a CD or the network server.

Backing up your computer files is simple and takes very little time. Your computer software will guide you through the steps. You can decide when, where, and how the computer backs up your files. Get your system in place and stick with it.

TIP

Create two sets of backup disks. Swap them out so that there is always one full set of backup disks. Store them offsite, such as in a safe deposit box or in your home.

There are two kinds of backups:

- **Full backup.** Full backup means just what it sounds like: You back up everything on your computer. Create full backups in accordance with how much and how often the data changes in your files. You can set the computer to do a daily, weekly, or even monthly full backup.

- **Selective backup.** Selective backups are useful if you are working on only special sections at a time. You can select entire drives for backing up, or you can choose individual files and folders. Selective backing up should be done on a daily basis.

CREATE A SYSTEM

Label and number your disks, CDs, or tapes in advance. We'll call them Set A and Set B for the sake of example.

Pick a day, such as Monday or Friday, to begin your backup cycle. Insert your Set A, and select the drives or files necessary for a full backup in your backup program. Do this again with Set B. Now you have two copies. Take Set A offsite for the week.

Insert Set B daily to perform a backup of selected files, those used most often. These will automatically become a part of the full backup.

At the week's end, bring back Set A and perform a full backup. Take Set B offsite for the week (it's fully up-to-date already). Repeat the weekly process.

You'll never have to fear a loss of data greater than one day's worth if you follow this system. Damaged or lost files can be easily restored, using the backup program's restore feature.

TIP

You can back up your files on the Internet. Some Web sites offer free space; others charge annual fees in the $100 range. Two top picks in 2000 by *PC Magazine* were www.connected.com and www.xdrive.com.

TIP

Don't get discouraged if you don't have all the "traits" of a leader. You don't have to be born with them, but you can use them as inspiration.

Cleaning Up Your Hard Drive

Clutter creates stress and wastes time. Computer clutter may be confined to the central processing unit, but it can be just as debilitating as an untidy office. There is probably junk on your computer that you don't even know about. That's why uninstaller utilities such as Norton's CleanSweep by Symantec or McAfee's Clinic can prove invaluable for getting organized.

Once installed, these programs go through your computer system and help you delete unwanted junk and duplicate files. They will remove orphans and redundant DLLs, and even tidy up the files that hang on after you've been Web browsing.

Begin implementing some of the concepts introduced in this chapter slowly. As you incorporate them into your daily life, you'll find that it's not taking more time, but less, to get things done.

The 30-Second Recap

- Create personalized task lists.
- Schedule time blocks to complete tasks.
- Build flexibility into your day.
- Plan for tomorrow today.
- Identify problems and take corrective action.

Finishing a Day's Work in Advance

In this section, you will learn how to lay out your day in advance, from wake up to lights out.

Getting Up to Go to Sleep

Nothing in life is perfect, and no day works completely the way we expect. There are just too many factors that we can't control. Even in the world of business, planning consultants recognize that their projects will not happen exactly as written.

But plans exist to give direction—and sufficient resources—to respond appropriately to the unplanned. That is called organization.

The same can be said for how we plan each day of the workweek.

TIP

The very nature of organization is to anticipate and prepare for change.

No one individual will have a day exactly like that of the next person. However, we can define certain tasks and determine how they are to be accomplished. We set them in motion.

WHAT TIME IS IT?

What may be the most important task of the day is deciding when to rise and meet the day. That's very simple. You will perform certain functions to prepare your body for the whole day, interact with other members of the home, and leave the house with sufficient time to promptly arrive at work. That is the hour for setting your alarm.

MORNING ROUTINE

Conduct a morning exercise to generate the body into action and to stay trim and fit. It may require getting up earlier, but it can set the tone for the whole day. For instance, you could get up at 5 A.M. daily to spend 45 minutes following an exercise video before the rest of the family awakes. The feeling of having accomplished something for your own good is invaluable.

The benefits of exercise in battling stress are well documented. Regular physical exercise can help reduce anxiety and mild depression, and can help fight disease. You don't have to undertake a heavy workout to benefit; a brisk 20- to 30-minute walk daily can be enough. Other types of exercise, such as yoga or tai chi, can also help revitalize your spirit along with your body.

CAUTION

Don't forget to eat—it's often said that breakfast can be the most important meal of the day. The body needs nourishment to begin the day.

E-Mail, Anyone?

The incredible onslaught of the computer age has made this machine a common sight in most homes. Be careful—don't make the mistake of getting caught up to the point that you leave late for work or get frustrated before you even leave home.

Office e-mail should remain there—in the office. If you're waiting for an important document, however, you may want to use an e-mail forwarding system, such as hotmail.com or desktop.com. (See "Managing Your Computer," on page 183 for more details.) This allows you to access important messages from home, while leaving a copy on the office server so that you'll be able to view it again at work.

TIP
Leave personal e-mail review for the evening when you have the leisure time to read and respond to it.

Dress for Success

Have your clothes ready the night before, and round up the dry cleaning for drop-off the next day. Paralyzed over what to wear? You're not alone, especially because 90 percent of all companies in America have adopted a casual dress policy. In fact, one third of those companies allows dressing down every day. But how casual can you go?

Mary Lou Andre, fashion consultant and president of Organization by Design in Needham, Massachusetts, has created a booklet titled *Making Casual Day Work*. She says the best bet is to aim for a classic look; this booklet is available at www.dressingwell.com. Some other fashion do's and don'ts include the following:

- Leave your printed T-shirts at home.
- Save sweats for the gym, and save beachwear for the beach.
- Keep shoes shined and scuff-free.
- Combine items from your business wardrobe with casual attire.
- Wear a vest instead of a blazer.
- Match your belt to your shoes for a polished, coordinated look.

Andre notes that a relaxed dress code has many benefits, including improved productivity, increased morale, and greater loyalty. So if you're a manager, you may want to institute a casual dress policy. If you're an employee, you still need to draw the line between casual and sloppy.

Off to the Races!

For most of us, driving to and from work can be the most stressful beginning to any day. There are ways to avoid the stress:

- **Turn on the radio.** Soft, soothing music or a humorous talk radio show is certainly more relaxing than the latest disaster news. Or find audio books at your library or bookstore.

- **Get a head start.** Leaving a little earlier and giving you more time to arrive greatly reduces that stress.

- **Discover new ways.** Why not get up a little earlier and take a less congested route? A change of scenery will make you feel less like a robot on its daily programmed mission.

TIP

Why not enhance your value to the company and boost your self-esteem by learning a new language during drive time?

You've arrived on time, nourished, rested, and relaxed. That's the way it should be. If you develop a well-organized routine as exemplified in the previous sections "Easy Organizing Basics," on page 156, your mind and body should be ready to take on the day.

Going Home

The time between the office and home may quite often be the only time alone you'll have in the day. Take your mind off the job now. Put that soothing music back on, or practice your foreign language verbs. Why jump back on the expressway? Don't take that stress home to the family. Take that quieter route.

It's fairly easy today to find out the traffic report before you leave the office. Even Web sites—including the New York/New Jersey/Connecticut tri-state regional traffic site, www.metrocommute.com, or the San Francisco Bay Area's www.travinfo.org—offer in-depth details.

Etak, a publisher of digital maps, has created a demonstration Web site called www.etaktraffic.com that will provide live, real-time traffic information online for metropolitan areas in the United States. The system eventually will be able to send e-mail and pages to commuters to let them know about problems in advance.

TIP

If you've planned it well, you may have something to pick up on the way home, such as dry cleaning, or you may have a workout appointment at the gym. Make the most of your drive time.

No Surprise

If you have planned this day beginning this morning, or the night before, there shouldn't be any surprises when you get home.

TIP

Make sure to greet each family member individually when you come home—it reestablishes personal contact.

When you arrive, everybody should be going about the job of fulfilling obligations of dressing down, going through the mail, preparing meals, doing homework, and then getting together at the dinner table. Eat, relax, and share your day with the rest of the members of your household.

CAUTION

Surf the Internet if that relaxes and entertains you, but don't get caught in a time warp. The idea is to relax.

Lights Out

The notion of a full night's sleep should not seem like a luxury. Go to bed at a time that allows you to get sufficient rest and sleep. And don't worry about the job or tomorrow's challenges. You can't do anything about tomorrow until it arrives. Remember, you are getting your life organized. You should begin to feel in control of your life.

Plan Ahead to Save Time

One of the best ways to succeed in getting organized is to be ready for what comes your way. By planning ahead, you avoid the panic and anxiety that can overcome you when the unexpected comes up. One of the first steps in planning is to identify your problem areas.

Tackle the Time-Wasters

Take a look at the results of the following survey, conducted by Pace Productivity, Inc., of Toronto, Canada. Pace surveyed more than 600 employees and entrepreneurs in North America to find out what they considered to be the top time-wasters in terms of their productivity.

These were the top 15 responses to the question of what things outside the respondents' control got in the way of productivity. We feel certain that you'll recognize them yourself:

Time-Waster	Number of Responses
Paperwork/administrative tasks	135
Customer requests	115
Phone calls/phone interruptions	101
Computer/system/equipment problems	86
No internal support/other department inefficiencies	58
Unspecified interruptions	45
Traffic/travel	43
Meetings—too many/too long/unnecessary	38
Volume of work/not enough time	38
Staffing issues/people absent	36
Requests from peers/other departments	31
Changing priorities/unplanned projects	29
Fire fighting/emergencies	27
Doing other people's jobs	26
Handling customers without appointments	23

How can you stop wasting time? Two words: Be ready. Let's use the top problem on the previous list as an example—paperwork.

TAKING STEPS

The most common time-waster is paperwork or administrative tasks. Although these tasks may seem like a waste of time, they are essential to keeping order and records of your business. Let's tackle them:

1. First, determine when your energy level is at its highest, and use that time to tackle those tasks that tap your brain the most. Put all those seemingly Herculean tasks on your to-do list at your peak energy times.

2. Second, call ahead. If you know that you have a weekly report to do, for example, gather the facts a few days before. A few minutes spent on the phone or sending e-mails to the right parties to assemble data could save you an hour. Place your notes in a file folder labeled "In Progress." When you're at your peak productivity time, you want to have the details at your fingertips.

3. Finally, streamline your process. Clutter creates stress. Select the tools that you use most often, and toss the rest. Don't waste precious time digging through desk drawers of files, scissors, pennies, and paperclips. According to Michael Fortino, a time management expert with the Efficiency Index, the average American spends a full year searching for misplaced objects in a lifetime. You can avoid some of that by having fresh pads of paper and several working pens ready, and also having your favorite word processing application shortcut ready on your computer screen desktop.

Self-Determination, Your Power Tool

In the section "Easy Organizing Basics" we created a task matrix. This is one of the best tools you can use to plan the week ahead. When you get into the task list habit, you'll become a better time manager, simply by trial and error. Here are some other time-planning techniques to add to your toolbox:

- **Own your own time.** You wouldn't let someone help himself to your cash, would you? Why let that person dig into your time? You can control interruptions by having a ready response, such as, "I'd like to help you with that problem. If you send me an e-mail/note/memo, I can give it the attention that it deserves when I'm through here."

- **Just say "no."** It's not easy to do, so we don't often say it. Here's an exercise to help you learn to be positive while delivering the negative. At the end of each week for four weeks, write down the requests that you should have turned down. Now write down why it didn't work out, or why you felt burdened by it. That's the reason that you'll give next time you get a similar request.

- **Prioritize and protect.** Ask yourself if you're working on the most important project. Have you scheduled enough time to do it? When you have created the time blocks outlined in the section "Easy Organizing Basics" on page 156, guard them. You can't make time go faster or slower, but you can keep a to-do list, freeing up your mind to tackle the work.

You can't manage every minute of your day, and no one is saying that you should. What's important is to plan ahead for the big chunks of time to get the work done. It's also important to give yourself a few breaks. Scheduling in 15 minutes for quiet reflection or a walk around the building can provide just the change in mental attitude that you need to be efficient in business and to continue to enjoy life.

THE 30-SECOND RECAP

■ Organized living allows flexibility in dealing with life's surprises.

■ Planning your day in advance can give you control of your life.

■ Rise early enough to perform a morning routine.

■ Exercise and diet ensure good mental and physical health.

■ Ease yourself to and from work to limit stress.

Using High-Tech Tools and Software

In this section, you will learn how to turn the gadgets of early twenty-first–century technology into powerful organization tools.

HIGH-TECH TOOLS

This era of explosive growth in information technology has had phenomenal impact on our lives, at home and at work.

Today's tools have dramatically increased worker productivity and the ability to communicate in manners considered unimaginable only 10 years ago.

CELL PHONES

Cell phones are convenient and portable, weighing from two ounces to four pounds. The most well-known brands include Ericsson, Motorola, NEC, Nokia, Sanyo, and Samsung. Prices are associated with three types of technology: analog, digital, or digital PCs, and cellular service that you lease.

Analog phones are the cheapest and oldest models. You can get them free with the service, but digitals, today's more common technology, can cost as much as $75 to $300. A monthly service can be had for around $15.

Finally, digital PCs is the latest technology, using a higher-bandwidth frequency than its predecessors. The cost of this phone can range from $50 to $200, and monthly phone service costs about $15. It is important to note that monthly cell phone services will vary from one place to the next, but the price trend is moving downward because competition in the cell phone service industry is intense.

DESKTOP COMPUTERS

Nowhere is the rapid evolution of information technology more evident than in desktop or personal computers. By the time you read this book, there will be bigger and faster models on the store shelves everywhere.

PC World, one of the most respected consumer magazines about computers, categorizes these computers by power, midrange, budget, and home PC models. The major distinctions are in processor speed, hard drive space, amount of RAM, and add-on hardware devices.

CAUTION

Most PCs come with a standard-size monitor. If you spend many hours a day at the computer, get a 19-inch monitor, even if it means an upgrade. It's worth it to avoid eyestrain.

Today's personal computer characteristics are as varied as the three major categories—power, midrange, and budget.

Type	Power PC	Midrange	Budget
Price	$2,500+	$1,500+	$900+
Hard Drive	20+GB	13+BG	10+GB
RAM	128MB	64MB	32MB
Processor	800Mhz	600Mhz	466Mhz
Monitor	19+ inches	17 to 19 inches	15 inches

The most notable difference is the lack of or reduced performance of extra features. Of course, price ranges are approximate and represent what *PC World* defines as "street prices," which can vary from one month to the next. Brand names are quite diverse, but the more well-known brands include Acer, Axis, Compaq, Dell, Gateway, Hewlett Packard, Micron, Micro Express, and Quantex.

The previous table reflects the three categories of computers as of this printing. It should be noted that prices and other features constantly change, reflecting the very short product life cycle in the computer industry. You would be advised to periodically review industry magazines such as *PC Magazine* (www.zdnet.com/pcmag/) and *Smart Business* (www.zdnet.com/smartbusinessmag/) for changes in prices and features.

PLAIN ENGLISH

RAM   Random access memory. The more RAM you have on your computer, the better the performance of your applications.

LAPTOP COMPUTERS

A must-have for many traveling executives, laptop computers (also called notebook computers) are diverse and have street price ranges of $1,200 to $3,200. Typical specification ranges include 366MHz to 650MHz processors, 64MB to 128MB of SDRAM, 4.3GB to 12GB hard drives, and 12- to 15-inch screens.

Apart from the well-known desktop brand names (Toshiba, Hewlett-Packard, and IBM), Chem USA, Enpower, and Twinhead are also notable among the notebooks. Apart from increased power, speed, and storage space, notebooks are adding CD-ROM and CD-RW drives. They have also made great strides in the viewing screen and built-in mouse features. The touch pad has become commonplace, and screens now have the technology to be viewed from all angles; they no longer require head-on vision.

PALM COMPUTERS AND WIRELESS APPLICATIONS

First introduced by Apple Computers in 1993, handheld and palm devices, from computers to connected organizers, have become incredibly popular only in the last year. The handheld PCs typically range in price from $400 to $3,200.

Operating on external power and batteries, these devices have processor speeds that can reach 750MHz, and their screen sizes average about 10 inches. Just three to five pounds in weight, they have docking stations for hooking up to your desktop and sharing data. Hard drives can now reach 1GB. Common brand names include IBM, Palm, Inc., 3Com, Compaq, and Dell.

TIP

Limit yourself to one or two compatible types of organizers. Otherwise, you'll spend a lot of time updating different systems.

Handheld Organizers

A step down from the handheld PC is the connected, handheld organizer, known as the *personal digital assistant* (*PDA*). These small machines, weighing in at as little as seven ounces, provide Internet and e-mail access, but they direct other applications to organize dates, phone numbers, addresses, and memos. Prices range from $250 to $500. The dominant operating systems for handheld systems are Windows CE and Palm OS, which come installed on the organizers. Newer versions of Windows CE now incorporate miniversions of the Windows office suite.

Accessories include the stylus, a penlike stick that substitutes for the classic mouse; a three-pack can be purchased for $40. If the handheld doesn't have a keyboard, foldable, full-size keyboards are useful—just slide the handheld device into the tray and being typing. The keyboard relies on the device for its power source and typically retails for $90 to $100. The dominant operating systems for handheld systems are Windows CE and Palm OS, which come installed on the organizers. Newer versions of Windows CE now incorporate miniversions of the Windows office suite.

Pocket Organizers

The predecessor to the handheld organizer, pocket organizers can now be purchased for as little at $10 to $40. They remain a very reliable, low-cost alternative.

Texas Instruments, Rolodex, Royal, Casio, and Sharp were leading brands when these devices reached their zenith of popularity. Still, they remain a very reliable, low-cost alternative for those on a restricted budget but who want to maintain ready access to names, addresses, phone numbers, calculators, calendars, a notepad, and memos. Powered by a lithium battery, they typically store up to 64KB of memory.

CAUTION

Pocket organizers are powered by lithium batteries and store up to 64KB of memory. Make sure that yours also has a backup battery included to avoid losing valuable data.

Software

Just as electricity is the fuel of the desktop, software is the steering wheel of the computer.

OFFICE SUITES

The Big Two in office suites have long been Microsoft Office (www.
microsoft.com) and Lotus Smart Suite (www.lotus.com). A full program can
cost from $100 to $690. The basic applications of all three suites include
word processing, spreadsheet, and presentation software.

But nothing stays the same. IBM no longer continues to develop Lotus, and a
newcomer has arrived. Called StarOffice, this full-fledged cross-platform
office suite is developed by Sun Microsystems and is available for free on the
Sun Web site (www.sun.com/staroffice).

MONEY MANAGEMENT

Personal finance manager software (*PFM*) has become much easier to learn
these days. Tools serve bookkeeping, accounting, investment portfolio management, and online banking functions. Microsoft Money, Intuit's Quicken,
and Peachtree Accounting are the proven leaders; the various versions range
in price from $20 to $220.

PLAIN ENGLISH

PFM   Short for personal finance manager software, such as
Quicken or Microsoft Money.

TIP

Don't overlook business-planning software as an organization tool.
It's designed to help you develop milestones, assignments, and
deadlines. Some well-known brands are Business Plan Pro (www.
paloaltosoftware.com), BizPlan Builder (www.jian.com), and Smart
(www.smartonline.com).

TASK AND CONTACT MANAGEMENT

Organize your contact and account information with full-fledged software
packages. Brand names for software include Day-Timer, Lotus Organizer,
Microsoft Outlook, Act!, and Select Phone; prices range from $50 to $180.

PLANNING SOFTWARE

Project-planning software can help you in planning, development, and monitoring projects. FastTrack Schedule, Primavera SureTrack (www.primavera.
com), Microsoft Project, and Visio (www.microsoft.com) are the most well-
known brands; depending on the complexity and requirements of the project,
the price range varies dramatically from $20 to $10,000.

Business-planning software is designed to lead you through the process of developing a comprehensive business plan; prices range from $50 to $100. The more well-known brands are Business Plan Pro (www.paloaltosoftware. com), BizPlan Builder (www.jian.com), and Smart (www.smartonline.com).

WEB CALENDARS

Put your calendar, to-do list, and address book on the Internet for easy access anywhere. These interactive online calendars will remind you to make appointments, gather data, file taxes, and even pay your part-time employees. Many, such as Outlook and Palm Pilot, will synchronize with your *PIMs*. You can log on to these Internet-based calendars anywhere you can find a computer with Web access. A few are now available, although some were in test stages at this writing:

PLAIN ENGLISH

PIM   Personal information manager. A software application that lets you enter dates, lists, and reminders. Most also include scheduling, calendars, and calculators. Check out Zdnet.com for the latest PIM reviews and downloads.

- **The Daily Drill (www.dailydrill.com).** A free online calendar and appointment book. You can customize a calendar to remind you of official or religious holidays, birthdays, and special events. The Drill will notify you of upcoming dates with a Web page alarm, send you e-mail, or page you if your pager is equipped with text messaging. At the bottom of each calendar is a to-do list. Fill it out, update it from anywhere, print it out, and carry it with you.
- **Day-Timer Digital (digital.daytimer.com).** A free, private calendar on the Web. You can view personal and public events at the same time. The service can remind you through e-mail or pop-up screens when you log on. This service will also add e-mail accounts in the future.
- **Excite Planner (planner.excite.com).** A free Web portal offering of calendar and day planner. The service can send e-mail and pager reminders, and it synchronizes with popular desktop and handheld organizers, including Palm devices, Microsoft Outlook, and selected Motorola, Nokia, and Ericsson wireless phones. You can also get your own toll-free number for voicemail and faxing.
- **Yahoo! Calendar (calendar.yahoo.com).** This free Web portal calendar has Time Guides, a feature that automatically overlays events such as sports games, co-workers' calendars, and stock splits on your

own personal schedule. You can keep track of earnings release dates, stock splits, and board meeting dates for companies in your portfolio.

You can also keep up with the rest of nation's calendars. For example, Yahoo! has condensed the key economic indicators from several government areas into an economic calendar at biz.yahoo.com/c/e. html. What makes this online calendar so distinctive is that it provides the links to the actual government report for those who want to read more.

- **IRS Calendar (www.irs.treas.gov/prod/tax_edu/tax_ cal/0100. html).** Free, but not personalized. Bookmark this IRS calendar on your computer to keep ahead on your tax obligations.

VOICE-RECOGNITION SOFTWARE

Voice-recognition software translates the spoken word into text in your word processing software, either by microphone or by specialized tape recorder. Some of the more common applications include Via Voice (www.ibm.com) and Voice Express (www.lhsl.com); they range from $40 to $230. Think about the captions on your TV screen when you hit the Mute button—now imagine the same technology on your computer with a software package. If you're not a typist, or if you always find yourself scrambling for pen and paper when the big ideas hit, this is for you.

TIP

Special versions of voice recognition software can be found for specific professions. Prices range from $200 to $800.

The tiny tape recorders slip easily into a pocket, ready when you are. After recording a day's worth of ideas, download the .wav files onto your computer. It takes a little bit of setup using a microphone plugged in to the computer, but it can be a real time-saver.

INTRANETS

One restricted-travel highway beyond the Internet is the *intranet.*

PLAIN ENGLISH

Intranet   A network designed for information processing within a company or organization.

Having your own intranet requires a software developer to access a series of tools (applications), including page editors, Web designers, code, and WYSIWYG (What You See Is What You Get) editors. The applications and costs are varied, so you should contact software developers to learn the specific costs based on your company's needs.

A Word About Low-Tech

High-tech tools and software are great, but there are mainstay items necessary to an organized lifestyle, including telephones, pagers, and tape recorders.

TIP

For the office, buy a phone with an answering machine. Other good features include two or more lines with Hold buttons, caller ID, speaker-phone capability, and remote message access.

Telephones

You have four categories from which to choose a telephone—corded or cordless, and with or without integrated answering machines.

Cordless systems enable you to move around without restrictions to location or distance, within limits. Typical brands include Panasonic, Sony, AT&T, V-Tech, Nortel, and Siemens. Prices typically range from $100 to $500.

In more recent times, the use of portable headsets has become very common among executives and SOHO environments. It allows you to communicate by phone, hands free, while performing some other function like typing, filing, and so forth.

CAUTION

If your home office has two telephone lines—one for Internet and the other for telephone/fax—portable phones can create frequency interference, depending on the quality of home wiring.

Pagers

Basic pagers have a numeric readout of the paging phone number. Prices range from $10 to $50. The next grade up offers numeric and word messaging with an average price of $80. Sophisticated pagers allow two-way word messaging and contact management software for prices up to $400.

TAPE RECORDERS

Tape recorders come in two varieties—cassette and digital. The traditional cassette format ranges from $40 to $80 dollars. Newer digital systems allow recording in separate files and feature compatibility with voice-recognition software. Olympus, Dictaphone, and Panasonic sell these items for between $80 and $260.

THE 30-SECOND RECAP

- Hardware and software applications are extremely valuable to an organization.

- Desktop and laptop computers should be compatible. Office suites provide a useful array of software.

- Web calendars and intranets can help keep distant and teleworkers in touch.

- With such a variety of choices in hardware and software, comparison shopping for compatibility and price is essential.

Organizing Your Office

In this section, you learn how to find the right products and arrange your office for maximum efficiency.

YOUR DESK AND CHAIR

The right furniture and filing systems can have a significant organizational impact on your productivity. Don't make the mistake of taking them for granted.

TIP

According to the feng shui theory, a high-back chair at your desk encourages decision-making because you have the leisurely feeling of leaning back while contemplating.

Your desk is most likely the center of your business activity. As such, all the necessary daily tools of your profession should be positioned in and around that desk for easy access. Recall the times that you often have to get up and retrieve an item two or three times a day.

Simple repositioning for easy reach can trim time and frustration. Key items include the telephone, the answering machine, writing utensils, note pads, in/out file trays, your favorite worry beads, and more. An L-shaped desk can offer additional positioning of your computer and printer.

THE SCIENCE OF ERGONOMICS

If you spend a lot of time behind the desk, you need a chair that is not only comfortable, but that also is ergonomically designed to reduce or eliminate any damage to your posture. No tool, however, will take the place of frequent breaks, if you spend considerable time working on your computer. Rest, exercise, and moderation can all help you avoid problems caused by repetitive motion.

Sitting for prolonged periods of time is also very stressful on the lower back and neck, according to Dr. William J. Murphy, a chiropractic physician practicing in South Florida. He has several ideas to take care of your "working body."

- Talk on the phone while standing, not sitting.
- Invest in a stand-up desk, originally invented by Thomas Jefferson.
- Keep your shoulders and chin back to combat the damage done over time by the posture you assume attending to tasks in front of you.
- Buy a clock that chimes every half-hour to remind you to take a stretch break.

Mini stretch breaks at regular intervals throughout the day can help improve circulation and comfort, and can reduce fatigue that can lead to repetitive stress injuries.

The following basic stretches are recommended by the University of Virginia Office of Environmental Health and Safety. Take a few minutes and work out your body. Just remember to start off easy, stretch regularly, and see your doctor if you have pain.

Whole body stretches:

1. Stand up with your arms at your sides, and then inhale and reach up with both arms. Hold this pose for five seconds.
2. Repeat three to five times.

Back stretches:

1. While seated or standing, clasp your hands behind your head. Press your elbows back, squeezing your shoulder blades together.

2. Relax and repeat three to five times.

3. While standing, place your hands on your hips and bend backward gently.

4. While sitting, bend forward slowly and touch the floor, if you can. Grasp your leg at your shin, and slowly pull your leg up to your chest. Repeat with your other leg.

Arm, wrist, and hand stretches:

1. With your arms and hands outstretched, slowly circle your wrists outward five times; then reverse the direction.

2. With your arms outstretched and your palms facing down, flex your wrists up to the ceiling. Hold for five seconds, and then reverse direction, with your wrists flexed to the floor. Hold for five seconds and then relax. Repeat two or three times each.

3. Flex your fingers and hands by opening and closing your fists five to ten times.

4. Interlace your fingers with the palms facing away from you. Straighten your arms and lift them toward the ceiling.

Neck stretches:

1. Tuck your chin to your chest. Tilt your head to one shoulder and then to the other. Repeat two or three times.

2. With your head upright, turn your head slowly from side to side, looking over your shoulder each time. Relax and repeat.

3. Remember to keep your head and neck aligned with your body. Do not jut your head forward while working at your desk.

Costing from $200 to more than $1,200, *ergonomic* chairs are known to eliminate back pain, fatigue, and increase productivity.

PLAIN ENGLISH

Ergonomics   Also known as human engineering, the science of designing and arranging things that people use for safe and efficient interaction.

CAUTION

A study done by Yale University revealed that persons who sit for more than half the day at work have a 60 to 70 percent greater risk of slipping a disk than their mobile co-workers.

DESKS

Chose portable desks that can be expanded. Permanent, built-in desk systems limit space arrangements and growth. Other considerations are to do the following:

■ Allow sufficient room for papers and desk accessories.

■ Place printers within easy reach.

■ Allow leg clearance under the desk to stretch your legs.

■ Provide a small step stool under the desk to elevate your feet and legs.

■ Train yourself on work habits that are ergonomically healthy for the body and mind.

CAUTION

In June 2000, the National Institute of Occupational Safety and Health (NIOSH) reported that working women have a higher risk level for musculoskeletal injuries on the job, suffering 63 percent of all work-related repetitive motion injuries.

COMPUTER DESKS AND CREDENZAS

Often, computer workstations do not accommodate space for much more than the computer and peripherals. You should use a separate chair for the main desk and computer, if you use both of them, for efficiency.

TIP

One NIOSH study showed that the use of ergonomic furniture increased worker productivity by 24 percent and increased job satisfaction by 27 percent.

Credenzas are like side tables for the office and are extremely accommodating for holding those items that you use only occasionally but that you want to have at arm's reach.

COMPUTER USAGE

Data entry and other tasks involving video-display units lead to ergonomic risks due to repetitive exertions and awkward postures. Musculoskeletal problems of the upper limbs, neck, and back, as well as eyestrain, are the result.

To avoid these problems, improve lighting and reduce glare. Pay attention to workstation design such as keyboard height and viewing distance and angle. Introduce wrist rests and detachable keyboards.

TIP

NIOSH recommends implementing a visual testing program and rest-break schedules for constant computer users.

LIGHTING

Lighting products should save energy consumption, assist productivity, and be aesthetically pleasing. In general, you should follow these tips:

- Take advantage of natural lighting where windows exist.
- Use task lighting, or lamps appropriate for the purpose.
- Maintain lighting fixtures to optimum performance.

For optimum computer screen viewing, you should do the following:

- Decrease background lighting.
- Arrange task lighting away from screen.
- Adjust curtains or blinds.
- Install a glare filter on monitors.

Good lighting is important to reduce eye fatigue. However, just as frequent exercise breaks can limit repetitive stress injuries to your body, eye exercises can reduce eyestrain. If you stare at the computer screen or documents all day, try the following exercise:

1. Focus on an object at least 15 to 20 feet away, and then look out the window or down the hall as far as you can.

2. Move your eyes from left to right, and then focus on other objects in the room before turning back to your screen or desk.

Remember to take frequent vision breaks throughout the day. Rearrange your task lights if you find yourself straining to focus when looking from desk to screen.

TIP

When filing, different types, color, and sizes of folders can be used to maximize the orderly placement of files.

FILING SYSTEMS

Develop a system that saves time, whether for personal, staff, or department use.

PLAIN ENGLISH

Document management   The system of converting and organizing paper-based information to make it accessible via the Web and corporate intranets. The process may include optical character-recognition (OCR) software.

Smaller filing systems can be coded by one color for each major category, with up to 11 colors available on the market today. Larger systems can use colors to subcategorize major categories.

Other points to consider include these:

- Place files subject to constant use in hanging file folders for ease of movement and extended durability of the folder.
- Use expanding files as working files when constantly sorting, using, and moving files for project or client use.
- Use color-coded expanding files for quick identification when several projects are underway simultaneously.
- Use a labeling starter/supply kit, or precut and packaged labels and a label software application, in your word processor software when tagging file folder tabs.

CAUTION

Never hand-write office file titles. Not everybody can read your handwriting, and the label system means orderly, easily accessed files.

Smead and Avery offer labeling systems and supplies that cost from $6 to $20 each. Smead, Pendaflex, and SCM are the more common brands of folders by size, color, and function. Prices vary widely, but per-unit cost of folders is reduced with bulk purchases.

TIP

Important, everyday files should be kept in a desk drawer or desktop holder.

FILING CABINETS

Implement filing cabinets and storage shelves according to the nature and type of item to be filed and stored.

Store stackable office supplies in shelving units that allow visibility and easy access. Select cabinets by need, function, and location. Use four-drawer upright or lateral units for large filing systems. Use two-drawer lateral units when space is at a premium, and use wheeled units for mobile files.

Color filing cabinet labels by type or function. Use magazine files for storing your industry publications. Label these files by name and dates of publication to be found in each file.

THE 30-SECOND RECAP

- How you position office furniture impacts productivity.
- Proper ergonomics promotes good health.
- Finding the right product can make a difference.
- A good filing system is critical to organization.

Managing Your Computer

In this section, you will learn how to create, move, copy, and organize computer files like an information technology (IT) professional.

HARDWARE

Knowledge of computers is a prerequisite for so many jobs. But do you know how to use computers to better organize your workday? Knowledge of hardware, software, and related accessories can save you time when creating, saving, and retrieving work.

The most important element of hardware, for organizational purposes, is the central processing unit (CPU). It's the box that contains your hard drive, floppy drive, and CD-ROM drive. Decades ago, CPUs encompassed entire rooms. With the advances in microelectronics, however, they have shrunk to small boxes that neatly fit on or underneath your desk.

HARD DRIVE

The hard drive is like the filing cabinet for your computer: It holds all the software applications and documents that you use.

You should be aware of the size of the hard drive and how much free space remains at any point in time. Older computers, with older hard drives, consume free space quickly. If you have Windows operating system, you can check available space by going to Explorer, clicking on the C drive, then choosing File on the toolbar, and selecting Properties. The pink wedge of the pie indicates free disk space, and the blue wedge shows what is already taken by files and applications.

HARD DRIVE FOLDERS

Every software application has a filename extension. Perhaps the most famous is .doc for Microsoft Word (myfile.doc).

File folders are also easily manipulated. Create a new file folder in your Word directory named My Documents. Call it My Project. Make note of the file path on your hard drive—the path is the drive, the directory (My Documents), and then the folder name (My Project). Then every time you want to save a document related to the project, you do so in the My Project file folder.

If you want, you can use a unique file extension to help segregate certain types of files for easy identification or organization on your hard drive. For example, say that John R. Smith wants to save certain Microsoft Word documents related to his project apart from others. When saving the document, he names it myproject.jrs. When looking for the file, he types in .jrs in the appropriate box, and only files with that extension will be listed on the screen.

Back up these files and folders on disks or a CD-ROM if they are important.

TIP

Today's hard drive sizes for power PCs can hold up to 20 or more gigabytes (GB).

CAUTION

Back it up! Computer crashes and viruses can destroy hard drives and data. Portable units or remote storage should be used for storing backups. Rotate weekly between two backup disks, and keep one copy offsite.

PORTABLE STORAGE UNITS

These are equivalent to hard drives but can be toted around, stored away, and then brought back out to hook up and use with the computer system.

Portable storage units include the following:

- **Iomega (www.iomega.com) Zip and Jaz drives.** Installed internally or externally, the disks hold 100MB to 250MB each. The units retail between $50 and $200.

- **Ecrix (www.ecrix.com/).** This device has a 66GB storage capacity at a record rate of 6MB/second. A VXA drive retails for $900.

- **Hewlett-Packard (www.hp.com/) SureStore DAT40.** This device stores data on digital audio tapes and retails for less than $1,200.

TIP

Portable storage units and drives, such as Iomega Zip drives, are great when you divide your time between different machines.

FLOPPY DRIVES AND DISKS

These previously were limited to 1.4MB of disk space, but drives have expanded to hold up to 110MB and 144MB of space. Expected to become the standards for future drives, these systems retail between $60 and $80. The LS-120 Monster Drive retails for between $60 and $80 respectively (www.tigerdirect.com). They are expected to become the standards for future floppy drives, with the 1.4MB floppy going the way of 8-track tapes.

E-mail file transfers and CD drives are rapidly eliminating the need for floppy disk storage.

CAUTION

CD-RWs cannot be universally read on all computers. CD-Rs can, but they can be written on only once.

THE CD-ROM DRIVE

The CD drive is evolving into a data storage system. Newer computers allow the recording, copying, and re-recording of data to a CD. Two types of CDs exist in this capacity: the CD-R (recordable or write once) and the CD-RW (rewriteable). Typically, CD-RWs store 650MB and more of data.

Which type of disc you use depends on how you will be using the CD and whether you want to use the CD on other systems. CD-RWs, which you can write and rewrite on, are replacing more traditional data backup system.

Hewlett-Packard, Creative Labs (www.creative.com), Iomega, Acer (www.acer.com), Samsung (www.samsung.com), and a host of other companies are hot into this product. Prices range from $120 to $350.

REMOTE STORAGE

A new alternative to local storage of data is remote Internet sites, where entire hard disks or company server data can be stored for ready access.

This is an extremely valuable resource to business travelers or offices with remote employees and teleworkers. Many services are free and allow you to upload important files right on to their servers. You simply sign up, pick a password, and create your own Internet office.

You can also provide staff members with passwords to selected areas so that they can view, add, or delete files. Try an Internet search for Internet storage, or go to About.com and search for Internet file space. This site also maintains a list of services and gives their pros and cons.

E-MAIL FOLDERS

E-mail folders are created for organization of e-mail and easy retrieval. Your software application dictates the manner in which that is done. It isn't hard to do in any e-mail application; if you do have a problem, just go to the Help menu for instructions.

Typically, your e-mail application will include *default* folders titled Inbox, Outbox, Sent Items, and Deleted Items. Use the same naming methods for your e-mail folders, such as Client Name, Product Type, Project, or Activity.

PLAIN ENGLISH

Default   A selection automatically used by a computer program if the user makes no specific choice.

For maximum efficiency, your organization might create a company filing system similar to your paper file system. Then office staff could be trained to follow the system. When office team members leave the company, their files should be easy to understand.

TIP

Some remote storage Web sites also collect e-mail from several accounts. Check out www.desktop.com and www.netledger.com.

SOFTWARE

Compression software compresses and stores large data files. The compressed files can even be stored on disks and compact disks. For retrieval and expansion back into normal format, just access them through the same compression software.

These applications from several manufacturers are easily accessible through the Internet. They include Nico Mak's WinZip (www.winzip.com) and PKWare, Inc.'s PKUNZIP (www.pkunzip.com).

You can download free, 30-day evaluation copies of compression software. Purchase price is about $30.

SYSTEM TOOLS

Just as with a car, your hard drive needs a periodic tune-up. Most operating systems have system tools to eliminate unnecessary data and organize the data and applications. Called defrag, scan-disk, and disk-cleanup, they tune your hard drive for fast retrieval and reduce software conflicts.

TIP

Use the "uninstall" feature on software applications to take them off your hard drive. It's cleaner and more efficient than using the Delete button.

PROTECTION

Surge protectors reduce the likelihood of electrical surges from damaging the computer and peripherals.

Universal power supply (UPS) units save the work in progress in case of a power outage. A battery pack allows your computer to remain operational for an extended period so that you can save and store work before shutting down the system.

BACK IT UP

Regardless of the size of your hard drive, you should back up valuable data and store it by way of one of the previously mentioned peripheral units.

If your hard drive crashes because of a computer system failure, or if it is destroyed by power surges, all stored data and software applications will be lost.

Protect your files by backing them up. A backup is a copy of your computer files stored on either a disk, a tape, a CD, or a network server.

Backing up your computer files is simple and takes very little time. Your computer software will guide you through the steps; you can decide when, where, and how the computer backs up your files. Get your system in place and stick with it. For more details on backing up your computer files, see "Easy Organizing Basics" on page 156.

Remember that you can back up your files on the Internet. Some Web sites offer free space; others charge annual fees in the $100 range. Two top picks in 2000 by *PC Magazine* were www.connected.com and www.xdrive.com.

The use of computers to communicate and send important data transcends photocopying and regular mail. We need to learn how to use the operating systems and software applications for saving, storing, and backing up copies of documents we create.

THE 30-SECOND RECAP

■ Carefully choose computer hardware to match your storage needs.

■ Back up work on a daily and weekly basis.

■ Keep one backup copy offsite.

■ Create and maintain a filing system in your computer.

■ Use remote storage for excess data or when traveling.

Going on the Road

In this section, you will learn how to make those business trips a little easier by understanding what to take and what to delegate.

PLANNING AHEAD

Everything begins with planning, and the same is true for going on the road. Poor planning results in having to buy a second copy of something you already have, the inability to get something done because something else was left behind, and the likelihood of being "called on the carpet" by your boss upon returning to the office.

Regardless of the level of personal and/or company high-tech capacities, each of the following issues should be addressed before going on the road:

■ Confirm all business appointments by phone and follow up with an e-mail before leaving.

- Confirm reservations (airline, car rental, hotel, restaurant, and so on) at least three days before traveling.

- Reschedule any local appointments while you're away. Otherwise, a negative image is cast on you and your company. The person whom you stood up will feel a lack of respect or will think that you are simply not interested.

- Delegate all regular and special assignments to staff before your departure. You don't want them constantly calling and interrupting your travel, meetings, and rest periods with requests for instructions.

- Assign a trusted staff member to create daily activity reports via e-mail. This keeps you updated and saves phone time. You don't want any surprises when returning to the office.

- Thoroughly review all documents needed while on the road. Be certain that a hard copy and a computer-generated copy remain at the office. If you lose one of those documents on the road, the staff can fax or send an e-mail attachment immediately.

- Make note of any extraordinary events occurring in the office while you're away. This affords you the opportunity to provide input that would otherwise not occur while on the road. Sometimes, face-to-face input simply is more influential than an e-mail or a phone call.

- Stock up on the tools of your trade that you may need while traveling. These include a combination of laptop or palm computer, power adapters, additional batteries and power supplies, personal organizers, address and appointment books (if you're not yet computerized), a portable tape recorder, writing instruments, a calculator, and note pads. Your company's level of computerization and the length and nature of the trip will dictate which items to take.

- Depending on company marketing and promotional strategies, you may want to take along an ample supply of brochures, novelty advertising items, and any other items used in company advertising and promotions.

- One of the most serious items to address is a list of all user names and passwords for computer, telephone, and ATM access. If you are bad at remembering these things, be careful where you place that information. You may want to place that in a palm computer or a personal organizer in a password access mode. This way, if the computer or organizer is stolen, it will require a hacker's skill to access that data. A very old alternative is to write this information on a sheet of paper. But where will you hide it?

■ Make three copies of your travel itinerary: one for you, one for home, and one for the office staff. Now all the significant people in your life know where to find you.

TIP

Wireless handhelds provide basic e-mail access and PIM software. For reviews of the latest versions, try ZDNet's *PC Magazine* at www.zdnet.com/pcmag/.

PACKING FOR THE TRIP

Today, attaché cases take on so many different shapes, sizes, and amenities. Have one that fills your needs. For example, some traveling business people like attaché cases that allow for the regular storage amenities and space for a laptop computer. Others prefer one case for the computer and one for the other necessities of their job. Here are some other matters to consider:

■ Place your airline tickets, car rental, and hotel reservation forms in one small container or bag that is easily accessible.

TIP

Electronic, or ticketless, ticketing can be a boon to the business traveler. All you need is your ID to board the plane. Keep a copy of your reservation for flight numbers and times.

■ Use one file folder or envelope for all hard-copy receipts of your business expenses.

■ Bring a floppy disk or CD (assuming that you have a CD-W) containing important business documents as backup to hard copies.

■ Take a map of the area. Highlight the hotel and restaurants that you'll be visiting. Highlight the planned route if you're traveling by car.

STAYING CONNECTED

Business travel is part of most management positions today. In fact, many people work only from their "virtual offices," consisting of a laptop computer and a packed briefcase.

With technology as part of your team, laptop included, time on the road can be well organized and efficient. Here are some options for staying connected, at home or away:

■ **Virtual desktop services.** These abound on the Internet. You can store files, forward e-mail, and access calendars and address books. Many allow sharing, so you can keep in touch with the office. Examples include www.desktop.com, www.halfbrain.com, and www.netledger.com. For e-mail centers, try Hotmail at www. hotmail.com, or Yahoo! at mail.yahoo.com/. Yahoo! also has a directory of virtual offices.

■ **E-mail *autoresponders*.** There are plenty of autoresponder services on the Internet, both free and for a fee. Go to www.emailaddresses. com/email_auto.htm for a directory of free services.

PLAIN ENGLISH

Autoresponder   A program that receives e-mail. It reads the e-mail address of the sender and automatically e-mails your reply. An autoresponder is useful for contact management and marketing.

■ **Laptop modems.** To take advantage of your laptop and stay connected to the office, have a modem installed on your laptop—or purchase one in the first place with that peripheral. Some airports and hotels provide phone line access for modems, but do be cautious if selecting a hotel specifically for modem access. Those using digital phone access can damage your modem; you need a regular tone line.

■ ***Remote access program.*** Install this type of software on your office PC and your laptop, and you're good to go. However, your laptop must be configured to function in a company-wide, intranet format. If you're on the road a lot and you visit other company facilities frequently or routinely, encourage the company to implement remote access formatting at all sites, to facilitate your ability to access your office PC from any company location worldwide. For reviews of the latest remote-control software, go to ZDNet's *PC Magazine* reviews at www.zdnet.com/pcmag/.

PLAIN ENGLISH

Remote access program   Enables you to connect to the office computer from your laptop. You can transfer and copy files and run applications.

■ **Voicemail.** Leave your departure and arrival times on your office voicemail message. Make sure to bring remote access numbers to

retrieve messages, or have an assistant transcribe messages and
e-mail them to you. You also might install a voicemail software
program offered by such companies as eFax (www.efax.com) and
Fax4Free (www.fax4free.com). They provide you a phone number
where voicemail can be sent, and then you access it via an e-mail
attachment. The service to you is free.

■ **Fax.** You can install the same software from eFax or Fax4Free, and
it also serves as a remote access for faxes. Someone can send you a
fax via the same phone number assigned for voicemail, and you are
forwarded that document via an e-mail attachment. Again, the software and the service are free. The alternative is to make sure that fax
services exist at your hotels while on the road.

CAUTION

Don't skimp on hotel costs. Look for one that caters to the business
traveler, such as Marriot or Hyatt hotels. You want at least a business center on the premises for fax, copying, receiving or sending
overnight packages and letters, and so on.

■ **Cell phone.** For some, this is a luxury; for most executives who do a
lot of traveling, it is a necessity. Regardless, don't be without it if the
budget allows. A cell phone keeps you connected with the office and
clients, if necessary, from anywhere and at any time, with no coins or
credit cards. Be certain to have the necessary accessories for various
types of plug-in access (if you have that type of phone) and a battery
charger.

■ **Dictation.** Voice-recognition software (see "Using High-Tech Tools
and Software" on page 169) for dictating and electronic downloading
can make a tape recorder out of your laptop. Hate transferring those
notes from paper or a traditional tape recorder? This software on the
laptop can eliminate another low-tech device from the business arsenal
that you carry on the road.

Furthermore, you can fall back on the following standards on a business traveler's to-do list:

■ **Business cards.** Take along a supply of business cards. Why? Very
simply, the phone numbers (office, cell, fax, and voicemail) and
e-mail addresses for contacting you or your company are provided
for the client or any other networking relationship. Today, the business card better serves the function of listing the various avenues of

communication rather than merely listing a name, address, phone number, and pretty logo. The client should know how to contact you. If you travel from one city to the next, given cell phone and/or remote e-mail access, it enhances customer service by allowing the clients to contact you instead of having to wait until you get back to your office. Furthermore, it is considered appropriate to first present your business card when conducting business in certain countries overseas.

TIP

In your business diary, the IRS wants to see four things for business entertainment deductions: the date, the place, names of people there, and what business was discussed.

TRAVELING ABROAD

Traveling abroad requires additions to your checklist of things to do before leaving. Some are mandatory, or you'll never leave the country:

- Have all visas and your passport validated well in advance of the trip. Naturally, you will have to go to the nearest consular office of that country to get a visa. Go to the U.S. State Department Web site at www.state.gov/, and click on the directory for consular offices to find the location nearest you.

- Check the U.S. State Department's Bureau of Consular Affairs Web site at travel.state.gov/ and click on the hyperlink for travel warnings.

CAUTION

Be extremely careful where you keep your password data. You don't want to instantly become the victim of a thief or a hacker with the drop of a wallet.

- If you're not fluent in the native language, learn some basic expressions, and take a language dictionary with you. Pocket versions of dictionaries are easily found in local bookstores, but electronic versions offer more languages. LingoTranslators (www.lingotranslators. com) provides dictionaries for 25 different languages. Phone-Soft (www.phone-soft.com) provides links to several online sites to locate these electronic dictionaries.

- Take the time to learn the customs and mores in the country of destination—it can mean the difference between business success and failure. For example, circling the thumb and index finger in the shape of an "o" to signal that things are okay is acceptable in the United States but is considered vulgar in Brazil. Two informative books to guide you in adjusting to other cultures are *Survival Kit for Overseas Living: For Americans Planning to Live and Work Abroad,* by L. Robert Kohls, and *U.S. Expatriate Handbook: Guide to Living and Working Abroad,* by John W. Adams, are easily accessible in the book category of amazon.com.

- Bring a power adapter for your business tools requiring alternate current.

- Learn the currency exchange rate, and bring a minimal amount of the currency with you.

- Don't forget any prescription medications.

For more tips about traveling abroad, go to the Small Business Knowledge Base at bizmove.com/. Another excellent, informative Web site for overseas travel is provided by America Online (AOL) at www.governmentguide.com/govsite/aol/0.

THE 30-SECOND RECAP

- Technology can make time on the road productive and efficient.

- Keeping in touch with the office through daily communications is essential.

- Prior planning and packing is essential to organization.

- Confirm everything before you go, from reservations to staff assignments.

Working at Home

In this section, you will learn how to manage the business end of telecommuting or independent contracting.

SUITING UP YOUR HOME OFFICE

It would seem sometimes that the ideal profession would let you work from the home. You never have to travel through rush hour, you can grab a cup of real home-brewed coffee, and you can dress the way you like.

But if you are not disciplined and organized, working from home can be paradise lost.

PLAIN ENGLISH

Telecommute   To work at home by hooking up to the main office by electronic means.

To work from home successfully, you'll need to refine some self-management skills:

- **Experience.** Be realistic about the jobs that you can do from home.
- **Project management.** Be results-oriented by setting goals for yourself each day. See "Easy Organizing Basics," on page 156, for more on organizing basics.
- **Time management.** Plan ahead, prioritize, and stick with your to-do list.

TIP

Don't forget to take breaks. With fewer office interruptions, you can accomplish a lot. But don't overdo the workload.

- **Self-discipline.** Create a home schedule so that you can begin and end your day at fairly regular times. Post it for family to see.

CAUTION

If you're a remote worker, always attend staff meetings when possible. Also encourage progress meetings with your supervisors.

SETTING UP YOUR HOME OFFICE

Outfitting a home office requires some extra features:

- Arrange for a separate telephone line for business.

PLAIN ENGLISH

DSL   Digital subscriber line. Consider installing a cable modem or DSL for faster computer access.

- A cell phone can double as a work line, as well as a portable phone to bring to office headquarters, if you can afford the fees.

▓ Have an answering machine installed with your office phone.

▓ Create a separate office space from the rest of the home, even if resources and space are limited.

KEEPING IN TOUCH

The independent contractor working from home doesn't have a brick-and-mortar environment to inspire or direct his or her attention to stay in touch with the outside world.

You *can* be forgotten. Here are some ways to stay in the mainstream:

▓ Network through chambers of commerce and other business organizations.

▓ If clients are local, make a habit of occasionally visiting them onsite, but don't show up unannounced.

▓ Sponsor community events and programs to get your company's name in the public eye.

▓ Make use of your e-mail to communicate with past and present clients. Communicate the desire to know how they are doing, and let them know that you are available if they need any further assistance.

The home office employee, or teleworker, should also establish certain routines:

■ Make an effort to visit the office at least once a week. Stay in the know about the unavoidable office politics.

TIP

Like it or not, office politics affect all of us. Even remote or teleworkers need to keep an ear open for changes in the work environment.

■ Communicate with specific employees who are always "in the know" about any upcoming programs and events. You don't want to be performing unnecessary tasks.

■ E-mail is a fast and easy way to communicate with the office, but don't avoid the telephone. You can learn more in a phone conversation, sometimes unexpectedly.

■ If you're uncertain about any element of a task to be performed, call your immediate supervisor for clarification. To do something wrong and waste time and money can give your employer second thoughts about the value of letting you work from home.

Pitfalls

Both authors have worked for years as independent contractors working out of the home, and they have experienced the joys and pitfalls that working from a home office can bring. We'd like to share a few tips with you:

■ Don't give in to the temptation to wake up later in the morning and quit earlier in the afternoon.

■ Lounging around in your pajamas may be a leisurely feeling, but it tends to suppress the urge to work.

■ Don't get glued to the TV. Avoid the urge to go to the family or living room, lounge on the sofa, and watch the tube. It's easy to get wrapped up in distractions.

■ Avoid the temptation to make up for work you didn't get done during the day by working at night. How do you feel the next day after not having enough sleep? This can be counterproductive.

■ Resist computer games. It's easy to switch over to a favorite game of Solitaire or Hearts when frustrated or stymied by the report that's due tomorrow.

■ Stay professional on the phone. If a client, vendor, or fellow employee calls, it doesn't reflect well on you for a family member to pick up the phone and say "Hi."

■ Minimize interruptions from others. If you're using the family room, you don't want people coming in while you conduct your business affairs. They shouldn't turn on the TV while you are talking on the telephone.

■ Your spouse and children can innocently come into the office and ask you questions in the midst of an extremely important phone call or thought process.

■ Stay in touch with the office. You don't want to find out that your recommendations to management, which initially were enthusiastically received, suddenly are rejected. Did you miss out on some event at the office that resulted in this change of heart?

We don't want to discourage anyone from working from home. However, there are pitfalls, and you must be prepared to overcome them.

SOME SOLUTIONS

Setting up an office in the home requires self-discipline, as well as support and cooperation from others living with you:

■ **Keep a schedule.** Arrange to speak with a staff member or fellow manager at the start and the end of the work day to help you get up early and put in a full day of work. Likewise, arrange for reports to be transmitted via e-mail early or late in the workday.

■ **Dress for work.** At the very minimum, dress in casual wear, but leave the pajamas in the bedroom.

■ **Avoid distractions.** Keep television as far away as possible from the home office. If someone else is home watching TV, shut your office door. Also, unless you are self-disciplined, take the game software off your computer. It can be too much of a distraction.

■ **Be disciplined.** Don't put off today's work for tonight. Prioritize!

■ **Get organized.** Internet companies can provide fax and voicemail at no charge to you. You can have the faxes and voicemail forwarded to you via your e-mail software.

■ **Keep separate phones.** Do not allow anyone other than you to answer the business phone. Otherwise, let the answering machine do its job. Likewise, keep all personal phone lines and answering machines out of your office area.

- **Learn to balance business and personal time.** If you have a family, let them know the limits of work and personal time. Don't take advantage of the home office to get ahead of the workload, either—you risk alienating your family. Besides, if you didn't have that home office, the report would have likely waited until the next morning to be completed.

- **Don't be a stranger.** For those who split time between the company and the home office, it is wise to visit the company facilities one to three times a week, depending on the nature of your work. You cannot possibly know everything happening at the office unless you are there or are having someone fill you in on those activities on a regular basis. In that case, you may spend more time "talking shop" than working.

Some of us are limited in resources and space for a home office, so here are some tips:

- If the room is available, designate it exclusively for business use, and renovate it to simulate an office environment and to accommodate office needs. Take the kids' boom box back to their room. Make room for your filing cabinet, desk, chairs, computer workstation, shelving, and other office equipment. Move the daybed somewhere else in the house.

- If you must share space with some home function, such as a family room, set up some form of perimeter, like a free-standing room divider, to mark the distinct boundary between your office and the family room.

- Enforce the law that no one is to use your office space and its content for personal reasons. Imagine a family member using a note pad to write a phone number and message from a friend; then you come home to find that your notes from the last staff meeting have disappeared.

Working from a home office can be a rewarding, but challenging, experience. Without the structured surroundings of a formal corporate office, it's especially important to remain organized. Remember to respect your work, and yourself for the work you do.

THE 30-SECOND RECAP

- Working from the home requires self-discipline and self-management.
- Setting up a home office requires, at minimum, a computer, an extra phone line, and an answering machine.
- Networking can help independent contractors stay in touch.

Motivating People

What Motivates People?

In this lesson, you get a foundation for recognizing what motivates people and understanding how people's motivations differ depending on their current needs.

Let's start with the basics: What motivated you to pick up this book? You probably want to elicit certain kinds of behavior in someone and are unable to do it, right? That frustrates you. That challenges you. Perhaps you're a manager with employees you want to motivate to enjoy their work more. Or maybe you have a particular problem employee who you want to motivate to perform better.

No matter why you bought this book or who you want to motivate, I won't kid you: Motivation can be a tricky thing. Not everybody is motivated by the same thing, and what motivates somebody one day might not motivate him the next. You can never rest on your laurels, either: One kind of motivation repeated many times becomes the expected behavior and loses its motivational quality.

In this chapter I'll provide you with an overview of motivation—what it is and how it works.

UNDERSTANDING MOTIVATION

The good news is that psychologists who have spent a lot of time studying what motivates people have come up with some tried-and-true guidelines that can help you motivate anybody. Throughout this book I'll provide information on some key theories about motivation that you can use every day.

 PLAIN ENGLISH

Motivation   An incentive, an inducement, or a stimulus for action. A motivation is anything—verbal, physical, or psychological—that causes somebody to do something in response.

But no matter how much experts would like to find one key to motivating people, the truth is that individuals are motivated by different things, and what motivates each of us changes throughout our lives. So using some combination of these theories might be your best bet in motivating people in the everyday world.

EVERYONE IS UNIQUE

Take this example. You have two employees, Ethel and Arnold. They make the same amount of money. They have the same size office with the same size window. They received the same year-end bonus. They were promoted through the ranks at the same speed. You gave them each a nice box of candy for Christmas and complimented their achievements at the yearly employee meeting.

But one is happy, while the other is miserable. How can that be? Simple: Different things appeal to different people, and what's good for the goose is not always good for the gander.

If you're trying to motivate a particular individual, the first piece of advice I can give you is to take a little time to get to know him or her. Notice what seems to make that person happy, excited, bored, or frustrated. And here's a neat trick to use whether you're dealing with an individual or a group: Just ask them what you want to know. Nothing is stopping you from sitting down with your employees and asking them to tell you what puts a shine on their shoes and smiles on their faces. Try a few of these questions to help you get a picture of a person's motivations:

- Why did you take this job?
- Why do you come to work in the morning?
- What do you like best about this job?
- What do you dislike about your job?
- What frustrates you?
- What makes you feel valued?
- What was the best job you ever had? Why was it so good?
- What do you expect from a job?
- What do you want from your life a year from now? What about five years from now?

TIP

If you're concerned that people won't answer your questions about their jobs and their levels of satisfaction honestly, make it an anonymous survey. If employees know that you can't identify which comments belong to which employees, they're more likely to respond frankly to questions such as "What do you dislike about your job?"

People's answers to these questions are likely to be diverse. One employee might come to work for the paycheck, another for the friendships with co-workers, and another for the challenge of taking on difficult projects. One person will thrive on change, while another will be threatened by anything but structure and the status quo.

MOTIVATING PEOPLE IN GROUPS

Does the fact that each individual feels motivated by different things mean that you can't motivate a whole group of employees at once? Not at all. There's nothing wrong with determining what kind of motivation the majority of people in an organization will respond to and then providing that motivation. But the key to motivating a group of people is to vary the kinds of motivation you provide. That extra day off for the holidays might not mean much to that single person without a family to visit and who lives to come in to work. Just make sure that the next perk you offer will be something that he or she will appreciate, such as an employee of the month award that recognizes his or her devotion.

PATTERNS OF MOTIVATION

Luckily, this variety of motivation among people doesn't mean it's random chaos out there. The good news is that there are patterns to what motivates people. Understanding those patterns can help you spot which kind of person or group of people you're dealing with.

MASLOW'S HIERARCHY OF NEEDS

One well-known theory that is very relevant to motivating people is Abraham Maslow's *hierarchy of needs*. If you took Psychology 101 in college, you probably remember this one: People have a hierarchy of needs that determines their actions. These needs start at the most basic level of physiological needs, which include such fundamental requirements as food and clothing. Once those needs are satisfied, people move on to the next level.

PLAIN ENGLISH

Maslow's hierarchy of needs   A theory stating that human beings have an innate order, or hierarchy, for the things they want. When one level of this hierarchy is satisfied, they move on to the next.

Take a look at Maslow's hierarchy, listed from the most basic at the bottom to the most advanced at the top:

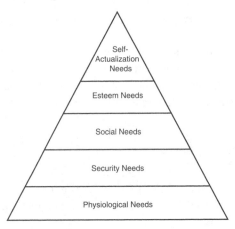

Spotting Examples Around You

Look around you; if your company is typical, you should see people being motivated at each of these levels:

- The mail clerk who's just out of school wants to pay off his car loan and make the rent every month (physiological needs).

- The single mother/junior executive works to provide medical and insurance benefits for herself and her child (security needs).

- The chatty man in accounting loves the people he works with and lives to organize the football pools (social needs).

- The middle manager works 70 hours a week to earn that next promotion (esteem needs).

- And there's sure to be somebody who does his job not for money, nor for friendship, nor for a fancy title, but because it fits his value system: This is truly what makes his life worthwhile (self-actualization needs).

You can easily use patterns that apply to individuals to identify group needs. Groups of people who do the same kind of work or perform the same level of work often share the same needs.

Here's an example of a way to identify a group need. What motivates employees paid by the hour is different than what motivates salaried workers. For example, let's say you decide to let people go home early on the day before a holiday, but you never indicate to the hourly people that it's okay for them to record those extra four hours on their timesheets so that they get paid for the time off. It's doubtful that the hourly workers felt it was a perk to lose four hours of pay just before a holiday. In this instance, time off was a motivator to salaried people but was a demotivator to hourly employees.

 CAUTION

Avoid using the same motivator over and over again. If you give the team a reward dinner every month rather than when they've performed exceptionally, that night out will become routine rather than motivating.

Motivations Change

So that's it, right? Recognize what kind of need motivates somebody to work and meet that need, and you're all set? Well ... no. Unfortunately, it's rarely that simple because people have different needs at different times in their lives.

For instance, once the mail clerk earns enough to cover the rent with money to spare, his physiological needs are met, and he may start to look for more job security (security needs on the Maslow hierarchy). Or he might jump to the esteem level and look for advancement within the company. Likewise, the person who has had years of promotions and who is respected by her peers because of all her hard work might stop and wonder if all these promotions are worth it if she doesn't have the time or energy to stop and smell the roses. That's when she'll move into the self-actualization phase and perhaps decide to chuck the big salary and impressive title in favor of consulting part-time from home and returning to school to study graphic design.

Not only do people progress through these levels, but they also may bounce back and forth among them. When a major company downsizes, someone who was concerned only with creating a social life at work might jump right back to the security level when he feels his job is threatened.

These different levels of need and the fact that people move among these levels throughout their lives are why it's so important that you get to know the people you work with. Understanding their positions in life and their positions within the company will help you identify the best way to motivate them at any given time.

The same principle of change and growth applies to groups of workers as well. At the beginning of a challenging project, social camaraderie and free pizza might be enough to motivate a group of people to work long hours. But it's likely that this same group will need more substantial recognition and tangible gestures of esteem, such as promotions or bonuses when you're a year into the project. Keeping in touch with the group—and learning to gauge its mood and its needs—is an important part of deciding how best to motivate it over the long haul.

Don't Mistake Your Motivation for Theirs

One of the biggest mistakes managers and supervisors make is to assume that what motivates them is what motivates their employees. That's just human nature. If you're motivated by things that bolster your self-esteem, you just can't imagine someone who simply doesn't need the promise of a raise or a promotion to keep her working. You might just have to walk a mile in her running shoes before you can relate to her perspective.

Here's an example: I once worked in a small company located in an office building with many other small start-up companies. One day, I ran into the office manager from the company next to ours in the parking lot. She had quit and was loading a box filled with her personal belongings into her car. When I asked her why she had quit, she told me that she felt uneasy because her boss kept giving her more responsibility and more promotions. I was amazed: I was craving more responsibility and more challenge from my job after climbing out of the ranks of assistantship, and you couldn't make me go back for all the tea in China.

But this woman had quit to take a job as a secretary, which was actually a demotion from her current position. Her boss hadn't recognized that this employee, though bright and capable, didn't want more responsibility. In fact, she was made insecure by the constant change in her job description and level of responsibility. If her boss had understood that, he might have been able to structure a job to better suit her needs and desires. This was a young, dynamic company, and I have no doubt he could have created such a position. But he couldn't imagine someone satisfied with her position and wanting to stay right there. Because he couldn't understand what motivated her, he lost a good employee.

TIP

Use employees' yearly performance reviews as a time to take stock of their current motivational needs. Ask each employee what he or she wants to get out of the job in the next year. If you see patterns of need among several employees, institute policies that address them so that you can motivate all employees to work more productively and be more satisfied with their jobs.

COMMON MOTIVATORS

To help you see the other person's point of view, take a look at this list of things that stimulate different people to perform their jobs well:

- Money
- Respect
- Challenge
- Structure
- An attractive work environment
- Praise
- Flexible work hours
- Feeling like part of the team
- Wearing casual clothing to work
- Contributing ideas
- Travel

- Not having to travel
- The chance to learn
- Promotions
- Camaraderie
- Recognition
- An award
- Telecommuting
- Free soda in the lunch room
- A discount on company merchandise
- A great retirement plan
- Independence
- Bonuses
- A creative environment
- Being thanked for extra work
- Believing in the job
- Working with other people
- Having set processes
- The boss's trust

TIP

To truly understand how motivations change, just think about what's motivating you to report to work every day. Is what motivates you today different than what motivated you a year ago? Five years ago? Ten years ago?

Now that you know something about the different forms and patterns that an individual's needs fall into, you could probably take this list and slot each item on it into Maslow's hierarchy. Keeping that hierarchy in mind will help you remember that people look for different things out of their jobs, and will help you become a better motivator.

As you read the other chapters in this book, you'll find many suggestions for ways to motivate people. Some will motivate an entire group; others will be more useful in dealing with specific employees. As you choose what you might want to try to motivate your team, keep in mind the guidelines in this chapter, and choose the right motivation for the right people and circumstances.

THE 30-SECOND RECAP

- People are motivated by different needs.
- People's motivations change over time.
- Maslow's hierarchy of needs helps you understand types of motivators.
- Understanding what motivates individuals helps you motivate groups.

Take Care of the Basics

In this lesson, you learn how employee motivation is tied to perceived equity in the way compensation is doled out by your company.

Okay, let's be honest. This is probably the one chapter in this book that you feared most. Salaries, benefits—they all add up to you having to pay people more money to get performance. And whether you control the budget or just administer it, you probably don't have money to burn, right?

Most people think that if they can't offer top-dollar salaries or hefty bonuses, people will be lazy and unmotivated. Well, don't worry. You should be less concerned about paying lavish salaries and more focused on giving your employees compensation that you consider fair. Indeed, I'm going to surprise you in this lesson because I believe that the size of the salary or yearly bonus is not always the key motivation for performance or loyalty. Let's take a look.

THE IMPORTANCE OF COMPENSATION EQUITY

In psychology, there is a whole set of *equity* theories of motivation. One key figure in this school of thinking is J. Stacy Adams. Adams states that it is human nature to compare ourselves with others. We compare our looks, our cars, and, most importantly, our salaries with those of our peers. The perception that there's an *inequity* in our compensation at work might seriously impact our motivations for performing.

PLAIN ENGLISH

Equity   The state or condition of being just, impartial, and fair.

Inequity   An imbalance or lack of justice.

Think about it: Does it sometimes seem as if your Human Resources department spends most of its time making sure that no one receives special treatment? It sounds petty at the time: "No, your star employee cannot get comp time for working 30 nights in a row. If he does, everybody else has to get comp time." The result: Nobody gets comp time, and your star performer never puts in another hour of overtime.

Whether it's well implemented or not, there's good reason for this policing of equity. One of the strongest motivational factors in the workplace today is whether employees feel that they are being fairly compensated compared with others in their workplace.

TIP

When you're assigned an employee to supervise, ask your Human Resources department for a salary history. This history can be like a roadmap to employee demotivation if you see that his compensation hasn't kept pace with a co-worker's.

REACTING TO INEQUITY

Whenever an inequity exists, either perceived or real, employees react in a few predictable ways:

- **They lower their performance.** "Well, if they're not going to pay me what I'm worth, why should I try so hard? I'll just coast like everybody else around here!"

- **They demand equity.** "I'm going in there to demand that I get what I deserve!"

- **They quit.** "I'm out of here! I'm going to a company that recognizes my contributions."

- **They demand that those they perceive as less valuable produce more.** "Martinez doesn't put in half as much overtime as I do, but he got the same raise I did. I demand that you make him put in the same hours I do!"

- **They realign their comparison process.** "Well, those guys make as much as I do because they're in the marketing department, and everybody knows that assistants there are way overcompensated. Compared to the assistants in finance and HR, I guess I'm doing okay."

Another condition that arises when an employee perceives an unacceptable situation is something psychologists call *cognitive dissonance*. This psychological phenomenon occurs when our perceptions of ourselves and the perceptions of the outer world are out of whack. A classic example of cognitive dissonance is the heavy drinker who, knowing that alcohol can be addictive and that his use of alcohol interferes with almost every aspect of his life, still believes that he isn't an alcoholic. Reality and his view of himself collide, so he simply denies that the situation exists.

PLAIN ENGLISH

Cognitive dissonance   A condition that arises when there's a conflict between one's perception of oneself and the way the world perceives one.

When cognitive dissonance occurs in the workplace, you'll see employees expressing disbelief or denial about a negative situation, or making excuses for themselves or others. For example, despite the fact that an employee *knows* she's doing a fantastic job, her employer fails to give her a raise. It's impossible for her to reconcile the fact that she can do a great job and not get a raise. So either she's not doing as great a job as she thinks or she will, in fact, somehow get that raise.

However, cognitive dissonance is only a short-term coping mechanism that masks a real problem that won't go away in the long term. The only real solution is to provide the equity employees seek in the first place.

SETTING COMPETITIVE SALARIES

It's important to understand that wanting to get a competitive salary means more than just receiving a higher paycheck: It is a way for employees to get a sense of their own value. They watch to see whether their input is more or less valuable than that of others as measured by their monetary compensation. They listen at the water cooler when a co-worker gloats about a recent raise, and they wonder what they need to do to earn that same raise. Although salary is just one indicator of their value, it's a measurable one.

TIP

If you have several offices, one key to understanding whether your salaries are fair is to measure them against the cost of living in each area. The salaries for similar positions in your San Francisco and rural Georgia offices might be very disparate. But they also might be fair because of the differences in the cost of living in each area. If a Georgia employee complains when she finds out she's making less than her San Francisco colleague, make it clear how much more it costs to rent an apartment in the Bay Area.

Needless to say, it's very important to understand that salary is tied to an employee's self-worth and motivation; understanding how people respond to perceived inequity is important. But the real world presents barriers to salary equity. Do you recognize any of these common compensation scenarios?

- A lab technician who started 10 years ago at $20,000 now earns $30,000 after receiving regular annual raises. But new lab technicians, right out of school, are getting $35,000 as they come in the door because of current industry demand.

- You spot an employee who is earning much less than others of similar rank in the company and ask the human resources department if you can raise his salary by $10,000. Human resources denies the raise, claiming that giving an employee such a large increase all at once would set a bad precedent.

- Although all employees were promised a minimum 5 percent raise this year, new management has instituted cost savings measures. Those measures include cutting that increase to 2 percent.

All these situations pose compelling challenges for managers. Indeed, it's rare that a manager has the chance to make a clean sweep and totally reset everyone's compensation in a way that he or she thinks is fair. If you find yourself in such a position, I suggest that you try to focus on one employee at a time.

Try this plan for achieving employee compensation equity:

- Evaluate each employee's merits, and help him or her focus on personal growth and performance rather than on what other employees in the company earn.

- Review each employee's salary history and performance evaluations.

- Request information from the human resources department on the industry salaries for each position, as well as information about what those in similar positions throughout the company make.

- After evaluating these factors, if you think there's an inequity in an employee's salary, work with human resources to find out how much—and how fast—you can adjust it.

- Communicate your findings to the employee in question. As long as he or she knows that you're trying to bring his or her salary in line within the constraints of company policy, he or she probably will appreciate the recognition and effort as much or more than the increase itself.

- If you can't adjust compensation, see if you can offer some other recognition of the employee's value to the company, such as a new job title, a promotion, or a special project assignment.

TIP

If you can't make changes now but indicate your desire to make things right down the road, employees are often grateful for the attention you're giving them, even if you can't deliver anything tangible right now. Just make sure you *are* working toward eventual change, not just saying you are!

REVIEWING YOUR BENEFITS PACKAGE

Besides salary, you have another weapon when it comes to winning the motivation/self-esteem battle in the workplace: the benefits package. Depending on the size of your company and your role in it, you may or may not have any influence over what these benefits consist of and who receives them.

If you do influence benefits, make sure that you or your human resources team knows what other companies in your industry offer and where you exceed or fall short of their packages. Survey your employees about which benefits are most meaningful to them. If you have a choice between offering vision care or dental insurance as part of your medical benefits, give your employees some say as to what they prefer.

If you don't have any control over benefits, you can at least arm yourself with information. Having this information will allow you to use it as an effective negotiating chip in hiring, setting levels of compensation for your employees, and participating in compensation discussions among employees.

You'll need to find out about these items:

■ The cash value of your benefits package. Often, the cost of benefits to an employer amounts to about half the employee's salary.

■ How your package stacks up against other companies in your industry or area.

■ The full range of benefits you offer. In addition to your medical package, be aware of programs such as matching 401(k) funds, tuition reimbursement, and long-term disability insurance.

TIP

An interesting 1949 study looked at what motivates supervisors and nonsupervisory workers. For supervisors, high wages ranked number one, while the amount of compensation merited only fifth place for workers. The lower your wage, the more important job security, benefits, and potential for advancement become in getting you to work every day. Once you've moved up in the ranks, those motivations hold less sway.

Providing Special Financial Incentives

Everybody earns a salary, and almost everybody receives benefits (except, perhaps, part-time employees and contract workers). But a bonus is one place that an employer or manager can use his or her discretion.

Companies today are setting up complicated formulas for calculating bonuses. What was once a way for an employer to show unexpected appreciation for excellence has now become a 10-page document that takes an hour to explain in employee orientation.

Still, the way you use bonuses remains an important motivating factor in today's workplace.

A Yearly Bonus: It's Expected

A once-a-year bonus, usually presented around the Christmas holiday season, has become the norm. This is the bonus that is usually based on those detailed calculations just mentioned.

If you're a manager with the power of the purse strings, here are a few things to consider in doling out this money:

- Make sure that people understand that these bonuses are usually determined not only by individual employee performance, but also by how the company or division as a whole has performed.

- If you're allowed to give a higher reward to people who have excelled, use that discretion wisely.

- The way you present the bonus can be as important as the few hundred dollars that goes into the envelope. Take time to personally present the check, and add a few words of appreciation and praise. An employee often values being singled out for praise more than he does the money itself.

Using Unexpected Bonuses

Expected bonuses are great and can certainly help pay for holiday overspending. But the unexpected bonus—especially one directly tied to performance—may be an even better motivator. Indeed, an unexpected $50 in a weekly paycheck for work well done could be more motivating than a $500 yearly bonus that an employee considers a given. These unexpected rewards simply make people feel special.

TIP

One motivational experiment isolated two groups of workers. One group was treated differently than other workers at the company; the other was treated just like everybody else. The results? Both groups performed better, simply because they had been singled out to be involved in an experiment, which made them feel special.

Here are some suggestions for formulating an unexpected bonus scheme for your company:

- Provide a birthday bonus for every employee. An extra $100 associated with their special day makes an employee feel special in the workplace, too.

- Tie bonuses to a company's profits. If your company has a remarkable quarter, see if you can share that success with your employees.

- Make use of any discretionary fund for employee entertainment. If you haven't used it all by fiscal year end, ask your management if you could distribute it by giving each employee in your division a $20 bill.

Not all companies will be flexible enough to accommodate these kinds of bonus plans, but it doesn't hurt to ask. The rewards of motivation can be great.

CAUTION

Never, ever promise something you know you can't deliver. The promise of a bonus at the end of a project might act like a carrot to a donkey, but if it never happens, you've done serious damage to that employee's belief in you, your sense of fairness, and your reliability.

Nobody's Business: Keeping Compensation Private

Now that you understand how important fair compensation is and have learned a few ways to help manage variables on the salary and benefits front, it's time to figure out how to prevent dissatisfaction over compensation from developing in the first place.

Every business has a policy that discourages employees from discussing their salaries with others in the company. Employers think this is just good management. Employees think that it's part of a bigger plot to keep them from finding out about all the unfair things management is doing to them. The outcome? Telling employees never to discuss their salaries with others often has the opposite effect.

If an employee chronically gossips about salaries and other confidential information, you might be able to bring disciplinary action against him or her, but you'll never be able to stop the occasional confidence.

To cut down on the problems that can ensue from such discussions, make sure that your company has such a policy against revealing compensation and that you explain the policy to employees.

If an employee comes to you complaining about another employee's compensation in relation to his or her own, try these methods of minimizing damage:

- Point out that every employee is different: Each starts at a different salary, which is determined by the general economy, the strength of your industry, and the success of your company *at the time they are hired.*

- Offer that employee an opportunity to change the inequity by meeting certain goals that would lead to higher compensation. Then it's in their control to obtain the higher salary.

- Refuse to compare that employee with the other employee point by point. Instead, move the discussion to a comparison of the employee's performance this year with his or her performance last year. Has there been an improvement? Has that employee received rewards other than an increase in salary, such as a promotion?

In the end, you're better off guarding against the sharing of salary information. If that fails, you should refuse to enter into a discussion about information the employee had no right to in the first place, while attempting to assuage discontent.

COMPENSATION ENVY: KEEPING UP WITH THE JONESES

If you have a human resources department, a large part of its role is to keep abreast of current compensation and benefits standards in your industry and geographical region. Work with them to educate yourself on these matters so that you can more effectively manage compensation equity for your employees.

But if you're in a smaller company and don't have legions of HR professionals at your beck and call, you can use other resources to keep yourself educated.

The Internet provides many discussion forums and professional association Web sites dealing with compensation for specific industries. A few good Web sites for general compensation information are these:

- WageWeb, run by Human Resources Programs Development and Improvement (HRPDI), at wageweb.com.

- Society for Human Resources Management (SHRM), at shrm.org.
- Institute of Management and Administration (IOMA). Their Salary Zone, at ioma.com/zone, is particularly helpful.
- American Compensation Association (ACA), at acaonline.org.

If you belong to any professional associations, ask them to forward any of their salary studies, or simply pick the brains of colleagues at association meetings to find out what compensation their companies offer.

TIP

Listen to people you are interviewing for job openings. They sometimes will give you clues as to what your competitors are offering in the way of salaries and benefits.

THE 30-SECOND RECAP

- Concerns about compensation might be less about the total dollars offered and more about the fairness of an individual's compensation in your particular organization.

- It's human nature for people to compare themselves to others, but those comparisons could cause them to spot perceived inequities quickly. Inequity is a great demotivator in the workplace.

- Work within the constraints of your company policies to get and maintain equality of compensation.

- Look for ways other than compensation by which to recognize people, such as changes of title, special bonuses, or assignment to special projects. Singling people out for special recognition goes a long way toward making them feel appreciated.

- Understanding your company's policies and how you compare to other companies gives you the facts you need to deal with unhappy employees.

Providing a Great Environment

In this lesson, you learn how pleasant surroundings and ergonomic conditions spur productivity.

I observed a very interesting motivational move when I worked for a small video consulting firm. We had just moved into new offices when the owner announced that he was going to buy some artwork to add some visual interest to the place. He went on to say that each of us could choose a picture we would like to display in our own office space. He got a huge catalog of artwork from a framing store so that we could make our choices. The company would pay to have the pictures nicely framed.

We all buzzed around for weeks choosing our pictures and their frames and mattes. We then waited expectantly for a few weeks while the framers did their work. Finally, all the pictures arrived and were hung. They looked great. Although the art soon faded from the topics of conversation around the lunchroom, it gave the office the interest and color it needed, and each office took on a personal look that reinforced the creative atmosphere. This artwork made people feel as if they were a real part of the company, and we all enjoyed coming to work in the morning just that little bit more.

So if you're looking for a new way to motivate your employees, consider how making your workplace more attractive might motivate better performance.

UNDERSTANDING MOTIVATORS AND DEMOTIVATORS

One researcher of personality and motivation, Frederick Herzberg, conducted a fascinating study from which he devised the concept of *maintenance factors* on the job. Herzberg asked thousands of people to talk about both moments when they felt good about their work and moments when they felt bad.

PLAIN ENGLISH

Maintenance factors   Things about a business that contribute to a healthy business climate, but that do not cause it. For example, a clean lunchroom may not motivate good performance, but if it's not clean, people will complain about it. In that sense, cleaning the lunchroom becomes a maintenance factor.

Out of that study came two lists: a list of things that satisfied people, and a list of things that dissatisfied people. Now you might assume that these lists would consist of opposites: What satisfies a person would be to have chance for advancement, and what dissatisfies that same person would be lack of opportunity. But that wasn't the case—in fact, there were hardly any matches at all!

Look at the top six items on each of these lists:

Satisfiers

- Achievement
- Recognition
- The work itself
- Responsibility
- Advancement
- Growth

Dissatisfiers

- Company policy and administration
- Supervision
- Relationship with supervisor
- Working conditions
- Relationships with peers
- Relationships with subordinates

Here's the conclusion Herzberg reached from this information: What it takes to motivate an employee is different from what it takes to build a complaint-free workplace. Although providing nice working conditions might prevent people from becoming completely dissatisfied, this benefit might not result in complete satisfaction, either. Even more important, it might not be a motivation for employees to perform or to excel.

TIP

Many companies find it useful to have outside agencies perform satisfaction surveys. These companies tally anonymous results, giving an overall picture of why employees are satisfied and why they are dissatisfied.

Think about this result for a moment and apply it to your own experience. Was your favorite job your favorite because of the company policies, or because you consistently received recognition for your efforts? Although a stingy company policy about comp time might have grated on your nerves, it's doubtful that a fair comp-time policy would rank up there with recognition of your contributions when it came to motivating you to work hard. Listen to the people in your office. You'll probably find that they complain most about things like the lack of parking spaces, bad coffee, the vacation policy, and the temperature of their offices. Solve those problems, and you might keep your workers from staging an in-office revolution—but you probably won't have a motivated workforce.

So is it worth dealing with the bad coffee situation? Yes! The better coffee will not necessarily affect performance, but your willingness to listen and then to take action will have meaning for your employees. Furthermore, by providing the finest Colombian blend instead of instant coffee, you eliminate a source of discontent, one that could be demotivating people in the workplace.

DESIGNING AN INTERESTING WORKSPACE

As you can see, this chapter is about the flip side of motivation: demotivation. Getting rid of things that demotivate people might not motivate them, but it helps you get past the more minor complaints about the lousy lighting and lack of parking spaces to find out what will really motivate workers, such as job growth and advancement.

When it comes to eliminating demotivators, one good place to start is with the general appearance of your workplace. I've often been amazed at the number of businesses I've visited that haven't had a single picture hanging on the walls. I've even worked at companies where displaying anything personal in a cubicle was against policy. Now, I realize that you have to work within the parameters of your own organization, but try taking the following inventory of your workplace to see how you stack up.

At my company, we ...

- Have artwork on display (and not just in the conference room or executive offices).
- Have workspaces with adequate daylight as well as artificial lighting.
- Allow workers to display personal items in their workspace.
- Have live plants around the work area.
- Use a color besides bright white or industrial green on some walls.

What about your workplace? If you weren't able to check at least three of these items as applicable to your company, this chapter is for you!

TIP

Been in your workplace so long you can't see it for the trees? How about bringing a friend or your spouse in and getting their reactions about whether it could use another coat of paint?

As you begin to institute some of the changes suggested here, keep in mind that the display of art and personal items will have its limits. Pictures that are offensive to some people, such as male or female pinups, are a no-no. Even cartoons or jokes that have sexual overtones posted on a bulletin board might be a problem. And needless to say, racist and sexist commentary—even if part of a "joke"—is wrong in any context.

CAUTION

Check with your human resources department to learn about some of the limits your company's sexual harassment and other policies might impose on your proposed changes.

THE COLOR ADVANTAGE

Many studies show that color affects mood and that using color wisely can help produce an atmosphere in which motivation, concentration, learning, and retention flourish. For example, lack of vivid color creates boredom, while too much color variation overstimulates people. Too much of any one color makes people irritable and impairs their ability to concentrate.

TIP

Ever hear the phrase "waiting in the green room"? A green room is where performers wait when they're not onstage. These rooms are traditionally green because green induces relaxation and soothes the performers' eyes, which can be strained by spotlights on stage.

Use this list to help you understand how different colors impact people and their moods:

- Green relieves stress and calms people.
- Blue is another calming color, said to help resolve conflict.
- Red encourages alertness and mental clarity, but in vibrant shades it also can make people slightly edgy.
- Yellow can create a feeling of harmony, but in bright shades it can make some people uneasy.

Now, whether use of color will make dull employees jump up and turn handsprings is debatable, but if nothing else, a little color makes a statement that management is willing to splurge a little on the employees' creature comforts.

So how do you add color to your office? You can provide color with artwork, or you can paint your walls in creative ways. This color need not be everywhere. In fact, painting three walls off-white and one wall with a strong accent color can be more effective than surrounding people with intense color. Your choices of carpet and fabric upholstery also influence the color tones of the workspace.

Finally, if you don't want to break out the paint cans and brushes, you can always buy a few plants or artificial flowers and sprinkle them around the place at little expense.

LET THERE BE LIGHT!

Light also influences how people perceive color. Fluorescent light amplifies cooler colors such as blues, but drains warmer colors such as red; that's why fluorescent light makes most humans look awful—it drains the pinks and oranges from our flesh color. Daylight or incandescent light works the opposite way: Cooler colors pale, while warmer colors become more vibrant.

In addition, light affects how people feel about their workspace. You may have heard about a condition called seasonal affective disorder (SAD), which causes depression in susceptible people who are negatively affected by the lack of bright light during the winter months. Likewise, a perpetually dark workplace can cause depression in some employees and can result in lethargy and despondency in others. In short, lighten up if you want to motivate your work force!

TIP

If cramped working quarters are a problem, use low-intensity colors. *Intensity* refers to the saturation of the color; for example, in the red hue, pink has less intensity than deep red. High-intensity colors make a room seem smaller. Darker shades of colors also make rooms seem smaller because they absorb light.

MUSIC, MUSIC, MUSIC!

Playing music in the workplace is a tricky thing. Music distracts some people, while others find that their productivity increases when set to a beat. If you decide to allow your workers to play music in the office, make sure that everyone is in agreement about the policy. If not, you'll have to ensure that those who *do* play music in their personal workspaces do so at a volume that doesn't carry to those nearby. Naughty lyrics could also push the sexual harassment envelope, so make sure that everyone understands the limits of personal taste.

Needless to say, music isn't a universal panacea. If you decide that background music throughout the workplace during the day is impractical, you might be able to compromise. For example, each week you could take a poll to find out what style of music your employees would like to hear and then pipe it in between 4 and 5 every Friday afternoon. This approach can work for several reasons, including these:

- Most people are ready to break out of the working mode on Friday afternoon.

- It's often dress-down day, so it fits the mood.

- Rarely are clients or visitors in an office at the end of the day on Friday.

- Playing upbeat music can leave employees feeling good about their jobs when they leave for the weekend, even if they've had a terrible week.

- Allowing employees to vote on the weekly selection gives them a sense of involvement and community.

- If somebody finds it hard to work with music playing, you've picked one of the lowest productivity hours of the week to affect him or her, so the damage will be minimal. Just reassure that person that not producing much during that time is not a problem, and thank him or her for being patient.

TIP

Don't have a CD player at work? Tune a radio to the local station that plays the kind of music you want that week. Yes, commercials are a bit annoying, but even they make for a refreshing change of pace.

Here's another extension of the music idea: If you throw an off-site Christmas party with live entertainment, consider taping the band (with its permission, of course). Then replay the tape on a Friday in August to remind employees of the fun they had the year before.

ERGONOMICS MEANS SAFE AND COMFORTABLE

Ergonomics has been a buzzword in business for many years now. Simply put, ergonomics is the study of how working conditions affect our bodies. Ergonomics in a factory setting relates not only to worker comfort, but often to employee safety as well. The addition of word processing and computing as almost constant activities for many workers has kept associated strains and ergonomics in the forefront of management thinking.

PLAIN ENGLISH

Ergonomics   The design and use of furniture and other tools to reduce physical strain on employees.

Providing a workplace with comfortable and safe physical conditions increases productivity and decreases absenteeism and workman's compensation claims. It also can make your employees feel that management cares about their health and safety, which is a big morale booster.

If you work at a large company, it's likely that your facilities department purchases chairs and other equipment that meet Occupational Safety and Health Administration (OSHA) requirements. However, there are some other tools and furnishings worth installing to help people feel more comfortable.

ERGONOMIC PERKS: HEADSETS, FOOTRESTS, AND MORE

If you work at a large company, it's likely that many things about your office setup will be generic and out of your control. But if you're the owner or manager, you usually have discretion over smaller purchases. If so, consider some of these items. Most of them cost $50 or less, but they will make work much easier on the body:

- A footrest, to ease lower back strain
- A headset, for those who spend hours on the phone
- A lumbar support cushion (a desk chair pillow that supports the lower back)
- A copy holder (whether stand-alone or mounted to the computer monitor), to reduce eyestrain

TIP

Here's something that will help your workers without costing you a dime: Recommend that they make a habit of moving about during the day. Getting up from their chairs, moving their eyes away from the computer screen, and adjusting their chair height now and then helps keep them from straining their bodies and from becoming stiff and inflexible.

COMPUTERS AND PRODUCTIVITY

One of the most talked-about ergonomic hot spots today is the computing station. The repetitive nature of many computing tasks, such as typing and clicking the mouse, can cause serious injury. Eyestrain is also a concern when a worker stares at light rays emanating from a screen most of the day.

You can implement many things to ease strain and keep workers happy while they compute. Here are just a few:

- A wrist rest
- An ergonomic keyboard
- A trackball mouse
- A touchpad
- A glare-reduction screen
- An under-the-desk keyboard drawer

TIP

If an employee suffers from carpal tunnel syndrome as a result of repetitive keyboarding, consider voice-recognition software. Although its functionality is still a little clumsy, this technology allows those unable to use computers because of injury or lack of skill to enter text by speaking into a headset microphone.

THE 30-SECOND RECAP

- Although getting rid of demotivators won't in itself motivate people, it can improve the morale of employees.
- Color and light can be used to subconsciously motivate productivity or to give a sense of space to employees.
- Musical interludes might be the perfect way to break up or end the work week.
- The right furniture and accessories can make repetitive work easier to handle and can keep employees more productive and healthy.

Giving Them What They Need to Succeed

In this lesson, you get some ideas about motivating your people by providing them with what they need to be successful.

Imagine this: You're on top of a ladder, you've got a mouthful of nails, you're juggling a stack of pictures to hang, and you realize that you left the hammer on the kitchen counter. That's kind of what it feels like when you've got work to do at the office and you don't have the proper tools.

One of the most demotivating things in the world is not having the knowledge or equipment to do what you have to do. This chapter looks at some of the things you can give workers to help them succeed.

TRAINING THE TROOPS: FROM ON-THE-JOB TRAINING TO A DEGREE

You hire people because they have certain qualifications. These qualifications might include a college degree or specific work experience, such as experience with certain software programs or pieces of equipment.

But nobody comes equipped with everything he or she needs to work at your specific company, with all its homegrown procedures and processes. And it's human nature to want to continually evolve and learn new things. So from the day you start working with an employee, that person will look to you for training to help her succeed and move forward in her career.

TIP

Try asking job candidates what training they would like when you interview them. Their answers can tell you whether they understand what skills are required for this position. You'll also learn whether they are forward-thinking about their future with your company.

THE RIGHT START

The first thing you owe an employee is the right training, starting on his first day at your company. Many people begin training an employee by lecturing him about company policies and procedures. Often, though, it's more efficient to ask a few questions first. Here are a few to get you started:

- Ask what the employee already knows about the company, his job, and the road ahead. Why waste time teaching what he has already learned?

- Ask how he learns best. Some people like to be shown; others like to try themselves. Some like to take all the manuals and guidelines for their job and lock themselves away in a cubicle for three days; others like to just walk around and observe for a while.

- Ask what processes he already understands but needs more practice to master.

- Ask how he did his job at his last place of employment. Not only might you get a few tips about how to improve your own processes, but you'll also figure out what the employee might have to unlearn to fit in with your crew.

After you have the answers to these questions, you can begin to train. Here are general techniques I recommend for effective training:

- Hold a meeting to go over the main responsibilities of the job, from manager to employee. During this discussion, provide a description of the main job responsibilities, give an overview of the processes involved, and be very clear about your expectations, both in general and as they apply to this employee.

- Assign a *mentor* to work with the new employee on a day-to-day basis. Have the new employee work alongside the mentor for a few days or a week, observing and taking notes.

PLAIN ENGLISH

Mentor   A trusted counselor or guide. Mentors impart knowledge to others based on their real-world experience.

- After the employee has observed the work for a few days, sit down again and go over everything you went over in your first discussion. You must repeat this information because you can't expect an employee to have grasped even 20 percent of what you talked about the first day—everything was too new to have stuck. However, by observing the job for a few days, the employee should now be able to absorb what you have to say and to ask intelligent questions.

- Assign some specific process, and have the mentor observe the employee as she performs it. Give her constructive feedback on her performance. If all goes well, the employee should be able to try that process on her own, but she should always feel free to come back to you or her mentor with questions.

CAUTION

If you're using mentoring in the workplace, be sure that you support those mentors. As their manager, you have to allow them the time they need to help others in addition to doing their own work. Mentoring can be rewarding if people are given what they need to do it right.

Of course, different jobs require different amounts and types of training. In general, though, following the pattern outlined here (giving an overview, allowing the employee to observe the work, providing another overview, and letting the employee try the process under supervision) helps most people get off to a good start.

CAUTION

Be sure to let a new employee know that you don't expect him to absorb all you're telling him on the first day. By telling him that you'll go over it all again, you take some of the pressure off and allow him to really listen to what you're saying.

LEARNING ON THE JOB

Don't make the mistake of thinking that learning stops once an employee masters his or her job. In fact, being able to pick up new skills on a regular basis is an important motivator that keeps people doing the same job at the same company for many years to come.

TIP

Always emphasize to employees that you welcome their questions and concerns. Many people don't learn new skills because they're afraid to ask questions.

You can structure ongoing learning into every job by using a few simple techniques. First, remember that doing one's job well often requires an understanding of other areas of the business. Allow your employees to interact with and observe other departments'—or even other vendors'—operations. By doing so, your employees will better understand what impact their work has on others. In addition, this exposure shows them options for their future growth in the company, which could lie in another department or type of work.

Second, practice stretching your employees' abilities. If they perform some tasks well, put them in situations in which they can excel. If they have supervised a small group of people on a project well, for instance, up the ante and have them supervise a larger group. If they successfully organized a meeting for 30 people, have them plan and coordinate a trade show. Even though these tasks might not be part of their regular job, try adding a few things to their responsibilities now and then to see whether they can handle them. People always learn in new situations.

Third, expose your employees to other people who might know techniques they don't. You started that on day one with a mentoring scenario. Remember that the appropriate mentor for an employee might change as time goes by; the person who knew more than the employee on the first day might not be the right mentor a year from now. Have other managers share their skills and experience with the people in your department. Observing people who are really knowledgeable in action is a great education.

TIP

Don't be so egotistical that you're afraid to admit your own weaknesses. If another manager at the company knows more about some area of your business or has a strength in an area you don't, swallow your pride and ask that person to share the knowledge with you and your staff.

Finally, make sure that you dedicate part of every performance review to a discussion of training. If an area of the employee's performance is weak, consider recommending that the person receive additional mentoring or take a class or seminar.

LEARNING ONLINE

Many companies today employ whole training departments that see to employees' classroom learning experiences. Many companies offer classes ranging from how to use a software product to negotiating skills, and from business ethics to sexual harassment policies. Sometimes on-staff trainers teach; other times, people attend an off-site training facility for a day or two.

TIP

When you get catalogs in the mail from training companies, don't toss them; save them in a folder. Then place the folder where all your employees have access to it so that they can get ideas for the training programs they would like to see the company offer.

Your employees might benefit from additional educational opportunities as well. Online training is an option that offers great convenience in these busy times. Also called *distance learning,* online training allows employees to take a course over the Internet from home, from their desks, or even from the road.

PLAIN ENGLISH

Distance learning   Any structured learning that takes advantage of communication media, such as computers and videotapes, to allow learners to study in a remote location but under the guidance of an instructor or educational institution.

Online training opportunities range from those that allow people to download and print information and submit tests by e-mail to live interaction between a remote trainer and student online. Many companies also run video conferences to train people in the field. Regardless of whether your company is willing to invest in certain technologies to enable distance learning or whether you simply encourage your employees to look for online courses they would like to take on their own time, this form of training is definitely the wave of the future.

TUITION REIMBURSEMENT

Today most companies offer some form of tuition reimbursement. Under this kind of program, the company reimburses an employee for all or some of the costs of tuition and textbooks. Reimbursement can be as informal as a manager okaying attendance at a one-day seminar on Windows to a formal program that helps employees get a college degree.

Tuition reimbursement is usually tied to two key factors: First, the coursework must be logically related to the employee's work responsibilities. Second, the employee must obtain an acceptable grade in the class.

Learn your company's tuition reimbursement policy, and make that information available to your employees. Make sure they know what they need to do to be eligible and how much reimbursement they can expect. Tuition programs are great perks that make employees more valuable to you and that help them get ahead in their careers. Unfortunately, people often don't take advantage of these programs just because they're in the dark about what's involved.

PROVIDING THE PROPER TOOLS

Training gives people the knowledge they need to do their job. But it's important that you also ensure that your employees have other things to help them succeed. These include a little peace and quiet and the right technology.

A LITTLE PRIVACY, PLEASE!

Some jobs require constant interaction. Others require complete concentration and quiet. But everybody needs a little peace now and then. Often you can't do much about the office setup and how private or public workstations are, but you can be sensitive to the need for getting away now and then. Try a few of these strategies to give your people some needed quiet time during the day:

- Allow flex time so that people can come in and leave early, or come in and stay late to get work done when it's quieter.

- Make an office available to people who have a project they need to concentrate on. If nothing else, make your office available on a rotating basis when you're at lunch or at a meeting.

- Allow people to work at home when they have to meet a tough deadline.

- Establish a quiet time one afternoon a week when people are not to disturb each other, unless it's a dire emergency.

TIP

One company I worked for gave out plastic disks that were green on one side and red on the other. If someone didn't want to be disturbed, he or she hung the red disk on the door or cubicle. If the green side of the disk was turned out, it was okay to talk to that person. This approach gave employees some control over their own privacy.

THE OFFICE MAMBO

Of course, the ultimate in private work space is an office of one's own. For many people, an office is like the Holy Grail of corporate America. The bigger the office, the more windows—and the better the view—the more successful they feel. Needless to say, there is both a practical gain of simply having more privacy and space to get work done and the psychological benefit that comes from having a bigger and better work space. It's a sign of status and success.

Even if you don't care what kind of space *you* work in, don't forget how your employees feel about their work space. Watch for opportunities to reward good performance with better accommodations. Moving from a cubicle into an office can work wonders in the motivation department. Moving from a small office to a bigger one can do almost as much.

TIP

At all costs, try to avoid giving someone a quality of work space that you have to take away at a later date. If you give someone a window office once, he or she will be totally demotivated if the window is lost when the company reorganizes or makes an office move.

PENS, PAPER, A 500MHZ PENTIUM?

If you think about it, you'll decide that a large part of being a manager or supervisor is being a glorified office supply sergeant. Even if handing somebody a $5 calculator might not seem particularly motivating, it certainly is if the employee needs it to perform his or her job. Indeed, management sends a very negative message if it does not provide its employees with the tools they need to succeed. You might not be able to procure state-of-the-art computers for everyone in your group, but you should make it part of your job to listen carefully to what people need and then to do your best to provide it.

Here is a checklist of items that might make your employees' work lives a little easier to manage:

- Current versions of software, such as Microsoft Office and Windows or Corel WordPerfect
- Additional memory or upgraded motherboards for computers
- Modems that allow faster access to the Internet
- A information manager, such as the Palm Pilot
- Contact-management software for busy salespeople or customer service folks
- A pager or cell phone to help people stay in touch if they're on the road a great deal
- Basic supplies such as a calendar or organizer, a Rolodex, and a phone with features they need, such as mute or conference
- Ergonomic items, such as a wrist rest and a footrest

TIP

If you can't get the go-ahead from management to purchase what an employee needs, consider sharing an item, such as a department laptop computer, among all employees. If nothing else, acknowledge that you appreciate the fact that it's challenging for an employee to work without the item.

THE 30-SECOND RECAP

- People need good training as they begin a job, in addition to ongoing learning opportunities.

- Training can occur in a class, on the job, or online.

- Online training can save time and be more convenient than attending classes in person.

- Work space can provide privacy, quiet for concentration, and status to motivate employees.

- Give people the tools they need to do their work successfully, from basic office supplies to high-tech equipment.

Go Team!

In this lesson, you learn the importance of team spirit in motivating employees.

This chapter concerns one of the most overused motivational strategies in business today: team-building. So many people are talking the talk of team-building without really building a team-oriented workplace that it has left employees somewhat dubious. How can you breathe fresh life into a technique that many employees have come to discount and even dread?

First, you have to remember that the basic concept of teamwork, fueled by the driving force of leadership, is a sound one. You simply have to understand how to make teamwork become more than just a label among your work-group. Once you really understand how team-building works, you can use some of the suggestions in this chapter to give this motivator a shot in the arm at your company.

TEAMWORK TODAY

Although it seems as though the concept of team-building has been lurking around the corporate hallways in the form of buzzwords and workshops for a long time now, it's a relatively recent addition. To a large extent, the workplace of 50 years ago was based on a vertical hierarchy in which rigid job descriptions defined one's contribution to the whole.

As society became more prosperous, workers became better educated, our economy offered more choices, and people began to question these rigid roles. Studies on team-building began in the late 1940s but really took off in the 1950s, when programs that assisted veterans in obtaining an education became widespread and there was less unemployment. People began to look to the workplace to do more than just provide a paycheck. In this more democratic working climate, team-building theories began to proliferate.

These theories aimed to motivate employees with several strategies and desired outcomes. Team-building is supposed to accomplish these goals:

- Make employees feel that their contributions are valued.
- Acknowledge that no goal is reached without the contribution of everybody working toward it, no matter what their positions are in the hierarchy.
- Generate loyalty by making employees feel that their team (company) is somehow better than others are.
- Encourage respect and trust among team members.
- Enable more effective communication.

PLAIN ENGLISH

Teams   Groups of people with a common goal who use the unique strengths of each member and the combined strengths of the group to achieve that goal.

But today, team-building is often a mandate handed down in a company memo to managers rather than a long-term commitment to sound team-building practices. Managers aren't trained in sound leadership and team-building practices (unless you consider a one-day workshop every few years to be training). The result is that a few managers with innate leadership abilities have made team-building work, while the majority of managers have stumbled around spouting bad sports analogies.

WHAT MAKES A GOOD TEAM?

Not all teams are created equal, although some team-building theories treat them as if they were. A brand-new team has different opportunities and challenges than an existing team riddled with conflicts and politics. Likewise, large teams are different than small teams. *Decision teams*, such as an executive committee that votes on policy decisions, have different mandates than *work teams*, which work together on day-to-day tasks to reach measurable goals.

PLAIN ENGLISH

Decision teams   Teams that function primarily to make decisions. An example would be a committee formed to review flex-time policies at a company.

Work teams   Teams that have to coordinate individual efforts on a day-to-day basis to perform tasks; a space shuttle crew is a work team.

But although teams may differ, successful teams are built on some basic precepts:

- **Trust.** Building a sense of trust among team members is vital to an open team structure.

- **Communication.** Opening up avenues of communication among members ensures that everybody understands the goals of the larger group and knows how his or her individual work fits in.

- **Involvement.** One key to creating a successful team is to obtain the commitment of all team members to key decisions. This doesn't necessarily mean that everything gets done by consensus, but each member should be aware of the decisions and should understand why they are made.

- **Conflict resolution.** Within good teams, conflict is brought into the open and is resolved as quickly as possible.

- **Feedback.** In a successful team, the manager or other team members provide feedback on a regular basis so that all members can work together to improve the team's performance.

CAUTION

One basic principle of team-building has been expressed this way: Team-building is a process, not an event. Don't expect to implement team-building in a day!

WHEN DOES A GROUP BECOME A TEAM?

Every team has a leader, and more will be said about the quality of leadership later in this chapter. But how else does a group of people differ from a team of people? Compare the qualities on this chart to understand this key difference.

Groups	Teams
No formal communications procedures	Communication procedures in place
No support for each others' activities	Support for each others' activities
No overriding vision	Vision and goals provided by the leader or by consensus
Subgroups formed randomly	Focus on working together as a single group
No group identity	Self-esteem formed through group identity
Individual contributions not encouraged	Individual contributions welcomed

A group does not automatically make a team. It takes some work on your part to ensure that you institute the characteristics of a team in any collection of people you work with. One of the most important vehicles for this is communication.

COMMUNICATION IS THE FOUNDATION

Communication is another buzzword in the business world. But cliché or not, good communication is the very foundation of good teams. In teams, communication serves several purposes, including these:

- **Common goals.** You must ensure that the team is in agreement about the goals and work to be performed.
- **Conflict resolution.** Make sure that conflicts are aired and resolved.
- **Problem resolution.** Catching procedural or task problems before they get out of hand.
- **Synergy.** Create a synergy of talents by using methods such as brainstorming to generate ideas and solutions that an individual alone might not be able to produce.

Good communication consists of a basic model. First, communication is initiated; for example, you send a memo to an employee. The employee receives the message, with varying amounts of noise getting in the way of understanding it. This noise can consist of things such as personal preconceptions, lack of context, or semantic interference. Finally, a response to the communication is generated, perhaps in the form of another memo or phone call.

TIP

You can reduce the chances of miscommunication by encouraging team members to repeat or paraphrase important information you present to them.

To create successful communication, you have to encourage a communications network—that is, a series of two-way communications that ensure the information perceived is the information that was intended. That requires a sense of openness and trust among team members, one that allows them to admit confusion or to ask for clarification. As you set up communications vehicles such as weekly staff meetings, regular reports, or online chatting areas, consider the underlying need for trust and openness in your communications model.

DOES YOUR TEAM COME WITH BAGGAGE?

Now that you have an understanding of some of the characteristics of teambuilding, how do you begin to use it on the job? One place to start is by understanding what has been done in the past to build team spirit at your workplace and how your employees feel about those efforts. Start with a little simple research:

- Talk to your Human Resources department manager to find out what efforts have been made along these lines in the past. How did these efforts go over? Did the company get employee feedback on them?
- Talk to your employees, and ask them what teamwork means to them.
- Assess whether you see the earmarks of teamwork among your group. It's easier to build on a few characteristics of teamwork that are already in place than to start from scratch.

Specifically, ask your employees these questions:

- What stops our group from being an effective team?
- How could we become a better team?

■ What are we doing now that is team-oriented, and how can we build on that?

Is "Team" a Dirty Word?

I once encountered a company that had grown rapidly from a small entrepreneurial group to a large public company, yet it clung desperately to the vestiges of its younger self. As the company became too large for the whole group to fit into a single conference room, management hired professional consultants to come in and run what they called Team-Building Days.

Team-Building Days consisted of scavenger hunts and other games in which group effort counts. People were forced to wear hats that had silly team names on them, such as "Cougars" and "Pythons." They were given assignments to think of clever solutions to stupid problems. Childish prizes such as yo-yos and water pistols were distributed throughout the day. If anyone missed Team-Building Day because he was trying to make a work deadline, he was severely reprimanded.

How did the employees feel about this enforced team-building? They hated it. They could see, better than senior management could, that the young company was feeling growing pains and the loss of its entrepreneurial childhood, and was trying desperately to live in the past. But searching for your entrepreneurial roots isn't team-building—and a once-a-year fun-fest doesn't build trust or lay the foundations for teamwork.

TIP

A whole subset of people resent teamwork not because of its concepts, but because of its language. Analyze your own speech for clichés and tired sports analogies (like comparing the last part of a project to the homestretch or final inning), and get rid of them!

The point is that teamwork is not something you can drag out a few times a year, and it's not something you can jam down people's throats. If you implement team-building practices on a daily basis and work with your employees to make sure they buy in, you will find a team environment to be a powerful motivator.

Make It Last

After you've polled your employees for their attitudes about teams, you need to assess the commitment of senior management to the concept. In 1994 one survey found that although most companies spouted team-building as a policy, only 22 percent actually had any kind of team-building program in place. Here are the most common reasons companies gave for not using team-building programs:

- Managers didn't know how to build teams.
- Managers didn't understand the payoff of spending time on team-building.
- Team-building efforts weren't rewarded in the company.
- People felt that their teams were doing okay; they didn't need team-building.
- People felt that management didn't support team-building.

Note the second, fourth, and fifth items. Each of these suggests that a manager runs the risk of employees questioning team-building efforts in an organization in which team-building isn't supported from the top.

Can you instill more team-oriented activity in your workgroup without broader support? Yes. By doing so, you might make productive changes in employee motivation and attitude. But, as with any motivational effort, the time a manager or supervisor spends on team-building is ultimately going to be supported or questioned by your management. Seeking support early on will not only make your task easier, it will also show employees that the team-building talk isn't only one layer of management deep.

TIP

You can find one big clue as to how teamwork is viewed at your company in your company mission statement (it's there in a memo at the bottom of your drawer or in the back of the employee handbook). See if teamwork is part of the greater mandate for your organization. If it isn't, suggest that it should be.

When you understand how management feels about team-building and have gathered your employees' attitudes about it, start to work the basic elements of team-building (trust, communication, involvement, conflict resolution, and feedback) into your workplace. Don't announce it at the staff meeting as a great new program. Do start to practice it on a daily basis!

LEADERSHIP: IT'S ESSENTIAL TO A SUCCESSFUL TEAM

Now this is the difficult part. Putting the precepts of teamwork up on a bulletin board doesn't make a team. The hard truth is that, to a great extent, a team is formed by the leadership it receives. Thus, the most serious work you can do to establish a team environment is to work on your leadership skills.

Some people are born leaders, and others have leadership thrust upon them. Regardless, you can cultivate certain characteristics of leadership.

INNOVATION IS KEY

Consider the words manager and leader for a moment. Here are definitions that might help:

- A manager is someone who maintains things. A manager is an administrator of processes, policies, and people.

- A leader is someone who has a vision and communicates it. A leader focuses on the long-term goal, not the day-to-day processes.

In short, a manager manages the present situation, and a leader leads the way into the future. A key part of that leadership is the willingness to innovate. Where a manager is a champion of the status quo, a leader asks questions and pokes at current policy and procedure to see if something better can be found. To a great extent, it's that willingness to be open to excellence and change, and to involve the team in those efforts, that motivates a team.

In the 1970s a team of researchers named Berlew and Burns talked about some key characteristics of leaders. A leader, they said, carries out the following actions:

- Establishes shared values among team members
- Instills confidence in followers
- Creates organizational excitement
- Isn't afraid of introducing major change
- Empowers followers
- Gives meaning and purpose to an organization

KNOW YOUR TEAM'S STRENGTHS

One other thing will help you become a good leader: Get to know your team. Quite often managers or supervisors get into the rut of seeing their workers according to their job descriptions. But each person on your team is complex; each has strengths and weaknesses. It's your job to really understand the best way to use the whole person to get the job done.

Now I'm finally going to resort to a sports analogy. Leadership is very much akin to the role a coach plays on a sports team. A good coach knows his or her players and watches carefully throughout the game to put each player in a role that will maximize that person's usefulness. Ask yourself these questions to see where your coaching skills could use improvement:

- Do I fully understand the strengths and weaknesses of each team member?

- Am I constantly aware of whether each team member is being challenged in his or her work?

- Have I created an environment in which each worker is willing to play the role that best ensures the success of the team? Am I willing to make shifts in assignments to utilize each person in the best way?

- Do I look for opportunities to help team members grow in their areas of weakness? Even if someone will never be the star hitter, that person still has to know how to hit now and then.

OFFICE TEAM-BUILDING

Even though team-building cannot be a once-a-year event, it's still possible to have some fun with your teams. If you've laid the foundation for a true organizational team structure, applying it to the dynamics of your group outside of day-to-day work can be a logical extension.

CAUTION

Don't insist upon participation in team activities outside the office. If several team members participate, that will be fine. The key is not to make this out-of-the-office team effort feel forced or allow it to become a burden to those who are too busy or not inclined to join.

SPONSOR A SPORTS TEAM

Cliché sports analogies aside, sports provide a model of teamwork that cannot be denied. The trust and communication players must have to maintain their focus and get a football from one end of a field to another, for example, provide a wonderful model for your office team. Allowing your employees to spend time outside the workplace building that kind of trust can have direct benefits back on the job.

Many offices sponsor sports teams to play other companies, or they have one department play against another. Doing so builds team spirit even among the team members who choose not to play because they root for their group to win. Ask your employees if they would enjoy such an activity—and remember, keep it fun. The last thing you need is to build cliques or personal conflicts on the playing field that spill over into your working team.

GET BEHIND A CAUSE

Less time-consuming than a sports team, but often every bit as good for team-building, is a cause that employees can rally around. Consider some of these group efforts:

- Sponsor an employee who is running in a charity race.
- Sponsor a poor family or child through a local or national agency. Post letters and progress reports on the company bulletin board, where everybody can read them and feel proud.
- Participate as a group in a volunteer activity. For example, man the phones for a local public radio station pledge drive.
- Organize a food or toy drive at Christmas time.
- Organize donations of food or clothing for a disaster relief effort.

TIP

The key to making support of a cause a team-building effort is to make sure that everybody is kept apprised of the contributions to date and the impact your efforts are having. Announce progress in the team meeting every week to keep people interested and involved.

TEAM PARAPHERNALIA

One other way to build team spirit is to engender a feeling of pride in your organization or department. You can do this by building brand loyalty, a tactic companies and sports teams have discovered with a vengeance in recent years. How is this done? Simply give people something they can wear, carry around, or display proudly on their desks that sports your company or team name or logo. In other words, give them *tchotchkes*.

PLAIN ENGLISH

Tchotchke   A Yiddish word, tchotchke has become a catchall phrase for small gifts or giveaways—such as notepads, pens, or key chains—that companies give to employees or customers.

Now, these things aren't free, but their ability to provide an ongoing reminder of your team is usually worth it. If employees wear or carry the items outside the office, it's also a nice form of free advertising.

Try to find interesting items; coffee mugs, caps, and T-shirts are old standbys, but get creative!

- Mouse pads
- A customized screensaver
- Cookies with your logo baked in
- Puzzle cubes
- Water bottles

TIP

Get together with your marketing department. These giveaway professionals might just be producing several hundred of some giveaway item for a trade show or for customers. If you can piggyback your order with theirs, that lowers the unit price for everybody.

Whatever you decide might make a nice gift, remember to make it a reminder of the intangible things you're doing to provide leadership and an environment where true team spirit can thrive.

The 30-Second Recap

- Team-building must be part of your everyday work environment and cannot be a short-term effort.
- Support for team-building from management is important for long-term success.
- Keystones of good teams are trust, communication, involvement, conflict resolution, and feedback.
- Good leaders provide innovation and understand how to use the skills of the team to best advantage.
- Team-building can be supported by out-of-work team efforts, such as a sports team or charity efforts.

Throw a Party!

In this lesson, you get some ideas for throwing successful office parties that involve and stimulate your workers.

Office parties are as inevitable as the seasons. When they go well, they're great motivators. They help people get to know each other, have a little fun, and feel relaxed with each other when they return to work. When they don't go well, they're about as pleasant as an IRS audit.

When was the last time you sat around a conference table staring at your co-workers while munching on stale cookies, trying to think of something to say? In this chapter, you'll get some insight into the role of office parties, learn some of the do's and don'ts of office parties, and discover some great ideas for how to spice them up.

THE WORKPLACE: MORE THAN WORK

Whether it's an emotionally healthy trend is debatable, but today many people depend on their offices for providing a hefty percentage of their interpersonal relationships. Many single people find that the office is the place they're most likely to meet a potential mate or form a new relationship. Even those already involved in a romantic relationship have trouble finding room in their schedules of childcare, house maintenance, and errands to socialize outside of work.

Let's face it: You spend 40 or more hours a week with these people. Not counting sleep time, you probably spend more time with co-workers than you do with your spouse or children. Few people have the luxury of having a full-time stay-at-home mate to organize their social life. So the *socialization needs* in today's office have taken on an importance they didn't have in years past.

PLAIN ENGLISH

Socialization needs   One of the stages of Abraham Maslow's hierarchy of needs; they involve personal fulfillment from social interaction (see "What Motivates People?" on page 202).

This is not to suggest that you have to become a social director. Work is work, and companies that waste too much time throwing little parties or organizing team games usually end up forcing people to put in overtime to get their real work done. But because occasional parties are part of your working reality, you might as well use them effectively to entertain and motivate your employees.

THE DYNAMICS OF SOCIALIZATION

One of the reasons we sometimes end up with dull, uncomfortable office get-togethers is that we fail to remember that people have different personalities and different social styles. In effect, we are forcing people to sit in a room together and have fun. When we organize an office party, we're often putting people who are party animals in a room with those who think that an office is strictly for work. The outcome can be unpredictable.

Outside of work, people usually choose the time and place for socializing, as well as the people to socialize with. So in essence, you're creating something of an artificial social scenario when you throw an office party.

With that in mind, consider applying some of these guidelines when you organize your next office event:

- Get as many people as possible involved in organizing the party so that each has a vested interest in its success.

- Plan a few topics of conversation or activities, or create a theme that will offer common ground to people with different personalities.

- Don't let the party go on forever. Aim to please the person with the lowest tolerance for socializing, and let people know it's okay to wander off even if the party is still in full swing at that time.

- If you can break up the usual office cliques so that people chat with new people, great. But people form their alliances for a reason, and if they choose to talk only to those people they talk to every day, so be it.

- Be prepared to be a facilitator. Have a few anecdotes on hand to tell in order to fill in the quiet moments. If you begin by sharing a personal story that's interesting or humorous, others will often be made to feel more relaxed and will chime in with their own stories.

- Don't overdo the party thing. Instead of giving a birthday party for every employee, for example, give a party every month for everybody with a birthday in that month.

TIP

Stuck for snappy material? Use the Internet. These days, stories, jokes, and anecdotes whiz around the World Wide Web like good wishes at a wedding. Borrow a few to relate at your next party.

HELPING PEOPLE OUT OF THEIR SHELLS

For people who love to socialize, parties will always be fun, and these people will be motivated to enjoy your workplace all the more because of them. But what do you do to make parties motivating to those who are less sociable? These work-oriented people often live to be efficient. Why not harness that efficiency to help organize the event? If these people set up the party themselves, they'll feel like it's their responsibility to make sure things go well. And remember, these people enjoy responsibility, so in their own way, they'll enjoy the party.

Make most parties optional for people who get less out of these events. Some parties will be required, but let these folks bow out of those that aren't. Even when their attendance is required, make sure they understand that they don't have to put in more than a token appearance.

AVOIDING OFFICE PARTY PITFALLS

Of course, there are some potential challenges to partying at work. You have to be concerned about the use of alcohol in the workplace, as well as the potential for sexual harassment and other inappropriate behavior that could develop.

The Department of Labor's Working Partners for an Alcohol- and Drug-Free Workplace has put together nine tips for office celebrations. They're worth repeating here:

1. **Honesty is the best policy.** Make sure your employees know your workplace substance abuse policy and that the policy addresses the use of alcoholic beverages in any work-related situations and office social functions.

2. **Post the policy.** Use every communications vehicle to make sure your employees know the policy. Prior to an office party, use break-room bulletin boards, office e-mail, and paycheck envelopes to communicate your policy and concerns.

3. **Reinvent the office party concept.** Why have the typical office party? Try something new—an indoor carnival, a group outing to an amusement park, or a volunteer activity with a local charity.

4. **Make sure employees know when to say when.** If you do serve alcohol at an office event, make sure all employees know that they are welcome to attend and have a good time, but that they are expected to act responsibly.

5. **Make it the office party of choice.** Make sure there are plenty of alternative, nonalcoholic beverages available.

6. **Eat and be merry!** Avoid serving lots of salty, greasy, or sweet foods that tend to make people thirsty. Serve foods rich in starch and protein, which stay in the stomach longer and slow the absorption of alcohol in the bloodstream.

7. **Designate party managers.** Remind managers that even at the office party, they have responsibilities for implementing the company's alcohol and substance abuse policy.

8. **Alternative transportation.** Anticipate the need for alternative transportation for all partygoers, and make special transportation

arrangements in advance of the party. Encourage all employees to make use of the alternative transportation if they have any alcohol.

9. **None for the road.** Before the party officially ends, stop serving alcohol and remove all alcoholic beverages.

CAUTION

If you do make alcohol available at your office party, check out your state laws regarding their use and your legal responsibilities.

PARTIES THAT MOTIVATE

You've looked at your party plans and whittled down the number of events you'll have in any given year. You've considered people's attitudes toward parties and thought about how to involve people in organizing events. You've learned some do's and don'ts about alcohol and behavior at parties. Now it's time for the fun stuff. Let's get into some great ideas for partying!

TIP

If you're organizing a really big affair, consider using a consulting company that specializes in organizing themed office parties. Search for one on the Internet using keywords such as "office parties" and "corporate events."

TAKE YOUR PARTY ON THE ROAD

One obvious way to spice up your parties is to take them out of the office. Here are some company parties I've been witness to that were extra special:

- One company rented an entire amusement park for a day to celebrate its tenth anniversary.

- Another company rented a large picnic area in an African-themed wildlife park. Employees picnicked near a lake, received glasses and Frisbees with the company logo, and then were given passes to wander around and ride the elephants and pet the llamas.

- While I was working in northern California, one of my bosses took the whole gang to a nearby cheese factory for a lunch-time picnic (wine optional).

- A company I worked for in Boston rented a creepy Gothic-looking building on a university campus for a blow-out Halloween party with employees, vendors, and customers in attendance.

Avoid the hotel meeting room or corporate meeting facility if you can. Take people someplace where there's something to do, whether it's an arts performance or a cooking class. These employees are used to doing things together, so bring those team-oriented skills into play and get them doing, not just talking.

CAUTION

Although many options, such as zoos or museums, are fun, avoid forcing your employees to perform childish or embarrassing activities, such as flinging water balloons at each other. Unless your group is a pretty homogenous party crowd, these activities are likely to fall flat.

FOCUS ON THE UNUSUAL

Finding a unique place to hold a party is one approach. Another is to set a fun *theme*, which can work both in and out of the office. You remember this from your high school prom, when you and your classmates chose "Paris Night," "Roaring Twenties," or "Evening in the Tropics" as your theme.

Depending on your group and the occasion, you can set a small budget with simple decorations and food, or you can go all out: Give souvenirs and prizes, and play music and games that fit the theme. The important thing is to be sensitive to your people and know whether they'll get into the spirit of a more elaborate theme party. If they won't, keep it simple.

PLAIN ENGLISH

Theme   A subject or topic of discourse or artistic expression. (So get artistic with your party themes!)

Here are some thoughts that might stimulate a theme for your next office party:

- Relate the theme to work. If you're launching a new product or service, for example, see if you can use its name to spark a theme. A new product called Summit Faucets, for instance, could revolve around famous mountains (summits). Have an ice sculpture of Mt. Everest, Mt. St. Helens canapés, and Pike's Peak punch!

- A theme can involve a place (such as Paris, for the opening of your first European office, with an Eiffel Tower-shaped cake and can-can dancer finger puppets) or an event (such as the American Revolution for the introduction of a revolutionary new product line; use red, white, and blue liberally).

- Have people wear costumes if you think they will be comfortable with that. Give prizes not only for the most imaginative costume, but also for creative categories such as the cheapest costume and the most outrageous.

- Use your theme to direct conversation or play a game. If the theme is Mardi Gras, play a trivia game about celebrations around the world.

TIP

Don't limit your themes to places and events on earth. How about a *Star Trek* party, a sixth-dimension party, or a come-as-your-favorite-space-alien party?

TEN GREAT PARTY IDEAS

Here are my 10 most creative ideas for a party. Borrow any you like:

1. Invite employees to bring their pets into the office (located in an easy-to-clean-up area such as your warehouse, in case of animal accidents). Hold a pet parade, a best pet story contest, or a pet obstacle course competition.

2. For your Christmas party, rent out a local indoor skating rink for an evening, and have the event catered.

3. To celebrate hitting a long-awaited goal, such as record sales numbers, throw a bingo party. The first one to get the record profit number on the card wins a prize!

4. Throw a funky movie party. Let employees vote on their favorite quirky movie from a list you provide, and then show the movie in your largest conference room or rent out a local movie theater. Provide fresh popcorn, and encourage people to goof on the movie all they want.

5. Choose a campy TV show of today or yesteryear, and throw a theme party. A *Monty Python* party, for example, would have people holding Ministry of Funny Walk contests, dead parrot competitions, and Spanish Inquisition quiz games.

6. If everyone complains about the fattening food you usually serve, get away from the cookies and chips and throw a healthy party. Supply fresh fruit, raw veggies with low-fat dip, and diet drinks. Rent out an exercise facility as the site of the party. Let people come in sweats and use the treadmills and other equipment during the event. Make sure it's all in fun and that everybody—no matter what shape he or she is in—has something to do.

7. Have a musical party. Let people bring in musical instruments and jam, hold singing contests, and run a *Name That Tune*–like trivia game. Be sure to include a wide spectrum of musical styles so those not up on current pop music have expertise to contribute.

8. Throw a founder's year party. Figure out the year your company was founded, and have everybody come dressed in clothes of the time. This works best if your company is more than 50 years old, but even a 20-year-old company will send employees researching trends and hot news stories of the 1970s and 1980s.

9. Hold a party on the birthday for the person who invented the product you make. If you make light bulbs, throw a Thomas Edison birthday party. If you publish books, honor Guttenburg. If you're a pharmaceutical company, try Madame Curie or Jonas Salk.

10. For a smaller group, buy one of those murder mystery party kits and have everybody play a part. Or write your own mystery revolving around a little-known new employee who is found dead of overwork in the lunchroom. Your employees' assignment: Find the manager who assigned such a deadly workload!

TIP

If you have the choice between several low-budget small parties and one bigger one, why not go for the bigger one and go all out? The promise of the bigger event several months ahead can be just as motivating in its anticipation as parties occurring every month or so.

By putting a little more creativity and thought into office social events, you can turn them from dreaded obligations to motivational energizers!

The 30-Second Recap

- If you plan them properly, parties can be a fun and motivating experience.

- Remember that people socialize differently, and people respond differently to the essentially enforced socializing of an office party.

- Be sensitive to the people who don't enjoy social events as much as others, and find ways to make them more comfortable with office events.

- Be careful when involving alcohol in a company event, and know your company's liabilities in such a situation.

- Spice up parties by holding them out of the office at a unique location or setting them to a fun theme.

Give a Gift

In this lesson, you get some ideas for gift giving that will keep your team spirit on track.

Giving gifts is an age-old custom in many cultures. In some countries, such as Japan, it's practically a science. A gift can be used to express respect, affection, gratitude, or appreciation.

Over the years, giving business gifts to motivate employees has become an accepted practice. As long as you take care to keep the gifts professionally appropriate, your gift incentives are limited only by the boundaries of your own creativity.

GIFT GIVING AS MOTIVATION

Think for a moment about Ebenezer Scrooge in the Dickens classic, *A Christmas Carol.* Remember when the Ghost of Christmas Past reminds him of the holiday parties his old employer used to throw? Scrooge grudgingly admits that even though they cost his employer only a few pounds, the happiness those parties brought the staff was immeasurable.

That's kind of how gifts work as motivators on the job. They don't have to cost a lot, but they say to employees that their management thinks of them as more than just workers. They show that the company pays attention to the employees when they go the extra mile and demonstrates that loyalty and hard work are valued.

CAUTION

Giving presents is not designed to be a substitute for providing a well-rounded work environment. Cookies get stale very quickly when salaries are low, opportunity is scarce, and policies are stifling.

THE RIGHT TIME

The appropriate occasions for giving a gift can be many and varied. A gift tied to performance or meeting a certain goal is a great incentive. A gift for no reason at all, especially when morale or energy is running a little low, often works wonders as well. Here are a few other times when giving a gift is a natural motivator:

- On each employee's birthday or working anniversary, or for everyone at holiday time.

■ When a team achieves a goal or milestone on a project (and you can give just one gift for the whole group).

■ Any time a customer takes the time to tell you he received great service from a particular employee.

■ When someone goes outside his or her own job description to help a co-worker. This discourages the dreaded it's-not-my-job attitude.

■ As a reward for a tedious or menial task well done, such as when a particular employee has ordered and picked up everyone's dinner during late-night sessions, when ordering dinner isn't part of anyone's job description.

TIP

People don't often think of it, but having employees give a gift to a manager is also an occasion for fun. At one job, I rallied my employees to put together a collage of relevant paperwork and framed it as a gift when my manager finished negotiating a very tough deal to our department's benefit. It was fun for them and was very appreciated by our manager!

GUIDELINES FOR GIVING

Here are some general do's and don'ts for gift-giving at work:

■ **Use discretion.** Be very careful not to give gifts that are unrelated to specific work performance to one individual. Not only does that suggest favoritism to this employee, but it also can suggest a form of sexual harassment to the recipient or to your human resources department.

■ **Variety is key.** Vary the gifts you give so that they don't become old hat. If you sent cookies last month, spring for coffee mugs with the team name on them next month.

■ **Don't use gifts as bribes.** Gifts are gifts—they don't come with strings attached. A gift should simply be your way of expressing appreciation.

■ **Do give appropriate gifts.** Anything that's sexually suggestive or in poor taste doesn't belong in your office and could land you in hot water.

■ **Don't overdo.** After all, this isn't a social club; it's work. When all is said and done, remember that an employee is likely to appreciate 10 minutes of your undivided attention to help him solve a problem more than a red rose on his desk every month.

■ **Be creative.** Have fun with gifts: Nobody needs six coffee mugs with the company logo when, for the same money, they could get tickets for a popular concert or a roll of quarters for an afternoon at the local video arcade.

Shopping for Gifts

Congratulations—you live in an age when you can buy anything and everything over the Internet. This use of *e-commerce* can be a tremendous saver of both time and money in the business gift-giving department. You can usually get things shipped for free, and they generally arrive within a few days of placing your order.

PLAIN ENGLISH

E-commerce   The buying or selling of anything online through the use of the Internet.

If you're not an online shopper, haunt your local mall. Check out those kiosks in the center of the mall. Some offer personalized gifts such as desk pen sets or glasses with employee initials, although these are much pricier than buying through catalogs or online. Also keep an office supply catalog handy; many include business gift items such as fancy pens or tins of caramel popcorn, and the companies usually deliver.

You might want to set a budget at the beginning of each year for gifts to your employees, and then buy some items at a discount store to save money. That way you'll have some things on hand to give at the spur of the moment.

TIP

To find great gift ideas, try searching the World Wide Web with the keywords "business gifts," "corporate gifts," or "promotional products."

Online Shopping

Probably hundreds of thousands of online sites have products that your employees might enjoy.

TIP

Try to deal with more reputable sites, especially when buying large quantities of items. Make sure they have good customer support, a reasonable return policy, and security for exchanging credit card information online.

To get you started, here's a small selection of Web sites you might want to explore for interesting business gifts:

- **Diamond Promotions, www.logomall.com.** This site features various customized business gifts such as pads, mugs, shirts, and so on. Check out the Promotional Idea Showcase for gift ideas, or read a copy of *Imprint,* a quarterly publication on promotional gift-giving.
- **Just Gift Baskets, www.justgiftbaskets.com.** Here you can select from coffee, tea, cookies, dried fruits, and baskets with assorted goodies.
- **Virtual Florist, www.virtualflorist.com.** This site offers both flowers and free electronic cards. There's even an Office Chat card selection with messages such as "Take the Day Off" and "What a Great Idea."
- **Promotional Products, www.promotionalproductss.net.** This site offers a wide assortment of customized business gifts, such as calendars, mouse pads, and so on, on which you can silk-screen your logo or company name.
- **Corporate Gifts Network, www.corp-gifts.net.** This one is slightly more sophisticated, with gift baskets including items such as wine and caviar, as well as the more typical fruit and cookie packages.
- **Music Gift Spot, www.musicgiftspot.com.** Want some real fun? How about ordering an assortment of toy musical instruments, such as musical spoons and finger cymbals for your next staff meeting?

TIP

If you're going to have items customized, remember that it might take a little more time, and you'll probably have to provide artwork if you want your logo included. Also, verify who pays for shipping before you place your order.

Gifts: From Apples to Zebras

So what kinds of things make good office gifts? Here are several ideas to get you going:

- Any kind of food, including cookies, candy, pizza ordered in for a lunch-time or late-night meeting, fruit, and almost anything chocolate.

- Computer accessories, such as mouse pads, screen savers, and wrist rests.

- Desktop toys, such as stress balls or mini-Slinkys. These have the added benefit of helping your employees relax or even think a little more creatively in the middle of a mind-numbing day.

- Personalized notepads, each with an individual employee's name on top. These have the added benefit of being practical personalized notes employees can include with correspondence to customers or vendors.

- Unusual business card or pen holders for employees' desks. Rather than the standard plastic holders, how about small wicker baskets you can buy cheaply at discount stores?

- Cool Pez dispensers.

- Tickets to events, such as sports, movies, or concerts.

- A visit from a masseuse. Set up the masseuse in a central location, and have people sign up to get a 10-minute neck massage.

- A $5 donation in each employee's name to a charity of their choice.

- A popular CD, book, or video. Just make sure there's nothing offensive to anyone in the contents of these items.

- A visit from a magician. Invite the magician to come to the office for a day and wander around, entertaining the troops as they work.

TIP

Don't forget to team up with your marketing department: They often order company-specific promotional items in bulk and can tack on your order for savings. You can also let them do the work of ordering and providing logo artwork.

FREE COMPANY STUFF

When choosing gifts, don't forget about your own company's products or services. Obviously, if you make nuts and bolts, a gift box of company products is less fun than if you're a toy manufacturer handing out free toys. But think about it: You might just have something employees want.

You either can offer these products or services free of charge, or you can give employees a great discount to purchase them themselves. If your company thinks to order a certain number of extra products, you'll reduce the manufacturing costs and keep the price low for your employees.

For example, I've worked for book publishers who make all their titles available to employees. One publisher let employees order one of every title for free (we're talking about more than 300 books here), and then charged them 50 percent off the cover price for additional copies. Another charged only the cost of manufacturing the book (often only a couple dollars for a $20 book). Another company I worked for owned a huge chain of video rental stores. Employees could order videos at a substantial discount. When I worked for a major national magazine, a free copy of the magazine showed up on my desk every week.

If you work for a service company, you can offer your company services to employees for free or at a discount. For example, if one of your services is carpet cleaning, offer employees a once-a-year free carpet cleaning, or perhaps an upholstery cleaning at 25 percent of the regular price.

TIP

After establishing good business relationships with suppliers or customers, you might be able to buy products that might appeal to your workers and then offer them at a discount. For example, you might make plastic grommets for sneakers, but the company you sell them to might offer your employees sneakers at a discount.

THANKING THE FAMILY

Most employers forget the fact that most employees have a family—a family who supports the employee when he or she works long hours or is under particular stress. A wonderful and often quite unexpected gesture is to take the time to thank the family of that employee for their support. Try some of these ways to show your appreciation:

- Write a thank you note to the employee's significant other after a bout of frequent travel or a few late nights of work.
- Send a turkey or cheesecake home with each employee at holiday time (many companies used to do this, but the tradition seems to have fallen off over time).
- Throw an open house for families, complete with refreshments and even entertainment. Invite spouses and children to visit the office during a slow period so that they can see what their father/mother/wife/husband/significant other does all day.
- Invite families to holiday parties. One company I worked for even flew in employees from remote locations, along with their spouses, for the holiday party.

- Offer to fly a spouse along on a business trip to a particularly fun spot.

Remembering to thank the family is just another way to tell your employee that you see him or her as a person, and not just a job title.

The 30-Second Recap

- Give gifts to show employees appreciation or gratitude.
- Make sure gifts are appropriate for a business setting.
- The Internet provides a great way to shop for business gifts.
- Consider whether your company's products or services might make good gifts or can be offered to employees at a discount.
- Try sending thank you notes or gifts to an employee's family in appreciation for supporting the employee and all he or she does for the company.

Getting Out of the Office

In this lesson, you learn about the benefits of getting people out of the traditional office setting.

Think about it: When you have only a week or two per year for vacation, do you sit around the same house you've been sitting around all year, or do you go somewhere else? When people want to renew or refresh themselves, many head for a change of scenery. Workers are no different—even the most attractive and pleasant workplace gets tiresome after a while. At some point, employees begin to measure the dynamics of the workplace by the number of feet they walk from their cubicle to the coffee pot, a number that never varies.

In this chapter, we'll explore some of the benefits of giving your employees a chance to work out of the office and get a new perspective on their careers.

Telecommuting: When Work Comes Home

Some call it *telecommuting,* others telework or flex work. Whatever you call it, it involves a decentralizing of your work force, allowing some of them to work part-time or even full-time from their homes.

PLAIN ENGLISH

Telecommuting (also called telework or flex work)   The practice of allowing workers to work from their homes, taking advantage of various technologies to connect them to other workers and information.

According to a recent survey, more than 12 million people telecommute today, making it clear that this way of doing business is here to stay. Advances in technology and telecommunications, especially in the area of computers and the Internet, have made this lifestyle possible.

Ironically, this practice is really nothing new. In the not-so-distant Industrial Age of the late nineteenth century, workers were pulled out of their cottage-based industries into factories. That means that only a hundred years or so divides us from a time when people didn't get up, knock back a cup of coffee, and run out the door to the office. Instead, they stayed at home and made products that they sold to a company or sold directly to their community. So telecommuting may be a lifestyle whose time has come—again!

THE BENEFITS OF TELECOMMUTING

Many debates have gone on about the pros and cons of telecommuting. But with technology providing more ease of communication and better access to centralized information, it's getting harder to argue against it.

The first thing most people consider to be a benefit of telecommuting is an increase in productivity, often cited in the 15 to 20 percent range. That productivity increase is thought to come from the less stressful environment found in one's own home, the lack of disturbances or downtime from casual chats in the hallway, and the removal of as many as a couple hours of high-stress commuting from the workday.

TIP

If you want to sell the concept of telecommuting in your workplace but think that you'll be left with an empty office when everybody stampedes home to work, don't worry. Many people can't stand the isolation; others lack the discipline to work from home.

Other benefits are financial in nature. True, most companies that allow telecommuting contribute to the cost of equipment, supplies, and phone bills of those working from home offices, and they also have to reimburse the high initial costs of setting up a telecommuting site. However, companies usually find that they save money in the long run. If people are working at home full-time, companies can downsize office space, and even the cost of setting up videoconferencing may be quickly offset by cutting down on the number of phone lines, parking spaces, and break room spaces needed for your in-office work force.

HOW TELECOMMUTING WORKS

A few variations on telecommuting exist. First, there's either a full-time or part-time telecommuting situation. In a full-time telecommuting scenario, the employee makes a weekly or monthly office visit. In the part-time telecommuting scenario, a worker works at home two or three days a week and is in the office the other days.

CAUTION

At first look, part-time arrangements might seem better to you because you'll still get significant face-to-face time with your employee. But beware: Part-time telecommuting means financial support of two offices instead of one and an office that sits empty and unproductive for a few days every week.

If an employee is a full-time telecommuter, that person actually might live in another state or even another country. In that case, companies must factor in costs of bringing telecommuters to the office every month or so.

Another consideration is deciding what expenses of the home office the company will cover and what the employee will pay for. Some employees, eager to move into the telecommuting lifestyle, will deal with setting up an area of their home, purchasing ergonomic office furniture, and even paying to install a second phone line. But ongoing costs, such as a computer, phone calls, monthly cost of the second phone line, an Internet account, software, and supplies, typically become the burden of the employer. In some situations, employers also are expected to pay a portion of an employee's home utility bill. Whatever the arrangement, make sure that you and the employee are clear about it from the start.

TIP

It might prove easier on your company to arrange for direct billing of some items, such as a second phone line and overnight shipping.

SETTING UP SHOP: THE TELECOMMUTING OFFICE

The existence of various technologies contributes greatly to the success of telecommuting. But each comes with an associated cost—and, in some cases, the time of your Information Services (IS) staff to support it. Be sure that your employee really understands all the things involved in setting up a home office before you both take the plunge.

Some items to consider in setting up a telecommuting situation include these:

- A docking laptop computer so that part-time telecommuters can take their office computer back and forth between office and home easily, negating the need for two computers
- A connection to your company network for access to information and an office e-mail account
- IS support for hardware and software used at home
- A fax machine
- An answering machine or voice mail
- A copier
- A second, faster phone line for Internet access
- Videoconferencing capability
- A two-line phone with hold, mute, and conference capabilities
- Access to an overnight shipping account and materials (consider providing software for generating shipping labels and tracking shipments)
- Supplies of company stationery and envelopes
- Office supplies
- New business cards with home office contact information

TIP

Make sure that your support staff faxes or e-mails documents to telecommuters well in advance of meetings in which they'll be participating by phone.

THE DOWNSIDE OF TELECOMMUTING

But it's not all roses on the road to telecommuting. Although this is a great solution for many employers and employees, and although it can offer clear-cut benefits in terms of productivity and morale, it also has its challenges.

First, your company will face the aforementioned start-up and ongoing costs. This includes the need for IS support for a remote location, which can be complicated and costly.

Be alert to the challenges the employee will face as well. Working at home involves a certain kind of loneliness because socializing and face-to-face interaction is limited or nonexistent. Many people find it difficult to motivate themselves and organize their time with a less rigid schedule and no one looking over their shoulders.

TIP

Take the time to call your telecommuting employee once in a while just to see how he's doing. Make it a policy when you're on the phone with him not to pick up other phone calls or talk with people in the office. This employee deserves a closed-door meeting with you from time to time, even though it's on the phone.

As a manager or supervisor, you'll have your own challenges in overseeing such an employee. You must have great trust in that person and the amount of effort he or she expends every day. You also are less privy to performance issues because you can't observe telecommuters in action. This can make performance reviews much more challenging because you might not be able to cite examples of behavior that you have observed.

Finally, you might face a concern that out of sight means out of mind. The telecommuter runs the risk of sidetracking his or her career. Without being physically present for meetings and other in-office encounters, telecommuters can have a less dynamic presence in the organization. They also run the risk of being left out of certain communications, such as the spontaneous hallway encounter or the lunch with fellow team members at which something important is decided, but nobody remembers to contact the telecommuter.

HOLD THAT MEETING OFF-SITE

Another option for motivating workers without taking the telecommuting route is to get them out of the office now and then for a meeting or other activity. If you remember how you felt when you took a field trip in school, you know the power of getting away from your usual stomping grounds.

TIP

Does an off-site meeting have to cost an arm and a leg? Not at all. If you hold it over lunch, many restaurants will provide a private dining room free of charge. If the weather's nice, you can simply go to a park.

What occasions work for an off-site meeting? Problem-solving and brainstorming sessions are naturals because new surroundings help you break out of your usual thinking. A quarterly company meeting or any gathering of a larger group of employees is often an occasion to go off-site because most companies don't have a conference room that can accommodate more than 25 to 50 people.

Whatever the occasion, once you've decided to get away, the next thing is to decide where.

THE RIGHT PLACE

Typical off-site meeting sites are hotel ballrooms, hotel meeting rooms, and conference centers. Those options are fine, and they usually provide the amenities of coffee break service and a business office to help with photocopying and taking phone messages. But if you have the luxury of doing something a little different, try one of these suggestions:

- **Go back to nature.** Head for a nature retreat or the administration building of a large park. These sites often have good-sized meeting rooms for community events. Even better, the beautiful surroundings can be stimulating and make for interesting walks during breaks.

- **Be dramatic.** Rent a local theater or symphony hall. Some of these ornate older buildings are quite lovely, and the acoustics are great. You can even attend a matinee in the middle of your meeting to support the arts and give your folks a breather!

- **Think art.** Many museums have member rooms or community event rooms available for rent. Once again, the ability to go schmooze with Picasso on a break can be very stimulating to good business ideas!

- **Think smart.** Rent some space from a local college, and ask a charismatic professor of business or marketing to give a little kick-off speech for your meeting. A college campus setting often provides more attractive surroundings than the typical business campus.

- **Get creative!** If you live in California, have a large picnic at a winery. If you are located near the beach, grab your towel and go! Got a racetrack nearby? Set aside a section of the restaurant and conduct your business between horse races (but set a limit of $2 per person to bet, please!). Talk to your local zoo keeper to see if there's a space in the dolphin house for rent.

CAUTION

When choosing an off-site meeting place, be considerate to your employees. Make sure there is ample parking, that employees know they will be reimbursed for any travel costs, and that the location is convenient for handicapped access.

Change More Than Location

One of the greatest benefits of getting out of the office for a meeting is that it breaks up the everyday routine. With that in mind, also realize that you'll get the most benefit from this experience if you also try to provide more than a change of scene.

Being out of the office provides a great opportunity for office workers to get to know each other in a different way and to break away from the confines of business as usual. Consider these techniques:

- Leave the hierarchy in the office. (If you're the manager, for instance, be sure you're the one to bring the bagels or make the coffee rather than leave it to an assistant.)

- Provide time to socialize so that people can chat about themselves outside of their job descriptions.

- Instead of running the meeting yourself, why not ask a bright young employee or group of employees to run part of it? Although you set the agenda, they can moderate, which will make them feel that they have a little bit of authority over the group.

- Even if your main purpose isn't brainstorming, start the day off with a free-form brainstorming session about anything, from the theme for the sales meeting to a new product name. This is a great way to get people involved and contributing equally.

- If you accomplish what you want to do early, give your employees the rest of the day off.

TIP

You can even take small meetings off-site. Try giving performance reviews out of the office; it can ease tension and make the process more relaxed and informal.

Trips as Perks

For anyone who has to travel a lot for work, this is no perk at all. But for employees who never get out of the office, an occasional trip can seem like winning the lottery.

Of course, if you can find a business reason for the trip, such as a trade show, a training class, or a visit to the plant to see how your products are made, so much the better. But sometimes a trip is useful just to improve relationships. For example, send the contracts clerk to the New York office to meet the reps she deals with every day on the phone. This will improve their relationships and communications from that day on. Or let your customer service rep visit a customer site. That also can improve customer relations and even help your staff identify other ways you can serve your customers better.

You can even use trips to scope out the competition. Are you in the hotel business? Send the VP's secretary to a competing hotel in the next city for a night, and have her report on what the competition did right and what they did wrong.

TIP

To make these trips most productive, ask employees to write a one-page trip report. That will let you see how they've benefited from the trip and make it easier to share any insights they have with co-workers.

THE 30-SECOND RECAP

- Getting people out of the office breaks routine and often stimulates creativity.

- Telecommuting can increase productivity and enhance morale, but it has costs and isn't for everybody.

- Holding meetings outside the office is a great way to motivate people; choose a creative location, and avoid dragging routine and hierarchy along.

- Sending employees who don't have to travel a great deal in their regular work on a trip can provide a motivating perk as well as business benefits.

Just Go Home!

In this lesson, you learn how to use flex time and other forms of nontraditional working hours to motivate employees.

If you're like 99.9 percent of the working world, your life has become more complex in recent years. You work long hours; you even work on your laptop computer while traveling on a plane or sitting in a hotel room. You're available by pager, cell phone, and Internet 24 hours a day. Oh, and by the way, you might also have a family, friends, and personal interests to juggle. That's not even mentioning those really fun chores like getting your driver's license renewed or your cable TV hooked up in your new apartment.

As William Hazlitt once said, "As we advance in life, we acquire a keener sense of the value of time. Nothing else, indeed, seems of any consequence." Well, take a look at your employees. If you could give them one gift that each and every one would treasure, what would it be? If you guessed time, go to the head of the class.

FLEX TIME: A HOT TREND

Now, we all know that it's impossible to give someone more than 24 hours in a day, and seven days in a week. You can't just go around giving people time off from work arbitrarily—nothing would get done. But you might be able to bend the structure of a typical workday just a bit, and that bending could help your employees a lot.

A growing trend in recent years, actually brought on by the desire to beat heavy traffic, is called *flex time*. Flex time started when companies wanted to avoid overloaded elevators and long commutes for employees, so they started adjusting start and end times into mini-shifts. Since then, flex time has become even more flexible: Today a flex-time employee's start and finish times are pretty much up to the individual, within some general parameters.

PLAIN ENGLISH

Flex time   A work scheduling system that typically mandates some core hours all employees must work and also requires that the same total number of hours be worked by each employee. However, flex time allows employees to choose their own start and stop times.

THE BENEFITS OF FLEX TIME

So how does flex time help, and therefore motivate, employees? It helps in several ways:

- Flex time helps employees avoid peak rush-hour traffic, making for a shorter commute.

- Flex time allows workers to work when their body clock dictates (those who aren't morning people don't have to drag themselves in at 8 A.M., and those who start to fade by 3 P.M. can come in early and leave early).

- Flex time enables employees to deal with personal demands that don't occur outside the traditional workday, such as day care center schedules, an afternoon class, or personal errands.

- Flex time empowers employees to take charge of their own time and productivity.

■ Flex time lowers stress due to worry over personal affairs that aren't being attended to.

CAUTION

In using flex time, be sure to have adequate coverage during non-core hours, especially in positions that involve customer interaction.

Particularly at a time when many households with children have both adults working full-time, this flexibility can be a great boon to balancing job and family.

CURRENT TRENDS IN FLEX TIME

In 1995 Virginia Slims conducted the American Women's Poll and asked questions about flex time and other factors in working women's lives. A couple of telling statistics came out of this poll.

People were asked what things would help working women balance job, marriage, and children better. Out of eight possible factors, both men and women polled chose men's involvement in chores as the most helpful; both men and women chose more flexible work hours as the second most helpful factor.

When asked if they were taking advantage of flexible working hours at work, 34 percent said they were (a much higher percentage than those taking advantage of job sharing, at 7 percent; part-time work, at 26 percent; working from home, at 8 percent; or maternity leave, at 3 percent).

A whopping 87 percent of women polled said some changes or major changes were needed in terms of workday flexibility in the next 10 years. A still impressive 77 percent of men said change was needed.

It's clear from these results that a lot of workers, both male and female, feel the need for some flexibility from their employers when it comes to scheduling their day.

FLEX TIME: TAKE THE SURVEY

Now it's time to take your own survey among your employees to see if flex time is wanted, and if so, what form it might take. Make it anonymous so employees don't feel uncomfortable giving honest answers.

Flex Time Survey

1. What is your most productive time of day?

    a. Morning

    b. Afternoon

    c. Any time I work outside of regular working hours

2. Do you ever find yourself being less productive at your job because you're worried about personal issues outside of work?

   a. Rarely

   b. Sometimes

   c. Frequently

3. How much time do you spend every day commuting to and from work?

   a. Under half an hour

   b. Half an hour to one hour

   c. Over an hour

4. Do you ever take work home?

   a. Never

   b. Sometimes

   c. Frequently

5. If you could work at home one day a week, how would it impact your job?

   a. I'd be more productive

   b. I'd be less productive

   c. I'd get the same amount of work done

6. If your employer would let you work four 10-hour days instead of five 8-hour days a week, would you want to do that?

   a. Yes

   b. No

   c. Not sure

7. Do you find the balance between your personal and work life …

   a. Healthy

   b. Slanted too much toward work

   c. Slanted too much toward your personal life

8. Do you ever eat lunch at your desk in a typical week?

   a. Yes, about once a week

   b. Yes, two or more times a week

   c. Never

Take a look at trends as you get a few different people to take this survey. One thing I'm sure you'll find is that most answers reveal a desire for a different approach to scheduling working time. The odds are you'll find trends in when people feel most productive (and it's unlikely to be between 9 and 5 exclusively), the inability to provide a balance between work and home life, and openness to nontraditional working schedules.

FLEX TIME AT WORK

Flex time can take several forms. Sometimes it involves variable start and stop times; in other forms, it involves working fewer days with more hours each day. Some companies even allow workers to work longer hours and take extra vacation time to compensate.

TIP

What are the politics of flex time? Labor unions are typically against it. Apparently, unions fear that employers might force workers to put in more hours per day without paying overtime. If you run a union shop, check with the union before exploring flex time.

Offering flex-time options helps employers recruit and retain workers. And by providing a mechanism for a healthier balance between personal and work demands, flex time can help reduce employee stress and make people more productive.

HOT FUN IN THE SUMMERTIME

Several companies offer variations on flex time to address seasonal variations in work demand. Some employers adjust hours in summer, for example, to let workers leave in the early afternoon on Fridays. This allows workers to take full advantage of nice weather and spend time with children during their school holidays.

TIP

Many employers find that throughout a seasonal flex schedule, almost every employee will work through a Friday afternoon now and then because of an important deadline. These workers often report how productive those afternoons are, with no co-workers around to disturb them!

One side benefit of granting shorter workdays in slow business times is that employees are more content to spend longer hours when the business demands it. They know there's a tangible reward at the end of the tunnel.

JOB SHARING

Another flexibility option is *job sharing*. The idea here is that two people share the responsibilities of a single job. Sometimes the two people are husband and wife employees who split childcare and work duties, but not always. Job sharing is often a short-term solution to outside challenges, such as a long-term illness in the family or an employee working on a second college degree.

PLAIN ENGLISH

Job sharing A team approach to work. Job sharing allows two people to split the responsibilities of a single job so that by each working part-time, they complete a full-time job.

Job sharers split not only the job responsibilities, but also the salary and benefits. Because many part-time jobs don't afford benefits, job sharing allows people to work less time at some point in their careers without giving up their position on the career ladder or giving up benefits they might not be able to do without.

TIP

Thinking of allowing job sharing? Don't forget one great benefit to employers: You almost always have someone to cover that job when one half of the team goes on vacation or calls in sick.

Benefits of job sharing to employees and employers include the following:

- Little absenteeism occurs because of family demands because those can be dealt with on off-time.
- Two individuals can develop on-the-job skills and expertise instead of one.
- Job sharers often help each other work through difficult challenges or problems.
- An employer gets two skill sets to call on instead of one.

CAUTION

The last thing you need is a situation where one worker begins placing blame for mistakes or work that doesn't get done on the other. Make sure job sharers understand that they share responsibility for the job being done right. If it isn't, they must solve any inequity between them if the job sharing is to continue.

Of course, you should set a few ground rules when establishing a job-sharing scenario. First, make sure that you have a written job description so that both individuals understand their responsibilities. Also, agree on the split of salary and benefits from the start. Finally, set a time frame for the trial arrangement that can be extended in the future if things are working well. In the event that one employee wants to switch to a full-time job, it's probably wise to designate which of the two people has first claim to the full-time position they are planning to share.

TIP

If the two people sharing a job have unique talents, it's okay to split up the work accordingly. For example, one person might do the phone calling while the other types out the invoices. However, make sure that each is willing to cover the other person's work in the event of an absence.

TAKING LEAVE

Netscape, a leader in the Internet browser market, has a policy that allows many employees to take a four-week *sabbatical* every four years. Should you follow suit?

PLAIN ENGLISH

Sabbatical   A leave without pay for research, travel, or rest. Traditionally, sabbaticals are granted every seventh year to professors at universities and colleges.

Allowing extended time off every few years has clear benefits, including helping to limit the burnout that may result from doing the same work week after week, year after year. Sabbaticals also allow good workers to refresh their skills by reading, taking a workshop, or just relaxing so that they can generate fresh ideas for their work.

Some companies encourage employees to use an extended leave to expand their job knowledge. In that case, this may be a paid leave. For example, let's say you're a magazine publisher and have a manager who purchases printing services. Why not let her spend three or four weeks apprenticing at a printing company to get to know more about the printing business? This makes for an interesting change of pace and broadens the employee's understanding of a key area for your industry.

TIP

Have an employee who loves to travel? Why not let that person spend a month at your branch office in San Francisco—or better yet, overseas? The employee gets to watch and learn from others doing the same job and also enjoys a change of scenery.

THE 30-SECOND RECAP

- Allowing employees flexibility in their working schedules lowers their stress, decreases absenteeism, and gives them a feeling of empowerment.
- Flex time allows people to avoid longer commutes and to work when their energy level is at its peak.
- Seasonal variations in the work schedule during slower business times rewards employees and motivates them to accept longer work hours during busier times.
- Job sharing is a great way of allowing employees to deal with demands on their time outside of work without losing either benefits or their place on the career ladder.
- Allowing employees to go on leave every few years helps them refresh their spirits and get a new perspective on work.

Recognizing Achievement

In this lesson, you learn how giving positive feedback and rewarding perform-ance can be great motivators.

It's human nature to pay more attention to the people around you when there are stresses and problems. We reassure each other in times of strife, but when times are good, we sometimes forget to give these same reassurances.

Unfortunately, it's also human nature to thrive on compliments and kudos on a pretty consistent basis. This chapter takes a look at providing positive strokes when things go right—so that successful employees stay motivated—and also giving input so that those who are struggling a bit get motivated to keep at it.

THE IMPORTANCE OF RECOGNITION

Psychologist Eric Berne developed a set of theories of *transactional analysis* that are relevant to this topic. Simply put, Berne looked at all interpersonal interaction as a transaction. A complete transaction involves a stimulus and a response that involves feedback.

PLAIN ENGLISH

Transactional analysis   A theory that states that all interpersonal interactions are basically transactions, each having a stimulus and response.

When employees exert extra effort, this should be a stimulus for you to respond to that work with some form of feedback. If you don't, you're leaving your employees to direct their energies into a void. That lack of feedback can frustrate even the most self-assured individual.

TIP

To be sure you're providing regular feedback, make it a habit to start or end your weekly or monthly evaluation meeting with a positive comment on something that person has done recently.

GIVING FEEDBACK

In my *Merriam-Webster Dictionary,* the first definition of *feedback* is "the return to the input of a part of the output of a machine." Feedback in this sense is the squeal you hear when you get a microphone too close to a speaker. But if you follow the model of transactional analysis, this mechanical definition isn't all that out of line. In an interpersonal transaction, your employee gives you input in the form of effort. You provide feedback by returning output based on that input—that is, a response appropriate to that effort.

PLAIN ENGLISH

Feedback   Defined by *Merriam-Webster* as 1) return to the input of a part of the output of a machine or system; 2) response about an activity or policy.

Now, all feedback isn't positive. But at the least, when it can't be positive, it should be constructive. Pure negative feedback without offering suggestions for improvement or solutions to problems is not only cruel, but it doesn't move you or your employee any closer to a solution.

SINGING PRAISES

Let's start with the positive side of feedback. Although you would think that saying nice things is a pretty easy thing to do, several factors or attitudes sometimes keep a manager from giving praise. Here are a few:

- Feeling that people shouldn't need to be coddled.
- Having the attitude that because employees are already getting paid to do a job, and that should be reward enough.
- Figuring that since your manager doesn't compliment you, why should you compliment your employees?
- Believing that good work should be its own reward.
- Finding it difficult to think of anything nice to say to your less-productive workers without sounding insincere.

I'll address all these objections with one argument: Whether or not you personally feel that compliments are necessary, the fact is that most people thrive on them. If everybody did what he or she was hired and paid for, and that level of performance was good enough, your company wouldn't need managers around to motivate the staff. Your job is to get employees not only to do their jobs, but also to enjoy their work and even excel at it. Given that mission, praise is a big part of your job as an effective manager. And believe it or not, even the poorly performing employee has to be doing something right; if he's not, he should be in another job.

 CAUTION

Providing positive feedback isn't a license to be insincere. People can sense hollow praise. You simply need to develop new radar to be on the lookout for good performance on a regular basis so that your praise can be meaningful.

Of course, the most often-quoted reason for not giving positive feedback on a regular basis is that you're just too darn busy to remember to do it. But consider this: Taking the time to give a little positive feedback each day might save you from taking lots of time to deal with a disgruntled employee—or training a new one—down the road.

PRACTICING POSITIVE FEEDBACK

Not every piece of positive feedback has to be a glowing "Gosh, you're doing a fantastic job!" In fact, feedback can be pretty low-key in both tone and message. To be able to provide compliments on a regular basis, you have to move from the generalized "great job" comment to some more specific comments.

Here are some statements that might help you find reasons to compliment members of your staff:

- Thanks for getting that report in so promptly.
- I can see you're improving in that area; keep up the good work.
- That was an interesting point you brought up in the meeting.
- I got your e-mail and appreciate your getting the information to me.
- You seem to know a lot about this area; I'd like to hear some more of your ideas sometime.
- You handled that situation nicely.
- Your contribution is really making a difference on this project.
- I've noticed that you've been putting in a lot of overtime during the crunch, and it's appreciated.

The point is that just letting someone know you've observed his or her efforts is often compliment enough.

THE ART OF GIVING PERFORMANCE REVIEWS

Now that you're giving positive feedback on a regular basis, let's take a look at the periodic appraisal of performance—called a *performance review*—that has become a staple of business management. Typically given once or twice a year, the performance review incorporates both positive feedback and constructive criticism.

PLAIN ENGLISH

Performance review   Part of a performance appraisal, or the process of identifying, observing, measuring, and developing human performance in organizations. Performance appraisal was introduced in a study by Carroll and Schneir in the 1980s.

Oddly enough, even good performance reviews can be difficult to deliver. There are a few reasons for this. First, you and your employee aren't used to sitting face to face and talking about him for an hour (although if you're providing good feedback year-round, you may help establish a comfort level for this). Reviews often get into emotional territory, including discussing the relative happiness and satisfaction of the employee, which is outside your typical working relationship. Finally, people tend to obsess about the negative; if 99 percent of the review is good, the employee will home in on that 1 percent problem area.

But there are some things you can do to make these sessions productive, professional, and positive. Let's get started.

KEEPING TABS

These days, most human resources departments require managers to document employee performance to justify any action that needs to be taken for poor performance. But beyond this basic requirement, keeping notes on an employee throughout the year will help you prepare for an accurate review with specific examples of both good and not-so-good performance.

Get into the habit of making a note when an employee either experiences a problem or does an exceptionally good job. It takes a few moments a week per employee, but if you think about the last time you struggled for two hours over an employee review at year end, you'll see that this will save you time overall.

TIP
Keeping notes will give you fuel for regular, positive feedback. Also, if you keep these notes in a computer file, you can quickly reorganize them and cut and paste them into a written review at the end of the year.

MANAGING BY OBJECTIVES

A good tool both for helping employees to improve their performance and for helping you to organize your performance review is *management by objectives,* often abbreviated to MBO.

PLAIN ENGLISH
Management by objectives   Introduced by Peter Drucker in the 1950s, this is a behavior-based system of joint goal setting by supervisors and employees.

MBO is the brainchild of management analyst Peter Drucker, who introduced the concept in the 1950s. Its popularity spread through the books *The One Minute Manager* and *In Search of Excellence.* The core concept of MBO is that a manager and an employee will jointly set goals for the employee. This process enables the manager to assign work to employees in a way that challenges individuals to grow. MBO lets employees understand what's expected of them and allows them to negotiate achievable goals so that they can succeed.

CAUTION

Don't let an employee get away with only easy-to-accomplish goals. Some challenge is good, even for the most complacent employee. On the other hand, don't push this type of employee with too ambitious a challenge—you'll only lay the foundation for failure.

Setting these goals at each year's performance review gives you a framework for tracking and reviewing the employee's activity over the next six months to a year.

Here are some characteristics of MBO to consider:

- MBO is behavior-based, not personality-based. Thus, an employee knows that there is a measurable way to succeed that isn't grounded in vague standards such as attitude or interpersonal skills.

- Because the company needs to get work done, some of the agreed-upon objectives might not be an employee's dream tasks or great career advancers. But be sure to balance the mundane with the challenging, and make sure that the employee buys into the need for this balance.

- Make the goals large enough that you're not outlining all the detailed specifics of getting the job done; keep them narrow enough that they are clear and measurable.

- If a goal has many variables outside the employee's control, it's important to add that to the description of the goal. For example, let's say that you want an employee to negotiate a new union contract. The goal might be to facilitate the process of negotiating a contract as efficiently as possible, rather than getting a contract signed by a certain day and date, which could be out of the employee's control.

- If you agree to a goal, be sure to provide anything the employee needs to succeed. If she needs funding, resources, or time, discuss these at the performance review before you each agree to the goal.

MBO supports employee self-esteem by involving employees in their own management and presenting them with interesting challenges that will help them further their careers if they succeed. Setting the general goal and trusting the employee to work out its successful implementation is a highly motivating scenario.

TIP

Be sure that when you agree on a goal with an employee, you also agree on how to measure its success. Specifying quantities, time frames, and quality of work will help you assess success at the yearly review.

BE CONSTRUCTIVE WITH CRITICISM

Of course, there are times either during the year or at the annual review when feedback is needed, but it isn't of the positive kind. You may be surprised to know that many employees get as much of a boost from constructive criticism as they do from praise. That's because constructive criticism, when correctly delivered, tells the employee that you're paying attention. This kind of feedback says you believe enough in the employee to spend your time helping him or her become better at the job.

The key word here is *constructive*. To be constructive, feedback first must point to a problem and then must either suggest a solution or involve the employee in a dialogue about the problem's solution. Here are the ground rules for constructive criticism:

- Reassure the employee at the outset that, in general, you're pleased with his or her job performance, but you want to focus on one area for improvement.
- State that your job is to help the employee succeed.
- Suggest specific things the employee can do to improve.
- Focus on improving the situation, not on excuses for why it exists.
- Don't make light of the situation, but don't spend more time on it than it merits. A lengthy discussion about a small problem can leave the wrong impression entirely.
- Listen.

Did you notice that last one? I hope so. Listening to the employee's input on why the problem exists is vital to providing useful feedback. We're not talking about excuses here, but about hard information on why this area is difficult for the employee and what you can do to help.

REWARDING EXCELLENCE

When an employee does great things, you should make a point of doing something more than commenting on it or including it in a review. Sometimes, based on the employee's capabilities, seniority, and company structure, reward takes the form of a promotion. But when a promotion isn't possible or appropriate, you can use other forms of recognition to reward excellence.

PROMOTIONS MOTIVATE

One of the most rewarding things for me as a manager was wholeheartedly endorsing an employee for a promotion and then getting approval for that promotion from senior management. Promotions are a tangible way to reward good performance in terms of salary, title, and responsibility.

But to be strong motivators, promotions must be given judiciously. If they come too quickly from you, they can cause future frustration when the next manager promotes more slowly. If a promotion comes before an employee is ready to take on greater responsibility, you can be setting him up for failure. If a promotion is delayed too long, you may be organizing that employee's going-away party as she sails away to a more rewarding workplace.

Use these guidelines in handing out promotions:

- Don't promote one person too frequently. Too many easy promotions begin to lose their meaning.

- Make sure a promotion fits in with organizational goals for this individual and provides the type of training and challenge that will continue to make this person valuable to the organization.

- Make sure you understand your employee's long-term career goals, and that the promotion fits those goals.

- Be sure that the employee is ready for the promotion and that he understands the responsibilities and expectations that go along with it.

- Don't discount a lateral move if that might be useful in broadening the employee's skill set to help her reach her eventual goals.

- Do announce a promotion right away, and specify the reasons for it. This ensures that others have a clear understanding of the new responsibilities of this person, as well as a model for what kinds of behavior can get them a promotion in the organization.

AWARDS AND GOLD STARS

Of course, it's not always possible, or appropriate, to give a promotion for great job performance. In those cases, you should begin to stockpile some other ways of recognizing people.

Here's a list of just some of the types of things you might do:

■ Authorize the employee and significant other to go out to a nice restaurant and expense the cost.

■ Implement an Employee of the Month program, and provide a set of perks to go along with it. These might be a designated parking space near the office entrance, a feature article in the employee newsletter, or an extra day off.

■ Buy a stash of gift certificates or small presents, and leave one on an employee's desk with a thank you note for a job well done.

■ Send flowers.

■ Take the employee out to a nice dinner.

■ Post the employee's picture on the company Web site. This boosts the employee's morale and shows customers that your company values having good employees to serve them.

■ Give two tickets to a sports or artistic event (many companies have seats for sporting seasons for clients that might be available to employees now and then).

Whatever reward you give, it's important that everyone understands that there was a specific accomplishment for which it was given. That stops people from accusing you of favoritism if one person gets a few rewards. Also, being clear about what sparked the reward tells other employees what will win them the same prize and thus motivates them to emulate that behavior.

TIP

Give rewards on a bell curve. That is, if one employee isn't exactly the star player, but she does do something above average relative to her abilities, give her a reward. Constantly rewarding the best people can be demotivating, so spread the rewards around and strike a balance.

THE 30-SECOND RECAP

■ Recognition is an important motivator and should happen on a consistent basis.

■ Transactional analysis theory suggests that every interaction is a transaction, and your response to good performance should be positive feedback.

- Feedback should be sincere and frequent.

- Performance reviews provide an opportunity for both positive feedback and constructive criticism.

- When an employee does something exceptional, you can reward him with a promotion or some other appropriate sign of recognition.

Involving People in Innovation

In this lesson, you learn how to get people involved in creative problem solving and how to recognize their contributions.

Allowing people to contribute to innovation in the workplace is a two-way street. Employees feel empowered and appreciated when their ideas are solicited and, even better, implemented. Employers get solutions and products that keep them on the leading edge in the marketplace.

THE FOUNDATION FOR ORGANIZATIONAL INNOVATION

Innovation itself isn't clearly defined. When you get a great idea and nobody acts on it, was it an innovation? Not really. Innovation involves both the development and the implementation of an idea. If you implement an idea and it flops, people don't often refer to it as an innovation, although by strict definition, it probably was. Innovation generally relates to new ideas that are implemented successfully.

Innovations can be small ideas for doing a job better, or they can generate new products that are a perfect fit for the marketplace. But it's generally acknowledged that some of the most successful companies support innovation at every level of their operations.

Social scientists have studied *organizational innovation* carefully over the years. Although nobody has discovered the magic pill that makes innovation happen, there are some good ideas about what kind of work environment fosters innovation.

PLAIN ENGLISH

Organizational innovation   Planned efforts by groups of people to develop and implement new ideas.

The first (and most obvious) point is that innovation occurs in contexts that motivate innovation. That motivation can come in the form of financial

incentives for great ideas or acknowledgement of one's part in the generation
or implementation of those ideas.

TIP

Interestingly, studies have shown that incentive pay is a weaker
motivator than simple recognition for one's contribution.

One organizational theory is that organizational segmentation and bureaucratic procedures constrain innovation. In simpler terms, the more you're
divided from other areas of the company, and the more layers of process separate workers from implementing their actions, the less innovative the organization is.

The following is a list of various conditions that studies have shown to foster
innovative behavior:

- Appropriate resources
- Communications across workgroup lines and among workers with
  different viewpoints
- Some level of uncertainty and the ability to focus attention on
  change
- Workgroups that are cohesive and resolve conflicts in a way that
  integrates creative people into the mainstream group
- Access to role models and mentors who are good at innovation
- Low turnover

Now, you may not be able to change your entire workplace to mirror this list,
but you can at least look for ways to implement these ideas in your own
group.

SOLICITING IDEAS

Most people have the ability and the potential to be creative and innovative.
They need only the structure that encourages it.

On an individual level, look for or create settings to solicit ideas from each of
your employees. Let people know that ideas are listened to and that, if successful, their contribution is recognized and rewarded.

On an organizational level, one of the most important things you can do to get
innovation going is to support an open communication model.

OPENING UP YOUR COMMUNICATION MODEL

Sometimes individuals come up with great ideas all on their own. But more often, the really good ideas come from group involvement. You can encourage that interaction by opening up communications, not just among those who think alike, but especially among those who totally disagree.

If you have created a good team environment among your people, they won't be afraid to bring conflict out in the open and resolve it. That's the foundation for a good communications model. When people with different ideas or opinions aren't afraid to express them, you discover different ways to approach a problem or question.

CAUTION

Although your own ideas may be very good, don't make the mistake of thinking it's a good thing when everyone in the group follows your lead all the time. They must know that you are open to having them disagree with you.

Take the time to ask people what they think about a problem or idea, even if it's not their area of expertise. Gathering different perspectives on a problem is key to innovative solutions. When you do get ideas from people, avoid these innovation-killing phrases at all costs:

- We tried that before, and it didn't work.
- That's not really your department.
- I appreciate your input, but it's out of my hands.
- Why don't you just focus on your job and leave this to me?
- That sounds way too risky.
- We've never done anything like that before.

Finally, encourage communication among different groups in your organization. They might have very different takes on an issue, and striking a logical balance between disagreement and cooperation can be tricky. But it's out of this balance that true innovation usually surfaces.

BE OPEN TO CHANGE

All the encouragement of open communication and solicitation of ideas won't amount to a hill of beans if your organization is afraid of implementing change. Even the most creative employee will stop offering ideas when nothing ever changes.

True innovation comes when companies are willing to take risks, when there is a model for change, and when people are willing to make a leap of creativity and faith.

One key to this risk-taking attitude is to clearly define what problem you're trying to solve with innovation. A great idea for its own sake is less likely to be implemented than a great idea that solves a specific problem. The problem becomes the motivator for the organization to make changes.

TIP

Recent studies have found that organizational change is most effective when it is multifaceted, affecting several subsystems and areas of the organization.

As much as possible, support a future-focused organization, one that is aware that change is inevitable and that looks for proactive ways to set a vision for the best future possible. When employees sense that structure and are encouraged to contribute to that vision, they are much more motivated to work harder and stay the course to see the outcome.

CREATIVITY TECHNIQUES

Okay, you've done what you can to examine your communications model, you've opened yourself up to change, and you generally support an environment that fosters innovation. Now, what specific techniques can you apply to get your people in a creative mood? First, let's take a look at what creativity is.

WHAT IS CREATIVITY?

At its most basic, creativity is simply the ability to create something. But most people add another element to this definition. The *Blackwell Encyclopedia of Management,* for example, defines creativity as "the generation of ideas or products that are both novel and appropriate."

The novelty in this definition relates to the originality or uniqueness of the idea. The use of the term *appropriate* refers to the way an idea relates to the need at hand, solving a specific problem or fulfilling a market need.

Some people consider creativity to be a personality trait. Others have said it is a process. In the context of this latter characterization, anyone can be creative by being involved in a creative process.

USING BRAINSTORMING AND SYNECTICS

The creative problem-solving process, devised in the 1950s, basically is a fancy name for what we all recognize today as brainstorming. Brainstorming consists of certain elements:

- Listing
- Forced relationships
- Delayed judgment
- Generation of large numbers of ideas

Missing out on one of these items could result in less effective brainstorming sessions. So effective brainstorming sessions involve long lists of ideas that are written down. No idea is thrown out, and no judgment on an idea's value is passed until late in the process. Finally, relationships between ideas are used to work toward a final solution.

Synectics is somewhat similar to brainstorming, but here the focus is on use of metaphor and analogy. The idea behind synectics is to try to look at things in a completely different way. If the typical response to a budget overrun is to cut back on staff, turn the problem upside down and consider what would happen if you added staff.

PLAIN ENGLISH

Synectics   A process using analogy and metaphor to look at things differently, thereby generating novel ideas.

In a business setting, the use of analogy or metaphor can take the group's thinking out of the workplace and help you see ways in which you would treat a problem in another setting that just might work at the office. Here's an example of how to use synectics:

> **Problem:** We can't seem to get customers to send in survey cards telling us how to improve our customer service.
>
> **Analogy:** When I'm trying to get my small children to do something, I make it into a game.
>
> **Solution:** What if we held a contest? Every time somebody submits a comment, that name is entered in a contest for free products.

ACKNOWLEDGING CONTRIBUTIONS

So now you've got everybody in your company creating and innovating like mad. You might have set up bonus incentive programs to reward contributions to innovation. But don't forget one other very important thing: Acknowledge individual and group contributions. Studies have shown that *intrinsic motivations* are much stronger than *extrinsic motivations*. That is, personal motivations such as interest in an activity or personal challenge are much stronger than outside motivations such as money.

PLAIN ENGLISH

Intrinsic motivations   Interior motivations, including personal challenge and involvement.

Extrinsic motivations   Motivations outside of oneself, such as financial or career rewards.

Acknowledgement of effort supports intrinsic motivation. You are publicly giving praise to someone for having achieved a personal goal or having been involved in and committed to an idea.

Acknowledgement can take many forms, such as the following:

- Publicly thanking people in a larger group meeting
- Making sure that a story about the achievement shows up in the employee newsletter
- Copying the employee on a memo or e-mail to senior management that commends his contribution
- Noting the contribution in the employee's yearly performance review

Whatever you do, do not take credit for others' contributions. First, it's unethical. Second, it usually gets found out. Third, your credit should come from the fact that you manage people in a way that allows them to be their most creative and productive.

THE 30-SECOND RECAP

- Innovation is a way for companies to stay ahead in the market and for employees to feel vested in the company's success.
- Innovation occurs in an organization that supports risk-taking and is willing to accept change and open communication.
- Communication involves openness about conflict and its resolution, as well as the interchange of ideas among people with different perspectives.
- Techniques for bringing out creativity include brainstorming and synectics, or the use of analogy and metaphor to place the problem outside the workplace setting.
- Never forget to acknowledge employee contributions of ideas or solutions.

Providing Challenge

In this lesson, you learn how providing challenge involves balancing goal-directed activity and goal fulfillment to keep employees motivated.

Think about the last time you started a new job. Everything was new, and you might have felt overwhelmed by the challenge of taking on the unknown. Now think about a job that you left because you had learned everything there was to learn and were bored to tears when you came in to work every day.

These are examples of the two uncomfortable ends of the spectrum of challenge. Neither too much nor too little of a challenge feels right. Your job as a manager is to strike a balance for each of your employees. This chapter tells you how.

UNDERSTANDING GOAL FULFILLMENT

Much of the time that you're working on a project, you're performing *goal-directed activity.* You are actually enjoying the anticipation of accomplishing your goal because it's tantalizingly just out of reach. Once you accomplish your goal, you are in the *goal-fulfillment* phase. Often, this phase is somehow less satisfying than the goal-directed phase because the challenge is gone.

PLAIN ENGLISH

Goal-directed activity   The tasks you perform in the expectation of reaching a goal.

Goal-fulfillment   The attaining of a goal.

In fact, if you think about the life cycle of any endeavor, you'll see that you usually generate much more energy toward the beginning than at the end. That's the power of expectancy.

THE EXPECTANCY THEORY IN ACTION

What you experience when you're more excited at the beginning of a project than you do when you're nearing its end is what the *expectancy theory* is all about. At its core, the expectancy theory claims that people's actions are based on their expectations. Most people do things not for a reward, but for the expectation of a reward; they put in effort because of their hopes and dreams rather than for tangible payoffs.

PLAIN ENGLISH

Expectancy theory   People perform tasks in expectation of success.

To understand the expectancy theory, consider this: Although you work hard on a major project for 200 days out of the year, you don't get 200 rewards. You work those 200 days in the expectation of a successful product launch or a great big bonus at the end of the project. You might not even get a bonus, but you work because you imagine you might.

Now, the motivation gained from expectancy isn't constant; it involves some cycles. For example, look at your favorite sports team. If the players are in the fourth quarter and are 20 points ahead, they might just start getting sloppy. If they're in the fourth quarter and are 20 points behind, they might give up. The best games happen when there's a good chance that either side might win. Then each side is deeply involved in the anticipation of winning rather than the surety of winning or losing.

TIP

Not convinced about the expectancy theory? Just ask yourself if you've ever left a game in the last inning. You left not because your team was losing, but because their win was so sure that it just wasn't interesting anymore.

This tendency to lose motivation as success seems imminent was documented by David McClelland and John Atkinson in the concept of what they call a 50 percent curve. When the probability of success is near zero, motivation is low. When probability of success approaches 50 percent, motivation increases. Finally, when probability of success gets higher than 50 percent, motivation begins to fall off.

CHALLENGING EMPLOYEES: IT'S A BALANCING ACT

Therefore, the key to challenging employees is to make sure they are neither too complacent in their work nor too unsure of their ability to succeed. Success must seem possible, but not a sure thing.

CAUTION

There's a difference between keeping your employees on the cutting edge of challenge and getting them edgy. Make sure they succeed often enough to feel the good side of challenge.

Read over these tips for using expectancy theory to strike a balance between goal-directed and goal-fulfillment activities:

- If you know that workers have passed the 50 percent probability of success on a project, encourage them to redouble their efforts; you can even raise the stakes a bit. Praise their efforts to date, and then define success a little more aggressively. (Be sure, however, that if you promised rewards at the initial success milestone, you provide them.)

- One theory states that three things must be available for expectancy: Someone believes his efforts affect performance, believes that performance determines outcome, and assigns a value to that outcome. Pay attention to the second item: If the outcome isn't attainable because of market factors or a lack of resources, motivation goes out the window.

- Allow your employees to share in the larger vision of the company. This plays to the nature of people to be motivated by what they imagine to be possible. Then make sure they understand that their actions relate to the success of that vision.

ASSIGN AN INTERESTING PROJECT

One of your jobs as a manager or supervisor is to distribute the workload among your staff. Your first priority is probably to get the work done. But right up there on your priority list should be to distribute that work in a way that challenges and stimulates your employees.

Now, some businesses are in constant flux, and new opportunities to take on projects abound. But other workplaces are pretty consistent, and the people you supervise might be required to do the same repetitive task every day. It's trickier to provide stimulation in this situation, but it's not impossible.

Even a factory worker with one assigned task to perform all day long might be able to help assess a new piece of equipment. Although a secretary must type and copy documents all day, you could give her a research project now and then. Look for unique activities to intersperse throughout each person's workweek, and you'll go a long way toward providing a challenging environment.

CAUTION

You should be aware that some people absolutely love routine and get scared to death when asked to take on something new. Learn to recognize those people, and give the interesting projects to someone else.

TRYING ON DIFFERENT HATS

Whenever somebody takes on a new responsibility, it's a challenge to his ability to learn and absorb new situations. That something new could be an entirely new type of work he has never performed before. It also could be a kind of activity he has done, but in a new setting, with new people, or with more responsibility or authority.

Remember, your job is not to assign brand-new activities on a daily basis, which would be inefficient in getting the company's business done. Your job is to find activities that balance new challenges with routine work. This ensures that an employee finds enough stimulation in the work to enjoy the workplace.

Here are some examples of challenging situations that can be incorporated into any employee's worklife:

- Ask a clerical worker to learn how to perform research on the Internet. Although he has done research before, he might never have used this tool, so he would be in a learning situation.

- Invite a factory worker to be involved in a project to improve working conditions in the plant. Although she might never have been part of a committee working with management, she knows conditions in the plant firsthand and can contribute that expertise in a new setting.

- Invoke a skill you know an employee has but that he or she has never used in a business setting. Let's say, for example, that Sally often gives talks on bird watching to a local nature club, but has never given a business presentation. You can have her transfer her existing skills to a business setting. Although she faces a new challenge, she'll have enough confidence about the skills involved to be pretty sure she'll succeed.

- Say that one employee has purchased printing services for years for your company. Now that you have more work to produce and need additional printing vendors, you might give her the job of meeting with possible vendors and giving her recommendations.

TIP

Sometimes managers hesitate to assign more responsibility to people because they're worried that those people will fail. It's always best to trust an employee to perform well, but if you have any doubts, work along with the employee on a project and observe his performance before letting him fly solo.

SKILLS BUILDING 101

Offering challenges to employees isn't purely to keep them amused on the job, although that is important in attracting and retaining good employees. Through challenging new situations, employees stretch themselves, learn new skills, and exhibit abilities that help you and them see the next logical step in their career paths.

You can develop many types of skills with special projects, including these:

- **Technical skills.** High-tech skills are the wave of the future, so consider letting your employees learn to use the Internet, a software product, or a new piece of equipment.

- **Management skills.** An employee can acquire management skills if you assign him or her the responsibility to train another person, to supervise another person's performance, or to give input for the budget for your department.

- **Communication skills.** Good communication is key in moving up the career ladder. Assign projects such as writing a proposal, speaking to a group, or giving a demonstration.

- **Interpersonal skills.** When you put an employee in with a different mix of people, he'll get to flex his interpersonal skill muscles. Put a worker on a committee with people from another department, or have her go along with a salesperson on a sales call. Although she's not in sales, she might be able to help the salesperson explain the features of the product to the customer better.

TIP

Part of providing opportunity for advancement is spotting skills that are transferable to other roles in the company. Is your assistant good in building relationships? Maybe there's a fit for her in sales or customer service.

LISTEN UP!

When you're trying to think of ways to provide challenge and variety to your employees, it's always important that you factor in their goals and interests. That's not hard to do if you simply listen to what your employees want.

Try these questions to discover what types of new situations or challenges might be best suited to your employees:

1. How do you feel about working on projects with other departments?
2. Do you enjoy picking up new skills? What skills do you think you would like to learn?
3. If you could find ways to use your existing skills in new ways, what might those be?
4. Are you interested in managing other people?
5. Do you like training or mentoring others in work that you're familiar with?
6. Do you enjoy familiar routines? Why?
7. Are there any activities you definitely do not want to be involved in (public speaking, managing people, traveling, and so on)?
8. What would be advantageous to you in having more authority over other people?
9. Do you have suggestions about ways in which you could do your job differently to improve productivity or allow you to be more creative?

PROMOTING FROM WITHIN

Although most companies profess to promote from within, some companies don't do so in practice. Why? In some cases, it's because it takes work on a manager's part to groom employees to add skill sets that make them promotable—some companies don't support managers spending their time that way. Some management types want only those with experience in higher-level jobs to do those jobs. Then there are some people who have prejudices. The sentiment "He's a clerical worker, and someone at that level could never handle this kind of responsibility," is more common than you like to think.

CAUTION

Never, ever let yourself hold an employee back because he or she is invaluable to you in a current role. Absorbing the headache of letting someone good move on and training a replacement is a fact of life for any manager. And eventually, anyone held back time after time will find the front door and walk.

So what are the motivational benefits of promoting from within? People have a natural tendency to want to grow and change throughout their lives. They work through stages of physical development, emotional development, and intellectual development. No matter how much you may want to keep people in the jobs they have today, they eventually will want change, and if you don't provide it, another employer just might. People like strides in their development to be recognized and rewarded.

TIP

Some companies give more credence to outside training than on-the-job training. If taking classes or getting a second degree will help management consider an employee in a new light, encourage people to try that route to promotion.

If people believe that effort and a broader skill set will win them the reward of growth through promotion, it provides tremendous motivation to work hard and try new things. If taking on new challenges isn't going to lead to growth, why bother? Meeting challenges for challenge's sake works for a while—maybe even years. But at some point, people want their efforts recognized.

THE 30-SECOND RECAP

- People often are motivated not by success, but by the expectation of success.
- If success is impossible or assured, motivation goes down.
- New challenges motivate employees because of the promise of possible success in a new endeavor.
- Challenging employees can help them acquire additional skills that will benefit both the company and the employees' career goals.
- Talk to employees to understand what kinds of challenges they are interested in.
- Promoting from within, as a policy, makes workers aware that taking on new challenges can lead to more than praise.

Share the Success!

In this lesson, you learn how sharing the benefits of success can motivate future effort.

When all is said and done, you and your co-workers are working to achieve success for the company. You do that so you will continue to have jobs, but also so that you will see some reward from all your hard work.

You can reward employees on a day-to-day basis with paychecks, parties, gifts, or recognition. But when the company's ship comes in, don't forget to invite the employees to the party on the dock. That's what this chapter is all about!

Ownership Isn't Just for Owners

Some companies forget that employees want to feel part of something bigger than their own daily responsibilities or their own careers. Because many employees are not involved with setting the course or overall vision for the company, those who are involved sometimes don't credit employees with major accomplishments. This is a big mistake. People have a natural inclination to want to belong to something bigger. And because their work makes your success possible, it's only right that you make them feel involved.

This investing of employees in your company's success goes beyond making them feel warm and fuzzy, or even sharing financially in success. If people feel involved in where the company is headed, they are likely to stay with the company longer and view their own efforts as more important in the scheme of things.

Share a Piece of the Action

As noted in other parts of this book, personal motivators such as challenge and involvement have been found to be more motivating than outside motivations, such as financial reward. But in the case of sharing the wealth in successful times, you're really appealing to both kinds of motivations: You're making employees feel involved by including them in the financial rewards.

Sharing Profit

Profit sharing falls under the category of variable compensation. This means that the amount you'll pay out to each employee varies depending on the performance of the company.

TIP

One benefit of having a profit-sharing program is that you can vote to reduce the profit-sharing margin if times get bad as a way of offsetting losses rather than laying off employees.

Three types of profit-sharing programs exist: cash, deferred, and a combination of cash and deferred. Cash plans pay a cash bonus either quarterly or annually, based on company financial performance. Deferred plans place an employee's payment in a tax-deferred fund. A *deferred profit-sharing plan* is basically a retirement fund. The combination program pays both a cash bonus and a payment into a retirement fund. 401(k) plans are a form of profit sharing in which an employee can contribute a portion of his pay into a tax-deferred fund, and the employer matches the contribution.

PLAIN ENGLISH

Deferred profit-sharing plans   Sharing plans that make payments into a tax-deferred fund. As long as the employee does not withdraw any funds, she does not pay taxes on the income.

Profit-sharing plans *vest* over a period of time. When vested, funds are available for an employee to access. The most common time period for vesting is seven years. This is a stepped process, with a certain percentage of the fund vesting each year until the 100 percent point is reached.

PLAIN ENGLISH

Vest   To grant or endow with a particular authority, right, or property.

Profit-sharing and 401(k) plans are very popular with employees. A 1999 survey by The Profit Sharing/401(k) Council of America (PSCA) shows that 87.4 percent of eligible employees participate in a profit-sharing or 401(k) plan. Average employee deferral contributions are around 5.5 percent of their salaries. On average, companies contribute 4.9 percent of their payroll to these plans.

TIP

For more information about these programs, visit the PCSA Web site at www.psca.org.

STOCK OPTIONS

Companies that have gone public can grant stock options to their employees. Stock options are basically shares of stock granted to an employee at a certain value. In future years, after the options vest and are available to the employee, that employee can exercise them by selling the shares at the current market value. The employee receives the difference between the option price and the current market price.

Companies can also set up a system by which employees can purchase additional stock options out of their paychecks with regular deductions.

Stock options are a great motivation for staying with a company because one has to wait a certain number of years to exercise those options. If an employee leaves the company, the options don't go with him.

TYING BONUSES TO SUCCESS

Most bonus programs also offer complicated formulas that relate the size of the bonus to the financial success of the company or the work unit. The benefit of tying a bonus to performance comes when employees believe that their own work performance can impact the overall performance of the company and, therefore, their bonus amount.

Although you might not be able to affect the percentage of salary an employee receives in the form of a bonus, you can impact the perception of whether individual effort results in company success. You can do that in several ways, including these:

- Keeping employees informed about company initiatives and successes on a regular basis.

- Initiating a two-tiered bonus structure that rewards both overall company performance and workgroup performance. This way, if other groups fail, your own group's success can still save the day—and the bonus—for your people.

- Setting group goals that are measurable and related to profit, such as number of units produced, new accounts opened, or an increase in the number of customer inquiries processed.

TIP

Senior management's communication with employees is very helpful. Suggest that senior managers hold a quarterly lunch with a handful of employees picked at random from different departments. Management can listen to their input and express appreciation for their efforts.

SPREAD THE GOOD NEWS!

When your department or the company as a whole achieves a success, it's vital that management inform employees as soon as possible. Employees often feel cut off from the larger initiatives that a company is involved in, such as negotiating mergers or going public when the first they hear of it is on the 6 o'clock news.

Some companies make the mistake of not following up after a big employee initiative. For example, if you've launched a new product, it probably took the efforts of hundreds of people from research and design, marketing, manufacturing, and so on. Yet many companies don't share sales results after the launch, so people don't really know whether their efforts paid off. They always hear if the product falls flat on its face, but they should also be told about a nice big order that came in from a major customer or an award that the product received.

Here are some mechanisms for sharing the word when success hits:

- Use a company Web site or newsletter to announce the news.
- Hold quarterly company meetings, and designate one section of the meeting just to announce good news.
- Throw a party, or send out a special bonus when an unusually important goal is achieved.
- Print buttons that say "We did it!" and distribute them in paycheck envelopes with a brief description of the accomplishment.

CAUTION

Some employers hesitate to share financial information or future plans with employees because such information is confidential. By asking employees to be involved in keeping this confidence, you express trust that makes them feel valued. Be sure to warn employees when information is not to be shared, though.

Now Get Out There and Motivate!

Well, that's the last theory I'll offer you about motivating people. But I can't resist one more list! Here are a few thoughts I'd like to leave you with:

- Remember, the very fact that you bought this book means that you are a caring and concerned manager. Give yourself a pat on the back for the effort you're expending on motivating your staff.
- Often, simply being more alert to how your employees feel about or react to a situation helps you find the solution. Let your people know you're in tune with what's happening to them and how it makes them feel. Whether you can do anything to change it or not this time, that recognition means a great deal.

- Think back to the very first chapter and remember that people go through phases of motivation, that different things motivate different people, and that they're not always the same things that motivate you.
- There is no replacement for day-to-day leadership, honesty, fairness, and integrity. All the gifts, parties, promotions, and bonuses in the world can't replace these.

If you implement many of the recommendations in this book, over time you'll find you have a more motivated work force and that your own job is more pleasant and fulfilling. Good luck!

THE 30-SECOND RECAP

- Making people feel involved in larger company successes reduces turnover and makes employees feel part of something bigger than their daily tasks.
- Profit-sharing and 401(k) plans reward employees for company and department financial performance.
- Tying bonuses to financial performance encourages people to put in effort for which they see a direct monetary reward.
- There are several ways to spread news about company successes, including newsletters, Web sites, and company meetings.

Leadership

What Is Leadership?

In this section you will learn the definition of leadership, see the qualities that leaders possess, and discover that leaders are not born, but developed.

DEFINING LEADERSHIP

When we think of successful, high-profile leaders, we think of people such as General Colin Powell, who led the American forces during the Gulf War; or Bill Gates, the Harvard dropout who founded Microsoft and became the richest man in the world.

In your own field, you can probably name one or two men or women who are successful leaders—people who seem almost visionary and have an intangible knack for getting things right and inspiring their subordinates.

Leaders are able to define a goal, persuade others to assist in achieving that goal, and lead their teams to victory. But what is the definition of leadership?

Leadership is crucial to managers in the business world, but it also plays an important role for coaches, teachers, and parents.

There is not one single definition of leadership. Understanding this is the first step toward becoming an effective leader. Some common definitions or beliefs about leadership include the following:

- A leader is the appointed head of a group, team, or organization.
- A leader is a charismatic person who is able to make good decisions and inspire others to reach a common goal.
- Leadership is the power to communicate assertively and inspire others.
- Leadership is the ability to influence others.

Not one of the preceding definitions is more correct than any of the others. All of the definitions, however, agree on one common fact: Leadership involves more than one person.

You cannot be a leader without a group of people following your direction and putting their trust in you. Remember, as a leader you have a responsibility to your employees, group, organization, or team to lead fairly and ethically. The title "Boss" or "Manager" does not automatically make you a leader.

To be a good leader, you'll need to fortify yourself by keeping up with the latest leadership trends, observing other leaders (including leaders in your own chain of command and leaders in the news), and recognizing that your own unique brand of leadership will change as you gain experience.

TIP

Keep up on the latest leadership trends by reading trade publications, watching the news, and observing successful leaders in your own organization.

LEADERSHIP QUALITIES

As defined in the preceding section, a leader is someone who inspires, who makes decisions that affect the organization in a positive way, and who can pull together a diverse team to work toward a common goal. But if all managers are not leaders, what are the qualities that set leaders apart?

Charisma is one quality that is often mistaken as the most important leadership requirement. However, you can attain charismatic leadership more easily if you work to develop the following qualities:

PLAIN ENGLISH

Charisma   An almost intangible quality that inspires loyalty and great results from subordinates.

- **Knowledge.** Know your facts and use them. A leader must know the details of the business in order to act for the entire organization.

- **Trust.** Don't micromanage. If your employees feel you are constantly peering over their shoulders, you will create an atmosphere of distrust. Be aware of what team members are working on, but don't make them feel like "Big Brother" is watching.

- **Integrity.** A leader will be ineffective if subordinates and superiors do not trust him. The organization soon learns to work around a leader who is untrustworthy or does not keep his word. For example, a leader who tells his employees one thing but does another could be viewed as untrustworthy—even if the difference seems inconsequential to you.

- **Standards.** As a leader, your public and private lives should be exemplary. Lead by example. A leader who expects a certain code of conduct from the employees but does not practice the same standards can suffer a loss of respect. A staff that does not respect the leader will suffer a loss in work quality.

- **Decisiveness.** Leaders are valued for their decision-making abilities, especially in high-pressure situations. When confronted with a tough decision, fall back on the knowledge mentioned earlier in this list.

The best decisions are decisions made with full possession of the facts.

■ **Assertiveness.** Leaders are chosen to lead a team, group, or entire organization. Often, you'll be in situations where your staff is not present—for example, high-level organizational meetings. Your assertiveness can and must represent the employees who have put their trust in you.

■ **Optimism.** Be realistic but not fatalistic. Your employees and your superiors may soon lose confidence if they are constantly confronted with pessimism or negativity from you. Situations aren't always ideal, but as a leader you're expected to find the best way to turn the situation around. Figure it out and concentrate on the positive.

■ **Results.** A leader has a track record of solid decisions and outcomes to point to. If you've been managing for some time, try to compile a list of successful decisions and events that you're responsible for. Not only can you point out these successes to others, but you can use them to build your own confidence in your abilities.

■ **Vision.** A leader is expected to set goals that will guide an organization in a specific direction. A leader must think broadly and far into the future to set those goals and help the team grow in the right direction.

■ **The appearance of power.** As "casual Friday" becomes "casual every day" at a growing number of companies, you still must give off the aura of power in your dress, carriage, and surroundings. In a traditional environment, men should wear suits and remain relatively conservative in their choice of tie and shoes. Women, too, should dress tastefully and err on the side of looking conservative. In a casual environment, both men and women should avoid wearing jeans and T-shirts.

TIP

The qualities that make a leader are charisma, knowledge, trust, integrity, standards, decisiveness, assertiveness, optimism, results, vision, and the appearance of power.

WHAT A LEADER IS NOT

A leader is not merely the manager who sits in the corner office, the person who controls quitting time and paychecks, or the person who can hire and fire people. Managers in this day and age must be flexible and willing to adapt to an increasingly more demanding and younger workforce that questions authority.

Technology companies have taken the lead in showing that a less autocratic chain of command can produce phenomenal results. Companies such as Bill Gates's Microsoft boast of campus-like atmospheres where permissiveness is no longer the exception, but the rule.

As a leader, you should avoid the following:

- **Micromanagement.** This will be addressed in the section "Avoiding Micromanagement," on page 351, but for now stop and consider whether you might be keeping too close an eye on your staff or handling too many of the responsibilities in your organization yourself. Are you viewed as overbearing?

- **Closeness.** Steer clear of getting too close to your staff. You are a leader, not your employees' best friend. It's hard to criticize or chastise someone you view as a friend, and even harder for that employee to see the criticism as unbiased.

- **Temper.** Put your negative emotions aside. We're all human, but as a leader you must avoid negative outbursts or personal attacks on co-workers.

- **Arrogance.** You are not a supreme deity. Remember that you wouldn't be a leader without a staff. Avoid autocratic behavior.

A leader is also not synonymous with a manager. Management involves specific business-critical functions such as tending to a budget, developing a product, and generating reports.

However, leadership is an important part of being a manager. A manager who works to improve his or her leadership skills can surpass the status quo to improve the unit's performance.

CAUTION

Don't confuse management with leadership. Management and leadership are not the same thing. Management involves specific organizational functions such as budgeting and producing a product. Leadership is one part of management that deals with how you communicate with the others in your organization.

BECOMING A LEADER

Some people would have you believe that the best leaders are born that way, and that if you weren't captain of the preschool debate club, you're out of luck when it comes to the ability to be a leader.

Many of the best leaders, however, will point to the fact that they were "C" students, sometimes as late as college. Usually there was a defining event or person in their lives that gave them the confidence to step out of the pack and start leading it.

For you, that moment has arrived. Now you must fortify yourself with knowledge and start thinking like a leader.

THE 30-SECOND RECAP

- There are several definitions of leadership, but a leader is generally considered a charismatic person who is able to make good decisions and inspire others to reach a common goal.
- Leadership qualities include charisma, knowledge, trust, integrity, standards, decisiveness, assertiveness, optimism, results, vision, and the appearance of power.
- Good leaders avoid micromanagement, negativity, and getting too close to subordinates.
- *Manager* and *leader* do not mean the same thing, although leadership is an important part of being a manager.
- The ability to lead is not something you are born with, but something you can develop over time.

The Traits of a Leader

In this section you'll learn how to use positive thought and talk to your advantage, develop vision, and build your own confidence.

POSITIVE THOUGHT, POSITIVE TALK

It isn't often that you hear a Super Bowl–winning coach quoted before the game as saying, "Well, I don't think we can win. What a long shot. If we do, no one will be more surprised than me."

Sports teams have made a science of practicing *positive thought* and *positive talk*. You're more likely to hear that Super Bowl–winning coach say, "We know it's going to be hard, but we know we can do it. We're a first-class organization, and this year the players have really honed their skills. It shows in their play."

Positive thought and positive talk are integral to thinking and functioning as a leader. You must learn to face head-on your fears about competition, your abilities, and the abilities of your team or group. Only then can you begin to win and to raise the quality of your team's work to a higher level.

Positive Thought

Just like the coach of that Super Bowl–winning team, you've got to visualize yourself winning. Visualizing the win will help you to take the right actions to achieve the outcome you want.

For example, Dave's group was assigned the high-profile project of redesigning a large part of his company's Web site. Dave had no experience in Web site design. He privately told a trusted friend outside the company that he wasn't sure he could accomplish this task because he had no idea where to begin.

Dave's friend, a practitioner of positive thought, told Dave to think again. He reminded Dave that he had five staff members who were skilled in HTML and Web design. He also reminded Dave that his background was in designing magazine layouts, at which he had been extremely successful. Dave agreed, completed the project successfully, and ended up winning an award for the site's design.

Here are some key steps in thinking positively:

1. Break a given problem down to its most basic components and deal with each separately.
2. If you deem something as a negative, figure out why: lack of experience? past failure?
3. Figure out what you can do to increase your chance of success. For example, if your concern is lack of experience, could you take a class or ask a colleague to help you learn about a particular topic or procedure?
4. View each challenge thrown your way as a chance to lengthen your list of successes.
5. Visualize yourself winning. In the preceding example, Dave could have thought, "I need to redesign this Web site. I've never done this before, but I've had similar experience and I'm eager to learn. I've got a talented staff, and I know we can do a great job."

TIP

Visualizing yourself winning does not have to apply to a specific situation. If you're new to leadership or striving for a leadership position, concentrate on your assets. You might think positively by saying to yourself, "I know that I am capable of being in a position of greater responsibility. I'm smart, have the right experience, and have great people skills."

POSITIVE TALK

Positive thought will help you visualize successes and increase your chance of success. To project that same confidence in your own abilities and the abilities of your group, however, you must also engage in positive talk.

To refer again to the example of the Super Bowl–winning coach: Not only did the coach feel that his team could win, but he was also quoted in the press as saying his team was going to win, and saying exactly why they were going to win.

Besides the obviously positive effect his words will have on his own coaching and his players' morale, he also inspired confidence in the team's owners and, the most important bosses of all, the fans.

As a leader of a team, group, or organization, you must learn to develop and regularly use positive talk. Positive talk is key to helping your group visualize a win.

When Dave's team heard they were going to redesign a high-profile area on the company's Web site, Dave wasn't the only person who was initially doubtful about their chances for success. The team members themselves were unhappy at having a different kind of work introduced into their routine. Although the team was skilled in HTML, they felt they had enough to do with merely updating the site content daily. One team member even said to the others, "I don't know why they asked us to do this. This is really going to be awful."

After Dave began thinking positively, he addressed his team's misgivings by saying, "I know this is a new challenge for us, but we're going to do this project and we're going to do it on schedule and make it the best site redesign this company has ever seen. This team has more combined Web experience than any other group in this company. We've been given the chance to set the pace, not just keep up. Let's get to work."

Dave's confidence in his team's abilities not only flattered his group, but it made them realize they could do more than they previously thought. Dave made it sound as if it was a given that the redesign would be successful and that it would be because of their contributions.

Dave also inspired the same confidence in his superiors when they asked how he felt the project was progressing. Instead of saying that his team was trying to figure out the redesign, Dave said, "I have to admit this project was a new challenge for my group, but my team loves a new challenge and thrives under pressure. Thanks for the opportunity to showcase my group's abilities."

CAUTION

Beware of negativity. Negative thoughts will undermine your leadership qualities. Minimizing negative thoughts and talk will help you to think and appear more like a leader. For example, avoid deprecating yourself in thought and talk with negative statements like, "I know nothing about this," "I'm so stupid," or "My opinion probably doesn't count for much, but ...." Such negativity will only erode your confidence and the confidence your superiors and subordinates have in you.

VISION

Another important leadership trait is *vision*. An argument could be made that it is impossible to be a true leader of a group, organization, company, or industry without having vision.

Vision is closely allied with positive thought and positive talk, but involves taking that positivity to the next level.

PLAIN ENGLISH

Vision   A leader's ideas and plans for an organization's future. Idealistic in nature, a vision gives a sense of the differences between the present and future states of an organization.

Visionary leaders are often noted for innovations within an organization or industry. For example, Bill Gates is considered a visionary for anticipating that the personal computer could be an indispensable part of every household and then developing the products to make it so.

A leader's vision is extremely important because it gives people something to strive toward: a view beyond the present, into the future of the organization.

DEVELOPING VISION

To develop your own vision, try the following exercises:

- **Start with your aspirations.** What are your aspirations? Is there some particular concept, process, or product that you want to develop?

- **Do your research.** Compare your ideas with others in your field by studying books, trade magazines, and Web sites.
- **Spend some time thinking about your organization.** What could you do to improve the organization? What is the single biggest hurdle to success in your unit or the organization as a whole?
- **Think about possible and necessary improvements.** What can you do to improve the organization or unit? Think about both the short term and the long term. This will enable you to set short-term and long-term goals to take steps toward realizing your vision.
- **Think about do-ability.** Are your goals realistic? If your vision points to goals that seem unattainable, is there a way to break down the vision into a simpler form?
- **Use your intuition.** Does your vision make sense?

COMMUNICATING YOUR VISION

Sharing your vision with others, be it your team or your superiors, is an important aspect of leadership. By sharing your vision with your team, you'll let them know they have a manager who is thinking of the organization's future, as well as theirs. By sharing your vision with your superiors, you'll let them know you are an innovative thinker who is not content with the status quo.

BUILDING CONFIDENCE

Confidence in yourself will be bolstered by both positive thinking and by the process of formulating your vision. Self-confidence, however, tends to be the result of measurable success.

To build your self-confidence, you might make a list of your assets and past successes, no matter how small they were. Some assets you might list are education or specialized training, the ability to communicate well with others, or a great sense of humor.

THE 30-SECOND RECAP

- Positive thought and positive talk are integral to thinking and functioning as a leader.
- A vision is a leader's ideas and plans for the future of an organization. To be effective, a leader must communicate his vision to his team members as well as his superiors.
- To build your self-confidence, make a list of your assets and past successes.

Leadership Styles

In this section you'll learn about several different styles of leadership, the merits and downsides to each, and how to determine which style is right for you.

NO TWO ARE ALIKE

Just as no two snowflakes are exactly alike, no two people lead in exactly the same way. This section, however, outlines several of the most common leadership styles.

Depending on the group he or she has to lead, a successful leader may adhere stringently to the rules of one kind of leadership or can combine aspects of different styles.

TIP

As you read about the different aspects of leadership styles, make notes about concepts that appeal to you or that you think might work in your situation. Don't feel compelled to adhere to one style's set of rules and boundaries. Be flexible.

DICTATORSHIP

You've probably run across a dictator in your life. Like the political leaders the name is borrowed from, dictators tend to keep decision-making power and most critical knowledge to themselves.

CHARACTERISTICS OF DICTATORSHIP

Here is a list of typical characteristics of a dictator:

- **No questions asked.** The dictator lays down the law in his or her group and expects individuals to perform without questioning his or her authority.

- **Knowledge is power.** The dictator rightly believes that knowledge is one of the keys to power. For this reason, the dictator will often keep most of a unit or organization's critical knowledge to himself and dole out only small portions of information on a need-to-know basis.

- **No mistakes.** The dictator expects performance to be of the highest quality at all times. Mistakes aren't tolerated. Mistakes usually result in dismissal or some other form of punishment for the individual.

WHEN THIS STYLE WORKS BEST

The dictator can be particularly effective when a group has gotten out of control and is making little or no effort to actually work. In such cases, the dictator can provide a wake-up call to team members that they are each individually responsible for carrying an equal share of the team's weight.

THE DICTATOR'S DOWNSIDE

The dictator style of leadership can be hard for both the leader and the team members. The dictator is not known for creating a creative, trusting work environment. The dictator also runs an incredibly high risk of being disliked by his unit.

The dictator will also not reap the benefits of his team's creativity. If the supervisor does not have knowledge of the team's status and objectives, team members may not be able to perform to the best of their abilities.

CAUTION

Be careful if you practice the dictator style of leadership. Because of the harshness required for this form of leadership, the leader is often perceived as oppressive and unfair.

THE "ALMOST" DEMOCRACY

The "almost" democracy is a bit more lenient than a dictatorship. The leader in this situation strives to make sure the group is well informed and participating in the direction of the team as a whole.

For example, Kate holds regular staff meetings each morning for her team. In the staff meeting, she outlines the agenda she has prepared for the day, then turns the floor over to the staff. The staff can then state their point of view about the agenda or propose an entirely different one. Kate then has the power to agree or veto the staff's ideas.

CHARACTERISTICS OF THE "ALMOST" DEMOCRACY

Here is a list of the characteristics of this type of leadership:

- *Participation.* The leader engages the team in most aspects of business, making sure that each team member is equally aware of what is going on throughout the unit.
- **Encouraging debate.** The leader recognizes the value of debate and competition and encourages team members to participate in setting new directions for the unit.

- **Veto power.** The leader's absolute power is what gives this style of leadership the "almost" in its title. Although the leader encourages participation, he or she ultimately will make the final decision on all matters of importance to the unit.

PLAIN ENGLISH

Participation   The act of allowing group members to take part in decision-making, as seen in the "almost" democracy and the partnership styles of leadership.

WHEN THIS STYLE WORKS BEST

The "almost" democracy works best when you're leading a highly innovative staff that still needs direction. Although they have tons of ideas, quantity doesn't always equal quality. The leader is responsible for determining right and wrong.

THE PARTNERSHIP

The partnership is a drastically different kind of leadership from the styles previously discussed in this section. Both the dictatorship and the "almost" democracy maintain a clear boundary between leader and group members. The partnership, however, blurs the line and requires the leader to become just one of the group.

CHARACTERISTICS OF THE PARTNERSHIP

Partnership characteristics include the following:

- **Equality.** The leader becomes just another group member, one who may have more experience, certainly, but one who doesn't really pull more weight than other individuals in the group.
- **Group vision.** All group members participate in decision-making and setting the direction for the unit.
- **Shared responsibility.** All group members are responsible for the results and consequences of the group's actions.

WHEN THIS STYLE WORKS BEST

The partnership is a style of leadership that works best with a small group of incredibly experienced or talented individuals. Trust, honesty, and belief in the staff's ability are key ingredients for a partnership to succed.

THE DOWNSIDE

The partnership style of leadership can be one of the most rewarding leadership experiences. Not only are you leading, but you are interacting with your group members as equals. However, this is not the style to use if you are concerned about your authority being undermined.

TRANSFORMATIONAL LEADERSHIP

Transformational leaders go beyond trying to keep individuals and teams performing at the status quo. A transformational leader is one who has the power to bring about change in team members and the organization as a whole.

PLAIN ENGLISH

Transformational leader   A leader who is capable of bringing about change in individuals and entire organizations, often helping troubled organizations turn around their performance.

CHARACTERISTICS OF A TRANSFORMATIONAL LEADER

Transformational leaders distinguish themselves through the following characteristics:

- **Charisma.** A transformational leader is one who has a clear vision for the organization and can easily communicate that vision to group members.

- **Confidence.** A transformational leader has a good business sense and is able to see what decisions will positively affect the organization. This enables the leader to act confidently, inspiring trust in team members.

- **Respect and loyalty.** A transformational leader inspires respect and loyalty in individuals by taking the time to let them know they are important.

- **Expressive praise.** A transformational leader is often expressive in praising individuals and the team on a job well done. Letting people know how much they contributed to one success will steel them for future challenges.

- **Inspiration.** A transformational leader is a master at helping people to do something they weren't sure they were capable of doing. This is achieved through praise and encouraging statements.

WHEN THIS STYLE WORKS BEST

Transformational leadership is the ideal style of leadership to use when you need to drastically improve the performance of an individual, group, or organization.

THE DOWNSIDE

Transformational leadership can be a particularly draining style of management. You are responsible for the vision and the means of accomplishing that vision. The transformational leader is also somewhat of a gambler, betting that his or her vision is the right one.

WHAT STYLE IS RIGHT FOR YOU?

You've read about the dictatorship, the "almost" democracy, the partnership, and transformational leadership. You may have found characteristics of each of those styles that correspond with how you have already been leading. Or you may have found some traits that you'd like to develop.

You may also find that as your group weathers challenges, successes, and changes in the organizational culture, you may need to be a partner one day and a dictator the next. As unpredictable as one individual can be, a group is even more so.

For example, Tom was a newly promoted manager in the sales division of a sporting goods manufacturer. He knew that his group had achieved phenomenal success in the past, but had recently been performing below average since a company-wide reorganization in which the group lost some longtime employees.

Since Tom was a new manager and relatively young, he entered the situation using the partnership method of leadership. He knew that several of the sales division's most decorated members were in his new group. He began by telling the group that their performance had slipped noticeably and let the employees know that he was there to help them regain their spot as the top sales team in the company.

Tom turned to the veterans in his group to find out how they had achieved their past successes and to help diagnose what was holding them back now. He found that they were eager enough to talk about how great and innovative they were in the good old days, but they repeatedly said they didn't have the energy to try again.

Once Tom had established a level of trust and loyalty with his staff, he became a dictator. He needed to jump-start his employees and let them know that they were all directly accountable for the group's success, or lack thereof, and that he expected them to work. Tom ended up having to fire one employee who continually defied his leadership and had never exhibited much skill in sales.

Once his team was working on at least an average level again, Tom morphed into the transformational leader. He inspired even the oldest veterans in the group to try new sales methods and to strive toward his vision of a 75 percent increase in the group's sales within six months.

By encouraging and stimulating his employees, Tom's group emerged as the leading sales team at the company. Both he and his employees were recognized for their innovation and contributions to the company's success.

DETERMINING YOUR STYLE

To determine which style of leadership will work best for you, make two lists: one with your natural leadership traits and one with the goals you need to accomplish within your group.

On the first list, you might include things such as sense of humor, ability to easily communicate, commanding presence, or innovative visionary. When your list is complete, try to see which style of leadership is most closely matched to your traits. You might use that style of leadership as a starting point.

On the second list, compile the goals—large and small—that you'd like to accomplish with your group or organization. What are the hurdles to those goals? Is your staff ineffectual or just in need of intellectual stimulation?

In practical use you'll discover, like Tom in the earlier example, that you will probably combine several leadership styles and aspects of those styles to create your own unique style of leadership.

Leadership style is not determined only by you, but also by the group that you are charged with leading. As stated in "What Is Leadership?" on page 300, you are not a leader if there is no one following you. Be sensitive to the unique challenges the individuals in your group face.

Above all, there are some traits that are always important in a leader, regardless of his or her style: fairness, integrity, honesty, and caring.

THE 30-SECOND RECAP

- No two leaders' styles are alike. Most leaders develop a unique style of leadership that is a combination of several general styles.

- The dictatorship is the harshest form of leadership, in which the leader holds all the power and knowledge. This form of leadership can be considered oppressive and unfair.

- Participation and debate characterize the "almost" democracy, while the leader still reserves most of the decision-making power.

- The partnership blurs the line between leader and subordinates and requires the leader to become just one of the group. All group members are equally responsible for decision-making and taking responsibility for successes and failures.

- A transformational leader brings about change in individuals and entire organizations, often helping troubled organizations turn around their performance.

- Your own style of leadership will be determined by your natural traits and the needs of your unit or organization.

Communicating as a Leader

In this section you'll learn how to communicate as a leader using effective language and nonverbal communication.

THE IMPORTANCE OF COMMUNICATION

One of the most distinguishing traits of a leader is the rare ability to communicate effectively. Knowing the right thing to say and how to say it can make or break your leadership tenure, your team, and your organization.

PLAIN ENGLISH

Communication   The ability to transmit information, thoughts, and ideas so that they are satisfactorily understood by a listener or listeners.

As a leader, you want to satisfactorily communicate information and ideas; however, you also want to communicate them in such a way as to achieve a desired outcome—for example, to convince, motivate, or persuade.

USING LANGUAGE EFFECTIVELY

The first communication tool to master is your own command of language. Practice distilling thoughts into clear, concise, and understandable phrases. Rambling, using slang, and mumbling are not effective.

Try to speak in an audible, clear voice and to speak forcefully in a consistent tone. Speaking forcefully suggests to the listeners that you have power. Mumbling has the opposite effect.

HIGH-IMPACT WORDS

Why settle for saying "We did good this year," when you can say "We exceeded performance expectations this year"? The phrases you use in everyday business communication can have a strong impact on the listeners.

Leaders are expected to motivate and inspire; therefore, a leader's use of words is important. Use words that give force to your speech and have an inspirational effect on your group.

To illustrate this, let's rephrase the following statements:

- Great job.
- Any new ideas, John?
- Maybe that other company just needs to watch out.
- I'm sure we'll figure out this sales problem soon.

The preceding statements may be factual, but they are far from being forceful or motivational. Here are the same statements, rephrased using effective language:

- Absolutely phenomenal job.
- Let's get creative. John, what are your thoughts?
- Our competition has good reason to be worried.
- We're on the verge of making a sales philosophy breakthrough.

The revised statements exude power and control of each situation.

BUZZWORDS

Corporate cultures, and even certain industries, are breeding grounds for buzzwords, or insider terminology that is used within a particular culture.

For example, *offline* is a buzzword recently inspired by Internet companies. "Let's talk about this offline," means that a certain topic should be discussed elsewhere, perhaps not in the context of a meeting, but in a more private setting.

Pay close attention to the buzzwords circulating in your company or industry. Using them correctly could identify you as a player who is aware of the latest trends.

CAUTION

Take care not to use outdated buzzwords. Doing so could result in a loss of credibility, and will probably at least guarantee you a roll of the eyes from listeners who are bored with the term.

USING ANALOGIES AND METAPHORS

Analogies and metaphors help effective communication by giving listeners a frame of reference for understanding a concept.

Analogies imply to the listener that if two situations or people agree in one respect, they are likely to agree in several others. The following are some examples of analogies:

- You remind me of Rocky. Sure, you started at the bottom, but you've got ambition and you're working your way to the top.
- Since every American household has a TV, books are going the way of vaudeville—no one is really interested anymore.
- Sure, your computer may have just blown up and you've lost the project you've been working on all year … but did Scarlett O'Hara give up when the Union soldiers burned down Tara?

A metaphor is a figure of speech that compares two objects not ordinarily associated with each other in order to put the first into context.

Here are some examples of metaphors:

- His business sense is impeccable; he's like a bloodhound that can't be shaken off the scent of his prey.
- We're swimming with the sharks now; watch your back.
- The company is being crushed by the weight of this debt. It's time to cut our losses and regroup.

TIP

You're a leader, not a poet. Don't get carried away with using analogies and metaphors in your speech. You might limit yourself to using them only when a listener is having a hard time understanding a particular concept.

ANECDOTES

Leaders often use anecdotes to weave past successes into inspirational appeals to their groups. Anecdotes are particularly effective because people tend to enjoy hearing them and will remember a point more easily if it's framed in an anecdote.

Subject matter for anecdotes might include the story of an individual whose efforts saved the unit or company from ruin or the effect the company's work has had on a particular customer's life.

The desired result of anecdotes is to inspire the listener(s) to believe that they are capable of achieving similar results. In the preceding two examples, the first lets the individual know that his or her contributions are important and can have a profound effect on the entire organization. The second example helps employees recommit to the idea that the company does provide a beneficial service to consumers and that all of the day-to-day struggles of the business are worth it.

SPEECHES

Leaders are often called on to make speeches. Public speaking can take place in several different settings. Managers routinely address their groups as a whole and are often required to give prepared presentations to peers or superiors. You may also be required to give a speech before a large group. For some sure-fire tips to great speeches and presentations, see "Successful Speeches and Presentations" on page 322.

NONVERBAL COMMUNICATION

Nonverbal communication is equally important as the ability to use language to your advantage. A leader's attitude, gestures, stance, and appearance all tell people that he or she is a leader.

PLAIN ENGLISH

Nonverbal communication   Conveying a message or idea without using words—for example, through facial expressions, gestures, stance, or appearance. Also called **body language.**

EXHIBITING ASSERTIVENESS

A leader must project an air of positive confidence. Part of that confident manner should be in the form of assertiveness. For example, assertive nonverbal communication includes firm handshakes, a relaxed yet forthright posture, and the ability to look other people in the eye.

Kelly was a new manager and wanted to quickly make her mark as a good leader. However, she often slouched during meetings and avoided shaking co-workers' hands. Her shyness also made it hard for her to look people in the eye. Kelly was nonverbally communicating that she was unsure of herself and therefore not assertive.

Jan, who did not have as much experience in the same business, was also a new manager who attended many of the same meetings Kelly attended. Jan made sure to shake hands with her new co-workers, and she always sat a little bit forward with her arms on the table during meetings. When talking, she was sure to meet the eyes of her listeners.

Although Jan didn't have the experience Kelly had, she was able to make a better impression on her new superiors and peers by making them feel confident in her abilities.

FACIAL EXPRESSIONS

Your eyes, mouth, and head convey your attitude more than any other part of your body language. To successfully communicate your leadership qualities, try the following:

- When talking to an individual, give that person your full attention. Looking past that person at another person or off into space will put them off.

- As stated previously, when addressing a group of people, make eye contact. This gives the impression that you really believe in what you are saying.

- Avoid sighing or rolling your eyes when listening to someone else talk. Sighing and eye-rolling give the impression that you are bored. You may be, but there's no need to communicate that fact.

POSTURE

Your posture also is a big indication of your assertiveness and self-confidence. In the preceding example, posture made all the difference in people's perception of Jan's power. When you're standing, stand straight up with your feet slightly separated and pointed outward. If you're sitting at a conference table, lean forward a bit. If you're sitting at a chair in a lobby or someone's office, relax, but cross your legs and use the chair's armrests. Avoid sinking or slouching in chairs.

HAND GESTURES

Hand gestures can be particularly effective at nonverbally communicating your feelings about a particular subject. The "thumbs up," for example, is universally recognized as conveying positive feelings. Some other gestures that may be worth using from time to time include the following:

- Clapping your hands together when things are going right or you hear about a recent success from a group member.

- Using a finger to lend increased weight to a point you're making.

- Gently, but forcefully, punching a fist down on a conference room table to lend weight to a point.

CAUTION

Avoid using negative gestures such as the middle finger in your business relations. Like profanity, such gestures are not appropriate for the workplace.

INTERPERSONAL DISTANCE

When speaking with one person, try to stay close enough to be able to speak in a normal conversational tone. If you're too far, you may give a standoffish impression. If you're too close, you may risk invading personal space, making your listener uncomfortable.

PERSONAL APPEARANCE

Your choice of clothes, hairstyle, and personal hygiene all make a statement about the type of person you are. Although this may seem superficial, a first impression is often made before you open your mouth to speak.

Leaders should dress appropriately for their position. Also, those who aspire to be leaders should dress for the level they aspire to. For example, if you want to be promoted to the director level at your company and all the directors wear khakis and golf shirts, wear the same type clothing to give them the sense that you are one of them.

The workplace has changed over the past few years, with dress codes loosening. No longer are most men required to wear a three-piece suit to work; nor are women required to wear suits or dresses. A general rule for both men and women is to wear clean, pressed clothes, whether they are formal business attire or casual clothes.

Here are some personal appearance tips for men:

- Avoid wearing jeans. Although jeans may be permitted in your workplace, a leader should avoid wearing them on a regular basis. You might limit yourself to wearing them on a light day, such as a day

before a major holiday when you are less likely to have to meet with
superiors or clients.

- T-shirts are not appropriate work attire, unless the T-shirt bears a
  company logo and is worn for a specific reason, such as a company
  barbecue.

- Hair should be kept clean and neatly trimmed. Many workplaces are
  accepting longer hair on men; however, even long hair should be
  neatly groomed and worn in a ponytail if it's long enough.

- In most cases, err on the side of the conservative. If you enjoy showing off your tattoos and wearing jewelry, limit this dress to evenings
  and weekends.

- Keep nails and teeth clean and maintained.

Most of the preceding rules apply to women as well. However, here are some
specific personal appearance tips for women:

- Avoid wearing revealing clothing in the workplace. Femininity is a
  good thing and should be highlighted; however, wearing incredibly
  short skirts or shirts with plunging necklines is not appropriate at
  work.

- Don't wear too much perfume. In moderation, perfume adds great
  flair to personal hygiene. But if you use too much, perfume can be
  annoying, distracting, and the object of ridicule.

Ultimately, use common sense when it comes to your personal appearance at
work.

THE 30-SECOND RECAP

- Communication is the ability to transmit information, thoughts, and
  ideas so that they are satisfactorily understood by a listener or
  listeners.

- High-impact words and buzzwords lend force to statements.

- To give an excellent speech, prepare ahead of time, take notes with
  you, practice, relax, and be ready for questions.

- Nonverbal communication is conveying a message or idea without
  using words. This includes facial expressions, gestures, posture,
  interpersonal distance, and personal appearance.

Successful Speeches and Presentations

In this chapter, you'll learn how to construct and deliver a successful speech and presentation. You'll also learn how to use visual aids to your advantage.

THE IMPORTANCE OF PUBLIC SPEAKING

Leaders are often called upon to make speeches. One measure of your success as a leader will be how effectively you can communicate, not only in a one-on-one situation, but also to large groups.

Public speaking can take place in several different settings.

PLAIN ENGLISH

Public speaking   The act of effectively addressing a large group to orally communicate a new idea or point to the audience.

For example, if you are the head of a product design group at a major car manufacturer, you may need to use public speaking skills in any of the following situations:

- Addressing your team as a whole to reinvigorate their efforts or communicate an important new initiative.

- Giving a presentation to your peers and superiors to share innovations or ideas generated in your group.

- Speaking at an industry convention to carry the banner for your corporation.

- Speaking to investors.

- Heading up an informative session presented to people outside your industry.

Addressing a large group does not only mean speaking in an auditorium. You might find yourself speaking in a conference room or informally gathered around a team member's desk.

SPEECHES

If you are in a position of leadership, the likelihood is that you'll be required to give a speech before a large group. In all cases, the following basic steps will ensure success:

1. **Preparation.** The old Boy Scout motto is a good idea for most situations, not just speeches. By preparing for your speech, you'll be sure to address all the major points you'll need to cover. Many people consider themselves skilled at speaking cold, or without any preparation. However, when speaking cold, an orator is liable to stray from the main point and actually forget to include some important information. This is especially true of those who are new to public speaking.

2. **Notes.** You're not required to make a detailed outline, but it probably won't hurt to carry a basic sketch of your main points on a notecard in case you do lose your train of thought.

3. **Practice.** The mirror is good for more than just checking for gray hairs. Make sure that you are keeping your head up and not focusing solely on those notes, maintaining an assertive posture and sticking to a self-predetermined time limit.

4. **Delivery.** Take a few minutes to relax before delivering your speech. Nervousness can cause a speaker to mumble or rush through words, both of which will detract from your credibility. Also, try to make eye contact with some audience members while speaking. Connecting with your audience is an important means of gauging their reaction.

5. **Embrace spontaneity.** Know your facts and be prepared to take questions from your audience, or modify your speech if you sense that a particular point is not hitting home. As long as you are well-versed in your subject matter, you should easily be able to make small deviations from your outline.

 TIP

A long speech does not necessarily a good speech make. Often, audiences get impatient listening to a speaker, no matter how good, talk about the same subject for an extended period of time. The quicker a case can be made, sometimes the quicker you can win the favor of an audience.

WHO ARE YOU TALKING TO?

In addition to the preceding step-by-step tips, make sure that you tailor your speech to the crowd you're addressing.

For example, Sandy works for an Internet company and needs to speak to two groups in the same day. Sandy needs to explain the importance of the online world to a group of first-graders, then to a group of senior citizens.

Although both of Sandy's speeches will likely contain much of the same information, she'll tailor each speech to make the most sense to the group she's addressing. She might stress the incredible educational resources to the first-graders, while highlighting the merits of e-mail for keeping in touch with far-flung friends and family to the senior audience.

CAUTION

The president and presenters at the Oscars have the benefit of a teleprompter when speech-making. Most of us do not. Don't type up your entire speech and read it to your audience word by word. As mentioned above, brief notes of key points should be enough to help you through your speech.

PRESENTATIONS

A presentation is merely a variation on a speech. What differentiates the two? A presentation usually uses some other medium or component to help along the point, not only relying on oral communication.

For example, in addition to a speech, someone giving a presentation may use visual aids such as prototypes of a product, audio clips, or visual aids.

VISUAL AIDS

Visual aids can be an effective way of selling your point. You can tell a group 50 different ways how new and exciting a product is, but until they see it for themselves, they're not likely to be completely swayed by your enthusiasm.

For example, Lana, a video-game designer, was giving a presentation about her group's newest game. She felt strongly that the game would be the next big thing in the gaming world.

Lana gave a presentation outlining the game's innovations in graphics, action and storyline. She explained to the marketing group how the game's characters were so cute and cutting edge that they'd be sure to have a huge market for crossover products like cartoons, toys, and lunchboxes.

Lana's audience listened patiently to her speech. Having heard the same enthusiasm from most group leaders, the audience was skeptical. It wasn't until Lana dimmed the lights and gave a fully functional demonstration of the game that she won over the crowd.

Visual aids can take on several forms, from the cheap and basic to the expensive and elaborate. The visual aid you choose to use will depend on your crowd, your subject matter, and your budget:

- **White board or chalkboard.** Both serve the same function of allowing you to illustrate a point graphically while giving your presentation. You might use a white or chalkboard to illustrate a design concept or make lists of ideas brainstormed by your audience.

- **Photocopied handouts.** A photocopied handout might contain the main points of your speech or be used to illustrate points with statistics or graphs. The advantage of a handout is that it gives your audience something to take away with them when the presentation is over. This will help your audience be able to more easily jog their memories or illustrate your point to others.

- **Prototypes or product samples.** If trying to sell a new or already existing product, you might pass around a real, tangible example of that product. For example, if you make stuffed animals and have a new unicorn doll to market, you might bring samples.

- **Audio and video.** A multimedia presentation might be the way to illustrate your point. Supporting material, like testimonials or examples of your concept or product in use could be highlighted using audio or video.

- **Overhead projector.** Stop picturing the prehistoric overhead projector from elementary school. The latest generation of overhead projectors can do everything from printing out what you've written on the overhead to projecting a computer screen.

- **Presentation software.** Several software packages, like Microsoft's PowerPoint, are designed to help you give a richer, fuller presentation. Not only can you create an outline and slides to carry you throughout your presentation on an overhead screen, but you can also print out the presentations to use as handouts. In addition, you can save the presentation to disk to send to far-away audiences.

CAUTION

Don't fall into the trap of thinking that a really neat visual aid will do all the work and carry your point for you. In the final analysis, your speech and subject matter must be the emphasis.

IF YOU GET NERVOUS

If you've ever experienced cold sweats and stuttering when giving a speech or making a presentation, you are not alone. It is common for unpracticed public speakers to get a case of nerves or an anxiety attack when confronted with a room (no matter the size) focused entirely on you.

Remember that the nerves usually only last for the first few minutes. Once you sense that your audience is responding to your presentation, you'll realize that the focus is on the subject matter, not you.

The following tips should also help you through a case of public speaking jitters:

- **Know your material.** Try to avoid getting in the situation of giving a speech or presentation on unfamiliar subject matter. If you know your stuff, you'll get past the few minutes of nervousness once the facts you so carefully studied come to your aid.

- **Relax.** Take a deep breath and don't rush yourself. Unless you're participating in a timed debate, there's no need to deliver your speech or presentation at break-neck speed.

- **Don't mention it.** Don't tell your audience about your case of nerves. They probably didn't notice it and if you mention something, you'll be alerting them to the fact that you're less than at ease.

- **Get more experience.** Try to practice public speaking, in small and large forums, as often as possible. For example, you might practice in front of the mirror or your family. Or better yet, make it a regular event to speak to your staff. This will give you the confidence of speaking to an audience while in a familiar setting.

The 30-Second Recap

- Public speaking is the act of effectively addressing a large group to orally communicate a new idea or point to the audience.

- Steps to giving a successful speech are prepare, make notes, practice, and embrace spontaneity.

- A presentation usually uses some other medium or component to help along the point, not relying on oral communication only.

- Visual aids include paper handouts, white and chalkboards, product samples, audio and video materials, overhead projectors, and presentation software.

- If you get nervous, relax and rely on the fact that you know your material.

Managing Performance

In this section you'll learn how to set goals for your group, how to encourage teamwork, how to manage telecommuters, and how to use feedback and rewards.

SETTING GOALS

As a leader, it is your job to have a vision for the work your unit or organization does and how that work is to be accomplished.

But how can you make sure that your vision becomes a reality? A large task, such as creating a new ad campaign or starting a new season for a sports club, can seem daunting. To ensure success, you will need to break that large task down into attainable *goals.* Breaking a job down into its simplest form makes it more probable that the job will be done and done right.

PLAIN ENGLISH

Goals   Specific metrics you set for your group to accomplish. Goals benefit an organization in two ways by giving you a way to measure performance and by creating a realistic, simpler way to accomplish large tasks.

For the manager whose team is working on that new ad campaign, that may mean setting a goal-oriented timeline that specifies that certain parts of the job be done in increments. For example, the outline of the advertising concept is due in week one, the copy in week two, the artwork in week three, and so on.

Or for the coach of the sports team at the beginning of a new season, it may mean tasking a particular player to improve his swing or kick by a small amount in that season. Improving even one player's performance by a small increment can have a huge benefit for the team as a whole.

GROUP GOALS

To ensure that your group is working to fulfill your vision, you must make sure that you have clearly communicated your expectations to them. A team cannot function without knowing your idea of the group's immediate and long-range goals and, if you work in a corporate environment, the goals and vision of the larger organization.

MISSION STATEMENTS

This is where a mission statement may come in handy. A mission statement is a small document that outlines the overarching business philosophy and ultimate goal of your organization.

If your company has a mission statement, make sure that you have a copy of it handy. You could post it in a common area that your group uses.

America Online's mission statement is "To build a global medium as central to people's lives as the telephone or television ... and even more valuable." This statement is posted throughout the company's offices on plaques. Although this is clearly not a goal that could be achieved in a year, employees are aware of what they are all working toward and can think about their work in relation to that mission statement.

If your company does not have a mission statement, or you are leading a smaller group or organization, try crafting your own mission statement.

THE MEASURE OF SUCCESS

Any industry has measures of success. If you're a sports team, you have a record of wins and losses. If you are a media company, you have your ratings in relation to other media companies. If you are a sales team, you have sales figures.

Don't keep the measures of success a secret from your staff. Hold regular meetings to let them know how successful their work is and what they'll need to do to improve their standings.

TIP

Give your staff the benefit of knowing your organizational goals through a mission statement or by sharing your unit's metrics with them. Remember, they can't do what you want until they know what you expect.

INDIVIDUAL GOALS

As stated previously, to function as a unit your staff must be aware of overall organizational goals. However, your people must also have individual goals.

As stated in the definition at the beginning of this section, goals give you a way to measure an individual's performance compared to other staff members and against his or her own past performance.

There are some rules for goal-setting that you should know before having the first meetings with your staff:

■ **Have a job description.** The most important aspect to goal-setting for individuals is to make sure they have a job description. It sounds simple, but many organizations don't think giving employees clear and detailed job descriptions is a priority; instead, they expect employees to figure it out on their own. This can result in lost time while an individual does the figuring out, as well as more lost time and resources when the individual arrives at the wrong conclusion.

■ **Have realistic expectations.** Make sure the goals you set for an individual are realistic. For example, Ken asked Sandra to write a 200-page report by the end of the week. This was an unrealistic goal.

■ **Be specific when assigning goals.** The method of measurement must be clear. For example, Charles asked Amy and Chris to each create 10 Web pages for the company site. Amy finished her portion of the pages in two weeks, whereas Charles finished only half of his work by then. Charles should not be penalized because a time limit was not set. To take this one step further, Amy may have seen time as the most important factor in the assignment, whereas Charles may have considered research and well-rounded pages to be the top priority. You must be as specific as possible when assigning goals.

■ **Distinguish between formal and informal goals.** There are several types of goals for individuals. It must be made clear whether a goal is formal or not and whether a specific reward is tied to the accomplishment of that goal. For example, are the goals written on paper and tied to a yearly review, or are the goals more abstract? An abstract goal might be asking an employee to casually learn more about a given aspect of the business.

Although goals can go a long way toward keeping your staff on track, mistakes will be made. Practice tolerance. Employees can often learn just as well from their failures and mistakes as they can from their successes.

Fostering Teamwork

Goal-setting can help an individual to realize a higher level of personal achievement. You should place an equal emphasis on encouraging teamwork within a group.

A healthy level of competition is good and can keep employees striving to do a better job. Taken too far, however, that competition can become a detriment as the various individuals that make up the whole fail to pull in the same direction.

To encourage and cultivate teamwork within a group, a leader might do the following:

- **Build trust among staff members.** Encourage honesty and the open expression of opinion among group members.

- **Reward people who contribute to the team.** A leader might make a point of the importance of teamwork in an individual's evaluation. Let employees know that they are not only judged on personal achievement, but also on their ability to sacrifice personal glory for the greater good of the unit.

- **Use terms like "we" and "us" when referring to your group's work as a whole.** This will reinforce the idea that they were an integral part of your unit's performance.

- **Handpick your team.** Nothing encourages teamwork like actually handpicking a team. Choose members of your group who you think could potentially work well together and assign a joint project to them.

CAUTION

Don't let teamwork stand in the way of dealing with an employee who is not performing up to the standards you've set. The team environment can make it difficult to recognize and correct subpar performance. Be aware of whether team members are pulling equal loads.

Managing Telecommuters

Personal computers, modems, and the Internet have made it possible for a growing percentage of the workforce to work from home. *Telecommuting* is particularly popular with part-time employees who may have more than one job, mothers who want to remain on the job while raising small children, and those who would just rather not deal with the hassle of a commute on a daily basis.

PLAIN ENGLISH

Telecommuter An employee who works from home, often linked to a central office by computer.

This new cyber workforce creates new challenges for today's leaders. It is difficult to ensure that employees with no immediate supervision will actually perform as well as employees in a typical work environment.

Give these employees a sense of teamwork and accountability in the following ways:

- Send e-mail and make regular telephone calls to keep the employee in the loop.

- Include these remote staffers in group meetings. Most conference rooms are now equipped with speakerphones. However, if geographically possible, ask your telecommuters to come in to the office for departmental meetings and other important events.

- Establish clear measures of success, since you can't be there to look over the shoulder of someone who is working from home.

- Request a weekly report from your at-home workers each Friday to keep up with what they've been working on.

FEEDBACK AND REWARDS

Although feedback and rewards are two different aspects of reacting to your employees' work, they are often tied together. For example, after landing a major new account, Jennifer's boss told her that not only was he pleased with how she performed, but that she would be receiving a bonus for her good work.

Both feedback and rewards give employees a sense of how well they've done their jobs in the eyes of their manager and the organization.

FEEDBACK

Feedback is vital to the health of a unit. A leader must communicate feedback effectively to a staff in order to get desired results and improved future performance.

As a leader and manager of people, you'll be required to give both negative and positive feedback. Both are necessary, although positive feedback may be the easier of the two to communicate.

Positive feedback should be given when an employee is performing a task right, innovating with success, or surpassing previous performance.

Be sure to give feedback that specifies exactly what was good. Avoid generalizations such as, "You're doing a great job." They may not sound believable, and they don't really let an employee know what he or she is doing right.

Negative feedback is also integral to molding or changing a group or individual's performance. Again, make sure that you are specific about the undesired action or behavior and avoid criticizing a person's personality traits.

For example, John continually makes the same mistakes, although his peers and his boss have corrected his work several times. Instead of telling John that he is hard-headed or just not getting it, his boss continues to tell him the exact nature of the mistake and gives him a cheat-sheet to use when performing the task in the future.

The cheat-sheet is an example of the other half of negative feedback. The feedback alone will tell a group member he or she has done something wrong. To correct that behavior, however, you must also explain how to fix the problem or teach the employee how to perform correctly.

TIP

You may also want to solicit feedback from your group members. This will help in promoting a teamwork atmosphere and let employees know that you value their opinions.

You should also draw a clear line between formal and informal feedback. Formal feedback is in the form of written yearly reviews that gauge an employee's performance and are tied to raises and promotions. Informal feedback most often takes the form of oral comments—for example, telling an employee he did a great job on a specific task and how.

You should try to give both positive and negative informal feedback often to keep your employees working in the desired manner.

REWARDS

Rewards for desired performance can take many forms. Along with feedback, rewards are how you let an employee know he or she has done something right.

Rewarding desired performance can motivate a group to push themselves. Rewards make extraordinary individual efforts and teamwork worth it for your staff.

Rewards can take several forms, including the following:

- **Promotions.** When an employee consistently performs up to the standard you have set and beyond it, you might consider promoting that employee. This rewards the employee by giving him or her increased responsibility and stature in the organization.

- **Raises.** Usually tied to yearly reviews, raises are the most common form of rewarding employees. However, most organizations are in the habit of giving raises to employees every year, regardless of performance. There should be a scale outlining a range of raises tied to specific performance. For example, you might give an employee who is reliable but not stellar a 3 percent raise, while giving your star performer an 8 percent increase in salary.

■ **Bonuses.** A bonus is standard in some industries, such as sales, where employees are given bonuses tied to the amount of business they pull in for the company. In others, bonuses are given at the holidays or to reward an outstanding achievement. If you or your organization has a policy on bonuses, make sure your employees are aware of that policy.

■ **Fame.** Complimenting an employee may not sound like a huge reward. However, complimenting an employee on a job well done at a staff meeting or in front of company officers can be extremely rewarding.

■ **Increased trust.** If an employee consistently performs outstanding work and meets individual and team goals, you might reward that employee by giving him increased trust. For example, Jim often accomplishes tasks before he's asked and has saved the company money by streamlining reporting protocol. Jim's boss not only rewarded him with a raise, but gave him the freedom to work in a more self-directed manner.

THE 30-SECOND RECAP

■ Individual and group goals give you and your employees a method for measuring success.

■ Goals can also break down large tasks into more basic tasks, which gives you a higher chance of success.

■ Teamwork makes a group more effective by ensuring that all are working toward the same goals.

■ Stay in regular contact with telecommuters to measure the amount of work done or their success in doing it.

■ A leader must communicate feedback effectively to a staff in order to obtain desired results and improved future performance.

■ Rewards take several forms, including promotions, raises, bonuses, fame, and increased trust.

Improving Your Team

In this section you'll learn how to give your team members more confidence, delegate, and advertise your group, as well as the importance of respecting seniority.

GIVING YOUR TEAM CONFIDENCE

In the section "Managing Performance," on page 327, you learned how to set goals and encourage teamwork in your group. Now you'll read about some more subtle methods of improving your team.

One important aspect of your team's performance is their level of confidence in their leadership, their goals, and their own work. One way that you can project confidence in your group is to show through offhanded actions and words that you believe in them.

For example, Samantha knew her department was capable of raising yearly sales levels by at least 15 percent. They had the products, the know-how, and the time to really pull it off. But she noticed a certain amount of uncertainty and self-doubt in her staff members.

At the next morning staff meeting, Samantha told her group they were getting close to breaking last year's sales record and said, "You guys are going to come in 15 percent over last year if you keep this up. Wow." By stating her desired and attainable goal as a given, Samantha let her team know how confident she was in their abilities.

You can project confidence to your group with blanket statements as well, such as telling an employee she always does a great job. The more specific you make these statements, the more believable they will be.

You can also project confidence in your team in several other ways, including the following:

- **Take ability as a given.** If you're convinced someone can do a particular job, but the person is not sure of his her own abilities, verbally acknowledge those abilities as a given. You might say, "I know you'll be great at this because ...."

- **Give compliments.** A leader should always compliment employees on a job well done. No task done well is too big or small to be recognized.

- **Assign confidence-building projects.** Assign smaller projects that will stretch a team member's responsibility a little bit at a time. The fact that the projects are smaller in scope will allow the team member to accrue successes quickly, building the individual's confidence.

- **Reinforce confidence.** People cannot live on confidence alone. Back up your confidence in your group by rewarding them with raises, bonuses, and promotions, or by recognizing their contributions publicly.

- **Acknowledge the winning team.** Let your employees know they are part of a winning team by referring to it as such. For example, tell them they really make you look good and that their hard work is not going unnoticed in the larger organization. This will redouble each individual's desire to perform and not let the team down.

CAUTION

Concentrate on building your team's confidence, but remember to be realistic. Never lead someone to believe that he or she can do something that is just not feasible. If an individual fails, your statements will have the opposite effect of shattering his or her confidence.

DELEGATING

Delegation is critical to the success of your unit or organization. A leader or manager must recognize that he or she cannot do all of the work alone.

PLAIN ENGLISH

Delegation   Sharing tasks and authority with your team to more effectively and quickly accomplish goals—for example, breaking a job down into simpler parts and assigning those parts to different people in your group.

To illustrate the point, let's look at two units in the same company. Both managers are faced with a tight deadline to get a certain project done for the company.

The first manager understands the critical time element involved. Because time is so tight, he won't have time later to go back to reconsider and recheck work. He's noticed a few mistakes his team members have made in the past, so he opts to do most of the project himself.

The second manager also understands the critical time element and that there isn't much time to review the work before turning it in. However, she feels she can accomplish more by breaking the project into specific parts and delegating each part to a member of her group. That frees her to check the work, since she, too, has noticed some mistakes from her group in the past.

Both managers turned in their projects at the same time. However, the second manager's project was much more complete, thoughtful, and effective than the first manager's, who overburdened himself and ended up sacrificing quality to just get the job done.

Most managers think that they already delegate responsibilities in their group. However, too often the tasks that end up being delegated are mundane, tedious, or extremely difficult.

To keep your group's interest level up, try delegating some of the more interesting and exciting tasks. Sure, it may mean that you have to give up something that you would have preferred to do yourself, such as attend a business conference in a tropical locale, but you'll raise morale by showing your team that you are willing to share the better assignments.

RESPECTING SENIORITY

Leaders often enter a new job situation with a specific idea of the direction they'd like to take and what they'd like to do with their human resources. However, a new leader can create problems by not recognizing the pecking order in an existing workplace and not listening to the voice of experience from employees who have been on the job for a long time.

For example, John had been the director of marketing for a Fortune 500 company for a month. He had a reputation for producing maximum quality in the minimum amount of time at his last job. On his first day, John told his team the results he expected from the group and reassigned each team member to new tasks. Two employees who had been with the department for years told John that his "new" plan had already been tried by a previous boss and that a couple of the people in the group were terrible at the tasks he'd assigned.

John considered himself a good manager and an even better leader, so he thanked the two employees—whom he considered a bit out of line—for their input but told them he would stick to his original plan.

By dismissing the advice of the senior employees, John made two enemies on his first day at work. Not only did he lose their initial support, but he lost the support of the rest of the staff, who respected the two senior employees.

As a result, quality did not immediately begin to rise in the department. John recognized this and decided things would go more smoothly with the senior employees on his side. He was right. Once he listened to their advice again, he realized it was good advice and modified his plan a bit. Quality rose and people were happy.

TIP

Seniority doesn't mean an employee has gray hair or has been with a company for 20 years. In today's fast-paced business world, a senior employee could be a 28-year-old who has been with a company for 4 years. Make friends, not enemies, out of these employees. Often they can speak to the performance history of a department and act as a barometer of the staff's morale.

ADVERTISING YOUR GROUP

Often it is not enough that a unit or group within an organization turns in top performance or provides a key component of the organization's success. If you don't advertise your successes, they could blend into the background of day-to-day corporate work. Advertising your group not only benefits you, but it also benefits your employees and department as a whole.

Senior managers are often not technically literate about the work that different departments in their organizations do. By advertising your group, a leader can make sure senior managers have some idea of the work that's being done.

In addition, if the senior management is aware of the contribution your department makes, it could help ensure that your department is not hit when the budget ax starts swinging.

Some ways to advertise your group include the following:

- **Share accomplishments.** When meeting with your superiors, be sure to mention a recent success your group has accomplished.

- **Share the spotlight.** Mention specific team members who contributed significantly to a success. Your superiors and your subordinates will value the fact that you are not just attributing the success to yourself.

- **Share success with superiors.** When acknowledging an individual or team's work on a particular success via e-mail, send a copy of the message to your superiors.

TIP

Make a point of not advertising your group every time you meet with your superiors. You don't want to give the impression that you are a braggart or insecure about your unit.

Hiring and Firing

As a leader, you are responsible for hiring and firing the members of your team. Although it may seem much easier to give a person a job than to take a job away from a person, both tasks are equally challenging.

Hiring

Like choosing a jury in an important case, hiring your team is a critical decision, one that can have a huge impact on your team's success. You need to be aware of how an individual will change the dynamics of your unit or organization.

When hiring, first consult your company's human resources department to see whether any seminars or company policies about interviewing are offered.

Here are some tips on successful hiring:

- **Interview and interview again.** Interview the promising potential job candidates at least twice. The second interview gives you the luxury of finding out whether you get the same impression twice. Some people will put all of their energy into one typical interview. The process of performing a second time may force a job candidate to give more than the usual interview answers.

- **Don't be the only interviewer.** Allow potential job candidates to talk to other members of your team while interviewing. The answers an interviewee gives to a junior member of the staff may be more relaxed and more enlightening. The group style of interviewing also gives potential employees a broader sense of the culture in your group.

- **Probe for results.** People often speak in broad generalizations about past performance. Ask job candidates to point to specific results they've achieved in the past.

- **Find out about the candidate's behavior and character.** In addition to asking job candidates about specific results, try to find out how their mind works and if their work philosophy will mesh with your team. (This is also known as behavioral interviewing.)

- **Limit your questions.** Remember, some questions are considered discriminatory in interviews. For example, questions about age, nationality, race, or sexual preference are considered inappropriate and could have legal ramifications. Consult your human resources department if you are not sure about a particular question.

CAUTION

The interview process can be as short or as long as you deem necessary. Some swear that a first impression is the right one, but take your time and interview thoroughly. Spending the time to hire the right person will keep you from having to deal with problems in the future.

FIRING

No matter how arduous the process of hiring employees may be, firing is something that most managers never get used to. But part of successful leadership is knowing when to cull the herd and taking the required action.

If you notice a member of your team is consistently not performing up to the standards of the group, first meet with the individual to determine the reason for the subpar performance. Employees can often be affected by trouble outside the workplace, such as a souring relationship, financial difficulties, illness, or a family member's illness. In these cases, the best course of action may be to simply let the employee know you are there and that you understand the conditions leading to their diminished performance.

In all other cases, such as good old-fashioned laziness or stubbornness, consider giving the individual a warning before taking the steps to terminate employment.

For example, Stacie was new to the department and had never been pushed to perform at her last job. She was consistently doing less work than the other employees, which was lowering the overall quality of work done by the department and creating resentment in the other employees.

Stacie's manager, Vince, decided to meet with Stacie to find the cause of her lack of commitment to her job and give her a written warning that she needed to improve her performance. Confronted with the written warning, Stacie realized that she needed to apply herself. Over the next six months, Stacie improved her performance considerably. Vince congratulated her on the improvement and let her know her job was secure.

If none of the preceding reasons or warnings work to improve an employee's performance, you may need to terminate that employee.

Again, consult with your company's human resources department if it has one. If not, you can find rules for terminating employment from local and federal government agencies or a lawyer who specializes in labor issues.

THE 30-SECOND RECAP

- To project confidence in your group, show through specific and offhanded actions and words that you believe in them.
- Delegating means sharing tasks and authority with your team.
- Advertise your unit's successes throughout your organization to ensure credit and recognition for your team.
- Hiring new employees is a critical decision, one that can have a huge impact on your team's success.
- To hire successfully, interview more than once, allow several group members to talk to the job candidate, and avoid discriminatory questions.
- When an employee's performance is not meeting standards, try to determine the cause of the trouble or give the employee a written warning.
- If you must terminate an employee, consult your human resources department, a lawyer, or the appropriate government agency to make sure you are terminating employment correctly.

Worst Leadership Mistakes

In this chapter, you'll learn about some of the common pitfalls people in a position of leadership fall into and how to avoid them.

Although a leader may strive to manage performance, inspire her team, and gain the support and trust of that team, things don't always turn out as planned.

 CAUTION

Don't overestimate yourself. If you go into a leadership situation thinking you're prepared for and capable of handling any and every situation, think again. A modest amount of egotism is inherent in any leader, but a true leader also recognizes the fact that she will learn as much from her team as her team will learn from her.

If a new leader, you may find yourself in a situation where you are expected to manage a team that has been allowed to become lethargic—in other words, a team that is not used to being led by an effective manager.

Or you may have an ideal team except for one problem employee. One bad apple may not spoil the whole bunch, but can go a long way toward derailing the goals of the whole bunch.

Last, the new leader may let his lack of management experience show by overreacting or letting his team see that they are capable of playing on his weaknesses.

Whatever the case, there will be bumps along the road for any manager or leader. Why? Because managing humans is much harder than managing the most sophisticated computers. Humans are complicated, diverse, and imperfect. While those diversities and imperfections are often things to be celebrated, they provide unlimited opportunities for friction.

This chapter touches on some of the most common mistakes made by leaders, new and old, and offers alternatives and solutions to help avoid these situations.

HEY, WE'RE ALL BEST BUDDIES HERE

A leader is put into a position of responsibility at the head of a team or organization to provide guidance and direction to that organization.

However, some leaders make the mistake of becoming too friendly with their team. While an amicable working relationship with a staff is better than a hostile one, overfriendly leader/subordinate relationships can backfire in several ways:

- **Lack of respect.** If team members view you as "just one of the gang," chances are their willingness to defer to your judgment will evaporate.

- **Lack of motivation.** Team members may start to slack off on accomplishing team goals and even mundane workday tasks. Why should they break their back to impress you when a "friend" wouldn't give them a bad review or withhold a raise?

- **Blurred lines.** The boundary between friendship and inappropriate relationships is a blurry and ever-changing mark. Being overfriendly, physically or verbally, could be construed as flirtation.

- **Leap-frogging.** While a leader may forget his place is at the head of the team, you can bet there's a team member who remembers and may try to quietly bring in a major project on his own. Of course, the first person he'll let in on the secret is your boss.

In the final analysis, no one wants to work for an ogre, but employees will be much happier working for someone who sets limits and does not try to be their best friend.

MICROMANAGING

Have you ever worked for someone who looked over your shoulder and seemed to always be ready to do your job for you? If so, you've been in the presence of a micromanager.

Micromanagement is the subject of the section "Avoiding Micromanagement," on page 351. So briefly put, micromanagement is the practice of exercising an undue amount of control over one's team. This usually stems from a lack of trust or a feeling of being out of control.

Micromanagement does not work. A leader's job is to identify a vision for the organization, set goals, and delegate authority and tasks to accomplish those goals.

The micromanager tries to accomplish everything himself and ends up with either subquality work or several unfinished tasks.

The solution? Learn to loosen the reins and delegate.

THIN SKIN

As a leader, your qualities must include the ability to stay above the fray. Don't take things personally, even if a team member baits you with a snide remark or hostile behavior.

For example, Dan had been the head of the textile department at a North Carolina furniture manufacturer for a year. In his short tenure, his department's productivity and quality had sky-rocketed, largely due to his unorthodox and easy-going management style.

However, one employee was always going after him during meetings. If Dan was giving a presentation to his group about a new process, Bret would interrupt and tell him in no uncertain terms that he thought the idea was bogus and that he had a better one.

Sometimes Bret was right, but even so, he needed to learn that there is a time, place, and polite way to debate with his boss.

After several such incidents, Dan lost his cool, called Bret into his office and told him he would be transferred to another department because Dan could not work with him anymore.

Needless to say, Dan reacted inappropriately. He mistook Bret's attacks as being directed at him, instead of at the subject matter of his presentations or ideas.

To defuse Bret's interruptions, Dan might have instituted a new policy of asking his entire team to hold all comments until the end of his presentations or even asked them to send their comments via e-mail.

As a leader, you do the getting along. Never let an employee see that she is capable of getting to you and pushing the right buttons.

Do as I Say, Not as I Do

A leader must be prepared to live by the rules she sets for her team. Asking your team to put in excessive hours or maintain certain standards will be meaningless unless you, too, work excessive hours and adhere to those standards.

TIP

Sometimes the best lesson a leader can give is to roll up her sleeves and show her team how she expects them to work. You may not even need to let them in on the fact that you're trying to get the same performance out of them. Often, the example stands on its own.

Don't Forget to Tip

If a waiter gives good service, the societal norm is to leave that waiter a tip. The better the service, the better the tip. The same applies to the work done by your team.

As discussed in the section "Managing Performance" on page 327, valued work behaviors must be outlined, then rewarded when achieved. Too often, employees strive to produce excellent results, only to find that the promise of a raise or increased responsibility will not happen.

Once employees realize that the raise is never coming or that you are trying to limit their careers by keeping them in the same jobs, they'll decide to move on.

My Cousin Vinnie

Sometimes the tendency for a new leader is to replace key employees with people that leader has worked with in the past.

Sure, you've worked with this person, so you know he'll work hard and probably deliver any objectives that you set before him.

However, if you assume leadership of a new group, then set about either firing existing employees to make room for your desired hires, or create new positions for those hires, you're likely to win one big prize: the animosity of the rest of the staff.

While they may have welcomed you with an open mind, they'll start resenting you if you immediately pass them over for promotions.

When you assume a new leadership position, take some time (if you have it) to evaluate the group you've been charged with leading. You may be surprised to find a group, or individuals, who work hard and are ready to take their efforts to the next level.

Don't Compete with Your Group

Some leaders make the fatal mistake of viewing their group as competition.

These leaders are constantly keeping vital information to themselves, only to spring it on the staff very late in the game, in the hopes that they will be able to one-up their staff.

Part of the leader/subordinate dynamic you set for your group must be to make sure that your employees understand they work for you, not for your boss.

Let them know that their job is to achieve the team objectives, not to achieve personal objectives. Your job is the same.

And, if you feel an employee is excellent at her work and really should move on, try to facilitate that step up the ladder. You'll be recognized as a true leader and not mistaken for a paranoid dictator.

The 30-Second Recap

Some leadership mistakes to avoid include:

- Being overfriendly with your team
- Micromanagement
- Letting employees get to you personally
- Asking employees to do tasks or perform up to levels you are not prepared to do
- Passing over an existing staff for new positions or promotions to bring in old friends
- Viewing staff as competition

Nonstandard Techniques

In this section you'll learn how to encourage and direct creativity, when to use humor, and how to ethically persuade and manipulate your team.

ENCOURAGING CREATIVITY

The old adage rings true: Two heads really can be better than one, especially when they're freed to think "outside the box."

Creativity can do wonders for an organization. New ideas coming from more than one employee can greatly benefit a company by harnessing the intellectual capital of a staff and encouraging conflict of ideas to arrive at the best possible outcome.

PLAIN ENGLISH

Creativity   Using your imagination to innovate or create something that is not an imitation of anything else.

Different employees are gifted in different ways. For example, whereas Mary may excel at customer service innovations, Scott's forte may be redesigning the way you present printed materials to your customers.

FOUR TYPES OF THINKERS

In a study, the Strategic Leadership Forum found four specific styles of thinking:

- **Knowers.** Best at facts and able to quickly sort data, knowers are good with numbers and technical systems.

- **Conciliators.** Conciliators are able, without words, to intuit things about people, projects, and the best way to do things. Conciliators often excel when they love what they are doing, but can lack discipline and have a hard time completing projects.

- **Conceptors.** Conceptors are able to actually conceive a logical way to accomplish a task that may sound far-fetched at first and then convince skeptics. If conceptors have enough self-discipline, they can go on to make industry breakthroughs.

- **Deliberators.** Most business executives tend to be deliberators. They have the ability to balance several routine tasks while maintaining a rational approach to the business at hand.

After you get a clear sense of your staff's strengths, you'll be able to leverage their thinking styles by allowing them to think creatively.

You may also want to group people who think differently into teams. For instance, Alice may conceive an ad campaign that she knows has the potential to be wildly successful, but as a conciliator she is unable to conceive how to actually pull it off. Realizing this, Alice's boss assigns Joe to help her. As a conceptor, he's able to figure out how to do it and convince the client to take a leap and try the new approach.

TIP

As a leader, you are responsible for figuring out your employees' thinking style, but it may be very beneficial to apply the same magnifying glass to yourself. If you find, like most managers, that you are a deliberator, you may want to spend more time leveraging the intellectual capital of the knowers and conceptors on your team.

HOW TO FOSTER CREATIVITY

So you've realized that you have some knowers, conciliators, conceptors, and deliberators on your team, but you need to get them to think beyond the end of the day.

First, you'll need to let your employees know that the rules are changing. By asking for their ideas or even asking them to think of new ways to do an existing job, you're acknowledging that you are human, you do not hold all the answers, and you're willing to ask for help.

In most cases, this has the added benefit of raising morale. Fostering creativity makes a staff feel appreciated as individuals. Now they'll work even harder to let you know you've made the right decision.

Your relationship with your employees also has to become more permissive, or open and flexible. Your staff needs to know that they can come to you with ideas.

Here is a sampling of some ideas that may help get your team thinking creatively:

- You might want to begin with a good, old-fashioned brainstorming session with a relatively general focus. For example, go around the room and ask each of your staff members to give one idea of a way to improve your unit or product.

- Ask your employees to push themselves to come up with one new idea a week—large or small. A boss once told me that I should be able to point to at least one innovative thing that I had done to improve our business every month.

- Keep your group informed of the challenges your business unit faces. Consistently ask them what they would do to solve a particular problem.

- Make it clear to your staff that no idea is too wild. Employees sometimes fail to innovate because they are scared to mention a good idea they may consider outlandish, inadequate, or silly.

- Let your staff know that it's okay to make mistakes. Not all ideas, regardless of how great they sound and how feasible they may be, end up working.

- Be sure to let the entire staff know when an employee's good idea is implemented.

CAUTION

Make sure your staff understands the difference between discussing a new idea and actually implementing that idea. Employees should never be encouraged to strike out on their own without management's knowledge and approval.

DIRECTING CREATIVITY

Three cheers for creativity, but creativity for creativity's sake could be a bad thing. As a leader, it's up to you to subtly keep your team thinking of your primary goals as a unit.

You might set an example to show your group what kind of ideas you're looking for. Or you might keep a list of the top ten creative ideas your staff has submitted. Last, you might hold a meeting to share innovations other businesses in your industry have accomplished, to get your team thinking outside their cubicle walls.

REWARDS

Consider setting up a financial rewards system, as outlined in "Managing Performance" on page 327, to further formalize the creative process in your organization. Letting your employees know their reward won't be just a pat on the back could get their creative juices flowing.

USING HUMOR TO GET RESULTS

Humor and laughter can be excellent additions to the daily grind. When people share a laugh, they begin to feel less formal and more comfortable with one another. Associating the positive feeling of laughter or happiness with the workplace has the added benefit of making a job or task enjoyable.

But how to introduce humor? Should you, as the leader, set up a microphone and perform a stand-up comedy routine each Monday morning? Probably not. Remember, you want your staff to laugh with you, not at you.

One way to bring humor into the workplace is to set an example by sharing some personal anecdotes with your employees. For example, chat with an employee about something funny your pet did.

TIP

Although a few "You won't believe what I did" anecdotes can be helpful, avoid ridiculing yourself too much when communicating with your employees. Letting them know you're human is good; letting them know you're too human could erode your power base.

BOUNDARIES

Over the weekend a buddy recounted an incredibly humorous but sexual joke to you on the golf course. You spent the rest of the weekend passing the joke on to more friends. However, stop and think before sharing the joke with your subordinates, and even your equals and superiors.

Although humor is welcome in most settings, the workplace is not the place to share certain comic material. A good way to test whether something is acceptable is to imagine telling the same joke to a group of children. Would it be appropriate? That's not to say employees are children, but often the same subjects that are taboo to raise with children are also taboo in the workplace.

Here's a list of topics to avoid in the workplace:

- Sexually explicit material
- Jokes dealing with gender or sexual orientation
- Ethnic or racial humor
- Religious humor

The 1980s and 1990s saw a huge rise in awareness of sexual harassment and discrimination based on gender, sexual orientation, race, and religion. Although a joke may seem harmless to you, it could be incredibly offensive to someone else.

HUMOROUS E-MAIL

The age of the Internet has brought with it a whole new humor outlet. On any given day, I probably get 10 to 15 humorous e-mails. Although these messages are often funny, it is best to avoid passing them along to your employees in most cases.

Many companies are penalizing employees for using e-mail systems for personal purposes. Forwarding humorous e-mail to your staff could be seen as setting a bad example.

SOCIALIZING

As a leader, you should expect your staff to do their jobs and work in harmony. If you had to stop and read that sentence again, you probably have leadership or managerial experience. Getting a staff to work in harmony, or *gung ho,* is easier said than done.

PLAIN ENGLISH

Gung ho   A Chinese term meaning "work together." The term was first adopted by U.S. Marines in the 1940s.

Using humor is one way to keep an organization in good spirits. Another way is to recognize people as individuals and to acknowledge that they have a life outside the organization.

You can do this by organizing semiregular social gatherings for your group. Even something as casual as declaring each Friday morning bagel day can produce the desired effect.

Giving your team the green light to communicate outside the context of their jobs will help to build camaraderie and relax the atmosphere.

HOW TO ENCOURAGE SOCIALIZATION

Large corporations often host holiday parties to reward employees for a job well done. However, there's no need to wait until December. Here are some ideas for encouraging organized socialization in your group:

- **Breakfast on the boss.** Once a week, or once a month, spring for bagels or doughnuts and/or coffee for your staff.
- **Timeout for birthdays.** Each month, have one small afternoon gathering for everyone in the organization who celebrates a birthday that month.
- **Make friends with newcomers.** Encourage older employees to take a new employee out to lunch. New employees can often feel like outsiders. Jump-start their inclusion in the workforce by giving them the opportunity to cultivate friendships with other employees.
- **BBQ on the boss.** If you have a small enough staff and feel comfortable with it, invite your staff to your house for a barbecue. However, both you and your staff will feel better if you set up rules. For

instance, instead of merely saying that the barbecue begins at 7 P.M., say the barbecue will last from 7 P.M. to 9 P.M. That way, they won't feel guilty for leaving and you won't have anyone in your house until 2 A.M.

How Not to Encourage Socialization

Although some social outlets are a good thing, make sure they remain the exception rather than the rule. Your group needs to continue to identify the workplace as just that: a place where work is done.

The Power of Persuasion and Manipulation

One of a leader's most powerful tools must be the power of persuasion. Some consider leadership to be solely the ability to make people want to do what they would normally not do on their own. Although it encompasses more than this sole quality, the power to *manipulate* your staff is the means to this end.

As a leader, you set goals. As a leader, it is your vision that is being fulfilled. And, as a leader, it is your job to motivate and persuade your group to fulfill those goals and to realize that vision.

Manipulation is often viewed as something untrustworthy or underhanded, and it certainly can be. However, you can safely use subtle manipulation to influence a person to do something that's in the best interest of that person and the organization as a whole.

PLAIN ENGLISH

Manipulation   The ability to skillfully and subtly manage something or someone to one's own advantage or the advantage of an organization. The word manipulate most often has a negative connotation.

Here are some techniques to use when you need to persuade a member of your group to do something:

- **Provide context.** Give a sense of the importance of a particular task or project to the organization as a whole. People can get so involved with a particular task that they forget where it fits into the big picture.

- **Feign ignorance.** If someone has missed a deadline or is not doing a job correctly, pretend you aren't clear about what she is doing and need to review. For example, Bess is a week behind in turning in some sketches that are critical to a big campaign. Her boss, Susan, asks her casually what deadline she had given Bess. Bess, of course, admits to being a week behind schedule. Susan then gives Bess a few more days to complete the project and checks to make sure she'll be able to complete the work in that amount of time.

■ **Make them think it's their idea.** Involve employees in decision-making, but influence them in the direction you've already decided to take. For instance, Frank wants to create a manual for how to work correctly on his team. He knows that Brian would be great for the job of writing it, but Brian does not take well to being ordered to do something. One day Frank mentions to Brian that he is a model employee and that every employee could benefit from his gift for imparting knowledge. Brian then suggests writing the guide himself.

■ **Hand out rewards.** Let an employee know that if he or she performs well on a given task, there could be a bonus, raise, increased responsibility, or even a promotion waiting for him.

Remember, as a leader you have the responsibility of gaining and maintaining the trust of your subordinates. Use your power to persuade and manipulate constructively, and the organization will benefit.

THE 30-SECOND RECAP

■ Creativity can greatly benefit a company by harnessing a staff's intellectual capital and encouraging conflict of ideas in order to arrive at the best possible outcome.

■ Appropriate humor allows employees to feel less formal and more comfortable with one another.

■ Encourage a moderate level of socialization in your group. Communicating about topics other than work can put employees at ease.

■ Manipulation is the ability to skillfully and subtly manage something or someone to one's own advantage or the advantage of an organization.

Avoiding Micromanagement

In this section you'll learn the definition of micromanagement, the characteristics of a micromanager, and how to trust your team and tolerate mistakes.

DEFINING MICROMANAGEMENT

As leaders, we like to think of ourselves as infallible, and often as the only person who has a full grasp of the work our teams do.

There is, however, a fine line between being aware of the work your team is doing and being an outright nuisance to the individuals in your group. If the second half of that sentence sounds familiar, you may be a micromanager.

PLAIN ENGLISH

Micromanagement   Excessively controlling the individuals in one's group. This often stems from a lack of trust or faith in employees' abilities.

Ted was the manager of a moderate-size group of 10 employees at a Web design firm. As an individual contributor, Ted had a track record of turning out incredible pages with innovative designs.

Ted's employees were also gifted Web designers. However, Ted rarely gave them free reign to come up with new designs. In fact, when a group member was assigned a new project, Ted would often tell that group member how the page should look when it was completed and what steps to take to get there. Then, Ted would continually check in with the employee to make sure the project was progressing according to his plan.

Ted's leadership style could only be described as micromanagement. His controlling actions affected his group negatively in several ways:

- Because Ted was treating all of his employees the same way, he constantly had too much on his own plate. By viewing their individual projects as his responsibilities, he consistently overwhelmed himself. This affected Ted's ability to effectively lead and manage his group.

- Ted's insistence on making all decisions and constantly correcting his employees stunted the group's natural creativity, skill, and innovation, the very qualities they were hired for.

- Ted's micromanagement alienated his staff members. Not only did they feel they were being babied, they felt as if their boss didn't have any faith in their abilities. This bred low morale in Ted's group as the employees started sharing their negative impressions of Ted with each other.

- Because Ted insisted on checking employees' work every step of the way, the amount of work his group completed was nowhere near the amount other groups were producing. Senior management noticed this, and it reflected badly on Ted's leadership abilities.

Ted was a micromanager. Paying too much attention to every single detail of the work being done in his group actually had an adverse effect on Ted, his employees, and the work done in his unit.

CAUTION

Micromanagement always backfires! Micromanagement is a trap that will leave a leader bogged down in a morass of details—truly an example of not seeing the forest for the trees. A leader needs to keep a more overall view of the work being done in the group or organization.

Spotting a Micromanager

If you think you may be a micromanager, or you simply want to know how to avoid becoming one, here are some clues to watch for:

- **Twenty questions.** You assign a project to a group member. Every evening on your way out the door, you stop by that individual's cubicle and quiz him mercilessly on the progress of the project.

- **The right way.** You continually check up on the work the individuals in your group are doing because you're convinced they'll botch the job. You feel constantly obligated to enlighten your employees with the correct way to do something.

- **Clock watching.** You keep track of what time each employee arrives for work and leaves, not to mention timing their lunch breaks.

- **My way.** You rarely ask group members for their opinions in meetings. Can you even remember the last time a group member was responsible for a new process in your department?

- **The weight of the world.** You feel as if you are alone at the helm of a group of children. Who are these people and how did you get stuck with such incompetence? Why don't they think more like you?

TIP

Sure, micromanagers pay too much attention to the details. But that doesn't mean that it is wrong or bad for a leader to be aware of the details of the work being done in the group. But when the leader's primary focus shifts from the big picture to the details, it can be troublesome.

Curbing Micromanagement

So you're a confirmed micromanager. How do you change your micromanaging ways and turn your department around at the same time?

To end your tendency to micromanage, try some of the following methods.

DISTANCE FROM DETAILS

It will be hard at first, but to curb micromanagement you must ease yourself away from the details you've been focusing on so closely. Remember, you cannot do everything yourself. You are a manager, a leader, not a team member. Your skills to delegate and manage others must be your prime focus now, even if you are incredibly experienced at the type of work the people in your group are doing.

ESTABLISH TRUST

If you're in the habit of checking up on each of your employees every day and correcting their natural work habits or tendencies, you need to learn to leave them alone. If you do this too much, they may start ignoring their natural business instincts and just think about what you would do in that situation. This stunts the development of an employee's own problem-solving abilities and will make creativity a rare commodity in your group.

To continue the preceding example, once Ted realized he was a micromanager, he swiftly set about changing his ways. To establish trust, he limited the checks of his staff's progress to weekly design meetings in which each employee reported on his or her progress and new proposals for projects.

This allowed the individuals to start showcasing and developing their talent. The meetings also encouraged healthy, competitive debate between the staff members and with Ted.

MISTAKES HAPPEN

Surely, in your years of experience, you've made a mistake. Instead of damaging your career, it is more likely that the mistakes have served as some of your best lessons. Mistakes are invaluable teaching tools that are often more memorable than successes.

You must allow your employees to make mistakes as well. This will give your employees their own experiences with right and wrong and will pay off in their future performance, much like your mistakes did for you.

 TIP

Mistakes can actually give a leader the chance to step in and help an individual who may have been struggling with his or her work. Whereas a micromanager is viewed as controlling by constantly correcting, a manager who waits until an employee makes a mistake is viewed as a coach, stepping in to help only when an employee needs it.

Give Others Confidence

One characteristic all micromanagers share is the belief that they can do any job better than their employees can. This has a crippling effect on the employees' confidence. As discussed in "Improving Your Team," on page 334, projecting confidence is an extremely important part of the development and success of individuals and the team as a whole.

Once Ted witnessed the resourcefulness of his staff in his weekly meetings, he set about building their confidence by complimenting them regularly, asking their opinions on decisions affecting the business unit, and saying things like, "That's a great idea. It never even occurred to me. Thanks."

Being a Macromanager

The key to ending micromanagement lies in learning to trust the individuals in your group and knowing how to delegate tasks to them, or being a *macromanager*.

Once you begin delegating the work, you'll find that you have more time to concentrate on higher-level leadership work, such as charting a course for your unit in the coming months and years.

The 30-Second Recap

- A micromanager is someone who excessively controls the individuals in the group. This often stems from a lack of trust or faith in the employees' abilities.

- Micromanagers constantly check and correct the work people in their group are doing.

- To curb micromanagement tendencies, try establishing trust in employees and understanding that mistakes will happen and are part of the learning curve.

- Macromanagement is a much more effective model for leadership than micromanagement.

Transformational Leadership

In this section you'll learn about transformational leadership, the qualities of a transformational leader, how to plan for long-term success, and how to achieve some relatively quick successes.

Defining Transformational Leadership

As mentioned in "Leadership Styles," on page 309, transformational leadership is the style of leadership a manager uses when he or she wants a group to push the boundaries and perform beyond the status quo or achieve an entirely new set of organizational goals.

When Lee Iacocca took the helm of the Chrysler Corporation, his vision and use of transformational leadership were integral to the renewed success of the American automobile company in the face of the almost uncheckable Japanese car industry of the early 1980s.

PLAIN ENGLISH

Transformational leader   A leader who is capable of bringing about change in individuals and entire organizations, often helping troubled organizations turn around their performance.

Qualities of the Transformational Leader

The qualities of a transformational leader include the following:

- **Charisma.** A transformational leader is one who has a clear vision for the organization and is able to easily communicate that vision to group members. For example, a transformational leader can easily detect what is most important to individuals and to the organization as a whole.

- **Confidence.** A transformational leader has a good business sense and is able to see what decisions will positively affect the organization. This gives the leader the ability to act confidently, inspiring trust in team members.

- **Respect and loyalty.** A transformational leader inspires respect and loyalty in individuals by taking the time to let them know they are important.

- **Expressive praise.** A transformational leader is often expressive in praising individuals and the team on a job well done. Letting them know how much they contributed to one success will steel them for future challenges.

- **Inspiration.** A transformational leader is a master at helping people do something they weren't sure they were capable of doing. The leader achieves this through praise and encouraging statements.

Working Toward Transformation

No matter how charismatic or innovative the leader, transformation of an entire organization, or even a unit, does not happen quickly. Most transformations involve changing the *corporate culture*—often from one of stale clockwatching and low risk to one of innovation, moderate risk, and competition.

PLAIN ENGLISH

Corporate culture   The average and accepted behavior, atmosphere, values, attitudes, dress, business practices, and philosophy in a given organization. Even if you aren't working for a large corporation, you'll recognize that cultures exist wherever people work together in teams.

Changing how a large group of individuals works and thinks is not an easy task. Calling a meeting and telling the organization en masse that they are expected to change will not work. To change the entire organization, a transformational leader must start with the building blocks of the organization: the individual contributors.

Individualized Attention

You have your vision for the future of your group, and your employees are aware of that vision. But no matter how lofty the goal, no matter how big the envisioned win, pep-rally–style speeches often do little to motivate the individual. This is because the individual is often motivated to change only when it is for the greater good of self, not for the greater good of the group.

A transformational leader must evaluate the individual contributors in the organization and discover how to motivate them by playing on their sense of self-interest. This does not mean that if you employ 2,000 people that you need to sit down with each of them and find out how to light a fire in them. However, you could meet with a representative sampling of those individuals.

Also, if you do employ 2,000 people, chances are that you have some intermediate-level managers who could also use some motivation. The philosophy that you pass on to your direct reports will trickle down to their direct reports.

Looking Beyond "Me"

Once you discover how to motivate your group by appealing to their self-interest, try to communicate to them what effect their work has on the entire organization.

Often, when a person realizes that his or her position really does make a difference, he or she will find a new respect for his or her place in the organization. Individuals will then be working for the benefit of themselves as well as the benefit of the organization.

MOTIVATING GROUPS

Figuring out the individuals who make up your unit is only half the battle. The successful transformational leader must also learn how to communicate to groups within the organization his or her vision and the need for change.

Danielle is responsible for running a chain of high-end bakeries. New to the job, she wants to turn the organization around and beat its only competitor. Although she recognizes that the individuals working at each store know their jobs well and have years of experience in the business, she wants to reinvigorate the group and get them to commit to new organizational goals that will position the company better in the increasingly competitive market.

Danielle is familiar with the individuals in her group, but now she must turn to some tactics that will help the group pull together as a team and bring about organizational change.

To do so, a leader can try the following motivators:

- **Rewards.** A leader can raise the group's awareness of rewards for bringing about positive change. For example, if you have a formalized reward system, such as merit bonuses, make sure your employees are aware of the policy. Also, you might make it clear to the group that their success will contribute to a larger win for the organization, which could result in increased business. Increased business, in turn, would come back to the employees in the form of increased prosperity.

- **Urgency.** An integral step in bringing about organizational change is helping your group recognize the sense of urgency for creating that change. A leader might say that if the organization does not change now, it may be too late in the future. For example, most companies in the mid-1990s needed to start paying attention to the Internet and how their businesses would integrate the Internet into their way of relating to the customer. Even companies that have nothing to do with media or communications have developed a strategy for embracing the Internet.

- **Excitement.** To bring about organizational change, a transformational leader must also discover a way to get people excited about being part of a sweeping organizational change—for example, helping the group to understand that their efforts will bring about an industry innovation.

THE 30-SECOND RECAP

- A transformational leader is capable of bringing about change in individuals and entire organizations, often helping troubled organizations turn around their performance.

- The qualities of a transformational leader include charisma and confidence, which allow the leader to influence and inspire the group.

- To inspire a group to organizational change, make sure your employees are aware of the possible rewards, then invest them with a sense of urgency and excitement.

Troubleshooting

In this section you'll learn how to recognize problems early, how to best resolve problems and confrontations, and how to win over a hostile group.

PREVENTING PROBLEMS

No matter how prepared the leader, no matter how grand the vision or inspiring the work, problems tend to crop up. No matter what business he or she works for, a leader is really in the business of people. The individuals and teams that make up an organization are often the most volatile and risky part of that operation.

CAUTION

Don't blame yourself! Just because all your plans aren't going off without a hitch does not mean that you are a bad leader. Remember, people are a volatile work material and do not always perform as expected.

Certainly, using a rigorous interviewing process can minimize problems. An individual's ability to work well with the team is as important as his or her skills.

Interviews give the leader a chance to preview the education, skills, and work experience of a potential employee. Equally important as a person's technical know-how is the candidate's ability to fit into the corporate culture of a given organization.

This means that before hiring someone, the leader must try to determine whether a potential employee can treat co-workers civilly, function as a member of a team, or be comfortable in a largely self-managed position.

Another preemptive step that's gaining popularity in today's corporations is giving seminars to let employees know what is appropriate workplace behavior. Seminars can cover all topics that relate to how employees conduct themselves within the organization—from warning employees about insider trading to asking them to refrain from telling discriminatory jokes in the office.

Even if you work in a smaller-scale company, you can benefit from conducting a seminar for your employees. You might include topics such as your mission statement, accepted behaviors, expected performance, and how team members are evaluated and rewarded.

Just be prepared to stand by the statements and to work under the same conditions that you ask your employees to work under. For instance, if you ask your employees not to wear shorts because they work around dangerous equipment, don't show up for work in shorts yourself. Even though you may not directly work with the equipment, you could be setting a double standard that will cause resentment.

TIP

Once your employees are aware of what is expected of them, try reinforcing that message by creating posters containing that information and hanging them around the work area. This will be a constant reminder of valued work behaviors.

RECOGNIZING PROBLEMS

Despite a rigorous interview process and the best-presented seminars, problems will crop up in any unit or organization. Beyond interviewing and letting your employees know the expected work behaviors, you must learn to recognize problems in the early stages.

The leader who fails to realize developing problems in the team, unit, or organization won't accomplish organizational goals and will probably suffer a loss of authority.

INDIVIDUAL PROBLEMS VS. SYSTEMIC PROBLEMS

You must also recognize the scope of the problem: Is it individual or systemic? Individual problems, as the name implies, are limited to one person—for example, a particular employee who is unable to understand a key business concept.

By contrast, systemic problems involve more than one person and often spread quickly. Examples of systemic problems include misinformation spreading throughout an organization and having a negative effect on morale, or a group of employees using company-owned equipment for a side business.

IDENTIFY THE SYMPTOMS

Some telltale signs usually accompany problems. The following signs apply to both individual and systemic troubles:

- **Negativity.** Employees exhibit a pessimistic attitude. For example, an employee may openly say, "I'll never finish this project on time. I just don't get it."

- **Gossip.** If something is going wrong, you can bet that more than one person in the group is aware of it. To err is human, but so is the tendency to discuss the ills of an individual or organization.

- **Loss in productivity.** Productivity often drops when an individual or unit is troubled. For example, when morale is low, employees can easily develop a hopeless attitude about work, leading to losses in quality and quantity.

- **Challenging authority.** If employees feel there is a problem, often they will attribute the cause of the problem to their leaders. Leaders are the ones who have the vision and set the organizational goals, so when things go wrong on a large scale, employees can lose confidence in the organizational leadership. Employees then begin to challenge the person they consider to be an ineffective leader.

- **Resignations.** Are employees jumping ship? If so, this could be symptomatic of a serious problem. The resignations are significant because the employees would rather quit than continue to work toward the organizational goals.

- **Concrete evidence.** Limited to problems such as embezzlement and workplace violence, concrete evidence includes keeping track of employees' equipment, corporate credit card accounts, and any reports of hostility or unprofessional behavior.

TIP

Keep the lines of communication open with your group members. Much as Sherlock Holmes believed a criminal would unwittingly confess his crime if he kept talking, group members often betray their doubts, fears, and gossip in casual talk with a leader.

Resolving Problems

Now that some of the telltale signals of problems have been discussed, how does a leader take the initiative to confront the problem and eliminate it?

As stated previously, behaviors including negativity, gossip, and a drop in productivity are symptoms of a problem. Be careful not to confuse the symptom with the real problem. A leader must be prepared to take the time to diagnose the real problem behind the symptom.

A Case Study

Bob noticed that his staff was growing increasingly pessimistic after his company announced a coming reorganization. He didn't understand the problem. His unit had continually surpassed its goals from quarter to quarter. And the hint of a coming reorganization had already pleased Wall Street, evidenced by a large bump in the company's stock price.

When Bob finally held a staff meeting to discuss the deteriorating group morale, he found that the employees were concerned that they would lose their jobs in the coming reorganization.

Armed with knowledge of the real problem, Bob assured them that because they were leading performers, upper management had already guaranteed that the department would keep all positions. Soon after the staff meeting, Bob found that his team's morale and productivity were back to their normal high levels.

CAUTION

Don't treat the symptom! When you notice a decrease in productivity or morale, spend the time to find out the real cause behind the symptom. If you take the quick route of treating only the symptom, problems are likely to crop up again later.

Problem-Solving Methods

Whether a problem is individual or systemic, once you've determined the core cause of the trouble it's time to take action and use your problem-solving skills to change a bad situation.

Remember, workplace problems are many and varied, so you will need to evaluate and deal with each one individually. For example, what may work to motivate one employee may have the opposite effect on another.

Some options include the following:

- **Positivity.** If negative attitudes and talk are permeating your team, first find out why. Then dissect the problem, finding a few positives to help turn around attitudes. For example, if a group is reeling from defeat by another unit or company, point out the positives about your team's work, emphasizing how easy it would be to win the next battle with a few minor changes.

- **Honesty.** Gossip can be a huge problem in any organization, having a huge effect on morale. However, gossip is usually a symptom of employees feeling that the leadership is up to something and not being straight with the employees. The best solution is to go to your direct reports and be as honest as you can without divulging sensitive material or strategies. Let your employees know that you are being straight with them.

- **Step-by-step.** Dropping productivity can often be a symptom that your group is unsure of how to proceed or doesn't understand the organizational goals and how their work fits into those goals. First make sure that your staff is aware that their hard work, creativity, and dependability are noticed and vital to the organization. Then try breaking a goal down into more easily accomplished steps. This will help give employees a sense of job satisfaction and teach them the pace at which they need to be working.

- **Don't cave.** If employees are pessimistic and not responding well to authority, don't give in to their whims and demands. A team always needs its leader to be strong, whether or not they currently appreciate that strength.

- **Cut losses.** Not all problems are solvable. If you have continually struggled with a problematic employee and he or she is failing to respond to your best efforts, it may be time to consider letting that employee go. A leader must be prepared for the eventuality of having to "cull the herd" from time to time to maintain a healthy and productive organization.

TIP

One important aspect of the problem-solving cycle is to keep detailed notes. You might make a file for each of your employees and add a note each time that employee is involved in creating or solving a problem. That way, you'll have a track record to refer back to when you need to judge an employee's good or bad work behavior.

CONFLICT RESOLUTION

Heated moments can often arise when a group is working together under stressful conditions. However, depending on an employee's temperament, confrontations can occur even on the best of days.

No matter who is at fault, it is up to the leader to resolve conflicts on the team. Whereas debate is healthy, conflict leads only to lowered morale. Often, a conflict involving only one subordinate can affect the entire team, galvanizing employees against the leader.

To resolve a conflict, use these steps:

1. **Remain calm.** The employee who initiated the conflict is likely in a very excitable, volatile state. If you are in the same condition, the chances of coming to a resolution are very small. You must remain in control of the situation and avoid giving the employee the sometimes-desired reaction of seeing you shaken.

2. **Seek privacy.** If the conflict was initiated in front of other group members, ask the employee to go with you to your office or a conference room to discuss the conflict out of the way of prying eyes and ears. The less disturbance the conflict creates for the group, the better.

3. **Determine the real issue.** When an employee feels strongly enough about something to act out, he may cloud the issue by making far-flung accusations and ultimatums. You need to get to the heart of the matter and find out what is really upsetting him. For example, an employee may personally attack your character because he is upset about his salary. Although you may think that he just dislikes you, the real issue is that he dislikes his salary.

4. **Meet the problem head on.** Don't dance around the issues. Now is the time to engage in the conflict and acknowledge any correct facts presented by the angry party. Then either agree or disagree with the party. In the example given in step 3, a leader might say, "You're right, your work is worth a lot more, but you haven't been here very long. You haven't even been through a yearly review yet."

5. **Solve the problem.** Work with the individual to figure out how to change his or her belief that there is a problem. Or if there really is a problem, work on how to alleviate that problem. You might ask the employee how he or she would solve the situation or what he or she would do differently to avoid the problem in the future. Again, to use the example in step 3, a leader might ask the employee to list the reasons his salary should be increased and ask the employee to make a convincing case for an early increase.

Winning over a Hostile Staff

If you are a new leader or are heading up a group that has just gone through a restructuring or layoffs, you are likely to encounter a hostile staff.

In addition to giving their skills and talents, people often make an emotional investment in their work environment. They get used to a particular routine or niche. They get very close to the individuals with whom they work. They also often feel as if they know more about the business than the leaders do.

When that world is rocked, they can become hostile toward the leadership. For example, an individual has been working in the same department for five years. Recently his company was bought by a competitor and his department was downsized. The remaining department was reorganized into a different division and he lost several co-workers.

The employee in question probably isn't thinking that the reorganization and layoffs have made the company leaner and stronger. He is thinking that things were fine the way they were and good friends are now out of a job.

Getting a hostile staff to understand new organizational goals and to return to productivity can be extremely difficult. A hostile staff delivers conflict on a grand scale, but many of the steps for dealing with individual conflict (listed previously) also apply.

Additionally, the following may help:

- Get the group together and let them know that they are still there because of their skills and professionalism.

- Help the group to recommit to old or new organizational roles by restating them and underscoring how the team will contribute to them in the future.

- Reward the group in some way. Have an offsite bowling party or take the entire staff to a movie.

- Take the time to talk to individuals on the team. You may find that when you talk to them one-on-one, employees have a hard time being as hostile as they are when in a group. Connect with each individual about something positive.

- Give the group time to heal. Company upheaval is a difficult time. Once the dust settles, employees will often resettle into a new routine.

The 30-Second Recap

- Interviewing rigorously and giving standards seminars for existing employees can help prevent problems before they start.

- If there are problems in your unit, you'll usually start to see symptoms, including negative attitudes, gossip, a loss in productivity, resignations, or even physical evidence such as missing equipment.

- Treat the real problem causing the symptoms, not the symptoms themselves.

- Some problem-solving techniques include positivity, honesty, breaking tasks down into simpler steps, remaining strong as a leader, and letting an employee go if repeated attempts at problem-solving have failed.

- To resolve a conflict with an individual, remain calm, diagnose the actual problem, meet it head on, and work with the individual to achieve a solution.

- To win over a hostile staff, try letting the staff know how important and recognized their work is to the organization, talking to each individual in the group separately, and attempting to connect with each person on something positive.

- Keep notes detailing when employees contribute to problems or problem-solving.

Nurturing and Mentoring

In this section you'll learn how to help your staff grow their talent, and how to be a role model and a mentor.

GROWING YOUR STAFF

Growing a staff is an important part of realizing your organizational vision and goals. Much like a plant needs water and nutrients to survive and bear flowers and fruit, employees must be nurtured and given the benefit of rich experience if they are expected to continually improve their performance.

PLAIN ENGLISH

Growing a staff The time and effort used to educate, improve, and empower your team.

For example, when you take over as the leader of a team, group, or organization, you are instantly at the helm of a ship staffed by a crew, large or small.

That crew may be getting the job done, but is it being done in the most effective way? Is the crew happy? Are crew members educated and motivated enough to figure out a better way themselves?

The reasons for growing a staff are many, benefiting the employees, you, and the organization. The reasons include the following:

■ **Skill levels.** By taking the time to mold your staff—as a group and as individuals—you'll improve the standard of the work being conducted. Employees will have more specialized knowledge, enabling them to make more specialized decisions.

■ **Happiness.** Employees feel best when they feel they are in motion. By giving them a chance to grow as individuals, morale will improve. Even if their job description remains the same, they'll be able to more creatively attack their work.

■ **Retention.** If an employee perceives that you are interested in his or her growth, you are likely to make an ally of that employee. Taking the time to nurture that employee can build loyalty and help keep a valuable staff member in place.

Empowering employees is a positive work experience, one that can transcend the organizational politics and improve the bond between you and your team.

Nurture, educate, care, and listen. Investing in your group members always guarantees a solid, exponential return.

CAUTION

As your staff's talent, ability, and grasp of the business improve, some group members are likely to realize their own high growth potential. You will probably suffer minor setbacks when losing a valuable group member to a better job or even another company. Be happy; this is one of the best indications that you are giving your employees important skills.

SUPPORTING EDUCATION

Education can take employees away from immediate job duties; however, corporations are quickly realizing the value of helping their employees acquire more and specialized knowledge.

By helping employees earn their GEDs, learn to speak English or a foreign language, learn a specific skill, or get a Master's degree, companies are demonstrating an increasing awareness of the benefits of more education.

INFORMAL SEMINARS

One form of education that is fairly easy to introduce into a unit or organization is a *seminar.* You may begin by dedicating one staff meeting a month to educating your staff on a specific topic.

For example, Angie wants to help her online magazine staff understand the qualities of a successful Web publication. Although all her employees have journalism backgrounds, only one has previous Internet experience. Angie decides to hold a regular Thursday staff meeting to concentrate on helping her staff to think in terms of the Web.

Each Thursday, Angie gives a presentation about a specific successful online publication. She uses an overhead monitor to give examples about what works on specific sites and also gives examples of absolute flops. She also engages her staff by asking them to rate the sites and to think about how some successful principles could be incorporated into their own site. From time to time Angie invites guest speakers who are experts in the field to talk to her staff.

As a result, Angie's staff are very aware of what plays well on the Internet and are also extremely interested in their work now that they have detailed knowledge of the myriad options available to them.

CORPORATE EDUCATION PROGRAMS

Some larger companies now house their own education departments. These in-house programs usually concentrate on topics relating to how business is done at the company. For example, at Angie's company, classes may range from basic HTML to how to use common Windows applications to how to conduct effective interviews.

The wider the opportunity for taking classes in the workplace, the more contented the workforce. Employees can point to the solid *transferable skills* they've acquired in the workplace, even if they have no intention of leaving.

PLAIN ENGLISH

Transferable skills   Skills learned at one workplace that would be beneficial for gaining employment elsewhere. For example, HTML is the most commonly used language for putting content on sites on the World Wide Web. A skill such as using HTML, which is not proprietary to one company, is a transferable skill.

EDUCATION REIMBURSEMENT

Another program gaining popularity in today's workplace is *education reimbursement.* Companies set up programs that pay for an employee's higher education tuition if their field of study is deemed work-related. Often the individual is required to make a certain grade-point average to be eligible for the reimbursement.

If you work in a large company, check with your human resources department to find out whether your company participates in a tuition-reimbursement plan. If you work in a smaller setting, perhaps raise the idea of starting a partial reimbursement program.

BE A ROLE MODEL

"Do as I say, not as I do" is not a sound practice for people in leadership positions. As the head of a team, group, or large organization, you are the most visible representative of your team—both within and outside your group.

Leaders often expect high quality out of employees and expect them to perform to certain standards without applying those same standards to themselves. Remember, being a leader does not make you exempt from work, fairness, or ethics. In fact, these qualities become even more important as you are looked to as an example.

TIP

Mixed messages occur when you say one thing but your actions reveal a different truth. For example, you say you value honesty, but an employee catches you in a lie.

Some of the valued behaviors for role models include the following:

- A leader should not shy away from work. If you know your employees will need to ignore the clock and work extra hours to get the job done, show your employees that you, too, are not afraid to stick around the office after hours. This example will communicate to your staff that you are committed to getting the job done, no matter how much overtime it means.

- A leader should also be aware of the kind of business the entire organization and the specific unit is engaged in. For example, leaders are often chosen because of their leadership abilities, not because they are specialists in a given business. Smart leaders make it their business to become specialists once they are on the job.

- Communication cannot be stressed too much. Today's professional has available so many different ways of communicating: traditional mail, the telephone, e-mail, instant messages, and good old one-on-one conversations. Show your employees that you are equally comfortable using several different communication media. A leader who confines his communication to e-mail could be perceived as cold and distant.

- A leader must also possess a certain amount of care and concern for his group members. Have respect for your team; remember that not every day is a good day.

- As mentioned previously, integrity is the foundation of any leader's ability to garner respect. As a leader, you have a responsibility to deal honestly and fairly with your subordinates. Employees owe a boss loyalty and obedience; however, respect is a quality that can only be earned.

MENTORING

Beyond offering education and being an ideal role model for a group, a leader can also greatly help some employees by serving as a mentor.

A leader should be constantly reviewing subordinates for those who can and should advance within the organization. Never fall into the trap of worrying that a bright subordinate will one day eclipse you. The reverse is true: You will be correctly perceived to be an excellent leader when you demonstrate the ability to debut first-rate protégés.

The group member who would respond well to a mentoring is not difficult to spot. You're looking for employees who continually surpass marks set by others, employees who think outside the box and are not afraid of sharing innovative ideas.

For example, John heads up a large unit in a mid-size company. He's responsible for over 20 employees, directly and indirectly. His unit is known for high-quality work, which he attributes to a dedicated group of employees who pull together as a team. However, lately he's noticed that one employee, Laura, has pulled ahead of the pack.

Laura innovates, works long hours without complaint, and patiently helps other team members who frequently come to her for help. John is convinced Laura would respond well to mentoring.

A *mentor* can be an incredible help to a developing employee. Much like the apprenticeship relationship in days of old, a seasoned, successful leader can impart significant on-the-job knowledge to the protégé.

PLAIN ENGLISH

Mentor   A person of higher rank or standing in an organization who takes a particular interest in helping to nurture, teach, and guide a promising employee.

A successful mentor fulfills the following roles for the protégé:

- **Coach.** A mentor must remain in close contact with the protégé to help him or her learn fine distinctions in day-to-day business dealings. This continual advice helps the protégé develop skills that would otherwise take years to acquire through trial and error.

- **Challenges.** A mentor will continually find new and exciting work for the protégé to perform. The challenges help the protégé learn new skills and learn how to handle responsibility.

- **Constant feedback.** Once you engage in a mentoring relationship, it is critical to provide constant feedback to your protégé.

- **Support.** The mentor must be prepared for successes as well as failures from a protégé. Try to be there to encourage your protégé to learn from the failures and get past them.

- **Protection.** In a fast-paced and competitive environment, a mentor can also run interference for the protégé, protecting him or her from hostile or difficult high-level managers or situations.

- **Promotion.** As a mentor, you are required to help advertise the merits of your protégé. Let your peers and superiors know how much faith you have in your protégé and what a great future you predict for him. This could help your protégé to be promoted or win increased respect from a wider audience.

CAUTION

So you've found a worthy protégé, and now you want to dedicate most of your time to coaching that person. Be careful! The rest of your team could suffer a loss in quality as a result of resentment. To alleviate this, choose more than one protégé, or pair some junior employees with more senior members of the staff for their own mentoring relationships.

THE 30-SECOND RECAP

- Employees must be nurtured and given the benefit of experience and education if they are expected to continually improve their performance.

- You can improve your team's performance by educating the team members using regular group seminars, a corporate training program, or a tuition-reimbursement plan for higher education.

- Transferable skills are skills learned at one workplace that would be beneficial for gaining employment elsewhere.

- Be a role model to your group. Don't send mixed messages by saying one thing when your actions reveal a different truth.

- A mentor is usually a person of higher rank or standing in an organization who takes a particular interest in helping to nurture, teach, and guide a promising employee.

Women in Leadership

In this section you'll learn about the special challenges women face in getting to and maintaining leadership positions.

WHAT DIFFERENCE DOES GENDER MAKE?

In the past few decades, women have made incredible strides in the workplace. The playing field is now more level than it has ever been in the past.

Women are achieving more and breaking into the higher echelons of management more often. For example, a woman became the leader at one of the country's biggest computer manufacturers in 1999. Carly Fiorina became president and CEO of Hewlett-Packard after her huge success in spinning off AT&T's Lucent Technologies.

Martha Stewart is another example of a woman who defied the odds to achieve incredible success. Stewart turned a catering business run from her basement into a huge empire including magazines, books, television shows, and specials and products bearing the Martha Stewart name. Martha Stewart Living Omnimedia went public in 1999 to great success, completely attributable to the strong woman leading the company.

Although the corporate gender landscape is changing, successful women leaders remain the exception rather than the rule.

TIP

If you want to be a woman leader, start taking the time to learn about other women leaders. Keep up with news about specific women leaders and studies about leadership and gender. You may learn something that will help you down your own path.

GETTING THERE

Women are increasingly taking management roles once mainly reserved for men. Thanks to the pioneering efforts of women such as Martha Stewart and Carly Fiorina, it is now generally recognized that women can and should be called upon to shoulder greater responsibility.

However, there are still some things you can do to help ensure that you are considered for a leadership position:

- **Be realistic.** Don't expect to be named VP simply because you are a woman. If you want to be considered an equal, make it your business to be an equal. This means immersing yourself in your work and improving your skills every chance you get.

- **Know your resources.** What is true for men is true for women, too. The road to success isn't that different for women, so use every resource available to hone your leadership skills. For instance, every chapter of this book applies to all leaders and potential leaders, not just men.

- **Find a mentor.** As mentioned in the section "Nurturing and Mentoring," on page 366, a mentor can be a valuable teacher, coach, and ally when you're negotiating the path to power. Seek out a mentoring relationship. It doesn't matter whether your mentor is a man or a woman.

- **Speak up.** A position of leadership isn't offered to a shrinking violet of either sex. Be forward. Speak up and let your superiors and peers know that you are resolute and innovative. Also, verbally remind your superiors of your past successes.

- **Come out and say it.** If you are ready for more responsibility, but you feel your superiors are not aware or not sure about your ability, nip their fears in the bud by telling them you are not only ready to lead, but ready to succeed. The more confident you are in your own abilities, the more confident others will be in you.

OVERCOMING GENDER BIAS

Hundreds of years of male-dominated leadership resulted in women being considered a more subordinate or submissive sex. Although rare, it is still possible to encounter direct or indirect *gender bias* in the workplace.

PLAIN ENGLISH

Gender bias   Prejudice or discrimination against a person based solely on the fact that the person is of a different gender.

Here's an example of gender bias: Jennifer and Matt started their jobs as assistant producers in the same week. Both were incredibly good at their jobs and worked well with other team members. Their boss, Ken, was equally pleased with the work both of them did.

Over a period of two years, Jennifer and Matt were each responsible for several key successes for their unit. When a senior producer left to join another company, Jennifer and Matt each felt they were the right candidate to be promoted to the open position.

Ken, their boss, didn't really spend much time deciding who would fill the open position. He knew Matt to be a great employee who would continue his success in the new position. He also liked Matt as a person. He could really talk to him, and often they had spent time bantering about work, sports, and life in general.

Without holding interviews, Ken met with Matt only once before announcing to the staff that Matt would take over the senior position.

Jennifer was floored. She felt that her work was equally good, if not better than, Matt's. She also thought it was unfair that the position was filled without giving everyone a chance to at least submit a resume or make a case for being promoted.

Jennifer was right. Ken's hiring of Matt without so much as a thought for Jennifer or other female employees was an instance of indirect gender bias. Ken didn't consciously want to keep Jennifer in a subordinate position. He just assumed that a guy, who he could relate to on a personal level, would be the best man for the job, so to speak.

EQUAL PAY

Let's take this example one step further. Suppose that Jennifer and Matt both had the same job titles, but Matt made a bit more on each of his paychecks than Jennifer. This would be another example of gender discrimination. If Jennifer and Matt perform an equal amount of work, both should be paid the same.

Although there is a federal law requiring equal pay, men continue to make more money than women do. It could be possible that gender stereotypes play a part in this discrepancy. Men are traditionally seen as the breadwinners of the family, and so employers think, perhaps subconsciously, that they deserve more money.

However, federal law also specifies that it is illegal to make employment decisions based on stereotypes or assumptions about the traits or skills of people based on their sex, religion, or race.

Challenges Women Leaders Face

Once a woman has achieved a promotion or has been welcomed into the higher echelons of management, she's won only half the battle.

A woman may have an excellent track record as an individual contributor; she may have a fail-safe vision for the future of her unit or organization; she may even consider herself easy to talk to and equal to the challenge of managing a group of people. However, any woman in a position of leadership must be prepared for certain challenges directly related to gender, such as the following:

- **Learning curve.** Your group may not be used to working for a woman. Give them time to get used to the concept of not only adjusting to a new boss with a new management style, but also to the fact that you are a woman.

- **Challenges to authority.** Some employees may not immediately warm to being directed by a woman. For hundreds of years, our society placed men at the head of the family and painted women as subordinate and not capable of high-level decision-making. Also, since women leaders are still in the minority, you may be the first female manager your employees have ever encountered. Take care to follow through on policies and assignments with which you have charged your group. This will show your team that you hold them accountable for following through on their work and respecting your authority.

CAUTION

Don't create problems for yourself! Don't assume that just because you are a woman, people will have trouble working for you. Don't let paranoia trick you into thinking a problem is gender-based. Most leaders experience challenges to their authority.

If All Else Fails

If you have exhausted every possibility and are confronted with a problem that is definitely gender-related, be sure to document the precise nature of the problem and keep a log of any attempts at mediation.

If a male employee is openly defying your group's goals and making suggestive, snide remarks about your gender, you have a legitimate gender-discrimination problem.

First you might attempt to speak with the employee in question yourself. Make sure that you choose a formal setting for this meeting, such as your office or a conference room, and that your positions relative to each other are in keeping with the power structure. For instance, you should be sitting behind your desk with the employee either standing or sitting somewhere on the opposite side of the room.

Explain that you consider his behavior unprofessional and ask for an explanation. Perhaps there is a deeper issue that is causing him to act out in this way. If all goes well, you may not have to take any further action.

If the behavior persists, however, mention the behavior to your mentor and see if she has any suggestions on how to resolve the situation. Second, make sure to contact your superior and your organization's human resources or legal department.

Human resources may have a standard procedure for dealing with workplace harassment. Human resources should also have Equal Employment Opportunity Commission (EEOC) material on what constitutes discrimination or harassment.

If resources within the organization fail to help, you might consider seeking outside help from the EEOC itself, a lawyer, or a family member or friend.

The best possible solution will be a speedy one. Don't hesitate to bring a close to the situation—whether it ends happily or with the employee being chastised or dismissed. If left unchecked, the employee could prove to be a major distraction for your group.

THE 30-SECOND RECAP

- If you want to be a woman leader, start taking the time to learn about other women leaders.
- Increasing your skills and finding a mentor could help you on the path to leadership and increased responsibility.
- Gender bias is prejudice or discrimination against one gender based solely on the fact that a person is of a different gender.
- Give employees time to adjust to having a woman leader.
- If you are experiencing discrimination or harassment based on your gender, get help from the EEOC, your human resources department, a friend, a family member, or a lawyer.

Young or Minority Leaders

In this section you'll learn about some special challenges that young and minority leaders face.

YOUNG LEADERS AND THE CHALLENGES THEY FACE

What difference does age make? You could argue that experience and the years required to rack up that experience are invaluable and worth as much, if not more than, incredible vision or traditional education.

In the past, the age structure in the workplace was predictable. Young people generally started at the bottom and worked their way up to the top. It took decades to reach the top, by which time they were no longer young. In the past few decades, however, the business world has been undergoing a change in philosophy in relation to age-appropriate roles.

It is probably no coincidence that younger leaders have become more common as technology and computers have become the second Industrial Revolution. Young people tend to be more comfortable with technology than their older peers because most people under age 40 have been using computers since at least their early 20s.

Bill Gates dropped out of Harvard in 1975 to found Microsoft. Considered an upstart by established computer companies such as IBM, he went on to build the most successful software company in the world. At the time this book was written, Gates was the richest man in the world, with an amassed fortune of $80 billion.

Young leaders can often be successful because they aren't held back by *traditional business practices,* certain ways of working in the system that are learned over time. Since young leaders often lack the years of experience, they forge new and different ways to get things done. Often these methods are more streamlined and quicker than traditional ways, which gives them an advantage over the competition.

PLAIN ENGLISH

Traditional business practices   The time-tested, set way of doing things. Traditional business practices are often ignored by young leaders in favor of finding a newer, quicker way of meeting the same goal.

Although all of the previous examples of young leadership have been positive, there are still some special challenges inherent to being a young leader.

The biggest challenge to a young person in a position of power is the very lack of experience that gives him or her the ability to ignore the old way of doing things. For example, Cindy was a newly minted vice president at a large advertising agency. Her group was in charge of several accounts related to products for infants. One ad campaign in particular was failing and in need of a complete overhaul.

Cindy had some great ideas for the new campaign and was eager to set things in motion to take her ideas through to actual advertisements. As a VP she knew she didn't have to wait for anyone to okay her plan.

Cindy thought that one member of her staff in particular was incredibly resourceful, so she put him in charge of the project. He, too, was new to the company, so they felt a bit of camaraderie.

Cindy and the employee in charge of the project pushed the project through to completion, only to find that it did not measure up to certain standards required by the ad agency.

Where did Cindy go wrong? Her first mistake was in assuming that she didn't need to bounce her ideas off of anyone else. Although approval wasn't required, Cindy should have presented her ideas to her staff and opened up discussion on what worked and did not work in the campaign.

Several of Cindy's employees had been with the agency for years and were well versed in what passed muster according to the agency's standards. Those same senior employees were also turned off by the fact that Cindy turned the project over to the newest member of the staff—someone who didn't know the proper channels to go through to bring a project to completion. If Cindy had paired the junior employee with another, more senior employee, the project might have been more successful.

So specifically, Cindy's problems were the following:

- **Inexperience.** Cindy was not aware of the traditional business practices in place at the ad agency. Before defying convention, it's a good idea to find out what the conventional methods are.

- **Lack of respect for seniority.** Cindy should have relied on some of the more senior employees to help her in the first few months of her job. By asking their opinion and enlisting their help, she would have made allies rather than enemies.

Regardless of how good of a young leader you are and how good your decisions are, there will always be a bit of friction from subordinates who are in the same age range or older than you. The best thing you can do in this situation is ignore it. Just continue to lead, making good decisions and relying on your group as normal. If you are a good and ethical leader, your age will cease to be the first thing your employees think about.

Rely on some of the methods discussed in "Improving Your Team" on page 334, for winning over your staff by giving them confidence, delegating, and giving feedback and rewards. Solid management practices should work for any leader, regardless of his or her age.

CAUTION

Don't get flustered! If a subordinate or peer challenges you solely because of your age, avoid confrontation. The other party is trying to draw you into a situation in which you lose your cool. If you lose your head and get involved in an argument, he is likely to say it's because you're young and can't handle pressure.

Try to seek out membership in an association tied to your line of work. You will meet other leaders there, young and old, who can give valuable advice.

You could also seek out a mentor to help you negotiate your first few years of management.

MINORITY LEADERS AND THE CHALLENGES THEY FACE

Minority leaders still face some of the problems faced by women in positions of power. Until the last few decades, women and minorities were a rarity in public office and in the boardroom.

The same challenges and solutions noted in "Women in Leadership" on page 372, apply to those of different races or ethnicities. Still, the best advice remains to let your track record, expertise, and successes speak for themselves.

If you find yourself confronted by an unfortunate situation in which you feel discriminated against simply on the basis of your minority status, first keep a detailed written account of the problem. Then contact your boss and the human resources or legal department to file a formal complaint. If this is no help, turn to resources outside your company.

A family member or friend could provide valuable advice and support. You may also want to contact a lawyer who specializes in discrimination cases. If you are unsure how to find one, you can contact the American Civil Liberties Union (ACLU) for a list of lawyers in your area.

Also, even if you don't experience a huge problem, it's a good idea to seek out a mentor in your company—someone who will help guide you through some of the stickier situations you may encounter.

The 30-Second Recap

▧ Younger leaders have become more common as technology and computers have changed the face of the workforce.

▧ Traditional business practices, often ignored by young leaders, refer to the time-tested way of doing things.

▧ The biggest challenge to a young person in a position of power is lack of experience.

▧ Young leaders should rely on senior staff members.

▧ If you find yourself confronted by an unfortunate situation in which you feel discriminated against simply on the basis of your minority status, first keep a detailed written account of the problem.

▧ Like most leaders, both young and minority leaders should seek out a mentor.

Where to Find Help

In this section we'll discuss some resources designed to further improve your leadership abilities.

No one leader has all the answers. Fortunately, most good leaders realize that having all the answers isn't the important part. The important part is knowing where to find those answers when you need them.

There are several resources you can use to help you improve your leadership skills. From classes and seminars to the World Wide Web, today's leader has no excuse for avoiding betterment.

Have Your Own Mentor

One of the most important allies you can have has already been discussed in detail. The section "Nurturing and Mentoring" on page 366, discussed mentoring from the standpoint of you mentoring a subordinate or peer. However, you should also seek out the reverse of that relationship. Even seasoned leaders admit that there is always someone who has been in the game for a few more battles than they have.

Classes and Seminars

Classes and seminars are a quick immersion technique for learning specific leadership skills. Some colleges and universities offer management and leadership courses in their business schools, realizing the importance of people skills intrinsic to a leadership position. An MBA does not guarantee that you can successfully motivate employees.

Other college courses can also be helpful to future managers. For example, public speaking is effective in teaching you how to organize thoughts and forcefully make a point.

Psychology is another class that may help you to handle leadership responsibilities. In contrast to the kinds of problems that occur when you're working with computers, managing people can be less predictable. Learning how to interpret body language and other signals can go a long way toward helping a leader handle human nature.

Some larger companies include some management classes in their corporate training catalog. For example, your company may offer classes on how to use your time more effectively, communicate better, encourage employees to meet goals, interview, or review an employee's performance. Companies often contract out such classes to companies that specialize in leadership training.

Leadership courses are available also from companies that specialize in leadership training outside the workplace. Some nationally recognized leadership training companies include the Franklin Covey Leadership Center and Frank Lee Associates. You can also find courses in your area by looking in your Yellow Pages under "Career Development" or "Career Training."

Associations

Several associations exist for the sole purpose of helping their members be better leaders. Other associations are more trade-specific, but can also be beneficial and offer some leadership or management help.

Networking is another good reason to seek out and join at least one association. Not only will you expose yourself to a greater chunk of the working world, but you'll also meet other people with goals and career aspirations that are similar to your own. Consult your local phone book or universities to find the associations in your field or geographic region.

The Internet

It would be irresponsible to leave out the vast resources afforded by the Internet. What was once a loose bundle of amateur sites posted by the techno-savvy has become an incredible network of information, offering everything from shopping to online churches.

There are myriad sites relating to leadership and management. To search on your own, use an online search engine such as Yahoo! (www.yahoo.com) or Google (www.google.com) and type search terms like *leadership*.

TIP

When you find a site you feel has accurate, worthwhile information, see if the site has a Links section that offers paths to other recommended sites. This might help you find the good sites a bit more quickly.

Here's a list of sites to get you started:

- **Ninth House Network (www.ninthhouse.com/).** Provides the latest news and resources related to improving leadership and management skills. Browse articles from other publications and keep up with the latest trends.

- **FastCompany.com (www.fastcompany.com/homepage/).** A monthly journal that features articles about leadership challenges and experience. Also offers online discussion forums.

- **The CEO Refresher (www.refresher.com/ceo.html).** A monthly newsletter concentrating on topics in leadership and high-level management.

- **The Harvard Business Review (www.hbsp.harvard.edu/ products/hbr/).** For those who want to delve a bit further into the latest research about today's workplace.

- **New Leadership (www.newleadership.com/frame.htm).** Online resources for women leaders.

The 30-Second Recap

- Having a mentor and taking classes or seminars can help to hone your leadership skills.

- Membership in a trade association will put you in touch with other leaders facing similar challenges to your own.

- The Internet is a vital resource for keeping up with leadership trends.

Organizational
Management
Basics

Organizing Your Staff

In this section, you will learn how to keep your employees focused and on target—and learn how to recognize when they're not.

CONDUCTING A SURVEY

Organizing staff to maximize efficiency requires a process. It begins with surveying, proceeds through an evaluation of the data, and is completed by implementing solutions.

CAUTION

If your organization and staff have a union contract in place, this survey will not likely be allowed. Consult with your immediate supervisor regarding the legal ramifications.

Manuals of organization and procedure may or may not exist in your organization. Regardless, your first objective is to determine the staff's perceptions of the organization's structure. Develop and personally distribute a survey to each member of your staff.

TIP

To remove suspicions or fear, be certain that all staff members understand that the survey intent is to improve the organizational productivity of the department.

The survey should request the following information:

- **Name.** Be sure that all staff members are assured confidentiality of the survey's content. You may want to include a statement to that effect at the top of the survey and not require a signature. Otherwise, it may be best simply not to request a name.
- **Departmental goal.** Let the staff member convey his or her perception of how the department fits within the total organization.
- **Departmental objectives.** This further defines the staff members' perceptions of the department's position within the total organization.
- **Job title.** This standard request often shows a lack of communication and understanding.
- **Immediate supervisor.** Often, this question may evoke an inaccurate response where formal and informal lines of authority are misconstrued.

TIP

Personality testing is one way to establish an employee's strengths. Unhappy employees may be in a position that does not match their natural talents.

- **Responsible for supervising.** You want the job title, not the name of the persons supervised by this individual. Again, this is another source of data for determining any misconceptions of organizational structure.

- **Qualifications for the position.** Let the staff convey their understanding of what qualifications should be required for employment in the position. This response can be insightful in identifying staff shortcomings of abilities required to perform the tasks of his or her position.

- **Responsibilities.** Leave sufficient space for the person to list perceived responsibilities.

- **Comments.** Allow people to convey any feelings and observations regarding the survey, its content, or any other issue. This can add information to help you evaluate the survey results.

Fill in one of the surveys yourself for each staff position based on your knowledge or perceptions in managing the department.

TIP

If none is available, you may also want to draft an organizational chart of your department. Then compare your perceptions with those of your staff.

EVALUATING SURVEY RESULTS

Evaluating survey results is perhaps the most critical stage in this three-step process. Poor evaluation makes the survey effort a waste of resources. Likewise, poor evaluation will likely result in poor decision-making toward any actions implemented to improve organizational structure and any improved productivity. Be patient, thorough, and objective when evaluating results.

Furthermore, your decisions will impact the work lives of your employees and the overall environment in the workplace. You are attempting to improve productivity, but simultaneously, you will inadvertently address workplace morale and relationships between employees at all levels of authority within your department.

When the surveys are returned, compare them to your manuals or personal survey. Look for consistencies and inconsistencies in these areas:

- Are job titles and descriptions understood, and do the responses reflect the nature of the job?
- Are lines of authority clearly understood, or does the informal organization have an adverse impact?
- Do your employees understand how the department fits within the total organization, or could there be signs of a lack of communication between departments?
- Are there signs of duplication of efforts?
- Are employee perceptions of job qualifications consistent with actual company needs?
- Do written comments demonstrate harmony and confidence, or suggest problems between employees?

These six items listed provide specific categories of evaluation. There may be more, depending on the nature of your organization. For example, if you work in a nonprofit environment, there may be issues of political affiliations and campaigning if the organization receives funding from a political entity.

Regardless, each category will represent a specific type or group of action plans. Whatever they may be, you must affirm or accomplish the following:

- Define or redefine the department's goals and objectives on paper.
- Define or redefine the organizational structure of the department on paper.
- Define or redefine each job description.
- Define any reduction or realignment of staff to eliminate any duplication of effort.
- Define any training needs.
- Define any personnel or employee relation actions to be taken to reduce or eliminate any tensions between staff members.
- Define and clarify any organizational policies that may be lacking regarding employee conduct on and off the job.
- Define the actions to be taken, lines of authority, and responsibility for implementation of each item.
- Define timelines and qualitative and quantitative results anticipated with the implementation of each action.

Again, as already noted, your action plan may be augmented by any specific issues and characteristics not covered in this text.

Finally, you may want to consider whether to evaluate the results with the assistance of your immediate supervisor or members of your own staff. It may or may not assist you to ensure a comprehensive evaluation and the foundation for implementing a proactive action plan. If given the option, you must judge the positive or negative impact of others' participation in evaluating survey results.

CAUTION

During the (re)organization process, show no people preferences. The well-being of the department takes priority over personal feelings and relationships with members of staff.

IMPLEMENTING SOLUTIONS

Implementation will test your leadership ability to influence and secure the cooperation of staff when implementing change. Clearly, you must ensure them that any change is for the better. Overcome their fear of change in the spirit of cooperation.

Additionally, this third and final step in (re)organization requires the cooperation and approval of the total organization, not just your department. Take the following steps to implement your action plan:

- If you have a large department, hold your first meeting with the supervisors. You need their involvement and support if any action plan is to succeed. Consider any suggested changes as equitable to all supervisors and consistent with company policy and procedure.

- Take the final document (action plan) to your immediate supervisor for review, revision, and approval. You cannot implement an action plan that is not consistent with company policy and that does not have the support of your upper management.

- Review the final document one more time with your supervisors. Inform them of what has been approved by upper management, and then decide how to present the plan to the line employees.

- Be certain that your supervisors understand their individual responsibilities regarding timelines, anticipated results, and contingencies to be implemented, if necessary.

- Encourage your supervisors to communicate any difficulties and provide them with solutions.

■ Likewise, instruct your supervisors to be equally supportive and open to suggestions from their line staff when implementing the action plan.

CAUTION

Avoid surprise changes in company policy. Ask staff for suggestions following the survey, and then begin an implementation process.

Implementation requires additional leadership skills in total communication, cooperation, and a willingness to be flexible in times of change. Likewise, your organizational skills will be tested from beginning to end.

THE 30-SECOND RECAP

■ The process of (re)organization of a department is potentially lengthy.

■ Begin with an orderly survey of your staff.

■ Use existing company policy and procedures to analyze and determine your tools of implementation.

■ Always find every acceptable way to incorporate your staff in the process.

Managing Your Budget

In this section, you will learn how to create, maintain, and review a budget to analyze performance.

COMPANIES AND BUDGETS

How you organize and manage a budget varies with the size of the company, your for-profit vs. nonprofit status, supervisory/management vs. ownership status, and start-up vs. existing conditions.

■ **Small organizations.** In smaller organizations, the budgeting process is generally limited to the highest-ranking persons and an accountant or bookkeeper. Unless you are one of these individuals, you should anticipate little or no involvement in the budgeting process.

■ **Large organizations.** In larger organizations, department managers and supervisors tend to be more involved in determining budgets.

Occasionally, there can be competition between departments, especially if funds are limited or cutbacks are on the horizon.

■ **For-profit companies.** In for-profit companies, management must generate a profit after taxes to allow for the distribution of dividends to the stockholders. In publicly held companies, financial statements are accessible by the public, but accessing departmental budgets may require some research. In privately held companies, financial statements and budgets are not disclosed to the public.

■ **Nonprofit companies.** For nonprofit agencies, profit is not an issue, but revenue from fund-raising and charges for services rendered must equal or surpass expenses. Typically, the executive director and trusted employees close to the director will be involved in the budgeting process. Furthermore, the financial statements and budgeting process are subject to arbitrary review by funding sources. If that includes government money (tax dollars), the entire process is subject to public scrutiny.

■ **Start-up companies.** Start-up organizations have little or no historical performance on which to determine budgets. Projections are based strictly on industry performance and assumptions about how this organization will perform. The development of a business plan is where the budgeting process is developed and elaborated.

■ **Existing organizations.** Existing organizations rely on historical performance and projected changes in performance in developing a budget. Clearly, it is a much easier position from which to determine a budget than a start-up.

UNIVERSAL PRINCIPLES

Regardless of the type of organization, universal principles apply in the organization and maintenance of a budget:

■ **Generally Accepted Accounting Principles (GAAP)** should be applied to the budgeting, bookkeeping, accountability, and projection process. These are published in the *GAAP Handbook of Policies and Procedures,* which you can purchase at most bookstores.

■ **Financial statements,** including balance sheets, income statements, and cash flow statements, are the primary documents analyzed to develop budgets. In a for-profit company, all three statements apply. In a nonprofit agency, with some exceptions, there is much greater reliance on the cash flow and income statements.

The higher your position of responsibility and the larger the organization is, the more likely you will be involved in the budgeting process. If necessary, you should become totally familiar with these principals.

TIP

Most community colleges offer basic courses in bookkeeping and financial statements.

RATIO ANALYSIS

Ratio analysis is a process whereby elements of the financial statements are combined in simple mathematical equations to determine financial performance and stability of the company. Banking institutions and private investors can apply 150 or more of these simple equations to analyze financial statements, historic and projected, to determine financial performance, stability, and feasibility.

Five categories of ratios are commonly used:

- Liquidity ratios determine a company's ability to use assets to meet liability demands.
- Coverage ratios determine the ability to cover debts.
- Operating ratios evaluate management's performance regarding profits, net worth, assets, and sales.
- Leverage ratios measure a company's level of vulnerability to industry downturns and the impact on fixed assets, liabilities, and net worth.
- Expense-to-sales ratios compare fixed asset expense and ownership compensation to sales.

Let's take a simple example of a ratio known as the current ratio. The most well known and used of all the ratios, this ratio measures the company's ability to use current assets to meet current liability obligations. Let's assume, on the balance sheet, that the company's total current assets equal $300,000, and total current liabilities equal $150,000. The formula is as follows:

Current Ratio = Current Assets ÷ Current Liabilities

CR = $300,000 ÷ $150,000 = 2.0

Simply stated, if you were to liquidate all current assets into cash to pay off current liabilities, you would have $2 of current assets to pay off each $1 of current liability. In any industry, that is a good ratio.

Industry performance for each of the five categories of ratios is compiled annually and published for use by the banking industry. The Risk Management Association (www.rmahq.com/), formerly known as Robert Morris Associates, is one of the most well-known institutions that compiles and publishes this data, which is categorized by each industry. Companies compare their ratios to the top quartile, middle half, and lower quartile of previous years' performance.

COST OF GOODS SOLD AND GROSS SALES

In the manufacturing and wholesale/retail environments, it is imperative to know the cost of goods sold (*COGS*) in the budgeting process. You must differentiate among categories of costs in the budgeting process. Knowing COGS also allows you to determine gross sales before deducting operating expenses. The formula—in this case, exemplified by a wholesale or retail environment—is best reflected by an examples:

	Sales	$200,000
Minus	Cost of materials/product	$50,000
Minus	Allowances and rebates	$5,000
Minus	Returns	$5,000
Equals	Gross sales	$140,000

The added-up deductions ($60,000) represent the COGS. Gross sales represent the total sales minus the COGS. The formula for a manufacturing environment is more amplified than this, though, so you are encouraged to purchase a good accounting textbook that defines and exemplifies all these formulas.

PLAIN ENGLISH

COGS   In a manufacturing environment include raw materials, manufacturing labor, packaging, depreciation expenses of manufacturing equipment, transportation of raw materials, and other expenses directly associated with the manufacturing process.

BREAKEVEN ANALYSIS

Breakeven analysis is a mathematical process in which you determine the level of sales required to pay off the costs of goods sold and operating expenses. The formula is as follows:

Total Fixed Costs ÷ (Unit Sale Price – COGS – Unit Variable Cost)

Total fixed costs represent those monthly costs that will be incurred, more or less at the same level, whether or not you make a sale. The unit variable cost represents costs that vary from month to month and are impacted by sales or other activities such as advertising, special events, and other nonmonthly activities.

Let's take the example of a company that projects next year's fixed costs to be $500,000; the sale price per unit of the product is $5, COGS is $2.50, and the anticipated per-unit variable cost will be $1. The breakeven analysis would be as follows:

$$\$500,000 \div (\$5.00 - \$2.50 - \$1.00) = 333,333$$

In other words, the point in time that 333,333 units of the product are sold is when the company will cover all anticipated costs for the year.

CAUTION

Breakeven analysis relies exclusively on projection of sales and expense. The level of accuracy of your projections directly correlates to the accuracy of your breakeven analysis.

AN EXAMPLE OF BUDGET ANALYSIS

Not every budgeting situation is the same. The following example, though rather simple, attempts to guide you through the learning process of analyzing departmental costs and their relationship to sales.

Assume that you are new to the organization. You need to learn about past performance as a guide to developing next year's department budget.

PLAIN ENGLISH

FY   Fiscal year, a 12-month accounting period.

Start with a table like the following example, which reflects a department staff of four and 10 line-item expenses. Assume that total department income in FY 1999 was $430,000 and is projected at $500,000 for FY 2000.

Line Item	Budget FY 1999	Percent of Total Budget FY 1999	Percent of Income FY 1999	Budget FY 2000	Percent of Total Budget FY 2000
Salary: Manager	$45,000	26.30	10.50	$48,000	26.20
Benefits Expense: Manager	$6,300	3.70	1.50	$6,720	3.70

Line Item	Budget FY 1999	Percent of Total Budget FY 1999	Percent of Income FY 1999	Budget FY 2000	Percent of Total Budget FY 2000
Salary: Secretary	$28,000	16.40	6.50	$30,000	16.40
Benefits Expense: Secretary	$6,300	2.30	0.90	$4,200	2.30
Salary: Service Rep 1	$39,200	21.70	8.60	$39,500	21.50
Benefits Expense: Service Rep 1	$5,180	3.00	1.20	$5,530	3.00
Salary: Service Rep 2	$32,000	18.70	7.40	$34,500	18.80
Benefits Expense: Service Rep 2	$4,480	2.60	1.00	$4,830	2.60
Travel expense	$5,000	2.90	1.20	$5,850	3.20
Office supplies	$4,000	2.30	0.90	$4,250	2.30
Total	$170,880	100.00	39.70	$183,380	100.00

You generate much more data with just a few sets of numbers. The sample table provides for several observations, including these:

- If the FY 2000 sales are met, the cost of sales will be lower than FY 1999, meaning increased department productivity. FY 2000 expenses of $183,000 would equal 36.6 percent of $500,000 in sales. That would represent a reduction of 3.1 percent in departmental costs to sales.

- The percent increase in sales exceeds the percent increase in expenses, as further proof of increased productivity. Sales would increase 16.2 percent, while departmental expenses would increase 7.3 percent.

- Salary expenses for the manager and service representatives, as a percent of total sales, will decline from 1999 to 2000. The secretary is getting a salary increase exceeding the percent increase of his or her salary to the percent of total sales. Is it justified?

- The salary for Sales Rep 2 increases as a percent of the total department budget, while Sales Rep 1's salary increase represents a lower percentage of the department budget. Is sales performance consistent with the increase of absolute salary and the change as a percent of the total departmental budget?

CAUTION

No expense should ever be considered unless it directly or indirectly has a positive impact on productivity, of which company morale is a consideration.

■ Benefit expenses are rising as a percent of total sales, but increased productivity will likely result in no reduction of this expense.

It doesn't take much to learn budgetary analysis, and your overall awareness of the budget increases your influence and control over the decisions leading to its approval.

THE 30-SECOND RECAP

■ The legal and business nature of an organization dictates how budgeting and accountability are approached.

■ Certain universal principles of bookkeeping and accounting should be followed.

■ Ratio analysis uses a set of simple equations to analyze historic and projected financial performance.

■ COGS and gross sales allow you to quantify sales costs, categories of costs, and their relationship to sales.

■ Breakeven analysis allows you to determine how much sales are necessary to cover expenses.

■ Significant budget analysis can be conducted with simple comparisons of departmental costs to sales.

Staying Focused Amidst Change

In this section, you will learn how to plan for the unexpected, such as cutbacks, mergers, social trends, and technological advances.

Flexibility and Discipline

Flexibility and discipline appear to be two very contradictory words. In reality, within the context of organization, flexibility requires discipline. Discipline is a fundamental organizational characteristic directed to an orderly process of developing methodology and procedure when producing blueprints, fulfilling tasks and responsibilities, completing projects and events, and dealing with lifestyle changes. Embedded in that discipline is the formation of contingency plans, in case your established procedure fails or you encounter overbearing change or unanticipated events.

Change and unanticipated events are inevitable. You must accept and be prepared for their eventuality. World War II brought on the emergence of women competing with men in the workplace. Two-income households are now more the norm than the exception. And those households rely on the two incomes to survive economically. The likelihood for acquisitions, mergers, closures, and related layoffs to affect one's job has increased two-fold for many homes.

Furthermore, the emergence of a more global economy means events outside national boundaries impact change, on the job and at home, more frequently than ever before.

CAUTION

The voicemail maze that clients are subjected to before reaching a human voice can be a turn-off for business. Many companies are reverting to human operators or answering services.

Evolving social mores have resulted in company health benefits extended from the workers to their families, and, in more recent times, to significant others in alternative family lifestyles.

Computers moved from rooms the size of office complexes to the palm of your hand. And all these dramatic changes have occurred in only the last 45 years.

To address maintenance of organizational skills in this context requires examination of your mind-set within the framework of changes affecting the modern workplace.

Using Computers

Many managers are willing to cut labor costs if a computer can provide the same function much faster, at reduced expense. The for-profit motive of capitalism and the obligations to stockholders require such analysis and response.

On the other hand, especially in businesses requiring much face-to-face encounters between the organization and the clients served, it may be wise to retain some personal contact instead of computerized telephone answering systems.

At home, with the apparently increased demands on time, a computer can be a blessing. For those eager to learn computers, the advent of online payments of accounts, mortgages, and the like can save time and money. You can make payment on an account in a matter of seconds. Whereas writing a check, putting it in an envelope, and addressing and stamping it can be boring and laborious. There is a sense of satisfaction in having made the payment via computer and saving so much time.

There are advantages to implementing computers and other high-tech applications in the workplace versus employing individuals:

- No compensation and benefits expenses will be incurred.
- You can simply contract out services when no one in-house is available or able to provide them.
- You pay less for office space and related utilities.
- A manager doesn't have to be as tactful and diplomatic when dealing with computers versus human beings.
- You avoid human errors.
- Computers can be as small as your laptop, and there is no added travel expense.

On the other hand, there are advantages to using a human being in the workplace:

- An employee is more flexible. The computer is often subject to reprogramming by a human being to adapt to change.
- An employee can provide creativity, whereas the computer is limited by the software.
- Very often, clients would much rather hear a human voice and see a human face than answer to a machine with automated voice recordings.

It would be a serious error to decide in favor of a machine simply because there are more advantages listed for computers versus human beings. The decision is best made on the basis of the nature of your organization, financial constraints, and customers needs.

TIP

Periodic surveys by computer-related magazines have indicated that many customers prefer human interaction with customer service when resolving hardware and software problems.

USING HUMAN HELP

A strong example of where computers can't supplant human beings is in the customer service area. Even on the Internet, consumers are not content with *FAQ* pages to solve problems with the installation and use of software applications.

For example, Internet service providers (ISPs) and Web hosting services are increasingly promoting the 24/7 concept of having real people, not computers, available to address customers' problems when accessing the Internet and e-mail, dealing with changes to the Web site, and other related issues.

PLAIN ENGLISH

FAQs   Frequently asked questions. Most Web sites have FAQ pages to answer common questions in text form.

A responsive and knowledgeable customer service department is key. Consumers are looking for value and strong relationships, and a company must be flexible to fit those needs.

SURVIVING MERGERS, ACQUISITIONS, AND LAYOFFS

In the last 20 years, American industry has undergone dramatic changes. As an example, three years ago, Barnett Bank was the largest banking institution in Florida. NationsBank, the major competitor to First Union Bank in the Southeast United States, then acquired it. Now those two names have disappeared from the banking landscape. The name holder of record is Bank of America.

Mergers, acquisitions, downsizing, and outsourcing are common household words today. The best way to respond to this ever-shifting environment is to think like an entrepreneur or a free agent:

- Regularly review the trade and business journals. Track the changes in your industry.
- Pay attention to major company contracts that may be pending approval.

Nobody likes to publicly admit that his or her individual well-being takes precedence over loyalty to the company. But when you legitimately suspect that your days of employment are numbered, it is justifiable to consider proactive measures. If you believe that change is coming, take the following into consideration:

- Anticipate layoffs.
- Expect expanded job responsibilities for those who remain.
- Realize that retraining may be necessary as a result of layoffs.
- Consider additional outsourcing of services once performed in house.
- Begin developing rudimentary reorganization plans.
- Review the local job placement ads for a parachute job. You may have to make a decision to leave the present job for a new position, even if the compensation package is smaller.

CAUTION

It may be worth looking for new work before the axe falls. Weigh the risk of accepting another job (maybe lower-paying) against the possibility of layoffs before you begin your search.

- Consider alternative professions that require skills, experience, and formal education that match your background.
- Consider starting your own business. Investigate the risks of such a venture.
- Talk to your family and significant others, but to no one else. They will be most directly impacted after you.
- Keep resumés and work portfolios updated.
- Polish computer, Internet, and other skills valuable in your profession.
- Network with professional associations to establish business contacts *before* you need them.

Nobody wants to leave an enjoyable job that provides good compensation and benefits. Take all steps necessary to make yourself invaluable to the company. On the other hand, be prepared for the possible layoff.

THE 30-SECOND RECAP

- Many cultural and technical changes are drastically reshaping the landscape of professional employment.

- Recognize these changes when they're underway in your company.
- Accommodate those changes to the benefit of the company and department staff.
- Take care of your own well-being by practicing good career management.

Streamlining Business-Specific Processes

In this section, you will learn how to streamline meetings and control communication overload.

THE MEETING

The high-tech information technology age put us in communication contact in more ways than we could have imagined. As with all other things in life, all processes have a limit. You must recognize when you're approaching excess, and then take corrective action to ensure that the right tools are implemented to keep balance with productivity and harmony in the workplace.

The idealistic motivation for meeting is to bring together a group of individuals, sharing common goals and objectives. The ideal outcome is to design an action plan and delegate the related responsibilities.

You may not always be able to reach the desired results. But the time spent and the manner in which you manage the meeting may help get you there:

- **Have an *agenda*.** Outline the intentions of the meeting, who is to attend, any documents or business tools to bring, date, time, location, and the order in which issues will be addressed.

- **Give a copy of the agenda to all participants.** Make sure that it's distributed well in advance for preparation. Be certain that each participant knows what specific elements of the meeting will require participation, guidance, or leadership. No one likes surprises—that can be humiliating.

PLAIN ENGLISH

Agenda   A list of things to be considered, or an underlying idea or plan.

▣ **Schedule the meeting for appropriate times.** If possible, try not to overlap departmental activities.

▣ **Schedule meetings for peak results.** Position regular meetings to best correspond to gathering and analyzing related data. For example, weekly meetings to plan the week ahead are best scheduled for Friday afternoons or Monday mornings.

▣ **Delegate a meeting leader.** Teamwork is nice, but the moderator needs to keep the meeting focused on the subject matter. The moderator can also serve as a mediator when differences of opinion arise.

▣ **Avoid impromptu meetings.** They wind up being counterproductive and take people away from scheduled tasks.

CAUTION

Encourage and promote the installation of firewall software applications at work and at home. These protect systems from unwanted and illegal intrusions into computer systems via the Internet.

INTERNET AND E-MAIL

Internet and e-mail have become two of the most worker- and company-productive tools of communication in the last 50 years. They have reduced overall communications costs, and they allow for near-instant communication response to clients and vendors alike.

However, Internet access and e-mail have also become a major source of irritation to people focused exclusively on work.

TIP

Install a proven antivirus program on your computer at home and work. Update it weekly with online downloads.

Here are some ways to tame the electronic tiger on your desk:

▣ Limit the time spent on the Internet at work, unless it's directly part of the job.

▣ Create folders for specific types of e-mail, such as by company or individual names.

▣ With some e-mail programs, you can use the Tool option in your e-mail software to include your name, your company name, your e-mail address, and the company's e-mail address at the bottom of each item sent. This saves time and ensures that e-mail you send is recognized instantly.

TIP

Take advantage of e-mail to advertise. In all client correspondence, include a company logo and a phrase or reference to a new product or service somewhere in the body of the e-mail. Don't send unsolicited mail, though (known as spamming).

- Encourage the use of e-mail communication within the organization. It saves time and resources.

- Review, edit, and spell-check all e-mail that you send. It is a reflection of you and your company.

- Print out a hard copy or create a backup copy to disk of all e-mail that you deem valuable to the conduct of your business.

- Use your e-mail software options to block e-mail addresses from which you have received irritating, unsolicited, and personally objectionable materials. For help or more details, ask your system administrator.

E-MAIL POLICY

Increasing legal value is being placed on e-mail communications. Watch what you write, and keep hard copies of your e-mails.

Anyone who paid attention to the Microsoft antitrust case knows the effect that e-mail had on the trial. Attorneys are now using e-mail the way they previously used interoffice memos when presenting evidence.

How do you protect yourself and your office from damaging e-mails? Set a company e-mail policy. Involve the legal, public relations, and information technology departments (if you have them) in its development. If not, use the company policy for memos as a standard for determining how long to keep incoming e-mails and how to express company mission when creating outgoing messages. Negative publicity gets around fast, especially when it's an e-mail coming from your firm that can be forwarded faster than you can say "lawsuit."

Just as you wouldn't denigrate a company colleague in an office memo, don't allow slanderous, negative material in e-mails. You don't promote sexual harassment in the workplace, so prohibit sexually explicit material in company e-mail. You don't send notes to family and friends on interoffice memos, so why allow it in e-mail?

Common sense will go a long way in creating an e-mail policy and will keep the level of unwanted, negative e-mail under control.

CAUTION

Be careful not to use e-mail to the point that face-to-face contact is compromised. Not all messages can be adequately communicated by the written word.

OFFICE HELP

Free fax and voicemail services can help you get organized by reducing the amount of equipment that you have in your office. They can also act as your electronic office secretary. With these types of online messaging services, you not only minimize the extra appliances, phone lines, and electrical outlets that you need, but you also gain communications flexibility:

- You can maximize your time spent online because you won't have to stop for calls or faxes.

- Confidential documents won't wind up in the company fax bin.

- All outside messages can be accessed at one time. You pick up your faxes and voicemail messages when you check your e-mail.

The following list presents services that offer fax receiving and voicemail. Some can send messages to your cell phone, and some have online calendars for organizing your online office. Choose the one with the best options for your work style and needs. Most of these companies also offer additional services and upgrades for small monthly fees:

- **CallWave (www.callwave.com)** offers FaxWave and the Internet Answering Machine. With FaxWave, you eliminate the need for a dedicated fax line—great news for home offices. Sign up for a private fax number, and faxes are automatically routed to your e-mail inbox. They arrive as e-mail attachments, and you can view them without any extra applications or software. Free faxes have an area code that you may not be familiar with, but CallWave plans to offer fax numbers within a chosen area code or with toll-free calling in the future for an additional fee.

  Internet answering machines such as the one offered by Call-Wave allow you to be online with a single phone line without missing important calls. These answering machines work with the "Call Forward on Busy" feature provided by your local phone service, and they also make it possible for you to hear the caller while you're online doing other work. You can order the call-forwarding feature from your local phone company. Callers won't hear a busy signal when you are online; instead, they will have the opportunity to leave a message—and you can hear that message instantly.

- **eFax (www.efax.com)** provides access to your faxes and messages when you're on the road or at the office. eFax Free service offers messages by e-mail or wireless notification of incoming e-mail. eFax Free numbers are assigned at random, but for a minimal monthly fee, you can upgrade to eFax Plus, which provides a local fax number and the ability to send faxes.

    You use the same eFax number for voicemail. Your messages can be received as voicemail or as voice-to-e-mail, and you can receive them by phone or computer.

- **Onebox (www.onebox.com)** offers free faxing and voicemail in numbers from more than 40 area codes serving metropolitan areas. You simply choose the fax number in an area code close to you. With Onebox, you can also stop typing and start talking with the voice e-mail service. Other features include a calendar, an address book, and a distinct Onebox e-mail address. Wireless Onebox can also send messages to wireless Web-enabled phones.

    The advantage to Onebox is the ability to neatly organize everything in one place. Faxes are delivered to your Onebox e-mail address, and all e-mail responses sent from the Web site are preset with your fax number and Onebox e-mail address. Future premium services should allow you to send faxes.

CELL PHONES AND PAGERS

Cell phones are becoming so popular that they're almost becoming a public menace. Some restaurants even have cell phone booths so that diners won't be distracted by phone conversations at nearby tables. The phones are convenient, though, if used judiciously:

- Don't carry cell phones or pagers into meetings with supervisors or clients.
- Don't give your company cell phone or pager number to anyone other than work-related contacts.

CAUTION

Cell phone usage while driving is against the law in some jurisdictions. Practice safe cell phone usage in the car.

▓ Don't use personal cell phones and pagers in company or client meetings. Make arrangements with personal associations to communicate with you via company or department phone centers.

TELEPHONE MANAGEMENT

The telephone is one of the greatest business tools we have, yet it can be the greatest source of interruptions in a day. That's where answering machines and voicemail come in. Here are some telephone-taming basics:

▓ Leave a detailed message on your outgoing voice message, stating office hours and when you're available to speak.

▓ In your message, direct callers to leave their own detailed message describing what they need, their phone number, and the best time for you to return the call.

▓ Write down the messages that you get—don't hope to remember who, what, when, and where.

▓ Make notes before you make a call. Know what you want to accomplish. Be prepared to leave a message so that you won't stumble over yourself when the machine kicks in.

▓ Make notes during important business calls. Number the steps that you need to take, or the steps that you ask another person to take, in order of priority. Do what you can as soon as you hang up. Make a note on your calendar to follow up if you've delegated a task to the other party.

TAKE BACK YOUR DESK

A desk full of paperwork may make you look busy, but it can also drain your energy. One glance at the mountains of paperwork is enough to discourage the heartiest of workers. Start a daily desk routine to establish an order to your chaos:

▓ **Avoid piles.** During the day, it may be okay to place paper in piles marked Urgent, Read, Incoming, or Outgoing. Better to have stackable trays for this. At day's end, put those papers in files (statistics show that 80 percent of filed papers are never looked at again), or address the issues and toss the paperwork.

▓ **Avoid news overload.** Are you really planning to read all those magazines, newsletters, and trade journals? Instead of stacking them up, put some in your briefcase for later, or clip the articles of real interest.

Important issues can be placed in stand-up magazine files organized by date for easy reference.

▥ **Manage contacts.** Eliminate pieces of paper by entering phone numbers and addresses immediately into your organizer. If you receive business cards, staple them to your Rolodex or into the pages of your address book, if you don't have a business card organizer.

At the end of each workday, a look around your office shows who's in control. You are, not the paper tiger on your desk.

THE 30-SECOND RECAP

▥ Limit meetings and reports.

▥ Implement "Robert's Rules" for your office to maximize meeting efficiency.

▥ Learn to tame the electronic tiger on your desk—namely, Internet and e-mail.

▥ Establish a company-wide e-mail policy.

▥ Create a telephone system to limit interruptions and make callbacks more productive.

▥ Organize your desk.

Hiring Employees

Analyzing the Position

In this section, you learn the importance of beginning at the beginning—with the job itself! You learn how to analyze a job to uncover what's necessary for an employee to succeed and how to reveal a profile of the candidate you seek.

BEGINNING AT THE BEGINNING

Beginning at the beginning is always the sensible thing to do. That's especially true when it comes to conducting employment interviews. But just where does the road to a successful job interview begin? The answer: with the job itself!

Begin by embarking on a systematic review of the job, a process known as introspective investigation. Your objective is to collect as much information as possible about how the job is done and what knowledge and skills are needed to perform it. Here are a few suggestions that will help you collect the information you need:

- Take a close look at the official job description, paying particular attention to established performance standards.

- Consider the environment in which the job is performed. Are there any special skills required? For example, a public relations or sales position will usually be performed in an environment requiring exceptional interpersonal skills and an ability to relate to people with diverse interests.

- Determine the product produced by the job and what is required to ensure consistent quality of that product.

- Examine business plans that may affect the position. Will the job change as a result of changes in business strategy? A few years ago a friend of mine was hired as west coast field sales manager by a large national insurance company. In six months he was asked to relocate to the home office located in the Midwest. The company was implementing a portion of its business plan that changed the way in which its products would be sold. Direct marketing would replace field sales. The business plan had been developed prior to the time my friend was hired, but no one bothered to inform him of the impending changes.

- Make note of any machines or tools that must be used to perform the tasks of the job.

- Solicit the input of the person who supervises the position.

- Talk with workers in the organization who regularly interact with the position to determine their perspective on what qualifications the successful applicant should possess.

- Don't forget to talk with those who have held the job in the past. What competencies and skills contributed to their success? Did the lack of certain competencies or skills cause or contribute to difficulties that they experienced on the job?

Through *introspective investigation,* you gather the information that you need to begin the hiring process. There are no shortcuts, but if you're serious about matching the right job with the right candidate, time invested in this task will be well rewarded.

PLAIN ENGLISH

Introspective investigation   The process by which an organization examines the position to be filled. The goal of introspective investigation is to identify essential competencies, skills, and abilities required for successful performance of the job.

ANALYZING THE POSITION

The objective of introspective investigation is to discover what skills and competencies are necessary for successful performance of the job. When you've identified these skills and competencies, organize them into the following categories: technical competencies, functional skills, self-management skills, interpersonal skills, and requirements of the corporate culture.

TECHNICAL COMPETENCIES

Technical competencies include any certifications, degrees, licenses, experience, and so on required to do the job. For example, an accountant position may require a degree in business as well as certification by a recognized board of accountancy. The job of personnel manager may require a human resources degree and experience in union/management affairs. Technical competencies are sometimes prescribed by law (as in the case of physicians, nurses, psychologists, teachers, lawyers, and so on).

What technical competencies, if any, are required to perform the job?

TIP

Don't be concerned about prioritizing the competencies and skills you've included in your list. The initial task is to list them; we'll prioritize them later.

FUNCTIONAL SKILLS

Functional skills are skills that help people function effectively on the job. To help identify functional skills, complete this sentence: "The primary responsibilities of the job include ____, ____, ____, and ____." List each functional skill that is required to do the job.

Here are some examples of common functional skills:

- Communication (written and verbal)
- Management
- Analysis
- Supervision
- Leadership
- Delegation
- Listening ability
- Independence
- Entrepreneurial approach
- Safety consciousness
- Risk taking
- Detail orientation
- Judgment
- Initiative
- Development of subordinates
- Service orientation
- Resilience
- Flexibility
- Adaptability
- Innovation
- Negotiation
- Sensitivity
- Planning and organizing ability
- Training
- Mentoring
- Sales ability
- Stress management ability
- Public relations ability

- Teamwork
- Equipment operation

The functional skills required for success in a typical organization vary widely depending on the job. For example, to be successful, a sales associate position may require someone with above average communication skills (both written and verbal) as well as highly developed time-management skills.

Functional skills are skills that can be learned. In fact, the acquisition of functional skills is usually an important goal of ongoing corporate training programs and postgraduate continuing education.

Functional skills are also transferable. *Transferable* means that an individual who has demonstrated specific functional skills in other employment or life situations can apply the same skills to the challenges of a new situation.

What functional skills distinguish top performers in the position under consideration? Remember to list them all, regardless of the degree of importance.

SELF-MANAGEMENT SKILLS

Self-management skills are personal characteristics that enhance one's ability to do the job. In this category, you'll want to include such characteristics as these:

- Creativity
- Dependability
- Ethics
- Honesty
- Loyalty
- Reliability
- Tactfulness
- Appearance
- Competence
- Helpfulness
- Popularity
- Accountability
- Self-sufficiency

Unlike functional skills, self-management skills are acquired over a period of time and often have their roots in childhood. Although it is possible for someone to alter personal characteristics, change in this area is often difficult and complex, usually requiring the assistance of a professional counselor.

Self-management skills are an important part of the overall hiring equation. Concentrating on functional skills and neglecting to consider the personal characteristics of the applicant is a recipe for failure. Avoid it.

List each of the self-management skills that the ideal candidate should possess. Consider asking others for suggestions.

INTERPERSONAL SKILLS

Interpersonal skills are "people skills." How people get along with each other, including how they communicate, is an important concern of any organization.

Good interpersonal skills include the ability to respect others, to be empathetic and caring, to listen attentively and respond accordingly, to maintain objectivity and refrain from emotionalism, and to communicate accurately and appropriately. These skills are rooted in a healthy understanding of oneself and others.

People with good interpersonal skills enjoy interacting with others. They recognize conflict to be a natural, normal, and sometimes even delightful part of life and are always prepared to explore ways to resolve conflict and reconcile differences.

Interpersonal skills help in any position. For some jobs, however, strong interpersonal skills are absolutely essential to success. For example, the success of a bean counter working in an obscure part of the office who rarely sees people will not be influenced much by his or her interpersonal skills. But the job of a sales and marketing executive who is responsible for conveying a positive company image as well as selling its products requires extraordinary interpersonal skills.

Consider the importance of interpersonal skills in the position under consideration. List any specific interpersonal skills that you feel apply to the position.

REQUIREMENTS OF THE CORPORATE CULTURE

What additional requirements (written or otherwise) are imposed on the position by the culture in which it exists? Every organization has a unique culture that must be considered.

For example, it is the unwritten rule of some organizations that executives should always wear suits and ties (some organizations even prescribe the color of the suit!). In other organizations, it is expected that employees, regardless of where they are on the corporate ladder, always be involved in continuing education, or that they regularly participate in extracurricular company activities, or that they volunteer for various community projects and endeavors.

As ridiculous as cultural expectations may seem, the fact is that success within the culture is dependent upon compliance with that culture. Like it or not, that's the way it is. The organizational culture is sacred, and you must take it into account when hiring a new employee.

List any cultural expectations of your organization that you need to consider when interviewing candidates for the job.

CAUTION

Don't underestimate the demands that corporate culture places on employees. A new employee cannot succeed with your organization unless there's a good fit with the existing culture.

MANDATORY SUCCESS FACTORS

Each of the competencies and skills that you've discovered through introspective investigation, and that you've listed under the categories outlined previously, is important. Together they provide a profile of the job as well as the ideal candidate.

However, in preparing for the interview process, it's helpful to narrow the focus to those specific competencies and skills that are absolutely necessary to the successful performance of the job. From your list of skills and competencies, select each factor that is an absolute must. These are the position's *mandatory success factors,* and they will form the foundation for the process of interviewing and selecting.

PLAIN ENGLISH

Mandatory success factors   Those specific competencies and skills that are absolutely essential to successful job performance. They are determined through a process of introspective investigation and provide a profile of the job as well as the ideal candidate.

In selecting the position's mandatory success factors, consider each of the categories listed above. Remember: These are the factors that are required for success in the position and are, therefore, the attributes that you'll want in your candidate of choice.

TIP

Ask two or three others familiar with the position to help you select the mandatory success factors. These may be the same individuals who will comprise your interview team.

CAUTION

Don't allow yourself to be rushed through the process of introspective investigation. Take the time that you need to find out just what is required for a new employee to succeed. This step alone will significantly increase your chance of hiring someone who will succeed. It's better to have an open position than to hire the wrong person for the job.

THE 30-SECOND RECAP

- Begin with a thorough analysis of the job.
- List each skill and competency even remotely associated with the job.
- From the list of skills and competencies, choose those factors that are absolutely essential to successful job performance.

The Resumé

In this section, you learn how to use a resumé to select candidates to interview.

BEGINNING THE SELECTION PROCESS

There's a job opening in your organization. You're responsible for hiring the right person—someone who will succeed in the job and remain with the organization for the long term.

You've done your homework. You've identified the mandatory success factors for the position and passed that information on to your organization's Human Resources department. The Human Resources department, in turn, announced the opening internally, placed appropriate advertisements in local newspapers, and notified area headhunters.

Suddenly, a deluge of resumés arrives on your desk. Now what?

It's time to begin the selection process.

First, don't panic. The fact that you've received a number of resumés is good news. Not only do you have a job that's of interest to a number of people, but you also have a large pool of potential candidates to select from. Consider yourself fortunate.

Begin reviewing resumés and selecting applicants for further consideration. Keep in mind that the more time you spend selecting applicants, the higher the quality of your final group of candidates (those who will receive an interview) will be.

CAUTION

A human resources professional should screen resumés before they reach the desk of the hiring manager. Information contained in the resumé that violates Equal Employment Opportunity Commission (EEOC) or Human Rights standards should be blacked out or otherwise eliminated.

CAUTION

Since photos included with a resumé provide an unwritten source of inappropriate information (gender, race, age, etc.), they should be immediately returned to the candidate by the Human Resource department.

THE RESUMÉ: WHAT IT IS—AND ISN'T

In Latin the words *curriculum vitae* mean "course of life." That's precisely what a resumé should be: the story of the applicant's life as it pertains to education and work experience.

The resumé is your first opportunity to identify an applicant who may have the experience and training you're looking for. A few words of caution are in order before you begin, however.

First, don't be too impressed with slick resumés that appear to have been professionally designed. The other day, I went to a local office supply store and counted 11 different pieces of resumé-producing software for sale. Each manufacturer boasted of its product's ability to produce print-shop quality resumés in a matter of minutes. Sharp-looking resumés are the norm today, not the exception. Anybody can produce one.

Second, don't be overly impressed with a resumé that's filled with fashionable buzzwords and terms that appear to have been written by someone of superior intellect. The truth is that in the cybersurfing age in which we live, anyone who is willing to spend a few minutes surfing the Web can easily glean all the *technospeak* necessary to write an impressive resumé.

PLAIN ENGLISH

Technospeak   Words and phrases that are particularly in vogue within special segments of society but that are not generally understood or recognized by outsiders. For example, in the field of human resource management, the term Bi-Polar refers to specific pairs of a candidate's core strengths; in the field of mental health, that same term refers to a specific mental health diagnosis.

Third, understand that statements made by an applicant on a resumé cannot always be taken as absolute truth. Remember that resumés have a natural bias in favor of applicants. To get their foot in the door, some applicants think nothing at all of spicing up their resumés by using highly imaginative ways to promote their perceived strengths, abilities, and competencies. In fact, some studies suggest that as many as 30 percent of all resumés contain information that is blatantly false and misleading.

Keep in mind that, from the standpoint of an applicant, the purpose of a resumé is to help him or her stand out in competitive hiring situations. Many job seekers today have been trained to think of their resumés as personal marketing tools designed to impress prospective employers.

Pertinent facts stated on a resumé, including degrees, licenses, and experience, ultimately need to be verified before an employment offer is made.

However, for initial screening purposes, in which the goal is simply to select applicants for further consideration, you should accept information provided in the resumé at face value and evaluate it accordingly.

THE RESUMÉ REVIEW GRID

The right tool always helps you to do a job well. That's certainly true when it comes to reviewing resumés.

I suggest that you develop a tool to help you with this important task. A simple Resumé Review Grid, with the candidate's name on the left and the selection criteria across the top of the page (as in the accompanying figure), will do the job.

Resumé Review Grid
Technical Competencies

Candidate	MBA Degree	Required Experience	Desktop Publishing	Training Experience	Hiring Experience	Budgeting Experience	Total
John Doe	x	x		3	3	5	11xx
Al Green		x	5	5	4	5	19x
Mary Smith	x	x	4	5	3	4	16xx
Paul Jones	x	x		4	2	3	9xx
Betty Brown		x	4	5	4	2	15x
Jim Peterson		x	2	3	3		8x

Functional Skills

Candidate	Analysis	Supervision	Management	Innovation	Total
John Doe	5	4	3	5	17
Al Green	3	5	4	4	16
Mary Smith	5	4	5	5	19
Paul Jones	2	1	3	4	10
Betty Brown	3	4	5	5	17
Jim Peterson	2	1	2	4	9

Recap

Candidate	Total
John Doe	28xx
Al Green	35x
Mary Smith	35xx
Paul Jones	19xx
Betty Brown	32x
Jim Peterson	17x

A sample of the Resumé Review Grid.

Under each criterion, allow room for a rating number of 0 to 5 (5 being the optimal score). Selection criteria that involve special education, licensing, or degrees would simply be checked in the appropriate area of the grid.

On the right side of the grid, designate a column for the total score achieved by the applicant. Check marks should be carried over and included with totals to indicate that, in addition to the numeric score, other specific selection criteria have been met. Leave the bottom of the sheet open for evaluator comments and notes.

Give each evaluator a copy of the resumé, together with the Resumé Review Grid. After evaluations have been completed, prepare a Master Resumé Review Grid for each applicant, showing the average score achieved for each selection criterion as well as an overall average score.

Offer personal interviews to those applicants who score highest. Note questions and comments made by the evaluators, and explore them further with the applicant in person.

NARROWING THE FIELD

At this juncture in the hiring process, narrow the field of applicants to those whose resumés demonstrate the likelihood that they possess the appropriate qualifications. Your time and the time of those who help you interview candidates is valuable. You don't want to waste it with applicants who obviously are not qualified to do the job.

But be careful about the reasons that you use to disqualify applicants from further consideration. Make sure that your reasons for rejection are firmly rooted in the requirements of the job, not in anything extraneous. Also, be sure to thoroughly document your reasons for disqualification. A copy of the Resumé Review Grid, together with any notes concerning the disqualified applicant's resumé, should be attached to the resumé and kept on file.

To ensure objectivity, ask those who will later serve on your interview team to help review resumés and select applicants. Not only will you be assured of a better, more objective result, but you also will make a legal challenge by a disgruntled applicant more difficult to conduct. Shared decision making, especially in hiring matters, is always best.

CAUTION

If the job requires a degree or other special education, make sure that such requirements are essential to the successful performance of the job. Requirements of this nature can be considered discriminatory because they may have a disproportionate impact to certain segments of the population. For example, the EEOC has held that employment decisions based upon the credit history of a candidate will have a disparate impact on minority candidates because a disproportionate number of minorities live below the poverty level.

ZEROING IN

You should consider three parts of the resumé in the preinterview selection phase:

- Education and training
- Experience
- Personal information

EDUCATION AND TRAINING

This portion of the resumé catalogs the applicant's formal education. Some applicants will also list seminars and workshops attended, especially when such programs have direct application to the job being sought. Applicants should furnish information concerning dates of graduation or completion, as well as dates that degrees were conferred.

Look for education and training that meets the requirements of the position. Be sure to note any questions or concerns that you may have so that you can ask the applicant for clarification or further information during the interview.

TIP

Consider whether the position really requires a degree. Filling a position with someone who is overqualified for the job ensures rapid turnover.

EXPERIENCE

Experience is the most significant portion of the resumé in the preinterview selection phase. Here you'll find the particulars about an applicant's work experience and qualifications.

In evaluating the experience of an applicant, be sure to do the following:

- Look for job descriptions that have particular relevance to the position that you hope to fill.
- Consider the level of the applicant's prior experience. Is it above or below that required for the job for which the candidate is applying?
- Is the applicant's experience written in a clear, concise manner, or are the terms used particularly vague and confusing?
- Based on the applicant's experience, does it appear that he or she possesses the mandatory success factors discussed in "Analyzing the Position" on page 408?

PERSONAL INFORMATION

Personal information contained in a resumé can be of exceptional value in your preinterview screening process. Information such as personal interests, extracurricular activities, and civic involvements provide a glimpse into a candidate's values and ambitions. Leisure pursuits and hobbies that relate to the responsibilities of the position suggest a candidate who is deeply interested and committed to the mission of the job.

GREEN FLAGS, RED FLAGS

A thorough review of most resumés is likely to produce some *green flags* as well as some *red flags*.

PLAIN ENGLISH

Green flags   Items on the resumé that clearly demonstrate positive achievement, especially in areas involving mandatory success factors.

Red flags   Items that indicate potential problems and mean either that further exploration with the applicant is necessary, or that the resumé can be rejected from further consideration outright.

GREEN FLAGS

Green flags are dazzling indicators that justify further consideration of the candidate. You will want to note any green flags present in an applicant's resumé and consider that information as you select candidates for interview.

Here's a list of some of the more important green flags that strongly suggest real achievement:

- **Career stability.** The candidate's resumé provides evidence of solid commitment to a chosen career path. Job changes have involved progressively more responsibility.

- **Contribution to organization.** The resumé not only discusses job responsibilities, but it also talks about contributions that the candidate made to organizations as a result of meeting or exceeding expectations.

- **Determination.** The resumé reflects the applicant's strong desire and ambition to move forward. Duties and responsibilities listed for previous work demonstrate that the applicant accepted challenges beyond those normally associated with the nature of the job.

- **Dreams and aspirations.** The resumé demonstrates that the candidate wants to accomplish something great and has the vision to realize his or her dreams. A resumé that states a career objective well above and beyond the position applied for can reveal a candidate whose dreams and aspirations are in focus.

RED FLAGS

You will also encounter some red flags as you review the resumés of potential candidates. That's to be expected.

Red flags signal possible problems. Note each red flag you find on the candidate's resumé review grid. Red flags may indicate a need for more information or clarification from the applicant. Or they may signal a genuine cause for concern.

Whatever you do, don't ignore red flags. Here are some common ones:

- Unexplained gaps in employment history. These may simply be errors in the chronology of the resumé, or they may signal the possibility of more serious concerns.

- Frequent job changes that are obviously not promotions or better opportunities may signal a variety of work-related problems. Does the applicant have difficulty taking direction? Or is there a problem getting along with co-workers?

- Overuse of terms such as "knowledge of," "experience with," "understanding of," "exposure to," and "familiarity with." These are terms frequently used by those who lack the kind of hands-on experience required.

- Experience or education listed in something other than chronological order. Resumés using functional formats in which prior experience is emphasized often ignore dates completely and are frequently used to hide significant gaps.

- Resumés that criticize former employers or supervisors may signal serious attitude problems. A resumé should be a vehicle used to sell the skills and experience of an applicant, not to trash former employers.

THE RESUMÉ AND THE INTERVIEW

The resumé is an important document. It provides pertinent information about qualifications of applicants for positions in your organization.

It's important to remember, however, that the interview itself should be devoted to behavioral questions that seek to measure a candidate's skills and abilities as they relate to the identified mandatory success factors. The interview is not the time to rehash the resumé point by point.

THE 30-SECOND RECAP

▦ Pizzazz is no substitute for substance—resumés should present an applicant's qualifications in a straightforward chronological manner.

▦ Develop a simple Resumé Review Grid that will help evaluators assess resumés fairly.

▦ The same team members who will participate in the interview process should also review resumés.

▦ Be sure to note all green flags and red flags that are uncovered in the initial review.

▦ Don't rehash resumés during interviews.

References

In this section, you learn how to obtain good reference information that will help you conduct a more meaningful interview. You also learn what questions you can legally ask and what areas to avoid.

WHY CHECK REFERENCES?

Of all the tasks associated with hiring new employees, checking references has historically ranked among the least favored. All too often, managers don't bother to contact former employers because they think that reference checks are an exercise in futility. Some studies by the American Management Association estimate that the references of as many as 70 percent of all new hires were never checked. Big mistake.

Here are the two best reasons I know for conscientiously checking the references of prospective employees:

▦ Reference checks help prevent lawsuits for negligent hiring.

▦ Reference checks help prevent costly hiring mistakes.

NEGLIGENT HIRING

Workplace crime involving assault, terrorism, fraud, arson, theft, and even murder is on the rise. In fact, statistical evidence from the United States Department of Labor identifies violence in the workplace as one of the fastest-growing causes of death on the job. Moreover, studies seem to demonstrate a strong correlation between past criminal activity and job-related crime.

Most states have already adopted the legal doctrine of *"negligent hiring"* and "negligent retention." These legal theories maintain that an employer is liable for the harmful acts of an employee if the employer knew—or should have known—of similar incidents in the employee's background. An employer's negligence is based on the fact that, had the employer done an adequate job of evaluating and investigating the applicant, the harm would not have occurred.

PLAIN ENGLISH

Negligent hiring   The failure to exercise a reasonable amount of care in recruiting and selecting a candidate for a job, which ultimately results in injury or damage to another.

In the past, employers were considered liable for the acts of an employee while performing the duties of the job. Today, under the tort of negligent hiring, employers are liable for the harmful acts of an employee even when those acts are beyond the scope of the job.

The legal adage remains true: The best defense is a good offense. Thoroughly checking an applicant's employment history and personal references is the best way to keep your workplace safe and avoid becoming embroiled in costly negligent hiring claims.

DECREASING HIRING MISTAKES

Hiring mistakes are expensive. They take a major toll on an organization's finances and employee morale.

CAUTION

Regardless of how impressive a candidate may seem, always verify academic credentials and check the references provided. No exceptions.

A few years ago, a Minnesota firm hired a chief financial officer whose resumé stated that he had graduated with honors from a prestigious Ivy League university with an advanced degree in accounting. The candidate had interviewed well and had impressed management with his prestigious background.

Management was so convinced he was the right man for the job that they immediately offered him an excellent salary and benefit package, and included some truly exceptional perks such as a liberal stock option arrangement. But in their rush to fill the position, no one bothered to verify the individual's educational credentials.

Almost two years later, a federally mandated audit revealed that the company's financial records were in a state of absolute disarray. That's when the board of directors decided to take another look at the resumé of their CFO. When they contacted the Ivy League university listed on it, they learned that the closest this individual ever got to the prestigious campus was, in all likelihood, driving down the freeway that passed nearby.

The result: embarrassed managers, an irate board of directors, a demoralized staff, the loss of a federal contract worth more than a million dollars, and an expense of $185,000 for an outside accounting firm to repair the company's financial records. And all of it could have been prevented with a five-minute phone call to the Ivy League university to verify a degree.

Will performing thorough reference checks keep you from making hiring mistakes? No. But your percentage of bad hires will decline significantly. In fact, some informal research conducted by my organization suggests that as many as 85 percent of hiring mistakes can be avoided by thorough reference checks.

Reference checks present a genuine opportunity to learn more about an applicant. Former employers are in the best position to provide useful information about a candidate's skills, abilities, prior work performance, and character.

TIP

Consider asking candidates to submit as many as 10 "personal" references that may include previous employers. That way, when you contact a former employer, you can truthfully explain that the applicant provided his or her name as a "personal" reference (instead of as a former employer or business reference). This approach usually yields better information, and more of it.

THE CONSPIRACY OF SILENCE

Getting previous employers to level with you about an ex-employee may prove difficult. Conspiracies of silence are very real. In many organizations, *disclosure agreements* make it next to impossible for previous employers to speak candidly about former workers.

PLAIN ENGLISH

Disclosure agreement   A legally binding agreement between an employer and an employee who is leaving the organization. The agreement purposely limits the information that can later be disclosed to prospective employers.

Whether or not employees leave under less than favorable circumstances, disclosure agreements are often used to limit the information that former employers can disclose. Some employers adhere to the "name, rank, and serial number" approach, providing only minimal information. It's not uncommon for such firms to restrict disclosable information to dates of employment, job title of the last position held, final salary, and a touch of murky narrative that has been carefully worded and mutually agreed upon concerning the character of the employee and the general quality of work that he or she performed.

The use of disclosure agreements is motivated by the fear of costly, and often well-publicized, defamation or invasion of privacy litigation. Ex-employees sometimes sue former employers, claiming substantial damages as a result of negative reference reports. Juries in many of these cases have been sympathetic to employees, handing down megadollar judgments against corporate defendants.

Here are some suggestions that will help you in your quest for meaningful reference information. Think about implementing them in your organization:

- Always have applicants complete an application that grants permission to contact references. A resumé is not an application. Be sure that your application contains an authorization permitting you to contact any and all former employers and others who have knowledge of the applicant's work history, experience and education, and that allows them to provide information about the applicant.

- Include a "hold harmless" agreement with your employment application that will prevent former employers from being sued by an applicant as a result of releasing reference information. Then send a copy of the signed agreement to each reference before contacting them. Hold harmless agreements can go a long way in lowering the guard of former employers.

- Check references *before* interviewing those you've selected for further consideration. Having done so will not only provide a better understanding of each applicant, but it may also direct you to areas that require further exploration.

- Check references yourself—don't assign the task to others. Managers will have more success talking with other managers. Also, by contacting references directly, the manager can *listen intuitively* to what is (and is not) being said.

- Be sure to ask each reference for the names of others in the organization who may be familiar with the qualifications of the applicant. It's astonishing how much information you can obtain from those whose names weren't provided by an applicant.

PLAIN ENGLISH

Intuitive listening   Being sensitive both to what is said and to what is not said. It is the message conveyed by a hesitation, a reluctance to discuss a matter, or an obvious desire to change the subject.

- Share the information received from reference checks with other members of the interview panel.

- Always contact colleges and universities to verify degrees. The most common form of deception involves applicants who overstate educational accomplishments. Colleges and universities are eager to provide information about the academic achievements of former students. It's fast and easy information to obtain.

- Document all information that you receive. Your documentation will be vital if you ever have to defend your actions.

- Don't contact only one or two references. Make it a practice to contact all of them, without fail. And be sure to ask each reference to provide you with the names of others who have knowledge of the applicant's skills and work experience.

THE RIGHT QUESTIONS

The quality of information that you receive from references depends upon how well you ask questions. Here are a few things to remember:

- Don't ask leading questions that provide the reference with the information given by the applicant. Instead of asking, "Mr. Peterson said that you worked in his unit for five years. Is that correct?" ask instead, "How long did you work for Mr. Peterson?" Let the reference provide the information.

- Don't ask closed-ended questions (questions that can be answered with a simple "yes" or "no"). You want to hear what the references have to say. Give them a chance to speak freely without limiting their replies.

- Be sure to ask questions that verify basic facts such as dates of employment, salary, title of last position, duties, and so on.

- Limit your questions to those that directly relate to an applicant's qualifications for the job (that is, the mandatory success factors—see "Analyzing the Position" on page 408).

QUESTIONS YOU CAN'T ASK

Some questions you can't ask when talking to references. Questions regarding any of the following categories are illegal:

- Age
- Race
- Religion
- Marital status
- Children or childcare arrangements
- Pregnancy or family plans
- Sexual orientation
- Parents of the applicant
- Medical status, disabilities, or impairments
- Psychological or physical well-being
- Residence
- Membership in social organizations
- Union membership
- Previous use of drugs and alcohol
- Arrest record
- Visible characteristics

In addition to these, a prospective employer is prohibited by law from asking a reference (including former employers) anything that the employer is prohibited from asking the applicant directly.

METHODS OF INTERVIEWING REFERENCES

There are three primary methods of interviewing references—by mail, by telephone, and through the use of a private search firm.

REFERENCES BY MAIL

Requesting references by mail (or e-mail) is decidedly the poorest method. It always results in the fewest responses. Those replies you do receive are likely to be written in an extremely guarded fashion.

Why? Written information about an ex-employee can easily be construed as demeaning and can become the basis for litigation against the former employer. Even when the intent was to provide a positive reference, certain words or phrases can imply something else. Most former employers simply avoid responding in this manner.

Use mail to send references a personal note informing them that John or Jane Doe has applied for a position with your firm and has given you their name as a personal reference. Inform the reference that you will be phoning in the next few days to talk about the qualifications of the applicant. Be sure to include a copy of the applicant's consent form and hold harmless agreement. This helps set the stage for the reference interview and knocks down barriers in advance.

REFERENCES BY TELEPHONE

The telephone is by far the most common way of obtaining references. It's fast, inexpensive, and effective.

Begin your phone conversation with a reference by referring to the letter that you sent earlier, together with the consent and waiver signed by the applicant: "John Doe gave me your name as a personal reference and asked me to phone you. Is now a good time to talk, or would you prefer that I phone later today?"

Get the details out of the way first. Start by asking questions that verify factual data. Ask for dates of employment, title of the applicant's last position with the firm, salary information, duties and responsibilities of the job, and so on.

After the preliminary information has been gathered, tell the reference a little about the job for which the applicant is being considered and the requirements of that job. Use the mandatory success factors that you developed in the section "Analyzing the Position," on page 408, to formulate specific *probes*. Consider these examples:

- Can you tell me about a time when Pete had to use his problem-solving skills? (problem-solving)

- What did Mary do to contribute to an environment of teamwork in your organization? (team-building)

- Can you tell me about a time when Helen positively influenced the action of others? (leadership)

- What was the most creative thing Bill did while he worked for your company? (creativity)

PLAIN ENGLISH

Probe   A question or request that seeks specific information, clarification, or confirmation from a candidate being interviewed. Probes may be open or closed depending on the purpose.

USING SEARCH FIRMS

Many firms today specialize in checking the backgrounds of applicants for employment. Many of them have an Internet presence, and their services can be obtained electronically.

Most search firms perform in-depth interviews with previous employers, check educational credentials, and confirm dates of attendance and degrees earned at any institution of higher education. Some will even check the credit of applicants, obtain motor vehicle reports, and perform criminal background checks (if appropriate).

Typically, these services are fast and relatively inexpensive, and provide professional reports of their findings. However, in my opinion, they are a poor substitute for personal contact by a prospective employer. Be careful about delegating this important task to an unknown investigator.

And incidentally, if you think that by using a professional search firm you somehow diminish your potential legal liability in a negligent hiring lawsuit, think again. A firm that you hire to help gather information about an applicant becomes your legal agent. You remain responsible for the completeness and accuracy of the information used to make employment decisions.

TALKING WITH PRESENT EMPLOYERS

It's common practice for applicants to ask you not to contact current employers. Until they find what they're looking for, applicants often don't want it known that they're searching for another job. That's understandable.

Although it's important to honor such a wish, it's also important to protect your interests. I suggest that in these instances, you make it clear to an applicant that any offer of employment would be contingent upon a satisfactory reference from the current employer. If the current employer provides a less-than-satisfactory reference, the offer would be subject to immediate withdrawal. Be sure to include language to this effect in any job offer and letter of confirmation.

Always follow up with a call to the present employer after a conditional offer of employment is made and accepted. Don't neglect talking to the person who has the most current information about your candidate and is in the best position to discuss his or her skills and abilities.

CREDIT CHECKS

If personal financial conduct is relevant to the job for which an applicant is being considered, consumer credit reports can be an important source of information. However, on September 30, 1997, the Fair Credit Reporting Act was amended to include strict notice requirements whenever credit reports for employment purposes are sought. Under present law, an employer must do the following:

- Notify an applicant in writing before a consumer credit report is procured, stating that such a report may be obtained for employment purposes.

- Obtain the applicant's written authorization to procure such a report.

- Provide the applicant with a copy of the report, together with a description of the applicant's rights under the Fair Credit Reporting Act *before* taking adverse action based in whole or in part on the report.

- Refrain from taking adverse action based in whole or in part on the report until the applicant has had sufficient time to respond to any discrepancies in the report.

An investigative consumer credit report that involves questioning friends and neighbors of the applicant may also be used to obtain important background information. A written notice must be sent to the applicant within three days of requesting the report. In addition, the applicant must be informed of his or her right to demand disclosure of the nature and scope of the investigative report and to receive a written summary of his or her rights under the law.

CAUTION

The use of consumer credit information in making employment decisions is legal. However, exercise extreme caution in using this information. Credit information can have a disparate impact on minority or women applicants and can provide a basis for litigation against employers. The likelihood of becoming embroiled in litigation is enhanced by the notice requirements of the law. Consult your corporate attorney before obtaining credit information and using it to qualify or disqualify an applicant.

PLAIN ENGLISH

Disparate impact A term used by the United States Supreme Court in a 1977 case involving the International Brotherhood of Teamsters. According to the court, disparate impact results from employment practices that appear to be neutral in their treatment of different groups, but that actually impact one group more harshly than another and cannot be justified by business necessity.

CRIMINAL BACKGROUND CHECKS

Obtaining information about an applicant's prior arrests can be problematic. Some states prohibit employers from accessing such information.

But the real concern is with the federal law. Members of minority groups have been effective in asserting that their groups are overrepresented in the population with arrest records. If this fact can be demonstrated by state or local statistical evidence, chances are good that inquiries into the arrest records of an applicant of the minority group involved will violate federal law.

Most states allow prospective employers to inquire about felony convictions. However, not all states allow employers to deny employment on the basis of a felony conviction.

Exercise care if you intend to use information about an applicant's record of arrest and conviction. Remember that you are likely restricted by state or federal law in the way you can use the information. Consult your organization's legal counsel to determine the advisability of performing criminal background checks and to learn what restrictions apply to you.

DRIVING RECORDS

If a prospective employee's duties include driving, checking motor vehicle records may be in order. But access to this type of information is often limited and difficult to obtain. And obtaining motor vehicle records in other states presents an even greater challenge since each state has its own regulations governing the release of such information.

THE 30-SECOND RECAP

- Thorough reference checks can prevent negligent hiring lawsuits and reduce hiring mistakes by as much as 85 percent.

- Ask for 10 "personal" references that may include former employers.

- Ask each preselected applicant to complete a formal job application that contains written permission for you to contact references and others having knowledge of previous work, and that allows others to release information to you.

- Consider developing (with the help of your legal department) a hold harmless agreement that would prevent former employers from being sued by an applicant as a result of releasing reference information.

- Make it a practice to phone each reference provided by the applicant before an interview.

- Network references by asking each reference for the names of others who have firsthand knowledge of the applicant's work.

- Make your job offer contingent on a positive reference from a present employer.

- Use credit checks, criminal background inquiries, and checks of driving records only after receiving legal guidance from your corporate attorney.

Testing

In this section, you learn to obtain factual data about how an applicant is likely to perform on the job by means of various tests.

THE MARVEL OF PRE-EMPLOYMENT TESTING

We live in a marvelous age. Almost every week we learn of wonderful new scientific discoveries to help us live longer or enhance the quality of our lives.

Employment testing has also benefited from years of scientific research. Today, pre-employment testing offers a valid, objective way to predict the suitability of a candidate for a particular job. And here's a bonus: Information obtained through testing will help you zero in on important areas to explore further during the interview.

CAUTION

If you opt for pre-employment testing, be sure to test each qualified applicant before the interview. Testing that is done following an interview and limited to only a few finalists may well be considered discriminatory.

You should know about five basic types of pre-employment tests:

- Aptitude and intelligence tests
- Behavior tests
- Technical skills testing
- Clinical evaluations
- Pop psychology tests

APTITUDE AND INTELLIGENCE TESTS

The purpose of aptitude testing is to predict an applicant's general level of future performance. Most of us have had experience taking some kind of aptitude test. For example, chances are, in high school you took the Scholastic Aptitude Test (SAT) to determine the likelihood of your success in college; before entering graduate school, you probably were required to take a Graduate Record Examination (GRE); if you went to law school, the Law School Admission Test (LSAT) was a requirement. Each of these aptitude tests predicted your performance in the future.

Tests of intelligence (or IQ tests) assess an individual's mental ability, as well as his or her intellectual capacity to reason and apply skills and knowledge. Two of the most widely used tests for this purpose are these:

- The Stanford-Binet test
- The Wechsler Adult Intelligence Scale

Administration of either of these tests requires specific training and, in many states, a license. Other tests of this nature are on the market today and can also do admirable jobs of measuring a candidate's intelligence.

Why are tests of intelligence important? In an article published in *Fortune* magazine, James Q. Wilson, professor of management at the University of California, Los Angeles, reviewed the book *A Question of Intelligence: The IQ Debate in America,* by Daniel Seligman (New York: Carol Publishing [Birch Lane Press], 1992). Professor Wilson wrote:

> People who mistakenly think that "intelligence is only what intelligence tests test" will be surprised to learn how powerfully IQ predicts not only school achievement but also job performance—even in jobs that don't require people to engage mostly in "mental" activities. Soldiers firing tank guns are more likely to hit their targets if they have higher IQs. Bright police officers make better cops than not-so-bright ones. Professor John E. Hunter of Michigan State concluded after surveying the abundant evidence on this matter that there are no jobs for which intelligence tests do not predict performance. Of course, other factors, such as personality and work habits, also make a difference, but IQ is emphatically not just a matter of being "good with words."

Intelligence tests are exceptional predictors of future performance. Consider taking advantage of them.

But be careful in your selection of tests. Be sure that the test you use to measure aptitude and intelligence has been professionally developed and that there is evidence that test results are *valid and reliable*.

PLAIN ENGLISH

Valid and reliable   These two words have special meanings in the world of testing. Validity refers to the extent that a given test actually measures what it is designed to measure. Reliability refers to the consistency of scores and measurement that is free of error.

BEHAVIOR TESTS

Behavior tests operate in the *soft area of measurement*. They predict an applicant's behavior on the job by exploring motivation, personality patterns or problems, and interpersonal skills. This information can be helpful in gaining a better understanding of the applicant and in preparing to interview him or her.

PLAIN ENGLISH

Soft measurements   Tests and inventories based mostly on self-reporting, beliefs and feelings, or past behavior. There are no right or wrong answers.

It is essential, however, to determine exactly what personality traits are applicable to the job. The mandatory success factors that you've discovered through your assessment of the job (see "Analyzing the Position" on page 408) will suggest personality traits and interpersonal abilities that should be measured.

Information about a candidate derived from behavior testing will help keep your interview focused on important issues. Concerns identified by testing signal the need to probe certain areas more thoroughly in the interview.

CAUTION

Although some employers insist on selecting and administering pre-employment tests themselves, psychological testing is best left to professionals. Industrial psychologists are trained to select testing that measures specific criteria (mandatory success factors), and are skilled in administering tests and interpreting results.

TIP

The cost of testing, compared to the value of the information received, is money well spent. The cost for testing alone is generally much less than the cost of a comprehensive psychological assessment.

TECHNICAL SKILLS TESTS

Technical skills tests are tests that are best performed in the natural work environment. These tests are designed to measure an applicant's ability to perform a specific task.

For example, a keyboarding test (formerly known as a typing test) measures an applicant's ability to produce a certain number of correct words per minute. Similar tests may seek to measure proficiency with various computer programs, or the ability to operate certain machinery or equipment.

CLINICAL EVALUATIONS

A comprehensive clinical evaluation by a licensed industrial psychologist involves a combination of tests and interviews with the applicant. These evaluations are usually reserved for applicants contending for key management positions with an organization.

Comprehensive evaluations are thorough and require a significant amount of professional time to complete. The cost is usually between $500 and $1,200, depending on location.

The employer furnishes the psychologist with a complete description of the job, along with its mandatory success factors. The psychologist selects tests and inventories that probe critical areas and performs in-depth interviews with applicants designed to confirm and supplement test results. Upon completion of the evaluation, the employer is usually provided with a multipage narrative report discussing the fitness of the applicant for the job.

POP PSYCHOLOGY TESTS

It never ceases to amaze me how many pop psychological tests appear on the market each year. Given the litigious nature of the society in which we live, it's difficult to imagine that anyone would risk using any instrument that has a questionable or nonexistent foundation in research.

Be careful. Pre-employment testing is, first and foremost, the practice of psychology. Let me say it again: Unless you have the requisite training and license, it's best to leave the practice of psychology to psychologists.

ARE PRE-EMPLOYMENT TESTS LEGAL?

The answer is not as uncomplicated as it may seem. Under present federal law, and in view of relevant Supreme Court decisions, it's fair to say that pre-employment tests are legal, provided that the following is true:

- The tests measure factors involved in the specific job for which the applicant is being considered. This point is important. A test that has only limited relationship or application to the job may result in a lawsuit for discrimination.

■ The tests have been professionally developed, and ample research exists demonstrating the tests to be valid and reliable in the testing of job candidates.

■ Testing is not conducted in a discriminatory fashion. All applicants for the job who pass initial screenings for qualification should be given an opportunity to demonstrate their competence and ability by participating in pre-employment testing.

CAUTION

Employers should also be aware that even when extreme caution has been taken to ensure that tests meet legal requirements, they could still be challenged under a disparate impact theory. An applicant can allege that test questions had a disparate impact on a protected group of which they are part (women, minorities, disabled individuals, people over 40 years of age, and so on).

The type of tests least likely to produce a legal challenge are tests that measure technical skills. These are easily validated and usually involve the measurement of skills directly related to the job. Validation of other, more subjective, tests is much more difficult and demands the services of a highly trained professional psychologist.

OTHER KINDS OF PRE-EMPLOYMENT TESTS

Listed here are a few other kinds of pre-employment tests and evaluations that employers often ask about. It's important to understand the potential legal consequences of using each of them in the selection process.

■ Medical examinations

■ Polygraph examinations

■ Drug and alcohol tests

■ Genetic tests

MEDICAL EXAMINATIONS

It is unlawful to require an applicant to take a medical examination in the *pre-offer stage* of the employment selection process. Prospective employers may not even so much as make inquiries into the medical history of an applicant at this juncture. That's because the EEOC broadly defines "medical examination" to mean any procedure or test that seeks information about an individual's physical or mental impairments or health.

PLAIN ENGLISH

Preoffer stage   That period in the selection process before the employer extends a conditional offer of employment to an applicant.

Questions concerning disability or about the nature and severity of a disability are also unlawful. Employers may ask questions about the applicant's ability to perform certain job-related functions, as long as the questions are not phrased in terms of a disability.

Also, employers may request applicants to perform physical agility tests that demonstrate their ability to do the job for which they are applying. However, any attempt to determine a physiological condition based on such a test would be considered a medical examination under EEOC guidelines and, therefore, would be prohibited.

In the *postoffer stage* of the selection process, an applicant can be asked to submit to a thorough medical examination. At this time, employers may also make disability-related inquiries.

PLAIN ENGLISH

Postoffer stage   That stage of the selection process when a conditional offer of employment has been extended to an applicant. Conditional offers are made when present employers have yet to be contacted, or when the offer is subject to the applicant passing a medical examination.

CAUTION

To avoid claims of discrimination, employers must treat all applicants the same. If one prospective employee is required to pass a medical examination before a firm offer of employment is extended, every applicant for a job in that same category must also be required to pass the same medical examination.

One more important consideration: If a prospective employee is eliminated as a result of medical or disability information, the criteria used to exclude the prospective worker must be job-related and based on business necessity. Furthermore, an employer must be able to demonstrate that the essential functions of the job could not be performed by the employee even with a reasonable accommodation on the part of the employer.

POLYGRAPH EXAMINATIONS

The use of polygraph examinations in the selection process has been the subject of litigation. Courts have consistently held that the use of polygraph examinations in this manner is illegal unless the employer is one that is specifically exempted by the Employee Polygraph Protection Act. The Act exempts employers who provide private security services and employers who manufacture, distribute, or dispense controlled substances.

Not long ago, the city of Long Beach, California, began a practice of requiring pre-employment polygraph examinations for all job applicants. City officials ordered the change in employment policy after discovering some money missing from city property.

The Long Beach City Employees Association sued the city but lost in Superior Court. However, the Supreme Court of California reversed the lower court's decision on appeal. The Supreme Court said that the city's policy on polygraph evaluations violated the prospective employee's right to privacy. The court further ruled that the city failed to prove a compelling interest to public safety that would necessitate polygraph testing, and questioned the reliability of the polygraph itself.

Polygraph examinations of existing staff are also prohibited. The Employee Polygraph Protection Act specifically prohibits demanding that present employees submit to polygraph examination. There are some exceptions, but they are few.

My advice if you're considering including a polygraph examination as a testing device: Forget it. Employers who violate the federal law are subject to a fine of $10,000 for each occurrence and, in addition, can be sued by the individuals involved.

DRUG TESTS

Drug tests are permissible in the preoffer stage as long as the employer provides prior written notice to applicants. Employers must also be prepared to demonstrate that a drug test is required of all applicants who reach the preoffer stage.

The EEOC has made it clear that anyone who is currently using illegal drugs is not protected by the Americans with Disabilities Act and may be denied employment (or fired, if already employed) on the basis of such use. Also, a test for illegal use of drugs is not considered a medical examination, and employers are not required to demonstrate that the drug test is job-related and consistent with business necessity.

If the testing laboratory notifies the employer that a drug test was positive for a controlled substance, the employer should discuss the result with the applicant to determine if there is some reasonable explanation (the applicant is taking prescribed drugs which are controlled substances under the care of a physician, for example).

If an applicant cannot provide a reasonable explanation for the positive drug screen, an employer is justified in withdrawing the conditional offer of employment.

CAUTION

Employers should consult their legal advisers about any changes that may occur in federal regulations pertaining to drug testing. State law may also dictate conditions under which drug tests may be required of prospective employees.

GENETIC TESTING

As I write this book, one of the greatest discoveries of our age was announced. Scientists involved in the Human Genome Project have announced that they have successfully "cracked" the human genetic code. This means that the locations and functions of human genes that code for inherited genetic traits have been discovered and mapped.

Although I'm no scientist, it seems clear that understanding the human genetic code has vast implications in the field of modern medicine. An individual's risk of falling victim to a genetically influenced disease may now be able to be identified early and treated proactively by altering the gene in question.

One of the unresolved issues that surrounds this discovery has to do with the use of genetic information in the workplace. Genetic information reveals predisposition to certain traits or disorders—should employers be allowed access to test results in considering applicants for employment? Should they be permitted to deny employment on the basis of genetic testing? Should employers be allowed to use genetic information to determine jobs best suited for an individual?

The legal and ethical implications of this research are overwhelming, challenging public policymakers to think beyond traditional legal and ethical paradigms.

Under current regulations, genetic testing would likely fall under the ADA's broad definition of "medical examination." If this is true, employers may require applicants in the postoffer stage to undergo genetic testing, as long as employers meet three basic conditions set by the ADA:

1. The employer must require that all new employees submit to genetic testing regardless of disability.

2. The employer must maintain a separate confidential file containing the results of genetic tests.

3. The employer can reject an applicant only if genetic test results clearly demonstrate that such a decision would be "job-related and consistent with business necessity."

All this seems like a page out of Aldous Huxley's *Utopia*, in which science controls the destiny of humankind and an individual's genetic blueprint determines his or her fate. Without doubt, there is a dark side to genetic testing.

THE 30-SECOND RECAP

- Pre-employment tests should be done before the interview to prevent claims of discrimination and to help focus the interview on important areas that may require further exploration.

- Aptitude tests, behavior tests, and intelligence tests are best selected and administered by a trained, licensed psychologist who specializes in employment testing.

- Pre-employment testing is legal as long as the tests involved are job-specific, are professionally developed, have proven validity, and are not conducted in a discriminatory fashion.

- Understanding what can be required of an applicant in the preoffer and postoffer stages of the selection process is important.

- Specific regulations apply to other forms of pre-employment tests, including medical examinations, polygraph tests, drug tests, and genetic tests.

Conducting a Job Interview

Interview Models

In this section you learn about the major types of interviews commonly used in the hiring process, and the advantages and disadvantages of each.

MUTUAL EXPLORATION

The primary purpose of a job interview is mutual exploration. The employer wants to discover more about an applicant's qualifications for a job; the applicant wants to discover more about the employer as well as the opportunity that the employer has to offer. The exploration is a learning process for both parties, each of whom develops understandings and expectations.

The employer can use several interview formats. Each, in its own way, fosters mutual exploration. Each format is designed to elicit specific information about a candidate's qualifications for the job while affording the candidate an opportunity to ask pertinent questions of the employer. However, the formats differ significantly in the way they accomplish these goals. As a result, the type and quality of information obtained can vary from format to format. Selecting the right format for an interview is crucial to hiring the right person for the job.

TYPES OF INTERVIEWS

The interview formats commonly used in the selection process include these:

- Telephone screening interview
- Traditional interview
- Stress interview
- Team interview
- Situational interview
- Structured behavioral interview

TELEPHONE INTERVIEW

> Hi, I'm Joan Peterson with XYZ Corporation, and I'd like to ask you a few questions about the resumé that you submitted for the position of sales associate with our firm. Do you have a few moments to talk?

TIP

Use telephone interviews as part of your "narrowing the field" activities.

Telephone interviews are primarily used in the preselection phase of the selection process. Their purpose is to narrow the number of applicants who will receive a formal interview by eliminating those who don't have the requisite education, experience, and skills to successfully do the job. Telephone interviews are used to obtain answers to any questions that may be posed by the applicant's resumé, and to obtain additional information about the skills and experience of an applicant.

One advantage of the telephone interview is that it can be accomplished quickly and economically. Without telephone interviews, organizations would be overwhelmed by the task of interviewing candidates face to face who could have been disqualified much earlier in the process.

In a typical telephone interview, the interviewer spends a few minutes explaining the position and how it fits into the organization. The interviewer then asks some predetermined questions about background and education, and attempts to clarify any inconsistencies in the resumé. Typically, the interviewer inquires whether the applicant has any questions about the position, and concludes the interview by explaining what the applicant can expect to occur next in the selection process.

Telephone interviews are usually highly focused and last about 10 to 15 minutes.

CAUTION

Remember that while you are evaluating applicants by phone, good candidates will also be evaluating you. Be sure to represent your organization well by remaining professional and courteous.

Advantages: Telephone interviews are fast, easy to accomplish, and cost-efficient. They are an effective way to narrow the field of applicants to those who will be offered a personal interview.

Disadvantages: Telephone interviews eliminate the possibility of evaluating an applicant's nonverbal behavior. In addition, it's easy for an interviewer to judge a candidate on the basis of "telephone presence" instead of mandatory success factors. People who would otherwise make excellent candidates may not have good telephone communication skills.

TRADITIONAL INTERVIEW

Tell us a little about yourself.

The traditional interview is the most common form of interview in small- to medium-sized organizations, and it's not all that uncommon in large organizations and government offices.

Here are some characteristics of the traditional interview:

- Questions are often vague, unfocused, and theoretical.
- Candidates are allowed to theorize and generalize about their background and experience.
- Very few questions have follow-up probes to obtain more specific information.
- Candidates who have become skilled at interviewing often gain control of the interview and tend to redirect attention to areas of their choice.
- Interviewers may take some notes during the interview, but note taking is not tremendously important.
- Interviews can easily drift into rapport-building sessions.

In the traditional format, questions are often predictable, allowing applicants an opportunity to rehearse their responses in advance. Here are some of the more common questions that are usually part of a traditional interview:

- Tell us a little about yourself. (Ninety-five percent of all traditional interviews begin this way.)
- What are your strengths and weaknesses?
- What do you hope to be doing five years from now?
- What are your long-term goals and objectives?
- Why did you choose this particular career path?
- Why are you interested in working with us?
- What is your greatest professional accomplishment to date, and your greatest professional disappointment?

And my all-time favorite:

- If you were a tree, what kind of tree would you be?

The traditional interview has always bothered me. Interviewers too often surrender control of the interview to the applicant, which is absurd. Moreover, interviewers seem resolutely determined to ask the kinds of questions that can easily be anticipated by candidates, many of whom have rehearsed their answers.

Then, too, there's the matter of honesty. Using the traditional interview format, there's absolutely no way of knowing whether a candidate is telling the truth or engaging in pure fantasy. Furthermore, the traditional interview offers the candidate who's well rehearsed or proficient in the art of interviewing a tailor-made opportunity to eclipse those who are better qualified for the position.

But the most irritating part of the traditional interview is the contribution it makes to poor hiring decisions. Because interviews of this type often lack substance, "gut feelings" frequently replace solid, objective judgements based on a candidate's strengths and competencies. Too often, the subjective information derived from the interview is used only to support and reinforce decisions based on "gut feelings."

CAUTION

Never confuse the quality of an interview with the quality of a candidate. A good interviewer seeks to match the skills and competencies of an applicant with the mandatory success factors of the job; a good candidate is one who closely matches what is being sought. A candidate with great interviewing skills is not necessarily a great candidate for the job.

Interviewers sometimes attempt to "structure" the traditional interview—ask the same prepared questions of every candidate—especially for civil service positions. While structuring the traditional interview may prevent claims of unfair hiring practices by unsuccessful applicants, they do little to solve the real problem of figuring out who's best for the job. The kinds of questions asked in the typical traditional interview usually result in hiring decisions based on unreliable and highly subjective information. And most attempts at structuring don't even include a uniform method of evaluating candidates based upon the job's mandatory success factors.

PLAIN ENGLISH

Unstructured interview   An informal process similar to a conversation with an applicant. In unstructured interviews, the interviewer asks questions about key areas of concern that may be different for each applicant. In a structured interview process, questions specifically relating to an open position are formulated in advance of the interview and each question is asked of each applicant. Structured interviews are more formal.

Advantages: The traditional interview provides an opportunity to engage in a rapport-building exercise that may be enjoyable.

Disadvantages: Numerous. In my opinion, the traditional interview, and the poor hiring decisions that it inspires, is a surefire way for an organization to guarantee itself a high percentage of hiring mistakes. The fact is, the traditional interview no longer works, and probably never did.

Stress Interview

> Do you see this paper clip I'm holding in my hand? Paper clips are useful little tools, wouldn't you agree? Tell me 12 uses for a paper clip. You have 60 seconds, beginning now.

The role of an interviewer drastically changes in a stress interview. The interviewer becomes more of an interrogator who deliberately asks questions designed to make an applicant feel uncomfortable and insecure.

The purpose of stress interviews is to discover whether a candidate can cope with difficult, demanding situations in which the best in performance is required even in the worst of conditions. Some jobs, after all, not only necessitate someone with the technical expertise to do the job, but also someone who can keep cool even in incredibly stressful situations.

TIP

Stress interviews have their place, but only in situations in which the position being sought is extremely demanding. Even then, a stress interview should be used only as a follow-up to the primary interview, and only finalists should be invited to participate.

Questions asked of candidates in a stress interview can often sound crude and offensive. They're designed to be. Questions are phrased to determine whether a candidate will react to the sarcasm and general nastiness of the interviewer, or maintain a sense of restraint and deal with questions in a noncombative manner. Will the candidate lose composure or maintain it in the midst of a stressful environment?

Stress interviews are justified when job-related questions like these need to be answered:

- Can the candidate survive the rigors of being part of a special services police unit where life and death situations are routine, or will the candidate come unglued and place his life and the lives of others in jeopardy?
- Can the candidate handle the extreme daily pressures of being an air traffic controller responsible for the lives and safety of unnumbered air travelers together with multiple millions of dollars in equipment?
- Will the candidate succumb to the strain of a large city newspaper where work is regularly done under the pressure of surrealistically compressed deadlines?

For these and similar occupations, a stress interview may well be an important part of the selection process.

Advantages: Stress interviews, although unpleasant for the candidate and the interviewer, are an effective method of determining whether a candidate can function professionally under extreme conditions.

Disadvantages: While stress interviews may help determine an applicant's ability to work under extreme conditions, it's important to remember that those with some rather severe types of personality disorders will also do well. Also, overly zealous interviewers can chase off all but the most confrontational (and therefore potentially unmanageable) candidates.

TEAM INTERVIEW

As you know, it's our unit's job to publish the monthly company newsletter. Tell us what publications experience you've had in your present and former jobs.

Team interviews are becoming increasingly popular. They operate on the premise that the more knowledgeable people who are involved in the hiring process, the better the hiring decision will be.

Using the team interview approach, selected members of a division, department, or unit where the job opening exists meet with the candidate either individually or as a group. Each team member is free to ask the candidate job-related questions.

Following the interview, team members discuss the candidate's strengths and weaknesses in relationship to the job and record their impressions.

Team interviews can be effective, but only when they're structured (all applicants are asked the same job-related questions) and team members use a common assessment guide to rate applicants. Unstructured interviewing by teams often degenerates into group conversations, with the hiring decision being based on "gut instinct."

Advantages: Team interviews involve people with a vested interest in selecting the right candidate for the job. After all, they are the people with whom the successful candidate will eventually work. An additional advantage is that employees are more committed to helping a newcomer succeed when they have had direct input in the hiring decision.

Disadvantages: Teams sometimes resist structure and, in doing so, destroy the real value of team interviews.

TIP

Team interviews work best when they are part of another interview format. For example, a team approach to interviewing candidates using the structured behavioral model (discussed later in this section) will maintain the advantages of team interviewing and include the structure and evaluation tools necessary to maintain objectivity.

SITUATIONAL INTERVIEW

Suppose on your first day at work with us the telephone rings. It's a call from an irate customer who is threatening to sue us unless we take back the equipment he bought from us and refund his money. What would you do?

The situational interview is similar to a traditional interview, with some important differences. The situational interview is usually structured and makes use of a common assessment guide.

Questions are *hypothetical* and designed to elicit responses that provide a glimpse into a candidate's thinking processes, personal values, creativity, and practical experience.

PLAIN ENGLISH

Hypothetical   Imaginary. Hypothetical interview questions attempt to discover how a candidate would act if a certain situation were to occur; both the question and the response are purely conjecture.

Hypothetical problems can also be given to candidates to analyze and solve as the interviewer (or interview team) looks on. This presents the opportunity to evaluate candidates as they attempt to solve problems that may actually occur on the job. Is the candidate completely befuddled by the problem? Has the candidate plunged headfirst into the problem only to offer a quick, simplistic solution? In wrestling with the problem, does the candidate demonstrate exceptional problem-solving skills, including analyzing and strategizing a solution? Does the candidate offer reasoned responses that display a unique combination of imagination, courage, and creativity?

The fundamental problem with the situational interview is that it deals only with the hypothetical. You can't assume that a candidate will be a highly creative problem solver on the job just because he or she solved a hypothetical problem in an interview.

Without a doubt, situational interviews provide some insight into the way a candidate thinks, feels, and acts. But they don't provide you with the objective information necessary to help you make an informed hiring decision. For example, one of the most critical deficiencies of the situational interview is that you learn what a candidate *could do* in the hypothetical situation being discussed, instead of what that person *has done* in different but similarly challenging situations in the past.

Advantages: Situational interviews provide some insight into a candidate's problem-solving skills, reasoning abilities, and creativity. They are interesting for the interviewer, and challenging for the candidate.

Disadvantages: By concentrating on the hypothetical, the interviewer never learns about how a candidate has actually behaved in the past when confronted with different but similarly challenging situations. Hypothetical solutions to hypothetical problems force a candidate to offer only conjecture about what could be done.

STRUCTURED BEHAVIORAL INTERVIEW

> Tell me about a time when you disagreed with a decision made by your boss. What did you do?

Structured behavioral interviewing is based on this simple premise: The most accurate predictor of future performance is past performance in a similar situation. This form of interviewing focuses on real-life job-related experiences, behaviors, knowledge, skills, and abilities.

Candidates are asked to talk about actual situations in which they've had to use certain skills and abilities. In answering behavioral questions, candidates draw from their past experiences at work, in school, as a volunteer, or even from extracurricular activities and hobbies. Structured behavioral interviewing is considered a modern business best practice.

In "Structured Behavioral Interviewing: Part 1" on page 450, we'll discuss structured behavioral interviewing at length. But for the purposes of this lesson, it's important to understand that structured behavioral interviewing can revolutionize your interviewing practices and, according to my research, improve your chances of hiring the right candidates by as much as 300 percent.

Advantages: Structured behavioral interviewing enables you to catch a glimpse of a candidate dealing with real-life situations that required the same skills and abilities that your open position requires. A structured behavioral format allows you to get "behind" the resumé and explore the depth and breadth of a candidate's experience and training. Job-related questions are prepared in advance, and the same questions are asked of each candidate interviewed. Combined with a rating system tied to the mandatory success factors that you're seeking, this model is an objective and highly effective way to select a candidate.

Disadvantages: Initially, adjusting to the structured behavioral model can be challenging, especially for those who have used the traditional interview model for years. With a little practice, however, you'll soon be comfortable with structured behavioral interviewing.

THE 30-SECOND RECAP

- Selecting the best format for an employment interview is one of the most important tasks in the selection process.

- Telephone interviews are an effective and inexpensive way to help narrow the field of candidates to a manageable number.

- The traditional interview usually results in traditionally high numbers of hiring mistakes.

- Stress interviews should be reserved for positions that involve extremely stressful conditions.

- Team interviews work well when they are part of a structured interview format.

- Situational interviews deal in the hypothetical; candidates offer conjecture about what they might do in a given situation.

- Structured behavioral interviews focus on the behavior of candidates in past situations requiring skills and abilities similar to those required by the position they're interviewing for.

Structured Behavioral Interviewing: Part 1

In this section you learn about structured behavioral interviewing and how a typical structured behavioral interview works.

WHY STRUCTURED BEHAVIORAL INTERVIEWING?

Whether you're searching for an entry-level employee or a seasoned executive, structured behavioral interviewing will help you select the best candidate for the job. The technique is based on the *behavioral consistency principle* that the best method of predicting future behavior is to determine past behavior under similar circumstances.

PLAIN ENGLISH

Behavioral consistency principle   Argues that the best predictor of future behavior is past behavior in similar situations.

Practically speaking, the behavioral consistency principle suggests that probes such as "Tell me about a disagreement you've had with your boss" will prompt more worthwhile information about an applicant than questions such as "If you were a tree, what kind of tree would you be?"

Behavioral questions force candidates to discuss real-life situations in which they use key skills to solve problems. As a result, interviewers are given a unique opportunity to look "behind" the resumé and discover a candidate's real potential.

TIP

Expect some candidates—those who rehearsed their answers in preparation for a traditional interview—to be surprised that the questions you ask require them to think and reveal real-life behaviors.

Structured behavioral interviewing has a proven track record of success. My informal research has shown that this method of interviewing improves the probability of hiring successfully by more than three times the rate of a traditional, less structured interview. Current employment literature reports similar findings and recommends structured behavioral interviewing as a best practice.

But that's not all. Consider these added benefits:

- Structured behavioral interviewing provides an orderly, efficient process of job-related assessment.

- Behaviorally based questions yield more valuable information about a candidate than questions normally asked in traditional interviews.

- Managers obtain and evaluate behavioral evidence of skills and abilities before making critical hiring decisions.

- Legal guidelines involving fairness in the selection process are respected.

- There is maximum assurance that a good match will ultimately exist between new hires and the jobs that they enter.

- Structured behavioral interviewing results in shorter new employee training time, higher initial productivity, and significantly lower rates of turnover.

Successful organizations use structured behavioral interviewing because it works. Hiring decisions based on behavioral evidence about a candidate's job-related skills are bound to be better decisions than those based on a "hunch" or "a gut feeling."

How Structured Behavioral Interviewing Is Different

Traditional forms of interviewing can enable some candidates to look good because they offer the ideal opportunity to display their presentation skills and knowledge of the subject matter. But talking in generalizations is one thing, and offering concrete examples is another.

Structured behavioral interviewing requires a candidate to talk about real-life situations in which they used the particular skill being evaluated. Using the structured behavioral interview model, it's not "Do you know how to do it?" but rather "Tell us how you've done it and the result that you achieved."

Structured behavioral interviews differ from traditional interview formats in a number of additional important ways. For example:

- Control of the structured behavioral interview always remains with the interviewer. Candidates are never allowed to redirect the focus of questions to areas of their own choosing.

- The interview is "structured," which means that the same job-related questions are asked of all candidates and that each question is based on a specific mandatory success factor of the job.

- Candidates are evaluated using a standard evaluation tool also based on mandatory success factors. "Gut feelings" and "hunches" are ignored.

- Candidates are not presented with hypothetical questions to answer or problems to solve. Instead of being asked to speculate on what they would do in certain situations, candidates are asked what they have actually done in similar situations in the past.

- Follow-up probes, similar to those used in more traditional types of interviewing, are used extensively to test answers for accuracy, honesty, and consistency.

- Interviewers take copious notes throughout the interview, as opposed to other forms of interviewing, in which taking notes is not as much of a priority.

A CONSISTENT INTERVIEW PROCESS

Consistency is important in the interview process. It ensures that interviewers perform quality interviews that elicit relevant information, and that candidates leave with a favorable impression of the organization.

The structured behavioral interview process is no exception. You'll need to consider the following consistency guidelines.

First, if you plan to use a panel of interviewers, be careful whom you select. This is especially important if the position being filled is a senior position. For most positions, however, a good rule of thumb is to invite all supervisors to whom the new employee will report, together with a peer or two from the department or unit in which the opening exists. These are the people who know what it takes to get the job done; their input will be valuable.

TIP

A panel interview offers the advantage of allowing several interviewers to question and evaluate a candidate. Consider assigning roles to members of the interview team: "hostile interviewer," "friendly interviewer," "company salesman," and so on. How a candidate responds to the various personalities can in itself be revealing.

Second, in developing the interview process, make sure that you allocate enough time for each interview, remembering that part of the time allotted must be devoted to evaluating the candidate following the interview. Usually the position to be filled will determine the length of the interview. (It's common for middle-management positions to require interview slots of two hours or more.) Don't short-change either the candidate or yourself by failing to provide an appropriate amount of time for the tasks to be accomplished.

Third, be sure to stay on schedule. Nothing communicates unprofessionalism quicker than interviews that always seem to be "running late." Start on time; end on time. In fact, it's a good idea to inform a candidate of an anticipated end time before the interview begins. Concern about time demonstrates regard for the candidate and for those participating in the interview.

Fourth, to the extent possible, arrange only morning interviews. It's a fact that neither candidate nor interviewer performs as well later in the afternoon. Give yourself and your candidates an opportunity to perform at peak levels.

Finally, try to avoid interviewing more than two to three candidates a day. It's difficult to do justice to more than that.

Plan Each Stage of the Interview

To ensure consistency in the interview process, be sure that your interviews contain three major parts:

- Opening
- Information exchange
- Closing

Although each stage is distinct and has a unique purpose, the overall process should be seamless. Moving from the opening to the information exchange and finally to the closing should be done smoothly and naturally.

TIP

Give each interviewer all the candidate's information well in advance of the interview. This will enable each participant to ask pertinent questions about a candidate's background, and generally will enhance the interviewer's ability to evaluate candidates.

The Opening

Interviews should open with a genuine attempt to put the candidate at ease. The interviewer (or primary interviewer, in panel interview formats) should use body language that conveys warmth and genuine pleasure in meeting the candidate—standing when the candidate enters the room, leaning forward to offer a handshake, and smiling are great ways to break the ice and establish instant positive rapport.

Once the candidate is seated, introduce him or her to everyone participating in the interview and ask each panel member to introduce themselves by name and position within the organization.

The opening of the interview is the time to talk about the interview process. Tell the candidate what to expect during the interview.

Begin by providing a context for the interview. You might say something like, "The purpose of our interview with you today is to provide you with an opportunity to learn more about our organization … and for us to learn more about you. We're particularly interested in learning whether you have the qualifications we're seeking for the position of sales manager."

CAUTION

In attempting to help a candidate feel at ease, it's tempting to ask a few personal questions that are irrelevant to the job. Resist the temptation! Even innocent questions about a candidate's family are prohibited and could be grounds for a discrimination action by an unsuccessful applicant.

The Information Exchange

The information exchange is the central part of the interview. During the information exchange, questions are asked and information is received that will lead directly to a decision to hire or not to hire. Don't hesitate to ask as many follow-up questions as needed whenever you feel that more information is required.

Be sure that all questions about the candidate's experience, education, and work history are asked and answered. Now is the time to explore any gaps in a candidate's employment history, and to confirm (if necessary) important information about education, experience, and job-related skills and abilities. Such questions should be limited; this is not a time to ask a candidate to make a verbal presentation of the entire resumé.

TIP

Practice the 80/20 rule: During the core part of an interview, the candidate should do 80 percent of the talking, and the interviewer should do only 20 percent. Resist the urge to help candidates who become stalled or who are searching for words to convey information.

To help put a candidate at ease, it's wise to ask easier questions first. Questions about the candidate's resumé or application having to do with experience or training work particularly well in the beginning of an interview, as do questions that elicit insight into a candidate's character and personality such as, "Of all the jobs you've held in the past, which was the one you liked best and why?"

As you move into the more difficult structured behavioral questions, be sure to allow the candidate time to think through each question and formulate a response. Allow periods of silence. Don't rush the candidate, either verbally or nonverbally.

Closing

The manner in which you close an interview will leave a lasting impression on the candidate. Interviews should be closed in a professional, unhurried manner. Ask one member of the team to "sell the company" by presenting the benefits of working for the organization and the opportunities that exist. Invite the candidate to ask any lingering questions. Finally, tie up any loose ends that need attention, and inform the candidate of what to expect next.

Don't forget to thank the candidate for participating in the interview. By standing and offering a handshake, you signal to the candidate that the interview has concluded.

A Consistent Evaluation Process

In the structured behavioral interview model, the process of evaluating candidates should also be structured. You should devise an assessment tool to help your organization evaluate candidates consistently.

The Assessment Tool

Design your assessment tool with simplicity and consistency in mind. The idea is to assess a candidate's behavioral evidence as it relates to the mandatory success factors required by the position. That's as technical as your tool should get.

> **TIP**
>
> Occasionally I've found assessment tools that appear to be very complicated and technical. With some of them, the math alone would probably frighten Einstein. Take my word for it, you don't need anything that complicated. I recommend that you construct your own assessment tool and keep it simple. Simple tools are usually the most effective.

In constructing an assessment tool, devise a system in which mandatory success factors identified within each skill set are weighted depending on importance. For example, if there are six mandatory success factors in the technical skills set, the most important of the six factors would be given a weight of 6; the second most important would be weighted 5; the third would be weighted 4; and so on.

Candidate performance scores for each factor, which may range from 0 (poor) to 5 (excellent), are then multiplied by the weight factor to arrive at an adjusted score for the factor being assessed. If several members of an interview team have rated the candidate, average the scores for each skill set to determine final candidate scores.

SOME ADDITIONAL IDEAS TO CONSIDER

Here are some additional ideas to consider as you develop a process for evaluating candidates following an interview:

- Don't wait. Make it a point to take a few minutes following each interview to complete the evaluation. The quality of evaluations sharply decreases when they are completed following a series of interviews.

- If you have used a panel of interviewers, hold off any discussion of a candidate's strengths and weaknesses until each member has completed the written evaluation.

- Instruct each team participant to focus on the evidence of important job-related skills. Don't allow "gut feelings" to play a role in the evaluation process.

- Be sure that all interviewer notes have to do with a job-related topic. Ignore anything that is not directly applicable to the job for which the candidate has applied.

- Make sure that interviewer notes are legible and that they contain complete sentences. Interviewer notes may become very important when it's time to make a hiring decision.

LOCATION OF THE INTERVIEW

Deciding on a location for the interview is an important part of the planning process. Choose a location suitable to the situation.

For example, if the position you're attempting to fill is, at the moment, confidential, choose a location away from the office. Private meeting rooms in hotels can work well in these instances.

But most of the time, candidates are interviewed in the workplace. For those situations, I recommend conducting interviews in an office or meeting room that is comfortable, well lit, and free of disrupting noise. Your objective should be an atmosphere that will help the candidate feel at ease.

If there's a telephone in the room, unplug it or turn off the ringer. Consider hanging a "Do Not Disturb" sign on the door during the interview to prevent unnecessary interruptions. Instruct members of the interview panel to turn off cellular phones and pagers. Advise secretaries and other office staff to disturb panel members only in cases of extreme emergency.

Also be mindful of seating arrangements. Panel interviews are sometimes set up so that the candidate, sitting alone, faces the interview panel, seated at a long table. This can be a very intimidating arrangement for the candidate (although effective if you want to observe a candidate's behavior in a tense situation). A less intimidating arrangement would be for the interview panel to be seated around a long table, with the candidate at one end.

CAUTION

Make sure that the candidate's chair is not lower than the chairs used by the panel members. Otherwise, the candidate may be intimidated unintentionally.

THE 30-SECOND RECAP

- Structured behavioral interviewing is based on the theory that the best predictor of future behavior is past behavior in similar circumstances.

- Structured behavioral interviewing examines behavioral evidence of a candidate's skills and abilities, and compares them to identified mandatory success factors of the job being sought.

- The process of structured behavioral interviewing should be well defined and communicated to all who participate so that interviews are conducted in a consistent manner.

- The primary purpose of the interview is to hear from the candidate, so be sure to follow the 80/20 rule—let the candidate do most of the talking.

- Scoring by evaluators should be completed immediately following each interview to preserve integrity of the data and to maintain consistency.

- Make location and seating arrangements part of your interview planning process.

Structured Behavioral Interviewing: Part 2

In this section you learn how to develop effective behavioral questions and follow-up probes that get behind the resumé to explore a candidate's competency in key areas.

LEARNING TO ASK QUESTIONS

Structured behavioral interviewing is designed to minimize personal impressions and focus instead on a candidate's actions and behaviors. That's important because successful hiring decisions are based on objective behavioral evidence demonstrating a candidate's proficiency with identified job-related skills—not on subjective impressions.

Learning to develop questions that explore a candidate's past behaviors is key. Become proficient at it, and your "successful hire" numbers will start to skyrocket.

PLAIN ENGLISH

Probe   A question or request that seeks specific information, clarification, or confirmation from a candidate being interviewed. Probes may be open or closed, depending on the purpose.

QUESTIONING CONSISTENTLY

One reason that structured behavioral interviewing is so effective is its use of consistent questions. You achieve consistency when you ask the same behavioral questions of each candidate and align each question to a mandatory success factor within a specific skill set.

Whether you're interviewing for chief executive officer or custodian, these are the skill sets that you'll want to consider:

- Technical skills (or competencies)
- Functional skills
- Self-management skills
- Interpersonal skills

CAUTION

In developing questions and follow-up probes, remember to keep them focused on the mandatory success factors of the job being sought. As tempting as it may be to wander into more personal areas, avoid doing so. Seeking information unrelated to the job is looking for trouble.

Analyzing a job to identify mandatory success factors for each of the skill sets is an important part of the interview process. Once identified, mandatory success factors are weighted by order of importance, and behavioral questions are developed for each factor.

The objective is to discover behavioral evidence of a candidate's level of competency in each of the skills required for success. Follow-up probes are used to ensure that each key skill has been thoroughly explored, and to confirm information or challenge inconsistencies.

DEVELOPING BEHAVIORAL QUESTIONS

Behavioral questions seek responses from candidates based on their real-life work experiences. Each response should demonstrate the practical use of key skills and abilities necessary for success in the job under consideration.

Asking each candidate the same behavioral questions ensures fairness and consistency in the interview process. But more than that, the procedure provides a fair and equitable means of objectively comparing each candidate's qualifications—and protects you from charges of illegal hiring practices.

OPEN BEHAVIORAL QUESTIONS

Prepare *open behavioral questions* for all identified mandatory success factors. Their purpose is to reveal key behavioral information by encouraging a candidate to talk about past situations in which the use of a particular skill was important.

PLAIN ENGLISH

Open behavioral questions   Questions that cannot be answered with a simple "yes" or "no." They require a candidate to discuss at length an incident from the past that required a working knowledge of specific skills.

Because open behavioral questions seek descriptions of real-life personal and interpersonal situations, they usually begin with phrases such as these:

- "Tell me about ..."
- "Describe a time when you ..."
- "Give me an example of a time in which you ..."
- "Describe the most significant ..."
- "What did you do in your last job when ..."
- "Describe a situation in which you ..."
- "Relate a personal story in which you ..."
- "Relate a scenario where you ..."
- "Narrate a situation in school when you ..."

- "Describe an opportunity in which you ..."
- "Tell me about an occasion in which you ..."

TIP

Don't worry about silences during the interview, when candidates attempt to think of appropriate behavioral responses to questions. Your questions are not only causing them to think, but to openly discuss areas that may be sensitive.

Occasionally a candidate will have to be prompted to provide more information about a disclosed situation or problem. You can accomplish this by using additional open probes such as these:

- "Oh?"
- "Tell me more."
- "Really?"
- "Please go on."
- "What happened then?"
- "I'd be interested in knowing more about that."

Probes such as these not only encourage a candidate to provide more information, but they also offer assurance that you're listening and interested in what's being said.

TIP

Structured behavioral interviewing is not designed to find a candidate with "all the right answers." In fact, the ideal candidate should be one who demonstrates a steady growth in competence and skill over time. Candidates who are courageous enough to reveal behavior that they now recognize to be faulty demonstrate growth and maturity.

FOLLOW-UP PROBES

Follow-up probes can be either open or closed, depending on the information that you seek. Open follow-up probes are used to search for further behavioral evidence of a skill, to provide more information about a specific event, or to resolve inconsistencies. Open follow-up probes can also be used to guide a wandering candidate back to the question at hand.

Because they are responsive to information provided by a candidate, open follow-up probes are always impromptu and usually begin with one of these phrases:

- "Tell me more about ..."
- "Help me to understand why ..."
- "Could you explain ..."
- "I'd be interested in hearing more about ..."
- "Let's talk more about ..."
- "I'd like to return to my original question, which is ..."

Closed follow-up probes are used to solicit very specific information. This kind of probe can usually be answered with a "yes" or "no" or with just a few words. Closed follow-up probes are used to obtain confirmation of important information or to clear up misunderstandings. Here are a few examples of closed follow-up probes:

- "You said that you are fully qualified for a state license to practice acupuncture?"
- "Did I hear you say that you think your present employer is a crook?"
- "Is it correct that you graduated from Dartmouth in June of 1992?"
- "When do you expect to take your CPA examination?"

EXAMPLE OF AN OPEN BEHAVIORAL QUESTION WITH OPEN FOLLOW-UP PROBES

"Tell me about a time when you were completely over your head with work on a particular project. How did you deal with the situation?"

The purpose of the question is to assess the candidate's ability to manage time. This question would be asked if being skilled in time management was one of the identified mandatory success factors.

Follow-up probes could include questions such as these:

- "That's interesting. Tell me more about what you did to get control of the situation."
- "How did you decide which task to do first?"
- "What was the outcome of your actions?"
- "What could you have done differently?"
- "How did the experience change the way you work today?"

Note that the purpose of each of these open follow-up probes is to more fully explore the candidate's personal thoughts, feelings, motivations, and behavior. Questions that begin with "why," "what," or "how" accomplish this objective particularly well.

Use open follow-up probes freely. In fact, it's helpful to continue to probe until you've discovered the result of a given action or learned how the situation turned out. And in some cases, it's entirely appropriate to ask the candidate what could have been done differently or better.

CANDIDATES WHO LIE

Occasionally follow-up probes make it plain that a candidate is not providing truthful behavioral information at all. ("You indicated in your answer that you began your research project in April of 1994; your resumé, however, indicates that during that period you were a full-time student. Could you please explain further?") Confronted with behavioral questioning, candidates sometimes attempt to fabricate stories rather than to discuss real-life situations. On catching a candidate in a lie, some interviewers politely end the interview and disqualify the candidate from further consideration.

How you handle a deceitful candidate is up to you. But if you elect to continue to interview a candidate who has been untruthful, at the very least make careful note of the situation so that the matter is taken into account in the evaluation phase of the process. Telling boldfaced lies in an interview reveals much about a candidate's character and sense of personal integrity. This kind of information should not be ignored.

CAUTION

Don't conclude that a candidate has lied to you unless the candidate actually confirms the falsehood. Unless confirmed by the candidate, opinions in this regard are dangerous and should not appear in the notes of the interview.

CONTRARY EVIDENCE QUESTIONS

At first, this type of question seems tricky and may feel uncomfortable to ask. But the intent of contrary evidence questions is not to trick or trap a candidate, but to drill down to reveal what's behind a candidate's past work experiences. Contrary evidence questions are an effective tool to use in exploring the degree and refinement of a candidate's skills.

Contrary evidence questions have two parts: The first part describes a situation that is somewhat negative; the second part asks for behavioral evidence that demonstrates action taken by the candidate that was contrary to the precipitating situation. The second part of the question is asked only after the first part has been answered. For example:

Interviewer: "What things make you angry?"

After candidates answer the question by telling the interviewer all the things that make them angry, the second part of the question is then asked:

Interviewer: "How do you deal with each of those situations?"

Here are a few more contrary evidence questions to consider:

- "Tell me about a time when you had to make a difficult decision about a matter that wasn't covered by a company policy. What did you do?"
- "Do you have job-related areas that you need to improve? Tell me about a time that illustrates your need for improvement."
- "What experience have you had dealing with subordinates with performance problems? Give me an example of a recent problem and how you resolved it."
- "What were the major obstacles that you encountered in your present job? Tell me how you overcame each of them."

At least one contrary evidence question should be included in every structured behavioral interview. The ability to positively impact negative situations is of vital importance. Questions that begin with behavioral negatives tend to take candidates off guard a bit, but result in excellent behavioral evidence that is very valuable.

CONTINUUM QUESTIONS

Another kind of question that provides valuable insight is the continuum question. Continuum questions place candidates between two positive qualities, one of which is an identified mandatory success factor and critical to the successful performance of the job being sought, the other of which is something that may be a commendable skill but not a mandatory success factor for the position.

Here are some examples of effective continuum questions (remember to ask for specific behavioral evidence for the answer):

- "On a continuum between being a team player and working independently, where do you see yourself?"
- "On a continuum between being a loner and being a people person, where do you fit?"

■ "On a continuum between hating new technology and loving it, where do you fit?"

Try using a continuum question to explore areas of personal preference. Use follow-up questions to explore responses thoroughly, and don't be afraid to ask for behavioral evidence for the answers provided.

SELF-APPRAISAL QUESTIONS

Self-appraisal questions present an opportunity to learn how candidates think others perceive them. Make an effort to include a self-appraisal question in every interview. The question asks a candidate to evaluate how others perceive his or her performance of a mandatory success factor. This can be very revealing.

Here's a typical self-appraisal question: "If I were to call your present supervisor, how would she describe your ability to meet deadlines on a timely basis?"

And here's a bonus for those who followed my earlier recommendation and already talked with the candidate's supervisor: You'll immediately be able to compare a candidate's response with the actual report of the supervisor. The supervisor may have also provided enough additional information about the candidate's work experience to know whether a more thorough assessment of other key areas is warranted.

But whether you contact references before an interview or afterward, the self-appraisal question is a valuable tool. It will help you assess whether there's congruity in the way candidates think they are perceived, and the way they're actually perceived by those who have supervised them and know them well. Lack of congruity in this regard could mean that the candidate may be out-of-touch with reality in some important way or simply attempting to mislead the interviewer.

Be sure to use follow-up probes to obtain behavioral evidence for a candidate's answer. "Why," "what," and "how" probes will help provide the necessary additional information. Be prepared to learn some interesting and useful information about a candidate using this style of question.

ANSWERING BEHAVIORAL QUESTIONS: THE STAR FORMULA

Behavioral questions are intended to make candidates think. Responses should tell a complete story with a beginning, a middle, and an end. You should expect stories of this nature to convey a considerable amount of factual detail. In fact, it's the lack of detail that often betrays those who attempt to fabricate behavioral stories.

TIP

Some candidates may lack on-the-job experience. In those instances, ask behavioral questions that explore real life experiences
from school or from volunteer service. Behavioral evidence of skills
used in these settings is also a valid indicator of a candidate's likelihood of success on the job.

I recommend using the STAR technique to ensure that a candidate's story is
fully probed. Here's how the STAR technique works:

- **S and T = situation or task.** A candidate should talk about a specific situation or task in which they had to use certain skills and abilities to deal with a real problem or concern.

- **A = action.** Find out what actions the candidate took to resolve the
  situation or perform the task. Actions are important because they
  reveal the extent of the candidate's ability to use many of the skills
  required in a new employee. This area requires thorough exploration
  through the use of follow-up probes.

- **R = results.** Don't forget to find out the result of the candidate's
  actions. Were the results those that were intended? What could the
  candidate have done differently or better?

This simple formula will help you explore behavioral situations completely
and obtain valuable information about a candidate's ability to use key skills in
practical ways. The formula also helps keep interviews focused and on track.

TIP

Limit your interviews to the very best candidates. Also limit the
number of candidates (six to eight is optimal) who will be offered
an interview. Remember, the shorter the short list, the quicker you'll
be able to fill the position.

Second Interview Strategies

Sometimes, depending on the position, the first round of interviews will result
in the selection of candidates for a *short list*. That means that a second interview eventually needs to take place.

But second interviews can be quite different from the first. A number of
strategies work well for second interviews. Each of these strategies attempts
to further evaluate a candidate's qualifications by having the candidate
become involved in some form of actual work experience.

PLAIN ENGLISH

Short list   A list of a few select candidates who achieved the highest scores in an initial interview and have been chosen to continue with the selection process.

PROJECT REVIEW

In this method of evaluation, candidate finalists are assigned projects. For consistency and fairness, each candidate is assigned the same project.

Projects should require specific criteria and should be based on the job being sought. For example, candidates for a sales manager position might be asked to present a plan for keeping the sales staff motivated. Candidates for a marketing manager position might be asked to develop a strategic marketing plan for a specific product or service.

Assignments have deadlines, and project review assignments are no exception. Candidates usually are allowed no more than two or three days to complete the task. When projects are completed, a second interview is scheduled in which candidates present their work and answer questions from the interview panel. Candidates are evaluated based on the quality and content of their presentations, and the final selection is then made.

ON-THE-JOB TRIAL

The on-the-job trial is a strategy that seems to be increasing in popularity. It offers employers an opportunity to observe a candidate as a functioning part of the unit, department, or division in which the job opening exists.

Candidates are invited to spend a day on the job with various members of the interview panel. During the day, the candidate is asked to perform specific tasks that relate to the highest-rated mandatory success factors.

Observers rate each candidate on demonstrated skill proficiency. But equally important are observations about the manner in which candidates relate to members of the panel and to those with whom they would be working.

THE SITUATIONAL PROBLEM

The situational problem is an interesting variation on the project review model. Instead of a project, a candidate is assigned a situational problem to solve. Problems are usually complex, requiring several issues to be addressed.

Candidates are asked to solve the situational problem by doing all the things necessary to achieve a favorable result. Candidates may have to write letters or internal memoranda, hold staff meetings, convene brainstorming sessions, or even conduct independent research. Consistency and fairness are maintained by giving the same problem to each of the candidates being evaluated.

Candidates submit their solutions within established deadlines, and their work is evaluated by members of the interview panel. This method of further candidate evaluation requires some planning, but the results are usually well worthwhile.

THE 30-SECOND RECAP

- Asking behavioral questions, which are linked to mandatory success factors, significantly improves your chances of hiring successfully.
- Use follow-up probes to seek further behavioral information.
- Use contrary evidence questions to explore the degree and refinement of a candidate's skills.
- Use continuum questions to explore areas of personal preference.
- Use self-appraisal questions to explore whether there's congruity in the way candidates think they are perceived, and the way they are actually perceived by others.
- Remember the STAR technique to guide candidates into providing complete answers to behavioral questions.
- When second interviews become necessary, consider the project review, on-the-job trial, and situational problem strategies.

Controlling the Interview

In this section you learn valuable techniques for maintaining control of the interview while obtaining the information that you need to evaluate candidates.

THE KEYS TO CONTROLLING THE INTERVIEW

Effective interviews are focused, yielding important information about a candidate in a specified amount of time. Maintaining control of the interview is a vitally important task. Following are some valuable techniques that can help you stay in charge of the interview from beginning to end.

PREPARATION

Controlling the interview begins with the interviewer being well prepared. Preparation is essential to good interviewing. The more time you spend preparing, the more likely you'll hire successfully.

When preparing for an interview, don't skip any bases:

- Research the job thoroughly to identify mandatory success factors.

- Make copies of the current job description to provide candidates that you interview.

- Talk with previous jobholders and others who are familiar with the requirements of the job.

- Choose interview panel members who have a stake in finding the right person for the job.

- Structure the interview by developing position-specific questions that will be asked of all candidates and that correspond to mandatory success factors.

- Develop an evaluation tool to rate each candidate on the basis of behavioral responses to questions.

REMEMBER THE 80/20 RULE

Don't forget the 80/20 rule. Let the candidate do 80 percent of the talking. The 20 percent of talking done by interviewers should be in the form of asking questions or using follow-up probes.

Many times during an interview you may feel tempted to abandon structured questions and simply converse with the candidate. Resist the urge. An interview (especially a behavioral interview) is not meant to be a casual conversation with a candidate. Its purpose is to obtain and assess specific behavioral information so that you can identify the best candidate for the job.

The 80/20 rule implies more for the interviewer than simply allowing candidates to do most of the talking. Interviewers should listen actively and intently to what a candidate says (and does not say) during the 80 percent of the time that they are not talking. Active listening provides you with a unique opportunity for insight into a candidate's behavioral patterns. Attentive listening also enables you to construct follow-up probes to further explore behavioral issues while keeping the interview on track. (See "Active Listening Skills" on page 487 for more on active listening.)

THE CLOCK IS RUNNING

During an interview, be mindful of the clock. Take responsibility for starting and ending on time and for accomplishing all that needs to be done during the course of the interview.

Don't let yourself run out of time or let the interview run long because you allowed candidates to respond to questions at length. Also avoid rushing through the last few questions because time is running out.

You provide adequate time for interviews by planning ahead. Estimate the time that candidates need to answer each set of behavioral questions and follow-up probes.

And don't forget to reserve time for evaluating the candidate after the interview has concluded. Both the candidate and the organization are shortchanged when evaluations are postponed to a later time.

PROBE IN DEPTH

Controlling the interview and obtaining the behavioral evidence that you need means following up each primary behavioral question with several follow-up probes.

Although it's true that some follow-up probes will be spontaneous, based on behavioral information provided by the candidate, you should develop several follow-up probes for each primary behavioral question before the interview.

Probe deeply to obtain all the behavioral evidence that's available. (See "Structured Behavioral Interviewing: Part 2" on page 458 for more information on effective probing techniques.)

SUPPORTIVE FEEDBACK

Use supportive feedback to calm and reassure candidates and to encourage sharing of important behavioral information. You should use supportive feedback throughout the interview, but it's particularly important early on, when the resumé-related exchange of information takes place. Helping the candidate to build confidence when easier questions are asked will pay off when the candidate is asked more sensitive questions.

Comments such as "That must have been very exciting for you" or "That must have been very difficult for you" provide the encouragement and support necessary for some candidates to talk freely. Supportive feedback is important for every candidate, to be sure, but it's essential for the candidate who's nervous or distressed.

TIP

The manner in which interviewers behave during an interview has a direct impact on a candidate. If a candidate displays nervousness, it's important for interviewers to remain calm and reassuring.

NONVERBAL ENCOURAGEMENT

As we've already discussed, in an ideal interview situation, the candidate speaks at least 80 percent of the time. It follows that during the course of an interview, interviewers will communicate with candidates in ways that are primarily nonverbal.

So just what is it that you want to communicate to candidates? Decide ahead of time. If your objective were to communicate skepticism and a certain degree of hostility, as in a stress interview, folding your arms and frowning while a candidate attempts to answer questions would convey the message. But if you're interested in encouraging a candidate freely and openly to provide behavioral evidence of his qualifications for the job, a much different nonverbal message is in order.

It's important to remember that nonverbal messaging begins before a candidate even enters the interview room. How a candidate is treated in waiting areas communicates much about the organization and the degree of importance that it places upon the position to be filled. Candidates who are ignored in waiting areas receive one message; those who are met with a smile and words of welcome, who are offered coffee or a soft drink, and whose arrival is immediately announced receive quite another message.

How a candidate is received in the interview room also conveys important messages about the organization and the open position. When the manager in charge meets the candidate at the door, extends a hand, smiles, and offers the candidate a seat, the message is one of warmth and welcome.

During the interview, smiles and nods from each member of the interview panel will also work wonders. Leaning forward in one's chair can also show interest in what's being said and offers significant nonverbal support.

An interviewer's nonverbal communication plays an important role in controlling the interview while simultaneously encouraging candidates to speak freely. Nonverbal communication is a powerful tool.

THE SOUNDS OF SILENCE

Interviewers sometimes panic during momentary silences in an interview. Big mistake. Just relax and let the silence happen.

Occasional lulls should be expected in every interview. Remember that structured behavioral interviewing requires the candidate to think. Thoughtful consideration requires silence.

Whatever you do, don't jump in to save a candidate with a follow-up question that attempts to make things easier or that changes the subject entirely. Instead, take the opportunity to observe how the candidate reacts to the additional stress.

Does the silence prompt the candidate to begin talking nervously to fill the void? Does the candidate try to change the subject? Does the candidate give up and confess his inability to answer the question? Or does the candidate use the silence to consider how best to answer the question? How a candidate reacts to silence can be revealing.

Momentary lulls do not mean that an interviewer has lost control of the interview. They are a natural part of the interview process. The interviewer loses control only when he or she panics and tries to fill the void.

TIP

Be careful how you act during silences. An interviewer who displays signs of obvious impatience will only add to the problem. Instead, reassure the candidate with comforting words, with a friendly smile, and with body language that conveys relaxation and acceptance. Remember, there's a difference between reassuring a candidate (in order to promote open communication) and jumping in to save a candidate by suggesting actions that might be taken, moving on to the next question quickly, and so forth.

MOVING ON

An interviewer's ability to keep the interview moving along is absolutely critical. But when should an interviewer move to the next question?

Use the STAR technique (see "Structured Behavioral Interviewing: Part 2" on page 458) to determine when you've thoroughly explored a behavioral situation and are ready to move on. Remember—every behavioral situation requires a number of actions; each action requires certain skills or competencies. Use follow-up probes to delve into each of these actions, the skills required to handle them, and, finally, what the result of each situation was.

Once you're satisfied that you have enough information about the specific competency to accurately assess the candidate's level of skill, move on! Whether the result was positive or negative, once you've used the STAR technique to probe it at length, you've accomplished your mission. Move on to the next question.

TIP

What to do when you find yourself interviewing someone who is clearly underqualified for the position? Don't just go through the motions. Explain to the candidate that it appears that he or she simply doesn't have the work experience or skills that you're seeking. Thank the candidate for his or her interest, and encourage the person to apply for other positions with your organizations in the future. Cut your losses early and move on!

THE NINE MOST COMMON MISTAKES INTERVIEWERS MAKE

Interviewing mistakes can be costly, especially if they result in the wrong candidate being hired. But the most common interviewing mistakes are entirely preventable. Knowing what they are is the first step in preventing them from occurring in your organization.

Here are the nine most common mistakes made by interviewers:

- Managers lack training in interviewing. Such lack of training can cause problems ranging from hiring the wrong person to being sued for asking illegal questions. Time, money, and effort invested in training managers to interview effectively pays immediate dividends and ensures quality hiring decisions.

- Interviewers fail to determine a position's mandatory success factors. If you haven't defined what it is that you need, how will you know it when you've found it?

- Panel members fail to prepare for interviews by meeting to discuss the process (discuss questions, decide who will ask what, etc.).

- Interview questions are not carefully prepared ahead of time, or they lack a behavioral component.

- The interview lacks depth as a result of inadequate follow-up probes designed to seek additional behavioral evidence.

- Interviewers surrender control of the interview to candidates who are skilled at interviewing and who redirect the course of the interview to areas that they're familiar with (and well-rehearsed in).

- In selecting candidates to interview, interviewers give little or no thought to the importance of diversity in the workplace.

- Interviewers compare candidates against each other instead of on the basis of mandatory success factors.

- Hiring decisions are made on the basis of "gut feelings," or "a twinkle in the eye," or "just a hunch."

Many of these mistakes may seem obvious, and they are. But as obvious as they are, they still occur. Avoid them, and you'll significantly increase your chances of hiring the right person for the job. Remember, it takes work to interview effectively, but the results are worth the effort.

FOUR TYPES OF CANDIDATE RESPONSES AND WHAT THEY MEAN

This chapter wouldn't be complete if it didn't include a brief section covering the four basic ways candidates respond to behavioral questions. To maintain control of the interview, you should be familiar with, and know how to react to, each.

Remember that a candidate will often employ more than one strategy during the course of an interview and can even attempt more than one strategy in answering a given question. Listen carefully for the type of response that the candidate uses, and react accordingly.

THE MOTOR MOUTH RESPONSE

The motor mouth response comes from a candidate who probably has little to say about a particular behavioral question. However, instead of pleading ignorance, this candidate attempts to gain control of the interview by talking incessantly. He or she hopes to redirect the interview to another topic of choice.

How to react: Try to gently bring the candidate back to the original question by using open probes. Failing that, don't hesitate to stop the candidate in mid-sentence, if necessary, and ask to return to the subject at hand. Sometimes it may be necessary to repeat the original question. Whatever you do, be sure to intervene. The motor mouth response is an attempt to impress the interviewer, but it's really a cover-up for a lack of competency. Don't be fooled by it.

THE SHORT STOP RESPONSE

This response is abrupt. The candidate answers a question with a short comment, sometimes consisting of just a few words, such as, "Whenever I had a problem, I'd ask my boss what to do, and then I did it." The interviewer, in an effort to draw the candidate out, uses follow-up probes that require a behavioral response with specific examples. But they, too, are met with terse responses. What's happening is that the candidate is extremely nervous, is attempting to hide something, or completely lacks the competency that you seek.

How to react: Use sufficient follow-up probes to be sure that you're dealing with a true short stop response and not just a nervous candidate. Once you're sure that you're dealing with a short stop, note the lack of responsiveness and move on to another question set dealing with the next mandatory success factor. If the pattern repeats itself, you may want to consider ending the interview. You're interested in obtaining behavioral evidence of key competencies; the candidate, for whatever reason, is interested in disclosing as little as possible. Proceeding further would likely be a waste of everyone's time.

THE GENERALIST RESPONSE

The generalist response is a clever attempt on the part of the candidate to cover up a real lack of competence. In fact, most of those who attempt a generalist response do so because the subject matter of the question is over their heads. Often, these are the candidates whose resumés contain a significant amount of "fluff."

The generalist response is similar to the motor mouth response in that candidates may opt to talk incessantly. However, unlike the motor mouth response, the generalist does not attempt to redirect the focus of the interview onto another topic. Instead, the generalist wants to provide general answers to specific questions.

For example, if asked, "Tell me about a time when your boss talked to you about a problem related to your work," the generalist might answer by talking at length about how employees in general can develop a positive working relationship with supervisors.

Often the information provided by a generalist response is quite good, and the candidate providing it may be very articulate. But notice how it misses the mark! The question in this example requires a specific behavioral response, not a general monologue on building rapport with one's supervisor. There's a big difference.

When pressed for specific behavioral evidence, candidates relying on the generalist response sometimes revert to providing interviewers with adjectives that describe how they see themselves in the situations being probed. For example, instead of providing behavioral evidence of being hardworking, a generalist response may be, "I'm a very hardworking person, and I always have been." But, again, note that the response is nonbehavioral and general.

How to react: Continue to press for behavioral evidence by using follow-up probes. If general responses continue, it sometimes helps to simply say, "But that's not what I asked. Let me restate my question." If after several attempts you still cannot make headway, summarize by saying, "I take it you have no examples you wish to share with us today." If after a few question sets the generalist response continues, consider ending the interview.

THE VALID RESPONSE

A valid response to a behavioral question or follow-up probe is a real-life account demonstrating how a candidate responded to a specific situation or task, together with an explanation of the actions taken and the results achieved (STAR). This response allows the interviewer to properly evaluate a candidate's level of competence with the success factor under consideration.

How to react: React by providing verbal and nonverbal support and encouragement. This is the kind of response that provides the information you need.

THE 30-SECOND RECAP

- Maintaining control over the interview is achievable by using a few simple techniques: prepare; remember the 80/20 rule; stay on time; probe in depth; use verbal and nonverbal supportive feedback; allow silence to happen; and, when it's appropriate, move on.

- There are nine common interview mistakes, each of which can be easily avoided.

- Candidates answer behavioral questions in four ways, each requiring an appropriate response by the interviewer.

Navigating the Legal Minefield

In this section you learn how to conduct a job interview without subjecting yourself and your organization to potential legal problems.

TAKING OFF THE BLINDFOLD

I'm always taken aback when I come across managers who haven't a clue about the legal aspects of interviewing. Interviewing without any knowledge of legalities is a little like insisting upon navigating a minefield blindfolded when the exact location of each mine has been marked with a big red flag.

The simple fact is that if you're going to be involved in the hiring process, you need to know where the legal mines have been planted. Their location has been well identified, but it's up to you to take off the blindfold and see them. Leave the blindfolds for the amateurs.

Remember that effective interviewing and legal interviewing are not mutually exclusive terms. It's both possible and desirable to plan interviews that not only are effective, but also avoid the legal pitfalls that abound.

CAUTION

Be advised that the author is not a practicing attorney, nor does he purport to give legal advice. Information concerning state and federal laws regulating employment practices as well as major court decisions is believed to be correct as of the date of publication. The law changes frequently, and every employment situation has its own unique legal concerns. Consult an employment attorney whenever questions arise, and review your organization's general hiring practices at regular intervals.

HIRING AND THE LAW

Numerous federal, state, and local equal opportunity and antidiscrimination laws regulate the application and interview process. Each of these laws was enacted to offer individuals and groups of protected persons legal protection against employment discrimination.

While state and local laws do not supersede federal legislation, they often are more restrictive or broader in scope. Managers must be aware of all laws affecting employment practices to prevent costly discrimination claims by unsuccessful applicants.

Here are just some of the federal laws that affect the hiring process:

- Title VII of the Civil Rights Act of 1964
- The Civil Rights Act of 1991
- The Americans with Disabilities Act
- The Immigration Reform Control Act of 1986
- Age Discrimination in Employment Act
- The Vietnam Era Veterans Readjustment Assistance Act
- The Rehabilitation Act of 1973
- The Equal Pay Act
- The National Labor Relations Act
- Executive Order 11242
- The Family and Medical Leave Act

This is just a sampling of the laws that determine what is appropriate and legal in the hiring process. In addition to federal law, each state has laws that also apply. To avoid problems involving legal liability, be sure to involve your corporate attorney in a regular review of your hiring practices and procedures.

TIP

For complete information about state laws affecting the hiring process, Nolo.com has a Web site that allows you to search the statutes of each state. Their address is www.nolo.com/statutes/state.html.

DISPARATE TREATMENT AND DISPARATE IMPACT

"Disparate treatment" and "disparate impact" are the two basic legal concepts at the heart of Title VII of the Civil Rights Act of 1964, as well as similar civil rights legislation. It's important to understand what these terms mean to avoid the consequences that come with breaking the law, knowingly or in ignorance.

In a landmark 1977 case, the Supreme Court defined these two concepts in this manner:

> **Disparate treatment** is the most easily understood type of discrimination. The employer simply treats some people less favorably than others because of their race, color, religion, sex, or national origin. Proof of discriminatory motive is critical, although it can in some situations be inferred from the mere fact of differences in treatment.

> **Disparate impact** involves employment practices that are facially neutral in their treatment of different groups but that in fact fall more harshly on one group than another, and cannot be justified by business necessity .... Proof of discriminatory motive, we have held, is not required under disparate impact theory.

In layman's terms, here's what the court said:

> Disparate treatment occurs whenever a double standard is used in a selection process. Treating one candidate appreciably different than another is considered discriminatory. For example, asking women, but not men, whether their responsibilities at home might interfere with their employment is disparate treatment. So is asking someone whether church activities might keep that person from fulfilling the duties of the job for which they're applying.

Disparate impact takes place when one group of candidates is affected by a question more harshly than another. For example, asking whether candidates would mind working as part of an all-male workforce would have disparate impact on female applicants.

TIP

The best way to avoid becoming ensnared in nasty and expensive litigation is to make sure that every interview question you ask a candidate has a clear and direct business-related purpose.

INAPPROPRIATE QUESTIONS

A number of subject areas ought to be avoided in every job interview. These are the landmines that we talked about earlier. Some of them are always problematic; some can be rephrased in ways that make them legally palatable; some can be asked only after an offer of employment has been made.

Most of the subjects listed are not only inappropriate (or downright illegal) to include in interviews, but they also should not appear on your organization's formal employment application.

CAUTION

You could be held liable for obtaining potentially discriminatory information even if the applicant gives it voluntarily. If that occurs, it's best to change the subject immediately without making any notation whatsoever of the voluntary information.

MAIDEN NAME

Examples of inappropriate questions include these: "What was your maiden name?" "What was your father's surname?" "What was the last name you were born with?"

Asking an applicant to furnish a maiden name can be considered discriminatory in that it forces a female applicant to disclose her marital status.

Consider asking the candidate whether she is known by any other name by her former employers so that her work record can be obtained. This attaches a clear and direct business purpose to the question and makes it legal.

AGE

Examples of inappropriate questions include these: "What's your date of birth?" "How old are you?" "What year did you graduate from high school?" "Are you near retirement age?" "Aren't you too old to be applying for this kind of job?" "Aren't you too young to be applying for a job that requires a good deal of experience?"

Asking an applicant to provide his or her date of birth, or asking how old that person is, focuses the interview on age rather than the qualifications of the applicant. Asking when an applicant graduated from high school enables the interviewer to calculate an approximate date of birth.

Although questions of this type are not expressly forbidden in Title VII, they could present formidable problems with candidates who are over 40 years of age and are thereby members of a protected class under the terms of the Age Discrimination in Employment Act.

If your purpose is to determine whether someone is of legal age for employment, ask if that person is 18 years of age or older. If you have any other purpose in asking the question, forget it. More than half the discrimination lawsuits filed in the United States each year are based on age discrimination. Don't become a statistic.

PLACE OF BIRTH/NATIONAL ORIGIN

Examples of inappropriate questions include these: "Where were you born?" "What's your nationality?" "What language do you speak in your home?" "What languages do your parents speak?" "Where did your family originally reside before coming to the United States?" "How long have you lived at your present address?"

Title VII of the Civil Rights Act of 1964 prohibits discrimination in the workplace on the basis of national origin. In 1986, federal legislation known as the Immigration Reform and Control Act imposed the restrictions of the law on businesses with as few as four employees. Questions relating to one's place of birth invite claims of discrimination by unsuccessful applicants. So do questions regarding the birthplace of an applicant's family. Also taboo is asking an applicant to furnish a copy of a birth certificate or other papers demonstrating citizenship naturalization.

If your primary concern is whether a candidate has the legal right to hold a job in the United States, you could ask, "If you were hired, could you provide us with verification of your right to work in the United States?" If you need information as part of the federal *I-9* process, you may legally request the applicant for the information required for that purpose.

PLAIN ENGLISH

I-9 Form   Section 274a of the Immigration and Nationality Act requires that employers verify that every employee hired after November 6, 1986, is authorized to work in the United States. This obligation applies to citizens and alien job applicants alike. Immigration and Naturalization Form I-9 outlines a formal process by which employers verify that candidates are legally able to work in the United States.

Also, employers may ask what languages a candidate speaks or writes fluently if there is a clear job-related purpose.

RELIGION

Examples of inappropriate questions include these: "What church do you attend?" "We often require our employees to work weekends—would that be a problem for you?" "What's the name of your pastor, priest, or rabbi?" "Do you observe any special religious holidays?"

Title VII of the Civil Rights Act of 1964 prohibits any form of discrimination against employees or candidates for employment on the basis of religion. In fact, the Equal Employment Opportunity Commission states that Title VII "creates an obligation to provide *reasonable accommodation* for the religious practices of an employee or prospective employee unless to do so would create an undue hardship."

PLAIN ENGLISH

Reasonable accommodation   For religious practices, reasonable accommodation (without limitation) may include special work schedules designed to enable the employee to attend religious services or participate in religious observances. It may even include the possibility of transferring the employee to another job if that becomes necessary to accommodate the religious needs of the employee or candidate.

Several years ago, when I applied for a professional job in state government, I was told that I was "ruled out" as a viable candidate because I was an ordained Lutheran minister "who belonged in church work, not government." I didn't pursue the matter, but I could easily have done so.

It's frightening how many employers can't seem to understand that how employees (or potential employees) practice their religion is simply none of the employer's business unless the employer is asked to provide a reasonable accommodation. Not only does Title VII make that clear, but so does the First Amendment to the Constitution of the United States: "Congress shall make no law respecting an establishment of religion, or prohibiting the free exercise thereof."

If you make it a practice to discriminate on the basis of religion, you eventually will be sued—and you'll lose.

Periodically, I've read the work of some consultants who recommend making it a condition of employment when weekend work is mandatory. I suggest caution, however. Unless you've discussed the matter with your legal counsel, who is absolutely convinced that you can demonstrate that any other alternative would present an undue hardship on the organization, you're inviting litigation for discrimination.

I think it's preferable in situations in which weekend work is occasionally necessary for an employer to make it clear that a reasonable effort will be made to accommodate the religious needs of employees. This kind of language is certainly less offensive and is more in keeping with the spirit and letter of the law.

RACE OR COLOR

Issues of race and color normally do not arise as a result of questions posed in an interview. However, because unsuccessful candidates can raise claims of racial discrimination, I have included it here for your review.

Title VII of the Civil Rights Act of 1964 makes it unlawful for employers (or prospective employers) to discriminate on the basis of race, complexion, or color. There are no exceptions.

Those who feel that they have been discriminated against because of their race or color not only have the right to sue, but, under the provisions of The Civil Rights Act of 1991, they also have the right to a jury trial as well as the right to collect punitive and compensatory damages if the claim of discrimination is found to be valid.

Do not allow race or color to enter into the evaluation process. To the contrary, make it a practice to actively recruit minority applicants for positions within your organization. Make sure that you have a written plan to correct any areas of serious racial underrepresentation through an ongoing process of recruiting, hiring, training, and promoting minorities. (If your organization participates in federal contracts either as a primary contractor or a subcontractor, Executive Order 11242 mandates that such a plan be in effect.)

Marital Status

Examples of inappropriate questions include these: "Are you single or married?" "Have you ever been married, divorced, separated, or widowed?" "Do you prefer being called Ms., Mrs., or Miss?" "What is your spouse's name?" "Do you have any children?" "Are you planning to have children within the next few years?" "If you were to be employed, would locating suitable childcare be a problem?"

Title VII of the Civil Rights Act of 1964, along with a number of state antidiscrimination laws, make this area of employer inquiry a dangerous one. Unless there is a clear work-related reason for questions of this nature, it's best to avoid them altogether. Historically, questions about marital status have been used to discriminate against women.

Even when a candidate is obviously pregnant, it's best to avoid commenting on the fact in the pre-employment phase of the selection process. In 1978, Title VII was amended to include protection for women who are pregnant. Questions such as those indicated previously invite charges of sex discrimination by an unsuccessful job candidate.

Unless there is a clear job-related purpose, it's best to completely avoid questions of this nature. If a candidate mentions her pregnancy, it is advisable to simply change the subject. Do not make note of what she has told you concerning her pregnancy or her plans for subsequent childcare.

However, employers may inquire whether a candidate would be willing to relocate, if necessary. And if travel is an essential function of the job, inquiries concerning the candidate's willingness to travel are appropriate as long as all candidates are asked the same questions.

Health and Disability

Examples of inappropriate questions include these: "Are you disabled?" "How many days of sick leave did you use last year?" "Do you have any significant health problems?" "Do you take prescription drugs regularly?" "Have you ever filed a workman's compensation claim?" "Do you have AIDS?"

The Americans with Disabilities Act of 1992 prohibits discrimination against qualified applicants whose disabilities would not prevent them from performing the essential functions of a job with or without a reasonable accommodation. This law applies to every business that employs 15 or more people, unless the business can demonstrate to the satisfaction of the Equal Employment Opportunity Commission that compliance with the law would present an undue hardship on the employer.

If you're concerned about whether a handicapped candidate can actually do the job, ask, "Are you capable of performing the essential functions of the job with or without an accommodation?"

After a conditional job offer has been made, an employer may require candidates to undergo a medical examination to determine their fitness for the job. Examination results can assist employers in determining specific accommodations that will enable the candidate to perform the essential functions of the job.

SEXUAL ORIENTATION

Examples of inappropriate questions include these: "Are you gay?" "Are you lesbian?" "Do you date other women (or men)?"

Although no specific federal laws prohibit employment discrimination on the basis of sexual orientation, several states offer legal protection for gays and lesbians. California, Massachusetts, Hawaii, Wisconsin, Vermont, Connecticut, New Jersey, and Minnesota have led the way.

Judge Sidney Asch of the New York State Supreme Court, Appellate Division, commenting on employment discrimination based on sexual orientation, said, "Where sexual proclivity does not relate to job function, it seems clearly unconstitutional to penalize an individual in one of the most imperative of life's endeavors, the right to earn one's daily bread."

It is only a matter of time before federal legislation makes this form of discrimination illegal. Unless you are prepared to demonstrate that being gay or lesbian adversely affects someone's ability to perform the essential functions of a job, don't inquire about sexual orientation.

ARRESTS

This is one example of an inappropriate question: "Have you ever been arrested?"

Although no specific federal laws prohibit inquiries about arrest records, several states have enacted legislation that would make this kind of question unlawful. Questions concerning a candidate's arrest record have been held to have an adverse discriminatory impact upon certain segments of the population. Under the disparate impact theory, questions about a candidate's arrest record could become the basis of a lawsuit for discrimination under Title VII of the Civil Rights Act of 1964.

While asking about the arrest record of a candidate for employment is risky business, employers may usually ask whether a candidate has ever been convicted of a crime. But be sure to check with your organization's attorney to determine whether the laws of your state may prohibit inquiries about an individual's conviction record, or whether state law limits the period of inquiry to a fixed number of months or years from the date of application.

CREDIT RECORDS

Examples of inappropriate questions include these: "Have you ever filed for bankruptcy?" "Have you ever had your wages attached?" "Are there any judgments against you?"

Such questions have been held to be unlawful when asked prior to a job offer being made. Employers may make an offer of employment contingent upon a credit check, as long as the employer abides by the conditions of all applicable state and federal laws, and can demonstrate that only those with good credit histories can perform the essential functions of the job.

Also, because some minority groups are economically disadvantaged, their credit histories tend to be adversely affected. Under the disparate impact theory, using credit information to make final employment decisions can be held discriminatory. Again, this is especially true when performance of the job is not affected by the poor credit history of the employee.

Be careful about using credit history. The burden of proof is clearly upon the employer to show a direct relationship between performance of the essential functions of a given job and the credit history of the employee. Be sure to consult your corporate attorney if you believe that credit checks are important to your selection process.

UNION MEMBERSHIP

Examples of inappropriate questions include these: "Do you belong to a labor union?" "Are you for or against labor unions?" "Have you ever been a member of a labor union?"

The National Labor Relations Act prohibits the discrimination of employees or applicants for employment who are members of labor unions, or who favor membership in labor unions. Furthermore, the act prohibits employers from questioning employees or prospective employees about their union membership preference.

Avoid this kind of question altogether.

MILITARY SERVICE

Examples of inappropriate questions include these: "Have you ever served in the armed forces of another country?" "If you've served in the U.S. military, did you receive an honorable discharge?"

Employers may ask about a candidate's U.S. military service but may not inquire about military service to another country. Questions about military service outside the United States may compel an applicant to disclose information about national origin, which may become the basis of a discrimination action.

When inquiring about a candidate's U.S. military service, frame your inquiries in such a way as to probe for skills and abilities acquired during the period that may have direct application to the job for which the applicant is being interviewed. The training that a candidate received as a member of the armed forces is usually valuable, and questions about it are always appropriate.

In Case of Emergency

Examples of inappropriate questions include these: "Please give us the name, address, and telephone number of your nearest relative whom we should notify in the event of an emergency."

Asking for the name of a *relative* could become the basis of a legal action for discrimination based on national origin, race, or even marital status.

The employer can't ask for a relative's name; limit this request to the name of "someone to contact in the event of an emergency." The candidate may provide the name of a relative in response to the question, of course.

Club Memberships

Examples of inappropriate questions include these: "What clubs do you participate in regularly?" "List all the lodges, societies, and clubs to which you belong."

Unless you can demonstrate that this information is somehow related to the essential functions of the job, it's best to avoid this line of questioning completely. Club memberships may indicate the race, color, religion, national origin, or ancestry of its members; that information can become the basis of a discrimination action by an unsuccessful candidate.

Personal Information

Examples of inappropriate questions include these: "How tall are you?" "How much do you weigh?" "May we please have a photograph of you to attach to your application?"

Each of these questions is an example of an illegal pre-employment inquiry. Although this kind of information may have been routinely requested in applications for employment decades ago, today this is a surefire way to become embroiled in messy litigation.

Employers may inquire about the height and weight of a candidate if there are established minimum standards that have been determined to be essential for the safe performance of the job. In all other situations, personal questions of this nature should be avoided.

HIRING WITHOUT BEING SUED

When managers don't ask the right questions (in interviews and in reference checks), their organizations run the risk of being sued for negligent hiring if the candidate is hired and later does something and someone gets hurt. Managers also run the risk of causing their organizations to be sued if they ask the wrong questions and learn things about a candidate that are unrelated to a candidate's qualifications and suitability for the job under discussion.

Managers must attend training seminars and workshops on hiring to help keep up to date with changes in employment and civil rights law. They should also work closely with their organizations' legal counsel whenever they have a question or concern about a hiring situation.

THE 30-SECOND RECAP

- Federal and state laws, as well as rulings from the courts, often regulate questions that can be legally asked of a candidate.

- Questions that are considered unlawful or inappropriate for interviews are similarly unlawful and inappropriate for use in employment applications.

- Interview questions should always be related to the essential functions of the job being sought.

- Avoiding potential legal problems involving claims of discrimination is the best strategy.

- Structured interviewing keeps the interview focused on job-related issues, thereby avoiding unplanned questions that can become the basis of discrimination claims.

Active Listening Skills

In this section you learn the importance of practicing good listening skills during the interview.

LISTENING ACTIVELY, TALKING FREELY

Several years ago, I completed a graduate program in therapeutic counseling. My hope was to be able to help people regain control of their lives after experiencing some type of psychological trauma.

One of the things I learned back then, and have since had reinforced more times than I care to count, is that counselors really can't help anyone until they know what the problem is—and counselors can't know what the problem is until clients tell them.

Active listening skills, one of the most important tools that a counselor has to work with, help encourage clients to talk freely and openly about problems and difficulties that they're facing. And the more freely a client talks about problems, the better equipped the counselor is to help. Getting people to talk about subjects that they may not want to discuss is the first step in any effective therapeutic intervention.

PLAIN ENGLISH

Active listening   An interview technique, with origins in the field of psychotherapy, that helps assure candidates that the interviewer is listening to them intently. Active listening involves encouraging candidates to talk openly and freely by often reflecting back to them the meaning of their communication, both verbal and nonverbal, in ways that promote further exploration and awareness.

Interviewing candidates for employment involves the same basic challenge. To hire the right person for a job, it's necessary to gain a real understanding of each candidate who applies. It's important to know who they are, how they think, what their goals and aspirations are, and whether they have the competencies needed to be successful in the job.

But to evaluate each candidate fairly and accurately, the interviewer must obtain the necessary information, and that means getting the candidate to talk even about subjects that may be uncomfortable to discuss (past failures, weaknesses, problems with former employers or co-workers, and so on). The more the candidate talks, the better the interviewer understands the candidate and can decide whether he or she is qualified for the position.

CAUTION

Be sure that your questions about a candidate's weaknesses or past failures have direct application to the job he or she is seeking. Past problems that involve a candidate's personal life are not appropriate for discussion during the interview process.

THE BENEFITS OF ACTIVE LISTENING

Active listening skills promote warmth and honest communication. But even more important, they help strip away superficial levels of *communication* by encouraging candidates to talk about skill-related experiences and the deeper personal meanings that often accompany them.

PLAIN ENGLISH

Communication   Any means (verbal or nonverbal) of giving information or news to another. One of the main functions of communication in the context of a job interview is to impart knowledge and provide job-related information.

Here are some of the benefits of active listening, along with some typical interviewer responses that help bring them about:

- Active listening demonstrates to a candidate that the interviewer is intensely interested in what's being said: "You seem to be saying that you have felt undervalued in your present employment and that you feel frustrated as a result."

- Even more important, it demonstrates that the candidate has not only been heard, but also understood: "If I'm hearing you correctly, you would like a chance to work for a company that would value someone with your skills and abilities."

- It provides an opportunity for the interviewer to discover and correct any misunderstandings or inaccurate interpretations that may develop during the course of an interview: "If I understand you correctly, you like the company you're presently working for, but you dislike your immediate supervisor. Is that correct?"

- It communicates unconditional acceptance to the candidate, which encourages further exploration: "You feel undervalued in your present work."

- It keeps the focus where it belongs—on the candidate and the specific behavior being probed: "It seems that you feel that your ability to lead others is being overlooked in your present employment, and that you want to find employment that will allow you to not only manage, but also lead. Is that correct?"

- It encourages deeper levels of communication: "You want to be recognized for your leadership abilities …. Tell me about a time when you were placed in a leadership role. What is there about it that you liked? What did you dislike?"

■ It encourages open and honest communication: "You say that you resent not having a leadership role in your present job, and you seem hurt by it."

HOW TO LISTEN ACTIVELY

Active listening, as the term implies, requires active participation on the part of the listener; the listener does more than just listen. It calls for the listener to become actively involved in the process of communication by periodically confirming understanding of what's being said by the speaker. Developing active listening skills demands practice.

When using active listening while conducting job interviews, there are several important points to remember.

First, be genuinely curious about what the applicant is saying. Even if you're tempted to tune out because you've heard the question and the usual response a hundred times, force yourself to be curious about what the candidate is saying.

TIP

Make an effort to engage with the candidate, and suddenly you'll find yourself taking real interest in what's being said. There's nothing more encouraging to a candidate than to have an interviewer really listen and to confirm that listening with appropriate questions or statements.

Second, don't be judgmental. When a candidate makes statements that you disagree with, don't voice your disagreement. Remember that this is the candidate's opportunity to tell a story about the use of a certain skill or ability, or simply to express an opinion. Reserve your judgment for the evaluation phase of the process—that's where it belongs. During the interview, focus only on making sure that you understand exactly what the candidate is saying.

Third, make a conscious effort to resist distractions, whether internal or external. Active listening requires total concentration on what's being said. Control those distractions that are controllable so that the concentration of everyone participating in the interview process remains unbroken.

Fourth, reflect content back to the candidate. When you tell candidates what you think they're saying, you encourage them to continue speaking, you show sincere interest in their presentations, and you demonstrate concern for the accuracy of the message they're conveying.

Fifth, listen for the emotions behind a candidate's words. Those emotions can include happiness, sadness, fear, disappointment, frustration, anxiety, and every other emotion. When you hear a candidate talking in emotional terms, learn more about why the emotional response is there by saying, "You sound frustrated with your present job. What is there about it that frustrates you most?"

Sixth, don't interrupt a candidate with a follow-up question. Sometimes while you're actively listening to a candidate, you'll suddenly think of an important follow-up question that simply must be asked. When that happens, jot it down and ask it later. Interrupting a candidate who's attempting to answer specific behavioral questions is a little like throwing cold water on a fire.

And seventh, while we're on the subject of note taking, plan to take plenty of notes about what the candidate says. Not only does note taking demonstrate the importance of what's being said, but it also will prove invaluable when it comes time to evaluate candidates.

FACILITATIVE AND INHIBITING INTERVIEWER RESPONSES

The manner in which the interviewer responds to a candidate will either facilitate communication or inhibit it. The following is a list of *facilitative responses* that will help you listen actively:

- Unconditional acceptance ("That must have been very difficult for you. Thank you for sharing your feelings with us.")
- Obvious open-mindedness ("That's an interesting way of looking at that situation.")
- Open behavioral questions
- Patience ("Take your time.")
- Reflective comments
- Positive reinforcement
- Empathetic remarks
- Support comments
- Structuring
- Supportive body language

Inhibiting responses will keep a candidate from speaking freely and deeply about important matters. Here are a few of the most common inhibiting responses:

- Criticism
- Rejection

- Moralistic responses ("I never would have believed that anyone would actually do something like that.")
- Self-indulgent disclosures ("Sometimes people ask me about the secret to my financial success in life and I tell them that since I was a lad I've always saved 10 percent of everything I earn, and I give another 10 percent to charity. I've always felt that if you can't live on 80 percent of your income, you can't live on 100 percent of it either.")
- Belittling statements
- Intolerance
- Dogmatic statements
- Sarcasm
- Obvious impatience
- Allowed distractions

PLAIN ENGLISH

Facilitative responses   The responses of an interviewer that encourage a candidate to talk freely about the areas explored in the interview.

Inhibiting responses   Those responses of an interviewer that prevent candidates from wanting to talk about important matters. Facilitative responses produce excellent interviews; inhibiting responses are destructive.

NONVERBAL CUES

Body language has become a hot topic in human resources circles over the past few years. Body language can be revealing, but sometimes an interviewer can get the wrong message entirely.

For example, some people routinely hold their chin in their palm hand when they're contemplating something important. But in an interview session, this kind of body language could easily be interpreted as suggesting someone who is unfocused and inattentive.

Over the years, I've developed the habit of sitting with my arms crossed while carrying on a business-related conversation. But in an interview situation, that kind of body language could be interpreted as evidence of closed-mindedness and defensive posturing.

TIP

Make an effort to examine your own unique body language, especially during interview sessions. Try to avoid body language that may conflict with the principles of active listening.

THE CANDIDATE'S NONVERBAL CUES

When you encounter a candidate whose body language seems to communicate one thing but whose verbal responses seem to communicate something else, it's usually best to check your interpretations of these nonverbal cues with the candidate. Do so in a way that doesn't cause embarrassment, but be direct. Ask the candidate if your interpretation of a certain body language is correct. ("It seems that whenever we discuss your present employment your body language appears to indicate a reluctance to discuss the matter in any detail. Is there a reason for that? Or, am I simply misinterpreting your body language?")

Also, remember that you have no idea of the context of the interview in the life of the candidate. A number of years ago, I interviewed a young lady for a professional position for which she seemed eminently qualified. During the interview, however, she became distracted and unfocused. Her body language suggested extreme anxiety.

I attempted to confirm the message from her body language by asking whether she was feeling anxious about the interview. The young lady began to sob uncontrollably. When I inquired what was wrong, she said that a few hours beforehand, she had received a telephone call from her sister telling her of her father's sudden death. In spite of the news, she attempted to muster up enough strength to complete the interview, but the news proved too overwhelming.

Had I relied only on the nonverbal cues presented by the candidate, I would have probably concluded that the job and the candidate were not a good match. But having inquired further, I learned that it was the context of the interview that was the problem, not the candidate. We rescheduled our interview for another time, and the young lady was eventually hired and today manages an entire division of the same firm.

Always confirm nonverbal cues with a candidate. Body language can be prompted by many things other than the interview—or, for that matter, nothing at all.

THE INTERVIEWER'S NONVERBAL CUES

From the standpoint of active listening, what's really important is the interviewer's nonverbal cues. To communicate acceptance, interest, and support, the interviewer should practice making eye contact with the candidate while leaning slightly forward from a seated position. Eye contact should be broken only when notes are being written or other members of the interview panel are being addressed.

Be careful not to convey boredom by paying attention to something other than what the candidate is saying, by yawning, or by constantly looking at your watch or a room clock. These kinds of messages can put a real damper on what might otherwise be a good interview.

When the interviewer mentally engages with the candidate and practices good active listening skills, nonverbal communication usually takes care of itself.

THE 30-SECOND RECAP

- Active listening is a technique that has its roots in psychotherapy and helps encourage candidates to talk freely and openly about behavioral situations.

- Active listening helps move an interview from superficial levels to deeper levels, giving the interviewer an opportunity to gain a better understanding of the person being interviewed.

- Among other important benefits, active listening provides the interviewer an opportunity to immediately clear up any misunderstandings or to obtain needed clarification.

- Interviewers should be constantly aware of the messages that they are giving applicants through verbal and nonverbal forms of communication. How an interviewer responds to a candidate (verbally and nonverbally) will be either facilitative or inhibiting.

Conducting the Interview

In this section you follow a general sales manager for XYZ Corporation step by step as he constructs a sample structured behavioral interview.

So far, you've learned to begin the interview process with an analysis of the job to determine the mandatory success factors; you've learned how to review résumés and to prescreen candidates to interview; you've learned about the process of structured behavioral interviewing; and you've learned how to develop behavioral questions that seek out essential competencies.

Now it's time to put it all to work to construct an actual interview.

THE MODEL

XYZ Corporation is about to lose an important member of its team. For the past 15 years, John Jones has occupied the position of district sales manager for one of the company's most profitable geographic regions. John is scheduled to retire in two months, and recruitment activities to find a suitable replacement are about to begin.

Pete Smith, the general sales manager for the company, provides direct supervision of each of the company's district sales managers, so he will take the lead in recruiting and evaluating candidates. Although the final hiring decision will be made by him, Pete decides to enlist the help of one salesman, one district sales manager, and one home office support supervisor to assist him in the selection process.

JOB ANALYSIS

Pete begins by taking a hard look at the job being vacated. He reviews the formal position description and talks at length with John to learn John's perspective on what it takes to succeed as a district sales manager, and to learn about any unique requirements that may exist in his particular district. He talks with members of John's sales team to obtain their input on what's needed in a new sales manager. He talks with other home office managers and support staff who regularly work with district sales managers to get their advice on what to look for in a new sales manager.

As a result of his investigation, and based on his own knowledge of the job, Pete has developed the following position profile.

TECHNICAL COMPETENCIES

The following company-mandated competencies are required of all district sales managers:

- A Bachelor's degree in business administration, sales administration, marketing, or a closely allied field

- A minimum of five years of successful experience managing a sales organization

FUNCTIONAL SKILLS

From his own observations, and from talking with others, Pete makes a list of the functional skills that the new district sales manager should possess:

- Communication skills (oral and written)
- Management skills

- Training and mentoring
- Leadership
- Independence
- Teamwork
- Initiative
- Customer service
- Sales ability
- Public relations ability
- Development of subordinates
- Detail orientation
- Listening ability
- Supervision ability
- Planning and organizing ability

SELF-MANAGEMENT SKILLS

In addition, here are some suggested personal characteristics that would help a district sales manager to succeed with the company:

- Ethics
- Honesty
- Loyalty
- Reliability
- Accountability
- Self-sufficiency

INTERPERSONAL SKILLS

For the position of district sales manager, good interpersonal skills are important to the successful performance of the job, especially the ability to do the following:

- Empathize and care about the concerns of others.
- Listen actively and attentively.
- Remain objective without becoming emotional.
- Communicate effectively with others.

THE CORPORATE CULTURE

XYZ Corporation prides itself in the professionalism of its employees. Although it's an unwritten mandate, the company really wants each of its key employees (district sales managers among them) to adhere to the following:

- Constantly be involved in some form of formal training that will contribute to their ability to perform quality work in a professional manner.
- Attend all sales conferences and seminars sponsored by the company.
- Actively participate in state and national associations in which the company holds membership.

DETERMINING MANDATORY SUCCESS FACTORS

Having identified the competencies, skills, and abilities that the ideal candidate would possess, it's time for Pete to narrow the field to those factors that are absolutely necessary for success on the job. With this in mind, Pete proceeds to rate each skill in order of its importance to job success, identifying the top five functional skills and the top two self-management skills from the other skills listed.

TIP

Rating skills in order of their importance to the successful performance of a job is also something that can be done by the entire selection team. This procedure may be a bit more time-consuming, but the extra input is well worth it.

Here are the results:

Functional skills:

1. Teamwork (weighted by 5)
2. Training and mentoring (weighted by 4)
3. Communication skills (weighted by 3)
4. Leadership (weighted by 2)
5. Customer service (weighted by 1)

TIP

For purposes of weighting each of the factors in the evaluation process, take the number of factors being considered (in this case, five), and assign that number to the most important factor. Weighting for functional skills indicated here would be: teamwork (5), training (4), communication (3), leadership (2), and customer service (1).

PLAIN ENGLISH

Weight factor   A number that is assigned to each mandatory success factor being evaluated. The score for each mandatory success factor is multiplied by the weight factor to determine the total number of points awarded.

Self-management skills:

1. Honesty
2. Reliability

TIP

You can identify as many skills in each category as you want. However, from a practical standpoint, it's best to identify a limited number of skills in each category.

The skills identified in this process are the mandatory success factors for the position of district sales manager. These are the factors that will guide Pete as he develops structured behavioral questions and associated follow-up probes; these are also the objective factors upon which he and his team will evaluate candidates.

Notice that technical competencies, interpersonal skills, and requirements of the corporate culture were not prioritized. That's because each of these requirements is already considered mandatory.

A review of the candidate's application and resumé will help determine whether the candidate possesses the required technical competencies. Specific questions concerning interpersonal skills (if not already covered in the functional skill area) will need to be developed, as will questions concerning the candidate's ability to assimilate successfully into the corporate culture.

CONSTRUCTING BEHAVIORAL QUESTIONS

Now that the mandatory success factors have been identified, it's time to begin constructing behavioral questions that will elicit real-life evidence of a candidate's level of competence with each factor.

TEAMWORK

This is the most important success factor identified. Teamwork involves working well with others for the purpose of accomplishing organizational goals, or to identify and solve problems.

Behavioral question: "Tell me about a time when you used a team approach to problem-solving."

Follow-up probes:

- "How did the team work?"
- "What solutions did you attempt before involving the team?"
- "What were your responsibilities on the team?"
- "What specific actions did the team take?"
- "What obstacles needed to be overcome by the team in solving the problem?"
- "What results did the team achieve?"

Notice that each of the follow-up questions is designed to guide the candidate's response. Remember the STAR formula: Behavioral responses should discuss a specific situation or task, provide detailed information concerning actions taken by the candidate, and conclude with a discussion of the result achieved.

TRAINING AND MENTORING

District sales managers for XYZ Company are responsible for training and mentoring new sales staff, as well as continually developing existing staff. This function involves formal training sessions at the district office. It also involves regularly working with each member of the sales team in field situations, providing one-to-one coaching and skill-building activities.

Behavioral question: "Describe a time when you hired a new salesperson who knew very little about how to succeed in selling your company's product. What kind of help did you provide?"

Follow-up probes:

- ▨ "What kinds of training techniques do you think work particularly well?"
- ▨ "What kinds of one-to-one activities have you participated in with new salespeople to help them achieve success?"
- ▨ "Tell us about a time when a salesperson refused to see things your way. What did you do?"
- ▨ "What is a mentor? Give us an example of a time when you mentored someone."
- ▨ "Tell us about the impact that your training and mentoring activities have had on your past success as a sales manager."

COMMUNICATION SKILLS

The job of the district sales manager for XYZ Company requires the ability to express ideas orally and in writing. Over the years, many of those who have failed in this job lacked the ability to communicate effectively.

Behavioral question: "Describe a situation in which you made an oral presentation of a written proposal that you prepared."

Follow-up probes:

- ▨ "What were the most important elements of the proposal?"
- ▨ "What are some things that you did to strengthen the presentation?"
- ▨ "What could you have done to make the presentation better?"
- ▨ "What kinds of things have you done since that time to enhance your communication skills? What do you intend to do in the near future?"
- ▨ "Tell us about the outcome of your proposal."

LEADERSHIP

The district sales manager must be a leader and must lead by example. At XYZ Company, sales managers succeed only when they are able to lead others to success.

Behavioral question: "If I were to call your present supervisor, how would she describe your leadership ability?" (For this factor, Pete decides to use a self-appraisal question.)

Follow-up probes:

- ▨ "Tell me about a time when your ability to lead really paid off."
- ▨ "What kinds of things do you do that mark you as a strong leader?"
- ▨ "What results have you achieved through your leadership abilities?"

CUSTOMER SERVICES

At XYZ Company, customer satisfaction is a high priority. Listening to the needs of customers, understanding them, and responding in an appropriate and timely manner is essential.

Behavioral question: "Tell us about the most difficult customer service experience you've ever had to handle."

Follow-up probes:

- "How were you made aware of the problem?"
- "What steps did you take to solve the situation?"
- "What could you have done better?"
- "What happened as a result of your intervention?"

BEHAVIORAL PROBES FOR SELF-MANAGEMENT SKILLS

Developing behavioral questions for self-management skills is accomplished in much the same way as it is for functional skills. However, follow-up probes are often noticeably different.

Because the self-management skill set usually involves strongly held beliefs and attitudes, follow-up probes tend to be more exploratory in nature. The STAR response is not always what's needed to properly assess this type of factor. This is especially true when questions are phrased as continuum or self-appraisal questions.

HONESTY

XYZ Company believes that honesty is the cornerstone of its business. The company prides itself in dealing honestly and fairly with its customers as well as its employees, and expects the same kind of treatment in return.

Behavioral question: "On a scale between being absolutely honest and absolutely committed to making things work at any cost, where do you fit?" (For this factor, Pete decides to use a continuum question.)

Follow-up probes:

- "Tell me about a time when you bent the truth a bit to accomplish an important goal."
- "Describe a situation in which telling the truth lost you the sale or caused you to lose in some other way."
- "Give us an example of a time when you discovered some dishonesty in someone reporting to you. What did you do?"

RELIABILITY

"A man's word is his bond." That's hardly a twenty-first century idea, and many might even consider it old-fashioned and antiquated. But at XYZ Corporation, it's more than a motto; it's a performance expectation.

Behavioral question: "Give us an example of a time when keeping your word to a customer or an employee meant having to endure a good deal of personal difficulty."

Follow-up probes:

- "What was so important about the commitment?"
- "What was required of you to keep your promise?"
- "What happened as a result of your efforts to keep your word?"
- "Tell me about someone you know who is absolutely reliable."
- "Are you always reliable?"

THE INTERVIEW PLAN

Now that the behavioral questions and follow-up probes for each mandatory success factor have been developed, the next step is to plan the interview process itself. Here's a step-by-step interview model that I've used several times and can highly recommend.

TIP

Be sure to make any modifications necessary to customize the interview plan for use in your organization. Also, times indicated are merely suggested and should be altered to fit the needs of a specific interview.

Introductory phase: 5 to 10 minutes

- Introduce the candidate to each member of the interview team and ask panel members to introduce themselves.
- Inform the candidate of how the interview will be conducted (who will be asking primary questions, follow-up questions, and so on).
- Inform the candidate of when you expect the interview to be concluded.
- Ask any questions necessary to clear up questions concerning the candidate's application or resumé.

Information-gathering phase: 1 hour

- Ask primary behavioral questions. (5 percent)
- Probe for specific actions. (65 percent)
- Probe for additional information or clarification. (20 percent)
- Probe for results. (10 percent)

Repeat this process until each of your mandatory success factors has been probed.

Position description phase: 5 minutes

- Provide the candidate with a job description.
- Explain the duties and responsibilities of the position.
- Offer specific examples of work performed.
- Offer to answer questions concerning the position.

Sell the company: 5 minutes

Be sure to assign one member of the interview team the responsibility of "selling the company" to the candidate. This should be a true sales effort outlining the major benefits involved in working for the company.

The closing phase: 5 to 10 minutes

- Ask if the candidate has any unanswered questions.
- Ask if the candidate is interested in pursuing the position.
- Inform the candidate of what the next step will be in the selection process and when a decision is likely to be made.

THE 30-SECOND RECAP

- Begin with an analysis of the job—be sure to solicit the input of others.
- Identify required technical competencies, "ideal candidate" functional skills, "ideal candidate" self-management skills, interpersonal skill requirements, and any special requirements of the corporate culture.
- Rate the "ideal candidate" functional and self-management skills to determine which of them are mandatory success factors.
- Develop behavioral interview questions and follow-up probes for each of the mandatory success factors, the interpersonal skill requirements, and the requirements of the corporate culture.

■ Develop an interview plan that will provide an agenda for the interview process and define general time allotments.

Critique and Fine-Tune

In this section you learn the value of constructively critiquing the interviews that you conduct to spot weaknesses and other difficulties that may need to be corrected.

INTERVIEW CHECKLIST

The price of building and maintaining good interviewing skills and techniques is eternal vigilance. After each round of interviews, it helps to take a few minutes to critique the interview process to detect what went right and what may need improvement.

Here's a checklist covering each of the major tasks involved in the interview process. Use it to help spot weak areas and to reinforce strengths.

PREINTERVIEW

■ A thorough analysis of the vacant position was performed, and mandatory success factors were identified.

■ The immediate supervisor of the position was asked to describe any special factors that may be required to succeed in the job, including those imposed by the corporate culture.

■ An interview panel was assembled, consisting of all supervisors to whom the new employee will report, together with a peer or two from the department or unit in which the opening exists.

■ Panel members met at least once to thoroughly discuss the interview process.

■ A resumé review tool, such as the Resumé Review Grid, was developed and used as part of the preinterview screening process.

■ Resumés were screened by more than one person.

■ Applicants eliminated in the initial screening process were notified in writing.

TIP

Remember that just because an applicant was eliminated from further consideration for one job doesn't mean you'll never be interested in hiring them. The next opening in your organization may be a perfect match. So take the time to contact each unsuccessful applicant, thanking them for their interest, and encouraging them to apply again (unless, of course, the reason for their elimination is something that will disqualify them from being employed in any capacity with your firm).

- Specific concerns about information contained in resumés were clearly flagged for further discussion with the candidate.

- All candidates selected for further consideration were notified in writing and were asked to complete company employment application forms, which included a clause permitting you to contact any and all former employers as well as others with knowledge of the applicant's work history, and a hold harmless agreement permitting all references to release information about the applicant.

TIP

Be sure to ask your corporate attorney to periodically review your company's employment application to ensure that you have the proper legal authority to "network" references—that is, to ask each of them to provide a name of someone else who is familiar with the applicant's work.

- Candidates were also asked to submit 10 "personal" references that included the names of former employers.

- Behavioral questions and appropriate follow-up probes were developed for each of the mandatory success factors identified in the job review.

- Any required testing was arranged for each candidate selected to be interviewed.

- References were contacted prior to interviews.

- Academic degrees were verified prior to interviews.

- Interviews were scheduled in advance, and sufficient time was allocated for each interview.

INTERVIEW

- Interviews were held in an area that was free from noise and interruption.

- Panel members were briefed about the candidate before each interview and were given a copy of the candidate's resumé, together with the comments of reviewers who initially reviewed it.

- Panel members were punctual and prepared for the interview process.

- An attempt was made to put candidates at ease before each interview.

- In the opening segment of the interview, candidates were told what to expect during the interview.

- Candidates were asked to explain any questions raised in the initial review of their resumé.

- The 80/20 rule was followed—the candidate did at least 80 percent of the talking.

- Each member of the interview panel practiced active listening skills during the interviews.

- Panel members maintained eye contact with each candidate.

- The behavioral questions developed for each mandatory success factor were asked of all candidates interviewed.

- Candidates were allowed sufficient time to answer questions.

- Candidates were given verbal and nonverbal encouragement during the course of interviews.

- The course of each interview was appropriately controlled.

- Interviews were focused on mandatory success factors and didn't drift into areas not related to the position being sought.

- Interview panel members took appropriate notes during the course of each interview.

- At the end of each interview, candidates were told what comes next.

- Candidates were given a positive impression of the company because one member of the interview panel took responsibility for "selling the company" to each candidate.

- During the closing segment of the interview process, candidates were given an opportunity to ask questions about the job and the company.

POSTINTERVIEW

- Evaluations of candidates were completed immediately following each interview, using an appropriate evaluation tool (see "Structured Behavioral Interviewing: Part 1" on page 450).

- The candidate of choice was hired, with the decision being promptly communicated to all remaining candidates, or a short list of top candidates was developed.

- Second interviews were scheduled for short-listed candidates utilizing alternative interview methods.

- Feedback from those involved in second interview situations was evaluated.

- The candidate of choice was hired, with the decision being promptly communicated to all remaining candidates.

MAKE IT A HABIT

Each part of the interview process is important. Whether you're new to structured behavioral interviewing or have been doing it for years, there's always room for improvement.

Make it a habit to regularly review the interview process and to make improvements whenever necessary. Continue to look for ways to develop your style of interviewing.

THE 30-SECOND RECAP

- Critiquing interviews helps the manager to fine tune the interview process for maximum effectiveness.

- Regardless of your personal experience with structured behavioral interview techniques, there's always room for improvement.

- Checklists, similar to the one outlined in this section, are a good way to objectively review the interview process.

- Remember that the objective is to find the best candidate for the job. So retain and improve whatever process steps help accomplish that goal, and improve or eliminate whatever gets in the way of it.

Improving Employee Performance and Development

Improving Performance

In this section you'll learn how to establish performance measures. You'll also learn about common mistakes associated with performance measures and how these measures promote continuous improvement.

MEASURING PERFORMANCE

The phrase "performance measure" is intuitively satisfying, yet frighteningly vague. Simultaneously, you feel comforted by the thought of being able to measure results and distressed by the prospect of having to create the measure. The key to avoiding this conflict lies in understanding how measures are created.

The natural tendency is to measure the end result. There are a couple of problems with this approach:

1. Not all results are measurable.

2. Other useful measures are overlooked.

NOT ALL RESULTS ARE MEASURABLE

Let's assume your goal is to improve employee morale. That's tough to measure. Sure, you can survey your employees before and after an initiative, but there are a lot of factors that influence morale besides your effort. One of the most important is your employee's frame of mind on the days surveyed.

Did the employee just fight with his spouse? How was traffic that morning? Are the kids ill? Did the car break down? Or did the employee wake up feeling that everything is right with the world? All these factors influence the employee's morale on the date surveyed. The presence of these external influences makes the value of the surveys suspect.

OTHER USEFUL MEASURES ARE OVERLOOKED

In recent years we've seen a dramatic increase in the use of *process mapping* and *activity-based costing* to define performance measures. Both tools are designed to identify redundancies and inefficiencies in systems and approaches.

PLAIN ENGLISH

Process mapping   A method used to examine the effectiveness of the current approach used in accomplishing a task. It's called process mapping because it provides a visual map of the various steps in a process. These steps are listed in the order performed, then analyzed with an eye to increasing efficiency.

PLAIN ENGLISH

Activity-based costing   A method used to view all processes involved in offering a product or service to your customers. It looks at the costs of everything from marketing, through delivery, to the final paperwork. Activity-based costing even examines the costs of billing the customer, the cost of slow payment, and the cost of processing vendor invoices and payments to the vendors.

These powerful tools are excellent for generating ideas for improving performance and establishing performance measures.

One of the reasons these approaches are so effective is that they allow you to create smaller projects. While it may take years to achieve your end result, it often takes only days or weeks to improve a step in the process.

Each success moves your team closer to its overall goal. Each success intensifies the team's belief that it will be successful on a larger scale. The combination of these two elements, success and confidence, will accelerate the achievement of the result you seek.

Now that I've identified some worthwhile tools for creating measures, here are the hallmarks of effective performance measures. They must be:

- Quantifiable
- Easy to understand
- Well balanced
- Easy to track
- Frequently published

QUANTIFIABLE

You must be able to represent the measure numerically. Time, error rates, retention rates, units produced, absenteeism, cost, and profitability are all measures that lend themselves to numeric representation. Most can be adapted to a variety of operating situations.

For example, retention rates can be applied to both customers and employees. Error rates can be applied to manufacturing and administrative functions. Speed is as useful in measuring responsiveness to customers as it is in gauging the timeliness of information from the accounting department.

The key is that all these measures are quantifiable. They may be stated in percentages, actual performance numbers, or time intervals. The form of the numeric presentation isn't nearly as important as the ability to quantify the measure.

TIP

If you're having trouble creating a quantifiable measure, you're typically looking at the wrong result. Often you're looking at a result that's too broad. Break this result into smaller components, and you'll find a result that you can measure.

EASY TO UNDERSTAND

One of my clients established an incentive compensation program for all production and administrative personnel. They used several measures to support their overall goal of increased profitability. One of the measures was "return on average capital employed."

I learned that they were using this measure when the vice president of human resources called to ask for my help in communicating the concept. It seems that his initial attempt generated more questions than understanding.

After helping him devise a communiqué, I offered an observation. I told him that there was no way the employees on the shop floor would be able to relate their daily work to the achievement of this measure. Two years later, he told me that my prediction had come true; the employees were viewing the incentive payments as holiday bonuses.

Your employees must be able to understand the measure and relate it to their daily work. If they can't, the measure will not help them improve performance.

WELL BALANCED

We've all heard horror stories that demonstrate the importance of well-balanced goals. I've seen companies set aggressive sales targets without considering the production, service, and financing aspects of their decision. The tragic consequence is that they lose the very customers they fought so hard to get. Why? They failed to honor the promises made in their sales and marketing efforts.

I've seen companies focus so narrowly on reducing the cost of their delivery operations that they angered customers. You can imagine the pain a customer using just-in-time inventory would feel if his deliveries were delayed.

To help you avoid these mistakes, I refer you to a book by David Norton and Robert Kaplan titled *The Balanced Scorecard*. It offers valuable insights into the art of establishing balanced goals. Don't be intimidated by the fact that the approach is designed for company-wide use. The concepts can be used at any level in the organization.

TIP

Make your employees aware of the danger involved in creating a goal without fully considering the implications of its achievement. It'll help them be more successful. It will also help you avoid dealing with problems that your employees inadvertently created.

EASY TO TRACK

You want to choose measures that facilitate daily, or at least weekly, tracking of results. There is a direct correlation between the frequency with which results are posted and the intensity of your employees' focus. If you only post results once a month, I can assure you that your employees will lose sight of their performance goals. With that thought in mind, let's identify some measures for tracking customer retention.

Customer retention is a worthy goal, but it is not one that lends itself to daily or weekly tracking. There are, however, many aspects of customer retention that do lend themselves to daily measurement:

- Responsiveness to customer inquiries
- Time involved in satisfactorily resolving customer problems
- Number of defective parts shipped
- Billing errors
- Shipping errors

Choose measures over which the employee has control. Then post the results daily.

CAUTION

Employees who are held responsible for results outside their control live in constant fear. It's difficult to be productive when you're worried about your future.

If you're wondering why daily tracking is so important, place yourself in the role of the employee. Your boss is posting your results daily. Where are you going to focus your energies? Of course it'll be on the measures being tracked.

The best tracking system is one that allows the employee to monitor his own performance. The value of a self-monitoring system is two-fold. First, it allows the employee to make daily adjustments as necessary to achieve his goals. Second, the employee tends to trust the results more when he can verify them himself.

FREQUENTLY PUBLISHED

You can establish the best possible measures, track them daily, and still not gain the performance improvement you seek. How? The information doesn't get posted. Here's what happened to one of my clients.

This client is a specialty manufacturer dealing in the design and manufacture of custom products for its customers. One measure used in the production department was "production efficiency," the percentage of work completed that day versus the work planned for the day.

Every day someone in the office calculates production efficiency and posts the results on a white board in the plant. The person assigned this task is also responsible for the computer network. One day he experienced problems with the network and forgot to post the results. The next day the same thing happened. The third day he simply forgot to post the measure. (Isn't it amazing how quickly good habits die?) Three months later we observed a decline in the company's profitability. Why? The lack of feedback caused the production employees to lose sight of their goal.

Another equally important reason for posting information daily is that it allows the employee to experience the sense of success more often. Every time we achieve a goal, we experience the feeling of satisfaction. Don't rob your employees of one of the most satisfying aspects of their job. Provide them with frequent feedback.

CURRENT PERFORMANCE

Now it's time to measure current performance. Here's an example.

A construction client's goal is to improve cash flow. A study of the production and billing processes shows that it takes three weeks to invoice the customer after the job is complete. Three weeks is the *current level of performance.*

PLAIN ENGLISH

Current level of performance   The result you're getting today. These results are the benchmark against which you and your employees will measure results from improvement initiatives. With each new success you raise the level of current performance and the benchmark used in your measurements.

DESIRED PERFORMANCE

Once you've identified current performance, you have a solid foundation for establishing improvement goals. You'll be asking yourself questions such as,

"How much improvement should I target?" or, "How do I know whether my target is aggressive or unrealistic?" The latter question is especially important.

When you establish unrealistic goals, you set your employees, your company, and yourself up for failure. I can't think of anything more devastating than a no-win situation like this. Here are a few ideas on how you can avoid this problem.

First, does the goal promote customer satisfaction? This may seem like a strange question if you're leading an accounts payable function. Yet your actions can affect both the price of the goods your company purchases and the timeliness of the delivery of those goods.

If you cause your vendors to do a lot of paperwork, slow their payments, or are unresponsive to their requests for payment, you limit your company's ability to get further price reductions. You also give vendors reason to place your company farther down on the priority list for shipments. Both of these results affect your company's ability to serve its customers well.

Second, do a cost-benefit analysis. If you're not comfortable doing this analysis on your own, get help from the accounting department. Your goal isn't realistic if the costs of achieving the goal exceed the benefits gained.

Third, are the time frames for accomplishing the goal realistic? Don't misunderstand me; you should choose aggressive time frames. Just make sure they are realistic.

How can you tell whether you've crossed the line? Look at the probability of success. I use 50 percent as my guide. If I have a 50 percent (or better) chance of achieving the goal, I consider it aggressive. If the probability of success is less than 50 percent, it's unrealistic.

 TIP

Ask your employees to participate in goal setting. Their familiarity with the work helps you avoid costly mistakes. Their participation in the decision increases their commitment to the goal's success.

Let's assume that your employee is successful and achieves the desired level of performance, then what?

CONTINUOUS IMPROVEMENT

So much is written about *continuous improvement* these days, and rightfully so.

PLAIN ENGLISH

Continuous improvement   The goal of becoming better at what we do every day of our lives. When applied to organizations, it includes all segments of the company's operations.

The importance of continuous improvement goes well beyond the competitive advantage it affords your company. It allows your employees to enjoy …

- Variety in their work.
- Learning opportunities.
- The satisfaction of conquering new challenges.
- The satisfaction of doing valuable work.
- The pride of being associated with a successful company.

Unless you raise the performance bar after each success, you deprive your employees of the opportunity to experience greater job satisfaction. You also rob your company of the financial success it deserves and yourself of the recognition you could earn as a valued leader in your organization.

Some employees may resist your attempts to raise the bar. You may even hear comments like "Why bother? Once we get there he'll just set a higher goal. It'll never end."

If you don't find ways to improve what you are doing, you will end up doing the same job every day for the rest of your career. You'll learn nothing new, and you won't experience a sense of accomplishment. Your value to the company and yourself will continue to decline and, ultimately, you'll threaten your own financial livelihood.

The language in this statement focuses on what's important to the employee: job satisfaction, employability, and financial success. By providing "selfish" motives, you increase the employee's interest in improving his performance.

The 30-Second Recap

Performance measures must be the following:

- Quantifiable
- Easy to understand
- Well balanced
- Easy to track
- Frequently published
- Specific to the individual employee's work effort

- Stated in terms of current and desired performance
- Raised as soon as the desired performance is achieved

Encouraging Employee Development

In this section you'll learn about your role as mentor and the performance appraisal's part in fulfilling that role.

BECOMING A MENTOR

Effective performance goals don't assure improved performance. Your employees must possess the skills necessary to convert these goals to reality. In today's fast-paced world, it's difficult for employees to meet deadlines and evaluate their skill development needs. That's why it's essential that you become a *mentor* to all your employees.

PLAIN ENGLISH

Mentor   A wise and trusted advisor. Mentors can be found both within and outside your organization. The key is finding someone who possesses skills that you want to develop.

There is more to mentoring than saving time. Mentors provide their protégés with opportunities to view themselves through another's eyes. This is important because it's difficult for us to see our own weaknesses. Often we don't realize that we've developed a bad habit unless someone is kind enough to tell us. Your employees are no different. That's why it's important that they have someone in their lives who cares enough about them to tell them what they need to know about themselves. In the work environment, that's you.

WISDOM

By definition, a mentor is wise. I'm not sure how many of you consider yourselves wise. You are more likely to think of yourself as someone who does a good job.

Your promotion indicates that you have the ability to anticipate what is needed, act based on that information, and produce results well in advance of your peers. Sounds like wisdom to me. Regardless of whether you consider yourself wise, you have a talent you can use to help others.

Your ability to anticipate is the key. You have an intuitive sense for what needs to be done in any situation. Simply apply this skill to your employees' circumstances. How?

Place yourself in the employees' shoes. Use what you know about your employees' strengths, skills, and job requirements to decide what you would do in their circumstances. This analysis provides a map for leading your employees to higher and higher levels of performance and job satisfaction.

TRUST

A mentor must also be trusted. Your employees know when you have their best interests at heart. What does it mean to have their best interest at heart? It means that you ...

- Want to see them succeed.
- Do everything in your power to help them succeed.
- Want them to have fun on the job.
- Want to see them recognized for their accomplishments.

If your employees sense that the only reason you are encouraging their personal development is to make yourself look good, they will resist your efforts. On the other hand, if they sense that you want them to succeed and that the benefits to you and the company are ancillary, they'll willingly follow your lead.

CAUTION

Some people have so little confidence in their own abilities that they trust virtually no one. They look for hidden agendas in every opportunity and every word of encouragement you offer. It's rare, but I recently had a client who experienced this phenomenon. Understand the reaction for what it is—a lack of self-confidence.

EVALUATING STRENGTHS

Now that you've demonstrated wisdom and earned your employee's trust, your next goal is to understand the employee's strengths. Here are some questions you need to ask:

- Which tasks does the employee perform well?
- Which tasks cause the employee to struggle?
- What performance measures do you use for each of these tasks?

- What skills will the employee need to improve performance on existing measures?
- Will new measures be required in the future?
- When will the new measures be employed?
- What skills will the employee need to achieve desired results using these new measures?
- Do other employees readily accept this employee's lead?
- Does the employee communicate well?
- Does the employee possess the patience to teach others?
- Does the employee demonstrate the desire to teach?
- Are the employee's motives selfish, selfless, or somewhere in between?
- How would you classify the employee's attitude: optimistic, realistic, or pessimistic?
- Under which conditions does this employee excel: structured, chaotic, or creative?
- Does this employee prefer team or individual efforts?
- How does this employee react to time pressure?
- When faced with new challenges, does the employee jump at the opportunity, hesitate, or run for the hills?

These are representative questions. They form a good foundation on which to build an understanding of your employees' strengths. The answers to these questions will undoubtedly raise other questions that are specific to the individual employee. In the end, you want a clear understanding of the areas in which your employee performs well and what her potential for growth is.

TIP

Give your employees time to answer these questions. You'll create a new awareness of what's important to their success and help them become more forward thinking.

EXPLORING EMPLOYEE INTERESTS

A friend of mine, a financial planner, shocked me when he told me he might pursue another career. Even though he hadn't been in business very long, he had achieved considerable financial success. When I asked why the change of heart, he responded, "Now that I have proven I can be successful, I have to decide whether this is what I want to do."

This was a real eye-opener for me. I assumed that because he was successful he was enjoying what he was doing. As I examined my career I realized that I had made similar decisions over the years. Apparently, those weren't the conscious decisions my friend was making.

CAUTION

Don't equate skills with interests. As the previous story demonstrates, to do so is a serious miscalculation; one that may cause an employee to fail because he lacks interest in the work.

The performance appraisal is an excellent tool for discovering your employees' interests. Here are a few questions to help you uncover those interests:

- What is your favorite part of your job? Why?
- What do you like least about the job?
- What would make the least attractive aspect of your work more enjoyable?
- Is there work that you aren't currently doing that appeals to you? Why?
- What skills do you think you'll need to do that work?
- Do your currently possess those skills?
- If not, how would you go about gaining those skills?

The last three questions are designed to measure your employee's level of interest. They'll help you decide whether she's simply dreaming or seriously considering a career change.

If your employee is simply dreaming, make her aware of what she's doing. One of the greatest sources of dissatisfaction in this world is the gap between dreams and reality. Next, get your employee to make a conscious decision. She's either going to pursue the dream or abandon it. The middle ground is fraught with frustration. Help your employees make conscious decisions about their dreams. You'll save yourself, and your employees, a lot of pain.

An employee who has already thought about how he might become involved in other types of work is often bored. There are a variety of ways to deal with boredom. You can ...

- Add new responsibilities that will challenge the employee.
- Get two employees who are experiencing boredom to change jobs for a while.
- Involve the employee in special projects.

■ Have employees examine each other's work to increase efficiency.

■ Temporarily trade employees with another leader who shares your leadership style.

Boredom is a thief that quietly robs your employee of her job satisfaction and you of her productivity. The performance appraisal can help you avoid this problem.

TIP

If restlessness persists, your employee is ready to move on. Don't stand in the way. If possible, help her find what she needs in your organization. It's better to lose a good employee to another department than to a competitor.

MATCHING STRENGTHS AND INTERESTS

As you examine your employee's strengths and interests, compare them to the workload she faces, then answer the following questions:

■ Are there mismatches between this employee's workload, skills, and interests?

■ Do mismatches exist with other employees as well?

■ Will work reassignment cure these mismatches?

■ Do the employees have the skills necessary to make reassignment feasible?

■ What impact will reassignment have on productivity, both short-term and long-term?

TIP

Favor interest over skills in assigning work. Over the years I've learned that it is much easier to teach skills than to generate interest. A highly skilled, disinterested worker typically does not perform as well as an interested, less skilled worker.

Before you announce a new and wonderful reassignment plan, meet with the employees who will be affected. These meetings give you a chance to ...

■ Confirm your understanding of their interests.

■ Gain insights into concerns they may have.

■ Help them overcome any fears they may have.

- Provide insights into how this plan benefits all parties: the employees, the company, and you.
- Change the plan if the design is faulty.

The success of the reassignment plan depends heavily on the employees' belief that they participated in its design.

THE NEED FOR A DEVELOPMENT PLAN

Now that you have a thorough understanding of the employee's strengths and interests and you've identified future skill needs, it's time to help your employee create a *development plan*.

PLAIN ENGLISH

Development plan   A plan that identifies the skills needed, resources available, and timetables for developing the skills.

How important is the development plan? You may as well ask how easy it is to drive to a new location without directions? The development plan is a guide in which you identify ...

- **The destination.** The skills the employee needs.
- **Available resources.** College courses, public seminars, internal training, or experience in other departments or on other projects and coaching.
- **Timetables.** Deadlines for acquiring the skills.

Assure that your employees have the skills they need. Help them create a development plan.

CREATING A DEVELOPMENT PLAN

There are two things you can do to increase the effectiveness of a development plan. First, allow your employee to participate in the plan's development. Her participation increases the likelihood that she will act on the plan.

Second, leave the employee to her own devices as much as possible. This means that if you and your employee have different approaches for developing a skill and both would work, allow your employee to choose her method. Why? Her choice will match her learning style, which, in turn, will speed skill development.

Let's take a look at the steps involved in creating development plans:

1. Ask the employee what skills she thinks she will need in the future.

2. Share your thoughts with the employee and ask her opinion.

3. Ask the employee how she would acquire these skills.

4. Encourage the approaches that make sense.

5. Offer other approaches or resources the employee might not have considered.

6. Leave the choice of approaches to the employee, if possible.

7. Agree upon deadlines for each phase of the development plan.

8. Establish rewards for the timely development of each skill.

9. Establish feedback systems that allow the employee to monitor her progress.

10. Use the deadlines as communication triggers for follow-up meetings.

11. Use the information gained in follow-up meetings, good news or bad, to amend the development plan.

TIP

Even though *development plan* is the commonly used terminology in performance appraisals, I believe it implies the "need" to improve. I prefer *future success strategies*. I believe this phrase implies current success.

The approach just outlined simplifies the development plan process, involves the employee in designing the plan, increases the likelihood that she will act on the plan, and provides for periodic follow-up on the employee's progress. It's easy to see why the employee development plan is such an integral part of the performance appraisal process.

THE 30-SECOND RECAP

- Performance improvement requires improvement of skills.

- Your role as mentor is to help your employees improve their skills.

- Employees are more likely to develop skills in areas that interest them.

- Employees are more successful when they participate in the creation of their own development plan.

Striving for Employee Satisfaction

In this section you learn about the benefits of employee satisfaction, factors that influence satisfaction, and the performance appraisal's role in making work enjoyable.

THE BENEFITS OF HAVING HAPPY EMPLOYEES

In their book *Raving Fans,* Ken Blanchard and Sheldon Bowles offer numerous examples of how ecstatic employees take customer service to stratospheric levels. In addition to being great ambassadors for your company, happy employees are …

- More likely to stay with the company.
- Are absent fewer days than unhappy employees.
- File fewer grievances.
- Complete their work more quickly.
- Produce higher-quality work.
- Find ways to improve their effectiveness.
- Share their enthusiasm with colleagues.

To help us understand the enormity of these benefits, let's look at each more closely.

RETENTION

Today's hottest business topic is employee retention. Globally, companies are experiencing high rates of growth coupled with low unemployment. Is it any wonder that leaders are focused on ways to retain their employees?

What are the ramifications of losing an employee? What does it cost financially? Psychologically? The initial cost comes in the form of lost productivity. When you lose a team member, your options are to …

- Ask the remaining employees to pick up additional work.
- *Outsource* some of the work to a temporary help agency.
- Reevaluate the workload of the entire team and determine what, if any, work can be eliminated or postponed.

PLAIN ENGLISH

Outsource   A term that describes the company's decision to use outside services rather than have employees perform the tasks. Companies outsource tasks such as payroll and training.

If you choose the first option, you run the risk of creating more unhappy employees and more retention problems. Even if you are a strong leader and unconcerned about further losses, you face heavy costs in the form of ...

- Additional overtime.
- Lower productivity due to fatigue.
- Higher absenteeism caused by illness associated with fatigue.
- Rework caused by errors resulting from fatigue.
- Missed deadlines.
- Lost momentum on new initiatives.

As you can see, it doesn't take long for the costs to mount.

TIP

If you choose to spread the work among your remaining employees, allow them to participate in the decisions about how work should be reallocated. This approach minimizes their dissatisfaction with the increasing workload.

Outsourcing brings its own set of costs. If you choose to use a temporary help agency ...

1. You or someone in your department has to spend time finding an agency with the right talent pool.
2. Someone has to take time to train the person.
3. Higher levels of supervision are required because the work is unfamiliar to the person.
4. Even with additional supervision, errors are going to occur more frequently, which increases the amount of rework and the total amount of work to be accomplished.
5. The additional demands on you and your team make it difficult to plan far enough ahead to keep the temporary person productive throughout the day.

By the way, items two through four have to be repeated when you finally hire a permanent replacement.

The third option, reevaluating the work, can be a benefit. The old adage, "Necessity is the mother of invention," is true. The loss of a team member often spawns some very creative ideas for accomplishing the work more quickly. How? By identifying redundant or trivial tasks that can be eliminated. The problem is that your team is trying to create these efficiencies when they are already burdened with extra work. The best time for this activity is *before* you lose an employee.

TIP

Wait until you're fully staffed and in the midst of your slow season (most businesses have one) to embark on a reevaluation of your team's work.

ABSENTEEISM

Employee absences are inevitable, and the number of absences is increasing. The "sandwich" generation, those people in their 50s and 60s today, find themselves caring for three generations: themselves, their children, and their parents.

Combine these additional care requirements with the plethora of dual wage-earner families and you have escalating absenteeism. Add the occasional car breakdown, ice or snowstorm, and parent-teacher conference, and you can see that employee absences are indeed inevitable.

What impact does an absence have? First, you've got to drop what you're doing to evaluate what needs to be done that day. Then you have to disrupt someone else's (maybe several other people's) schedule, explain what needs to be done, make yourself available to answer their inevitable questions, then follow up frequently to make sure that deadlines are met.

You are easily facing losses of one to two hours for each person involved. That's a loss in productivity of 15 percent or more, and we haven't even discussed the costs associated with overtime, lost momentum on new initiatives, or the wear and tear on those who are handling the additional workload.

Employees who enjoy their work find ways to minimize their absences. They realize the burden it places on their teammates and they do everything in their power to avoid hurting the team.

Conversely, employees who are unhappy look for reasons not to come to work. I recently completed work with a client who was spending $84,000 a year for overtime and another $39,000 for temporary help to cover employee absences. Virtually all of the $123,000 could be traced to absences associated with employee dissatisfaction. That's a hefty price tag.

GRIEVANCES

If you work in a union environment, you know that the *grievance* process is expensive. You spend time researching your position, creating a defense, involving the legal department or an outside attorney, and testifying at the proceeding. All these activities take you away from your primary responsibilities.

PLAIN ENGLISH

Grievance   A formal complaint filed by a union employee against the employer, which is supported by the union. Some nonunion companies have similar procedures for dealing with employee complaints.

Even if you win, you face the possibility of retribution from the employee and, possibly, his co-workers as well. Usually acts of retribution are crafted to create problems without violating the terms of the contract. I don't need to calculate these costs for you. You know they're huge.

Happy employees file grievances only when someone in management violates the contract. Unhappy employees look for reasons to file grievances. They really don't care whether their claim is ultimately deemed frivolous. They have accomplished their goal: creating problems for you.

TIP

If you have an employee who is frequently filing grievances, ask him to participate in making decisions. It's difficult to complain about a decision that you helped make.

PRODUCTIVITY AND QUALITY

You need to look no further than your own performance to evaluate the impact happiness has on productivity and quality. Think of a task that you don't enjoy. Are you happy when you're doing the work? Since the work isn't pleasant, do you tend to postpone it? When you finally get around to tackling the job, are you bumping up against the deadline? Does the delay cause you to take shortcuts to meet the deadline? Have these shortcuts resulted in errors? Did the errors result in your having to redo the work? This picture is getting really ugly, isn't it?

Now let's look at a task you enjoy. This work gets priority status because you enjoy it. Deadlines aren't a problem; you usually complete the work early. You seldom make errors, so the need for rework is virtually eliminated. This simple comparison makes it easy to see how important employee satisfaction is to productivity and quality.

INCREASING EFFECTIVENESS

Unhappy employees will do a reliable job, if you're lucky. At best, they'll do what is asked of them. Generally they'll do enough to retain their jobs, nothing more. Today's competitive environment requires a commitment to continuous improvement from every employee. You're not going to get that commitment from an unhappy employee.

Conversely, people who enjoy their work typically look forward to new opportunities. They look for ways to accomplish their work more quickly so that they can learn and grow. They are committed to continuous improvement.

TIP

The effectiveness of your team depends heavily on your ability to assure each employee's satisfaction with his or her job.

ENTHUSIASM

Happiness and unhappiness share a common quality: They are both contagious. Think of someone, a friend or co-worker, who is always complaining. How do you feel when you're with that person? Does he sap your energy? Does life seem a little less worthwhile? Worse yet, does he destroy your good moods?

Now contrast the feelings you have when you're with an upbeat person. Do you laugh more often? What happens to your energy level? It soars! Do you experience a renewed zest for living? You bet you do.

Your employee's satisfaction with the job is going to determine his impact on co-workers, customers, vendors, and you.

How expensive is the lack of enthusiasm? What's the value of a customer? How important is the vendor to your ability to honor commitments to your customers? What's the cost when an unhappy employee drives away happy employees? What's it worth to you to work with people who are upbeat and committed to success?

Now that you've seen how valuable employee satisfaction is, let's see what it takes to ensure their happiness.

What Makes Employees Happy?

All right, let's be honest. How many of you think money makes employees happy? It's the one thing that everyone desires. Even billionaires like Bill Gates, Warren Buffett, and Michael Dell want more money. Not because they have unsatisfied lifestyle needs; they can afford any creature comfort they desire. Their desire is for greater success. Money is just the way they keep score.

For those of us who may not be able to dream quite that big, money holds the promise of a more comfortable lifestyle. Is it logical, then, to conclude that more money will make an employee happy? It may be logical, but it isn't factual. I know from personal experience that having more money doesn't lead to greater happiness.

Years ago, I was on the verge of quitting when the boss offered me more money. I thought the money would compensate for the less desirable aspects of the job. It didn't. Three months later I hated the job even more and felt guilty for having thoughts of leaving. The allure of money is great and it often clouds our judgment. Don't delude yourself into thinking that you can buy your employees' happiness with money.

What role should money play in an employee's happiness? As mentioned earlier, its greatest value is as a means of keeping score, a reward for success. Tie your employees' compensation to their performance, give them the ability to track their own progress, then reward them financially for achieving their goals. That's how you use money to promote employee satisfaction.

Variety

I recently worked with a group of data entry personnel to improve morale. Their work is very repetitive and *boring,* yet it is vital to the company's operation. One of the things we did was allow the employees to bring headsets to work so that they could listen to their favorite radio station or play CDs. We saw an immediate increase in productivity and drop in the absentee rate. Why? Variety was added to their daily routine.

You can accomplish similar results by periodically shifting work between employees, involving them in new projects, or possibly trading employees with another department for short periods of time. The method you choose isn't as important as assuring variety. After all, boredom is the bane of productivity.

TIP

Over the years I've found that nonmonetary aspects of the job—things like variety, learning, growth, and recognition—are more important to most employees than the money.

GROWTH OPPORTUNITIES

People don't enjoy the status quo. If you doubt that, think about one of the important achievements in your life. How long was it before you began to think about your next goal? The satisfaction that comes from goal achievement is fleeting. You enjoy it only for a few days or weeks, then you look for the next challenge to conquer.

I'm sure that some of you are thinking, "But that isn't true of all my employees. There are some who are very content doing the same job day in, day out." I believe you.

People who don't aspire to leadership roles are often very happy in their support roles. That doesn't mean they aren't interested in growth, it simply means they aren't interested in moving up the organization chart.

There is another type of growth that's available even in today's *flatter organizations*. That's growth within the job. This type of growth allows the employee to learn new skills and take on new responsibilities in his present position. Personal growth is both emotionally satisfying and financially rewarding.

PLAIN ENGLISH

Flatter organizations   Businesses that have reduced the number of layers of management. In the 1960s and 1970s many companies had six or more layers of management. Today that number is four or less.

It's emotionally satisfying because the employee enjoys feeling that he is becoming better every day. It's financially rewarding because he is making himself more valuable to the company. Help your employees understand the importance of growth, not just for the company, but for themselves. You'll dramatically increase their enjoyment of the work.

LEARNING

If you look at *Fortune* magazine's list of the "100 Best Companies to Work For," you'll find that all these companies invest heavily in training. Why? Their leaders recognize that employees ...

- Must improve their skills for the company to thrive.
- Feel good about themselves when they learn.
- Appreciate, respect, and readily follow leaders who regularly invest in their personal growth.

Your company doesn't need the training budget of a Fortune 500 company to provide learning. In fact, you don't have to have a training budget at all. That may sound like heresy from someone who offers training as part of his consulting work, but the reality is that learning comes in many forms. You can ...

- Involve employees in projects requiring new skills.
- Use cross-training to teach new skills.
- Have one of your best performers demonstrate the techniques that make him successful.
- Use book reviews to promote the learning of new skills.

The opportunities are limitless.

 TIP
Don't feel compelled to come up with these ideas on your own. Ask your employees what they would like to learn.

PARTICIPATION

Are you the master of your own destiny? Do you want to be? Of course you do. Ever since the age of two you've been asserting your independence. That's why you become irritated when your boss tells you what to do, when to do it, and how it should be done. Your employees feel the same way. That's why it's important to involve them in decisions regarding their work.

Ask your employees to participate in establishing performance measures, deadlines, goals, and priorities. Allow them to choose their own approaches to the work. Give them the opportunity to build their own development plans. They'll enjoy the job much more knowing that they participated in making these decisions.

RECOGNITION

Is there any greater reward than public recognition? Who among us hasn't dreamed of having our name in lights? Yet most of us view the odds to be roughly the same as winning the lottery.

CAUTION

Many people lose their desire to improve simply because their results aren't recognized.

It doesn't have to be that way for your employees. You control the spotlight. Shine it on their successes. Let them know that you are aware they're doing a wonderful job.

One of the more common mistakes leaders make is recognizing only top performers. There are employees who do a marvelous job yet get little, if any, recognition for their efforts. Here's how one of my clients addressed that issue. Every day he would list both the top performers and those who had achieved new personal bests. I love this concept. The people, who would never be able to achieve the title "Best," still have an opportunity to be recognized for their accomplishments.

You can add a team dimension to this recognition system by celebrating days when the team sets a record for new personal bests. The celebration can be as simple as ordering pizza or bringing in ice cream. I've let my team off an hour early on Friday afternoon when they have had an incredibly successful week. The form of recognition isn't as important as the recognition itself. Don't overlook this opportunity to make your employees' jobs more satisfying.

SECURITY

Is security a thing of the past? Many employees fear that it is. The merger and acquisition activities of the past decade seem to indicate that they're right— that is if you view security as continued employment with the same company.

There is another form of security that you can offer your employees that is just as valuable. The key is to help them understand the "new" definition of security.

The only real security is ability—specifically, the ability to produce results. If employees understand this and they use the performance appraisal to guide their success, they'll contribute significantly to their future employability. That's important, considering the likelihood of falling victim to a merger or acquisition.

Will increased employability remove the pain and fear associated with a job loss? Absolutely not! It can, however, minimize the time it takes to find comparable employment.

During the performance appraisal process, emphasize that hitting performance targets and development plan goals is as important to their future employability as it is to the company's success.

EMPLOYEE DIFFERENCES

Life would be simple if all employees valued all the job satisfaction factors equally. Alas, it is not to be. Some employees are driven by money. Others value recognition above the other factors. To some, security is the top priority.

TIP

Differences between employees are part of the variety of your job. Don't bemoan them. Your job would be very boring without them.

One of the advantages of performance appraisals is that they enable you to explore each employee's wants and needs. One approach is to simply ask your employees to rank each of the satisfaction factors in order of importance.

A less direct approach is to ask the employee how each factor influences his job satisfaction. It'll be easy to tell which factors are important by the sheer volume of ideas they express. The factors that elicit no ideas aren't important; those that generate 5 ideas in 15 seconds are.

THE 30-SECOND RECAP

Employee satisfaction is a key element of performance improvement. Factors that influence employee satisfaction are as follows:

- Variety
- Growth
- Learning
- Participation
- Recognition
- Security

Compensating Employees

In this section you'll learn about the connection between compensation, performance, and performance appraisal.

A COMMON OCCURRENCE

It's time for your performance appraisal and salary review. As you reflect on the past year, you realize that ...

- You haven't missed any work.
- The only deadline you missed was caused by another department's failure to provide the information you needed.
- Your boss has not criticized your performance; in fact, you have received a few compliments during the year.
- The few errors you made did not result in major rework; besides, the boss didn't seem concerned about them.
- You get along well with your co-workers.
- You have good working relationships with colleagues in other departments.
- You pitched in and helped your boss with a couple of projects when asked.

Overall, you're proud of your performance and you think that your raise is going to be on the upper end of the scale.

Your boss calls you into her office, hands you a copy of the appraisal, and gives you a few minutes to read it. You're delighted to see that her appraisal is closely aligned with your thoughts. Then you see it, a comment at the bottom of the last page. It says that you don't demonstrate initiative. It goes on to say that you have leadership potential, but you aren't assuming the role of a leader.

This is the first time you've heard these comments. You had no idea the boss saw leadership qualities in you. You certainly have never viewed yourself that way. You're flattered that someone would consider you a leader, then you realize that this comment is a criticism of your performance. You wonder whether it's going to affect your raise.

Your question is answered almost before its formed. The boss says that your raise will be the standard raise for someone at your level in the organization. She goes on to say that if you had taken the initiative to assume a leadership role that your increase would have been much higher. She hopes that you will take that initiative in the coming year.

How do you feel? Do you think you've been treated fairly? Would you have assumed the leadership role had you known it was expected of you? Do the compliments you received during the course of the year mean anything to you now? Of course not!

At this point, you feel betrayed. You cannot believe that your boss evaluated you on an expectation she hadn't communicated. You also find it hard to believe that you're being penalized for missing a goal you didn't know existed. Yet the penalty is there in the form of a lower raise.

At this point, what's your attitude toward the coming year? Are you excited about your prospects or are you wondering how you'll be blindsided next year? Do you have an interest in your boss's success? Are you considering other employment?

Your satisfaction with the job is rapidly approaching zero. I don't care how well your boss used the employee satisfaction factors listed in the section, "Striving for Employee Satisfaction" on page 524; everything she gained from those efforts just evaporated.

TIP

It's easy to anticipate an employee's reaction to any situation: Simply put yourself in her place. There's a commonality to our humanity that allows us to use our experiences to anticipate the reaction of others.

AVOIDING PROBLEMS

Besides communicating more effectively, what can you do to avoid these problems? One solution is to chronologically separate performance appraisals from salary reviews. I prefer a six-month interval between the two. Here's why.

The performance appraisal gives me an opportunity to think about my employees, how they can improve, and what I expect from them. During the performance appraisal meeting the employee and I discuss future levels of performance and reach an agreement on what that performance should be. We also discuss compensation for each level of performance. Then I monitor his performance for six months.

I use a six-month time frame because it allows me to evaluate behavioral changes. Most employees can change their behavior for a month or two, long enough to get a raise, then they revert to old habits. If they change their behaviors for six months, they've formed new habits. When the new behaviors produce the desired results, the salary review becomes a cause for celebration.

Even when the employee isn't completely successful, the salary review is easier for both parties. Both of you know what the goals are. Both of you agreed what the salary increase will be for each level of performance. As long as the tracking system allows the two of you to monitor the employee's progress, there should be no disagreement over the amount of the increase.

CAUTION

Here's another reason to be specific in the performance measures you use: Lack of clarity in the results to be measured invites conflict.

THE VALUE PROPOSITION

Compensation is a reward for producing results. The value of the result must exceed the amount of the reward, or the company loses money. This is a simple concept, right? Then how is it that so many companies have people on their payrolls who are "overpaid"?

Here are some of reasons why compensation and results get out of synch. Leaders …

- Don't quantify the value of results.
- Fail to raise expectations.
- Place too much emphasis on past performance.
- Don't require employees to think in terms of value.

Let's look at each of these in more detail.

QUANTIFYING VALUE

Value and improvement don't always go hand in hand. For example, the difference between a good print job and a great print job is imperceptible to most customers. For that reason, most customers won't pay for the extra quality. The same can be true for other types of improvement.

Here's another example. The collection department's responsibility is to assure that customers pay on time. Let's assume that, on average, customers are taking 33 days to pay their invoices. The company's terms are "Net 30," which means that the invoice is due 30 days after the invoice date. In essence, customers are paying three days late.

Let's say that you want the collection department to bring the average collection period down from 33 days to 31 days. What questions do you need to ask to determine whether that improvement has value? Consider the following:

1. How much will we collect by reducing the collection period by two days?
2. How will that money be used?
3. If it's used to repay loans, how much will we save on interest charges?

4. If the additional cash is used to invest in the company's growth, what kind of return can we expect?

5. Will we need more collectors to accomplish this goal? If not, will there be any overtime associated with the extra effort?

6. What's the likelihood that we'll antagonize our customers by calling so quickly after the due date on the invoice?

7. How much will it cost us if we lose a customer because of the heightened collection efforts?

8. How much lost business does it take to overcome the benefits of a shorter collection period?

TIP

Whenever you are evaluating a performance measure for possible improvement, ask yourself these two value questions. What will it cost to achieve this higher level of performance? How much profit or savings will the improvement generate?

I realize that many of you are not accustomed to converting performance measures into dollars and cents. If you struggle with these "value" questions, go to your company's controller and ask for help. One of the accounting department's functions is to help operating managers understand the financial impact of their decisions.

CAUTION

Improvement ideas can be exciting. Excitement can cause you to overlook the value questions. Whenever you feel yourself becoming enamoured with an idea, take a deep breath and ask the value questions. You'll save yourself at lot of headaches.

FAILING TO RAISE EXPECTATIONS

Often this mistake is made with your best performers. These people make your life so easy that you hate to rock the boat by suggesting they do more. Truthfully, you do them a disservice by failing to raise expectations. You rob them of opportunities for variety, growth, learning, and greater success. Often you create compensation problems as well. Here's how.

Even good performers reach performance plateaus, stages at which they find it difficult to see improvement opportunities. Unless you established performance goals during the last appraisal, you may not realize that your employee has hit a plateau. She still contributes significantly to the team's success, so you give her a substantial raise.

Again, you resist raising expectations because "she's doing such a fine job." The second year, performance hasn't increased, but it's still solid. You grant another substantial increase. You can see where this is headed. Without your help, expectations aren't raised, and the employee becomes a mediocre performer when measured against the salary she's getting. That's a problem you can avoid: Raise expectations every year.

EMPHASIZING PAST PERFORMANCE

Loyalty is a wonderful quality, until you allow it to cloud your judgment. I see this happen all too often. A leader knows an employee's performance is declining, but finds it difficult to address the issue because the employee contributed so much in earlier years. The leader compounds the problem by giving the employee an annual raise. Now there's a losing proposition: declining productivity and increasing costs.

Unfortunately, I've seen this practice continued for years, with both the leader and the employee becoming increasingly disenchanted with their relationship. The solution is obvious. First, don't give raises unless performance has improved. Second, tell your employee about performance problems as soon as you recognize them. That's the correct way to demonstrate loyalty.

TIP

Don't postpone the handling of problems. I've never seen them get better on their own.

HELPING EMPLOYEES UNDERSTAND VALUE

It's not enough that you understand how to value a performance improvement opportunity. You must teach your employees to do the same.

Earlier I discussed the fact that you were promoted to help others develop the skills that make you so successful. Teaching your employees to understand the value of performance improvement is one of those skills.

If you take the time to teach your employees how to quantify value, you accomplish two goals. First you enable them to work with greater autonomy, which means that you'll spend less time supervising and more time planning the future. Second, you'll enable your employees to create greater value with less effort. That'll make both of you look good.

Conversely, your failure to teach employees how to quantify value is an invitation for them to act on improvement ideas without understanding the idea's full impact. That's a risk neither of your careers can afford.

You can see how easy it is for compensation and performance to get out of synch. You also have a better understanding of the link between value and compensation. Now let's examine the two most common forms of compensation, base pay and incentive pay.

BASE PAY

Since most leaders have little influence over the benefit component of base compensation, we are going to limit our discussion to salary and salary increases.

Most employees, other than salespeople, are paid a base salary or an hourly rate. Many of these employees are satisfied with annual increases that allow them to keep pace with inflation. In other words, they want an increase that's large enough that they don't have to reduce their lifestyle. Employees first became aware of the connection between salary and inflation in the late 1960s and early 1970s when union leaders pushed for cost-of-living increases.

A problem occurs when employees focus on inflationary increases. They limit their success. Their "decision" to be satisfied with a minimal increase causes them to "decide" on the minimum level of performance necessary to get that increase. Don't let your employees fall into this trap. Help them realize their full potential from both a performance and a compensation standpoint.

LARGE VS. SMALL ORGANIZATIONS

In *large organizations,* your ability to grant raises is limited. Usually salary ranges are associated with job categories. Each category also has a range of allowable base pay increases.

PLAIN ENGLISH

Large organization   An organization that has more than 200 employees.

If you have an employee whom you want to reward with a larger increase, you'll probably need to get approval from above. You can improve your odds for getting the increase by demonstrating the value of your employee's performance. Your best employees earn the right to higher compensation. When you fail them, you invite their departure.

Smaller organizations face a different set of problems. Often formal pay structures don't exist. Raises are granted more on the employee's ability to negotiate than on the merits of his performance. One of the complaints I hear most often in smaller organizations is inequity. The employees' displeasure stems from ...

- A lack of performance measures.
- The leader's fondness for one employee over another.
- The dependence of the amount of the increase on the employee's negotiating skills.

Performance appraisals provide the means to increase fairness in compensation decisions.

INCENTIVE COMPENSATION

The form that incentive compensation takes is limited only by your imagination. Several factors are critical to the success of an incentive compensation program. They are ...

- A clearly defined, well-communicated goal.
- A realistic possibility of success.
- Knowledge of the value to be created by achieving the goal.
- An idea of the percentage of value you wish to share with your employee.
- A feedback system that prevents unpleasant surprises.
- An agreement as to how the incentive will be calculated and when it will be paid.

If your incentive program contains these critical elements, you have an excellent chance of achieving the goal and retaining a valuable employee.

TIP

I advise clients that once they've outlined the program, they need to switch hats. Take off the leader's hat and put on the employee's hat. Now look for ways to abuse the system.

Unfortunately, I've seen leaders abandon incentive programs because they couldn't prevent abuse. Don't forgo the advantages of an incentive program simply because one or two people may abuse it. You're much better off removing the abusing employees than abandoning a worthwhile incentive pay program.

The 30-Second Recap

- Do not combine performance appraisals and salary reviews.
- Not all performance improvements are valuable.
- Learn to quantify the value of performance improvements.
- Teach your employees how to calculate the value of performance improvements.
- Tie compensation to the value produced.

Conducting Performance Appraisals

Improving Communication

In this section you'll learn about the importance of communication skills to your employee's performance. You'll also learn about the role of communication in your success as a leader.

THE IMPACT OF POOR COMMUNICATION

How does the pace of today's world impact communication? Think about your e-mail. Have you gotten into the habit of writing partial sentences? In your haste, do you sometimes forget the salutation?

In communications with employees, how often do you feel like saying, "Just do it this way"? How often do you actually use that approach?

Time pressures cause us to place greater emphasis on "doing" than on "communicating." Unless we're working we feel that we're falling farther behind. Our employees feel the same way. Yet if I were to ask you and your employees to identify the single greatest cause of workplace problems, your answer most likely would be poor communication, and you'd be right.

TIP

When you are tempted to use shortcuts in your communiqués, ask yourself how long, it will take the person to redo the job if it's done incorrectly. Then ask yourself how long it will take you to give the proper instructions.

The vast majority of rework performed is the result of poor communication. It's not that employees' skills are inadequate, it's that they don't understand what's being asked of them. Rework is a drain on productivity. In a world where speed is a competitive advantage, there is no time for rework.

So far I've focused on your communications with your employees. It is equally important for your employees to communicate well with you, their teammates, and co-workers in other departments. Every employee has the potential to create rework through poor communication. It's your job to help them improve their skills. The performance appraisal can help. To see how, let's examine the impact that communication has on our lives.

The dynamics of personal interaction are affected by the way we communicate. We can ingratiate ourselves with others and in doing so garner cooperation whenever we need it.

We also have the ability to offend others. How much cooperation do you give people who've offended you? Do you do just enough to keep yourself out of trouble? That's a natural reaction, but it certainly doesn't promote a constructive work environment.

We could spend time discussing how poor communication creates frustration, adds stress, promotes conflict (sometimes to the point of violence), but you already know these things. Let's focus on how the performance appraisal can help your employees become better communicators.

TIP

Model the type of communication that you want your employees to use. Your actions are more powerful communicators than your words.

THE KEYS TO EFFECTIVE COMMUNICATION

Here are some of the things that you should be observing in order to improve your employees' communication skills:

- Completeness of their communication
- Their ability to listen while communicating
- Respect for others
- Style: dictatorial, cooperative, submissive, or parental
- The impact their mood has on their communications
- The tone of the communiqué

Let's explore each of these in more detail.

COMPLETE COMMUNIQUÉS

Does the employee regularly communicate all that the listener needs to know? If not, what types of information does the employee fail to communicate? The answer to the latter question will provide powerful insights into your employee's motivation.

Usually incomplete communications are quite innocent. The speaker simply credits the listener with more knowledge than he has. The absence of malice doesn't alter the fact that this assumption has the potential to create a lot of problems.

Lost productivity is a problem we've already discussed. Another problem is the effect this error has on the relationship between the two parties. The listener may feel betrayed, set up for failure, even though there was no such intent.

This attitude is contagious. The listener tells other members of the team of the betrayal and warns them to be alert so that it doesn't happen to them. The effect on morale is devastating. Amazing, isn't it? A nasty situation like this can arise from an innocent mistake.

Make your employees aware of the disastrous effect incomplete communiqués have on themselves and their co-workers.

CAUTION

A person who is trying to overcome the habit of incomplete communication will often go overboard and provide too much detail. The risk here is that the listener will feel that his intelligence is being insulted. Help your employees strike a balance between too much and too little detail.

LISTENING

How often have we heard that a good communicator is also a good listener? The questions and comments we get in response to our communiqués are the keys to effective communication. That's the good news. The bad news is that listeners offer us a wide array of feedback other than questions and comments.

Listeners who lack confidence don't often ask questions. They are afraid of appearing stupid. Instead, they'll restate what you said. Paraphrasing is their technique for eliciting more information. If the restatement is broad, they're struggling with the whole concept. You need to start over. Explain the goal and each step that you envision in accomplishing that goal.

If the restatement is specific to one area of your communiqué, then you need to elaborate only on that area. Attempts to review the whole concept will be viewed as condescending and reinforce the listener's feelings of inadequacy.

As strange as it may seem, overly confident listeners also don't ask questions. Their problem is that they don't think about the approach they'll use. They simply act. If you know that your listener has this tendency, make your communiqué more detailed than you might normally. You cannot rely on this listener's feedback to assure effective communication, so don't.

TIP

If an employee isn't asking questions and you're not sure whether he lacks confidence or is overly confident, try to recall the employee's actions toward similar types of activities. His past performance will help you identify his current mindset.

One of the most unusual situations I encountered as a leader involved one of my best employees. Her performance was solid and she was happy to do anything asked of her, but whenever I gave her a new project I'd have to repeat the entire instructions at least twice. It was maddening. We discussed this problem in earlier performance appraisals, but unfortunately neither of us could pinpoint the source of the problem.

Since this was the only individual on the team who posed this problem, I kept wondering what I was doing differently in my communications with her. One day while we were discussing a new project, I noticed that she was looking at the outline I'd provided. She didn't seem to be listening to what I was saying. From the look on her face it appeared that she was forming questions that she wanted to ask. That's when I realized what was happening.

Her mind was so busy developing questions that she didn't have the ability to listen effectively. That's why I had to repeat everything to her twice. I stopped my instructions and shared this insight with her. She quickly confirmed what I'd surmised. At that point we both knew what the problem was. Here's the solution we created.

I promised to allow her as much time as she needed to ask any questions she might have. In return she promised to focus her attention on my instructions as I provided them. It worked beautifully. We were both relieved of frustration that had plagued us for a couple of years.

My point in relating this story is that not all feedback is verbal. Pay attention to facial expressions, hesitation in the voice, and posture to help you evaluate the clarity of your message. Then teach your employees these skills.

RESPECT

We have a right to be respected until we fail to respect others. Are your employees respectful of the feelings of others? Do their communications ...

- Indicate a respect for the other person's abilities?
- Credit others with the ability to learn quickly?
- Indicate an interest in the other person's welfare?
- Recognize that the ideas of others have value?
- Attempt to elevate others or tear them down?

These questions should be asked and answered in the performance appraisal.

CAUTION

If you have an employee who enjoys kidding others, make sure that you let him know when his kidding becomes disrespectful of his co-workers.

STYLE

People exhibit four styles of communication:

- Dictatorial
- Cooperative
- Submissive
- Parental

TIP

Each of us exhibits all these styles at one time or another. What you need to look for is the style the employee exhibits most frequently.

Dictators dominate conversations and demand that their ideas be accepted. Dictators tend to irritate, frustrate, and incite to riot those with whom they work. If your employee exhibits this style, take action immediately. This person's development plan should have persuasion skills as the top priority. It's your job to teach your employees that communications that influence are more powerful than those that control.

Employees who demonstrate a natural instinct for cooperative communication are golden. Theirs are the voices of sanity in times of disagreement. They are the ones who find the common ground, gain agreement, and move the team forward. This is the style that you want to see in all your employees.

The submissive style is at the opposite end of the spectrum from the dictatorial style. Employees who prefer this style often suffer silently, allowing others to impose their will on them. On the top of their development plans should be assertiveness training. Get them the help they need to develop a cooperative style. Their current style robs them of job satisfaction and deprives you of ideas that might enhance your team's success.

Most of us hate the parental style almost as much as we do the dictatorial. Parents tell us what to do. This is fine when we're small children and don't have a lot of experience from which to draw. It's condescending and downright irritating when we're adults. If you see an employee exhibiting this style, explain to him what he is doing and the reaction others have to this style.

MOOD

A person who is normally upbeat and supportive might, on a bad day, become abrupt, insensitive, and sometimes downright belligerent in his communication. If you see this happening, simply say, "It appears that you're having a rough day. We all do from time to time. I'm not asking you to put on a false face, but do you think it's right to take your frustration out on your team-mates?" Usually this is enough to get the person to ease up on his co-workers. It may even help change the troubled employee's mood.

People who are regularly in a bad mood exhibit the abruptness, insensitivity, and belligerence mentioned above; they also discourage communication. The absence of communication will inevitably lead to errors, missed deadlines, and a diminution of team effectiveness.

Foul moods are also contagious. If you don't take action, you'll see your absentee rates rise, a can-do attitude replaced with a can't-do attitude, and a rapid decline in productivity. You also risk the loss of your best performers.

Why? Top performers gain energy for others who share their upbeat outlook on life. It's important to their success. They're not going to get that from someone who is riding an emotional roller coaster.

Identifying the cause of mood swings is generally beyond the expertise of most leaders. Your responsibilities include ...

1. To make the employee aware of the problem.

2. To suggest counseling.

3. If your company employs resources for this purpose, make the employee aware of these resources.

4. To tell the employee that this behavior will not be acceptable in the future.

5. To tell the employee that you are always available should she want a friendly ear.

6. To do nothing more than listen if the employee takes advantage of the offer in number 5.

7. To make mood improvement a focal point in performance appraisals.

TIP

If the employee demonstrates a pattern of mood swings, don't wait until the next performance appraisal to address the problem. Take action immediately. Tolerating this behavior sends a message that it is acceptable.

Tone

Is the tone of your employees' communication upbeat and encouraging, factual and unemotional, or critical and discouraging? Obviously, you prefer the tone to be upbeat and encouraging. You can tolerate factual and unemotional. The critical and discouraging part must change.

People who consistently criticize others are often burdened by their own feelings of inadequacy. Tearing others down is, in their minds, a way of making themselves look better. This is another situation in which counseling may be needed. I suggest using the same approach outlined for frequent mood swings.

Transforming employees who prefer the factual, unemotional tone into encouragers isn't difficult, but may take a little time. First, model the behavior you would like to see them adopt. Second, ask the employees the following questions:

■ How do you feel when someone encourages you?

■ Do you enjoy working with people who encourage you?

■ Are you more likely to help someone who is encouraging?

■ Is that how you would like others to view you?

The key is to get your employee to see how he reacts emotionally to someone who is encouraging. That makes it easy for him to understand how others react to this style. This approach, getting people to examine their own reactions, is one of the most powerful I've ever employed.

TIP

The technique of asking questions that help others understand their emotional reactions is one that will serve your employees well in their communications with others. Add the acquisition of this skill to their development plans.

Now that I've identified the aspects of communication that should be evaluated in performance appraisals, let's see how performance appraisals improve communication with employees.

THE ROLE OF COMMUNICATION IN PERFORMANCE APPRAISALS

The performance appraisal is your safety net in the world of communication. It allows you to recover when you drop the ball by failing to …

■ Recognize your employees' accomplishments.

■ Correct recurring errors.

■ Communicate expectations.

■ Indicate your interest in their success.

■ Provide guidance on their personal development.

The performance appraisal is a time to rectify these failings. Please don't misinterpret that statement. I am not suggesting that you wait until the performance appraisal to communicate with your employees. Performance appraisals are no substitute for the daily communications your employees need. You must communicate new expectations, provide feedback on performance, recognize success, and help them deal with their problems each and every day. Once every six months is not enough.

Having said that, I realize that even the best leaders are going to drop the communication ball from time to time. There will be some aspect of performance that should have been communicated, but wasn't. Performance appraisals give you the opportunity to correct this oversight.

Communication triggers are valuable tools, especially for those of you who have not developed the habit of communicating on a regular basis. Here are a few suggestions for their use:

1. Use multiple triggers

2. List the triggers on your calendar

3. Follow up religiously on all communication triggers

PLAIN ENGLISH

Communication triggers   Dates, performance goals, or other quantifiable measures that, when reached, require you to communicate with your employees.

Over the years, I've witnessed a lot of pain and heartache caused by the failure to use multiple triggers, specifically the failure to combine performance goals and deadlines. I can assure you that if left unstated, your deadline and your employee's deadline will be completely different.

Here's an example of how to combine performance goals and deadlines. The goal is to have our department's budget complete within three weeks. All proposed budgets will be completed by the end of the first week. By Wednesday of week two, the individual budgets will be combined into a departmental budget. At the end of week two we will evaluate the departmental budget in light of strategic goals and the targets set in our initial meeting. All budget revisions must be submitted by Wednesday of the third week. The budget will be finalized at the end of week three.

There are five communication triggers in this budget process: the end of week one, the middle of week two, the end of week two, the middle of week three, and the end of week three. Each of these offers you the opportunity to monitor your team's progress on the budget. Each creates another reason to communicate with your employees.

I'm not suggesting that you constantly look over your employees' shoulders. No one likes that. I'm saying that you have reasons for communicating on each of these dates.

Obviously, you'd prefer to see your employees report to you on those dates. If they don't, you have good reason to follow up with them.

TIP

It's important for your employees to know that you want advance notice if they are having problems. Tell them that you'd much rather take time to help them solve their problems than have them miss the deadline.

If one of your employees fails to tell you that he's having trouble, the communication triggers help minimize the damage, but only if you follow up. Mark the triggers on your calendar, then follow up religiously. You'll save yourself and your employee a lot of unnecessary pain.

Here's another reason for following up. If you don't, you send the message that the deadline is frivolous and you invite the slide of all future deadlines. Employees don't like having their time wasted with deadlines that appear to be whimsical. It's insulting to them and makes you look like a power monger.

TIP

The behavior of others is dictated more by our behavior than by our words. If our words and behavior diverge, others will take their cue from our behavior.

Encouraging Success

We've already discussed the importance of tone in communication. I'm not going to revisit the entire topic again, but I do want to include a reminder here. I cannot emphasize enough the importance of letting your employees know that you want them to be successful.

The more you praise your employees' abilities and encourage their growth, the more likely they are to respond favorably to your leadership. Take advantage of every opportunity to make them feel good about themselves. They'll appreciate you for it and they'll take an interest in your success as well.

The 30-Second Recap

▦ Good communication is vital to good performance.

▦ Communication is an aspect of performance that should be evaluated in the appraisal.

▦ Every personal development plan should include communication skill improvement.

▦ Performance appraisals allow you, the leader, an opportunity to correct any errors you've made in communicating expectations, providing feedback, or recognizing success.

Looking at Sample Questions

In this section you will learn about the design of a performance appraisal form and a variety of performance factors; you will also see sample evaluation statements.

Appraisal Form Design

Previous sections have discussed performance from a number of perspectives. Now it's time to develop an approach to evaluating the employee's current level of performance.

Even if you aren't involved in the design of your company's appraisal, please don't skip this section. There are some valuable insights to be gained even though you may be using an existing form.

Numeric Measures

Most performance appraisals ask for both numeric measures and comments. Here's an example of numeric measures:

How often does the employee meet deadlines?

Never	Occasionally	Usually	Frequently	Always
0	1	2	3	4

Comments:

There are as many variations on this format as there are evaluation designers. Some leaders prefer a 10-point scale. They believe that the larger scale provides greater precision.

Personally, I hated teachers who used pluses and minuses (C+, C, C–) in grading. C+ was disappointing because I just missed a B. C– was distressing because I barely dodged a D. Neither of these grades evokes a positive emotion. That's one of the problems with a 10-point scale. Obviously, I am expressing a personal preference. Your preference is as valid as mine.

I prefer odd-numbered scales, five or seven points, because there is only one number that represents average performance, and that's the *mean* number.

PLAIN ENGLISH

Mean   In a numerical sequence, the number that has an equal number of values above and below it. For example, in the series 3, 5, 7, 9, 11, 7 is the mean because there are two values before it, 3 and 5, as well as two values after it, 9 and 11.

When you have only one number representing "average," it's much easier for the employee to understand the ranking. I prefer a five-point scale, where performance is lousy, below average, average, above average, or great. Most of us find it easy to deal with these concepts. We may not agree with the evaluator, but we understand what she's saying.

In the previous scale, the ratings range from 0 to 4. Many designers choose to use a 1-to-5 scale rather than the 0-to-4 scale. They prefer not to use a 0 rating believing that no one's performance is worthless. I've had one or two employees in 25 years who might refute that argument, but generally it's true. If you have an employee who warrants a 0 rating, I have to ask, "What's she still doing there?"

I use the 1-to-5 scale for the psychological effect that the "five" rating has. Over the years we've heard about five-star restaurants and five-star hotels. This is the elite class. I want people to believe that they can be elite-class performers. You may think that the employee has nothing to look forward to once she achieves a "five" rating. That's why the appraisal includes a comment section and personal development plan. I never use the "five" rating without raising expectations for future performance. There are, in fact, varying degrees of excellence. You need to make that clear in the development plan and comments.

Another issue in performance appraisal design is whether to use a 1-to-5 scale or a 5-to-1 scale, with one being the lowest level of performance and five being the highest.

Some performance appraisal designers feel that people are discouraged when the first measure they see is negative, as it is on a 1-to-5 scale. Others argue that the positive language of a 5-to-1 scale may cause the evaluator to be less objective. I don't place much credence in either argument.

TIP

Whether you like it or not, everything you do or say has a psychological impact. If you're not anticipating the reactions you'll be getting, you're setting yourself up for problems.

I do, however, believe that the evaluator saves time when using the 5-to-1 scale. Your goal as a people developer is to have your employees score four or five on each question. Why, then, would you want the scale to start at one?

Comment Section

Now that we've explored the numeric ratings, let's shift our attention to the comment section. Comments are crucial for several reasons. First, as you decide on a numeric measure you should know why you didn't give this employee a higher evaluation. You need to have a clear understanding of what the next level of performance represents before you can communicate it to your employee. Once you have this understanding, make sure that it is included in your comments.

Your comments should communicate that your employee is building on an already solid base of performance. The language you use is essential for assuring that the appraisal is encouraging, not discouraging. Choose your words wisely.

TIP

Even when you're careful in the selection of your language you can inadvertently offend your employee. If that happens, admit your mistake, apologize, and move on. Your employee will respect your integrity and forgive the offense.

The second reason for using the comment section is that it formalizes your thoughts. Let's face it, the pace of today's world makes it difficult to remember what we did five minutes ago. Don't risk forgetting key elements of your employee's future success; write them down.

Writing down your thoughts is even more important if you take my earlier advice and allow six months between the performance appraisal and the salary review. It can be a challenge trying to remember what you and your employee agreed to six months earlier. You can save yourself a lot of time and avoid the possibility of conflict by capturing your thoughts in the comment section.

A third reason for using the comment section is as an aid in creating the employee's personal development plan. The comments form a ready reference for prioritizing improvement initiatives and establishing an approach to improvement.

Captions for Numeric Measures

Before we move on to examples of performance criteria, there is one more element of performance appraisal design I would like to discuss with you. That's the language that appears above the numeric measures. I've seen all the following:

Excellent	Above Average	Average	Marginal	Poor
Exceptional	Exceeds requirements	Meets requirements	Meets most requirements	Fails performance requirements
Exceptional	Favorable	Satisfactory	Unsatisfactory	Poor
Always	Often	Usually	Sometimes	Seldom
Great	Solid	Okay	Needs improvement	Poor

To me, the captions used for numeric measures are second in importance only to the comment section in appraisal form design. If you doubt that, ask yourself these questions: "How do I feel when my boss says that my work is satisfactory or that it's average? Do I immediately translate the performance evaluation into a personal evaluation? In other words, do I feel that my boss is saying that I'm average or satisfactory?" I'll bet you do. Your employees feel the same way.

My preference is to use the terms *always, often, usually, sometimes,* and *seldom.* These terms are specific to behavior. I've never known them to be used in judgment of an individual as a person.

 CAUTION

Some employees are more sensitive than others. These employees tend to view judgments about their performance as judgments of them. You need to be very specific in your language when dealing with these folks.

Now that we have a sense of the form that most appraisals take and the reasoning behind their design, let's look at some of the things you need to evaluate.

PERFORMANCE

There are four aspects of performance: speed, quality, service, and value. These are not the only factors we might measure, but they form a good foundation on which to build. Let's look at some criteria that can be used to evaluate an employee's performance in each of these areas.

TIP

The more clearly you define the various aspects of performance, the easier it is for your employees to understand what's expected of them. To help them become successful, be specific when defining performance.

Note: In the interest of saving space, I will not be listing the scale for each of the criteria considered. For the remainder of this section, please apply the following scale to the criteria being measured.

Always	Often	Usually	Sometimes	Seldom
5	4	3	2	1

SPEED

Speed is vital to your company's competitive advantage. Here are some statements to help you evaluate your employees' understanding of the importance of speed:

- The employee's actions indicate an understanding of the importance of speed in today's competitive environment.
- The employee does a good job of balancing speed and quality in the performance of his work.
- The employee completes tasks ahead of schedule.
- The employee looks for ways to accomplish routine work more quickly.

QUALITY

Quality cannot be sacrificed for speed. How well do your employees understand this concept? The following statements can help you make that determination:

- The employee takes pride in her work.
- The employee does work correctly the first time.
- The employee looks for ways to improve the quality of her work.

SERVICE

The advantages of speed and quality are easily lost to poor service. You can evaluate your employees' service attitude with the following statements:

- The employee's actions indicate an understanding of the importance of serving both internal and external customers.
- The employee demonstrates the desire to serve others well.
- The employee responds to customers in a timely fashion (within two hours).
- The employee provides customers with more than requested.

TIP

Teach your employees how to place themselves in their customers' shoes. It will help them improve their customer service.

VALUE

Understanding value is vital to buying decisions, goal setting, establishing priorities and work effectiveness. Are your employees good at identifying value? The following statements will help you make that judgement:

- The employee's actions indicate an understanding of the concept of value.
- Value is something the employee considers in her decisions.
- When the employee doesn't see value in an effort she makes the appropriate authorities aware of her concerns.

Obviously, there are many more statements that you can use to evaluate these performance criteria. I hope these examples provide you with a good starting point in the development of your evaluation statements.

Next, I'd like you to take a moment to reflect on the previous statements. Did you notice a common thread running through them? They are all positive, aren't they? The language of these statements attributes desirable qualities or behaviors to the employee. The numeric rating indicates the level of quality or consistency of behavior achieved.

Performance appraisals must be encouraging, otherwise the employee will have no desire to improve. The language you use will determine whether your employee leaves the appraisal feeling good and wanting to do better or disappointed and wondering why she should bother trying. The choice is yours. Choose wisely: Your employees' success and your reputation as a people developer are at stake.

OTHER EVALUATION CRITERIA

There are factors that influence employees' performance that aren't directly related to the work they do. These factors are just as important as the factors mentioned above, which means they should be given equal weight in the evaluation process.

INTERPERSONAL SKILLS

The phrase "playing nice with others" is often used in conjunction with "interpersonal skills." With the following statements, you will be evaluating your employees' ability and willingness to consider the needs of others—coworkers, bosses, subordinates, customers, and vendors:

- The employee demonstrates concern for the feelings of others.
- The employee uses language that is encouraging to others.
- The employee willingly helps others.
- The employee genuinely celebrates the success of others.

SUCCESS MENTALITY

"Is the glass half-empty or half-full?" Do your employees "believe" that they can succeed or do they "hope" they can succeed? Here are some statements that will help you evaluate your employees' attitudes toward success:

- The employee possesses a can-do attitude.
- The employee is looking for ways to expand her knowledge.
- The employee is looking for ways to broaden her experience.
- The employee is realistic in her assessment of her abilities.

TIP

The importance of a success mentality cannot be overstated. None of us can succeed without the belief that we *can* succeed.

OPENNESS TO CHANGE

Many people resist change, others accept it willingly. What are your employees' attitudes toward change? Here are some statements that assist in answering this question:

- The employee willingly accepts change.
- The employee looks for new ways to accomplish old tasks.
- The employee's actions indicate an inquisitive nature.
- The employee views her role as one that is continuously evolving.

CREATIVITY

Creativity can take many forms. Some people are most creative when working with a "blank canvas." Others are very creative when improving existing systems. Still others find their creativity best suited to problem situations. Whatever the arena, creativity is a vital component to your employees' success. Let's look at some statements that are designed to identify your employees' creative talents:

- The employee displays creativity in problem-solving.
- The employee demonstrates the ability to see connections between seemingly unrelated issues.
- The employee can take an abstract concept and develop it into one that's workable.
- The employee applies her creativity to her daily work.

COMMUNICATION SKILLS

In "Improving Communication" on page 544, you learned how problems are easily created through poor communication. Here are some statements to use in evaluating your employees' communication skills:

- The employee presents ideas logically in easy-to-understand language.
- The employee voices disagreement without creating conflict.
- The employee writes using clear, concise language.
- The employee uses language that is encouraging.

INITIATIVE

Do your employees initiate improvement efforts or do they wait for someone to assign those efforts to them? Your greatest success, as well as that of your employees, comes when they demonstrate initiative. Here are some statements that will help you evaluate your employees on this vital trait:

- The employee makes herself available to help others when her work is complete.
- The employee seeks involvement in new projects.
- The employee works on skill development outside the workplace.
- The employee is a source of ideas for performance improvement.

CAUTION

If an employee has an extremely hectic schedule for several weeks, and then experiences a slowdown, don't expect her to exhibit the initiative she normally would. She probably needs a little time to rejuvenate herself. Give her that time. Just don't let it become a habit.

PLANNING AND ORGANIZATION

Do your employees plan their futures or react to what the future brings? Can they readily find what they need or do they lose numerous hours each week trying to locate things they need to do the job? The answers to these questions will give you insights into your employees' performance. Here are a few statements that help you assess your employees' planning and organizational skills.

- The employee creates a personal work schedule.
- The employee works the schedule.
- The employee decides on the approach to task before beginning work.
- The employee can easily locate information in her files.

TIP

People who don't have good organizational skills may be in the wrong job. Take a look at their skills and see whether they can be better used in less-structured work.

I hope these criteria and sample evaluation statements will generate even more ideas that you can use in the design of your performance appraisal.

For those of you using existing appraisal forms, I suggest that you evaluate the appraisal language. You may have to alter your verbal communications and write more comments to overcome the appraisal's negative language. Here's an experience I had with an existing appraisal form.

Do you remember my story about the employee who was formulating questions when she should have been listening to instructions? Well, the appraisal form had a statement that dealt specifically with the issue of instructions. The evaluation statement said, "Employee readily understands instructions." I had no choice but to rate her low on this statement. Her failure to listen frequently caused me to repeat instructions.

In the comment section I noted that she needed to listen more carefully and that when she listened to instructions, she had no problems understanding them. When she saw my comment, she thanked me. She said, "This rating makes me sound like I'm retarded, but your comment let me know that you don't feel that way."

Frankly, the word *retarded* is the one that came to my mind when I read the statement. That's why I had so much trouble deciding on a rating. If I hadn't written the comment she would have mistakenly thought that I considered her dim-witted.

Emotions are powerful and they surface very quickly when we feel we're being criticized. When you're completing an appraisal, look for language that might offend your employees. If you find offensive language, use the comment section to remove the sting from poorly designed statements.

360-DEGREE FEEDBACK

Many companies today are using an appraisal technique called *360-degree feedback*.

PLAIN ENGLISH

360-degree feedback   The appraisal system that elicits appraisals from your boss, your peers, and your subordinates. The term 360-degree refers to the fact that you are being evaluated by people all around you. Your boss is above you, your peers are at your side, and your subordinates are below you.

The primary advantage of the 360-degree feedback system is that it allows multiple perspectives on performance. It also makes it difficult for the employee to dispute her failings when they are being observed by a number of people rather than just her boss.

Everything we discussed in this section can be applied to 360-degree feedback. You may need to make slight adjustments in the wording of the evaluation statements to reflect differences in perspective between bosses, peers, and subordinates. Otherwise, the approach is the same.

THE 30-SECOND RECAP

- The two most important design components of the performance appraisal are the comment sections and the captions above the numeric measures.

- The captions *always, often, usually, sometimes,* and *seldom* make it more difficult for the employee to translate performance ratings into personal judgments.

- The use of odd-numbered scales makes it easier for both the evaluator and the employee to visualize the concept of "normal" or "average" performance.

- Evaluation statements should incorporate language that indicates success.

- If you are forced to use an existing appraisal form, look for statements that generate negative emotions. Use the comment section to overcome the negative tone of these statements. You may have to adjust your verbal communication as well.

- 360-degree feedback systems require only slight modifications in the evaluation statements to reflect the differing perspectives between bosses, peers, and subordinates.

Three Approaches to Performance Appraisals

In this section you'll learn about three of the more common approaches used in conducting performance appraisals.

APPROACH ONE: FAVORS THE EVALUATOR

The most common approach is to prepare the appraisal, invite the employee into your office, give him a few minutes to read the appraisal, then begin a dialogue. I've never felt that this was fair.

As the evaluator, you get to take all the time you want preparing the appraisal, while the employee gets only a few minutes to absorb what you've written before responding. It's particularly unfair to employees who have difficulty thinking on their feet or who are easily intimidated.

APPROACH TWO: A BALANCED APPROACH

Fairness can be built into the system quite easily. Continue to take as much time as you like, but give the employee two working days to review the appraisal and get back with you.

You may be wondering, "Why two days, why not three days or a week?" First, two days is ample time for the employee to reflect on the evaluation and his behavior.

A request for more time is often an indication that he disagrees with your appraisal. If that's true, additional time won't diminish his displeasure. Quite the contrary; given more time, the employee's unhappiness can escalate to anger, bitterness, and resentment. By requiring the employee to discuss his appraisal within two days, you avoid this escalation of ill will.

A second, more selfish reason for selecting two days is that you don't have to reconstruct your thoughts. If more than two days elapse between the completion of the appraisal and the meeting, you may forget some of what you intended to say to the employee. The time spent trying to remember is unproductive. In effect, you're doing the same work twice. If the meeting occurs within two working days, you avoid this waste of time and do a better job of helping the employee.

How do the employees feel about this approach? They like it. First, they don't feel pressured. Second, they have time to organize their thoughts. Third, they have time to reflect on the comments and their own behavior. This approach avoids a lot of the pressure created with "evaluator favored" approach. Here are a few more reasons for adopting this approach.

Regardless of how skilled you become as a communicator, what you say or write can easily be misconstrued. If the employee's gut reaction to your comment is disagreement, the additional time allows him to reread your statement. Often the second reading helps him get past a word or phrase he finds objectionable.

Similarly, a low rating will initially trigger a defensive reaction. Again, the additional time allows the employee to reflect on his behavior. If your rating is accompanied by a comment that illustrates the reason for your rating, the employee will find it easier to accept. Many of the negative reactions we see in performance appraisals can be avoided by simply allowing the employee more time to review the appraisal.

APPROACH THREE: EMPLOYEE PARTICIPATION

A friend of mine offered this approach. I haven't had a chance to try it, but I love the concept. She provides the employee with a blank appraisal form and asks him to rate himself. She also asks him to write improvement ideas in the comment section. Simultaneously, she pencils her appraisal of the employee.

At a mutually agreed upon time, they provide each other with copies of the appraisals they've prepared. She allows two days for reflection, then they meet to discuss each item on the appraisal.

CAUTION

When using this approach, you will be tempted to bypass the items on which there is agreement. Don't do it. If you do, you'll forego opportunities to praise your employees and to raise performance expectations for them. These are two integral components of a successful performance appraisal.

There are a couple of advantages to this approach. First, people tend to be more critical of themselves than others are. That means that you'll have opportunities to tell your employee that he's better than he thinks he is. That's a lot more fun than criticizing, isn't it?

Second, you have a chance to reevaluate your ratings. I'm not suggesting that you waffle endlessly on your decisions. That will cost you your employee's respect. I am saying that there are times when new information will influence your thinking.

CAUTION

If you tend to vacillate on decisions or are easily intimidated by an employee, you may find this approach less effective than approach number two.

Approach three opens the door to new information in the form of your employee's perspective. This occurs before the appraisal is finalized. That's why my friend uses a pencil on the initial appraisal; it's easier to make changes when warranted.

The "balanced" and "participative" approaches both provide time for reflection—a critical element in the success of the appraisal. Allow your employees time to think about the ratings, your comments, and their behavior. These approaches remove a lot of the stress normally associated with the appraisal process.

A FEW REMINDERS

The more successful you are at communicating expectations, using communication triggers, and maintaining feedback systems that allow employees to monitor their own progress, the more your ratings and those of your employees will converge.

Agreement is the foundation for future success. Employees who agree with their performance appraisals are open to suggestions for improvement. They are also more likely to act on those suggestions. Their continued success and improvement make all future performance appraisals more enjoyable.

The opposite is true as well. For employees who can't monitor their own progress and who don't get regular feedback, criticism comes as an unpleasant surprise. Employees experiencing these surprises feel that they have been blindsided.

How do you feel about situations like this? Do you want to discuss ideas for improvement? Do you feel that your boss is really interested in your success? I doubt it.

There is another advantage gained by allowing your employees to monitor their own progress. It reduces the amount of time you have to spend on the performance appraisal.

The easier it is for the employee to monitor his progress, the less likely he is to disagree with his evaluation. Appraisal meetings progress more quickly when you don't have to spend time resolving disagreements. You can turn a previously unpleasant task into an enjoyable and rewarding experience by simply creating feedback systems that allow your employees to monitor their progress.

THE 30-SECOND RECAP

- Allow employees two days to review your appraisal before discussing it with you. Most won't take the full two days, but they appreciate the option.
- Have employees rate themselves; often they are more critical of their performance than you are.
- The easier it is for the employees to monitor their progress, the less likely they are to be surprised by the appraisal.
- Fewer surprises result in fewer conflicts. The potential for conflict is what causes us to dread the appraisal process.

Preparing for the Meeting

In this section you'll learn about some of the things you need to consider in preparing for a successful appraisal meeting.

PROCESS VS. PROJECT

First, I want to repeat an important point made in "Three Approaches to Performance Appraisals" on page 563. The success of your performance appraisal depends heavily on the things you do during the interval between appraisals. Make sure that you ...

- Communicate your expectations.
- Use communication triggers.
- Establish feedback systems that allow the employees to monitor their progress.

These tasks, performed well, will do more to create a positive tone for the meeting than anything else you might do. Now let's look at some of the other things that contribute to your meeting's success.

YOUR STYLE

How would you describe your natural style: encouraging, neutral, or critical? If you have a naturally encouraging style, you're fortunate. Setting a positive tone for the meeting will be easy for you. That doesn't mean that you are home free. You've got challenges to overcome, just as managers with other styles do.

First, your enthusiasm can easily be overdone. Excessive enthusiasm is displayed in two ways:

- Ratings higher than warranted by the employee's performance
- Sugar-coating bad news

Who pays the price for these mistakes? Everyone does. Your employee doesn't get the feedback needed to improve. You end up living with substandard performance because you weren't candid in your appraisal. The company doesn't get the performance it needs to remain competitive. There are no winners in this game. If you have a naturally encouraging style, make sure that your ratings and the associated praise are warranted.

TIP

After you've completed the evaluation, go through each evaluation statement again and ask yourself these questions: "What does this employee need to do to improve performance?" "How much effort will be required: significant, average, or little?" "Does my rating accurately reflect the amount of effort this employee must put forth to improve?"

The neutral style is easier to demonstrate than explain. One of my brothers had a neutral style. When you asked how he enjoyed his vacation he'd answer, "Okay." If you asked about a problem, he'd say, "Not a big deal." Things never got better than "okay" or worse than "not a big deal."

Can you imagine being his employee? You feel like you've done a great job, yet your ratings say your performance is "okay." What a disappointment! At best, you'll feel unappreciated; at worst, betrayed.

Conversely, if your performance stinks, you may not get the feedback you need to improve. Without feedback, you're severely limited in your ability to achieve a secure future.

If your natural style is neutral, you are going to need to find ways to become more encouraging.

TIP

After you've completed the evaluation, go through each evaluation statement again and ask yourself these questions: "What praise can I offer this employee?" "What do I expect from this employee that I'm not currently getting?" "Does my rating accurately reflect the gap between my expectations and the employee's performance?"

If you are critical by nature, you've got a different set of challenges. The success of performance appraisals hinges on your ability to see the good in others and build on that good. That's not natural for you.

It's much easier for you to see what's wrong than what is right. That doesn't mean that you can't see the good; it simply means that you see the bad first. My advice to you is, "Don't fight your nature." Allow yourself your natural tendency, then ask yourself what good you can find in the individual's performance.

TIP

After you've completed the evaluation, go through each evaluation statement again and ask yourself these questions: "Now that I've determined where the employee needs to improve, what has he done right?" "Do my ratings accurately reflect all the good the employee has done?" "How can I make the language I use more positive so that it reflects the results the employee has achieved?" "Are my comments written in a positive or critical tone?"

You'll notice that regardless of the style you possess, I have not asked you to change that style. Rather, I'm offering ways to balance your natural style with the employee's need for an honest and encouraging appraisal.

Is it possible to change your style? Yes, but it often takes years to accomplish. Your style is natural for you, which makes it difficult to change. Does that mean you shouldn't try? Of course not. I believe that each of us needs to strive to become better every day of our lives.

If you choose to change your style, remember that you still have to do a good job today of appraising your employees' performance. Use the balancing techniques I've described until you feel that you've achieved the right blend of encouragement and honest evaluation.

Now that you've evaluated your style, let's examine the impact the employee's style has on the appraisal meeting.

TIP

Just a reminder that both you and your employees will from time to time exhibit all these styles. What you're looking for is the style you or they use most frequently.

EMPLOYEE'S STYLE

Employees also possess one of the three styles just discussed: encouraging, neutral, or critical. Each style poses special challenges in creating the right tone for the meeting.

ENCOURAGING STYLE

An employee who exhibits the encouraging style is upbeat and confident, invites change, and possesses a can-do attitude. The focus of your attention has to be on her realism. Are her expectations of herself and others realistic? Does she often set herself up for failure by being overly optimistic? Is she a good judge of her strengths and weaknesses? Does she only see the good, never the failings?

If the answers to these questions indicate that the employee is realistic, consider yourself lucky. Realistic people appreciate honest, open discussions about their abilities, their potential, and what the future holds for them. Their appraisals will be some of the most enjoyable that you'll experience as a leader.

If the individual is overly optimistic, you've got a little work ahead of you. With overly optimistic employees the challenge is to reign in their enthusiasm without dampening it. You must get them to evaluate their performance more realistically.

Usually, overly optimistic employees expect higher ratings than they get. The disappointment in their ratings will be obvious in their demeanor. This emotional state prohibits the kind of dialogue that's so vital for their future success.

Your ability to predict this reaction is the key to dealing with it. Expect their disappointment. When you know it's coming, you can prepare yourself to accept the reaction without emotion. As long as one of you remains objective, the door remains open for a solution.

Be prepared to tell your employees that you know they are dissatisfied with some of the ratings. Ask where they would have rated themselves higher. Ask for their rationale. Rather than disagree with them, ask them questions that will cause them to view their performance through your eyes. Use questions such as ...

- What skills would an employee need to get the top rating?
- What should the person getting a top rating be able to do?
- If any employee was accomplishing this level of performance and you knew she had the ability to achieve considerably more, would that alter your rating?

Questions like these cause the employee to consider the ratings more objectively and with less personal attachment.

TIP

Use role-playing. Ask the employee to assume the role of the leader. Ask him questions based on the criteria you used in your evaluation. Then allow him to evaluate the fictitious employee's performance using these new criteria.

NEUTRAL STYLE

Employees demonstrating the neutral style usually won't dispute your ratings unless they are really low. The challenge with these employees is to get them excited about doing more. Often they are quite comfortable with the status quo. Career advancement isn't important to them. They simply want to do a good job, get paid fairly, and enjoy their personal lives.

The key here is to get them to see that job enrichment is an important aspect of total life enjoyment. Your discussions with the neutral types need to focus on how the improvement will make their jobs more fun, not how it will advance their careers.

CRITICAL STYLE

Employees who are naturally critical don't accept criticism well. Often, they are plagued with low self-esteem and little self-confidence. When praised, they tend to discount the praise as flattery because they don't see themselves in that light. I witnessed one case where the employee's self-doubt was so severe that he ascribed selfish motives to the boss's words of encouragement.

Favorable ratings are usually a pleasant surprise to employees who exhibit the critical style. However, the ground gained by these ratings and celebratory comments is often lost when the discussion turns to opportunities for improvement.

TIP

Don't offer performance improvement suggestions to employees who exhibit the critical style. Rather, ask them what would make them better at what they do. Then use their comments as an opportunity to praise both their current performance and their insights into how they might improve.

BLENDING STYLES

Understanding your employee's style will help you anticipate her reactions. The ability to predict behavior gives you a couple of advantages in the meeting. First, it removes the element of surprise that often hinders your effectiveness. Second, when you get the reaction you anticipated, your self-confidence gets a boost and you feel more comfortable. When you're comfortable, it's easier to make your employee comfortable.

Understanding your style allows you to narrow the gap between your style and the employee's. If the employee has an overly optimistic encouraging style and you have a neutral style, you're going to have to increase your enthusiasm so that you don't disappoint the employee.

If your employee has a critical style and you are an encourager, you know that your praise must be well founded or the employee will suspect you of, heaven forbid, flattery. Actually, she'll suspect insincerity, which will cost you credibility in your future dealings with her.

These are examples of why it's so important to blend your style with those of your employees. This is one of the more difficult aspects of performance appraisals. It's also one of the most important to the success of the appraisal meeting.

THE 30-SECOND RECAP

When preparing for the appraisal meeting ...

- Evaluate your style: encouraging, neutral, or critical.
- Evaluate your employee's style using the same three categories: encouraging, neutral, or critical.
- Use your understanding of both styles to anticipate employees' reactions and plan your responses.

The Meeting

In this section you'll learn about the psychology at work in an appraisal meeting, as well as techniques and language for improving the emotional climate of that meeting.

FACTORS INFLUENCING EMPLOYEE COMFORT

There is a "natural" psychology that employees experience when entering an appraisal meeting. It's a blend of confidence and fear. Most employees are confident that they've done a good job, yet fear the unknown. Simultaneously, they expect a good appraisal, but wonder if you have an expectation that hasn't been met.

These mixed emotions create discomfort. It's your job to provide comfort at the outset of the meeting. Let's look at some of the factors that influence the employee's comfort.

PARTICIPATION IN SETTING GOALS

If you've allowed your employees to participate in establishing their performance goals, they'll approach the meeting with less fear. Why? Their involvement allows them to feel more secure in their understanding of these goals.
Comfort is the companion of knowledge; fear accompanies uncertainty. The
level of fear that your employees bring to the appraisal meeting is a function
of their knowledge of the goals.

SELF-MONITORING FEEDBACK SYSTEMS

We've already discussed the importance of allowing the employee to monitor
his performance. If the employee knows what's expected of him, and the two
of you use the same information to monitor his progress, there should be no
disagreement about his performance. Again, knowledge removes uncertainty
and fear.

Even if your employee knows that he hasn't performed well, he will not experience fear. He doesn't fear low ratings; he expects them. In this situation, you
don't have to overcome fear; you have to find out why the fear of failure
doesn't motivate this employee. In essence, you have to determine why, in the
face of poor performance, this employee didn't change his behavior. Some
possible explanations are that the employee ...

- Doesn't enjoy the work.
- Feels that he has been treated unfairly in the past; poor performance
  is his way of balancing the scales.
- Is in over his head and lacks the confidence to ask for help.
- Is lazy.
- Dislikes you or your management style.

These are some of the more common reasons why employees ignore the
warning signs provided by performance feedback. Are these the only reasons?
Certainly not, but I doubt that I could come up with an all-inclusive list if I
tried.

TIP

If you find yourself in this situation, begin by exploring the reasons
previously mentioned. Usually the real reason will surface. Only
once in 25 years have I terminated the employment of a poor performer without learning the reason for his failure.

Employee Self-Confidence

I'm sure it doesn't surprise you to hear that an employee's self-confidence determines the level of fear experienced. We know that people who lack self-confidence are always concerned about what others think of them. Since they feel inadequate, they live in constant fear of disappointing others. So it's natural that the performance appraisal process engenders an inordinate amount of fear for them.

What may surprise you is that even very confident employees experience some fear. Let's be honest. Each of us cares about what others think of us. The possibility that someone may think poorly of us is disconcerting. Oh, I'm sure you've known people who insist that they don't care what others think; you may have even made that statement yourself once or twice. When I hear someone disavow interest in the opinion of others, I'm reminded of the line, "Me thinks he doth protest too much."

The question isn't "Will the employee come to the appraisal with or without fear?" The question is "How much fear will the employee bring to the table?" The employee's level of self-confidence is a good indicator of the amount of fear you should expect.

Your Style

As we discussed in an earlier section, there are significant differences between encouraging, neutral, and critical styles. The farther toward the critical end of the spectrum you are, the more likely the employee is to fear the appraisal meeting. The greater the fear, the more work you have in front of you.

CAUTION

Fear is the single greatest obstacle to an effective performance appraisal.

Your Approach

The section "Three Approaches to Performance Appraisals" on page 563 discusses the following approaches to performance appraisals:

1. Allowing the employee a few minutes in the meeting to review the appraisal before beginning a dialogue.

2. Allowing the employee two days to review the appraisal before initiating the appraisal meeting.

3. Asking the employee to evaluate himself; then allowing two days before the meeting for each of you to review the other's appraisal.

Two of these three approaches allow the employee to privately review the evaluation in advance of the meeting. Employees who have the opportunity to consider the evaluation and prepare their responses are more confident when entering the appraisal meeting. In our discussion of self-confidence we learned that there is an inverse relationship between confidence and fear. The more confidence someone has, the less fear he experiences, and vice versa.

I have noted that fear accompanies uncertainty. Until the employee sees his evaluation, he is uncertain about your opinion of his performance and his future. While you cannot separate fear from uncertainty, you can change the venue for dealing with it.

By permitting the employee to review the appraisal in advance of the meeting, you allow him to deal with his fears privately, rather than in the "public" environment of an appraisal meeting. Most people find it easier to deal with their fears in private than in public. You can remove a lot of the fear from the appraisal meeting by simply allowing the employee to review the evaluation in advance of the meeting.

SETTING THE TONE OF THE MEETING DCF

Now that we have a sense of the psychology at work, let's look at the things we can do to create a better emotional climate. In particular, notice the language that is being used. Modify the language to suit your style or use it verbatim, whichever you prefer. Just make sure that the language is encouraging.

CAUSE FOR CELEBRATION

Let the employee know that this meeting is designed to celebrate his accomplishments since the last appraisal and position him for even greater success in the future.

> **TIP**
>
> After telling the employee that the purpose of the meeting is to celebrate his accomplishments, begin with a recap of his more significant successes. It solidifies the celebratory tone.

PERFORMANCE APPRAISAL, NOT PERSONAL APPRAISAL

It's important to let the employee know that you are judging his performance, not him. The more your language focuses on achievements, behavior, and skills, the less likely you are to hurt the individual's feelings. We often hear this advice in parenting classes when we are told to first make sure the child knows he's loved, then tell him how he could have behaved more appropriately. The same concept applies here.

Candor and Disagreement

Two important elements of the appraisal process are candor and disagreement. First, you must be candid with your employees. That means you don't sugar-coat low ratings or offer excessive praise with high ratings. As soon as your language diverges from your beliefs, you lose the respect of your employees.

Similarly, you have to let employees know that you expect candor from them, especially when they disagree with you. Let them know that disagreement is the foundation for future agreement. Assure them that they can disagree with you without fear of retribution. Finally, remind them that you are going to speak only of their performance and not of them as individuals. Tell them that you expect the same consideration when they disagree with you.

Accepting Responsibility

During the performance appraisal, it's not unusual to learn that you've con-tributed to an employee's performance problems. The natural tendency is to become defensive. Don't! You will gain a tremendous amount of respect from your employees when you take responsibility for your actions.

Ask the employee for ideas on how you can prevent a recurrence of this prob-lem. Reach a conclusion that makes sense to both of you. If the problem is the result of a lifetime habit, ask the employee to remind you whenever he sees you adopting the old habit. Let him know that you will appreciate his help. Not only will you gain the respect of this employee, but more than likely, he'll tell his co-workers of your integrity, and you'll gain their respect as well.

TIP

Nothing quite elevates an employee's desire to help you succeed as your willingness to credit him for his contributions.

Separating Appraisals and Salary Reviews

Your employee is going to be a lot more open to your suggestions for improvement if he isn't worrying about his salary increase.

Here's what happens when you try to combine salary reviews and perfor-mance appraisals. Every time you indicate a need for improvement, the employee is thinking, "What's this going to do to my raise?" With that thought in mind, he can't help but resist or at least trivialize your improve-ment suggestion.

Contrast that with an improvement suggestion accompanied by the promise of a future salary increase. It's a no-brainer, right? You don't mind accepting new performance targets as long as you will be rewarded financially for achieving those targets. If you want your employees to be open to improvement suggestions and new performance targets, separate the appraisal from the salary review by six months.

JOINT DECISIONS

You didn't get your promotion by seeing problems without seeing solutions. Similarly, you don't see improvement opportunities for your employees without seeing approaches for them to employ. That's as it should be. There are, however, serious dangers involved in telling your employees how to improve.

First, no one likes being told what to do. If you tell your employees what approach they should use to improve performance, they'll resist. It doesn't matter how good your approach is, you will create resistance by requiring them to use it.

The second danger is that your approach may not lend itself to the employee's style. For example, I'm an auditory learner. I learn by listening. If I have an employee who learns by doing and I ask him to use an audio program to acquire new skills, I'm throwing an obstacle in his way. I am asking him to employ a learning style that's unnatural for him. He may be able to acquire the skill this way, but it certainly isn't an effective approach.

 TIP

To get a better sense for how uncomfortable it is to use someone else's approach to a job, try it. Get someone to show you how he approaches a task. Make sure that it's different than the approach you would use. Then perform the task. You'll get a sense of how frustrating it is to do something unnatural.

The third danger is that you might be overlooking approaches that could be even more effective. I have yet to meet anyone who has all the answers. The reality is, there is a plethora of approaches that will work, and we don't know them all.

These are compelling arguments for allowing your employees to choose their own devices for improving performance. Only when you know that their approach won't work, should you intervene in this decision. You owe your employees suggestions on how to improve performance. You also owe them the benefit of your experience and insights in evaluating alternative approaches. You shouldn't, however, make the decision for them. After all, it's the result you're after, not the approach.

TIP

When people make decisions for themselves, they feel that it's the right decision. That simple reality increases their commitment to the decision.

As you employ the techniques described in this section, you'll find that the appraisal meeting is energizing. You and your employees will develop a stronger bond. Together you've set the stage for your mutual success, and that of your company as well.

Your willingness to hear your employees' thoughts, ideas, and opinions will ingratiate you to them. Your ability to admit your failings and your desire to improve serve as models for them.

There is one more very important benefit you'll gain. Future appraisals will be much easier—easier for you because you've become more adept at them, and easier for your employees because they know they're going to be encouraged, not criticized.

THE 30-SECOND RECAP

The "natural" psychology of the meeting is influenced by ...

- The employees' participation in setting goals.
- The use of self-monitoring feedback systems.
- Employee self-confidence.
- Your style: encouraging, neutral, or critical.
- The amount of time you allow for your employees to review the appraisal before the meeting.

Keys to creating an encouraging atmosphere in the meeting include ...

- Celebrating employees' successes.
- Appraising performance, not the individual.
- Being candid with your employee and expecting candor from your employee.
- Allowing disagreement without the threat of retribution.
- Taking responsibility when you've contributed to a performance problem.

- Allowing six months to elapse between performance appraisals and salary reviews.
- Permitting the employee to choose his own devices for improving performance.

Gaining Your Employees' Trust

In this section you'll learn about the importance of trust in the appraisal process. You'll also learn what you need to do to engender your employees' trust.

THE IMPORTANCE OF TRUST

The section "The Meeting" on page 572 discusses the importance of candor to the appraisal process. Candor cannot exist without trust. If your employees have any concerns about your motives, they will not trust you.

If you doubt the last statement, recall your experiences with two very different salespeople. The first salesperson gives the impression that her only interest is in the sale. The second demonstrates a genuine interest in helping you make the right decision. Which of the two do you trust? Do you respond as openly to the questions of both salespeople? Of course not!

With the first salesperson, you weigh your responses. You expect her to use everything you say to serve her purpose, making the sale. The way you protect yourself is to withhold information. In other words, your responses lack candor.

Does the second salesperson elicit the same cautious responses? No, your responses are open and honest. In fact, you usually provide more information than the salesperson needs. Why? You know the information will be used to help you, not hurt you.

Your employees react in the same way. When they trust you, they are candid with you. When they don't trust you, they withhold information. It's virtually impossible for you to succeed in your leadership role when employees withhold information about their fears, interests, goals, and reward preferences. That's why it's so important that you gain your employees' trust.

TRUST—RIGHT OR PRIVILEGE?

A leader's strength is measured by the trust her employees place in her. Trust is not a right; it's a privilege that must be earned every day of your existence.

Sadly, trust earned over a period of years can be lost in a few seconds. An ill-chosen word or a senseless act is all that it takes to lose trust.

Fortunately, your employees don't expect you to be perfect. In fact, most employees are very forgiving, if you've earned the right to be forgiven.

Employees forgive mistakes that might otherwise cost you their trust when your past acts and words consistently show you to be worthy of trust. When you normally behave in ways that elicit trust, workers recognize mistakes for what they are. Employees find it easy to forgive the occasional failing. They find it almost impossible to forgive a violation of trust.

Now that we have a sense of the importance of trust, let's see what we have to do to earn that trust.

BE INTERESTED IN THEIR SUCCESS

Your employees must believe that you are genuinely interested in their success. As I tell people in my seminars, "That should be easy. After all, it's you who looks good when your team is successful."

RECOGNIZE THEIR CONTRIBUTIONS

Your employees need to know that you will tout their successes for them. Everyone desires recognition, but most people are reluctant to brag about their successes. By publicly stating your employees' accomplishments you assure them the recognition they deserve without the risk of being labeled a braggart.

Here are some of the benefits you'll realize when you recognize your employees' success:

1. Your employees continue to strive for success.
2. Your employees view you as someone so comfortable with your success that you don't need to "steal" anyone else's.
3. Your employees respect your integrity.
4. Your interest in your employees' success will stimulate their interest in your success.
5. Your employees will be completely candid with you. Their candor makes it easier for you to succeed.

TIP

When presenting an idea, make sure that you credit the employee who came up with the idea. Even if your employee isn't present at the meeting, word will get back to her that you recognized her contribution in front of others. This simple act endears you to your employee and gives her an additional incentive to come up with more ideas. Recognition is a powerful motivator.

CRITICIZE PRIVATELY

While it's important to recognize employees' accomplishments publicly, it's equally important to discuss their shortcomings privately. You know what it's like when someone speaks poorly of you in public. It's embarrassing. You won't gain your employees' trust by embarrassing them in public.

Even though you know better, you can easily fall into the trap of discussing an employee's performance with others. Here are a couple of the more common traps.

You want to vent your frustration before discussing the problem with the employee. The last thing you want to do is begin this type of discussion when you're angry. If that's the case, wait until the end of the day, vent with a loved one who doesn't know the employee, and then go back the next day and discuss the problem with your employee.

At other times, you want the counsel of others on how to deal with this specific performance problem. That's fine, just make sure that you choose counselors who honor confidences. The sting of betrayal will be just as great whether it comes from your lips or those of your advisors.

If you want your employee's trust, discuss her performance only with her and only in private.

TIP

Remember our earlier discussion of encouraging and critical styles. You are far more likely to see performance improve if you encourage your employee rather than criticize her.

TREAT YOUR EMPLOYEES AS PEERS

How do you feel when someone gives you the impression that she is better than you are? Does the fact that she possesses more talent than you alter your feelings? Absolutely not! An attitude of superiority is insulting even when the individual possesses incredible skills.

It's easy for leaders to develop an attitude of superiority. To understand why, let's assume that your boss just announced your promotion. In effect, she said, "This person has demonstrated abilities greater than those of her peers. I am rewarding her by giving her authority over you." Pretty heady stuff.

Is it any wonder that you feel superior to your new charges? Of course not! If you choose to allow that feeling of superiority to persist, you'll lose your employees' interest in helping you become successful. If, however, you overcome these feelings, you'll win their respect and trust.

CAUTION

If your employees sense that you feel superior, they will set you up for a fall. They will find ways to let you know that you aren't as good as you think you are.

Avoid Comparing Employees

Your employees need to trust that you won't compare them to their co-workers. I don't know whether you've ever had your skills or abilities compared to someone else's. I have.

Experience has taught me that in a comparison like this, one person is treated favorably, the other unfavorably. In other words, there is a winner and a loser. No one likes to be the loser. Even winners cringe at the comparison. Why? They don't like being used as an instrument of criticism.

Often, comparisons are made without your realizing what you're doing. You might make a comparison like this: "Jim has found this technique to be particularly helpful; you might want to give it a try." I don't care how pure your motives are, you just told this employee that his technique isn't as good as Jim's.

Do you trust people who cast you in an unfavorable light? Do you trust people who repeatedly belittle you by using others to demonstrate your failings? Then use your experience to guide your actions. Treat each employee as the individual she is.

CAUTION

When you compare one employee to another you risk divisiveness in your department. The employee who loses in these comparisons eventually resents the employee who wins.

Admit When You're Wrong

Nothing endears you to your employees more than a willingness to admit when you're wrong. You know what it's like to deal with someone who knows she's wrong and won't admit it? You hate it. You also lose respect for the individual. Her actions indicate a lack of integrity. Integrity is an important component of trust, so she also loses your trust. Is that how you want your employees to view you? If not, then be willing to admit when you're wrong.

Allow Your Employees Their Own Devices

Micromanagement is a term we hear all too often these days. Those of us who have had the misfortune of working for a micromanager know how frustrating this can be. We'd like to ask, "Why don't you find a machine to do this?" or, "Why don't you do it yourself?"

PLAIN ENGLISH

Micromanagement   A managerial style in which the manager controls minute details of the effort.

You can avoid this reaction by allowing employees to choose their own devices or approaches to doing the work. Here's what the employee "hears" when you allow her to choose the approach:

- "I trust you to do a good job."
- "You know what you're doing; you don't need my help."
- "Your method is as good as mine."

These statements indicate respect for the individual and trust in her abilities and judgment. It's much easier for people to trust you if you trust them. Trust your employees! Leave them to their own devices!

Matching Words and Actions

Your words and actions need to match if you want others to trust you. I'm not talking just about the big things; I'm talking about everything.

If you tell an employee you'll help him with a problem later in the day, make sure you help him before the day is out. If you promise to provide information he needs, don't make him ask a second time. If you set a deadline, follow up to make sure the deadline is met.

It's actions like these that tell your employees how good your word is. If your word is your bond, they'll trust you to mean what you say. If you don't honor your word, they'll treat your words as lackadaisically as you do. The choice is yours.

TIP

When you honor your word, you earn the right to expect others to honor theirs. If you have an employee who isn't careful with the promises she makes, it's much easier to discuss the problem with her when you are modeling the proper behavior yourself.

THE 30-SECOND RECAP

You must earn your employees' trust every day of your existence. The amount of trust you earn is determined by …

- Your interest in their success.
- The public recognition you give their accomplishments.
- Your ability to keep their failings private.
- Your success at treating employees as peers.
- Your ability to avoid comparing one employee to another.
- Your willingness to admit to being wrong.
- Your success in avoiding the micromanagement trap.
- Your ability to match your actions to your words.

Forging Agreements

In this section you'll learn about the types of agreements you need from your employees. These agreements lay the foundation for future appraisals.

LEVELS OF AGREEMENT

Agreement occurs at two levels. *Logical agreement* is the easier of the two to achieve. *Emotional agreement* is more difficult to acquire. It's also more powerful.

PLAIN ENGLISH

Logical agreement   When your mind accepts the premise.

Emotional agreement   When you desire to act on the idea.

I'm sure you've had an employee agree with your ideas, yet never act on them. It's frustrating, right? Why didn't the employee act? You achieved only logical agreement; you didn't get to the emotional agreement needed for action.

There is an old sales adage that says, "People buy with their emotions, then justify the decision with logic." Why? We buy emotionally because that's the way we're built. There's no magical insight here; that's just the way we are.

Why do we use logic to justify our decisions? We don't want to appear whimsical or foolish. We're afraid that if we admit to allowing our emotions to rule our decisions our intelligence will be suspect. That's why we use logic to mask the emotions involved in our decisions.

What does this mean to you as a leader? It means that your employees aren't likely to achieve their performance and development goals unless they agree emotionally to those goals. This reality places an additional burden on you. You not only have to get agreement, you have to gauge the level of agreement you're getting.

To help you understand what's involved in getting emotional agreement, let's look at the types of agreement you need.

AGREEING ON YOUR EMPLOYEE'S STRENGTHS

You need agreement on your employee's strengths. This may seem like a ridiculous exercise. After all, the employee knows his strengths, doesn't he? Not necessarily.

Every employee has some tasks that he accomplishes with such natural ease that he doesn't realize that other people struggle with the same work. This is a common occurrence. You need to highlight their strengths to make sure they are aware of them. This awareness is crucial to their ability to teach these skills to co-workers.

TIP

Have your employees share their skills with each other. It's one of the most powerful, inexpensive, and readily available methods for helping your employees achieve their development goals.

When discussing your employees' performance, begin by agreeing on their strengths. It's a wonderful place to start. Not only does it set a positive tone for the meeting, it makes it easy for you to gain emotional agreement very quickly. The more quickly you open the door to agreement, the easier future agreements become.

Discussing Improvement Opportunities

The key to successfully discussing improvement opportunities is to avoid losing the ground gained while discussing strengths. This is not as easy as it might sound. Implicit in the need to improve is an admission that we're not as good as we should be. No one likes to admit that.

The need to improve shouldn't trouble us, but it does. Once again, we're facing the logic-versus-emotion argument. Logically, we know that we're not perfect, that we will never be perfect. Since perfection isn't possible, there is always opportunity for improvement. Intuitively we know this. We can even accept it logically. That doesn't mean we have to like it.

Emotionally, we despise the thought of being less than perfect. We hate admitting shortcomings. The mere thought of inadequacy brings us down emotionally.

Your employees wrestle with the same emotions we do. It is easy to trigger these emotions in your employees by using the wrong language in discussing improvement opportunities. Once lost, the emotional high gained from reviewing strengths is almost impossible to regain. How can you be sure that you're using the right language? Avoid discussing "the need to improve." Rather discuss the "desire to improve."

Here are some examples of language you can use:

- Instead of asking, "How do you think you can improve your skills?" ask, "What's the next level of success you want to achieve with these skills?"

- Rather than ask, "What are your weaknesses?" ask, "How can you build on your strengths?"

- Don't ask, "Why do you struggle with this type of work?" Ask, "What would make it easier for you to accomplish this task?"

You get the picture.

When discussing improvement opportunities, you can either build on the momentum gained in your discussions of strengths or lose that momentum through ill-chosen words. The choice is yours.

CAUTION

There are lots more agreements to gain. Drop the ball at this early stage, and you've set yourself up for a long, difficult, and often unproductive appraisal meeting.

APPROACHES TO IMPROVEMENT

Once you've achieved emotional agreement on what needs to be improved, you and your employee have to agree on the approach to use. In an earlier section we spoke of the importance of leaving employees to their own devices. Let's revisit the emotional aspects of leader-directed versus employee-directed approaches.

Place yourself in the role of the employee. Let's assume that you and your boss have decided that you need to become more organized. Last year your boss attended a wonderful seminar on organization skills. He suggests that you attend the seminar.

You don't like group education. You prefer audio programs for several reasons. First, you feel that you learn better in a quieter environment. Second, you aren't the type of person who likes to participate in exercises, nor do you ask a lot of questions. Third, you enjoy the ability to rewind and review anything that didn't quite register the first time. Finally, you consider yourself a slow learner. It's not that you are stupid, it's just that sometimes it takes a little longer for you to grasp a concept than it does your co-workers.

Now let's assume that your boss insists that you take the seminar. What's your commitment likely to be? Are you likely to postpone action on this approach? If you do agree to attend the seminar, will your agreement be logical or emotional? How will the level of your agreement affect the benefit you gain from the seminar? How likely is it that your organizational skills will improve? The answers are obvious.

Am I suggesting that you give your employees carte blanche? Absolutely not! When you see that your employee's approach isn't going to work, you have a duty to convince him that it won't work. It's your job to prevent his failure.

Again, be precise in the language you use. Don't say, "That won't work." A statement like this puts the employee on the defensive. You know the odds of gaining emotional agreement when the employee is being defensive.

You're better off asking, "What's this approach going to do for you?" By using this question you get the employee to reexamine his decision. If you're right and he has overlooked something important, he will find the mistake during his analysis. If he doesn't see his error, ask follow-up questions that allow him to examine aspects of the decisions he hasn't considered. When he realizes his error he'll abandon his approach in favor of one that holds out the opportunity for success.

There are two keys to gaining emotional agreement on approaches:

- Allow the employee to choose his own devices.
- If the employee's approach won't work, use leading questions to help him reach the conclusion that it won't work.

Measures of Improvement

When it comes to measuring improvement, emotional agreement hinges more on the *amount of improvement* than on the *performance measure* used.

PLAIN ENGLISH

Amount of improvement   Relates to the level of success. Should the desired level of improvement be 10, 30, or 70 percent?

Measures of performance   Speed, number of defects, number of errors, and volume produced.

It's much easier for the employee to agree on the measure to be used than on the amount of improvement to be targeted. The key here is realism. Employees tend to be more conservative in their estimates than leaders do. Why?

First, employees are the ones who are committing to the goal. Since no one wants to fail, they naturally become cautious. Second, depending on your style, they may get the idea that you're trying to build a career on their results and you really don't care how it affects them. Third, there is the confidence issue. Some employees don't possess confidence commensurate with their skills. In other words, they underestimate their own abilities.

You have a much better chance of achieving emotional commitment to improvement measures if you ask your employees ...

- For their estimate of what's realistic.
- What obstacles stand in the way of greater improvement.
- To help devise a plan for overcoming these obstacles.

Their participation in this process is the key to gaining emotional agreement.

If you're working with an employee whose fear simply won't allow him to agree to the performance measure you need, there is one more approach you can try. It's worked well for me when I've had an extremely cautious employee.

The approach is a combination of statements and questions that are designed to elicit agreement. Once again, pay particular attention to the language. The language is designed to help the employee remove the emotional constraints imposed by his comfort zone. Here's the approach:

- I know that I'm asking you to stretch beyond your comfort zone.
- I realize that you don't want to fail.

- I don't want you to fail either.
- If we agree that this lower level of performance is acceptable, will you try to achieve the higher level?
- I promise you that missing the higher target won't negatively impact your next appraisal or your salary.
- Achievement of the higher goal can, however, improve your next appraisal and offers the benefit of a higher increase.
- I know that you have concerns about the more aggressive target, but I believe that you can achieve it.

CAUTION

You have to walk the talk. You cannot express disappointment, withhold praise, or adjust the salary increase because the employee doesn't hit the more aggressive target. If you do, you violate his trust. Trust lost is difficult to regain.

My experience is that when I take the pressure off employees and state confidence in their abilities, they typically achieve the more aggressive goal. To me, that's proof of their emotional commitment to the goal.

DEADLINES FOR IMPROVEMENT

All the same fears and concerns that we discussed with improvement measures hold true for deadlines. When you develop the skills to deal with one, you equip yourself to handle both.

REWARDS FOR IMPROVEMENT

In particular, you want to gain agreement on the amount of increase that the employee will receive if he achieves his goals. The "amount" can be a percentage increase over his current base pay.

The key here is to emphasize the relationship between performance improvement, the value of the improvement, and the amount of increase. The clearer the employee's understanding of the value gained by the improvement, the less likely he is to demand unrealistic increases. People understand the concept of value. They employ it every day in their buying decisions. They also understand that the company is purchasing their services. If, for some reason, the employee forgets this simple fact, don't hesitate to remind him.

By using this value approach, you'll gain another valuable insight into your employee's character. How? You'll learn his definition of fair.

An employee who is greedy will ask for a disproportionate share of the value he generates. His willingness to "settle" for less depends on the importance he places on money and the presence of other aspects of job satisfaction.

CAUTION

Be aware that employees who "settle" for less than they want often balance the scales by reducing performance. That's contrary to your goal of improving performance.

For most employees the importance of salary declines if ...

- There is significant investment in their education.
- They have a sense of being a part of something bigger than themselves.
- Their ideas are welcomed and acted upon.
- Their contributions are recognized publicly.
- They can choose their own devices in accomplishing goals.
- They like their leader.

Those of you who have taken a job for more money and later found these satisfaction factors missing know exactly what I mean.

By providing more of the intangible aspects of job satisfaction you minimize the importance of money for most employees. This makes it easier for the two of you to agree on monetary rewards.

THE 30-SECOND RECAP

- Agreement must occur at the emotional level if it's going to drive action.
- Without action there is no improvement. Your employees' development depends on your ability to gain their emotional agreement.
- Areas in which you need agreement are the employees' strengths, improvement opportunities, approaches to improvement, measures of improvement, deadlines for improvement, and rewards.

Feedback Systems and Recognition Programs

In this section you'll learn about feedback systems and recognition programs for various areas of the operation.

FEEDBACK SYSTEMS—THE MISSING LINK

Feedback is the often-overlooked component of performance improvement. This may seem strange, but it's true. To help you understand how this happens, let's look at a typical exchange between leader and employee.

You're the leader. You and your employee agree that you want to reduce the cycle time on billing by two days. You also agree that the employee's focus is going to be on procedures rather than on technology. Both of you feel that the goal can be achieved within two months. Your employee leaves the meeting ready to begin the procedural analysis.

What's missing? Deadlines? Communication triggers? Progress reports? Essentially, you and your employee failed to establish a feedback system. Why didn't it get developed?

Very simply, the existence of an agreement and your trust in your employee cause you to overlook the need for a feedback system. When your employee leaves the meeting you are convinced that she …

- Has a clear understanding of what needs to be done.
- Understands the importance of the improvement initiative.
- Knows the deadline and its importance.
- Will honor her agreement to achieve this goal.

Wouldn't life be grand if it worked that way? The reality is that during the two months preceding the project's due date, this employee …

- Has a "normal" workload to complete.
- Will certainly encounter problems in dealing with the "normal" workload.
- Will be asked to participate in new initiatives.
- Will make numerous priority decisions regarding work flow.
- May have to deal with family crises.
- May have to fill in for absent employees.

In other words, there are a lot of things that can distract your employee from the agreed-upon goal. You can help her remain focused on the goal by establishing a feedback system. Here's an example of a simple feedback system:

- **Week two.** The employee submits procedural changes that have the potential of reducing the billing cycle by two days.

- **Week four.** The employee presents the reactions of employees who will be affected by the changes.

- **Week six.** The employee provides procedural updates including oral and written communications to the affected employees and launches the improvement effort.

- **Week eight.** The employee reports on the early stage success, the obstacles confronted, and the solutions created.

TIP

Your feedback system needs to align specific results with a very clear deadline to be effective.

The existence of these interim goals and deadlines intensifies the employee's focus throughout the two-month time frame. This simple step dramatically improves the employee's odds of being successful. If the employee becomes distracted and loses sight of this goal, you'll know it much sooner. You'll also be able to take corrective action much earlier than you would without the feedback system.

I know that we've discussed this before, but it bears repeating. When you establish a feedback system, be sure that the employee can monitor her progress. In the feedback system just outlined, you can see that it's easy for the employee to determine whether she ...

- Identified procedural changes.

- Obtained the reactions of affected employees.

- Provided written procedures and oral instructions to each affected employee.

- Obtained information on the success and problems her coworkers experienced.

- Met the deadlines.

Now that you have a sense for the more common mistakes made with feedback systems, let's look at a variety of operating areas and determine what your feedback systems can measure.

MARKETING

There are two goals in marketing. The first is to create general market awareness; does the public know that we exist?

That's why you see pharmaceutical companies running ads touting their prescription medications. It's also the reason why you see the "Intel Inside" logo on every computer that includes Intel chips.

The second goal of marketing is to elicit orders. General awareness ads run by a pharmaceutical company won't influence the physician who is making the buying decision. He needs study results, drug interaction information, a clear understanding of possible side effects, and the cost of the medication. It's obvious that these marketing goals require different approaches and, consequently, different feedback measures.

GENERAL AWARENESS MARKETING

Let's use the pharmaceutical company example. The company is marketing a cholesterol-reducing prescription medication. How will the company determine the success of its general awareness ads? What feedback systems can it employ?

1. The company can survey people within the age group that is at greatest risk of heart disease. These people are likely to have their cholesterol tested on a regular basis. The company's survey can include questions such as ...

   - Are you familiar with the names of these medications?
     (Provide a list that includes your medications and those of your competitors.)

   - What is the purpose of each of these medications?

   - Based on the ads you've seen, which medication would you consider most effective?

   - Would you ask your physician about this medication if you had high cholesterol?

   - If you had a loved one who had high cholesterol, would you suggest that she ask her doctor about this medication?

   This information will tell the marketing people how successful they are in gaining public interest in their products.

2. The company can survey physicians with questions such as ...

   - What percentage of your patients with high cholesterol asks about a specific medication?

- ▨ Which cholesterol-reducing medications are generating the most interest with your patients?
- ▨ Which medication produces the most inquiries? Which medication ranks second? Third?
- ▨ Do patients who inquire seem to have a preference for one medication over another? If so, what's the reason for their preference?

Measurements from the physicians' survey may be less precise than the public survey. That's because doctors don't often track the frequency of patient requests for a medication. They do, however, remember their patients' questions. That's enough to help the pharmaceutical companies gauge the effectiveness of their market awareness campaign.

TIP

Make sure you understand the level of precision that exists in the measures you use. A lack of precision doesn't eliminate value, but it may diminish value.

With the information from these two surveys, the marketing team can assess its current level of success and establish goals for improvement. Assume that the surveys show that 37 percent of the public knows the name, but only 8 percent ask their physicians about the product.

There are several improvement opportunities available. The marketing team can pursue an increase in public awareness from 37 percent to, let's say, 40 percent. It can target higher rates of patient inquiry off the existing 37 percent awareness. Or the marketing group may pursue some combination of the two. The feedback from the initial effort provides the basis for new goals, new marketing messages, and new feedback. That's the cycle of continuous improvement worth employing.

ORDER ELICITING MARKETING

Some of the things you want the feedback system to track are …

- ▨ The number of contacts with the physician before an order is received.
- ▨ A ranking of the physicians' concerns about the medication; this information can reduce the number of contacts needed.
- ▨ Whether physicians respond most often after a mail piece, a phone call, an office visit, or attending a seminar.

TIP

You'll notice that all of this feedback is measurable. Feedback must be quantifiable to be useful.

SALES

There are many activities involved in selling, most of them are easily quantified. Here are some feedback measures used in sales management:

- Number of telephone contacts in a day
- Number of appointments made in a day
- Number of appointments cancelled or postponed each day
- Percentage of appointments that result in sales on the first call, second call, and so on
- Average size of the sale
- Profit margin on the sale
- Percentage of sales that come from existing customers versus new customers

CAUTION

Averages can be misleading. When evaluating the average size of the order or the average profit margin, make sure that you understand the magnitude of the range included in the averages.

PRODUCTION

Production efficiency involves a lot of measures including quality, speed of delivery, material costs, labor costs, equipment costs, error rates, and rework costs. Here are some measures that address the various aspects of production:

- Material costs
- Your vendors' defect rate on parts supplied
- Time required for each phase of production
- Reject rates
- Rework costs
- Percentage of shipments that go out early, on time, or late
- Number of units produced by shift
- Number of shipments returned by customers
- Credits given to customers for poor quality

If you're experiencing high numbers on the last two items, you've got some serious problems. It's probably the result of not having feedback on the other items in the list.

CREDIT AND COLLECTION

You want your credit and collection function to strike a good balance between increasing business and improving cash flow. The following measures will help you achieve that goal:

- The percentage of "new customers" who don't qualify for credit (This will give you insights into whether your sales force is targeting the right customers.)
- The percentage of customers who are delinquent
- The dollar amount of delinquent receivables
- Which industries produce the highest level of delinquency
- Which customers represent the greatest percentage of delinquent receivables
- How many collection calls your staff makes in a day
- How many calls it takes to collect the money
- What percentage of receivables get sent to outside collection services
- The amount spent on outside collection services
- Which outside collection service is most effective

CAUTION

Collection is one area of operation in which you need to pay particular attention to how improvement affects the customer. If further shortening of the collection period is going to irritate customers with good payment histories, it's not a worthwhile improvement.

HUMAN RESOURCES

Human resources is responsible for the hiring, retention, and development of good performers. Mistakes in any of these areas are very costly to the organization. The following measures can be used to evaluate the human resource function's performance:

- Employee turnover rate
- Cost of hiring an employee

- Cost of terminating an employee
- Length of time required for hiring a new person
- Percentage of new hires that leave after a month, three months, six months, a year
- Employee participation in discretionary training offered by the company
- Effectiveness of training
- Number of grievances filed
- Win/lose percentages on grievances
- Number of grievances filed against each leader
- Types of grievances filed

TIP

To gain greater insights into how to evaluate training, read Donald Kirkpatrick's book *Evaluating Training Programs: The Four Levels*.

FINANCE

One of the finance group's responsibilities is reporting financial information to operating managers and the general public. The finance group is also charged with paying bills and monitoring the company's cash situation. Here are a few items that the finance group might track to measure its performance:

- Number of days required to provide financial statements to operating managers
- Number of adjustments required before publishing the financial statements
- Number of corrections required after the statements are published
- Cost of processing vendor invoices and paying bills
- Cost of billing customers and making deposits
- Number of transactions processed per person
- Cycle times involved in handling receivables and payables
- Timeliness of expense reimbursements

Certainly, these are not all-inclusive lists. Nor do they cover all areas of operation. There are many more measures that can be tracked in each of these feedback systems.

The keys to a successful feedback system are as follows:

- A specific performance goal exists.
- The goal must be measurable.
- Results must be posted frequently, preferably daily.
- Results should be posted where the work is done and in high-traffic areas.
- Each employee is able to gauge his contribution to the result.

One of the greatest benefits you'll gain from a feedback system is focus. With all the demands made on us and our employees, it's easy to lose sight of what's important. Feedback systems provide focus and the means to maintain that focus every day.

TIP

In my 25 years of experience in leadership roles, I've found that the reason more people aren't successful is that they lose focus. Feedback systems allow you to help your employees retain the focus they need without having to continuously look over their shoulders.

RECOGNITION PROGRAMS

Feedback guides success, recognition rewards success. Some say that success is its own reward. There is some merit to that statement, but the greater reward lies in recognition. Think about the satisfaction you feel when you achieve a goal. Now compare that feeling with the one you get when someone comes to you and says, "I just heard that you cut two days out of the billing cycle. That's incredible."

Which of these two "rewards" is more enjoyable? The latter, right? That's why it's so important to build recognition programs into your daily activities.

It may seem that we are drifting away from the performance appraisal topic, but we aren't. Remember, the goal of the performance appraisal is to help your employees become more successful. That success isn't going to occur unless you help them stay focused on their goals, allow them to monitor their performance, and recognize their accomplishments during the interval between appraisals. Now that we see how recognition programs fit into the appraisal process, let's look at different approaches to recognition.

I've seen organizations post employees' accomplishments on bulletin boards, banners, and, yes, in the electronic age, on the company's *intranet.*

PLAIN ENGLISH

Intranet   A software network similar to the Internet except that its access is limited to the company's employees, customers, and vendors.

Some companies offer financial incentives, cash awards, trips, sports tickets, merchandise, or vehicles. The possibilities are endless. Others give gag gifts to add another dimension of fun to the celebration.

Still others bring in pizza or ice cream so that the whole team can join in the celebration. A reward that employees really enjoy is getting out early on a Friday afternoon. If my team had an unusually successful week, I'd send them home at 3:30 or 4:00 in the afternoon. It's amazing how much longer the weekend seems when you miss rush-hour traffic.

The form of recognition isn't as important as being recognized. Your employees know you care about them when you make time to celebrate their successes. The more that you demonstrate your interest in their welfare, the more they'll care about yours.

CAUTION

Recognize an employee's personal best. The tendency is to recognize only top performers. If you recognize only your top performers, you risk having the majority of your employees lose interest in improving their performance.

THE 30-SECOND RECAP

- Feedback is essential to performance improvement. Good feedback systems provide information that is quantifiable, timely, and easily monitored by both you and your employee.

- Feedback is essential for helping employees maintain focus on their goals. Lack of focus is the primary cause of missed goals. In effect, feedback guides success.

- Recognition is the reward for a job well done. It's essential to the employees' ability to remain motivated during the time between performance appraisals.

- The more opportunities your employees have to celebrate success, the more they'll desire success. After all, everyone loves to celebrate.

You Can't Win 'Em All

In this section you'll learn that regardless of how adept you become at performance appraisals, some just won't take.

THE PROBLEM

First I want to share my attitude toward performance. I believe that employees have to do more than their "job." They have to find ways to do the job more effectively. Whether you agree or disagree with that definition, my employees know that's what I expect of them.

Not all performance appraisals produce the results that you desire. Read on to learn about one of my more glaring failures ....

I had an employee who wasn't performing to expectation, yet she wanted a double-digit salary increase. These were the days before I learned to separate appraisals and salary reviews. Now that I think about it, this appraisal may have been the reason I separated the two.

This employee did her "regular" work well. The problem was that whenever I asked for anything new from her, she responded, "I can't do that." When I asked why not, she'd say, "It's too complicated for me." I reminded her that she had handled more complicated tasks in the past, but she insisted that my new requests were beyond her abilities.

One day I overheard her telling some of her co-workers how wonderful her husband was. She said, "Last night I was going to help him with the lawn. He told me that it was too hard for me, that he would take care of it." She went on to describe several other situations in which her husband did the work because it was "too difficult" for her. She admitted that she enjoyed being pampered in this way.

Obviously, this arrangement was working well for them in their marriage. That's great! It's not my place to tell others how their marriages should work. At the same time, I can't allow one employee to get by saying it's too hard without offering the same consideration to all employees.

As you can imagine, the appraisal meeting wasn't much fun. She contended that she was doing a good job on the work she had been assigned. I agreed, but reminded her that I had always expected continuous improvement. She said that anything more than what she was currently doing was just too difficult. I retorted by saying that I thought she was underestimating her abilities. She disagreed.

This discussion went on for more than an hour with no progress. I suggested that we postpone our discussion until after lunch. I expressed my hope that the break might help us resolve our differences. When I came back from lunch her appraisal was on my desk. Across the front of the appraisal, in big red letters, she had written "Bull——!" She never came back from lunch.

I'm not proud of this result. I wish that I could have found a way for us to reach an agreement. My reason for sharing this failure is simply to help you understand that you won't always be successful. There are many reasons why the appraisal process fails.

TIP

When you strive for perfection you become more successful. When you expect perfection, you set yourself up for failure.

WHEN AN EMPLOYEE DOESN'T VALUE PROFESSIONAL GROWTH

Some employees aren't interested in a career. All they want is a job that pays well enough to allow them to enjoy their leisure time. I've done a lot of work in the construction industry. I can tell you that when deer season opens, even foremen call in sick if they can't get time off any other way.

Other employees lose the desire to grow when their careers reach a plateau. Sometimes that plateau is a personal choice. They enjoy the work and don't want to advance beyond that point.

Often the decision is made for them. They are passed over for promotions, and they realize that regardless of how much effort they put forth they aren't going to rise to the next level. These employees suffer from a malady known as "retirement on the job." It's difficult to regain the interest of someone who has the attitude, "Why bother?"

Lifestyle changes also influence the employee's attitude toward growth. In the example of my failure, marriage encouraged the employee's attitude of "it's too difficult." Chronic health problems often rob a person of his desire for career growth. So can a large inheritance, winning the lottery, or simply getting older. All of these factors influence the employee's desire for personal growth.

POOR MORALE

A promotion often includes inheriting a staff. The good news is you don't have to scramble to find people, and you have lots of experience from which to draw. The bad news is you may inherit morale problems.

Twice in my career I "inherited" people who felt that ...

- They were the dumping grounds for all the nasty work in the company.
- No one appreciated their contributions.
- Their salaries weren't adequate.

It's virtually impossible to turn around an employee with these beliefs. If you've found an effective way to do this, call me. In 25 years, I have not found a remedy for this malady.

TIP

Don't assume that an employee with poor morale is experiencing these feelings. There are other causes of morale problems that can be cured.

CONFIDENCE

The importance of confidence is discussed in the sections "Preparing for the Meeting" on page 567 and "The Meeting" on page 572. If an employee possesses low self-esteem and little confidence, the appraisal process is going to be difficult. Still, I'd much rather deal with a confidence problem than with the morale issue. Why? I have a chance at success when dealing with confidence problems; I don't with morale.

You see, with confidence, I can structure the work so that the employee experiences a series of successes. With each success comes confidence. Only if the employee lacks the confidence to try do I have an insurmountable problem. Other than the failure I described earlier, I've never met an individual who wasn't willing to try at some level.

WHEN AN EMPLOYEE DOESN'T ENJOY WORK

In recent years we've seen a significant increase in the number of workers expressing interest in changing careers. I doubt that the interest itself is new, rather I believe that several cultural changes encourage employees to act on their interests.

One change is the workers' attitude toward security. Most employees no longer view security as lifetime employment with one company. The plethora of *mergers* and *downsizings* of the past two decades have taught workers that they can't rely on the company for employment, they have to depend on their abilities. So many people have lost jobs in recent years that the stigma once associated with frequent job changes is gone.

PLAIN ENGLISH

Mergers   When two companies combine into one.

Downsizings   Significant reductions in a company's workforce. They usually represent a cost-cutting move.

Education is another important ingredient. Our workforce is one of the best educated in the world. Many people, especially those in midlevel management positions, find that their skills and knowledge have application well beyond their current jobs. The transferability of their skills makes career changes easier. If your employee is serious about wanting a career change, it's going to be difficult to interest him in improving performance in his current job.

Obviously, each of these situations threatens your success in helping your employees improve performance. How do you deal with them?

First, avoid the temptation to act as a parent. As parents, we instruct children about what's right. That's fine for children; they don't have a great deal of experience to draw upon. For an adult it's condescending.

You know how much you resist the attempts of others to treat you like a child. Your employees will react the same way. If you adopt a parental mindset with your employees, your attempts to help them will almost certainly fail.

THE SOLUTION

Now that I've discussed what not to do, let's look at each of the previous situations with a focus on success.

WHEN AN EMPLOYEE DOESN'T VALUE PROFESSIONAL GROWTH

You can generate or rekindle interest in professional growth by asking the employee what he and his family would do with extra income. Get him to dream. The more he thinks about what he wants, the easier it is for you to tie performance improvement to those dreams.

TIP

This approach is useful for all employees. The more you frame what you want in terms of what they want the more likely you are to get action. With workers who've lost interest in their work, it's mandatory.

I realize that this approach isn't going to work with employees who win the lottery or receive large inheritances. Frankly, you don't have to worry about improving their performance; they're not likely to remain in your employ.

POOR MORALE

As I said earlier, if you have an effective way of dealing with the employee's perception of years of mistreatment, please let me know. I haven't found the answer. The best I've been able to accomplish is to guide them to leave on their own.

You'd think that it would be easy to convince an employee with morale problems to leave, but it isn't. Why? The employee is already pessimistic about the future. He's been treated poorly in the past, and he has no reason to believe that will change.

When he considers other employment, his negative frame of mind causes him to look for the things that could go wrong in another job, not at what might be good about that job. That's why these employees tend to resist help in finding other work.

Your only alternative may be to discharge the employee. If you can't get him turned around in a couple of months, make the decision and move on. You'll both be better off. If you doubt that, let me remind you that I inherited two people with precisely these attitudes. In both cases, I had to fire them. They were both extremely angry with me for adding to their problems. In both cases, these people saw me about a year later, came up to me, and thanked me for letting them go. They had both found jobs that they enjoyed and were making more money than before.

In both cases, I experienced mixed feelings. Simultaneously, I was happy for them and angry with them. I was happy to hear that they were enjoying their work again. They were good people with the skills necessary to do a very competent job.

At the same time, I resented the fact that they didn't leave on their own. I hated having to be the one to make the inevitable decision. I wished they had made it on their own. Now I realize that their feelings of unfair treatment caused them to have a pessimistic attitude toward life. I can see that it would have been very difficult for them to overcome this pessimism and make the decision they needed to make. If you ever find yourself in this situation, I hope you'll remember my experiences and make the difficult decision. You really are helping your employee as much as yourself.

CONFIDENCE

We've already discussed the handling of confidence issues. The only thing I would add is that if the employee is so deficient in confidence that he's unwilling to try, you need to suggest counseling. The individual needs the help of a trained professional.

Even if you have the training necessary to counsel the employee, I recommend outside professional help. Why? The time required to help this person will prevent you from helping the rest of your employees become more successful. It's simply not fair to penalize them for another employee's problems. Use outside professional help for really difficult situations.

CAUTION

Don't confuse caution with confidence. Some employees are very thorough because they want to be sure they understand what's expected of them. That's caution, not lack of confidence.

WHEN AN EMPLOYEE DOESN'T ENJOY WORK

If the employee has lost interest in his work, find out what interests him now. I'm assuming that this employee was, at one time, a productive worker. Make sure that the new interest is not just a passing fancy, but a sincere desire to fill an emotional need in his life.

Once you ascertain the genuineness of his desire, look within your department for work that might meet his needs. If you can't provide the opportunity he wants, assure him that you'll help him look elsewhere within the company to accommodate his needs. It's better to lose a good worker to another department than to lose him to another company, especially if that company ends up being a competitor.

When you help him find a job in another department, arrange a trial period for both your employee and his new leader. Why? I've seen too many employees who thought a job would be "fun" learn very quickly that it isn't. Leave the door open. If the new job doesn't work, not only will your employee be grateful to have his old job back, he'll be very interested in improving his performance. The new leader will be glad that he doesn't have to decide what to do with an unhappy employee.

TIP

When discussing a trial period for the new job, agree on a reasonable time frame. Remind him that your team can't work short-handed forever, nor can the new leader afford to invest in an employee who may not remain with the department.

CAUTION

Don't allow your employee to decide frivolously that he wants to try something new. That's a formula for chaos. It's easy to tell whether or not he's sincere. If there's passion in his voice, a sparkle in his eye, and he becomes animated as he describes his newly found interest, he's sincere.

There is one last piece of advice I have for situations like those just described. Don't spend an inordinate amount of time with poor performers. When you do, you diminish your ability to help those who have earned the right to benefit from your time and talents.

Good performers deserve success. It's your job to see to it that they enjoy success for many years to come. You can't do that, baby-sit poor performers, and plan for the future. There simply aren't enough hours in the day. Use your time wisely; spend most of it with your good performers.

I'm sure some of you are wondering, "How do I minimize my time with poor performers? After all, they are the ones causing me the most problems." Here's an approach that's always worked well for me:

1. Set expectations, with or without his agreement.
2. Establish deadlines, with or without agreement.
3. Create a self-monitoring feedback system.
4. Tell the employee that the ball is in his court; he can choose to produce or not as he sees fit.
5. Let the employee know that his choice will determine his future employment.

You won't believe how liberated you'll feel when you place the responsibility for the employee's future employment where it belongs, with the employee.

Another reason for using this approach is the impact it has on the rest of the team. You win the respect and support of good employees when they see that you aren't …

- Wasting time with an unwilling worker.
- Shifting work to them that should have been done by a poor performer.
- Tolerating ill-humor or poor performance.
- Hesitating to eliminate a poor performer who refuses to get with the program.

Even though employees know that life isn't fair, most of them like to see some measure of equity in the workplace. It allows them to feel good about themselves and the environment in which they work. The approach I've just outlined gives your employees a sense that you're fair in your dealings.

There are other advantages to this approach. Employees who feel that everyone is being treated fairly are more productive. For one thing, they don't spend their days trying to figure out how to balance the scales.

I've seen people who wouldn't think of taking a paper clip from the office, slow their production because they didn't feel they were being compensated fairly. There's no malice intended, it's a natural reaction to the perception of inequity.

TIP

Employees who are balancing the scales are often unaware of what they're doing. If you see this happening, help your employee see the error of this strategy, then work together to remove the inequity they perceive.

Another advantage of this approach is that employees who feel they are being treated fairly approach their work with greater verve, which increases their productivity, and with it their performance. All of these advantages come from placing the responsibility for the poor performer's employment where it belongs, on his shoulders.

THE 30-SECOND RECAP

- Try to find out why an employee doesn't have an interest in improving performance.
- If the employee lacks confidence or has become bored with the work, you can often salvage the employee. To deal with a lack of confidence create a plethora of opportunities for the employee to succeed. Each success will build confidence. For the bored employee, add some variety to his work.
- If the employee's attitude toward the company is poor or if he has simply lost interest in the work, you're probably going to have to help him find other employment.
- One of the biggest mistakes you can make is spending a lot of time with people who aren't interested in improving their skills or performance. It's the ones who are interested who deserve your time and energy.

Pulling It All Together

In this section you'll review the performance appraisal process. You'll also receive some checklists that will help make your performance appraisals more successful.

PERFORMANCE APPRAISAL—A PROCESS

I've covered a lot of ground since the introduction, where General Electric CEO Jack Welch says that he spends his time on people, not strategy. Now it's time to pull everything together into a cohesive performance appraisal process.

I'd like to begin by emphasizing the word *process*. Too many leaders view performance appraisals as projects that require attention once or twice a year. This approach explains most of the failings that occur with performance appraisals.

Performance appraisals are ongoing processes that encompass …

- An evaluation of the employee's current performance.
- Goals for improving that performance.
- The definition of future rewards for achieving the goals.
- Feedback systems that allow both the leader and the employee to monitor her performance.
- Periodic meetings between the leader and the employee to discuss the employee's progress toward her goals.
- Corrective action when the employee is struggling to achieve her goals.

Each and every one of these components is vital to performance improvement.

- Employees can't improve their performance unless they know their current level of performance.
- Their goals must be quantifiable so that they can measure their success.
- Knowing what rewards to expect enhances their interest in achieving goals.
- The ability to monitor their progress helps the employees remain focused on their goals.

- Periodic meetings increase the likelihood that the employees will use the feedback systems to monitor their own progress.

- The requirement that employees report their results in periodic meetings reduces the likelihood they'll miss their targets. After all, no one likes to admit failure.

- Corrective action is best determined in discussions that identify the reasons for the employees' failure to meet goals.

On the surface, this process appears to require a great deal of time. That doesn't have to be the case.

TIP

My experience has been that every hour I invest in these activities saves me at least three to four hours of follow-up, problem solving, and scrambling to meet deadlines.

TIME COMMITMENTS

The initial appraisal meetings can be accomplished in a couple of hours per employee. In these meetings you'll identify the current level of performance, establish improvement goals, create tracking systems, and define future rewards. If you handle the rest of the process well, your subsequent appraisal meetings can be completed in as little as a 45 minutes to an hour.

The next investment in time comes in the form of establishing feedback mechanisms. In the initial meeting you identified the measures to be used when you established the goals. All that's left is to put a reporting system in place. Keep it simple!

As discussed in "Feedback Systems and Recognition Programs" on page 591, the results can be posted on a bulletin board, a white board, or the intranet. The medium isn't as important as the message. Just make sure that both you and your employees are able to monitor their performance from the same system.

Once the system is in place, the tracking and reporting should take only a few minutes per day. Often you can assign this task to someone other than the employee being evaluated. Don't feel compelled to do all the work yourself.

TIP

If your tracking and reporting systems are complex, you probably have the wrong measures. Your best results come when you focus on activities where the results are easy to measure.

Your only other time commitment in this phase is the time you spend creating fun ways to celebrate your employees' success. The interesting thing is that the more successful your employees become at managing themselves, the more time you have for these activities.

The time invested in periodic meetings is determined by the success of the employee. If the employee stays on target, you need only spend five minutes a week or a half-hour per month discussing their progress. A few minutes spent letting them know how that you care about their success and that you're happy to see them succeeding means a lot to them. It can also save you countless hours of supervision.

If the employee isn't succeeding, you'll need to spend more time meeting with her to help her get back on track. If that doesn't occur within a reasonable time frame, use the approach outlined in the section "You Can't Win 'Em All," on page 600, and place the responsibility for her future employment where it belongs, in her hands.

ESTABLISHING TIME FRAMES FOR CORRECTIVE ACTION

What's a reasonable time frame? That depends on the goal. If the task is one that should be accomplished in days, then a reasonable time frame is a week. If it should be accomplished in a few weeks, then a month is a reasonable time frame. You'll notice that I am allowing a little more time than should be needed. There are two reasons for this.

First, I want to give the employee every opportunity to succeed. I am truly interested in her success. There are times when the likelihood of success is enhanced by taking pressure out of the situation. In this instance, I'm removing time pressure.

Second, if the employee chooses not to take corrective action, I don't want her to have the opportunity to say that I established unrealistic time frames. Quite the opposite, I want to be able to demonstrate that I gave her every opportunity to succeed.

If the employee fails, I want the failure to clearly be her failure. If termination is warranted, I want the decision to be viewed as her decision. How? By allowing her failure to become evidence of her lack of desire to continue her employment. I'm not going to waste my time trying to help someone who won't help herself.

You can see that it doesn't require much of your time to assure the success of your appraisals. In fact, time spent wisely in the interval between appraisals can actually reduce the time you spend in future appraisal meetings. Since your employees are going to be more successful using this approach, your future meetings will also be more enjoyable. Now that's a winning combination: less time, more enjoyment.

One last reminder: Make sure that the language you use reflects current success and increased success. That way your employees won't feel that they're being criticized.

Now that you have an overview of the system, let's look at some checklists that'll help you keep the appraisal process on track.

TIP

Some people view checklists as a crutch to help someone with a poor memory. I view checklists as a tool to help me develop and maintain good work habits. I hope you'll adopt the latter view.

DAILY CHECKLIST

- ❑ Have the feedback systems been updated?
- ❑ Have I reviewed the feedback?
- ❑ Have I publicly recognized all achievements?
- ❑ Have I honored my commitments to periodic meetings today?
- ❑ Did I earn my employees' trust today?
- ❑ Were there any performance problems that I neglected to address today?
- ❑ Are there any concerns that I have that I haven't expressed to my employees?
- ❑ Are there any expectations that I haven't communicated to my employees today?

WEEKLY CHECKLIST

- ❑ Have I spent at least a few minutes with every employee this week?
- ❑ Have I recognized every employee at least once this week?
- ❑ Did I find some interesting ways to celebrate my employees' success this week?
- ❑ Do any of my employees appear to be behind schedule in achieving their goals?
- ❑ For the employees who are falling behind, did I take time to discuss their problems and help them get back on track?

❏ Are any of these employees exhibiting signs of lack of interest or boredom with their work?

❏ If an employee is developing a morale problem, did I discuss it with her?

❏ If I've had more than two discussions with an employee about morale, did I employ the approach defined in "You Can't Win 'Em All," on page 600, and place the employee's future employment in her hands?

CAUTION

Occasionally failing to accomplish an item on the checklist does not make you a bad leader. It simply means that you're human. Just don't allow yourself to get in the habit of skipping items.

These simple checklists will help you stay focused on your primary responsibility, which is developing your people. They also help your employees remain focused on their goals, which assures improved performance. When your employees are more productive the company benefits as well. Everyone wins, which is the way it should be.

The performance appraisal is one of the most powerful tools available to you. Use it wisely, and it'll simplify your life and help you become recognized as master at developing people.

THE 30-SECOND RECAP

▪ Businesses are always looking for leaders.

▪ People who have the ability to develop leaders are rare.

▪ The performance appraisal will help you develop the skills necessary to become one of those people.

▪ When that happens, you become invaluable; you can write your own ticket. My wish for you is that you achieve that level of success.

Effective Business Presentations

Become an Effective Speaker

In this section you learn about the importance of effective public speaking and about several skill sets that will make you a better presenter.

A young manager once told me that he'd started to move up in his organization only after he'd overcome his fear of public speaking. It had always scared him to death. Once he mastered those feelings he began to work on developing his speaking skills, and found out that he was actually a very good presenter.

STAND UP AND SPEAK

One of the best ways to turn public speaking into a more positive experience is to consider all the advantages you bring to the table:

- You probably know more than anyone in the audience about your topic.

- If you leave something out or forget something, the audience will never know. Remember, they didn't know what you were planning to say in the first place.

- Most listeners would much rather be sitting where they are than standing where you are. So they feel for you and empathize with your situation.

- The audience usually wants you to succeed; they're in your corner, not rooting against you.

- Many other people in the room probably wish that they could do what you're doing, so relax and enjoy being a star.

You undoubtedly have more going for you than you think.

ACKNOWLEDGE THE PERSUASIVENESS OF PRESENTATIONS

When Carleton Fiorina took over as CEO of Hewlett-Packard (HP), which had recently fallen on hard times, the first thing she did was to start communicating with her employees. She traveled to work sites around the globe and addressed more than 20 large meetings in 10 different countries. The new CEO had an important message to deliver, which involved revitalizing HP and making it successful; the means she chose was oral communication.

Whether you're the CEO of a large organization or the supervisor of a small work team, you must know how to communicate effectively. When you stand up to speak, you instantly become a voice of authority and your audience is waiting to hear what you have to say. The words you use can have several purposes. They can ...

- **Inform.** Sometimes you only want to give your audience information. For example, you may want to tell them about the past week's production figures or the results of your meetings with several important customers.

- **Explain.** Perhaps the purpose of your talk is to briefly explain a new process or procedure, like how to file a health insurance claim or conduct a performance evaluation. Generally, talks that explain also provide information.

TIP

Many speakers believe that they are simply presenting information. In reality, they want their listeners to use that information to take action, so their talks are actually persuasive. It's important to know your purpose when you stand up to speak.

- **Persuade.** These are usually the most difficult types of presentations. Carleton Fiorina, for example, was trying to persuade her employees to make a change in their organization. Speakers like Fiorina usually use information and explanation in the service of persuasion.

If you are clear in your purpose, it's easier to organize your presentation and to deliver it.

Use Persuasive Talks Regularly

Most persuasive talks do not involve changing the direction of a major corporation. Nor are you likely to be put in the position of Winston Churchill who used his words and distinctive speaking style to help convince the British people to keep fighting during the dark days of World War II. Nevertheless, your presentation could make a significant difference.

While the world may not move from a state of war to a state of peace, your department or business unit may make an important change. Perhaps it will decide to embark on a quality improvement process or enter a new consumer market or streamline its R&D procedures. As the person who suggested this change, you have an unusual opportunity:

- To make an impact on your organization and change the minds of employees.

- To stand out and be remembered as the person who advocated a new direction.

- To advance your own career within your department or company.

Take advantage of opportunities to speak effectively about changes and developments you've initiated to those who will be affected by them.

TRIUMPH OVER STAGE FRIGHT

What runs through your mind when you think about public speaking? Perhaps you remember an incident from your childhood when you appeared in a school play and forgot one of your lines. Or you may recall standing in front of an audience at a PTA meeting and looking at 100 eyes that seemed to be staring back at you—and staring and staring and staring.

It's enough to send chills up and down the spine of even the most courageous person. Indeed, most people admit that they'd rather do anything than give a presentation. And that includes root canal procedures, getting fired from a job, and even dying.

Stage fright is a normal feeling for anybody who has to get up in front of an audience. Even great actors suffer from it.

PLAIN ENGLISH

Stage fright   A natural anxiety most people feel when they get up and speak before a large group of listeners.

There's an old saying, "He who hesitates is lost." The same may be said for anyone who is afraid to get up and speak. The people who move ahead in an organization are the same ones who seem capable of distinguishing themselves from their colleagues. Often this means that they know how to get up on their feet and deliver a clear, persuasive message.

If you can give a powerful talk, not only can it catch the attention of your listeners, it can focus much of that attention on you, showcasing your ideas and showing your listeners that you are someone who knows how to be a leader.

CAUTION

Don't fire before you aim. A successful talk will help you stand out, but an unsuccessful one could damage you. Make sure you've thought about what you want to say before you start speaking.

AIM FOR A MEMORABLE PRESENTATION

A young engineer once told me that many of the meetings he was attending were becoming depressingly similar. Employees would sit down, listen to the speaker for a few brief moments, then begin doodling and daydreaming. It seems extremely impolite, until you remember how many meetings some people must attend in the course of a day and how excessively dull the speakers usually seem to be.

Most of us have learned to accept a pretty low level of performance in business presentations. After all, you tell yourself, the topic is usually not very scintillating; what else can you expect? But every once in a while, you hear a speaker who is far better than average. Suddenly your expectations are raised again, and you remind yourself of what's actually possible.

Once I heard a speaker deliver a presentation that he routinely gave to new salespeople who had been hired by his organization. He spoke about five different types of customers and how to convince them to buy his product. I've never forgotten that presentation because of the effective way it was delivered. I demand the same things from myself whenever I speak. Here are my six rules:

1. Make the message clear so no one will misunderstand what you're saying.

2. Sound as if you mean it; so many speakers seem to have very little interest in what they're saying.

3. Be yourself. Don't try to play a part or mimic the mannerisms of another speaker. It won't work.

4. Personalize the presentation. Let your personality stand out and put its stamp on what you're saying.

5. Connect with your listeners. Try to turn the presentation into a one-on-one experience for them.

TIP

Think about presentations that made a strong impact on you. Taking the point of view of an audience member, expect of yourself the kind of presentation you would hope to hear.

6. Tell the audience why they're there and why they should listen to you; otherwise they won't.

Follow these six rules and you'll be on your way to delivering memorable presentations.

SPEAK POWERFULLY ON ANY OCCASION

You may be asked to speak in a variety of situations. Sometimes you'll be given plenty of notice and have an opportunity to prepare; sometimes you won't. You'll be required to speak almost on the spur of the moment. In each case, you should try to make a powerful impression on your audience.

STREAMLINE YOUR INTRODUCTIONS TO SPEAKERS

Perhaps you're not the main speaker for an event but have been asked to introduce someone who will give the keynote address. Here are several elements to remember when you give your introduction:

- **Keep it short.** Remember that they've come to hear someone else—not you. Forty-five seconds to a minute is long enough.

- **Introduce the title or topic of the talk.** That's the thing most listeners want to hear first.

- **Relate the speaker's topic to the group.** Explain how it's relevant to the listeners so they'll pay attention.

- **Describe the speaker.** Discuss his or her qualifications to speak on the subject.

- **Tell the audience the speaker's name, and sit down.**

The speaker will be grateful, and so will the audience.

PRESENT AWARDS WITH STYLE

You may be asked to speak at a retirement dinner or present an award to an individual or team for an outstanding accomplishment. Remember the following key guidelines:

- Be brief but not so brief that you are too vague about the recipient's unique characteristics.

- Give legitimate, honest praise but don't overdo it.

- Specifically mention what the recipient has done and why the recognition is being given.

- Personalize your presentation so it doesn't sound as if it could apply to anyone.

- Prepare for your talk by gathering information about the recipient of the recognition or award.

TIP
Learn about the person you're recognizing from published information and from colleagues and friends.

Giving recognition is an important role. These guidelines will ensure that you do it with distinction.

BE AN ORGANIZED MEETING FACILITATOR

Most of us spend too much time in meetings because they usually seem very poorly planned. Generally the leader or facilitator does not have a clear program in mind for the meeting. If you are the facilitator, remember the following:

1. Try to accomplish only one objective and be clear with participants about what that objective will be.
2. Carefully lay out the agenda at the beginning of the meeting.

PLAIN ENGLISH
Agenda   A list of things to be decided or acted on at a meeting.

3. Set a firm time limit on the meeting and try to keep it short.
4. Come to clear decisions and action items at the end of a meeting. Otherwise nothing will ever get accomplished. Remember these guidelines and you'll keep your meeting focused and action oriented.

PREPARE AND REHEARSE FORMAL PRESENTATIONS

Sometimes you're asked to give a formal presentation in front of a large group. Each of the chapters in this book contains detailed information that will help you with this type of presentation. For now, here are a few general guidelines to keep in mind:

- **Prepare.** This can't be stated too strongly. Too many speakers leave their preparation until the last minute.
- **Keep it simple.** Don't overwhelm your audience with information just because you have it at your fingertips. They won't remember it anyway.
- **Practice.** Give the talk to colleagues or family members before you deliver it, and iron out the kinks.

These are the basic guidelines that will ensure an effective presentation.

LEARN THE PRESENTATION SKILL SETS

No matter what type of talk you give, there are three skill sets that you should always use. Together they will enable you to become a powerful speaker. These skill sets, known as the "three Vs," are verbal, visual, and vocal.

PERFECT YOUR VERBAL SKILLS

Most of our time in preparing for a talk is spent perfecting our verbal skills. These include ...

- Developing a clear message for the presentation.
- Making the presentation relevant to the audience.
- Analyzing your listeners.
- Outlining the main ideas.
- Gathering evidence to support your ideas.
- Organizing your information.
- Creating visual aids to present verbal information.
- Involving the listeners with open-ended questions.
- Holding a question-and-answer session.

Your organization of the material makes the information easier to understand and more persuasive.

ADVANCE YOUR VISUAL SKILLS

Visual skills do not refer to visual aids. Visual skills are the visual images that you create as a speaker. The more interesting you are to watch, the more likely the audience is to pay attention throughout your entire presentation. Visual skills include ...

- Making eye contact to connect with each of your listeners.
- Using gestures to describe and emphasize ideas.
- Using facial expressions to communicate your feelings and attitudes.

Often these skills are not incorporated and their absence can make the presentation much less interesting than it should be.

DEVELOP YOUR VOCAL SKILLS

Your voice is a key part of your tool kit as a presenter. Vocal skills include ...

- Raising and lowering your voice level for emphasis.
- Changing your pacing to stimulate the interest of your listeners.
- Using pauses to make important points.

Your success as a speaker will be determined by how well you use all of these skills to make a powerful impact on your listeners.

THE 30-SECOND RECAP

In this section you learned how to make public speaking a more positive experience. You've gained perspective on the importance of giving business presentations, and you've been introduced to the skill sets that will make you a better speaker.

Define the Central Message

In this section you learn how to develop the central message of a presentation and at what point to deliver it most effectively.

A humorous cartoon depicts a man thrashing around in the middle of a large pond. On the shore sits a dog watching its master. The man calls out: "Fido, get help!" The second panel of the cartoon shows the dog in a veterinarian's office being examined by the doctor. Clearly the animal had misunderstood its master's message.

How often does the same type of thing occur during a presentation? The speaker walks to the podium and begins talking. He or she presents a long series of colorful slides, filled with statistics, pie charts, and complex graphs. You try to follow along in the package of handouts distributed at the start of the presentation. While the information is interesting, the sheer quantity of it seems overwhelming. About halfway through the talk, your mind begins to wander and you start thinking about that partially finished project that's still sitting on your desk back in the office. Finally the speaker concludes and thanks the audience.

As the speaker leaves the podium, you ask yourself: What point was he or she trying to make? Perhaps it was buried somewhere in all the data and you just missed it. Sometimes the speaker's point isn't clear or easy to spot, but far more often, the speaker never really makes a point at all.

DEVELOP THE CENTRAL MESSAGE

The *central message* is part of your verbal skill set. Developing this message is the most important step in creating a successful presentation. Without a message, a presentation simply doesn't hang together. With a message, the entire presentation is like a great piece of music: All the notes fit harmoniously together around a central theme.

Focus on the Substance

Studies show that a few days after attending a presentation, most of us remember only about 5 percent of what we've heard. It's not surprising. With all the information we receive in a week, it's a wonder that any of it really sticks with us. Information is constantly being thrown at us in meetings, company reports, magazine and newspaper articles, television and radio programs, and on the Internet. Sometimes it's hard to remember what you read yesterday, to say nothing of last week or last month.

Make sure you consider this whenever you prepare a presentation. If your listeners are only going to remember 5 percent of what you tell them, you want to be certain that it includes your central message. It is the core of your presentation. Everything else is just supporting data.

The central message should be clear and simple. No one in the audience should come away having missed it.

Highlight Your Central Message

It's important not to confuse your central message with the subject of your presentation. The subject is usually a large circle of information. An example of a subject might be improving customer service in your department. That's a large subject, and there are many things you might talk about during your presentation. Your job is to focus on a single point within that subject; call it a point of light in the circle if you like. That point is your central message. It's what you want to say about the wide subject of improving customer service.

For example, your central message might be: We need to hire three more customer service representatives; or, we need to streamline our database so we have more information about each of our customers; or, we need to answer each customer's call by the second ring.

Of course, delivering a central message usually requires that you take a position and even stick your neck out. But that's often what it means to be a successful speaker.

Try this exercise. Select two of the following subjects and develop a central message around each of them.

- Your organization's niche in the marketplace
- The company's earnings in the most recent quarter

- Your organization's Web site
- The current method of giving performance evaluations
- An on-site day care center for employees
- The amount of rework in the manufacturing area
- Flextime in your department
- The speed of your organization's R&D process
- The quality of the written communications via e-mail
- Your organization's recruitment programs on college campuses

You should now have a clear sense of how to frame the central message in the subject.

INTERPRET YOUR MESSAGE'S SUPPORTING DATA

So many speakers seem to believe that their mission is to tell you everything they know about their topic. What they're giving you is nothing more than a data dump. As effective speakers, we owe our listeners much more. Our responsibility is to analyze that data, interpret what it means, explain what all of it adds up to. That's our central message.

CAUTION

Don't make your presentation a data dump. Include only information that relates to your central message, and tie the information to the message throughout your talk.

PRESENT YOUR CENTRAL MESSAGE

Good leaders are not expected to mire themselves in detail. We want them to make sense of those details for us. Great speakers present a vision. Just recall John F. Kennedy's inaugural address or Martin Luther King Jr.'s "I Have a Dream" speech.

As a speaker you're supposed to present your vision—your central message: how you see the facts, what they mean, your opinion about them, and your position on what action should be taken on them. To present your vision, or the central message of your presentation, is to lead your listeners to take the action or follow in the direction you propose.

CONSTRUCT A ONE-SENTENCE CENTRAL MESSAGE

Developing your central message is critically important. Too many speakers simply gather information, quickly create some visual aids, then stand up and deliver their presentation. They never ask themselves: How does all this information fit together? What does it all mean? What do I want my listeners to get out of it?

TIP

For each minute that you intend to speak, spend 5 to 10 minutes planning and preparing your presentation.

If you're asked to make an impromptu presentation about developments in your work unit to a group of visiting customers, you won't have much time to prepare. When you do have advance notice, however, and you're free to select the subject yourself, deciding what to talk about should be your first step.

For example, you may be slated months in advance to speak at the local Rotary Club about an important issue that is currently confronting your organization. Start thinking about your central message. What point are you going to make? If the listeners are only going to remember 5 percent of your presentation, what do you want to make sure they remember?

When you have very little time to prepare a presentation, this type of planning is even more important. The central message becomes an organizing principle that allows you to quickly select information that relates to your message and forget everything else. Leave that material for another talk and another central message.

Once you've decided on a central message, you may want to write it down in a single sentence or two. This way you won't forget it. Even more important, you can constantly refer to this sentence as you collect information to present in your talk. All this information should relate to the central message. If it doesn't, leave it out.

CAUTION

Keep it short. If the central message is longer than a sentence or two, then it's too long. Look at it again. You should be able to compress your main point into a few well-chosen words. These may be the same words you use to present your message to the audience.

Present a Single Central Message

Speakers often wonder whether a lengthy presentation should have more than a single central message. Typically your audience will find the talk confusing. Listeners expect you to make a single point and deliver it in as few words as possible. All your other ideas should be subordinate to the central message and provide support for it.

Most speakers say too much. In a presentation, shorter is generally better. No one will criticize you for keeping the talk short. Very few speakers have ever been so good that the audience wants them to keep talking. They'll thank you for getting to the point and sitting down.

Begin with the Central Message

A human resources manager once told me that he liked to "load the cannon." I asked him what he meant by that phrase. The manager explained that he preferred to start by giving his audience a lot of background information and supporting evidence. Once they had digested it, he would make his main point. He called that loading the cannon with data, then firing it—delivering his message.

Engineers and other technical people often present information the same way, and the approach may work well in technical and academic settings, but not in the business world. By the time you "fire the cannon," the audience may already be tuned out and not hear the main point of your presentation.

Suppose you're taking a trip. You pack your bags and load them in the car. Your family jumps in the car with you and you head off down the street. But you don't tell them where you're going. "It's a surprise," you laugh. "You'll find out when we arrive." Most families would want you to stop the car right there. They'd demand to know their destination.

It's the same when you give a presentation. Your audience wants to know the point of the whole thing, where you're taking them. Otherwise they won't be able to follow your talk, nor will they want to.

TIP

Get to the point. Giving a presentation is not the same as writing a mystery story. Listeners don't want you to save the most important information until the end. They want you to get to the point sooner rather than later.

All the preliminary evidence or supporting material won't make any sense unless they know why you're delivering it. Tell them your central message, and then you can tell them everything else.

Make Your Point—Fast

If you bury the central message in the body of your presentation or save it until the end, the audience won't wait for you to get to it. They'll start growing restless, drift off into daydreams, and even fall asleep.

One speaker, the supervisor of a manufacturing cell in a large engine plant, made exactly this mistake when she gave her presentation. She began by giving her audience some background information about the cell. She explained how it had grown in staff and productivity since she had joined the company 10 years earlier.

Then she went on to describe the current functions of the cell. The supervisor discussed the amount of overtime that her team was putting in each week. She mentioned the productivity awards the cell had won in the past.

The speaker pointed out that customer complaints about the cell's products had been increasing recently, and this problem had to be solved as soon as possible. At the end of her talk she finally presented her central message: The cell needed more people to do its job effectively.

Unfortunately, long before she reached her central message, the audience had lost interest in what the supervisor was saying. They had no idea why she'd presented all the preliminary information, what point she was trying to make, or what she wanted them to do.

Present the central message at the beginning of your presentation with sentences like these:

- The main point I want to make today is …
- The one thing I want to emphasize is …
- My central message is …
- My purpose in speaking to you is …

Only if you give your listeners a clear direction of your presentation at the outset can you hope to have them with you at the end.

Get Your Central Message Across

Every successful central message has several key attributes. It should be:

- Simple
- Short
- Clear
- Delivered at the beginning

The central message is crucial; don't be afraid to repeat it several times during the presentation.

The 30-Second Recap

In this section you learned how to develop a central message and when to deliver it so that it will provide structure for your presentation.

Know Your Listeners

In this section you learn about the importance of the audience and how to perform a listener analysis so you can make your presentations more effective.

Every business presentation involves a speaker and at least one listener, if not an entire group of them. This seems pretty obvious. But you'd be surprised at how many speakers seem to operate as if their audience didn't exist. They stare at the floor, speak in a boring monotone, and show very little passion for what they're saying. Not surprisingly, their presentations usually fall on tuned-out ears.

Effective speakers don't speak to thin air; they speak to their listeners.

Remember to Whom You're Speaking

Most of us probably don't look forward to preparing a business presentation. It's easy to become completely absorbed in the process of gathering information, preparing visual aids, and creating handouts. As a result, you may forget about the most important issue of all: What does your audience want to know?

This problem becomes especially noticeable when a speaker introduces a new policy or procedure. Generally the information is presented from the speaker's point of view, not the listeners'.

TIP

Remember the audience. The most important person in any presentation is not the speaker, but the listener.

A speaker I recall began by describing a new quality management program that he and his team had developed and explaining what the new program would accomplish. This was his central message, and, quite rightly, he introduced it at the beginning of the talk.

Then he gave a long background description of each step that his team had taken to decide on the elements of the new program. While this information may have been interesting to him, since he was involved in the process, it held little or no interest for his listeners. What they wanted to find out was how the new program would impact their jobs.

But the speaker did not introduce this information. Instead, he contrasted the new program with the old way of doing things. He pointed out that the quality of the company's products had been suffering in the past. Because many of his listeners believed that they had been doing a quality job, they found his words highly insulting.

Finally the speaker tried to explain the advantages of the new process and how it would impact the listeners. This is what they had been waiting to hear. But it came far too late in the talk—after the audience had been told they were not doing quality work. The result was that most of the listeners were so upset that they had already stopped paying attention by the time the speaker made his point.

The speaker had violated a cardinal rule of good presentations: Always put yourself in the shoes of the listeners and give them the type of talk you would want to hear. Ask yourself how your words would sound to you if you were listening to them. Then decide what you're going to say and how you'll say it.

GIVE THEM THE MEANING

Perhaps you're familiar with the acronym WIIFM. It stands for "What's in it for me?" That's the key question on the minds of your audience as they sit down to listen to your central message. They want to know ...

- How will it benefit me?
- How can I use this information in my job?
- Why is the central message relevant to my life?
- What does it mean to my future here?
- What is the impact of the message on how I do my job?

Another way to describe WIIFM is the *meaning of the message,* which you can find out more about in the part in this section called "Begin with the WIIFM."

PLAIN ENGLISH

Meaning of the message   How the central message relates to the listeners and what they're likely to get out of it.

Make the Message Meaningful

As part of the planning stage for every presentation, you should begin by developing a central message. (See the section "Define the Central Message" on page 621.) After that, determine a second element that describes the meaning of your message to the listeners.

Practice this by doing the following exercise:

1. Decide who your audience will be for a presentation.
2. Select two of the following topics and write a central message for each.
3. Write an additional sentence to express the meaning of the message for your listeners.

The sample topics include …

- Cycle time on the manufacturing floor
- Moving allowances for transferred employees
- Employee participation in community service projects
- Better safety programs at your plant
- Improving tuition assistance programs
- E-marketing on the company Web site
- Sabbatical leaves for managers

You're ready to decide when in your presentation you should state the meaning of the central message.

Begin with the WIIFM

When should you introduce the WIIFM, or the meaning of the message, in your presentation? At the beginning, along with the central message. Listeners want to know what's in it for them as soon as possible. It's the best way to ensure that they'll pay attention for the rest of the talk.

CAUTION

Don't keep the audience in suspense. Always look at your talk from the listeners' perspective. They want to know what's in it for them. You should deliver this information just before your central message or just after it.

To introduce the meaning of the message, you might use sentences like these:

- This is how the (central message) will affect you. As of next Monday ...
- How would you like to make your job easier and more interesting?
- These are the ways this will benefit you.

This may sound like an unsubtle way to introduce the meaning of the message, but your audience will rarely criticize you for being too clear or too straightforward. Communicate the meaning of the message as directly as possible. Next to the central message, it is the most important part of your presentation. Indeed, a statement about the message's benefits may be even more important than the message itself: It may persuade the audience to support your vision.

TIP

Give your WIIFM statement impact. Make the meaning of your message as powerful as possible. Remember: The audience will only listen if they think your message relates to them.

UNDERSTAND YOUR LISTENERS' PRIORITIES

Since the listeners are the most significant people in any business presentation, you should try to know as much about them as possible. This will enable you to present your information in a way that is most likely to appeal to them and hold their interest.

How do you find out about the characteristics of your listeners? Many talks are given to internal audiences, so you may already know many of the key players. If not, talk to colleagues in the organization who may know them. Find out what they are expecting from your presentation.

Preparing a speech for an external audience can be more difficult. Your listeners may be potential customers, employees in another company that is merging with yours, a civic group, or a professional organization. In that case, you may need to: Look for material about your audience in business publications or on the Internet; network to key people in the organization; or if you've been asked to address a civic group, get as much information as possible from the person who invited you about the group and what they're expecting.

RESEARCH AUDIENCE ATTITUDES

The material you gather about your audience should be aimed at answering some key questions.

Are they in your corner, against you, or straddling the fence? This information is critical if you're trying to persuade them to adopt your point of view. You'll need to work a lot harder if most of the audience doesn't see things the way you do.

CAUTION

Make sure you get off on the right foot, by describing any benefits that the audience might derive from supporting your position. If your message is about new procedures, frame your criticism of the current system carefully to avoid offending people who produced the work.

If the key players are resistant, what would convince them to support you? Sometimes you can find out the main reasons why some of the key players in your audience might not support you. It may help to structure your entire talk around dealing with their objections.

How much does the audience know about your topic? Many speakers must address audiences where there are different levels of knowledge and sophistication on a subject. Always pitch your presentation to the lowest common denominator.

What are their positions in the organization? Clearly you would give a different type of talk to peers or subordinates than you would deliver to a meeting of the board of directors of your company.

How do they like their information presented? Some people are persuaded by numbers. They like pie charts and line graphs. Others remember anecdotes or a speaker's personal experiences. The best approach is to vary the way you present information. In a mixed audience, there should be something for everyone.

How long do they expect you to speak? Find out how much time you'll be given. This will enable you to plan the presentation. No one likes a speaker who runs on too long. On the other hand, if the program planner has given you 20 minutes, she wants to make sure you fill the time slot so she's not left with an embarrassing hole in the schedule.

What are they likely to wear? You should always dress appropriately for the occasion. Don't show up in business casual attire if the entire audience is wearing suits. A good rule of thumb is to dress one level above your audience. For example, if they're wearing work clothes, you should be dressed in business casual. That way, you won't feel awkward but you'll still stand out from the audience, as befits a speaker.

Determine Your Goal

As you plan a presentation and think about your audience, ask yourself: What do I want them to do as a result of my presentation? In short, what is your goal? Speakers who fail to ask themselves this question fall far short of achieving their goal.

Perhaps your goal is simply to deliver information to your listeners. You may be giving them a progress report on the installation of a new computer system or you may want them to know about the benefits of a new employee assistance program.

Your goal could be more ambitious. You want to explain a new procedure, step by step, so your listeners will be able to carry it out. It may involve something as simple as the action to be taken in case of a fire drill. Or it may involve something more complex, like the standard procedure for writing technical reports.

Sometimes your goal may be to entertain an audience. If you're speaking at a roast or a retirement dinner, for example, your talk would remain light and humorous.

The most ambitious goal of all is to persuade, or to convince an audience to take action. You may want the listeners to fund a new research project. Getting a key decision-maker to write a check can be difficult because the money might just as easily be spent on something else. You must plan your talk carefully and deliver it forcefully to achieve such ambitious goals.

Continually Measure Your Presentation's Effectiveness

Whatever your goal may be, you can tell whether you're achieving it by examining the faces of your listeners. As you look out at each one of them ...

■ Do they seem to understand what you're saying? Or do they look confused?

■ Are they paying attention? Or do they seem to be daydreaming or slipping off to sleep?

■ Are they nodding in agreement? Or are they shaking their heads as you make your key points?

Whether you realize it or not, each of us is a salesperson as we stand up in front of a group and make a presentation. We must present our information or deliver our explanations in a way that will make them credible and believable to the audience. We must present our persuasive arguments so convincingly that the audience will take action on them.

As good speakers, we're in the business of making a significant impact on our listeners. And we measure success one listener at a time.

THE 30-SECOND RECAP

In this section you learned the importance of delivering a talk that will appeal to your listeners' interests and priorities.

Energy for Effectiveness

In this section you learn how to use energy to add power to your presentations.

One of my colleagues, a communications consultant, serves on the board of a local nonprofit organization. Recently he was asked to become a member of the fund-raising committee. Knowing next to nothing about fund-raising, he decided to take a course at a well-known training institute.

The program was taught by a woman widely respected in philanthropic circles because she had raised millions of dollars for charity. My colleague arrived early in the morning and took his seat along with 20 other people from various charitable agencies in the area. Many of them were new to fund-raising, and they had come to learn the latest techniques from a recognized expert.

The course was very well structured, the information based on the instructor's own fund-raising experiences. It was presented clearly, and it related directly to many of the issues my colleague was grappling with at his own organization. At first, all his attention was focused on the speaker, and he tried to learn as much as possible.

As the morning wore on, however, his concentration started to flag. He thought about a problem he was trying to solve for one of his clients. Then he thought about a suspense thriller he'd seen over the weekend.

At first the lapses in his concentration lasted only a few seconds, but gradually they became longer. At one point, he realized that the speaker had presented several important ideas and he hadn't heard any of them. In fact, he was struggling to stay awake.

Finally, the training program broke for lunch. "Perhaps the afternoon session will be more interesting," he thought. Sadly, it wasn't. About 2:30 P.M., the instructor signaled a break. My colleague decided to take advantage of the opportunity; he collected the materials that had been handed out at the beginning of the class and headed for the door—never to return.

"As I left the building," he recalled, "I tried to figure out why I didn't want to stay for the entire session. The information was clear, and I was very interested in learning more about fund-raising. Then I realized that it was the speaker. She lacked any enthusiasm for her subject. In fact, she was deadly boring!"

SPEAK WITH ENERGY

If you want to be a good speaker, it's not enough simply to present a clear central message. Nor is it sufficient for you to make the message relevant to your listeners so that they'll be interested in it.

Effective speakers do more: They bring a passion and commitment to what they're saying. This passion is infectious. It spreads to the audience and keeps them involved and excited about the speaker's topic, even through a long presentation. This excitement is called *energy.*

PLAIN ENGLISH

Energy   Enthusiasm and passion for your message. Energy should fill your entire delivery so the audience will more readily remain focused on you and what you have to say.

SUPPLY THE ENERGY COMPUTERS CAN'T

Computers are very versatile instruments that can deliver entire presentations, complete with magnificent visual aids. But there's at least one thing they can't do and you can: bring energy and enthusiasm to a presentation.

Unfortunately, many speakers seem to forget this fact. They spend all their time on the verbal component of a presentation—the words. Then they stand up and deliver their material in a boring monotone, with their eyes focused on the back wall instead of on the audience.

They think that words alone, as long as they're clear and 100 percent accurate, will hold the interest of the listeners.

Why not deliver the presentation via e-mail? It would have the same impact and save the speaker and the listeners a great deal of time.

TIP

Say it with energy. One of the best ways to add value as a presenter is to use energy when you deliver a talk.

Energy makes all the difference between a boring presentation and an effective one because ...

- Energy is the human touch that you bring as a speaker.
- Energy gives the audience a reason for assembling and listening to you instead of reading a report about your topic.
- Energy is one of the key differences between a great speaker and a mediocre one.
- Energy will ensure that you, and your message, are remembered by the audience.

Energy involves two of the skill sets that were introduced in the "Define the Central Message" section on page 621. They are your visual skills and your vocal skills.

USE VISUAL ENERGY TO STIMULATE

Many people who take a public-speaking class for the first time recall that a teacher in school once told them not to use their hands when they speak. Gestures, they were warned, might be distracting and make them look like used-car salespeople. As a result, they stand in front of a group with their hands locked together or possibly playing with a ring.

CAUTION

Pay attention to your hands. If you find your hands are doing things that have no relation to what you're saying, stop. These gestures may only distract the listeners from your talk.

When used effectively, gestures can add a great deal of energy to your presentation.

Facial expressions are also part of your visual tool kit, but too many speakers seem content to adopt one deadpan expression throughout their entire presentation. Speakers who smile at appropriate moments, raise an eyebrow, or show some enthusiasm on their faces add immeasurably to the impact of their presentations.

REINFORCE YOUR MESSAGE WITH GESTURES

We live in a visual age. Most of us are accustomed to being stimulated by the colorful images on television, in films, and on the Internet. We expect the same things from speakers.

As a presenter, you can use gestures to create powerful visual images that reinforce the words you speak before a group. The more visually interesting you can be, the more likely you are to stimulate and hold the attention of your audience.

TIP

Remain the focus of attention. Effective gestures help ensure that your listeners will concentrate on you throughout an entire presentation. You'll be too visually interesting for them to tune out and ignore.

The next time you deliver a presentation, try the following approach to using gestures:

1. **Face the audience and plant your feet firmly and slightly apart.** Some speakers like to pace back and forth in front of their listeners. But the pacing rapidly becomes a distraction.

2. **Start with your arms at your sides.** This should be their resting position. From this position, it's easy to raise up your arms and gesture. If you lock your hands, they tend to stay there and never come apart.

3. **As you make an important point, use one or both hands for emphasis.** Don't repeat the same motion continually or you'll rapidly become boring.

4. **When you describe something, use your hands to create a visual image.** If employment figures are going up, for example, indicate this by raising an arm. If inflation is declining, show it by lowering your arm.

5. **Make your gestures as expansive as possible.** Don't look like you're addressing an audience from a phone booth. Enlarge your gestures and extend your arms. Don't worry, you won't look like a carnival barker.

6. **Don't try to plan your gestures.** A former U.S. president was told to improve his speaking style by using gestures. Unfortunately, they looked too planned and artificial, which only made his presentations worse. Most of us use gestures naturally in normal conversation. Apply the same principles when you stand up in front of a group.

TIP

Become aware of the way you use gestures in conversation. Most of us are pretty animated. You need even more animation when you speak to a group because it's larger and you must stimulate more people.

7. **Move out of your comfort zone.** As you start using more gestures in a presentation, it will seem uncomfortable at first. You'll feel as if you're overdoing it. If possible, videotape yourself as you rehearse your presentation. You'll probably be surprised to discover that you weren't as animated as you thought and can use even more visual energy in your presentations.

HUMANIZE PRESENTATIONS WITH FACIAL EXPRESSIONS

Recently I was on a flight from Houston and watched a sitcom on the television monitor without putting on the headphones. It was amazing to discover how much I could figure out about the story simply by watching the characters' gestures and facial expressions, their body language was so demonstrative.

Good speakers use the same approach with their audiences. It's another way to humanize a presentation and make a connection with your listeners.

Show a human face. Look at your listeners, and don't be afraid to smile or grimace when you speak. Audiences generally like to know that there's a real person standing up there with real feelings that show up on your face.

USE VOCAL ENERGY FOR POWER

When you're speaking to another person, especially about a topic of great interest to you, your voice generally demonstrates that enthusiasm. However, many of us seem to believe that a different approach is necessary when we run a business meeting or deliver a formal presentation. Somehow these activities seem to call for a dry tone of voice that remains at the same level from start to finish.

Who says business presentations are supposed to be this way? If you want to ensure that your audience tunes you out, speak in a monotone. It will have the same effect as listening to soothing music designed to lull you to sleep.

A speaker I once heard had the kind of voice a hypnotist would use to put a patient in a trance. Unfortunately, when he delivered his key points, his audience was far too glassy-eyed to hear them.

CAUTION

If you're unfortunate enough to speak directly after lunch, you need to work even harder to keep your listeners awake. Don't speak in a monotone. You must use your voice to inject as much energy as possible into your talk.

To keep your audience's attention and get your message across, use these elements in your vocal skill set:

- **Loudness.** You should raise and lower the level of your voice during your presentation. Varying the level helps ensure that your audience stays awake. By raising your voice, you can also add emphasis to important points.

- **Pacing.** Changing the pacing is another way to add interest to your presentation. Speak a little faster during one section, although not so fast, of course, that the audience can't follow you. Then slow down as you get to an important point.

- **Pausing.** Many good speakers have learned how to use pauses very effectively. As they reach a key statement, they pause just before delivering it. This keeps the audience wondering what's coming next.

- **Tone.** You can communicate volumes about the words you speak by the tone of voice you use. Tone can signify approval or disdain, enthusiasm or disappointment.

Start strong, moderate your vocal energy in the body of the talk, and then end with the highest energy you can muster.

Be Passionate to Be Persuasive

You can't hope to persuade your listeners to change the way they do things unless you sound convinced yourself. Energy puts passion into your presentations. The best speakers know how to combine visual and vocal energy to deliver their words.

In short, all three channels—visual, vocal, and verbal—are open and operating together in an unforgettable presentation.

The 30-Second Recap

In this section you learned how to use visual and vocal skills to add power to your presentations.

Eye-Contact Communication

In this section you learn about the value of eye contact in communicating with your listeners.

Think about all the people you're likely to meet throughout your career; many more than your parents or grandparents, who may have gone to work for an organization and stayed there until retirement. Each time you start another job and meet new colleagues, the ritual is usually the same. You extend your hand, look the other person in the eye, and introduce yourself.

Perhaps you were one of those people who was told repeatedly by your parents, "Always look someone in the eye when you shake hands." It's a way of being polite, of showing respect, and it can even help you remember someone's name after you first meet.

INTERACT THROUGH EYE CONTACT

Eye contact is part of human interaction, whether you're communicating one to one or speaking in front of a group. Studies show that we receive more than 50 percent of our information visually.

Consider what your eyes tell you about other people. You can read their body language and find out if they're feeling comfortable with you or tense and awkward. You can look into their eyes to determine whether they communicate empathy and support or cold indifference.

A major difference between e-mail and in-person communication is that your eyes can pick up subtle signals and hidden messages that e-mail will never reveal. It's one of the reasons why world leaders want to meet face to face, so they can take the measure of each other.

You can also use your eyes to make closer contact with the people in your audience. Your eyes can communicate a wide range of emotions. You can also use your eyes to focus attention on individual listeners and make them feel special and important.

In short, eye contact is part of the added value you, as a good speaker, bring to a presentation.

TIP

Establish eye contact with your listeners from the beginning of your talk to enhance your effectiveness as a presenter.

Avoid Eye-Contact Blunders

When it comes to making eye contact with an audience, speakers use a variety of approaches. Those you should beware of using are ...

- **Peekaboo.** Some speakers like to put their laptop computers on the lectern to project slides. Then they stay hidden behind the computer and deliver the entire presentation without ever making eye contact with their audience.

- **I'm too busy!** The speaker is completely preoccupied reading a prepared text or a set of notes and never looks up and acknowledges that the audience is in the room.

- **Please, help me!** These speakers spend much of the time looking up at the ceiling as if they're hoping for divine intervention to help them through their talk.

- **I'm reading the eye chart.** Similar to the last approach, except that this time the speaker is staring at the back wall as if reading an eye chart throughout the presentation.

- **I'm not worthy to stand in front of you.** These presenters keep their eyes cast down at the floor as they speak. They seem to be saying that they're unqualified to address the audience.

- **Watching a tennis match.** Some speakers try to make eye contact by *scanning* the room. Their heads are constantly moving back and forth as if they're watching a tennis match.

PLAIN ENGLISH

Scanning   A method of eye contact in which the speaker's eyes are continually moving from one person to another. This approach will leave your eyes tired, your neck aching, and the audience wondering what you're trying to accomplish.

Speakers who adopt one or more of these techniques usually do so because they're nervous and afraid to look at any individuals in the audience. Unfortunately, any of the preceding approaches prevent you from making real contact, whether it's in a conversation or with your listeners. You risk having the people you're talking to feel ignored—or even worse—unappreciated and insulted.

Use the Three-Step Approach

As you may recall from earlier sections, eye contact is one of the techniques in your visual skill set. Used correctly, your eyes can significantly increase your impact as a speaker. Here's an approach that has proven to be quite successful:

1. **Find a pair of eyes.** As you begin your talk, look for one person in the room and speak directly to that individual.

2. **Deliver a thought.** Continue looking at that person until you have communicated a complete thought. How long is a thought? It can be an entire sentence. Or it can be much shorter—the information between the commas in a sentence. For example, suppose you were saying: "We need to expand our sales in Europe, in Latin America, and in the Far East." You might deliver only the opening of the sentence (the information before the first comma) to one individual.

3. **Pause and look at someone else.** After you finish delivering a thought to one person, pause and move your eyes to someone else. Then communicate your next thought.

CAUTION

Keep your eyes focused on your audience. Never deliver a thought unless you are speaking to a pair of eyes.

Use this approach throughout your entire presentation. It enables you to make person-to-person contact with individual listeners in your audience.

You may be thinking that this technique might work with small audiences, but you couldn't possibly look at each person in an audience of 100 or more. That's true, but you don't have to look at every person who's there. When you look at one of them and deliver a thought, the people sitting nearby imagine that you're looking at them, too.

Remember that you're probably standing some distance away, so it's difficult for your audience to be sure of whom, exactly, you're really looking at.

Find Your Eye-Contact Pattern

As your eyes move from one listener to another, avoid a regular pattern of making eye contact. For example, if people are sitting in a U shape, don't start with a listener at one end and work your way from person to person around the room. Start with a listener on one side, then look at someone on the other side, then look at a listener in the middle. This will prevent listeners on the far end from dozing or daydreaming because they figure you'll have to go around the entire room before you look at them.

It may take you some time to grow accustomed to using eye contact effectively, but if you make a conscious effort to speak to one person, pause, then speak to another, you'll reap huge benefits as a presenter.

EYE-CONTACT QUESTIONS AND ANSWERS

Here are the answers to some of the most common questions people have about eye contact:

How long should I look at a person? I don't want to stare and make the individual feel self-conscious. Use your own judgment. About six seconds spent looking at one person usually seems long enough. But if you have several allies in the audience and want to spend more time making eye contact with them, then do so.

Should I try to spend about the same amount of time looking at each person during a presentation? Obviously you can't time it exactly. Try not to shortchange anyone. Sometimes, people sitting in the back or on the far side of a room feel as if the speaker is paying no attention to them. Be sure you don't overlook those listeners.

How should I deal with a key decision-maker? You'll probably want to focus more eye contact on this listener because he or she has more power than anyone else. But make sure you know who the real decision-maker is. Some speakers have been fooled, and they've given too much of their attention to the wrong person.

As you've gathered, there is no fixed pattern for making eye contact, but if you practice the advice in this section your use of eye contact will become more effective with every presentation.

CONTROL PACING THROUGH EYE CONTACT

It may sound counterintuitive, but your eyes can actually control the pace of your presentation.

Most of us have a tendency to talk much too fast. Perhaps it's only a reflection of the speed at which events seem to move in the twenty-first century. Perhaps you also find yourself with too many job responsibilities, so you constantly feel the need to hurry through each activity.

Many speakers talk too rapidly out of nervousness and a natural desire to get the presentation over with as quickly as possible. But whatever the reason, speaking too fast can make it very difficult for an audience to follow what you're saying.

Using the proper method of eye contact can eliminate this problem. Deliver a thought to one listener, pause as you switch your eyes to another listener, then—*and only then*—deliver your next thought. This will reduce the pace of your presentation. Your audience will thank you for it.

TIP

Since patterning eye contact is not something we naturally do when making a presentation, it will take practice. But you'll quickly discover that pausing in between thoughts will not only work wonders on your pacing, it will give you a little extra time to think about what you're going to say next.

Get Feedback Through Eye Contact

Eye contact opens an important two-way channel of communication between you and your listeners. Not only can you communicate your interest in them, they can give you critical feedback on your performance as a presenter.

Here are some of the signals to look for and what you can do in response:

- **Some listeners already have their eyelids at half-mast.** Your energy level is probably too low. Raise your visual and vocal energy.

- **Your listeners look confused after you explain a key point.** Your explanation or visual aid was probably not clear enough. Go over the information again.

- **A key decision-maker is shaking her head from side to side.** You obviously failed to convince this person. It's time to roll out a more persuasive argument.

- **Your supervisor starts reading his mail.** You're probably boring him. Maybe you can inject some information—an anecdote, for example—that will interest him. Or perhaps your talk has already gone on too long and you should bring it to a speedy close.

- **Your audience is watching you with rapt attention.** Great! Whatever you're doing is working well. Keep up the good work.

TIP

Plan ahead. Your audience analysis should help you figure out what will and won't work with your listeners. But sometimes you can be wrong, so prepare an additional story or slide or some backup statistical data to use if you're losing your listeners.

Person-to-person eye contact is a way to get an instant evaluation from your listeners. You can read it in their eyes and in their body language. If what they're telling you is negative, you can often react quickly to put your presentation back on track.

PRACTICE YOUR NEW PRESENTATION SKILLS

So far you've been introduced to a variety of verbal, vocal, and visual skills. Clearly it's difficult to practice all of them at once. You're probably already spending enough time on the words for your presentation. The vocal and visual skills, on the other hand, may be new to you. So you'll need to spend more time on them.

At first, using gestures, vocal energy, and eye contact may take you out of your comfort zone. It's just like trying any new skill. Concentrate on only one skill at a time and use it as much as you can in your next presentation. Then keep adding more of the skills to your repertoire as you give additional presentations. Soon you'll be using all of them successfully.

THE 30-SECOND RECAP

In this section you learned about using eye contact to improve your presentations.

Gather Your Evidence

In this section you learn how to collect material to support your central message.

Where do business leaders get their information? Generally, it comes from reading great amounts of information, drawing on their own past experiences—successes as well as failures—and, perhaps most important, talking to many different people.

For example, Michael Bonsignore, chairman and chief executive of Honeywell International, spends two weeks each year traveling to the company's plants and holding town meetings with employees. For Bonsignore and leaders like him, this information becomes the raw material for their presentations. They know where to look for important, new ideas; how to organize this material logically; and how to present it persuasively to their audiences.

UNDERSTAND THE IMPORTANCE OF EVIDENCE

If every talk consisted of only a central message and the meaning of the message, it would be very short—perhaps no more than a minute or two. You may be thinking that this would be a welcome change from all those long-winded presentations that you currently suffer through every week. And you're right.

Yet without supporting *evidence,* the central message would be like a gossamer floating on air. It's simply your opinion and nothing more. Good evidence is essential because it …

- Grounds your central message and gives it a structural framework.
- Logically supports your point of view.
- Confirms that you've done your homework on your topic.
- Demonstrates your expertise as an authority on the material that you're presenting.

PLAIN ENGLISH

Evidence   Data that either proves or disproves a viewpoint, like the material presented in a court of law to prove a person's innocence or guilt.

Evidence is an essential element in a presentation, but before you get down to the tough business of gathering it, you'll have to do some preliminary work.

MIND-MAP YOUR MATERIAL

One of the most effective approaches to gathering evidence is a process called *mind-mapping.* Here's how it works:

1. Draw a circle in the middle of a piece of paper.
2. Inside the circle write your central message.
3. Think of ideas that will support your message. You may have gathered these from your reading or from conversations with other employees.
4. Write a brief description of each idea on a line that radiates out from the circle.

PLAIN ENGLISH

Mind-mapping   A process of brainstorming ideas related to your central message and graphically displaying them so you can decide which ones are relevant and important.

Don't discard any idea; include everything that comes to mind.

Your paper will look something like a spider's web. Now go back and examine all the ideas that are in front of you. Some may seem irrelevant or trivial and can easily be eliminated. Others may seem related to each other and can be grouped together.

Finally, you should have several important ideas that support your central message. These will become your primary pieces of evidence.

Don't regard the mind-mapping process as final. Think of yourself as an explorer. While putting together your presentation, you may uncover another key idea that should be included. Add it to your talk, like a new river being drawn on an explorer's map.

Choose Three Supporting Ideas

Presenters often wonder how many supporting ideas they should include in a presentation. Another way to look at this question is to ask yourself: How much can my listeners remember?

Perhaps you're planning to include handouts in your presentation, so you decide that it's safe to present a great amount of material because the audience can always review the handouts later. Don't kid yourself. Most people may never look at those handouts again.

It's best to operate as if the only information your listeners are likely to remember is what you say. Recall the 5 percent rule, which studies show is the amount of information that listeners will retain after a presentation. Perhaps they'll remember as many as five to seven key ideas, but more likely it'll be only about three.

There's something about the number three. All of us are familiar with the three musketeers and the three blind mice. Most presentations consist of three parts—an opening, a body, and a conclusion. Three of anything seems to be a quantity that's easy for us to remember.

TIP

Try to use the power of threes in your presentations. Present three key ideas as supporting evidence. Under each idea, introduce no more than three related concepts.

Present Your Ideas Creatively

Most of us recall ideas best when they're presented not simply as abstract concepts but in a form that we can see—at least in our mind's eye. In literature, among the most popular devices are metaphors and similes. An author will take an abstract emotion like fear and describe it as a "gnawing at the pit of the stomach," for example. That gives readers a way to relate to the idea of fear.

You can do the same thing as a speaker: Dress up your ideas in bright clothes and present them in interesting ways to bring them to life for your listeners. Here are a few ways to do it:

- **Analogies.** These are like metaphors and similes, which suggest comparable qualities of things. For example, a speaker might compare the current structure in his organization to a patchwork quilt without any clear design. Another speaker might make a comparison between the company's manufacturing process and a smooth-running automobile. Analogies help listeners to visualize what the speaker is talking about.

- **Statistics.** Many business presentations are filled with statistics— sometimes to the exclusion of everything else. Obviously statistics are appropriate if you're delivering a financial report to the CEO, but they can be overdone with other audiences that may not think in statistical terms.

- **Quotations.** Quotes from a recognized expert in a field can lend the voice of authority to what you're saying. They can come from articles in magazines and newspapers, and many publications also host online forums where you can find out what other people are thinking about your topic. In addition, some speakers like to use quotations from their peers, subordinates, or customers to give credence to a central message.

- **Examples.** These can come from almost anywhere. Perhaps you've used examples from other companies in your field to provide support for your key points. You might also draw examples from vendors and customers. Each time you can cite a "for instance" it strengthens your arguments.

TIP

Variety broadens the appeal of your material. Some listeners relate best to statistics, while others may prefer analogies or anecdotes.

■ **Anecdotes.** Personal stories from your own experience or from someone else's seem to be retained by many listeners long after a presentation has ended. Introduce a concept, then follow it with an anecdote to illustrate your point. Or tell your story, then draw a moral or a point from it. Either approach can be extremely effective.

Try to include as much variety as possible in the way you present your ideas. Variety is one way to keep your audience interested and involved in your presentation.

PLAN YOUR INFORMATION-GATHERING PROCESS

Collecting information for your presentation may stretch out over several days or several weeks, depending on when you start working on a scheduled speech. Make sure you leave enough time to do an adequate job.

As you come across articles or other data that look promising, store them away in a file. You'll probably collect far more than you need. But this will give you a broad range of material from which to make your final selections.

Draw from your own experiences. Before you start collecting data, don't forget to mine your own experiences for possible quotations, anecdotes, and so on. Spend some quiet time thinking about things you know that could support your ideas, and expect some useful thoughts to occur to you while you're taking a shower, jogging, or commuting to work.

APPLY CRITERIA FOR INCLUDING EVIDENCE

Since you'll probably have more information than you need, how should you decide what to include and what to omit? Use the five-C test:

■ **Correct.** The material must be accurate. You don't want to present anything that has flaws in it. This will only be an embarrassment.

■ **Complete.** Make sure that the information, especially statistical data, is complete, and there are not any important points missing.

CAUTION

Don't take any chances with your evidence. All of it should conform to the five-C criteria. Otherwise, you may risk undermining the strength of your arguments and losing your audience.

■ **Clear.** An analogy or anecdote should be easy to understand and clearly relate to your central message or supporting evidence.

- **Consistent.** The evidence you present should be consistent with the expectations of your audience. One speaker I recall opened her presentation with an off-color joke that seemed completely inappropriate to the occasion. The audience was turned off for the rest of her talk.
- **Clever.** Try to select examples that will stimulate your audience, not boring, overused material.

Once you've gathered information, you're ready to take a first stab at an outline for your presentation.

CREATE A PRELIMINARY OUTLINE

You now have the ideas and the supporting evidence to create a preliminary outline.

1. Write out each of your main points.
2. Under each point, list the supporting information that you have collected.
3. Evaluate the material in terms of the five criteria described in the preceding section.
4. Decide whether any point appears to be weakly supported and needs more data. If so, go back to your file and look for more information. If none is there, you may have to do additional research. Company publications may be helpful, especially if you're speaking to a group of employees about an internal problem.

 TIP

Most presentations have very tight deadlines so there usually isn't much time to find more research material if you need it. The quickest approach is the Internet. Use one of the search engines, type in your topic, and see what comes up.

The best presentations include enough evidence to convince even the most skeptical listeners.

THE 30-SECOND RECAP

In this section you learned how to collect, sift, and organize supporting evidence for the ideas in your presentation.

Organize Your Material

In this section you learn how to present information in six organizing patterns so your listeners can remember it more easily.

According to a recent business survey, more and more chief information officers—the people in charge of the computers—are being promoted by their companies to CEOs. If we ever needed further proof that information is the most valuable resource an organization can possess, this is surely it.

As speakers, we operate like chief information officers, taking raw data and turning it into useful information that our listeners can use. This process involves organizing our data into points which form patterns.

LEARN THE SIX ORGANIZING PATTERNS

By creating patterns, we give shape to the data we use to support our central message. It's the same as taking the pieces of a jigsaw puzzle and fitting them together to form a picture. We enable our listeners to see that picture; that is, we bring them to a conclusion (our central message) based on the information that we present.

TIP

Develop a pattern. The pattern is like a formal outline for a talk. It will not only help you arrange your facts and points in a logical order, it will also help you remember all of them when you deliver your presentation.

The material that you deliver in a presentation can generally be organized into six different patterns. Each of them presents information in a clear, logical way.

The six patterns of organization are as follows:

- The whole and its parts
- Chronological order
- Problem-solution
- Spatial order
- The news reporter approach
- The best alternative

One pattern will probably work better than the others in organizing your facts for the presentation. However, you might also decide to use more than one pattern to organize different parts of the same talk.

THE WHOLE AND ITS PARTS

This is probably the most common type of pattern and the simplest one to execute. You present your central message, then break it into individual subtopics, or points, and discuss each of them.

Central Message: New, young managers are not remaining with our company for more than a year. There seem to be three reasons for this problem.

Points:

> Eighty-hour work weeks
>
> Too much travel
>
> Compensation packages that are smaller than those our competitors offer

CAUTION

Lead with your best shot. In the whole-and-its-parts pattern, don't leave your most important point until last. Always present it first. In case any of your listeners need to leave before you finish, or lose interest in your talk partway through, at least they've heard your most important argument.

Central Message: We need to improve our tuition assistance program for employees.

Points:

> Companies need a highly trained work force to be competitive in the marketplace.
>
> A good tuition assistance program encourages employees to broaden their skills so they can do more than one job, making them far more valuable to our organization.
>
> A generous program will enable us to retain more employees.
>
> An effective program will enhance the reputation of our organization, attracting a higher number of talented young people.

CHRONOLOGICAL ORDER

Speakers often use this pattern to describe a series of past events that have led up to or caused a current situation. The events follow each other in a specific chronological order. In your presentation, you'd often use time order words: *first, then, next; in 1998, in 2000; in the first quarter, in the second quarter,* and so on.

Central Message: Our current manufacturing problems have resulted from a series of events that began more than two years ago.

Points:

> First, we took on a large new contract without enough employees to carry it out.
>
> Then, our vice president for quality left for another organization and was never replaced.
>
> Next, we put too much emphasis on meeting production quotas instead of manufacturing quality products.
>
> Finally, our major customer left us for another vendor.

Speakers also use the chronological pattern to describe the steps in a process. These steps must be presented in a specific sequence or the process will not work correctly.

 TIP

Fill in with details. These patterns provide the basic structure for a presentation. Under each subtopic, or point, you can add as many details as necessary to fully explain it.

Central Message: In case of a serious chemical spill, you must follow these steps:

Points:

> Evacuate the area upwind of the spill.
>
> Put on the proper personal protective gear.
>
> Return to the spill area and begin cleaning up the chemical.
>
> Put all cleanup materials in an approved receptacle.
>
> Hose down the area to remove any remaining chemical.

PROBLEM-SOLUTION

This type of speech usually contains three parts: a description of the problem and its impact on your organization, a discussion of the causes that created the problem, and a presentation of your solution.

Central Message: There have been too many accidents on the manufacturing floor during the past year, and we must do something to deal with the problem immediately.

Points:

> Several types of accidents have occurred: falls from ladders, burns, severe electrical shocks.

Causes Include:

> Inadequate knowledge of safety procedures
>
> Lack of proper training
>
> Safety procedures given too low a priority in the plant

Solutions:

> A new safety training program
>
> Regular presentations by the plant manager and his staff emphasizing the importance of safety

Central Message: Our organization must bring products to market much more rapidly.

Point:

> The problem is causing us to lose market share to our competitors.

Causes Include:

> A culture that has been research driven, not market driven
>
> Past dominance in our field with very little competition
>
> An unwillingness to learn from our competitors

Solutions:

> Streamlining the R&D process
>
> Benchmarking our competitors
>
> Creating teams that include research and marketing people

SPATIAL ORDER

This pattern works well when you're trying to create a visual picture for listeners. Suppose you want to explain the layout of a new facility, or the geographical distribution of your company's retail outlets. This information can be easily organized into a spatial pattern.

TIP

When you use a spatial order pattern, your talk will probably include various signal words, such as: *front, back, center, left, right; north, south, east, west;* or specific geographic locations such as: Atlanta, Houston, and so on.

Central Message: We're adding more stores in the South in response to increased customer demand for our products.

Points:

Building plans for the Atlanta region

Acquisition plans for existing store chain in Tampa area

Construction of new stores in Charlotte region

New store openings in greater Houston

THE NEWS REPORTER APPROACH

In this organizational pattern, a speaker provides answers to the five Ws: *who, what, when, where, why,* and sometimes *how.* This pattern will seem very familiar to your listeners because they read newspaper and magazine articles and watch news reports on television.

The *what* is often contained in the central message, and the rest of the presentation tries to answer the other questions.

Central Message: There is too much downtime because of smoking breaks.

Points:

Who: Employees from every department are leaving their desks to smoke a cigarette.

When: These breaks are occurring at regular intervals throughout the day, more of them for people with a heavy cigarette-smoking habit.

Where: The smokers are congregating outside the building. Some of them must travel five floors to the smoking area. This extends their downtime.

Why: This is an important issue because we are losing too much productivity and something must be done about it.

TIP

Following this presentation, you might then open the meeting to a discussion about the issue and possible solutions.

Central Message: We should hold a company-wide event to celebrate our substantial sales increases in the past quarter.

Points:

When: The event could be held next Friday.

Where: The company cafeteria would provide food and drinks.

Who: All employees would be invited. But the event would recognize those teams that contributed to our increased sales.

Why: A recognition event sends all employees the message that increased sales have a very high priority in our company.

THE BEST ALTERNATIVE

This is similar to the problem-solution pattern discussed earlier. The speaker presents a problem, then considers several solutions. Each one is eliminated, in turn, until only a single, best solution remains.

Central Message: We need to improve the quality of materials that we are receiving from several of our vendors.

Points: So far we've tried various approaches to improve vendor quality:

Letters to the vendors asking them to make improvements

Visits by our CEO and her staff to vendor plants

Quality training programs for vendors sponsored and paid for by our organization

None of these approaches has been completely successful. Quality problems still exist.

Best Alternatives:

Call in vendors and threaten to end their relationship with us.

Set a three-month time limit for them to make improvements that meet all our quality standards.

If standards are not met, cancel our arrangements with the vendors.

WARM UP TO PATTERN-MIXING

Don't worry if one of the patterns doesn't seem to fit your presentation. It may organize itself into several of them. Or your material may be best organized as simply a series of related topics. These should be presented in order of importance, from most important to least important.

THE 30-SECOND RECAP

In this section you learned about six methods of organizing information for your presentation.

Create Successful Presentations

In this section you learn how to develop an effective opening, body, and close for your presentation.

If your opening sentences are delivered in a dull monotone and they're dry as dust, the audience may decide that this is just another boring talk and they can think about something else. Hook the audience in your opening, and you can hold them in rapt attention through your entire presentation.

Listeners should not be required to work hard to figure out what you're talking about. Ease your audience through the transition from the opening to the body of your presentation by summarizing points made in the opening and sketching the outline of the body.

Your presentation shouldn't just end; close with a call to action and a specific follow-up agenda: "I'd like you to get back to me with your comments on my proposal by next Wednesday," or if you're making a financial request, direct it to the key decision-maker: "Can I look for your approval by the end of the week?"

Every good presentation should be tightly structured. It should take listeners on a straight path from the opening, through the body, to the conclusion and a call for action. Follow the advice in this section and you'll have the keys to a successful presentation.

OPEN WITH A FLOURISH

There's an old saying that "first impressions are lasting impressions." Your listeners form an impression of you immediately, from the first words that you speak. If you start with a high level of energy and your ideas are interesting, you're likely to have the listeners' attention.

TIP

The most important part of any presentation is the first 60 seconds. If you don't capture the attention of your listeners then, they may decide to tune out for the rest of your talk.

It may sound pretty harsh to suggest that a presentation can be made or broken in the opening. After all, you might have spent several days putting together a 30-minute talk, designing visual aids, and printing handouts.

Unfortunately, the listeners probably don't care about all your hard work. If they aren't hooked in the opening minute, they may not hear much of what you're going to say afterward, and all your hard work will be for nothing.

Listeners are much like surfers on the Internet, clicking on and off Web sites. An audience can click you on and off just as easily. One manager explained that when he went to meetings, some of the attendees would routinely begin reading their mail a few minutes after the speaker started talking. They had already lost interest. You certainly don't want the same thing to happen when you stand up to talk.

CONSIDER FIVE SUCCESSFUL OPENINGS

There are several effective ways to open a presentation. The approach that you decide to use will depend on a couple of things:

- **Your listener analysis.** What will work best with your audience.
- **Your material.** What seems most appropriate for the information you're presenting.

OPENING ONE: CENTRAL MESSAGE AND MEANING

Every presentation should have the central message and the meaning of the message in the opening. Sometimes this is all the opening needs, especially if the central message comes as a surprise to your audience.

Suppose you were speaking to a group of Wall Street analysts who were expecting fourth-quarter earnings at your company to be down. Instead, you told them that earnings were up by 5 percent. That's a startling central message that will certainly grab their attention.

CAUTION

Don't be like speakers who spend their time preparing the details of their talks and forget about the opening. Remember that every good talk must be listener-centered. Your listeners want an opening that will knock their socks off.

The meaning of the message can also be quite an attention-getter. This is where the audience finds out WIIFM (what's in it for me?—see "Know Your Listeners" on page 627, for more on WIIFM). If the benefits are substantial—

for example, an increase in pay, more stock options, shorter work hours—
your audience is sure to listen to everything you tell them.

Opening Two: An Analogy

Some presenters like to begin their talks with an analogy. Analogies can be
valuable in relating a theoretical concept to something that's familiar and easily understandable to your audience.

The more unusual the analogy, the more likely your listeners are to remember
it. For example, a series of books has been published over the past few years
that take the leadership skills of great historical figures and apply them to the
workplace.

Among these famous leaders are Attila the Hun and General Ulysses S. Grant.
Since most of us might not immediately think of Attila when looking for
ideas to guide a modern CEO, the analogy attracts our attention and might
even persuade us to buy the book.

TIP

If you begin your presentation with an analogy, make sure it's an
appropriate one that relates to your central message. Then tie the
analogy and the message together for your listeners.

Opening Three: Voice of Authority

Another way to open a presentation is to cite an authority. This may be a
quote from the president of your company, some benchmarking information
from a survey you conducted of competitors in your field, or it might be some
information from a newspaper or magazine article.

The more unusual and startling the information is, the greater the impact is
likely to be on your listeners. Whatever material you decide to present should
also be directly related to your central message.

You can present the message first, followed by the quote from the president or
a statistic from the article. Or you can reverse the order and begin with the
information from your authority.

Suppose you are speaking on the importance of a college education in an
individual's career. You might begin with an article from *The Washington Post*
that reports that seven years ago a majority of Americans believed that we had
too many people with a college degree. But today 75 percent of all adults
believe that we should have as many college educated young people as
possible.

OPENING FOUR: TELL A STORY

Nothing is more powerful than beginning a presentation with a story that illustrates your central message. Former President Ronald Reagan was a wonderful storyteller—one of the skills that made his speeches so effective.

You can draw on a story from your own personal experience, from something you've read, or from the experiences of other people.

CAUTION

Don't be long-winded. If you plan to open your talk with a story, make it short. There's nothing worse than an anecdote that goes on and on and never seems to get to the point. The audience grows impatient and stops listening.

One of the best presentations I ever heard was delivered by a clergyman who told the story of a governor in one of the Southern states. The governor had been an orphan as a boy, and been ridiculed by children who had parents, but he worked hard, put himself through college, and eventually rose to the highest office in the state. As the governor often told other people: "I knew I was a child of God and I could do anything." This was the minister's central message.

OPENING FIVE: ARTFUL HUMOR

Speakers often wonder whether they should use a joke to open a presentation. The answer is: *It depends*—on several factors:

- **How skillful are you at telling jokes?** Some speakers forget the punch line or mix it up with the beginning of the joke, and it falls flat.

- **How well do you know your audience?** If you're going to use a joke, you must be sure that your audience will respond well to humor. Even more important, you must know what kind of humor they like. Many a speaker has told a joke that he thought was funny but the audience didn't.

CAUTION

Play it safe: Avoid off-color humor. Ribald stories are generally inappropriate for business presentations and may even offend many listeners. You'll immediately lose their support for your message.

- **How does the joke relate to your central message?** Speakers sometimes open with humor to break the ice, but the joke has nothing to do with their central message. Be sure there's a clear connection between your joke and the message, or the listeners may become confused and may not fully comprehend the message when it's delivered.

Transition the Talk with Summaries

Once you've completed the introduction, segue into the body of your talk. This information should be organized according to the patterns discussed in the last section. Before you jump directly into the body of your talk, however, it's helpful for the listeners to know what you're planning to do.

For example, if your central message is the need for a new transportation facility, you might lead off the body of your talk by saying: "I'm going to tell you three reasons why we need to build this new facility." Then present the reasons.

After you discuss each reason, it's a good idea to briefly summarize what you said before going on to the next one. These summaries give your listeners a little breathing space, which allows them to briefly recall what you've already explained before moving on to the next point.

You might even use phrases such as, "Let me briefly review what I've covered," or, "Let's take a moment to summarize the first reason we need a new facility."

After you finish with the second reason, summarize again and briefly recall the first reason, then you can continue with words like, "the third reason we need this facility is."

Keep it simple and streamlined. If your speech becomes too complex or confusing, the listeners will probably stop paying attention.

TIP
The structure of your presentation should be as tight as possible, with no extraneous ideas or unnecessary points. Try to relate each summary to your central message.

By telling your listeners what you plan to say and using frequent summaries, you can lead them gently to the conclusion of your presentation.

Close with a Call to Action

The closing of your presentation is often the last opportunity you'll have to make an impact on your listeners. You want that impression to be as powerful as possible, so here are the elements to build into your close:

1. End the presentation with as much energy as possible.

2. Repeat your central message and the meaning of the message.

3. If you want your listeners to do something after leaving your presentation, make sure to give them a call to action.

Too often, meetings end without any of the participants knowing what the next step should be, or what they ought to do. As a result, meetings are often a waste of time and no action is ever taken.

The call to action, which wraps up your talk, is just what it says. You ask the listeners to do something based on what you've told them and you give them a deadline for taking action.

THE 30-SECOND RECAP

In this section you learned about how to develop the opening, the body, and the conclusion of a talk.

Interact with Audiences

In this section you learn how to increase audience participation.

A children's book author was recently asked to address a group of young people and their parents on the subject of writing biography. The author decided not to deliver a lecture, which he thought would bore the audience. Instead he opened his talk with a few words about biography, then asked the children some questions. He wanted to involve them in the presentation as much as possible.

The author began by asking them what interesting biographies they had read lately. Then he wanted them to tell him why they like biographies. He also knew that some of the children were writing their own biographies about family members, so he asked them to tell him about their research.

At the end of the presentation, one of the parents came up to the author. "You know," she said, "that talk was just like having a conversation in your living room. Everybody had a chance to participate."

GET YOUR LISTENERS TALKING

Most speakers take their responsibility very seriously. Many believe that the entire burden of making a presentation should be squarely on their shoulders; in short, that they should do all the talking.

Where is it written that all the time allotted to your presentation should be filled with the sound of your own voice? Why should you put so much pressure on yourself? Wouldn't it be much easier if you could take a break from speaking and let the audience participate?

Shakespeare said that "brevity is the soul of wit." Good speakers know when to stop talking and pass the baton to members of the audience so they can become involved in the presentation.

CAUTION

Don't hog the limelight. Very few speakers are so compelling that they can fill 30 minutes or an hour completely by themselves. The audience needs a break from your voice; let them have a chance to speak. They'll thank you for it.

This turns the talk from a "you-they" to an "us" situation; all of us are involved in the presentation. The audience will be flattered at being asked for their thoughts.

Avoid the Close-Ended Question

The purpose of asking a question is to initiate a dialogue with your listeners. You want them to talk. Unfortunately, certain types of questions will elicit little or no response from your listeners. These are called *close-ended questions*. They include …

- A question that can be answered with a show of hands.

  Example: How many people here enjoy public speaking?

- A question that has a yes or no answer.

  Example: Do you think the company should improve its health benefits program?

- A question that has only one correct answer.

  Example: How many sales offices do you think our organization operates in the United States?

PLAIN ENGLISH

Close-ended questions   Questions that have only one correct answer or a brief one- or two-word response.

The last question may elicit no response at all; unless people are positive of the answer they're not likely to raise their hands for fear of looking foolish.

CREATE DIALOGUE WITH OPEN-ENDED QUESTIONS

If you want to begin a dialogue with your listeners and elicit a meaningful response from them, you must ask *open-ended questions.*

PLAIN ENGLISH

Open-ended questions   Questions that have no right or wrong answers or one-word responses. They ask for listeners' opinions, attitudes, feelings, and experiences.

For example, one speaker was talking to an audience about ways to expand the use of their telephones at home. This would enable them to do more work from a home office.

He discussed such things as using the phone for fax transmissions and Internet access, and adding an answering machine. After presenting his central message, the speaker asked his listeners a question:

> How are you currently using your telephone?

This was an open-ended question. Everyone in the audience could answer it because all of them could talk about their own experiences using the telephone. There was no right or wrong response.

Another speaker was delivering a talk on fire safety. She asked her audience this open-ended question:

> When you hear the alarm for a fire drill, how do you respond?

Each person in her audience had been in this situation at one time or another and could answer the question. This enabled the speaker to find out how her listeners were dealing with fire drills, which was the topic of her talk.

TIP

Dialogue questions are part of your verbal skill set. Although they may not work in every situation, you should think about using them as you prepare a talk. It's a good way of keeping your listeners involved.

INCORPORATE DIALOGUE QUESTIONS EFFECTIVELY

Have you ever attended a cocktail party and found that you didn't know a single person in the room? The feeling can be overwhelming. One way to deal with it is to walk up to someone who is standing alone, extend your hand, introduce yourself, and ask a question: "What brings you to this party?" And after you've talked about that topic, you might ask: "What kind of work do you do?"

We call these questions *ice-breakers*. Some people go so far as to make a fairly long mental list of them. If one question doesn't work, they try another.

PLAIN ENGLISH

Ice-breakers   Questions that begin a dialogue, or interaction, between a speaker and listener(s).

One place to use a dialogue question is at the beginning of your presentation, as an ice-breaker. You can start with a question that's related to your central message, elicit a response from your listeners, then introduce the message. Or you can begin with the central message, then ask the question.

Open-ended questions can also be used almost anywhere in the body of a presentation where they seem to work.

You might even ask an open-ended question in the closing of your presentation. Then restate your central message and follow up with a call to action. This is a powerful sequence for your listeners to experience just before they leave the presentation.

PLAN AND REFINE DIALOGUE QUESTIONS

If you decide to use dialogue questions in your presentation, here are a few points to keep in mind:

- Prepare the questions carefully during the planning stage of your presentation. Think about your audience and what types of open-ended questions will work best with them.

- Remember the difference between an open-ended and a close-ended question. Sometimes you can ask a close-ended question and follow it up with an open-ended question.

  Examples: How many people think they could be better speakers? From your own experience, what skills would make each of you a better speaker?

- When you present an open-ended question, give your audience time to respond. Sometimes it takes that long for your listeners to realize that you've just asked them to participate in your presentation. Then they need time to formulate their response.

- If no one says anything, don't just wait a split second and immediately move on with the rest of your talk. Give the listeners time to say something.

■ Sometimes an audience may be hesitant to speak. If so, respond to the question with your own experience. This will "prime the pump" and often the audience will begin talking.

TIP

The best television interviewers, people like Barbara Walters, know how to ask the right questions to get people to talk about themselves. Study their techniques to help you formulate open-ended questions.

■ Remember, this is not a question-and-answer session. You don't need to respond to a listener's experience except to say something like, "Thank you," or, "That's very interesting." Then move on to someone else.

■ After several people have answered the question, segue back into your presentation. At this point, it's probably a good idea to summarize what people said.

After your summary, repeat your central message, or the last key point in the body of your presentation; then introduce any new ideas.

USE DIALOGUE QUESTIONS ADVANTAGEOUSLY

One of the most important goals of every good speaker is to keep the audience awake. Once they start nodding off, everything you say is a waste of time— yours and theirs—because they won't hear it.

Dialogue questions are one way to keep your audience involved in a presentation. It's pretty hard for them to daydream if they're busy answering your questions.

A dialogue question will usually take most listeners by surprise. It's the last thing most people expect during a presentation. They were assuming that your talk would be just the same as everyone else's—that you'd do all the speaking, not them.

The element of surprise is often enough to pick up the pace of your talk. Indeed, if you see people are beginning to lose interest in what you're saying, an effective way to bring them back again is to ask a dialogue question.

TIP

Hold something in reserve. Prepare one or two extra dialogue questions just in case your talk begins to run out of gas. Audience participation is an effective way to add renewed energy to your presentation.

The primary purpose of a dialogue question is simply to involve your listeners. But sometimes a question can do even more. It can help put the audience on your side, which can be very useful, especially if you're delivering a persuasive presentation. It can also give you a better feel for the listeners' concerns, and for what they need to hear.

Suppose you're delivering a talk on expanding the usefulness of your home telephone, like the speaker in an earlier section of this chapter. You know, from your listener analysis, that most of the audience currently uses the phone for very limited purposes. Therefore, an open-ended question can open the door to your central message: Your home telephone can be far more versatile than the way it's currently being used.

One word of caution: Don't expect too much from your open-ended questions. It's enough to use them to produce audience participation.

THE 30-SECOND RECAP

In this section you learned how to use open-ended questions to produce a dialogue with your listeners.

Make It Simple

In this section you learn how to speak in clear, simple language so your audience will immediately comprehend your message.

Political leaders often open themselves to criticism because they talk in doublespeak so no one can understand what they're saying. While these standards may be all that we expect from politicians, we should expect far more from ourselves whenever we give a business presentation.

Our goal should always be to present even the most difficult ideas as clearly as possible. A formal presentation doesn't mean that you should resort to ponderous, $50 words that go over the heads of your listeners.

Newspaper reporters are taught to write at a sixth-grade reading level, not because their entire audience is at that level, but so that readers can grasp the meaning of what they read quickly and easily.

The same thing goes for your presentations. When good speakers phrase a sentence or select a word to deliver to their listeners, their guide is: Keep it simple and short.

Speak Naturally

One manager began his presentation this way:

> A vulnerability comparison of the basic and upgraded chemical spill response system was performed to address a DOT requirement and to examine the impact of the system upgrades on the vulnerability of this facility in case of a chemical incident.

If you're wondering what the speaker was saying, so were the listeners. The message was, in fact, quite simple, but the speaker used far too many complicated words to deliver it. Compactly phrased, the message was ...

> We compared the new chemical response system with the old one to see if the new system was better.

Instead of using 40 words, the speaker could have said the same thing in only 19—less than half that number. Instead of using words like *upgraded, vulnerability,* and *chemical incident,* the speaker could have communicated in a simple, conversational style.

 CAUTION

Don't impress—express. Don't try to impress your listeners with the extensiveness of your vocabulary. Just express yourself in everyday, conversational language.

A talk is just that—talking, so you should speak just as you would if you were talking to another person across the desk. Speeches should be like conversations, not filled with pompous-sounding, ambiguous words that leave the audience trying to guess your meaning.

Use the Active Voice

Most business communication seems to occur in the passive voice. The subject is being acted on by the verb.

Examples:

> The *man was hit* by the girder.

> The new *project was started* by the team in the second quarter.

Many speakers not only use the passive voice, they also like to depersonalize their information as much as possible.

Example:

> A decision was made to reduce our marketing budget.

Perhaps the speaker doesn't want us to know who made the decision. That way, in case something goes wrong, no one will be blamed for it.

There is nothing inherently wrong with using the passive voice. If, however, you're trying to persuade your audience to take action, the passive won't do it; it's much too weak. Instead, you need to speak in the active voice.

When you use the active voice the subject is doing the acting.

Here are two examples comparing the passive and active voice.

>**Active:** The manufacturing team should put on a third shift to handle the increased workload.
>
>**Passive:** A third shift should be put on by the manufacturing team to handle the increased workload.
>
>**Active:** The company should spend more money to market its new products in Europe.
>
>**Passive:** More money should be spent by the company to market its new products in Europe.

In each case, the active is stronger and more forceful than the passive. It also uses fewer words. If you expect to do any convincing, especially if your listeners are skeptical, use the active voice. It will give your words far more impact.

WATCH OUT FOR JARGON

Many presentations are filled with a form of language called *jargon*. It's English, all right, but the words don't really mean very much because they've been so overused. You've heard some of these words:

>*synergy, bottom line, paradigm shift, proactive, touch base, think outside the box, win-win, leverage, reengineering the company*

PLAIN ENGLISH

Jargon   The obscure and often pretentious language of a special activity or group. There's no need to resort to meaningless business jargon when you speak. Use standard English. The English language is filled with a great variety of powerful words.

One organization became so tired of listening to these words that several employees designed a jargon bingo game. Each time a speaker at a meeting used jargon, participants marked it off on their bingo sheet. The first one to fill in five squares vertically, horizontally, or diagonally won. It was something they did to pass the time while they tried to concentrate on a boring presentation.

SHOULD YOU AVOID ACRONYMS?

Every profession and organization uses technical terms and *acronyms*. While acronyms cannot be avoided, don't assume that everyone will understand what they mean when you include them in your presentation.

PLAIN ENGLISH

Acronym   A word formed by the first letters of words in a phrase. For example, radar is an acronym for radio detecting and ranging.

Whenever you introduce an acronym, explain what each of the letters represents. There's nothing worse than listening to a speaker who sprinkles a speech with acronyms and never tells the audience what they stand for. Some listeners will feel left out, excluded from those "people in the know" who supposedly understand what you're saying. As a result, they ignore the rest of the presentation.

MAKE IT CONVERSATIONAL, WITH PRONOUNS

Many speakers make their presentations unnecessarily formal by never using a personal pronoun. They constantly talk about "the company," "the organization," and "the department."

In the military services, speakers were accustomed to using phrases like "the command has recommended," and "the facility has decided." You'll be delighted to know that, according to recent directives in the armed forces, speakers are now expected to use more informal language in their presentations to make them more listener-friendly.

CAUTION

If your presentation has very few personal pronouns, or none at all, chances are it's much too stiff for the occasion.

Personal pronouns like *we, our, I,* and *you* are supposed to be part of every communication, whether oral or written. Perhaps it's time for people who work in the private sector to address a group as if they were talking to someone across the lunch table, and keep their language informal and conversational.

DEFLATE YOUR VOCABULARY

Why use big words, when you can say something in plain English? Evaluate your next presentation to determine whether you're planning to use any of the words in the following list. If so, replace them with ones that are simpler.

TIP

The next time you attend a presentation, listen carefully to the speaker's choice of words. Does he or she try to impress you with high sounding words and phrases or rely on down-to-earth language? Which approach works better for you and communicates the message most effectively?

Big	Simpler	Big	Simpler
accompany	go with	accomplish	do
accorded	given	accrue	add
adjacent to	next to	advantageous	helpful
allocate	give	apparent	clear
ascertain	find out	attain	meet, reach
caveat	warning	comprise	include
commence	begin	component	part
deem	believe	designate	choose
effect changes	make changes	employ	use
enumerate	count	evident	clear
expiration	end	facilitate	help
finalize	finish	function	act, role
identical	same	implement	carry out
inception	start	in order to	to
initial	first	in proximity	near
interface with	meet	in reference	regarding to
magnitude	size	methodology	method
optimum	best	promulgate	issue
pursuant to	by, per	remuneration	pay
subsequent	next, later	terminate	end
transmit	send	utilize	use

REMOVE NONWORDS FROM YOUR TALK

Some speakers punctuate their presentations with nonwords, including: *ah,* *um,* and *you know,* between each thought. The constant use of such nonwords can become very distracting to listeners. One of the best ways to eliminate this problem is by practicing effective eye contact. Instead of saying *um,* pause between thoughts for a second of silence. Move your eyes from one listener to another, then start speaking again. You'll reduce the number of nonwords in your talk almost immediately.

CHOOSE YOUR WORDS CAREFULLY

From time to time, I hear speakers make embarrassing mistakes by using one word when they mean to say something else. Sometimes the same mistakes show up on a visual aid. Practicing your talk in front of a friend or family member can help you catch errors like the following.

Common Errors

affect	have an influence	**effect**	result; to bring about
allusion	reference to something	**illusion**	a mistaken perception
anecdote	story, personal experience	**antidote**	medicine to fight disease
appraise	measure, assess the value	**apprise**	inform in detail, notify
desert	dry, sandy area	**dessert**	final course of a meal
formally	in a dignified manner, according to the rules	**formerly**	previously, in the past
ingenious	clever, very skillful	**ingenuous**	innocent, naïve
moral	good; the lesson of a story	**morale**	spirit, sense of well-being
personal	individual, personal	**personnel**	the employees in a department
uninterested	not interested, neutral	**disinterested**	not caring

THE 30-SECOND RECAP

In this section you learned how to select the best words to deliver the information in your presentation.

Banish Those Butterflies

In this section you learn how to deal with stage fright when you give a speech.

The CEO of a large communications firm once explained how she dealt with pressure situations, like standing up and giving formal presentations.

As a child, she recalled, she played competitive tennis and somebody would always tell her, "You have such composure." At least that's how she looked on the outside. "Inside, I was dying, either because it's the beginning of a match and I'm so nervous I want to get sick, or I'm thinking, 'I'm about to lose this match in the third set.'"

Through competitive sports, she added, "I learned how to manage the balance between the adrenaline, which is helpful, and the wanting to be sick." It's that burst of adrenaline that she still relies on to pump her up whenever she has to address a large group of people.

THINK OF BUTTERFLIES AS ADRENALINE

Mostof us feel butterflies when we stand before an audience. The founder of a large nonprofit organization, who had addressed hundreds of groups, admitted that she always felt very nervous before the start of her speech.

The butterflies, or *stress,* we feel also produces the adrenaline rush that can help us become successful. It gives us a quick burst of energy that we can channel into delivering our presentations. The trick is to let the adrenaline do its job and not let the sick feeling in the pit of our stomach overcome us when we look out at the room full of listeners who seem to be hanging on every word.

PLAIN ENGLISH

Stress   A heightened mental state produced in response to a threat, either real or imagined, like thinking that the audience may start laughing when you start to speak.

Don't worry about your dry mouth and moist palms. Remember that hundreds of people have been exactly where you are. They overcame it and so can you. There's a five-step process that will help you beat the butterflies and deliver a successful presentation.

STEP ONE: PREPARE, PREPARE, PREPARE

When it comes to preparing for a presentation, many people much prefer to procrastinate. Then, at almost the last minute, they start to panic. That panic carries over into the actual delivery itself and reduces its effectiveness.

Earlier sections have outlined all the stages in planning a presentation. These include defining your central message and the meaning of the message, which you may accomplish quickly. Others, like gathering evidence, organizing the material, and developing your visual aids, are far more time-consuming. To stay focused, develop a schedule for your presentation.

First, figure out how many hours or days you need for each step. Many speakers discover that they should have started their preparation much sooner, and they may already be short on time. And remember to be generous in case some unforeseen emergencies arise. For example, you may need to take a business trip that will cut into your preparation time.

Then work backward from the day of the presentation to the date where you should begin working on it. Put each step on the schedule in the order in which it should be done.

 CAUTION

Use a schedule and stay on it. Try to schedule a short block of time every day to prepare your presentation. Make it a high priority. Preparation usually takes far longer than you think it will.

You may work on some steps, like preparing your visual aids, while you're developing the opening, body, and closing of your talk.

The planning stage is the most important part of any preparation. By rushing through it, you can easily make embarrassing mistakes that will lessen the impact of your presentation.

Remember this rule: Don't procrastinate: Plan and prepare! It's the best way to reduce your nervousness on the day of the presentation.

STEP TWO: PRACTICE YOUR DELIVERY

Make sure you leave enough time in your schedule to practice your presentation before delivering it. If something doesn't sound quite right when you give your presentation, it's too late to do anything about it. Chances are that your stage fright will get worse, and everyone will know it by your quavering, shaky voice.

A much more effective approach is to build in one or two practice sessions for yourself a day or two before the presentation. Stand in front of a mirror and rehearse your delivery, using the verbal, visual, and vocal skills.

If you feel awkward delivering your central message, change the wording. If your gestures look weak, raise your energy level.

To evaluate your strengths and weaknesses you may want to videotape yourself and review the tape, making any necessary adjustments in your delivery.

Another option is to practice in front of colleagues or family members who can give you immediate feedback. Several practice sessions may be necessary until you've eliminated any serious problems and brought your delivery to a high level of excellence.

 TIP

If you don't have a video camera, try taping yourself on an audio-tape recorder. You'll be able to evaluate your vocal energy and verbal skills and make any necessary improvements in advance.

There's an adage that practice makes perfect. That may be an overstatement, but practice will certainly make improvements in your presentation. It'll help you feel more comfortable with your delivery and reduce your stage fright on presentation day.

Step Three: Meet the Audience

If I'm feeling nervous before speaking to an unfamiliar audience, I often try to chat with a few people as they enter the room. I introduce myself and try to find out something about them. By getting to know some of my listeners, I'll see some familiar faces in the audience when I stand up to speak. When I deliver my opening I try to concentrate on these listeners, who seem almost like friends.

The opening, of course, is the most important part of the presentation. This is when you can least afford to sound nervous. Yet the beginning of a talk is also when you're most likely to feel unsettled.

Arrive early to a presentation and meet a few of your listeners informally before the talk begins. You'll feel more at ease as you start to speak.

Step Four: Unleash Your Energy

The stress that comes from looking out at a large audience awaiting the start of your presentation unlocks adrenal energy in your system. It can take the form of sweaty palms and rubbery legs, or you can use that adrenaline far more productively. Simply channel it into your gestures and use it to increase your visual energy.

Channeling adrenal energy accomplishes two things: It dissipates much of your nervousness, and it enables you to open the presentation with a high level of energy. That will capture the attention of your audience.

CAUTION

Don't let nervousness paralyze you. The vocal and visual energy you need in your opening will not be high enough. Unfortunately, this can create a poor impression with the audience and undermine the effectiveness of the entire presentation.

If you're feeling nervous at the start of a talk, the last thing you may want to do is increase your energy level. It will probably take you out of your comfort zone. But raising your energy works.

Use your gestures to emphasize key points and to describe important concepts in your talk. You'll be carried along on a high wave of enthusiasm that will immediately make you feel better while adding extra power to your presentation.

Step Five: Use Eye Contact

If you want to increase your level of nervousness, try scanning the audience at the beginning of your talk. Your eyes will be taking in so much visual stimulation that your brain will rapidly feel overwhelmed.

All those people, all those eyes will be staring back at you. It's enough to activate our primitive fight-or-flight response. Since we can't fight, our first inclination is to run out of the room as fast as possible. Of course, you can't do that either. So you just become more and more nervous.

Remember the principles of eye contact discussed in the section "Eye-Contact Communication" on page 639. Pick a single set of eyes, perhaps someone you know or a person you met before the beginning of the presentation. Then start speaking. That turns your presentation into a one-to-one conversation. You're just talking to another person. It's the same as having a dialogue across the desk.

Keep repeating the same procedure throughout your talk. As if by magic, the rest of the audience seems to disappear, at least momentarily, and you're concentrating on just one person at a time.

Many speakers admit that this is the technique they find most helpful in decreasing their level of nervousness. They also remind themselves that the people in the audience are usually on their side. Listeners don't enjoy seeing anyone fail. Especially if many of them are speakers themselves, they usually have empathy for you and want you to succeed just as much as you do. Keep this in mind, and it will help boost your confidence when you make a presentation.

THE 30-SECOND RECAP

In this section you learned a five-step process for dealing with stage fright.

Dealing With the Details

In this section you learn the importance of handling the logistics of your presentation: being on time, checking the audiovisual equipment, and arranging the room.

All of us have probably experienced that momentary panic when we realize that we may not have left ourselves enough time to travel to an important appointment. Then we get caught in traffic, and we know that we'll be late. This is especially embarrassing if you're scheduled to speak at a large conference.

There's nothing more nerve-racking than rushing into a room full of people who have been waiting impatiently for you to arrive. Your entire talk gets off on the wrong foot. Instead of beginning with a powerful opening, you're forced to apologize to your listeners for being late.

One of the most important responsibilities of any speaker is knowing the schedule and keeping to it.

TIME FLIES

No matter how carefully you've prepared and rehearsed your presentation, it won't be as effective if you arrive late to deliver it. Arriving on time should be a top priority. The following suggestions may sound fairly obvious, but you'd be surprised how many speakers overlook them.

■ Make sure you know the date of your speech. You wouldn't be the first speaker to get confused and miss the date of your talk or arrive a day early. Remember to call a week or so in advance just to confirm the date. Sometimes dates are changed and the conference planners forget to inform everyone.

- Leave yourself plenty of time to arrive at a speaking engagement. Call ahead to find out how long it should take you to get there. Then add at least a third more time in case of unexpected delays.

- Be sure you know where you're supposed to speak. So many hotels and conference centers sound the same that it's easy to mix up one place with another and arrive at the wrong location.

- Get a good set of directions to your destination. Call the event planner or consult one of the services on the Internet that can map out a route for you.

TIP

Try to arrive at your speaking engagement early enough to give yourself time to check out the room as well as any equipment you may be using during your presentation.

CHECK OUT THE ROOM

When listeners are comfortable, they're far more likely to pay attention to your presentation. Their comfort is often determined by the conditions in the room where you're speaking. Before the day of your presentation, call ahead and ask some questions about the room, such as ...

- **How large is it?** The room should be big enough to easily accommodate the number of participants that are expected to attend your talk. If the room is too small, they'll be uncomfortable.

- **Where are the restrooms located?**

- **Can I control the temperature?** There's nothing worse than a room that's too hot or too cold, especially when there's nothing you can do about it. Ideally your room should have its own temperature controls that you can operate yourself. If not, you should know how to contact a service technician who can adjust the temperature in the room for you.

- **Will there be refreshments?** If you're scheduled to give a lengthy presentation or a half-day workshop, you may want to take periodic breaks. When light refreshments are available near the workshop room, the breaks become far more enjoyable. Refreshments not only reinvigorate your audience, they can give you a renewed burst of energy to continue your presentation.

■ **What is the seating arrangement?** There are several ways to arrange the seating in a room. Some speakers want a classroom arrangement, with all the chairs in long rows. For a smaller group, you may prefer a few tables arranged in a more intimate U shape. However, if you're planning team activities, separate tables with chairs grouped around them may be the best arrangement for your presentation. Have the room set up to your specifications in advance.

CAUTION

Keep your cool. Sometimes there's little you can do to change a room that doesn't meet your expectations. Explain the problem to your listeners and ask them to work with you to make the best of a difficult situation.

There's no guarantee, of course, that the room conditions will always conform to your requests. But by arriving at your presentation substantially ahead of schedule, there may be time for you to make some adjustments; for example, changing the seating arrangement or finding a larger or smaller room if necessary. It will make the presentation far more pleasant for your listeners while giving you a far greater chance of success.

Double-Check the Equipment

Many presentations have broken down because of some kind of equipment failure. While you can't eliminate every problem, anticipating them can save you a great deal of trouble later while you're giving your talk. When it comes to equipment, Murphy's Law is always operating. Here are a few steps to help you deal with it:

■ **If you're planning to use an overhead projector, take an extra lightbulb with you.** Overhead lightbulbs have a way of blowing out just when you need them the most. Some projectors have a backup bulb.

■ **Arrive at your speaking engagement early to check out the projector.** Find out whether it has two bulbs and if both of them are working. If one bulb is already bad, replace it with the spare you brought.

■ **If you've decided to present a series of slides with a laptop computer, as a safety measure, create a backup slide presentation on an extra disk.** Sometimes slide programs develop a glitch on the day you're supposed to show them. Test out the disk in advance to make sure it's running smoothly.

■ **Try out the projection equipment for the slides before beginning your presentation.** If there's any problem, find an audiovisual technician and obtain new equipment.

TIP

If you use overheads, number the transparencies. In case you drop them and they get out of order, it will help you put them back in sequence.

■ **If you're using a microphone, try it out in advance to make sure it's operating properly.** It may be attached to a podium, or it may be a small, portable device that you can pin onto your clothing. Some microphones produce loud feedback, which interferes with your presentation; it can be very annoying when you're trying to speak. Adjust the microphone or, if you can't, ask an audiovisual technician to provide a replacement.

REMEMBER THE LITTLE THINGS

Don't overlook the details that go into planning a presentation. It's easy to become so involved in developing your message or preparing your visual aids that you forget about a little thing that's necessary to deliver them effectively.

Remember to check those mundane details, such as when and where you're supposed to speak, the setup and size of the room, and the reliability of the equipment you'll be using. All these factors are essential to making your presentation a success.

THE 30-SECOND RECAP

In this section you learned about some important logistical considerations to remember whenever you give a presentation.

Ten-Point Presentation Primer

In this section you learn how to deliver a presentation that will get you an ovation from your listeners.

Successful oral communication depends on a three-step process:

- **Preparation.** Includes defining your central message and its meaning to the listeners, gathering and organizing your evidence, designing dialogue questions, and creating visual aids.

- **Practice.** Involves rehearsing your presentation in front of a mirror, video camera, tape recorder, or small audience of family or co-workers.

- **Presenting.** Is the actual delivery of your talk—applying all the efforts you made in the presentation's development stages when you stand up to address your listeners.

Perhaps the best way to describe the last step, presenting, is to compare it to playing a round of golf after you've finished hitting balls on the driving range. When you finally get up on the first tee, you're not entirely sure you'll be able to duplicate those long, straight drives you may have been hitting in practice. Relax. Even the pros feel nervous in tournament play. When they do, professionals concentrate on all the fundamentals they've learned on the golf course. Do what they do: Recall all the key points in this book, learn and practice the 10 points described in this section, and soon, hearing applause will be par for the course.

TAKE THE ROUTE TO SUCCESS

When you're getting ready to speak, focus on the task at hand and remind yourself that you've done everything possible to make the presentation a success. You'll probably still experience some nervousness, which is only natural. Remember to use that adrenal energy to your advantage by injecting more power into your presentation.

TIP

Most listeners come to a presentation ready to give you their attention, at least for a few minutes. But that may be all you have, so make the most of it. Start your talk at a high energy level.

As you begin to speak, these 10 pointers will help ensure that not only your message, but you, the speaker, will make a lasting impression on your audience.

POINT ONE: MAKE EYE CONTACT

As you approach the podium, it's easy to feel momentarily overwhelmed when you look out at all the people in your audience. Direct your attention to one person and a single set of eyes and turn your presentation into a one-to-one conversation.

Speak to a single person, even while you're saying words that are meant for the entire audience. Don't forget that while you're looking at one person, others seated nearby believe you're looking at them, too. Once you've completed the first sentence, find another set of eyes and continue speaking.

It's easy to forget this technique and try to look at everyone. Don't; your talk won't be as powerful.

POINT TWO: OPEN THE CHANNELS

Many speakers focus on the words. They want to make sure that everything they say comes out just right. Studies reveal that what listeners remember most is not the words, but your delivery. Audiences are far more forgiving than you think. They will tolerate stumbles, pauses, and hesitations. So start your presentation by opening up all the channels—the verbal, the visual, and the vocal.

Beginning with your hands locked together and your voice at the level of a dull monotone is no way to command the attention of your audience. Let them know at the outset that they're in the presence of a powerful speaker, one who commands authority. You undoubtedly know more about your subject than they do. Speak with all the energy you can muster!

POINT THREE: CREATE A RHYTHM

Unless your talk is extremely short, it's impossible to maintain a high level of energy throughout it. You'll be exhausted and your audience will be worn out, too.

Good talks are like the tides that ebb and flow. Your energy should be high at the opening. This is the time to make a good first impression. High energy also helps dissipate your *performance anxiety*.

PLAIN ENGLISH

Performance anxiety   That natural uneasiness we feel before performing any difficult task in front of other people.

Throughout your talk, however, the energy level can go up and down. This enables you to emphasize certain key ideas that the audience should remember.

Close your talk at a high level of energy, especially as you repeat your central message and deliver a call to action.

POINT FOUR: ENERGIZE WITH GESTURES

If you look at your listeners and they seem to be losing interest, your energy level has probably begun to sag. Increasing your gestures can pick up the entire presentation.

It's very difficult to speak in a monotone while you're gesturing emphatically. A high level of visual energy will increase your vocal energy. Suddenly your presentation seems reinvigorated, the audience is brought back to life, and you are their center of interest again.

Unfortunately, you can't wait too long to apply this technique. A talk that proceeds at the same slow, quiet pace far into its body may be beyond rescue. By the time you reach the conclusion, all the energy in the world may not succeed in resuscitating your listeners.

Don't expect that the verbal channel will carry you through a presentation. Your listeners need stimulation for their eyes and ears as well. Give them what they need.

POINT FIVE: USE DIALOGUE QUESTIONS

Dialogue questions can serve a variety of purposes if you let them. They get the listeners involved in your presentation. By hearing what your audience says, you can also gauge their temperature: how they stand on the issue and what they think of your ideas. Perhaps it confirms your opinion that they're eager for a change, or you may pick up some hesitation in a few of your listeners. That may indicate that you need to work even harder to "sell" your message.

CAUTION

Don't be a control freak. You don't have to know exactly what the audience may say, and it's usually quite easy to summarize their responses with a general statement and segue back to your talk.

After you listen to their responses, summarize them briefly. You might use phrases such as: "I can see you have a wide range of opinions on this subject," or, "It helps me to know how you feel about this issue." Then go back to your talk.

POINT SIX: DON'T PANIC

Sometimes your talk may be flowing along smoothly and suddenly you can't remember your next idea. It's easy to push the panic button, but it's the worst thing you can do to your presentation. Instead, take a second or two and refer to your notes. Or if the next idea is sitting on a visual aid, turn and look at it. It gives you a little breathing room.

Don't be afraid of silences or feel you must apologize to your audience for them. They weren't expecting perfection, anyway. A brief pause will appear only natural to them, although it may seem like an eternity to you.

POINT SEVEN: GO WITH THE FLOW

Suppose you're the third or fourth speaker on a program and the conference planner asks if you can shorten your talk substantially because the other presenters ran too long. That's not a difficult problem if you've organized your talk around a central message. Open with your message. It is the key idea that you want to deliver, and everything else is just supporting information.

Then cut down the amount of evidence you plan to deliver and make sure that your most important supporting data come first in the presentation. You can easily fit your talk into the new time slot.

POINT EIGHT: KNOW THE EQUIPMENT

There's nothing more upsetting than presenting your audiovisual aids and fumbling with the hardware as you try to operate it. Overhead projectors never seem to have the on-off button in the same location, and brands of projection systems for PowerPoint slides run differently.

The message is simple: Familiarize yourself with the audiovisual equipment before you start to use it. If you look like a klutz up there with the technical hardware, your credibility and professionalism may be damaged in the eyes of your audience.

POINT NINE: NEVER MEMORIZE PRESENTATIONS

Trying to memorize a speech will almost surely land you in trouble. You're likely to forget a line, which will throw off the rest of your talk, and you may draw a blank on what you're supposed to say.

Concentrate on the thoughts you want to deliver, not the words. The likelihood is that if you present a speech more than once, some phrases will remain in the talk; others will disappear, to be replaced by better ones.

The audience will remember very few of your words; they'll remember your ideas. Write them out as notes and refer to them as necessary.

TIP

Some speakers rely on memory aids such as acronyms created out of a series of words that summarize or begin their main ideas. This approach may help you the next time you deliver a talk.

POINT TEN: EVALUATE YOURSELF

After you finish a talk, take stock of your delivery. Evaluate your mastery of the three channels of communication.

Don't criticize yourself. Begin by focusing on what you did right. Then look at areas where you may need improvement. Set goals for yourself. Perhaps you should try to double your vocal energy next time you speak.

Solicit feedback from listeners who attended your presentation. Don't simply ask them whether they liked the talk. Most people will say yes because they don't want to offend you. But this tells you nothing.

Instead, ask them to comment specifically on your use of eye contact, the clarity of your central message, your energy level, your visual aids, and so on. A little probing will often result in some useful feedback that will help you the next time you give a talk.

The goal, of course, is to realize your full potential and become the best speaker you can be, to even receive a standing ovation when you finish your presentation.

THE 30-SECOND RECAP

In this section you learned about 10 points that can improve your delivery of a presentation.

Handling Questions and Answers

In this section you learn how to handle a question-and-answer session in a way that will impress your audience.

The tall, gray-haired CEO had just completed a nearly flawless presentation about the company's reorganization plan. Then he opened the floor to questions.

A listener in the front row put up his hand. "You've told us everything except what we want to know most of all," he said. "How many of us are going to lose our jobs in the reorganization?"

The CEO attempted a smile but he was clearly uncomfortable. He tried to deal with the question, but his response sounded vague.

The listener shot back. "You're not leveling with us. What are you trying to hide?"

The CEO's face became flushed. He denied the listener's accusation and spoke in glowing terms about the upcoming changes and how they would improve the company. "I hope I've answered your question," he said.

"No, you haven't," the listener said angrily, rising from his seat. "All of us are still waiting to hear about the numbers. How many jobs are you going to eliminate?"

"Frankly, there's been no decision, yet," the CEO said. But the employee in the front row wasn't satisfied. He started to ask another question.

"I'm sorry," the CEO said, backing away from the podium. "I have to go." And with that, he hurriedly left the room. His entire presentation had become a shambles.

ANTICIPATE THOSE QUESTIONS

A question-and-answer session following a presentation can make or break your entire performance. If you're not ready for the questions, you can look like a fool; or worse, a dissembler. And you can lose control of your entire talk to someone in the audience who is trying to get the better of you.

As you prepare for a presentation, don't forget to rehearse for questions and answers. That means trying to anticipate the questions and develop credible answers to them. You can usually guess what some of the questions are likely to be, so there's no excuse for not being ready to answer them.

You can do something as simple as jotting down a list of possible questions and composing your answers. You can also rehearse the session with family members or co-workers.

TIP

Imagine that you're the president of the United States about to hold a news conference. With the help of your advisors, you prepare by anticipating the questions you're likely to be asked, and rehearsing your answers.

Remember, the very last impression that the audience will have of your presentation is likely to be the question-and-answer session that comes at the end of your talk. It should be just as strong as the rest of yourperformance.

LEARN THE FIVE-STEP APPROACH

Rehearsing for a question-and-answer session will make you feel more comfortable when you stand in front of an audience. When it actually comes time to deal with their questions, here's a five-step approach that can be very helpful.

STEP ONE: THE OPENING

Begin the session by telling your audience that you have a specific amount of time to handle questions—5 minutes, 15 minutes, whatever it is. Then ask the listeners if they have any questions.

As you do so, raise your hand. That indicates to the audience that you'd also like them to raise their hands when they ask questions instead of just shouting them out. This technique gives you greater control over the session.

STEP TWO: LISTENING

The question-and-answer session is one of the few times in a presentation when you're expected to listen instead of speak. As the first listener asks a question, listen all the way through.

As speakers, our tendency is to begin composing an answer before the listener has finished asking the question. Perhaps it comes from our days in elementary school, when some of us raised our hands to answer a question before the teacher had finished asking it. If the question wasn't what we thought it would be and the teacher called on us, it was very embarrassing if we didn't know the answer.

Don't start thinking about your answer until the listener has finished asking the question. It may not be the question you're anticipating, or you may not understand it, especially if the listener is not entirely fluent in English.

If you're not sure what the question means, say so. Then, ask the listener to repeat it.

STEP THREE: REPHRASING THE QUESTION

Before you answer a question, rephrase it. This enables anyone in the room who may not have heard the question to know what it is. There is nothing worse for your audience than listening to your answer without having heard the question. The answer rarely makes very much sense.

In addition, rephrasing the question gives you several additional seconds to frame your answer. This may help you sound more knowledgeable.

Rephrasing does not mean repeating. For instance, if you presented a new program, someone may ask: "You haven't outlined the costs of what you propose. Are they likely to be high or low?" It takes too long to repeat the entire question. Instead, you can simply say: "You asked about costs," or, "regarding the costs of my program," or just "costs." This sums up the question in a few key words for your listeners.

Suppose a listener has asked you a provocative question. Then you should try *neutralizing* it.

PLAIN ENGLISH

Neutralizing   To answer a question removing the pejorative terms—neutralize them—and answer the question in the way that suits your purpose. This does not mean changing it. Your listeners will immediately recognize what you are trying to do and you'll lose credibility.

We all know the old story about a senator who was asked by a reporter: "Senator, when did you stop beating your wife?" Trying to answer that question would make it seem like there was some truth in it. Instead, the senator rephrased and neutralized the question: "You asked about the relationship I have with my wife."

STEP FOUR: ANSWERING THE QUESTION

Begin your answer by making eye contact with the listener who asked the question. Then involve other members of the audience by making eye contact with them. As you come to the end, don't look back at the person who asked you the question. Finish your answer by making eye contact with someone else. This may be a difficult technique to remember but it can be extremely useful. Why?

If a listener has asked you a provocative question, and you complete your answer by making eye contact with the questioner, it's an open invitation for him or her to try to embarrass you again. The best tactic is to ignore the questioner, and it's much easier to do if you're looking at someone else when you finish your answer. Otherwise, the entire session can become a repartee between you and the questioner, who may eventually get the upper hand. Remember the employee at the beginning of this section who drove the CEO from the podium.

CAUTION

If the key decision-maker wants to keep asking you questions, you may have no choice but to keep going back and answering them. This person must be fully satisfied or your presentation may not be successful.

STEP FIVE: COMPLETING THE SESSION

Once you've come to the end of the session and answered the final question, you might say: "That's all I have time for today." At this point, you should do one more thing: Repeat your central message as well as your call to action, if you have one. Listeners remember only a small part of a presentation. You want to make sure they don't forget your most important idea.

Instead of closing with the last answer to the last question, close with your central message and call to action.

NEVER PRETEND

Adequate preparation and an effective approach to fielding questions can make you a star at every question-and-answer session, but there still may be some questions you can't handle. If you don't know the answer to a question, say so.

Never try to pretend that you have the information. Someone in the audience is likely to realize that what you're saying is incorrect. If this happens to be a key decision-maker, the credibility of your entire presentation will immediately be undermined.

Simply tell the listener that you don't know the answer but you'll find out and get back to him or her with that information within a specific time period.

TIP

Be as responsive as possible. If you need to do further research to answer a question, don't procrastinate. Get the data as soon as you can and communicate with your listener even earlier than you promised. This shows that you're trying to be responsive.

NEUTRALIZE HOSTILE QUESTIONERS

Sometimes a member of the audience may try to provoke you with a question that has nothing to do with your central message. It's simply designed to make you look uncomfortable and enable the listener to score some points or pursue his or her own agenda.

The other listeners usually know what's going on and they expect you to deal with the situation. Without being unpleasant, you can simply tell the listener that you'd be happy to take up this issue at another time after the presentation is over. But this session is not the time or the place to do it. As you finish your statement make sure you're not making eye contact with the questioner, who will try to keep talking.

In some especially heated question-and-answer sessions, a listener may stand up while asking a question and begin to approach the speaker. That is a clear attempt to take over the presentation. If this happens to you, immediately put up your hand. Then ask the listener to return to his or her seat. When someone realizes that you're not going to give up control, it's usually enough to persuade the person to sit down. The audience will usually be on your side.

Suppose a listener asks you an embarrassing question and, before you can answer it, tries to gather support for his or her position from other members of the audience. Perhaps the person says: "I know everyone here agrees with me," or specifically names several other people and says: "Tell everybody here what you think." That is another blatant attempt by a listener to take over your presentation. Before the person can go any further, make it clear that you'll only deal with his or her problem, and that if anyone else has concerns, you'll be happy to address them one by one.

STAY IN CONTROL

This is your question-and-answer session, and you should stay in charge of it at all times, whenever it occurs during your presentations. Some managers report that their listeners will not wait until the end for questions, but ask them throughout a presentation. In such cases, you must be ready to answer everyone, but after you finish each answer, always segue back into your presentation. Repeat your central message and remind your listeners of the previous points you covered before going on to introduce any new information.

The key is to always land on your feet as you answer each question and to demonstrate to the audience that this is your presentation and you know what you're talking about.

The 30-Second Recap

In this section you learned a proven approach to handling question-and-answer sessions successfully.

One-to-One Presentations

In this section you learn how to deliver one-to-one presentations.

Most of us don't have the opportunity to deliver a stand-up presentation every day, or for that matter, even once a week. However, we do have plenty of occasions to speak one-to-one with co-workers: at the water fountain, in the cafeteria, or across the desk. Each is a situation for practicing the skills of effective communication.

Suppose you come up with an idea for streamlining the operations in your unit. First you might decide to walk down the hallway and try it out on one of your colleagues. If your presentation is convincing and your colleague gives you a thumbs-up, you might then present the same proposal to your supervisor.

When you talk to your supervisor, a clear, concise delivery is critically important. It's not only the best way to win approval for your proposal, it can enhance your image in the supervisor's eyes.

Perhaps you regularly make sales presentations to describe new products or services. If you want to be successful, your message must be short and easy to understand, with plenty of benefits for the potential customer.

Apply what you've learned from this book about group presentations, and follow this section's advice on how to make an effective one-to-one presentation.

Put Your Best Foot Forward

One-to-one presentations may be less formal than stand-up speeches. They can also be less stressful because you're usually sitting down, and you're not speaking to a big audience. Nevertheless, the criteria of good oral communication are no different.

TIP

Remember to prepare. One-to-one presentations require preparation just like formal speeches do. Work on the verbal, visual, and vocal components of your communication so they'll be as sharp as possible when you deliver your information to a listener.

In every case, you must put your best foot forward and effectively apply the same skills that you'd demonstrate in front of a large group.

PRESENT FIRST THINGS FIRST

Whether you're presenting to your supervisor, a co-worker, or a customer, one thing is almost certain. They're busy people without much extra time to listen, so you need to get to the point, and get there quickly. That means that the first step in preparing any one-to-one communication is to define your central message. Instead of sounding vague and uncertain when you speak, you'll know exactly why you're speaking and what you want to accomplish. Your listener will, too.

If you want your supervisor to fund your proposal, or a customer to buy your product, make sure they know what's in it for them (WIIFM). Sometimes, it even helps to lead off with this information and follow up with the central message. You're almost always guaranteed to get the listener's full attention.

KNOW WHAT APPEALS TO YOUR LISTENERS

Your listener analysis is relatively easy in a one-to-one presentation. But if you get it wrong and don't know what kind of evidence is most likely to convince your listener of your position, you're probably not going to accomplish your goal.

If the listener is a numbers person, include statistics. If he or she is likely to be impressed because a major competitor is doing the same thing, be sure to mention it. Always present your most important evidence early, in case you run out of time at the end.

Some listeners need a picture to persuade them. One of the most effective visual aids is a PowerPoint slide on your laptop computer. Keep the visual simple. Then, as you present it, follow the same approach that you would use in a formal presentation. Apply what you learned from earlier sections:

- Give the listener an overview of the visual aid.
- Describe each of the details.
- Don't talk to the visual, talk to the listener.

Remember to only use visuals that can make your point better than you can do it orally.

CAUTION

Don't push the laptop computer to the listener's side of the desk; it may be interpreted as an invasion of his or her space. Keep the computer on your side of the desk and under your control. The same rule applies if you're using a transparency.

Make Your Points with Energy

Energy is essential in a one-to-one presentation. Otherwise the listener won't believe that you're committed to what you're saying.

Most of us naturally use gestures when we speak to another person, but we usually use our visual energy less than we do when we speak to a large group. Keeping our hands in front of us is appropriate for a one-to-one situation.

TIP

Many speakers seem to forget about energy when they make one-to-one presentations. Perhaps they're afraid of coming on too strong and overwhelming the listener. Nevertheless, a high level of energy—but one appropriate to the situation—is important if you want to make your case.

Vocal energy is also important to add emphasis and meaning to your words when you're presenting one-to-one. Once again, the volume is much lower than it would be in front of a big audience. Nevertheless, the listener should never be in any doubt that you feel strongly about your message.

Practice Eye Contact

Eye contact is a valuable visual skill when you're making a presentation across a listener's desk. If you're looking around the room as you talk, the person is likely to think that you're not interested in him or her, or, worse yet, that you're trying to hide something.

CAUTION

Eye contact may be more important in one-to-one conversations than it is when you're speaking to a large group. It's more notice-able to a single listener if you seem hesitant to look him or her in the eye. You can easily appear to be bored or indifferent and the listener will stop paying attention.

On the other hand, you can't stare at the listener throughout the entire presentation. This will only make the person feel uncomfortable; you should stop talking and break eye contact at appropriate intervals. Look down at your notes, to one side, or refer to your visual aid. Then resume your conversation.

REMEMBER TO LISTEN

One-to-one presentations don't need to be continuous monologues by the speaker. You may decide to ask an open-ended dialogue question to involve your listener or solicit information from the person. Your presentation may also leave your listener with some unanswered questions that can only be handled in a question-and-answer session.

In both of these situations, your role is to listen so that you understand the questions and can deal with them effectively. The answers may be critical to convincing your listener that your idea or your product is worth trying.

Don't fumble the presentation at the question-and-answer stage. Try to prepare yourself for possible questions. An "I don't know," or an "I'll have to find that information for you," may only leave the listener feeling that you're not really in command of your subject.

Finally, repeat your central message at the end of your presentation. If you have a call to action, make it; if you're trying to make a sale, ask for the order. Otherwise, your entire effort may have been totally useless.

MAINTAIN YOUR PERSPECTIVE

One-to-one presentations may seem more informal and relaxed than stand-up speeches, but they can be just as vital to your future. A client once explained that each talk you give is like a job interview—you're being evaluated by your audience. Keep this perspective in mind as you make a presentation across the desk. It will help you stay sharp and in charge during your delivery.

THE 30-SECOND RECAP

In this section you learned how to use your verbal, visual, and vocal skills to give one-to-one presentations.

Listening

In this section you learn how to improve your listening skills.

"You aren't listening!" is a common complaint made by many people who are trying to communicate with someone else. Unfortunately, some people prefer to do all the talking and none of the listening.

In every successful communication, the speaker and the listener have had the opportunity to play both roles. While it may seem a bit unusual in a book on business presentations to include a lesson on listening, listening is an essential part of every presentation. We must listen during dialogue questions and question-and-answer sessions in order to handle them effectively.

In addition, effective listening skills enable us to read the audience and determine their reactions to our message.

CONSIDER THE VALUE OF LISTENING

As children, all of us learned the importance of *listening.* If your parents said, "Don't touch that hot stove," and you didn't pay attention you suffered the consequences. For most of us, "learning things the hard way" seemed to be a natural part of growing up. That usually meant not listening when an adult told you to do something.

PLAIN ENGLISH

Listening   Paying attention to sounds; hearing with thoughtful attention.

School was a listening laboratory. Teachers stood at the blackboard and lectured. Coaches taught us the rules of a game and how to play it. Most of the information we gathered came from listening.

As an adolescent, perhaps you worked at an after-school job. Learning how to do that job usually meant getting a set of instructions, practicing what you were told, receiving feedback from a supervisor, and, you hoped, mastering the work.

Your success depended on listening. We apply the same listening skills in every job we do as adults. Studies point out that almost 50 percent of our time at work is spent listening; that nearly equals the hours we spend in reading, writing, and speaking combined.

LEARN THE LISTENING PROCESS

Human sounds bombard us from every direction. We sit in meetings, pick up voicemail messages, watch television, and receive information over the radio. We hear these sounds, but we don't always listen to them.

Listening involves processing the sounds through our brains. First, the messages we hear must hold some interest for us. Otherwise, we simply ignore them. Much of what occurs in meetings, for example, falls into this category.

Second, we must begin to process these messages, which means visualizing what they mean, putting them into our own words, and thinking about them.

Then we begin to connect the new messages with other material: information we've heard in the past, or seen, or read about in a variety of sources such as company reports, periodicals, television, conversations with co-workers, formal presentations, and so on.

With our past knowledge and our unique experiences we put our own "spin" on the material we receive. Suppose you're attending a presentation and the speaker has just made an important statement. You might use this new idea to …

- Change your perspective or reinforce your current perspective.
- Decide to do further research to find out more information.
- Respond to what you've heard by saying something to the speaker.

TIP

Listening involves not only your ears, but your brain and your eyes as well. To respond appropriately you must hear what a person is saying, read his or her body language, and process what the person is communicating.

These are exactly the same responses we're called on to provide during a question-and-answer session. We must follow the same listening process, using precisely the same skills, to handle these sessions effectively.

OPEN ALL CHANNELS

Listening occurs on many levels. It begins with the words that someone else is using.

Suppose you've just completed a presentation on a pension and retirement health plan for your organization, and someone from the audience raises his or her hand and asks a question. It involves coverage for prescriptions. The listener could say:

> Will our prescriptions be fully covered under the new plan?

Or ...

> This sounds like an attempt by management to shortchange retirees and I bet our prescriptions won't be fully covered any more, will they?

In both cases the questioner is looking for the same information, but the words are entirely different.

Something else may be different, too: the questioner's *affect.*

PLAIN ENGLISH

Affect   The feeling or emotion connected with what a person says.

The first question, for example, may be delivered in a neutral tone of voice by a questioner simply looking for clarification. Or there may be a hint of skepticism in the questioner's tone. The affect will tip you off to the person's attitude and how you choose to respond to it.

You have to be listening "between the lines" to pick up the affect. Otherwise, you may fumble your response during the question-and-answer session.

The affect of the second question, of course, is much more obvious. There will certainly be an edge to the questioner's voice, and there may be resentment or even anger in the person's tone. So you must be prepared not to ruffle the feathers of a hostile questioner.

Read the Body Language

When people talk, their body language often speaks volumes—sometimes far more than their words can ever say. Take the example of a woman recounting a seemingly unimportant incident that happened many years in the past. Her mouth may begin to droop, her eyes may grow sad, and she may start twisting the ring on her finger. This body language tells you that the event is still very much alive for her and still casting a dark shadow over her life.

Watch the body language of your listeners during the dialogue questions or question-and-answer sessions in your presentation. As they're speaking, what do you see on their faces? Sometimes their facial expressions may reveal that an organizational problem is far more serious than their words are revealing, or than you could ever have imagined. Focus your attention on the speaker, and observe with your eyes as well as your ears, and you'll get all, not just part, of the message.

As pointed out in an earlier chapter, reading an audience's body language can also tell you how they're reacting to your message during a presentation:

Is one listener smiling and nodding his or her head?

Is another listener taking assiduous notes as you speak?

Did a key decision-maker respond to your last visual aid with a look of knowing appreciation?

If so, then your message is having a positive impact on the audience.

BECOME A BETTER LISTENER

Although we spend a great deal of our lives listening, most of us have never taken a course in it. We learn the fundamentals of other communications skills—writing, reading, even public speaking—but not listening.

LISTEN RESPECTFULLY

Good listening begins when you put yourself in someone else's shoes. How many times have you caught yourself growing impatient while someone is relating an experience or asking a question? You want him or her to hurry up and finish. Try to imagine that you're that person. How would you like to be treated? Respond to that person the same way.

TIP

Most people speak at 160 words per minute. But you can listen at a rate that's three times faster. During dialogue or a question-and-answer session wait for the person who's speaking to finish. Fight the tendency to stop listening, cut the person off, or let a look of impatience cross your face.

Have you ever found yourself basing your reaction to people on their surface appearances? The way they're dressed? The accents in their voices? All of us have probably been guilty of doing it from time to time. Unfortunately, the tendency to jump to conclusions can undermine the quality of our listening. It's too easy to write off people because they're different from us, and to fail to give them our full attention when they ask questions.

Give every listener the same thing you'd expect: your complete interest in what they're saying.

OVERCOME DISTRACTIONS

Effective listening can only take place in the absence of distractions; the distractions can be external or internal.

Perhaps two people in the audience are talking to each other while someone else is asking a question. One way to deal with the problem is to position yourself so that you can look at them; making eye contact with one of them may be enough to stop their conversation. If not, you might also say: "Excuse me, I can't quite hear the question." That's usually enough to handle the problem.

Some distractions can be internal. As a listener is asking a question, you may be thinking about something else. Consequently, you may not hear the question and may give a response that's incomplete, or even completely irrelevant. This will reflect badly on you. Remember, often your presentation doesn't end until you've dealt with all the questions from your audience. So banish the distractions and don't start thinking about your next meeting before you've finished with the current one.

Listening is a critical component of every successful talk.

THE 30-SECOND RECAP

In this section you learned about effective listening skills.

Mastering the Media

In this section you learn how to use your presentation skills to participate in effective interviews.

While you're working in an organization, you may be called by a member of the press for an interview. It might be conducted over the telephone and used in a radio broadcast, or the information from your interview might appear in a newspaper or magazine article.

You may be interviewed on camera, and your responses aired on local or national news. Interviews can be conducted for a variety of purposes:

1. To provide background information for a news story
2. To supply general material on your specific organization
3. To focus on a controversial decision or project that involves your company
4. To provide information about you

When a reporter calls and requests an interview, your natural reaction may be negative. It's easy to imagine yourself on a program like *60 Minutes* being grilled by a hard-nosed interviewer who's out to expose some mistake you've made. Just remember that interviews can also give you an opportunity to make a positive impact.

Giving an interview is a presentation just like any other. The same public-speaking skills apply here, plus a few others, and they'll enable you to conduct a successful interview.

PREPARE FOR THE INTERVIEW

The most important thing in any interview is to realize that this is your show, not the reporter's. Always try to stay in control, even if the reporter tries to throw you.

Once you've received the invitation to be interviewed, begin planning for it. Most interviews are short, and you'll probably have an opportunity to deliver a single central message.

After you answer each question, return to your central message so the interviewer will be sure to remember it.

TIP

Know your objectives. Start the interview with a central message and three pieces of evidence you want to get across. Then stay on track.

Anticipate the questions, just as you would if you were preparing for a question-and-answer session. You'll probably have a pretty good idea of what the reporter is likely to ask. If you need help, talk to your colleagues and rehearse your answers with them.

Be prepared with three questions that you'd like to be asked. Good interviewers will ask if there are any questions you'd like to address during the interview. When one doesn't, you can work your questions into the conversation. For example, you might answer the interviewer's question, then say, "and there's a related question that I think is equally important." Then deal with it.

ANSWER QUESTIONS WITH CARE

Once the interview begins, there are some key points to keep in mind. Whether you're on camera or being interviewed in person or over the telephone, they'll help make your interview a success.

- Most reporters are smart, outgoing people who want you to be a good interviewee. You'll get along fine as long as you're open and straightforward.

- Fill your answers with specific examples and anecdotes that illustrate your key ideas. Interviewers appreciate anecdotes because they add texture to a story.

- "No comment" is never a good answer. If you don't want to answer a question, say so, and explain why. Example: "It's up to the courts to decide, and it would be inappropriate for me to make a public statement."

- Avoid convoluted, jargon-filled language, and don't make any claims that you can't support.

- Look upon the interview as a business meeting, not a combat situation, and act as you would in any business setting.

CAUTION

Accentuate the positive. Don't try to knock down someone else's position during an interview. Instead, concentrate on making your own case as strong as possible.

Remember that you can do much more than just avoid mistakes; you can successfully promote your central message.

BE PREPARED FOR ON-CAMERA INTERVIEWS

On the day of a television interview, wear traditional, conservative clothing. Avoid a white blouse or shirt. It's a color that shines in the camera. Select a softer color, such as blue.

You should also leave any large jewelry at home. Showy jewelry pieces can create flares in the camera lens and distract from your message.

A technician will probably pin a microphone to your clothing. Don't touch the microphone or tap your fingers on the table or desk you may be seated at. Microphones are very sensitive, and they will pick up low-level sounds.

When you're being interviewed, unless you're asked to do otherwise, look at the reporter, not at the camera.

TIP

Try not to be distracted by the camera; the camera operator knows how to position the equipment so that you'll appear natural to the audience. Whether you're on camera or off, be as relaxed as possible and don't make exaggerated gestures.

Keep your answers short, 60 seconds or less. Avoid rambling or making long digressions. The audience will find them boring.

Finally, be yourself, not some television personality you've seen on camera; you'll make a much better impression on the viewers.

BE READY FOR COMMON PROBLEMS

Interviews may not always run smoothly, especially if you're being asked to deal with a controversial issue. Here are a few common problems and how you can handle them.

PROBLEM ONE: YOU'RE ASKED A "ZINGER"

If the interviewer asks you a tough question, don't overreact. Before you answer the question, analyze it in your mind. If necessary, ask the interviewer for clarification and for the grounds on which he or she is basing the question. Try to throw it back in the interviewer's court before you begin your answer. Then rephrase the question to neutralize it, if necessary, and provide an answer.

PROBLEM TWO: YOU DON'T KNOW

If you don't know the answer to a question, there's nothing wrong in admitting that you're not the expert on the subject. Suggest someone the reporter might contact for the best information. Above all, don't try to wing it. The interviewer, who probably knows the answer, may point out your mistake and embarrass you on camera.

PROBLEM THREE: YOU MAKE A MISTAKE

If you make a mistake, don't be afraid to say so in the middle of the interview. Then go back and correct yourself. No one is expecting you to be perfect. But if you leave an incorrect impression in the mind of the interviewer or the television audience, it may hurt your message and your organization.

PROBLEM FOUR: YOU QUESTION THE QUESTION

If you think the interviewer's question is not quite right, restate it more clearly, or mention a related question that you feel is closer to the mark and answer it.

PROBLEM FIVE: THE INTERVIEWER PROVOKES YOU

If the interviewer tries to provoke you, don't demonstrate your anger. Show your willingness to discuss anything in an objective, calm way, and make sure any disagreements with the interviewer are factual, not emotional.

Use All Your Skills

Your words will carry you part of the way during an interview, but always remember the other channels of communication. They enable you to add emphasis and power to what you're saying.

Use hand gestures, especially when you're appearing on camera. Research shows that people who talk with their hands on camera are perceived as being more honest and direct than those who don't. But television magnifies movements, so be sure to reduce the energy of your on-camera gestures by half of what you would use in a large conference room.

When you talk with your hands, your facial expressions become more natural. Visual energy also enables you to dissipate some of the nervousness you may be feeling as the interview begins.

Make It *Your* Interview

Media interviews enable you to reach a broad audience. But you can only be successful if the interview accomplishes your goals.

- Know your key message before you begin the interview, and stick to it.
- Make sure the message is relevant and interesting to the audience that you're trying to reach.
- Keep your answers relatively short and always tie them back to the central message.
- Use energy to enhance the credibility of your ideas.
- Conclude the interview by reemphasizing your central message.

Practice the strategies and techniques in this section, and the interviews you give will be more successful every time.

The 30-Second Recap

In this section you learned how to use your presentation skills to handle media interviews.

Continuous Improvement

In this section you learn how to keep your oral communication skills finely tuned.

A colleague of mine has this to say about becoming an effective public speaker: "There's some good news," he explains, "and some bad news."

The good news is that making presentations is based on a set of skills, not some innate genetic ability. Anyone can develop and refine these skills so they become better presenters.

But that's also the bad news. Once you learn these skills, you need to constantly practice them. Otherwise, like a good golf swing or accomplished piano technique, the skills atrophy and decline.

Use Your Presentation Skills

It's easy to read a book and try to incorporate a set of skills into your next few presentations. You can work on the verbal channel, refining your central message, making it relevant to your listeners, and using clear, simple words to deliver your ideas.

You can open up the visual channel, using eye contact to connect with each of your listeners and obtain feedback from them during your speech. You can also raise your energy level, with gestures that describe and reinforce your message.

Finally, you can unclog the vocal channel. The human voice is a marvelous instrument that can add passion and power to your words by changing its tone and volume. Pauses and silences can also punctuate a presentation, giving it greater meaning.

Each of these skill sets can make you a better speaker, but only if you constantly remember to use them. Otherwise, your presentations won't continue to improve, they'll decline almost to the level at which they started before you read this book.

Practice Every Day

As you begin this section, you may be saying to yourself: "I can't give a presentation every day. So how can I expect to become a better speaker?"

TIP

It's possible to become a better speaker, but you must be willing to practice. Think of public speaking as part of your job. It's something you need to work at constantly so you can be the best.

Simple: You can practice your presentation skills every time you talk. Suppose you're having a conversation with one or two people in your office. Instead of simply focusing on your words, concentrate on your body language.

Are you practicing effective eye contact? Are you using gestures and vocal energy to reinforce your ideas? What are your facial expressions saying to your listeners? What is their body language telling you?

Raise your level of awareness as you talk to friends and family members. Each situation presents an opportunity for you to sharpen your skills.

The more conscious you are of using the three communication channels on every occasion, the more likely you'll be to open them up when you give a stand-up presentation in front of a large audience.

Don't Hide: Speak

When your supervisor asks for a volunteer to give a presentation, don't shrink into a corner; use the opportunity to improve your presentation skills.

CAUTION

Don't shrink from agreeing to give a presentation when asked because the idea makes you anxious. Agree to do it, and if you immediately say to yourself, "What have I done?" well, you've just given yourself a chance to become a better speaker.

There are many types of talks that you may be called on to deliver, and they're not all high-pressure situations.

The Job Description

This usually consists of describing your job, or what your functional area does, to a group of visiting customers, vendors, or others. It's a fairly low-risk presentation. All you have to do is talk about what you know best.

The Team Presentation

Team presentations have become very common in most organizations. Usually you'll appear onstage with other members of your team. Each person will be responsible for only one aspect of the presentation, so you'll only need to speak for a short period of time. In addition, you have the support of other team members during your delivery.

One team member is generally designated to lead off the presentation. If you feel comfortable in this role and want to deliver your talk as soon as possible, volunteer to be the first speaker.

Generally, you'll be asked to deliver the central message. Then you'll introduce the next presenter.

Meeting or Workshop Facilitator

Being a facilitator doesn't require you to give a long presentation. You generally set the agenda, give a short introduction, and then solicit input from other members of the meeting or workshop.

TIP

Try out low-risk situations where you can make a presentation. Gradually increase the level of difficulty until you feel comfortable standing up in front of a group.

One psychologist says she loves this type of environment because it plays to her strength. She enjoys asking open-ended dialogue questions and encouraging participants to speak. At the end, she summarizes what's been said, and if it seems appropriate, she formulates an action plan.

Running a Booth

Many companies have booths at large conventions or trade shows. They may be run by salespeople as well as other employees who are technical experts.

Standing in a booth for an entire day gives you an opportunity to talk to a variety of people, one-to-one, or in small groups. In this situation you can use all your presentation skills.

Take Advantage of Volunteer Activities

One of the best things about volunteer activities is that they give you an opportunity to try something new in a low-risk situation. Your job and your future don't depend on your performance.

Volunteering also gives you a chance to stretch yourself. You can experiment with an activity or work in a field that's far removed from your regular routine. If it turns out to be enjoyable, you can continue. If not, you can do something else.

Volunteering often provides excellent opportunities to sharpen your speaking skills. You really have very little to lose when you ...

- Introduce a guest speaker at a club luncheon. It's short, easy, and the spotlight is not on you, but on the speaker.
- Work as a *docent* in a museum or historic site, giving tours. You can describe paintings and artifacts, and provide historical information to groups of visitors.

PLAIN ENGLISH

Docent   A person being trained to become a teacher or guide.

- Read to groups of schoolchildren. You can practice your vocal and visual skills as you tell a story.
- Coach a sport and use your enthusiasm to motivate a team.
- Lead nature walks and describe the flora and fauna along the trail.
- Teach a course in your area of expertise at a local high school.
- Run a committee at a club or civic organization.

All of these activities will help you become a better speaker.

ENROLL IN PUBLIC-SPEAKING PROGRAMS

Many courses are available in public speaking. One of the best is the Focus Communications Executive Communications Program. Their Web site is www.focuscommunications.com.

Look for courses that include the following elements:

- Plenty of opportunities for you to stand up and speak. Lectures by an instructor will not help you become a better presenter.
- Feedback from the instructor and other students. You won't improve unless you know your shortcomings.
- Videotaping. If you can see yourself on camera, it will enable you to correct problems and make improvements much faster.
- A step-by-step approach. This enables you to learn about a skill, practice it, then add an additional skill. At the end of the session, you should be able to put all the skills together in a single presentation.
- Printed materials. Books, handouts, and other materials give you a ready reference source during the course and after you complete it.

Once you've finished a program, look for articles about public speaking in magazines and newspapers. You may also decide to read additional books on the topic.

Make presentation skills an area in which you're constantly learning and trying to build your expertise. You can be sure that you'll become a better speaker.

THE 30-SECOND RECAP

In this section you learned how to constantly improve your skills as a speaker.

Creating Effective Visuals

Visual Aids

In this section you learn the uses of visual aids and the fundamentals of developing effective ones.

In the past decade, speakers have relied on more and more visual aids to present their information. The first visual aid goes up to introduce the topic of their presentation and it's followed by a lengthy series of visuals, each one repeating almost word for word what the speaker is telling his audience. This is a clear case of role reversal: The overhead projector is now the presenter, and the speaker has become the aid.

Good speakers recognize that they need very few visual aids to make their key points. In fact, Louis Gerstner, the chief executive of IBM, speaks to analysts and investors every year without using any visuals. It's just Gerstner onstage, sitting on a stool, with a glass of water beside him. As one analyst commented: "It's a performance worth seeing."

Of course, visual aids can be used effectively. They can make a point better than you can make it verbally, or present complex data in a way that makes it much clearer to your audience. The key is: Less is more. Don't clutter up your presentation with visual aids just because "they're there." Use them thoughtfully and sparingly, and they will enhance your presentation.

EVALUATE YOUR VISUAL AIDS NEEDS

Developing visual aids is part of the planning stage for many presentations. Studies show that an audience remembers more when they *see and hear* something than when they only hear it. So visuals can help you get your point across. But before you decide to use them, consider the following:

Why are you using them? Visual aids should only be used when they make a point better than you can do it by yourself. Yet some speakers admit that visual aids are their crutch. They don't want to stand up and face an audience, so they let the projector do the work for them.

If you want to make sure you're *not* remembered by your listeners, turn on the projector as you begin your talk and read one slide after another. This approach is guaranteed to put your audience to sleep.

TIP

Make an impact. If you want your visual aids to make an impression, use as few as possible. With visuals, less really is more.

What do your listeners want? The audience doesn't come to look at your visuals. Frankly, you could e-mail hard copies just as easily and save them and yourself all the time a presentation takes. The listeners come to hear you. Your performance, not your visual aids, will make or break your talk.

What kinds of visuals should you create? Recently the CEO of a major manufacturing company directed his subordinates to stop using so many word slides. He was tired of looking at them. He wanted speakers to rely more on pictures—charts, diagrams, and cartoons—that could say more and deliver a message more clearly than words alone. This is really the purpose of visual aids.

How much can my visual aids tell the audience? Here again, less is always more. Too many speakers try to load their visuals with far more information than the audience can possibly absorb. Like your presentation, each visual aid should contain only one central idea, or message.

DESIGN EFFECTIVE VISUALS

Most of us have probably attended presentations where the speaker puts up a visual aid and tells us: "Now, I know you can't read this but …" If a speaker needs to apologize for a visual, why use it in the first place? It simply detracts from the presentation.

As you design visual aids, make sure they enhance your presentation. Effective visuals have these characteristics:

- **The information is readable.** The rule of thumb is this: Project the slide onto a screen and stand in the back of the room. If you can read the information easily, then the type is large enough. Use a type size of 16 to 24 points. Also, keep the typeface simple. Usually a *sans serif* works best.

PLAIN ENGLISH

Sans serif   A simple typeface that does not have little lines (serifs) projecting from the top or base of the letters. The text in this box is sans serif.

- **The colors are simple.** Desktop presentation programs like Power-Point give you such a wide variety of colors to use in your visual aids that the choices may seem overwhelming.

  Simpler is generally better. Don't mix more than two or three colors on the same slide. It will look much too busy.

■ **Stick with high contrast.** The color you select for your type or charts should contrast with the background color on your slides. Use light colors for type (such as yellow, white, and gold) with darker backgrounds (such as blue, green, and red).

■ **Make your titles short.** Every slide needs a title to introduce it. But don't get carried away; a title should contain only a few words, or it's no longer a title. You may choose to use a special color for the title that's not used in the body of the slide so it stands out.

■ **Select a design and stay with it.** Desktop presentation programs offer a variety of designs for your slides. They look so attractive that it's easy to find yourself trying out a different design for each slide. This simply distracts your audience.

You don't want people focusing on the appearance of your visual, but on the information you present with it. Use the same design for every slide and keep it as simple as possible.

■ **Proofread when you finish.** Carefully read your visual aids after you complete them. There is nothing more embarrassing than presenting a visual with a mistake in spelling, punctuation, or grammar.

A computer spelling check will not pick up every spelling mistake. For example, *there* and *their* are spelled correctly but mean different things. If you use one incorrectly in a sentence, the spelling check won't highlight it—unless you misspell it.

DECIDE ON TYPES OF VISUALS

Speakers commonly use several types of visuals in a presentation. These include words, pie charts, bar graphs, line graphs, and diagrams.

WORDS

The most widely used visual aids consist of bulleted points. If you decide to use one of these bullet slides, keep the lines short—no more than five to eight words. It makes each line easy to read. The most effective visuals usually contain no more than five or six lines. Otherwise the slide starts to look crowded.

CAUTION

Be sure to keep the grammatical structure consistent. On bullet slides, for instance, if the first line starts with a verb, the other lines should begin the same way.

Example:

- Make the central message clear.

- State it at the start of your talk.

- Repeat it during your presentation.

PIE CHARTS

These visual aids enable you to show the parts of a whole. Sometimes speakers try to cut the pie into too many pieces, showing 15, 20, or more parts. This is usually far too much for an audience to absorb.

Keep the pie chart simple; show only a few pieces. You might use one color for the chart, another color for type, and a third color for background to make the visual stimulating for your audience.

BAR GRAPHS

These visual devices enable you to compare several items either at a single point in time or at multiple points.

Vertical bar graphs show how several items compare with each other at various time periods. For example, you might show plant production at one facility during each month of the past year. Along the horizontal axis, you could indicate the months. On the vertical axis, you could show the units of production in thousands. Twelve bars would indicate the amount of production for every month of the year.

LINE GRAPHS

These graphs also show change over time, but as a continuous flow or line. Your graph can display the changes in one quantity, such as profits, or compare several items, such as costs of production and units sold.

Try to keep your graph as simple as possible. Don't draw in lines showing 15 or 18 different items and try to compare them. Your audience will never be able to follow what you're telling them.

DIAGRAMS

These visuals are especially valuable to show your audience a complex piece of equipment, the layout of a plant or other facility, and even the organization of your company (organization chart). A picture can truly be worth 1,000 words by showing how parts relate to each other in a way that words alone could not explain.

As with all visual aids, try to keep them as simple as possible. If you include too many labels on a piece of machinery, the audience will find the visual too complicated. Instead use several diagrams to show different parts of the machine.

USE THE POWER OF POWERPOINT

Today many desktop presentation programs enable you to create stunning visual aids on your computer. And no program is more popular than Power-Point. This program gives your visual aids a professional look that you just can't create on your own.

With PowerPoint you can produce colorful bullet slides or design charts and graphs in far less time using one of the AutoLayouts in the program. You can also add art to your word slides by using the clip art files that come with PowerPoint. Or you can create your own drawings.

The PowerPoint program also allows you to arrange slides in one sequence, then move them around easily from place to place if you change your mind. One of the most useful parts of the program is the collection of templates. These offer a variety of different designs for your slides. Once you've selected a *template* and inserted your text and graphics, it's easy to move them around and change their dimensions.

PLAIN ENGLISH

Template   A master slide that creates a design and applies it to all your visuals. Templates use effective color combinations and graphics.

Some speakers also take full advantage of the transitions that PowerPoint lets them create. For example, you might decide to develop a build, which means showing one piece of information on the first slide, then adding to it in successive slides until all the information is on the screen. This approach can be very effective if you only want to talk about one item at a time.

While most slides simply cut from one to the next, PowerPoint also permits you to transition by dissolving from slide to slide, which looks much smoother. In addition, you can fly in type from the right or left of the screen, or from the top and bottom. Some truly adventurous speakers also use animation to give their presentations additional sparkle.

PowerPoint visuals can be shown in a variety of formats. They can be projected as slides from your laptop computer. They can also be printed on transparencies to be displayed from an overhead projector. In addition, you can make hard copies of the visuals to hand out to your audience.

PowerPoint has become one of the most useful tools in the speaker's toolkit.

CONSIDER YOURSELF THE PRINCIPAL VISUAL

Many speakers get carried away with PowerPoint. It's easy to become so enamored of it that you forget one of the cardinal rules of presentations: *You are the most important visual.* What you create with your gestures, your facial expressions, and your eye contact are far more effective than any visual aid.

What's more, you can't cover up a lack of content with colorful visuals, no matter how many of them you use.

Recently General Henry H. Shelton, chairman of the Joint Chiefs of Staff, had to remind his subordinates to stop using so many Power-Point visuals in their presentations and get back to basics. They were packing their presentations with so many pictures of rolling tanks and animated artillery pieces that they were forgetting to present the facts. In fact, a pejorative term in the military is the *PowerPoint ranger,* someone who's better at making slides than developing content. Don't let yourself fall into that trap.

THE 30-SECOND RECAP

In this section you learned how to use visual aids effectively in your presentations.

Presenting Your Visuals

In this section you learn the best method of introducing your visual aids and working with them during a presentation.

Studies show that if you're trying to present new, complex information, 85 percent of the learning by your audience will occur visually, through their eyes. So visual aids can be extremely useful if you avoid cluttering your presentation with them and include only those that serve a clear purpose.

A variety of visual aids is available for speakers. The section "Visual Aids" on page 710, covered the process of evaluating the number and types of slides for your presentation. In this section we look at how to present your visuals most effectively.

MAKE YOUR VISUALS WORK

Whether you use traditional visuals such as flip charts and models, or the cutting-edge technology of PowerPoint, how you present them is key to how well they work in your presentation.

LEARN TO PRESENT TRADITIONAL VISUALS

If you handle them properly, props, models, and flip charts can be good choices, depending upon the subject of your presentation and the size of your audience.

PROPS AND MODELS

A speaker explaining the improvements in one of the parts of an aircraft engine demonstrated by holding up the old part and comparing it to the new one. After he completed his explanation, the speaker passed around the parts to his audience so they could see the improvements more closely.

Props and models are sometimes the best way of making a visual demonstration. Architects, for example, create models of new buildings they're planning and show them to their clients to help them visualize how the proposed structure will look. This makes it much easier for clients to see and understand what the architects are proposing and ask questions or make suggestions at an early stage.

Props work best with small groups of listeners. A large audience would be unable to see a small engine part held up by a speaker in a large auditorium.

Props or models can be cumbersome for a speaker to carry to a presentation. Nevertheless, under the right conditions, they can make an enormous impact on your audience.

TIP

The size of an audience often determines which visual aid will work best. Props, models, and flip charts are most effective with small groups in informal settings. Slides and overheads are a better choice for larger audiences.

FLIP CHARTS

Like props, flip charts also work very effectively with smaller groups. A colleague of mine who teaches technical writing uses a flip chart extensively to put down key points in his presentation. He also uses it to write down feedback from his listeners as they critique writing samples in the class.

Flip charts have several key advantages:

- They can help a speaker to interact with an audience. As you ask open-ended questions and receive important information, you can write it on the flip charts.

- They add spontaneity to a presentation. They're created on the fly in front of your listeners.

- They're flexible. The information on the chart can easily be changed and updated.

- They're colorful. If you use bold, dark colors—red, green, blue—the charts will be visually appealing.

- They can be displayed easily. Pages from the charts can be torn off and taped on the walls of a room so the audience can refer to them throughout a presentation.

 CAUTION

Use only the top two-thirds of a flip chart. When you tear off a page and paste it on the wall, the information will be much easier for an audience to see, no matter where they're sitting.

Of course, flip charts created during a presentation may not look as professional as slides and overheads prepared in advance. But you don't need any special equipment for charts—equipment that can sometimes break down and disrupt your talk.

OVERHEADS AND SLIDES

Although the technology is now decades old, overhead projectors continue to be the most widely used audiovisual equipment in the business world. In addition to projecting overheads, a projector together with a liquid crystal display (LCD) can also display slides from your laptop computer. Other projection devices are also available for showing computer-generated slides.

There are many benefits to using slides and overheads:

- They are easy for large audiences to see.

- They give your presentation a professional look, which showcases your knowledge and expertise to their best advantage.

- They present information in clear type and crisp colors instead of relying on the speaker's handwriting.

- Slides enable you to build in easy transitions so you can move smoothly from one visual to the next with the click of a button.

- Overheads can be flexible; if your handwriting is legible, you can create effective overheads during your talk.

Of course, overheads and slides are not without their disadvantages. These can be summed up in a single word: *equipment.* A bulb may burn out in an overhead projector, bringing your entire presentation to a complete standstill while someone searches for a replacement.

Your computer may also decide, on the day of the presentation, to develop glitches, which can stop any show dead in its tracks. Then you have to be ready to continue without the visual aids.

You should know how to deliver a powerful presentation without visuals, if necessary.

CAUTION

Don't be like some speakers, who become so dependent on their visual aids that they can't operate without them. If there's an equipment breakdown, they can't remember the information in their talk. Learn to deliver a presentation so you are always prepared, no matter what happens to the equipment.

NEVER FORGET THESE FOUR STEPS

So many speakers begin a presentation with high energy and good eye contact only to forget these essential skills when they start to present their visual aids. Somehow all their energy disappears, and instead of looking at their audience, they focus all their attention on the visual aid, talking to it with their backs to the listeners.

There is a far more effective way to work with visual aids, which enables you to continue using all your presentation skills. This process includes four steps, which are described as if you were using overheads or slides, since these are the most common visual aids.

1. **Project your first visual and walk back to the screen.** As you talk about a visual, you should always stand next to the screen. This accomplishes two things:

    a. You will not be blocking the view of anyone in the audience. If you stand next to the overhead projector or other projection device, it's easy to prevent someone from seeing the screen.

    b. By standing next to the screen, you and the visual aid present one unified image. The audience doesn't need to look back and forth to focus on the visual, and it will become the center of attention.

2. **Introduce the visual aid.** Before you talk about any of the details in the visual, give your audience an overview of what they're looking at. It's like introducing your central message before you deliver the rest of your talk, and it will make the details far more meaningful.

    Frequently the central message of your visual aid is contained in the title.

3. **Talk to a listener.** As you describe the visual, always talk to your listeners. If you need to refresh your memory about what is on the visual aid, pause, look at the visual, then look back at a listener and continue talking.

    This is the hardest thing to remember when you work with visual aids. Most of us have a tendency to look at the visual when we discuss it, but that breaks our contact with the listeners.

TIP

Try to stand to the right of a visual aid (to the left, from the audience's point of view). The reason is that listeners read from left to right. That way, their eyes start with you, and you remain the center of attention as they read the visual.

4. **Avoid the Statue of Liberty position.** As you introduce the visual, it's a good idea to point to it, but most visuals should be simple enough so that you don't need to continue to point to them as you discuss them.

    Too many speakers get locked in a Statue of Liberty position, which is extremely tiring and often prevents them from using gestures. If you have a bullet slide, simply refer to each point as "bullet one" or "bullet two."

If you're using a graph or chart, you can tell the audience where the information is located by saying: "in the upper corner," or "on the top." Or you can point to it periodically instead of keeping your arm locked in the Statue of Liberty position.

CAUTION: POINTERS AND LASER LIGHTS

Speakers regularly use pointers and laser lights to focus the attention of their listeners on specific aspects of a visual aid. Unfortunately, these devices are often far more trouble than they're worth.

Many speakers begin twirling their pointers like batons, when they aren't using them, which can be distracting to their listeners. It also prevents the speaker from using gestures effectively to add energy to a presentation.

While laser lights can be useful, they're a dead giveaway for any speaker suffering from nervousness: The laser beam will shake when the speaker points it toward the visual aid. The attention of the audience is now drawn away from the visual to the speaker's case of nerves.

CONSIDER HANDING OUT HARD COPIES

Presenters often ask whether they should distribute hard copies of their visuals at the start of a presentation. In some cases, the audience may be expecting hard copies, so you have little choice but to meet their expectations.

Where you do have a choice, however, don't hand out copies of your visual aids before you begin speaking. There are good reasons for avoiding this practice:

- Listeners will invariably start reading your handouts instead of paying attention to you. This undermines your effectiveness as a speaker.
- Listeners often look ahead and begin reading the hard copy of a visual aid before you reach it in your presentation. They may interrupt and ask questions about the visual before you're ready to deal with it.
- If you wanted to leave a visual out of your presentation it would be almost impossible if the audience already had copies of your visual aids.

If you want to distribute handouts, wait until the presentation is over. You don't necessarily have to provide a full set of hard copy visuals; many speakers include only the most important ones. It's a good way to make sure your listeners remember the main points of your talk.

Don't Use Visuals as Notes

Some speakers use many visual aids because they rely on them as notes. The unfortunate audience is then forced to look at far too many boring visuals.

If you need notes, use them. Write down a few key words for each idea you plan to deliver, then put the notes on the podium and refer to them as necessary. This will enable you to drastically reduce the number of slides you use in a presentation and save your listeners from visual burnout.

The 30-Second Recap

In this section you learned the best methods of working with visual aids in a presentation.

Running Effective Meetings

Effective Meeting Basics

In this section you learn the basic components of a successful meeting.

Successful meetings are not lucky accidents. Whether it's a regularly scheduled staff meeting, a faculty retreat, a meeting to launch a new product, a sales conference, or a meeting to introduce a new employee benefits plan, every meeting requires thoughtful planning and advance preparation. An effective meeting has an outcome, a desired result, and leaves the participants satisfied with the process that led to that outcome. To plan and execute a successful meeting, it is important to understand the basic components.

BASIC COMPONENTS

A comprehensive list of components of successful meetings includes …

- An objective that defines the purpose of the meeting.
- An expectation of what is to occur by the end of the meeting.
- A reasonable cost for the expected benefit.
- A list of attendees.
- An appropriate physical environment.
- Participant roles and responsibilities that are clearly defined.
- An agenda and advance preparation of materials.
- A distinction between content and process.
- Presentation skills to inform, influence, or motivate participants.
- A trusting and open environment that welcomes and values all participants' contributions.
- A clear understanding of where power and authority reside.
- *Facilitation,* all the actions taken to manage the successful progression of the agenda.
- Win-win approaches to decision-making.
- Pacing to keep the meeting on track.
- A means to determine, track, and assign action items.
- Follow-up after the meeting.

PLAIN ENGLISH

Facilitation   The act of making easier or helping to bring about a desired outcome. In a meeting, it includes helping all participants to contribute, handling problems, making sure that group dynamics remain positive, and pacing. It is seeking information and participation to reach an optimal outcome.

Some components will vary with the purpose of the meeting. For example, not all meetings require a presentation or present a problem to be solved. Some components are always present, such as cost; every meeting has a cost, even if it is only the *opportunity cost* of the participants' time.

PLAIN ENGLISH

Opportunity cost   The cost of making an investment that is the difference between the return on one investment (participating in a week-long sales conference) and the return on an alternative (making 20 more sales calls that month). The opportunity cost is the sales lost due to fewer sales calls.

CONTENT

The objective, the expectation, the materials providing information for the meeting, and the action items are all components of the content: *what* the meeting is about. The following list details each of these items:

- The **objective** must be clearly stated and communicated to participants: Why are we assembled here? It can be a list to be constructed in the meeting, a budget approval, a list of problems, a problem to solve, or information to be disseminated.

- The **expectation** must be something attainable: a minimum level of new product knowledge sufficient to begin selling, a list of final job candidates, or a decision to change vendors or purchase a new computer system.

- The **information** available for the meeting must be accurate and available, as it may be the foundation for any decisions made during the meeting or the action steps resulting from the meeting.

- The **action items** are the "next steps" to occur as a result of any meeting. They must be assigned (with due dates) before the end of the meeting and followed up.

TIP

Providing the objective, expectation, and information required for a meeting to all participants well in advance of the meeting is always a good idea. It gives participants an opportunity to think about the issues, read and absorb information, and make any preparations of their own.

PROCESS

The agenda, facilitation, presentations, approaches to decision-making, pacing, and follow-up are all components of process: *how* the meeting is run. How the work of the meeting gets done is important to reaching the objective, determining the quality of the outcome, and satisfying the participants.

- The **agenda** sets the stage for the meeting: It lists the items the meeting will address and often the time frame for each agenda item. It also lists the participants.

- **Facilitation** often involves taking on the role of facilitator yourself (if you are the meeting planner) or delegating it to a colleague, subordinate, or resident expert in the topic being addressed. A facilitator is not a leader imposing a solution or pre-determined decision on a group.

- **Presentations,** if there are any, are one way to provide information, *institutional memory,* or alternatives to be considered. They can be one person talking, a team lecture, a Microsoft PowerPoint slide, or a video or Internet presentation.

- Methods used for solving problems and making decisions (for meetings other than straight presentations of information) will determine both the quality of the solution or decision and the participants' satisfaction with the process.

  For example, **approaches to decision-making** will affect whether or not a meeting in which decisions have to be made has win-win outcomes. Some decision-making methods, such as voting, have win-lose outcomes; others, such as riots, have lose-lose outcomes. Consensus, achieved through collaboration and problem solving, is the win-win approach. Consensus is the judgment arrived at by most of those concerned, which requires group critical reasoning and may involve negotiation.

- **Pacing,** or keeping a meeting on track, demonstrates respect for the participants and maintains the energy in a meeting. One component of trust is ending the meeting at the announced time.

■ A meeting without **follow-up** is a meeting wasted. Identifying and assigning action steps is only as good as the follow-up to ensure the action steps are taken.

PLAIN ENGLISH

Institutional memory is the cumulative, retrievable, and collective knowledge possessed by an organization about its history, processes, products, business practices, markets, and competitors. Organizations are said to have no institutional memory when such knowledge resides in only one employee and is lost when that individual leaves the organization.

CAUTION

To make your presentation effective, remember to tailor it to your audience. For example, a presentation for the marketing team for a new prescription drug cannot discuss its effectiveness with the same level of complexity desirable for pharmaceutical chemists.

PARTICIPANTS

Identifying participants, assigning clear roles and responsibilities for each, establishing trust and openness, and outlining a clear understanding of who has authority in the meeting are all critical components of determining the participants: *who* will contribute to the meeting.

TIP

As you make up the list of participants, ask yourself these two questions: What will this individual contribute to this meeting and what will the impact be if this individual is not present?

Selecting participants involves addressing issues of inclusion, exclusion, influence, attitude, trust, and control. Here are some considerations:

■ **Identifying participants** sounds obvious, but the wrong choices can derail a meeting. Some advance thinking can help you steer clear of the potential problems. Do you need a full committee for a particular meeting or are certain members key? Do you have the right expertise in the room for the situation at hand? Are the constituencies affected by the actions to be taken in this meeting represented? Are there valid reasons to exclude a person or group from this meeting?

- **Identifying clear roles and responsibilities** for each person should be easy if you've chosen the participants well. Make sure roles and responsibilities are clearly understood before the meeting begins.

- **Trust and openness** are necessary for any productive exchange to take place in a meeting. Your track record as a facilitator—or your lack of a negative track record if this is your first meeting—is an important factor in establishing trust and openness in a meeting.

- **A clear understanding of who has authority in the meeting** is required for any action, resolution, or decision to occur. Getting to the right decision is useless if those who make it do not have the authority to execute it. This is information that should be clearly communicated to all participants.

CAUTION

Without trust and openness, participants may feel the meeting has a foregone conclusion, and nothing they say will be heard. Participants will not feel free to introduce new ideas, nor will they hear what is being presented. A lack of trust and openness will sabotage a meeting.

ENVIRONMENT

The physical—or virtual—environment of a meeting is a critical and often underappreciated component in the success of a meeting (see the sections "The Importance of Environment" on page 748, and "Meetings Without Meeting" on page 818). Whether formal or informal, in the usual workplace or off-site, environment helps to set the scene for successful interaction, focus, and pacing. Location, seating, audio-visual and electronic aids, arrangements for break times, refreshments, and an absence of interruptions and distractions impact success.

- **Location** sets the scene for a meeting and communicates to the participants how formal (or casual) and how important a meeting will be. A meeting in the office is less elaborate than one off-site and usually more formal. A meeting in a conference center is more formal than one at a resort. You must choose a location based upon the tone and function of a meeting: Idea generation may occur more readily in a relaxed, low-key setting; a crisis management meeting may need to be in an organization's headquarters in order to put decisions into effect instantly.

- **Seating arrangements** impact how people interact and where the energy in a meeting is concentrated. Options include circular, oval, rectangular, semicircular, and small groups around tables.

- **Audio-visual and electronic aids** often add clarity, break up lecture formats, or introduce material best presented visually. They are used more and more frequently as awareness about different learning styles has migrated from the schoolroom to the meeting room.

- Details as small as **break arrangements** can affect the productivity of a meeting. Establish protocols by announcing break arrangements. In a two-hour meeting, for example, no formal break may be scheduled, but participants may excuse themselves for restroom breaks or to refill coffee cups at any time. For all-day meetings, a morning and afternoon break are the minimum. For meetings at resort locations, working all morning and reconvening each evening allows participants to enjoy their surroundings and take a real break in the afternoon.

- The provision of **refreshments** will also affect productivity and the perceptions of participants. Caffeine, water, and alcohol will produce different levels of attention in participants. Healthy snacks and menu options for special diets (vegetarian, diabetic, low-fat, salt-free, Kosher) show consideration for the "human capital" in the meeting.

- **An absence of interruptions and distractions** goes a long way toward keeping the meeting on track and focused. Halfway through an afternoon meeting in a hotel is not the time to discover a disc jockey is setting up in the room one folding door panel away from your meeting. Interruptions can be minimized by having a message board outside a meeting room to prevent intrusions except in emergencies.

THE 30-SECOND RECAP

- Successful meetings require thoughtful planning and advance preparation.

- A successful meeting has a positive result, and its participants are satisfied with the process of reaching that result.

- Success depends upon managing the content, process, participants, and environment utilized in a meeting.

Types of Meetings

In this section you learn about different types of meetings and how they differ based on their purpose.

Although successful meetings share many elements, structures vary with the purpose and the tools chosen to accomplish its success. Five common types of meetings will be discussed in this section: informative, team-building, negotiation, project scheduling and management, and problem-solving. Some meetings will have multiple purposes. For example, a sales conference may present new products, solicit sales representatives' input in order to develop a marketing plan, and build enthusiasm and team morale. Issues and methods of each type of meeting are also addressed.

INFORMATIVE MEETINGS

Informative meetings have a primary purpose of education. They include conferences where new products' characteristics and competitive advantages are taught to sales representatives (for example, textbooks with new pedagogy) or prospective customers (for example, new drugs being introduced to doctors), as well as training meetings (for example, on new sales methodology, a performance evaluation system, use of a new surgical instrument, or changes in next year's health benefit plans).

Issues to be considered in planning a successful informative meeting include …

- Differing levels of premeeting knowledge mastered by participants.
- Different *learning styles* of participants.

PLAIN ENGLISH

Learning style   Individual differences in understanding information based on its method of transmission. Some people can easily grasp concepts by reading about them or hearing a speaker talk about them; others need visual representations; and still others need to act them out through practice exercises.

- Unequal benefits to participants of mastering new material. Learning a new sales technique will be more helpful in sales territories not dominated by a competitor than in those where one competitor predominates.
- The need to tailor the information transfer to the specific audience for this meeting.

Methods to consider utilizing in an informative meeting include the following:

- Premeeting handouts
- Lectures and presentations
- Visual aids
- Demonstration
- Role plays

TEAM-BUILDING MEETINGS

Team-building meetings have a primary purpose of building or rebuilding group focus, momentum, morale, and enthusiasm. Examples include staff meetings; meetings called during or after a merger, acquisition, or downsizing; meetings after a key employee leaves an organization; and meetings to *incent* or recognize exceptional achievement.

PLAIN ENGLISH

Incent   To motivate someone to achieve a desired outcome. Managers may devise bonus plans tied to market penetration, sales targets, project deadlines, product performance, financial targets, or recruitment goals, for example.

Issues to be considered in planning a team-building meeting include …

- Understanding the concerns of group members so appropriate incentives are offered.
- Identifying and overcoming barriers for successful team-building.
- Ensuring incentives offered do not create unintended consequences.
- Ensuring your ability to deliver promised incentives.
- Ensuring clarity of expectations, processes, and rewards.

Methods to consider utilizing in a team-building meeting include …

- Exercises rewarding group over individual effort.
- Activities that bond team members.
- Open discussion asking for grievances, obstacles, and complaints.
- Presentations of team expectations and rewards.

TIP

You must be an active listener in any team-building exercise or event to establish the legitimacy of the activity. Be sure each participant contributes and is heard by addressing and assessing each point raised and insight offered.

NEGOTIATION MEETINGS

Negotiation meetings have a primary purpose of finding a mutually satisfactory outcome. They include union contracts, joint ventures, vendor disputes, and purchase and outsourcing contracts, just to name a few.

Issues to be considered in planning a negotiating meeting include …

- Clarifying negotiating authority of participants.
- Establishing trust.
- Calculating fallback positions.
- Obtaining access to decision-makers not present.

Methods to consider utilizing in a negotiating meeting include …

- Proposal presentation and review.
- Offer and counter offer.
- Strategize and bluff.

PROJECT SCHEDULING AND MANAGEMENT MEETINGS

Project scheduling and management meetings have a primary purpose of keeping projects on target, on time, and within budget. Projects encompass new product development, new product launch, software development, conversion or implementation, staff development programs, work flow analysis, process reengineering, and any management initiative such as cross-training or installing a performance evaluation or supply chain management system.

Issues to be considered in planning a project scheduling and management meeting include …

- Identifying functions and players affected by changes that might result from the meeting.
- Conflicting priorities of mutually exclusive projects.
- Understanding capacity and resource constraints.
- Understanding performance factors.

- Understanding cost factors.
- Identifying individual agendas that may interfere with successful negotiation.
- Ensuring *buy-in* by all participants.

CAUTION

Failure to ensure buy-in, the full trust and participation of each participant, leads to meeting failure. A participant may promise effort she or he will not make or an outcome in which she or he has neither ownership nor confidence. Take the time to identify barriers to buy-in and resolve them before the meeting.

Methods to consider utilizing in a project scheduling and management meeting include ...

- Status reporting on the progress of each step or process.
- Test run analysis, to measure performance under a simulated or live "road test."
- *Benchmark* review of progress against preset criteria.

PLAIN ENGLISH

Benchmark   A measure of performance against a specification or schedule. Most projects have performance, schedule, and cost benchmarks that are checked during the course of the project to ensure timely, accurate, and budgetary completion.

- Specifications change request, review, or analysis based on client or user feedback.
- Schedule delay review to ascertain if lost time can be made up.
- Risk analysis of future obstacles.

PROBLEM-SOLVING MEETINGS

Problem-solving meetings have a primary purpose of fixing something that is not working, such as a product defect, a client relationship, an ethical dilemma, or an ineffective marketing campaign. Problem-solving meetings may address one of, some of, or all of these steps: problem identification, analysis, solution criteria development, alternative solution generation, evaluation, and decision-making.

Issues to be considered in planning a problem-solving meeting include ...

- Identifying steps that can be completed during the meeting.
- Choosing suitable approaches to each step undertaken.
- Assigning problem ownership.
- Identifying steps that will have to be done outside of the meeting, such as research.

Methods to consider utilizing in a problem-solving meeting, depending on the steps to be undertaken in this particular meeting, may include presentation of symptoms, possible causes, and alternative solutions.

The following table is a guide to assist you in preparing for different kinds of meetings with different kinds of outcomes, content, and processes, but one common criterion: Does the benefit of this meeting exceed its cost?

Different Types of Meetings and Their Characteristics

	Inform	Team-Build	Negotiate	Project-Manage	Problem-Solve
Objective	Transfer info	Build common purpose	Resolve differences	Keep on track	Identify and solve
Expectation	Learn	Work together	Agree	Deliver on time	Fix or interim step
Who	Whoever has or needs info	Team	Both sides	Players affected	Players affected
Agenda	Present, demo, role play, and test	Exercises reward group behavior	Present offer and counteroffer	Test-run analysis, status, and benchmark review	Identify, analyze, develop, and decide
Prepare	Assess participants' level of knowledge and benefits	Learn concerns, develop incentives, and identify barriers	Estimate cost of contract and determine fallback positions	Gather right info	Choose steps and tools
Pacing	Timeline to cover material discussed	Allow for input from all	Strategic	Allow time for adjusting	Allow for full discussion
Action Items	Retest	Address grievances	Unresolved items	Spec and schedule changes	Research and develop damage control
Follow-Up	Measure performance	Communicate	New proposal	Assess impact	Test

THE 30-SECOND RECAP

■ Different types of meetings raise different issues and call for different tools.

■ The five common meeting types are informative, team-building, negotiation, project scheduling and management, and problem-solving.

■ Issues common to most meetings are the varying levels of knowledge participants have prior to the meeting, the need for clarity about the expectations for the meeting, the need to keep a meeting's cost in line with the expected benefit, the need to identify the proper participants, and the needs for preparation, pacing, and follow-up.

■ Issues unique to different types of meetings must be recognized and addressed in planning your meeting.

■ Choosing appropriate tools for your meeting will enhance the probability of success.

Is This Meeting Necessary?

In this section you learn how to decide if a meeting is the best tool to achieve the result you need in a given situation and to identify and assess alternatives to a meeting.

As much as teamwork is hailed as necessary to the success of most ventures in today's world, it is important to think through any proposed meeting before committing resources to it. Why do you want to meet? What do you want to accomplish? Is a meeting the best way to accomplish that objective? The act of meeting does not guarantee *efficacy*.

PLAIN ENGLISH

Efficacy   The power to produce an unquestionable, decisive, or desired effect without waste, delay, or unnecessary cost.

When you call a meeting, you want to ensure a high probability of productivity, and you want participants to like the process and, therefore, not devalue or discard the outcome. There are many situations in which a meeting may not be productive. When a meeting is proposed, there are criteria that should be met before deciding to proceed.

To avoid poor decisions, assess what input is needed to achieve the desired result and what sources can provide you with that input; next, assess what barriers to success might result in an unproductive meeting. Review the basic components in "Effective Meeting Basics" on page 724.

There are good reasons *not* to have a meeting, and they should be examined. This section identifies several of these reasons.

MEETINGS AS A SUBSTITUTE FOR ACTION

If you have all the information you need, possess sufficient expertise to assess the information, are authorized to make a decision, and have the buy-in of others whose cooperation is necessary, why is a meeting needed?

A little self-evaluation is a good idea here. Are you postponing an action you are reluctant to take? Calling a meeting to "study" a possible action in hopes it will die on the vine, or attempting to transfer a responsibility that is clearly yours to a group is not going to enhance your track record for effective meetings. If there is no group consensus on the premise of the meeting, the likelihood of a successful outcome is reduced.

CAUTION

It's easy to gloss over these assessments and to *assume* you have the necessary information, expertise, authority, and consensus; but mistakes in your assessment can be costly and visible. By acting alone, you assume sole responsibility for the outcome.

MEETING FATIGUE

In some organizations, meetings may have become a habit. If there is a track record of meetings without outcomes, meeting fatigue might set in, creating a self-fulfilling prophecy that meetings are a waste of time.

If you are facing meeting fatigue, one solution is to change the structure of your meeting so it will not be mistaken for "one more monthly yawn session." Here are some suggestions:

- Change the agenda to show the expected outcomes
- Change the order of events
- Change the room
- Change the format from structured discussion to brainstorming
- Throw in an ice-breaker to engage participants who have attended previous meetings as observers

- Invite an outside guest
- Assign every participant a premeeting exercise designed to contribute to the topic of the meeting

MEETING GRIDLOCK

Will any factors crimp the free flow of ideas, such as antagonistic participants or power plays? Is the issue so tense that conflicts arising in a meeting would be destructive? Alternatives to consider under these circumstances include moving sensitive agenda items off-line, changing the participants invited, and getting participants' agreement to ground rules, such as discussing only issues and positions, not individuals, that will preclude destructive behavior.

MEETING RESOURCES

Having considered real barriers to a good meeting, you will also want to consider the adequacy of resources.

Is there sufficient expertise in-house to tackle the issue? How do you know? Do you have to reach outside the organization to find the necessary expertise or information to bring into a proposed meeting? Can the outside expertise or required information be made available for the meeting?

Can the essential participants travel, if necessary, to attend this meeting?

Are there funds available for this meeting? You may have all the other factors required, but if there is no budget or if the cost of the meeting exceeds the expected benefit, you do not have the financial resources needed to hold a meeting (unless you can present an argument compelling enough to divert funds from other approved needs).

TIP

In assessing the benefits versus the costs of a meeting, consider how long-term, noncash, and hard-to-measure benefits, such as increased morale and better training, are valued by the decision-makers in your organization. Similarly, consider opportunity costs such as staff time and distraction from other valuable endeavors.

MEETING SALIENCE

You may have all the resources needed for the meeting you desire, but there are still other factors to take into account, and they include the likelihood of implementation of any decisions or actions resulting from the meeting.

Does the team you plan to invite to a proposed meeting have the authority to make the decision(s) or take the action(s) required? Even if the answer is yes, are there forces inside (budgetary, policy, pending merger, capacity constraints, and so on) or outside the organization (raw material shortages, regulatory, competitive, political, and so on) that would prevent implementation?

ALTERNATIVES TO MEETINGS

What if your analysis results in the decision that an in-person meeting is not warranted or possible? What are the alternatives?

CAUTION

If negotiation is the purpose of your planned meeting, writing may not be an effective substitute for in-person negotiation. "Negotiating by contract draft" almost invariably makes each party's position look less negotiable than it might be, and it is cumbersome.

- **Individual action.** Write out your analysis of the situation and the rationale for your decision or other action.
- **A conference call.** While telephone calls do not solve the problem of necessary individuals working in different time zones, they can provide group input and discussion without the expense and time of travel to an in-person meeting.
- **E-mail correspondence.** E-mail has the advantage of creating a record and allowing participants to communicate at different times, but it does not facilitate group process.
- **Real-time electronic meetings.** This type of meeting is conducted on an intranet Web site or dedicated "chat room" (really a variation of an in-person meeting; see the section "Meetings Without Meeting" on page 818).
- *Asynchronous* **meetings.** These meetings are conducted on a secure Web site when time zones prevent in-person meetings. They capture participants' contributions in an organized way, such as having a specific location for comments on each agenda item.

PLAIN ENGLISH

Asynchronous   Digital communication in which there is no timing requirement for transmission. An asynchronous classroom or meeting is one in which participants communicate electronically as time is available, and the communications are shared with other participants for response.

Other alternatives to meetings include ...

■ Surveys, additional data collection, or data reporting that might provide more information.

■ Identification and solicitation of the additional expertise the topic requires.

■ Deferral of any action unless or until factors change to more favorable conditions for an effective meeting.

 TIP

Now that you have read this section and assessed whether or not this meeting is necessary, ask a trusted colleague to review your assessment. She or he may be able to see salient points you've missed or offer corrective information.

THE 30-SECOND RECAP

■ Meetings do not automatically generate action, decisions, or a sequence of meaningful events. It's important to consider whether or not a planned meeting is the best method of achieving the desired outcome.

■ Before calling a meeting, assess whether you have sufficient information, expertise, authority, and buy-in to determine if you should act alone, call the meeting, or need to defer the meeting until these conditions are met.

■ Also assess any possible barriers to its success. If everyone is tired of meetings, change your meeting so that it is not recognizable as "same old, same old."

■ Consider whether an alternative to a meeting, such as individual action, a conference call, electronic correspondence, further data collection, or expert solicitation, might be a better course of action to obtain the outcome you desire.

Planning Your Meeting Strategically

In this section you learn to plan each component of an effective meeting to maximize the probability of obtaining the outcome you seek.

Ineffective meetings often result from a lack of strategic planning. Sometimes there is a total absence of planning: Someone decides it's a good idea to have a meeting, haphazardly invites the people she or he wants to attend, sets the time based on his or her own convenience, and makes room arrangements based only on proximity, not capacity to hold the number of participants. The individual or group initiating the meeting may give no thought at all to the process, to group interaction, or to the ability of the group to reach the desired outcome.

In other meetings, everything is prearranged, giving the semblance of planning, but nothing is thought through, leading to an overly ambitious agenda, incomplete information for decision-making, participants who do not have the authority to make the desired decision, poor attendance because of competing demands on participants' time, and an inappropriate choice of presentation and/or problem-solving tools. The result is a meeting with unrealistic expectations and unmet objectives. To plan an effective meeting, you need to think strategically about how each component will contribute to the outcome you desire.

FINDING A RATIONALE

There are four sequential steps to determine the rationale for a meeting:

1. **Identify the purpose of the meeting you are considering.** What is the objective? Review the types of meetings discussed in "Types of Meetings" on page 730, and then write down your specific objectives for this proposed meeting. For example: "Review first batch of resumés received for the position of purchasing agent."

2. **Determine what the expectation is for this meeting.** To continue with the same example, the expectation might be "Identify 20 candidates to contact for telephone screening interviews."

3. **Evaluate whether or not a meeting is the best method of accomplishing your objective and expectation.** Review the section "Is This Meeting Necessary?" on page 736, and assess the particular situation. In the previous example, if you are the Director of Supply

Chain Management, have sole authority to hire, were promoted from purchasing agent and possess sufficient knowledge to assess candidates, and have an urgent need to fill the job to prevent shutting down a production line, do you really need a meeting to identify promising candidates? On the other hand, if there is a search committee for this job or a new competency required by changing technology that you need other experts to assess, acting alone may be the inappropriate method and a meeting is necessary.

This example is a simple one, but the concepts can be applied to more complex situations.

CAUTION

Taking shortcuts in determining the rationale for the meeting may sabotage your decision-making prowess. Write down your arguments for choosing to hold the meeting you are considering, and then argue the opposite viewpoint. Having played devil's advocate with yourself, does your original argument remain sound? Don't proceed until you're sure.

4. **Measure the meeting's estimated cost versus the expected benefit.** Components of cost include *out-of-pocket* costs, such as travel, hotel and conference site, meals, materials to be distributed before the meeting or prepared for the meeting, and speakers' fees; *sunk* costs, such as staff who will be paid the same amount whether they are in this meeting or another activity; and *opportunity* costs. These are the hardest to measure. What other opportunities are being foregone in order to hold this meeting? For example, if you take 100 sales representatives off the road for a weeklong sales conference, the opportunity cost is the new accounts not signed or products not sold because of the resulting reduction in sales calls.

KNOWING WHO TO INVITE

Now that you are satisfied the rationale for your meeting is sound, who needs to participate? The answer may be obvious as in the previous example: If there is a search committee already selected, you know whom to invite. The same is true for standing committees, faculty meetings, and sales force meetings.

For many meetings, however, selecting participants is trickier. In an informational or training meeting, one consideration is the optimal size of the group. A meeting of shareholders or a sales force may predetermine the size; a training meeting may be limited to the number of computer terminals available in a laboratory or the number that can participate in exercises led by one facilitator. In a negotiation meeting, too many players may impede the process, and you may have to appoint one representative to speak for the group.

In project scheduling and management meeting or problem-solving meetings, or other meetings unique to your organization, determine who should participate by asking these questions:

- Who has the **information** necessary to conduct this meeting?
- What **roles** need to be filled in this meeting, and who can fill them? Beyond decision-makers, this list may include those who can provide institutional memory and historical context, a facilitator, a union representative, and a recorder to *memorialize* the steps taken and future action steps assigned in this meeting.

PLAIN ENGLISH

Memorialize   To summarize, record, and communicate the events of the meeting, the action steps assigned, and the next steps planned. This is a vital role in building institutional memory, so the history of a decision process does not depend on individual memory or leave the organization.

- Who has the **authority** to make any decisions necessary in this meeting? Decisions include approval or disapproval of contemplated specification changes, schedule changes, spending, advertising campaigns, staff increases, contract terms, and so on.
- Who has the **expertise** to take the actions contemplated in this meeting? For example, an e-commerce retailer trying to solve the problem of processing a seasonally high volume of orders during the holiday season needs to know who has the knowledge to forecast the peak volume, determine how many temporary order takers to hire, and figure out how many more shipping boxes to order.
- Who must be invited for **political** reasons? In some situations, someone without an operational role may need to be included to satisfy a policy directive about participation.

CAUTION

Very small groups—under five people—may not have the requisite information, expertise, and authority to produce the desired outcome. However, the larger the group, the more complex the task of ensuring participation and synthesizing the discussion. More than 10 or 12 participating attendees may be unwieldy.

Considering all you have learned in this section, make a list of whom to invite. Note that some of these roles may overlap. Information, expertise, and the authority to make a decision may reside in one individual.

Facilitator _____

_____

Information providers _____

_____

_____

Expertise providers _____

_____

_____

Decision-makers _____

_____

"Politically required" invitees _____

_____

_____

Recorder _____

_____

DETERMINANTS OF TIMING

When to hold your meeting depends on several factors. Obviously, the availability of those you wish to invite—all essential players or they wouldn't be on your list—is key. In some situations, such as an emergency meeting in response to a crisis, you may have to call a meeting immediately and instruct the essential participants to drop whatever they are doing and get on the next plane. You may have to take action without perfectly accurate information or complete expertise.

TIP

Some criteria are more important than others. The driver for the timing of most meetings will be *when do you need the expected outcome of the meeting to occur?* Training completed two weeks after it's needed or the right decision made too late to be implemented defeats your objective.

For most meetings, you will have to determine when to hold them based on the following criteria:

- **Availability of participants, inside and outside your organization.** For some meetings, you may have to make staff available by reprioritizing their other work obligations. If electronic scheduling is available for an internal meeting, solving this problem is easier.

- **Internal and external deadlines.** Internal deadlines are budget deadlines, management mandates, and project completion deadlines. External deadlines include investment community expectations about profit projections, grant application deadlines, tax return deadlines, legal notice periods, and competitive deadlines.

- *Seasonality.* It makes sense to take your sales force off the road or convert your order processing system during the slowest month of the year.

PLAIN ENGLISH

Seasonality   Varying in occurrence according to the season. In business, this refers to sales or production volume and may not correlate to a calendar season: A new swimsuit line is shown to store buyers, ordered, and manufactured long before summer.

- **Holidays.** It's rarely effective to hold a meeting just before a holiday when people are likely to be focusing on projects they need to finish before the break or on their plans for the holiday.

- **Cost.** Smart planners take large meetings to ski country in August when off-season hotel rates are in effect. Breakfast meetings are cheaper than lunch meetings, which are cheaper than dinner meetings; meetings ending well after working hours may incur taxi and car service charges in certain cities and industries.

TIP

If you are a novice at planning a large, off-site meeting, hire a conference planner. They have expertise in managing events cost effectively, auditing master bills and per-head charges, obtaining discounts, and heading off problems before they occur.

■ **Productive times of day and meeting duration.** Early morning meetings leave time for action steps to occur the same day but may not take flex-time schedules into account. Meetings starting too close to the middle or end of the day risk the loss of attention, as participants with lunch dates or train schedules focus on departure. Most office meetings lose productivity after an hour or two. All-day or multiday meetings should allow for significant breaks for relaxation. Few people can concentrate with the attention required in a meeting for a seven-hour stretch even with lunch and coffee breaks. One productive all-day format, especially at an off-site location with recreational facilities, is to meet from 8 A.M. to 12 P.M. and reconvene from 4 to 6 P.M., leaving the afternoon for relaxation, beach time, exercise, and socializing.

■ **Process duration.** Most of a meeting's process will be under your control, but a particularly complex presentation or exercise may have to be broken into two parts or require advance preparation by the participants in order to be workable in a meeting.

DETERMINANTS OF PLACE

Where you hold your meeting will depend upon your purpose, meeting size and duration, travel considerations, need for equipment, and budget. Assess your needs: a computer lab? a neutral space in which to negotiate? a conference room with auditorium-style seating? an off-site location to foster informality and prevent interruptions? a central location to reduce travel time and cost?

CAUTION

Be sure to budget your meeting, including accommodations, meeting space, travel, meals, equipment, and entertainment, before committing to contractual arrangements. Large, off-site meetings involving conference center or hotel space often require 12 to 18 months' lead time, substantial deposits, and cancellation penalties.

DETERMINANTS OF PROCESS

Choosing the process of your meeting depends on both its purpose and the tools most effective in reaching the outcome desired. An agenda and an advance briefing of participants, both discussed in the section "Preparation Time" on page 755, will lay the groundwork for the process of your meeting. Before you can do either, you need to evaluate and select processes appropriate to your meeting:

- How will you introduce the meeting? The participants? The topics?
- How will information be presented? Orally? In a written narrative? Graphic handouts? Electronic display? Group exercise?
- At what point will discussion occur, and how will it be facilitated?
- What tools will you use for problem identification? For assigning problem ownership? For problem analysis and solving?
- What decision-making method(s) will you use?

THE 30-SECOND RECAP

- A clear rationale for your meeting is critical to successful planning.
- Determining who to invite requires identifying who has the necessary information, expertise, and authority to act in a given situation, as well as who can facilitate and record the meeting.
- The timing and length of your meeting will vary with the availability of participants, urgency of action, seasonality of your organization's activities, internal and external deadlines, cost, productive times of day, and process duration.
- The ideal location for your meeting depends on its purpose, the meeting size and duration, travel considerations, equipment needs, and budget.
- The process of your meeting needs to be thought through before setting an agenda or briefing participants.

The Importance of Environment

In this section you learn how to choose the location, physical space, and room setup to contribute to an effective meeting.

The environment you select for a meeting will impact its success. In the context of a meeting, environment includes every factor that affects the thinking, feeling, and behavior of the participants. Environment consists of the type of facility, site location, room size and shape, seating and work space, lighting, temperature, ventilation, colors, freedom from interruptions and distractions, and, for lengthy or multiday meetings, food service, overnight accommodations, and availability of recreation.

In some situations, the purpose of the meeting will determine where some meetings are held. For example, when a problem requires an emergency meeting, it will be held immediately in the facility where participants are located; if a meeting includes a tour of a manufacturing facility, it will be held in or near that facility; and a hands-on training meeting in new software will be held in a computer lab. For many meetings without such urgency or constraints, you have choices about where to hold them. Paying attention to elements you can control will make your meeting more productive.

For any meeting that will incur out-of-pocket costs, the first step in choosing a location is to determine your budget. Develop your cost estimate and measure it against the benefit of the meeting, adjust the estimate up or down as appropriate, and obtain the necessary approval to spend the planned amount.

CAUTION

Even if you included a meeting's costs in your (approved) annual budget, it is important to get any approval necessary before making spending and contract commitments. As revenue forecasts change and unforeseen events occur, spending on meetings may be cut or increased to meet a strategic objective.

Ordering sandwiches and cookies for a lunchtime meeting obviously requires a different level of planning and approvals than a 10-day national sales conference, but don't ignore this stage of your planning.

LOCATION, LOCATION, LOCATION

A meeting's location immediately communicates information to participants about the tone of the meeting. Location sets the scene for information sharing, learning, negotiation, team building, problem solving, and social interaction. The longer the meeting, the longer the *window of opportunity* in which to have an impact on participants and the more important the location.

PLAIN ENGLISH

Window of opportunity   A finite time period during which some action, not possible before or after this period, becomes possible. In a two-hour training meeting, the window of opportunity for direct experiential learning is only two hours, although reinforcement may occur later and the benefit may be permanent.

Location telegraphs tone, seriousness, investment, and purpose. Factors in determining location also include the size and length of the meeting, accessibility to public transportation and distance participants have to travel, and needs for equipment, meals, overnight accommodations, and entertainment.

Here are some typical meeting locations:

- For short, partial, or full-day meetings, **on-site locations**—office, conference room, factory floor, computer lab—signify a get-down-to-business attitude and a level of formality correlative to that of the organization.

- **Hotel meeting rooms** are an option for accommodating a large group (when on-site space is too small), planning a meal break for lengthy meetings, removing staff from the distractions of day-to-day work in the office environment, gathering telecommuting or field sales representatives in a central, often urban, location, or creating a neutral space for negotiation between two parties that gives neither a "home court" advantage.

- For multiday meetings, **conference centers,** often set in nonurban locales or attached to university campuses or even religious retreat facilities, demonstrate a seriousness of purpose and a desire to create a distraction- and interruption-free environment. While the dress may be casual, the structure of the meeting day may be quite elaborate and formal. Business and food services run from rudimentary to outstanding, but entertainment options may be limited.

- **Resorts,** most often used for longer meetings that entail team-building, social interaction, lengthy training, and sometimes rewards for outstanding performance, set a casual tone that remains purposeful because the cost is significantly higher than other locations, especially for large groups.

TIP

If you are planning a meeting in a resort setting, set and clearly communicate your organization's policy on bringing family members and/or domestic partners. Your staff may see the meeting as a company-paid family vacation, when your need may be for a highly focused meeting interspersed with relaxation and team-building.

Some prominent hotel chains specialize in business conferences in a resort setting and can provide smooth, worry-free setups even for very large groups. You choose such a setting when there is a strategic reason, such as a need to break up long days of new product introductions, to provide a variety of interesting things to do and places to visit during down time, such as a beach, a wildlife refuge, a casino, or lavish entertainment events. Examples of events range from ski-lift-to-the-mountain-top barbecues to catered sunset sails to theme balls requiring participants to pack costumes.

I once attended a sales conference where one evening's entertainment included mini-training at a nationally renowned clown school followed by a circus performance in which many of the 100 conference attendees participated in full makeup and costumes along with the professional trapeze artists and fire-eaters. Arrangements for entertainment at this level require not just a conference planner as suggested in the section "Planning Your Meeting Strategically" on page 741, but a *destination management company*.

PLAIN ENGLISH

Destination management company   A company that specializes in planning events for clients traveling to their locale. These organizations have extensive knowledge of local attractions and facilities and experience at tailoring an event for your group that you or your conference planner cannot buy "off the shelf."

See "Out of the Boardroom" on page 803, for additional location ideas.

MEETING ROOM BASICS

Across all of these locations, certain basics that seem obvious can cause havoc when they are not evaluated in the meeting planning process. Check out these items in choosing meeting rooms:

- **Room size and shape.** Choose a room large enough to accommodate the number of participants comfortably, but not so large that the group will feel lost in it. A room that holds 50 comfortably auditorium style may hold 25 at seated work spaces. Crowding will dilute concentration as well as comfort. Square rooms promote physical and psychological cohesion, which is important in group work. Long, narrow rooms create distance and problems of seeing and hearing participants at the other end.

■ **Audio-visual and electronic tools capability.** Overhead projectors and flip charts are fairly portable, but additional and newer tools may be desirable. Can you get microphones and sound systems set up? Is there a hookup for computer network and Internet access? Are extensive, fold-out white boards available for list making? Are televisions and VCRs readily available? Are the walls designed for taping up the results of small group brainstorming on flip chart pages for group discussion?

■ **Work space.** If you need work space for your participants, what is available? Tables? Computers? Linen-covered banquet tables?

■ **Lighting.** The longer the meeting, the more light matters: the kind of light, placement, and intensity.

■ **Temperature and ventilation.** This sounds like a no-brainer until you hold a Saturday meeting in January in a large office building, but forget to inform building management that you need the heat turned up past its weekend setting. If the hotel meeting room is in a basement, ventilation may be nonexistent or incapable of solving the problem. Typically, 68° is generally accepted as cool enough to keep participants alert and warm enough to keep them comfortable and focused.

TIP

For an on-site meeting, make sure you understand whose responsibility it is to assure heat or air-conditioning will be turned on. Offsite, visit a potential location and satisfy yourself that adequate and functioning heat or air-conditioning and ventilation will be available.

■ **Color.** You can't repaint the conference room to accommodate your meeting, but all other things being equal, choose a room in neutral colors. For long meetings, bright colors add energy. Dark walls, carpet, drapes, and furniture induce drowsiness, do not reflect light, and convey a feeling of being closed in.

■ **Noise level.** Nothing kills concentration faster or more effectively than competing noise. Noise may be easiest to control in your own office building or facility and hardest to control next to a manufacturing facility or in a hotel hosting multiple meetings. I have attended meetings suddenly competing with a dance band in the next room and heard speakers whose presentations contain unintended audio effects from a sales-meeting-cum-pep-rally on the other side of a room divider. Be sure to specify your need for quiet and request that rooms next to the one you reserve not be used at the same time as your meeting—especially in a hotel where the event next to yours could be a wedding reception or a job fair.

CAUTION

If you are planning a meeting in an off-site facility, put in your contract that there will be no contemporaneous events scheduled in rooms contiguous to yours, and make sure there is a financial penalty and a "Plan B" in place, just in case.

SEATING DYNAMICS

Seating arrangements matter. Issues impacted by seating arrangements include ease of communication, group energy, level of participation, group interaction, concentration, and control. Factors that determine seating arrangements include room shape, table and chair options, meeting format and activities, and relative status of participants. Your objective in choosing seating arrangements is to *optimize* the impact of seating on the work of the meeting despite any constraints on obtaining the setup that is ideal for your purpose. Typical constraints are having no table options except a narrow, rectangular table or a need to adapt to a cultural norm, for example, to seat by age because age confers status in Asia.

PLAIN ENGLISH

Optimize   To find a method to make a system, design, or a decision as flawless, effective, or productive as possible under implied or specified conditions. To optimize seating for a meeting is to create the most favorable positioning for positive interaction.

Here are some basic criteria to help choose a seating pattern:

- A speaker or facilitator needs to be able to see and hear everyone in the room.
- Each participant should be able to see and hear everyone in the room and have a clear view of any aids used in visual presentation, such as

projection screens or flip charts. The angle between a participant and the visual aid is as important as the distance.

▓ If at all possible, aim for movable seating. Movable seating allows people to move comfortably closer or further away from a table or computer. It also allows the facilitator to set up subgroup discussions or team exercises easily.

▓ Participants need sufficient room between them so they won't feel crowded, but not to be so far apart or distant from the facilitator or speaker that they feel excluded from the group.

▓ No participant should be seated facing a door, which draws the eye away from the speaker or facilitator or group member who is speaking.

▓ If a meeting room has windows, participants should not be seated facing them during a meeting held in daylight. The back lighting effect makes it hard to look at the presenter or facilitator, not to mention the distraction of scenery.

TIP

The longer the meeting, the more comfortable the chairs need to be in order to maintain concentration. Hard plastic chairs are only easy on the budget. Upholstered chairs should be the minimum; armrests, adjustable backs, and swivel chairs all help participants to sit more comfortably for long periods.

Seating options vary by facility; an auditorium rarely has removable seats, and many boardroom tables were not designed for frequent disassembly to create alternative seating. Possibilities and the impact on group dynamics are as follows:

▓ A **rectangular or oval conference table** is the most common setup in meeting rooms and boardrooms, and the least helpful for group work. Sitting opposite someone promotes confrontation; sitting next to a facilitator or leader suggests a stronger alliance than with more distant participants; and sitting at a corner suggests ambivalence about participation. A facilitator sitting at one end focuses attention on that individual rather than the issues of the meeting and has the undesired effect of placing some participants much more distant from the leader than others. If you must use a rectangular or oval conference table, the facilitator should sit in the middle of one side rather than at one end. Seating exceptionally talkative participants on either side of the facilitator assists the facilitator in focusing on other participants to ensure everyone contributes.

▨ **Round conference tables or circles** result in circular seating, which provides the most direct face-to-face interaction possible, making this style ideal for full-group discussion. Circular seating without chairs intensifies the directness of the interaction and allows you to arrange two circles, one inside the other for a *fishbowl discussion.*

PLAIN ENGLISH

Fishbowl discussion   A discussion in which one subgroup is observed by one or more other subgroups, as when you observe fish through their tank. Fishbowl discussions can also be set up with a rectangular or square table (one side of the table conducts a discussion) or at groups of small tables.

▨ A **square conference table** has many of the benefits of a round table as people are equally distant from others and can see and hear each other, unlike at a rectangular table.

▨ A **U-shaped setup** is a great configuration for a moderately large group (10 to 25 people) because it allows the facilitator or speaker to make eye contact with each participant more easily than in a configuration that positions participants directly on either side of the facilitator. The U-shaped setup also expedites handout distribution and allows a clear view of both a speaker and any visual aids.

▨ In the **classroom style,** straight rows of seats facing a facilitator or speaker should be avoided. Arrange chairs and tables in a *chevron* configuration or a *semicircle* to increase participants' vision range and sense of being in a group. This configuration, like auditoriums and computer labs, is most often used for informational and training meetings rather than those with much discussion. Immobile chairs limit options for spacing or small group work, so if this is your only option, ask participants to gather front and center to create group coherence.

PLAIN ENGLISH

Chevron   An object or pattern having the shape of a V or inverted V. Here, it refers to an inverted V seating configuration facing the facilitator or speaker.

- The **amphitheater style,** a circle with the leader in the middle, can be used effectively for large groups. All energy is directed toward the person in the center.
- The **banquet or breakout style,** small tables spaced far apart, facilitates small group discussion and problem solving.

THE 30-SECOND RECAP

- Creating an appropriate environment is critical to the success of your meeting because it impacts thought, emotion, and behavior.
- Environment includes the type of facility, site location, room size and shape, audio-visual capability, seating and work space, lighting, temperature, ventilation, colors, freedom from interruptions and distractions, food service, and for multiday meetings, overnight accommodations and availability of recreation.
- Location options include on-site offices, conference rooms, computer labs, hotel meeting rooms, conference centers, and resorts.
- Large, complex, and lengthy meetings, especially in distant locations, require professional planners.
- Seating dynamics impact ease of communication, group energy, participation, interaction, concentration, and control.

Preparation Time

In this section you learn how to structure an agenda and plan for audio-visual and electronic aids.

Structuring your meeting in advance is a critical element to ensure its effectiveness. Communicating that structure to participants in the form of an agenda, along with any materials they need to review in advance, helps to manage the expectations of the group for the meeting and ensure that all participants will come to the meeting prepared to participate appropriately.

The section "Effective Meeting Basics" on page 724 discussed the need to identify the objective or purpose of a meeting, the expectation of what is to occur by the end of the meeting, and the information needed for this expectation to be met and steps to go forward (for the post-meeting action). I also discussed the process, or how the meeting will take place, based upon its purpose. (Types of meetings were introduced in the section "Types of

Meetings" on page 730.) Having ensured this meeting is the right tool for the job at hand in the section "Is This Meeting Necessary?" on page 736, selecting participants was discussed in the section "Planning Your Meeting Strategically" on page 741.

In this section, I build on these discussions by putting these elements—content, process, and participants—into an agenda and discuss planning any audio-visual and electronic aids.

ORDER OF TOPICS

An agenda's first task is to remind participants of the upcoming meeting: the date, time, and place.

Providing a list of participants helps attendees tailor their advance materials or remarks to the knowledge level and *need-to-know* status of other participants. This list can be as brief as "Executive Committee; Guest Outsider Venture Capitalist" or, for a national professional association meeting, as elaborate as an addendum providing name, contact information, and professional affiliation for thousands of attendees.

PLAIN ENGLISH

Need-to-know   A designation of whether or not to share information with an individual in order to obtain an expected outcome. Restricting information dissemination on this basis assures both security and confidentiality of sensitive information and reduces the amount of information received by someone who won't be acting on it.

Next, the agenda should clearly state the purpose of the meeting and the expected outcome(s). Even a regularly scheduled staff meeting will have different topics based on current projects whether they involve production cycles, grant applications, staffing levels, sales targets, employee morale, or accounts receivable.

Example 1: Weekly Production Meeting 2/1/02 (for a Book Publisher)

Agenda Items	Expected Outcome
Shorten schedule for first e-book	Guarantee 3/1 pub date (tie in to movie release date, moved up from 6/1)
Status of April 2002 Publications	Correct bindery delays
Status of May 2002 Publications	Approve cover art
Estimate of Fall 2002 List	Approve production budget
Review of book packager contracts	5 percent cost reduction

In this example, the order of agenda items is determined by the up-coming publication dates of the books, so that the most timely issues are addressed first. That's an obvious order, but not necessarily the only one. The most urgent (approve the cover art before the artist leaves for Milan on the 4 o'clock plane), most complex (the budget for the publisher's first 5-color book or list of 200 titles that exceeds the contracted printer's capacity), or most controversial (attempting cost reductions from a vendor) item may consume most of the time, energy, and effort of the participants. When in the meeting should such an item be discussed?

Urgent issues are probably *not* the first item on the agenda, although the cover art approval in Example 1 might jump to the top of the queue. You should get announcements, routine items, and simpler items out of the way before tackling more difficult issues. On the other hand, difficult and important items need to be scheduled early enough in the meeting to ensure they are addressed.

Another determinant of the order of topics is logical flow: In problem-solving, step x has to come before step y. Although some components overlap, the problem-solving sequence is generally as follows:

1. Problem identification and description
2. Problem ownership
3. Problem analysis
4. Solution criteria development
5. Alternative solution generation
6. Solution evaluation
7. Decision-making
8. Action steps to implementation
9. Follow-up to measure success of solution chosen.

In any one meeting, one or all these steps can be on the agenda.

In a training meeting or information-sharing meeting, it's just as important as in a problem-solving meeting to prepare an order of topics and outcomes:

Example 2: Employee Benefits Open Enrollment Meeting for 2003 Agenda

Topic	You Will Understand
Health plan benefit changes	Options A, B, and C
Premiums, deductibles, and co-pays	Costs of Options A, B, and C
Flexible spending plans	What they are and how they work

continues

Example 2: Employee Benefits Open Enrollment Meeting for 2003 Agenda *(continued)*

Topic	You Will Understand
Health club membership benefit	A new benefit for 2003
Addition of new fund for 401(k)	A higher-risk and higher-return investment vehicle
Test on 2003 benefits	How well you understand them
Question-and-answer period	Answers to questions you didn't get answered previously
Assistance in filling out enrollment forms	How to obtain the coverage chosen

CAUTION

In any presentation of information that is going to increase out-of-pocket expenses for an employee, cause production delays, or produce any other negative result, be prepared for criticism and discuss action taken to mitigate, offset, or prevent repetition of that negative result, such as looking for cheaper or more reliable vendors.

When determining your list of agenda items, in some situations such as staff meetings, you may want to solicit regular participants for items they would like to put on the agenda. Alternatively, you can schedule an "Open Forum" time near the end of the meeting for people to bring up topics.

For especially sensitive or important meetings, your agenda preparation may include asking colleagues or selected participants to review your draft agenda; asking selected individuals for their agenda ideas or to advise you on their views of issues on the agenda to avoid surprises; and having a "dress rehearsal" of key elements, such as presentations.

CAUTION

Opening up an agenda for unplanned topics may be risky (or it may be a value of your organization's culture). It lessens your control over the meeting. Set a policy about introducing topics during the meeting (that may mean obtaining consensus about what the policy should be) and stick to it.

DISCUSSION LEADERS

Just as critical as the order of topics is the assignment of discussion or exercise leaders and presenters. This sounds obvious—whoever owns the project or has the expertise should lead the discussion or present the material. However, in many situations it may not be clear who is responsible for a given problem. In this instance, it might be wiser to assign discussion leaders for what you *do* know about the problem, such as symptoms or manifestations, or to assign a leader just to facilitate an open discussion in order to assemble relevant facts.

In other situations, there may be reasons to select a discussion leader other than the obvious one or the highest-level participant from a given department or function. A meeting might be a good opportunity to assign a discussion leadership role to a promising employee or one usually in the background, both for that employee's professional development and to develop an organization's *bench strength*.

PLAIN ENGLISH

Bench strength   A team's depth of talent; if a member is ill or injured, a substitute can take over her or his role with no reduction in the team's performance. The term comes from sports but is equally applicable to any organization with highly differentiated functions.

In groups of peers with similar roles in the organization, such as a regional sales meeting, discussion or activity leaders can be chosen on a rotational basis, alphabetically, by sales performance, by birthday, or at random, because the goal is shared responsibility and the capability is, by and large, equivalent.

For a discussion of the assignment of roles to participants in your meeting, see the section "The Mechanics of Facilitation" on page 764. You may also want to assign roles in advance and distribute them with the agenda.

TIME ALLOTMENT

Your primary tool to ensure that your meeting is effective in the designated time frame is to allot time for each item on the agenda. To do this well, you need reasonable assessments of the amount of time needed for each discussion, presentation, exercise, assignment of action items, and recap.

How to do this? If your total time frame is locked in, choose only agenda items that can be accomplished within the total time, and select postponable items for deferral to another meeting. If the project or agenda items are going to determine the length of the meeting, you still want to allot time to each of the items to ensure that you cover what you plan (and announce).

How do you determine how long each agenda item will take?

■ **Experience.** If you've run weekly staff meetings for a long time, you know, roughly, how long it takes to have a discussion of the pros and cons of proposed changes to the faculty reappointment review process in a meeting of 10 people. If you run the meetings to decide whether or not a new drug is ready to be presented to the Food and Drug Administration for approval, you know how long it usually takes to present and decide if a drug has met the benchmarks and criteria your firm requires for submission. If you are planning to lead your umpteenth brainstorming exercise, you know about how long it takes for the size of group that will be participating.

■ **Practice.** If you're the presenter, time your presentation; if not, ask any presenter how long he or she needs. If you think that amount of time is unfeasible, suggest shortening or lengthening it and explain why. If it's your first time leading an exercise or doing a slide presentation, do a "dry run" beforehand and time it.

■ **Ask an expert.** If you hire a professional facilitator for your meeting, part of what you hire is her or his advice on timing the agenda items. If you're a novice at running a meeting but have attended similar ones, look at the previous agenda and assess the adequacy of the time allotments. If you're a seasoned meeting leader, holding a meeting featuring exercises you've never done or a problem unlike any previous ones analyzed, ask someone who's had similar experience for guidance.

■ **Set parameters.** In a team-building exercise, the process of ensuring participation by each member may be as important an objective as the content of the exercise. So you may have to arrive at an estimated time by allowing one to five minutes for each participant to speak (times the number of participants) plus a few moments for the introduction and summary. In a negotiation meeting, you may allot a certain amount of time for each item on the table and move to the next item no matter how much progress has been made on the current one. Alternatively, you can set a limit on the length of the meeting and agree not to leave an agenda item until resolution has been achieved even if you get through only some of the agenda items in the meeting.

You are making an educated, informed estimate. If an unusual development occurs in the meeting, you can adjust the agenda accordingly (see the section "Pacing the Meeting" on page 778).

CAUTION

An agenda is a guide, and there are times when part of your "road map" should be discarded. Be prepared to be flexible and adaptable, to continue a discussion that is too productive to stop, to cope with the unexpected absence of a presenter, or to deal with an equipment failure.

ADVANCE HANDOUTS

In theory, all handouts should be distributed before the meeting so participants can come to the meeting having read relevant material. This chore has been made much easier for the sender since e-mail eliminates both reproduction and transit time, although more tedious for the recipient who has to print it. In reality, handouts often include material or information so recently gathered or acquired, such as yesterday's sales figures, that an advance handout would contain stale information. So the real-world compromise is to send in advance all material except last-minute data and to distribute the hot-off-the-press material to participants' chairs or workspaces just before the meeting begins.

Extensive handouts should be organized and labeled by agenda item and sent with the agenda. Call it *Agenda Topic 1, Participant Preparation.* Such a handout might include ...

- Background reading, such as resumés of candidates for a search committee's review.

- Reports by other participants since a previous meeting.

- Assignments participants are to complete before the meeting, including follow-up on action items assigned at a previous meeting.

- Items to bring to the meeting, such as writing materials if not provided.

- Discussion questions to think about before the meeting.

TIP

Spelling, grammar, punctuation, and syntax checkers in word processing programs are fallible, and nothing saves you from word usage hell ("pubic policy" for "public policy," "ethically diverse" for "ethnically diverse," "there" for "their") except careful proofreading. Also, check for missing or out-of-order pages that occur in collation.

Audio-Visual and Electronic Aids

It's so simple, yet there are so many opportunities for something to go wrong. Ensuring audio-visual and electronic aids actually appear on cue and work properly is taking care of many different details, and if one goes wrong, you have the old Christmas tree string of lights that all go dark when one bulb wears out. I have experienced virtually all of these snafus; don't let them happen to you. To avoid them, answer these questions as soon as you know what equipment you need:

- Is the equipment you need available? If your vendor needs you to supply a laptop, don't agree to provide one until you know that the only one your organization owns is working, and not with a professor on sabbatical in Kenya.

- What is the *lead time* to reserve equipment? What is the lead time to reserve an audio-visual technician to run the video camera if you are recording the meeting? How much time do you have to allow for set up of microphones and speakers?

PLAIN ENGLISH

Lead time (pronounced *leed* not *led*)   The amount of advance notice required to obtain something or complete some action. For equipment and staff, it may be determined by departmental or organization policy; for purchases, a vendor may charge you air freight to shorten the wait.

- If you need access to the Internet for the presentation to work, is there a dataport in the room in which you are meeting? Is the dataport turned on or does that take a week's advance notice?

- Is every component and cable compatible with each other? Is there a working bulb in the overhead transparency projector? Whose responsibility is it to provide blank videotapes?

- Do you know how to use the configuration of equipment you have requested? In one meeting I witnessed, no one could find the volume knob on the television on which a benefactor's address was being played on a VCR. It was like watching a silent movie except embarrassing.

- If you are reserving a computer and the presenter's presentation requires certain software to run it, does the computer you are using have the necessary software program? I once attended a meeting where a senior official was unable to make his presentation because three successive computers brought by the audio-visual department did not have PowerPoint installed.

TIP

The only way to know your computer presentation, videotape, slide projector, or audio system will work is to try it out. There are no shortcuts and no exceptions. If a meeting starts early in the morning, have all the equipment set up and tested the night before.

- If using a flip chart, do you know how to change the pad (pressurized grip, wing nut, and screw)? How to assemble a portable flip chart stand? Where the flip chart presentation is? Do you have a blank flip chart pad if needed? Do you have flip chart markers in a variety of colors and in a quantity sufficient for the exercise planned?

THE 30-SECOND RECAP

- Advance planning for a meeting increases the likelihood of having an effective one.
- The topics for the agenda, their purpose, and the order in which they are listed will affect participants' expectations and suggest an active, productive meeting.
- Designating discussion leaders divides up responsibility for agenda items and offers opportunities for different members of the group to demonstrate and develop skills.
- Time management is facilitated by allotting finite amounts of time to each agenda item.
- Soliciting advice and feedback on the agenda helps to shape the meeting productively.
- Distributing the agenda and handout materials in advance prepares participants for their roles in the meeting.
- Setting up and testing all audio-visual and electronic equipment well in advance of the meeting is the only way to ensure everything will work as planned.

The Mechanics of Facilitation

In this section you learn how to define and assign roles to meeting partici-pants, prepare a meeting room, handle breaks and refreshments, and avoid distractions and interruptions.

Successful facilitation begins with thinking ahead of time about every detail, and then executing those details well. This section deals with *tangible* details that, if done well, support the process of the meeting and allow the facilitator to concentrate her or his efforts on the art of facilitation during the meeting, which is discussed in "The Art of Facilitation" on page 770.

PLAIN ENGLISH

Tangible   Something perceivable but not necessarily physical. It is used here to mean physical, practical acts of meeting preparation and to differentiate those acts from those involving interpersonal skills, such as guiding problem-solving or conflict resolution.

Once you master these practical details, they will become second nature to you in planning future meetings or delegating these tasks.

ASSIGNMENT OF ROLES

One powerful tool for planning an effective meeting is assigning roles and responsibilities to participants, often in advance; however, in small, informal meetings it's sometimes done at the start of the meeting.

These roles are important to virtually every meeting:

- As the individual who initiated and planned a meeting, your role is often a **manager.** You "own" the meeting and are ultimately respon-sible for its outcome. You set the agenda, choose the attendees and the process of the meeting, urge participants to accept roles in the meeting, and take follow-up assignments. You may make final deci-sions or be part of a team with that authority. In an informational, training, or negotiating meeting, you may be the discussion leader, presenter, or lead negotiator.

- The role of the meeting manager may or may not include the role of **facilitator.** The facilitator's role includes ensuring that all partici-pants are engaged and contribute, the chosen process takes place, pacing is controlled and the agenda met, follow-up tasks are assigned, and all participants agree on the outcome of the meeting.

This may include testing participants to verify what was learned in a training or informational meeting, doing a *process check,* and ensuring that assigned tasks are completed before the next meeting.

The facilitator's role often includes deflecting hidden agendas, resolving conflicts, and clarifying participants' statements or other contributions; these topics are covered in the section "The Art of Facilitation" on page 770. In order to perform this role successfully, a facilitator has to remain neutral, and therefore gives up both contributing and evaluating ideas.

PLAIN ENGLISH

Process check   An evaluation of a series of actions or operations conducive to a particular end. It is often done at the end of a meeting when participants' experiences are fresh.

- Another role is **recorder,** someone whose primary role is to capture and memorialize the ideas presented and discussed as well as the arguments or contributions that led to decisions.
- The role of **active participant** is to engage in the meeting as an active listener receiving information or training, or as a contributor and evaluator of ideas.

CAUTION

Assuming attendees know what is expected of them often results in participants not knowing that their contributions are required or how they are valued. Set forth the expectations at the start of a meeting. Listing the "rules" on a flip chart keeps them available to all during the meeting.

ROOM PREPARATION

Preparing a meeting room includes every physical element, including …

- **Seating and work spaces.** If the room you are using is not permanently set up for the seating and work space arrangements selected, allow plenty of time for the changes to be made, whether an in-house facilities staff actually does the changes or you have to round up office volunteers to do the job. Disassembling a large boardroom table and removing it via a freight elevator, for example, can take hours, not minutes.

Check to make sure the room is immaculate—food and papers from previous meetings have been removed, work surfaces and carpet are clean, and there is a coatroom or coatrack available.

TIP

Aim to have the meeting room completely ready one hour before the meeting, and any food deliveries completed at least 30 minutes before they are scheduled to be consumed. That way, if some unforeseen event causes a delay, you have some time to remedy it.

■ **Signage.** If you're having a large meeting in a hotel, conference center, or resort facility, signage includes having your meeting listed on the "Events of the Day" board in the lobby (which may be electronic), near any lobby elevators or stairs to the meeting room, and just outside the meeting room(s). If you are planning a professional association meeting for which corporate sponsorship was solicited, be sure to credit the sponsor; for example, "Afternoon coffee break sponsored by Company Name." This signage may require significant *lead time* in order for the print shop to create, enlarge, and mount the sign on poster board.

Signage also may include *tent cards* for speakers or presenters and sometimes for participants who are unknown to each other. These can be printed from most word-processing programs—but you want to have them printed on pre-scored, heavy-weight stock, so here, too, advance planning counts.

PLAIN ENGLISH

Tent cards (called so because when folded in half lengthwise and put on a flat surface they create an inverted V that looks like a tent) are used to identify speakers on a dais or participants in a meeting and are especially useful in interactive meetings.

■ **Lighting.** Check lighting and where the switches are in case the room will be dimmed for a slide, VCR, or computer presentation. Check temperature and ventilation in advance of the meeting so there is time for adjustments. Remember that a room will warm up as people fill it, so start with a slightly cooler, rather than warmer, room.

■ **Audio-visual and electronic aids.** These were discussed in the section "Preparation Time" on page 755, but it's always a good idea to test run the actual videotape, slide show, or computer presentation just before the meeting and hang up a prepared flip chart if using one.

■ **Individual writing materials.** These should be placed at each seat in advance, along with a copy of the agenda and any handouts not predistributed. Place any other props out of sight until needed: blank flip chart pads, masking tape if hanging group work on the walls, plenty of markers, index cards, and whatever is required for the activities of your meeting.

AVOIDING DISTRACTIONS

Planning ahead and setting meeting *protocols* will go a long way toward minimizing distractions.

PLAIN ENGLISH

Protocols   Rules of etiquette, convention, and procedure unique to a type of meeting, the nature of an exercise, a branch of diplomatic or military service, or a culture. In a meeting setting, participants are expected to agree to these rules for the good of the meeting.

Some meeting protocols should be provided in advance to participants, such as how to send messages so participants can instruct their staff (and families) how and when to reach them when necessary. By stating or restating these protocols at the start of the meeting, it is more likely that participants will honor them. Other protocols are just formal procedures that ensure certain tasks are accomplished, such as census-taking, that can prevent backtracking or reconstructing events after the fact.

Examples of protocols include …

■ Using sign-in sheets for census, attendance, or quorum purposes.

■ Starting and ending the meeting on time.

■ Taking formal steps required for certain meetings, such as approving minutes or proposing and seconding of motions.

■ Announcing how long will be devoted to a step, topic, or process and keeping to that time frame.

■ Setting time limits for any one participant's contribution or evaluation.

■ Returning from breaks on time.

■ Asking that cell phones and pagers be turned off or at least muted and not responded to until a break.

■ Ensuring that all materials needed for a meeting are in the room prior to its start to avoid both delays and interruptions for deliveries.

■ Arranging for snacks and meals to be in a separate room from the meeting to avoid interruptions and distractions of set up and clean up.

TIP

For a long meeting with a large number of participants, arrange for a message board just outside a meeting room where participants can receive messages and place them for fellow participants.

BREAK ARRANGEMENTS

Most people's attention spans don't last much longer than an hour and a half. Even in three-hour workshops that I run for graduate students, filled with interactive exercises, I try to schedule a formal 10- to 15-minute break halfway through to maintain productivity, and suggest that everyone leave the room during that break.

In a longer meeting, one of the breaks may include a "stretch in place" exercise, led by the facilitator, to prevent sore backs, necks, and legs.

In multiday meetings, planners are increasingly aware the *law of diminishing returns* applies to a series of seven-hour days. Even a three-day conference will be more productive if at least one of those days, there is no formal meeting time for at least a half day. People may use that time for planned or spontaneous recreational events, especially in a resort location. Another use of this time is for individual meetings and relationship-building and camaraderie between participants.

PLAIN ENGLISH

The law of diminishing returns   States that beyond a certain point, additional investment will not produce proportionate results. In meetings, participants cannot absorb information or problem solve at the same rate in hour seven as they could in the first hour.

REFRESHMENTS

Refreshments can be totally absent in a brief meeting, as simple as pitchers of ice water and glasses, or as elaborate as a themed five-course meal. Consider the length of the meeting, cost, and precedent for the type of meeting in the organization. As noted in the section "Effective Meeting Basics" on page 724, refreshments will affect both the productivity and perceptions of the participants. Caffeine in coffee and soft drinks may provide a burst of energy after a mid-morning or mid-afternoon break, while alcohol served at lunch may impair judgment and interpersonal effectiveness all afternoon.

CAUTION

If you do choose to provide alcohol, ensure two things: Participants under legal age do not have access to alcoholic drinks and any adult choosing to consume alcoholic drinks has alternative transportation to driving after imbibing.

The refreshments you serve send messages to participants whether you are serving a major sponsoring client's branded snacks or putting together a full meal. It is considerate to provide healthy options, such as fruit and low-fat cereal, along with breakfast pastries, and to offer decaffeinated coffee and tea. Offer fruit and vegetable snacks alongside the gourmet cookies at break, and juices as well as soft drinks. If your budget can't support refreshments, direct participants to places they can purchase them.

Meeting meals are not the time for exotic menus; no matter how much *you* like shellfish in green curry, there's a strong likelihood some participants won't. Additionally, special dietetic needs must be taken into account. For a small meeting, you can survey participants in advance and request appropriate meals, but for a large meeting, menu options need to be available for diabetic, low-fat, low-salt, vegetarian, and Kosher requirements.

Meeting refreshments can reflect a consistent belt-tightening throughout an organization, a thoughtfulness about participants' preferences and needs, and a flair for choosing tasty, appropriate foods. They can be a component in rewarding performance or accomplishment, or a celebration. Done well, they can add to the effectiveness of a meeting.

THE 30-SECOND RECAP

- Assigning roles (manager, facilitator, recorder, active participant) and articulating expectations for each provide clear guidelines and accountability.
- Preparing a meeting room in advance includes every physical element: seating and work spaces, cleanliness, signage, lighting, audiovisual and electronic aids, and individual writing and exercise materials.
- Setting protocols regarding messages, honoring time limits, and sources of interruptions and distractions help to keep participants focused and productive.

- Providing breaks appropriate to the length of the meeting increase productivity.

- Refreshments can improve productivity but also convey messages of respect, consideration, reward, or celebration to participants.

The Art of Facilitation

In this section you learn how to manage the interactions of participants to assure clear communication and to remain focused on the subject, process, and objectives of the meeting.

The art of facilitation is the application of interpersonal skills to situations that arise in a meeting. These situations are less foreseeable, more variable from meeting to meeting based upon the personalities of the individuals present and the nature of the meeting, and therefore less able to be *scripted* in advance than the tangible mechanics of facilitation.

There are, however, tools that can guide you or your designated meeting facilitator in applying interpersonal skills to the interactions that might come up in the course of the meeting. First, make a clear distinction between the roles of facilitator and manager or leader.

PLAIN ENGLISH

Scripted event   Event for which a carefully prepared dialogue has been written, as in the script of a play that is followed precisely in a production.

FACILITATION VS. LEADERSHIP

The art of facilitation implies a personal, creative power. So does leadership. How do they differ?

Leadership is directive: Its intention is to influence, to govern, and to introduce new information that would not otherwise be provided in a meeting, such as a teacher introduces new concepts into a classroom. Leadership is a role of active guidance. This role is deliberate and effective in meetings to convey information, such as staff briefings and training meetings, and where persuasion is a goal, such as negotiations. The authority to make decisions is a necessary feature of leadership.

CAUTION

Leadership is not authoritarianism, and confusing the two concepts is a common mistake. Authoritarianism is about control; leadership is about direction and motivation. The end result of authoritarianism is knowing what the rules are; the end result of leadership is a commitment to the course of action chosen.

Facilitation is nondirective: Its intention is to elicit contributions without influencing the content of what is contributed. Facilitation is a role of enabling others to work through a process and to develop the required outcome. Facilitation in a meeting requires laying out the process, and then stepping back to let the group guide the discussion. Interventions of a facilitator are solely to ensure all participants are engaged and contribute, conflicts are resolved, the chosen process is followed, the meeting stays "on point," and the pace is maintained in order to cover the agenda. A facilitator does not make decisions but assists the group in coming to a specified outcome. This role is deliberate and effective in meetings where there is a need for participants to own the process, such as problem-solving meetings, project management meetings, and team-building meetings.

TIP

The role of facilitator is especially necessary in meetings called to discuss emotionally charged issues, such as the possible cancellation of someone's pet project, or who to lay off and who to retain when staff cuts must be made. A neutral facilitator will help keep the meeting from disintegrating.

Leadership and facilitation are not mutually exclusive; both roles may exist in the same meeting. Both roles may even be assumed by the same individual in a meeting.

CAUTION

While one person can act as both facilitator and leader in a meeting, this risks confusion in participants as to which role the person is in at any given moment. Which comment is a leader's signal of a direction to follow, and which is a facilitator's course-correction tactic?

Facilitation and leadership are both dynamic roles that rely on highly developed interpersonal skills. If one person must perform both roles, this individual must announce which role is being used with every intervention. I will focus on important facilitation skills and the tools used to deliver them.

INTERPERSONAL TOOLS

Facilitating a meeting does not mean turning yourself into a robot that jumps in to make interventions according to a set of rules. Be yourself, keep a sense of humor, and create a meeting culture that invites the free exchange of ideas. To establish this culture, demonstrate your trust in the group's ability to accomplish the objectives of the meeting. Successful facilitators use the following tools and strategies:

- Use open-ended questions and invite suggestions to demonstrate openness to new ideas.

- Reinforce the group's energy by encouraging universal contributions to engage each person in the business of the meeting.

- Model behavior that honors individuals: Avoid interrupting speakers, discarding suggestions, and ignoring someone who wants to speak.

- Solicit and protect differing opinions and ideas. This is a critical facilitation skill that prevents a meeting from turning into a pep rally for a preconceived notion or the most widely held view.

- Ask for feedback on both the content and the process of the meeting.

TIP

Observe each participant's eye contact with you and the group as well as their body language and oral contributions. Averted eyes, crossed arms, inattentive posture, and sidebar conversations are all signs that a person is not buying into the premise or process of a meeting.

Cultural expectations also color the usage of leadership versus facilitation roles. In the United States, the chair of a meeting is expected to drive the process of the meeting and to direct its outcome. A chair-person who wants to ensure participation and creative innovation may assign the role of facilitator to another participant to reduce the expected influence her or his position as chair confers. In Japan, the role of the chair is to achieve consensus, and the trade-offs made by the chair and the participants to achieve consensus may have unintended consequences, such as a failure to fully air and evaluate competing alternatives. This method impairs the quality of decisions made. The chair may have to adapt a more assertive role in order to elicit dissenting but valid ideas.

CLARITY AND REFLECTIVE LISTENING

One of the most important skills of a facilitator is ensuring clarity in everything that is presented, discussed, analyzed, or decided on in a meeting, so that all participants agree on the outcome.

As human beings we tend to assume a word, phrase, or concept clear to us is universally understood exactly as we understand it. In meetings there is often an assumed mindset that "everyone is on the same page." The facilitator is responsible for verifying that the message sent by a speaker or presenter is heard, whether the message contains information or presents a theory or supporting data. Here are some of the ways messages lose clarity and how a facilitator can overcome them:

- **Use of acronyms.** If a speaker or presenter does not provide the name represented by the acronym the first time it is mentioned, listeners may be left clueless. Even the AARP, which has changed its name to just that series of letters, refers to itself as "AARP, formerly the American Association of Retired Persons," so no listener misses the identity of the group. Likewise, a facilitator should explain acronyms used by a participant or ask, "Is everyone clear what AARP is?"

- **Use of lingo.** Many organizations use terms familiar to their members or professional shorthand to identify projects, processes, regulations, departments, and concepts. In a meeting, they may forget the lingo is unintelligible to those who don't know it. Examples: LIFO (last-in, first-out method of inventory accounting), 501(3) (IRS category for qualifying organizations exempt from taxes), galleys (first pass of a typeset manuscript). The facilitator's role is to translate the lingo into plain English, or if necessary, ask the participant who uses it to explain it in everyday language.

- **Use of nonliteral language,** such as idioms and metaphors. Wordsmiths like me think they are adding clarity by using idiomatic and symbolic language to build analogies and explain concepts. The danger is in assuming that the idiomatic terms and *tropes* are understood, especially with nonnative speakers of English.

PLAIN ENGLISH

Trope   The use of a familiar word or expression to express an idea other than the term's usual meaning. For example, "her voice was music to my ears" conveys not that the speaker was singing, but that her speaking voice brought pleasure to the listener.

The facilitator should not attempt to squeeze all the color out of participants' speech, or meetings would be very dull indeed; but he or she should be alert for any misreading or confusion.

- **Verbosity and excess detail.** The point of any discussion can get lost in long expositions and minutiae. To encourage concision, a facilitator can limit the amount of time devoted to any one speaker or topic both in the agenda and by adjustments made during the meeting.

- **Oversimplification.** Conversely, the "keep it simple" rule can result in glossing over critical items, and the role of the facilitator is to ensure that does not occur. Asking "Are those all the points we should be addressing?" or "Do we have a complete picture?" may help prevent this error.

- **Sidebar conversation.** The facilitator may have to close off any individual conversations as they distract other participants and effectively disengage those individuals from the meeting.

- **Assumed understanding.** Silence is not confirmation of comprehension; it may be speechlessness caused by confusion.

One of the best tools for assuring clarity is *reflective listening.*

PLAIN ENGLISH

Reflective listening   The act of confirming what was said. It is the "playback" mode of interaction in the words of the listener rather than the speaker.

As a facilitator, you model reflective listening. When anything is said that is not common knowledge to the group, you as facilitator can ask questions, such as "Do you mean _____?" "Are you saying _____?" "This is what I heard; did I get it right?" "Are you making the same argument Sam made a few minutes ago?" "I'm not sure what you mean; could you give us an example?" Asking such questions will encourage others to ask them, identify misconceptions and elicit clarifications, and contribute to the understanding of all participants.

CONFLICT RESOLUTION

Conflicts and controversy are common in meetings. They arise from different perspectives, different agendas, competition for organizational resources that may be allocated as a result of a meeting, and significant but differing impacts of the outcome of a meeting. Reasonable people differ: This kind of conflict is necessary to arrive at good decisions, and the facilitator's responsibility is to manage it toward that outcome.

However, conflicts also can be caused by personal antagonism, personality clashes, a lack of trust and openness, hidden agendas, and plain rude behavior. Here a facilitator's role is to defuse the tension so the meeting can move forward.

Conflict avoidance will fail; conflict management is the role of the facilitator. The facilitator has to anticipate conflicts and be prepared to address and resolve them in order to prevent the sabotage or failure of a meeting. Stifling conflict or allowing it to surface and create tension without resolution are counterproductive.

CAUTION

Be careful not to draw the focus of a conflict to you as the facilitator. You can squelch a conflict but that is not solving it. Your role is to assist the conflicting parties in resolving the conflict or controversy themselves.

The facilitator's role is to avoid polarization; having clear goals and looking for commonalities in differing goals are the first steps as is acknowledging those goals which are mutually exclusive or incompatible. Having objective criteria for decision making is equally important.

The focus is on the ideas being discussed and not the individuals who disagree. Keeping the focus on the issues and not the personalities also helps you as the facilitator remain emotionally removed and objective.

Sometimes, breaking down the disagreement into smaller components and finding some which the group can agree helps to defuse tension and establish that at least partial consensus is possible.

Using all the tools discussed earlier in this section to attain clarity may not prevent a meeting from disintegrating if conflict develops. Plan what you will do if conflict occurs, perhaps finding a mediator or meeting individually with the *saboteur(s)* will help. Even if the best outcome is only that you "agree to disagree," having arrived at that point may help the next meeting to go forward.

PLAIN ENGLISH

Saboteur   Someone inside a group or organization who engages in intentional destructive or obstructive behavior in order to undermine a collaborative effort. This behavior may not be overt or visible to others in the group.

TRAFFIC FLOW

A well-planned agenda with allotted times for each agenda item is the first line of defense against having your meeting bogged down. Smooth logistics, discussed in the section "The Mechanics of Facilitation" on page 764, will prevent unwanted delays, snafus with audio-visual and electronic aids, and avoidable distractions.

But to keep a meeting moving productively, a facilitator also needs to be attentive to blocks put up, unwittingly or intentionally, by participants. Prepare to be alert to the signs that are "red lights" to honest discussion. How do you recognize them?

Listen for phrases that block the critical examination of ideas either by pushing for one speaker's point of view or by belittling or discarding another participant's idea without considering it. Take a look at the following examples:

- "I've been telling you this is the problem for six months."
- "The solution is so obvious; I don't understand why we don't just do it without further discussion."
- "No one ever listens to what the engineers say until the production line breaks down."
- "This detail is not that important; let's move on."

Also observe participants for signs they are not really listening: impatiently waiting for a speaker to finish so they can say what they have been preparing to say next; jumping to conclusions; and assuming other participants have already agreed with them.

When you encounter such blocks, defuse them by stopping the discussion and explaining the need to air all sides and defer judgment. Question the speaker, ask for patience, and ask for opposite points of view.

TIP

As the facilitator, stay neutral and intervene only enough to get the discussion back on course. Use tone, body language, and choice of words to signify your neutrality.

HOW TO STAY ON POINT

Diversions to topics not on the agenda, digressions to tangential issues, and anecdotal asides all undermine the productivity of a meeting by reducing the time actually spent on discussing, informing, negotiating, analyzing, team-building, and deciding.

A facilitator's tools for staying on point include the following:

- Agree to schedule the "off point" topic for a future meeting.
- Ask how a tangential issue is pertinent to the agenda item under discussion.
- Remind speakers time is almost up for their input.
- Cut off speakers who talk past the allocated time.
- Add a period for rebuttal and summary at the end of the discussion period so participants feel heard.
- Ask participants' views on agenda adjustments that may have to be made as the meeting progresses.

Above all, stay flexible and adaptable as you work toward the common goal of staying focused on the topic and process chosen.

THE 30-SECOND RECAP

- Facilitation is distinct from leadership; facilitation is nondirective and helps participants reason critically, while leadership's purpose is to influence participants.
- A facilitator has to adapt her or his intervention style to accommodate cultural expectations other than her or his own.
- Facilitation tools include using open-ended questions, encouraging everyone to contribute, protecting minority opinions, explaining unclear language, engaging in reflective listening, and asking for feedback.
- Conflict and controversy are necessary where different points of view must be brought into consensus. Conflict resolution tools include focusing on issues rather than personalities, articulating clear goals and objective criteria, and breaking down conflicts into smaller components where some agreement may be found.
- To keep the meeting moving, a facilitator needs to be alert to barriers to honest discussion, which push or discard others' points of view.
- The facilitator also needs to intervene to table "off-agenda" or tangential issues and limit speakers to their allotted time in order to keep the meeting on point.

Pacing the Meeting

In this section you learn how to start, run, and end a meeting so that adequate attention is devoted to each agenda item.

Pacing a meeting for maximum productivity requires making an agreement with participants that you, as the facilitator, will honor time constraints, and they, as participants, will give their undivided attention and effort to the content and process of the meeting. This agreement may sound somewhat obvious and unnecessary, but meetings have acquired a bad name in many organizations because of starting late, rushing through agendas, getting bogged down on agenda items or off point or on tangential issues, and running over the allotted time.

Start by shaping the expectations for your meeting when you provide an advance distribution of the agenda. Make this contract explicit by stating in the agenda the meeting will start and end on time if everyone is prompt and arrives committed to the goals and objectives of the meeting. Commit to ensuring that you, as facilitator, will deliver on that promise.

GETTING STARTED

If your group, committee, organization, or leadership has established a precedent of late or sloppily run meetings, announcing that this meeting will be different may be met with skepticism on the part of participants. If you are planning a meeting of a new group or if the culture of your organization supports on-time, well-run meetings, your role is to live up to the expectation of a well-run meeting.

You do this by *modeling* good meeting behavior.

Good meeting behavior begins with starting the meeting precisely on time, which can happen only if all the preparation has been executed flawlessly, such as room preparation, delivery of meeting materials, and set up of refreshments (see the section "The Mechanics of Facilitation" on page 764). For example, for a breakfast meeting, you may want to announce in the agenda breakfast will be available 20 minutes before the start of the meeting to allow everyone to fill their plates and get settled.

PLAIN ENGLISH

Modeling   Setting an example, worthy of imitation, for others to follow. This example can be a pattern, process, style of behavior, or even a positive attitude.

Starting the meeting on time signals to participants and latecomers your meeting will get down to business quickly and use the time well, and suggests the meeting will end on time. Setting this precedent demonstrates your respect and appreciation for those who arrive on time. This is a positive way to begin.

TIP

The first thing to model is being on time: As the facilitator, be early, and not just because you have to eat *before* the breakfast meeting begins. Others will notice your arrival, and some will copy it; all will be on alert that this meeting will start on time.

Both to allow for stragglers, who should become fewer at each subsequent meeting if a series is anticipated, and to preempt questions about meeting mechanics, start your meeting with a brief welcome and thanks for promptness. Introduce any guests not known to the participants.

Next, provide information about "housekeeping" issues. These include ...

- Announcing break times and meal or refreshment arrangements.
- In an off-site facility, identifying location of rest rooms, telephones, and the hospitality suite; contact information for the meeting planner; and required reservations or sign-up lists for entertainment activities.

TIP

For large, multiday meetings, you may want to prepare a daily news bulletin announcing which entertainment events still have available slots, meeting room or time changes, recommended attire for the kayak trip through the Everglades, and departure times for the courtesy van to the airport.

- Announcing how, where, and when messages for participants can be retrieved.

Recap the purpose of the meeting, objectives, and expected outcomes even though they are on the agenda.

Introduce the process of the meeting. Is it an instructional lecture followed by a quiz? A workshop using *role play* exercises to practice good selling techniques? A negotiation where each side will present a proposal for a negotiating point? A problem-solving or decision-making process?

PLAIN ENGLISH

Role play   The simulation of a real situation that puts people in the position of acting out an interaction. An example is trying out a sales closing technique on a resistant client.

Set ground rules. For example, maintain confidentiality, participate, ban side conversations, focus on issues and not people, agree to disagree when necessary, and stay in the meeting until it is over.

When participants know what to expect and what their role is, there will be higher cooperation and engagement than if they plunge blindly into the content of the meeting.

Adjusting the Agenda

Strict adherence to the time allotments on the agenda is not always possible or even desirable. No one writes an agenda with a crystal ball, and even years of experience facilitating meetings can't guarantee the progress of your meeting. If you had perfectly accurate knowledge, you wouldn't have a rationale for a meeting!

Therefore, flexibility and adaptability are hallmarks of a good facilitator. You have to listen for signs that an agenda item is not moving forward, and then evaluate the cause.

If a participant is speaking too long, is she or he just long-winded or has she or he raised an issue that needs further discussion? You have to decide, or find a mechanism for a group decision, if this meeting is the right forum for that particular discussion or if it should be an action item for a subcommittee.

If each contributor to a discussion is speaking too long, have you lost control of the meeting and can you retrieve it by shortening time for those who have not yet spoken without causing offense or lessening the merit of their contributions? "Too long" is not just longer than the number of minutes you allotted; a longer discussion may be necessary because you underestimated the complexity of the discussion or because more layers and issues arise in the discussion that are worthy of spending extra time.

If a discussion, analysis, or presentation is completed ahead of schedule, you can suggest the meeting be shortened or an additional item or step can be addressed later—or survey the participants, if appropriate, on what adjustment should be made.

If a discussion gets bogged down for lack of information, you can call a short break, move the item to a later spot in the agenda (if the missing information is quickly retrievable), or table the item for a future meeting.

If a discussion stalls or has to be halted due to heightened tension or argument, you can try to intervene to defuse it (see the section "The Art of Facilitation" on page 770). You may decide to call an unannounced break, and speak one-on-one with those in conflict. Tabling the item for a future meeting again gives you an unexpected opportunity to adjust the agenda.

TIMING FOR MAXIMUM PRODUCTIVITY

The energy level in a meeting is not constant; it ebbs and surges based upon the participants' interest in a particular topic, the biorhythms and blood sugar levels of those present, the ability of the facilitator to engage each individual and still move the meeting along, and the personalities in the room. The energy level is not a factor over which you, as the leader or facilitator, will have total control.

However, understanding there are phases common to many meetings and remaining flexible to make adjustments during the meeting will help you to maximize productivity. These common phases can be categorized as follows:

■ **Premeeting social time.** Humans are social beings. Some crave more interpersonal activity than others. Encouraging participants to gather in the meeting room a few minutes early, serving refreshments, and engaging in small talk with individuals prior to a meeting all allow people's varying needs for social interaction to be met without spilling over into the meeting itself where it can be distracting.

CAUTION

Be wary of formalizing any premeeting time at the risk of killing spontaneity: No agenda here! Keep this premeeting time unstructured so individuals can use it as they wish, to catch up with a colleague, discuss a topic unrelated to the meeting, or share a story about their just-completed vacation.

■ **Engagement.** At the start of the meeting, bring everyone's attention to the business at hand, introduce guests and newcomers, and move to the first agenda item soliciting universal participation as promptly as possible so as to not lose your audience.

■ **Presenting, problem-solving, and negotiating.** Energy levels are higher early in the meeting than later, which you can use to quickly cover less critical agenda items to make more time for the main event or alternatively tackle the most difficult items early so sufficient energy is devoted to them.

- **Decision-making.** Good decisions arise from good problem-solving tools, decision methods, accurate information, solid reasoning, and reasonably fresh minds. This stage must not be rushed; it is better to table this step than do it poorly.

- **Follow-through and implementation.** Energy levels, concentration, and patience are at their lowest near the end of many meetings, and it can be tempting to skip the recap, identification and assignment of action steps, and recording steps. Perceptions being far from uniform and memories being fallible, it's wise to take these steps.

If you have to adjust the balance of an agenda because it was necessary to expand or contract the time spent on one item or step in your planned process, you will have to prioritize the remaining agenda items or steps. This requires *triage.*

PLAIN ENGLISH

Triage   The process of assigning priority to projects in the order in which resources can be used to provide the best outcome. The term comes from World War I battlefields, where medical teams had to choose which wounded soldiers to treat in order to maximize the number of survivors.

In the context of a meeting with predetermined desired outcomes, each not-yet-addressed agenda item or step would be evaluated to see if it was critical to a desired outcome. If not, that item could be tabled for another meeting. If so, could the item be included but shortened? What is the impact (and the alternative) if the meeting outcomes cannot be met with an adjusted agenda?

Whether you suggest the adjustments to be made to the agenda or ask participants to help you, aim for consensus in the adjustments chosen.

ENDING THE MEETING

Ending your meeting well is just as important as starting it well. Two important tasks precede recording and assigning action steps—the concrete acts that ensure the results of your meeting are remembered and acted on.

The first task is to validate the *content* of the meeting—was the information transmitted learned; was the contract point negotiated to mutual satisfaction; and did everyone concur on what the problem is, what the alternatives are, and what the implementation plan is? As facilitator, you need to plan a mechanism to test the group's understanding. This may be a quiz on information taught, a rewritten contractual clause read back to the group, or a request that one participant explain in his own words what was concluded or decided, before it is recorded. As facilitator, you may recap a conclusion or decision and ask the group if that is accurate.

CAUTION

If, as the facilitator, you provide the recap of a meeting's main conclusions or decisions, be wary of having your statement interpreted as an imposed decision. Your tone must be neutral and questioning—"Did I get it right? Does this fairly represent the group's action?"

The second task is to validate the *process* of the meeting. A process check can be brief, but without it you may not learn how participants feel about the process that was utilized to arrive at the actual outcome. The danger is if the participants do not feel the process was objective, accurate, fair, or enlightening, they may not believe the outcome was optimal or even valid: The consensus you thought you achieved as facilitator may be *lip service.*

PLAIN ENGLISH

Lip service   An avowal of belief, advocacy, or compliance, contradicted by actions; a false promise.

Your process check can be an oral survey of participants, but to get a more honest evaluation and useful feedback, consider an evaluation form, filled out anonymously. This form can include questions about the process steps and a Likert scale (a ranking of effectiveness from 1 to 5, where 1 is least effective and 5 is most effective) as well as space for additional comments and critique.

The recording process is discussed in the section "Creating Group Memory" on page 784, and the identification and assignment of action steps are discussed in the section "Meeting Outcomes and Follow-Up" on page 790.

THE 30-SECOND RECAP

- Set expectations in advance by stating in the agenda the meeting will start and end on time if participants commit to it.
- Model good meeting behavior by starting precisely on time.
- Provide information about housekeeping issues, recap the purpose of the meeting and expected outcomes, introduce the process of the meeting, and set ground rules.
- Anticipate changes in energy levels and adjust your pacing accordingly.

- Listen for the signs an agenda item is not moving forward, evaluate the cause, and be flexible and adaptable in order to take appropriate action. Prioritize remaining agenda items before deferring or eliminating them.
- Validate both the content and the process of the meeting before it ends.

Creating Group Memory

In this section you learn how to capture and build on information brought into a meeting, developed in the meeting, and resulting from the meeting in order to create and record a uniform group understanding of events and decisions.

It is entirely possible to have a meeting in which a problem is solved to everyone's satisfaction, a decision is made in which attendees feel they participated, a new level of camaraderie is established in which every trainee masters the material presented, or all parties believe a negotiating point was resolved, and still have that meeting fail. Failure occurs when an organization's apparatus for maintaining and utilizing its institutional memory is not working, functions but is underutilized, or does not exist.

Any knowledge known only to one person is lost to the group or organization when that person leaves or becomes incapacitated. Knowledge common to all participants in a meeting but not recorded is not retrievable or actionable to either the participants or others who need it.

A lack of institutional memory can hinder the success of your meeting in three ways:

1. Failure to record meeting outcomes may result in information and the lessons of past experience being unavailable to prepare for or bring into a meeting.
2. Failure to record during a meeting what is decided on and how those decisions were reached creates irretrievable, unactionable information.
3. Failure to record meeting results invites conflicting memories of events, decisions, and next steps.

Let me address each of these potential pitfalls and how to avoid them.

RECORDING HISTORICAL INFORMATION

One of the greatest advantages of information technology is its capacity to record and identify historical trends of an organization's activities and transactions, and to permit analysis and forecasting of future outcomes. Even the most rudimentary *management information system* (*MIS*) provides standardized data enabling more easily recognized patterns and changes in pattern, whether of financial, sales, human resources, research, survey, manufacturing, chemical processing, product performance, marketing, or fulfillment and distribution activity. In organizations that undervalue the speed and accuracy of computerized information, historical information may not be available or utilized as a foundation for analysis, or decision-making, or forecasting.

PLAIN ENGLISH

Management information system (MIS)   Any methodical compilation of data providing information that can assist in decision-making. Today it refers to computerized systems that have replaced manual and paper record-keeping systems in all but the smallest organizations.

As a leader or facilitator, you want to have the full benefit of historical information available to those who have premeeting assignments and also to meeting participants who will need to refer to such information in order to make informed judgments.

CAUTION

Don't allow yourself to be surprised by unexpected gaps in critical data. It is a good idea to survey what historical information is available in advance of the meeting, especially if you are new to an organization or a project.

Historical information includes not only raw data about activity in your own organization over time, but internally and externally developed information to help your meeting have "real world" relevance, such as the following:

- **Internal analysis of activity,** such as product launch, ad campaign, or moving customer service from telephone to Internet support. How successful was this effort and what lessons were learned?

- **Internal policies and guidelines,** which if not consulted, can result in contracts your organization does not want to honor or other outcomes in direct conflict with the will of management.

■ **Knowledge of existing constraints,** including contracts, production capacities, client relationships, political environments of countries in which you do business or operate, and the presence or absence of *mission-critical* competencies.

PLAIN ENGLISH

Mission critical   When something is so important to an undertaking that the desired activity cannot occur without it. For a simple example, you cannot make coffee without both coffee and water, so both are critical to the mission of a morning cup of java.

■ **Competitive analysis,** including analysis of competitors' market positions, products, talent, access to capital, and agility in fending off threats.

■ **Industry standards** for metrics of performance, such as staff retention, inventory turnover, DSO (days outstanding, a measure of how promptly revenues are received after billing), sales-per-hour-per-employee, or percent of income spent on administrative costs (a visible benchmark for nonprofit organizations).

■ **"Best practices" surveys** of organizations like yours.

■ **Information about external changes** since the last time you or the organization examined the topic at hand. For example, improvements in "call center" technology, changes in the regulatory or political environment, supply and demand for talent, cost and availability of raw materials, tax laws affecting philanthropy, or client demographics.

Providing each participant access to relevant historical information during the meeting helps the group to stay focused on the data under discussion.

TIP

Consider having historical information accessible via a computer in the meeting room whether from an organization's own database or via the Internet. This allows a larger amount of information to be available for reference or display to the group. A summary or a smaller subset of information can then be selected for reproduction and paper distribution.

BUILDING ON EXPERIENCE

To successfully utilize historical information to build institutional or group memory requires the information be interpreted and understood. Individuals or groups with expertise must evaluate the information, assess its validity, articulate its meaning, and apply the insights gleaned to the problem or task of the meeting. If these assessments are given orally during a meeting, and not recorded, they may be unreliably remembered in the future, and thus are lost to the organization.

Therefore, creating a group memory of the experience of a meeting takes a more comprehensive effort than just the task of taking minutes. The role of the recorder is as critical as that of the facilitator (and may be combined with it) or the leader. In assigning the role of recorder, look for the following characteristics:

- A good listener, with the ability to ask for clarification of anything not clear to her or him or the other participants.

- The ability to restate others' positions and statements accurately and succinctly, synthesize similar ideas, and organize their presentation.

- The capacity to identify patterns as well as commonalities and draw out inconsistencies and *non sequiturs* (statements that do not follow logically from anything previously stated).

- The ability to stay neutral, so that participants do not feel manipulated to support the recorder's position, thus invalidating the process.

Creating group memory requires the identification and provision of historical information, as discussed earlier, and the interpretation of that information by the organization's and/or outside experts participating in the meeting.

The additional required steps are recording the process and the results of the meeting; they are very different actions with different purposes.

RECORDING DURING THE MEETING

Recording during the meeting to create group memory is not an attempt to capture every word uttered by participants; if that is a goal, videotaping is the tool. Rather, the task of recording during a meeting is part of the process of presenting information, consensus-building, problem-solving, decision-making, or negotiation.

In an information meeting, participants who learn through hearing, seeing, or role playing, and then write down what they learn are recording functions as both a record of what was learned and a reinforcement of that learning.

For other types of meetings, recording statements, opinions, ideas, proposed contractual language, alternative solutions, or facts brought out in the meeting (in a place where all participants can see them without having to recall them) both facilitates their discussion and creates a permanent record. With this information right in front of all participants, it is easy to point out contradictory or conflicting points or conclusions and immediately resolve or correct them.

The designated recorder—sometimes but not necessarily the facilitator—can use a variety of tools to accomplish this task. Writing on a computer or overhead transparencies projected on a screen or a flip chart works well.

TIP

Use different color markers to categorize different types of information; numbered lists for easy reference; large, clear handwriting using a broad marker for readability across the room; and uppercase letters for emphasis. Leave lots of white space for readability, clarification, and additional ideas.

Categorizing items into several lists, hung from the meeting room walls with masking tape, is another low-tech tool.

Having participants write on Post-it notes and categorizing by sticking the note to the appropriate sheet is another method. Having once written a nonprofit organization's mission statement as a member of the Board of Directors by this method, I learned that this tool is only useful if someone collects and transcribes the notes.

Inputting data into a computer-modeling program to immediately assess the impact of changed assumptions, or *sensitivity analysis,* and saving each iteration is a high-tech recording instrument.

PLAIN ENGLISH

Sensitivity analysis   Forecasting what outcome can be expected to occur when one variable in a model is changed but others are held constant. For example, if an airline increases the price of a flight from New York to Los Angeles, what is the expected reduction in seats sold?

Whatever method is used to record actions during the meeting, it must meet the test of instant retrieval, so participants can review, challenge, or verify what was said.

RECORDING RESULTS OF THE MEETING

Recording during a meeting captures process; recording the results captures outcomes. Again, this could not be more different from the who-said-what act of minute-taking.

Recording the results of a meeting includes summarizing majority and minority opinions or conclusions, decisions made, decision methodology, analytical process, and obtaining consensus about what was agreed to.

Equally important, the recorder should capture the next steps assigned during the meeting, to whom they were assigned, and when the assignment is due to be completed.

Here's a guide to some of the headings you might include in your meeting summary:

Name of Group

Name of Meeting

Date and Time of Meeting

Participants

Names/Titles/Role in Meeting

Presentation Title

Summary of Presentation

Topic for Discussion

Summary of Discussion

Problem Statement

Problem Analysis

Solution Criteria

Alternative Solutions

Decision Analysis

Post Meeting Tasks/Assignees

Next Meeting Date

TIP

Decide what should be recorded as though preparing material for an outsider to review without the guidance of anyone present at the meeting. The reader should be able to follow the critical reasoning of the group and find the supporting information.

Have the draft of this summary e-mailed to participants for comment (in decision-making or negotiation meetings) before being finalized, and distribute the final summary as soon as possible. Waiting until a future meeting to have "minutes" approved could result in a misstep in many situations in a wired world.

Also, determine where the organization maintains its institutional memory, and make sure the record becomes part of the appropriate information archive.

THE 30-SECOND RECAP

- Accurate historical information is available, even from very basic management information systems, and is more reliable and retrievable than information drawn from individual memory.

- Historical information includes knowledge external to an organization that is helpful in assessing the competitive, regulatory, and political environment in which your organization operates.

- The role of recorder requires good listening, synthesis, and organizational skills. It also requires the capacity to identify patterns, commonalities, inconsistencies, and *non sequiturs* as well as neutrality.

- Recording during the meeting captures the process as well as the content of the meeting and makes this information visible to all participants for immediate retrieval and clarification.

- Recording the results of the meeting captures outcomes, including post-meeting assignments and next steps.

Meeting Outcomes and Follow-Up

In this section you learn how to set objectives and expectations, identify and assign the action items that result from a meeting, and follow up after the meeting to ensure a successful outcome.

A completely successful meeting can quickly turn into an unsuccessful one if no action results. Excellent training meetings are wasted if the newly acquired skills are not applied and reinforced; negotiation meetings are only as good as the documents that memorialize the agreements made, to give just two examples of why follow-up is so important.

Establishing Objectives and Expectations

Ensuring that something actually happens as a result of a meeting starts well before the meeting, because planning requires you to establish one or more objectives and expectations. Establishing objectives and expectations helps you to determine who can contribute to achieving them and decide how the meeting will proceed. When you set meeting objectives and expectations in advance and communicate them to participants, you are building a framework for everything that will occur during, and as a result of, that meeting.

What's important in setting objectives and expectations?

- **An objective is a *purpose*.** It needs to be compelling enough to justify a meeting, not trivial. Periodic staff meetings can be wasteful. On the other hand, if they are the vehicle by which work is assigned or projects are managed or team-building occurs, they can be exceptionally productive.

- **An objective needs to be *clear*.** "We're having a meeting to talk about next summer's sales conference" is a purpose, but what does "talk" mean? Determine the budget? Site selection? Cancellation? Whether or not to invite independent reps as well as staff? Changing the format? How do participants prepare for a meeting with so much undefined content?

- **An objective needs to be *explicit*.** Unless the agenda is a surprise team-building activity (see the section "Unusual Means to Create Successful Meetings" on page 810), tell participants exactly what the purpose of the meeting is.

- **An expectation is an *actionable deliverable*.** It has to be describable and specific: "By the end of this meeting we need to have narrowed the list of candidates for the Director of Advertising job to three finalists to pass on to the hiring manager."

- **An expectation must be *feasible*.** A college admissions committee is unlikely to decide on 100 applications in an hour-long meeting; a workflow consulting team meeting a department's staff for the first time is not going to be able to develop new job descriptions by the end of the meeting, although I've seen one try.

TIP

Set a reasonable expectation for your meeting, and then aim to overdeliver. If you are assigned an impossible expectation for your meeting, something so ambitious it's unlikely the group can attain it, say so and renegotiate the assignment rather than fail.

■ **An expectation must be *measurable*.** "The expectation is to persuade the vice president to authorize 20 hours of overtime a week
and the hiring of a temporary paralegal until this case is over, and to
be able to tell her the estimated duration and expense of this
decision."

IDENTIFYING ACTION ITEMS

Action items are those activities that need to occur after a meeting in order for
anything to change: for a decision to be put into effect or a solution to be
implemented, for example.

With a meeting objective and expectations in place, some action items are
known going into the meeting. In the preceding example of a measurable
expectation, if authorization is obtained, the action items are predictable: a
memo authorizing the overtime signed by the vice president, the preparation
of an authorization to hire a temporary paralegal to be signed by the vice
president, the assignment to the recruiter to find the last good temporary paralegal who worked in the department, and an adjustment to the expense forecast for the duration of the case to cover the cost.

Some actions will only be identified during the course of the meeting. For
example, a workflow consulting team may have an objective of becoming
familiar with a department's staff with the expectation of producing a list of
major tasks that department performs. In the course of the meeting, the team
may discover that one task has been *outsourced* and another is about to be
eliminated due to new automated equipment; the team can produce a list, but
unanticipated action items may include visiting the outsourcing vendor and
observing a test run of the expected equipment in order to move to the next
step in the analysis.

PLAIN ENGLISH

Outsourced   A task or function that an organization has determined
can be done better, faster, or cheaper by an outside provider and
therefore contracts to have done off-site. Commonly outsourced
functions include telemarketing, auto-parts manufacturing, benefits
administration, and conference planning.

Identifying action items to take place after the meeting means setting additional, sequential expectations. In identifying actions, clearly state …

■ The specific action to be taken.

■ The level of detail or standard of performance required.

- The deadline for completion.
- In what form the action is to be delivered: e-mail? diagram? excel spreadsheet? formal report? phone call? product delivery? in-person meeting?

ASSIGNING ACTION ITEMS

It's not enough to identify action items; they must be assigned to specific individuals during the meeting. Doing so will eliminate any confusion about what the action item is and what is required, as well as concerns about feasibility from those assigned. Public assignments allow meeting participants to see logical and fair allocation of assignments, as well as the opportunity to volunteer their own expertise.

CAUTION

In some situations the logical person to undertake an item isn't in the meeting, perhaps because the action item involves different functions than those represented by the attendees. If you assign an action item to someone not present, make sure the assignment is conveyed promptly.

The meeting recorder should write down each action item, its assignee, and deadline. This information should become part of the minutes.

FOLLOWING UP

The first follow-up item is the creation and distribution of meeting minutes whether by the recorder or another designee.

TIP

For sensitive or controversial topics, circulate the draft of the minutes only to key participants for review before distributing a final version to all. As with any document you wish to limit distribution of, do not use e-mail for this draft version.

If you did not do a process check at the end of the meeting, or want a formal evaluation as feedback on both process and content, do it as soon after the meeting as possible, while memories are fresh. A meeting evaluation form (paper or electronic) is frequently provided at the end of workshops and member association conferences, but can be a useful tool to measure the success of almost any meeting in the eyes of participants.

Typical components of an evaluation form are ...

- Identification of the meeting by date, topic, facilitator.
- An open-ended statement of the participant's expectations for the meeting, and the degree to which they were met.
- A ranking of the value of the components of the meeting.
- A *Likert scale* of overall satisfaction of the meeting.
- A request for suggestions on how the meeting could have been improved.

Evaluation forms are most often filled out anonymously in order to generate constructive criticism and honest evaluations.

PLAIN ENGLISH

Likert scale   A numerical ranking where 1 is the lowest ranking and 5 or 10 is the highest ranking of a particular activity. It is used to quantify participants' level of satisfaction and to compare the effectiveness of group facilitators or presenters.

Regarding action steps, waiting until a future meeting to learn if action steps have been completed is common and can undermine the success of your meeting. Ask for a progress report, or contact assignees halfway between the meeting date and the assigned deadline.

Following up after a meeting also may entail ...

- Reporting to others in the organization besides the participants, in a more or less formal way than through meeting minutes.
- Reviewing evaluations and/or process checks for improvements in future meetings.
- Figuring out if another meeting is required.
- Turning over a project to a different group and ensuring a smooth transition.
- Hiring an outside expert to pursue topics raised in the meeting.

THE 30-SECOND RECAP

- Establishing objectives and expectations before the meeting provides the framework for effective follow-up.
- Objectives need to be clear and explicit, and expectations need to be feasible and measurable.

- Some action items are predictable but others may develop during the meeting.

- Action items must be assigned to a specific individual with a clear description of what is required and a deadline, and this information should be recorded in the minutes.

- A process check or evaluation form will help you measure the success of the meeting.

Handling Common Problems

In this section you learn how to handle common meeting problems that can undermine a group's ability to progress towards its objectives.

There are some problems that occur in meetings so frequently they are almost predictable. If you anticipate that one or more is likely to appear in a meeting, and know what to look for and how to offset or overcome them, you will reduce the risk of meeting failure.

GROUPTHINK

While research indicates group decisions are often better than those made by individuals—due to the variety of points of view and the benefits of exploring issues with others, who have different expertise—there is a tendency of groups to fall into *groupthink*.

PLAIN ENGLISH

Groupthink   A pattern of thinking that stifles critical reasoning and leads to artificial consensus. It is caused by conformity to group or organizational values and is characterized by self-deception and subconscious suppression of dissenting views.

The danger of groupthink is highest in groups with high morale. High morale fosters a sense of the group's ability and likelihood of success in meeting the objectives and producing the expected deliverables. The difficulty is this sense of success may be unwarranted if it is not supported by objective analysis. This concept was popularized by Irving L. Janus in 1982 and is now widely understood to undermine group decision-making, especially in particularly cohesive groups.

The danger is increased by a group's tendency toward self-justification and polarization, which can lead to it becoming more entrenched in a given course of action and stifle a more objective examination of the issues. Self-censorship reduces contributions of differing ideas. The time pressures inherent in a meeting exacerbate this tendency.

As a facilitator, you have to balance the group's confidence in its ability to analyze evidence and weigh information objectively with the tendency toward groupthink that overconfidence brings. This problem shows up in groups when everything seems to be going well: That's a signal to be observant and alert for groupthink.

Symptoms of groupthink include comments such as "We all know that won't work"; "Let's not let the finance guys see this, it'll slow the project down three months"; "Can't we hurry up, we basically agree on this and I have to leave in 10 minutes"; or "This suggestion is so great, why look at anything else?"

Some of the tools available to a facilitator to prevent groupthink you already learned in the section "The Art of Facilitation," on page 770, such as maintaining neutrality, fostering minority points of view by legitimizing disagreement, and seeking contributions from all participants. Here are some additional ideas for avoiding groupthink:

- During the meeting, ask participants to present arguments against the prevailing point of view. You may even assign one or more participants to the role of *devil's advocate*.

- Review and critique the group process being utilized. Is it generating a free flow of ideas? Is everyone contributing? Are participants reasoning points in depth? Is anyone dominating the discussion? You may need to switch to a different technique or process.

PLAIN ENGLISH

Devil's advocate   A role taken on to champion and critically examine the evidence for a minority or unpopular point of view or course of action.

- Gather information, ideas, or suggestions anonymously (either before or during the meeting) to make it "safe" to introduce novel, minority, or even maverick approaches and ideas.

- Encourage the group to think through an idea more than once to avoid superficial, cursory analysis and prevent a rushed decision.

- Invite an outside expert to the meeting for the specific purpose of critiquing planned actions based on the prevailing point of view.

- Introduce an open debate into the meeting—even if it's not on the agenda—in order to examine opposing points of view.

- Assign someone, as a formal action item, the responsibility of identifying possible problems with favored solutions and reporting back to the group in a future meeting.

Which of these tools you choose will depend on which stage of problem-solving or decision-making your meeting is addressing. If groupthink is seriously skewing your group's deliberations, it may be necessary to suspend the meeting until one of these interventions can be undertaken. This is not meeting failure but a pause to prevent a bad judgment from affecting meeting outcomes.

CAUTION

Be sure to inform the group the action you are taking is to promote objective thinking, and remember to use neutral language to reinforce objectivity. Otherwise, participants may think you are advocating for the minority point of view or unpopular action, a perception that could polarize the group into opposing camps.

Your facilitation style is also a factor in avoiding groupthink. The more supportive, neutral, and collaborative you are, the lower the risk to damaging group morale or cohesiveness.

CONFUSION BETWEEN CONTENT AND PROCESS

In the section "Effective Meeting Basics" on page 724, you learned that the content of a meeting (what is acted on) includes the objective, expectations, materials, and action items. The process (how the content is acted on) includes the agenda, facilitation, presentations, approaches to decision-making, pacing, and follow-up. I defined an effective meeting as one in which participants are satisfied with both the results of the meeting (the objectives of the meeting are met) and the process by which those results were accomplished.

As a facilitator, you want to be able to distinguish problems of content from problems of process in order to make a successful intervention and get the meeting moving again.

Some process problems are easy to fix because they are relatively easy to change. As a facilitator, you can add or subtract agenda items, direct discussion to stay on point and avoid distractions, adopt different problem-solving techniques, slow down a discussion, or execute follow-up effectively.

Other process problems require less mechanical solutions, such as participants' perceptions of whether or not their contributions are heard and valued and skepticism that anything will change as a result of the meeting. Problems such as bias, anger, personal agendas, indecision, and manipulation require a facilitator to stop discussion and return attention to the issues of the meeting before such problems contaminate the group's faith in the process.

Sometimes, arguments over content are masked as arguments over process, and the group really does not have a common goal. Changing the process won't work because some participants don't agree on the objective. For example, if the purpose of your meeting is to identify 20 positions to be eliminated to cut expenses, and some participants want to find another way to cut costs other than reducing the number of employees, it doesn't matter what your process is. Some participants are going to be dissatisfied with the outcome. In this situation, the layoffs may be decided by executive decision over the objections of some participants, or the facilitator might change the objective by challenging participants to come up with other expenses to cut to meet the targeted savings.

NONPARTICIPATION AND DOMINATION

Nonparticipation reduces the sense of legitimacy in a meeting and threatens the success of its process.

Participatory exercises can be used in training meetings as a way for participants to practice what they are learning. In problem-solving and decision-making meetings, assigning participants to orally present different points of view, factual evidence, or an expert opinion spreads participation among more individuals. In team-building meetings, group exercises demonstrate interdependence and build camaraderie. See the section "Unusual Means to Create Successful Meetings" on page 810, for ideas on team building and group activities in meetings.

Domination by an individual or a faction within a meeting is another common problem and can intimidate or suppress group participation.

PLAIN ENGLISH

Domination   The exercise of a controlling influence over others. It is behavior based on assumed power and not superior ideas.

Domination includes taking up too much "air time" in discussion, belittling others' contributions, excluding information that contradicts a favored position, and attempting to short-circuit discussion in order to direct an outcome.

As facilitator, your role is to prevent and eliminate domination by anyone in a meeting. In extreme cases, this may mean excluding an individual or group from your list of participants or utilizing an alternative other than a meeting to reach your objective. In most cases, you can avoid or reduce domination significantly by using some of these tactics:

- Set clear rules for discussion in the meeting, such as limiting contributions to rounds in which every participant must speak before anyone can offer a second contribution.

- Limit each speaker to a certain amount of time and enforce the limit.

- Instruct anyone monopolizing a discussion to refrain from contributing for a certain period of time during the meeting in order to provide offsetting time for a contrasting presentation or argument.

- Enforce the free generation of ideas without any concurrent evaluation at this stage, which will reduce a dominant speaker's ability to influence or suppress contributions by others.

- Ask a dominant participant to argue the opposite side of the question. You are harnessing her or his intelligence, persuasiveness, tenacity, and ability to articulate to give heft to an opposing view, which creates some balance.

TIP

Do not hesitate to interrupt or cut off a participant who breaks the rules. Demonstrate your own respect for the process and your commitment to enforcing the rules for the good of the group, and create time for additional points of view to be heard.

The more equally a facilitator can distribute participation, the more respect participants will have for the process.

DATA OVERLOAD

Data overload is counterproductive. It can be unintentional or a tool to intimidate participants into caving under too much raw data or organized information. As facilitator, your role starts with screening the amount and type of material distributed in advance for participants to read in preparation.

In reviewing information to be utilized in a meeting, look for these factors:

- Is the information too complex for the participants to easily comprehend? For example, engineers may present statistics that nonengineers cannot understand. Ask that such information be translated into layman's terms.

- Are you getting raw data rather than information? Three months' worth of daily production tallies is information overload. Instead, ask for an interpretive summary.

- Is there simply too much material for participants to read before a meeting? If you send out a book, chances are no one will have the time to read it.

- If a presentation will contain information projected onto a screen, how can you ensure it's an absorbable amount? Limit the number of words on a slide or screen. I once attended a meeting in which the presenter tried to project a legal document onto a screen; no one could read any of it. If a presenter needs to share that level of information, it should be in a handout.

- Why is this information needed for this meeting? What would be sacrificed if this information were not presented?

Answering these questions will help you limit information to what is actually useful in meeting the objectives of the meeting.

CAUTION

Make sure you are not contributing to the problem by structuring too much time for information presentation. Even an appropriate amount of information can be too much if a meeting is unbroken by mental breaks and physical activity. Fifteen to thirty minutes is about the limit before attention begins to wander.

PERSONALITY CONFLICTS

Personality conflicts present a special challenge to running an effective meeting. Participants who dislike each other can bring a discussion to a halt pretty quickly. The role of a facilitator here is not about airing differing points of view but about assisting people in hearing and respecting each other. Keep the focus on the information, evidence, or argument to deflect it from the individual.

Many personality conflicts are driven by differences in interpersonal style. What we hear is influenced by how we prefer to hear information from others. Some people value information presented sequentially, completely, and in great detail; others value information delivered succinctly and in summary; others need to be persuaded of your commitment to your argument; and still others need to see the "big picture" conceptualization behind your conclusion. David Keirsey's book *Please Understand Me II* is a good resource to learn more about interpersonal style.

To help participants who seem to grate against each other hear and listen more effectively, you, as facilitator, can act as a sort of translator. One way to do this is to assess the speaking styles of the two individuals whose personalities clash and to *reframe* their statements for the group and for each other.

PLAIN ENGLISH

Reframe   To express an idea or convey information in a different way. It involves restating it at more length, in fewer words, in less complex language or using examples, metaphors, or analogies in an attempt to bridge the gap between a speaker's meaning and a listener's comprehension.

You can do this by asking a participant to reframe or by reframing yourself. The objective is to present the thought in a less alien way to the listener. Assessing two individuals' interpersonal styles takes some skill, but you can increase your skill by careful observation. You are trying to get from "unlike" to "like" speech either by restating a speaker's thought yourself or coaching a speaker to restate in a way more like her or his antagonist.

For example, here are four speakers trying to get the same point across: A proposed budget should be adopted today. Here's how each might present it:

> *Speaker A:* "This is a strategically driven budget. Here is the 25-page report of the economic and business assumptions behind the strategy. Here's the revenue and expense budget with projected outcomes that show possible upside and downside scenarios. Here's a bridge analysis between last year's actuals and this year's budget. Here are 376 supporting schedules ..."

> *Speaker B:* "This budget meets the target the president asked for. Carl has the strategic summary and supporting schedules for anyone who'd like to see them. Any questions?"

Speaker C: "Let me take you through the big picture on this budget. We're trying to increase the brand identity of the company, and that's going to be an evolving process over the next five years. It's really exciting to see our name become more familiar to consumers. I have a really interesting study on brand identity in my office I'd be happy to share with you. This budget will put us on the right track."

Speaker D: "Let me share with you how happy the division managers are with this budget. I really feel good about how participatory this process has been. We've increased the understanding of how the budget works throughout the organization and we can all be proud of that accomplishment."

It is very possible that each of these individuals prepared a sound budget and is analytical, conceptual, and responsive to the need to act quickly, and cares about the people in the organization. Getting them to talk to each other about the budget without conflict, however, would be difficult. None of the other three speakers can really hear what the fourth is saying. A facilitator who knows these individuals or hears them in the meeting should ask each to tailor their presentation to the concerns of the others.

The underlying content—a solid budget—doesn't change; its presentation does, and presentation can change perception and therefore improve communication.

Differing interpersonal styles are of course not the only cause of personality conflicts. Psychological traits and individual differences in the ability to relate to others unlike themselves cause negative meeting behavior, such as manipulation and power plays, and being judgmental, closed-minded, and insulting. As a facilitator, you can't change participants' personalities or psychological makeup, but you can refuse to tolerate inappropriate behavior.

THE 30-SECOND RECAP

■ Groupthink, an artificial consensus common in highly cohesive groups, can be reduced by a facilitator who demonstrates a commitment to hearing and having the group objectively consider contradictory opinions.

■ To work effectively, groups must agree on both content and process, unmask disagreements on objectives (content) that seem like process problems, and identify process disagreements that are perceived (in error) as content disagreements.

- Nonparticipation can be overcome by establishing trust and utilizing exercises that foster contributions. Domination requires clear rules from the facilitator that limit monopolization and premature evaluation of ideas.

- The decision to screen information (based on its necessity and appropriateness for a meeting) will assist in avoiding data overload.

- Personality conflicts can be mitigated by a facilitator's mediation of different interpersonal styles and a refusal to tolerate inappropriate or offensive behavior.

Out of the Boardroom

In this section you learn about the advantages and challenges of meetings held outside of your office or conference facilities.

Meetings don't have to be held in traditional settings. With the increased informality and structure of organizational life, from "dress-down" policies to *virtual offices* to *hotelling,* almost any setting you can imagine can be appropriate for a particular meeting.

PLAIN ENGLISH

Virtual office   An electronic connection to a physical headquarters (albeit the CEO's den) from wherever one works: car, airplane, or hotel.

Hotelling   The practice of maintaining cubicles or offices for rotating employees.

Holding meetings off-site allows you to do things differently, add a sense of novelty or fun, relax the corporate or organizational hierarchy, and build more collegial and deeper relationship with colleagues. Removed from more formal settings, groups often discover they are more creative and innovative in generating ideas and solving problems.

OUTDOOR MEETINGS

You don't have to travel very far from the office to create a different experience for your meeting at low cost: Just move the meeting outside. For many organizations in suburban office parks, this isn't a new idea: The "corporate campus" may include well-landscaped sites intended for outdoor meetings.

Nobody has to travel, you're close enough to the office to use the facilities, and lunch can be ordered from the cafeteria or catered.

Outdoor meetings immediately transform participants' perceptions of place. Even in an office park, you're looking at the office from the outside; the pleasures and distractions of nature are unavoidable. Of course, if you choose to hold your meeting in a park or on a beach, you have even more material to work with. Birds, breezes, scenery, and fresh air relax most people and provide a sense of anticipation about the meeting, at least until the novelty wears off: What else will be different about this meeting from ordinary meetings?

Capitalize on both the informality and sense of anticipation by making sure something is different about this meeting. Here are some suggestions:

- Consider assigning a different facilitator, recorder, discussion leader, or presenter if it's a regular staff or committee meeting and people have settled into their roles.

- Assign the least senior person from a given area to present, report, or lead a discussion. This is a great staff development tool in any meeting. Make this staff development assignment in advance and include the function's most senior person and the assignee's immediate supervisor in your plans.

- Assign participants to different groups to discuss various aspects of an issue on the agenda and have them report back to the group.

- In an outdoor meeting, include at least one group activity or exercise that utilizes the outdoor location. For example, introduce the idea-generation or problem-solving technique of *mapping*.

PLAIN ENGLISH

Mapping   Recording the ideas of the group in a visual, nonlinear format, such as a diagram, which fosters creativity and aids visual thinkers who can draw what they know but may be less able to articulate it in words.

Why not draw your diagram on the beach or in the park with a stick? (The meeting recorder could photograph the diagram instead of copying it on paper.)

CLIENT SITE MEETINGS

Client site meetings are most frequently done to present a sales pitch, advertising campaign proposal, or progress report to a client of your organization.

As leader or facilitator of such a meeting, you have two primary issues: how to manage with the loss of control that occurs when you don't control the location, room preparation, and perhaps not even the scheduling, and how to ensure a good organizational fit with your client.

The answer to both of these problems is planning. Establish a liaison with the person who is managing the meeting at the client's site, and assume that no detail is too small or unimportant.

If at all possible, meet with that person well in advance to jointly plan the meeting and review the room preparation, audio-visual requirements, and schedule.

Ask your contact how her or his organization likes to run its meetings and what the protocols are for meetings with outside vendors or organizations that have a relationship to it similar to yours. You'll observe some things about the organizational culture through your interactions with this individual, see the dress code or lack of one, and pick up on the level of energy, pace, degree of formality, and hierarchy.

Next, you need to prepare your team to function in this environment. You won't have the degree of control you do in a meeting you plan yourself, but you will build confidence that your team will know what to expect and how to adapt to suit the client's needs.

CAUTION

Tread lightly. Be sure not to give the impression that you want to take over the planning of this meeting, even if you do. It's the client's site, and the client has assigned someone it views as competent to this job. Defer to that person gracefully and work within the preferences of the client.

HOME MEETINGS

The home meeting, like outdoor meetings, signals a relaxed atmosphere and sets the expectation for something different.

Meeting in an individual's home, even if it's that of the chief executive, the dean, or the executive director, really skews the participants' senses of hierarchy and formality. Not only are you not meeting in the office or a conference center—where hierarchy and formality can easily be maintained—but the group is probably dressed more casually.

The relaxed hierarchy and informality of a home meeting can foster openness and enable participants to get to know each other as people, with fewer of the artificial barriers of rank getting in the way. Hanging around a swimming pool in bathing suits is a great equalizer; such activities just foster different conversations.

A home meeting is a great opportunity for team-building exercises, brainstorming, and concentrated time away from the organization's normal schedule. It's a great location for a board of directors' retreat, a staff meeting, or a confidential meeting.

Planning again is key. Here are some problems unique to home meetings:

- **Transportation.** If you're leaving the public transportation system your office depends on to travel to an executive's home in West Snowshoe, you may need to arrange for car pools, taxis, or a car service.

- **Weather.** You've planned a great meeting by the host's outdoor pool. What is Plan B if it rains? If you can't easily move the meeting indoors, you may have to have a "rain date" or an alternate site.

- **Seating.** Having enough seating can be a problem—for the last home meeting I attended, the host borrowed chairs from a church. Chairs can be rented from a party planner but not in West Snowshoe.

- **Food.** Food can be a challenge. Is the host's spouse a gourmet cook? Do a potluck supper? Have food catered? Bring in an executive chef? Order pizza? Poll the group in advance and make arrangements for dietary restrictions.

CAUTION

Alcohol can be a different challenge. A downside of increased informality in a home meeting is the possibility participants will overindulge. If the host plans to serve alcohol, discuss postponing it until after the business of the meeting or restricting the time it is available, and assign designated drivers.

A home meeting can be a bonding and memorable experience for a group, but it does require careful planning for elements you don't have to worry about in a more conventional setting.

CAPTIVE MEETINGS

Captive meetings are those designed to remove a group from the normal distractions of the office and daily life for a sustained period in order to concentrate on the purpose of the meeting. Labor contract negotiation meetings are often held in hotels or other neutral spaces for this purpose and run late into the night, or all night, to wear out or out-pressure the opposing group. Religious revivals are another example of captive meetings. For most organizations, captive meetings are chosen to foster unusually concentrated effort.

In planning a captive meeting, your role is to maximize the concentrated focus on the tasks of the meeting, minimize distractions and interruptions, and take advantage of the locale for building camaraderie and good will among participants.

If you choose a distant or exotic locale, the sense of displacement does help to concentrate efforts on the meeting. A Caribbean island or a hotel in a distant city is not the office: All energy can be focused on the meeting because you don't have two more following it and a mound of paperwork to do at night.

The local attractions are in a sense a distraction, but in a meeting of several days' length, they can be planned distractions and a welcome break from concentrated intellectual effort.

TIP

Plan events for off-hours that take advantage of the unique attributes of the location you are in. See the section "The Importance of Environment" on page 748, for examples of such events.

Reducing distractions during meeting time is more difficult; pagers, cell phones, and wireless Internet connections may work even internationally. It's always a good policy to banish those items and make other arrangements for emergencies. Locations where wired telephone service is unreliable may require several attempts to place even one call to home or office, and you can be more out of touch than intended.

GO-WHERE-THE-ACTION-IS MEETINGS

Sometimes the best meeting site is where participants can see the effects of the problem they are trying to solve or put their hands on the resources you are trying to train them to use.

Here are some suggestions that may provoke you to think of others suitable for your purpose:

- Can't find the bottleneck in the accounts payable process? Have your meeting begin in the mailroom or around the computer screen where vendors' electronically submitted invoices appear. Declare that in this meeting the group will play the "I Am an Invoice" game.

Have the group literally walk the path an invoice would take, from time-stamped receipt; to allocation to an accounts payable clerk; to match up with a purchase order; to coding to the proper account; to approval for payment; to the queue for check writing, signing, and mailing or funds transfer; to appearance of the transaction in the accounting system. The recorder writes down every procedure and the position of every individual who is involved in the transaction.

Spend the second part of the meeting, or a subsequent meeting, analyzing the observed process and devising alternative solutions. You can copy this tactic for any paper processing or workflow mystery.

- Consider holding a training meeting in a computer lab, so trainees can have a "hands-on" experience with new software. If you want to train and demonstrate targeted Internet research, you can take this idea two steps further by holding your meeting in a public library's computer lab and bringing in experts in the field you wish to train participants to research and/or reference librarians. I recently did this for graduate students on electronic career and job search. The bonus for holding it in a large public library: Students gained exposure to commercial databases that academic libraries often cannot afford.

- Go where the "best practices" in your field of endeavor are acknowledged to take place and arrange for your group to observe them by *shadowing*. Your group may be broken up for this information-gathering type of meeting, but can reassemble to report what each subgroup learned and consider how to transfer that knowledge to your organization.

PLAIN ENGLISH

Shadowing   The practice of observing the daily activities of someone performing her or his job—most often when the observer is exploring career alternatives of which she or he has little knowledge.

- Go on a field trip. The field trip meeting is another alternative that enriches participants' contextual understanding of a project. For example, if your firm just won the contract to repair the stained glass windows in a church, the first meeting to frame out the project could be held in the church. The repair team could examine the damaged stained glass in place, observe how the natural light affects each pane, compare original glass to previously repaired pieces and complementary pieces not being removed for repair, view the whole rather than just the parts that need repair, and plan how to dismantle and transport the windows.

Reality Training

Reality training refers to structured group activities that attempt to put participants in situations that test and develop the skills needed to perform as a team and as leaders in organizations. They often teach the necessity of interdependence. You don't lead this kind of a meeting—you hire it. The physical challenges can be risky and the psychological experiences stressful. Make sure you choose a trainer with an established track record and proper insurance.

Consultants and organizations provide these experiential learning training events, sometimes to groups of senior executives, and sometimes to entire organizations one group at a time. The events often involve tests of physical endurance and group discipline and can be almost paramilitary in nature. Think of *Survivor* without the cameras, the $1 million prize, and the talk show appearances.

Some alumni rave about these experiences. Others resent having to participate or quit their jobs to avoid them.

TIP

Consider taking a camera or assigning a meeting photographer, and handing out film to encourage participants to snap shots of board retreats, home meetings, and especially multiday meetings in exotic locales. After the meeting, collect photos, assemble a collage, and send copies to participants.

The 30-Second Recap

- Outdoor meetings provide many advantages at little cost. Use the opportunity to assign roles to different people and introduce an activity that incorporates the outdoor setting.

- Client site meetings challenge you to plan a meeting not totally under your control and to ensure a good organizational fit between representatives of both organizations.

- Home meetings generally reduce barriers of rank and provide opportunities for team building, brainstorming, and concentrated time away from the office. They can also present some logistics problems.

- Captive meetings remove groups from home for a sustained period of concentrated effort.

- Go-where-the-action-is meetings take you to the site of a problem or resource and give your group first-hand observation of events.

■ Reality training is a type of experiential meeting that instills teamwork, leadership, and the value of interdependence but should be run by a professional trainer specializing in this type of work.

Unusual Means to Create Successful Meetings

In this section you learn out-of-the-ordinary ways to capture participants' attention, decrease meeting stress, improve performance, and build camaraderie, while taking cultural differences into account.

Well-planned meetings are purposeful events that are expected to produce a return on the investment of participants' time. They do not have to be predictable, plodding, glum, or boring. In fact, if a meeting has these characteristics, the effectiveness of the meeting is compromised. In the section "Out of the Boardroom," on page 803, you learned about alternative environments that can enliven meetings and increase creativity and innovation. Now I'll look at other techniques that can contribute substantively to increasing participants' energy, interest, focus, ability to concentrate, and capacity to *think outside the box* during a meeting.

PLAIN ENGLISH

Think outside the box   To conceptualize or analyze without the constraints of precedent, rules, historical frameworks, and generally accepted assumptions.

The ideas in this section are not about creating entertainment in between long meeting sessions. These suggestions are about incorporating unusual elements into your meeting's agenda that further the purpose of the meeting. Some of them may "push the envelope" on what is appropriate for your organizational culture, so be sure to consider how senior managers or leaders in your organization will view any unusual means you choose to use in your meeting. What appears to you as innovative may be perceived as welcome in one environment, uncomfortably strange but acceptable in another organization, and unbusinesslike and weird in a third.

CAUTION

If you have any doubt about whether an activity is appropriate for this particular meeting or this organization, talk it through with your manager or a senior person in the organization first.

As you consider innovative activities to bring into your meeting, evaluate how they might be used to accomplish a meeting objective.

THE ELEMENT OF SURPRISE

A sure-fire way to break the predictability of a meeting, especially a group that meets regularly, is to introduce an unexpected element. Think of how a fire drill interrupts the momentum (or sometimes the lethargy) of a meeting. The resulting loss of concentration can be annoying, but a few minutes of physical activity and fresh air often have the effect of rejuvenating the group and increasing the energy in the room.

The difference between a surprise event at a meeting and a fire drill is that the surprise you plan should have something to do with the purpose of the meeting.

The surprise can be as mild as introducing a new problem-solving tool into a meeting. This will break the routine thought patterns of a group and perhaps provide an intellectually interesting challenge.

A surprise exercise that will also change thought patterns is to ask a group to approach an issue or a problem as though it was a competitor (for a client, for a grant, for shelf space in the cereal aisle, for a vote, or for a prospective student or job candidate). Have the group assume the competing organization's resources, talent, historical strengths and weaknesses, reputation, and position in the market. This exercise will change the way the group views the issue or problem, and may generate new ways to approach it for your organization.

A different kind of surprise is created when a guest is brought into a meeting. Here are two examples. At a sales conference dinner, my boss introduced a "mystery guest" who turned out to be a highly regarded former colleague. What ensued was a fun-filled reminiscence and catch-up on industry events and trends.

The second example was a training meeting for existing staff on a new method of delivering services that was being resisted. Three unannounced guests were invited to that meeting, all of them prospective hires. The leader announced that any current staff member who didn't embrace the new method should look for new employment—their replacements were being trained along with them. Not a warm and fuzzy message, but a clear one.

Another form of surprise is to use a memorable example to illustrate a principle you are trying to teach or a point you are trying to make. During a presentation of a new college textbook at a sales meeting, an author explaining a psychological principle, automatism (meaning that reflexes cannot be controlled), asked a sales rep to come to the front of the room. He then asked the sales rep to order his (own) body to do something that cannot be done by will power. No one in the room is ever going to forget the principle, because the illustration was so hilarious.

Destination Stress Busters

Long trips to distant sites for lengthy meetings, combined with expectations of performance at some such meetings and sustained interaction with people, usually without the presence of one's family, can induce meeting stress.

CAUTION

Don't overplan so that every minute of a long meeting day is filled with mandatory activity. Some people need daily time alone to regroup. Allow time for mental rest.

Stress reducers include ice breakers and other social events where people can get to know new participants and relax; however, you should also plan for unstructured time during multiday meetings so that unplanned, informal encounters can occur.

Meditation may sound like an unusual means to create a successful meeting, especially in a business setting, but that is where I first encountered *guided meditation.*

PLAIN ENGLISH

Guided meditation   A supervised form of contemplation or reflection in which a trained leader talks a group through the process of emptying the mind of all thoughts and feelings, and relaxing.

Introducing meditation to a group of individuals unfamiliar with it may meet initial resistance. Several employers were paying for the training meeting I attended, and I'm not sure the National Park Service or Wall Street firms knew the agenda included meditation. It's not for every group. My group of skeptical forest management professionals and buttoned-down executives ultimately agreed that not only did it reduce stress, it also provided increased focus later in the meeting.

The best stress reducers involve physical activity: Plan a volleyball game, hike, or morning workout. At a professional association meeting I attended, the best-attended off-hours activities were an early morning yoga class (taught by a participant) and an early morning aqua-exercise class in the hotel pool.

TIP

Stress occurs in shorter meetings closer to home, too. If your desti-nation is no farther than the conference room in your office, take a break, have everyone stand up and do exercises in place or walk around the room.

Another stress reducer is humor. Plan some activities just to make participants laugh. For example, ask each participant to bring a baby picture anonymously, and put them in a scrapbook, unlabeled. Then pass it around the group and ask them to guess which picture represents which adult in the room.

Make the work of the meeting fun wherever you can. Introduce a new market-ing slogan by playing charades, or write a song around it and have a chorus of participants deliver it. Demonstrate a new sales technique in a skit with char-acters dressed in outlandish costumes. You will reduce stress and utilize the element of surprise at the same time.

CAUTION

Not everyone finds games, pep rallies, and contests fun or appropriate. People raised outside the United States may find such activities a turnoff, childish, or offensive, however valid the business goal is. Know your participants before you impose any activity that can be viewed as unprofessional or alien to the culture of your participants.

TEAM-BUILDING CHALLENGE EVENTS

Break your meeting group into two or more teams and assign an agenda item to each. Then, reconfigure the teams and repeat the exercise. You can also use a game unrelated to your meeting's agenda but specifically designed to demonstrate the power of teamwork over individual effort, such as the "Lost on the Moon" game devised by the National Aeronautics and Space Administration and cited by Michael Doyle and David Straus.

These are not contests to see who reaches the goal first or devises a better solution. They are exercises to build camaraderie and the healthy interdepen-dence that is a hallmark of good teamwork, and to help a group bond in a positive way.

CONTESTS

There are also out-and-out contests you can plan for meeting participants. Two guidelines:

- **Make them real.** Draw a new corporate logo, decorate a T-shirt with a picture that illustrates a new marketing campaign, or choose a title for a book.

- **Make the prizes attractive.** Offer theater tickets, $100 to spend on the indulgence of your choice, or an extra day off.

There isn't an idea in this lesson that hasn't been tried successfully in meetings; I've witnessed everything suggested here. The only limits are your imagination, your budget, avoiding illegal activity, and the culture of your organization.

CULTURAL EXPECTATIONS

The section "The Art of Facilitation" on page 770 introduced cultural expectations that color the role of facilitators and leaders in meetings. To understand how individuals behave in group situations such as meetings, it is also important to consider cultural differences and international business protocols.

ORGANIZATIONAL CULTURE

Effective groups are participatory, open, and free to come to an independent consensus. Meetings and other group activities do not take place in a vacuum, and your success in creating an effective group may be enhanced or constrained by the *organizational culture* in which the meeting occurs.

PLAIN ENGLISH

Organizational culture   The set of shared values, goals, practices, and management styles that characterize an organization and are expected to be reflected in its public face and its members' behavior.

If the organizational culture is participatory, democratic, and open to dissenting views, and if individuals are valued for their ideas as well as their task completion, interdependence and trust may be pre-established and natural to the group you assemble for your meeting.

Other organizational cultures are common, and they may be less supportive of the kind of climate you are trying to create. Many organizations are hierarchical, autocratic, bureaucratic, or tradition-bound. They may stifle unsolicited contributions and frown on dissent. Any organization may be a hybrid, advocating participatory management but stuck in bureaucracy so that executing good decisions is difficult, or one that solicits ideas but retains all decision-making power in a few people.

As a meeting leader or facilitator, assess the organizational culture in planning your meeting.

- **Know the organizational culture.** If this is your first meeting in this organization, for example, if you just joined the organization or are an outside consultant, read all the material you can find about the culture of this organization. Talk to your supervisor or the person engaging you about how decisions are made and how meetings have been run in the past.

TIP

Review the minutes of the most recent meeting in this organization similar to the one you are planning. Talk to its leader or facilitator and, if possible, a few participants not in a leadership role in that meeting.

- **Demonstrate your past success.** If you have a proven track record, give examples of your experience and effectiveness in facilitating groups in the kind of meeting you are going to run, especially if your process or style will be a radical change from what the organization is used to.

- **Prevent yourself from being seen as a maverick.** In the meeting itself, if you are unknown to the group, arrange to be introduced and have your credentials presented by someone in the organization to let the group know you have credibility.

- **Modify your style.** If your style is different, try to move closer to that of the organization. It may mean being more or less formal than you usually are, or more or less directive in leading discussion. Expect more questions from the group about process and more skepticism about outcomes in organizations with less participatory cultures.

- **Go slowly.** Build the group's confidence in your facilitation or leadership one success at a time. The first interaction in which you request feedback or solicit a minority opinion in an organization where either action is unexpected will set the stage.

CAUTION

Do not promise what you cannot deliver. If the desired outcome of your meeting is a recommendation on next year's budget for new equipment, but the organization's practice is to prioritize recommendations for the president's sole decision, you cannot promise that the recommendation will be accepted.

CULTURAL IDENTITY AND INTERNATIONAL DIFFERENCES

In addition to organizational cultural differences, *cultural identity* and international differences affect group behavior.

PLAIN ENGLISH

Cultural identity   The customary beliefs, social structure, and attitudes to which individuals subscribe by virtue of their self-defined racial, ethnic, religious, or social group.

If you are planning a meeting that includes participants from one or more cultures other than your own, be sure to research the cultural expectations and business protocols of the participants. Consult colleagues who have worked with these cultures, or a consultant on cultural acclimation.

Opportunities for confusion and gaffes abound in everything from language (for example, General Motors prepared to sell its Nova model in Mexico without changing its name, *No va,* which means "No go" in Spanish) to hand gestures that are innocuous in the United States (such as pointing at someone with a forefinger), but vulgar on another continent (in Malaysia people point only at animals, never at other people).

If you are not well versed in cultures other than your own, you may misinterpret meeting behavior by individuals from other cultures. An excellent book on this topic is *Kiss, Bow, or Shake Hands: How to Do Business in Sixty Countries,* by Terri Morrison, Wayne A. Conway, and George Borden (Bob Adams, Inc., 1994). The following is only a brief sampling of cultural factors that may affect group behavior in the setting of a meeting.

- Conformity rates are lower in individualistic cultures, such as that in the United States, than in cultures where the good of the group—family, employer, neighborhood—is more highly valued, such as Japan.

- Small talk at the beginning of a meeting is not a nicety in certain Asian, Latino, and African cultures; it is a necessity, and omitting it is both an affront to participants and a barrier to conducting the business of a meeting. It makes some Americans uncomfortable to be asked about their families' well-being, but this is an expression of courtesy, not a personal intrusion.

- Angry exchanges and people walking out of meetings—behavior that may look like the breakdown of a meeting to an American—is a common, often planned behavior in Russia. Avoid overreacting; they will be back.

- In a social setting, such as a reception for spouses of meeting participants, Americans are advised not to ask anyone what they do for a living. This is a United States component of small talk, but considered terribly rude anywhere else, where who you are is not defined but what kind of work you do.

- If entertainment is planned during a long meeting or after one, make sure it is culturally appropriate. You can commit sins of omission (as well as commission) in this area. Omission: In a multicultural group attending a three-day meeting with entertainment planned each night, I overheard a Latino participant exclaim, "How can they plan entertainment for a group that includes Latinos without any music?" Commission: Lawsuits have been won over male employers taking female sales representatives to go-go bars as "entertainment."

CAUTION

Make no assumptions about a participant's cultural identity or country of origin. There are few appropriate or legal reasons to ask. If you are planning a meal after a meeting, for example, ask "Any suggestions for a good restaurant?" rather than "Ms. Wong, can you recommend a Chinese restaurant?"

The guiding principle in adapting to different cultural and business protocols is to do what makes those in your group comfortable.

THE 30-SECOND RECAP

- Predictability, boredom, and stress compromise the effectiveness of a meeting. The element of surprise will reinvigorate a meeting.

- Effective stress reducers include ice breakers, unstructured time, meditation, physical activity, and humor.

- Team-building challenge events are not contests but exercises that build camaraderie and an appreciation of the healthy and productive interdependence of teams.

■ Contests will grab participants' attention but need to be serious attempts to produce something of benefit to the organization, and rewards need to be attractive in order to generate significant effort.

■ Organizational culture may support or inhibit the functioning of effective groups, and a facilitator or leader can take steps to increase the success of the group.

■ Cultural identity and international differences affect group behavior and need to be understood in order to make all meeting participants comfortable.

Meetings Without Meeting

In this section you learn about effective alternatives to face-to-face meetings.

There are situations where you really need to have a meeting in order to accomplish an objective, but there are constraints of time, budget, and/or availability that might work against an in-person meeting. Thanks to advancing technology, there are now mechanisms becoming widely available that enable you to conduct most or all of the kind of interpersonal exchanges that occur in a meeting without the physical presence of participants.

Some of these mechanisms have been around for some time and may be familiar, such as teleconferencing and videoconferencing, while e-mail and other electronic tools may be familiar, but their applications to the needs of a meeting are new. Most require significant one-time and/or recurring investments, which should be carefully evaluated and road-tested before they are adopted as a replacement for any given meeting.

In organizations that are not already familiar with these technologies, you may have to advocate for their use as a viable substitute for a physical meeting. In low-tech organizations and organizational cultures that are not *change hardy,* persuasion may be a particularly daunting task.

PLAIN ENGLISH

Change hardy   Conditioned to embrace change because human nature is change resistant. Change-hardy organizations are proactive in their quest for organizational effectiveness, and build in rewards for responsible risk-taking. The speed of change in the twenty-first-century economic environment is forcing most organizations to become change hardy to survive.

If you have to persuade your group or management to try one of these meeting alternatives, look for a similar team or organization that has used the alternative you are considering successfully, or create a test-run simulation to demonstrate how the elements work to create the same group interactions a live meeting would.

TELECONFERENCING

The conference call is the alternative to in-person meetings that has been around the longest. It is low-tech, low-cost, readily available, and doesn't throw up technical barriers to its use by first-time participants.

Teleconferencing is most effective for exchanges of small amounts of quantitative information, group decision-making based on qualitative data, and for small groups. I haven't seen it used effectively for groups of more than six people. It becomes unwieldy very quickly with large numbers of participants for a number of reasons.

To make a conference call as effective as a meeting, plan it just as you would a physical meeting. Schedule it in advance, prepare and distribute an agenda and premeeting materials, and ask all participants to arrange not to be interrupted during the call.

There are additional considerations to planning and facilitating a teleconference meeting. Because of the absence of nonverbal cues from the facilitator and a recorder to track what is said, people tend to speak longer and more slowly during a teleconference to make sure their point is understood and retained. As facilitator you need to limit speaking time so that participants can absorb what is said, and frequently recap what was said for the group.

TIP

To prevent the common problem of several people starting to talk at once, the facilitator should announce a speaking order, and then designate who should speak next in each round of discussion, as in "Marj, would you give us your opinion next?"

If you permit speakers out of sequence, set a rule that each must identify her- or himself each time, so that everyone knows who is speaking.

Whether you are the recorder or have designated another participant that role, because the group can't see what the recorder is writing, it is important to get confirmation from the group as to what has been stated or agreed to.

Here's an example of a successful conference-call meeting. I am a member of a professional association diversity advancement committee that annually awards two conference scholarships to a student and a new professional in our field. The committee members are scattered throughout the Northeastern United States, and holding an in-person meeting to decide the winners is out of the question.

The co-chairs collect and distribute all the applications to the full committee by fax a week before the conference call, with an assignment to read, evaluate, and rank the applicants in order of preference. The conference-call agenda is restated at the start of the call and the decision process is explained. Each committee member introduces her- or himself briefly; it is not uncommon that committee members, who change each year, have never met. Each applicant is discussed by all members, within a time limit, with frequent recaps and clarifications requested or provided by the co-chairs. Then the rankings are compared and sometimes amended by the committee until a consensus is reached.

A benefit of this teleconference is that when we actually meet at the annual conference two months later, the committee members already "know" each other just as if there had been a physical meeting.

VIDEOCONFERENCING

Videoconferences are run similarly to teleconferences, with two main differences: the cost and availability of the technology are significant deterrents, and the addition of a visual dimension to the meeting.

As with any new technology, the cost of videoconferencing equipment has fallen since introduction, technology has improved, and availability is increasing. Desktop video—real-time video transmitted from one participant's computer to those of other participants—is now possible, if not prevalent.

The issues in deciding whether or not to try videoconferencing include *cost-benefit analysis* as well as availability and user acceptance.

PLAIN ENGLISH

Cost-benefit analysis   A measure of expected expense compared to expected benefit that takes into account financial and intangible costs, underlying assumptions, the time value of money, and the financial and nonfinancial benefits of a given action.

Videoconferencing has been most frequently used to interview prospective job candidates in national searches in order to save on the travel costs of bringing candidates to a central interviewing site while maintaining the visual advantage of face-to-face interviews. It also adds speed to the process.

In the mid-1990s, Dell Computer utilized videoconferencing at a computer industry show in New York City. Representatives at the show accepted resumés from job applicants, faxed them to headquarters in Texas, and asked applicants to return in an hour for a decision whether or not they would be interviewed by videoconference. Over the course of a several-day conference, Dell hired several recruits for jobs with six-figure salaries, significantly reducing both recruiting costs and the time needed to fulfill the jobs.

Negotiation meetings, problem-solving and decision-making meetings, informational meetings, and training meetings all lend themselves to videoconferencing, providing an opportunity to save both travel time and money for situations where these costs exceed the cost of the technology.

VIRTUAL MEETINGS

Computer-mediated communication (CMC) exploded with the expansion of the Internet to the general population.

PLAIN ENGLISH

Computer-mediated communication   Any type of communication in which a computer is utilized, including electronic organizers, e-mail, groupware such as LotusNotes, and proprietary software systems accessible over the Internet.

E-mail is the simplest of these tools. A virtual meeting can be as simple as creating a list serve of participants and exchanging e-mails along a given agenda within a given time frame.

The next innovation in virtual meetings was the chat room, a dedicated site on the Internet where admitted participants can exchange ideas either within a given time frame or at a previously scheduled time.

These tools are helpful, but provide little if any structure for a meeting or control by a leader or facilitator.

CAUTION

In an in-person meeting where comments are made orally, there is an immediate ability to mitigate or withdraw statements before they are permanently recorded. In e-mail, chat rooms, and other cyberspace communication, one's words are irretrievable, providing a challenge for participants and facilitator alike.

E-mail and chat rooms are fast, cost effective, allow for a high level of participant control, and are an equalizer that provides the same level of access to all participants. They are also faceless and voiceless, which may impede the development of cohesiveness within a group.

THE DELPHI METHOD

One computer-assisted decision-making method that became popular in the 1990s is the Delphi Method. It allows participants to address issues or solve problems by anonymous responses via e-mail filtered through an administrative staff. Two rounds of questions are prepared, the second summarizing the results of the first and asking for clarification, agreement or disagreement, and prioritization. A final report is then prepared and distributed.

CUSTOM SOFTWARE

Electronic meetings utilizing proprietary software are proliferating. An organization may establish such software for a variety of purposes. Within the academic environment, for example, custom software has been developed for distance learning, in which students take classes that undertake all assignments electronically and meet for only part of the course or not at all.

Advanced systems allow participants to upload documents, digital files, audio- and video-clips as well as art, and to create hotlinks to Web sites as part of their contributions.

The disadvantage of custom software is its cost. The software has to be flexible enough to allow a meeting facilitator to incorporate different processes into different meetings, but also be tailored to a specific set of predetermined applications. Many organizations will find the cost prohibitive or unwarranted for the benefit it provides.

SYNCHRONOUS ELECTRONIC MEETINGS

Synchronous electronic meetings are those that occur in real time, when participants are all electronically present concurrently.

The advantage of synchronous meetings is that they provide the energy of an in-person meeting or class, where a facilitator or teacher guides the discussion. The disadvantage is that participants in different time zones have difficulty attending.

ASYNCHRONOUS ELECTRONIC MEETINGS

Asynchronous electronic meetings occur in these proprietary systems as set up by the facilitator. Participants log on at any hour of the day or night. They receive instructions and assignments, view other participants' contributions and feedback, and write their responses or ideas where other participants and the facilitator can review them.

The advantages of asynchronous electronic meetings are inclusion of participants independent of the time zone in which they live, and the ability to reflect and prepare contributions off-line and save them for later transmission. Most systems allow participants to upload files.

The disadvantage of asynchronous meetings is the inherent loss of immediacy. The specific tailoring of each meeting's process that custom software provides, however, allows for group bonding and cohesiveness, and energy is higher than in e-mail or chat room formats.

THE 30-SECOND RECAP

- You may have to advocate for nontraditional alternatives to meetings.
- Teleconferencing is a low-cost, low-tech, familiar alternative but requires the same planning as a face-to-face meeting and additional facilitation of voice exchanges in order to be effective.
- Videoconferencing adds a visual dimension to long-distance meetings, but at higher cost and with limited availability.
- Virtual meetings can be devised using e-mail, chat rooms, groupware, and customized software.

Business Writing

Effective Business Writing Matters

In this section you learn how to overcome the fear of writing, how effective writing serves as a leadership tool, and how clear thinking is the foundation of effective writing.

WRITE WITHOUT FEAR

For many professionals, the thought of writing a business document generates anxiety and procrastination. If you are among these people, you're not alone. Becoming anxious or procrastinating at the thought of expressing yourself in a permanent medium is quite natural, for several reasons.

First, you may not have the confidence to write well because when you were in school, the importance of expressing ideas often got lost in the pursuit of proper grammar or style requirements. Remember the English teacher who asked you to write a five-paragraph essay with five sentences in each paragraph? Or the college professor who asked you for a 15-page paper? Although these objectives served a purpose, they did little to distinguish the importance of the thinking behind the writing.

Second, you may not be clear about precisely why you need to write a certain document or specifically what you need to say in it. This is a common stumbling block among our Effective Business Writing workshop participants. The anxiety sets in for them because they're trying to write too soon—they've skipped the first, most important step, namely clarifying their thinking.

Third, you may fear that by putting words to paper your flaws as a writer will be exposed to the world, including your bosses and colleagues. Speaking in public may be the number one fear among professionals, but writing surely is a close second. The situations are strikingly similar; once your written document has been distributed, you are, in a sense, speaking to the recipients.

CAUTION

Procrastinating due to fear will only increase your anxiety as the deadline approaches. Find some way to make progress on your document, even if you're not sure how to finish it.

TIP

If you're procrastinating because you're afraid the final document won't be good enough, write a "throw-away" draft you'll never show anyone. That will give you a base from which to write the final version.

This section about business writing breaks down the writing process into manageable steps and provides the framework to structure your document and clarify your thinking. By treating the content and thinking behind a document separately from its style and grammar, the process eliminates anxiety, enabling you to write without fear.

TIP

Being anxious about writing a business document does not imply your inability to write it. In fact, caring how you come across—which is most likely what's causing your anxiety in the first place—is the first important ingredient in writing effective documents.

EFFECTIVE WRITING IS A LEADERSHIP TOOL

Poorly written documents can cloud issues and distract people's thinking. If you as the writer don't clearly articulate a point of view, the reader will have a hard time not only sorting through what's being said, but also understanding the issue in the way you'd like for him to.

PLAIN ENGLISH

Leadership   Having a vision for what you'd like to happen, and setting in motion the events that will realize your vision. It doesn't mean you must necessarily command the forces that execute the plan—merely that you guide the thinking that eventually causes the plan to be executed.

PLAIN ENGLISH

Poorly written document   A document in which the thinking is hard to follow, the point is hard to find, or the writing has mistakes or other flaws that distract and detract from the main message.

Well-written documents clarify issues, assist people's thinking, and ultimately build consensus. When you're able to focus the reader's thinking on the key issues, and concisely lay out why your point of view is a valid one, you've assumed a leadership role. In addition, you've created the framework for how the issue will be discussed.

PLAIN ENGLISH

Well-written document   A document in which the main message is clear and compelling and the writing itself—the style, grammar, and logic flow—doesn't distract the reader from the point being made.

TIP

Try to use every document you write as an opportunity to focus the attention of the reader on the specific business goals you've been charged with. You can use even documents of seemingly minor importance to begin laying the foundation for persuading others to share your business vision. For example, monthly "activity reports" can be a vehicle to highlight where improvements in procedure could improve results, sowing the seeds for a later recommendation to change the procedures.

CLEAR THINKING LEADS TO EFFECTIVE WRITING

The foundation of effective business writing is clear thinking. Grammar and style matter, but critical thinking is even more important.

Consider the following example. While these two memos are on the same subject, one demonstrates clear thinking and the other doesn't. Which would you rather read? Which would you rather send? Most important, which do you believe would be more likely to be acted on?

CAUTION

Big or important-sounding words that don't clarify your message detract from, not add to, the quality of your document. Clarity of thought is more impressive than a big vocabulary.

MEMO A

To: Division President

From: Division Manager

Subject: Data Collection

Our division has a problem. We have a major sales force reorganization project to develop and there are no computers in our division to accommodate the data collection that will be necessary to carry out what we have in mind. We are wondering if Corporate will help us. The secretaries in the various divisions currently all have computers and it is our understanding that these computers have significant processing capabilities. Cheaper alternatives for secretaries' word processing needs can be found in other ways. As employees, we object to using powerful computers for this purpose. Regardless of what may be planned for the secretaries' computers, we believe that these computers would meet our requirements and would be convenient to our sales force. Our sales force would be able to quickly add the programs needed to the new computers. Our budgets would accommodate the switch-over, too. We would be able to maintain the sales force data collection needs. It would be very much appreciated if a decision on this issue were forthcoming at the earliest possible date. If there are any further questions or comments, please don't hesitate to call me.

MEMO B

To: Division President

From: Division Manager

Subject: Proposal to Improve Division's Data Collection Capabilities

This recommends replacing the computers of 23 company secretaries with networked terminals, in order to give the freed-up CPUs to the Division Sales Force to improve their data collection capabilities. The MIS personnel concur with this recommendation.

The MIS Department agrees that the corporate network is capable of meeting all secretarial computing needs, eliminating the need for separate CPUs for each secretary.

The approved sales force reorganization will require approximately $200,000 in computing equipment. However, most of this need could be filled by the CPUs now used by the company's secretaries, saving the company over $150,000.

With your approval of the plan, I will work with the MIS department manager to implement the change and develop the appropriate training for the secretaries.

In the preceding examples, the writer wants something—more computing capability for the sales force—and sees a way to acquire it: Reallocate the computers currently used by company secretaries. In the first example, however, the writer uses a "stream of consciousness" style to describe the situation, forcing the reader to read through the entire document to figure out what the writer wants and why.

In the second example, the writer has thought about what she is asking for, what information the reader needs to make the decision, and what steps must be taken to make the plan happen. The second example starts by clearly stating the purpose of the document ("This recommends replacing the computers ..."), provides evidence that the plan will work ("The MIS Department agrees ..."), and states the benefits of the plan ("... saving the company over $150,000"). Finally, the writer describes what will happen next ("... I will work with the MIS department manager to implement the changes ...").

This clearly laid-out, step-by-step explanation helps the reader to easily understand what's being asked for and why, making it much easier to agree to the request—and not incidentally, be impressed with the writer's depth and clarity of thinking.

TIP

When working on your document, focus first on thinking and content. Concentrate on grammar and style after your critical thinking is complete.

EFFECTIVE WRITING CAN BE LEARNED

Writing effectively for business is something that can be easily learned. We've seen in our Effective Business Writing workshops that when people focus on the thinking first, and are given a simple framework in which to do so, they immediately become more effective writers.

The framework, which this book details, enables you to break down the writing process into a number of manageable pieces—setting your objective, or purpose, for writing; framing your thinking by organizing your thoughts into discrete "chunks" corresponding to specific sections of the document; and then easily assembling the pieces into an effective business document.

THE 30-SECOND RECAP

- If you become anxious at the thought of writing a business document, you're not alone.
- Effective business writing is a critical leadership tool.
- The foundation of effective business writing is clear thinking.
- Writing effectively for business is something you can easily learn.
- Working within a framework can reduce the natural fear of writing business documents.

Start with a Purpose in Mind

In this section you learn to start with a clear purpose in mind. You also learn the key questions to ask yourself before beginning to write, and how to advance your business objectives.

UNDERSTAND YOUR PURPOSE

Understanding why you're writing is the most important factor in creating an effective business document. Although you may think this point is obvious, our experience in teaching effective business writing says otherwise. Most of the poorly written documents we've seen stem from writers who have no clear purpose in mind.

TIP

A clear, well-thought-out purpose will adhere to the "SMART" principle. SMART stands for ...

Specific. Your purpose focuses on a single, well-defined issue.

Measurable. There is a way to measure whether the objective is achieved.

Actionable. Achieving your purpose is within the control of you or others in the organization—i.e., you needn't rely on outside, uncontrollable factors to achieve your purpose.

Rewarding. Achieving your purpose has value for you and your organization.

Terse. The purpose can be stated in a few simple words.

We'll begin the discussion of purpose by focusing on the business memo. The reason we focus first on *memos* is that they are the most common form of business communication, perhaps the most important one, and the principles outlined in the memo sections apply to all forms of business communication.

PLAIN ENGLISH

Memo (short for memorandum)   Any written interoffice communication, including most e-mail correspondence. The most common memos are recommendations and summaries.

ASK QUESTIONS TO FOCUS YOUR WRITING

Asking a few simple questions before you write will help you clarify your objective.

WHY ARE YOU WRITING?

In some cases, the immediate answer to the question, "Why am I writing?" may be, "Because my boss asked for this report," or, "Because we write this report every month." As you think more deeply about why you're writing, the purpose will probably fall into one of the following categories:

- To clarify important facts about your business (e.g., a meeting summary, monthly/interim progress report, other informational memo).

- To suggest/propose/convince others to do something (e.g., a request for additional resources).

- To request permission or inform others about action you're taking (e.g., a proposal to change operating procedures in your department).

CAUTION

Beginning to write with only a vague purpose in mind, such as "Something needs to be done about our accounting system," may result in your trying to wrestle with too many possibilities and hamper your ability to write a clear, concise document. By contrast, a clearer purpose, such as "We need to install the XYZ accounting system by January 1," will focus your thinking and make your memo-writing go much more smoothly.

PLAIN ENGLISH

Resources   The money, materials, or people needed to advance your business objectives.

WHO IS YOUR AUDIENCE?

Once you know what you want to make happen, consider the people to whom you're addressing the memo. First, are these the people who can take the action you want? If not, should you send the memo to different people, or do you need to rely on the recipient to forward it to the appropriate parties? In either case, consider not only the immediate recipient, but also all those who will eventually read and take action on your document.

To write effectively for your audience, consider the following:

- What is their position in the company?
- What impact can they have on the issue you're writing about?
- How much do they already know about the issue you're writing about?
- Do they already have a point of view about your request or proposal, and if so, do you need to address that point of view in your document?

TIP

Your business objectives will only be achieved when someone takes action. Therefore, try to spend your time on memos or other communication that effect action.

What Do You Want Them to Do?

Every person to whom you send a memo should be getting it for a reason—either you want him to take action, or give his approval for you to take action, or you'd like to persuade him to understand/agree with your point of view, in order that he may later agree to some action. To be effective, your document should be clear about what action you're requesting the recipient to take.

CAUTION

Be judicious in sending documents. Your potential readers are busy people, so send them written information only if they need to know about, agree with, or take action on your subject.

Why Should They Agree?

Now that you've identified why you're writing, who should receive your document, and what you want them to do, take the time to understand your recipients' perspective on the issues at hand. Ask yourself the following:

- What is your readers' understanding of the issues involved?
- How will your recommendations affect your readers' success, failure, or day-to-day operations?
- What are the risks associated with your readers' taking action?

Be sure to keep your audience's perspective in mind and attempt to address their concerns as you write your document.

Through the course of the book, we'll discuss in detail ways to structure your document to best address your audience's concerns. The first step, however, is to recognize that those concerns exist and to know what they are.

ADVANCE YOUR OBJECTIVES

Part of writing with a purpose is to view every business document as an opportunity to advance your business objectives. This is most obviously true for documents in which you're recommending a specific proposal or a change in how your business is operated. However, you can use even seemingly routine documents such as meeting summaries or monthly progress reports as vehicles for framing the thinking on important business issues, and laying the groundwork for later recommendations.

For example, suppose you're the division sales manager for your company, and you've recently begun testing a new order-tracking system that you believe will provide better customer service. Following are segments from two potential monthly progress reports. Note how the second memo, while still summarizing the monthly sales events, clearly lays a foundation for later recommending full-scale implementation of the new order-tracking system.

TIP
Recognize that any written communication gives you the opportunity to lead others' thinking.

MEMO A

To: National Sales Manager

From: Division Sales Manager

Re: Monthly Progress Report

This summarizes monthly sales in the Eastern Division.

- Sales are up 2 percent from the previous month, and up 4 percent from a year ago.
- We opened three new accounts, including Acme Company, the largest user of our type of products in the Eastern Division. As you know, we've been trying to open this account for more than six months.
- On-time shipments were 98 percent, up 3 percent from the previous month, and up 5 percent from a year ago.

Starting with a clear purpose will make the writing process much less difficult. As you think about why the document needs to be written, who needs to read it, and why they should agree with what you're writing, you will become much better prepared to decide what information needs to be included in the document and how that information should flow.

If you would like your writing to be consistently effective in helping you achieve your business objectives, you must have clearly in mind, each time you write, what effect you wish to have. Therefore, taking a few minutes before beginning any document to review in your mind what your objective is for writing—beyond just completing the "assignment"—will pay dividends both in terms of how much less difficult it is to know what to write, and how much more effective the final product will be in enabling you to lead the organization in the direction you want it to go.

MEMO B

To: National Sales Manager

From: Division Sales Manager

Re: Monthly Progress Report

This summarizes monthly sales in the Eastern Division.

- Sales are up 2 percent from the previous month, and up 4 percent from a year ago.

- We opened three new accounts, including Acme Company, the largest user of our type of products in the Eastern Division. As you know, we've been trying to open this account for more than six months. In our most recent presentation to the Acme buyer, we explained the new order-tracking system and the positive effect it would have on on-time shipments.

- On-time shipments were 98 percent, up 3 percent from the previous month, and up 5 percent from a year ago. This on-time shipment number is the best we've had in the past 18 months, and appears to be directly attributable to the new tracking system. The sales force also reports that complaints about delayed or incomplete shipments are down significantly since we began testing the tracking system.

THE 30-SECOND RECAP

- Before you start writing, be clear about why you are doing so.

- Identify the appropriate audience for your document based on your objective, and understand this audience's perspective before writing.

- Remember, every memo gives you the opportunity to lead others' thinking and advance your business objectives.

Framing Your Thinking

In this section you learn the value of using a standard framework when writing your memos and are given a framework used for the most common types of business documents.

THE IMPORTANCE OF A FRAMEWORK

Starting with a standard framework when writing a business document jump-starts your thinking and consequently your writing. By knowing the sections you should include in your document, you can easily identify missing information and ensure you incorporate all the data you need to make your document as effective as possible. The framework also enables you to quickly organize your thoughts and evaluate your logic. Using the framework consistently trains your mind to write more efficiently and effectively. The framework also assists your readers because they know where to find specific information.

We will provide a "standard memo framework" for writing most kinds of business memos. This model is appropriate for virtually all the memos you will write; however, you may wish, over time, to modify the standard framework to better suit your personal style and specific business situation. Regardless of whether you adopt the standard framework, a slight modification of it, or a framework of your own creation, beginning with the underlying structure in mind before doing any writing will be a significant aid to your thinking.

TIP

If you're going to create your own framework for documents, keep your typical reader in mind. What kind of information is she expecting to see? What logical flow of information is most likely to be persuasive? What organizational structure for your memo will make it easiest for her to find what she's looking for quickly and easily?

Think of a document framework as you would the framework for a new house. The framing in the home-building process provides the outline for what materials are needed and where they're to be placed. The document framework does the same for your logic and data.

Some people dismiss a document framework because they believe it is restrictive. We have found in our careers and in our workshops quite the opposite. The framework provides the structure writers need to be thorough and creative. The framework is a tool, a starting point. Use it to start your writing process, and tailor it to your situation as you see fit.

RECOMMENDATIONS AND SUMMARIES

The most common business documents written are recommendations and summaries. Use a recommendation when you're asking the reader to take some action or to approve your taking some action. Use the summary to convey information to the people who need it. Both follow a similar framework. For the purposes of this book, we call this framework the "standard memo framework."

THE STANDARD MEMO FRAMEWORK

The standard memo framework consists of the following five sections: the Overview; the Background; either the Recommendation or the Conclusions, depending on whether your memo is a recommendation or a summary; either the Rationale (for a recommendation memo) or the Key Findings (for a summary memo); and the Next Steps. The contents of these sections are ...

- **Overview.** Two or three sentences that provide a synopsis of the entire memo, including a brief statement that summarizes your conclusions or recommendation.

- **Background.** One or two paragraphs describing the business situation relevant to why the recommendation is being made or the conclusion is being given.

- **Recommendation.** A brief description of exactly what you want to have happen. This would typically include what needs to be done, what it would cost, and how quickly it could be done.

- **Conclusion.** A brief description of your interpretation of a business analysis, research analysis, or other information analysis.

- **Rationale.** Three to five paragraphs, each of which provides a reason for the reader to agree to your recommendation, and the support needed to back up each reason.

■ **Key Findings.** A list of facts obtained from business analysis, research analysis, or other information analysis.

■ **Next Steps.** What needs to be done, by whom, and by what date.

THE STANDARD MEMO FRAMEWORK IN ACTION

To better understand how you can use the framework to create an effective business recommendation, consider the following recommendation memo. (We'll take a look at a summary memo in "The Opening Is the 'Bottom Line'" on page 842.)

To: General Manager

From: Brand Manager

Subject: Acme Shampoo Sampling National Expansion Recommendation

Overview

This requests management agreement to execute a broad-based sampling program during the second year of Acme's national expansion. The key element of this program is mailing sample-size product to 20 percent of U.S. households in late June of this year, followed by a 25¢ coupon insert in newspapers to 50 percent of U.S. households in mid-July to secure follow-up consumer purchase and retail support. No incremental budget dollars are needed for this program.

Background

Acme entered the test market two years ago using a sample mailing to 30 percent of market households to gain initial trial of the product, followed by a coupon insert to 60 percent of households. After the initial sample and coupon drops, Acme share remained relatively stable. Acme expanded nationally one year later using the same sample and coupon effort. Year-one national results are in line with year-one test market results.

In year two of the test market, shipments and share increased 26 percent and 22 percent respectively, following a second wave of samples and coupons. Year two of the national expansion begins next month.

Recommendation

The purpose of the recommended national sampling initiative is to broaden Acme trial and purchase. We will accomplish this by mailing samples to an additional 20 percent of national households, bringing the total Acme sampling effort to 30 percent of U.S. households over 18 months.

In line with the test market, sampling will principally be a mailed effort. Beyond the sampling, consistent with our test market plan, we will execute a

25¢ freestanding coupon insert in newspapers three weeks after sampling, in order to encourage consumer purchase while providing a focal point for retail support.

Rationale

Year-two sampling substantially builds the business. Specifically, since the second wave of sampling in the test market, business results have been strong with shipments and share up 26 percent and 22 percent respectively, vs. year-one base.

Sampling effectiveness research showed significant increases in trial and purchase behind test market year-two sampling. Specifically, past three months' usage and purchase were significantly up among sampled vs. nonsampled households, as shown in the following table.

	Sampled Households	Nonsampled Households
Past four weeks brand usage	15%	9%
Past three months brand usage	23%	13%
Past three months brand purchase	19%	12%

The Promotion Department sampling payout model confirmed Acme year-two sampling is a financially sound initiative. Specifically, the model projected the year-two sampling to generate a volume increase of 18 percent over year one and payout in 12 months, based on the purchase levels seen in the sampling effectiveness research.

Next Steps

With management approval for the national execution of the year-two sampling effort, we will proceed on the following timing:

Start of sample filling	March 1
Start of sample pouching	April 1
Sample drop	June 30
Coupon drop	July 17

May we have agreement?

TIP

Clearly delineating the sections of your document—for example, by printing your headings in a different font and larger type size—can make your memo more inviting to read, and make the information in your document easier to find.

The preceding memo lays out a fairly complicated plan with detailed explanation of why the plan is right. Writing such a memo could be very difficult and confusing, and reading it could be equally confusing, if there was no clear framework for both the writer and reader to follow. The standard framework, then, gives the writer a road map for laying out the discussion, and the reader a similar road map for following it:

- The Overview tells exactly what the memo is about, and what the reader is being asked for (e.g., approval of the plan).

- The Background gives the reader relevant information about events that have already occurred—in this case, the test market results.

- The Recommendation section tells the reader the specifics of what is being recommended—the details of the sampling plan—amplifying what's been stated in the Overview section.

- The Rationale section lays out, point by point, why the recommendation is sound. In this case, both test market results and other research are cited to support the recommendation.

- Finally, the Next Steps section describes what the Acme brand manager will do, and when he'll do it, if the recommendation is approved.

CAUTION

Try to avoid putting too much detail in the Background section. You need to include enough so that your reader can understand the situation; additional detail will bog down the reader before he ever gets to the "meat" of the memo (the recommendation or conclusion). If the background information doesn't apply directly to the recommendation or conclusion being made, leave it out.

COMPLEX RECOMMENDATIONS

Some recommendation memos are more complex. To keep these memos easy for your reader to understand and agree to, it's best to add the detailed information on how the action plan works in a later section, and keep the recommendation section at a summary level. In these cases, the standard memo framework may be expanded to include How It Works and Risks sections as follows:

- Overview
- Background

- Recommendations
- Rationale
- How It Works
- Risks
- Next Steps

TIP

If your Recommendation section is more than two or three paragraphs of four to six sentences each, consider adding a How It Works section, and summarizing the recommendation in the Recommendation section.

The two sections added enable you to easily outline in detail how the plan you're recommending will work and how you have addressed the associated risks. Note that these sections may be added as appropriate, and are not necessarily required to be added together.

- **How It Works.** Several paragraphs that outline in logical detail how a recommendation will be implemented. Specifically, this section details who will do what, when, and how for the entire plan. This section is optional and is needed only for complex recommendations.

- *Risks.* Two to three paragraphs describing what risks may be associated with implementing your recommendation. This section should usually be accompanied by a brief explanation of why the risks are small, or how the risks can be mitigated. This section is optional and should be used only for high-risk recommendations.

PLAIN ENGLISH

Risk   Something important enough to be included in a Risks section is a threat to the success of the plan that is unique to this situation or significant in some way. The "usual" risks, such as possible competitive response or unforeseeable disasters, wouldn't generally qualify, since those risks are assumed to be there in all cases, and needn't be pointed out each time you write a recommendation.

Suppose in the previous memo example that the sample and coupon program required $6 million more spending than has been budgeted. The Acme brand manager would likely need to add more financial detail based on the test market results and the sampling payout model in order to justify the additional spending. The manager would likely outline the incremental spending and volume projections in a How It Works section, and compare Acme revenue and profit based on implementing the sampling plan vs. not. In addition, the brand manager would need to ask for approval not only for the sample and coupon expansion, but also for the incremental funding associated with it.

A framework helps guide your thinking before you begin writing, and guides the reader through the completed document. This makes it easier to do your job of determining what information to include and where to include it, and makes it easier for the reader to find and understand the information you've provided.

The 30-Second Recap

- Using the standard memo framework helps clarify your thinking before you start to write.

- Using the standard memo framework enables your audience to stop reading the document once it has enough information to agree or approve your recommendation.

- You can use the standard memo framework as a starting point to evaluate your logic and strengthen your argument, then tailor the final document format as appropriate for your purpose.

The Opening Is the "Bottom Line"

In this section you learn how to begin your document in a way that most helps your reader, and what information to include in the overview.

Respect Your Audience

Most good stories build some kind of suspense for the reader: What will happen next, how the hero will save the day, whether the butler really did it. Logical arguments, such as proofs of mathematical theorems, also begin with the information available and lead gradually to the conclusion.

Some people, therefore, believe that in a business document you should build your case before clearly stating your conclusions or recommendations. But writing an effective business document requires reversing the order of presentation: Conclusions or recommendations should come first, followed by the supporting arguments.

Your purpose when writing in business is to efficiently and effectively transmit what you know and have concluded to the people who need the information. In this sense, business writing is much like journalism.

Newspaper articles begin with the most important piece of information and proceed to the least important. Readers may stop at any point, knowing that they've read the most important part of the article.

The first sentence or two of a newspaper article will usually succinctly sum up the key points of the entire article. Similarly, the first few sentences of a business document should sum up the key elements of the entire document. This section is called the Overview.

TIP

Don't lead up to your conclusion or recommendation—start with it.

WHAT IS THE OVERVIEW?

The Overview section of a memo is the first paragraph—two or three sentences that sum up the content of the document. The Overview enables the reader to make the most efficient and effective use of her time. After reading this section of your document, your reader should ...

- Know exactly what the document is about.
- Know what is being proposed or what the reader will learn from reading the document (that is, what information is contained in the document).
- Know specifically what action you want or expect from her.
- Know your point of view on the subject.

By providing this information at the beginning of your document, you enable the reader to make an immediate decision on how to proceed. For example ...

- If the reader doesn't need the information you're presenting, she may set the document aside without wasting further time on it.
- If the reader doesn't need the information now, but may need it at a later date, she may file the document for later retrieval.
- If the reader must act on or react to the information, she knows she must read the document now. She knows exactly what she is expected to do once she has read it.

TIP

To write a good overview, imagine that you have only ten seconds of your readers' time to convey as much important information as possible on the subject you're writing about. What do you tell them in that 10 seconds?

What's in the Overview?

There are several key elements to the overview that you should include:

- A simple statement of purpose—why you're writing the document (to summarize a meeting, to recommend a course of action, and so on).

- What you want from the reader—what you hope or expect the reader will do.

- Your opinion or point of view on the information being presented—what you've learned based on this information that the reader needs to know.

CAUTION

An overview that goes on for six or seven sentences—or contains several thoughts in each of three or four sentences—has too much information in it. You can probably move much of that information to other sections of your document.

TIP

The first paragraph may be labeled "Overview"; however, in most contexts, the reader will understand and expect the first paragraph to be an overview whether it's labeled or not.

The Overview in Action

Suppose you're the marketing manager for your company, and your advertising agency, at the direction of your company's vice president of advertising, has recently created a new campaign for your product. You've tested the campaign with consumers and must summarize the results.

Your supervisor, the vice president of marketing, will make a final decision on whether to air the advertising. The vice president of advertising is in charge of delivering a campaign that will be both memorable and persuasive.

In addition, the vice president of sales has asked to be kept informed about any new marketing initiatives that may eventually affect his sales presentations. Following are the first few lines from your summary.

To: Vice President—Marketing

From: Marketing Manager

Re: New Ad Campaign Test Results

Cc: Vice President—Advertising, Vice President—Sales

This summarizes results of awareness and persuasion testing for our new advertising campaign titled "Singing Orangutans." Overall, the campaign is less effective than expected, despite obtaining extremely high awareness scores. Awareness was 83 percent, compared to average awareness scores in our category of 36 percent. However, persuasiveness was only 17 percent, compared to an average score of 46 percent, and the company's guideline for a threshold acceptable persuasiveness score of 33 percent.

The remainder of this summary would lay out the test results in more detail, including information on why the ad was so memorable yet so unpersuasive.

CAUTION

While you need to keep the overview brief, it shouldn't leave out critical information. Don't let the reader be surprised by an important fact later in your document.

RESPONDING TO THE OVERVIEW

The three people who receive this document will each have very different needs regarding it. The vice president of sales may be interested in the results, but these results are not his top priority. After reading nothing but the subject line, he can decide to skip reading this document for the moment, saving it until he has some time to catch up on reading not directly related to sales.

The vice president of marketing has all the information she needs after the first four sentences—she must make a go/no-go decision on this campaign, and the answer in this case is clearly no, since the ad does not meet company standards with respect to persuasiveness.

The vice president of advertising, however, can tell after the first three sentences that he will need to read and digest all of the information in the entire memo. Since his job is to direct the creation of a campaign that is both memorable and persuasive, he'll need to get into the details of the document to see what consumers found memorable, and why they didn't find the ad persuasive.

TIP

Make sure the subject line fully encompasses the topics discussed in the memo so your readers will know the memo is important to them.

For each of the document's recipients, the first few sentences provide the reader with a clear idea of what the document is about, what key information is contained in it, and what he or she needs to do right now in response. This "quick read" is a significant time-saver for each reader. Even the vice president of advertising, who would need to read the entire memo, benefits from the overview—he knows what he's looking for and what he's going to need to do with the information (in this case, try to maintain memorability while improving persuasiveness in the next version of the advertising).

PLAIN ENGLISH

Effective business document   A document that truthfully conveys all the important information on a subject in a way that convinces the reader to do what you'd like him to do.

CAUTION

If you don't know what you want your reader to do with the information you're presenting, you can't write an effective document.

An effective business document begins with an effective Overview section. A well-written overview tells all the recipients exactly what to expect in the remainder of the document, and allows them to make a quick but informed decision on what to do with the information you're presenting. The important elements of the overview are your statement of purpose (why you're writing), what you want from the reader, and what your point of view is on the information you're providing.

TIP

Collect samples of documents you believe are especially well-written, particularly ones that deal with the same kinds of issues you deal with in your business writing. Then you can emulate the structure of those well-written documents in your own writing.

THE 30-SECOND RECAP

■ State the intent of your document in the first two or three sentences.

■ Make sure the reader knows what he's supposed to do with the information you're presenting.

■ Provide a brief statement of why the information is important or the recommendation should be accepted.

Give Your Reader Sufficient Background

In this section you learn what to include in the background section of your document to appropriately set the stage for the balance of your memo.

WHAT IS THE BACKGROUND?

The background of a memo immediately follows the overview and provides the facts and assumptions relevant to the subject of your document. These facts and assumptions enable your reader to react to your recommendation or conclusions appropriately. After reading the background, your reader should …

■ Quickly understand the current or historical context necessary to evaluate your recommendation(s) or conclusion(s), regardless of the level of prior familiarity.

■ Clearly understand what portion of information included is based on data and what portion is based on your assumptions or hypotheses.

■ Accurately understand your frame of reference for the recommendation(s) or conclusion(s).

By providing your summary of the situation before your recommendation or rationale, you enable your reader to appropriately evaluate your recommendations/conclusions and rationale/key findings.

Providing background information aids several types of readers:

■ If the reader is not familiar with the situation, you have equipped her with the necessary background to continue reading.

■ If the reader has an understanding of the situation that differs from yours, you have enabled her to consider the upcoming information based on your point of view.

■ If the reader has an understanding of the situation that differs from yours and is the basis for disagreeing with your recommendation or conclusion, you have maintained some level of credibility.

The background is typically one paragraph. For complex issues or major recommendations, you may expand the background to several paragraphs. Also, in cases where you include assumptions based on your analysis of the situation, you should clearly indicate that these are your assumptions and why they are relevant.

WHAT'S IN THE BACKGROUND?

There are two key questions to consider when deciding what information to include in the background and what information you may safely omit. The first question concerns what facts are pertinent to the subject of the document. The second concerns how much knowledge the reader already has, and thus doesn't need to have repeated.

Adequately addressing these two questions is a balancing act. The correct balance depends on the complexity of the issues your document addresses, the importance of the document, and whether the document is likely to be distributed further by the original recipients.

As a rule of thumb, the more complex, more important, and more likely to be forwarded the document is, the less you should assume your audience knows about your subject, and thus, the more information you should provide in the Background.

THE BACKGROUND IN ACTION

Suppose you're the manager of the leading brand of shortening used for baking and frying foods. You're writing a memo to recommend a specific action plan to increase shortening usage in both baking and frying. Volume in the shortening category has been declining steadily for many years, and although your brand is dominant in the category, the brand's volume has been declining at roughly the same rate as the category. This information is probably well known to anyone in the management of the company, particularly since it's been going on for many years, and is therefore probably not an important fact to include in the background of your document.

PLAIN ENGLISH

Action plan   The set of steps you plan to take to achieve some specified goal. The steps should follow one another in sequential order, and proceed logically to establishing the goal.

However, suppose category-wide use of shortening in baking has recently begun declining much more rapidly than its use in frying. While people who work directly with your division may know this, it's likely that people in the company who are not as closely aligned with the division may not, and thus, the rapid decline in baking usage may be an important background fact.

Using this same example, suppose a competitor, in the past six months, introduced a new shortening product that directly competes with yours for both baking and frying. At the same time, suppose the American Butter Institute has begun a nationwide campaign that promotes the use of butter in baking.

Clearly, both of these developments are important to the brand. The competitor's entry into the market is unlikely to have had a negative effect on the category's volume, but may have an effect on your brand's volume. If so, you should include this information.

TIP

If your background section seems too long, check to ensure that your document focuses on a single important issue. If you discover you're writing about two or more separate issues at once, break the document into separate ones—each focused exclusively on a single issue.

On the other hand, use of butter in baking could clearly impact shortening use in terms of category volume. So for the purpose of this memo, the American Butter Institute's marketing campaign should probably be included in the background, whereas the competition's new product may not need to be mentioned.

USING FACTS AND ASSUMPTIONS

The background may include both facts and important assumptions. In the previous example, you may have included certain facts about the decline of the shortening category such as, "Frying volume is down 2 percent versus last year, whereas baking volume is down 11 percent." At the same time, you may also have included certain assumptions about the business—in this case, "We believe the recent campaign by the American Butter Institute has significantly increased the use of butter in baking at the expense of shortening."

When you state facts, you should, as often as possible, cite the source of the facts. In the preceding example, the sentence would read, "According to Nielsen data for this year, frying volume is down." Citing your source lends credibility to your statements and gives the reader a place from which to do further research.

When you state assumptions, label them as such to let the reader know that, while you believe these statements to be true, they are not facts. The assumption about increased butter usage in the previous example ("We believe the recent campaign by the American Butter Institute has significantly increased the use of butter in baking at the expense of shortening") was signaled by the opening words "We believe."

In addition to labeling your assumptions, whenever possible support them with corroborating evidence. Such corroborating evidence for the butter/shortening example might be, "Nielsen share data show that butter use for baking is up 19 percent since the beginning of their marketing campaign, while shortening for baking use is off 11 percent in the same time period." While this fact doesn't prove your assumption that the campaign has increased butter usage at the expense of shortening, it certainly provides strong circumstantial evidence to support your belief.

TIP

After you've written a draft of your document, check the statements made in the recommendation or conclusions section. Are all of these statements supported by information included in the document? If not, you may need to expand the background to include the support needed.

WHAT TO OMIT FROM THE BACKGROUND

To ensure that your background contains enough information, you may include more information than is needed. Too much information makes inefficient use of the reader's time, and can be confusing if the reader is expecting all the information in the background to be relevant to the rest of the document.

There are a number of categories of information that should not be included in the background:

- **Unsupported or controversial assumptions.** The background should be the foundation for the rest of the document, a section that all relevant parties agree on. If you include assumptions in this section that many of the document's readers may legitimately disagree with, you undermine the rest of the arguments in the document. In the background, statements should be self-evident or easily supported. The place for arguments in favor of a controversial point of view is in the main body of a document devoted to that subject, not the background of a document on a different subject.

- **Extraneous information.** Information that may be true but does not have any impact on the subject of the document should not be included anywhere, including the background.

  For example, you may have recently tested a new package made of lightweight plastic that is a 10 percent cost-savings compared to the current package. You believe the company should immediately switch to the new package, in order to save money. However, that cost-savings effort is not relevant to the subject of the memo—increasing shortening usage—and thus should not be mentioned in the current document.

- **Information that is not general knowledge or has not been previously reported.** If you have recently acquired information that provides important perspective relative to the main subject of your document, that information should be either reported in a separate summary specifically on the subject, or potentially, included in the main body of the document at hand. The general rule here: If the information you're reporting will be "news" to your readers, it probably does not belong in the background.

  For example, suppose you discovered this morning in reading the just-released bimonthly sales report that your sales are declining more rapidly in the Western Division than in the Eastern Division. You believe there may be several reasons for this phenomenon, some of which could be related to the overall category decline, and some of which are probably not. However, the plan you're recommending in the memo at hand is a nationwide plan, and does not attempt to address differences among regions. While the difference in sales results between the Eastern and Western Divisions is an important subject, it needs to be addressed in a separate memo exploring the issue and possible causes. If you mention it for the first time in the background of the memo you're writing now, your reader will appropriately want to know much more about the issue—how severe is the difference, what are the key causes, how long has the difference been going on, and so forth. All of these questions will detract from your reader's attention to the document at hand, which concerns the nationwide plan.

CAUTION

Too much information in the background is just as problematic as too little. Your reader may not sift through the unimportant data you've presented in order to find what is important.

The material to include in a background section is very dependent on the subject of the document, and the key issues that have the most impact on the subject. You must evaluate the need to ensure that your reader is informed on all important aspects of the subject, balanced by the need to keep your document concise and focused.

CAUTION

Don't try to "sell" your recommendation or conclusions in the background—use it for laying out the facts. Use the recommendation or conclusions section to convince your reader to agree with your proposals.

THE 30-SECOND RECAP

- The background lays the foundation, or "sets the stage," for the rest of the document.

- The background should include enough information so that readers previously unfamiliar with the situation can become knowledgeable enough to make informed judgments on the topic.

- The background should exclude extraneous information, unsupported assumptions, and "news"—previously unreported or unknown information.

Making Your Recommendations or Conclusions

In this section you learn how to frame your recommendation or conclusion(s) so that your readers clearly understand what you're asking them to do or to believe.

THE IMPORTANCE OF RECOMMENDATIONS AND CONCLUSIONS

A Recommendation section is used in documents in which you're asking your reader to agree to or approve your proposal. A Conclusions section is used in documents that summarize or analyze data, but do not seek specific agreement or approval to a course of action.

In memos asking for agreement to a proposal, the Recommendation section lays out the specifics of what you're seeking approval to. In summaries and analyses, the Conclusions section is where you'll provide your point of view regarding what the information means.

WHAT IS A RECOMMENDATION?

The recommendation of a memo immediately follows the background and tells your reader exactly what action you're asking her to agree to or approve. After reading the recommendation of your document, your reader should ...

- Understand the plan of action you're recommending and the parameters of the recommendation.
- Understand specifically what you're asking her to do with regard to the recommendation.
- Understand the benefits of the plan of action.

By providing the recommendation immediately after you've set up the background, you show respect for your reader's time. She can now respond accordingly:

- If your reader agrees with your recommendation based on the background, she doesn't need to read further.
- If she needs more information before making a decision, she now has the appropriate understanding with which to evaluate your rationale.

TIP

Try to make your recommendation as clear and simple to understand as possible. Since you're asking the reader to do something, it's especially important that the reader understand what you're asking for.

WHAT'S IN THE RECOMMENDATION?

There are several key elements you should include in the recommendation:

- **The recommendation itself.** Depending on the complexity of the plan you're recommending, you may or may not include the details of how to implement it. The key is to keep the "what" here at a summary level. For example, you may be recommending that your business implement a national marketing plan based on the test market plan you implemented. You wouldn't include the details of the national plan here, but you would include an overview of the important attributes. However, if the action plan is relatively simple, you may include it here.

- **The person or group you're asking approval or agreement from.** For example, you may be asking for your manager's approval, or you may be asking for the executive committee's approval. Be specific.

- **The benefits of your recommendation.** For example, the benefit may be increased market share, better shelf presence, shorter lead time, or reduced expenses. Don't go overboard with the benefits in the recommendation, though. You'll defend your recommendation in the next section (see "Providing Rationale for Your Recommendation" on page 858).

PLAIN ENGLISH

Benefit   Something positive that will happen for the organization as a direct result of implementing the recommended plan.

WRITING THE RECOMMENDATION

Suppose you're the marketing manager for a shampoo product that was successful in the test market and has received the general manager's final approval to launch nationally. At the time the general manager approved the expansion, she delayed final approval of the marketing plan until further business results and consumer usage and attitude data were available. Those results are now in, and you are writing a memo to gain final approval to the marketing plan for national launch.

Given the complexity of your recommended action plan, you will not want to weigh down the recommendation with detail. So your recommendation will be fairly straightforward. However, given the importance of the plan, you will need to provide specifics as to how the plan will be carried out later in the document, after you've made your case.

Before stating your recommendation, you've set the stage with the background, reminding your readers of the test market success, the approval for launch, and the decision to delay marketing plan approval pending new data. Your recommendation might look something like the following.

> **Recommendation:** This seeks management agreement to national Brand X marketing plans. Specifically, we would expand the identical plans on the identical timing as in test market. The same marketing plans and timing are warranted given the significantly higher than objective business results and consumer adoption.

After this recommendation you would go on to support your recommendation in the rationale section (see the section "Providing Rationale for Your Recommendation" on page 858), which would likely include in this case specifics on volume, share, usage, and other results based on the test marketing plan.

WHAT ARE CONCLUSIONS?

Conclusions are similar to a recommendation in that they are the "bottom line," or your ultimate reason, for writing in the first place. Conclusions typically outline your interpretation of information, one that you want the company to accept. The conclusions immediately follow the background of your document. After reading the conclusions, your reader should ...

- Understand your interpretation of specific information (business results, research results, and so on).

- Understand why the information and your conclusions are meaningful.

CAUTION

Avoid conclusions that are merely summaries of the data. Conclusions should go further—they should explain what the data mean for your organization.

By providing the conclusions immediately after you've set up the situation through the background, you show respect for your reader's time. She can now respond accordingly:

- If the reader understands the conclusions in the context of the background, and does not need the detailed information your conclusions are based on, she does not need to read further and can safely set the document aside.

- If the detailed information in the document is something the reader doesn't need now, but may need at a later date, she may file the document for later retrieval.

TIP

Use summaries and data analyses to begin to lay the foundation for a future recommendation by presenting conclusions that will later be used to support your recommendation.

What's in the Conclusions?

There are several key elements you should provide in the conclusions:

- The conclusions themselves. For example, you might conclude from business analysis that coupon drops no longer lead to incremental stocking and merchandising in national accounts. Your conclusions should be directly tied to your analysis or research objectives. Unlike a recommendation, which should focus on a single topic, you may wish to make several conclusions based on the information you're summarizing or analyzing.

- A sentence or two describing the data you used to reach each conclusion. Since you'll be providing the data in detail later in the document, you should only very briefly summarize it here.

- Any caveats or mitigating information needed to ensure that your reader knows whether your conclusions may be based on less-than-complete information.

CAUTION

Make sure your conclusions are supported by the data you're summarizing or analyzing. Making unsupported conclusions can damage your credibility in the organization.

Writing the Conclusion

Suppose you're the financial analyst for your company, which sells standard lighting fixtures for commercial buildings and residences, and customized lighting for industrial settings. The customized light business is smaller than that of standard fixtures, but generates a much higher profit margin per unit. The Sales team is currently examining ways to increase sales of customized lighting, and you've been asked to analyze the financial implications of the various pricing and promotion plans the sales team has developed.

At this stage, you are not prepared to recommend one plan over any of the others. However, you are in a position to report on your analysis of whether the plans may result in increased profitability for the company.

In the Background section, you've described each of the plans and estimated what each would cost to implement. With that background, your conclusions might appear as follows:

Conclusions

1. The "Half-Price" Promotion plan would be the most expensive to implement, and unless it generated significantly more repeat business among new customers than we presently obtain from current customers, it would be unprofitable to implement. The promotion eliminates our profit margin on the initial sale, requiring two additional sales at full price to establish an acceptable total profit margin.

2. The "New Distribution" Plan, while carrying the most risk, has the potential to be the most profitable. Hiring new salespeople to call on companies in industries we've never called on before will require significant up-front investment. However, if these new salespeople are as effective at selling our products in the new industries as our competitors are, we will dramatically increase customized lighting sales and overall profitability.

3. The "Sales Incentive" Plan carries the least risk, and may be effective in focusing sales force effort on customized light. If it does, as Sales Management believes it will, this plan will increase company profitability.

Although the test is not complete and you are not ready to recommend any specific plan, you want the brand and sales teams to understand initial results, including the plusses and minuses of each plan. In essence you're laying the foundation for a future recommendation.

After these conclusions you would go on to support them in the key findings section, which would likely include in this case specifics on each test plan, results to date, and projected end-of-test results.

THE 30-SECOND RECAP

- Recommendations tell your reader exactly what actions for which you're asking agreement or approval.

- Recommendations should include the specifics of the plan, who you're seeking approval from, and the benefits of accepting your recommendation.

- Conclusions tell your reader your interpretation or analysis of information presented in the document.

- Conclusions should include your analysis of the information, the data you used to reach your conclusions, and any caveats the reader needs to know about to effectively evaluate your conclusions.

Providing Rationale for Your Recommendation

In this section you learn how to structure your rationale in a persuasive, logical manner and how to clearly articulate key findings from your interpretation or analysis of data.

WHAT IS A RATIONALE

The rationale of a memo immediately follows the recommendation and provides three to five key reasons that support the recommendation.

After reading this section of your document, your reader should ...

- Understand the logic behind your recommendation.
- Be confident that your logic is based on facts or reasonable assumptions.
- Be persuaded to agree with or approve your recommendation.

RATIONALE POINTS

You should try to get into the habit of providing three to five rationale points for any significant recommendation. Ensuring that you have three to five *rationale points* forces you to separate your reasoning into narrowly focused, easily supportable elements. Such separation is important so that your reader can easily evaluate the strength of each rationale point and quickly identify the advantages of accepting your proposal.

PLAIN ENGLISH

Rationale point   One specific reason why accepting your proposal makes sound business sense.

If after separating your reasoning into narrowly focused, clearly supportable elements, you have fewer than three reasons your recommendation should be accepted, either you have not clearly thought through all the advantages of your proposal, or the recommendation isn't very important. Keep in mind that your recommendation asks the organization to begin doing something differently than it is today. This may have ramifications throughout the company.

For example, in the national expansion recommendation cited in "Making Your Recommendations or Conclusions," on page 852, the marketing department will have to implement the plan, the sales department will have to sell it to customers, the manufacturing department will have to make more product, and so on. With this much at stake, you should be able to provide a number of reasons the organization should be willing to make the changes required.

If you have more than five rationale points, you need to prioritize them in order of importance, and list only the top three to five. Although you may have more than five reasons to support your recommendation, a "laundry list" of rationale points tends to detract from the importance of any one reason. Your objective in the rationale should be for your reader to consider each rationale point as meaningful by itself. Having too many points detracts from this objective.

Also, including more than five rationale points may be taking more of your reader's time than necessary. If you haven't convinced the reader to accept your recommendation after providing the three to five most important reasons to do so, additional reasons are unlikely to be any more persuasive.

TIP

Even for less important recommendations, digging deeply enough to provide at least three strong reasons to accept your proposal is valuable. Acquiring this habit can significantly improve your persuasiveness and your ability to think logically about why you want to do what you're recommending.

WHAT'S IN THE RATIONALE?

In the rationale you not only must have key points to support your recommendation, but must present them in a persuasive, easy-to-read format. A good rationale contains the following elements:

- A topic sentence for each point that clearly and succinctly states the information to be considered. The topic sentence of a rationale point is generally set apart from the rest of the paragraph by using italics or bold print.

- Supporting data or corroborating information that demonstrates the validity of the topic sentence of each point. This corroborating information may be a chart of numbers or a brief summary of previous learning. If the supporting data take up too much room in the main document, you may wish to use a sentence or two to summarize the point, and include the complete data set as an appendix.

- The rationale points listed in order of importance, from most important to least. While you may be tempted to "save the best for last," giving the most powerful and persuasive reasons first shows respect for your readers' time and their interest in quickly understanding exactly what you want to do and why you want to do it.

TIP

When you append material in your document to support key points, be sure to refer the reader to the respective appendix at the appropriate place in the main document.

CAUTION

Large charts filled with numbers can be very difficult for your reader to understand and extract the important information from. Try to include in your document only the numbers that are most important, and put the entire chart in an appendix, if necessary.

WRITING THE RATIONALE

Recall the example recommendation document in "Framing Your Thinking," on page 836, where the Acme Shampoo brand manager recommends the national expansion of a sampling program that was successful in test market. Note how each rationale point is supported by the appropriate data.

These rationale points support your recommendation that the sampling plan used in test market should be implemented nationally. You've given the reader several different measures of the plan, and provided the data that confirms its effectiveness. At this point, your reader should be ready to approve your recommendation.

Rationale

Year-two sampling substantially builds the business. Specifically, since the second round of sampling in test market, business results have been strong with shipments and share up 22 percent and 26 percent respectively, compared to the year-one results.

Sampling effectiveness research showed significant increases in trial and purchase after the test market sampling program in year two. Specifically, past three months' usage and purchase were significantly up among sampled vs. nonsampled households, as shown in the following table:

	Sampled Households	Nonsampled Households
Past four week brand usage	15%	9%
Past three months brand usage	23%	13%
Past three months brand purchase	19%	12%

The promotion department's sampling payout model confirmed the sampling program is a financially sound initiative. Specifically, the model projected the sampling program would generate a volume increase of 20 percent over year one, and pay out in 12 months, based on the purchase levels seen in the sampling effectiveness research.

WHAT ARE KEY FINDINGS?

Memos that summarize or analyze data without making a recommendation would of course not require a section providing the rationale for the recommendation. Summaries and analyses will instead generally have a section containing conclusions, as discussed in "Making Your Recommendations or Conclusions" on page 852. This type of memo will have findings following the conclusions. Key findings are the most relevant facts that come from your analysis of data, research, or other business events. Key findings accompany conclusions in the same way that rationale points accompany recommendations.

After reading your key findings, your reader should ...

- Understand that your conclusions are based on facts.
- Be confident that the facts you've presented are adequately supported by the data you've collected and summarized.
- Be persuaded to agree with your conclusions.

The principles discussed earlier that apply to developing rationale points also apply to key findings. With that in mind, when developing your key findings you should ...

- Put them in order of importance, starting with the most important.
- Include only those key findings that tie in directly to your conclusions. Don't include stray findings. If a finding doesn't support a meaningful conclusion, leave it out.
- Start your key finding with a topic sentence, followed by the corroborating data.

Occasionally, when the findings do not require a significant amount of supporting data—that is, each finding can be encapsulated in a sentence or two without additional support—you may wish to combine the conclusions and key findings sections. Do this by stating a conclusion as the *topic sentence* of a paragraph, and list the findings that support that conclusion as the remainder of the paragraph. Typically, you would only combine these sections for analyses with a small number of fairly straightforward conclusions.

PLAIN ENGLISH

Topic sentence   The first sentence of a paragraph and that states the main point. Additional sentences in the paragraph should support the point made in the topic sentence.

Writing the Key Findings

Suppose you're the marketing director of a small software company that is preparing to launch a desktop publishing product called *Publish It* and a clip art/graphics product called *Imagine It.* Your department recently conducted packaging communication research to confirm that the packaging communicated key messages. Your research summary concluded that the new product packaging direction communicates key messages effectively. Your key findings from the research might look something like the following.

CAUTION

Avoid making conclusions or stating an opinion in a finding. Findings should be statements of fact, based on the data being summarized or analyzed.

Rationale points for recommendations, or findings for summaries or analyses, are the "guts" of a memo—the factual foundation on which the recommendation or conclusions must rest. For that reason, this section of your document should clearly and concisely lay out the key facts you need the reader to know in order to understand and agree with the rest of your document.

Key Findings

Publish It *packaging communicates the product's key attributes as well as the desktop publishing software market leader,* Publisher 98. When asked how to rate their product expectations based on the package design, target consumers rated *Publish It* and *Publisher 98* the same on all attributes except brand reputation. This is not surprising given that *Publisher 98* is the third version of *Publisher*, and the *Publisher* software product line has been in the market for more than six years. For perspective, 50 percent of the respondents own and use some version of *Publisher*.

Product Ratings on a 7-Point Scale

7 = Excellent and 1 = Poor

	Publish It	*Publisher 98*
Overall quality	5.9	6.0
Fun to use	5.6	5.6
Easy to use	5.5	5.7
Easy to get started	5.6	5.6
Compatible with other software I have	5.8	6.0
Has a good reputation	5.4	6.3

Imagine It packaging communicates the product's key attributes as well as the clip art software market leader, Click Art. When asked how to rate their product expectations based on the package design, target consumers rated *Imagine It* and *Click Art* the same on all attributes. For perspective, 45 percent of the respondents own and use *Click Art*.

Product Ratings on a 7-Point Scale

7 = Excellent and 1 = Poor

	Imagine It	*Click Art*
Overall quality	5.5	5.4
Fun to use	5.7	5.5
Easy to use	5.6	5.5
Easy to get started	5.5	5.4
Compatible with other software I have	5.8	5.6
Has a good reputation	5.4	5.4

THE 30-SECOND RECAP

■ The rationale of a document should provide three to five well-supported reasons that the recommended course of action is the right one.

- Rationale points should begin with a topic sentence describing the important information, followed by supporting data that demonstrate the validity of the topic sentence.
- The key findings section of a document should list the most important findings supporting your conclusions about the data or research.
- Each key finding should be supported with the data that demonstrate the validity of the finding.
- Both rationale points and key findings should be listed in order of importance, beginning with the most important.

Add Information as Needed

In this section you learn to include additional sections in your document when necessary, what information those sections should contain, and how to present them logically to maintain the flow of the document.

WHEN TO INCLUDE ADDITIONAL SECTIONS

As we've seen in the previous section, the framework for a document you might write to request approval to a proposal includes the overview, background, recommendation (or conclusion), and rationale (or key findings). Once you've stated your recommendation and reasoning, it often remains only to describe what needs to happen next assuming the recommendation is accepted. Sometimes, however, there are additional issues that should be addressed but that do not fit easily into any of the previously mentioned sections of your document.

EXHIBITS AND APPENDIXES

The most common way to include needed information without interrupting the flow of your document is by using exhibits or appendixes. Include an exhibit when you wish to show the reader graphical or visual information that would be impractical or inconvenient to include in the main body of the document.

For example, suppose you want to refer to a map of the United States that is shaded in green, yellow, or red according to whether your product has the leading market share, the second or third highest share, or is not one of the top three brands in that state. Rather than insert the entire map into your document at the point you want to write about it, you might attach it as Exhibit 1, and reference it as follows: "We have the leading market share throughout most of the South and Southwest, but are trailing in the Northeast. See Exhibit 1 for details."

Appendixes are similar to exhibits, but generally include written data or charts of numbers, rather than visual or graphical data. For example, if you were writing a memo on how the company should respond to consumer complaints, you might attach the list of recent complaints as an Appendix and quote from it in your document: "Customers are dissatisfied with the quality of our instruction manual. One typical comment is 'I've tried several times to make your product work by following the manual you provided, but the instructions are hopelessly muddled and confusing.' The complete list of complaints in the past three months is included as Appendix 1."

Appendixes should also be used for charts of numbers that are too large to include in the main body of the document. For example, suppose you're writing a memo summarizing sales results for each of your company's products over the past 12 months. You have a chart with 12 columns (one for each month) and 25 rows (one for each of your company's 25 products) in which each number shows the quantity of that particular product that was sold in the relevant month. While the entire chart contains information that is valuable to your reader, in your document, you only wish to discuss two specific products' sales over the 12-month period. In that case, you could include in the main document just the two rows for the products you plan to discuss, and reference the fact that the entire chart is included as an appendix.

Beyond the use of exhibits and appendixes, there are occasions when you have information to impart that is awkward to include in one of the sections of a standard document.

For example ...

■ When the plan you're recommending is complex or requires a significant amount of explanation to understand completely, you might want to add a section that describes how the plan works.

■ When the plan you're recommending carries significant risk or possible repercussions that are hard to quantify and address briefly, you might want to add a Risks section.

■ When you've considered other plans designed to accomplish a similar objective, and need to provide some explanation of why the other plans are not as appropriate as the one you're recommending, you might add a section describing other considerations.

In cases where you need to address one or more of these issues but can't do so in a sentence or two in either the recommendation or the rationale, it is appropriate to add a section specifically to address these concerns. We'll examine each type of additional section previously described separately.

THE HOW THE PLAN WORKS SECTION

If the plan you're recommending is complex or requires a significant amount of explanation to understand completely, you may wish to include a How the Plan Works section. Since a detailed explanation of the plan could disrupt the flow of the recommendation and the corresponding rationale points, you should include this section after the rationale.

WRITING A HOW THE PLAN WORKS SECTION

In "Making Your Recommendations or Conclusions," on page 852, we discussed a proposal to nationally expand a marketing plan that had been successfully tested in a small part of the United States. The Recommendation section read as follows:

> **Recommendation:** This seeks management agreement to national Brand X marketing plans. Specifically, we would expand the identical plans on the identical timing as in test market. The same marketing plans and timing are warranted given the significantly higher than objective business results and consumer adoption.

Clearly, in this example, the details of the marketing plan will be an important part of the decision-making process, and should be included in the document. However, the plan specifics don't have an impact on the rationale for the recommendation, as the rationale focuses on share and shipment results and other relevant information about how the plan was performing in the test market. In this case, the specifics of the plan aren't the issue—the plan as a whole is working, and that's the basis on which the recommendation to expand is made. Therefore, your memo will flow more smoothly if you wait until after your rationale to provide the plan details.

 CAUTION

Even when including a section to describe how the plan works, you should still try to make the plan description as clear and succinct as possible. If the plan is too confusing, your reader may not fully understand it and be less ready to accept it.

TIP

If the plan you're recommending has more than four or five main elements, or your description of the plan requires more than two or three paragraphs, consider summarizing the plan in the Recommendation section and adding a How the Plan Works section to provide the details.

How the Plan Works

The following is the marketing plan currently being tested:

Advertising Copy

The purpose of our advertising copy is to maximize awareness of the new Brand X by communicating that it is (a) a revolutionary, breakthrough technology, and significantly different than the old Brand X. We will expand nationally with the executions currently in test market (storyboards are attached as Exhibit 1). Test market research confirms these executions are strong, with "related recall" scores double those of old Brand X (40 percent versus 22 percent), and with 60 percent awareness of the key selling message.

Media

The objective of the media plan is to create awareness and maximize comprehension of Brand X's product news among the physically active target consumer (people aged 13 to 34). The strategy to meet this awareness/comprehension objective during the introductory months will be to (a) spend most of our advertising dollars in the first three months of the introductory period; use 45-second commercials to fully communicate how Brand X works; and spend the majority of our budget (70 percent) on the introductory-oriented execution. This replicates the plan tested.

Promotion

The objective of the Brand X promotion plan is to maximize trial by leveraging the Brand X technology strength among consumers. To accomplish this, we plan to execute the three introductory events used in test market.

The first event (30 percent household sampling via in-store single-brand delivery) is proven to be key to initial Brand X purchase. Specifically, households that received in-store samples had significantly higher purchase and intent-to-purchase levels than households that did not receive samples (see Exhibit 2 for complete research results).

PLAIN ENGLISH

Storyboard   A collection of sketches similar to panels in a cartoon strip, used by advertising agencies to present the idea of a television commercial to their client prior to actually filming the commercial.

As you can see from this segment of a section describing how the plan works, each plan element should contain ...

- The objective of the plan.

- The strategy and tactics being used.

- Data, as available, to support your reasoning for using this particular strategy and tactics.

THE RISKS SECTION

Virtually all recommendations carry some risk—the most obvious being the cost of the plan to the company if it doesn't meet expectations. Occasionally, however, you may recommend a plan that carries greater risks than usual, or one whose risks aren't immediately obvious. In such cases, you should bring those issues to light and indicate, where possible, how your plan will address the risks in order to mitigate them.

WRITING THE RISKS SECTION

Suppose you are the product development manager for a coffee company, and you've created a process called "fast-roasting." Fast-roasting has several advantages compared to the method your company (and your competition) currently employs. Fast-roasting expands the coffee beans in such a way that you can use 20 percent fewer beans to make an equally good-tasting cup of coffee. This means you can produce a product that tastes the same, comes in the same size container, and is measured and used in the same way as your current product, with a raw materials cost reduction of 20 percent.

You're recommending that your company implement the fast-roasting procedure for all its coffee brands. However, you recognize that this plan carries unusual risk. Because fast-roasting expands the beans, your containers will contain fewer coffee beans and consequently weigh less. If your competition or an outside party, such as a consumer advocate, publicizes that your container, although it is the same size as your competitors', contains less coffee (by weight), consumers may react negatively. You should address this in a risks section, immediately following the rationale.

As in the preceding example, in the case of significant or unusual risk you should ...

- Clearly state what the risk is.

- Describe efforts you've made to quantify the risk.

- Describe what steps you've taken to mitigate the impact if the risk actually occurs.

■ Provide the worst-case scenario, if possible, and how that compares to the best case or most likely one.

Risks

Coffee manufacturers are required by law to print the weight of the contents on the front of the container. If we implement this plan, our standard size can will state "13 oz.," whereas competitors' identically sized cans will read "16 oz." Depending on how this difference is handled by the media, our competitors, and our own public relations department, the disparity in weight could be perceived by consumers as an attempt to take "too much" profit, since the plan does not include a price reduction. We view this risk as acceptable, and recommend proceeding with the plan as proposed, for the following reasons:

■ The company has already converted "High Ground" brand coffee, the division's lowest-share brand, to fast-roasting. In the six months of national distribution, we have received only seven questions about the reduced weight on the company 1-800-number consumer hot line. Each of these consumers was satisfied with the explanation given him on the hot line, and has continued to use the product.

■ We have worked with the marketing department and the company's public relations department to develop a response to a public "consumer advocacy" story or a competitor's negative announcements about the weight reduction. In consumer focus group testing, the response we've developed was effective in allaying consumer concerns. We would only use this response if there is a significant story or competitor announcement about our product.

■ In the "worst-case" scenario, the largest possible negative impact would be $2.5 million. This includes the cost of reverting to conventional roasting technology and the cost of consumer promotions the marketing department estimates would be needed to regain any share loss we might incur. This worst-case loss of $2.5 million compares to the annual savings we estimate of more than $5.5 million, assuming the conversion goes as expected.

CAUTION

Listing a great many risks, even if you address them all, can make your reader reluctant to accept your proposal. Try to include only the most important or serious risks.

THE OTHER CONSIDERATIONS SECTION

Occasionally, you will recommend one plan among several. While the bulk of your memo will address the important elements of the recommended plan and the reasons it is an appropriate choice, you may wish to include a section on why this particular plan was chosen over the alternatives.

WRITING THE OTHER CONSIDERATIONS SECTION

Suppose you're the new vice president of sales for a company with four major automotive accessory product lines and four key distribution channels—hardware stores, auto parts stores, auto repair shops, and discount retailers (such as Wal-Mart and Target). Until now, each sales representative had a territory, and could choose whether or not to call on any type of distributor within his area, and choose which of the product lines to sell. You're recommending a major restructuring of the sales force along distribution channel lines. This restructuring means that each sales rep will be responsible for all four product lines, but will call on only one type of distributor within his territory.

In your Rationale section, you've stated that this reorganization will improve coverage of important distribution outlets, make training new sales reps easier and more effective, and enable sales management to more effectively monitor and manage their sales reps' performance.

You considered reorganizing the sales force along product lines, with each sales rep carrying only one product line and calling on all types of distributors in his territory, but chose not to recommend that option. You might then write an Other Considerations section like the one that follows.

Other Considerations

An alternative to reorganizing along distribution channels is to reorganize along product lines. Since sales reps would be calling on all types of distributors, each representative could have a much smaller territory than under the recommended plan, saving on travel time and expense. In addition, each rep could become more expert on the single product line he carried, facilitating his ability to answer customer questions about the products he carries.

However, we believe these advantages are more than offset by the following:

■ The different-distribution-channel customers have vastly different needs and expectations. Many of the skills required to sell to one type of distributor do not necessarily transfer to others. On the other hand, the product lines we carry are similar enough so that the skills required to sell one line are readily transferable to selling other lines. Therefore, it will be much more effective and efficient from a training standpoint for sales reps to specialize in a single distribution channel rather than a single product line.

- Many of our customers make buying decisions for all their outlets from a district or regional headquarters. If we organize along product lines, a large number of the outlets will be in a different sales territory than the headquarters. The territory sales rep will be unable to affect the purchase decisions of the outlets in his territory. Conversely, by organizing on distribution channels, we can more closely match sales territories to our customers' buying territories.

- Most of the current sales force already specializes to some degree on one or two distribution channels. For a variety of historical reasons, the majority of our sales representatives call on only one or two different types of distributors in their territories, despite being allowed and encouraged to call on all types of distributors. Therefore, reorganizing along distribution channels will cause the least disruption in the current sales force's operation, thus significantly reducing the amount of lost sales we may incur during the transition from our old organization to the new one.

TIP

If you're recommending a different course of action than the one your management is expecting, you may want to include an Other Considerations section that mentions the other plan and the reasons you chose the one you did over the one they had expected. Otherwise, your management will probably not accept your plan until they understand why the other plan was rejected.

Note that in the Other Considerations section, you should include …

- A brief description of the alternative considered.
- Advantages the alternative may have to the recommended plan.
- The key reasons the recommended plan was chosen over the alternative.

Each of these additions to the "standard" structure—exhibits or appendixes, or sections that describe how the plan works, risks associated with the plan, or other considerations—can be used to include important information in your document without interrupting its flow. As you write your memo, begin with the basic structure, but keep these possibilities in mind if you find that the organization of your memo is becoming cumbersome or hard to follow.

THE 30-SECOND RECAP

- If you have information that needs to be included in your document, but it doesn't fit easily into the background, recommendation, or rationale, you may include an additional section after the rationale.

- You may also add a section after the rationale to present information that would disrupt the logical flow of your document if you included it elsewhere.

- Standard kinds of additional sections are How the Plan Works, in the case of complicated plans; Risks, in cases of significant or unusual risks inherent in the plan; and Other Considerations, when you've considered but rejected alternatives to the plan you're proposing.

Specify What Should Happen Next

In this section you learn how to end your memo with an action plan that details what needs to happen based on the rest of the information you've presented.

THE NEXT STEPS SECTION

When you've written a recommendation, the final section of your document, called the Next Steps section, should lay out the action plan you will follow if the recommendation is accepted. The plan should include the following information:

- What, specifically, needs to happen next.
- Who is, or should be, responsible for ensuring the completion of each step.
- When each step will be complete.

WRITING THE NEXT STEPS SECTION

Consider the recommendation discussed in "Making Your Recommendations or Conclusions," on page 852, to nationally expand the marketing plan that had been successfully tested in a small part of the United States. If management agrees to fund the national expansion, there are a number of things that need to happen right away. These include …

- Immediately increasing production of the test market shampoo in order to have enough inventory on hand to supply national distribution needs.

- Updating the materials the sales force will use to sell the shampoo to your customers.

- Buying the media time needed to air your commercials nationally.

Given these immediate requirements, your next-steps section could look like this:

Next Steps

With approval to the recommendation, we will do the following:

- Manufacturing (John Smith) will ramp up production of Brand X, in order to have 50,000 units in inventory by June 1.

- Marketing (Tom Roberts) will work with sales merchandising (Mary Thompson) to develop and produce revised sales materials by May 15.

- Marketing (Tom Roberts) will work with the advertising agency media department to purchase media for the introductory period. We will have a schedule prepared for final approval by May 1, and purchase the media time by June 1.

Note that the preceding example does not include much detail—just the task to be completed, the date it will be done, and the names of the people who are responsible for it. The level of detail you include in the Next Steps section depends on how much detail your readers need. If the readers need only to be assured that you've thought of the required steps and assigned responsibility for them, a very brief section like the preceding example will suffice.

CAUTION

Don't assume everyone knows what steps are needed to complete the plan and who is responsible for each step, even if it seems obvious. Include all the steps needed so your memo can serve as a guide for the appropriate people.

TIP

Be sure to send a copy of your memo to everyone who is responsible for a next step. This will serve as a reminder to them about their responsibility, as well as documentation of who's supposed to do what.

In some cases, however, you may want to spell out the specifics of the plan in more detail. For example, producing and inventorying Brand X in sufficient quantities to support a national rollout may entail significant coordination of manufacturing schedules, and thus require a much more detailed action plan, such as the following.

PLAIN ENGLISH

Sell-in   The period at the start of a new product introduction in which the product is first sold into the stores that will carry it. Since stores must usually build up an inventory of a new product, the sell-in can be a significant percentage of total sales for a new product introduction.

Manufacturing Plan

Date	Activity	Responsibility
March 1	Develop initial quantity estimates for sell-in	Sales (Mary Thompson)
March 15	Develop production plan to meet estimated need	Manufacturing (John Smith)
April 1	Move production of Brand Y to alternate plant to accommodate increased Brand X production	Manufacturing (John Smith)
April 15	Complete testing of equipment to ensure quality control of Brand X in national quantities	Product development (Sue Wilson)

In cases where a detailed plan is needed, you may wish to put a brief description in the Next Steps section and include the more detailed plan as an appendix. You would, of course, reference the appendix in the appropriate place in the Next Steps section.

CAUTION

If you don't specify who's responsible for making sure each of the steps occurs, you run the risk of everyone assuming it's someone else's job and nothing getting done.

TIP

Before you assign responsibility for ensuring that your next steps are completed, make sure the people you're assigning have the ability and resources to do the job—and that they agree to be responsible for seeing that it gets done.

THE INDICATED ACTIONS SECTION

When you write summaries or analyses of data, you won't be requesting that specific steps be taken, since you're not recommending a plan. However, there are usually some actions that appear to be appropriate next steps, based on the information you've presented in your summary or analysis.

WRITING THE INDICATED ACTIONS SECTION

Suppose you're the market research director of a company that organizes and manages golf tournaments. You've recently completed research on what spectators most like to see at golf tournaments, and you wrote the research summary.

CAUTION

Be careful when you set deadlines for next steps or indication actions to ensure that those deadlines are realistic, particularly for items not directly in your control. Your reader will probably expect you to meet the deadlines you set, and be disappointed if you don't.

TIP

When listing next steps or indicated actions, use a bulleted or numbered list. Use bullets if the order of the actions isn't important, and numbers if the actions need to be in a specific order.

Let's assume your findings are as follows (in part):

Findings

- Spectators prefer to watch holes that have considerable risk and offer significant reward vs. holes that are merely difficult for all players. For example, spectators prefer par 5s where going for the green in two requires hitting the second shot over water in front of the green, rather than very long par 4s on which the average score may be 4.5, but there is no significant obstacle to reaching the green.

- Spectators like to see players facing a variety of challenges around the course. Specifically, while spectators want there to be some "risk" on every hole, they'd like to see a variety of risks throughout the course—for example, a narrow landing area for the drive on some holes, water hazards in play on some, pin placements that punish inaccurate approaches on some, and so on—but not all of these risks on any one hole.

- Spectators want to see players hitting shots that require great skill, but do not like "gimmicky" shots. Specifically, the following table details the types of shots they like and don't like.

These and other findings may have some implications for how you set up the golf courses you use for your tournaments. While this memo is intended to summarize the research findings, not to recommend a plan to improve spectator enjoyment of your tournaments, you may wish to provide a preview of the kinds of actions you believe would be appropriate. The place to do this is in the Indicated Actions section. In this example, your Indicated Actions section may look like this:

Indicated Actions

- We may wish to investigate how we can increase the risk/reward factor on several of the holes at our Duluth and Tacoma tournaments. I will work with our course architect and the club professionals at these venues to develop a proposal by April 1 on how we could most effectively do this.

- The bunker we inserted into the middle of the eighth green in Spokane may be seen as a gimmick, and thus be unappealing to spectators. My assistant director, Mark Johnson, will contact the tournament director in Spokane to see if she's had any feedback about that hole, and if so, work with her to determine a plan of action before the next Spokane tournament in July.

Notice that you've cited specific actions you may wish to take based on what you've learned. As with Next Steps sections, you've also laid out who will be taking the initiative to complete any actions indicated, and when those actions will be taken.

TIP

Sometimes you can't initiate the actions indicated by your findings. Nonetheless, you should describe what you plan to do, even if it's only to bring your findings to the attention of the individuals in the organization who can initiate action.

By writing a thorough, well-documented Next Steps section as outlined in this section, you can ensure that your recommendation is carried out the way you planned. You've not only provided a step-by-step process for each responsible individual to follow, but also created a written record of who is supposed to do what and by when.

THE 30-SECOND RECAP

- For memos in which you propose a plan of action, conclude with a Next Steps section.
- Your Next Steps section should include what needs to be done to implement the plan, who is responsible for doing it, and when it will be complete.
- Conclude summaries and analyses with an Indicated Actions section.
- Your Indicated Actions section should describe actions that may be appropriate for the organization to undertake, based on the findings or analysis you've done.
- The Indicated Actions section should lay out what you plan to do to initiate each action, along with when you plan to do it. If you are not the person initiating the action, you should state who that person is.

Outline Your Thinking

In this section you learn how to outline your memos based on the writing principles and the memo framework discussed in the previous sections.

WHY OUTLINE?

Writing an effective business document is easier if you take time to outline your document before you write. We are surprised at how many of our workshop participants choose not to outline first. They believe that outlining takes too much time. But outlining actually streamlines the writing process, makes the writing easier, the logic of your document flow more smoothly, and therefore can save you time.

PLAIN ENGLISH

Flow of a document   The ease with which the reader can move from one statement to the next. In a document that flows well, each statement follows logically from the previous ones, and each subsequent statement is the one the reader expects to see, based on what he's already read.

GETTING STARTED

Start the outlining process by clearly defining your purpose and writing it down. Next think of all the critical pieces of information related to your purpose. Write each piece of information on paper. Don't worry about editing your thoughts or stating them in complete sentences. The goal at this stage is to get your thoughts on paper so that you can sort them.

Using the framework described in earlier sections, sort your thoughts by placing them in the appropriate section, identifying which thoughts are background data, which thoughts are rationale points, which thoughts support your rationale points, and so on. I typically do this visually on a chart pad or large white board, but some writers prefer to do it on a writing pad.

After you've placed all of your thoughts in the appropriate memo section, identify any gaps in your logic or any data you need to support your rationale. Once you obtain that data or fill in your logic gaps, you're ready to start writing.

PLAIN ENGLISH

Gap in logic or information   A point in your document that requires additional information for your reader to accept the validity of your statement. If you have a gap, you need to discover what information will close the gap, then ensure the needed information is included somewhere in your document.

WRITING THE OUTLINE

Suppose you're the brand manager for a premier, yet stagnant, brand of bathroom tissue named Fluffy. During the previous 12 months you have worked closely with managers from product development and market research to develop a product upgrade and new positioning for the brand. You are now ready to recommend the upgrade (Fluffy Q) for test market and need to write the recommendation for the general manager.

Your first step is to state your purpose. Your next step is to put all of your thoughts about the test market recommendation on paper.

TIP

If you're having trouble beginning to outline, just start by writing down any fact, conclusion, or statement you think you will eventually want to include in the document. When you've written down four or five of these, sort them into the document framework. This will give you an excellent start on your outline, and should make completing the outline easier.

CAUTION

Try not to procrastinate on the outlining process. If you try to outline when you're under time pressure for the finished document, you can often short-change the outline, causing difficulty for the final document as well.

Purpose

■ Develop Fluffy Q for test market.

Related thoughts (everything you know that may be relevant to the document)

■ Fluffy share has declined steadily for the past 10 years from 9.8 percent to 6.6 percent.

■ Fluffy Q uniquely meets consumer needs.

■ The Fluffy Q positioning and product is unique and ownable.

■ Fluffy had a significant thickness advantage when it was introduced in 1970.

■ Fluffy Q is financially attractive.

■ Fluffy no longer has a thickness advantage in the category.

■ The Q technology gives Fluffy the opportunity to regain thickness advantage.

Use the Framework to Sort by Memo Sections

Now that you have your thoughts on paper, sort them by the appropriate memo sections outlined in previous sections.

Overview

Recall from the section "The Opening Is the 'Bottom Line'" on page 842 that the overview is two or three sentences that sum up the content of the document. Given the summary nature of the overview, it is most appropriately written last—after you've completed the rest of the document. For this reason, you do not need to include it in your outlining process at this point. You may, however, wish to come back to the overview when you've completed your outline to note what the main point of your document will be.

Background

■ The Q technology gives Fluffy the opportunity to regain thickness advantage (roughly 50 percent).

■ Fluffy share has declined steadily for the past 10 years from 9.8 percent to 6.6 percent.

- Fluffy had a significant thickness advantage when it was introduced in 1970.
- Fluffy no longer has a thickness advantage in the category.

Recommendation

- Develop Fluffy Q for test market.

Rationale

- Fluffy Q is financially attractive.
- Fluffy Q uniquely meets consumer needs.
- The Fluffy Q positioning and product is unique and ownable.

Next Steps

The next steps should come directly from your understanding of what's needed to complete the plan you're recommending. You may wish to include these in your outline at this point, but since they don't affect the flow or the organization of information in the document, you may safely omit them until you write the final draft. Whenever you include the next steps, however, you should be sure they're complete, in the sense that they should suffice to execute the plan you're recommending.

TIP

Keep copies of outlines and final drafts of documents you feel are well written and well-thought-out. You can then use these outlines and drafts as guides to help you write similar documents in the future.

CAUTION

It's easy to leave out information in the outlining process, figuring you can fill it in as you write the final draft. Try to avoid this, because you can forget to include it, or discover that the new information means the final draft doesn't flow like you thought it would, and you need to do an extensive rewrite.

START WRITING

Now that you've developed the logical sequence for your document, your
writing should flow easily.

To: General Manager

From: Brand Manager

Subject: Fluffy Q Test Market Recommendation

This requests your agreement to the development of Fluffy Q.
Specifically, we are seeking agreement to the $1.2 million needed in
process and product development support. This spending is accounted
for in the current forecast.

Background

Fluffy was introduced in 1970 with a significant thickness advantage
(50 percent) vs. the premier segment leaders. Fluffy share grew to a
high of 9.8 percent, but since 1980 has declined steadily to a 6.6 percent
share as the segment leading brands have closed the thickness gap. With
the Q technology, Fluffy has the opportunity to regain a thickness
advantage of roughly 50 percent and to enhance this product advantage
with a distinct and ownable positioning.

Recommendation

Develop Fluffy Q for test market. Fluffy Q offers a distinct product and
positioning that uniquely meets current unmet consumer needs.

Rationale

Fluffy Q uniquely meets consumer needs. From research we know
consumers …

- Need to get clean without pain.
- Believe to do the job right they should not use too much tissue.
- Find doing both is not always achievable.

While most premium tissues focus on cleaning without pain, Fluffy Q
offers consumers resolution to this conflict with a "thicker, more-
absorbent-so-you-can-use-less" tissue.

**Fluffy Q provides a distinct and ownable product and positioning
for the brand.** Both the Q product and the more absorbent/useless positioning are clearly distinct from the premier segment leaders, and are
significantly more appealing to consumers than the current Fluffy

("Research Study Number 254"). Fluffy Q delivers on the positioning with a unique and ownable product design. Using the Q technology, we can increase thickness without compromising softness. Other manufacturers are not capable of making a significantly thicker and heavier tissue without compromising softness.

Fluffy Q is financially attractive. A financial analysis of Fluffy Q using a conservative volume estimate projects a 10 percent to 15 percent rate of return. For perspective, the company standard is 10 percent and our internal category target is 15 percent. We believe 15 percent is achievable based on initial concept and use results and consumer reaction to the product.

Next Steps

We need to qualify the process.

We need to confirm the product design of plant-made product.

The outlining process can save you time in the long run, by helping you organize your thoughts, collect the information you need, and enable you to begin filling in the framework of the document you're writing. Taking this time up front allows you to quickly catch any gaps in your information or flaws in your logic, and correct them without having to rewrite the entire document.

THE 30-SECOND RECAP

- Always take time to outline before you begin writing.
- Start by stating your purpose for writing.
- List everything you know related to your purpose without worrying about sentence structure.
- Sort your thoughts by the memo sections found in the standard framework.
- Write your document based on your outline.

Writing Business Letters

In this section you learn the fundamentals of writing business letters and see how several of the principles of good internal communication also apply to external communication.

CREATING A BUSINESS LETTER

Crafting a well-thought-out business letter can be equally as or more important than crafting a well-reasoned internal memo. In a business letter, you represent the company to someone outside the organization. Your letter will affect the reader's perception not only of you, but of your company as well. Since the reputation of the company is important, you want your letter to be perceived in the best, most professional light.

There are a host of books devoted to the subject of writing business letters; in this section, we'll cover the key principles that will enable you to communicate more effectively in your letters.

 CAUTION

Don't use stilted, formal language in your business letters—or any language that you wouldn't use in actual speech. Your letter should be part of a dialogue between you and the recipient, and should "sound" like a dialogue as well. "Enclosed please find the revised requisition form #841. Vendors must use the aforementioned form in connection with all purchase orders pertaining to machinery" should be re-written to be more conversational—for example, "I've enclosed a new requisition form. Please use it whenever you submit a purchase order for machinery."

In previous sections, we thoroughly examined the principles behind writing effective internal documents. Many of these same principles apply when writing a letter to be sent outside your organization. In the section "Start with a Purpose in Mind," on page 831, we described several key questions you should ask yourself when beginning to write:

- Why are you writing (what's your objective)?
- Who is your audience?
- What do you want them to do?
- Why should they agree?

Each of these questions is also important when writing a business letter.

WHY ARE YOU WRITING?

Before beginning to write your letter, be sure you've thought out all the reasons you're writing. For example, suppose you're a consultant and are drafting a letter to someone who has been an excellent customer for years, but who has not paid the invoice you sent him several months ago. Of course, you'd like to receive payment. However, you probably have a number of other goals for your letter. You might ask yourself:

- Is there a good reason for his delay in paying? He may have never received the invoice, or he may believe it has already been paid. A simple reminder may be all that's needed. On the other hand, he may be waiting for a payment owed to him from a third party relating to work you did; in that case, you may be willing to discuss payment options with him.

- Does this delay signal a growing dissatisfaction with your company, or is it a one-time occurrence? If the delay is an "early warning" signal, you'd like to not only get your payment, but also understand the source of any dissatisfaction so that you can eliminate it.

- Are there new circumstances in your client's organization that may be to blame for the late payment? For instance, they may have put a new bill-payment system in place with revised reporting requirements that you'll need to address in future invoices. Your client may have a new management chain of command that must approve your invoices, in which case you'll need to allow for that in your planning.

You probably won't try to cover all these possibilities when you write your letter. However, if you have a strong understanding of why you're writing, you'll be more likely to achieve the result you want. As the preceding possibilities illustrate, the "why" is rarely as simple as it might first appear.

WHO IS YOUR AUDIENCE?

Just as it's important to know your audience when composing an internal memo, you should keep your recipient in mind when writing a business letter. You might ask yourself:

- Does she prefer a formal style, or a more relaxed one?

- What kinds of arguments are most likely to be persuasive with her (for example, do analogies work better than data in proving your point?)?

- What does she value most highly in a business sense (for example, increased sales, reduced costs, or higher cash flows)?

PLAIN ENGLISH

Style   The manner of expression of a letter—for example, formal as opposed to conversational, or stiff as opposed to relaxed.

TIP

Whenever possible, confirm your recipient's title and the correct spelling of his or her name. People notice and appreciate it when you take the time to get their personal information correct.

Whatever you know about your recipient can help you craft your letter. Of course, you may sometimes write to people you've had no previous contact with. In these cases, use reasonable judgment in assuming what is most likely to motivate them. For example, if you're writing to the head of the accounting department, he may be most interested in reducing costs, whereas the sales manager will most likely be interested in higher sales volume.

WHAT DO YOU WANT THEM TO DO?

As with internal memos, you should be clear in your mind about what actions you want your recipient to take. In the example of the delinquent client, you'd like your client to pay his invoice. However, you'd also like to understand more about why the invoice wasn't paid earlier. Therefore, your letter will most likely be an inquiry for information, rather than a stern request for payment.

WHY SHOULD THEY AGREE?

When you write a business letter, you have a purpose in mind. In some cases, you may only want to impart information to your recipient. For example, if you're writing a letter to a supplier who's done an especially good job over the past year, you're sharing information—namely, that you believe the supplier has done a good job.

In other cases, you'll want something from the recipient. For example, you'll want him to physically do something—fill your order, send your invoice, refer you to another client, and so on. In those cases, you should bear in mind that, he will want to have a reason why it's in his interest (not just yours) to do so.

In the example we've been using, getting your client to provide you with information about why he hasn't paid your invoice may help him get better service from you—either an improved invoicing system, or better consulting service, or other solutions that address the issues that prevented him from paying your invoice on time.

STRUCTURING YOUR LETTER

As the mechanics of how to lay out a business letter are available in a number of reference sources, as well as many word processing programs that provide a variety of preformatted templates, we'll focus here on the organization, or flow, of your letter, including the following:

- The opening
- The body
- The closing

Each of these sections corresponds in a general way to similar sections of an internal memo.

TIP

Be as concise as possible in your business letters without being abrupt. Your reader will appreciate your taking up no more of his time than necessary.

THE OPENING

In the first paragraph of your letter, you should immediately state your reason for writing. As you write this paragraph, refer to the thinking you've done about your purpose, or objective. This paragraph is similar to the overview of an internal document, discussed in "The Opening Is the 'Bottom Line,'" on page 842. As with the overview, there are a number of key elements in the first paragraph of your letter. After reading your opening paragraph, your recipient should know …

- Why you're writing.
- What you're asking for.
- What kind of action you will take or want your recipient to take.

WRITING THE OPENING

Referring to our example of the late payment, the first paragraph of your letter might look like this:

November 2, 2001

Eric Smith
Vice President, Marketing
Top Notch Manufacturing Co.
123 Main Street
Atlanta, GA 30300

Dear Eric:

As you may recall, I sent you an invoice for the Brand X Relaunch
Project in late July. I'm concerned about the fact that I haven't yet
received payment on that invoice, and am writing to ask for your help in
understanding the delay. Please let me know a convenient time I can call
for us to discuss this matter.

An opening paragraph that spells out the reason you're writing and what you
want from the recipient enables him to quickly understand and process your
request. Being mindful of your recipient's time is as important in communicating externally as it is internally.

THE BODY OF THE LETTER

In the paragraphs following the opening, you will go on to explain what you
want to happen, or what information you have. Depending on the complexity
of your subject, this part of your letter may be from one to several paragraphs.
Keep in mind, however, that, unless it is of vital importance to him, your
reader is unlikely to want, or have time for, a several-page letter.

WRITING THE BODY OF THE LETTER

Following the opening paragraph, the body of the letter to your client might
look like the following box (see the next page).

Notice that in these three paragraphs, you've provided the detail necessary for
your client to track down the invoice within his organization. In addition,
you've given him two possibilities for what you believe may have happened,
which you will want to discuss in the follow-up phone call you requested in
the opening paragraph.

TIP

When writing to request something, give your recipient as much
information as possible to assist him in giving you what you need.
Not only is it considerate to help your reader out as much as you
can, it will make it more likely that you will get what you want.

I mailed Invoice #3106 to your attention on July 24. Since you have always been very prompt in responding to my previous invoices over the course of our seven-year association, I was surprised not to have received payment in August, or September at the latest. I know there was significant restructuring of your department in August, and other departments may have been restructured at that time as well. Because of this, there may be new requirements for how I should invoice you; if so, perhaps you could refer me to someone in your accounting department for more information.

Because of our mutual travel schedules, we haven't had the opportunity to "debrief" after the Brand X Relaunch Project, as we normally do after each of our major projects. While I don't imagine the delay in paying the invoice is related to any dissatisfaction you might have with how the project went, I'd like to get your feedback on it in any case. The Relaunch Project was, as you know, an extremely complex one, and your perspective on what went right as well as what went wrong will be very beneficial to both of us as we go forward on future projects.

Of course, the payment delay could be for some other reason entirely. In any case, understanding the cause for the delay will enable me to give you better service in the future so that we don't have this sort of issue again.

THE CLOSING

The final paragraph of your letter is similar to the Next Steps or Indicated Actions section of an internal document. In this paragraph, you will want to ...

- Conclude, or sum up, your letter.
- Request or agree to initiate a specific action.
- Provide a specific time by which the action will or should occur.

WRITING THE CLOSING

The closing paragraph of the letter to your client might look like the following:

> I have enjoyed our association to date, and look forward to many more years of working with you. To that end, I would like to clear up the confusion around my invoice for the Relaunch Project as quickly as possible. I'll call your assistant later this week to arrange a time we can discuss the issue.
>
> Sincerely,
>
> Eric Smith

In this case, you need help from your recipient (information about why the payment is delayed), so it makes sense for you to be the one who takes the next action step (in this case, calling his assistant).

CAUTION

Angry letters can make the recipient angry and defensive in turn. If your objective is to get some action from him—correcting his mistake, for example—keep in mind that the tone of your letter will have an impact on how well received it is, and how likely your recipient is to take the action requested.

Following the steps to completing a business letter—in much the same way as you've followed similar steps to complete an internal memo—will enable you to write clear, effective letters. While you probably won't label the various sections of your letter as you would in a memo, you'll still want to impart much of the same kind of information in much the same order.

THE 30-SECOND RECAP

- Writing a successful business letter requires using most of the same principles as writing a successful internal memo.
- In writing a business letter, ask yourself the same questions you would for an internal memo: Why are you writing (what's your objective), who is your audience, what do you want them to do, and why should they agree?
- In the opening paragraph, clearly explain why you're writing.
- In the body of the letter, provide all necessary detail.
- Close the letter with specific action steps, including who should take them and when.

Writing E-Mail

In this section you learn general principles for making your internal e-mail communication more effective, including ways to make initiating, sorting, and responding easier for you and your recipient.

THE E-MAIL PHENOMENON

Ten years ago, e-mail was unheard of outside a few technical and academic circles. As few as five years ago, e-mail was an unusual form of internal business communication. Today, of course, e-mail is ubiquitous, both in personal and business settings.

In the business environment, the use of e-mail has spread like kudzu, threatening to overwhelm and virtually eliminate other forms of communication. The reasons for the rapid proliferation of e-mail are obvious: The same message can be sent to all relevant parties simultaneously, you can read and respond to e-mail on your own schedule (whether that be 3 o'clock in the afternoon or 3 o'clock in the morning), and it combines the instantaneous nature of voice communication with the permanence of written communication.

The spread of e-mail is a mixed blessing, however, as anyone who has arrived in his office on Monday morning to see 135 messages waiting for him can attest. It is now so easy to send anyone (and everyone) in the organization a message that a huge and growing number of messages are poorly thought out, hard to read and respond to, or simply irrelevant to the recipient.

In this section we'll provide some guidelines to ensure that your messages are not among the poorly thought out, hard-to-read, or irrelevant ones, as well as some help for reducing the clutter in your inbox.

We'll consider three basic topics:

- Composing an e-mail message
- Responding to an e-mail message
- Reducing message clutter

COMPOSING AN E-MAIL MESSAGE

When composing an e-mail message, you'll want to ask the same questions you'd ask when composing any other written communication:

- Why are you writing (what's your objective)?
- Who is your audience?

- What do you want them to do?
- Why should they agree?

We've covered these elements at length in other sections; however, there are a few points worth noting that are specific to e-mails.

CAUTION

Keep in mind that e-mail, while having the immediacy of voice communication, can also have the permanence of written communication. Don't write anything in an e-mail you wouldn't write in a memo—it may become more public than you'd like.

WHY ARE YOU WRITING?

Since it's so easy to send e-mail, it is easy to fall into the habit of sending it without considering why the content of the message matters, and who it matters to. This wastes both your time and that of your recipients, if it results in your sending messages that didn't really need to be sent at all.

Similarly, a *telegraphic subject line* is even more critical in e-mail than in other communication—it will enable your recipients to quickly understand why this e-mail—among the many in their inboxes—is important, and should be read and acted on immediately.

PLAIN ENGLISH

Telegraphic subject line   One that very succinctly conveys the subject and nature of the message.

Assuming you decide that the content of your message does matter, you can take one additional step to ensure that your communication is as effective as possible: namely, ask yourself whether you need to send this e-mail or can achieve your objective in some other way. If a quick phone call or short conversation with the intended recipient is easier, quicker, and will suffice to meet your objective, you may decide to forgo e-mail in favor of other forms of communication.

WHO IS YOUR AUDIENCE?

As noted, one of the tremendous benefits of e-mail is that it is so easy and efficient to send copies to numerous recipients simultaneously. However, this benefit carries a risk. Be careful not to send copies to someone just because it's easy. Take the time to assess whether each person on your copy list really needs the information you're sending. In this way, you'll avoid cluttering people's inboxes with unnecessary reading, and you'll avoid having your inbox cluttered with responses from people who didn't need the information to begin with.

Don't always assume that someone has read your e-mail, especially if he's one of a large number of recipients. You probably skim or skip some of your mail; others do, too. If you get into the habit of sending e-mail messages only to the people who really need what you're sending, your recipients may realize over a period of time that they should be sure to read your messages when they arrive.

PLAIN ENGLISH

Copy list or **distribution list**   All the people to whom the message is being sent.

WHAT DO YOU WANT THEM TO DO?

Keep in mind that if you don't know what you want from your recipients, they are not likely to know either, and will consider your e-mail a waste of their time. Thus, it's important to try to be specific about what you're expecting each of the recipients to do with the information you're sending.

At the same time, don't assume they'll do what you want them to do—they may not have even read your message (as discussed earlier in this section). If you request action, ask for confirmation that they've read and agreed to the note, and that they're initiating action.

WHY SHOULD THEY AGREE?

On many occasions, you'll probably use e-mail for simple, direct questions or comments, rather than a more complex issue like making a recommendation or summarizing data. Even in those cases, however, you and your recipient will both benefit from your taking a few moments to consider your objective and how best to address it.

CAUTION

Be careful when sending charts via e-mail; some mail programs convert your message to a different font, which may dramatically affect how the chart looks.

WRITING THE E-MAIL

Suppose you're the division vice president of a company, and you've scheduled a meeting to discuss recent cost overruns in various departments in the division, and ways to reduce costs in the future. Three department heads must attend the meeting, since their departments have cost overruns. The other two department heads may attend to learn and share tips on reducing costs, but their attendance isn't mandatory. You could send a single e-mail such as the following to all five department heads:

To: All Department Heads

From: Division Vice President

Re: Cost Overrun Meeting

There will be a mandatory meeting for the heads of Departments A, B, and C on June 2 from 2 P.M. to 4 P.M. in Conference Room 1 to discuss cost overruns in those departments. Other department heads may attend the last hour of the meeting or send representatives to learn and share tips on reducing costs, but attendance is not mandatory. Please confirm your attendance by return e-mail.

While this note conveys the necessary information, it is less effective than it could be. With just a few extra moments, you could send separate, more effective e-mails to the relevant groups. Here is an example of the first e-mail you might send.

To: Heads of Departments A, B, and C

From: Division Vice President

Re: Mandatory Meeting on Cost Overruns

Please confirm by return e-mail your attendance at the following mandatory meeting to discuss cost overruns in your departments and how those overruns can be reduced.

Date: June 2

Time 2 P.M. to 4 P.M.

Place: Conference Room 1

Here is an example of the second e-mail you might send.

To: Heads of Departments D and E

From: Division Vice President

Re: Optional Meeting on Cost Reduction

I will be meeting with the heads of Departments A, B, and C to discuss cost overruns in those departments and how they can be reduced. You may find our discussion of cost reduction ideas valuable, and are welcome to attend or send a representative from your department to that part of the meeting, which should occupy the last hour of it. Meeting specifics are:

Date: June 2

Time 2 P.M. to 4 P.M.

Place: Conference Room 1

Note that, in the second example, the request is much clearer than it was in the original example, and what the recipient must do with the information is better delineated.

TIP

If you want to use different fonts and type faces to make your document visually appealing, consider writing it using a word processing program and sending it as an attachment to your e-mail.

RESPONDING TO E-MAIL

There are a number of guidelines for responding to e-mail that will save time and "inbox clutter" for both you and the people with whom you're corresponding.

- Respond only when a response is needed. For example, if you've been sent information you'll use in a separate document you're working on, you may not need to respond directly to the e-mail you were sent. The fact that the information shows up in your subsequent document will be enough indication that you've received and used the information given.

- When you do respond to an e-mail for which you were one of several recipients, don't automatically send a copy of your response to everyone on the original distribution list. In many cases, only a few of the original recipients will need to know your response. By copying only those people who need to know, you'll reduce the inbox clutter for the others.

■ After several iterations of responses, the subject line is often no longer relevant to the topic discussed in the body of the message. In that case, change the subject line as appropriate. For example, suppose the Vice President of Sales sent an e-mail to all District Managers, including you, discussing recent sales trends in each district, titled "District Sales Reports." You responded to his message, describing several steps you'd taken to achieve the excellent results he'd noted in your district. He responds to you, asking that you describe more fully each action you'd taken, and the effect you think that had on sales. At this point, the subject line of the e-mail you're sending one another still reads something like "Re: District Sales Results." The actual subject of the e-mail, however, is "Actions taken to increase sales in District 4." In this situation, you should change the subject line to reflect the actual content of the e-mail.

■ Most e-mail programs automatically attach the entire original message to your response. However, you can and should delete the portions of the original message that are not relevant to your response. This will cut down on the portion of the message the recipient must read.

■ While you needn't necessarily quote the entire message, you should be sure to include all relevant passages when responding, so that your recipients will have easily available the information you're responding to. Don't assume all recipients remember the original message.

■ For short responses, use the subject line to telegraph your intent, but also include the response in the body of the message, since many people open mail without looking at the subject line.

TECHNIQUES FOR REDUCING CLUTTER

Most of the topics discussed so far concern how you can ensure that your e-mail doesn't add to the clutter in other people's mailboxes. Unfortunately, this doesn't immediately solve the problem of how to deal with the clutter in your own mailbox. While much of that clutter can only be controlled by getting the senders to change their e-mailing habits, there are a few things you can do on your own to "clean up" your mailbox and make your handling of e-mail more efficient and effective.

The most powerful tool available to you is the option on most e-mail programs to automatically sort your mail according to instructions you provide. If you don't know how to access this capability, try to get instruction from someone who does, or if the program is publicly available (such as Microsoft Outlook or Outlook Express), find a book explaining its features. When you know how to use the sorting capability, you can use it to ...

- Sort messages based on who they are from. Thus, for example, you can put messages from your subordinates in one folder, and those from your boss in another. Since I use my e-mail address for both business and personal mail, I have my mail program sort messages from friends and family into a separate folder, enabling me to read those at my leisure.

- Sort messages based on the topic in the subject line. Suppose, for example, you regularly receive messages from one person regarding two different projects. For one of these projects, you have an active role, and must make daily decisions based on the information you receive. For the other project, however, your role is advisory, and you do not need to be as up to date on the issues associated with that project. In this case, you could sort messages into folders based on the project being discussed, and be sure to read all messages concerning the first project immediately.

- Copy messages to several folders based on content. I have a colleague with whom I work on several projects. He often sends me one e-mail that contains information about a number of different projects. To ensure that I keep track of what's going on with each of the projects we're working on, I have my mail program put a copy of his mail in the folder of each project he mentions. While this increases the total number of e-mail messages in my inbox, it organizes them in a way that allows me to know, when I open a message from him, that there is information in that message pertinent to the project on which I'm currently working.

TIP

Try to standardize the subject line of your e-mails if you send the same type of message regularly to the same recipients. For example, if you post a weekly budget review, get in the habit of always labeling it "Weekly Budget Review—Week of (date)." This makes communication faster and saves your recipients' time.

In addition to reorganizing your mailbox to improve your efficiency in handling your incoming mail, there are two things you can do to reduce the volume of incoming mail you see:

- Ask senders to remove you from group mailings that are not relevant to you.

- Instruct your mail program to automatically delete messages that you're certain are not relevant or important to you, either based on who the sender is or what the subject is.

E-mail has become a primary method of communication in most offices. With the benefits of e-mail have come a number of concerns, including proliferation of messages and less attention being paid to structure and style, resulting in poorly written documents. However, by using the information presented in this section, you can ensure that you use e-mail as the powerful communication tool it can be.

The 30-Second Recap

- Just as you would with any other written communication, before you write an e-mail message, think about what you want to accomplish.

- Consider who needs to receive your message, what you want from them, and what's in it for them in order to structure your message most effectively.

- Use your mail program to sort your mail, enabling you to handle it more efficiently.

Writing a Presentation Document

In this section you learn the general principles for writing a presentation document, including ways in which a presentation is similar to or different from a written document.

Uses for a Presentation

There are a wide variety of presentations and reasons to give one. We will focus in this section on internal presentations (that is, presentations to people within your organization); however, most external presentations follow the same principles.

There are two general types of internal presentations:

- Persuasive presentations
- Informative presentations

Persuasive presentations are similar to recommendation memos—you're asking your audience to agree to something you're proposing. Informative presentations more closely follow the structure of a summary or analysis, in which you are providing information your audience did not previously have.

STRUCTURING YOUR PERSUASIVE PRESENTATION

In general, you should structure your persuasive presentation similarly to the way you would structure a memo on the same subject. Specifically, when you wish to persuade your audience to do something (for example, you wish your company's board of directors to fund a new plant) the structure should follow the form of a recommendation memo, with the following sections:

- Overview
- Background
- Recommendation
- Rationale
- Additional Information Needed
- Next Steps

In the overview, you will tell your audience what the presentation will be about, and what you're asking them to do. You would then go on to provide any necessary background the audience needs to understand your recommendation and why you're making it. Next comes the recommendation itself, and then the reasons why the recommendation is sound (the rationale). If necessary, in the Additional Information Needed section you would include any significant issues or concerns with this proposal, and how you're addressing them. Finally, you would conclude your presentation with your Next Steps section, a brief listing of what needs to happen next, along with when it needs to happen and who's responsible for making it happen.

TIP

Just as you would outline an important memo, you may find that outlining your presentation makes the actual writing faster and easier.

STRUCTURING YOUR INFORMATIVE PRESENTATION

Similarly, if you're preparing an informative presentation, your deck would
follow the summary or analysis structure:

- Overview
- Background
- Findings and conclusions
- Indicated actions

PLAIN ENGLISH

Presentation deck   The written form of a presentation—the "deck"
of pages that you show your audience as you go through your presentation. A page of a deck is sometimes called a slide.

The Overview and Background sections would be the same as for the persuasive presentation. Exactly how the Findings and Conclusions sections are
structured will depend in part on the nature of your conclusions.

For example, suppose you are the marketing manager of a line of leather
products (wallets, attachés, organizers, and so on). You've just completed a
major survey of a competitor's marketing activities, including differences by
region, by month, and by major product line, and are going to present these
findings to two different groups. The first presentation of your competitive
analysis is to your company's senior management. They are interested in the
broad overview of what competitors are doing, and how that generally affects
the company. For that presentation, you might present only one or two overarching conclusions, supported by a number of important findings. (Three findings are listed here for illustration; in actuality, you might have several more.)

Conclusions

- Establishing a strong brand name among consumers has enabled
  Company A to obtain strong sales without the high level of promotional expenses other competitors, including us, must incur.

- Our smaller competitors use their higher profit margins in lines we
  don't carry, such as belt and other apparel accessories, to fund
  aggressive marketing tactics in the more competitive categories such
  as wallets and attachés.

Findings

1. Companies A and B spend approximately 8 percent of their whole-sale revenue on promotional support, versus an average of 12 percent for all other competitors.

2. Company A has the highest brand-name recognition among consumers, with 78 percent unaided awareness. No other company has more than 52 percent unaided awareness.

3. More than 80 percent of leather goods purchasers say they prefer to purchase a brand they know.

4. (And so on ...)

Alternatively, your second presentation of the same material is to the regional marketing managers, who must implement tactics in their own regions. For that presentation, you may wish to present a number of "smaller" conclusions specific to various regions or seasons of the year, rather than one or two overarching ones. If so, an appropriate format is to present each conclusion, followed immediately by findings supporting that conclusion:

Conclusions and Findings

Company A has a dominant position in the Midwest region, allowing them to spend less in promotion.

- Company A market share is 60 percent in the Midwest.
- Their total promotional spending is 75 percent of competitive average.
- Promotional spending per unit is 30 percent of competitive average for Company A.

Companies C and D are vulnerable in the East Region due to low brand awareness.

- Brand awareness for C and D is 12 percent and 15 percent, respectively.
- Both companies' promotional spending is increasing annually.
- Market share for both C and D is declining.
- Wallets and organizers represent a strong profit opportunity in the West Region.
- (And so on ...)

As with a written summary of analysis, end your presentation with an Indicated Actions section, based on your conclusions.

THE MECHANICS OF THE PRESENTATION DECK

While the framework for your presentation deck should follow along the same general lines as a memo, some of the mechanics will be different. We will examine four important aspects:

- Brevity
- Charts and graphs
- Other visuals
- Handouts

BREVITY

In a written document, the words on the page must carry the entire load—they must deliver your information, provide the support for that information, and persuade the reader to accept your message. In a presentation, however, you have the opportunity as speaker to shoulder some of that burden. This allows you to be judicious in how much written material you put on each page (or slide) of a presentation deck.

Two other factors contribute to the need for brevity. The first is that you want your audience to pay attention to you, rather than the slide; you don't want them to be reading more than they have to. The second is that presentations filled with pages of tightly packed prose are uninviting to read, so your audience may tune it (and you) out.

CAUTION

Your audience has a limited attention span. It's easy to create presentations that run too long—be sure to keep yours short enough to hold your audience's attention.

Therefore, try to limit your slides to the "headlines" of your presentation. A good rule of thumb is that more than 25 to 30 words will start to overcrowd the page.

Let's look at how the previous presentation example would look in slide format:

Slide 1

Conclusions:

- Developing a strong brand name with high awareness drives volume without high promotional support.

- High margin niches fuel smaller competitors' aggressive spending
  against us.

Slide 2

Finding 1:

Promotional support as a percent of wholesale revenue:

Companies A and B: 8 percent

All others: (average) 12 percent

Slide 3

Finding 2:

Brand-name recognition (unaided awareness):

Company A: 78 percent

All others: less than 52 percent

Slide 4

Finding 3

(And so on ...)

Notice that there is not much information on any single slide—generally only
one or two important points. In this way, you can lead the presentation by
focusing your audience's attention on the single point under discussion, rather
than allowing your audience to "read ahead."

CAUTION

Don't overwhelm your audience with too many visual effects such as
complex slide transitions and zooming text. Be sure the content of
your presentation is what is remembered, not the "slide show."

Charts and Graphs

Charts and graphs can be effective tools in a presentation, allowing you to quickly demonstrate your point. As with words on a page of the deck, however, you must avoid trying to cram too much information into a single page or chart. Edit as much as you can to allow your chart or graph to show clearly the single point you're trying to make.

Consider the competitive analysis discussed in this section. Here's one possible slide:

Finding:

Company A is dominant in the Northeast

Market Shares (Percent Total Market)

Company	Southeast	Southwest	Northeast	Northwest	Central	Midwest
A	24	27	63	17	31	19
B	18	11	22	18	14	15
C	8	5	n/a	7	5	21
D	11	21	12	16	n/a	3
E	4	3	1	2	4	1
F	3	8	1	5	11	4
G	6	2	n/a	15	3	3

A better alternative to showing all the information is to just show the relevant information:

Finding:

Company A is dominant in the Northeast

	Market Shares (Percent Northeast Region)
Company A:	62
Company B:	22
Company C:	12
All others:	4

In the first chart, your audience will have a difficult time picking out the relevant information and potentially will be distracted by trying to analyze the share numbers for the other regions. The second chart is preferable because it distills the data into exactly what is needed to make the point you wish to make.

TIP

If you *must* include a large array of numbers on a single slide, use boxes, arrows, bold print, or underlining to highlight the few numbers you want your audience to focus on.

OTHER VISUALS

Similar to the use of charts and graphs, the use of other visuals, such as a copy of a competitor's print advertising in a discussion of how successful that advertising is, can be effective in a presentation. As with charts and graphs, be judicious in your use of visuals, to avoid overwhelming your audience with pictures and causing them to lose sight of your key messages.

TIP

Practice your presentation several times to be sure you know what you're going to say, how you're going to verbally transition between slides, and how long the presentation will be.

HANDOUTS

After your presentation is complete, you will often want to give audience members handouts of the presentation deck that they might refer to later. In general, the handout can be merely a close copy of the deck you used in your presentation. Occasionally, however, you may wish to include backup or supporting data for some of the key points made in the presentation. These can be added as appendixes to the deck itself. Since these appendixes are not part of the main presentation, they can contain more data than a chart or page in the regular deck.

Effective presentations follow essentially the same format as effective memos, for exactly the same reason—to deliver the information you wish to present as efficiently and effectively as possible. The presentation format gives you the additional flexibility of including charts, graphs, and other visual aids that are more difficult to include in written memos, as well as the opportunity to orally expound on the data you're presenting. For these reasons, the presentation can be an effective tool if used properly.

THE 30-SECOND RECAP

- Structure presentation decks similarly to how you structure memos.
- Keep individual pages of your deck brief, with at most one or two points and about 25 to 30 words per page.
- Use charts and graphs to present data; as with other pages of your deck, streamline charts and graphs to focus on only a single piece of information.
- Use other visuals to illustrate key points, but don't overwhelm your viewer with so many visuals that he loses sight of the point of your presentation.

Avoid the Grammar Minefield

In this section you learn the most common grammatical mistakes made in business writing and how to avoid them.

KNOW YOUR GRAMMAR RULES

In this section we'll examine the grammatical mistakes we see most often in our workshops.

There may be times when you choose to break some of the following rules or other rules of grammar. For example, you may choose to end a sentence with a preposition because the options for correct grammar are more awkward. We suggest that you do so only occasionally. Don't lose credibility in your writing by ignoring good grammar.

USE PROPER SENTENCE STRUCTURE

Proper sentence structure is critical to effective business writing. If you don't already know the fundamentals of good sentence structure, review the following rules and practice using them.

MATCH YOUR NOUNS AND VERBS

Singular sentence subjects require singular verbs, and plural sentence subjects require plural verbs. Match the verb tense to the subject tense. Don't be confused by other nouns in the sentence.

Incorrect

The list of promotions to be implemented next year are listed in the marketing plan.

Correct

The list of promotions to be implemented next year is listed in the marketing plan.

The subject of the sentences above is *list*, not *promotions*. Therefore, the appropriate verb is singular.

BEWARE OF DANGLING WORDS AND PHRASES

A phrase at the beginning of a sentence must refer to the subject of the sentence.

Incorrect

In developing the human resources budget, the distribution budget was used as a model.

Correct

In developing the human resources budget, the CFO used the distribution budget as a model.

Keep related words together so that your communication is as clear as possible.

Incorrect

The company's first retail store opened October 1st with shoe samples from multiple designers in a hanging display case.

Correct

The company's first retail store opened October 1st with shoe samples from multiple designers. The samples were displayed in a hanging display case.

In the preceding example, the samples, not the designers, were in the hanging display case.

PLAIN ENGLISH

Dangling modifier   A word (or phrase) that appears to modify an inappropriate word in the same sentence.

PUNCTUATE

Correction punctuation is an important component of clear communication.

COMMAS

Commas help you clarify meaning. If you can remove a comma and maintain sentence clarity, then you don't need the comma. Following are the most useful comma rules to remember.

Commas separate words in a series.

- In a series of three or more words, use a comma after every word before the conjunction (and, or, but).

    Incorrect

    The company reimburses meal auto air and lodging expenses incurred on authorized business trips.

    Correct

    The company reimburses meal, auto, air, and lodging expenses incurred on authorized business trips.

- In a series of modifiers, use a comma after each modifier except the last.

    Incorrect

    The sales team asked for a simple focused effective plan.

    Correct

    The sales team asked for a simple, focused, effective plan.

Use a comma to separate clauses joined by a conjunction if the clauses have different subjects.

Incorrect

The VP of Human Resources requested the performance ratings and I submitted them on Friday.

Correct

The VP of Human Resources requested the performance ratings, and I submitted them on Friday.

Use a comma to separate clauses joined by a coordinating conjunction such as "but" or "yet."

Incorrect

We wanted to run the advertising but we had no budget to cover the expense.

Correct

We wanted to run the advertising, but we had no budget to cover the expense.

SEMICOLONS

Use semicolons to separate word series that contain other punctuation and to join related independent clauses not joined by a conjunction.

Word series

The board of directors includes Virginia Coleman, Voilà Cosmetics President; Alice Burns, GW Transport Chief Financial Officer; and David Michael, BFS Vice President of Sales.

Joined independent clauses

The tax attorneys reviewed all possible deductions; only three were legal.

The last example could also be written with a conjunction:

The tax attorneys reviewed all possible deductions, but only three were legal.

Use the comma and conjunction if the tone is casual or the clauses are short. Use the semicolon if the tone is formal or the clauses are long.

PLAIN ENGLISH

Independent clause   A group of words that can stand alone as a complete sentence.

COLONS

Use colons to introduce a list or a quote, or a related thought to an independent clause.

List

We created three new positions: Office Managing Partner, Integrated Solutions Director, and Business Development Director.

Quote

The president began the meeting with this mantra: "Work hard. Work smart. Take risks. Have fun."

Related thought

The shelter exists for one reason: to serve the homeless.

Quotation Marks

Use quotation marks around words quoted from someone or something. Also use quotation marks around a word you intend to define.

Quote

The president began the meeting with this mantra: "Work hard. Work smart. Take risks. Have fun."

Definition

The brand scored below industry average for "unaided awareness." The unaided awareness score is the percentage of people polled who stated they had heard of the brand when asked the following question: "What brands have you ever heard of in the BLANK category?"

Commas and periods should always be placed inside the quotation marks. However, question marks are only placed inside quotation marks if they are part of the quoted material.

Take Possession

To make a singular noun possessive, add an apostrophe and s, even if the noun already ends in s. For plural nouns that end in s, add an apostrophe.

Singular nouns

Jane   Jane's report

Bess   Bess's report

Plural nouns

Directors   Directors' stock options

Absolute personal possessive pronouns (hers, his, ours, yours, theirs, mine) do not use an apostrophe.

Note that the personal pronoun "it" does not use an apostrophe in the possessive form. The possessive is "its"; the contraction "it's" is used in place of "it is" or "it has."

Use Parallel Structure

When you have more than one thought to express in a sentence, express those thoughts in parallel structure. Parallel structure is not only grammatically correct, but also more persuasive because it suggests order and thoughtfulness on the part of the writer. Consider the following examples.

Not parallel

The new commercial is persuasive and a 15-second spot.

Parallel

The new commercial is persuasive and short.

Not parallel

The research will identify within the facial tissue category

- Consumer attitudes.
- How consumers purchase.
- If consumers use products more heavily than others depending on time of year.

Parallel

The research will identify within the facial tissue category

- Consumer attitudes.
- Consumer purchase patterns.
- Consumer usage patterns.

TIP

Don't change tenses in the middle of a sentence or a paragraph. Pick a tense and stick to it.

THE TROUBLE WITH "IT"

My college editing professor, David McCann, brought to class one day a wooden sculpture of the word "it" and loudly placed the sculpture on his desk. He began the day's lesson by stating that, going forward, any time his students began a sentence with the word "it," he would assume the students were referring to the sculpture on his desk, for there was nothing else "it" could modify as the first word in the sentence. Consider the following examples:

It comes as no surprise. (Well, I was surprised to see the sculpture on the desk.)

It should never have turned out this way. (The sculpture looked fine to me.)

It's a mystery to me. (But I understand now thanks to my good professor.)

Professor McCann probably had no idea that this student would remember the "it" lecture and be tortured by the word for 15 years now (and counting).

Sadly, I see "it" beginning a sentence in almost everything I read: the news-paper, business documents, even novels. You may choose to torment me by starting sentences with it. But do so cautiously. Try to find a clearer sentence structure. This reader, and yours, will thank you for doing so.

Incorrect

It appears that we will meet both sales and profit numbers this year.

Correct

We will meet both sales and profit numbers this year.

We will likely meet both sales and profit numbers this year.

Incorrect

It is not essential to the plan's success.

Correct

The plan will be successful with or without the flyer.

PAY ATTENTION TO SPELLING

As business writers, we are fortunate to have the spelling tool in word pro-cessing software. The spelling tool will tell you if you have misspelled words, and will sometimes tell you if you have used a word inappropriately. But the tool is not a perfect one. Consider the following examples. The spelling tool reads each sentence below as correct.

We will file the document on you're system (vs. "your system").

We depend on the spelling tool 100 percent of the thyme (vs. "time").

We rely on the grammar tool, to (vs. "too").

The grammar tool, although useful, is also not perfect. For example, the tool recommends changing the verb "rely" in the last sentence to "relies."

TIP
Be sure to proof your work, and don't always rely on the software's artificial intelligence to make spelling or grammar decisions for you.

COMMONLY MISUSED WORDS AND PHRASES

Following are some commonly misused words and phrases.

Affect and Effect

The word *affect* is a verb that means "to influence." The word *effect* can be used as both a noun and a verb. The noun *effect* means "result." The verb *effect* means "to bring about or accomplish."

We hope to affect the outcome.

We will not be able to measure the program effect until next year.

Among or Between

Among is the appropriate word to use when three or more people or things are involved. *Between* is the appropriate word to use when only two people or things are involved.

The program cost will be allocated among the five participating brands.

The issue is between sales and marketing, and does not involve other departments.

Ensure and Insure

Ensure means "to make certain." *Insure* means "to protect against loss."

We need to ensure the program's success.

We will insure the company against any liability associated with the summer promotion.

Farther and Further

The word *farther* is used to describe physical distances. The word *further* is used to describe conceptual progress.

San Francisco is farther than Kansas City.

Further analysis is needed to understand the issues.

Fewer and Less

The word *fewer* refers to the number of people or things involved. The word *less* refers to the degree involved.

In business writing, fewer words are better.

The project required less effort than we expected.

IMPLY AND INFER

Imply means "to suggest or indicate." *Infer* means "to deduce or to assume."

The buyer implied that he would not purchase the new product line unless we offered significant promotional spending to support it.

The sales representative inferred from the conversation that the buyer would not purchase the new product line unless we offered significant promotional spending to support it.

IRREGARDLESS OR REGARDLESS

Always use *regardless. Irregardless* is not a word.

We will share the research with the sales team, regardless of the results.

MORE THAN AND OVER

The words *more than* refer to the number of people or things involved. The word *over* refers to the degree of things involved or the spatial relationships of things involved.

The book contains more than 500 entries (not "over 500 entries").

The reports are located in the filing cabinet over my desk.

UNIQUE

Never modify *unique* in your writing. Phrases such as "The idea was very unique" are grammatically incorrect. *Unique* means "one of a kind"—having no like or equal—and therefore, cannot be modified.

His idea was unique.

CONSENSUS

Never use *general* to describe "consensus." "General consensus" is a redundant phrase. A consensus is, by definition, general.

The consensus was to retain the agency for another year.

TIP

Keep at least one writing reference in your desk or on your bookshelf to use when you're writing. Knowing where to look up the rules is as important as knowing the rules.

The 30-Second Recap

- Always proof your writing for correct spelling, word usage, and grammar after using the spelling- and grammar-checking functions in word processing software.

- Don't begin a sentence with the pronoun "it," because there is no subject for "it" to modify.

- Be aware of the most commonly misused words and phrases so that you may use them correctly.

Style Facilitates Effective Communication

In this section you learn key writing principles that will immediately make your documents more effective and inviting to read.

An Overview of Style

While the thinking behind your writing is more important than your writing style, you can sabotage the communication of your best thinking by not paying attention to a few key style principles.

Most of these principles might seem like common sense. Yet as obvious as they are, using them consistently is not easy. Applying them to your writing requires effort and practice. We continue to be amazed in our writing workshops by how obvious these principles seem to the participants, but how few of them actually apply them to their business writing.

You may also recognize the following principles because they consistently appear in style guides, writing courses, and books on writing. While many style principles exist that can help you be more effective, we have included in this section those most appropriate to business writing. For more in-depth instruction on style, we recommend *The Elements of Style,* by William Strunk Jr. and E. B. White.

PLAIN ENGLISH

Style   *How* you communicate, not *what* you communicate.

STYLE PRINCIPLE ONE: BE CONCISE

Concise writing communicates more clearly, shows respect for the reader's time, and builds the writer's credibility. If you apply only one principle to your business writing, make sure it's this one.

Professor William Strunk Jr. makes the point eloquently in *The Elements of Style:*

> Vigorous writing is concise. A sentence should contain no unnecessary words, a paragraph no unnecessary sentences, for the same reason that a drawing should have no unnecessary lines and a machine no unnecessary parts. This requires not that the writer make all of his sentences short, or that he avoid all detail and treat his subjects only in outline, but that every word tell.

With Professor Strunk's advice in mind, consider the following example.

Not concise

The key objective of the Brand X promotion plan is to maximize trial in order to leverage the Brand X technology strength that provides super performance among consumers. To accomplish this, we plan to execute the identical three introductory events used in test market.

Concise

The Brand X promotion plan objective is to maximize consumer trial, leveraging the product's superior performance. We will execute the three introductory events used in test market.

Notice how the example with fewer words communicates more clearly.

Look for, and delete, phrases that overshadow the thinking you have worked so hard to clarify. We cringe when we see them. Your readers do, too. So if "The truth is," "The fact that," or "We think that" appear in your first draft, delete them when you edit.

For perspective, let's review some examples. Which version of each do you find easier to understand?

Not concise

The truth is that this plan carries significant risk.

Concise

This plan carries significant risk.

Not concise

The fact that we were successful in test market indicates that we will be successful nationally.

Concise

Our test market success indicates we will be successful nationally.

Not concise

We think that the plan will eliminate communication barriers and improve productivity.

Concise

The plan will eliminate communication barriers and improve productivity.

CAUTION

Don't use "I feel" or "We feel" in your writing. In business, what you think is critical, what you feel is not.

TIP

Use "I think" in business writing only when you are distinguishing your point of view from another's point of view. If you are merely stating your case, say what you think, not that you think it.

Style Principle Two: Be Specific

Your writing will be much more persuasive if you write the way you talk. Don't use flowery language just because you're putting pen to paper. Remember, your readers are busy people. They don't have time to translate or interpret, nor should you expect them to.

Not specific

We are very excited to be having this session, as we hope to achieve three very critical goals that feed next year's corporate Web presence. They are ...

Specific

We appreciate your attendance at the corporate Web presence planning session. We have three meeting objectives. They are ...

Not specific

We hope that each of you finds Friday to be a very beneficial, and enlightening, working session. This is only the beginning. The results of this session will be incorporated into an overall strategic framework that will guide the prioritization and implementation planning for next year's initiative.

Specific

You should find Friday's working session beneficial. We will refine the initiative's strategy and plan based on the results we generate at the session.

Being specific is also critical when you're presenting data tables. Be sure to accurately label the tables. Assume that at least one of your readers is not familiar with the data or sources you're presenting.

Finally, don't use jargon or cliches; they communicate the writer's lack of clarity or vocabulary. Find the right word and use it.

TIP

Don't use vague modifiers such as "very." These modifiers clutter your writing.

STYLE PRINCIPLE THREE: USE THE ACTIVE VOICE

Using the active voice will make your writing more inviting, and likely more concise and specific. Concise and specific writing leads to clear communication. If you're presenting a recommendation for approval, or a point of view for adoption, the clearer your message, the more likely it is to be adopted.

Consider the following examples of passive and active sentences. Which would you rather read?

Passive

What we need are your ideas for the new sales plan.

Active

We need your ideas for the new sales plan.

Passive

Mistakes were made.

Active

We made mistakes.

Passive

The results were reviewed by the executive committee members.

Active

The executive committee reviewed the results.

TIP

The passive voice can be effective when you don't want to embarrass a third party. "A mistake was made" may be better than "My boss made a mistake."

STYLE PRINCIPLE FOUR: AVOID REDUNDANCY

Using redundant words and phrases makes your writing appear sloppy and erodes your credibility.

■ "The reason is because"—this all-too-common phrase is not only the style equivalent of nails on a chalkboard, but is also grammatically incorrect. Also avoid "the reason why"—this can often be reduced to just "the reason."

Redundant (and grammatically incorrect)

The reason why sales declined is because of poor merchandising.

Better

The reason sales declined is poor merchandising.

Best

Sales declined because of poor merchandising.

Or ...

Poor merchandising caused sales to decline.

TIP

Your ability to clearly communicate is based to some extent on your vocabulary. As your vocabulary grows, so do your opportunities to be precise in your writing.

Style Principle Five: Be Gender-Neutral

Several years ago I received a cover letter and resume for an open position. The cover letter was addressed to the "Hiring Manager," but the salutation was "Dear Sir." I was stunned. That this person clearly assumed the Marketing Director was a male stunned me. I did keep the resumé and cover letter on my desk for a couple of days, but only to show my colleagues. I did not consider the writer fit for my department and did not respond to his application.

Using gender-neutral language not only keeps you from alienating your readers, but also makes your writing more specific.

CAUTION

Your writing style communicates not only your ideas on a specific subject, but also how you think in general. Be careful not to use sexist language.

Final Thoughts on Style

Although the style of your writing is not as important as your thinking, it can increase your persuasiveness. By paying attention to these key style principles, you enhance not only your writing, but also your perception among others.

The 30-Second Recap

- Be concise. Concise writing communicates more clearly, shows respect for the reader's time, and builds the writer's credibility.

- Be specific. Your readers are busy people. They don't have time to translate or interpret, nor should you expect them to.

- Use the active voice. It will make your writing more inviting, and likely more concise and specific.

- Avoid redundancy. Redundant writing sounds sloppy and erodes your credibility.

Problem-Solving and Decision-Making

All Are Smarter Than One

In this section, you learn how groups work and how to utilize basic knowledge of group interaction and behavior.

Meetings occur on the premise that individuals have something to contribute to an organization that is best tapped in a group effort, or that they will learn more effectively and efficiently in a group than in one-on-one instruction. In order to generate successful learning or collaboration in a meeting, a facilitator needs to understand the basic elements of *group dynamics.*

PLAIN ENGLISH

Group dynamics   The behavior of individuals in small groups and the scientific study of this behavior and underlying personality, attitudes, and motivation in order to learn more about the nature of groups, how they develop, and what happens in them. It is part of the larger field of social psychology.

People behave differently in groups than as individuals. Because humans are social beings, the presence of others influences an individual's behavior.

UNDERSTANDING HOW GROUPS WORK

Assembling a lot of brainpower in a meeting is not enough to ensure successful learning, negotiation, problem-solving, or decision-making. Attitudes, beliefs, and feelings affect our reactions even to factual material. Some of the effects of group dynamics help to produce the desired "all are smarter than one" synergy in meetings; other effects appear to derail strong individual contributors and wreak havoc with group problem-analysis, decision-making, and team-building. Let's examine some basic concepts of group behavior.

In a group, there is a human tendency to avoid rejection and gain the approval of others in the group. This impulse can cause us to clap at something we don't agree with because the group is clapping, to eat because the group is eating rather than because we are hungry, to feign understanding of something we don't comprehend, or to "see" something we don't agree with at all. In social psychology, this is called normative social influence. We will adjust our behavior or thinking to bring it in line with that of a group. Also, when participants anticipate that a group may provide information valuable to them, individuals are more accepting of others' opinions. This is called informational social influence. While these adaptations can be viewed as the grease that makes civilization possible, they can produce skewed results in a meeting.

CAUTION

Making assumptions about any individual's susceptibility to social influences is risky. The more you know about participants' opinions and positions on the topics of the meeting, their feelings about being in the group, and their expectations, the better you will be able to obtain objective input during the meeting.

As a facilitator or leader, be aware that suggestibility and conformity increase just by virtue of being in a group (more than two people) and having others observe your behavior. These conditions also increase conformity:

- When participants are made to feel incompetent, powerless, or insecure.
- When the group is perceived to have high status by the participants.
- When the group is homogenous.
- When participants enter a group without a commitment to a preconceived conclusion.
- When an organization's culture fosters and rewards conformity and obedience rather than dissent and a free exchange of ideas, risk-taking, and original thinking.

There are other effects of being in a group that influence participants' behavior in a meeting. Individuals tend to do what they do well even more strongly in the presence of others than when alone, and to do poorly or not be able to do at all in a meeting what they find difficult alone. This effect, called social facilitation, may be a double-edged sword: It allows a facilitator to feel confident that someone who can lead another individual one-on-one through an analysis can be assigned to lead a problem analysis in a meeting, but it also makes it more difficult to use a meeting as a developmental opportunity for someone who may be able to analyze and write exceptionally well but has difficulty presenting his ideas, evidence, or arguments orally.

A factor to be aware of is minority influence. Just as a strong-opinioned, directive leader can exert so much power over a meeting that no substantive discussion may take place, a small number of individuals holding a minority opinion consistently over time may influence the thinking of the majority group.

Another effect is the tendency to diminish one's effort in a group activity, what the social psychologist Bibb Latané calls social loafing, because people acting as part of a group may feel less accountable for their individual contributions. This is one of the reasons why it is so important for a facilitator to ensure every participant is engaged in the meeting.

Yet another effect of group interaction is group polarization, the tendency of initial differences between groups to increase over time and the intensifying of a group's prevailing tendencies. This can be a positive effect in motivational and team-building meetings, but a detriment in negotiations or if a group's tendencies are leading them to ignore evidence that challenges a *hypothesis* or prevailing view.

PLAIN ENGLISH

Hypothesis   An interpretation of an event that leads to an action, or a tentative assumption or theory made in order to examine or test its logical or real-world outcomes.

The degree to which any or all these phenomena of group behavior are present in any given meeting ranges widely. Your awareness of these effects on behavior will increase your observational skill as a participant as well as a facilitator.

CREATING EFFECTIVE GROUPS

In his book *Emotional Intelligence,* Daniel Goleman states that the key to a high group IQ is social harmony, not the sum of talent alone but the ability of the group to harmonize. Think about that term, harmonize: You do not want to create a group that speaks with one voice (conformity), but to have different voices sing together creating music no one voice could produce by itself.

If you fail to establish this harmony in a meeting, you will have what David and Frank Johnson call a pseudogroup (*Joining Together: Group Theory and Group Skills, Seventh Edition*), a roomful of people who have been assigned to work together but have no interest in doing so. To push the analogy further, what you get without social harmony is noise, not music.

So how do you create a group that is eager to work together in a meeting? Some of these steps you learned in "Effective Meeting Basics" on page 724, and "Planning Your Meeting Strategically" on page 741. Here you can see how these steps and other suggestions support the establishment of two critical elements of successful group work: healthy *interdependence* and trust and openness.

PLAIN ENGLISH

Interdependence   The quality or state of reciprocal and equal reliance on another. It suggests trust as opposed to enmeshment, which means an unhealthy entanglement and a state of being trapped. Interdependence is walking hand in hand; enmeshment is walking bound to someone with handcuffs.

ESTABLISHING TRUST AND INTERDEPENDENCE

Here are the components required to create trust and openness, and healthy interdependence in the group:

- **Examine your belief in the value of group work.** As leader or facilitator, if you don't believe the success of a group depends upon the efforts of all of its members, you will have difficulty instilling this belief in others.

- **Establish clear group goals for the meeting.** Setting group goals lets the participants know that the group, not individuals, is expected to deliver outcomes; therefore, they will all be held accountable.

- **Demonstrate your own commitment to these goals.** Expect and evoke a high level of commitment in the group. This may require participants to mentally "clear the decks" of competing tasks or to actually clear their calendars to make time for preparation, participation, and follow-up assignments.

- **Model expressing a minority opinion.** You will legitimize questioning and critically examining what is presented in the meeting. Encouraging structured disagreements and eliciting controversy increases the opportunity to address, mediate, negotiate, and resolve conflicts during the meeting. Unresolved conflicts will survive to sabotage meeting outcomes.

- **Create effective interaction and communication.** Even in a training or informational meeting, communication cannot be all one way—just from the leader or trainer to the participants. If you don't want their active involvement, why are they here? Failure to do this provokes a response I once heard at a sales conference from a senior sales representative: "I didn't need to be at this meeting—next year just send me the videotape."

- **Acknowledge the value of each individual's contributions.** This should be done during the course of the meeting. When participants' ideas or suggestions are ignored, time is not provided to hear them, or input is discouraged, they feel that their contributions are dispensable.

TIP

Immediately after a participant offers a comment or other contribution, say "Thank you, _____." A simple but personal recognition reinforces for the entire group that *each one matters*.

- **Distribute power.** Create participation by structuring the meeting so everyone contributes, and share leadership by assigning roles such as discussion leaders, subcommittee leaders, and presenters across the group of participants.

- **Recognize all contributions.** This should be done while in the process of determining the outcomes of the meeting as well as in follow-up actions. If encouraging contributions is just *lip service* and the actual contributions are discarded or ignored, you have undermined the participatory process set forth here. Such insincerity destroys trust.

THE 30-SECOND RECAP

- An understanding of group dynamics will help you to generate successful learning or collaboration in a meeting.

- Elements of group dynamics include increased suggestibility and conformity, influence of minority opinion, reduced accountability for individual actions, and group polarization.

- The ability to create effective groups requires establishing healthy interdependence, and trust and openness.

Problem-Solving Overview

In this section, you learn the aspects of problem-solving in a meeting.

Most people think of a problem as something gone wrong, something that needs to be fixed, and such situations are often the major agenda item for a meeting. A broader meaning of the word problem, as *Merriam-Webster's Collegiate Dictionary, 10th Edition* defines it, is "a question raised for inquiry, consideration, or solution." In other words, a problem *is* a situation you want to change, but it may be an opportunity to discover a possible outcome you want to create. I will use the word problem to mean both negative and positive situations that require action.

Whether you are faced with correcting a negative situation or exploiting an unexplored opportunity in your meeting, there are several distinct phases to problem-solving:

- Problem perception and identification
- Problem ownership
- Problem analysis
- Solution criteria development
- Alternative solution generation
- Evaluation and decision-making
- Solution implementation

This approach to problem-solving, stated slightly differently by John Dewey in 1910 in *How We Think,* is known as the *standard agenda* and is based on his research on how the mind works when faced with a problem. Each of these phases will be addressed, implicitly or explicitly, as the group works through the problem.

Within this framework, however, there are many different techniques for problem-solving. There is no perfect method, no universal technique that will work equally well for all situations. Leading a group in problem-solving is a facilitation skill. Understanding group dynamics and having knowledge of a "tool kit" of problem-solving and decision-making methods will enable you to try a different approach if one is not working and help the group get "unstuck" if the process bogs down.

Techniques for group problem-solving are discussed in "Problem-Solving Tools" on page 933 and "Decision Methods and Implementation" on page 939. First, it is important to develop a good understanding of problem-solving basics.

PROBLEM PERCEPTION AND IDENTIFICATION

Human problem-solving is informed trial and error, and the first step, finding a common and accurate understanding of what the problem is, can derail your meeting.

TIP

Ask the meeting participants to state aloud their definition of the problem or opportunity on the agenda, and ask the recorder to write them down as stated, without challenging their views. This exercise allows different problem definitions to surface and be saved for future reference, preventing premature discards of ideas.

If you ask everyone present in a meeting to define a given problem—or opportunity—as they understand it, you might have as many definitions as participants. The first thing most people perceive about a problem is a symptom or result, not the problem itself.

For example, if one sales territory delivers a significantly smaller *market share* than others, the problem could be any of the following:

- Novice or poorly trained sales representative
- Entrenched competition
- Unique product specifications a competitor has chosen to meet but to which your company has not tailored its product
- Bankruptcy of a major client in that territory

If the problem is bankruptcy of a major client, retraining a sales rep isn't going to help.

PLAIN ENGLISH

Market share   One company's percentage of the total sales of a given product or industry. For example, Kellogg's has a large market share of the breakfast cereal sold in the United States.

Identifying the real problem or opportunity is critical to solving the problem or exploiting the opportunity, and misidentification is a common occurrence. When this happens, resources are wasted attacking symptoms that will recur until the cause is found.

PROBLEM OWNERSHIP

Problem ownership has two components. One, does the group buy into a common understanding of the problem and recognize it as a situation it wants to change? If the group can't admit there is a problem, or agree on what the problem is, it won't be able to come up with a solution that satisfies the group.

Two, whose problem is it? The group assembled in your meeting may have a clear understanding of the problem, but may not include those responsible for the problem. For example, the sales manager may report and understand a manufacturing flaw, but only the production manager, who may or may not be present at the meeting, can correct it.

Problems are often viewed as something negative that people wish to avoid, so none of the problem "sticks" to them. Unexploited opportunities may also be viewed negatively as an unsolicited source of more work or as a risk that could result in a failure for an individual or the group. The culture of your organization may foster problem and risk avoidance or reward those who take on problems and accept some risk as the price of innovation and success. Assess the group's comfort level as a starting point.

Your role as the facilitator is to understand the organizational culture and, within that context, create a supportive, sympathetic, and uncharged meeting environment. Your task is to legitimize problem ownership and educated risk-taking so problem-solving can occur. If people are hesitant, tense, or seem to be skirting talking about the problem, encourage open discussion by bringing up a past problem that was successfully solved by introducing your own perception of the problem as "one among many different personal perceptions we'll hear today" and by using positive, friendly body language.

CAUTION

The more urgent the problem, the more tempting it is to rush into problem analysis and solution evaluation in hopes of coming up with a quick resolution. The risks in skipping the problem identification and ownership phases are (1) addressing symptoms, not causes and (2) devising solutions to others' problems that are not able to be implemented by the group.

PROBLEM ANALYSIS

Problem analysis consists of answering the question "Why is this a problem?" by looking at all the components or contributors to a problem and identifying how they relate to one another. This analysis will only be as good as the data that supports it. If data is missing and not readily retrievable, the analysis may have to be *tabled* until a future meeting when it is available.

PLAIN ENGLISH

Table an agenda item   To postpone it to another time. This step is taken for lack of information, because a key participant is absent, or the item has become a source of irresolvable conflict. If this last case is true, the item may be better handled by a subcommittee or individual.

The basic questions in problem analysis are not unique to group problem-solving; they frame the work of journalists, detectives, scientists, and analysts in almost every kind of inquiry:

- Who?
- What?

- Where?
- When?
- Why?
- How much?
- How big?
- What additional questions need to be answered in order to see the whole problem clearly?

Ask the recorder to write these headings on a storyboard, flip chart, or computer being displayed to the group, so information that comes to light in the group discussion can be recorded under the appropriate headings and everyone can see it.

Then break down the problem into logical parts that can be addressed one at a time. For example, a problem of shipping delays could be broken down logically into ...

1. Order entry.
2. Order processing and transmittal to the warehouse.
3. Picking the order's items out of inventory.
4. Packing the order.
5. Routing and preparing the shipment (weighing, labeling, postage, and so on).
6. Shipping the order (damage *en route,* customs clearance, and so on).
7. Customer delivery.

CAUTION

In a society accustomed to "quick fixes," it is tempting to skip or rush through the problem analysis phase. Problems are increasingly complex and few exist in a vacuum. The risk is devising solutions that may be based on unexamined assumptions about the components or ramifications of the problem.

SOLUTION CRITERIA DEVELOPMENT

Before attempting to generate alternative solutions, it is helpful to establish solution criteria against which the alternatives will be evaluated. When this step is taken, individuals will compare possible solutions to the established criteria before presenting them to the group. When this step is not taken, individuals may present solutions, and then become defensive when their ideas are challenged by the group, setting up a win-lose atmosphere.

Criteria are value judgments. Setting solution criteria in advance puts objective criteria in place for the group and gives a leader a forum for articulating criteria of particular importance. Establishing objective criteria will make the group test old assumptions and assess what is different from the past. Decisions are more likely to be consistent.

One of these criteria is to avoid, as much as possible, a solution that will fall afoul of the *law of unintended consequences.*

PLAIN ENGLISH

Law of unintended consequences   Undesired and unforeseen outcomes will follow actions designed to produce a desirable result, and not all of those consequences can be avoided.

Typical criteria for evaluating alternative solutions are cost, limited resources, time to implement, and performance measures. The facilitator's role is to ensure that solution criteria are appropriate and that those affected by the problem are heard.

ALTERNATIVE SOLUTION GENERATION

Generating alternative solutions is the creative part of problem-solving. Sometimes people are eager to begin this process but they can also dread it. For example, if orders are 25 percent above production capacity, that's a good problem to have. If orders are 25 percent under budget and that dictates cutting expenses, the choices may be painful (cut research funding, lay off staff, close a plant, and so on).

Solution generation in a group can be fun and more productive than working alone, as one individual's idea generates another's and then a third person's. Proposed solutions to difficult problems are more likely to be perceived as fair and evenhanded if developed in a group where objective criteria are established.

The facilitator's role is to make sure all ideas are received equally and not dismissed prematurely, to keep the group from evaluating solution alternatives at this stage, and to help the group move forward if they get stuck. It's easy to get fixed in one point of view; as the facilitator, you can look at the problem from a different view or change an assumption in order to generate more or different ideas.

TIP

If the group's solution generation is hampered by limited knowledge or expertise in the group, it may be wise to postpone solution development until a future meeting when individuals possessing that knowledge or expertise can participate.

EVALUATION AND DECISION-MAKING

Evaluating solution alternatives is easier if you have preestablished solution criteria, but it is not a rote process. Some criteria are more important than others and have to be ranked. Some solutions may be counterintuitive and have to be reexamined. Solutions that "feel right" may not match up well against the criteria chosen. Criteria may have to be changed or abandoned.

Additionally, the decision-making process has to be one that participants accept as valid, or they will feel all their efforts have been devalued. For more details, see the section "Decision Methods and Implementation" on page 939.

SOLUTION IMPLEMENTATION

A solution is only a concept until it is put into effect. Implementation requires a plan, resources, a budget, a timetable, and monitoring both   the completion of the project and the outcome after implementation is complete. The problem isn't solved until the solution works.

Solution implementation won't happen in most problem-solving meetings because the problem exists outside of the meeting room. Being aware of the need to plan the implementation, however, and making it an action item for follow-up after the meeting is crucial.

THE 30-SECOND RECAP

- A problem is a situation you want to change, so problem-solving can be an opportunity to make something good happen as well as to fix something not working.
- There are several phases to problem-solving: perception and identification, ownership, analysis, development of solution criteria, generation of alternative solutions, evaluation and decision-making, and implementation.
- People often skip problem identification, setting solution criteria, and even analysis in their eagerness to jump to solution development. A good facilitator will keep the problem-solving phase of the meeting on track.

- No one problem-solving technique is perfect or equally applicable to all problems, and the group may have to try more than one.
- Problem-solving involves asking and answering "who, what, where, when, why, how much, how big," and any additional questions needed to see the whole problem clearly.
- Each phase of problem-solving is a problem in itself, and some problem-solving techniques can be used in more than one phase.

Problem-Solving Tools

In this section, you learn a range of techniques for group problem-solving.

No single system for problem analysis, solution development, and decision-making could possibly be all things to all problems. There are too many variable factors for a universally applicable system. There are many problem-solving techniques. This section will introduce you to the most common techniques for group problem-solving. Because each phase of problem-solving is a mini-problem in itself, several techniques can be used for more than one phase.

Before discussing a variety of techniques, here is a simple exercise to help the group focus their attention on the problem to be solved in your meeting. Frame your questions as looking at the consequences of solving, or not solving, the problem at hand.

Ask the group, "Let's assume we solve this problem. What's the best possible outcome? What's the worst possible outcome if we solve the problem? What's most likely to happen if we solve it?"

Next, ask the same questions about what will happen if the group chooses to ignore the problem or fails to solve it. "What's the best that can happen if we do not correct this problem or exploit this opportunity? The worst? The most likely outcome?"

There may be an occasion where the consequences of not solving the problem are so inconsequential the group decides not to act, and that may be the right response to the situation. Most of the time, if the problem has made it to an agenda item for a meeting, the reaction will be to see both the importance of solving the problem and that solving it has little downside. Willingness to tackle the problem is thus increased.

Scientific Method

Dewey's *standard agenda* for problem-solving, introduced in "Problem-Solving Overview" on page 926 is based on the scientific method taught in high school science class. Because it is familiar to most people schooled in western educational systems and it is a straightforward, linear approach to finding the cause of a problem and identifying actions that would cause the situation to change, the standard agenda framework is the most commonly used discussion format for group problem-solving in American businesses. Many problem-solving techniques work within this framework. Its success is dependent on the *critical reasoning* skills of group participants.

PLAIN ENGLISH

Critical reasoning   The ability to think logically and to undertake causal analysis. Because of the likelihood of multiple causes, it is also the ability to sort out principal causes from contingent causes and symptoms.

The standard agenda framework forces a thorough, information-rich, and time-consuming analysis. If adhered to by a group, it can prevent or mitigate the common tendency to race past the problem identification and analysis stage into solution development, a tendency that leads to solutions based upon untested and frequently false assumptions.

Rational Problem Identification

One technique for identifying a problem is the Is-Is Not exercise developed by C. H. Kepner and B. B. Tregoe and published in their book *The Rational Manager*. I learned this exercise in graduate school, and it has become second nature in identifying problems.

On a flip chart, storyboard, or computer screen that will project what you type so everyone in the group can see the evolving lists, make two columns captioned "Is" and "Is Not." Ask the group to offer known facts about the problem: when it occurs, under what circumstances, and what the effects are. List them in the "Is" column.

Next, ask the group to give facts that the problem is known not to entail: when it does not occur, the circumstances under which it does not occur, and what is not affected. List those in the "Is Not" column.

For example, here is such a list for a problem with malfunctioning e-mail in an organization:

Is	Is Not
Incoming and outgoing e-mail messages are delayed on Friday afternoons and occasionally at other times.	E-mail messages are always delayed.
Delays occur in sending e-mail outside the organization's system and receiving e-mail from outside the system.	All e-mails are affected.
Anyone checking e-mail has no way of knowing the system is experiencing delays.	Incoming or outgoing e-mails are lost.
E-mail is time-stamped at the time it was written, not transmitted, and received even if appearance in the addressee's received mail is delayed.	E-mail is time-stamped with the actual time the message was transmitted or appeared in the addressee's received mail.

TIP

You can help this process along by suggesting possible Is-Is Not statements for the group to identify as factual or not true. For example, if you say "No e-mail delays occurred before April 7," this statement can quickly be contradicted by participants who may have experienced delays earlier, thereby establishing the date of first incidence.

When reviewed collectively, these statements help a group to define a problem clearly using known facts instead of assumed facts.

IDEAL SOLUTION FORMAT

Developed by Carl Larson in 1969, this approach starts with characterizations of the ideal solution and works backward to discover how to achieve them. This method shares a focus on the desired outcome with *management by objective*.

PLAIN ENGLISH

Management by objective   A tool for directing a business; it is especially effective in supervising and measuring the performance of employees based upon setting targets for business activities or professional development, allocating resources to efforts that further the objectives, and assessing the degree to which they are achieved.

The ideal solution format consists of asking questions of the group in sequence:

1. Ask if participants agree on a common definition of the problem.

2. Solicit each participant's statement of the ideal solution.

3. Ask what could be changed to achieve the ideal solution.

4. Last, ask participants which of the proposed available solutions comes closest to the ideal outcome.

This approach devotes little time to problem identification and analysis, but is helpful in evaluating solutions from the different viewpoints of group participants and keeping the focus on the results desired.

CREATIVE IDEATION

Creative ideation is a fancy term for brainstorming, a simple and effective idea-generating tool. There are many elaborations on the basic concept of generating a large volume of ideas unconstrained by any evaluation of them.

The facilitator asks for ideas and encourages participants to *free-associate,* or build on the ideas others present.

PLAIN ENGLISH

Free-associate   To report the first thought that comes to mind in response to a stimulus without pausing to consider the value of the idea.

Set a time limit and a target number of ideas: "Let's see if we can get 50 ideas on the board in 10 minutes." The recorder writes down all ideas. For this approach, it's a good idea to assign two recorders in order to ensure all the ideas are captured, because they will come fast under this scenario.

Any praise, criticism, or evaluation ruins the free flow of ideas necessary for brainstorming, so the facilitator must not only refrain from any comments but must also clearly state the need for participants to avoid commenting on any ideas presented.

CAUTION

Unless everyone is heard, the process won't seem fair. Participants who like to talk or dominate a meeting may generate ideas nonstop and drown out others. Encourage those who have not spoken or appear reticent to share their ideas. If necessary, limit speakers to one idea at a time until everyone has contributed.

At the end of the exercise, ask the group to label each idea as worth keeping, a possible alternative, or "hold." This is not a formal evaluation—just a quick check to gauge the group's reaction to the ideas generated.

NOMINAL GROUP TECHNIQUE

The nominal group technique, developed by Delbecq, Van de Ven, and Gustafson in 1975 (see Appendix A), has become a popular tool for group problem-solving. It combines individual contributions with group discussion.

The steps in the nominal group technique are ...

1. The facilitator poses a question to the group, and participants individually write down their response. For example, "What are the three characteristics of this product we should mention in every advertisement?"

2. Only after they have been silently generated and written down, each participant orally states his or her written answers. The meeting recorder writes them, in the individual's own words, on the flip chart, computer display, or other mechanism chosen to be visible to all participants.

3. After all participants have contributed, the facilitator leads a discussion in order to clarify, but not critique, the ideas and arguments proposed. Duplicates are eliminated.

    While it is intentional that no criteria for evaluating ideas has been introduced until this point, this is a logical time for the facilitator or leader to propose prioritization or solution criteria before the next step.

4. Now the facilitator asks each participant to choose a limited number of the most important items from those listed. If there are 10 participants who each provided 3 characteristics in the preceding example, there may be 20 to 25 possible characteristics to choose from after duplicates are eliminated. Participants rank their choices individually and silently in order of preference, and the group then votes anonymously on the preferred choices.

5. The facilitator leads a discussion of the preliminary vote. If there are significant variances in ranking, they are explored fully to bring out any inconsistent, underlying assumptions or misinformation.

6. The facilitator has the group take a final vote using rankings or ratings.

CAUTION

Be particularly alert to unstated assumptions. Disparate or untested assumptions are most likely to occur when groups jump to solution development without having defined and analyzed the problem first and also in groups inexperienced in this type of application of critical reasoning.

This can be a time-consuming procedure for multistep problems, but is appropriate for complex ones. It is the combination of individual, anonymous voting followed by group discussion that makes this technique effective. It can be applied to problem identification, development of solution criteria, and solution development.

Force Field Analysis

This popular method of problem analysis was developed by National Training Laboratories (NTL). It consists of looking at the factors that *sustain* a problem from getting worse and at the factors that *restrain* a problem from getting better. Once these factors have been identified, the group works toward the objective of increasing the sustaining factors and decreasing the restraining ones.

For example, let's state the problem as declining enrollment in a particular training program. Sustaining factors might be a high conversion rate of inquirers to enrollees, a price advantage compared to competing programs, and referrals from graduates. Restraining factors might be a decreasing pool of candidates who've completed prerequisites for this program, a decreasing demand for the skills taught in the program, and a decrease in employers' training budgets or tuition reimbursement rates.

The analytical task for the group is to figure out which of the sustaining factors can be increased and which of the restraining factors can be decreased. The next step is to come up with alternative solutions as to how those factors can be changed in the direction you wish.

Morphological Analysis

Sometimes called the *checkerboard approach* because it utilizes a matrix, morphological analysis is a systematic way to look at two sets of variables. It works with almost any sets of intersecting variables, that is, variables that affect each other.

Let's use the example of planning a job fair. The problem is to maximize both revenue and the number of employers who exhibit. Across the top of the matrix are different price structures, and down the side of the matrix are different services to be offered to employers exhibiting at the fair (full-page ad in the program, banner on the Web site, exhibit booth with Internet hookup, table without electric outlet, and so on). Looking at the intersections where price and service packages meet, the group is forced to evaluate and alter pricing or service to attract the maximum number of exhibitors and obtain the maximum revenue.

THE 30-SECOND RECAP

- It is helpful to articulate with the group the best, worst, and most likely consequences of solving and not solving the problem.

- The standard agenda for problem-solving, based upon the scientific method, creates a framework usable with many problem-solving techniques.

- Some widely used techniques are rational problem identification, ideal solution format, creative ideation, nominal group technique, force field analysis, and morphological analysis.

Decision Methods and Implementation

In this section, you learn how to evaluate alternative solutions to an assigned problem and assess different decision-making methods in order to increase the likelihood your meeting will produce optimal decisions. You also learn about implementation tools to ensure those decisions result in action.

Your group has identified the problem and its ownership. The group has analyzed the problem using appropriate tools and developed solution criteria and alternative solutions. The next steps, evaluating alternatives, making a decision, and planning the implementation, should flow logically from the solution criteria. In group problem-solving, where process is as important as content so that all participants can live with both the process and the result, these last steps require some additional consideration and facilitation.

EVALUATION

Assessing alternative solutions against previously determined objective criteria sounds straightforward but is a little more complicated than assigning scores to each proposed solution against the criteria on which your group has agreed. Check out these additional considerations:

■ **Not all criteria are equal.** Some are more critical than others and have to be ranked in importance. You can use the checkerboard method (morphological analysis) described in "Problem-Solving Tools" on page 933 listing alternative solutions across the top and ranked criteria down the side. An alternative solution that ranks highly against most critical criteria but comes up short in even one critical criterion has to be evaluated for the impact that shortfall will have on the desired outcome.

■ **Not all alternatives "feel right."** The alternative solution that scores well against even carefully weighted criteria may be counterintuitive and not "feel right" to the group causing a reexamination of criteria and possibly requiring additional alternatives be generated.

■ **Some alternatives won't do.** There is always the possibility that no alternative solution generated by the group scores well against the preset criteria. Again, back to a reexamination of criteria and perhaps a second round of solution development.

■ **Some precedents are worth revisiting.** While as the adage has it, "Precedent is no excuse for not thinking," precedents may offer insights that suggest a newly formulated alternative solution has a high chance of success or failure.

■ **Personal criteria may cloud your vision.** Personal criteria, although minimized by the process of presetting objective solution criteria before generating alternative solutions, can surface subtly or blatantly in the evaluation process.

TIP

When personal criteria show up, such as "Solution C worked last time and I'm comfortable with it," move the focus to the characteristics of the ideal solution and the factual issues of this particular problem (such as the recurrence of the problem Solution C solved once) and away from the position of any individual.

■ **Concerns about certain solutions may not be apparent at first.** An additional tool in evaluating alternative solutions is to list the likes and dislikes each member of the group has for each solution. This helps to identify criteria and concerns that may have been unapparent to participants until after the alternative solutions were generated.

- **Some criteria may call for testing.** "Road testing" may be required by regulatory agencies, as in the development of new pharmaceutical drugs or food additives. Such testing may be desired to generate real-world outcomes but be prohibitively expensive, cumbersome, or unfeasible. Or such testing may be a step taken before a decision will be made, as when a direct mail marketer mails the same offer to a sample list of prospective clients at three different prices to see which generates the most orders.

- **Not all alternatives are equal.** Before the group moves on to decision-making, you may want to rank the alternative solutions in the order the group prefers them.

CAUTION

If you ask the group to vote on their preferred alternative solutions, be clear that this vote is for ranking purposes only and does not constitute a decision.

In evaluating alternative solutions, it is important that the voice of each participant be heard, so the trust of the group is not violated. With that trust intact and the idea generation and evaluation completed, the group can move on to decision-making.

DECISION-MAKING

The most common decision-making methods are executive decision, minority control, democratic participation, parliamentary procedure, and consensus-building.

EITHER/OR VS. COLLABORATION

The great divide that differentiates group decision-making methods is whether or not participants feel they were able to *collaborate* on the decision made.

PLAIN ENGLISH

Collaborate   To labor together, particularly on an intellectual endeavor, with others who may have different insights or even opposing points of view, to arrive at a common goal.

The point has been made throughout this guide that a successful meeting is not only one in which the objectives of the meeting are met but one in which all participants rank the process as effective. Let's examine different decision-making methods for their capacity to deliver decisions on which participants truly agree not just "throw in the towel" to arrive at a decision.

LOSE-LOSE METHODS

Some decision-making methods create no winners: Everybody loses. Riots and labor actions, such as work slowdowns, "sick-outs," and strikes are obvious "lose-lose" methods of pressing for change, but they are not likely to occur in the context of a meeting.

The decision-by-default method of decision-making is a lose-lose method that can occur when a group fails to make a decision. Often, inaction leads to not just the continuation of the problem but to a worsening of the situation. For example, if a new product development team cannot decide on a course of action to speed an eagerly anticipated product to market ahead of a competitor, the competitor may not only launch its product first but capture enough market share to create a much higher barrier to entry to that market: The problem is "solved" by default because the opportunity is gone.

WIN-LOSE METHODS

Many long-used, decision-making methods divide a group into winners, those whose preferred solution was adopted, and losers, those whose preferred solution was abandoned. This is an undesirable outcome because losers will often resist providing assistance or even cooperation in implementing the "opposition's" solution.

Executive decision is a predominant method of decision-making. If the group's mandate is to come up with alternative solutions and recommend action to an executive who will make the actual decision, the group does not have control over the decision-making process. The executive decision or authoritarian method is common in hierarchical organizations in western societies. The group assigned to problem-solving in a meeting may be able to develop alternative solutions and evaluate them collaboratively, and then pass a recommended course of action on to the executive with decision-making authority. Depending on the organizational culture, the group may be satisfied with this level of influence on the ultimate decision or may still resent its exclusion from the actual decision-making. Individual decisions are often fast but have a higher risk of being wrong than group decisions.

Another authoritarian method is minority control, such as in a family-owned business or in any group where a minority of dominant individuals can persuade or force others. The issues are the same as with the executive decision.

As discussed earlier in this section, voting is a way to take a reading on a group's preferred solutions but is not the most effective decision-making method. Voting produces a majority of winners and a minority of losers. The losers obviously do not agree on the decision made. Majority rule does, outside of parliamentary procedure, involve participatory democracy in all phases of problem-solving, making it more effective than executive decision.

CAUTION

Majority rule also promotes either/or decisions rather than promoting the crafting of a hybrid solution that includes the best parts of several alternatives.

Voting leaves group participants feeling the decision process was "us vs. them," and the losers may have difficulty supporting the majority decision.

Parliamentary procedure, as described in *Robert's Rules of Order,* is common in boards of directors of all types as well as government entities and *horizontal organizations* and is another win-lose method of arriving at decisions.

PLAIN ENGLISH

Horizontal organizations   Also called flat organizations, those organizations with equally shared responsibilities rather than a hierarchy in which most power is concentrated in a few individuals at the top.

Debate is the only discussion permitted in parliamentary procedure, which calls for no analysis of problems but only for the proposal of solutions stated as resolutions for the group to debate and vote on.

Negotiation may appear to be a decision-making method that delivers a solution everyone in a group can live with, but it is bargaining between opposing camps with polarized positions. The result is that neither side gets everything they want, and the atmosphere is not collaborative but oppositional: How little do we have to give to get what we want, to "win"?

WIN-WIN METHODS

Win-win methods are those in which all parties to a decision agree to work together until they find a solution no one has major objections to. All win-win decision methods are based on consensus-building, not compromise. The "us vs. them" or "either/or" mentality is avoided from the beginning of the process. The facilitator who is able to prevent polarization of positions during the problem identification, analysis, and development of solution criteria and alternative solutions will have created an environment in which decision-making, if the group has the authority to make the decision, will also be collaborative.

Sometimes a different group is charged with making the decision among alternative solutions generated and evaluated by an earlier group. If your group is the decision-making group in this situation, you, as the facilitator, may have to establish consensus-building as a method.

 TIP

If your solution-generating group is turning over recommendations to a group charged with making the decision, tell the decision-making group about previous problem-solving steps utilizing consensus-building to reinforce the desirability and successful outcome of collaboration.

To generate consensus-building, a group has to be genuinely collaborative in order to prevent the process from turning into minority control or bargaining. Genuine collaboration occurs naturally in groups that have a history of successful collaboration on projects and problem-solving and an organizational culture that values and supports collaboration. Japanese business is the model for the consensus-building method of decision-making.

As a facilitator or leader, you can foster collaboration in these ways:

■ Announce to the group the decision will be by consensus, and define it as "unanimous agreement on a course of action that all participants can support." Point out that consensus is not coercion or compromise of critical values.

■ Give examples of previous successful decisions made by consensus to which the group can relate.

■ Express your enthusiasm that this group can reach consensus.

■ Set clear rules:

   1. Limit time for the decision to be made.

   2. Stress that no participant should yield to a position that is not objective and logical.

   3. Look for the next most acceptable alternative or combination of alternatives if discussion reaches a stalemate. You are looking for synthesis and integration.

■ Understand that consensus-building is a time-consuming process because the Japanese model includes consulting with all individuals affected by a decision. In group decision-making, the best case may be that affected individuals are all represented in your meeting.

- Know that reasonable people differ. Allow for full discussion of disagreements. The quality of the group's decision will be higher if different views and information are fully examined rather than discounted.

- Use language that supports convergent, not divergent thinking: "If someone loses, everyone loses," "Everyone has a part of the truth," or "Everyone has to be able to sleep at night after this decision."

All these steps will reinforce genuine collaboration toward consensus-building.

SOLUTION IMPLEMENTATION TOOLS

Planning for solution implementation may be a part of the work assigned to your problem-solving meeting. It may call for a separate, subsequent meeting of your group. Frequently, problem-solving is divided among several groups, and the group responsible for solution implementation may not be the group that made the decision or developed and evaluated alternative solutions.

There are several implementation tools to help your group deal with implementation alternatives and complex, multistep solutions.

CAUTION

Don't assume the solution implementation team is predisposed to love the decision it has to implement. If your group is the one charged solely with solution implementation, you may have to get buy-in from this group and establish collaborative consensus building from scratch.

EXAMINING COMPETING IMPLEMENTATION ALTERNATIVES

There may be more than one path to successful implementation of the chosen solution, which means implementation can include developing and evaluating alternative scenarios: more problem-solving! Here you are comparing competing ways of implementing a decision. Posting the competing implementation mechanisms and listing their advantages and disadvantages was formally suggested by Norman R. F. Maier. For example, let's imagine the solution decided on after a summer of brownouts that caused a manufacturing plant to lose several days of production was to increase the amount of power available to the plant (discarded solutions could have been moving the plant or reducing energy consumption). Posting using Maier's listing method would look like this:

Implementation Alternatives to Increase Power for Manufacturer

Sign a long contract with a backup provider.	Buy a generator.
Advantages	*Advantages*
Lower overall cost next year	High certainty of power
No initial outlay	Future costs are known
No investment in expertise	
Disadvantages	*Disadvantages*
No price protection on contract expiration	Initial outlay of money
Dependent on outside vendor	Need to hire expertise

Because the group has to list advantages and disadvantages for both alternatives, this tool provides a way to manage the discussion of competing ideas in an objective way.

CHARTING IMPLEMENTATION PLANS

Implementing complex solutions is multitasking on a grand scale. To do it effectively, your group needs a master plan. The most popular implementation planning tools are variations of PERT (Performance Evaluation and Review Technique), credited to G. M. Phillips. PERT attempts to capture all critical steps and their interdependence in an implementation. It starts with the desired outcome, whether it's a finished product or a marketing campaign, and works backward through each step or process required to reach that outcome.

Here are the basic steps in PERT:

1. List all events that must occur.
2. Chronologically order them in a diagram.
3. Determine which events are simultaneous, which are serial, and how events are interdependent.
4. List what has to occur between each pair of events.
5. Estimate the best, worst, and most likely times needed to complete each of these intermediate events.

6. Calculate expected completion times for each activity as well as the whole project.

7. Assess completion times for feasibility.

8. Specify and allocate resources to support the critical path of these events.

PLAIN ENGLISH

Critical path   The plan to undertake a group of specific steps in specific time frames to reach a desired outcome. It is the educated "best guess" of the successful route through a complex project.

The more complex the project, the greater the need for some adaptation of this planning tool to ensure that implementation occurs. Such close attention to the project, including evaluating intermediate deliverables (benchmarking), helps the implementation team keep on top of budget, performance, and deadline issues.

THE 30-SECOND RECAP

- Process is as important as content in determining the success of a meeting; so evaluation, decision-making, and implementation require careful facilitation.

- Scoring alternative solutions against previously determined criteria is insufficient. Unequal criteria need to be ranked; favorite solutions may score poorly, and participants may not support high-scoring solutions. Criteria and assumptions may have to be reexamined and additional alternatives developed.

- The most-used decision-making methods—executive decision, minority control, and voting—are win-lose methods that polarize a group and preclude unanimous agreement. Parliamentary procedure and negotiation are also win-lose methods.

- Win-win decision-making methods all generate consensus building through genuine collaboration.

- Solution implementation is project management and requires planning of every event and the interdependence of those events.

Project
Management

So You're Going to Manage a Project?

In this section, you learn what a project is, essential skills for project managers, and what it takes to be a good project manager.

THE ELEMENTS OF A PROJECT

What exactly is a project? You hear the word used all the time at work, as well as at home. People say, "I am going to add a deck in the backyard. It will be a real project." Or "Our team's project is to determine consumer preferences in our industry through the year 2010." Or "I have a little project I would like you to tackle. I think that you can be finished by this afternoon."

TIP

When you boil it all down, projects can be viewed as having four essential elements: a specific timeframe, an orchestrated approach to co-dependent events, a desired outcome, and unique characteristics.

SPECIFIC TIMEFRAME

Projects are temporary undertakings. In this regard, they are different from ongoing programs that obviously had a beginning, but may not have a desired end, at least for the foreseeable future. Projects can last years or even decades, as in the case of public works programs, feeding the world's hungry, or sending space crafts to other galaxies. But most of the projects that you face in the workaday world will be somewhere in the range of hours to weeks, or possibly months, but usually not years or decades. (Moreover, the scope of this book will be limited to projects of short duration, say six months at the most, but usually shorter than that.)

A project begins when some person or group in authority authorizes its beginning. The initiating party has the authority, the budget, and the resources to enable the project to come to fruition, or as Captain Jean-Luc Picard of the *Starship Enterprise* often said, "Make it so." By definition, every project initiated is engaged for a precise period, although those charged with achieving the project's goals often feel as if the project were going on forever. When project goals are completed (the subject of following discussion), a project ends and, invariably, something else takes its place.

Tip

Much of the effort of the people on a project, and certainly the use of resources, including funds, are directed toward ensuring that the project is designed to achieve the desired outcome and be completed as scheduled in an appropriate manner.

Along the way toward completion or realization of a desired outcome, the project may have interim due dates in which "deliverables" must be completed. *Deliverables* can take the form of a report, a provision of service, a prototype, an actual product, a new procedure, or any one of a number of other forms. Each deliverable and each interim goal achieved helps to ensure that the overall project will be finished on time and on budget.

Plain English

Deliverables   Something of value generated by a project management team as scheduled, to be offered to an authorizing party, reviewing committee, client constituent, or other concerned party, often taking the form of a plan, report, prescript procedure, product, or service.

AN ORCHESTRATED APPROACH TO CO-DEPENDENT EVENTS

Projects involve a series of related *events*. One event leads to another. Sometimes multiple events are contingent upon other multiple events overlapping in intricate patterns. Indeed, if projects did not involve multiple events, they would not be projects. They would be single *tasks* or a series of single tasks that are laid out in some sequential pattern.

Plain English

Task or **event**   A divisible, definable unit of work related to a project, which may or may not include subtasks.

Projects are more involved; some may be so complex that the only way to understand the pattern of interrelated events is to depict them on a chart, or use specially developed project management software. Such tools enable the *project manager* to see which tasks need to be executed concurrently, vs. sequentially, and so on.

Plain English

Project manager   An individual who has the responsibility for overseeing all aspects of the day-to-day activities in pursuit of a project goal, including coordinating staff, allocating resources, managing the budget, and coordinating overall efforts to achieve a specific desired result.

Caution

Coordination of events for some projects is so crucial that if one single event is not executed as scheduled, the entire project could be at risk!

Effective project management requires the ability to view the project at hand with a *holistic* perspective. By seeing the various interrelated project events and activities as part of an overall system, the project manager and project team have a better chance of approaching the project in a coordinated fashion, supporting each other at critical junctures, recognizing where bottlenecks and dead ends may occur, and staying focused as a team to ensure effective completion of the project.

Plain English

Holistic   The organic or functional relations between the part and the whole.

A DESIRED OUTCOME

At the end of each project is the realization of some specific goal or objective. It is not enough to assign a project to someone and say, "See what you can do with this." Nebulous objectives will more than likely lead to a nebulous outcome. A specific objective increases the chances of leading to a specific outcome.

Plain English

Objective   A desired outcome; something worth striving for; the overarching goal of a project; the reason the project was initiated to begin with.

While there may be one major, clear, desired project objective, in pursuit of it there may be interim project objectives. The objectives of a project management team for a food processing company, for example, might be to improve the quality and taste of the company's macaroni dish. Along the way, the team might conduct taste samples, survey consumers, research competitors, and so on. Completion of each of these events can be regarded as an interim objective toward completion of the overall objective.

In many instances, project teams are charged with achieving a series of increasingly lofty objectives in pursuit of the final, ultimate objective. Indeed, in many cases, teams can only proceed in a stair-step fashion to achieve the desired outcome. If they were to proceed in any other manner, they may not be able to develop the skills or insights along the way that will enable them to progress in a productive manner. And just as major league baseball teams start out in spring training by doing calisthenics, warm-up exercises, and reviewing the fundamentals of the game, such as base-running, fielding, throwing, bunting, and so on, so, too, are project teams charged with meeting a series of interim objectives and realizing a series of interim outcomes in order to hone their skills and capabilities.

The interim objectives and interim outcomes go by many names. Some people call them goals, some call them *milestones,* some call them phases, some call them tasks, some call them subtasks. Regardless of the terminology used, the intent is the same: to achieve a desired objective on time and on budget.

Plain English

Milestone   A significant event or juncture in the project.

Time and money are inherent constraints in the pursuit of any project. If the *timeline* is not specific—the project can be completed any old time—then it is not a project. It might be a wish, it might be a desire, it might be an aim, it might be a long-held notion, but it is not a project. By assigning a specific timeframe to a project, project team members can mentally acclimate themselves to the rigors inherent in operating under said constrictions.

Plain English

Timeline   The scheduled start and stop times for a subtask, task, phase, or entire project.

Caution

Projects are often completed beyond the timeframe initially allotted. Nevertheless, setting the timeframe is important. If it had not been set, the odds of the project being completed anywhere near the originally earmarked period would be far less.

Although the budget for a project is usually imposed upon a project manager by someone in authority, or by the project manager himself—as with the timeframe constraint—a budget serves as a highly useful and necessary constraint of another nature. It would be nice to have deep pockets for every project that you engage in, but the reality for most organizations and most people is that budgetary limits must be set. And it is just as well.

Tip

Budgetary limits help ensure efficiency. If you know that you only have so many dollars to spend, you spend those dollars more judiciously than you would if you had double or triple that amount.

The great architect Frank Lloyd Wright once said, "Man built most nobly when limitations were at their greatest." Since each architectural achievement is nothing more than a complex project, Wright's observation is as applicable for day-to-day projects routinely faced by managers as it is for a complex multinational undertaking.

UNIQUE CHARACTERISTICS

If you have been assigned a multipart project, the likes of which you have never undertaken before, independent of your background and experience, that project is an original, unique undertaking for you. Yet, even if you have just completed something of a similar nature the month before, the new assignment would still represent an original project, with its own set of challenges. Why? Because as time passes, society changes, technology changes, and your workplace changes.

Suppose you are asked to manage the orientation project for your company's new class of recruits. There are 10 of them, and they will be with you for a 3-week period, just like the group before them. The company's orientation materials have been developed for a long time, they are excellent, and, by and large, they work.

You have excellent facilities and budget, and though limited, they have proven to be adequate, and you are up for the task. Nevertheless, this project is going to be unique, because you haven't encountered these 10 people before. Their backgrounds and experiences, the way that they interact with one another and with you, and a host of other factors ensure that challenges will arise during this three-week project, some of which will represent unprecedented challenges.

Plain English

Project   The allocation of resources over a specific timeframe and the coordination of interrelated events to accomplish an overall objective while meeting both predictable and unique challenges.

PROJECT PLANNING

All effectively managed projects involve the preparation of the project plan. This is the fundamental document that spells out what is to be achieved, how it is to be achieved, and what resources will be necessary. In *Projects and Trends in the 1990s and the 21st Century,* author Jolyon Hallows says, "The basic project document is the project plan. The project lives and breathes and changes as the project progresses or fails." The basic components of the project, according to Hallows, are laid out in the following figure.

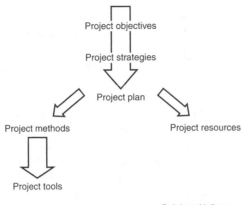

© Jolyon Hallows

Basic project components.

"With the plan as a road map, telling us how to get from one point to another," says Hallows, "a good project manager recognizes from the outset that a project plan is far more than an academic exercise or tool for appeasing upper management. It is the blueprint for the entire *scope of the project,* a vital document which is referred to frequently, often updated on-the-fly, and something without which the project manager cannot proceed."

Plain English

Scope of the project or **scope of work**   The level of activity and effort necessary to complete a project and achieve the desired outcome as measured by staff hours, staff days, resources consumed, and funds spent.

Prior to laying out the project plan (the subject of the section "Laying Out Your Plan" on page 975), the manager starts with a rough pre-plan—this could take the form of an outline, a proposal, a feasibility study, or simply a memorandum. The preplan triggers the project.

From there, a more detailed project plan is drawn up that includes the delegation of tasks among project team members, the identification of interim objectives, which may also be called goals, milestones, or tasks, all laid out in sequence for all concerned with the project to see.

Once the plan commences and the project team members, as well as the project manager, begin to realize what they are really up against, the project plan is invariably modified. Hallows says that "all plans are guesses to some extent. Good plans are good guess, bad plans are bad guesses." No plans are analogous to horrible guesses.

Tip

Any plan is better than no plan, since no plan doesn't lead any-where.

IMPLEMENTATION

Following the preparation of a formal project plan, project execution or implementation ensues. This is where the excitement begins. If drawing up the project plan was a somewhat dry process, implementing it is anything but. Here, for the first time, you put your plan into action. You consult the plan as if it were your trail map, assigning this task to person A, this task to person B, and so on. What was once only on paper or on disc now corresponds to action in the real world. People are doing things as a result of your plan.

If your team is charged with developing a new software product, some members begin by examining the code of previous programs, while others engage in market research, while still others contemplate the nature of computing two years out.

If your team is charged with putting up a new building, some begin by surveying the area, others by marking out the ground, some by mixing cement and laying foundation, others by erecting scaffolding, while yet others may be redirecting traffic.

If your project involves successfully training your company's sales division on how to use a new type of handheld computer, initial implementation activities may involve scheduling the training sessions, developing the lesson plans, finding corollaries between the old procedures and the new, testing the equipment, and so on.

Tip

Regardless of what type of project is at hand, the implementation phase is a period of high energy and excitement as team members begin to realize that the change is actually going to happen and that what they are doing will make a difference.

CONTROL

From implementation on, the project manager's primary task becomes that of monitoring progress. Because this is covered extensively in the following sections, suffice it to say here that the effective project manager continually examines what has been accomplished to date; how that jibes with the project plan; what modifications, if any, need to be made to the project plan; and what needs to be done next. He or she also needs to consider what obstacles and roadblocks may be further along the path, the morale and motivation of his or her staff, and how much of the budget has been expended, vs. how much remains.

Caution

Monitoring progress often becomes the full time obsession of the project manager intent on bringing the project in on time and on budget. In doing so, however, some managers lose the personal touch with team members.

Steadfastness in monitoring the project is but one of the many traits necessary to be successful in project management, and that is the subject of our exploration in "What Makes a Good Project Manager?" on page 958.

POSSIBLE PROJECT PLAYERS

The following are the types of participants you may encounter in the course of a project:

- **Authorizing Party.** Initiates the project. (Often called a sponsor, an unfortunate term, since after initiation, many "sponsors" offer very little sponsorship).

- **Stakeholder.** Typically someone like a senior manager, business developer, client, or other involved party. There may be many stakeholders on a project.

- **Work Manager.** Responsible for planning activities within projects and servicing requests.

- **Administrative Manager.** Tends to the staff by assuring that standard activities, such as training, vacation and other planned activities are in the schedules.

- **Project Manager.** Initiates, then scopes and plans the work and resources.

- **Team Member.** A staff member who performs the work to be managed.

- **Software Guru.** Helps install, run, and apply software.

- **Project Director.** Supervises one or more project managers.

THE 30-SECOND RECAP

- A project is a unique undertaking to achieve a specific objective and desired outcome by coordinating events and activities within a specific timeframe.

- The project plan is the fundamental document directing all activities in pursuit of the desired objective. The plan may change as time passes, but nevertheless, it represents the project manager's continuing view on what needs to be done by whom and when.

- Planning leads to implementation, and implementation requires control. The effective project manager constantly monitors progress for the duration of the project. For many, it becomes a near obsession.

What Makes a Good Project Manager?

In this section, you will learn the traits of successful project managers, the reasons that project managers succeed, and the reasons that they fail.

A DOER, NOT A BYSTANDER

If you are assigned the task of project manager within your organization, consider this: You were probably selected because you exhibited the potential to be an effective project manager. (Or conversely, there was no one else around, so you inherited the task!) In essence, a project manager is an active doer, not a passive bystander. As you learned in the section "So You're Going to Manage a Project?" on page 950, a big portion of the project manager's responsibility is planning—mapping out how a project will be undertaken; anticipating obstacles and roadblocks; making course adjustments; and continually determining how to allocate human, technological, or monetary resources.

If you have a staff, from 1 person to 10 or more, then in addition to daily supervision of the work being performed, you are probably going to be involved in some type of training. The training might be once, periodic, or nonstop. As the project progresses, you find yourself having to be a motivator, a cheerleader, possibly a disciplinarian, an empathetic listener, and a sounding board. As you guessed, not everyone is qualified to (or wants to) serve in such capacity. On top of these responsibilities, you may be the key contact point for a variety of vendors, suppliers, *subcontractors,* and supplemental teams within your own organization.

Caution

Whether you work for a multibillion-dollar organization or a small business, chances are you don't have all the administrative support you would like to have. In addition to these tasks, too many project managers today also must engage in a variety of administrative duties, such as making copies, printouts, or phone calls on mundane matters.

If your staff lets you down or is cut back at any time during the project (and this is almost inevitable), you end up doing some of the tasks that you had assigned to others on top of planning, implementing, and controlling the project.

Plain English

Subcontract   An agreement with an outside vendor for specific services, often to alleviate a project management team of a specific task, tasks, or an entire project.

MANY HATS ALL THE TIME

The common denominator among all successful project managers everywhere is the ability to develop a "whatever it takes" attitude. Suppose that ...

- Several of your project team members get pulled off the project to work for someone else in your organization. You will make do.
- You learn that an essential piece of equipment that was promised to you is two weeks late. You will improvise.
- You discover that several key assumptions you made during the project planning and early implementation phases turned out to be wildly off the mark. You will adjust.
- One third of the way into the project, a mini-crisis develops in your domestic life. You will get by.

Caution

Chances are that you're going to be wearing many hats, several of which you cannot anticipate at the start of a project.

Although the role and responsibility of a project manager may vary somewhat from project to project and from organization to organization, you may be called upon to perform one of these recurring duties and responsibilities:

- Draw up the project plan, possibly present and "sell" the project to those in authority.
- Interact with top management, line managers, project team members, supporting staff, and administrative staff.
- Procure project resources, allocate them to project staff, coordinate their use, ensure that they are being maintained in good working order, and surrender them upon project completion.
- Interact with outside vendors, clients, and other project managers and project staff within your organization.
- Initiate project implementation, continually monitor progress, review interim objectives or milestones, make course adjustments, view and review budgets, and continually monitor all project resources.
- Supervise project team members, manage the project team, delegate tasks, review execution of tasks, provide feedback, and delegate new tasks.
- Identify opportunities, identify problems, devise appropriate adjustments, and stay focused on the desired outcome.
- Handle interteam strife, minimize conflicts, resolve differences, instill a team atmosphere, and continually motivate team members to achieve superior performance.
- Prepare interim presentations for top management, offer a convincing presentation, receive input and incorporate it, review results with project staff, and make still more course adjustments.
- Make the tough calls, such as having to remove project team members, ask project team members to work longer hours on short notice, reassign roles and responsibilities to the disappointment of some, discipline team members as may be necessary, and resolve personality-related issues affecting the team.
- Consult with advisors, mentors, and coaches, examine the results of previous projects, draw upon previously unidentified or underused resources, and remain as balanced and objective as possible.

PRINCIPLES TO STEER YOU

In his book *Managing Projects in Organizations,* J. D. Frame identifies five basic principles that, if followed, will "help project professionals immeasurably in their efforts."

Be Conscious of What You Are Doing

Don't be an accidental project manager. Seat-of-the-pants efforts may work when you are undertaking a short-term task, particularly something you are doing alone. However, for longer-term tasks that involve working with others and with a budget, being an accidental manager will get you into trouble.

Remember that a project, by definition, is something that has a unique aspect to it. Even if you are building your fifteenth chicken coop in a row, the grading of the land or composition of the soil might be different from that of the first 14. As Frame points out, many projects are hard enough to manage even when you know what you are doing. They are nearly impossible to manage by happenstance. Thus, it behooves you to draw up an effective project plan and use it as an active, vital document.

Invest Heavily in the Front-End Spade Work

Get it right the first time. How many times do you buy a new technology item, bring it to your office or bring it home, and start pushing the buttons without reading the instructions? If you are honest, the answer is all too often.

Caution

Jumping in too quickly in project management is going to get you into big trouble in a hurry.

Particularly if you are the type of person who likes to leap before you look, as project manager you need to understand and recognize the value of slowing down, getting your facts in order, and then proceeding. Frame says, "By definition, projects are unique, goal-oriented systems; consequently, they are complex. Because they are complex, they cannot be managed effectively in an offhand and ad-hoc fashion. They must be carefully selected and carefully planned." Most important, he says, "A good deal of thought must be directed at determining how they should be structured. Care taken at the outset of a project to do things right will generally pay for itself handsomely."

Caution

For many project managers, particularly first-time project managers, investing in front-end spadework represents a personal dilemma—the more time spent up front, the less likely they are to feel that they're actually managing the project.

Too many professionals today, reeling from the effects of our information-overloaded society, feeling frazzled by all that competes for their time and attention, want to dive right into projects much the same way they dive into many of their daily activities and short-term tasks. What works well for daily activity or short-term tasks can prove disastrous when others are counting on you, there is a budget involved, top management is watching, and any falls you make along the way will be quite visible.

ANTICIPATE THE PROBLEMS THAT WILL INEVITABLY ARISE

The tighter your budget and timeframes, or the more intricate the involvement of the project team, the greater the probability that problems will ensue. While the uniqueness of your project may foreshadow the emergence of unforeseen problems, inevitably many of the problems that you will experience are somewhat predictable. These include, but are not limited to the following:

- Missing interim milestones
- Having resources withdrawn midstream
- Having one or more project team members who are not up to the tasks assigned
- Having the project objective(s) altered midstream
- Falling behind schedule
- Finding yourself over budget
- Learning about a hidden project agenda halfway into the project
- Losing steam, motivation, or momentum

Frame says that by reviewing these inevitable realities and anticipating their emergence, you are in a far better position to deal with them once they occur. Moreover, as you become increasingly adept as a project manager, you might even learn to use such situations to your advantage. (More on this in "Learning from Your Experience" on page 1063.)

GO BENEATH SURFACE ILLUSIONS

Dig deeply to find the facts in situations. Frame says, "Project managers are continually getting into trouble because they accept things at face value. If your project involves something that requires direct interaction with your company's clients, and you erroneously believe that you know exactly what the clients want, you may be headed for major problems."

Caution

All too often, the client says one thing but really means another and offers you a rude awakening by saying, "We didn't ask for this, and we can't use it."

One effective technique used by project managers to find the real situation in regard to others upon whom the project outcome depends is as follows:

- Identify all participants involved in the project, even those with tangential involvement.
- List the possible goals that each set of participants could have in relation to the completion of the project.
- Now, list all possible subagendas, hidden goals, and unstated aspirations.
- Determine the strengths and weaknesses of your project plan and your project team in relation to the goals and hidden agendas of all other parties to the project.

In this manner, you are less likely both to encounter surprises and to find yourself scrambling to recover from unexpected jolts.

My friend Peter Hicks, who is a real-estate developer from Massachusetts, says that when he engages in a project with another party, one of the most crucial exercises he undertakes is a complete mental walk-through of everything that the party …

- Wants to achieve as a result of this project.
- Regards as an extreme benefit.
- May have as a hidden agenda.
- Can do to let him down.

The last item is particularly telling. Peter finds that by sketching out all the ways that the other party may not fulfill his obligations, he is in a far better position to proceed, should any of them come true. In essence, he takes one hundred percent of the responsibility for ensuring that the project outcomes that he desired will be achieved. To be sure, this represents more work, perhaps 50 percent or more of what most project managers are willing to undertake.

You have to ask yourself the crucial question: If you are in project management and you aim to succeed, are you willing to adopt the whatever-it-takes mindset? By this, I don't mean that you engage in illegal, immoral, or socially reprehensible behavior. Rather, it means a complete willingness to embrace the reality of the situation confronting you, going as deeply below the surface as you can to ferret out the true dynamics of the situation before you, and marshaling the resources necessary to be successful.

BE AS FLEXIBLE AS POSSIBLE

Don't get sucked into unnecessary rigidity and formality. This principle of effective project management can be seen as one that is counterbalanced to the four discussed thus far. Once a project begins, an effective project manager wants to maintain a firm hand while having the ability to roll with the punches. You have heard the old axiom about the willow tree being able to withstand hurricane gusts exceeding 100 miles per hour, while the branches of the more rigid spruce and oak trees surrounding it snap in half.

Tip

The ability to "bend, but not break" has been the hallmark of the effective manager and project manager in all of business and industry, government and institution, education, healthcare, and service industries.

In establishing a highly detailed project plan that creates a situation where practically nothing is left to fortune, one can end up creating a nightmarish, highly constrictive bureaucracy. We have seen this happen all too frequently at various levels of government. Agencies empowered to serve its citizenry end up being only marginally effective, in servitude to the web of bureaucratic entanglement and red tape that has grown, obscuring the view of those entrusted to serve.

Increasingly, in our high-tech age of instantaneous information and communication, where intangible project elements outnumber the tangible by a hearty margin, the wise project manager knows the value of staying flexible, constantly gathering valuable feedback, and responding accordingly.

SEVEN WAYS TO SUCCEED AS A PROJECT MANAGER

Now that you have a firm understanding of the kinds of issues that befall a project manager, let's take a look at seven ways in particular that project managers can succeed, followed by seven ways that project managers can fail.

- **Learn to use project management tools effectively.** As you will see in the sections "Choosing Project Management Software" on page 1033 and "A Sampling of Popular Programs" on page 1042, such a variety of wondrous project managing software tools exist today that it is foolhardy to proceed in a project of any type of complexity without having a rudimentary understanding of available software tools, if not an intermediate to advanced understanding of them. Project management tools today can be of such enormous aid that they can mean the difference between a project succeeding or failing.

■ **Be able to give and receive criticism.** Giving criticism effectively is not easy. There is a fine line between upsetting a team member's day and offering constructive feedback that will help the team member and help the project. Likewise, the ability to receive criticism is crucial for project managers.

Tip

As the old saying goes, it is easy to avoid criticism: Say nothing, do nothing, and be nothing. If you are going to move mountains, you are going to have to accept a little flack.

■ **Be receptive to new procedures.** You don't know everything, and thank goodness. Team members, other project managers, and those who authorize the project to begin with can provide valuable input, including new directions and new procedures. Be open to them, because you just might find a way to slash $20,000 and three months off your project cost.

■ **Manage your time well.** Speaking of time, if you personally are not organized, dawdle on low-level issues, and find yourself perpetually racing the clock, how are you going to manage your project, a project team, and achieve the desired outcome on time and on budget? My earlier book, *The 10 Minute Guide to Time Management,* will help you enormously in this area.

■ **Be effective at conducting meetings.** Meetings are a necessary evil in the event of completing projects, with the exception of solo projects. A good short text on this topic is *Breakthrough Business Meetings* by Robert Levasseur. This book covers the fundamentals of meetings in a succinct, enjoyable manner, and can make any project manager an effective meeting manager in relatively short order.

■ **Hone your decision-making skills.** As a project manager, you won't have the luxury of sitting on the fence for very long in relation to issues crucial to the success of your project. Moreover, your staff looks to you for yes, no, left, and right decisions. If you waffle here and there, you are giving the signal that you are not really in control. As with other things in project management, decision-making is a skill that can be learned. However, the chances are high that you already have the decision-making capability you need. It is why you were chosen to manage this project to begin with. It is also why you have been able to achieve what you have in your career up to this point.

Tip

Trusting yourself is a vital component to effective project management.

■ **Maintain a sense of humor.** Stuff is going to go wrong, things are going to happen out of the blue, the weird and the wonderful are going to pass your way. You have to maintain a sense of humor so that you don't do damage to your health, to your team, to your organization, and to the project itself. Sometimes, not always, the best response to a breakdown is to simply let out a good laugh. Take a walk, stretch, renew yourself, and then come back and figure out what you are going to do next. Colin Powell, in his book *My American Journey,* remarked that in almost all circumstances, "things will look better in the morning."

SEVEN WAYS TO FAIL AS A PROJECT MANAGER

Actually, there are hundreds and hundreds of ways to fail as a project manager. The following seven represent those that I have seen too often in the workplace:

■ **Fail to address issues immediately.** Two members of your project team can't stand each other and cooperation is vital to the success of the project. As project manager, you must address the issue head on. Either find a way that they can work together professionally, if not amicably, or modify roles and assignments. Whatever you do, don't let the issue linger. It will only come back to haunt you further along.

■ **Reschedule too often.** As the project develops, you can certainly change due dates, assignments, and schedules. Recognize, though, that there is a cost every time you make a change, and if you ask your troops to keep up with too many changes you are inviting mistakes, missed deadlines, confusion, and possibly hidden resentment.

■ **Be content with reaching milestones on time, but ignore quality.** Too often, project managers in the heat of battle, focused on completing the project on time and within budget, don't focus sufficiently on the quality of work done.

Caution

A series of milestones that you reach with less than desired quality work adds up to a project that misses the mark.

■ **Too much focus on project administration and not enough on project management.** In this high-tech era with all manner of sophisticated project management software, it is too easy to fall in love with project administration—making sure that equipment arrives, money is allocated, and assignments are doled out to the neglect of project management, taking in the big picture of what the team is up against, where they are heading, and what they are trying to accomplish.

■ **Micromanage rather than manage.** This is reflected in the project manager who plays his cards close to his chest, and retains most of the tasks himself, or at least the ones he deems to be crucial, rather than delegating. The fact that you have staff implies that there are many tasks and responsibilities that you should not be handling. On the other hand, if you should decide to handle it all, be prepared to stay every night until 10:30, give up your weekends, and generally be in need of a life.

Caution

Micromanaging isn't pretty. The most able managers know when to share responsibilities with others and to keep focused on the big picture.

■ **Adapt new tools too readily.** If you are managing a project for the first time and counting on a tool that you have not used before, you are incurring a double risk. Here's how it works. Managing a project for the first time is a single risk. Using a project tool for the first time is a single risk. Both levels of *risk* are acceptable. You can be a first-time project manager using tools that you are familiar with, or you can be a veteran project manager using tools for the first time. However, it is unacceptable to be a first-time project manager using project tools for the first time.

Plain English

Risk   The degree to which a project or portions of a project are in jeopardy of not being completed on time and on budget, and, most importantly, the probability that the desired outcome will not be achieved.

■ **Monitor project progress intermittently.** Just as a ship that is off course one degree at the start of a voyage ends up missing the destination by a thousand miles, so, too, a slight deviation in course in the early rounds of your project can result in having to do double or triple time to get back on track. Hence, monitoring progress is a project-long responsibility. It is important at the outset for the reasons just mentioned, and it is important in mid and late stages to avoid last-minute surprises.

The 30-Second Recap

- Project managers are responsible for planning, supervising, administering, motivating, training, coordinating, listening, readjusting, and achieving.

- Five basic principles of effective project management include being conscious of what you are doing, investing heavily in the front-end work, anticipating problems, going beneath the surface, and staying flexible.

- Project managers who succeed are able to effectively give and receive criticism, know how to conduct a meeting, maintain a sense of humor, manage their time well, are open to new procedures, and use project management support tools effectively.

- Project managers who fail let important issues fester, fail to focus on quality, get too involved with administration and neglect management, micromanage rather than delegate, rearrange tasks or schedules too often, and rely too heavily on unfamiliar tools.

What Do You Want to Accomplish?

In this section, you learn how important it is to fully understand the project, what kinds of projects lend themselves to project management, and why it is important to start with the end in mind.

To Lead and to Handle Crises

Project managers come in many varieties, but if you were to boil down the two primary characteristics of project managers they would be ...

- A project manager's ability to lead a team. This is largely dependent upon the managerial and personal characteristics of the project manager.

■ A project manager's ability to handle the critical project issues. This involves the project manager's background, skills, and experience in handling these and similar issues.

If you could pick only one set of attributes for a project manager, either being good at the people side of managing projects or being good at the technical side of managing projects, which do you suppose, over the broad span of all projects ever undertaken, has proven to be the most valuable? You guessed it, the people side.

In his book *Information Systems Project Management,* author Jolyon Hallows observes, "Hard though it may be to admit, the people side of projects is more important than the technical side. Those who are anointed or appointed as project managers because of their technical capability have to overcome the temptation of focusing on technical issues rather than the people or political issue that invariably becomes paramount to project success."

Tip

If you are managing the project alone, you can remain as technically oriented as you like.

Even on a solo project, given that you will end up having to report to others, the people side never entirely goes away. Your ability to relate to the authorizing party, fellow project managers, and any staff people who may only tangentially be supporting your efforts can spell the difference between success and failure for your project.

KEY QUESTIONS

On the road to determining what you want to accomplish, it is important to understand your project on several dimensions. Hallows suggests asking key questions, including ...

■ Do I understand the project's justification? Why does someone consider this project to be important? If you are in a large organization, this means contemplating why the authorizing party initiated the assignment and whom he or she had to sell before you were brought into the picture.

■ Do I understand the project's background? It is unlikely that the project exists in a vacuum. Probe to find out what has been done in this area previously, if anything. If the project represents a new method or procedure, what is it replacing? Is the project a high-priority item within your organization, or is it something that is not necessarily crucial to continuing operations?

- Do I understand the project's *politics?* Who stands to benefit from the success of the full completion of this project? Whose feathers may be ruffled by achieving the desired outcome? Who will be supportive? Who will be resistant?
- Do I understand who the players are and the role they will take? Who can and will contribute their effort and expertise to the project? Who will be merely bystanders, and who will be indifferent?

Plain English

Politics   The relationship of two or more people with one another, including the degree of power and influence that the parties have over one another.

Hallows says that projects involve "the dynamic mix of people with different interests, philosophies, values, approaches and priorities. One of your main functions as a project manger," particularly in regards to what you want to accomplish, is to "ensure that this mix becomes coherent and drives the project forward." He warns that, "the alternative is chaos."

Caution

Project management is not for the meek. At times, you will have to be tough and kick some proverbial derriere. As a project manager, you become the human representative for the project. Think of the project as taking on a life of its own, with you as its spokesperson.

OKAY, SO WHAT ARE WE ATTEMPTING TO DO?

A post mortem of projects that failed reveals that all too often the projects were begun "on the run," rather than taking a measured approach to determining exactly what needed to be accomplished. Too many projects start virtually in motion, before a precise definition of what needs to be achieved is even concocted.

In some organizations, projects are routinely rushed from the beginning. Project managers and teams are given near-impossible deadlines, and the only alternative is for the project players to throw their time and energy at the project, working late into the evening and on weekends. All of this is in the vainglorious attempt to produce results in record time and have "something" to show to top management, a client, the VP of product development, the sales staff, or whomever.

In properly defining the project, Hallows suggests a few basic questions, including the following:

- **Have I defined the project deliverables?** The deliverables (as discussed in "So You're Going to Manage a Project?" on page 950) could also be analogous to outcomes, are often associated with project milestones, and represent the evidence or proof that the project team is meeting the challenge or resolving the issue for which they were initially assembled.

Tip

Teams that start in a rush, and accelerate the pace from there, run the risk of being more focused on producing *a* deliverable instead of *the* deliverable. The solution is to define precisely what needs to be done and then to stick to the course of action that will lead to the accomplishment of the goal.

- **Have I established the scope—both system and project?** This involves determining exactly the level of effort required for all aspects of the project, and often plotting the scope and required effort out on a wall chart or using project management software.

- **Have I determined how deliverables will be reviewed and approved?** It is one thing to produce a deliverable on time, and quite another to have the air kicked out of your tires because the reviewing body used criteria that were foreign to you. The remedy is to ensure at the outset that everyone is on the same page in terms of what is to be accomplished. In that regard, it pays to spend more time at the outset than some project managers are willing to spend to determine the deliverables' review and approval processes to which the project manager and project team will be subjected.

Tip

Abraham Lincoln once said that if he had eight hours to cut down a tree he would spend six hours sharpening the saw.

TASKS VS. OUTCOMES

One of the recurring problems surrounding the issue of "What is it that needs to be accomplished?" is overfocusing on the project's tasks, as opposed to the project's desired outcome. Project managers who jump into a project too quickly sometimes become enamored by bells and whistles associated with project tasks, rather than critically identifying the specific desired results that the overall project should achieve. The antidote to this trap is to start with the end in mind, an age-old method for ensuring that all project activities are related to the desired outcome.

Tip

By having a clear vision of the desired end, all decisions made by the project staff at all points along the trail will have a higher probability of being in alignment with the desired end.

The desired end is never nebulous. It can be accurately described. It is targeted to be achieved within a specific timeframe at a specific cost. The end is quantifiable. It meets the challenge or solves the problem for which the project management team was originally assembled. As I pointed out in my book *The Complete Idiot's Guide to Reaching Your Goals,* it pays to start from the ending date of a project and work back to the present, indicating the tasks and *subtasks* you need to undertake and when you need to undertake them.

Plain English

Subtask   A slice of a complete task; a divisible unit of a larger task. Usually, a series of subtasks leads to the completion of a task.

Tip

Starting from the ending date of a project is a highly useful procedure because when you proceed in reverse, you establish realistic interim goals that can serve as project target dates.

TELLING QUESTIONS

My co-author for two previous books, *Marketing Your Consulting and Professional Services* (John Wiley & Sons) and *Getting New Clients* (John Wiley & Sons), is Richard A. Connor. In working on projects with professional service firms, Richard used to ask, "How will you and I know when I have done the job to your satisfaction?"

Some clients were disarmed by this question; they had never been asked it before. Inevitably, answers began to emerge. Clients would say things such as …

- Our accounting and record-keeping costs will decline by 10 percent from those of last year.

- We will retain for at least two years a higher percentage of our new recruits than occurred with our previous recruiting class.

- We will receive five new client inquiries per week, starting immediately.

■ Fifteen percent of the proposals we write will result in signed contracts, as opposed to our traditional norm of 11 percent.

Richard Connor's question can be adopted by all project managers as well.

"How will my project team and I know that we have completed the project to the satisfaction of those charged with assessing our efforts?" The response may turn out to be multipart, but invariably the answer homes in on the essential question for all project managers who choose to be successful: "What needs to be accomplished?"

Desired Outcomes That Lend Themselves to Project Management

Almost any quest in the business world can be handled by applying project management principles. If you work for a large manufacturing, sales, or engineering concern, especially in this ultra-competitive age, there are an endless number of worthwhile projects, among them:

■ To reduce inventory holding costs by 25 percent by creating more effective, just-in-time inventory delivery systems

■ To comply fully with environmental regulations, while holding operating costs to no more than one percent of the company's three-year norm

■ To reduce the "time to market" for new products from an average of 182 days to 85 days

■ To increase the average longevity of employees from 2.5 years to 2.75 years

■ To open an office in Atlanta and to have it fully staffed by the fifteenth of next month

If you are in a personal service firm, one of the many projects that you might entertain could include the following:

■ To get five new appointments per month with qualified prospects

■ To initiate a complete proposal process system by June 30

■ To design, test, and implement the XYZ research project in this quarter

■ To develop preliminary need scenarios in our five basic target industries

■ To assemble our initial contact mailing package and begin the first test mailing within 10 days

If you are an entrepreneur or work in an entrepreneurial firm, the types of projects you might tackle include the following:

- To find three joint-venture partners within the next quarter
- To replace the phone system within one month without any service disruption
- To reduce delivery expense by at least 18 percent by creating more circuitous delivery routes
- To create a database/dossier of our 10 most active clients
- To develop a coordinated 12-month advertising plan

Finally, if you are working alone, or are simply seeking to rise in your career, the kinds of projects you may want to tackle include the following:

- To earn $52,000 in the next 12 months
- To be transferred to the Hong Kong division of the company by next April
- To have a regular column in the company newsletter (or online 'zine) by next quarter
- To be mentioned in *Wired* magazine this year
- To publish your first book within six months

THE 30-SECOND RECAP

- Too many project managers have an inclination to leap into the project at top speed, without precisely defining what it is that needs to be accomplished and how project deliverables will be assessed by others who are crucial to the project's success.
- Project managers who are people-oriented fare better than project managers who are task-oriented, because people represent the most critical element in the accomplishment of most projects. A people-oriented project manager can learn elements of task management, whereas task-oriented managers are seldom effective at becoming people-oriented managers.
- It pays to start with the end in mind, to get a clear focus of what is to be achieved, and to better guide all decisions and activities undertaken by members of the project team.
- To know if you're on track, ask the telling question, "How will you and I know when I have done the job to your satisfaction?"

Laying Out Your Plan

In this section, you learn the prime directive of project managers, all about plotting your course, initiating a work breakdown structure, and the difference between action and results (results mean deliverables).

No Surprises

For other than self-initiated projects, it is tempting to believe that the most important aspect of a project is to achieve the desired outcome on time and on budget. As important as that is, there is something even more important. As you initiate, engage in, and proceed with your project, you want to be sure that you do not surprise the authorizing party or any other individuals who have a stake in the outcome of your project.

> **Tip**
>
> Keeping others informed along the way, as necessary, is your prime directive.

When you keep *stakeholders* "in the information loop," you accomplish many important things. For one, you keep anxiety levels to a minimum. If others get regular reports all along as to how your project is proceeding, then they don't have to make inquiries. They don't have to be constantly checking up. They don't have to be overly concerned.

> **Plain English**
>
> **Stakeholder**   Those who have a vested interest in having a project succeed. Stakeholders may include the authorizing party, top management, other department and division heads within an organization, other project managers and project management teams, clients, constituents, and parties external to an organization.

Alternatively, by reporting to others on a regular basis, you keep yourself and the project in check. After all, if you are making progress according to plan, then keeping the others informed is a relatively cheerful process. And having to keep them informed is a safeguard against your allowing the project to meander.

What do the stakeholders want to know? They want to know the project status, whether you are on schedule, costs to date, and the overall project outlook in regards to achieving the desired outcome. They also want to know the likelihood of project costs exceeding the budget, the likelihood that the schedule may get off course, any anticipated problems, and most importantly, any impediments that may loom, or that may threaten the ability of the project team to achieve the desired outcome.

Tip

The more you keep others in the loop, the higher your credibility will be as a project manager.

You don't need to issue reports constantly, such as on the hour, or even daily in some cases. Depending on the nature of the project, the length, the interests of the various stakeholders, and your desired outcome, reporting daily, every few days, weekly, or biweekly may be appropriate. For projects of three months or more, weekly is probably sufficient. For a project of only a couple of weeks, daily status reports might be appropriate. For a long-term project running half a year or more, biweekly or semimonthly reports might be appropriate. The prevailing notion is that the wise project manager never allows stakeholders to be surprised.

THE HOLY GRAIL AND THE GOLDEN FLEECE

Carefully scoping out the project and laying out an effective project plan minimizes the potential for surprises. A good plan is the Holy Grail that leads you to the Golden Fleece (or the gold at the end of the rainbow, or whatever metaphor you would like to substitute). It indicates everything that you can determine up to the present that needs to be done on the project to accomplish the desired outcome. It provides clarity and direction. It helps you to determine if you are where you need to be, and if not, what it will take to get there.

Any plan (good or bad) is better than no plan. At least with a bad plan you have the potential to upgrade and improve it. With no plan, you are like a boat adrift at sea, with no compass, no sexton, and clouds covering the whole night sky so you can't even navigate by the stars.

FROM NOTHING TO SOMETHING

Perhaps you were lucky. Perhaps the authorizing party gave you an outline, or notes, or a chart of some sort to represent the starting point for you to lay out your plan. Perhaps some kind of feasibility study, corporate memo, or quarterly report served as the forerunner to your project plan, spelling out needs and opportunities of the organization that now represent clues to as to what you need to do on your project.

All too often, no such preliminary documents are available. You get your marching orders from an eight-minute conference with your boss, via e-mail, or over the phone. When you press your boss for some documentation, he or she pulls out a couple of pages from a file folder.

Whatever the origin of your project, you have to start somewhere. As you learned in the last section, the mindset of the effective project manager is to start with the end in mind.

■ What is the desired final outcome?

■ When does it need to be achieved?

■ How much can you spend toward its accomplishments?

By starting with major known elements of the project, you begin to fill in your plan, in reverse (as discussed in "What Do You Want to Accomplish?" on page 968), leading back to this very day. We'll cover the use of software in the section "Choosing Project Management Software" on page 1033 and "A Sampling of Popular Programs" on page 1042. For now, let's proceed as if pen and paper were all you had. Later, you can transfer the process to a computer screen.

A Journey of a Thousand Miles ...

In laying out your plan, it may become apparent that you have 10 steps, 50 steps, or 150 or more. Some people call each step a task, although I like to use the term event, because not each step represents a pure task. Sometimes each step merely represents something that has to happen. Subordinate activities to the events or tasks are subtasks. There can be numerous subtasks to each task or event, and if you really want to get fancy, there can be sub-subtasks.

Tip

In laying out your plan, your major challenge as project manager is to ascertain the relationship of different tasks or events to one another and to coordinate them so that the project is executed in a cost-effective and efficient manner.

The primary planning tools in plotting your *path* are the *work breakdown structure* (WBS), the Gantt chart, and the PERT/CPM chart (also known as the critical path method), which represents a schedule network. This section focuses on the work breakdown structure. We'll get to the other structures in "Gantt Charts" on page 1007 and "PERT/CPM Charts" on page 1014.

Plain English

Work breakdown structure   A complete depiction of all of the tasks necessary to achieve successful project completion. Project plans that delineate all the tasks that must be accomplished to successfully complete a project from which scheduling, delegating, and budgeting are derived.

Plain English

Path   A chronological sequence of tasks, each dependent on predecessors.

You and Me Against the World?

So here you are. Maybe you are all alone and staring at a blank page, or maybe your boss is helping you. Maybe an assistant project manager or someone who will be on the project management team is helping you lay out your plan.

Caution

Not getting regular feedback is risky. If there is someone working with you, or if you have someone who can give you regular feedback, it is to your extreme benefit.

Depending on the duration and complexity of your project, it is darned difficult to lay out a comprehensive plan that takes into account all aspects of the project, all critical events, associated subtasks, and the coordination of all. Said another way, if you can get any help in plotting your path, do it!

In laying out your plan, look at the big picture of what you want to accomplish and then, to the best of your ability, divide up the project into phases. How many phases? That depends on the project, but generally it is someplace between two and five.

Tip

By chunking out the project into phases, you have a far better chance of not missing anything.

You know where you want to end up; identifying the two to five major phases is not arduous. Then, in a top-down manner, work within each phase to identify the events or tasks, and their associated subtasks. As you work within each phase, define everything that needs to be done; you are actually creating what is called the work breakdown structure.

The Work Breakdown Structure

The WBS has become synonymous with a task list. The simplest form of WBS is the outline, although it can also appear as a tree diagram or other chart. Sticking with the outline, the WBS lists each task, each associated subtask, milestones, and deliverables. The WBS can be used to plot assignments and schedules and to maintain focus on the budget. The following is an example of such an outline:

1.0.0 Outline story

    11.1.0 Rough plot

        11.1.1 Establish theme

        11.1.2 Identify theme

        11.1.3 Link Story events

    11.2.0 Refine plot

        11.2.1 Create chart linking characters

        11.2.2 Identify lessons

2.0.0 Write story

    12.1.0 Lesson 1

        12.1.1 Body discovered

        12.1.2 Body identified

        12.1.3 Agent put on case

        12.1.4 Family

    12.2.0 Lesson 2

The following figure is particularly useful when your project has a lot of layers—that is, when many subtasks contribute to the overall accomplishment of a task, which contributes to the completion of a phase, which leads to another phase, which ultimately leads to project completion!

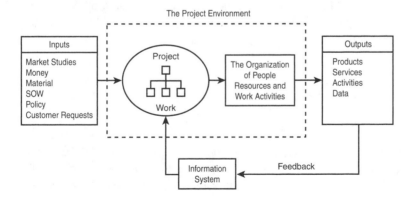

A Tree Diagram, such as the one shown here, represents another form of work breakdown structure (WBS).

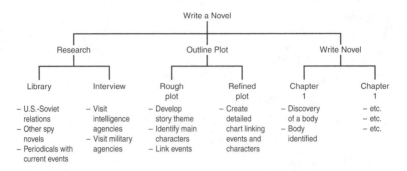

A project outline.

Keeping in mind that in many circles, deliverables are relatively synonymous with milestones, which are relatively synonymous with tasks, the WBS gives you the opportunity to break tasks into individual components. This gives you a firm grasp of what needs to be done at the lowest of levels. Hence, the WBS aids in doling out assignments, scheduling them, and budgeting for them.

DETAILS, DETAILS

How many levels of tasks and subtasks should you have? It depends on the complexity of the project. While scads and scads of details may seem overwhelming, if your work breakdown structure is well organized, you will have positioned yourself to handle even the most challenging of projects, such as hosting next year's international convention, finding a new type of fuel injection system, coordinating a statewide volunteer effort, or designing a new computer operating system. By heaping on the level of detail, you increase the probability that you will take care of all aspects of the project.

Caution

The potential risk of having too many subtasks is that you become hopelessly bogged down in detail and become overly focused on tasks, not outcomes!

Fortunately, as you proceed in execution, you find that some of the subtasks (and sub-subtasks) are taken care of as a result of some other action. Still, it is better to have listed more details than fewer. If you have not plotted out all that you can foresee, then once the project commences, you may be beset by all kinds of challenges because you understated the work that needs to be performed.

Tip

While the level of detail is up to you, as a general rule, the smallest of subtasks that you would list in the WBS would be synonymous with the smallest unit that you as a project manager need to keep track of.

Team-generated subtasks? Could your project management team end up making their own subwork breakdown structures to delineate their individual responsibilities, and, hence, have a greater level of detail than your WBS? The answer is yes. Ideally, you empower your staff to effectively execute delegated responsibilities. Within those assignments, there is often considerable leeway as to how the assignments are performed best.

Your good project team members may naturally gravitate toward their own mini-WBS. Often, good team members devise subtask routines that exceed what you need to preside over as project manager—unless of course the procedure is worth repeating with other project team members or on other projects in the future.

THE FUNCTIONAL WBS

In the following figure, the WBS is divided based on separate functions. This method of plotting the WBS is particularly effective for project managers who preside over team members who may also be divided up into functional lines. In this case, the WSB gives a quick and accurate snapshot of how the project is divided up and which teams are responsible for what.

As you may readily observe, each form of WBS, outline and tree diagram, offers different benefits and has different shortcomings. For example, the outline is far more effective at conveying minute levels of detail toward the achievement of specific tasks.

Caution

When many subteams within an overall project team each have individual responsibilities, the outline can be a little unwieldy because it doesn't visually separate activities according to functional lines.

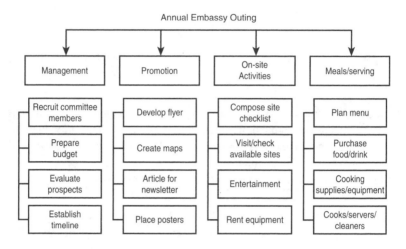

A combination tree diagram and outline WBS.

The tree diagram WBS (see the following figure) does a magnificent job of separating functional activities. Its major shortcoming is that to convey high levels of task detail, the tree diagram would be huge. It might get too big for a single piece of paper or single computer screen, and hence would have to be plotted on a large wall chart. Even then, all the tasks and subtasks of all the players in all of the functional departments would necessitate constructing a large and complex chart indeed.

Such a chart is actually a hybrid of the detailed outline and the tree diagram. Nevertheless, many project managers have resorted to this technique. By constructing both an outline and tree diagram WBS and then combining the two, however large and unwieldy the combination gets, you end up with a single document that assures the totality of the entire project.

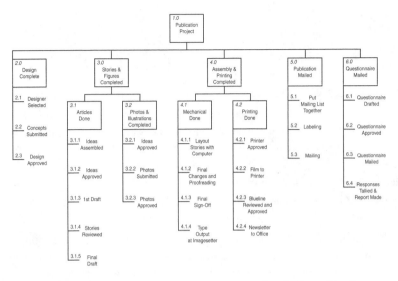

Here's an example of a segment of an outline and tree outline WBS combined.

MORE COMPLEXITY, MORE HELP

With this potential level of detail for the project you have been assigned to manage, it is important to get help when first laying out your plan. Even relatively small projects of short duration may necessitate accomplishing a variety of tasks and subtasks.

Eventually, each subtask requires an estimate of labor hours: How long will it take for somebody to complete it, and what will it cost? (See the next section.) You will need to determine how many staff hours, staff days, staff weeks, and so on will be necessary, based on the plan that you have laid out. From there, you will run into issues concerning what staff you will be able to recruit, how many hours your staff members will be available and at what cost per hour or per day.

Preparing your WBS also gives you an indicator of what project resources may be required beyond human resources. These could include computer equipment, other tools, office or plant space and facilities, and so on.

If the tasks and subtasks you plot out reveal that project staff will be traveling in pursuit of the desired outcome, then you have to figure in auto and airfare costs, room and board, and other associated travel expenses. If certain portions of the project will be farmed out to subcontractors or subliminal staff, there will be associated costs as well.

Tip

Think of the WBS as your initial planning tool for meeting the project objective(s) on the way to that final, singular, sweet triumph.

WHAT SHOULD WE DELIVER?

Completing project milestones, usually conveyed in the form of a project deliverable, represents your most salient indicators that you are on target for completing the project successfully. Deliverables can take many, many forms. Many deliverables are actually related to project reporting themselves. These could include, but are not limited to, the following:

- A list of deliverables. One of your deliverables may be a compendium of all other deliverables!

- A quality assurance plan. If your team is empowered to design something that requires exact specifications, perhaps some new engineering procedure, product, or service offering, how will you assure requisite levels of quality?

- A schedule. A schedule can be a deliverable, particularly when your project has multiple phases and you are only in the first phase or the preliminary part of the first phase. It then becomes understood that as you get into the project you will have a more precise understanding of what can be delivered and when, and hence the schedule itself can become a much-anticipated deliverable.

- The overall budget, estimates, your work plan, *cost benefit analysis,* and other documentation can all be deliverables as well.

Plain English

Cost benefit analysis   A determination of whether to proceed based on the monetary time and resources required for the proposed solution vs. the desirability of the outcome(s).

Another type of deliverable has to do with acquisition and procurement. A government agency or a large contractor could empower a project manager and project management team to develop requests for proposals (RFPs), invitations to bid or requests for estimates as project deliverables. Once the proposals or bids come in, proposal evaluation procedures have to be in place.

The following are examples:

- Software evaluation plans
- Maintenance plans

- Hardware and equipment evaluation plans
- Assessment tools

The wide variety of other deliverables might include the following:

- Business guidelines
- Lexicon or dictionary
- Buy-vs.-make analysis
- A phase-out plan
- Training procedures
- Product prototype
- Implementation plans
- Reporting forms
- Application
- Product specifications
- Close-out procedures
- Documentation
- Code
- Experimental design
- Test results
- Process models

IT's RESULTS THAT COUNT

In preparing the WBS and associated deliverables, focus on results and not activities. The plan that you lay out and eventually develop becomes the operating bible for the project team.

One project manager on a new software project requested that team-member programmers develop a certain number of lines of code per day in one phase of a project. He felt that this would be a useful indicator of the level of productivity of his individual project team members. In their efforts to be productive members of the project team, the programmers developed scads of new lines of code each day. The resulting program, however, was fraught with errors and was insufficient for completing that phase of the project. It put the overall project drastically behind schedule and behind budget.

Rather than making task and subtask assignments related to the number of lines of new code developed, the tasks and subtasks should have reflected code that accomplished a specific, observable capability. Then, project programmers would have concentrated on code efficiency and potency, as opposed to volume.

Tip

Remember the old adage that sometimes it's quality, not quantity, that counts.

SUPPORTING TOOLS

Undoubtedly, when laying out your plan, you will have many starts and stops, erasures, redirections, and second thoughts. If you are lucky enough to have a white board, where you can simply write down your current thoughts to have them stored to disc and printed later, then you know that this is a valuable tool indeed.

Many people simply use stick-em pads, which now come in various dimensions as large as three inches by five inches. An event or task can be confined to one stick-em note with associated subtasks on that same note or an attached note. These can then be moved around at will, as you are plotting out your plan.

Stick-em pads can even be used in combination with a white board. Simply stick them in place (or the best place you can determine at the moment). If you don't have a white board, you can also use a copying machine to take a snapshot of your current thinking.

To further ease your burden, you can use colors. These could include different colored stick-em notes, colored dots, or magic markers, flares, and highlighters. Each event or task could be a different color, or like subtasks could be a uniform color. The options are unlimited and are basically your choice.

Many project managers find it useful and convenient to use colors to track the responsibilities of individual project team members. For example, everything that Scott is responsible for will be in orange.

Many project managers also find it convenient to number tasks and subtasks.

Caution

Keep it simple when numbering tasks or subtasks. You don't want to end up with outline structures such as 1–1.2.34. This ends up being more confusing than not having them numbered at all.

Bounce Your Plan Off Others

After you've laid out what you feel is a comprehensive plan that will accomplish the mission, bounce it off others, even those that for one reason or another were not available to participate in its construction.

▓ You want people to give it a critical eye.

▓ You want to have them play devil's advocate.

▓ You want them to challenge you.

▓ You want them to question you as to why you went left instead of right. Maybe they immediately see something that you flat-out missed. Maybe they can suggest a way to combine several subtasks into one.

Caution

You don't want to fall so in love with your WBS that you can't accept the input of others, or worse, never even see the flaws. The more involved your project is, the easier it is to miss something.

In the next section, we add flesh and blood to your WBS, and focus on assigning staff, timeframes, and a budget to your WBS.

The 30-Second Recap

▓ Regardless of how worthy your project and how brilliant your plan, keeping others informed along the way, as necessary, is your prime directive.

▓ Carefully scoping out the project and laying out an effective project plan minimizes the potential for surprises, indicates what needs to be done, provides clarity, and offers direction.

▓ The work breakdown structure (WBS) is a primary planning tool in plotting your path.

▓ The WBS lists each task, each associated subtask, milestones, and deliverables and can be used to plot assignments and schedules and to maintain focus on the budget.

▓ You don't want to fall so in love with your WBS that you can't accept the input of others and miss major flaws.

Assembling Your Plan

In this section, you learn how to further refine your work breakdown structure (WBS), whether your labor should be part of the WBS, the importance of re-integrating project staff as the project winds down, and distinctions between the WBS and other planning tools.

THE CRITICAL PATH FOR COMPLETING THE WBS

Before a project was assigned to you, an authorizing party or committee determined that it needed to be executed. They allocated resources to the project. At the least, initially this included costs of your services. They may have also formally or informally made assignments of plant, equipment, and human resources to the project.

Plain English

Critical path   The longest complete path of a project.

At some point you were summoned. You discussed the desired objective, how long the project would take, the key events in pursuit of the final objective, and whether or not the project should have distinct phases. Perhaps a feasibility study was already done. Maybe there were notes and other documents that enabled you to get a running start as to what you would be required to do. Often, your initial assignment is to define your own role and present your definition to the authorizing party or committee.

Once the decision was made to launch the project, and once you were given the formal go-ahead, laying out your plan, developing the WBS, and presentation to your superiors became the order of the day, such as that depicted in the following figure.

Item:	J	F	M	A	M	J	J	A	S	O	N	D
Project Launch	——											
Sponsor Approval	—											
Plan Development			—									
WBS					—							
Presentation and Approval						-						
Implementation							——————————					

Laying out the plan.

The basic activities involved to complete the WBS are as follows:

- Identify the events or task and subtasks associated with them. They are paramount to achieving the desired objective.

- Plot them using an outline, a tree diagram, or combination thereof to determine the most efficient sequence.

- Estimate the level of effort required (usually in terms of person days) and start and stop times for each task and subtask.

- Identify supporting resources and when they can be available, how long they are available, and when and how they must be returned.

- Establish a budget for the entire project, for phases if applicable, and possibly for specific events or tasks.

- Assign target dates for the completion of events or tasks known as milestones.

- Establish a roster of deliverables, many of which are presented in accordance with achieving or are analogous to milestones.

- Obtain approval of your plan from the authorizing party. See the following figure.

Item:	J	F	M	A	M	J	J	A	S	O	N	D
WBS			—									
Task			–									
Precedences			–									
Assignment			–									
Resources			–									
Budget			–									
Approval			—									

Laying out your plan.

THE CHICKEN OR THE EGG?

Preparation of your work breakdown structure (WBS) and the actual commencement of project activities is a chicken-vs.-egg issue. For example, many experts advise that you first identify staffing resources and then proceed with the work breakdown structure. Following that approach, the opportunity to allocate staff as necessary comes first, followed closely by budget allocations.

Caution

Until you plot exactly what needs to be done, you can't allocate staff hours.

Some experts advise creating the WBS *independently* of staff allocations. First, you identify what needs to be done, and then you assemble the requisite staff resources based on the plan that you've devised. I recommend the latter, because it is a more pure approach to laying out and assembling your plan—you identify needs first and then allocate appropriate staff resources.

When does it make sense to start with the staff in mind?

- When they are all full-time
- When the project is relatively short
- When the project is labor intensive or requires a lot of expensive equipment
- When you are relatively certain that you have all the skills and experiences you need within the existing allocated staff

IS PLANNING ITSELF A TASK?

Another chicken-vs.-egg issue to consider is whether or not planning itself represents a task to be included on the WBS. Experts argue that especially for large and involved projects, planning can represent a variety of tasks or events or even subtasks. Planning can even be synonymous with a project phase. For example, depending on what you're trying to achieve, the outcome of Phase I might be to develop a plan which will be crucial to the execution of Phase II.

Still, some critics argue that while planning consumes time and budgetary resources, it is not appropriate to incorporate it into the WBS. They say that the WBS and any other type of planning document merely represent the outcomes of the planning process. A plan is only considered completed when the project actually begins. Thus, the work of the project itself is separate from the plan that enabled the work to commence.

On this particular chicken-vs.-egg issue, you decide whether you want to include the planning of the project as a task or event in itself or simply have it represent a prelude activity for the actual work of the project.

Caution

You can't skirt chicken-vs.-egg issues, as they could make a significant impact on your budget and overall project plans if you don't consider them.

What About Your Hours?

Should your activities and contributions to the project as project manager be listed in the work breakdown structure? Some experts say no. They argue that project management represents pure management—it is there from the beginning; it will be there at the end, and …

- It is ongoing.
- It isn't a task.
- There are no milestones or deliverables attached to it.
- There are no events or activities that are dependent upon project management per se.

Those who argue that project management should be plotted in the WBS point out that although all the above may be true, the act of managing a project is a vital project input and …

- It involves labor.
- It consumes resources.
- It helps to achieve outcomes.
- It is clearly a valuable resource.
- It is part of the overall budget in the form of the project manager's salary.

For these reasons, I advocate that the project management function of a project be included in the work breakdown structure.

Internal Resources vs. External Resources

As arduous as it may seem, constructing a WBS is relatively easy when all of the resources are internal, such as your staff, equipment, and other components supporting project efforts. What about when you have to rely on external resources, such as outside vendors, consultants, part-time or supplemental staff, rented or leased facilities, and rented or leased equipment? Then the job becomes more involved.

Caution

External project resources are more difficult to budget, schedule, and incorporate at precisely the right time.

It can also be argued that monitoring the work of outside vendors, consultants or supplemental staff is more challenging than working with internal staff. However, external human resources who bill on an hourly or daily basis have a strong incentive to perform admirably, on time, every time.

HELPING YOUR STAFF WHEN IT'S OVER

In perfecting your WBS, have you accounted for the reintegration of your project staff back into other parts of the organization as the project winds down? This is an issue that even veteran project managers overlook. On some projects most of the staff work a uniform number of hours for most of the project. If the project veers, perhaps they work longer until the project is back on course. Sometimes, project staff work steadfastly right up to the final project outcome.

Since by design your project is a temporary engagement with a scheduled end, it is logical to assume that the fate and future activity of project team members needs to be determined before the project ends.

Caution

The project manager who overlooks the concerns of project staff who are wondering about their immediate futures will find that as the project draws to a close, project staff may start to lose focus or display symptoms of divided loyalty.

Project staff justifiably are concerned about what they will be doing next, whether it is moving on to a new project, or finding their way back to their previous positions. You can't blame them, because they have their own career and own futures to be concerned with.

Abrupt changes in job status, such as working full bore on a project to a nebulous status, can be quite disconcerting to employees. Equally challenging for the project manager, however, is the situation where the brunt of the project work occurs sometimes before the actual completion date. Thus, many project staff members may be in a wind down phase—having worked more than 40 hours a week on the project at its midpoint and now perhaps spending 20 or less a week on it. They now devote the rest of the time to some other project or back at their old position.

In such cases, the project manager needs to account for issues related to diverted attention, divided loyalties, and the nagging problem of having several project staffers simply not having their "heads" in the project anymore.

Tip

The WBS needs to reflect the added measure of staff meetings, reviews, and "tête-à-têtes" that are often vital to maintain performance near the end of a project.

What Kinds of Tasks Comprise the WBS?

Whether you employ an outline, tree, or combination WBS, it is useful to point out some distinction among tasks. *Parallel tasks* are those which can be undertaken at the same time as other tasks, without impeding the project. For example, you may have several teams working on different elements of the project that are not time or sequence related. Hence, they can all be making progress without impeding any of the other teams.

Plain English

Parallel tasks   Two or more tasks that can be undertaken at the same time. This doesn't imply that they have the same starting and ending times.

Dependent tasks are those that cannot begin until something else occurs. If you are constructing a building, you first have to lay the foundation. Then, you can build the first floor, the second floor, and the third floor. Obviously, you can't start with the fifth floor and then move to the third, not in three-dimensional space as we know it.

Plain English

Dependent task   A task or subtask that cannot be initiated until a predecessor task or several predecessor tasks are finished.

Predecessor task   Task that must be completed before another task can commence.

The WBS is not the best tool for identifying the relationship between interdependent tasks. When preparing a WSB outline, you want to proceed in chronological order, much as you want to do with the tree approach. When you combine the outline and tree diagram type WBS, you end up with an extended outline describing the tasks and subtasks associated with the elements on the tree diagram. Thereafter, you can alter the position of the boxes to be in alignment with what takes place and when. Hence, parallel tasks are on the same position on the chart. As you can see in the following figure, some items, such as assignment and resource, occur at the same time.

Item:	J	F	M	A	M	J	J	A	S	O	N	D
Task A			————————									
Task B							———————					
Task C							———————					
Task D									———			

Adding detail to the WBS sequence.

Dependent tasks necessarily have to have staggered positions. These can be joined by the arrows that indicate the desired path of events or activities.

Milestones don't necessarily require any time or budget, as they represent the culmination of events and tasks leading up to a milestone. A milestone may or may not involve a deliverable. Nevertheless, milestones are important, particularly to project team members, because they offer a visible point of demarcation. They let team members know that the project is (or is not) proceeding according to plan. They represent a completion of sorts from which the project staff can gain new energy, focus, and direction for what comes next.

KEEPING THE BIG PICTURE IN MIND

In refining the WBS to get it to its final form, it is useful to revisit the basic definition of a project as first introduced in "So You're Going to Manage a Project?" on page 950. The project is a venture undertaken to achieve a desired outcome, within a specific timeframe and budget. The outcome can be precisely defined and quantified. By definition, the project is temporary in nature. It usually represents a unique activity to the host organization.

The challenge of establishing an effective WBS in many ways is likened to meeting a series of constraints. For example …

- Staff resources may be limited.
- The budget may be limited.
- Equipment and organizational resources may be limited.
- Crucial items on order may not arrive on time.
- Deliverables that you do prepare on time may be delayed by committees that have to go through various approval procedures.

Meanwhile, you have a project to run and can't or don't want to spend the time waiting for committee members to get their act together.

Caution

Even when deliverables are not the issue, there may be delays when you simply need to have a yes or no answer. Key decision-makers may be unreachable or too bogged down with other issues to get back to you in what you consider to be a timely manner.

Perhaps the most troublesome and hardest to plot on your WBS is the situation where progress on your project is dependent upon the activities of some other department within your organization or the success and timely combination of some other project.

Caution

If your project is delayed for days on end because some other project team has not conveyed a key deliverable to you, you can quickly find yourself in a touchy situation.

As you assemble your plan, you have to account for delays in the time that outside parties get back to you, even though they promised that such delays would not occur!

Tip

From a planning standpoint, if a group is supposed to get back to you in two days, consider their turnaround time to be four days. Only then would you build into your plans a series of announcements and reminders focused on getting them to respond.

The Big Picture vs. Endless Minutiae

In your quest to assemble a comprehensive WBS, you may run the risk of going too far. As mentioned in "What Do You Want to Accomplish?" on page 968, many a project manager has made the unfortunate error of mapping out too many tasks. When you subdivide tasks into too many subtasks, the WBS could possibly become more restrictive than useful.

Caution

Some project managers have been accused, hopefully unfairly, of charting bathroom breaks for staffers.

You want to maintain control of the project and have a reasonable idea of what each project team member is doing on any given day. In assembling your project plan, however, you don't want to go overboard. Beware if you have hundreds of items listed for each event or task area, and dozens and dozens of items scheduled each day for each staffer!

Micromanagement isn't pretty—particularly when you get into the nitty-gritty details of what otherwise competent project team members should be responsible for. What is worse, micromanagement techniques often focus on the wrong issues all together.

The goal in constructing a suitable WBS and being an effective project manager is to help your staff members achieve predetermined milestones in pursuit of an overall desired project outcome. From a mathematical standpoint, the longer the lists you have, generally the more difficult it will be to complete everything on the list. In addition, the complexity of your job as project manager increases many-fold.

What number of subtasks in support of an event or task represents the optimal? Nine is probably too many and two is not enough. Someplace between three and five is probably optimal.

FROM PLANNING TO MONITORING

Oncethe WBS is approved, your major responsibility for the duration of the project becomes that of monitoring progress. This involves a variety of responsibilities including the following:

- Keeping tabs on the course and direction of the project, noting any variation from the desired path.
- Modifying task descriptions as may become necessary as the project proceeds. Taking immediate corrective action if it appears that the project is veering while continuing to adhere to overall schedules and budgets.
- Working with team members, enhancing their understanding of their respective roles, team-building, offering praise and criticism, and incorporating their feedback.
- Controlling the scope of the project, which includes making sure that the desired level of resources are expended on tasks and subtasks according to plan.
- Ensuring that roadblocks and barriers are effectively overcome and that you don't end up winning some battles at the cost of losing the war—sometimes you can expend too much effort in one area and end up leaving yourself in a weakened position someplace else.
- Maintaining effective relationships with the authorizing party and stakeholders, keeping them informed, maintaining a "no surprises" type of approach, and incorporating their feedback.

The following section, "Keeping Your Eye on the Budget," examines the importance of expending resources carefully including dealing with budgetary constraints, equipment constraints, and other potential roadblocks. Thereafter, in the sections "Gantt Charts" on page 1007, "PERT/CPM Charts" on page 1014, "Choosing Project Management Software" on page 1033, and "A Sampling of Popular Programs" on page 1042, we discuss how to manage more involved projects.

THE 30-SECOND RECAP

- In assembling your WBS, there are several chicken-vs.-egg issues that must be resolved, such as whether to plot your own activities as a project manager and whether to include planning itself as a task.

- Project managers have an easier time maintaining control of internal resources including staff, equipment, and facilities, than managing external resources including consultants, rented equipment, and leased facilities.

- Your WBS needs to reflect realistic delays in getting feedback from committees following their reception of your scheduled deliverables.

- Once you nail the WBS, you shift from a planning to a monitoring mode.

Keeping Your Eye on the Budget

In this section, you learn how optimism gets in the way of controlling expenses, effective approaches to budgeting, how to combine top-down and bottom-up budgeting techniques, and the importance of building in slack.

MONEY STILL DOESN'T GROW ON TREES

One of the primary responsibilities that you have as project manager is to keep close reins on the budget. Your organization or whoever is funding the project enjoys hearing about cost overruns about as much as having a root canal.

Too often the monetary resources allocated to a project (perhaps even before you stepped aboard) have been underestimated. Why? Because of the irrational exuberance that the authorizing party or stakeholder may have as to what can be achieved at what cost. This is not to say that project managers don't have their own hand in underestimating cost.

The project manager often is charged with determining the project budget, as opposed to being handed some figure from above. In such cases, it always pays to estimate on the high side. This is true for many reasons:

■ In most organizations, no matter how much you ask for, *you can count on not getting it all.*

Tip
You might as well ask for slightly more than your best calculations indicate, thereby increasing the probability of getting close to the amount you actually seek.

■ No matter how precise your calculations, how much *slack* you allow, or what kind of contingencies you have considered, chances are your estimate is still low.

Plain English
Slack   Margin or extra room to accommodate anticipated potential shortfalls in planning.

Plain English
Murphy's Law   The age-old axiom stating that if something can go wrong, it will go wrong.

Parkinson's Law   Work expands so as to fill the time allotted for its completion.

■ In ever-changing business, social, and technological environments, no one has a lock on the future even three months out, let alone three years out. You simply have to build into your budget extra margins beyond those that seem initially commensurate with the overall level of work to be performed and outcome to be achieved.

Is it foolhardy to prepare a budget that merely reflects the best computation as to what the sum ought to be? Probably.

EXPERIENCE PAYS

Your level of experience as a project manager plays a big part in your ability to understand the real monetary costs in conducting the project. For example, a highly skilled laborer may be able to work wonders with less than top-of-the-line equipment, whereas an entry-level laborer is likely to be less productive in the same situation.

DISTORTED EXPECTATIONS

Another problem is related to your own competence. The more competent you are as a project manager and as a career professional in general, the greater the tendency for you to underestimate the time necessary for project staff members to complete a job. You tend to envision the completion of a job through the eyes of your own level of competency. Even if you discount for newly hired and inexperienced staff, you still tend to regard jobs in the way that you might have tackled them when you were newly hired. Hence, you end up underestimating the time required to complete the job with the staff that you *do have* by 5, 10, 15 percent or more.

The preceding phenomenon has a corollary in professional sports, particularly in NBA basketball. Many of the superstars who went on to become head coaches failed miserably because they could not budget for the lower competency levels of players on their current rosters. Such coaches thought back to their own days and what they were able to achieve, perhaps even thought of competent teammates and competent players from other teams. When coaching their current teams, they couldn't shake their preconceived notion of what a player was supposed to be able to do, the rate at which a player learned, and the skill level that the player could acquire.

HIDDEN COSTS

An experienced project manager also knows that any time you rely on external sources to proceed on a project, such as subcontractors, there are hidden costs involved. The subcontractor may work for a flat fee or lump-sum amount, and, if so, it's easy to pinpoint that figure and plug it into the overall budget. However, what about your time and effort, or project team members' time and effort, in carefully preparing guidelines for subcontractors, working with them to ensure smooth operation, and consuming time in extra meetings, phone calls, and e-mails? What about the extra reporting and other administrative tasks associated with working with outside vendors? Such factors ultimately impact the budget.

Caution

The cumulative impact of underestimating time can quickly put your project in jeopardy. Even if you apply a safety margin to your estimate, the level of safety margin is applied through the eyes of your own personal competency. Hence, you need to get help when preparing the budget.

CRISES WILL HAPPEN

The experienced project manager expects that one or more crises will occur in the course of the project. The inexperienced project manager may have been forewarned, but still is unprepared. Even experienced project managers know that sometimes you reach a point of desperation in the project—you must have something done by a certain time and need to move heaven and earth to do it. You may have to pay exorbitant short-term costs to procure a vital resource, work around the clock, plead for added help, make thinly veiled threats, or scramble like a rabbit in the brush to keep the project on time. All such instances have a potentially dramatic effect on the budget.

TRADITIONAL APPROACHES TO BUDGETING

If you're managing a project that remotely resembles anything else anyone has managed in your organization, you may be able to extract some clues as to how to prepare a real-world budget for your project. Obviously, you never want to merely lift the cost figures from one project and apply it to yours.

Tip

There may be cost elements of a previous project that are akin to some elements of your project, so that's as good a place to start as any.

Many industries have already codified cost elements associated with various jobs. Printers have elaborate cost estimate sheets. Their estimators can plug in the particulars of a customer's request and quickly yield a cost estimate for the customer. With the many variables involved in estimating the cost of a printing job, however, the estimator can end up underestimating the true costs and hence diminish his profit.

In construction, the cost estimator has comparable tools for the construction industry. The estimator may know the costs for each 2×4-foot, brick, cinder block, and glass panel.

Still, you hear stories about printing jobs that ended up costing 50 percent or more of the original estimate, of companies taking a bath on projects because the final costs were so out of whack with reality. Particularly in civic and civil engineering projects, cost overruns in the millions of dollars make for regular news features in every community. What is going on here? Why would experienced organizations that have the most sophisticated cost-estimating software, and undoubtedly have performed hundreds of jobs for clients and customers, be off the mark so often and sometimes so wildly? It all comes down to the skill of the person doing the budget estimate, the assumptions he or she relies upon, and the approach he or she takes.

Tip

By knowing the dimensions of the building, the number of floors, and all the other attributes via project blueprints to the best of his ability, the experienced estimator determines the overall cost of the construction project.

TRADITIONAL MEASURES

Let's discuss some traditional measures for preparing a budget, followed by a look at the cost estimation traps that you don't want to fall into.

TOP-DOWN BUDGETING

Using this approach, a project manager surveys the authorizing party or committee, stakeholders, and certainly top and middle managers where relevant. The project manager would also conduct a massive hunt for all previous cost data on projects of a remotely similar nature. He would then compile the costs associated with each phase (if the project is divided into phases), specific events or tasks, or even subtasks.

To further hedge his bet, he might even enroll project management staff if they have been identified in advance, and get their estimates of the time (and hence cost) for specific tasks and subtasks. He would then refine his own estimates, which now may be somewhat higher than the figure his peers may have arrived at. In any case, he would represent his data to the authorizing party.

Tip

More often than not, the wise project manager lobbies for a larger budget than the authorizing party feels is necessary.

Even if the project manager ends up yielding to the wishes of the authorizing party (and when hasn't this happened?) and accepts a lower budget figure, there are some safeguards built into the top-down budgeting approach. The judgments of senior, top-level, highly experienced executives and managers likely already factor in budgetary safety margins and contingencies.

In addition, the project manager may be one project manager of many calling on the top manager or executive. Hence, the amount allocated for his budget is probably in alignment and consistent with the overall needs of the department, division, or entire organization. A highly persuasive project manager may be able to lobby for a few percent more in funding, but probably not much more unless there are extraordinary circumstances.

Bottom-Up Budgeting

As the name implies, this approach to budgeting takes the reverse course. After constructing work breakdown structure, the project manager consults with project staff members (presumably pre-identified) who offer highly detailed estimates of the budget required for each task and subtask at every step along the way. In fact, the project manager routinely surveys the staff once the project begins to continue to formulate the bottom-up budget, which he then submits to the higher-ups. The project manager keeps a sharp eye on trends—possibly on a daily basis, more likely on a weekly or biweekly basis, and certainly between one task and another.

As project team members proceed up the learning curve, they are often able to achieve operating efficiencies that enable the overall project team to proceed on some aspects of the project with much greater productivity, and hence lower costs. This isn't to say that the project won't hit a snag or is otherwise immune to the potential cost overruns as discussed throughout this section.

The bottom-up budgeting approach holds great potential but also carries great risk. Potentially, a highly detailed, reasonably accurate compilation of costs can be achieved using this method. The danger is that if the project manager does not include all cost elements of the project, then the cost estimate understandably can be off by a wide margin.

 Caution

In *Project Management,* Meredith and Mantel state, "It is far more difficult to develop a complete list of tasks when constructing that list from the bottom up than from the top down."

In addition, if project management staff suspects that top management is on the lookout to cut budgets, then they may resort to overstating their case. This results in the project manager presenting a sum to the higher-ups that is larger than would otherwise be derived. In turn, the potential for the project budget being whittled away increases. What a process!

Nevertheless, as more and more organizations request that their project managers engage in project management, it makes sense to regularly solicit the input from those who are actually doing the work. Line workers in any industry have a first person, hands on connection to what is occurring—whereas staff usually are somewhat distant observers often relying on compiled information.

When project staff gets to participate in the preparation of budgets, if those budgets are cut, at least they had some role in the process and hence "will accept the result with a minimum of grumbling," according to Meredith and Mantel. "Involvement is also a good managerial training technique, giving junior managers valuable experience in budget preparation as well as the knowledge of the operations required to generate a budget."

TOP-DOWN AND BOTTOM-UP BUDGETING

Perhaps the most effective approach combines the two budgeting techniques discussed thus far. It involves gathering all the data and input from top executives and then soliciting input from project management staff and adjusting estimates accordingly.

Caution

Despite some wonderful benefits, most organizations and most projects do not rely upon bottom-up budgeting. Top managers are reluctant to relinquish control of one of their chief sources of power—allocating monies—and sometimes mistrust subordinates who they may believe routinely overstate project needs.

Regardless of the approach, one needs to account for the ever-present disparity between actual hours on the job and actual hours worked. No project staff person working an eight-hour day offers eight hours of unwavering productivity. There are breaks, timeouts, lapses, unwarranted phone calls, Internet searches, and who knows what else going on. Hence, you may wish to apply a 10 percent to 15 percent increase in the estimates submitted by project management staff in regard to the amount of time it will take them to accomplish tasks and subtasks.

If a particular task initially was determined to cost $1,000 (the worker's hourly rate times the number of hours), you would then allocate $1,100 or $1,150 dollars to more closely reflect the true costs to the organization. Taking the midpoint of your calculation, $1,135 dollars, you would plug that into the figures you then present back to top management.

Reverting back and forth between top management and line workers in the quest to pinpoint accurate costs is not a rare phenomenon among project managers. In many respects, budget approvals require a series of periodic authorizations. Depending upon how your organization views project management and earlier protocols established, your project may only proceed based on a constant flow of budgetary checks and balances. The following table is one example of a project budget with actual and budgeted amounts recorded.

Tip

Virtually all the project software programs available (see "Choosing Project Management Software" on page 1033 and "A Sampling of Popular Programs" on page 1042) offer relatively easy-to-use, comprehensive budgeting calculation routines, spread sheets, and other supporting tools.

Project Budgeting

	Actual Variance	Budget Percent
Corporate-Income Statement		
Revenue		
30 Management fees		
91 Prtnsp reimb—	410.00	222.00
property mgmt	188.00	119.0
92 Prtnsp reimb—	.00	750.00
owner acquisition	750.00–	.0
93 Prtnsp reimb—rehab	.00	.00
94 Other income	.00	.00
95 Reimbursements—others	.00	.00
Total revenue	410.00	972.00
	562.00–	74.3
Operating Expenses		
Payroll and P/R benefits		
11 Salaries	425.75	583.00
	57.25	85.0
12 Payroll taxes	789.88	458.00
	668.12	51.7
13 Group ins & med reimb	407.45	40.00
	387.45–	135.3
15 Workmens' compensation	43.04	43.00
	.04–	100.0
16 Staff apartments	.00	.00
17 Bonus	.00	.00
Total payroll and	1668.12	1124.00
P/R benefits	457.88	83.5

Systematic Budgeting Problems

When you consider all the potential costs associated with a task or subtask, it's easy to understand why some costs may not be budgeted accurately.

Suppose you are charged with managing a project to design some new proprietary software system that will be one of the leading products for your company. Consider the following:

- There will be a variety of system development costs including defining system requirements, designing the system, designing infrastructure, coding, unit testing, networking, and integrating, as well as documentation, training materials, possibly consulting costs, possibly licenses, and fees.

- Maybe you have staff costs as well to identify, configure, and purchase hardware, to install it, and to maintain it. Similar staff costs may accrue to acquiring software.

- There could be staff travel, transportation, hotel and meal expense, conference room and equipment fees, fees for coffee service, snacks, and other refreshments.

- There are costs involved in having top management, outside vendors, and clients and customers attend briefings.

- There could be costs associated with testing and refinement, operations, maintenance, refinement, debugging, beta testing, surveying, and compiling data.

Caution

Little or no prior data may be available that the project manager can draw upon to help estimate such a multifaceted project. Budgets from previous projects may serve to confuse and complicate issues, rather than clarify and simplify them.

In particular, look out for these estimation *faux pas:*

- Inexperienced estimators who don't follow any consistent methodology in preparing estimates overlook some cost items entirely, or tend to be too optimistic about what is needed to do the job.

- If you are managing a project that has a direct payoff for a specific client, you have to consider that your organization had to bid very tightly against considerable competition. Perhaps they bid too tightly to get the job done (low-balled to win a contract award). It now becomes your responsibility to work within these constraints. In such cases, you find yourself trying to trim costs every step of the way, even when there is nothing left to trim.

Sometimes organizations intentionally bid on projects they know will be money losers. They do this in the hopes that it will establish a relationship with the customer that will lead to other, more lucrative projects. This is little solace for you if you are the one trying to grind out every ounce of productivity you can from an already overworked project staff or having to use plants and equipment to the max.

■ In some organizations the most careful and comprehensive project budgets end up being slashed by some senior managers or executives who are operating based on some agenda to which you are not privy. In his book *The New Project Management,* author J. D. Frame says, "Political meddling in cost and schedule estimating is an everyday occurrence in some organizations." The best antidote against such meddling, says the author, is "the establishment of objective, clearly defined procedures for project selection ..." which should be set up so that no one, "no matter how powerful, can unilaterally impose their will on the selection process."

The issues raised in this section point to the ever-present need for project managers to build an appropriate degree of slack into their estimates. This is not to say that you are being dishonest or disloyal to your organization, but rather are acknowledging the ruthless rules of project management reality—you hardly ever get the funds you need, and even then, stuff happens!

The 30-Second Recap

■ Because of irrational exuberance, too often the monetary resources allocated to a project (perhaps even before you stepped aboard) have been underestimated.

■ In most organizations, no matter how much you ask for, *you can count on not getting it all.*

■ Perhaps the most effective approach to budgeting combines the top-down and bottom-up techniques.

■ Build an appropriate degree of slack into your estimates!

Gantt Charts

In this section, you learn what a Gantt chart is, why it is so useful in project management, variations you can devise, and how to use Gantt charts to keep your project on schedule.

CHART YOUR PROGRESS

Henry L. Gantt, for whom the Gantt chart is named, was employed at the Aberdeen Proving Grounds (part of what is now the U.S. Department of Defense—then called the War Department) in Aberdeen, Maryland—as an ordinance engineer during the First World War. Although nearly a century has passed, the Gantt chart remains widely recognized as a fundamental, highly applicable tool for project managers everywhere. A Gantt chart enables you to easily view start and stop times for project tasks and subtasks.

Tip

Gantt charts are derived from your work breakdown structure (WBS).

If you use an outline for your WBS, the Gantt depicts each of the tasks and subtasks in chronological order. For tasks that begin at the same time and run concurrently, the Gantt chart is a highly convenient tool. However, overlapping tasks and subtasks can easily be depicted on the Gantt chart as well.

A WBS is created from tree diagrams, which also lend themselves to depiction on a Gantt chart—although the process is a bit tricky when it comes to determining overall project sequence and start and stop times. (More on converting tree diagrams to critical path analysis in "PERT/CPM Charts" on page 1014.)

Two basic forms of Gantt charts are depicted here. The following chart uses bars extending from left to right along the horizontal axis to denote starting and ending times for events or activities. Greater detail could be added if you wish to add subtasks. Color-coding allows you to pinpoint which project workers are handling which tasks and subtasks. The following figure offers a simple plan for depicting the planned sequence of events vs. the actual (the shaded bars). It is a rare project indeed where the brunt of the planned events or tasks are closely mirrored by the actual performance and completion of them:

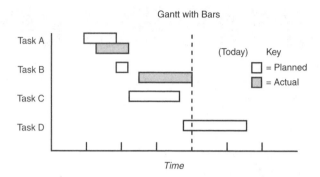

A Gantt chart with bars.

The next figure is merely an alternative to the previous one. Rather than using bars to depict start and stop times and shaded bars to depict actual performance vs. planned performance, this chart uses …

- Unshaded triangles pointing up to depict plan start time
- Unshaded triangles pointing down to depict plan end time
- Shaded triangles pointing up to depict actual start time
- Shaded triangles pointing down to depict actual completion time

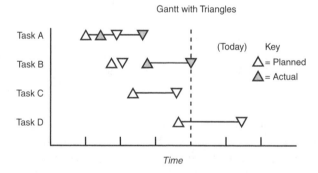

A Gantt chart with triangles.

One of the advantages of preparing a Gantt chart in this format is that tasks and subtasks, and planned vs. actual timeframes can be depicted on a single line emanating from the left of the chart, extending out along the horizontal axis to the right.

The two variations of the Gantt chart presented earlier (there are many others), offer a snapshot of a project's progress based on timeframes.

In the first figure, although Task 1 didn't start on time, its duration was roughly equal to the original planned time.

In Task 2, however, the start time was not only delayed, but the actual completion time for the task was far greater than originally planned. This could signal potential budgetary problems or human resource bottlenecks here or at other points as the project progresses.

If the start of Task 3 is not dependent upon the results of Task 2, then the manager can make a decision to initiate Task 3 as scheduled or even earlier, since delays in starting Task 2 may indicate the availability of idle resources.

If Task 3, however, *is* dependent upon the completion of Task 2, or at least the brunt of it, then the project manager may have no alternative but to have Task 3 start late as well. You can see that the delays in Task 1 and Task 2 may have a cascading effect which puts all project activities behind schedule unless the project manager is able to reallocate resources so as to pick up the slack where possible.

VARIATIONS ON A THEME

The Gantt chart in the following figure for a construction project depicts an eight-week period that includes four events, three of which are actual tasks and one representing completion of the project. Each of the three tasks has between four and six subtasks. Virtually all project activity is dependent upon maintaining the sequence of events as depicted.

The coding at the bottom of the chart indicates critical and noncritical progress related and management critical events.

- Scheduled start and stop times for the duration of tasks are earmarked by solid, downward-pointing triangles emanating from the start and end of progress bars.
- Milestones are depicted by dark diamonds.
- More detail could be added to this chart in the form of other kinds of lines and symbols.

The project manager for this chart probably found this level of coding to be useful and convenient for his purposes.

Tip

Each of the three Gantt charts depicted thus far represent plainly evident ways of illustrating overall project status while including the status of each task. Thus, they serve as valuable tools for keeping project team members abreast of activities, as well as the authorizing party, committees, top managers and executives, and other stakeholders.

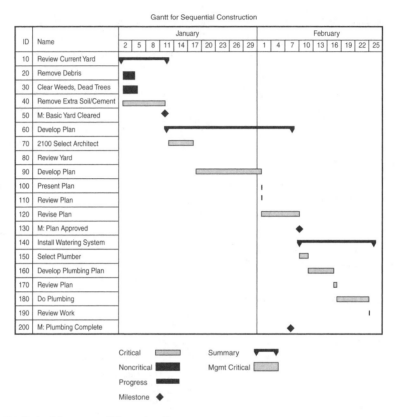

A Gantt chart for sequential construction.

EMBELLISHMENTS OFFER DETAIL

The more tasks involved in your project and the more important the sequence between tasks, the greater your propensity to embellish your Gantt chart. The next figure contains some highly useful added columns.

Gantt with Multiple Predecessors

ID	Name	Duration (Days)	Predecessors	Jan	Feb	Mar	Apr
21	Project Mgmt.	4					
22	Needs Analysis	11					
23	Specifications	7	22				
24	Select Server	8	23				
25	Select Software	14	23				
26	Select Cables	5	24				
27	Purchasing	4	25, 26				
28	Manuals	15	7				
29	Wire Offices	23	7				
30	Set Up Server	5	7				
31	Develop Training	16	8				
32	Install Software	5	10				
33	Connect Network	5	9, 12				
34	Train Users	10	11, 13				
35	Test/Debug	15	13				
36	Acceptance	6	14, 15				

Critical ■■■■■   Noncritical ▭▭▭▭

A Gantt chart with multiple predecessors.

- Column 3, "duration," lists how many days each task is scheduled to take.
- Column 4, "predecessors," identifies what needs to be completed before this task can be initiated.

Often the previous task needs to be completed, but this isn't always the case:

- For the purchasing Task 7, both Tasks 5 and 6 need to be complete.
- For Tasks 8, 9, and 10, only Task 7 needs to be complete, as Tasks 8, 9, and 10 all start at the same time.
- For Task 12, "install software," Task 10 needs to be complete, but Task 11, which is scheduled to start after, does not.

You may wonder, "Why not switch Tasks 11 and 12 in the Gantt chart?" The answer is that Task 11, "developed training," follows directly from the completion of Task 8, "manuals"—whereas Task 12, "install software," directly follows from the completion of Task 10, "set up server." They are listed in sequence on the Gantt chart *based on what they follow, not based on when they start.*

One of the benefits of listing the task duration in days is that it also gives you a strong indicator of required levels of staff support. In the simplest example, if all staff members have the same capability, and a 10-day project requires one staff person per day, you could simply add the total number of days in the duration column and get a total number of staff days necessary for the project.

Caution

Leave yourself (as project manager) *out* of the duration computation, because you are fully involved in management and not engaged in any individual task.

The challenge gets more complex when two, three, four, or more staff people are needed per task for each day of a task's duration, or when varying numbers of staff people are needed per task, per day. It gets complicated further if the skill levels of project staff vary widely.

Tip

Project management software solves many issues related to multiple resource complexity. First, however, you have to understand the basics with paper and pencil, just as you have to learn the fundamentals of math on your own before being able to successfully use a calculator.

GETTING A PROJECT BACK ON TRACK

Whenever you find yourself falling behind in one area, you have to make managerial decisions as to how you will compensate to keep the overall project on track. This involves a shuffling of resources, altering the scope of selected tasks or subtasks, or changing sequence of tasks. Let's visit each of these.

- **Reallocating resources.** It happens to the best of project managers. You launch into a task, and soon enough you find yourself underresourced. You didn't know that a particular task or subtask was going to be so challenging. If it's critical to the overall project, it makes sense to borrow resources from other task areas.

- **Reducing the level of effort on tasks or subtasks.** Just as you discovered that some tasks clearly mandate greater staff resources, you may also find tasks and subtasks that could be completed with *less* effort than you originally budgeted. Perhaps some subtasks can be combined, or skipped all together. For example, if you're doing survey work, perhaps you can get a reasonable result with eight questions instead of 10. Perhaps you can reduce the total number of interviews by 10 percent.

■ **Altering the task sequence.** Another possibility when faced with roadblocks is to change the sequence of tasks or subtasks. Can you substitute easier tasks for more challenging ones until some of your other staff resources are free? Perhaps you can devise a sequence that enables some of your more experienced staff members to manage multiple tasks for a brief duration.

THINKING AHEAD

The Gantt chart is a useful device for engaging in "what-if" questions. As you look at the sequence of events, their duration, and the number of allotted staff days, sometimes you see opportunities to make shifts in advance of the need. Such shifts may help things to run more smoothly down the road.

Tip

If you find that the first several tasks or subtasks to your project are already falling behind, a Gantt chart can help you identify where else this may happen given your operating experience. Hence, you can begin crafting alternative scenarios—alternative Gantt charts that may prove to be more effective for managing the duration of the project.

You may have the pleasant experience of having tasks and subtasks completed in far less time than you had originally plotted. So, use the Gantt chart to reschedule subsequent events, moving them up and taking advantage of the temporary gains that have already been realized.

In summary, the ease of preparation, use, alteration, and sheer versatility of Gantt charts makes them a marvelous tool for both managing your project and depicting your progress to others.

THE 30-SECOND RECAP

■ The Gantt chart is widely recognized as a fundamental, highly applicable tool for project managers to enable one to easily view start and stop times for project tasks and subtasks.

■ The more tasks involved in your project and the more important the sequence between tasks, the greater your propensity and desire to embellish your Gantt chart.

■ The Gantt chart helps answer "what-if" questions when you see opportunities to make shifts in advance of the need.

PERT/CPM Charts

In this section, you learn why projects get increasingly complex, the fundamentals of PERT and CPM charts, why PERT and CPM charts are inexorably linked, and how to use the critical path method to conserve resources.

PROJECTS CAN GET COMPLEX

Complexity happens more often than we care for it to happen. Take the case where you are managing a two- or three-person team. If it is you and another person, you have only one other connection between the two of you. With three people on a project you have three connections. One between you and person A, another between you and person B, and one between person A and B (see the following figure). Oh, if only things stayed that simple.

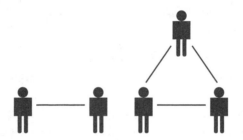

Two people, one connection and three people, three connections.

When there are 4 people on a project there are 6 connections, and with 5 people, there are 10 connections, as shown in the following figure.

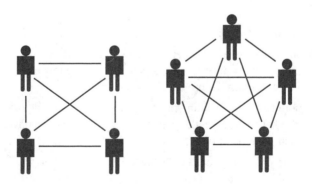

Four people, six connections and five people, ten connections.

When there are six people on a project there are 15 interpersonal connections, and when there are 7 people on a project there are 21. This simple mathematical algorithm reveals that on a project beyond four or five people, the number of interconnections grows rapidly and can even become unwieldy. Now suppose that you have a vital piece of equipment that needs to be shared among several of your project staff. Throw in some other resource constraints as to when they can use that piece of equipment, when the equipment needs to be maintained, and the probability of it being unavailable for repair time.

Now add a second resource, such as another piece of equipment, access to a database, or reliance upon a survey in process. Pretty quickly, with a lot of people on your project team, and with time, money, or resource constraints, effective management can get very involved in a hurry. Throw in some tasks that are dependent upon completion of previous tasks and you have the recipe for bottlenecks, roadblocks, and potentially massive project inefficiencies.

Tip

Complexity as project resources grow is not anybody's fault. It is just the nature of numbers, interconnectedness, restraints, and dependencies.

The Gantt chart, discussed in the "Gantt Charts" section on page 1007, is a valuable tool particularly for projects with a small number of project team members, the project end approaching, and few *project constraints*. For larger, longer-term projects involving many people, resources, and constraints, project managers need more sophisticated tools for maintaining control.

Plain English

Project constraint   A critical project element such as money, time, or human resources, which frequently turns out to be in short supply.

ENTER THE PERT AND CPM

The Program Evaluation and Review Technique, widely referred to and hereafter exclusively referred to as PERT, offers a degree of control that simply becomes essential for many projects. Using PERT, a project manager can identify a task or set of tasks that represent a defined sequence crucial to project success.

A second project management technique whose fundamental approach is close to PERT is called the Critical Path Method, or CPM. The critical path in a project is the one that takes the longest to complete. So, the critical path never has any slack. If you fall behind along the critical path, the whole project falls behind schedule.

Tip

Even if you never have to engage in PERT/CPM analysis, it's good to know the fundamentals.

PERT was developed by Booz—Allan Hamilton and the Lockheed Corporation in participation with the U.S. Navy on their Polaris Missile/Submarine project back in 1958. CPM was developed by Dupont Incorporated around the same time. While each approach has individual features, for our purposes they are close enough to treat them as virtually one and the same, so hereafter, we will refer to PERT/CPM as a unified approach to project management.

Tip

Project managers have used PERT/CPM to compress project schedules by identifying which tasks can be undertaken in parallel, when initially it may have appeared that they needed to be undertaken sequentially—a valuable capability.

PERT/CPM enables a project manager to address issues such as ...

- What will happen during the project if a *noncritical task* slips by two weeks?

- What will happen if a *critical task* slips by a few days and ends up starting at the same time as another critical task?

- If I have to keep project staff on one task for an extra three days, how will it impact all remaining tasks?

Plain English

Critical task   A single task along a critical path.

Noncritical task   A task within a CPM network for which slack time is available.

A SHORT COURSE

By definition, the critical path always represents that path that takes the most time to complete. So, the critical path never contains any slack. Delays along the critical path impact the entire project. Tasks not on the critical path, by definition, always have some slack in their completion time.

Caution

Those assigned to noncritical path tasks don't have to work quite as diligently as those on the critical path. If they are not careful, however, their total duration can exceed that of the critical paths, and thus they could put the project behind as well.

Let's look at how you could use PERT/CPM to manage a simple project. We'll keep it to 10 events or tasks, including a start and an end, so only eight tasks require attention. There will only be two people on this project, you and a friend.

1. Create a work breakdown structure for the project. The following figure will serve as our example:

Word-Breakdown Structure for an Outing			
	Task	Duration (mins.)	
1.	Start	6	
2.	Make drinks	30	Bill
3.	Prepare sandwiches	20	Erika
4.	Prepare fruit	4	Erika
5.	Prepare basket	4	Erika
6.	Gather blankets	4	Bill
7.	Gather sports gear	6	Erika
8.	Load car	8	Bill
9.	Get gas	12	Bill
10.	Drive to outing	40	Erika
11.	End	0	

Work breakdown structure (WBS).

In this example, the path that takes the most time is Task 10, the drive to the outing site.

2. Using the information in the WBS, create a flow chart such as that depicted in the next figure. Notice that in this flow chart some tasks can occur simultaneously. The tasks that Bill works on are depicted above, and the tasks Erica works on are depicted below.

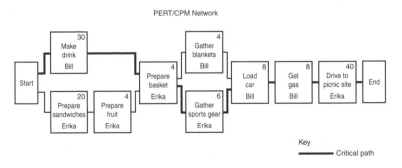

PERT/CPM network.

The relationships between the boxes are indicated with dark or fine lines. For example, "prepare desert" and "prepare casserole" are connected by a thin line. Bill's task "make drinks" connects to "load up food basket" with a thick line, which we will get to in a moment.

Both Bill's and Erica's tasks lead to "fill up food basket."

3. Because "make drinks" takes 30 minutes and Erica's tasks take 20 minutes and four minutes respectively, "make drinks" represents the critical path in this project—hence, the black line between Bill's first and second activity.

Erica's path has six minutes of slack built in. If she starts a few minutes late or takes a minute or two between tasks, she will still finish before Bill, as long as her total slack does not exceed six minutes. Conceivably, she could take her time on each project, adding a minute or two to each and still finish before Bill, and if her slack equals six minutes, she will finish at the same time as Bill.

4. The critical path for the entire project as depicted above can be traced by …

    1. Noting which tasks occur simultaneously.

    2. Noting which ones take longer.

    3. Routing the critical path through them.

    4. Summing the entire length of the critical path.

In the preceding case, the entire project would take 100 minutes. It all sounds straightforward so far, doesn't it?

5. For this or any other type of project, look at the earliest times that critical tasks need to start. Then determine the earliest times that noncritical paths could start. Column 2 of the next figure indicates the earliest start times for all of Bill's and Erica's individual, as well as combined, tasks.

Task	Early Start	Late Start	Slack
Make drinks	0	0	0
Prepare sandwiches	0	6	6
Prepare fruit	20	26	6
Prepare basket	30	30	0
Gather blankets	34	36	2
Gather sports gear	34	34	0
Load car	40	40	0
Get gas	48	48	0
Drive to outing	60	60	0

Roster of events, with start, stop, and slack time.

Column 3 shows the latest start times for Tasks 2, 3, and 6, the first two handled by Erica, and the latter handled by Bill. The *total slack time* for Tasks 2, 3, and 6 respectively are six, six, and two minutes as depicted in Column 4.

Plain English

Slack time   The time interval in which you have leeway as to when a particular task needs to be completed.

Total slack time   The cumulative sum of time that various tasks can be delayed without delaying the completion of a project.

In calculating the latest start times, you simply work from right to left. Focusing on the critical path, if the overall project takes 100 minutes, the latest start time for the last project ("drive to the family outing site") occurs at the 60th minute. This is derived by subtracting 40 minutes of driving from 100 total project minutes.

In a similar fashion, "filling up the tank" and "cleaning the car windows" should commence by the forty-eighth minute. The drive begins at the sixtieth minute and the service station stop lasts twelve minutes. Hence, 60 minus 12 is 48. All the other values can be computed similarly.

6. The computation for determining the latest start times for noncritical times also proceeds from right to left, similar to that described earlier. A slack time is simply computed by subtracting the earliest determined start times from the latest possible start times. Said alternatively, simply subtract the values in Column 2 from the values in Column 3 and the resulting value in Column 4 represents your slack time.

Tip

Notice that there is only slack time when both project team members are simultaneously engaged in individual projects. When both work on the same project, there is no slack time—in this example, joint project activities are on the critical path.

WHAT IF THINGS CHANGE?

By chance, if Bill finishes Task 2, "making the drinks," in less than 30 minutes and Erica has done her job as scheduled, up to 6 minutes could be reduced on the overall project critical path. If Erica starts at the earliest times indicated, works diligently, and finishes at the 24th minute mark as planned, conceivably, she could help with some of Bill's subtasks that lead to the successful completion of Task 2. It may save a few minutes off the total project time.

Just the reverse may happen, however. In her attempt to help Bill, she may end up spilling something, mixing the wrong ingredient, or otherwise causing a delay. If so, you would add back minutes to the critical path determination commensurate with the length of the delay caused.

Because all tasks' durations represent estimates, and very few will go according to plan, the overall project time may vary widely from what Bill and Erica first estimated. They may save one to two minutes on Tasks 5, 8, and 9. Conversely, there may be a traffic backup this fine Saturday morning, and instead of 40 minutes the trip takes an extra 10.

Tip

While time saved sometimes compensates for time lost, on many projects, invariably some tasks throw the project manager for a loop, and require 20 percent to 50 percent more time than budgeted. The project manager who has consulted with others (see "Laying Out Your Plan" on page 975 and "Assembling Your Plan" on page 988) and engaged in both top-down and bottom-up types of planning hopefully can avoid such wide variances. Don't count on it.

I FEEL THE NEED, THE NEED FOR SPEED

Along the critical path, adding more resources to the mix potentially shortens the overall timeframe. If a friend helps Bill and Erica load up the car, a minute may be saved. This is not a dramatic example, but think about the effect of having one person help another move from one apartment to another. The addition of a second worker yields dramatic time savings, especially for bulky, oblong, or heavy items that one person could not easily handle.

When additional resources are allocated for a particular task, this is called crashing (a funny name for a beneficial phenomenon). Crash time represents the least amount of time it would take to accomplish a task or subtask with unlimited resources with which to approach the task—all the equipment or all the money you could ask for.

In *Project Management,* authors Meredith and Mantel estimate that less than 10 percent of the total activities on real world projects actually represent critical activities. Interestingly, most models and most discussions of PERT/CPM depict projects where critical activities outnumber/outweigh noncritical activities!

Most tasks have several subtasks associated with them. So the PERT/CPM network depicted in 8B offers only a broad-brush look at a rather simple project. Examining Task 1 further, suppose that one of the subtasks involved is to add sugar. As Bill mixes up the drinks, he puts in a tablespoon of sugar and then tastes the drink. Is it sweet enough? His answer is subjective, but nevertheless it will be *yes* or *no.*

If it is *no,* then he has a new subtask: adding more sugar. He then makes the taste test again and eventually concludes that the sweetness is just right. At that point, he proceeds onto packing up the drinks. This activity can be depicted by the following figure.

If we were to incorporate the simple loop we have created in the "make drinks" flow chart (see the preceding figure) into the overall PERT/CPM chart depicted earlier in this section, we would have additional boxes with additional lines with additional arrows coming from Task 1, "make drinks," thus complicating our chart.

Likewise, all other tasks may have subtasks associated with them that involve *yes* and *no* questions and repeat loops until a condition is satisfied, hence, the introduction of more delays and the increasing complexity of our PERT/CPM diagram.

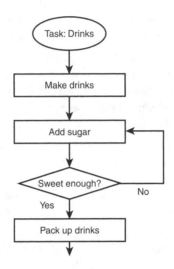

Flow chart of "make drinks" event.

LET'S NETWORK

A complete depiction of tasks and subtasks expanding on the chart in the PERT/CPM figure would be called a Network Configuration or a *network* for short. The project software tools available today assist greatly in this area. In manually constructing the network for simple projects, and to enhance your understanding of critical path charts, you could easily end up sketching and re-sketching the network until you get it right. You would then bounce this off of others, challenge your assumptions, and make sure that you haven't left out anything vital.

Tip

Experienced network diagrammers sometimes add what is called a dummy activity wherein nothing is actually done but which helps to depict relationships between two events. Additionally, there are other charting options, all of which project management software enables you to apply to your particular model.

Plain English

Dummy task   A link that shows an association or relationship between two otherwise parallel tasks along a PERT/CPM network.

ME AND MY ARROW

A highly convenient variation to the chart depicting the PERT/CPM network is called the activity-on-arrow PERT/CPM network and is depicted in the following figure.

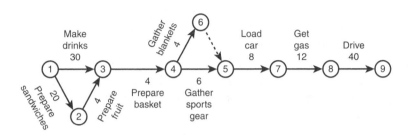

Activity-on-arrow PERT/CPM network.

Notice in this case that the critical path line is constant, starting from Task 1 and proceeding to Task 9, and noncritical activities represent diversions off the critical path. Tasks are represented by the bars with arrows. (Hence, the name "activity-on-arrow.") Events, which represent the beginning or end of a task, are depicted by numbers with a circle around them.

Gathering blankets, Task 6 leads to Event 6, which then must be connected by a dummy task, as already described. This is depicted on the chart as an arrow with a broken line leading to Event 5 (refer to the preceding figure).

Of the two possible diagrams for PERT/CPM networks, either will do. It all depends on your personal preference.

Done manually, updating a PERT/CPM network whenever there is a change in the known or estimated duration of a task can be a true pain. With software, the updating is instantaneous. If you've ever worked with spreadsheet software, you know the feeling. You plug in some new figures and, presto-chango, all the monthly cash totals and the year-end cash total change immediately to reflect the latest modifications.

Tip

Once you introduce new data to your project management tools, a new critical path configuration immediately appears on your screen.

DON'T FALL IN LOVE WITH THE TECHNOLOGY

Mastery of charting processes can lead to problems, particularly among technically oriented project managers.

Caution

Too many project managers fall in love with technology. The tools at their disposal become intoxicating, even addictive.

Managers become overly concerned with the charts and printouts at the cost of ...

- Managing the project team
- Serving as a liaison to top managers and executives and stakeholders in general
- Meeting the needs of the customer or client who needs interim psychological stroking as well as ensuring that the final desired outcome will be achieved.

Caution

Studies of managed projects reveal that the most frequent causes of failure are nontechnical, such as the lack of commitment among project team members, hidden political agendas, and the inability of the project manager to effectively communicate project results (the subject of the next section).

So use work breakdown structures, Gantt charts, and PERT/CPM networks for all their worth, but keep your eye on the people-related dynamics of the project.

THE 30-SECOND RECAP

- Managing a project of five people is far more complex than managing a project of three people. With each new person, or each new resource, far more lines of interconnectivity occur.
- For any given project there is a critical path that the project takes, and a delay in any activity along the critical path delays the overall project.
- Crashing a project means allocating additional resources to a particular task so that it is completed in less time than originally allotted. Thus, the entire project is completed in less time.
- It is easy to fall in love with the charts and technical tools available for project management today, but most project failures are a result of neglecting the human dynamic.

Reporting Results

In this section, you learn why it is getting more difficult to report your results, how to effectively use communication tools and techniques, the importance of giving credit to your team, and the importance of assuming any blame alone.

MORE COMMUNICATIONS CHANNELS LEAD TO LESS ACCESSIBILITY

In this age of the Internet, intranets, e-mail, pagers, faxes, cell phones, and whatever else is available next, you would think that it would be easier than before to communicate your progress as you proceed on your project. Yet it is just the opposite. The increasing number of communication vehicles have resulted in making it more difficult to get the time and attention of those to whom you must report, even when they are waiting for your report! Does this seem like a paradox?

Everyone in the working world today feels inundated by too much information at least several times during the week—if not every day and all of the time. Think back to yesteryear, when most of today's communication devices were not available. How did the typical project manager convey reports to his boss? Chances are, they worked within shouting distance of each other.

Many communication vehicles muster considerable impact for a time following their widespread acceptance in the marketplace. Twenty-five years ago, it truly was a big deal to receive a FedEx package in the morning. Now, think about how exciting it is when express packages from any vendor arrive. More often than not, they simply add to the burden of what you have already received.

Against this backdrop, is it any wonder that project managers have a more difficult time reporting results at both scheduled intervals and at random times throughout the course of their projects?

Caution

Even in this era when you can fax or e-mail skillfully developed WBS, Gantt, or PERT/CPM charts, there is no guarantee that your intended recipient will view them, or at least review them as scheduled.

Starting with the least technical, least involved method of communication, one person talking to another, let's proceed through widely available communication options at your disposal—with an eye on how to make them work for you to their best advantage.

In-Person Communications

For scheduled meetings where you have to report your progress, the key word is *preparation*. Have all your ducks in a row. Have your charts made out, your notes in order, and make bullet points of what you want to say. Chances are that the person to whom you are reporting is ultra-busy. This project may be one of many issues he or she needs to contend with.

Caution

If your live report is to a committee, preparation becomes even more important. Committees are more critical and less understanding than a single person. If you are using presentation software, such as Corel Presentations, PowerPoint, or any of the other popular programs, restrain yourself!

It is far too easy to go on and on, showing slide after slide in brilliant color with words that shake and sounds that go boom. This only extends the length of your presentation and takes you off the mark of what you need to be reporting.

■ If you have a video to present, make it 12 minutes or less. Four minutes or less would not be too short, depending on your project, how far along you are, to whom you report, and other dynamics of your organization.

Tip

Brevity is the soul of wit when it comes to making an audio-visual presentation.

■ If you're using a flip chart, wall chart, white board, or other presentation hardware, prepare in advance. For flip charts and wallboards, map out and complete what you can *before* the presentation begins.

■ For white boards and other media which you compose on the run, work from comprehensive notes and schematics prepared in advance so that you don't end up meandering all over the place.

Informal Person-to-Person Meetings

In informal person-to-person meetings, the same guidelines apply, except in spades. Be brief, be concise, and be gone! Don't attempt to collar anyone in the lunchroom, the hallway, the lavatory, or any other informal setting unless prior protocols for this kind of interaction have been established. You want to catch people when they are sitting down. That is when they can make notes, pick up the phone, click a mouse, staple something, whatever! When someone is standing, these types of follow-up and feedback activities aren't nearly as viable.

If you are informally asked to say a few words in a group meeting, stand and face the entire group while they are sitting. No matter what you say, this will give you a tad more authority. Again, be as concise and brief as possible. Be open to insights and take criticism. Thank the group for their attention and depart gracefully and quickly.

TELEPHONE CONTACT

Maybe your project calls for you to phone your boss several times a day, daily, several times a week, or only every now and then. Regardless, try to schedule the actual time of the call. It is far too easy to end up with voice mail or an answering machine. This can be highly frustrating if you need an interactive conversation then and there.

If you or your boss carry a pager or cell phone and you have exchanged contact numbers with one another, hopefully you both respect each other's needs not to be unduly interrupted during the day. Such devices are excellent in situations where immediate feedback is crucial and are entirely helpful for alerting each other as to when a formal telephone meeting has been scheduled. Otherwise, they are a true pain in the neck, representing open invitations to interrupt somebody anytime or with anything.

Why is scheduling so important? Studies show that the likelihood of getting through to someone you have called at random is now less than 28 percent and falling. If you do end up talking to a machine, here are some guidelines for being as effective as you can be in that circumstance:

- Aim for a message somewhere between 35 and 55 seconds. Too short, and the other party is likely to discount the importance of your message—unless, of course, it is something like "Get out of the building! It's about to blow!"

- Longer than 55 to 60 seconds and you are likely to raise the ire of the other person, who undoubtedly has been receiving messages from other people all day long.

- Speak concisely, for indeed everyone else in the world speaks hurriedly. Leave your phone number at a speed at which it actually can be written down by the respondent on the first listening. A good way to do this is to pretend that you are writing your phone number in the air with your finger as you announce it over the phone.

- Offer some gem in your message. Simply saying, "Please give me a call back," or "get back to me," is not nearly as effective as, "We need your feedback regarding what to do about the extra shipment we ordered."

E-MAIL

E-mail grows more powerful with each new version released. Popular programs such as Outlook Express, Netscape, Eudora, and Claris offer more than enough options, benefits, and features.

If you think an in-person report or phone conversation is warranted, you're probably right. Go ahead and follow through.

Tip

If you need a "yes" or "no" answer to a project-related question and have leeway as to when you need to get the answer, e-mail is a great tool. If you need to easily transmit report data to others waiting for it specifically via e-mail, then e-mail can also be a highly convenient reporting tool.

In general, here's a brief roster of appropriate project-reporting uses of e-mail:

- Approval or disapproval
- Forwarding vital information to appropriate parties
- Data, charts, summaries, estimates, and outlines specifically requested by recipients

Sometimes e-mail can be inappropriate for reporting purposes, such as conveying ...

- The overly complex.
- Outlandish, highly novel, or earthshaking ideas.
- Items requiring major discussion, clarification, or delicacy.
- Emotionally charged information.

Dr. Jaclyn Kostner says that e-mail is better than voice mail when ...

- A written record is needed.
- Language is a barrier. In multilanguage teams, written words are frequently easier to understand than spoken ones, especially when accents are heavy or language skills are less than fluent.
- The team's normal business day hours in each location do not match.
- You've been unable to reach the person interactively, but know the person needs the details right away.

Conversely, leave a voice mail or answering machine message when ...

■ The sound of your voice is key to understanding your message.

■ The recipient is mobile. Voice mail is easier to access than e-mail in most cases.

■ Your message is urgent.

FAXES, MEMOS, AND INFORMAL NOTES

A hard-copy note in this day and age sometimes gets more attention than voice mail and e-mail. Moreover, don't underestimate the impact of a hand-written, friendly note that states something as simply as, "Making good progress on Task 2, anticipate completion by tomorrow afternoon and smooth transition to start Task 3."

If you do write by hand, be sure to use your best handwriting. It is of no value if your handwriting looks like a flea fell into an inkwell and then staggered across the page before dying.

Caution

Poor penmanship has cost businesses millions of dollars due to misunderstandings, disconnections, rewrites, and revisions.

FORMALLY COMPOSED DOCUMENTS

Whether you type and print a letter to be hand-delivered, sent by fax, sent by mail, or delivered by courier, be sure that you have proofread your own document. This is particularly crucial if the document is a deliverable offered in association with achieving a milestone on the project. Undoubtedly, the document will make the rounds, be copied, and eventually be seen by stakeholders. Any little typo or grammatical error that you haven't corrected, even if small and not critical to your overall understanding of the document, tends to diminish your status somewhat.

As with person-to-person meetings, keep your document focused—short is better than long, concise is better than rambling. Although this varies from organization to organization and project to project, it probably makes good sense to have all of your contact information on any document that you submit to project stakeholders. This would include your name, address, phone, fax, e-mail, cell phone, pager number, car phone, and whatever other electronic leashes ensnare you.

TELECONFERENCING

Teleconferencing might take place between you, your project staff, and those to whom you are reporting, or it may simply be you alone reporting to others. They are listening on some type of speakerphone. Hence, your words need to be as clear and concise as you can practically offer.

You need to slow down your pace just a bit and make sure that words and sentences have clear endings. Even the most sophisticated speakerphones today designed for top executives and teleconferences still have major short-comings. Not all words are clear; some words, despite the claims of manufac-turers, still seem to get clipped. There is a small degree of channel noise, although this is diminishing all the time as newer and newer models appear.

Whatever you do, don't speak into a speakerphone on your end. It will sound like you are in a tin can, or at the bottom of a well. Pick up the phone and speak into the receiver or use a headset, which is widely available in office supply stores. Have your notes laid out in front of you, in sequence, so that you can offer a sequential, easy-to-understand telephone presentation.

Tip

Be prepared for the same round of observations, insights, and criti-cisms that you might experience in person. Teleconferencing partici-pants are somewhat less reticent to speak up as they would be in person, but the potential is still there.

Teleconferences today often are conducted in conjunction with online presen-tation materials. For example, the committee hearing your report can follow your slide show in the exact sequence that you are presenting it. This can be done by uploading your presentation to the post location in advance and sim-ply referring to each slide as numbers 1, 2, and so forth. Or, you can use a variety of Internet vendors who will assist in facilitating the transaction in real time. Check out www.MentorU.com, the leading online "faculty for hire," offering training in all manner of presentation skills. MentorU uses combina-tion teleconferencing and online presentation technology to the utmost.

WEB-BASED PRESENTATIONS

Depending on the dynamics of your situation, you may be able to fulfill the formal aspects of your reporting requirements via Web pages. Again, the watchword here is conciseness. It is far too easy to splash lavish colors and audio and visual effects onto a Web page that really distract from, rather than enhance, the overall message you want to deliver.

Tip

The page can be buried someplace within your company's Web page, part of your company's intranet placed on an independent server, or simply delivered in HTML or other hyperlink software via an e-mail attachment.

The beauty of those big computer screens that are populating people's desks these days is that the charts and slides that you send over look as magnificent on their end as they do on yours.

Oh, Them Golden Bullets

In their book, *Project Management for the 21st Century,* the authors say that "messages are golden bullets—you use them sparingly."

Too often, project managers *overcommunicate.* They spend too much time with verbiage and too little time addressing the issue at hand. Before preparing a report or delivering a presentation to any project stakeholders, consider the following:

- Will the message have strong impact, and what will be its after affects? Will someone misinterpret what you have said? Have you been as clear as you can be?

- Contemplate in advance who the receiver of your message is. This includes all receivers, those present at the time you first delivered it and anyone else who will encounter the message later.

- To the degree that you have leverage, decide on the best medium to deliver your message and the best timing. After your organization has received bad news is not a good time to convey additional bad news.

- Stick within the boundaries that have been established. If your report is supposed to be three pages or less, keep it to three pages. If it is supposed to be delivered via fax, deliver it via fax. If it is supposed to be free of graphics, keep it free of graphics, and so on.

- Seek feedback on your message. What value is it to you if you deliver a report and then don't get a timely response? You may head off in a slightly different direction because you didn't get the needed input in a reasonably timely manner.

Incorporate the Thoughts of Others

Whenever you are making a report to others, either in person or via cyber-space, in real time or delayed, try to incorporate others' opinions and ideas into what you are doing. For example, you could say, "As John suggested to us the other day, we went ahead and did XYZ. This turned out quite well for all involved."

As often as possible, relate within your report how you are doing. This may also dovetail with what other divisions or departments are doing and how the work may benefit the organization as a whole. Feel free to accent the mile-stones that you have achieved and the deliverables that you have offered, but don't go overboard.

It makes great sense to share the credit and praise for a job well done with as many people as you can. Always try to bring credit to your team, even if you did the brunt of the work. Upper management tends to know what is going on regardless. The upshot is that you look like a team player and somebody who is worthy of promotion.

Conversely, accept the blame for what didn't go so well without trying to cast dispersions. You will look like a "stand up" guy or gal, and people have a secret appreciation for this.

Be entirely honest in the report when it comes to addressing your own perform-ance. There is some leeway for tooting your own horn, but only if it is an *accurate* toot. No one likes a braggart. No one likes to read a report filled with fluff, and no one likes to be deceived. Stay on the up and up and develop your reputation as a project manager of integrity.

The 30-Second Recap

- The increasing number of communication vehicles makes it more difficult to get the attention of those to whom you must report.
- For scheduled presentation of any variety, the key word is *prepara-tion*.
- A hard-copy note in this day and age sometimes gets more attention than voice mail and e-mail.
- As PC screens get larger and sharper, your reports including charts and slides that you send over look magnificent.
- Incorporate the words of others and give credit to the group, but per-sonally accept blame. Be entirely honest when it comes to addressing your own performance.

Choosing Project Management Software

In this section, you learn the kinds of software that are available, the capabilities of software, which software functions are crucial, and guidelines for selection.

WITH THE CLICK OF A MOUSE

Project management software today is available at a variety of prices, offering a wide variety of functions. You can use software to plan, initiate, track, and monitor your progress. You can develop reports, print individual charts, and at the push of a button (or a click of a mouse) e-mail virtually any aspect of your project plans to any team member, top manager, executive, or stakeholder.

Whereas earlier versions of PM software focused on *planning, scheduling* and *results,* tools for *analyzing your progress, finding critical paths,* and *asking "what if" questions* were lacking.

Caution

Today, there are so many options in and among so many vendors that the problem is finding your way through the bewildering choices.

Bennett Lientz and Kathryn Rea observe in *Project Management for the 21st Century* that project management software has at least five distinct differences from more widely known and used word processing, database, and spreadsheet software:

- PM software is used far less often than other categories of software.
- Fewer people use PM software, although project participants and stakeholders usually do see the generated output.
- PM software allows for more customization than many other types of software.
- PM software tends to be more expensive than commonly used, widely known types of software.
- Fewer people in your work sphere are likely to know how to use PM software.

LEAVE A GOOD THING ALONE

Project management software went from being expensive and crude, to less expensive and highly functional, to even less expensive but confusing. When Harvard Project Manager was launched in 1983, it represented a breakthrough in PM software. Its main focus was on project budgeting, scheduling, and resource management. With Harvard Project Manager you were able to generate Gantt charts, PERT/CPM charts, and a variety of other charts and tables. It was considered an integrated project planning and control package and sold for as little as 30 percent of the price of its clunky, less functional predecessors.

In the two decades that followed, competition among PM software vendors heated up, prices came down, and functionality went sky high. Many packages now are harder to learn and use. Consider your own experience in using word processing, database, or spreadsheet software. Aren't there earlier versions of current programs that were easier and more convenient? You were able to pop them in, learn them in a day or so, and go on your merry way.

Today, with expanding megabyte counts, it seems that the vendors need to have everything plus the kitchen sink. This gives them the opportunity to design splashy ads listing umpteen features. Realistically, how many people are true power users who would use all of the advertised features?

Caution

Whereas the Harvard Project Manager could be learned in as little as a day if you were diligent, current PM software can take as much as five days of your time, if you are starting from square one and have no PC guru or mentor nearby to steer you along.

WHOSE CHOICE IS IT?

Certainly, if your organization, department, or division already uses or prefers a certain type of software, then your decision is already made. Your quest becomes mastering that software—or at least the parts of it that are crucial for you to know.

Tip

If a brand of PM software is the preferred choice in your workplace, and other projects employ such software, you are relatively fortunate. Other project managers or staff will know how to use it and can serve as *ad-hoc* software gurus to you.

With no experienced users in your work setting, some important questions arise:

■ **What kind of software should be chosen?** In choosing PM software, a rule of thumb is to choose a popular and very well-known package. The price is likely to be highly competitive, people around you will have either heard of the vendor or heard that the software is widely known, and you won't have to spend a lot of time defending your decision!

■ **Who should learn it?** If you and you alone will have responsibility for learning the software, you need to build time and expense into your budget—it will take you time to learn it or to take a course, and your time has a cost.

Tip

The Project Management Institute at www.pmi.org and the Project Management Control Tower at www.4pm.com each offer a wide variety of books, audio-visual materials, training guides, classroom training, seminars, and increasingly, online training. Also, PMFO-RUM at www.ProjectManager.com offers a host of career opportunities for project managers or those seeking to enter the profession.

While it may seem obvious that you as the project manager should be the primary user of PM software, you may need to rethink that assumption. Depending on what you are managing and the dynamics of your organization, if you were to be the primary software user, you might spend the brunt of your time working with the software and have precious little time left for forming and building your team, maintaining reporting requirements, and offering the overall kind of day-to-day project management that the venture requires.

Recognizing the danger of having a project manager become too immersed with project management software, some organizations have established support groups or provide internal software gurus. These gurus are the in-house experts and are often loaned to project management teams for the duration of the project.

The gurus work directly with the project manager, incorporating his feedback, answering his questions, and undertaking whatever types of analysis the project manager requests. They routinely maintain schedules, budget reports, and track the allocation of resources. An experienced software guru knows how and how often to share project-related reports with project staff and project stakeholders in general.

What's Your Pleasure?

Assuming that you're not in a position where your organization will loan
someone to you who will handle the brunt of PM software activities, and assuming that there is no particular program of choice yet established, how do
you go about selecting software?

First, establish what kind of user you're going to be, which is largely determined by two elements: the size of your project and how technical you are.

For tiny projects of zero to two staff for a project of a few months or less, it's
possible that no project management software is necessary! How so? You may
already possess all the software and software knowledge you need to be effective in managing a small project. We're talking about spreadsheets, word
processing, a graphics or drawing program, and the functionality to generate
tables, graphs, flow charts, and other diagrams.

Tip

Though somewhat makeshift, the combination of reports and exhibits that you can muster with your current software and skills
might be more than adequate for your project needs.

Your current software may be entirely adequate if the basic work breakdown
structure (WBS) and a Gantt chart or two is all you need, and you don't necessarily have to create a critical path.

For projects involving four or more people, extending several months or
longer, with a variety of critical resources, it makes sense to invest in some
type of software. Again, it doesn't necessarily need to be PM software per se.
Many calendar and scheduling software programs come with built-in functions. You can produce tables, Gantt charts, and even maintain a schedule for
4 to 10 people. Increasingly, you can do this on handheld computers.

Tip

With a total project management team of four people, extended over
several months, employing dedicated PM software may make the
most sense.

Dedicated PM Software

The competition among dedicated PM software vendors is keen. Major vendors in the field include PlanView, Inc., Primavera, Microsoft, Dekker
Welcome, and Artemus. (An overview of PM software with descriptions can
be found in the next section.) There are also lower-end programs that will
help you generate plans, project reports, and basic charts that don't require as

much learning time. Products such as Quick Gantt, Milestone Simplicity, and Project Vision sell for less than $100 and are available at office superstores as well as retail software stores.

Tip

Inexpensive PM software may be your best option if you don't have anyone else in the organization who can serve as guru, but you do wish to automate, rather than manually generate, critical reports and charts.

Suppose that you are managing many people over many months, and have a thousand or more tasks and subtasks to complete. Here, you would look at PM software for midrange project managers. You can spend anywhere from $200 to $6,000 using the more feature-laden versions of software named previously. Most packages will give you the full range of tools sought by even veteran project managers on multiyear projects.

The problem with software at this level is that you can quickly become a slave to it. For example, will you decide to schedule and track all subtasks and tasks based on identified start times and stop times, for each staff member, all the time? Or will you continually rely on your staff to give you estimates of task and subtask completion times?

- Relying on the input of your staff helps to build a team, but it takes more work.

- Using the software is arduous at first, saves time later, and keeps your head in front of a PC screen more often—away from the people and the events happening all around you.

High-end project management software is designed for the very largest, longest-duration, most involved types of projects. If you are a high-end user, you wouldn't have picked up this book. Here, we are talking about software that can range from a few thousand to several thousand dollars. Learning such packages could take weeks. The software selection process alone could take weeks or months.

Caution

Even if at the high end there are so many programs available, made by such vendors as Cobra, Semantic, Instaplan, Klavis (for Mac users), Open Plan, Prima-vera, Microsoft, Enterprise PM, Microplanner, and others, that you would need a consultant to make such a selection.

Regardless of your level of PM software knowledge, your selection could be one of the most important factors in overall project success. Many project managers have found that the software in force is too complex and too unwieldy to use for the entire project. Some end up using only an element of the software, such as budgeting or scheduling; some use it only for making charts; others end up abandoning the software midstream. Undoubtedly, a whole lot of scrambling follows because whatever the software was used for now needs to be done manually.

How Will You Use PM Software?

The first time, modest users obviously won't use PM software the way that an experienced pro will. Nevertheless, there are levels of usage worth differentiating:

- **Reporting.** Here the project manager uses the software to generate Gantt or, possibly, PERT/CPM charts. She may use other software programs such as word processing and spreadsheets to supplement her project graphs and produce reports.

- **Tracking.** The software is used to compare actual vs. planned progress. As the project staff completes tasks and subtasks, the results of their efforts are logged so that the *project tracking* effort stays current.

Plain English

Project tracking   A system for identifying and documenting progress performance for effective review and dissemination to others.

- **What-if.** The PM software is engaged to identify the impact of shuffling resources, changing the order of subtasks, or changing tasks' dependencies. What-if analysis is kind of fun, because you get immediate feedback.

Caution

Change one variable at a time to have a full grasp of its impact. If you change too many variables at once, the picture becomes cloudy.

- **Cost control.** Project managers use PM software to allocate costs to various project resources. This is usually done by figuring out how much resource time and effort is consumed. Lientz and Rea observe that "most project management software systems lack flexibility in handling costs as well as interfaces into budgeting and accounting systems." Thus, the cost computations that a project manager makes generally don't plug into the overall cost structures the accountants in her organization work with.

- **Clocking.** By adding project team member hours expended on various tasks and subtasks on a regular basis, project managers can then generate reports showing actual vs. scheduled use of resources.

CHECKLISTS AND CHOICES

It's hard to generalize what type of software various levels of users may require, but here are some general criteria worth considering:

- **Ease of use.** Is the software easy to plug in, are there good help screens, is there a tutorial, is there strong customer support, and is the software menu driven and intuitive? Is it easy to move things around, and are the commands as standard as possible and easy to learn? Is there an accompanying manual that is easy to read? Are you able to get started on some functions quickly?

- **Reporting functions.** Does the program allow for individual revising of report formats, can these be easily imported into other software programs, and can they easily be saved, added to, combined, and read?

- **Charting capacity.** Does the software offer the basic project management charts (virtually all do), is there automatic recalculation, are there easy-to-use options, and are there drag-and-drop capabilities? Can charts be imported and exported easily, are supporting graphics easy to see and to use, and can charts readily be changed into other forms?

- **Calendar generators.** Does this software allow for calendars of all durations, in a variety of formats, for different aspects of the project and project staff, with the ability to mark particular days and times, with holidays and other nonworking days preprogrammed, and are these calendars also easily importable and exportable?

- **Interfacing.** Can you easily connect with telecommunication systems, and is information easily shared with others who require online access? Is it efficient in terms of byte space consumed?

- **Report generation.** Can a variety of report formats be selected, with quick-changing capabilities and easy transference to word processing software?

In addition, consider these attributes:

- Shows onscreen previews of reports prior to printing
- Offers a variety of formats for Gantt and PERT charts
- Works with a variety of printers and other equipment
- Enables several projects to share a common pool of resources
- Conveys cost data by task or by time
- Allows printing of subsections of charts
- Accepts both manual and automatic schedule updates

Most of the vendors you will encounter have such capabilities. Hence, you need to go beyond a strict comparison of software functionality and consider the attributes, benefits, and services of using a particular vendor as well. In fact, for any major purchase it's advisable to have a good set of questions. The following is a list adapted from my book *The Complete Idiot's Guide to Managing Stress*. Ask the vendors whether they …

- Offer any corporate, government, association, military, and educators' discounts?
- Have weekly, monthly, or quarterly seasonal discounts?
- Offer off-peak discounts?
- Guarantee the lowest price?
- Accept major credit cards?
- Accept orders by fax or e-mail?
- Have a money-back guarantee, or other guarantee?
- Use a 1-800 ordering fax line?
- Guarantee shipping dates?
- Have a toll-free customer service line?
- Avoid selling, renting, or otherwise using your name and ordering information?
- Insure shipments?
- Charge for shipping and handling?
- Include tax?
- Have any other charges?
- Have demos?
- Offer free or low-cost upgrades?
- Have references available?
- Keep a list of satisfied customers in your area?

- Have been in business long?
- Have standard delivery times?
- Warranty the product?

MAKING A LIST, CHECKING IT TWICE

After you've established your own set of selection criteria in consideration of all the things that your project entails and in consideration of the various attributes, benefits, and features of working with each vendor, engage in a useful exercise: Decide on paper what you *must have* vs. what would be *nice to have* vs. what is *not needed*, but you will take it if it is offered.

Then, using articles, product reviews, and the vendors' Web sites, make a preliminary survey of the various packages available and how they stack up. A simple matrix or grid with the vendors listed across the top representing columns, and the important attributes to you down the left side of the page will suffice.

Caution

Selection processes can be brutal. You may encounter 10 or 12 possible vendors, but try to knock down the list early to three to five. Sometimes, a particular feature is so outstanding that it outweighs other mediocre elements of a vendor's overall package.

Most vendors will readily offer you product demonstrations. Downloadable product demos often are available at the vendor's Web site. Otherwise, demos can often be observed over the Internet.

Tip

Some vendors allow you to download a full package, available for a limited duration.

If you've narrowed the field to three or four vendors, you have a fighting chance of identifying the one that best meets your needs.

Tip

If at all possible, observe the software *actually in use* either in your own organization or someplace else.

Observing software in use is most telling. Someone in the field actually using the software can provide first-person input as to where the software shines and doesn't shine. You get far richer information than you can get from a Web site, or for that matter, a product demo.

THE 30-SECOND RECAP

- PM software has become more sophisticated and more bewildering. Many packages will do the jobs you need to do, but are so difficult to learn and to master that you waste valuable resources, namely your time. Worse, you end up abandoning the package.

- Many organizations loan software gurus to a project or have other project managers who can supply ad hoc mentoring. If this applies to you, consider yourself fortunate.

- Don't get so immersed in software that you lose contact with your project team and the environment that surrounds you.

- Choosing the right software may be vital. Predetermine your selection criteria so that you're not buffeted by an endless array of options, benefits, and features.

A Sampling of Popular Programs

In this section, you learn which software programs are popular, what vendors have to say about their own programs, and how to get in touch with vendors.

YESTERDAY'S NEWS

As each day passes, any software program evaluation presented in any book ages and soon becomes obsolete. Consequently, the surveys and review of products listed in this section are presented for the sake of example only!

A survey titled "Tools of the Trade: A Survey of Project Management Tools" appeared in the September 1998 issue of the *Project Management Journal*. The *Journal* evaluated what the authors called "Top Project Management Tools." Some 159 project managers responded to survey questions, out of 1,000 managers initially contacted. The typical respondent had slightly more than 10 years of project management experience and slightly more than 12 years' experience in the field of information systems. Hence, this was a select group of veteran project managers.

The 159 respondents cited 79 different project management tools that they either were using currently or had used within three years. Of note, the top

10 of these 79 tools were identified by three quarters of the respondents. The top 10 tools in order were ...

1. Microsoft Project
2. Primavera Project Planner
3. Microsoft Excel
4. Project Workbench
5. Time Line
6. Primavera SureTrak
7. CA-SuperProject
8. Project Scheduler
9. Artemis Prestige
10. FasTracs

Microsoft Project was the most frequently used PM software at the time of the survey. This is somewhat understandable. In the late 1990s, Microsoft dominated all channels of software advertising and promotion.

Artemis Prestige, Primavera Project Planner, and Project Scheduler were cited as being used more often for projects lasting six months or longer. However, for overall satisfaction with project management software, the ratings were close, with Project Scheduler first, followed by Primavera Project Planner, Project Workbench, Microsoft Excel, Primavera SureTrak, and CA-SuperProject. Thereafter, the score began to fall off a bit.

These programs were rated as to content, accuracy, format, ease of use, and timeliness, and then given an overall rating. The top five or six choices in terms of overall satisfaction closely matched the top five or six software packages for which project managers routinely received the most training within their organizations.

However, FasTracs was one product for which managers routinely had no hours of training, and yet it received a remarkably high score. This was especially true in terms or "overall adequacy" when respondents were asked how many months they had been working with the various software products, and how many hours a week they spent using them. Thus, based on this one study, FasTracs would be the product of choice for the first-time or light user, if all things could be held constant.

Tip

Not surprisingly, the training time that project managers received for the various software packages (that they were charged with learning) influenced how adequate they thought the software to be. Stated another way, the more training you have to work with a particular type of project management software, the higher you tend to rate that software.

ARMED AND ONLINE

Flash forward to today, when more and more project management tools have an online component. The power and capability of such programs is awesome.

The following is but a snapshot in time as to what is available now, largely in the words of the vendors themselves.

Caution

The array of software options available today is even more bewildering than that of years ago.

PLANVIEW

PlanView provides all-browser software within a Windows environment for managers, employees, and others throughout the enterprise—as well as partners, vendors, and service providers in the extended enterprise. The software helps manage projects and other work, update employee information, and manage the workforce. PlanView optimizes the staffing of multiple projects by taking into account the skills and true availability of your workforce. Thus, PlanView enables an enterprise to measure all work and to manage to its full capacity.

PlanView is delivered by user role. That could be managers, employees, and others throughout the enterprise—as well as partners, vendors, and service providers. PlanView Online is an integrated project and workforce management system, is 100 percent Web software, and features ...

- Personalized Web portal
- Self-administration by staff
- Collaborative critical path engine
- Support for your project office
- Viewing workforce capacity
- Integrated time and expense tracking
- Project delivery model

PlanView uses an enterprise Web portal to manage workplace access to information and applications. The enterprise portal is the workers' interface to the PlanView intranet or extranet. The features available to each role are tailored for each customer.

Managers, employees, and business partners sign on to PlanView through a dynamically built Web page called HomeView. Each person's HomeView portal reflects his rights to the information in the central repository and the unique needs of his role in the enterprise.

When the user signs on to the system, his or her profile is recalled, and a unique set of features is placed on the menu for his or her use. PlanView calls these FeatureSets, and they provide access to the rest of the functions of the PlanView suite. For instance, a project manager has access to her project portfolio, the scheduling engines, and approval of status information. A contributor will report time, expenses, and remaining work and update his skills.

Users' favorite Web links for discussion groups, project or department Web sites, as well as executables for key software such as virtual meeting software, project sites, and methodology content providers are all easily accessed.

Tip

Reminders let users track events with knowledge of current time, to inform them when events are due.

DEKKER

Dekker TRAKKER project management software offers many enhanced features, such as enhanced integration with Oracle and SQL Server for complete enterprise control, and enhanced human interface to simplify data entry through spreadsheet views. The software also does the following:

- Provides the ability to utilize Microsoft Access for Work-group and offline data requirements.
- Increases system performance.
- Provides user-defined three-dimensional bar charts.
- Provides configurable milestone and bar colors.
- Enables enhanced curve loading.
- Yields real-time calculation.
- Offers ABC and Gantt view screens.

The Gantt view screen, for example, offers selectable three-dimensional activity bars, user-defined bar style, customizable colors, configurable columns, integrated baseline control, interim milestones on a single line, user-defined milestone symbols, fiscal and standard time scale, and real-time calculation. The ABC View Screen offers selectable data row, values in heads, quantity dollars, burdens, configurable columns, the new Trakker spreadsheet view for familiar data entry, integrated baseline control, real-time calculation, and complete cost and schedule integration.

PRIMAVERA

Primavera SureTrak Project Manager recognizes a project team's need for constant, timely project communications and updates. Primavera bolstered its SureTrak with Web publishing enhancements that lets users quickly and easily save project layouts and reports in HTML format. The Web Publishing Wizard can then group and sort the tabular and graphical HTML reports and layouts from all your projects, into a single, easy-to-read project Web site that can be conveniently viewed by the whole team.

Based on extensive usability testing, SureTrak simplifies project management for mainstream use by addressing the ease-of-use needs of novice project managers, while delivering project management applications for small- to medium-size projects. Its rich feature offering includes advanced organization of project plans, activities, and team members; Project KickStart for step-by-step project plan creation; Progress Spotlight for easy updating of project activities and Web Publishing Wizard for enhanced online communications among team members.

The Variable Timescale feature lets users zoom in on a portion of the project time scale. For example, activities scheduled for the next month can be displayed in days, while the rest of the project is displayed in weeks or months. This feature presents the details for one period of interest, while still displaying the entire project on one page.

To give project teams greater insight into the sequence of interrelated project tasks, SureTrak 3.0 includes an intuitive PERT Timescale display.

SureTrak builds on existing customization capabilities, by enabling users to modify an individual or group of bars based on activity attributes. By combining new display options with colors and patterns, project managers will be able to graphically communicate valuable project details and status for analysis.

SureTrak includes several other new capabilities, designed specifically to simplify use of the software. In addition to an updated user interface that adheres to accepted 32-bit operating environments, users will find they are more productive when analyzing alternative what-if scenarios for their projects, by taking advantage of new options for using project filters and display layouts.

OTHER PRIMAVERA PRODUCTS

With P3e you can manage the entire project lifecycle. P3e is a total project management solution, encompassing all aspects of the project lifecycle. It combines all of the in-depth project management capabilities required by project-driven managers.

Through costs, schedule, and earned value thresholds, or variances, P3e automatically generates issues when thresholds are exceeded by project elements. Project managers can prioritize resulting issues and let P3e send e-mail alerts to the responsible parties to ensure prompt resolution. To make sure that project risks are properly identified and quantified, P3e also integrates risk management and assesses the impact of those risks. P3e quickly performs what-if simulation to determine the schedule and cost exposure of project risks based on estimated impacts and probability factors.

Tip

Risks can be categorized and risk control plans can be documented as part of the overall project plan.

Prima Progress Reporter provides full workgroup support and coordination of project resources with minimum training and hassle. Each team member receives activity assignments—even across multiple projects. Team members use Progress Reporter to communicate timesheet and activity status to the project manager and project database via the LAN, remotely via e-mail, and over the Internet.

Primavera Portfolio Analyst provides unparalleled project summary and tracking information to executives, senior managers, and project analysts through a rich set of graphics, spreadsheets, and reports. The Project Portfolio Wizard groups together any number of projects, based on project attributes or hierarchy, for comparison and analysis. Portfolio Analyst's interactive interface allows quick drill-down to see information at any level of detail for clear presentation and discussion.

P3e combined with Portfolio Analyst and Progress Reporter forms the most advanced solution for managing all projects within an enterprise.

WELCOM

Welcom offers "Project Management for a Changing World." Welcom is a global distribution of project management software, providing leading tools to corporations worldwide. The Welcom product line includes totally integrated and versatile software for managing both in-house and enterprise-wide projects.

Welcom has joined Pacific Edge Software to define the XML (Extensible Markup Language) schema for project management.

Tip

The flexible business-to-business schema will enable intelligent project data exchange between an organization's information systems.

MICROSOFT

The best way to manage your projects is to have the information you need right in front of you. Microsoft Project 2000 gives you that information by providing flexible tools for organizing, viewing and analyzing project data and by allowing your team members to update their status through the Web—another way of making The Business Internet work for you.

Since the most accurate status information comes from those doing the work, Microsoft Project 2000 includes a simple, Windows-based interface that team members can access from their Web browsers to provide collaborative input. It's called Microsoft Project Central, and it can give you up-to-the-minute data that will help you to make the best decisions for your business.

PROJECT KICKSTART

Project KickStart is a powerful but easy-to-use planning tool that helps you design, organize, and schedule *any* project. Project KickStart's eight-step planning process focuses your attention on the structure of the project, the goals, resources, risks, and strategic issues critical to your project's success. Your plan is ready in 30 minutes.

Schedule your project using the pop-up calendar and Gantt chart. Print out a to-do list or one of the seven presentation-ready reports. Or, for added versatility, "hot link" your plan into Microsoft Project, SureTrak, P3, FastTrack Schedule, Super Project, Project Scheduler 7, Time Line, Milestones Etc., WBS Chart, Word, WordPerfect, and Excel.

Some of the features and benefits include ...

- The ability to work with any size project up to 750 tasks and 75 resources.
- Sample projects packed with information, and ready to use.
- Drag-and-drop hints from libraries of goals, phases, and obstacles.
- Gantt chart for "big picture" scheduling.
- Seven presentation-ready reports.
- Saving as HTML—post project plans on your Intranet.

- Hot-link to Word, WordPerfect, and Excel—include project plans in proposals and business plans.
- Hot-link to other PM software.
- Free technical support.

Project KickStart requires no project management training to use and comes with a helpful (and knowledgeable) "advisor" and free, friendly telephone support.

Tip

By working through the program's icons and organizing your project step by step, you'll develop a clear overview of the project and what it will take to complete it. You become totally in control—more efficient, more effective, more successful.

The next time your boss asks for a project plan or your staff demands a marketing strategy, just click on Project KickStart. This breakthrough program will help you design, organize, and schedule your project in only 30 minutes.

- It's fast and easy—no training required. Your plan is ready in minutes!
- Plan with complete confidence. With Project KickStart, nothing is overlooked. Nothing is forgotten.
- Schedule the way you want. It is your choice. Use Project Kick-Start's built-in Gantt chart for small- to medium-size projects. Or hot-link data to Microsoft Project and other software for added functionality.

THE 30-SECOND RECAP

- PM software changes so rapidly that no book is published fast enough to review the latest software.
- The more training a project manager has with a particular type of PM software, the more highly he or she tends to rate that software. Hence, training is important!
- Many vendors now offer total online project management capabilities.
- Many vendors offer software support, and with the complexity of the programs they sell, support is crucial.

Multiple Bosses, Multiple Projects, Multiple Headaches

In this section, you learn how to keep your wits on multiple projects, help your bosses not to overload you, handle multiple reporting structures, and be assertive when overload seems unavoidable.

PARTICIPATING ON MORE THAN ONE PROJECT AT A TIME

Sometimes you're asked to manage this and asked to manage that. Managing more than one project at a time is more difficult than managing a single project, but it is not impossible. People do it all the time, and with a few observations and insights, you can become good at it as well.

Sometimes organizations assign smaller projects to up-and-coming managers, such as you, as a form of on-the-job training. By letting you get your feet wet on small fleeting projects, you are better prepared to tackle larger ones. Some companies also assign newly hired staff to serve as project team members on small projects so that they will have a wider view of company operations and, in time, manage some of the smaller projects themselves on their path to leading larger projects.

As you will see in "Learning from Your Experience" on page 1063, all the skills that you acquire and all the insights and experience you gain represent grist for the mill.

Tip

When managed properly, small projects (even one-person projects) still contain some of the essential elements found in the largest of projects.

By its nature, project management is a short-term, challenging endeavor. The opportunity to tackle small projects and even a series of small projects simultaneously is a worthwhile career challenge.

As you hone your planning, monitoring, and overall organizational skills, you become a far more valuable employee to your organization. After all, they have had other projects in the past in which managers failed to achieve the desired outcome, budgets were overrun, time frames were missed by a mile, morale dropped to zero, and chaos ruled.

Tip

Reframe your focus about participating in or even managing multiple projects as opportunities worth mastering.

COMPLEXITY HAPPENS

Suppose you're not formally assigned the task of managing two projects at once or having two projects overlap in terms of time interval. Chances are that you still face general issues related to managing multiple priorities. If so, you are not alone. An increasing number of career professionals seem to be affected by this same phenomenon.

Why is it that things seem to be getting more complex? The increase in both size and usage of the Internet means that information is disseminated at much greater speeds and volumes than at any time before. Information is power, as you've rapidly learned, and people use it to market or sell goods, construct new organizations, or create new ways to get a jump on the competitor.

In addition, the increasing use of technology in our society ensures that you will have more to contend with. In North America today, we face a major technological breakthrough every 17 minutes. This is as much as 3 or 4 an hour, 70 to 80 a day, and thousands per year. We will soon be in an environment where there are 17 technological breakthroughs every minute, with hundreds of associated services.

Perhaps most onerous for the project manager, as we proceed into the future and society becomes more complex, more stringent documentation is often required by the government, customers, and others. No project goes unscathed. It's unfortunate, but it seems it's getting harder and harder to do anything without documentation. Hiring or firing someone, buying a product, selling something, expanding, merging, casting off—almost any business function you can name requires more documentation, which contributes to each of us having to handle an increasing amount of work.

A DIFFUSE PATTERN

In many organizations, you may encounter scores and scores of small- to medium-size projects with various starting and stopping times throughout the year. Often, some of these projects are not large enough or complicated enough to require the services of a full-time project manager. In such cases, somebody may be asked to manage a project while still maintaining much of the responsibility for their principle role in some other department or elsewhere in the organization.

Such project managers may also find themselves in charge of several small projects whose timeframes overlap by varying degrees. If you're put in charge of a variety of small projects, you need to mentally separate them and to stay focused on each.

A TALE OF TWO OFFICES

My friend and fellow speaker, Al Walker from Columbia, South Carolina, managed two projects a few years ago with aplomb. As a professional speaker, Al had the continuing task of preparing for his roster of scheduled speeches coming up. In such cases, he had to ensure that flights were made, project materials were delivered to the meeting planner in plenty of time, all hotel accommodations were made, and so on. On top of that, he was elected to the presidency of the National Speakers Association, a post that lasted one fiscal year.

Tip

Managing multiple projects may be less of a burden than you anticipate. After all, in your own career, whether you can call them projects or not, you probably have already perfected techniques for handling a variety of simultaneous issues or priority items.

Al took on the responsibility admirably. He knew that more than 3,200 members of the organization were counting on him for effective leadership. To establish a separate focus, Al rearranged his corporate offices so that he had a distinct and separate office for his speaking business and for his role as NSA president.

As he walked from one office to another, his focus and attention shifted dramatically in seconds. He even had different phone lines installed and duplicate supporting equipment so that he did not have to shuttle items back and forth between the offices.

Tip

The key to managing multiple projects is to maintain a clear and separate focus so that when you are working on Project 1, Project 1 is the only thing on your mind, and likewise when you are working on Project 2.

EXTRAVAGANCE IS NOT NECESSARY

Al's approach may sound extravagant. After all, you have to have both the space to set up an additional office and the resources to stock both offices adequately for the projects at hand. Yet most people can do something nearly the same. Who doesn't have doubles of certain types of office equipment? Nearly everyone has the room to carve out additional space, perhaps not in a physically distinct office or cubicle. Yet somewhere else within your office, or organization, home, vacation home, or other physical space, you have.

Startup procedures and the associated burdens for creating a second office or work area are more than offset by the mental clarity and emotional resilience you engender. Once you're able to maintain the two work areas, managing two projects becomes more viable.

Caution

Does this mean that if you are managing three projects it would be advisable to create a third office? Not necessarily. You can carry this concept too far.

When faced with two major projects of fairly equal weight and complexity, the "two office spaces" approach works as well as any.

REPORTING TO MORE THAN ONE BOSS AT A TIME

Related to the issue of managing multiple projects is having to deal with multiple bosses—either on one project or on several projects. The immediate recognizable challenge is that either boss is likely to encroach on the schedule you have already devised in pursuit of the assignments doled out by the other boss.

Understandably, you may experience a range of anxieties and concerns when having to relay to one boss that plans may have to be delayed because of other activities you are involved with. Relations with all bosses in the case of a multiple boss situation need to be handled delicately. After all, depending on your organization, bosses may …

- Have the power to fire you on a moment's notice without consulting anyone else.
- Conduct performance appraisals of you that dramatically impact your ability to advance in the company.
- Define your job responsibilities. Indeed, they may personally have written your job description.
- Schedule your work activities. In this respect, your boss may have control over each and every hour that you spend at work, what you work on, how quickly you have to work, and what resources you're provided.
- Have leverage over what benefits you receive.

You may find yourself having to become professionally assertive with your various bosses. Stay open and candid with them so that you *don't end up promising everything to everybody and thereby creating incredible pressure on yourself!* Here are some suggestions for dealing with each of your multiple bosses:

- Praise your bosses when they merit praise. Many employees forget that the boss is a person, too, and one who needs psychological strokes just like everyone else.

- Assemble your evidence. If you have a point to make, come in armed with supporting artifacts.

- Don't dump on your boss. Your boss is not a shoulder to cry on for what went wrong at home or on the project.

- Pace your communications. Don't overwhelm your boss with more than he or she can comfortably ingest. Your project may be only one of many.

- Take personal responsibility for any department-wide activities or projects in which you're participating.

- Don't drone on. Present your situation or problem as succinctly as you can, while maintaining an effective level of interpersonal communication.

WORKAHOLIC FOR HIRE

What about the situation where you are flat out asked to do too much, take on too much work, stay too many hours, or handle more than you're comfortable handling? In such cases, the ability to assert yourself becomes a valuable one. Suppose you work for a boss who's a borderline workaholic. No, make that a full-fledged workaholic. How do you keep your job, turn in a good performance, maintain sufficient relations, and still have a life? As I pointed out in *The Complete Idiot's Guide to Assertiveness,* you say *no* without making it sound like *no:*

- "That is something I'd really like to tackle, but I don't think it would be in our best interest since I'm already on XYZ."

- "I can certainly get started on it, but because of the DEF deadline and the XYZ event, I'm certain I won't be able to get into it full-swing until the middle of next month."

- "If we can park that one for a while, I'm sure I can do a good job on it. As you know, I'm already handling the HIJ and wouldn't want to proceed unless I could do a bang-up job. If you're eager to have somebody get started on this right away, I wouldn't hesitate to suggest Tom."

- "Hmmm, help me here; I'm not sure what level priority this should be in light of the lineup I'm already facing ...."

DON'T WIMP OUT ON YOURSELF

Too many professionals today, fearful that they may lose their jobs as well as their health and other benefits, suffer various forms of work-related abuse because they lack the ability to assert themselves.

The following is some additional language, mildly more forceful, that you may need to draw upon depending on circumstances:

- "I'm stretched out right now on Project A to the full extent of my resources, and if I take this on, not only will I not be able to give it my best effort, but the other things I'm handling will suffer as well."

- "I'm going to request that I not be put on Project D, if that's okay with you. I've been going long and hard for several months now, and if I don't regain some sense of personal balance I feel I'm putting my health at risk."

- "Is there anyone else right now who could take on that project? I need to get a better handle on what I'm already managing."

- "I wish I could—I've been burning the candle at both ends on Project A, and if I start to burn it in the middle, there will be nothing left."

ASSERTING YOURSELF IN DIRE SITUATIONS

Suppose despite your protestations to the contrary, your boss or bosses keep piling on the work and responsibilities. No matter how effective you are at asserting yourself and how often you do it, you seem to be besieged with more assignments and more projects. Here are the basic options:

- You can push for a compromise situation where you take on *some* of the new work. Or you can take all of it on, but you'll have to receive additional project resources, such as more people, bigger budget, or more equipment.

- You can knuckle under and simply take on the added assignments with no additional resources. (Avoid this!)

Instead, compute how many staff hours will be necessary to tackle the added assignment, how much that would cost, and what the overall return would be. Likewise, if you need a bigger budget in general, new equipment, or other project resources, figure it out and ask for it!

THE 30-SECOND RECAP

■ Constant advances in technology make us constant multitaskers. This is a valuable and marketable skill. Managing more than one project at a time is achievable if you can successfully separate your responsibilities—mentally and maybe even physically.

■ Remember that your bosses are human, too—and at least as busy as you are. Respect their time by being concise and organized in your communications, but don't hesitate to issue kudos and praise when they are due.

■ Sometimes, you have to assert your own rights, as a person with a life, and you have to be assertive in declining additional responsibilities or requesting more support.

■ When you still are asked to take on more than you can comfortably handle, don't hesitate to ask for a compromise, or additional resources, or both.

A Construction Mini-Case

In this section, you learn how a thorough initial research phase can pay off handsomely for your project, that open and easy communication is critical to your project's success, the difference between getting by and excelling, and that simple solutions often are best.

HELPING CONSTRUCTION SITE MANAGERS TO BE MORE EFFECTIVE

Bob works for a large metropolitan construction firm that handles anywhere from 20 to 40 projects in a given year ranging from new home construction, office buildings, and parking lots, to assorted public works projects. Each project is headed by a project foreman who has various assistants and has anywhere from 5 to 25 crew members who perform the heavy labor.

Much like any company in the construction field, the company has had its ups and downs over the past several years. Regional weather patterns, shrinking municipal budgets, new competition in the market place, and a host of other factors keep upper management on their toes.

One of the biggest bugaboos in the business, as noted by the owner, is due to declining profitability per job even as the company matures. It was the owner's belief that as a cadre of highly experienced, well-trained foremen were established, the profit potential on jobs should improve somewhat.

Tip

A good plan executed by a knowledgeable foreman with sufficient labor should add up to overall corporate profitability.

Yet things didn't seem to be working. Even on construction jobs that represented fourth or fifth jobs for a regular client, where all parties involved were relatively old hands at various processes, profits were down.

A thorough audit of the company's practices revealed that the critical issue was high turnover among labor crews. All other factors, such as slight increases in cost of materials, increases in wages, licenses, permits, bonding, insurance, and the dozens of other issues that go hand in hand with initiating new construction were handled relatively well. In fact, compared to other comparably sized companies in the field, this particular company was above average in many categories.

LET'S ASSIGN IT TO A PROJECT MANAGER

Bob was put in charge of a project authorized directly by the owner to determine why the company was experiencing higher than normal turnover rates among its construction crews, and then, most importantly, to develop a strategy that would lower turnover rates to the industry and regional standards.

Using the very same software that the company employed to manage individual construction projects, Bob initiated a project of his own, called "Overturning Turnover," or "OT" for short. Bob was the solo staff person on the project. No one reported to him; all responsibilities were up to him. On top of that, the owner had precious little time to spend with Bob, as he was often up at the state capitol to lobby on certain issues and was the chief marketer for the company as well as the chief purchasing officer.

So Bob laid out a plan on his own based on his experience in the industry. He knew that he would need to talk to each of the foremen to get their views, several of their assistants, and the onsite crew chief and vocal leaders.

Tip

Bob chose to eyeball each of the construction sites and talk to all the players involved face to face, as opposed to using the telephone, even though many of the foremen would have opened up to him over the phone.

Bob felt certain that the key to successfully completing this project and devising a strategy that would overturn turnover would be found largely at the sites themselves. In the days that followed, Bob made the rounds, carved out some time with all of the participants he thought to be important to speak to, and carefully logged in his notes.

ARM CHAIR ANALYSIS VS. ONSITE OBSERVATION

After just his third visit to a construction site, Bob had what he thought was a breakthrough, but wanted to confirm his findings and continued to maintain his visitation schedule. Bob's major observation was that the project foremen were largely white, Anglo-Saxon, English-speaking males (this was no surprise to Bob), whereas over the years, there were increasing numbers of foreign-born workers who comprised the construction crews.

The company's far-flung empire stretched out over several counties and included projects in major urban and suburban areas from which the company recruited its labor. In past years, there had been many Spanish-speaking laborers, many of whom knew sufficient English to get by. Moreover, among any crew with five or more Spanish-speaking laborers, at least one of them spoke fluent English. So, the language barrier did not seem to be a problem among Hispanics, even between the foreman and a non-English–speaking worker, because there was always a liaison person nearby.

As the entire region began to be inhabited by a more diverse population, construction crews themselves became more diverse. It was not uncommon for a single crew to have several Spanish-speaking workers, as well as natives from Korea, Vietnam, Malaysia, India, Afghanistan, several countries from the Middle East, and various Eastern Europeans including Albanians, Greeks, Poles, Czechs, and Romanians.

Many workers also came from the Gold Coast, Guiana, war-torn Sierra Leone, and West Africa, as well as Somalia, Ethiopia, Uganda, and Kenya. From the Western Hemisphere, it was not uncommon to have Brazilians, who speak Portuguese, workers from any of the Latin or South American countries, and from French Canada.

In essence, the company's construction crews on many sites represented a virtual United Nations. When there were several crew members speaking the same tongue and at least one had reasonable fluency in English, foremen-to-crew relations went reasonably well. But, most often this wasn't the case. Composition of crew members varied widely from site to site, project to project, and even from season to season.

TOWER OF BABEL

After delving into the project at length, Bob realized that slightly increasing turnover rates were due at least in part to the inability of project foremen to communicate directly with individual crew members.

Tip

Even kind or caring project foremen can be less effective at their jobs when language barriers diminish effective communication.

Bob thought about the history of humankind and the legions of disputes that had occurred between peoples of different nations who did not speak each other's tongue. If countries sometimes ended up going to war with one another over misunderstandings, then it made sense to believe that workers might be departing at higher rates because of their inability to express themselves adequately, to be heard and understood, to be able to appropriately express frustration or grievances, and, conversely, to receive appropriate feedback or even praise.

When Bob presented his findings to the owner, at first he was met with a rather cool reception. It couldn't be that; we have had foreign-speaking crews for years. Bob persevered and explained that with more sophisticated project management software and advancing construction methods, down time and slack time in many projects (other than the owner's task of adequately replacing the workers and getting new crew members up to speed), were at an all-time low.

Construction projects were literally being completed at a quicker pace each year, and the timing, coordination, and precision compared to past operations was a marvel to behold. In other words, operating at a more efficient pace with little or no slack also meant that there was less overall time for bonding and conversation in general. Perhaps the modern management efficiencies resulted in some type of crossing of the threshold when it came to maintaining the human touch.

After a while, the owner bought into Bob's analysis, and, then of course was most interested in the strategy that Bob had come up with to overturn the turnover. As a result of making his rounds and collecting the input of many others, and collecting articles in construction industry magazines on this very same topic, Bob developed a multipart strategy that was inspired, though rather simple and inexpensive—and the owner liked it!

Bob's plan involved having each of the foremen attend a short training program that he would design personally. The program would only take an hour and a half and only require one handout with printing on both sides of the page. The following was Bob's handout.

MOTIVATING THE SHORT-TERM CREW MEMBER

Enrique is 19 years old. He came to this country when he was 11, never graduated from high school, and has only a rudimentary grasp of English. Enrique works on one of your crews. He is a good worker, is seldom late, and hardly ever complains. You can feel it, though: He is not going to be at your establishment very long. He will pick up a few dollars and then move on—to where, you will never know.

Can you increase the job length for workers like Enrique? Indeed, can you motivate someone who, quite bluntly, toils for long hours for little reward? The answer is a resounding "Yes." It will require a little effort and ingenuity on your part; still, after all is said and done, Enrique and others in his situation may still depart on short or no notice. The odds that they will remain with the job longer, however, will increase if you follow some of the guidelines for motivating these employees.

Check your attitude. You need to check your attitude before any motivation program can succeed. As human beings, we broadcast messages all the time. What are you broadcasting to your crews? That they are replaceable? That you are not concerned with their needs?

It's easy for the supervisor who has watched dozens of laborers come and go to develop quickly the view that "It's the nature of the business; why fight it?" It is partly that attitude that perpetuates the massive turnover in the industry. Resolve that you can take measures to increase the average longevity of low-paid laborers and your attitude and initiative will make a difference.

An encouraging word. How long would it take you to learn some key phrases in Vietnamese, or the language of your low-paid laborers? Whether they speak Spanish, Korean, or Farsi, it won't take long to master some short conversational pleasantries. Many bookstores are stocked with dictionaries providing various language translations. Even easier, sit down with one of your key crew members. On a piece of paper, jot down the phonetic spelling of phrases such as "How are you?" and "You're doing a good job."

Unannounced breaks. Periodically throughout the day, and particularly on challenging days, give your workers unannounced breaks. Augment these mini-vacations by distributing snacks. The few dollars you may spend will pay off in terms of greater productivity that day. These breaks will also enhance longevity among low-paid crew members. It pays to offer little perks.

Rotating leadership. Rotate leadership among some crews. For instance, on four consecutive days, make sure that crew members each have one day as "foreman." For some of your workers, this may represent their first taste of leadership. Rotating leadership is most effective when the crew members are unfamiliar with each other.

Awards system. Make "contests" short in duration and high on visuals. For example, you could keep a chart on the wall or other visible location indicating who has had the most consecutive days without being absent or tardy. Which crew performances have prompted words of praise from customers? Who has gone above and beyond the call of duty in the last week?

You can easily chart and share these achievements with crew members on duty. People like to see their names on a chart followed by stars or other performance indicators. The chart could be language-proof, for instance. Everyone recognizes their own name in English, and stars or dollar signs can indicate the bonuses you'll offer. After posting the charts, set up a simple system of rewards, which could include cash or more time as a team leader.

Develop mentors. Look for leaders among your crew members who can serve as mentors to newly hired staff. This alleviates having to break in each crew member. Those individuals selected as mentors will be pleased with this special status and will not only assist in achieving smoother operations, but will help alleviate quick departures among new employees.

Use a checklist. Here's a checklist to help you determine whether you are raising or lowering morale, increasing or decreasing crew members' length of stay, and serving as a leader, not just as a manager:

- ❑ Do I make sure employees understand how to properly complete a job?
- ❑ Have I clearly indicated what results I expect?
- ❑ Do I offer adequate and ongoing support?
- ❑ Do I cultivate positive relationships?
- ❑ Do I show concern for crew members as individuals?
- ❑ Have I established appropriate recognition and reward systems?
- ❑ Do I take the time to learn and dispense encouraging phrases for enhanced communication?

Even if you practice all of the above recommendations, you still will not eliminate quick turnover or enhance crew motivation. Yet, if you can induce the seasonal crew member to stay on an extra week or encourage crew members to finish a big job on time, then you have made your job a little easier, and have contributed to the profitability and long-term viability of the company.

AFTER THE HANDOUT

Bob covered the entire sheet during this session and then required each fore-man to employ at least one of the measures with each crew member at least once a week. So if the foreman had 15 crew members on a project, he was responsible for one of the following measures per crew per week, or in other words, an average of three such instances a day:

- Offering an encouraging word in the crew member's native tongue
- Giving workers unannounced, on-the-spot breaks
- Rotating leadership among some groups, and so on

Each project manager would then report back to Bob at the end of each week so they could assess progress. As it turned out, progress was readily visible from the first day on.

Tip

Foreign-born crew members start perking up immediately when people say a few words or phrases to them in their native language.

At the end of the first week, most foremen reported an increased level of vibrancy, higher morale, even possibly higher energy level. At the end of several weeks, the foremen were convinced that the program was sound.

At the end of several months, as they looked at the data on a project-by-project basis, the owner and Bob could see that the turnover rates were dropping. Workers were staying on longer, and they didn't need to be replaced, hence project profitability was rising. And both Bob and the owner felt great about that outcome.

THE 30-SECOND RECAP

- Researching your problem, talking to everyone who might be able to provide insight, and being observant of your environment and their environment are strong ways to be sure at the outset that your project is headed in the right direction.
- Meeting with your sources on their turf can make them more candid and open, and can help you see aspects of the project you might have overlooked entirely.
- Even the most qualified, expert professionals are only as good at managing as they are good at communicating with their teams.
- Morale and motivation among the troops can come as much from the positive attitude of management as anything else. Even a menial job can be worthwhile if there is positive reinforcement for a job well done.

Learning from Your Experience

In this section, you learn how to keep your role as project manager in perspective, the value of mastering project management software, why it pays to keep your eyes and ears open, and how to get ready for what is next.

LIFE IS LEARNING, AND SO ARE PROJECTS

Whether you volunteered to head up your current project or were assigned to it, whether you eagerly anticipate going to work the next day or dread it, it is highly important to keep your goal as project manager in perspective. Managing a project and managing it well routinely leads to other things. These include managing larger projects, being promoted as a supervisor, manager, or department head, and earning increases in pay, bonuses, and other perks.

Maybe you were given the role of project manager because no one else was around, but more often than that, it is because someone higher up in your organization believed that you could do the job. Perhaps you are being groomed to take on even greater levels of responsibility.

Tip

Any project can be viewed as a stepping stone along your long-term career path.

No project is too inconsequential, too low a priority, or too outside of your immediate interest area to not manage effectively. Some represent large steps, some are tiny. In each case, you have several opportunities:

- Undoubtedly, you will learn things along the way that you can use at other times and places in your career. What learning opportunities might develop? Learning new software, getting along with diverse groups of people, selling skills (please remember that as a project manager you are always selling one thing or another at every point along the way), and a greater appreciation for your organization's processes.

- When you work with a project team, you develop bonds with individuals that have potential future value as well. Perhaps they will work with you on other projects. Perhaps you will be reporting to them on projects. Their skills and interests ultimately may impact the direction that your career path takes.

Tip

If you can't stand some or all of your project staff, you can cultivate your ability to manage others effectively. Realistically, there will be lots of other times in your career when you have to work with less than "bosom buddies." You might as well hone your skills now.

■ Working on a project that represents a departure from what you were doing previously exposes you to new vistas. Perhaps you get to see another aspect of your organization. Perhaps you get to deal with external elements that represent new and challenging ground for you. Perhaps you become more in tune to your own weaknesses as a manager, as a career professional, and as an individual. Many a project manager has decided to enroll in a course or get additional training as a result of tackling a challenging project.

■ You potentially get to step into the batter's box, where all eyes are focused on you. Taking on a project means that others are counting on you for specific performance over specific intervals. Hence, the authorizing party and stakeholders have a vested interest in your progress.

Tip

Being the object of constant or semi-constant scrutiny means that you also have the opportunity to shine in ways that otherwise might be difficult to muster if you were simply doing routine work as part of the rank and file.

In short, consider the opportunity to manage projects, large and small, desirable and undesirable, as the wonderful opportunities they invariably secretly represent.

MASTER THE SOFTWARE

Project management software, discussed in "Choosing Project Management Software" on page 1033 and "A Sampling of Popular Programs" on page 1042, is applicable to far more than the project at hand. Whatever software skills you develop on this project will be of value on future projects, both for your organization and those you may elect to take on individually.

Most people don't learn software unless it is critical to their performance, status, and livelihood. When everyone else was switching from typewriters to personal computers, career professionals had no choice but to learn some word processing software just to keep pace with society in general and their own industry in particular.

Today, as more people learn more Internet applications or effective ways of accomplishing tasks, society is poised for an era of unprecedented productivity. Yet, the majority of people who mastered traditional PC software skills such as word processing, database management, spreadsheet applications, and communications don't necessarily encounter project management software. They aren't aware of its vast applications for managing all aspects of one's professional and personal life.

At home, you may discover the ability to use what you've learned on the job to do the following:

- Maintain a greater level of control of household expenditures
- Plot the path that you need to take in order to retire by a desired age
- Coordinate personal travel plans as never before
- Map out a plan that will carry your child to the finals in academics, sports, or the performing arts

KEEP YOUR EYES OPEN

How projects are initiated in your organization—by whom, when, and for what result—tells you much about the workings of your organization. Are projects routinely initiated as a result of deadlines or competitive pressures? Or, do they represent customer service initiatives undertaken by the organization to enhance its overall project or service offerings even when there is no immediate, visible pressure to do better? Forward-thinking organizations always operate according to the latter.

Tip

Forward-thinking organizations don't wait for dire circumstances to surface; they operate in a "managing the beforehand" mode, recognizing that proactive organizations stay in the lead by routinely taking leading, decisive actions.

Whether you are working for an organization that operates in a crisis mode, a leading-edge mode, or someplace in between, as a result of your observations as a project manager, you undoubtedly will come across other opportunities for your organization.

The execution of your project in pursuit of the desired outcome, if you keep your eyes open, inevitably will lead to insights worth reporting back to your authorizing party and stakeholders. It also tends to lead to the formulation of new projects which, quite conveniently, probably are best managed by you.

Think of it as a Machiavellian win-win situation where you are selfishly identifying what else you want to be working on, which happens to coincide with that which will benefit your organization. In this regard, you begin to take on far more control over your career path than seemed within your grasp before initiating your current project.

Tip

Effective project managers often create their own path by identifying one project after another. Such projects both help their organizations and further the project manager's own career.

Along the way, everything that worked well, added to all the roadblocks, obstacles and flat out failures, becomes grist for the mill. While you don't want to incur a series of frustrations on your current project, if you have the wherewithal to recognize that everything you experience is a lesson for another day, and can ultimately serve to benefit you in one way or another, then the current ordeal need not seem so bad.

PREPARING FOR THE NEXT PROJECT

Since the effective execution of one project undoubtedly will lead to another one, what are you doing along the way to improve your capability and readiness to tackle new projects? For example, are you

- Maintaining a notebook or file on your hard drive of key project insights?
- Denoting the skills and capabilities in detail of the project staffers who contributed to the project in some way?
- Compiling a resource file of books, audio-visual material, software, Web sites, supporting organization, and any other resources that could possibly be of use on future projects?
- Establishing relationships with vendors, suppliers, consultants, and other outside product and service advisors?
- Establishing relationships with stakeholders, be they top managers, the authorizing party, clients, customers, other project managers, other project team members, department or division heads, as well as controllers, accountants, and administrative staff?

Are you pacing yourself to a practical degree so that if you are requested to jump into something else immediately after completing this project you will be more or less ready? This involves taking care of yourself, eating balanced meals, perhaps taking vitamin supplements, getting adequate rest, exercising, practicing stress reduction techniques and, in general, allowing yourself to have a life even during the course of the project? In closing, it may be appropriate to refer to the words of Rudyard Kipling in his classic poem, "If":

If

If you can keep your head when all about you
Are losing theirs and blaming it on you;
If you can trust yourself when all men doubt you,
But make allowance for their doubting too;
If you can wait and not be tired by waiting,
Or, being lied about, don't deal in lies,
Or, being hated, don't give way to hating,
And yet don't look too good, nor talk too wise;
If you can dream—and not make dreams your master;
If you can think—and not make thoughts your aim;
If you can meet with triumph and disaster
And treat those two impostors just the same;
If you can bear to hear the truth you've spoken
Twisted by knaves to make a trap for fools,
Or watch the things you gave your life to broken,
And stoop and build 'em up with worn-out tools;
If you can make one heap of all your winnings
And risk it on one turn of pitch-and-toss,
And lose, and start again at your beginnings
And never breathe a word about your loss;
If you can force your heart and nerve and sinew
To serve your turn long after they are gone,
And so hold on when there is nothing in you
Except the Will which says to them: "Hold on!"
If you can talk with crowds and keep your virtue,
Or walk with kings—nor lose the common touch;
If neither foes nor loving friends can hurt you;
If all men count with you, but none too much;
If you can fill the unforgiving minute
With sixty seconds' worth of distance run—
Yours is the Earth and everything that's in it,
And—which is more—you'll be a Man, my son!

—Rudyard Kipling

The 30-Second Recap

- Managing a project well often leads to managing larger projects, being promoted as a supervisor, manager, or department head, and earning increases in pay, bonuses, and other perks. Any project holds the potential to become a stepping stone along your long-term career path. Hence, avoid regarding any project as too inconsequential, too low a priority, or too outside of your immediate interest area to be managed effectively.

- Effective project managers often create their own path by identifying one project after another. Such projects both help their organizations and further the project manager's own career.

- At all times pace yourself so that if you are requested to jump into something else immediately after completing this project you will be more or less ready!

Customer Service

Customer Service: What's It All About?

In this section you learn about basic customer service principles that are true in any situation, and about customer service myths that prevent some companies from enjoying the success that could be theirs.

THE IMPORTANCE OF CUSTOMER SERVICE

In their book *Built from Scratch,* Home Depot founders Bernie Marcus and Arthur Blank discuss at length how they built their $30 billion business on an absolute commitment to customer service. Home Depot currently operates more than 800 stores and is growing by more than 20 percent each year. By 2002 the organization expects to have over 1,600 stores.

The Disney Company is one of the most admired companies in America, according to a recent survey conducted by *Fortune* magazine. For years, Disney's commitment to customer service has enabled it to grow by leaps and bounds. New employees are required to attend several days of customer service training before they start work, and ongoing customer service training is mandatory for everyone. The result of Disney's emphasis on customer service is customer satisfaction, customer loyalty, and an awesome financial return.

But in spite of the obvious success that an unyielding commitment to customer service has brought to these companies and others like them, customer service remains the single most overlooked and underutilized weapon in the strategic arsenal of business in the twenty-first century. In fact, in America, customer service at most firms is appalling.

A few years ago, The Research Institute of America conducted a study for the White House Office of Consumer Affairs. The results of that study demonstrate just how costly it is for a business to be apathetic toward customer service. Here are just some of their findings:

- The average business will hear nothing from 96 percent of unhappy customers who receive rude or discourteous treatment.

- Ninety percent of customers who are dissatisfied with the service they receive will not come back or buy again from the offending organization.

- Each unhappy customer tells his or her story to an average of nine other people.

- Only 4 percent of unhappy customers ever bother to complain. For every complaint brought to the attention of a company, 24 others go unreported to the company—but are indeed reported to other potential customers.

- Of the customers who register a complaint, between 54 percent and 70 percent will do business again with the organization if their complaint is resolved. That figure rises to 95 percent if the customer feels that the complaint was resolved quickly.

- Sixty-eight percent of customers who quit doing business with an organization do so because of company indifference. It takes 12 positive incidents to make up for 1 negative incident in the eyes of customers.

CUSTOMER SERVICE: WHAT IS IT?

Customer service is the art of serving a customer. It is by far the most important marketing strategy a business can use in its quest to capture and retain market share.

PLAIN ENGLISH

Customer service   A way of life that involves putting the customer first in every aspect of the business. It is characterized by an obsession to achieve complete customer satisfaction in each and every encounter. It is an obsession that is shared by everyone in the company from the chairman of the board on down.

The objective of customer service is to understand and meet the needs of customers, whatever those needs may be. Its importance stems from an understanding of one of the basic tenants of free enterprise so simply stated by the late Sam Walton: "There is only one boss: the customer. And he can fire everybody in the company from the chairman on down, simply by spending his money somewhere else."

Customer service isn't the product of "smile training"; it isn't a scripted, predetermined response to a menu of anticipated customer complaints; it isn't a magical transformation that occurs as a result of a one-shot corporate training program; and it doesn't happen because of corporate lip service, or directives and mandates from upper management demanding that customers be treated with respect and dignity.

Customer service is a way of doing business that is born out of genuine concern for the customer, and it involves every person in the company, from the chairman of the board to the custodian. It's not just a way of doing business; it's a way of life.

IT'S A CULTURE, NOT A PROGRAM!

Effective customer service begins with an understanding and commitment by top management, who get directly involved in hands-on customer service activities. It's one thing to demand that your employees attend customer service workshops; it's another when the chairman of the board attends and actively participates in the training! When a company's top bosses live and breathe customer service, the rest of the firm is inspired to do the same. Conversely, most customer service programs fizzle because either top management doesn't understand their value or they're just too busy to roll up their shirtsleeves and get involved.

But that's not the case at Southwest Airlines. Here's what Herb Kelleher, the company's chief executive officer, has to say about the value of a customer service culture:

> The culture of Southwest is probably its major competitive advantage. The intangibles are more important than the tangibles because you can always initiate the tangibles; you can buy the airplane, you can rent the ticket counter space. But the hardest thing for someone to emulate is the spirit of your people.

The customer service culture at Southwest Airlines has had a major influence on the company's performance record. Consider this: Southwest is the fourth-largest carrier of passengers in the United States; the company has shown a profit over the past 27 years; it is twice as profitable as United Airlines; its record of on-time service is one of the best in the industry; and the company has never experienced a strike.

Companies that have developed outstanding customer service cultures share some important characteristics:

- Top management defines customer service as job number one and is actively involved in customer service activities.
- Line managers are thoroughly trained in quality customer service techniques and serve as coaches and trainers to those who report to them.
- Every employee understands that, first and foremost, he or she is in the service business.
- Customer service training activities are ongoing, and everyone participates.
- Employees are valued, and important customer service accomplishments are recognized in meaningful ways.

- Employees are empowered to solve customer service problems on the spot, with some companies authorizing employees to spend as much as $2,500 in order to resolve problems quickly or prevent repeat occurrences.

- Measurements of customer service outcomes, in which customer opinions are solicited (both formally and informally), are regularly used to monitor quality and make adjustments as needed.

THE QUALITY OF CUSTOMER SERVICE

The customer is the final arbiter in all matters involving customer service. It is the customer who will ultimately judge the quality of an organization's customer service efforts, and that judgment is based solely on the customer's perception, regardless of the facts.

Whenever customers become involved with an organization, even if only peripherally, they quickly perceive the quality of the service they are receiving and, based upon that perception, they judge the organization and its products. This means that *quality of service* is a moving target that can, and will, be uniquely defined by each and every customer.

PLAIN ENGLISH

Quality of service   The customer's perception of the service that an organization provides. It is a perception that is re-evaluated by the customer with each succeeding contact, wherever in the organization those contacts occur, from the executive level to the loading dock.

INFERIOR QUALITY

Inferior customer service always produces dissatisfied customers. These feelings of dissatisfaction lead customers to react in ways that have harmful long-term effects on the organization.

You can bet that your organization has customer service problems if …

- Customers are often hostile and threatening to representatives of the company.

- Supervisors regularly spend an inordinate amount of their time "stomping out fires," attempting to resolve highly charged disputes between customers and the company.

- Employee productivity is low because employees are spending too much time trying to resolve problems.

- Customer loyalty is low.

- Managers spend little or no time training employees in the area of customer service.

- The business budgets very little time and money for ensuring customer satisfaction and instead commits more of its resources to providing a steady stream of new customers.

- The work environment has become unusually stressful and negative.

- Employee turnover is high.

- The business lacks credibility in the marketplace—and employees begin to notice that the company seems to be advertising its shortcomings.

CAUTION

Whenever you spot customer service problems, regardless how minor they may appear, act immediately to correct the problem. Major customer service problems are often those that originally appeared insignificant. Treat every customer service problem with a sense of urgency.

From the customer's perspective, an organization's reputation for customer service is determined in two ways: from the customer's own firsthand experience and from comments heard from others. A customer who has heard negative things about an organization's products or services is likely to be negatively predisposed to the organization. What's more, negative predispositions are just as damaging (and just as costly) as firsthand negative experiences. Conversely, a customer who has heard positive remarks about a company is often positively predisposed to it, resulting in a significant payoff for the organization.

TIP

According to studies conducted by the United States Office of Consumer Affairs, it costs seven times more to acquire a new customer than to keep an existing one. A solid customer service program within any organization is simply good business practice.

CAUTION

Be sure of the accuracy of your company's claims to excellence. Customer service excellence shouldn't be emphasized in an aggressive advertising campaign unless fundamental changes have been made that ensure service excellence. Companies that make claims about something that doesn't exist do irreparable damage to their reputations in the marketplace.

Mediocre Quality

I mention the mediocre category of customer service only because so many companies seem to believe it exists. They're wrong. In customer service, you either do it right or you do it wrong; there's no middle ground.

High Quality

Organizations that routinely provide high-quality customer service have an important edge in today's competitive global marketplace. That edge can easily make the difference between success and failure. It's a fact: Exceptional customer service results in positive customer perceptions, customer satisfaction, and customer loyalty—and that's the stuff success is made of.

But make no mistake: High-quality customer service involves more than merely hiring good people; it requires more than offering a training session now and then.

Businesses that are serious about developing ongoing high-quality customer service must make a major commitment to shape and mold a corporate culture in which customer-oriented values and beliefs are supported by the entire organization. Top management needs to become so obsessed with high-quality customer service that the customer becomes the heart of every operational policy, procedure, and process.

In a high-quality customer service culture, everyone—from the janitor to the chairman of the board—has a clear understanding of the importance of the customer to the success of the enterprise. At every level of the organization there is an appreciation of the requirements and needs of the customer.

TIP

Employees who make it a practice to meet the needs of customers are generally happier and more productive, and enjoy a greater sense of fulfillment in their jobs. That's because employees who make customer service a top priority are often the beneficiaries of the thanks and praise of satisfied customers. Employees, like customers, have a basic need to be appreciated and valued by others. One of the effects of customer service training is higher employee morale.

A high-quality customer service culture has the following characteristics:

- Company representatives at all levels maintain a courteous and responsive attitude toward customers and want to be of real assistance to them.

- Top management is fully committed to maintaining a program of high-quality customer service (and the commitment is real, not just lip service).

- All persons in the company know that they are in the service business—not the manufacturing business, the banking business, the insurance business, the real estate business, or anything else.

- Every manager knows exactly what the customer expects and has developed the systems and processes necessary to meet those expectations (as well as established measurements of customer outcomes in order to monitor employee performance).

- There's substantial flexibility in meeting the needs of customers.

- Employees treat customers as "partners" rather than adversaries.

- The product or service is continuously improved to meet the changing needs of the customer.

- Prevention-based, or proactive, management has replaced reactionary, after-the-fact management.

- Corporate leadership relies on customer satisfaction, market share, and long-term profitability as measures of performance instead of immediate bottom-line financial results and quick return on investment.

- Quality of products or services is defined in terms of the customer's requirements and needs rather than the organization's standards.

- Important decisions are customer-driven instead of product-driven.

- Employees are involved in ongoing customer service training that introduces new ways of helping customers, and at the same time repeats and reinforces basic principles.

SOME COMMON CUSTOMER SERVICE MYTHS

Here are five of the most common myths about customer service, along with the facts that dispel them:

1. **Myth:** The only effective customer service happens when you're in a position to say "yes" to every customer request. For those organizations that can't always say "yes," high-quality customer service is just a pipe dream.

   Fact: I've never encountered an organization that is always able to say "yes" to every customer request. High-quality customer service can take place even when you have to say "no" to a customer—as long as saying "no" is done in a manner that preserves the dignity of the customer. In such situations, providing optional solutions helps customers feel respected and in control. High-quality customer service means providing the best service possible. It doesn't mean customers always get what they want.

2. **Myth:** I don't have to be concerned with customer service since I don't deal with the customers of my company.

   Fact: Regardless of the kind of work you perform within an organization, you have customers who need to be satisfied: those who depend on you. Your organization will never be able to meet the needs of its external customers until the needs of its internal customers are met.

3. **Myth:** Our organization provides excellent customer service, but the perception in the field is that we don't. That's just the way it is.

   Fact: If the perception of the customer is that your organization's customer service is poor, you need to take a hard look at what you're doing, and not doing, to satisfy customer needs. Remember that it is the customer who defines the quality of your customer service efforts. If the customer says they're poor, they're poor.

4. **Myth:** Customer service in our organization is better than that of any of our competitors. If our customers don't like what we offer by way of customer service, let them try our competitors. They'll be back.

   Fact: Don't count on it. Maybe one of your competitors has read this book and has already made a commitment to improve customer service. But the real problem behind this particular myth is a "Take it or leave it" attitude. Organizations that have that kind of attitude toward their customers will sooner or later either change their attitude or be left in the dust. Another problem with this myth is that it's based upon an erroneous comparison. How an organization's customer service quality compares with that of its competitors means nothing; how it is perceived by the customer means everything.

5. **Myth:** Our organization can't afford to offer high-quality customer service to our customers. We'd go broke.

   Fact: It's more likely that you'll go broke if you continue to ignore the value of high-quality customer service. According to the U.S. Department of Commerce, the average American business loses half of its customer base every five years, 60 percent of whom leave because of poor customer service. The same government agency has determined that it costs seven times more to acquire a new customer than to keep an existing one. Your organization, regardless of the products or services it sells, can't afford to ignore the financial benefits that result from offering high-quality customer service.

THE 30-SECOND RECAP

▦ Most business firms don't understand the value of quality customer service.

▦ The customer, not the company, defines the quality of an organization's customer service.

▦ Mediocre customer service (service that's just so-so) doesn't exist—you're either doing it right, or your customers are looking elsewhere.

▦ Highly successful enterprises recognize that they are in the service business, not the manufacturing business, the insurance business, the banking business, or the real estate business.

▦ Customer service is a culture, not a program—it's a way of life.

▦ Superior customer service provides a significant competitive edge to those firms that achieve it.

Who Are Your Customers— and What Do They Want?

In this section you learn to identify three levels of customers, and you see how each affects the success of the company. You also learn about the most common customer complaints and the six basic wants of customers everywhere.

WHO'S THE CUSTOMER?

Perhaps my broad definition of the term *customer* as any person or group who receives the work output of another surprises you. Most business people I talk to about customer service initially have a much narrower definition in mind—one that includes only those who finally purchase their product or service.

PLAIN ENGLISH

Customer   Any person or group who receives the work output (product or service) of another.

There are, however, three levels of "customer" in the typical organization, and each level is important to the success of the enterprise. To develop the kind of customer service that puts wheels under your company and wings alongside it, the needs, wants, and priorities of customers at each level cannot be ignored; they need to be defined and incorporated into the business strategies of the organization.

THE EMPLOYEE-CUSTOMER

In the first act of *Hamlet,* William Shakespeare wrote: "This above all: to thine own self be true." Those words had special meaning in Shakespeare's play, and they have special meaning in the world of customer service.

The first level of customer is the *employee-customer* who participates in the research and development, manufacturing, or sale of a company's product or service. Each first-level customer has ownership of a process for which he or she is responsible. These *process owners* are motivated by a desire for excellence and are satisfied with their work only when the product or service is of such quality that it evokes a sense of personal pride.

Characteristics of the employee-customer include a positive attitude about the product or service, an obsession with quality and self-inspection, a preoccupation with personal performance, and a commitment to personal improvement.

PLAIN ENGLISH

Process owners   Employees, or groups of employees, who are responsible for a specific aspect of the finished product or service of an organization.

THE INTERNAL CUSTOMER

Internal customers are those who receive work output (product) from internal process owners. For example, not far from where I live, the Boeing Company has a large plant that manufactures airplane wings. This particular plant is the internal customer of several other Boeing facilities that manufacture the parts needed for the construction of airplane wings. At the same time, the wing-manufacturing facility is also a process owner whose internal customer is another Boeing facility that assembles airplanes for delivery to customers worldwide.

The primary objective of each process owner is to satisfy its internal customers by providing top-quality products and services. Product quality, timeliness of delivery, and cost are among the most important factors influencing internal customer satisfaction.

Excellence in internal customer service is reflected in the quality of the finished product; the better the internal customer service quality, the higher the product quality.

It's also true that if internal customers are dissatisfied, the final customer— the one who purchases the product—will be dissatisfied, too. Use *prevention-based management* to ensure customer satisfaction throughout the entire process.

THE EXTERNAL CUSTOMER

The *external customer* is the ultimate recipient of the finished product or service. He or she is the final arbiter of quality, value, excellence, and *service*. More than any other single factor, the judgment of the external customer determines the success or failure of the enterprise.

MOST COMMON CUSTOMER COMPLAINTS

Whether you sell widgets or washing machines, when something goes wrong, customers have a right to expect someone from the company to demonstrate appropriate concern and solve the problem immediately. Unfortunately, that doesn't always happen.

Here's a list of common customer complaints:

1. **There seems to be a total lack of interest in the customer's problem.** This is without a doubt the number-one complaint in the field of customer service. "The company representative as much as told me

that he just didn't care!" When your company lacks real interest in customers' problems, employees verbally and nonverbally communicate an attitude of indifference, even contempt. A customer has a right to expect that the same company that sold the product will be genuinely interested in doing whatever it takes to make sure the product does what it's supposed to do. Nothing will irritate a customer quicker than an attitude of "I don't care, it's not my problem."

2. **No one wants to "own" the problem** (otherwise known as the "customer service shuffle," previously known as "passing the buck"). A customer with a problem is told, "I'm sorry, I don't deal with those matters. That's just not my area of responsibility. You'll have to talk with Mr. Jones about that." A high-tech version of this same problem occurs when a customer who needs help phones a company and is immediately confronted with voice mail and a seemingly endless series of menu options—which may or may not lead to a human being. Voice mail systems may be efficient and effective in some ways, but from a customer service perspective they're public enemy number one.

3. **The company representative uses condescending language that patronizes or belittles.** Have you ever experienced difficulty with a product and then contacted the company's customer service center, only to find yourself being talked to like a nine-year-old? No one likes to be patronized. It's demeaning and embarrassing. But it's one of the most common complaints of customers, who understandably like to be regarded with dignity and respect.

4. **The company is unresponsive to the customer.** Some companies have the mistaken idea that if you ignore the problem, it'll go away. The truth is that if you ignore the problem, your customer will go away—for good! Customers want a response to their problem, and they want it immediately. And if a commitment is made to a customer, it should be considered a sacred obligation. Putting people off with promises of future service may solve an immediate problem, but it creates an even worse problem if those promises aren't kept.

5. **The company provides the customer with wrong or inaccurate information.** No one likes to look stupid. But the fact is, none of us is able to provide the right answer every time. We all encounter problems that we simply don't know how to solve. When that happens, some representatives elect to provide the customer with wrong or incomplete information rather than admit they aren't sure and call for assistance. Only one thing is worse than providing a customer with no information, and that's giving him the wrong information.

6. **The company treats the customer rudely.** Customers will not allow you to treat them rudely for any length of time. Company representatives who treat customers rudely cost their companies an incredible amount of money per hour (the higher the profit margin, the more they cost). Like most people, I simply refuse to be treated in this manner. I consider rudeness a personal invitation to immediately stop doing business with a company and never return. I doubt that you're much different.

7. **The representative uses company policy and procedure as an excuse for not providing service.** It's amazing how frequently customers make this complaint—and rightfully so! To succeed in today's competitive business environment, companies need to be driven by customer needs and wants, not by internal policy and procedure. Companies who think of customers as anything but the most important people in the company need to make a paradigm shift before it's too late.

PHRASES THAT AROUSE ANGER

There are numerous phrases that exasperate customers. If you're interested in resolving problems and satisfying customers, you'll avoid these phrases:

- "You're going to have to ...."
- "What did you do?"
- "It's company policy that ...."
- "You can't ...."
- "You'll have to talk with ...."
- "Why are you talking to me about ...?"
- "I'm new here."
- "That's really not my department."
- "We can't do that!"
- "You should have ...."
- "You must have ...."
- "That's not my problem!"

When internal customers encounter service-related problems, the result is anxiety, tension, a breakdown in morale, and a final product that is of diminished quality. In the words of world-renowned management consultant Tom Peters: "I can think of no successful company that has found a way to look after external customers while abusing internal customers. The process of meeting customer needs begins internally."

By the time customer service problems affect external customers, the company is in real trouble. We live in a global business environment that is filled with competitive entrepreneurs, many of whom have a keen understanding of the value of customers and know how to provide the service they need.

To be successful in business today, you need a real sense of commitment to the customer at every level. You need to practice proactive management to prevent internal and external customer service problems whenever possible, and you need to quickly and aggressively solve the problems that occur in spite of your best efforts.

THE McDONALD'S ATTITUDE

Ray Kroc, founder of McDonald's, built his multi-billion-dollar company with customer service as a primary value. Long ago, McDonald's developed "10 commandments" for customer treatment. The customer service commitment expressed by these commandments remains at the heart of the company's day-to-day operation.

1. The Customer is the most important person in our business.
2. The Customer is not dependent on us—we are dependent on the Customer.
3. The Customer is not an interruption of our work, but the purpose of it.
4. The Customer does us an honor when calling on us. We are not doing the customer a favor by serving him or her.
5. The Customer is part of our business, not an outsider.
6. The Customer is not a cold statistic, but flesh and blood: a human being with feelings and emotions like our own.
7. The Customer is not someone to argue with or match wits with.
8. The Customer is deserving of the most courteous and attentive treatment we can provide.
9. The Customer is one who brings us his/her wants. Our job is to fill them.
10. The Customer has the right to expect an employee to present a neat, clean appearance.

McDonald's commitment to customer service has made the company one of the genuine success stories of the twentieth century. Theirs is a model well worth emulating.

What Your Customers Want

Excellence in customer service translates into significant sales and significant growth. Before you can deliver consistently excellent customer service, you must first understand what your customers want.

CAUTION

Some companies confuse advertising with a commitment to excellence in customer service. Don't embark on expensive advertising campaigns that tout your exceptional service until you've committed yourself to developing a customer service culture and have initiated the processes that ensure excellent performance. Don't promote what you don't have. False claims in advertising undermine trust and can do your company irreparable harm.

Here are six qualities that customers want and expect in organizations with which they do business:

- **Respectful treatment.** A good rule of thumb is: Do for your customer what you would want done if you were the customer. Treating customers with respect and dignity is where customer satisfaction and customer loyalty begins.

- **Responsiveness.** Customers want your immediate attention. They want you to be receptive to them and empathetic about their needs or problems, whatever they may be.

- **Technical excellence.** Customers expect company representatives to be knowledgeable about the company's product or service—in other words, to know what they're doing. Few experiences are as frustrating as talking to someone about a customer service matter only to learn, late in the conversation, that the person has absolutely no idea what you're talking about. Employees who represent a company with customers should not be newcomers to the organization, nor should they lack the experience and skills necessary to fully represent the products sold by the company. In fact, they should be among the friendliest and most knowledgeable people in your company.

- **Focus on problem-solving.** When there's a problem, customers want it solved—fast! They expect the person helping them to remain totally solution-focused. Nothing intensifies a service problem faster than a representative who finds reason after reason for the company's inability to solve the problem immediately.

- **Flexibility.** Customers with a problem want to deal with someone who can be flexible and creative in finding solutions. A "one-size-fits-all" approach to customer service is a design for disaster.

Customers expect you to be able to overcome roadblocks and cut through whatever red tape exists so that their problem can be solved without further hassle.

■ **Prompt recovery.** When mistakes happen, customers expect prompt *recovery*. They're not interested in knowing who or what is to blame. They don't want long, drawn-out explanations about why the mistake occurred. What they do want is an acknowledgment of the mistake, an apology, a resolution of the problem, and an assurance that it won't happen again.

PLAIN ENGLISH

Recovery   The process used by a company with its customer to rectify a mistake or solve a problem caused by the company. The goal of recovery is complete customer satisfaction.

TIP

Consider furnishing each employee with a copy of this book. Understanding the basics of customer service will help each employee become a better "process owner" and "internal customer" and will also help ensure the satisfaction of the final, or "external," customer. Educating employees about customer service is an excellent first step toward developing the customer service culture discussed in "Customer Service: What's It All About?" on page 1070.

IGNORE THE BASICS, PAY THE PRICE

There are many examples of companies that have ignored the basics of customer service and paid the price for their ignorance. The following story is just one example for you to consider.

A few years ago, *USA Today* ran a story titled "Bank Gets Million Dollar Lesson." It began when John Barrier went to Old National Bank in Spokane, Washington, to cash a $100 check.

When Barrier attempted to get his parking ticket validated (to save 60 cents), a bank receptionist refused to validate it because he hadn't conducted a transaction that qualified. "You have to make a deposit if you want us to validate your ticket," the receptionist told him. "That's the bank's rule and I'm not permitted to waive it."

Barrier told the receptionist that he was a "substantial depositor" with the bank. Nevertheless, that fact made no difference to the receptionist and he was told, "Rules are rules."

Barrier asked to see the bank manager, but the manager stood by the bank's rule that prohibited validating a parking ticket unless a deposit was made.

The next day, Barrier went to the bank headquarters determined to withdraw his $2 million-plus unless the manager apologized for the error and made things right. He was told that the manager was actually just doing his job; that it was fiscally responsible to control these kinds of bank expenditures.

"So the next day I went over and the first amount I took out was $1 million. But if you have $100 in a bank or $1 million," he said, "I think they owe you the courtesy of stamping your parking ticket."

THE 30-SECOND RECAP

- There are three levels of customer: the employee-customer, the internal customer, and the external customer.

- To improve customer service immediately, begin by eliminating those situations that consistently incur customer complaints, and train employees to avoid phrases that arouse customer anger, such as those outlined in this chapter.

- Make sure that you and your employees know what a customer wants and expects from your company.

- Whatever you do, don't ignore or underestimate the value of customer service to the success of your company. Remember: Regardless of what you sell, you're really in the service business!

Your Only Competitive Advantage

In this section you learn what the fundamental values of excellent customer service are and how to design an effective customer service delivery system—one that will transform customer service into the most powerful marketing tool your company will ever discover.

GAINING THE COMPETITIVE EDGE

There was a time when the life of a businessperson was simple. Sales of products or services were generated by salespeople or through various forms of advertising, and advantage over one's competitors was gained with the right combination of price and product quality.

Business has become much more complex. In today's global marketplace, competitive pricing and high-quality products or services are no longer enough to win customers over—they're just the price of entry for companies seeking to join the game of earning customer loyalty. Today, if you want to gain a competitive edge over your competition, excellence in customer service is an absolute requirement.

Providing top-notch customer service is the key to finding and keeping customers. And providing service that's better than the competition is what keeps the profits rolling in.

CAUTION

Even though pricing and product quality are no longer enough to win the competitive war, they remain important to the overall effort. High-quality products that are competitively priced, together with top-notch service quality, are the recipe for success in today's global marketplace.

THE FINANCIAL VALUE OF A CUSTOMER

In case you're wondering whether you're doing everything necessary to develop a customer service culture in your company, consider the following scenario.

Store A sells a widget to Customer A for $100. The profit margin for widgets is 40 percent, or $40, on the sale.

The typical customer buys 10 widgets a year. This means that if Store A offers excellence in customer service, the customer is likely to buy 9 more widgets from Store A during the year, bringing in another $360 in profit, for a total annual profit of $400. That's the annual value of one typical widget customer. Over a 5-year period, the value of Customer A is $2,000.

If Customer A tells 10 friends how satisfied he or she is with Store A's widgets and service, and each of the 10 friends in turn buys 10 widgets a year from Store A, over 5 years the value of Customer A becomes $22,000.

Whatever amount of effort and money your company invests in customer service, you can be sure that it will bring an excellent return. Conversely, failing to invest in customer service can mean the loss of significant profits over time.

AMAZON.COM AND CUSTOMER SERVICE

A few years ago, Jeff Bezos enrolled in an introductory course in book-selling offered by the American Booksellers Association. He was captivated by a customer service story told by his instructor, who owned a small bookstore in Mississippi.

The instructor recounted an incident in which one of his customers became upset and angry when dirt from a second-story flowerpot was accidentally spilled onto her car, which was parked outside his store. To solve the problem, the instructor rolled up his sleeves and personally washed the customer's car. The customer was so impressed by this gesture of goodwill that she returned to buy numerous books and told all her friends to do the same.

That kind of commitment to excellence in customer service is what Bezos insisted be the guiding principle of his company, Amazon.com. Last year, Amazon.com had sales of $1.6 billion dollars, representing 15.4 percent of all commerce conducted over the Internet.

The three keys to Amazon's success are competitive pricing, quality of product, and excellence in customer service.

PLAIN ENGLISH

Customer service   Meeting the needs and expectations of the customer as defined by the customer.

THE FOUNDATIONS OF EXCELLENCE

There's a principle of successful living my mother taught me years ago that has always fascinated me. It's so simple that many people seem to miss it altogether. It's this: You get back from life what you put into it!

We see that principle at work every day of our lives. People who skim by, who do only what's absolutely necessary and no more, and who settle for less than they are capable of, usually receive very little from life in return. They often end up feeling that life has somehow shortchanged them.

On the other hand, people who always give 110 percent of themselves to everything they're involved in seem to get much more out of living. The casual observer may be tempted to attribute these people's zest for living to "good fortune" or "luck," when the truth is they're just reaping what they've sown; their investment in life continues to bring them the best that life can offer.

Over the years, I've learned that this particular principle isn't true only in the lives of people; it's also true in the lives of corporations and other forms of organized business.

When a business attempts to do as little as possible to ensure customer satisfaction, and worries more about profits, it rarely rises above the level of mediocrity. That's true even if the business spends a fortune on advertising and has products that are of high quality and are competitively priced.

Excellence in customer service requires five important core values to which everyone in the company must genuinely strive to adhere:

- Commitment to building a culture
- Willingness to pay the price
- Desire to exceed customer expectations
- Obsession for excellence
- Eternal vigilance

COMMITMENT TO BUILDING A CULTURE

Famed Green Bay Packers coach Vince Lombardi once said, "The quality of a person's life is in direct proportion to their commitment to excellence, regardless of their chosen field of endeavor." Excellence in customer service has its roots in an unyielding commitment by top management to create a culture of customer service in which every facet of the business is customer-driven.

WILLINGNESS TO PAY THE PRICE

Excellence in any endeavor is not automatic. Excellence in customer service is no exception. As Dr. Stephen Covey, author of *The Seven Habits of Highly Effective People,* says, "Real excellence does not come cheaply. A certain price must be paid in terms of practice, patience, and persistence."

Building a culture of customer service requires patience over time. And persistence is necessary to continue moving forward toward excellence in customer service, even when it would be less time-consuming, less demanding, and less costly to be less than excellent. Once established, successful customer service techniques must be practiced both internally and externally—and everyone in the organization needs to be involved.

DESIRE TO EXCEED CUSTOMER EXPECTATIONS

Consistently exceeding customer expectations is a challenge to go a step beyond the usual. It involves giving a little more than is required or expected. It's not necessarily doing an extraordinary thing; rather, it's doing an ordinary thing extraordinarily well.

Smuckers, the jam and jelly maker, has a policy of filling its containers with a bit more product than the official weight indicates. Most customers never weigh the jar and consequently are never aware of the bonus. But giving the customer more than is expected is part of the Smuckers service to its customers. It's their practice, whether people are watching or not. Is it any wonder that Smuckers has captured a huge share of the jam and jelly market?

OBSESSION FOR EXCELLENCE

Winston Churchill once said, "I am easily satisfied with the very best." Your customers are, too. It's been my experience that when companies consider their customer service efforts "good enough," the reality is that their service is usually somewhere between mediocre and horrible.

The definition of a company's customer service quality will ultimately become the definition of the company itself. Hallmark cares enough to send "the very best." How do you know? The quality of their product says so.

ETERNAL VIGILANCE

If you're serious about wanting to provide *excellence in customer service,* and thereby maintain your competitive edge in the marketplace, the price you must be willing to pay is eternal vigilance.

L.L. Bean president Leon Gorman has defined customer service as "just a day-in, day-out, ongoing, never-ending, unremitting, persevering, compassionate type of activity." But however you define it, customer service is always a journey, not a destination.

PLAIN ENGLISH

Excellence in customer service   A way of doing business that involves going beyond the call of duty, stretching perceived limits, and empowering everyone in the organization to maintain the highest standards, pay attention to details, and go the extra mile. Take a lesson from Mother Goose: "Good, better, best; never rest till 'good' is 'better' and 'better' is 'best.'"

YOUR SERVICE DELIVERY SYSTEM

John Goodman, president of TARP, Inc., once said, "Eighty percent of customers' problems are caused by bad systems, not by bad people." He's right. Most of the service problems your customers encounter in trying to do business with you occur because your delivery systems (the systems you rely on to serve customers) are either antiquated, too complex, or just plain unfriendly.

PLAIN ENGLISH

Service delivery systems   The means, methods, and procedures used to provide a product or service to the public and to provide other customer assistance as deemed necessary by the customer.

For example, most dysfunctional systems include telephone technology that features such customer "displeasers" as call director or voice-mail systems with frustratingly lengthy menu options, or caller-hold features that entertain callers with annoying elevator music from the *Twilight Zone*. (Some organizations even dare to interrupt the entertainment with an occasional commercial message.)

To add insult to injury, when a customer finally reaches a real person, too often that person has little knowledge of the company's products and no power to solve the customer's problem or fix what's wrong. Such telephone technology costs companies millions in lost customers.

SEVEN CHARACTERISTICS OF EFFECTIVE DELIVERY SYSTEMS

It's true that each company's customer service delivery system is somewhat unique. But among highly functional systems, there are seven identical characteristics.

To be world class and capable of achieving customer service excellence, your service delivery system needs to be …

- **Customer-driven.** Your customer service delivery system should be designed as a partnership with the customer. Remember, the purpose of your company is to satisfy the needs of your customers and potential customers; never make the mistake of thinking that your company exists simply to produce and sell goods or services. So think of your customer as a partner. Take a walk in your customers' shoes. What kind of service delivery system would please you?

- **Available.** Open the way for customers to do business with you. Make it easy for customers to purchase your goods or services. When you encounter obstacles that prevent your customers from easily and conveniently doing business with you, make it a priority to remove those obstacles. If you're going to succeed, you need to be available to your customers.

- **Responsive.** Design a service delivery system that gets you up-close-and-personal with your customers. Know your customers' needs, desires, and expectations; and make them the standard against which you monitor your organization's efforts. Companies that make it a practice to know their customers as if they were family members are companies that are responsive to their customers. Customer loyalty rises or falls based on your ability to respond appropriately to their needs, desires, and expectations.

- **Correct.** Customer service delivery systems should consistently provide customers with accurate information. This is particularly true when it comes to technical aspects of products and information about warranties, price, delivery, billings, and so on. Customers are quick to perceive when the person helping them knows less about a product than they do.

- **Integrated.** Customers should be able to obtain all of the information they need from one source within your company. It is unnecessarily frustrating when customers are asked to obtain service in a piecemeal fashion by talking with several people in your company.

- **User-friendly.** The process that the customer uses to access your company's services should be friendly, uncomplicated, and accessible. Avoid using voice mail whenever possible.

- **Fast.** Customer service delivery systems should provide assistance to customers quickly. Customers perceive speedy help as excellence.

CAUTION

Remember that customer service doesn't just belong to the "customer service department." It's everyone's business. In developing a customer service culture, it's absolutely necessary to involve everyone in the company. Customer service isn't a job title; it's a way of life for everyone in your company from the chief executive officer to the part-time window washer. It's an all-or-nothing proposition.

THREE KEYS TO EXCELLENCE

In addition to building a firm foundation of customer-centered core values and designing a customer delivery system that makes doing business with your company convenient and easy, you need good people to make it all work. Excellence in customer service doesn't just happen because our hearts are right and our program design is good; it happens because good people working in *customer-centric* environments make it happen.

PLAIN ENGLISH

Customer-centric   Anything that is centered entirely on the customer. The more "customer-centric" an organization becomes, the more it is aligned with the needs, wants, and desires of the customer.

In the section "Hiring a Service-Oriented Attitude" on page 1095 we'll talk much more about how to find, hire, train, and keep good people. But for the purposes of this section, let's focus our attention on three specific characteristics of highly effective customer service staff:

- Technical quality
- Human interaction
- Empowerment

These are the keys to excellence in customer service, and they will give your company the competitive advantage it desires.

TECHNICAL QUALITY

Technical quality is what enables you to compete in the marketplace. Your *frontline employees*—those in your company who directly interact with customers—must be able to provide assistance in ways that demonstrate a high degree of technical competence.

PLAIN ENGLISH

Frontline employees   Those who deal directly with the customer—the purchaser of the product or service.

Excellence in customer service not only requires a top-notch product, but also requires that those serving the customer be knowledgeable about the company, its products, and their applications—or that they know where to go to find the necessary answers. Customer satisfaction soars when employees know what they're doing, *like* what they're doing, and are entirely absorbed with the company's purpose and mission.

Here are a few of the most important characteristics of employees who strongly influence a customer's assessment of technical quality. Excellence is conveyed by employees who …

- Consistently provide customers with accurate information about the company and the product it sells.

- Know the internal processes required to resolve customer problems or complaints (and how to cut through the red tape whenever necessary).

- Understand the way in which the company's products are used by customers and know how potential problems associated with the product can be avoided.

- Are effective problem-solvers—they know what to do.

- Can solve a customer problem, or resolve a complaint, quickly and efficiently.

HUMAN INTERACTION

There's a human side to the customer service equation, and it's important. People want to be treated as human beings, as unique and important people who deserve the very best you and your company have to offer.

In any type of enterprise, human interaction is what separates the excellent from the good. And it's human interaction that wins customers and keeps them over time.

Here are some examples of ways in which human interaction can be used to create excellence in customer service:

- Customers are greeted politely and courteously. Service representatives are courteous even when customers aren't, and they remain calm in the face of anger and chaos.

- An atmosphere of friendliness prevails throughout each customer interaction. Friendliness is not just a slogan; it's a way of doing business.

- By their words and body language, your staff conveys a deep respect for customers and demonstrates that respect with warmth in each interaction regardless of type (telephone calls, walk-in visitors, letters, sales contacts).

- Empathy and understanding for a customer with a problem or complaint is communicated in genuine ways that are not judgmental or critical but that demonstrate acknowledgment and appreciation of the customer's feelings.

- Information—even of a technical nature—is communicated in understandable ways without making the customer feel ignorant or put down in any way.

- Customers are treated fairly in every interaction with the company.

EMPOWERMENT

Dr. Benjamin Schneider, professor of psychology at the University of Maryland, is credited with this wise observation: "Treat your people like gold—or dirt—and they'll treat your customers accordingly." An empowered employee is an important key to providing excellence in customer service.

Empowered employees are authorized to solve customer problems on the spot in predetermined ways. For example, Horst Schulze, president of the Ritz-Carlton Hotel Company, allows any employee working on a customer service issue to spend up to $2,500 to resolve the matter and to prevent a repeat occurrence. According to a recent J. D. Power survey, 94 percent of Ritz-Carlton customers report that they are well satisfied; the Ritz-Carlton's best competitor for the same period received only a 57 percent rating.

Empowering your employees to meet the needs of customers is not just a good idea, it's absolutely necessary if your goal is excellence in customer service. An empowered employee ...

- Solves customer problems quickly and efficiently.
- Builds partnerships with customers that are based on mutual understanding and respect.
- Speaks volumes about the entire company's commitment to excellence in customer service.
- Provides an atmosphere of high morale in which employees take ownership of outcomes and customers are "treated like gold."

THE 30-SECOND RECAP

- The true financial value of a customer cannot be measured in terms of one sale, but rather in terms of the purchases the customer is likely to make over time.
- In today's global marketplace, the three keys to success are competitive pricing, quality of product, and excellence in customer service.
- For excellence in customer service, everyone in the company must share five core values: commitment to building the culture, a willingness to pay the price, a desire to exceed customer expectations, an obsession for excellence, and eternal vigilance.
- Develop customer service delivery systems that make it easy for people to do business with your company.
- The three keys that unlock the potential of your company's frontline customer service staff are technical quality, human interaction, and empowerment.

Hiring a Service-Oriented Attitude

In this section you learn the importance of people in creating and maintaining a customer service culture. You also learn which specific qualities to look for in candidates and how to use behavioral interviewing techniques to discover whether candidates can succeed in a customer service environment.

WINNING THE WAR

When David Frost interviewed General Norman Schwarzkopf, commander of the Allied Forces in the Gulf War, he asked the general, "What's the greatest lesson you've learned out of all of this?"

The heroic general replied, "I think that there is one really fundamental military truth. And that's that you can add up the correlation of forces, you can look at the number of tanks, you can look at the number of airplanes, you can look at all these factors of military might and put them together. But unless the soldier on the ground, or the airman in the air, has the will to win, has the strength of character to go into battle, believes that his cause is just, and has the support of his country ... all the rest of that stuff is irrelevant."

Technologies, systems, protocols, procedures, processes, strategies, and plans all provide the means. But only individuals, properly supported, well trained, and motivated by the mission, win the war.

That statement is also true in modern business, where the battlefield is the global marketplace, the battle objective is to gain market share, and victory is profitability. It takes the combined effort of top-quality people who are thoroughly trained, properly motivated, and continuously supported to achieve that victory.

HIRING QUALITY PEOPLE

J. W. "Bill" Marriott Jr., Chairman and CEO of the Marriott Corporation, puts it like this: "You start with good people, you train and motivate them, you give them an opportunity to advance, then the organization succeeds."

Building and maintaining a winning customer service culture in your company begins with hiring good people who can build positive relationships with customers. The success of your organization depends on your ability to hire well.

MISTAKES ARE COSTLY

Hiring mistakes can be very costly to your organization. In fact, some studies have shown that the direct costs alone can equal as much as four times the annual salary for the position.

But the indirect costs of hiring mistakes can be even more staggering. In addition to lost productivity, the drain on management, and the harm done to employee morale, the wrong employee can alienate some customers and substantially damage customer relations in general.

In "Your Only Competitive Advantage" on page 1086 you learned about the financial value of a customer over time. If we again consider the example of Customer A, who buys 10 widgets a year, each of which produces $40 in profit to Company A, then losing Customer A would produce an annual loss of profit to the company of $400. Over a 5-year period, the loss of profit would amount to $2,000. And if Customer A tells 10 friends—each of whom also buys 10 widgets a year—how badly he or she was treated by Company A, the potential loss to the company over a 5-year period is $22,000.

If 10 customers are alienated, and each customer tells 10 others, the potential profit loss now grows to $222,000! And that's if you're selling widgets. Imagine what the loss would be if the products were cars, construction equipment, computers, or other widely purchased products.

Hiring the right person for the job is critically important to the future of your company.

DON'T SETTLE FOR A "WARM BODY"

Finding the right person for the job takes time and effort. Unfortunately, most businesses today spend more time buying a new copy machine than they do choosing the right employee. And, too often, jobs that involve dealing directly with customers are given to the first "warm body" that promises to show up for eight hours each day of the workweek. The results are predictably disastrous.

Companies that consistently outperform their competition in quality of product and service delivery never settle for warm bodies. They know the value of hiring top-quality people. And they never allow the process of finding and hiring the right people to be rushed.

Several years ago, Seattle-based retailer Nordstrom opened its first store on the East Coast, in McLean, Virginia. To adequately staff the new operation, Nordstrom needed to hire 400 employees to serve in frontline positions. According to a story in the March 4, 1988, edition of *USA Today,* over 3,000 people were screened and interviewed to find the 400 who would complement the Nordstrom customer service culture. Nordstrom values its customers—and its employees. No wonder it's one of the most successful retailers in America.

THE HIRING PROCESS

Hiring is a process that involves …

- Analyzing the job opening to determine *mandatory success factors.*
- Recruiting candidates internally and externally who possess the desired qualifications.
- Screening resumés for further consideration.
- Checking references.
- Developing appropriate interview questions.
- Conducting interviews.
- Selecting the best candidate for the job.

PLAIN ENGLISH

Mandatory success factors   The specific competencies and skills that are absolutely essential to successful job performance. They are determined by thoroughly analyzing the job and by providing profiles of the job and the ideal candidate.

ANALYZING THE JOB

What skills or competencies are required to be successful in the job? That's an important question. Unless you know exactly what it takes to succeed in the job, it's impossible to know what to look for in job applicants.

Here are some typical questions to ask as you analyze the open position:

- What *functional skills* are required to do this job well?
- What technical competencies (degrees, certifications, licenses, and so on) are necessary?
- What *self-management skills* are needed?
- What *interpersonal skills* are required?
- What are the requirements of the corporate culture?

PLAIN ENGLISH

Functional skills   Skills that help people function effectively on the job. They include the ability to communicate, to listen, to lead, and to be flexible.

Self-management skills   Personal characteristics that help people do the job successfully. Included are such skills as creativity, honesty, competence, appearance, and helpfulness.

Interpersonal skills   "People skills." Such skills are particularly important to consider when interviewing for frontline positions. Good interpersonal skills include the ability to respect others, to be empathetic and caring, to listen attentively and respond accordingly, and to maintain objectivity and refrain from emotionalism.

CAUTION

Attitudes that reflect a genuine love of people and a burning desire to be helpful to others are particularly important for frontline staff. People can be trained to be proficient in most of the areas necessary for successful job performance, but attitudes are difficult to change. The attitude you hire is usually the attitude you'll have to live with during the tenure of the employee. Be careful.

A thorough analysis of the open position will result in a clear profile of both the job and the ideal candidate. Once you know what you're looking for, you're ready to start your search.

RECRUITING CANDIDATES INTERNALLY

Now that you know exactly what you're looking for, begin your search by making existing staff aware of the position and the qualifications being sought. Asking existing employees for referrals and recruiting within the organization by posting the job are cost-efficient ways to fill vacancies.

Seeking applicants from within has another important advantage: It tends to build morale. Employees appreciate knowing that their employer values them, and nothing communicates that message more clearly than offering to existing staff the first new opportunities.

RECRUITING CANDIDATES EXTERNALLY

There was a time when the chief means of locating candidates for employment outside the organization involved placing a "help wanted" advertisement in the local newspaper. Today, the task of external recruiting has become much more complex.

At the time this book is being written, unemployment rates within the United States are the lowest in history, and wages are at their highest levels ever. Attempting to recruit externally in an economy this robust requires innovative and aggressive strategies.

Most major employers today do not rely on single-source recruiting efforts. Instead they solicit applicants from a number of sources, such as ...

- Newspaper advertising.
- Advertising on the company Web page.
- Internet job search services.
- Employment or recruitment agencies.
- College-graduate placement services.
- Public job services.

Successful candidates can come from many different sources. It's a good idea to communicate the job opening to a lot of sources simultaneously for maximum results.

TIP

Be sure to offer candidates several options for submitting their resumés (in person, mail, e-mail, fax). Some organizations even allow applicants to apply online at the company's Web site. Make it easy for prospective candidates to send you their applications.

SCREENING RESUMÉS

The objective in screening resumés is to select applicants for further consideration. You want to narrow the field of applicants to those whose education and experience appear to fit the identified mandatory success factors.

It's a good idea to ask others to help you screen the resumés that you've received for an open position. Develop and use a standardized evaluation tool so that each resumé can be rated against specific criteria.

Once the screening process is complete, notify by letter those who have been disqualified from further consideration. Be sure to thank them for applying for the job, and encourage them to apply for future openings with your company.

CAUTION

Resumés rejected by evaluators should be kept on file, along with accompanying notes and evaluations. To defend yourself against possible litigation, it's important that your reasons for rejecting an applicant be firmly rooted in the requirements of the job, not in anything extraneous. Your documentation should clearly identify job-related reasons for screening out the applicant from further consideration.

CHECKING REFERENCES

Once you've narrowed the field of candidates, it's a good idea to check references. I know what you're thinking: reference checks *before* the interview? Why would I want to do that?

For two important reasons: First, the process of checking references helps employers gain a better understanding of the candidates under consideration—and that's an important objective of the evaluation process. Second, during the reference checks, employers often discover areas of special concern that require further exploration during the interview.

But whether you check references before the interview or after, be sure to check them. Some business journals have estimated that the references of as many as 70 percent of all new hires are never checked. That's asking for trouble.

CAUTION

After the interview and reference-check stages, have successful applicants complete a company application that contains broad written permission allowing you to talk with those who have firsthand knowledge of their abilities and experience. I also advise clients to consider including a "hold harmless" clause that prevents former employers from being sued by an applicant as a result of what they divulge. Consult your legal department about the company's employment application. Your legal counsel can also provide you with information about the questions that legally may, and may not, be contained in an application.

DEVELOPING APPROPRIATE INTERVIEW QUESTIONS

Developing interview questions that elicit specific information related to one of the mandatory success factors is a critical part of the selection process. The trouble is, the questions that are asked during most interviews don't yield the information needed to make a reasonable hiring decision. In fact, the number-one "question" asked in interviews today is "Tell us a little bit about yourself." Ninety-five percent of all interviews begin this way.

In developing interview questions, consider using structured behavioral interviewing techniques that will provide you with evidence of a candidate's ability in a specific area. *Behavioral interviewing* is based upon the behavioral consistency principle that the best predictor of future behavior is past behavior under similar circumstances.

Developing questions that are behavioral in nature will give you the information you need to make an informed decision about a candidate. And employing behavioral interviewing techniques will significantly improve your chances of hiring successfully.

The following is an example that demonstrates the difference between a standard question and a behavioral question in a job interview. Assume that the objective of the interviewer is to learn more about the candidate's attitude toward customer service. Which of these two types of interview questions do you think is more effective?

STANDARD INTERVIEW QUESTION

In a standard interview, an interviewer seeking information about a candidate's customer service attitude might ask: "How do you feel about customer service?"

The question might produce some interesting commentary that may, or may not, reveal the level of hands-on experience a candidate has with customer service. In the course of answering the question, if the candidate describes his or her own involvement in actual customer service situations, this may reveal the candidate's attitude toward customer service.

BEHAVIORAL INTERVIEW QUESTION

In a behavioral interview format, however, the candidate is asked to provide behavioral evidence that substantiates his or her claim of possessing the skills identified as mandatory for job success. An interviewer seeking information about a candidate's attitude toward customer service might ask the following behavioral question: "Tell me about the most difficult customer service problem you have ever encountered. What was involved? What did you do?" The candidate's response to the question will tell you about his or her attitude toward customer service in general and will give you a glimpse of his or her level of skill in handling difficult customer service situations.

The behavioral interview question will elicit real-life information about "the most difficult customer service problem" ever faced by the candidate. By listening closely to the answer and probing for additional information, not only will you gain important insights about the candidate's attitude toward customer service, you'll also be given a firsthand view of how well the candidate is able to translate attitude into action.

CONDUCTING INTERVIEWS

Once you've formulated your interview questions, you're ready to begin interviewing candidates. I recommend that you invite others who are stakeholders in the final hiring decision to also participate in the interviews.

Plan your interviews to have an opening, an information exchange, and a closing. The *opening* is the time you use to put the candidate at ease. Tell the candidate what to expect during the interview and provide some idea of the time required. The opening is also a good time to ask any specific questions about the applicant's education or experience that remain unanswered.

During the *information exchange,* ask the candidate your planned behavioral questions (each candidate is asked the same questions) related to specific mandatory success factors. Take all the time you need with each question. Probe whenever you feel the need to explore further.

The *closing* of the interview should include a company "sales pitch" delivered by one of the members of the interview team. Whether or not the candidate will be the one selected for the position is irrelevant; your objective should be for each candidate to leave the interview with the understanding that yours is a great company to be part of.

The closing of the interview is also the time for you to explain to the candidate what happens next—when a decision will be made and how he or she will be notified. It's also the time to ask whether the candidate has any unanswered questions about the job or the company.

SELECTING THE BEST CANDIDATE FOR THE JOB

Before you begin selecting the best candidate for the job, develop a candidate evaluation tool so that you will be evaluating each candidate on the same factors. Immediately after each interview, have each member of the interview team complete an evaluation.

The hiring decision should ultimately be based upon the evaluations of the candidate. Unless there is very good reason to do otherwise, the candidate who receives the highest ratings by evaluators should be offered the position.

The successful candidate is usually notified by telephone, but be sure to follow up with a letter confirming the details of the offer. Be sure also to write each of the remaining candidates to let them know that a decision has been made and to encourage them to apply again in the future.

THE 30-SECOND RECAP

- Employees are vital to the success of any enterprise. Top-quality people produce top-quality results.

- Hiring mistakes are costly—they hinder your company's quest to develop the kind of customer service culture that will cause phenomenal growth and success.

- Develop and maintain a hiring process that identifies the mandatory success factors of a position and helps to select candidates who possess the requisite skills and competencies.

- Each new employee changes your corporate culture for better or for worse. Take as much time as you need to do a thorough job of selecting.

Keeping a Service-Oriented Attitude

In this section you learn how to retain top-quality employees and how to use high-quality, ongoing training as a guarantee that your employees remain committed to providing the very best in customer service.

THE MICROSOFT EXAMPLE

With all the legal hullabaloo over the Microsoft antitrust suit, I've concluded that the world is divided into two camps: those who would like to see Microsoft broken apart (and taught a lesson—how dare they be so successful!) and those who think Microsoft is the best thing since the invention of the abacus. I consider myself part of the latter group. Here's why.

I enjoy great American success stories. I especially like those that feature a company that had its beginnings in a family garage and that became a wildly successful, multinational powerhouse within only a few decades. Such stories are inspirational as well as just plain interesting.

That's the story of Microsoft. Bill Gates and Paul Allen started their business a number of years ago in the Gates family garage. The company grew so fast and became so successful that Gates had to drop out of Harvard to devote all of his time to it. Today, Microsoft is one of the largest publicly held companies in America, with gross revenues exceeding those of many governments throughout the world.

One major contributor to Microsoft's success has been its understanding of the importance of customer service. However, at the heart of Microsoft's philosophy of customer service is another very important business truth: its treatment of employees.

Microsoft makes it a practice to treat its employees the same way it expects its employees to treat customers. The result: The company experiences high *employee retention* and high levels of employee and customer satisfaction. Employees are treated very well. They, in turn, pass that treatment on to customers. It's a win-win proposition. Learn from Microsoft.

PLAIN ENGLISH

Employee retention   An integrated process, not a series of isolated events or programs. The process of retention (keeping top-notch employees from going elsewhere) begins at the time of recruitment and is embedded in employment policies and practices that affect the employee throughout his or her career.

RETAINING TOP TALENT

But what does it take to retain good people? More than you might think.

When a company recognizes that there is a direct correlation between losing good employees and losing customers, it gets serious about employee retention. Creating a customer service culture in which good employees are highly valued assets is a fine beginning. But retaining good people and helping them achieve corporate service objectives also means making some basic management decisions that will keep them from leaving for the competition.

Following are a few areas that managers need to consider with regard to employees.

SALARY AND BENEFIT PACKAGES

Never let it be said that money solves the entire problem of employee retention; it solves only a substantial part of it. While money isn't a good substitute for major deficiencies in the company (bad reputation, inferior product quality, poor management, and so on), it is an important consideration in hiring and keeping good people.

Competition for good people in the new world order of the twenty-first century is fierce. Many companies today offer prospective employees a financial package that combines an excellent salary with such perks as stock options, 401(k) plans, profit sharing, early retirement options, club memberships, healthcare, student loan repayment options, paid sabbaticals, company-paid daycare, cars, and so on.

If you want to attract and keep good people who, in turn, will be profit generators, it's essential to offer a compensation package that expresses your estimate of their worth.

Some companies claim that money and benefit packages aren't all that important to employees. They're wrong. Certainly there are other important considerations, but it's been my experience that money and benefits are always high on most people's list.

ADVANCEMENT OPPORTUNITIES

Keeping good people also requires that there be real opportunities for advancement within the company and that the company promote from within whenever possible. A promotion is the greatest reward you can give to someone who is doing a good job.

But be careful how you promote. Top-quality employees want to work for a company that promotes fairly—and for the right reasons.

Be sure that the people you promote reflect the values that are important to the future growth and development of the company. In terms of values, what you promote is what you'll get.

The truthfulness of this statement lies in the fact that other employees soon become aware of what's really valued by the company. For example, when a company claiming to be customer-driven promotes people only on the basis of longevity, employees get the message that customer service is less important than remaining with the company and staying out of trouble. Such a message causes many employees to begin looking elsewhere. The reverse is also true: If a company promotes those whose customer service skills are exemplary, employees get the clear message that serving customers well is the pathway to success.

CAUTION

What do you value? It's true that a manager will hire and promote people whose values correspond to his or her own. Think of the last three people you promoted. What values did you promote along with the people you promoted?

FAVORABLE WORK ENVIRONMENT

One of the most important factors in retaining good people is a favorable work environment. And nothing is more conducive to a favorable work environment than supervisors and managers who value their employees.

It's been my experience that one of the most common reasons people leave their jobs for greener pastures is that they have somehow become disconnected with their bosses as well as with the work itself. Good bosses—those who embody your company's vision and who consider employee satisfaction to be a priority—make a big difference in employee retention.

Companies that are serious about retaining good workers need to be careful about whom they select and train to be supervisors and managers. Good people won't continue to work for a jerk.

And here's the real payoff: Study after study has shown a direct relationship between employee job satisfaction and customer service satisfaction.

TIP

Some companies have found that turnover is reduced when a portion of a manager's pay is tied to retention. When managers are rewarded for good retention stats, and penalized for high turnover, they develop innovative strategies designed to keep people happy in their work.

CHALLENGING WORK ASSIGNMENTS

To keep good employees, it's important that assignments be challenging, rewarding, and motivating. However, over time any job can become stagnant and boring. That's why, even in the best work environments, people sometimes need to change jobs.

Companies with the best records of retention have developed programs that allow employees to move laterally. Lateral movements often involve temporary or developmental job assignments that allow the employee to become revitalized. These opportunities not only offer new challenges, but also allow employees to gain a fresh perspective on the organization's mission.

Experiencing different positions within the company also affords employees an opportunity to explore their strengths and interests. Finding a job that best suits each employee is a key factor in retaining them, and lateral movement within the company fosters that kind of exploration.

REWARDS AND RECOGNITION

Recognition and reward are two powerful motivators for inspiring job excellence. Some studies have demonstrated that these two factors are even more important to job satisfaction than salary and benefits.

When you formally recognize employees for good work, you publicly acknowledge their value to the company and you demonstrate that their efforts have not gone unnoticed. People tend to stay in situations that provide ample amounts of personal satisfaction.

CAUTION

Managing is much like parenting: Be careful what actions you praise or reward, because you're sure to get a lot more of the same.

TIP

Be sure to recognize people for work accomplishments, not just for their longevity with the company. Recognition for real work accomplishments is rewarding to the employees being recognized and is motivational to others.

EMPOWERMENT

Empowerment means encouraging employees to take ownership of their jobs and to use creativity in meeting performance objectives and solving problems along the way. And employees who take ownership of their jobs are much more likely to remain with the company.

But empowerment doesn't just happen because you want it to. Empowerment requires companies to invest time and money in meaningful training activities that teach employees about the mission of the company and provide them with technical information about the company's product or service. Empowerment also requires that employees have the right tools to perform their jobs well and that they know how to use those tools.

Empowered employees not only are likely to remain with a company long-term, but will have a major effect on customer service as well. Empowered employees feel that customer satisfaction is a personal responsibility and will resolve customer issues on the spot.

TRAINING AND RETENTION

Training is a life-long experience. In his book *Life on the Mississippi*, Mark Twain wrote, "Two things seemed pretty apparent to me. One was that in order to be a Mississippi River pilot, a man has got to learn more than any one man ought to be allowed to know; and the other was that he must learn it all over again in a different way every 24 hours."

PLAIN ENGLISH

Training   A lifelong experience that has three primary objectives: to give employees a basic understanding of their job and a vision of the mission of the company, to provide the skills and tools necessary to perform the tasks of the job correctly and efficiently, and to keep people functioning at high levels throughout their careers.

The need for training never ends. Evolving technology, developing markets with special needs, continually improving methods of ensuring quality and service, and the frequent introduction of new products and services make training in the twenty-first century of absolute importance. Time spent in meaningful training activities is profitable for the employee and the company alike.

POOR TRAINING MEANS POOR PERFORMANCE

It's sad but true that the primary reason for poor employee performance is lack of basic training. The next time you're faced with a poor-performance problem, ask yourself whether specific kinds of training may be needed. By answering the following simple questions, supervisors and managers can quickly diagnose whether additional training will solve the problem:

- Does the employee know the primary purpose of his or her job? (For example, the primary purpose of a hotel doorkeeper is to assist customers who are arriving or leaving the hotel; it's not simply to call for cabs.)

- Does the employee understand the process—that is, the steps required to do the job well? (When people don't understand what they are supposed to do, they can never meet expectation levels. People need to understand the process required to do their jobs successfully.)

- Does the employee possess the necessary technical skills to perform each required task? (For example, a grocery store clerk may understand the entire process of assisting customers at checkout; but unless the clerk understands how to find the price of an item that won't scan, he or she is not well trained.)

CAUTION

Don't make the mistake of using training as a punishment. Training should never be used in a negative way. Send people to training in order to help them grow and develop as employees and as people.

Training Shapes Attitude

There's an important link between training and employee retention. Employees who are involved in ongoing training that is focused on helping them do their jobs better are more satisfied, and therefore more likely to remain with the company.

Training shapes employee attitude and behavior, and motivates workers to provide the very best in customer service. Training is the catalyst for positive change in any company; it is far and away the most powerful culture-building tool you have.

Developing and maintaining a positive service culture in which employees thrive and turnover rates are low depends to a great extent on the quality of training you provide. All training—even technical training—should be delivered from a customer service perspective and have clear behavioral objectives relating to internal and external customers.

All training should result in ...

- An understanding by employees that their number-one responsibility is serving customers (internal or external).
- Inspiring employees to aim beyond customer satisfaction—causing customers to say "Wow!" in response to the quality of service received.
- Learning specific problem-solving techniques that help satisfy the needs of customers and that effectively and quickly handle customer problems.
- A better understanding of the corporate vision and the individual mission of the employee.
- Enhanced internal cooperation and a better appreciation of teamwork.
- A more customer-centric organization.
- Greater employee empowerment to serve the customer better.

Mentoring and Coaching

But providing formal training opportunities isn't enough. To capture the full value of formal training, one more step is necessary—a step that's often overlooked.

Real learning takes place where the rubber meets the road: on the job. That's where the knowledge and ideas gained from formal training activities must be translated into actual practice. How? With an ongoing program of *mentoring* and coaching employees.

PLAIN ENGLISH

Mentoring   The act of counseling and advising an employee in the area of career development. Mentors not only advise employees on specific work tasks, they help them to assimilate into the corporate culture.

Supervisors and managers need to redefine their roles to include creating an environment of learning and growing that involves mentoring, coaching, equipping, sustaining, and nurturing those who report to them.

Effective training doesn't happen only in the classroom. Successful training programs include a mentoring/coaching component that helps employees do their best where it counts—on the job.

THE MAZDA SOLUTION

Consider the training commitment that the Mazda Company makes to its production-line workers.

When the Mazda automobile company opened its first American plant, it made a substantial commitment to training its production workers. Mazda attempts to hire workers 10 to 12 weeks before they are actually placed on the assembly line.

For the first few weeks, Mazda provides new workers with "soft training," which consists of classroom activities designed to teach the basics of team-work and the company philosophy and vision. Following this initial training period, new workers are assigned to various parts of the plant and given a combination of classroom and hands-on training in performing actual work functions, such as welding and painting.

Once new workers have completed their initial training activities, they are placed on the job. A mentor/coach is assigned to help them perform their jobs well and, by helping them, foster their ongoing growth and development as Mazda employees.

Mentoring/coaching is a necessary part of a customer service culture. And it is effective in meeting the needs of both internal and external customers.

TIP

Consider creating a company library consisting of books, videotapes, and audiotapes on subjects of interest to your employees. Topics of special interest would include communication, customer satisfaction, conflict resolution, assisting the difficult customer, problem solving, negotiating, and quality management.

Don't underestimate the power of customer service training that includes ongoing mentoring and coaching by supervisors and managers. Your company's customer focus, or lack of it, will determine the degree to which your company ultimately succeeds. Training that helps employees serve customers better also helps reduce employee turnover by making jobs more satisfying and rewarding.

Investing in customer-focused training is just good business.

THE 30-SECOND RECAP

- Retaining service-oriented people and retaining customers go hand-in-hand.

- Retaining good employees requires a substantial commitment from management to provide the kind of environment that encourages people to stay.

- Ongoing training is an important key to developing and retaining service-oriented employees.

- Ongoing coaching and mentoring are part of any successful customer service training program.

What's Your Vision?

In this section you learn the importance of developing an inspirational, customer-centered vision for your business. You also learn how to communicate your vision in ways that cause employees to approach their jobs with enthusiasm and a sense of adventure.

ESTABLISHING THE VISION

The first step in developing a customer service culture in which customer satisfaction is valued above everything else is to establish a *customer-centered vision* for your company. This vision is what you want your company to become. It is customer-focused and customer-directed.

THE CARLSON COMPANIES

My home state of Minnesota is the birthplace of several prominent international enterprises that began with ambitious customer-centered visions. One such enterprise is the Carlson Companies, whose owner, Curt Carlson, started the business in 1938 with a $55 loan and his customer-directed vision.

To help other companies maintain customer loyalty, Carlson introduced the concept of trading stamps. In the 1960s and 1970s, Carlson branched into the hospitality industry by buying and expanding the Radisson Hotel chain, and later added other hospitality companies to his holdings, such as T.G.I. Friday's, Mr. Foster Travel Agencies, and Country Kitchen Restaurants.

Today, the Carlson Companies is one of the largest travel and hospitality companies in the world. It is also one of the most successful privately held corporations in America, with operations in more than 140 countries and 188,000 employees. In 1999, the combined sales of all the Carlson subsidiaries amounted to $31.4 billion.

Carlson's business philosophy was simple: "Whatever you do, do with integrity; wherever you go, go as a leader; whomever you serve, serve with caring; whenever you dream, dream with your all; and never, ever give up."

Curt Carlson, who died in 1999, attributed his success to his ability to envision how things can be without being distracted by how things are. And his visions, inspired and directed by customers and potential customers, always involved ways of serving people better.

FEDERAL EXPRESS

In the early 1970s, Fred Smith wrote a paper for his economics class at Yale University. The paper discussed Fred's vision of creating an air-express delivery system that would be capable of transporting urgent packages overnight anywhere in America. His professor considered the subject of the paper to be impractical and awarded him a "C" for the effort. The paper outlined what would ultimately become Federal Express.

Smith's business philosophy is simple, clear, and customer-oriented:

> We will produce outstanding financial returns by providing totally reliable, competitively superior global air-ground transportation of high-priority goods and documents that require rapid, time-sensitive delivery. … Control of each package will be maintained utilizing real-time electronic tracking and tracing systems. A complete record of each shipment and delivery will be presented with our request for payment. We will be helpful, courteous, to each other (internal customers) and to the public (external customers). We will strive to have a completely satisfied customer at the end of each transaction.

Today, Federal Express is one of the most successful companies in the world. It is also consistently ranked among the best places to work in America. And it all started with a vision of providing a service to customers throughout America.

The spectacular success of this outstanding company has everything to do with its customer-centered and customer-directed strategies. Achieving total customer satisfaction by finding new and better ways to serve customers continues to be the vision of Federal Express.

THE PURPOSE OF A CUSTOMER-CENTERED VISION

Your customer-centered vision is not just a clear picture of how you will serve your customer's needs in the future, but an image of what your organization will eventually become. Your customer-centered vision serves two important purposes:

- It's a source of inspiration.
- It's a guide for decision-making.

INSPIRATION

People today are in search of purpose. Your employees are, too. They want to know that their job is important and relevant, more than just a way to earn a paycheck. For most people, work is tied to their identity, self-image, and sense of worth.

Your company's customer-centered vision should inspire your employees to action. Employees should see themselves as important stakeholders in the development of your company. Inspiration occurs when employees are involved as owners of a customer-centered vision and are empowered to do whatever it takes to move from vision to reality.

Employees who are inspired by your company's customer-centered vision will be energized, motivated, and challenged to excellence by its power. The vision will also provide a single unifying purpose that will help develop a sense of teamwork.

DECISION-MAKING

Important decisions affecting the company's future are sometimes difficult to make. Having a clear customer-centered vision of the future helps to provide a context. Everyone benefits when important individual and corporate decisions are made with the company's customer-centered vision guiding the way.

A well-defined customer-centered vision also acts like an organizational constitution. It guides the organization and unifies its functions to conform to a single goal. It becomes the point of reference by which everything else in the organization is ultimately evaluated. During times of conflict, it is the highest authority and becomes the final judge.

SCANDINAVIAN AIRLINE SYSTEMS

In 1981, Jan Carlzon became president of Scandinavian Airline Systems and within one year turned a $17 million loss into a $54 million profit. He transformed the airline by creating a customer-centered vision that made customer satisfaction a top priority.

"The only thing that counts in the new Scandinavian Airline Systems," said Carlzon, "is a satisfied customer. We are going to be the best airline in the world, and that means putting the customer first in everything we do."

The vision was preached, taught, and lived by airline executives and managers. Before long, every airline employee had caught the vision and knew exactly where the company was headed.

TIP

I encourage you to read Carlzon's book, *Moments of Truth* (HarperCollins, 1989). This is an excellent book on leadership and has much to say about adapting to the new customer-driven economy.

The vision became a guide and a rule for all decision-making. Employees were encouraged, empowered, and excited by a vision that became their own. The result was one of the most successful turnaround stories in the annals of modern business.

Great customer-centered visions have tremendous power for change.

TIP

It's important to appreciate the difference between strategy and vision. Strategy is like a blueprint: It provides builders with a detailed description of each component of a project. Vision deals with a future in which important goals and objectives have been met, resulting in success for the company and opportunity for everyone involved. By its very nature, strategy can be uninspiring to some people. But great customer-centered visions are charged with excitement and result in inspiration and enthusiasm among workers.

Developing a Customer-Centered Vision Statement

Developing a customer-centered *vision statement* isn't as difficult as it might seem. The objective isn't to create an impressive document that will wind up gathering dust on your managers' shelves. Customer-centered vision statements need to inspire, excite, and mobilize your entire workforce.

PLAIN ENGLISH

Vision statements   Statements that briefly describe a company's commitment to customer service. They communicate, in a few well-chosen words, important company philosophy that undergirds practice.

Effective customer-centered vision statements are down-to-earth and easy to understand. Take a look at six of the most successful customer-centered vision statements ever produced:

- "Quality Is Job One!" (Ford Motor Company)
- "Sell good merchandise at a reasonable profit, treat your customers like human beings, and they'll always come back for more." (L.L. Bean Company)
- "Quality, Service, Cleanliness, Value." (McDonald's)
- "Putting People First." (British Airways)
- "Kyakka shoko" ("Best service"). (Nippon Telephone)
- "I have one, and only one, ambition for Chrysler; to be the best. What else is there?" (Lee Iacocca, Chrysler Motor Company)

TIP

Consider creating a special work group to draft a customer-centered vision statement for approval by management. In preparing the statement, encourage the work group to talk with employees, supervisors, managers, and especially customers.

To develop an effective customer-centered vision of your own, begin by talking with customers to get their ideas on what your organization should look like in the future. What will they need from you? How could you serve them better? What could be done to make doing business with you easier and more efficient?

Then sit down with your management team and ask the following questions:

- What kind of company do we want to build? (Describe in as detailed a manner as possible what you want the company to look like in the future—in 1 year, 5 years, 10 years, etc.)

- How will our customers view us when we've achieved our vision? (In what ways will we serve them better? How easy will it be for them to do business with us? In what ways will we outperform the competition in terms of customer service?)

- How do we want to be known? (When people hear our company name, how do we want them to think of us?)

- What will our customers need from us in the future? (How will we meet those needs?)

- What do we value most? (What do we really care about? How will our vision for the future affect each of these values? How do these values relate to the needs of our customers?)

- How will our customer-centered vision change the way we operate internally? (How will our vision affect our practices?)

- Does everyone in the company have a part to play in the future vision of the company? (What will we do to motivate employees to help achieve the vision? How will we keep the momentum going?)

Remember that you're not attempting to write a book, just a customer-centered vision statement that will encompass your company's customer-centered vision for the future. Keep your statement clear, concise, and meaningful to everyone in the company.

CAUTION

Examine your present mission statements and slogans to make sure that they are consistent with your customer-centered vision for the future. Are they aligned with your company's values and linked to the needs of your customers? If your present statements and slogans no longer fit, replace them with something fresh that communicates an exciting, meaningful vision for the future.

ARTICULATING THE VISION

Once you've developed your customer-centered vision, impart it to management and staff. Your objective is to articulate the vision in a way that results in a shared commitment by everyone.

Commitment to the vision requires two important and ongoing functions:

- Communication
- Training

COMMUNICATION

Now that your customer-centered vision is developed, the most important thing you can do as a leader is to talk about it and encourage your managers to do the same. Call a general staff meeting and tell your employees about the company's vision that many of them helped produce; talk about it in board meetings, staff meetings, and meetings with customers or clients; write about it in official company newsletters, brochures, or other periodicals. Don't let a day go by without communicating the vision.

As you begin to formulate a strategy, set challenging goals and objectives that will help achieve the vision. Communicate those goals and objectives in ways that demonstrate how every employee is an important contributor. Emphasize the vision, and make it real.

Celebrate milestones on your way to achieving the vision. Reward exceptional effort on the part of individuals and teams, and do it publicly. Make each celebration a time of renewal of individual commitments to the vision. Communicate over and over the idea that the success of the company, and the success of each employee, depends on achieving the vision.

And most important, communicate commitment to the vision by your personal actions and those of your managers and supervisors. Walk the walk; don't just talk the talk. Communicate by your actions that things really are going to be different from now on.

Do you really mean what you say? Seeing is believing.

TRAINING

To achieve your customer-centered vision, your managers and staff will need training—lots of it. In fact, every formal or semi-formal gathering of employees should include some form of training that relates directly to the customer-centered vision. Unit meetings, departmental meetings, general staff meetings, all present important opportunities for training.

Here are some of the best topics included in most successful ongoing customer-centered training programs:

- Product knowledge (including customer applications)
- Telephone skills and etiquette
- Helping the difficult customer
- Expressing empathy
- Achieving mutual agreement in problem-solving
- De-escalation techniques in dealing with angry customers
- Active problem-solving
- Assertiveness training
- Managing conflict with co-workers
- Promises and follow-up
- Selling with service
- What you can do when you can't say "Yes"
- Saying "No" without offending the customer
- Teamwork

Of course, there are many more topics that can be used in customer-focused training. Search them out and use them.

When your employees know what's expected (through training), why it's expected (to achieve the vision), and what their reward will be for achievement (company and individual success), they are much more likely to see themselves as key players. That's what it takes to achieve their commitment.

TIP

Consider selecting a team made up of employees and managers to formulate training activities over the period of a year or two. Make sure that employees have direct input into the planning process to avoid having the plan labeled "the boss's."

Devote whatever time it takes to develop, communicate, and reinforce your company's customer-centered vision. A company's success in the marketplace is in almost direct proportion to its ability to define itself internally and externally by a well-crafted, customer-centered vision statement.

THE 30-SECOND RECAP

- Every great company started with a great company vision.

- Your company's vision should be customer-centered and specific about how the company will outperform the competition in the area of customer service.

- Your company's customer-centered vision will inspire and guide you every step of the way.

- Once your company's customer-centered vision is developed, you need to preach it, teach it, and practice it publicly.

What's Your Business?

In this section you learn how to gain an advantage over the competition by recognizing that service is the real product of your business. You also learn 10 common ways in which companies tell their customers they're not important.

EXCEPTIONAL SERVICE IS THE KEY

Knapp's Restaurant is an institution in the city of Tacoma, Washington. It's my family's favorite restaurant, even though getting a table sometimes means waiting in line for 10 minutes or more. And Knapp's is always busy, no matter what time of day or night you arrive.

Over the years, Knapp's Restaurant has gained an outstanding reputation for excellent food, generous portions, and prices that are among the lowest in the area. But the real secret of their success is that years ago Knapp's recognized that they weren't in the food and beverage business—they were in the service business! Excellent food and low prices were just a few of the ways they could serve their customers, means to an end. Knapp's learned early on that their principal product was service, and this understanding has made all the difference. It's the very heart of their success and is the reason their customers walk away thinking "Wow!"

Whatever your business—banking, manufacturing, investments, travel—it's critical to your success to understand that, first and foremost, you're in the service business. And when you provide excellence in service, sales results inevitably follow. Exceptional service creates increases in sales, and sales result in growth for your business.

DEVELOPING EXCEPTIONAL SERVICE

Developing exceptional customer service in your business isn't difficult. It doesn't require a knowledge of advanced business principles, nor does it demand the use of complex and sophisticated formulas and planning mechanisms.

CAUTION

Resist the idea that customer service is a "job function" or "department" within the company. The development of exceptional customer service in your company requires a real commitment on the part of everyone to make service your company's principal product.

What it does require is the completion of three important tasks:

- Knowing "why"
- Managing customer impressions
- Knocking down the barriers

Coupling these three tasks with a commitment to reorient your thinking and that of your employees to the idea that service is your principal product will lead your organization to customer service excellence.

KNOWING "WHY"

Have you ever noticed that people never make real changes in their lives until they have a personal investment in making a change?

I used to be a smoker. When I began smoking, cigarettes were considered fashionable. Everybody smoked, or so it seemed. Few people were concerned about the health hazards of smoking. On the contrary, most people thought it was a safe and satisfying pastime. The fact that some cigarette companies advertised their particular brand as being preferred by most physicians supported that view.

Then came the research proving that cigarette smoking was causing life-threatening illness in epidemic proportions. Medical science proved that there was a link between cigarette smoking and cancer, emphysema, heart trouble, and a host of other maladies. But I, and thousands of others like me, continued to smoke, despite the evidence.

Why did I continue to smoke? For the same reason that some businesses continue to treat customer service as a "function" or a "department" or a "task." In spite of the clear evidence that customer-focused companies achieve exceptional results, some businesses refuse to apply that evidence to themselves. They understand the principle but ignore it.

I eventually stopped smoking when I was diagnosed with cancer. Suddenly, the research had very personal meaning for me. I knew exactly why it was important for me to quit smoking. And the reason was compelling; my life was in the balance.

People need compelling reasons to make significant changes—and those reasons need to have personal meaning for them. That's why most people think about dieting when spring and summer months approach. Why? Because most people want to look good in bathing suits and in other summer fashions. Looking good is a compelling reason to endure the difficulties that come with dieting.

Exceptional customer service means that you and your employees are going to have to work harder and do more to please your customers. Everyone must go beyond the call of duty to ensure that customers are pleased enough to say "Wow!"

What are the compelling reasons for your employees to perform in this manner? What are the personal benefits attached? Why should they do the things that will cause customers to remain loyal and tell others about your business?

Give your employees the "why" for exceptional customer service by rewarding them and recognizing them accordingly. Behavior that is rewarded is repeated. Think about featuring a customer service employee of the month in your company newsletter. Tell your people exactly what special customer service the employee provided to receive the honor. Provide that person with a dinner for two, or a special parking slot for the month, or some other tangible expression of your appreciation. And don't forget to include an employee's customer service skills in regular employee evaluations. Make it clear that there is a direct relationship between customer service excellence and raises or promotions with your company.

Managing Customer Impressions

Customer impressions of your company are important. The customer service goal of every company should be to favorably impress a customer every time he or she comes into contact with any aspect of the company, regardless of how seemingly insignificant or remote. And this goal should apply to both internal and external customers (see "Who Are Your Customers—and What Do They Want?" on page 1078 for a discussion of internal and external customers).

Managing customer impressions means identifying *moments of truth*— potential points of customer contact—and identifying ways to favorably impress the customer at each of those points.

Moments of truth can occur anytime and anywhere customers, or potential customers, have contact with a representative of your company. When a potential customer asks a financial advisor what's involved in an IRA rollover, that's a moment of truth for the company that stockbroker represents. When an irate customer arrives at your company's doorstep, there's a moment of truth that begins with the first individual he or she meets.

Each moment of truth involves a very short period of time (40 seconds or less) during which a customer forms an impression of the quality of service provided by your company. This impression governs the remainder of the customer contact. What's more, studies have shown that it takes as long as two years before people forget the impression formed by their first moment of truth with a company.

PLAIN ENGLISH

Moment of truth   A customer service term created by Jan Carlzon of Scandinavian Airlines. Carlzon defined a moment of truth as "an episode in which a customer comes in contact with any aspect of the company, however remote, and thereby has an opportunity to form an impression."

Considering each moment of truth in your business, what does it take to make your customers say "Wow!"? What would it take to ensure that this level of service would be consistently offered? What are you willing to do by way of providing reward and recognition for this level of customer service?

TIP

Why not ask your employees to help define what it takes to favorably impress customers at each moment of truth? Make your employees a real part of designing exceptional strategies for customer service.

KNOCKING DOWN THE BARRIERS

In your quest to develop exceptional customer service, you will inevitably encounter barriers along the way. Don't panic, and, whatever you do, don't let barriers discourage you. The only path that has no barriers is the path that leads nowhere.

You may encounter three kinds of barriers:

- People
- Policy
- Process

PEOPLE

It's unfortunate, but true, that some people in your organization will resist becoming more service-oriented in their thinking and work. These are the same people who will not favor the creation of a customer service culture, and who may even work to undermine the customer-centric efforts of the company.

When these people make themselves known, my advice is to encourage them to find employment elsewhere. Their attitude toward the company's customer service efforts will be the attitude they show your customers. This kind of employee is too costly to keep.

Make sure your employees understand that your new approach to customer service isn't just a flash in the pan, that it's more than just another new program designed to make them work harder and longer. It's vital that employees recognize the real commitment on the part of management to create a customer-centered and -driven organization. And make sure that your employees understand that the company's success, as well as their personal success with the company, depends upon how well customers are treated.

TIP

Involve your employees in helping to identify barriers to exceptional customer service within your organization. Once the barriers are identified, ask employees to suggest ways to overcome them.

POLICY

If yours is the kind of business governed by formal policies, review them. Oftentimes, formal policy statements interfere with providing exceptional customer service. Be particularly mindful of policies that disempower employees, inflexible policies that prevent efficient customer service, and policies requiring numerous approval points that create a restrictive bureaucracy frustrating to employees and customers alike.

When you encounter policies that restrict the ability of your employees to provide exceptional customer service, eliminate those policies. If a policy can't be eliminated, change it so that it's no longer in opposition to your customer service objectives.

Remember: Your most important policy is to provide the customer with exceptional service. Every other policy in your organization must conform itself accordingly.

PROCESS

How easy is it for customers to do business with you—before, during, and after the sale? That's an important question and one you'll need to answer if your goal is to provide exceptional customer service.

Examine your company's processes that directly involve customers. Are they customer-friendly? Do they involve miles of red tape? Are they unnecessarily complex? Do they help, or hinder, your efforts to provide exceptional customer service?

Don't do what a friend of mine, the chief executive of a major governmental entity, used to do. He offered members of various community groups the opportunity to bring their problems and concerns directly to him. That sounded great, but the truth of the matter was that it was nearly impossible to reach him by phone. So he instructed his staff to redirect callers to the appropriate people, depending upon the nature of the call.

My friend had attempted to improve customer service by offering an "open door" to any constituent with a problem. What he ended up creating was a customer service nightmare. People who had been promised direct access to the boss were shuffled off to underlings, and were offended by that kind of treatment.

The matter was finally resolved when my friend's staff provided him with a brochure listing each department head, together with a description of the services they provide and their phone numbers. He could still promise that problems would be resolved quickly, but instead of directing people to himself he sent them to the people who needed to get involved.

Re-engineer and retool every process that complicates life for your customers and hinders the resolution of their problems quickly and efficiently. Make your processes work for you by designing them with your customer in mind. Design the kind of processes that cause your customers to say "Wow!"

WAL-MART'S COMMITMENT TO EXCEPTIONAL CUSTOMER SERVICE

In 1962, when Sam Walton opened his first store in Rogers, Arkansas, he never dreamed that his company would become one of the largest corporations in America. But that's exactly what happened.

As I write this book, Wal-Mart's total annual sales are about to overtake the sales of General Motors, the largest company in America. Wal-Mart's domestic sales for the fiscal year ending in January 2000 amounted to $142 billion (that's more than 6 percent of the total annual retail spending in America if automobiles and boats are subtracted).

Walton's business philosophy was simple: If you structure a retail sales organization around the customer by providing top-quality merchandise at low everyday prices, with unquestionable customer service, the company is bound to succeed. And it is this same wise customer-centered business philosophy that continues to guide and propel Wal-Mart into the twenty-first century.

Wal-Mart's commitment to customer service is more than just lip service or ad copy. This company really understands that service is their chief product. And Wal-Mart goes out of its way to ensure that its service to customers is exceptional beyond measure.

Consider the depth of Wal-Mart's customer service commitment. In order to provide customers with quality merchandise and the best possible price, Wal-Mart gets deeply involved with its more than 65,000 suppliers, helping them to streamline their operations and cut costs. Wal-Mart examines every penny that their suppliers spend. Lee Scott, Wal-Mart's chief executive officer, says he is committed to "driving unnecessary costs out of businesses."

The result: Wal-Mart's suppliers benefit from the management expertise of America's premier retailer; Wal-Mart benefits because it's able to offer products at the best possible prices; and customers (most of whom never even realize the effort Wal-Mart has made in their behalf) benefit from the savings. Everybody wins.

With that kind of customer-centered commitment, it's no wonder that Wal-Mart is America's top retailer. Service really is their principal product.

Ten Ways to Tell Your Customer "We Don't Care!"

Wal-Mart's situation also happens in reverse: Many companies started with the idea of becoming one of the largest corporations in America but ended up falling flat on their corporate posteriors. They were long on dreams but short on real customer-centered focus and commitment. What's worse, most of them, in one way or another, told their customers "We don't care!"

Here are 10 common ways that companies tell their customers "We don't care":

1. **They take their customers for granted.** Even simple courtesies like saying "Good morning," "Let me know if I can be of help," or even "Thank you! We appreciate your business" are absent. Customers interpret the lack of these niceties to mean that the company has come to expect their business or doesn't need it. The message is clear: "We don't care!" Stop showing your customers that you appreciate and care about them, and they'll go away in droves.

2. **They make it difficult for customers to do business with them.**
   You don't have to look far to find an abundance of companies that
   have acquired real skill in this regard. Recently, I wanted to secure a
   second business line for my consulting practice. I phoned our service
   provider and was greeted by an automated telephone routing system
   that had me on the line for over 20 minutes. When I finally reached
   the end of their annoying list of menu options ("Press 1 if you're still
   there"), I received a recorded announcement telling me that the
   office had closed 10 minutes earlier and would I please call back
   tomorrow. Their message to me was clear: "We don't care!" I never
   ordered that second line.

3. **They don't listen to their customers.** Customers are told what they
   should want and why they should want it. Customers are never asked
   for feedback, and only rarely are they consulted about what they
   really want. Customers will tell you how to please them if you just
   let them do so. But you'll never hear what a customer wants unless
   you're willing to listen. When you fail to listen to your customer,
   your message is clear: "We don't care!"

4. **They run ads that say customer service is their strength, but the
   reality is something else.** This becomes evident to a customer
   almost immediately. The message is as insulting as it is ludicrous:
   "We don't care about what you think—we can buy a reputation for
   customer service excellence." But that strategy always fails. An
   abundance of companies in the boneyard of broken dreams have
   learned that lesson the hard way.

5. **They depend heavily on voice mail.** Humans don't answer the
   phone—at least, not most of the time. Customers leave messages and
   never receive timely calls back. My own experience has demonstrated repeatedly that, in terms of lost customers, a voicemail system is one of the most expensive pieces of equipment a company can
   own. The vast majority of customers hate it! Customers are given the
   impression that they're not important enough to be put in contact
   with a "real person." The message is: "We don't care!"

CAUTION

If you use a voicemail system, be sure to monitor how it's being
used by employees. Phones that aren't answered by the third ring,
systems in which talking with a live person isn't an option, complaints from customers indicating that phone messages aren't being
answered—all are red flags that should prompt further investigation.

6. **They treat customers with disrespect.** Disrespectful staff can cost your business everything. Whenever a customer leaves an encounter with your business without his or her dignity intact, the likelihood of that person remaining your customer is slim. Even when customers are obviously wrong, they deserve to be treated with respect. Arguing with a customer is a fatal error. You can win the argument, but you will lose the customer. Not much of a win, in my book. Showing disrespect for a customer is saying "We don't care!"

7. **They judge customers based on their perceived importance.** Nothing tells a customer that you don't really care faster than the second-best treatment. Instead of making every customer feel special and important, some companies cater to a particular market—for example, the extremely wealthy—and make everyone else feel inferior. Their message is clear: "We don't care!"

8. **They aren't proactive about problem-solving.** Customers want you to care about them. When you discover a problem that you know will affect them, they expect you to take the initiative and notify them of it. When that doesn't happen, and customers find out you knew about the problem, the message is clear: "We don't care!" As I write this book, Firestone tires used on Ford Explorers are in the news. Not only does the tire have a long history of failing, especially in warm climates, evidence has now surfaced that the manufacturer knew about the flaw for years and chose to do nothing. It will be a long while before the public forgets the message conveyed by Firestone's actions.

9. **They don't train their staff.** Staff who don't understand the product and haven't been trained to serve customers can do serious damage. When you don't train staff, you set them up for failure—and set your customer up for substantial irritation. Untrained staff send a clear message: "We don't care!"

10. **They allow staff to serve the customers while ignoring them.** My wife and I have changed grocery stores simply because the checkout clerk insisted on carrying on a conversation with a fellow employee while scanning our order. That's inappropriate and rude. Customers deserve the full attention of the person serving them. When that doesn't happen, the message is unmistakable: "We don't care!"

Be conscious of the underlying message you're giving your customers. Make sure that it represents the way you really feel about them.

THE 30-SECOND RECAP

■ Regardless of what business you're in, service is your principal product.

■ Developing exceptional customer service requires a paradigm shift in which you redefine your business as a service business.

■ Knowing why changes should be made, managing customer impressions, and knocking down barriers are tasks that lead to exceptional customer service.

■ Be careful of the underlying message your company is sending to customers. Make sure the message is "We really care about you. You're the most important person in our company!"

Meeting (and Exceeding) Customer Expectations

In this section you learn the importance of communicating with your customers, and the six steps for turning complaints into opportunities that can strengthen your relationship with customers.

LEARNING FROM CUSTOMERS

What do your customers think about your product or service? You'll never know until you ask them. Learning how customers and potential customers feel about your product is where your quest for exceptional customer service begins.

HARLEY-DAVIDSON

Some years ago, the Harley-Davidson Company was experiencing a severe drop in sales. In spite of the quality of their motorcycles, people weren't buying them. Management was baffled.

Vaughn Beals, Harley-Davidson CEO, decided to find out why the company's motorcycles were no longer selling. Beals asked his senior management team to dress like bikers and join him on the road. Their journey took them to biker rallies and other events where they talked with customers and potential customers about what people really want in a motorcycle.

When the executives returned home, they had an abundance of fresh new ideas that were based on the expectations of bikers from coast to coast. Willie G. Davidson, vice president of styling, selected the best of those ideas and incorporated them into a plan for redesign. Some of the changes that would be made included more chrome, a shorter chassis, and sculpted gas tanks.

By learning exactly what bikers wanted, and by adapting the product to meet their expectations, executives turned around sales of Harley-Davidson motorcycles. Before long, the company had secured 60 percent of the domestic motorcycle market. It's no accident that today the name Harley-Davidson is synonymous with "exceptional quality" and "fine workmanship."

DISCOVERING WHAT CUSTOMERS EXPECT

If you don't know what your customers expect of your organization and its products, you'll never be able to give it to them. Meeting customer expectations—and exceeding them when possible—is what enables your organization not only to survive but to prosper.

Your customers are your best source of ideas and suggestions for improving product and service quality. They will tell you how you're doing as a company; about what works and what doesn't; about how their needs are changing and what your company can do to meet those changing needs; about who in your company is "doing it right" and who needs additional training. Think of your customers as a source of guidance that will help you direct the future of your company.

There are several ways to determine what your customers expect: surveys, focus groups, advisory boards, conversations, and complaints. You may choose to use any of these methods or, better still, several methods simultaneously. How you tune in to your customers isn't what's important. Listening to what they have to tell you is.

SURVEYS

Surveys can be a useful source of customer service information. If they are administered correctly, they can help you monitor the pulse of your company. But unless you have staff with advanced degrees in statistical analysis, consider engaging the services of a professional marketing company.

PLAIN ENGLISH

Customer satisfaction   A survey construct that compares what actually takes place in a given situation with what a customer thought would happen. Typical customer responses include comments like, "What I received was not what I expected to receive";

continues

continued

"I can always count on your company to do what's right"; "Your product didn't do for me what your advertisements said it would." The purpose is to determine whether your product or service met your customer's expectations.

Here are some important questions you'll need to answer before you can develop a survey that will yield worthwhile data:

- **What do I want to measure?** For example, if you want to gauge *customer satisfaction,* construct a survey that compares your customer's opinion of how well you performed with the customer's predictive expectations. If you want to measure *perceived quality,* construct a survey that compares your customer's perception of what happened with his or her ideal expectations (what should have happened).

- **Whom do I survey?** Some companies limit survey activity to external customers only. However, many more have learned the value of including internal staff in customer service surveys. The reason is simple: Employees who feel they are treated well by their employers will usually treat customers in the same manner.

- **What kind of survey do I want to conduct?** There are many types of surveys that your company may want to consider: *customer exit* surveys that focus on asking customers questions as they leave your premises; *targeted* surveys that measure specific types of accounts; *random* customer surveys in which randomly selected customers are asked to respond; *internal attitude* surveys that provide a measurement of internal satisfaction among employees; and *lost-account* surveys directed to customers who no longer do business with your firm.

- **Which method should I use?** There are several possibilities: *face-to-face interviews* (excellent, but costly); *telephone interviews* (not quite as costly, but time-consuming); *questionnaires* by mail (the least costly, but response rates can be problematic). Alternatively, some companies have found that the best results are achieved when a number of survey methods are used simultaneously.

- **Who should administer the survey?** This is the most important question of all, and one you should consider carefully. Unless you have staff who are trained in the science of constructing and conducting surveys, you should consider using a consultant or marketing firm. It's true that doing so increases the cost of surveying, but the quality and reliability of the information you obtain will usually be worth the cost. Remember that information obtained from a professionally conducted survey is critical to the future of your business. View this expense as an investment in your company's future.

PLAIN ENGLISH

Perceived quality   A survey construct that attempts to compare the customer's perception of what happened with what the customer feels should have happened ideally. Customers express perceived quality with statements like, "Ideally, you should have ..."; "When I booked my meeting at your five-star hotel, I expected ..."; "I expected more from a company considered the best in the business." The purpose of the construct is to determine whether your product or service meets your customer's ideal expectations.

FOCUS GROUPS

Focus groups usually consist of a small number of customers (8 to 10) who participate in a roundtable discussion about specific service-related issues. The company is represented by one or two managers who act as moderators for the session. Discussions normally continue for a predetermined length of time, rarely extending beyond two hours.

It's been my experience that focus groups work best when they are held off-site. Participants always seem more at ease in hotel meeting rooms or other neutral locations. Be sure to have plenty of refreshments on hand, and consider including a breakfast or lunch with your meeting. Combining a meal with your focus group meeting is a great way to thank participants. Most hotels offer meeting space at no cost to groups that include a meal function.

If you hire a consulting or marketing firm to gather information from customers, be sure to include a representative of that firm in every focus group meeting. Ask the consultant to suggest questions that will help you assess the level of customer satisfaction while exploring ideas for improvement and growth.

TIP

Employee focus groups are also beneficial. Product- or service-related questions and problems are identified and discussed, together with other issues affecting the workplace. Employee focus groups are especially effective when they are part of an ongoing staff survey project that seeks to keep a finger on the company's pulse, both internal and external.

ADVISORY BOARDS

Advisory boards offer the company a unique and powerful way to communicate with customers. These boards are made up of selected customers who regularly meet with company representatives to identify and resolve service-related problems. Advisory boards often become sounding boards for the company and unofficial (but powerful) advocates for all customers doing business with a company.

CONVERSATIONS

Knowing what's important to customers in general is vital to the success of your business. But knowing the details about a specific customer's needs, wants, and desires gives you the ability to provide exceptional service. One-on-one conversations are the best way to discover those important details.

Ichiorou Suzuki, the chief engineer in charge of designing the Lexus for Toyota, understood the value of one-on-one customer conversations. Suzuki insisted that, as an integral part of the design process, several weeks needed to be spent talking with the company's customers in the United States.

Suzuki wasn't attempting to determine the level of customer satisfaction with Toyota. Instead, he wanted to learn some personal information about his U.S. customers: what they liked and disliked, what their hobbies were, what they valued, and so on. Based on the information he obtained through those conversations, Suzuki concluded that the American consumer was more hard-working and conservative than the company had believed. As a result, he designed the interior of the Lexus to provide a soft and comfortable environment.

Lexus understands the value of one-on-one contact. In fact, maintaining one-on-one communication with its customers is so important that Lexus requires each of its U.S. employees to talk with at least one Lexus owner each week. The information obtained from customers as a result of these calls helps Lexus to continually improve its product.

The Ritz-Carlton Hotel chain is another company that prides itself on one-on-one customer contact. Every employee of the hotel is asked to document the unique requirements and special requests of each guest. This information is entered into the hotel chain's computer system and is accessible by every Ritz-Carlton hotel throughout the world.

As a result of the Ritz-Carlton's one-on-one dialogue with guests, service can be tailored and personalized to meet the specific needs of each customer. As the guest's needs change, those changes are input into the system for future reference by other hotels in the chain.

It's no accident that the Ritz-Carlton is a winner of the prestigious Baldrige Award for world-class service. The organization prides itself on building and maintaining relationships with its customers through ongoing one-on-one dialogue. Five-star customer service is the result.

COMPLAINTS

Complaints are misunderstood by many businesses today. Instead of considering a complaint as an opportunity to engage in meaningful dialogue with a customer, many companies view it as a menace to be avoided at all costs. That kind of thinking is not just unfortunate; it's more costly than the average company realizes.

A few years ago, the Travelers Insurance Company conducted an in-depth study of customer complaints. The study concluded that only 9 percent of those who did not complain about a defective product or service costing $100 or more would ever do business with the company again. But 82 percent of those who complained, and whose complaints were dealt with quickly and satisfactorily, would continue to patronize the business.

What does this mean? It means that complaints are unmistakably an opportunity that needs to be understood and exploited.

Complaints not only offer an opportunity to engage in meaningful dialogue with a customer, but also provide the company with valuable information about its products and services. Complaints signal the need to refine a product or develop something new. They also furnish insight about service-related difficulties that need to be corrected.

Well-managed companies today do more than welcome complaints; they invest in them. They understand that for every customer who complains there are approximately 26 who don't, most of whom will never do business with the company again. As a result, these companies actively solicit customer complaints and make it easy for customers to be heard.

Some companies install dedicated toll-free telephone lines to help customers complain. Others solicit complaints by phoning customers to ask if they're having problems with the company's products or services. These companies have learned that investing in customer complaints is good business.

General Electric has been a pioneer in soliciting customer complaints. Every General Electric appliance now comes with a service manual that lists a toll-free number to call if customers have questions or need help with any kind of problem. Not only has this effort resulted in significant goodwill, but the company has benefited from warranty savings as well. What's more, callers frequently purchase additional products as a result of information provided during their conversation with the company.

General Electric estimates that each toll-free call costs between $2.50 and $4.50. But savings in service calls and profits from new sales generated as a result of the program offset the costs involved and provide an additional center of profit.

When complaints are handled expeditiously and with skill, most customers will be satisfied and remain loyal. That's important because, according to a study done by the U.S. Office of Consumer Affairs, it costs seven times more to acquire a new customer than it does to keep an existing one. What's more, according to a multi-industry study conducted by Harvard Business School, increasing a company's customer retention rate by as little as 5 percent can boost company profits by as much as 85 to 100 percent!

YOUR CUSTOMERS' EXPECTATIONS FOR RECOVERY

When things go wrong, your customers have expectations about what you need to do to recover. How you recover when a mistake has been made is vital to your company's future.

Service recovery is so important that every frontline employee should be thoroughly trained in it. Furthermore, given the importance of recovery to your company, recovery procedures should be reviewed and reinforced often.

When mistakes are made or when customer feedback indicates that a problem has been experienced with your product or service, the manner in which you respond can turn a negative situation into a positive one. Turning disappointment into customer satisfaction is what service recovery is all about.

SIX STEPS TO EFFECTIVE RECOVERY

An effective and customer-satisfying service recovery involves six steps:

1. **Listen empathetically and actively.** The key word is "listen." Step out of your role as a company representative and view the problem from the customer's standpoint. Be nonjudgmental—don't talk about what the customer should have done to avoid the problem. Practice *active listening* skills, and ask *open questions* that encourage the customer to talk. Be understanding and compassionate; demonstrate that you care about making things right. Allowing customers to vent their frustrations is a vital part of recovery.

PLAIN ENGLISH

Open questions   Questions that can't be answered with a simple "yes" or "no." They often begin with phrases such as "Tell me about ..." or "Describe what happened when ...." The purpose of open questions is to obtain the information necessary to solve a customer problem by encouraging the customer to talk freely.

2. **Apologize to the customer.** Someone once said, "Eating crow isn't pleasant, no matter how much mustard and ketchup you put on it. But the sooner you eat it, the less unpleasant it is to the taste." Tell the customer you're sorry for whatever mistake has been made. By saying "I'm sorry," you acknowledge responsibility and support the customer, two critical steps in recovery.

3. **Fix the problem.** After you've listened to your customer's explanation of the problem, allowed him or her to vent frustrations, and apologized, it's time to fix what went wrong. Let your customer tell you what it will take to make things right. Tell your customer, "We value your business and want to keep you as a customer. What can we do to solve the problem and make things right?" Then quickly resolve the problem in a way that satisfies your customer. Remember that the more quickly you resolve the matter, the more likely you'll keep your customer.

4. **Offer a value-added atonement.** In addition to fixing the problem, give your customer something. Even if your value-added gift is more symbolic than valuable, it's important. The customer will remember your extra consideration, no matter what it is, long after the problem has been forgotten. Exceeding a customer's expectations communicates a message that you value the customer and want to do what's right.

5. **Keep your promises.** When promises are made to customers, they must be kept. Making promises that can't be kept not only adds fuel to the fire, but also wipes out your other efforts to resolve the issue and causes your customer to defect. Make absolutely sure that your employees understand what they can, and cannot, deliver.

6. **Follow up.** Nothing demonstrates concern and commitment more than a follow-up contact after the problem has been resolved. A simple phone call to the customer, checking to see that a problem has been resolved to his or her satisfaction, is impressive. Unfortunately, follow-up contacts are often viewed as optional—a nice thing to do if time permits. Big mistake. A short follow-up call is an important part of the recovery process and should never be neglected.

Remember that in the eyes of the customer, you and your business are only as good as your last interaction. Your company may have provided exceptional service in the past; however, if the most recent interaction was negative, your customer will think of your business in negative terms.

Mistakes do happen. But when they do, you have the ability to manage your company's recovery. Exceed your customer's expectations by following the steps in this section, and show that you really care. That's how to turn a negative situation into a positive encounter.

THE 30-SECOND RECAP

- Discovering what your customers expect is the first step in developing products and services that they want.
- Maintaining a dialogue with your customers is the best way to keep abreast of potential service problems and to learn about changing needs in the marketplace.
- No matter how diligent your efforts, mistakes will occasionally happen. But when they do, it's imperative that the company recover quickly and professionally.
- There are six steps to recovery that will ensure exceptional customer service.

Keeping Your Customers in the Driver's Seat: Part 1

In this section you learn how to design a down-to-earth service delivery process that is totally customer-centric. You also learn about 10 tools for building intimate, mutually beneficial, long-term customer relationships.

Not long ago, the national news carried a story about a little-known crate-and-barrel manufacturer from Connecticut that was closing its doors after having been in business for over 100 years. In its heyday, this manufacturer was considered a major employer in the state in which it operated. Now, the payroll had shrunk to only eight people, each of whom was an old world–style craftsperson. Most had started with the company as apprentices and were now nearly ready to retire.

At one time, the company was busy meeting the needs of its customers. Customers had to place their orders with the company well in advance to ensure an adequate supply of packaging materials, and for years the demand exceeded supply and the business thrived.

But as the years went by, fewer and fewer companies used wooden crates and barrels for packaging. Reinforced cardboard had gradually absorbed the market once controlled by the manufacturers of wooden crates and barrels.

The company responded to its dwindling market by downsizing through attrition—not replacing workers who retired or who left for other reasons. But finally, in late 1999, it became clear that the day of the wooden crate and barrel had passed into history. It was time to close shop.

The needs of customers who once packaged their products in wooden crates and barrels had changed, but the crate-and-barrel maker hadn't changed along with them. In the final year of the twentieth century, this company was still committed to nineteenth-century business practices. The failure of the enterprise was inevitable; even a casual observer could have predicted it many years before.

Responding to the changing needs of customers is essential to the survival of any enterprise. *Putting customers in the driver's seat*—letting their changing needs dictate the future of your company—is just good business!

TEN TOOLS FOR CONTINUED EXCELLENCE

You've done your homework. You know exactly what your customers expect from your company. You understand what it takes to make them happy and what will encourage them to remain loyal. And you've made a commitment to build a customer-directed business by putting your customers in the driver's seat—because you've learned that without your customers, there would be no need for your business.

Now comes the tough part: keeping your customers in the driver's seat by meeting their changing needs in a marketplace that is ever more competitive.

To accomplish this goal, you'll need to do a lot of things right. For example, you'll need to remain committed to providing exceptional customer service over the long haul; you'll need to form intimate partnerships and alliances with your customers that will help you develop innovative products to meet their changing needs; you'll have to ensure exceptional quality in each transaction; and you'll need to streamline your service delivery process by continually monitoring your performance and making adjustments when necessary.

Keeping your customer in the driver's seat means making a genuine commitment to exceptional customer service. It means real devotion to building a customer-focused culture and customer-friendly systems. And it means continually improving every aspect of your business so that meeting and exceeding your customer's expectations will always be job number one.

That kind of customer involvement in the future of your business requires hard work. It may also involve a paradigm shift in the way you and your employees view the customer.

Nevertheless, the rewards are well worth the efforts. Keeping your customers in the driver's seat means that you'll experience sustainable growth, perform at your very best, build unwavering customer loyalty, and never have to worry about becoming obsolete.

Following are the ten most important keys to keeping your customers in the driver's seat and building long-term relationships with them.

UNDERSTAND THE ROLE OF CUSTOMER PERCEPTION—AND MANAGE IT

From the preceding sections, you know that your customers have specific service expectations of you and your firm. Generally, those expectations are based on several things: previous experience with your company, a general understanding of the competition, and what customers have heard about your firm from others.

Every encounter you have with a customer is an experience. If that experience meets or exceeds their expectations, the experience is positive and the customer is happy. But if the experience does not meet expectations, the customer will view the experience as negative.

That makes sense. But now comes the ingredient that makes life a bit more complicated: Perception enters the equation.

Every experience is filtered by a customer's perception of the situation. A customer's sense of reality is based on perception rather than fact. And, regardless of the facts, you sink or swim based on your customer's perception. For example, when a customer returns a defective item, a cheerful replacement may not be perceived as excellent customer service without an accompanying apology. It's always good to inquire with a customer to determine exactly what it will take to satisfy him or her.

Perception defines your customer's experience with your company. Managing the service delivery experience, therefore, requires an understanding of the role of perception and a commitment to helping each customer achieve a positive experience.

EMPATHIZE WITH YOUR CUSTOMERS

Empathy is an important tool. It helps you manage service delivery by enabling you to see situations from your customers' points of view. The key to success in customer service is simple: Know what your customers expect; then provide it in a way that not only meets but exceeds those expectations.

CAUTION

Know what your customers expect before attempting to provide service. Customers will define their expectations if they are asked. Defining expectations is a vital part of customer service. Don't neglect it.

But to see what your customers see—to be empathetic—requires some real effort. It's not enough simply to act empathetic; you need to really understand and feel what your customer understands and feels. That requires work. Surveys, one-on-one interviews, focus groups, and so on can provide you with the kind of information you need to empathize with your customers (see "Meeting [and Exceeding] Customer Expectations" on page 1128).

Customers know when you're truly empathizing with them and when it's just an act. Make every effort to see things from their standpoint. You'll become a more effective advocate for them, and you'll find yourself creatively seeking solutions to their problems.

UNDERSTAND THE RULES

Knowing the rules of your organization (and the flexibility you have in altering them) is another important tool. Customers are impressed when companies bend or even break rules to make them happy.

Every organization has rules, policies, and procedures. But it's been my experience that some of those rules are more flexible than others.

Type "A" rules in organizations are the ones that must be followed to the letter, without exception. Included in this group are state and federal laws, matters of public safety, restrictions imposed by government regulators, and other rules that management has determined to be absolutely necessary for the well-being of the business and its employees. Don't even try to circumvent, bend, or in any way violate rules in this category.

Type "B" rules, on the other hand, are much more flexible. Examples of type "B" rules may include such policies as "We charge $25 on all returned checks," "Business hours are 8:00 A.M. to 5:00 P.M.," or "Refunds or exchanges cannot be processed without proof of purchase."

While type "A" rules must be obeyed, your frontline employees should be given discretionary authority to circumvent type "B" rules whenever doing so would help resolve a customer service matter quickly and efficiently.

TIP

If a type "A" rule is consistently preventing you from satisfying customers, change it if possible. Otherwise, establish some kind of compensating offering. For example, Seattle is one of the most expensive places on earth to park a car. Parking fees are not optional; failure to feed the city's parking meters results in severe fines. For years, downtown businesses have unsuccessfully attempted to change the city's parking ordinances. Finally, the problem was resolved by providing shoppers with free parking in a less congested area of the city, and free bus service to and from downtown.

ESTABLISH COMMON OBJECTIVES

Too often, the customer perceives that it's him or her against the company. It's important to eliminate that kind of barrier as quickly as possible.

One way to remove the barrier is to actively look for areas of agreement between you and your customer. Take time to explore the situation and discover areas of agreement. Once you've found them, look for solutions that you and your customer can agree upon.

When you and your customer work toward the same objective, two important events occur: First, the "them versus us" barrier is eliminated and the customer views you as an ally instead of an enemy; second, you've defined what the customer perceives to be necessary to make his or her experience a positive one. Take the time to seek common ground.

GIVE YOUR CUSTOMERS CHOICES ALONG THE WAY

The ability to offer choices to customers is a powerful tool. Use it frequently. Give your customers options in your journey to reach common objectives.

Most customers resent the loss of control that they feel when they encounter a problem with a company's product or service. Offering choices to your customers is empowering because it puts them in control of the situation.

But a few caveats are in order:

■ Don't offer choices that you can't actually provide. Know in advance what you're authorized to offer and don't transgress those boundaries. For example, don't tell a customer that if he or she doesn't like the vehicle they buy they can return it within 30 days for a full refund unless you are absolutely sure you can make good on your offer. If you've been authorized to make that kind of commitment, great; if not, don't offer it just to make a sale.

■ Make sure that your customer fully understands the implications of each of the choices you offer. Fully disclose the downside to each so that the customer can make an informed decision.

■ Don't twist the customer's arm attempting to "sell" the advantages of a particular option. High-pressure sales tactics don't work very well today, and probably never did.

■ Be fair. If you offer one customer something special, other customers will likely remind you of the fact. Will you extend the same offer to others?

■ Finally, remember that there are some people who simply don't want to make decisions. This kind of person usually knows exactly what he or she wants and will tell you ("Here's what I want, do you have it?"). Offering choices to this kind of customer will usually frustrate both you and the customer. My best advice: When you encounter that kind of attitude, don't use the tool.

ALWAYS DELIVER WHAT'S EXPECTED—AND A LITTLE MORE

This technique works miracles with customers, and it's yours, compliments of my mom. Years ago she taught me to "always do just a bit more than what's expected and you'll always be in demand." She was right. The technique worked well when I was a teenager mowing lawns for a few dollars, and it has worked well in my adult business life.

Customers today are tired of getting ripped off by businesses that promise something of value but deliver less. In fact, most customers today sincerely appreciate just getting what they were promised.

But when they receive more value than they expected, they are completely in awe. Many times they express their delight with words like "Wow!" And it's the "Wow!" that ought to be your target.

When you "Wow!" a customer—and keep on "wowing" him or her—chances are good that you'll keep that customer for life. Giving a customer a bit more than what he or she expects will keep the customer in the driver's seat—and keep the profits rolling in.

MAKE CUSTOMER SATISFACTION PART OF YOUR EMPLOYEE PERFORMANCE EVALUATION

To emphasize that your customers are in the driver's seat, include a customer satisfaction element in your employee performance evaluations. Base your evaluation of this dimension on feedback received from customers as well as the employee's compliance with established service standards.

It's a fact: You get the kind of performance you expect only when you're diligent about inspecting the kind of performance actually delivered. Let your staff know that the company is watching. Customer satisfaction is absolutely necessary to the future of the company and its employees.

Solicit comments from customers about the manner in which they were treated by employees. Let customers know that your employees are being evaluated on their customer service skills.

MAKE YOUR CUSTOMERS YOUR PARTNERS

Partnering with your customers is one of the most powerful ways of keeping them in the driver's seat. Partnering involves more than simply satisfying your customers' needs. It involves becoming so involved with them that you take responsibility for their results, and your customers assume responsibility for developing the kinds of products and services necessary to do the job.

Black and Decker, Microsoft Corporation, Baxter International, CIGNA Corporation, Levi-Strauss Associates, and Wal-Mart are just a few of the major companies who have led the way in customer partnering. All of these companies, and many others like them, have learned that by helping to create new value for their customers, they also create value for themselves.

Taking a stake in your customers' ultimate successes doesn't mean entering into an unhealthy dependent relationship. On the contrary, partnering gives both parties a fresh perspective on old concerns and problems. Partnering with your customers creates a dynamic *synergy,* which often results in new potential and greater opportunity for both parties.

PLAIN ENGLISH

Synergy   The powerful force that occurs when two or more entities work together jointly. The total effect is greater than the sum of their individual effects when acting independently.

Companies who lead in world markets today are those who have made their customers' problems their own. They constantly think about their customers. They get involved with their customers to the extent that they actually assume responsibility for initiating change and development.

Partnering gives you a competitive leg up. By partnering with your customers, not only do you keep them in the driver's seat, but you help them drive.

PLAIN ENGLISH

Partnering   To partner with a customer means becoming so involved in the customer's business that you make your customer's success a matter of personal concern. Boeing, for example, not only works very closely with customers worldwide to design airplanes that accommodate their needs, it often goes the extra mile to help its customers run more efficient and productive airlines. Boeing will often lend its management expertise to customers who are experiencing growing pains. The result: Customers succeed and, as a result of their success, they buy more airplanes from Boeing.

RECOVER WITH STYLE

Whenever I think of what it means to recover with style, I recall an incident that occurred when I was eight years old. I had purchased a box of Cracker Jack, only to discover that the box did not contain the little prize.

In my indignation, I wrote the Cracker Jack Company a stinging letter complaining that my expectation as a customer had not been met (I used different words then, of course). I told them that I had worked hard for the dime I had spent on their product and that I had come to expect more from them than just a box filled with Cracker Jack—I wanted my prize!

Two weeks later, a small box arrived in the mail addressed to me. It was from the Cracker Jack Company and it was filled with little prizes. A letter accompanied the box apologizing for the mistake, telling me how much the company appreciated my business (I was only eight, for Pete's sake!) and expressing their hope that I would continue to buy their product. Talk about recovering in style!

Service recovery is an important part of any business operation. When you blow it—and you will blow it occasionally—you need to recover quickly and with style. How you respond to mistakes makes the difference between keeping customers in the driver's seat and losing them altogether.

Effective service recovery involves five steps, each of which must be carried out with sincerity:

1. Apologize to the customer. Practice the skill that your mother taught you years ago: Say, "I'm sorry, Mr. _____."

2. Accept responsibility for the mistake: "That was our mistake, Mr. _____. It should never have happened."

3. Repair the damage by making the customer whole. If an item arrived damaged, give the customer a new, undamaged item.

4. Give something of added value to the customer to make up for his or her inconvenience. "As a way of demonstrating our regret, we're sending you, at no charge, a _____. We really appreciate having you as a customer."

5. Follow up with the customer to make sure that he or she is satisfied.

That's it. That's all it takes to recover in style and to keep your customer in the driver's seat. Make service recovery an occasion to demonstrate how much you value your customers. It works wonders.

MAKE IT YOUR PASSION TO BE THE VERY BEST (AND LET YOUR CUSTOMERS TELL YOU HOW)

The quest for excellence will be a hallmark of the twenty-first century. Excellence requires a passion to be the very best. But it's when passion and unique ideas come together that real excellence results.

Many companies today, such as Wal-Mart, Boeing, and Microsoft, have a passion for excellence. They want to be the best of the best. These companies continually solicit employees' ideas and suggestions for improving the organization or its products and services.

But companies in which customers are in the driver's seat don't stop there. Not only do they generate ideas for improvement internally, but they generate ideas and suggestions from their customers as well.

Customers are gratified and empowered when they're asked to provide input. So ask them! In fact, consider formalizing a process to reward customers whose ideas have been implemented by the company.

There's no reason for customers to be in the driver's seat unless they can assist in steering the company on its course to excellence.

In Part 1 of this section, you've been given the tools to make your business more customer-centric; in Part 2 of the section, you'll learn how to stay on course.

THE 30-SECOND RECAP

- The needs of your customers change over time. Successful companies respond to those changing needs by providing quality products and services that are competitively priced.

- An effective service delivery process requires an understanding of the role of customer perception and a commitment to helping each customer achieve a positive experience.

- Perception defines your customers' experience with your company, and there are specific ways to ensure that the customers' perception is positive.

- Remember the value of empathizing with your customers, partnering with your customers, and recovering with style.

Keeping Your Customers in the Driver's Seat: Part 2

In this section you learn about customer feedback and measurement strategies for evaluating your company's services, and about the value of benchmarking.

WORLD-CLASS DELIVERY

Keeping your customers in the driver's seat requires management strategies that will ensure the proper functioning of your service delivery systems. Management models for world-class service delivery include:

- Methods of gathering specific information about the quality of service delivery, including both customer feedback and objective measurement

- Measurement results that are compared against established benchmarks

- Results that are scoreboarded (made visible to every employee of your organization) so that every internal stakeholder has an opportunity to evaluate his or her performance and correct deficiencies

- Opportunities to learn from your customers what you need to improve on

- A means of identifying and solving problems, concerns, weaknesses, and deficiencies on an ongoing basis

Remember that the delivery management process is ongoing. A process of ongoing measurement, evaluation, learning, and adjustment will keep your customers in the driver's seat and provide you with the information you need to respond to service delivery problems or changes in your customer's needs.

CUSTOMER FEEDBACK AND MEASUREMENT

The first step in an effective delivery management process is actively soliciting customer feedback. Feedback enables you to develop *customer-focused measurements* and standards that let you know exactly how you're doing. Feedback is not a one-time or every-now-and-then exercise, but an ongoing process. Here's why:

Only 4 percent of customers who experience service problems with your company will tell you about them. That means that 96 percent of your dissatisfied customers will suffer in silence as far as you're concerned. However, it doesn't mean they won't tell others.

PLAIN ENGLISH

Customer-focused measurement   The comparison of customer expectations with actual company performance. For example, if customers expect deliveries within 24 hours of purchase, that number is compared with the actual delivery time and a determination is made of the number of times that the 24-hour expectation was actually met.

Research has repeatedly demonstrated that this dissatisfied group of customers tells an average of nine other people about the "horrible" service they experienced the last time they did business with your company. And those nine people will each tell another five people about the "horrors" of doing business with your company.

I shudder to think of the numbers of people who will eventually share the "nightmare" with others—and how the "hellish experience" will grow in negativity along the way.

CAUTION

Here's one of the most important principles of customer service: If a customer thinks there's a problem, there's a problem. Learn this principle, understand it, and teach it to every employee in your organization. And remember that problems are a matter of customer perception. You may or may not agree with your customer's perception.

Too often, problems perceived by a customer go unresolved simply because no one in the company knew they existed. The customer said nothing but stopped doing business with your firm. Unresolved customer problems result in more and more of your customers being lost to the competition.

To avoid losing customers because of unresolved service problems, it's important to develop both formal and informal ways of soliciting and encouraging customer feedback. Although research shows that most customers who experience service problems will defect rather than complain, it also demonstrates that companies who solicit feedback from customers break down the barrier of silence. When problems identified in this manner are resolved quickly and fairly, customers remain loyal.

Use Formal Feedback Methods

It's a fact that you get what you inspect, not always what you expect. Measurement is a means of inspection. It is a method of feedback that helps you determine whether your organization is doing the things that will meet customer expectations.

Measurement is also an effective way to determine what your customers think about the service you provide. It also provides an opportunity for customers to let you know if there's a problem. Measurement is an intelligence-gathering mechanism that helps your company stay on track.

In addition to the methods of obtaining customer feedback outlined in "Meeting (and Exceeding) Customer Expectations" on page 1128, it's important to formally and continually measure key performance factors and compare them to the customer-focused standards set by the company. For example, if your company has established the standard of answering the telephone by the third ring, a measurement should be established that monitors the standard.

PLAIN ENGLISH

Customer-focused standards   The internal regulations that govern how a job is done. Transactional standards deal with customer interaction and are often expressed in such guidelines as "Reassure the customer that the problem will be resolved" or "Be friendly and courteous." Outcome standards focus on outcomes: "The customer

continues

continued

complaint can be considered resolved only when ..."; "Twenty-four-hour delivery means that our product is actually in the hands of the customer within 24 hours."

Customer-focused standards are established by the company to ensure excellence in the treatment of its customers. Responding to mail from customers within 36 hours is a customer-focused standard, and one that is monitored by logs of incoming and outgoing customer mail.

Transactional standards are equally important but much more difficult to measure since they involve the face-to-face dimensions of customer contact and include such aspects as being friendly and helpful, being empathetic, using active listening methods, and so on. Transactional standards are often measured via supervisory observation ("Your call may be monitored for customer service purposes").

Outcome standards are objective and easily measurable. They can be measured quantitatively (using numbers) and qualitatively (using subjective opinion and perception).

Two Areas of Quality Measurement

There are two general areas of measurement that help organizations monitor their quality of customer service: systems quality measurements, and customer quality measurements. Both types of measurement should be ongoing.

CAUTION

Many companies have elaborate systems quality measurements but few, if any, customer quality measurements. Although systems measurements are important indicators of how internal procedures and processes are functioning, they provide no information on customer perception. And it's the customer's perception about your service quality that determines your company's destiny. Internal systems should be defined by the needs of your customers and should support your efforts to satisfy customers.

Systems quality measurements help ensure that established processes continue to work effectively. They should be used in conjunction with customer quality measurements. Systems quality measurements are internal and seek information such as ...

■ Was the customer's call answered on the first ring, the second ring, or the third ring?

■ Was the item ready for shipment within four hours of taking the order? Was it shipped within eight hours of taking the order?

■ What was the total turnaround time on the order?

Customer quality measurements relate directly to how well your company is meeting the expectations of its customers. Such measurements provide vital intelligence for corporate growth and development. These measurements are used to measure the quality of performance in areas defined by the customer as being essential, and to seek answers to questions such as ...

- How easy was it for the customer to do business with us? What obstacles made doing business with our organization difficult for the customer?
- Did the customer receive the product within 24 hours of taking the order?
- Was a shipment tracking number given to the customer along with verbal confirmation of the order?
- Was the billing presented in an understandable manner?
- Was the product well-packaged for shipment?

BENCHMARKING

We live in a rapidly changing business environment. Never in the history of modern business has change occurred so rapidly.

With continuous change in the marketplace comes continuous change in operating practices. Companies desiring to become leaders in their industry can no longer afford to think they have all the answers, nor that they're capable of inventing the solutions necessary to meet marketplace challenges.

PLAIN ENGLISH

Benchmarking   An ongoing process of investigating and studying practices that produce exceptional results. Often, the task of benchmarking involves the careful examination of the competitors' practices.

In today's high-velocity marketplace, it's suicidal to attempt to reinvent what others have already learned to do. Leadership in the marketplace requires companies to "Adopt, adapt, and advance"—and to do so creatively!

Benchmarking studies the practices of other companies—including competitors—that have discovered how to perform a critical task in some manner that is qualitatively different and better than the way your organization performs the same task. When you've discovered a practice that will help you improve your product or service, borrow it and adapt it to fit your purposes. Benchmarking is a way to find new ideas to serve your customer better.

Benchmarking is the managerial tool that facilitates "creative adaptation." It's a catalyst that enables an enterprise to learn and improve quickly.

In some companies, benchmarking teams actively search for better operating systems that are targeted to specific critical functions such as billing, order entry and fulfillment, distribution, and the like. Benchmarking is also an advanced business concept with applications for high-level functions such as restructuring, financial management, and joint-venture management.

If you're not using benchmarking in your business, you're missing a powerful management tool that can help you achieve breakthrough performance improvements. You keep your customers in the forefront by providing them with the best of the best.

Benchmarking is a highly practical tool that is easily taught and easily grasped. It doesn't deal with abstract suppositions and concepts but focuses on finding real-world solutions to everyday business problems.

Here's an example of how benchmarking has been used:

In his book *Made in America,* Sam Walton wrote about the part that benchmarking played in the formation of Wal-Mart:

> The discount idea was in the future. We had only two choices: stay in the variety store business and be hit hard by the discounting wave, or open a discount store. So I started running all over the country, studying the concept, from the mill stores in the East to California, where Sol Price had started his Fed-Mart in 1955. I liked Sol's Fed-Mart name, so I latched right on to Wal-Mart. On July 2, 1962, we opened Wal-Mart No. 1 in Rogers, Arkansas, right down the road from Bentonville. We did a million dollars in a year.

Performance management is the process of managing and improving operations and involves both benchmarking and benchmarks. Benchmarking seeks new and better ways to serve your customer; benchmarks measure the performance of specific practices or systems. Top-performing companies rely on both benchmarking and benchmarks.

BENCHMARKS

Benchmarks are the operating measurements by which two or more systems or functions are compared and evaluated. Performance benchmarks involve comparison at several levels. Here are a few of the most common levels of comparison:

- Best-in-world
- Best-in-country
- Industry leader
- Industry norm
- Industry standard
- Best-in-company

PLAIN ENGLISH

Benchmark   An operating measurement that defines the level of
performance of any given practice or system. Benchmarks can help
identify hidden opportunities to innovate and improve performance.

The most critical functions to benchmark are those core functions that are of
the highest strategic importance to the company. These benchmarks reflect
best-in-class performance (best-in-industry, best-in-country, best-in-world,
depending upon whether the business competes in national or global markets).
Federal Express, for example, has identified 12 core functions that, according
to their customer research, are of the utmost strategic importance. The company developed a measurement system based on these 12 functions, which it
calls its Service Quality Indicator (SQI). Those measurements are watched
very closely by managers at every level in order to ensure total customer satisfaction.

Other functions that are less strategically significant may also be bench-
marked, but the benchmark level is usually less (best-in-company, industry
standard, or norm). Benchmarks for support functions not critical to an organization's strategic advantage are often just internal measurements.

MEASURE WHAT'S CRITICAL TO SUCCESS

You can't measure every aspect of your business, but it's important to measure the aspect that is critical to the success of your business. For example, at
Starbuck's Coffee, management recognizes that inconsistent product quality
and slow service are the two operating failures that could destroy their business. Starbuck's, therefore, diligently measures and monitors these two significant performance factors.

What are the most important operating functions of your business? Why not
establish appropriate benchmarks for those processes, systems, or functions?
Then monitor and measure actual performance against established benchmarks.

Here are some helpful examples of critical performance benchmarks for customer service:

- Customer retention rates
- Customer repurchase rates
- Customer defection rates
- Customer satisfaction/dissatisfaction measures
- Customer ratings of sales and service personnel
- Customer ratings of delivery timeliness
- Customer ratings of product quality
- Customer ratings indicating the ease of doing business with the company

TIP

Through a program of ongoing measurement, you will identify those people who are doing an outstanding job of serving customers. Be sure to formally recognize those people in some meaningful way. Performance that's rewarded is repeated.

SCOREBOARDING

Scoreboarding is not just keeping score; it's broadcasting results so that everyone concerned is aware of what took place.

Make critical customer performance measurements available to everyone in your company. Whenever possible, break down these measurements into meaningful levels. For example, critical measurements will have special interest to company management, but you need to make them meaningful to the line worker as well. Therefore, in addition to measurements reflecting overall company performance in critical areas, let each division, section, and unit know how it measured up as well. For example, when Federal Express breaks down its late delivery numbers to the various workgroups directly involved, it gives line staff and managers the information they need to make necessary improvements.

When important measurements are scoreboarded by operational unit, employees are given the chance to take ownership of the results. By directly observing his or her contribution, an employee can help maintain present levels of functioning or assist in correcting deficiencies. This kind of scoreboarding also can result in competition for excellence among operating units, which will help achieve even better results.

LEARNING

Managing the service delivery process involves a commitment to continuous learning. As a result of customer feedback and formal measurement, your customers will tell you what it is they want and whether you're providing it; they'll tell you what needs to be continued and what needs improvement; they'll tell you who is doing a good job and who isn't; and they'll tell you what you need to know in order to plan for the future.

Learning is a never-ending process. To achieve success today and in the future, you need to learn all you can about your customers and how your products or services can be modified to meet their changing needs. You need to learn about your competition—in depth—so that you know how they respond to the needs of customers and what they do to meet the same problems and challenges you encounter.

CONTINUOUS IMPROVEMENT—MAKING THE NECESSARY ADJUSTMENTS

Competing, surviving, and winning in the competitive business economy of the twenty-first century require an absolute commitment to continuous improvement. This commitment must come from top management and from every employee of the company.

Continuous improvement is not just a buzzword or a fad. It's a way of thinking, planning, working, and striving for excellence in every aspect of the business. It's a way of life.

Continually improving is like running a race with no finish line. It's an adventure that is both demanding and satisfying; demanding because it's a never-ending journey, and satisfying because through each journey you discover new and innovative methods to enhance skills, processes, systems, procedures, and technologies, all of which ultimately enable you to serve your customer better, improve your market share, reduce cost, and improve your effectiveness.

Serve, measure, scoreboard, learn, and improve. This is the formula to successful customer service management—and the way to ensure that your customers remain in the driver's seat of your enterprise.

THE 30-SECOND RECAP

- Ninety-six percent of your dissatisfied customers will never tell you about their dissatisfaction, but they will tell an average of nine people about it—and those nine people will tell an average of five others.

- Develop a process for managing customer service delivery that ensures quality customer service by establishing methods of customer feedback and measurement.

- An effective model for managing service delivery includes ongoing measurement of core functions; benchmarking for best practices and benchmarks that provide target operational objectives; scoreboarding to communicate results; learning; and continuous improvement.

Participative Management

In this section you learn that exceptional customer service is everyone's job— from the CEO to the frontline worker—and that participative management techniques can promote a strong customer service culture.

World-class businesses recognize the importance of exceptional customer service. They also understand that in order to provide exceptional service, everyone in the company needs to realize the importance of the customer and share in the commitment to excellence.

The Wal-Mart Company makes sure that new employees clearly understand the importance of customer service and that they share in Wal-Mart's commitment to excellence. Whether they've been hired as a store manager or a stock clerk, each new employee makes the following pledge:

> From this day forward, I solemnly promise and declare that whenever a customer comes within 10 feet of me, I will smile, look them in the eye, and greet them, so help me Sam.

New employees are then reminded of the immortal words of Sam Walton, the founder of Wal-Mart: "Remember, a promise we make is a promise we keep."

EVERYONE'S RESPONSIBILITY

Achieving excellence in customer service doesn't happen by itself. It requires planning, training, and effort. But more than anything, it requires everyone in the organization working together to achieve the common goal of total customer satisfaction.

Exceptional customer service can't be achieved without teamwork, employee commitment and involvement, a sense of ownership in the final product, and a healthy working relationship between management and employees. Participative management is the key.

What Is Participative Management?

Participative management is a process in which managers and employees work together as peers to produce exceptional products and services that exceed customer expectations.

Participative management eschews typical lines of authority and enables employees to make decisions that affect the product purchased by the customer. Participative management stimulates productivity and innovation, and increases employee commitment to customer service throughout the organization. It also encourages employees to modify the functions of their work units in order to allow them to perform better for the sake of the final output. The result is a happier work force producing a better product, and improved customer service to boot.

PLAIN ENGLISH

Participative management   A process in which managers and employees work together as peers to produce exceptional products and services that exceed customer expectations.

Customer Service and Participative Management Techniques

Establishing a customer service culture that involves everyone in the company means a significant change will take place in your organization. Change is always difficult.

Most people want to feel in control of their environment. They will resist change unless they understand what is being changed and why, and have some input in the change process.

Informing employees of your intent and commitment to enhance the customer service emphasis of the organization is important. Basic education and training about the impact of customer service on the future of the company and its employees sets the stage.

Here are some important participative management techniques that will help bring about change in your organization:

- Communicate, communicate, and communicate. Hold all-staff meetings to talk about customers and their role in determining the future of the company and its workers. Make sure these are dialogues in which everyone has an opportunity to share ideas and thoughts. Make sure that customer service is on the agenda every time there's a scheduled unit, departmental, or section meeting. Use every opportunity to talk about the importance of exceeding customer expectations.

- While everyone in your organization is responsible for exceptional customer service, frontline employees will be most affected by any change in customer service philosophy. Make them part of the changes by including them in every aspect of the process.

- Form a customer service management team made up of frontline employees and representatives from management. Give the team the responsibility for recommending process changes to help the company achieve its customer service objectives. Sponsor training events for employees, and keep customer service matters paramount in the minds of employees.

- Empower frontline workers to solve customer problems quickly and effectively. Empower supervisors to recognize and reward exceptional customer service and to address problems effectively and promptly. Make it a point to "catch people doing something right," and reward them accordingly.

In addition to the preceding techniques, management has some special tasks to perform in order to promote a customer service culture. Management needs to ...

- Articulate its absolute commitment to building a customer-focused organization. Management needs to communicate levels of expectation and give overall direction to the effort.

- Communicate its vision for the future with its new emphasis on customer service. Talk about what that change will mean for the company and each of its employees. Demonstrate to employees why becoming a customer-driven company is important.

- Measure your organization's progress. Monitor results of your enhanced customer service efforts by using appropriate benchmarks (see "Keeping Your Customers in the Driver's Seat: Part 2" on page 1145). Make the results visually available to your entire organization (scoreboarding).

- Make adjustments or corrections when they're needed. Use benchmarking techniques to constantly be on the lookout for new and better practices that bring higher degrees of customer satisfaction.

- Motivate employees by focusing on job enrichment, empowerment, and decision-making, and foster a participative environment in which innovation and creativity flourish.

- Provide everyone with the tools and skill-building training needed to do the job. Positive change will not occur unless those who must make the change are well equipped and properly prepared. Remember, too, that training for enhanced customer service shouldn't be viewed as a "one-shot" experience, but as an ongoing one. Companies should consider spending 10 percent of their annual advertising budget on customer service training.

- Inform your service providers of your customer service expectations. Tell them that you intend to hold them accountable for the outcomes outlined in your contracts with them. Develop a mechanism for monitoring the compliance of your service providers to ensure they're meeting your standards and outcomes are being met.

- Publicly reward those who do the job well. Take appropriate corrective action when necessary.

- Demonstrate management's commitment to customer service in ways that are worthy of employee emulation.

- Establish a working environment in which communication is unrestricted. Actively listen to others' concerns and ideas about any aspect of the business. Empathize with the feelings, suggestions, and requests of others.

- Care about your employees by providing the necessary support mechanisms. For example, when it becomes obvious that employees need to improve performance, provide the necessary counseling, training, and feedback to correct the situation. Employees should be selected for specific jobs on the basis of skill and past performance; employees who are given jobs beyond their present skill levels are set up for failure. Employees desiring to advance should be offered job rotations along with classroom and on-the-job training, and mentoring and coaching from more experienced workers.

Be kind. Work with your people. Understand that a change of this magnitude isn't made overnight. Understand also that every employee will have a different rate of acceptance. The common psychological stages of change are fear, anxiety, confusion, acceptance, and energy. And it takes some people longer than others to move from fear to energy.

THE TEAMWORK ADVANTAGE

In developing a customer service culture within your company, take advantage of the special benefits that come with teamwork. Teamwork not only assists in the process of change, but also provides an immediate vehicle for improved customer service.

Customer service, after all, works best as a team activity. Teamwork fosters interdependence and interaction with others who are working to achieve the same goal. Through team participation, everyone in the company can have a role in providing exceptional service.

TIP

Management studies have consistently shown that the optimum number of participants for effective teamwork is between five and seven.

Here are some special advantages that teamwork offers:

- Teams tend to unify people, helping them to share common goals, objectives, values, and vision.

- Teamwork helps break down the barriers that sometimes exist between work units (sections, divisions, departments, etc.). Teams provide an opportunity for people throughout the company to work together to achieve a common objective.

- Teams provide a sense of direction—where the organization is going and what part each employee has along the way.

- Teams are fertile ground for new ideas and provide a fresh perspective on existing problems.

- Teamwork gives the customer a perception of good service. The organization appears well-organized and completely able to meet the customer's expectations.

- As stakeholders in outcomes, team members share responsibility and accountability for the tasks assigned to each, thereby helping to ensure the success of the effort.

TIP

Teams tend to spend more time planning than implementing what's been planned. That's because less time is needed to introduce change, since team participants are already in agreement. Change that occurs without teams usually requires less time in the planning stage, but more time is needed for implementation.

- Teams offer a venue for effective delegation of work assignments and for monitoring the progress of work underway.

- Regular team meetings and the distribution of team minutes offer an opportunity for increased communication with all employees.

- Teams make better decisions than individuals because there is more reliance on innovative and *proactive problem-solving*.

PLAIN ENGLISH

Proactive problem-solving   Anticipating problems and obstacles associated with a particular task and solving them before they're actually encountered.

EFFECTIVE TEAMS

Here are some important characteristics of effective teams:

- Effective teams know what their mission is and are committed to achieving it; team members—regardless of positions held in the organization—are regarded by one another as peers who share responsibilities and team roles.

- Effective teams are empowered by the company to complete an assigned mission; members are empowering to one another and to others within the company with whom they have contact.

- Effective teams operate in ways that are informal and people-friendly.

- Effective teams always encourage open and spontaneous communication among members; there is no fear of reprisal.

- Effective teams seek win/win solutions to problems.

- Effective teams welcome an opportunity to explore new ideas that initially present themselves as conflicts or differences of opinion.

- Effective teams have a leader, a secretary, a facilitator, and a time-keeper, and these roles are rotated among team members to avoid domination of the team.

- Effective teams make decisions by *consensus* of the members.

PLAIN ENGLISH

Consensus   After deliberating on every viable alternative, all team members agree on a specific course of action. Although each member may not prefer the course of action, each supports it.

THE 30-SECOND RECAP

- Providing exceptional customer service is the responsibility of everyone in your organization—from the CEO to the frontline worker.

- Participative management techniques help to establish and promote a customer service culture in which the needs of the customer are paramount.

- Team participation is a good way to involve both management and line staff in service-related tasks and projects.

Service Delivery Skills and Techniques

In this section you learn important techniques and skills for improving the interaction between yourself and your customer.

Service delivery skills and techniques are what make exceptional employees exceptional. They are the little things that together persuade your customers to think well of your entire organization.

Most of these time-tested skills and techniques are easy to learn and use. Each should be included in your training menu for frontline workers. Consistently using these skills and techniques will pay off tremendously for your company in the form of customer satisfaction.

COMMUNICATION

Communication is one of the most powerful tools available for providing exceptional customer service. It's a skill that is perfected by training and practice.

Your employees' ability to successfully interact with your customers is vitally important to the future growth and development of your business. And it's your employees' ability to communicate that determines the quality of customer interaction.

Communication doesn't just involve talking or writing; it's much more than simply sending a message. In fact, talking and writing constitute only one third of the process. Listening and understanding are equally important in the process of creating a shared meaning—a message held in common.

PLAIN ENGLISH

Communication   From the Latin root *commune,* which means "something held in common." In the context of customer service, communication is a process of sharing information with a customer in such a way that you understand what the customer is saying, and the customer understands you.

Remember our discussion concerning "moments of truth" in the section "What's Your Business?" on page 1119. The typical customer forms a lasting impression of your company's quality of service in 40 seconds or less. That impression governs the remainder of the customer's contact. If the "moment of truth" is mostly positive, chances are good that the customer will have a favorable impression of your organization; if it's mostly negative, that impression will likewise be negative.

Your employees' ability to communicate effectively with your customers will generate positive "moments of truth" and will help the customer form a positive perception of your organization. That's worthwhile!

Here are some ways to improve one-to-one communication with your customers:

- **Use your customer's name.** Don't take this suggestion for granted. Customers like being referred to by name. Why? Because calling someone by name is a way of demonstrating that you care about him or her as a person. When you address a customer by using his or her name, you start things off on the right foot—your "moment of truth" begins with a positive!

- **Smile sincerely.** Customers perceive someone who smiles sincerely, and often, to be friendly, approachable, and capable. Words spoken by someone who smiles are much more likely to be perceived as beneficial and helpful. A sincere smile will have a major positive impact on every "moment of truth."

- **Look them in the eye.** My grandfather used to say, "If someone can't look you in the eye, they're not to be trusted." Most people still feel that way, especially when they're making a purchase or attempting to deal with a problem. When you're talking with a customer, look them in the eye whenever possible. But never stare at customers. Staring causes feelings of intimidation and anxiety in the customer.

- **Don't cross your arms.** Crossing your arms sends a message to your customers that your mind is closed and that you are unapproachable. Even when your verbal message is friendly, warm, and helpful, if your body language sends a conflicting message your customer will be confused and will be less likely to perceive the experience in positive terms.

- **Respect your customer's personal space.** No one wants his or her personal space invaded. Personal space may be defined in various ways, but a good rule of thumb is one arm's length in all directions. People feel intimidated—even threatened—when their personal space is violated.

- **Lean forward when listening.** This is a simple, but powerful, nonverbal technique that tells your customer that you're really interested in what he or she is saying. And if there's one thing that's important to your customer, it's assurance that you're listening!

- **Show agreement with your customer.** Whenever possible, indicate your agreement both verbally and nonverbally with your customer. A good nonverbal method of showing agreement is by nodding. Nodding indicates that you've been listening to what the customer has said and that you agree.

- **Watch your appearance.** What they see is what they think they'll get. When you're dealing with customers, what you say will be filtered by how you look. Employees who look like they spent the night in jail won't inspire confidence in their customers. Appearance may not be everything, but it has an important role in creating a positive perception in the minds of customers.

ACTIVE LISTENING SKILLS

Years ago, I completed a graduate program in therapeutic counseling. My career goal at that time was to be able to help people who had experienced some kind of significant psychological trauma.

One of the first things I learned in my program was that counselors are unable to help anyone until they know what the problem is; and the only way to discover what's wrong is by listening intently to what patients have to say. Active listening skills are one of the most important tools a counselor can possess.

Active listening skills are also among the most important customer service tools available. Helping customers to talk openly and freely about their needs, expectations, problems, and concerns is where real customer service begins. Active listening promotes warmth and honesty in communication.

Here are some active listening techniques that can help you help your customer:

- **Tune in to the customer.** Be genuinely curious about what the customer says. Make a conscious decision to listen intently to what your customer tells you. Tune out everything else. Concentrate on what your customer is telling you verbally and through body language.

- **Be nonjudgmental.** Deliberately suspend your internal self-talk. Allow your customer's message to sink in without making decisions about it. Don't jump to conclusions about what your customer is telling you.

- **Resist distractions.** Don't allow external or internal distractions to disturb your focus on what the customer is saying.

■ **Wait to respond.** Be sure your customer has finished talking before responding to what he or she has said. And avoid superficial responses—they will only frustrate your customer further.

TIP

As your customer is speaking, mentally repeat to yourself those words that the customer uses to describe feelings and facts. This will help you stay focused on what the customer is saying and prevent your mind from wandering. Asking questions to clarify feelings and facts will further help define the problem.

■ **Reflect content.** Listen for feelings and facts; then reflect back to the customer what you hear him or her saying. For example, "You're angry because you paid extra for overnight delivery, but your item was sent parcel post." This technique communicates understanding (or offers an opportunity to correct misunderstanding.)

■ **Provide supportive cues.** Supportive cues are nonverbal ways of communicating support. Good eye contact and an occasional nod of the head demonstrate that you understand what the customer is telling you.

■ **Listen for solutions.** When customers are allowed to express the facts and feelings that surround a problem, they will also tell you what they expect you to do to resolve it. Use direct questions to ask customers what they would like you to do to make things right. (Use the recovery skills taught in "Keeping Your Customers in the Driver's Seat: Part 1" on page 1137.)

■ **Confirm the solution.** When your customer has finished explaining the problem and defined what he or she expects to be done, restate the proposed solution so that there's no misunderstanding.

Remember that listening is an important part of communication. Active listening enhances communication by demonstrating to customers that they not only have been heard, but have been understood.

CUSTOMER HOT BUTTONS

We all have *hot buttons*—words, attitudes, phrases, or comments that set us off. Whenever one of these hot buttons is pushed, especially when we suspect that it's been done deliberately, we react in negative, nonproductive ways that usually make a bad situation worse.

A customer also has hot buttons, and they're particularly easy to push when
something has gone wrong and the customer is already upset. Be aware of the
danger that hot buttons represent, and be sensitive to your customer's level of
anxiety when problems have occurred.

Here are a few suggestions that will help:

- Empathize with your customer; don't force the customer to see the
  problem from your perspective.

- Don't finger-point. Telling a customer that the problem is really his
  or her own fault is a sure way to add insult to injury.

- Don't scold, insult, or call the customer names. Initially, I hesitated
  to include this warning; then I remembered the number of customer
  service situations I've witnessed over the years in which company
  representatives actually resorted to these kinds of tactics. The only
  thing that's accomplished by scolding, insulting, or calling names is
  further damage. Encourage employees who habitually relate to customers in this way to seek other employment.

- Be careful of the phrases you use. Statements like: "I'm sorry, but
  it's against our policy to …"; "I'll have to check with my supervisor
  and I'll give you a call when I know more"; or "That's not my job"
  are sure to push your customer's hot buttons. Avoid them.

How to Handle Mistakes

Ronald Reagan once said, "By the time you reach my age, you've made
plenty of mistakes, and if you've lived your life properly, so you learn. You
put things in perspective. You pull your energies together. You change. You go
forward."

Mistakes are inevitable. That's why pencils still have erasers. But the things you do to minimize mistakes, and how you handle them when they do occur, make all the difference.

When mistakes occur, it's important that you understand what happened from your customer's standpoint, that you adequately demonstrate your concern, and that you recover in style:

- **Understand what's happened.** Let the customer vent. Use active listening skills to discover what actually went wrong. Confirm your findings with the customer so that there is no misunderstanding as to the mistake involved.

- **Demonstrate your concern.** Show the customer that you really care about what's happened by saying something like, "That's awful; I can't believe we did that" or "What a mess this has been for you." Be genuine, and remember to look your customer in the eye when you're communicating your concern.

- **Apologize.** Tell the customer that you're sorry for the mistake. Say, "I'm sorry that happened to you" or "That sort of problem should never happen. I'm very sorry it happened to you." When your company makes mistakes, it's only right to apologize on its behalf. Say you're sorry and be sincere about it.

- **Recover with style.** Use the skills you learned in "Keeping Your Customers in the Driver's Seat: Part 1" on page 1137 to recover with style.

HANDLING CUSTOMER REQUESTS

Responding to customers who request information is an important part of serving them. Handling customer requests requires knowledge of the company's products and services as well as the ability to skillfully interact with customers.

Here are the steps involved in responding to customers with requests:

- **Understand what's being asked.** Use your active listening skills to fully understand what a customer is requesting. Restating the request to the customer sometimes prevents misunderstandings.

- **Don't guess when answering customer questions.** If you don't know the answer to questions asked by the customer, say so. Immediately attempt to bring a supervisor or some other knowledgeable employee into the conversation so that the customer's questions can be answered. But whatever you do, don't guess at answers to customer questions. You run the very real risk of turning a bad situation into a disaster.

- **Provide accurate and current information.** This means that you must thoroughly know your company's products and services. Again, if you don't know, immediately find someone who does and bring that person into your conversation with the customer.

- **"A promise we make is a promise we keep."** Everyone who deals directly with customers should echo those words, originally spoken by Sam Walton. If you promise something, deliver on the promise. If there's any doubt about being able to deliver, don't promise it!

- **Learn how to say "no" in a customer-friendly manner.** That's not as difficult as it might seem. Sometimes you have no choice; you must say "no." But saying "no" doesn't have to be a negative situation. Begin by empathizing with the customer and demonstrating that you understand the problem. Tell the customer why you aren't able to do what he or she is asking. Then, offer alternatives—give your customer some choices of things that you *can* do.

- **Sometimes it's okay to say "maybe."** Customers may sometimes ask for things that may or may not be possible. If you aren't sure, say so, but reiterate what it is you can do. Say, "Here is what we can do immediately. We may be able to do something different in your case and if you'd like me to do so, I'll pursue it further." This gives the customer an immediate answer while demonstrating a willingness to serve the customer further by advocating on his or her behalf.

UNDERPROMISE AND OVERDELIVER

One of my wife's first ventures into the world of e-commerce involved the purchase of an inexpensive item from Eddie Bauer. When she made the purchase, she gave her credit card information and was told that the item would arrive in 10 days to three weeks.

Two days later, the item arrived via Priority Mail. I've rarely seen someone so excited. Her e-commerce adventure had proven worthwhile. She was downright thrilled by the wonderful service she had received from Eddie Bauer and vowed to make much more use of this very convenient method of shopping.

I can't tell you how many people my wife told about the great service she had received from Eddie Bauer. I wonder how many of those people told others the story about Eddie Bauer's great service? (After all, she told *me,* and look what happened—I included it in a book on customer service!)

Underpromising and overdelivering is arguably the world's greatest technique for ensuring customer satisfaction. Make it a regular part of your company's customer service practice.

THE 30-SECOND RECAP

- Communication is the most powerful customer service tool that exists.

- Communication is not just talking; it also involves listening and understanding.

- Moments of truth are effected positively or negatively, depending on your organization's ability to communicate effectively.

- Active listening helps to isolate the facts of a situation as well as what will satisfy the customer.

- Beware of your customer's "hot buttons" as well as your own.

- Saying "no" can be done in a customer-friendly manner.

- Underpromising and overdelivering should be an objective in every customer service situation.

Handling Difficult Customers

In this section you learn the importance of handling angry customers with confidence and professionalism.

THE ANGRY CUSTOMER

We've all dealt with customers who are angry, demanding, and sometimes downright nasty. Such customers sometimes even engage in personal attacks against the company representative trying to help them. Assisting these kinds of customers is a situation that requires skill, ability, and a cool head.

Your goal in handling difficult customers is to turn a potentially negative interaction into a positive one by solving whatever problems are presented and making sure your customer is satisfied. That's not always an easy task.

SERVING THE ANGRY CUSTOMER

Most anger begins when a person feels hurt and disappointed by the actions of another. Instead of admitting the hurt and doing something to correct the situation, some people keep it inside. If anger continues to grow, it ultimately leads to acts of revenge—sometimes overt, as when angry customers verbally attack anyone attempting to help; sometimes covert, as when customers don't tell the company what happened but make it a point to tell everyone else. In rare instances, revenge can even take the form of destructive criminal actions.

How you choose to react to angry customers will determine whether the situation will be resolved or whether it will escalate. If your goal is to provide the kind of exceptional customer service that turns an angry customer into a happy and satisfied one, you'll have to possess the requisite skills.

Here are a few important facts you need to know about serving angry customers:

- Conflict and disagreement are part of life. They cannot be avoided.

- Customers who engage in personal verbal attacks are angry with the company, not the person attempting to help them.

- Irate customers can't be helped until they calm down.

- Communication is the key—helping customers to express what they feel, what they want, and what they think is the pathway to resolving the problem.

CAUTION

Unfortunately, a few people seem to enjoy being angry. For whatever reason, these people thrive on what they consider unsolvable problems and have no real desire to find resolution. When you encounter this type of customer, simply do your best to solve his or her problem. Exceptional customer service doesn't always result in the customer getting what he or she wants, but it should always involve the obligation to give the best service possible.

THE LARSON APPROACH

Following is a successful technique for handling angry customers. I call it the LARSON approach, with each letter representing an important step of the technique.

L = LISTEN

Listen to your customer. Let him or her vent. Practice active listening, *empathizing* with the customer often. When you speak, use words and phrases that reassure the customer that you hear what's being said and that you want to help. Listen to your customer in the same way you would want to be listened to if you were in the customer's position. While you're listening, take notes of important facts. Note-taking helps you remain focused on what the customer is saying, and observing you take notes helps the customer focus on the facts of the situation, not just the emotion surrounding it.

PLAIN ENGLISH

Empathy   The ability to walk around in the shoes of a customer in order to know how he or she feels in them; it's the process of attempting to understand, from the customer's point of view, the thoughts and feelings he or she has about something of personal importance.

Sympathy   This occurs when one becomes so associated with another individual that he or she reacts or responds to a situation in much the same manner. Sympathy usually results from becoming so enmeshed with another person that objectivity and reason no longer play a functional role in problem-solving.

A = AGREEMENT

Find areas of agreement. "I certainly have to agree with you, Mr. Smith; we really blew it this time!" When you agree with an angry customer, you begin to defuse the anger as well as any form of verbal revenge. Remember, the irate customer expects you to engage in a power struggle of sorts (which would only escalate the problem). When you voice your agreement with some of the customer's accusations, his or her perception of you immediately changes from that of an enemy to a possible friend who can help.

TIP

If a customer yells at you, respond by talking softly. Use words that are kind and considerate as you talk in a voice that is soft, but not so soft that the customer can't hear what you're saying. This is one of the most effective techniques I've found for defusing angry situations.

Empathize with your customer. Say something like, "You've got every right to be angry, Mr. Smith. I'm really sorry that this happened to you. I can certainly understand why you'd think that no one from XYZ Corporation cares about you. I'm so sorry that happened; we can't afford to offend good customers like you." Try it—it works wonders.

TIP

Remember that there's a big difference between empathy and sympathy. Empathy means seeing a situation from the customer's standpoint. Sympathy means becoming overly enmeshed in the customer's situation. Empathy is objective and positive, and fosters solutions to problems; sympathy skews objectivity and can be extremely nonproductive.

R = Repeat, Restate

Using the words of your customer, repeat what he or she perceives to be the problem. Be as accurate as possible. Ask your customer to correct you if you state something that's wrong. Repeating and restating communicates to your customer that you are listening intently to what he or she is saying and that you're committed to solving the problem, whatever it may be.

TIP

Correcting misunderstandings and answering customer objections are situations that require special handling. Correct customer misunderstandings by offering the correct information. Answer customer objections by offering proof. In dealing with irate customers, be sure that you have sufficiently de-escalated the customer's anger before attempting either technique.

S = Seek Resolution

Once your customer is sufficiently calm and focused, ask what he or she would like you to do to solve the problem. When you seek resolution, you communicate your desire to act in the customer's behalf. That goes a long way toward defusing anger. Say something like, "Now that you've helped me understand the problem, tell me what you'd like me to do to solve it for you." Or say, "I'm very sorry that this happened to you. I can certainly understand why you're upset. Here's what I can do right now ...."

O = Offer a Sincere Apology

Offering an apology is another act that defuses anger. By offering an apology, you communicate that you've accepted blame for the situation. Apologies should not be partial ("I'm sorry for whatever part we played in creating the problem"), nor should they be conditional ("If you can show me that we caused the problem, we will certainly accept responsibility and do whatever it takes to correct the situation"). Many times, a sincere apology is what really turns the tide; it's a very powerful tool.

A second offering should be made to compensate the customer for all of his or her trouble. This offering can take many different forms (a discount on a future purchase, a dinner for two at a special restaurant, the gift of a product). Your offering of something tangible makes your apology much more meaningful.

N = Now!

Take action now! Once you've defined what needs to be done to solve the problem, and you've offered a sincere apology to the customer, take whatever action is necessary to solve the problem—and do it immediately!

Your ability to turn a negative situation into one that's positive depends on your ability to solve the problem that has upset your customer. Frontline employees should be empowered to solve problems on the spot, without having to obtain administrative approval. In instances where the entire problem cannot be remedied immediately, they should be empowered to solve as much of it as they can on the spot and seek a supervisor's assistance to solve the rest.

Solving major customer problems is a bit like triage at a busy urban hospital emergency room: It's not always possible to cure the problem immediately, but it's important to stop the bleeding without delay.

Some Important Caveats

The LARSON technique for handling irate customers works well. But as with all techniques, there are some caveats to keep in mind:

- Never allow yourself to be drawn into the customer's negativity. When this occurs, you lose any hope of effectively correcting the situation.

- Never argue with the customer or engage in power struggles. These will only escalate the customer's anger and diminish your chances of coming to a resolution. Remember, you're not engaged in a contest with the customer; your job is to help solve a problem to your customer's satisfaction.

- Never blame the customer for any part of the problem ("This would never have happened if you hadn't …").

- Never use sarcasm with a customer. Sarcasm has a way of creating ill will faster than anything I know. And when it's used with irate customers, it's akin to pouring gasoline on a bonfire.

- Never get caught up in the emotionalism of the encounter. Your job is to listen to the customer and to solve the problem. Stay focused on problems and potential solutions.

- Never personalize the situation ("If you just calm down, we could make some progress" or "If you would stop calling me names, maybe I could find a way to help you").

■ Never continue working with a customer if he or she threatens physical violence. In these situations, instruct your employees to disengage with the customer immediately and report the incident to you. If the customer, in turn, threatens you with physical violence, call the police. ("Excuse me, but I don't think we can continue working on this problem today. I'd really like to help you at a time when we could discuss the situation without resorting to threats.") Threats of physical violence should be taken seriously.

FOLLOW UP WITH YOUR CUSTOMER

Be sure to follow up with your customer. Your customer will be positively impressed if you take the time to phone a few days later to ask if he or she has any further concerns.

Some people think of following up as "looking for trouble." That's nonsense. Exceptional customer service includes contacting customers who have experienced problems to make sure you've satisfied them.

USING THE LARSON TECHNIQUE

For years, my family has owned a bookstore that specializes in rare and vintage books. It's not at all uncommon for a first edition of a classic title to sell for $1,000 or more. Some of the store's customers are established book collectors who know the true worth of a rare book based on its condition and the "points" that make it a true first edition. But many of the store's customers are new collectors who may be well-read, but who lack knowledge about rare books.

A few months ago, a customer purchased a first edition of *A Farewell to Arms,* by Ernest Hemingway. The book was in very good condition, but lacked a dust jacket. Nevertheless, the selling price was $575. The customer was delighted with his purchase.

A few days later, however, he returned the book and demanded a refund. He was livid. He accused everyone involved of "conspiring" against him and perpetrating a fraud. "How dare you take advantage of people like this! What kind of people are you anyway? I trusted you and you deceived me." (He said lots more, but for the sake of brevity—and good taste—I'll forgo the complete dialog.)

THE TECHNIQUE IN ACTION

Employing the LARSON technique in working through the problem, our representative's first objective was simply to **listen.** As difficult as it was to be the subject of insults and accusations, it was more important to allow the customer an opportunity to vent his concerns and frustrations.

Our representative used active listening techniques to help the customer get to the heart of the matter. "You feel that we cheated you by selling you a book that is not a true first edition?" The customer replied, "That's right! I took this book to my wife's brother, who really knows his books, and he told me that this is definitely not a first edition; that a true first edition has a disclaimer by the publisher printed on one of the first pages of the book! I didn't know that, and you took advantage of me for not knowing! My wife wasn't happy about me spending $575 on a book in the first place. And now that her brother has told her that I was cheated, my life at home is a living hell!" Allowing a customer to vent serves a two-fold purpose: It de-escalates the situation and enables you, through the application of active listening techniques, to discover the source of the customer's concern.

The second step in the LARSON technique involves **agreement** with the customer. This can sometimes prove challenging, especially when (as in this case) the customer's complaint is founded on poor information. It's important to remember that the irate customer expects you to engage in an argument or a power struggle with him or her. Instead, if you're following the LARSON technique, you will listen, clarify, and agree with the customer in some meaningful way. Here's what our representative said to show agreement with the customer: "I can understand why you're angry with us, Mr. Jones. Collecting rare books is an expensive hobby and it's important to be able to trust those with whom you do business." Soft-spoken and friendly statements of agreement spoken with sincerity normally result in the complete de-escalation of an irate customer.

The third step in the LARSON technique is to **repeat** or **restate** the primary complaint of the customer that you discovered in step 1. Repeating or restating the problem is a further attempt to clarify it in terms that both you and your customer understand and agree with. Our representative in this situation attempted to clarify by saying, "So if I understand you correctly, Mr. Jones, you are angry with us because you believe that the book you purchased was not the first edition of the work that we claimed it to be. Is that correct?" Mr. Jones agreed; the real problem behind all the anger and the accusations was clear: His wife's brother (a would-be rare-book expert) had given our customer some bad information. Our customer had accepted his advice at face value and concluded that we had cheated him, and his anger with us was fueled by an angry wife.

Because the customer's complaint involved a **misunderstanding,** we needed to correct that matter before going further. The customer believed, based on erroneous information, that a true first edition of the famous Hemingway novel contains a disclaimer. That's untrue—in fact, the disclaimer didn't appear until the second printing of the book. "Let me review the points to look for in a true first edition of *A Farewell to Arms,*" our representative told Mr. Jones. "First, the first edition was published by Charles Scribner's Sons and has a black cloth cover with gold printed paper labels on both the front cover and the spine; the copyright date is 1929 and the Scribner's seal is included on the copyright page; there are 355 pages; and there is no disclaimer included as a preface to the book."

Immediately, our customer raised an **objection.** "My brother-in-law has been collecting books for some time and he knows what he's doing. He insists that the disclaimer must be present in order for the book to be considered a true first edition!" Objections require proof, so our representative retrieved the store's copy of *Book Collecting 2000: A Comprehensive Guide,* by Allen Ahearn and Patricia Ahearn (Putnam Publishing Group), explaining to our customer that the book is used by book sellers and buyers worldwide to identify and value rare books. The guide recited each of the first edition points our representative had explained to the customer.

When the customer was finished reading the information, our representative made a copy of the page for him so that he could correct his brother-in-law. With his objection answered, our customer was satisfied and even apologetic. We assured him that we were happy to have been of service and invited him to consult with us whenever he had a question concerning a rare book—even if he was considering purchasing it from someone else.

CORRECTING MISTAKES

If, however, we had unknowingly misrepresented a book to a customer, we would have proceeded using the LARSON technique. Our next step would have been to **seek resolution** to the situation by asking, "What can we do to solve the problem?" Customers usually know what it takes to resolve the matter. If, for example, we had sold the disclaimer version of *A Farewell to Arms* as a first edition, we would have said, "I'm sorry this happened to you; it's clearly our mistake. I can certainly understand why you're angry. What would you like me to do to make things right?" The customer could ask for a refund, or may wish to keep the book at a reduced price (one that is fair for a second printing of the work). By seeking resolution, you refocus the customer's attention to the solution rather than the problem. It also provides the customer with a strong signal that you're really on his or her side.

The "O" in the LARSON technique stands for your **offer** of a sincere apology for a situation that should not have occurred. Saying "I'm sorry" may sound trite, but to a customer who has been offended by something your organization said or did, those words are like sweet music. Had our little store misrepresented a book, we would have sincerely apologized and offered a special customer discount certificate (50 percent off the next purchase) as evidence of our sorrow over the matter and as a token of our appreciation for the customer.

The final step in the LARSON technique is to resolve the situation by taking action **now.** Be sure that your employees have the authority to properly handle customer problems and complaints. From your customer's standpoint, there's nothing worse than to fully explain the nature of a grievance to a company representative only to be told, "I'm sorry, but you'll just have to come back tomorrow when the owner will be here." Solving problems immediately is an important key to exceptional customer service.

THE 30-SECOND RECAP

- Angry customers deserve to be treated with respect and understanding.
- In dealing with angry customers, your objective is to determine what happened and to fix it in a way that meets the customer's needs.
- Use the LARSON technique to deal with angry customers.
- Make sure that you understand which tactics you should avoid during an encounter with an angry customer.
- Follow up with the customer after the problem has been solved to ensure that he or she is satisfied.

Glossary

360-degree feedback A performance appraisal system that elicits input from an employee's boss, peers, and subordinates.

acronym A word formed from the first letters of words in a phrase, such as *RADAR* (radio detecting and ranging).

acquisition The process of one company taking over another.

action plan The set of steps you plan to take to achieve some specified goal. The steps should follow one another in sequential order, and proceed logically to establishing the goal.

active listening An interview technique, with origins in the field of psychotherapy, that helps assure candidates that the interviewer is listening to them intently. Active listening involves encouraging candidates to talk openly and freely by often reflecting back to them the meaning of their communication, both verbal and nonverbal, in ways that promote further exploration and awareness.

active voice When the subject is doing the acting.

activity-based costing The process of assigning costs to the various activities involved in offering a product or service to your customers.

adrenaline A hormone secreted by the adrenal glands that acts as a powerful stimulant in times of stress.

aerobic In the presence of oxygen.

affiliating Associating yourself with others of the same interests or goals.

agenda A list of things to be considered, decided, acted on, or an underlying idea or plan.

alarm response The initial recognition of a threat or demand; the first stage of the stress response.

analogy Implies to a listener that if two things agree in one respect, they are likely to agree in several others.

analytical approach Overcoming challenges by chunking them down into divisible elements to better comprehend each element and ultimately resolve the issue in contrast to the systems approach.

anecdote A story used to illustrate a particular point.

aromatherapist A professional using essential oils and herbs to treat clients' specific health and stress-related conditions.

aromatherapy Use of essential oils and herbs to treat specific health and stress-related conditions.

asynchronous A type of digital communication in which there is no timing requirement for transmission. An asynchronous classroom or meeting is one in which participants communicate electronically as time is available, and the communications are shared with other participants for response.

audio book   A voice recording of a book onto cassette tape.

autoresponder   A program that receives e-mail. It reads the e-mail address of the sender and automatically e-mails your reply. It's useful for contact management and marketing.

backup system   An established procedure whereby you help to reinforce established goals.

being organized   Arranging one's possessions, time, or life so as to remain comfortably in control.

bench strength   A reference to a team's depth of talent; if a member is ill or injured, a substitute can take over her or his role with no reduction in the team's performance. The term comes from sports, but is equally applicable to any organization with highly differentiated functions.

benchmark   A measure of performance against a specification or schedule. Most projects have performance, schedule, and cost benchmarks that are checked during the course of the project in order to ensure that completion is timely, accurate, and within budget.

benchmarking   An ongoing process of investigating and studying specific practices that produce exceptional results. Often the task of benchmarking involves the careful examination of a competitor's practices.

body language   The use of gestures, mannerisms, and movements to communicate, either alone or accompanying speech. It includes posture, facial expressions, hand movements, and repetitive motions such as toe tapping, muscle tightening, and eye blinking. The formal study of the relationship between these movements and communication is called kinesics.

bots   Software enabling you to automatically extract and receive information gathered from the Web based on your parameters or specifications.

burnout   A specific type of stress that involves diminished personal accomplishment, depersonalization, and emotional exhaustion.

buzzwords   Insider terminology, used within certain corporate cultures.

cardiovascular   Pertaining to the heart and blood vessels.

carrier oils   Odorless extracts from plants used to dilute essential oils.

cellular intelligence   The ability of the body to respond to stimulus in the immediate environment down to the cellular level.

central message   The main point of your presentation.

chakra   A concentration of energy in the human body, located along the spinal cord to the top of the head.

change hardy   Conditioned to embrace change because human nature is change resistant. Change-hardy organizations are proactive in their quest for organizational effectiveness, and build in rewards for responsible risk-taking. The speed of change in the twenty-first-century economic environment is forcing most organizations to become change hardy to survive.

charisma   An almost intangible quality that inspires loyalty and great results from subordinates.

chevron   An object or pattern having the shape of a V or inverted V. It refers to an inverted V seating configuration facing the facilitator or speaker.

chronic stress   Long-term, unrelenting, potentially health- or life-threatening stress that often is unrecognized by the victim. Continuous and unremitting demands on an organism to change.

close-ended question   A question for which there is only one correct answer or a brief one- or two-word response.

clutter   An unorganized accumulation of items the collective value of which is suspect.

cognitive dissonance   A condition that arises when there's a conflict between one's perception of oneself and the way the world perceives one.

collaborate   To labor together, particularly on an intellectual endeavor, with others who may have different insights or even opposing points of view, to arrive at a common goal.

communication   The ability to transmit information, thoughts, and ideas so that they are satisfactorily understood by a listener or listeners.

communication triggers   Deadlines, events, or results that cause you and your employee to get together to discuss performance.

compensation   A payment or remuneration.

compromise   A settlement in which both sides make concessions, or a solution that is midway between two alternatives.

computer-mediated communication   Any type of communication in which a computer is utilized, including electronic organizers, e-mail, groupware such as Lotus Notes, and proprietary software systems accessible over the Internet.

conflict management   Strategies for the resolution of sharp disagreements, of interests or ideas, or emotional disturbances.

consensus   The unanimity that results when all members of a team, after deliberating on every viable alternative, agree upon a specific course of action. Even though each member may not prefer the course of action, each supports it.

construct   A concept, model, or idea that is used to accomplish a specific business purpose.

consultant   An expert who gives professional advice or services.

contingency plan   A backup course of action in the event that the originally proposed course of action encounters significant barriers or roadblocks.

continuous improvement   The goal of becoming better at what we do every day of our lives.

corporate culture   The average and accepted behavior, atmosphere, values, attitudes, dress, business practices, and philosophy in a given organization. Even if you aren't working for a large corporation, you'll recognize that cultures exist wherever people work together in teams.

cost-benefit analysis   A measure of expected expense compared to expected benefit that takes into account financial costs and intangible costs, underlying assumptions, the time value of money, and the financial and nonfinancial benefits of a given action.

creativity   Using your imagination to innovate or create something that is not an imitation of anything else.

critical path   A plan to undertake a group of specific steps in specific time frames to reach a desired outcome. It is the educated "best guess" of the successful route through a complex project.

critical reasoning   The ability to think logically and undertake causal analysis. Because of the likelihood of multiple causation, it is also the ability to sort out principal causes from contingent causes and symptoms.

critical task   A single task along a critical path.

cultural identity   The customary beliefs, social structures, and attitudes to which individuals subscribe by virtue of their self-defined racial, ethnic, religious, or social group.

culture   The lifestyle and prevailing beliefs of a population within a political unit, such as a community, organization, state, or nation or within an association, cyber community, or other method of affiliation.

current performance   The result you're getting today.

customer   Any person or group who receives the work output (product or service) of another.

customer-centered vision   A clear picture of how your business will serve the needs of customers in the future. According to Richard Whiteley of the Forum Corporation, a customer-centered vision is a vivid picture of an ambitious, desirable future state that is connected to the customer and is better in some important way than the current state.

customer-focused measurement   The comparison of customer expectations with actual performance by the company. For example, if customers expect deliveries within

24 hours of purchase, a customer-focused measurement should be used to determine how often that expectation is being met.

customer-focused standards   The internal regulations that govern how a job is to be done. Customer-focused standards are composed of *transactional standards,* which deal with customer interaction, and *outcome standards,* which focus on outcomes. *See also* transactional standards; outcome standards.

customer satisfaction   A survey construct comparing what actually takes place in a given situation with what a customer thought would happen. Typical customer responses include comments such as, "What I received was not what I expected to receive"; "I can always count on your company to do what's right"; "I was expecting the same service I've always received but didn't get it"; or "Your product didn't do for me what your advertisements said it would." The purpose of the construct is to determine whether your product or service met your customer's expectations.

customer service   Meeting the needs and expectations of the customer as defined by the customer.

cycle time   The amount of time needed to complete an activity.

dangling modifier   A word (or phrase) that appears to modify an inappropriate word in the same sentence.

date stamping   The process of fixing a date to items as they arrive, and preferably before they are filed.

decision teams   Teams that function primarily to make decisions. An example would be a committee that is formed to review flex time policies at a company.

default   A selection automatically used by a computer program if the user makes no specific choice.

deferred profit-sharing plans Plans that enable employees to make payments into a tax-deferred fund. As long as the employee does not withdraw any funds, he or she does not pay taxes on the income.

delegate   To assign authority or responsibility to another person.

delegation   The act of sharing tasks and authority with the team in order to more effectively and quickly accomplish goals—for example, breaking a job down into simpler parts and assigning those parts to different people in your group.

deliverables   Something of value generated by a project management team as scheduled, to be offered to an authorizing party, a reviewing committee, client constituent, or other concerned party, often taking the form of a plan, report, prescript procedure, product, or service.

democratic leadership   A democratic leader strives to make sure the group is well informed and participating in the direction of the team as a whole.

dependent task   A task or subtask that cannot be initiated until a predecessor task or several predecessor tasks are finished.

destination management company A company that specializes in planning events for clients traveling to their locale. These organizations have extensive knowledge of local attractions and facilities, and experience in tailoring an event for your group that you or your conference planner cannot buy "off the shelf."

development plan   This is a detailed approach designed to help an employee develop new skills.

devil's advocate   A role taken on to champion and critically examine the evidence for a minority or unpopular point of view or course of action.

dialogue question   An open-ended question that encourages listeners to share their experiences, attitudes, or feelings on a subject.

diaphragm   A muscular partition between the chest and the abdominal cavities.

diaphragmatic breathing Breathing from the partition at the base of your lung cavity. As the diaphragm expands and contracts, it creates a vacuum effect, using force from the middle abdomen to draw air into the lungs. Expanding and contracting the diaphragm, rather than lifting the shoulders and chest cavity, to breathe deeply.

dictator   A leader who expects individuals to perform commands without questioning authority.

discipline   The act of gaining control by enforcing order.

disclosure agreements   Legally binding instruments between an employer and an employee who is leaving the organization. The agreement purposely limits what can later be disclosed to prospective employers.

distance learning   Any structured learning that takes advantage of communication media, such as computers and videotapes, to allow learners to study in a remote location but under the guidance of an instructor or educational institution.

document management   The system of converting and organizing paper-based information to make it accessible via the Web and corporate intranets. This process may include optical character recognition software (OCR).

domination   The exercise of a controlling influence over others in a meeting. It is behavior based on assumed power, not superior ideas.

downsizings   Significant reductions in a company's workforce designed to cut costs.

DSL   Digital subscriber line. An Internet connection that allows high-speed access over existing copper telephone wires from a switching station to your home or office.

dummy task   A link that shows an association or relationship between two otherwise parallel tasks along a PERT/CPM network.

EAP   Employee assistance program. A program offered in the work place that helps identify and resolve personal or other problems that can affect employee job performance.

e-commerce   The buying or selling of anything online through the use of the Internet.

effective business document   One that truthfully conveys all the important information on a subject in a way that convinces the reader to do what you'd like him to do.

efficacy   The power to produce an unquestionable, decisive, or desired effect, without waste, delay, or unnecessary cost.

elicit   Encourage, attract, and make part of.

emotional agreement   A level of agreement in which the agreeing party is inspired to act.

empathy   The ability to put yourself in someone else's shoes and feel what he or she does.

employee retention   Keeping good employees from defecting to the competition by providing a satisfying environment. Employee retention is an integrated process, not a series of isolated events or programs. The process of retention begins with recruitment and is embedded in employment policy and practice throughout the employee's career.

energy   An enthusiasm and passion for your central message.

environment   One's surroundings; in the context of the workaday world, one's office and surrounding offices and, in general, one's work place.

equity   The state or condition of being just, impartial, and fair.

ergonomics   The science of designing and arranging things that people use for safe and efficient interaction. Also known as human engineering.

essential oils   Liquid, concentrated extractions from flowers, fruits, trees, herbs, and resins used for therapeutic purposes. Derived exclusively from the plant; not diluted or mixed with another substance.

evidence   Data that either proves or disproves a viewpoint, like the material presented in a court of law to prove a person's innocence or guilt.

eustress   Beneficial stress that enables you to function more effectively, maintain concentration, strive to meet challenges, or seek thrills or excitement.

excellence in customer service   A way of doing business that requires going beyond the call of duty, stretching perceived limits, and empowering everyone in the organization to be responsible for maintaining the highest standards, paying attention to details, and going the extra mile.

exhaustion   A state in which the body's resources have been used up, tired out, or completely emptied or drained, and the body is no longer capable of remaining alert.

expectancy theory   A theory that states that people perform tasks in expectation of success.

experiential learning   Learning that takes place through observation of or participation in an event. Observation and participation are powerful because they demonstrate rather than tell whatever point a presenter is trying to make. To see a chemical reaction is more credible than to read about what *should* occur.

extrinsic motivations   Motivations that lie outside of oneself, such as financial or career rewards.

facilitation   The act of making easier or helping to bring about a desired outcome. In a meeting, it includes helping all participants to contribute, handling problems, making sure that group dynamics remain positive, and pacing. It is seeking information and participation to reach an optimal outcome.

facilitator   The person charged with forwarding the action in regard to a particular event.

FAQ   A frequently asked question. Most Web sites have FAQ pages to answer common questions in text form.

FCC   The Federal Communications Commission. An independent U.S. government agency that regulates interstate and international communications.

feedback   Communication to individuals and groups that specifies whether a job is good or bad. Positive feedback reinforces valued behaviors, whereas negative feedback can help to change an individual's performance.

feng shui   Means "wind and water" in Chinese; the ancient study of the natural environment. Placement of objects in a person's surroundings is believed to have a positive impact on the energy in that person's life.

fight-or-flight response   Automatic response to stimuli, real or perceived, that enables the human body to deal with a threatening situation. Mobilization of an organism's resources to deal with a threat or challenge physically, or to run away from a threat or challenge.

financial statements   Balance sheets, income statements, and cash flow statements.

fishbowl discussion   A type of discussion during which one subgroup in the discussion is observed by one or more other subgroups, as when you observe fish through their tank. Fishbowl discussions can also be set up with a circle within a circle, with a rectangular or square table (one side of the table conducts a discussion), or at groups of small tables.

flat organizations   Companies that have fewer than four layers of management.

flex time   A work-scheduling system that typically mandates some core hours all employees must work;

it also requires that the same total number of hours be worked by each employee. However, flex time allows employees to choose their own start and finish times.

flow   The ease with which the reader can move from one statement to the next. In a document that flows well, each statement follows logically from the previous one, and each subsequent statement is the one the reader expects to see, based on what he's already read.

free-associate   To report the first thought that comes to mind in response to a stimulus, without pausing to consider the value of the idea.

frontline employees   Those who deal directly with the end customer—the purchaser of the product or service.

full path   The charted route on a critical path diagram for a project from the first task to the final outcome.

functional skills   Skills that help people function effectively on the job, such as communication, listening, flexibility, and leadership.

fund-raiser   A social event held for the specific purpose of raising money.

FY   Fiscal year; a 12-month accounting period.

Gantt chart   A linear, visual tool for measuring progress made in pursuit of various activities over the course of time.

gender bias   Prejudice or discrimination against a person based solely on the fact that the person is of a different gender.

goal   Specific metrics you set for your group to accomplish. Goals benefit an organization in two ways by giving you a way to measure performance and by creating a realistic, simpler way to accomplish large tasks.

goal-directed activity   The tasks you perform in the expectation of reaching a goal.

goal-fulfillment   The attaining of a goal.

green flags   Specific items in the resume of an applicant that clearly demonstrate positive achievement, especially in areas involving identified mandatory success factors.

grievance   A formal complaint which is filed by a union employee, and supported by the union, against the employer.

group dynamics   The behavior of individuals in small groups, and the scientific study of this behavior and underlying personality, attitudes, and motivation in order to learn more about the nature of groups, how they develop, and what happens in them. It is part of the larger field of social psychology.

groupthink   A pattern of thinking that stifles critical reasoning and leads to artificial consensus. It is caused by conformity to group or organizational values and is characterized by self-deception and subconscious suppression of dissenting views.

growing a staff   The time and effort used to educate, improve, and empower your team.

guided imagery   The intensified use of visualization techniques to achieve a long-range goal.

guided meditation   A supervised form of contemplation or reflection in which a trained leader talks a group through the process of emptying the mind of all thoughts and feelings, and relaxing.

gung ho   A Chinese term meaning "work together." The term was first adopted by U.S. Marines in the 1940s.

habit   A pattern of behavior acquired by repetition. Psychologists and behavior experts say that it takes about 20 to 70 days to form a new habit.

holistic   The organic or functional relations between the part and the whole.

horizontal organizations   Organizations with equally shared responsibilities rather than a hierarchy in which most power is concentrated in a few individuals at the top. Also called flat organizations.

hotelling   The practice of maintaining cubicles or offices for rotating employees. *See also* virtual office.

hypothesis   An interpretation of an event that leads to an action, or a tentative assumption or theory made in order to examine or test its logical or real-world outcomes.

hypothetical   Situations that are imaginary. Hypothetical interview questions attempt to discover how a candidate would act if a certain situation were to occur; both the question and the response are purely conjecture.

ice-breaker   A group exercise whose sole purpose is to engage every participant in the meeting. It may include introducing newcomers or soliciting previously unknown information about participants; it has the flavor of a game rather than an agenda item. An icebreaker must be fun.

incent   To motivate someone to achieve a desired outcome. Managers may devise bonus plans tied to market penetration, sales targets, project deadlines, product performance, financial targets, or recruitment goals, for example.

independent clause   A group of words that can stand alone as a complete sentence.

inequity   An imbalance or lack of justice.

institutional memory   The cumulative, retrievable, collective knowledge possessed by an organization about its history, processes, products, business practices, markets, and competitors. Organizations are said to have no institutional memory when such knowledge resides in the brain of only one employee, and is lost when that individual leaves the organization.

interdependence   The quality or state of reciprocal and equal reliance on another. It suggests trust, as opposed to enmeshment, which means an unhealthy entanglement, a state of being trapped. Interdependence is walking hand in hand; enmeshment is walking bound to someone with handcuffs.

Internet   The Internet (also known as the World Wide Web) is a technology that allows people and companies throughout the world to connect with one another using their computers.

interpersonal skills   "People skills." These are particularly important to consider when interviewing people for frontline positions. Good interpersonal skills include the ability to respect others, to be empathetic and caring, to listen attentively and respond accordingly, and to maintain objectivity and refrain from emotionalism.

intranet   This is a network technology similar to the Internet that has been constructed by a company for its own benefit. Usually access to a company's intranet is limited to its employees, customers, and vendors.

intrinsic motivations   Interior motivations, including personal challenge and involvement.

introspective investigation   The process by which an organization thoroughly examines a position to be filled. The goal of introspective investigation is to identify essential competencies, skills, and abilities that are required for successful performance.

intuitive listening   Being sensitive to what *is* said and what *is not* said. It is the message conveyed by a hesitation, a reluctance to discuss a matter, or the obvious desire to change the subject.

job sharing   A team approach to work. Job sharing allows two people to split the responsibilities of a single job so that, with each working part-time, they complete a full-time job.

job stress   The physical and emotional response to harmful working conditions, including circumstances in which the job requirements exceed the capabilities, resources, or needs of the worker.

just-in-time inventory   This is a system designed to bring in only those materials needed for the current day's production. This allows the company to minimize its storage and handling costs.

key employee   An employee who provides a service that will not be performed as easily or as well when that person is absent.

law of diminishing returns   States that beyond a certain point, additional investment will not produce proportionate results. In meetings, participants cannot absorb information or problem-solve at the same rate in hour seven as they could in the first hour.

law of unintended consequences
States that undesired and unforeseen outcomes will follow actions designed to produce a desirable result, and not all of those consequences can be avoided.

lead time   The amount of advance notice required to obtain something or complete some action. For equipment and staff, it may be determined by departmental or organizational policy; for purchases, a vendor may charge you air freight to shorten the wait.

leader   A charismatic person who is able to make good decisions and inspire others to reach a common goal.

leadership   Having a vision for what you'd like to happen, and setting in motion the events that will realize your vision. It doesn't mean you must necessarily command the forces that execute the plan—merely that you guide the thinking that eventually causes the plan to be executed.

learning style   Individual differences in understanding information based on its method of transmission. Some people can easily grasp concepts by reading about them or hearing a speaker talk about them; others need visual representations; and still others need to act them out through practice exercises.

Likert scale   A numerical ranking where 1 is the lowest ranking and 5 or 10 is the highest ranking of a particular activity. It is used to quantify participants' level of satisfaction and to compare the effectiveness of group facilitators or presenters.

lip service   An avowal of belief, advocacy, or compliance, contradicted by actions; a false promise.

logical agreement   The acceptance of the rationale behind your idea by another person.

maintenance factors   Things about a business that contribute to a healthy business climate, but that do not cause it. For example, a clean lunchroom may not motivate good performance, but if it's not clean, people will complain about it. In that sense, cleaning the lunchroom becomes a maintenance factor.

management   Specific organizational functions such as budgeting and producing a product. Leadership is a part of management.

management by objective   A tool for directing a business; it is especially effective in supervising and measuring the performance of employees, based upon setting targets for business activities or professional development, allocating resources to efforts that further the objectives, and assessing the degree to which they are achieved. A behavior-based system of joint goal-setting by supervisors and employees; introduced by Peter Drucker in the 1950s.

management information system (MIS)   Any methodical compilation of data providing information that can assist in decision-making. Today it refers to computerized systems that have replaced manual and paper record-keeping systems in all but the smallest organizations.

mandatory success factors   Those specific competencies and skills that have been identified to be absolutely essential to successful job performance. Mandatory success factors are determined through a process of introspective investigation and provide a profile of the job as well as the ideal candidate.

manipulation   The ability to skillfully and subtly manage something or someone to one's own advantage or the advantage of an organization. The word *manipulate* most often has a negative connotation.

mantra   A sacred word or phrase repeated in the course of meditation as a means to focus.

mapping   The act of recording the ideas of the group in a visual, non-linear format such as a diagram, that fosters creativity and aids visual thinkers who can draw what they know but may be less able to articulate it in words.

market share   One company's percentage of the total sales of a given product or industry. For example, Kellogg's has a large *market share* of the breakfast cereal sold in the United States.

Maslow's Hierarchy of Needs A theory stating that human beings have an innate order, or hierarchy, for the things they want. When one

level of this hierarchy is satisfied, they move on to the next.

mass customization   This is the process of customizing your product or service to meet the individual customer's needs while serving thousands of customers every day.

massage therapist   A professional who is trained and skilled in kneading and rubbing parts of the body to promote circulation and relaxation.

master people developer Someone who is expert at helping others develop their skills and improve their performance.

mean   In a numerical sequence, the number that has an equal number of values before and after it. In the sequence 3, 5, 7, 9, 11, 7 is the mean.

meaning of the message   How the central message is relevant to the listeners and what they are likely to get out of it.

meditation   Quieting the conscious mind and allowing it to roam freely without intentional direction. Or, allowing the mind to focus on a single thought or sound; intended to provide mental rest and enlightenment.

memo   Short for memorandum; any written interoffice communication, including most e-mail correspondence. The most common memos are recommendations and summaries.

memorialize   To summarize, record, and communicate the events of the meeting, the action steps assigned, and the next steps planned. This is a vital role in building institutional memory, so that the history of a decision process does not depend on individual memory or leave the organization.

mentor   Usually a person of higher rank or standing in an organization who takes a particular interest in helping to nurture, teach, and guide a promising employee.

merger   This occurs when two companies combine operations to form one company.

metaphor   A figure of speech that compares two objects not ordinarily associated with each other in order to put the first in context.

mettle   Value or worthiness, particularly when tested by challenging conditions.

micro culture   A culture within a department, division, branch or project team or within an entire corporation itself.

micromanagement   A managerial style in which the manager controls minute details of the effort.

microsleep   A 10- to 15-second indiscernible sleep episode in the middle of the day.

milestone   A significant event or juncture in the project.

mindfulness   The practice of focusing on the positive in all aspects of life.

mind-mapping   A process of brainstorming ideas related to your central message and graphically displaying them so you can decide which ones are relevant and important.

mission critical   Anything that is so important to an undertaking that the desired activity cannot occur without it. For a simple example, you cannot make coffee without both coffee and water, so both are critical to the mission of having a morning cup of java.

mission statement   A brief written statement summarizing the overarching business philosophy and ultimate goal of your organization.

modeling   Setting an example, worthy of imitation, for others to follow. This example can be a pattern, process, style of behavior, or even a positive attitude.

moment of truth   A customer service term created by Jan Carlzon of Scandinavian Airlines. According to Carlzon, "A moment of truth is an episode in which a customer comes in contact with any aspect of the company, however remote, and thereby has an opportunity to form an impression."

motivating stress   Stress that stimulates and challenges you, as opposed to preventing you from accomplishing tasks.

motivation   An incentive, an inducement, or a stimulus for action. A motivation is anything—verbal, physical, or psychological—that causes somebody to do something in response.

Murphy's Law   The age-old axiom stating that if something can go wrong, it will go wrong.

need-to-know   A designation of whether or not to share information with an individual in order to obtain an expected outcome. Restricting information dissemination on this basis assures both security and confidentiality of sensitive information, and reduces the amount of information received by someone who won't be acting on it.

negligence   The failure to exercise a reasonable amount of care, which results in injury or damage to another.

network   A group of computers and associated devices connected by communications facilities for the purpose of exchanging services or information among groups, individuals, or associations.

neurotransmitters   Chemical messengers that trigger the brain to dispatch information that controls brain-wave activity and patterns, blood pressure, breathing, heart rate, glandular activity, hormonal production, and—you guessed it—stress levels.

neutralizing a question
Removing pejorative terms so you can deal with the question the way you want to.

noncritical task   A task within a CPM network for which slack time is available.

nonverbal communication
Conveying a message or idea without using words—for instance, through facial expressions, gestures, stance, or appearance. Also called *body language.*

objective   A desired outcome; something worth striving for; the overarching goal of a project; the reason the project was initiated to begin with.

open behavioral questions
Questions that cannot be answered with a simple "yes" or "no." They require a candidate to discuss at length a specific incident from the past that required a working knowledge of specific skills.

open questions   Those that cannot be answered with a simple "yes" or "no." They often begin with phrases like "Tell me about …" or "Describe what happened when …." The purpose of open questions is to encourage the customer to talk freely so that you can obtain the information you need to solve his or her problem.

opportunity cost   The cost of making an investment that is the difference between the return on one investment (participating in a weeklong sales conference) and the return on an alternative (making 20 more sales calls that month). The opportunity cost is the sales lost due to fewer sales calls.

optimize   To find a method to make a system, design, or a decision as flawless, effective, or productive as possible under implied or specified conditions. To optimize seating for a meeting is to create the most favorable positioning for positive interaction.

organizational culture   The set of shared values, goals, practices, and management styles that characterize an organization and are expected to be reflected in its public face and its members' behavior.

organizational innovation
Planned efforts by groups of people to develop and implement new ideas.

organize   To arrange something or things into a united whole through systematic planning and effort.

outcome standards   Customer-focused standards that deal with on outcomes: "The customer complaint can be considered resolved only when ..." or "Twenty-four-hour delivery means that our product is actually in the hands of the customer within 24 hours." *See also* customer-focused standards.

outsource   To contract for services rather than have employees perform the work.

outsourced task or **function**   A task or function that an organization has determined can be done better, faster, or cheaper by an outside provider and therefore contracts to have done off-site. Commonly outsourced functions or parts of functions include telemarketing, auto parts manufacturing, benefits administration, and conference planning.

overpacking   Taking more items than necessary while traveling; toting extra baggage that overburdens you and consumes more time and energy to handle.

parallel tasks   Two or more tasks that can be undertaken at the same time. This doesn't imply that they have the same starting and ending times.

Pareto's Principle   An observation about the relationship between inputs and outputs, essentially that 80 percent of one's effectiveness is derived from 20 percent of one's activities.

Parkinson's Law   "Work expands so as to fill the time allotted for its completion."

participation   The act of allowing group members to take part in decision-making, as seen in the "almost" democracy and the partnership styles of leadership.

participative management   A process in which managers and employees work together as peers to produce exceptional products and services that exceed customer expectations.

partnership   A style of leadership that blurs the line between leader and subordinate, requiring the leader to become just one of the group.

passive voice   When the subject is being acted upon.

path   A chronological sequence of tasks, each dependent on predecessors.

PDA   Personal digital assistant. Pocket-sized devices that allow access to the Web, your calendars, and contact information.

perceived quality   Another construct used in customer service surveys. Perceived quality is an attempt to compare the customer's perception of what happened with what the customer feels should ideally have happened. Customers articulate perceived quality with such statements as, "Ideally, you should have ..."; "When I booked my meeting at your five-star hotel, I expected ..."; or "I expected more from a company that is considered the best in the business." The purpose of such a construct is to determine whether your product or service meets the ideal expectation of your customer.

perfectionism   The need to be in control of situations; fear of making mistakes and looking like a failure.

performance anxiety   That natural uneasiness we feel before performing any difficult task in front of other people.

performance appraisal   The process of identifying, observing, measuring, and developing human performance in organizations. Performance appraisal was introduced in a study by Carroll and Schneir in the 1980s.

performance reviews   Part of performance appraisal.

personal digital assistants   *See* PDA.

Personal information manager   *See* PIM.

PFM   Personal finance manager software, such as Quicken or Microsoft Money.

physiological   Consistent with an organism's normal or expected functioning.

physiological stress   Demands on bodily systems.

physiology   The science that deals with processes and functions of living organisms.

PIM   Personal information manager. A software application that enables you to enter dates, lists, and reminders. Most also include scheduling, calendars, and calculators.

politics   The relationship of two or more people with one another, including the degree of power and influence that the parties have over one another.

positive talk   Speaking in terms of success before actually achieving a given success will help your team achieve a particular goal.

positive thought   Visualizing a success to help take the right actions to achieve the desired outcome.

postoffer stage   The stage of the selection process when a conditional offer of employment has been extended to an applicant. Conditional offers are made when present employers have yet to be contacted, or when the offer is subject to the applicant passing a medical examination.

precedence   If the completion of one event has priority over another, then that event has precedence over the other.

predecessor task   A task that must be completed before another task can commence.

preoffer stage   The stage of the selection process before an employer extends a conditional offer of employment to a candidate.

prereader   Someone who serves as an information scout for another, paring down voluminous reading materials to their essence.

presentation deck   The written form of a presentation—the "deck" of pages that you show your audience as you go through your presentation. A page of a deck is sometimes called a *slide*.

prevention-based management
The supervision and control of systems and processes that have been designed to prevent customer dissatisfaction and to eliminate the need for recovery. Prevention-based management is proactive and attempts to identify problems before they affect customer perception.

priorities   The things that are most important to you.

priority list   A simple roster, preferably easy to access, that names a handful of things in life important to you.

proactive   Making choices and determining your own attitude, as opposed to being *reactive* and letting circumstances control you.

proactive problem-solving
Anticipating problems and obstacles associated with a particular task and solving them before they're actually encountered.

probe   A question or request that seeks specific information, clarification, or confirmation from a candidate being interviewed. Probes may be open or closed, depending on the intended purpose.

process check   An evaluation of a series of actions or operations conducive to a particular end. It is often done at the end of a meeting, when participants' experiences are fresh.

process mapping   A method used to examine the effectiveness of the approach currently used in completing a task.

process owners   Employees, or groups of employees, who are responsible for a specific aspect of the finished product or service of an organization.

procrastinate   To put off doing a task, to delay an activity or task, or to ignore something that demands your attention.

project constraint   A critical project element such as money, time, or human resources, which frequently turns out to be in short supply.

project director   The individual to whom a project manager reports. Project directors maintain a big-picture focus and not a day-to-day focus on project activities on par with the project manager. Project directors may have several project managers reporting to them and hence require a series of briefings at specified intervals.

project environment   The political, legal, technical, social, economic, and cultural backdrop within which a project team operates.

project manager   An individual who has responsibilities for overseeing all aspects of the day-to-day activities in pursuit of a project, including coordinating staff, allocating resources, managing the budget, and coordinating overall efforts to achieve a specific, desired result.

project tracking   A system for identifying and documenting progress performance for effective review and dissemination to others.

protégé   The person being mentored (*see* mentor).

protocols   Rules of etiquette, convention, and procedure that may be unique to a type of meeting, the nature of an exercise, a branch of diplomatic or military service, or a culture. In a meeting setting, participants are expected to agree to these rules for the good of the meeting.

quality of service   A term that refers to the customer's perception of the service that a company provides. It is a perception that is re-evaluated by the customer with each succeeding contact, regardless of where in the company those future contacts occur, from the executive level to the loading dock.

quiet time   An interval during the day in which you are not subjected to noise.

RAM   Random access memory. This is the temporary storage area that allows the data to be fed to the computer processor at high speeds. The more RAM, the faster the applications can move.

rationale point   One specific reason why accepting your proposal makes sound business sense.

reasonable accommodation   The legal requirement that employers find ways to provide equal opportunity to protected classes of employees, including those with disabilities and those who require special accommodations for religious practices. It may even include the possibility of transferring the employee to another job if that becomes necessary to accommodate the religious needs of the employee.

recovery   A customer service term that means correcting a perceived performance problem. Recovery involves a process of quickly satisfying a customer who is ready to defect to the competition. It is a skill that requires the ability to see a situation through the customer's eyes and to resolve the problem with empathy, sensitivity, and good judgment.

recruiting   The process of locating, evaluating, and hiring new employees.

red flags   Those factors in a resume that indicate danger and require further exploration with the applicant, or that support rejection of the resume from further consideration.

reflective listening   The act of confirming what was said. It is the "playback" mode of interaction, in the words of the listener rather than the speaker.

reframe   To express an idea or convey information in a different way. It involves restating it at more length, in fewer words, in less complex language, or using examples, metaphors, or analogies in an attempt to bridge the gap between a speaker's meaning and a listener's comprehension.

reinforcement   Strengthening by providing additional assistance, information, or support. In an army, reinforcements are fresh or additional troops. In a presentation, they're ideas, arguments, and hypotheses that need to be supported in order to be heard, understood, and retained.

relaxation response   An organism's return to a state of low arousal, analogous to turning off the stress response.

reliability   Refers to the consistency of scores and measurement that is free of error.

remote access program   A program that enables you to connect to the office computer from your laptop. You can transfer and copy files and run applications.

resources   The money, materials, or people needed to advance your business objectives.

respiratory system   Your lungs, bronchi, trachea, and nasal passages.

return on average capital employed   A financial ratio that compares profits generated to assets employed. The ratio is often adjusted to reflect that some of the assets are financed by non interest-bearing debt.

reward   Valued performance is recognized and reinforced with a reward. Rewards can be verbal, monetary, or in the form of a promotion.

rework   The process of redoing a task to correct an error.

risk   The degree to which a project or portions of a project are in jeopardy of not being completed on time and on budget, and, most important, the probability that the desired outcome will not be achieved.

role play   The simulation of a real situation that puts people in the position of acting out an interaction; for example, trying out a sales closing technique on a resistant client.

sabbatical   A leave, without pay, for research, travel, or rest. Traditionally, sabbaticals are granted every seventh year to professors at universities and colleges.

saboteur   Someone inside a group or organization who engages in intentional destructive or obstructive behavior in order to undermine a collaborative effort. This behavior may not be overt or visible to others in the group.

sandwich generation   People in their 50s and 60s who find themselves caring for three generations: themselves, their children, and their parents.

scanning   Reviewing any lists, charts, or exhibits in a book; reviewing the index, the table of contents, some of the chapter leads, and an occasional paragraph. A method of eye contact in which the speaker's eyes are continually moving from one person to another.

scheduling tools   Palmtop organizers, electronic calendars, time management software, day planners, and any other device that supports one's use of time and productivity.

scope of work   The level of activity and effort necessary to complete a project and achieve the desired outcome as measured by staff hours, staff days, resources consumed, and funds spent.

scripted event   An event for which a carefully prepared dialogue has been written, as in the script of a play that is followed precisely in a production.

schedule   A planned sequence of events.

scheduling tools   Project management software, organizers, electronic calendars, time management software, day planners, and any other device that supports one's use of time and productivity.

seasonality   Varying in occurrence according to the season. In business, this refers to sales or production volume and may not correlate to a calendar season: A new swimsuit line is shown to store buyers, ordered, and manufactured long before summer.

self-management skills   Personal characteristics that help people do the job successfully. Included are such skills as creativity, honesty, competence, appearance, and helpfulness.

sell-in   The period at the start of a new product introduction in which the product is first sold into the stores that will carry it. Since stores must usually build up an inventory of a new product, the sell-in can be a significant percentage of total sales for a new product introduction.

sensitivity analysis   The act of forecasting what outcome can be expected to occur when one variable in a model is changed but others are held constant. For example, if an airline increases the price of a flight from New York to Los Angeles, what is the expected reduction in seats sold?

service   Any product-based interaction between a customer and a company. Service requires genuine concern for the customer by a representative of the company who is technically capable of offering assistance. Service requires that the company representative possess both the desire and the ability to treat each individual's problem as unique, even though the representative may have dealt with the same problem on countless other occasions.

shadowing   The practice of observing the daily activities of someone performing her or his job, most often when the observer is exploring career alternatives of which she or he has little knowledge.

short list   A list of a few select candidates who have achieved the highest scores in an initial interview and have been chosen for further consideration.

skimming   Reading only the first few sentences of each paragraph within an article in a magazine or on the Web, or in a chapter of a book.

slack   Margin or extra room to accommodate anticipated potential short falls in planning.

slack time   Time interval in which you have leeway as to when a particular task needs to be completed.

sleep debt   The amount of time you add to a typical night's sleep to make up for missed sleep.

Socialization Needs   One of the stages of Abraham Maslow's Hierarchy of Needs; Socialization Needs involve personal fulfillment from social interaction.

soft measurements   Tests and inventories based mostly on self-reporting beliefs and feelings, or past behavior. There are no right or wrong answers.

stage fright   A natural anxiety that most people feel when they get up and speak before a group of listeners.

stakeholder   Those who have a vested interest in having a project succeed. Stakeholders may include the authorizing party, top management, other department and division heads within an organization, other project managers and project management teams, clients, constituents, and parties external to an organization.

storyboard   A collection of sketches similar to panels in a cartoon strip, used by advertising agencies to present the idea of a television commercial to their client prior to actually filming the commercial.

stress   A heightened mental state produced in response to a threat, real or imagined.

stress response   The physiological reaction when an organism is exposed to change; the mobilization of bodily resources and changes in bodily functions that occur when you perceive jeopardy or a threat.

stressor   An undesirable or unpleasant situation to which the body responds with fight-or-flight reactions.

subcontract   An agreement with an outside vendor for specific services, often to alleviate a project management team of a specific task, tasks, or an entire project.

subtask   A slice of a complete task; a divisible unit of a larger task.

Usually, a series of subtasks leads to the completion of a task.

survey construct   The assembled part of a survey designed to obtain specific information from a group of individuals.

synectics   A process using analogy and metaphor to look at things differently, thereby generating novel ideas.

systems approach   A far-reaching cohesive way to approach problems involving varied and interdependent relationships, standing in contrast to the analytical approach.

table (an agenda item)   To postpone the agenda item to another time. This step is taken for lack of information, because a key participant is absent, or because the item has become a source of irresolvable conflict. If this last case is true, the item may be better handled by a subcommittee or individual.

tangible   Something perceivable, but not necessarily physical. It can also mean the physical, practical acts of meeting preparation and to differentiate these acts from those involving interpersonal skills, such as guiding problem-solving or conflict resolution.

task   A piece of work that has been assigned to be completed within a certain time frame.

tchotchke   A Yiddish word that has become a catchall phrase for small gifts or giveaways—such as notepads, pens, or key chains— that companies give to employees or customers.

team   A group of people with a common goal who use the unique strengths of each member and the combined strengths of the group to achieve that goal.

technospeak   Words and phrases that are particularly in vogue within special segments of society but that are not generally understood or recognized by outsiders.

telecommuter   An employee who works from home, often linked to a central office by computer.

telecommuting   The practice of allowing employees to work from their homes, taking advantage of various technologies to connect them to other workers and information; also called telework or flex work.

telegraphic subject line   One that very succinctly conveys the subject and nature of the message.

template   A master slide that creates a design for each of your visual aids.

tent cards   Cards that when folded in half lengthwise and put on a flat surface create an inverted V that looks like a tent. Used to identify speakers on a dais or participants in a meeting and are especially useful in interactive meetings.

theme   In terms of a party, a theme is a subject or topic of discourse or artistic expression.

time and motion studies The attempt to elicit greater productivity from workers by closely examining their workstations, movements, and available resources.

timeline The scheduled start and stop times for a subtask, task, phase, or entire project.

think outside the box To conceptualize or analyze without the constraints of precedent, rules, historical frameworks, and generally accepted assumptions.

topic sentence The first sentence of a paragraph, and states the main point. Additional sentences in the paragraph should support the point made in the topic sentence.

total slack time The cumulative sum of time that various tasks can be delayed without delaying the completion of a project.

trade-offs Options regarding the allocation of scarce resources.

traditional business practices The time-tested, set way of doing things. Young leaders in favor of finding a newer, quicker way of meeting the same goal often ignore traditional business practices.

training An ongoing experience that has three primary objectives: to give employees a basic understanding of their job and a vision of the mission of the company; to provide the skills and tools necessary to perform the tasks of the job correctly and efficiently; and to keep people functioning at high levels throughout their careers.

transactional analysis A theory that states that all interpersonal interactions are basically transactions, each having a stimulus and response.

transactional standards Customer-focused standards that deal with customer interaction and that are often expressed in guidelines, such as "Reassure the customer that the problem will be resolved" or "Be friendly and courteous." *See also* customer-focused standards.

transferable skills Skills learned at one workplace that would be beneficial for gaining employment elsewhere. For example, HTML is the most commonly used language for putting content on sites on the World Wide Web. A skill such as using HTML, which is not proprietary to one company, is a transferable skill.

transformational leader A leader who is capable of bringing about change in individuals and entire organizations, often helping troubled organizations turn around their performance.

triage The process of assigning priority to projects in the order in which resources can be used to provide the best outcome. The term comes from World War I battlefields, where medical teams had to choose which wounded soldiers to treat in order to maximize the number of survivors.

trope The use of a familiar word or expression to express an idea other then the term's usual meaning. For example, "her voice was music to my ears" conveys not that the speaker was singing, but that her speaking voice brought pleasure to the listener.

urgent   That which cries out for attention independent of its importance, typically announcing itself much like a microwave beeping when it's time to take the food out of it.

valet   Traditionally, a personal attendant; hotel/business services that pick up and drop off garments and other personal items.

validity   Refers to the extent that a given test actually measures what it is designed to measure.

value   That combination of quality and price that allows the buyer to feel that she's getting more than she is paying for.

vest   To grant or endow with a particular authority, right, or property.

virtual office   The concept of not having a permanently assigned space in an organization's facility. A virtual office implies an electronic connection to a physical headquarters (albeit the CEO's den) from wherever one works: car, airplane, or hotel. *See also* hotelling.

vision   A leader's ideas and plans for an organization's future. Idealistic in nature, a vision gives a sense of the differences between the present and future states of an organization.

visualization   The practice of forming a mental image to foster a sense of calm and to more readily focus on tasks.

volunteering   Willingly giving of one's time or effort.

vulture capitalist   A venture capitalist who specializes in offering high-interest financing to companies in financial distress (the image is of a bird of prey picking the flesh from the dying), rather than providing financing to start-up ventures.

WBS   *See* work breakdown structure.

window of opportunity   A finite time period during which some action, not possible before or after this period, becomes possible. In a two-hour training meeting, for example, the window of opportunity for direct experiential learning is only two hours, though reinforcement may occur later and the benefit may be permanent.

white noise   Frequencies and amplitudes of a droning, nondisruptive blanket of sound.

work breakdown structure (WBS) Project plans that delineate all the tasks that must be accomplished to successfully complete a project from which scheduling, delegating, and budgeting are derived. A complete depiction of all of the tasks necessary to achieve successful project completion.

work statement   Detailed description of how a particular task or subtask will be completed, including the specific actions necessary, resources required, and the specific outcome to be achieved.

work teams   Teams that coordinate individual efforts on a day-to-day basis to perform tasks; a space shuttle crew is a work team.

yin and yang   The two coexisting forces in the universe—the negative and the positive.

yoga   Means "union," referring to the union of the mind and body.

your life's priorities   That which is most important to you.

Management Resource List

Agnes, Michael, and Andrew N. Sparks. *Webster's New World College Dictionary, Fourth Edition.* Indianapolis: Hungry Minds, Inc., 1999.

Archibald, Russell. *Managing High-Technology Programs and Projects.* New York: Wiley, 1998.

ARMA International Standards Filing Systems Task Force. *Alphabetic Filing Rules, Second Edition.* Kansas: Association of Records Managers, 1995.

Baker, Sonny, and Kim Baker. *On Time—On Budget: A Step-by-Step Guide to Managing Any Project.* Paramus, NJ: Prentice-Hall, 1992.

Balch, James, and Phyllis Balch. *Prescription for Nutritional Healing.* Garden City Park, NY: Avery Publishing Group, 1997.

Barkley, Bruce, and James Saylor. *Customer-Driven Project Management.* New York: McGraw Hill, 1994.

Baugh, L. Sue. *Essentials of English Grammar: A Practical Guide to the Mastery of English, Second Edition.* New York: Passport Books, 1994.

Benson, Dr. Herbert. *The Relaxation Response.* New York: Avon, reissue, 1990.

Bhajan, Yogi, Ph.D., and Gurcharan Singh Khalsa, Ph.D. *Breathwalk: Breathing Your Way to a Revitalized Body, Mind, and Spirit.* New York: Broadway Books, 2000.

Blanchard, Ken, and Sheldon Bowles. *Raving Fans: A Revolutionary Approach to Customer Service.* New York: William Morrow & Co., May 1993.

Blanke, Gail. *In My Wildest Dreams: Living the Life You Long For.* New York: Simon & Schuster, 1998.

Brown, Simon. *Practical Feng Shui for Business.* London: Ward Lock Ltd., May 1999.

Bruce, Debra, and Harris McIlwain. *The Unofficial Guide to Alternative Medicine.* New York: Macmillan General Reference, 1998.

Burns, Robert. *Making Meetings Happen.* Warriewood, NSW, Australia: Business + Publishers, 2000.

Bykofsky, Sheree. *500 Terrific Ideas for Organizing Everything.* New York: Budget Book Service, 1997.

Cathcart, Jim. *The Acorn Principle.* New York: St. Martins Press, 1998.

Cleland, David. *Project Management: Strategic Design and Implementations.* New York: McGraw Hill, 1998.

Clough, Richard, and Glenn Sears. *Construction Project Management.* New York: Wiley, 1991.

Cousens, Gabriel, M.D., with Mark Mayell. *Depression Free for Life.* New York: Morrow, 2000.

Daniels, Aubrey, Ph.D. *Bringing Out the Best in People.* New York: McGraw-Hill, 1994.

Davidson, Jeff. *Breathing Space: Living & Working at a Comfortable Pace in a Sped-up Society.* New York: Mastermedia, 2000.

————. *The Complete Idiot's Guide to Managing Stress.* Indianapolis: Alpha Books, 1999.

————. *The Complete Idiot's Guide to Managing Your Time.* Indianapolis: Alpha Books, 1999.

————. *The Complete Idiot's Guide to Reaching Your Goals.* Indianapolis: Alpha Books, 1998.

————. *Joy of Simple Living.* Emmaus, PA: Rodale Books, 1999.

————. *Market Your Career and Yourself.* Holbook, MA: Adams Media, 1999.

Dawson, Roger. *13 Secrets of Power Performance.* Paramus, NJ: Prentice Hall, 1994.

Delbecq, A. L., A. H. Van de Ven, and D. H. Gustafson. *Group Techniques for Program Planning: A Guide to Nominal Group and Delphi Processes.* Glenview: Scott, Foresman and Company, 1975.

Devi, Nischala. *The Healing Path of Yoga.* New York: Three Rivers Press, 2000.

Dewey, John. *How We Think.* Boston: D.C. Heath & Company, 1910.

Dinsmore, Paul. *The AMA Handbook of Project Management.* New York: Amacon, 1993.

Domar, Alice, Ph.D., and Henry Dreher. *Self-Nurture: Learning to Care for Yourself as Effectively as You Care for Everyone Else.* New York: Viking Press, 1999.

Doyle, Michael, and David Straus. *How to Make Meetings Work.* New York: Jove Books, 1982.

Drucker, Peter, Ph.D. *The Effective Executive.* New York: Harper & Rowe, 1967.

DuBrin, Andrew J. *The Complete Idiot's Guide to Leadership.* Indianapolis: Alpha Books, 1998.

Dyer, Wayne, Ph.D. *Staying on the Path.* Carson, CA: Hay House, 1995.

Farr, Mary. *The Heart of Health: Embracing Life with Your Mind and Spirit.* New York: John Wiley & Sons, 2000.

Faust, Julius. *Body Language.* New York: MJF Books, Fine Communications, 1970.

Felton, Sandra. *Messie's Manual.* Grand Rapids, MI: Fleming A. Drevel, 1983.

Fisher, Roger, William Ury, and Bruce Patton. *Getting to Yes: Negotiating Agreement Without Giving In, Second Edition.* New York: Penguin Books, 1991.

Frame, J. D. *Managing Projects in Organizations.* San Francisco: Jossey-Bass, 1995.

————. *The New Project Management.* San Francisco: Jossey-Bass, 1994.

Fritz, Robert. *Path of Least Resistance.* New York: Ballantine Books, 1989.

Furtwengler, Dale. *Making the Exceptional Normal.* St. Louis: Peregrine Press, November 1997.

Glenmullen, Joseph. *Prozac Backlash: Overcoming the Dangers of Prozac, Zoloft, Paxil, and Other Antidepressants with Safe, Effective Alternatives.* New York: Simon & Schuster, 2000.

Goleman, Daniel. *Emotional Intelligence.* New York: Bantam, 1995.

Gretz, Karl F., and Steven R. Drozdeck. *Empowering Innovative People.* Chicago: Probus Publishing Company, 1992.

Grossman, John. *The Chicago Manual of Style: The Essential Guide for Writers, Editors, and Publishers, 14th Edition.* Chicago: University of Chicago Press, 1993.

Gurmukh. *The Eight Human Talents.* New York: Cliff Street Books, 2000.

Hallows, Jolyon. *Information Systems Project Management.* New York: Amacom, 1997.

Hobbs, Charles. *Time Power.* New York: Harper & Row, 1987.

Hunter, Dale, Anne Bailey, and Bill Taylor. *The Zen of Groups: The Handbook for People Meeting with a Purpose.* Tucson: Fisher Books, 1995.

Israel, Richard, Helen Whitten, and Cliff Shaffran. *Your Mind at Work.* London: Kogan Page Ltd., 2000.

Janus, Irving L. *Groupthink: Psychological Studies of Policy Decisions and Fiascos.* Boston: Houghton Mifflin, 1982.

Johnson, David W., and Frank P. Johnson. *Joining Together: Group Theory and Group Skills, Seventh Edition.* Boston: Allyn & Bacon, 2000.

Johnson, Will. *Aligned, Relaxed, Resilient: The Physical Foundations of Mindfulness.* New York: Shambhala, 2000.

Jolles, Robert L. *How to Run Seminars and Workshops: Presentation Skills for Consultants, Trainers, and Teachers.* New York: John Wiley & Sons, Inc., 1993.

Kaner, Sam. *Facilitator's Guide to Participatory Decision Making.* Gabriola Island, British Columbia: New Society Publishers, 1996.

Kaplan, Robert, and David Norton. *The Balanced Scorecard.* Boston: Harvard Business School Press, 1996.

Keirseye, David. *Please Understand Me II: Temperament, Character, Intelligence.* Del Mar, CA: Prometheus Nemesis Book Company, 1998.

Kelly, Patrick. *Faster Company.* New York: John Wiley & Sons, Inc., 1998.

Kepner, C. H., and B. B. Tregoe. *The Rational Manager.* New York: McGraw-Hill, 1965.

Kerzner, Harold. *Applied Project Management.* New York: Wiley, 2000.

———. *In Search of Project Management.* Wiley, 1998.

Kezsbom, Deborah, et al. *Dynamic Project Management.* New York: Wiley, 1989.

Kimeldorf, Martin. *Serious Play, A Leisure Wellness Guidebook.* Berkeley: Ten Speed, 1994.

Kirkpatrick, Donald L. *Evaluating Training Programs: The Four Levels.* San Francisco: Berrett-Koehler Publishers, Inc., 1998.

Klenke, Karin. *Women and Leadership: A Contextual Perspective.* New York: Springer Publishing Company, 1996.

Koch, Richard. *The 80/20 Principle: The Secret to Success by Achieving More with Less.* New York: Doubleday, 1999.

Kostner, Jaclyn, Ph.D. *Knights for the TeleRound Table.* New York: Warner, 1994.

Kraynak, Joe. *The Complete Idiot's Guide to Computer Basics, Second Edition.* Indianapolis: Alpha Books, 2002.

Krucoff, Carol, and Mitchell Krucoff, M.D. *Healing Moves: How to Cure, Relieve, and Prevent Common Ailments with Exercise.* New York: Harmony Books, 2000.

Krueger, Otto, and Janet M. Thiesen. *Type Talk at Work.* New York: Dell Publishing Company, 1993.

Lakein, Andrew. *How to Get Control of Your Time and Your Life.* New York: Wyden Books, 1973.

Levasseur, Robert. *Breakthrough Business Meetings.* Holbrook, MA: Adams Media, 1994.

Lewis, James. *The Project Manager's Desk Reference.* New York: McGraw-Hill, 1999.

———. *Fundamentals of Project Management.* New York: Amacom, 1995.

Lientz, Bennett and Kathryn Rea. *Project Management for the 21st Century.* San Diego: Academic, 1998.

MacCleod, Dan. *The Office Ergonomics Kit.* Boca Raton: CR Press Lewis-Publishers, 1998.

Mackenzie, Kyle. *Making It Happen: A Non-Technical Guide to Project Management.* New York: Wiley, 1998.

Magnan, Robert, and Mary Lou Santovec. *1001 Commonly Mispelled Words, First Edition.* New York: McGraw-Hill Professional Publishing, 2000.

Maharishi Mahesh Yogi. *Transcendental Meditation: Serenity Without Drugs.* New York: Signet, 1963.

Maier, Norman R. F. *Problem Solving Discussion and Conferences.* New York: McGraw-Hill, 1963.

Markham, Ursula. *The Elements of Visualization.* Rockport, MA: Element Books, 1989.

McCay, James. *Management of Time.* Paramus, NJ: Prentice Hall, 1959.

Meredith, J. R., and Samuel Mantel. *Project Management.* New York: Wiley, 1995.

Miller, Lyle, Ph.D., and Alma Dell Smith, Ph.D. *The Stress Solution.* Washington, D.C.: American Psychological Association, 1997.

Mitchell, Stewart. *The Complete Illustrated Guide to Massage.* New York: Barnes & Noble Books, 1997.

Moore-Ede, Martin, Ph.D. *The Twenty-Four Hour Society.* Reading, MA: Addison Wesley, 1993.

Morrison, Terri, Wayne A. Conaway, and George Borden. *Kiss, Bow, or Shake Hands: How to Do Business in Sixty Countries.* Holbrook: Bob Adams, Inc., 1994.

Moskowitz, Robert. *How to Organize Your Work and Your Life.* San Diego: Mainstream Books, 1981.

Mosvick, Roger K., and Robert B. Nelson. *We've Got to Start Meeting Like This! A Guide to Successful Meeting Management, Revised Edition.* Indianapolis: JIST Works, Inc., 1996.

Myers, David G. *Psychology, Fourth Edition.* New York: Worth Publishing, 1995.

Oliver, Joan Duncan. *Contemplative Living.* New York: Dell Books, 2000.

Ornish, Dean. *Program for Reversing Heart Disease.* New York: Ivy Books, 1996.

Ornstein, Robert, and David Sobel. *Healthy Pleasures.* Reading, MA: Perseus Books, 1998.

Pelletier, Kenneth R. *The Best Alternative Medicine: What Works? What Does Not?* New York: Simon & Schuster, 2000.

Phillips, G. M. *Communication and the Small Group.* Indianapolis: Bobbs-Merrill, 1966.

Provost, Gary. *100 Ways to Improve Your Writing.* Denver: Mentor Books, 1985.

Quigley, Joseph V. *Vision.* New York: McGraw-Hill, Inc., 1993.

Ralston, Patricia, and Caroline Smart. *Collins Gem Yoga.* New York: HarperCollins, 1999.

Rea, Kathryn, and Bennett Lientz, eds. *Breakthrough Technology Project Management.* San Diego: Academic, 1998.

Richardson, Donna. *Let's Get Real: Exercise Your Right to a Healthy Body.* New York: Pocket Books, 1998.

Rush, Anne Kent. *Bodywork Basics: A Guide to the Powers and Pleasures of Your Body.* New York: Dell, 2000.

Salsbury, Glenna. *Art of the Fresh Start.* Deerfield Beach, FL: Health Communications, 1995.

Scholtes, Peter R., Brian L. Joiner, and Barbara J. Streibel. *The Team Handbook, Second Edition.* Madison: Oriel Inc., 2000.

Seigel, Joel. *GAAP Handbook of Policies and Procedures, 2000.* New Jersey: Prentice Hall Trade, December 1999.

Shank, David. *Data Smog.* New York: HarperCollins, 1997.

Sharma, Robert S. *Monk Who Sold His Ferrari.* San Francisco: HarperCollins, 1998.

Silberman, Mel. *101 Ways to Make Meetings Active.* San Francisco: Jossey-Bass Pfeiffer, 1999.

Silver, Susan. *Getting Organized to Be Your Best!* California: Adams Hall Publishing, June 2000.

Simmons, Michael. *New Leadership for Women and Men: Building an Inclusive Organization.* Brookfield, VT: Gower Publishing Limited, 1996.

Spear, William. *Feng Shui Made Easy.* San Francisco: Harper, October 1995.

Stoll, Andrew, M.D. *The Omega-3 Connection: How You Can Restore Your Body's Natural Balance and Treat Depression.* New York: Simon & Schuster, 2001.

Strunk, William Jr., and E. B. White. *The Elements of Style, Fourth Edition.* Boston: Allyn & Bacon, 2000.

Thomsett, Michael. *The Little Black Book of Management.* New York: Amacom, 1990.

Tomlinson, Cybèle, and Vimala McClure. *Simple Yoga.* Berkeley, CA: Conari Press, 2000.

Toms, Michael, ed. *The Power of Meditation and Prayer.* Carlsbad, CA: Hay House, 1997.

Tracy, John. *How to Read a Financial Report.* New York: John Wiley & Sons, February 1999.

Tullier, L. Michelle, Ph.D. *Networking for Everyone.* Indianapolis: JIST Works, Inc., 1998.

Verzuh, Eric. *The Fast Forward MBA in Project Management.* New York: Wiley, 1999.

Weiss, Joseph, and Robert Wysocki. *5-Phase Project Management*. Boston, MA: Perseus, 1992.

Whicker, Marcial Lynn. *Toxic Leaders: When Organizations Go Bad*. Westport, Connecticut: Quorum Books, 1996.

Wieder, Marsha. *Doing Less Having More*. New York: Morrow, 1998.

Williams, Paul. *Getting a Project Done on Time: Managing People, Time, and Results*. New York: Amacom, 1996.

Zeer, Darin. *Office Yoga: Simple Stretches for Busy People*. San Francisco: Chronicle Books, 2000.

Zelinsky, Marilyn. *Practical Home Office Solutions*. New York: McGraw-Hill Professional Publishing, 1998.

Zimmerman, Neal. *Home Office Design*. New York: John Wiley & Sons, 1996.

Sample Interview Questions

Here are some sample behavioral questions, along with a few suggested follow-up probes, that you can use in future interviews. Feel free to adapt them to fit your unique situation. You'll also want to expand the number of follow-up probes that you use.

Because these questions are behavioral in nature, there are no right or wrong answers. They're meant to help you discover behavioral evidence of a candidate's ability to successfully perform the job in question.

Remember to use the STAR formula (see "Structured Behavioral Interviewing: Part 2" on page 458) to gather the information that you'll need to make an accurate evaluation of the candidate's skills and abilities (situation or task, actions taken, results).

ACCOUNTABILITY

- Tell me about a time when a project or task under your direction didn't measure up to expectations. What happened? Who was at fault?

- Give me an example of a time when you were accountable for the subpar work of others. How did you respond to the situation with your superiors? In what ways did you hold those working for you accountable?

ADAPTABILITY

- Describe a time when you had to adapt to a wide variety of people, situations, and environments. How difficult is it for you to adapt to new situations? What techniques have you discovered to be helpful?

- *(Continuum)* On a scale between liking constant sameness and liking constant change, where do you fit? Tell me about a job you've had in the past that involved a good deal of change.

ANALYTICAL SKILLS

▪ Relate a story in which you were given a work assignment that involved lots of analysis. What did you do to gather the needed information? What kinds of help did you need to complete the assignment?

▪ *(Self-appraisal)* If I were to ask your present supervisor about your analytical skills, what would she tell me? What does it take to perform good analysis? How did you develop your analytical skills?

ASSERTIVENESS

▪ We've all been involved in situations in which we've had to speak up to get our point across. Tell me about a time when you had to be assertive. What was at stake? What risks did you take in being assertive? How difficult is it for you to become assertive in a situation?

▪ Describe a time when you felt that something at work was happening that was unfair to yourself or others. What did you do? How did others perceive your action? What did you accomplish?

CLOSING TECHNIQUES

▪ Describe a time when you were working with a difficult customer but ended up closing the sale. What did you do to make it happen? What closing techniques do you use effectively? How many times should one attempt to close a sale before giving up altogether?

▪ Describe the most difficult sale you've ever made. Why were you successful? What's the most common objection you face in sales? How do you overcome it? How do you handle objections based on misunderstanding?

COMMUNICATION SKILLS

▪ Tell me about a time when you were asked to make a presentation on a business-related topic. What was the topic? How did you prepare? What things did you do to make your presentation interesting and effective? Did you use visual aids? Are you familiar with Microsoft PowerPoint?

▪ Relate a story about a work situation in which your communication skills were really put to the test. How important of a role have communication skills had in the development of your career? What types of communication do you feel you are particularly good at?

CONFLICT MANAGEMENT

- Recall for me a time when you had a disagreement with your boss. What prompted the disagreement? What did you do to convince your boss that your position was the correct one? How was the situation resolved?
- Tell me of a time when you had a conflict with a co-worker. What was involved? How did you handle it? Was compromise a part of your solution?

CONFRONTATION

- Give me an example of a recent confrontation that you had with an employee whose results were unacceptable. What did you do to prepare for the confrontation? Where was the physical location of the confrontation? What was your objective in confronting the employee and was it achieved?
- Tell me about the last time that a superior confronted you with a problem. What was involved? How did you handle the situation? How was the matter resolved?

CREATIVITY

- Describe a time in which you were allowed to be completely creative in your work. How did it feel? What about the project did you find energizing? Give me a few examples of creative projects that you've been involved with in the past.
- Tell me about the most significant creative presentation you've made. What was there about the presentation that worked? What could you have done better?

CUSTOMER SERVICE SKILLS

- Tell me about the most difficult customer you've ever encountered. What did you do to satisfy the customer? Was it enough? What could you have done better? What do you think is the most important principle governing customer service? What kinds of things do you do to ensure that this principle is always followed?

■ Describe a situation in which you dealt with a customer who insisted that he was right when you knew that he was wrong. Were you successful? What did it take? What is your philosophy of customer service? Considering your present employer's customer service policies, tell us about the ones that work well.

DECISION-MAKING

■ Tell me about a situation in which you were forced to make a decision about something not covered by company policy. How did you go about making the decision? How did you involve others in the process?

■ Describe the most difficult business decision you've ever made. What was at stake? Who was involved? What resources did you use in making the decision?

DELEGATING

■ Give me an example of a time when you were assigned a major project. How did you select those who would participate with you? How did you manage those to whom project assignments were given?

■ Tell me about a time when you delegated work to someone who didn't complete it in an acceptable manner. How did you handle the matter?

DEPENDABILITY

■ Give me an example of a time when you had to go above and beyond the call of duty to get the job done. What was at stake? What was the payoff? Where did the extra energy come from?

■ Tell me about a time when you had to sacrifice personal plans to complete a job-related task. Was anyone other than you affected by your sacrifice? If so, how would that person rate your dependability?

DETAIL ORIENTATION

■ Tell me about a time when you were in charge of a major project involving a multiplicity of detail. How did you manage the project while paying attention to each detail? How important to the outcome are the details of a project?

■ The last time you were assigned a major project, how did you go about planning the work to be done? What tools did you use? What methods did you rely upon to ensure quality work completed in a timely manner?

DISCIPLINE

■ Tell me about the last time you disciplined an employee. What was involved? How did you proceed? What was your objective? What success did you achieve?

■ Considering the last time you had to terminate an employee, what could have been done to prevent the termination? What could the company have done better? What could you have done better?

EDUCATION

■ Of all your past educational experiences (formal and informal), which ones were most helpful in qualifying you for this job? What kinds of skills did you acquire as a result of that training?

■ Describe a time when your education made a significant difference in your accomplishments on the job. Be specific.

EMPATHY

■ Relate a story about a time when your ability to empathize with an employee or customer really paid off. How well can you know what someone else is feeling? What's the difference between empathy and sympathy?

■ *(Continuum)* On a continuum between being empathetic to others and being dogmatic about policy and procedure, where would you fit?

ENJOYMENT

■ Recall for me a job or a project that you particularly enjoyed. What was there about it that you found enjoyable? What do you enjoy about your present job?

■ Tell me about the businessperson you most admire. What is it that this person enjoys about his or her job? If you could create your dream job, what elements would you include that would give you enjoyment?

ENTHUSIASM

- Tell me of a time when you needed to motivate others. How did you do it? What is the best way you've found to motivate others?

- Relate a personal story about a time when you simply couldn't become enthusiastic about a project or a task. Did you proceed in spite of your lack of enthusiasm? Was the work completed successfully? How did your lack of enthusiasm affect others?

ETHICS

- Tell me about a time when your personal ethics would not permit you to obey the direction of a superior. How did you handle the situation? What were the risks? What was the result?

- *(Contrary evidence)* What things do you consider unethical? Tell me about a time when you've become aware that someone you knew acted unethically in one of the ways you just described.

EXPERIENCE

- Tell me about the experiences you've had with your present employer that you feel are most valuable to you. What have you learned? How would you propose to share the same experiences with those who will work for you?

- Describe how your previous work experiences qualify you for the job you're seeking. Be specific.

FACT FINDING

- Describe a project that involved a good deal of fact finding. How did you approach the task? In what ways did the fact-finding mission contribute to the success of the project?

- Describe a time when you gathered facts from many different sources to create something important. What forms of research did you use to discover the facts that you needed? How did you organize your search? What did the final product look like?

FAIRNESS

- Give me an example of a situation that involved absolute fairness in dealing with a problem employee. What was involved in treating the employee fairly? What extraordinary things did your commitment to fairness cause you to do? What did fairness achieve?

- Relate a personal story about how you were treated unfairly by a former employer. When did it occur? What was involved? How did that treatment affect your attitude toward that employer?

FLEXIBILITY

- Describe a situation in which extreme flexibility was important to the successful performance of your job. How important do you think it is to be flexible in the job you're seeking? Why? What's the downside to being extremely flexible?

- Tell me about a situation in which your lack of flexibility hurt your overall job performance. How did you correct the situation? Tell me about a situation in which being flexible was difficult for you in some way.

FOLLOWING DIRECTIONS

- *(Continuum)* On a scale between working creatively and following the directions of others, where do you fit?

- Tell me about a time when you disagreed with something that you were told to do, but did it anyway. To whom did you voice your disagreement? What was that person's response? Would you have handled the matter any differently had you been in charge?

FORESIGHTEDNESS

- Give me an example of a time when you averted a major problem by using foresight. What does foresight on the job involve?

- Tell me about a time when a failure at work could have been avoided had you only used a little foresight. What did you learn from the experience?

FRUSTRATION

- Describe the most frustrating aspect of your present job. What could be done to make your job less frustrating? Have you suggested changes? What do you do to cope with the frustrating aspects of your present job?

- Tell me about a time when someone at work was frustrated by something you did. How did you find out about the frustration? Could you do anything to correct the situation? If so, what did you do? If not, what would you do differently?

HELP

- What did you do in your last job to help new employees get started on the right track? Did your efforts accomplish your objective?

- Tell me about a time when you needed the help of a more experienced manager to help you accomplish an important mission. How did you know whom to ask for help? When was the last time another manager asked for your help?

HIRING

- Tell me the biggest hiring mistake you've made as a manager. When were you first aware that a hiring mistake was probably made? In hindsight, were there any indications in the interview process that there may be problems with this particular candidate? If you had it to do all over again, are there areas that you would have probed more intensely in the interview process?

- Tell me about your use of structured behavioral interviewing. What do you see as the strengths of this method over conventional models? Are employees who have been selected using this interview method more likely to be successful on the job? Why, or why not?

HONESTY

- Relate a situation in which your sense of personal honesty defined the manner in which you accomplished a particular task. Is absolute honesty in business affairs possible?

- Tell me about a time when it appeared that someone's dishonesty seemed to benefit him or her in some significant way. Did that person's influence change the way you approached similar situations? When dishonest people succeed, how does an honest person reconcile the matter internally?

HUMOR

■ Relate a personal story that demonstrates the value of a sense of humor in business. Do you have a sense of humor? How important is humor in your life? Give me an example of humor misused.

■ Give me some examples of ways in which you handle stress and tension at work. Does humor play a role? How does it help? When is it appropriate? What special cautions are warranted?

INDEPENDENCE

■ Describe the amount of independence that you have in your present job. What do you like about working independently? What do you dislike about it? How important an issue is independence in the job you're seeking?

■ Describe the amount of independence that you allow those working for you. Do you allow different levels of independence to workers based on some qualifier? What does it take to qualify? What happens when those you've allowed to function independently abuse the situation?

INITIATIVE

■ Give me an example of a time when you took the initiative to lobby for changes in corporate policy or procedure. What were the risks? How did you approach the situation? What did you do to convince others that changes were needed?

■ Give me an example from your work experience that demonstrates how your personal initiative helped you move to positions of greater responsibility. Where does your initiative come from?

INNOVATION

■ Tell me about the last innovative suggestion you made about the work you do. To whom was it made? What happened as a result of the suggestion? Was your suggestion given a fair hearing?

■ Tell me about a time when you took the initiative rather than waiting to be told what to do. What was involved? What were the risks? What did your initiative accomplish?

INTERPERSONAL SKILLS

- Give me some examples of the contributions that you've made to create a team environment. What does it take to create a sense of team? What things are important to maintaining a team spirit? How do you deal with those who simply refuse to be team players?

- From your experience, give me an example of the importance of interpersonal skills to the success of a manager. What things do you say or do that reflect good interpersonal skills? In hiring new employees, what value do you place on finding people with good interpersonal skills? Why?

INQUISITIVENESS

- *(Continuum)* On a continuum between independently seeking information and depending upon others to provide you with the information you need to do your job, where would you fit?   Why?

- Give me an example of a project that you've worked on in which being inquisitive was a real plus. How did it help? What did being inquisitive produce in terms of results?

INTERNET SKILLS

- Give me an example of the way in which you have used the Internet on the job. How did you learn to use the Internet? What applications do you think the Internet has for our business in the future?

JUDGMENT

- Give me an example of a time when your good judgment helped solve a major problem. What was involved?

- Tell me about a time when you used your best judgment in a situation and later found that you were wrong. How did you discover you were wrong? What did you do to rectify the situation? How costly was the error? What did you learn by it?

KNOWLEDGE

- Tell me about a time when your technical or professional knowledge made an important difference. What were the circumstances?

■ Describe a time when it became obvious that you possessed a greater knowledge of the technical aspects of your job than your supervisor. How did you make the discovery? How did that alter your relationship with your supervisor? If you knew more, why weren't you the boss?

LEADERSHIP

■ Of all the projects you've worked on during the course of your career, which one best exemplifies your leadership skills? How often do you have an opportunity to provide real leadership in your present job? What's the difference between leadership and managership, and which of those two terms best describes your approach to business?

■ Recall the first time you were placed in a position of leadership within a company. What did you do right? What could you have done better? In your opinion, what's the most important key to effective leadership?

LISTENING

■ Give me an example of a situation in which good listening skills were required of you. How did you develop your listening skills? Why is it important to be a good listener? What are some of the situations in which good listening skills are a must?

■ Tell me about a time when you would have made a different decision if you had been practicing better listening techniques. What did you learn from the experience? In what ways have you become a better listener since that time?

LOYALTY

■ Recall for me a time when you weren't as loyal to your company as you should have been. What did you do? How did it feel? What should you have done differently?

■ Tell me about a time when, because of a subordinate's loyalty to the company, and particularly the department you supervise, a significant piece of work was accomplished. What kinds of things do you do to inspire loyalty?

MANAGEMENT

■ Tell me about the most unpopular management decision you've ever made. What steps did you take in evaluating alternatives? How did you gather the facts that you needed? How did you explain your decision to employees? How did you deal with negative reaction?

■ Tell me about the things you've done to build morale in the department that you now manage. How important is employee morale? How do you go about "catching" employees doing something right?

MARKETING

■ Tell me about a strategic marketing plan that you developed and the result of its implementation. What research was necessary before developing the plan? Who was involved? What changes did the plan make in the way your organization does business?

■ Tell me about a recent marketing questionnaire that you developed. What was its purpose? What did you learn? What is your experience with focus groups? What other marketing research tools have you used?

MENTORING

■ Tell me about a mentoring situation that you arranged that worked particularly well. Is mentoring a regular part of new employee training? What are the benefits of a good mentoring program? What are the drawbacks?

■ Give me an example of someone who failed in spite of having the benefit of a mentor. What went wrong? What could have been done differently? How did that incident change your mentoring program?

MOTIVATION

■ Think of a time when things were not going well. How did you keep yourself going? What do you typically do to help motivate yourself? What do you think is the most motivating aspect of your present job? What is there in the job you're pursuing that you would find motivational?

■ Tell me about the most significant failure you've experienced as a manager. How did you handle it? How did the failure affect your personal motivation? How did you overcome it? How did the situation affect the motivation of other members of the team? What did you learn by it?

NEGOTIATION

- Give me an example of a particularly difficult negotiation in which you participated. What was involved? Was it a successful negotiation? How so? How often in your present job have you been in the position of negotiator?

- Tell me about a time when you attempted to negotiate something, to no avail. What was involved? What were the problems? What could you have done differently, or better? What is your approach to negotiation?

NURTURING

- Tell me about the last time you found yourself nurturing a customer, client, or employee. What did you hope to ultimately gain? Is time spent in this way well invested? What kinds of activities are included in your nurturing efforts?

- Describe how you train supervisors under you to nurture new employees. What's the payoff?

OBJECTIVITY

- Tell me about an emotionally charged situation in which it was difficult for you to remain objective. Did you remain objective? How did you accomplish it? How did your objectivity help calm the situation or solve the problem?

- Recall a time when you were dealing with a problem at work in which you lost objectivity and made an emotional decision. What happened? Had you remained more objective, what kind of decision would you have made? What lessons did you learn from the situation?

OBSERVATION

- Relate a situation from your present job that demonstrates the importance of being observant. What do you hope to discover? What do you do with the information that you obtain in this manner? How did you develop this skill?

- Tell me about your ability to be observant of others. How has that ability helped you in your present position? How do you think that ability would help you in the job you're seeking?

Open-Mindedness

- *(Continuum)* On a continuum between favoring established methods of doing business and being completely open to new ideas, where would you fit?
- Tell me about the last time that a subordinate came to you with a new idea. What did the idea involve? How did you respond? What do you do to promote an atmosphere of "out-of-the-box" thinking among employees reporting to you? Was the employee's idea implemented?

Output

- Tell me about a time when your team broke records in terms of production quantity. What was involved? Was breaking the record a defined objective of the team? How did you keep up enthusiasm? What were the most important steps that led to success?
- Give me an example of the last time that you intervened in a situation involving poor employee productivity. What was happening? How did you learn of the problem? What did you do to solve the problem? What could you have done better?

Ownership

- Describe an incident that demonstrates that those who report to you really take ownership of their team and the work they accomplish individually and together. How is the attitude of ownership instilled? Do those to whom you report take the same kind of ownership for their work?
- Tell me about a time when it was difficult to take responsibility for something at work. What was the problem? What did taking ownership of the situation mean in practical terms? What did you learn from the experience? What did those who report to you learn?

PATIENCE

- From your management experience, tell me about a time when patience really paid off for you. How patient an individual are you normally? How did you develop your ability to be patient? Does patience ever get in the way of progress?

- Tell me about a time when you simply lost your patience and demanded that something happen immediately. What were the circumstances? What was the reaction to your demand for immediate response? What did you learn from the situation? When, if ever, should a manager set aside patience for the good of the organization?

PERCEPTIVENESS

- From your business experience, tell me about a time when your perception helped you in some significant way.

- *(Self-appraisal)* If I were to ask your references how perceptive they think you are, what would they tell me?

PERSISTENCE

- Relate a scenario in which your persistence really paid off. What was at stake? How did you demonstrate persistence?

- Describe the most difficult sale that you ever made. What were you selling? What was the competition? What did you do by way of planning the sale? What role did persistence play?

PERSUASIVENESS

- *(Self-appraisal)* How persuasive are you? If I were to ask your present supervisor to comment on your persuasive abilities, what would she tell me? Where did you learn how to be persuasive?

- Sell me the product that you now represent. In terms of sales ranking, where do you stand in relation to other members of your company's sales force?

PLANNING

- Tell me about a time when inadequate planning caused a major mess. What was involved? What role were you playing in the project?

What elements of planning were inadequately addressed? What was the result?

■ Describe a situation in which you were in charge of planning a major project or event. How did you approach the task? What steps did you take to ensure that an adequate job of planning would be done? When you finished your task of planning, how did you communicate the final product? What difference did your plan make?

POLITENESS

■ Tell me about a time when simply being courteous made a major difference. How important is courtesy in your present job? How important do you think it is in the job you're seeking? Why?

■ *(Self-appraisal)* If I were to ask your references about your courtesy to others, what would they tell me?

PRACTICALITY

■ Describe a situation that required you to be very practical in the way you approached it. Why did it matter? Why is it important to be practical in business matters?

■ Give me an example of a training situation that you offer new employees that emphasizes practicality. Why is that important? What steps do you take to ensure that practicality is part of every training program?

PRECISION

■ Give me an example of a time when your ability to be precise made a significant difference in an assigned task or project. How did you develop the skill to be precise? How often are you required to be precise in your present job?

■ *(Continuum)* On a scale between being concerned about precision and being concerned about quantity of work completed, where do you fit?

PRESENTATION

■ Give me an example of a recent presentation that you gave. Was it successful? Why do you think so? What did you do to plan the presentation? What elements of the presentation were particularly important? What did the presentation accomplish?

- Describe the elements of a good sales presentation that you recently made. Why are each of these elements important? How many presentations does it take to make a sale? What's the norm for a salesman with your present company?

PROCESS FOLLOWING

- From your experience in your present job, give me an example of the value of an established process in conducting business. Why is process so important? Should a process be flexible or inflexible? Why?
- Tell me about a primary process that's involved in performing your present job. Are there any parts of the process that could work better? When did you last suggest changes to the process? What was the result?

PRODUCTION

- Give me an example of a sales situation in which you outproduced other members of your team. How did you do it? How important is it to be a top producer? Why?
- *(Continuum)* On a continuum between being a thinker and being a producer, where would you fit?

PROGRESSIVENESS

- Tell me about a time when you recommended a major improvement to your present company's management. What needed fixing? What would your recommendation accomplish?
- Describe a time when someone who reports to you recommended the adoption of a new method or invention to improve the quality of the work product. What did you do as a result of the suggestion? Was the suggestion implemented? Why or why not? What do you do to encourage progressive thinking among members of your team?

PROJECT MANAGEMENT

- Tell me about a successful project that you've recently managed. What kind of planning is involved in a major project? What is a project milestone? When you assign a project, what steps do you take to ensure that the project will be completed on time?

■ Tell me about a time when a project that you were managing began to exceed budget expectations. What steps did you take? Whom did you involve? Were you able to correct the problem?

PROSPECTING

■ Give me an example of the way in which you go about finding new customers. Is it effective? On average, how many prospects does it take to produce one sale?

■ Tell me about the kind of people you normally like to sell to. Why this particular group? Have you always preferred this kind of buyer? What kind of person do you least like to sell to? Why?

PUBLIC RELATIONS

■ Tell me about a recent work experience that demonstrates your commitment to public relations. How important is public relations to your present firm? From your experience, what are the most important factors for good public relations?

■ Relate a situation in which the issue of public relations was not given the consideration that it deserved. What was the impact? What did you learn from the situation?

PUNCTUALITY

■ Tell me about a situation at work in which very few seem to be concerned about promptness. Are you prompt? Why is that important to you? What do you do to ensure your own promptness?

■ Tell me how you encourage the promptness of others when they're working on projects that you've assigned them. What happens when someone fails to be prompt?

QUALITY

■ Tell me about a time when work performed by those reporting to you did not meet your expectations for quality. What was happening? How did you discover the problem? What steps did you take to correct the situation?

■ Describe a situation that demonstrates your commitment to customer satisfaction. How do you inspire that same commitment in others? Why is quality and customer satisfaction important to your business?

QUOTA MAKING

■ Tell me about the last time that your monthly sales were below expectations (or quota). What happened to produce the problem? What did you do to get back on track?

■ Recall a time when your sales team was functioning below expectations. What did you do to turn the situation around?

RELIABILITY

■ *(Self-appraisal)* If I were to ask your references to tell me how reliable of an employee you are, what would they say?

■ Recall a time when you had to deal with a subordinate over the issue of reliability. What was happening? How did you approach the issue? What kind of plan did you mutually develop that addressed the issue of becoming more reliable?

REPORT WRITING

■ Tell me about the last major report that you wrote. What did you like least about it? How do you prepare to write a major report? What are the important elements of a good report? What steps do you take to ensure accuracy and readability?

■ How important is report writing for those who presently report to you? Tell me about a situation that demonstrates the need for good report-writing skills. What report-writing assistance do you offer those who report to you?

REPRIMANDING

■ Tell me about the last time that you had to formally reprimand a subordinate. What prompted the reprimand? How did you proceed? What was the result of the reprimand?

■ Give me a few examples of the kinds of work performance issues that have prompted you to formally reprimand a subordinate. What kinds of corrective action did you attempt before the formal reprimand? In your experience, have formal reprimands been helpful in correcting employee misconduct? Does the threat of reprimands prevent misconduct?

RESEARCHING

- Describe your last major research project. How many people were involved? What was the objective of the project? How did you organize the project? How were results compiled?
- Tell me about a time when your instincts were proven wrong by research data. What was involved? How did you confirm the accuracy of data? How did you present your findings?

RISK TAKING

- Tell me about the last time you took a major risk and it paid off. What was at stake? What made you think that taking the risk was the right thing to do? In practical terms, what would have happened had you been wrong?
- Tell me about risks that those who report to you may occasionally take. What latitude do you provide subordinates who are assigned a specific task or project? How do you react when a subordinate takes a risk and fails?

SELLING

- Tell me what you dislike most about selling. How have you tried to overcome this dislike? What do you do to make it tolerable? How has this dislike affected your ability to sell?
- Tell me about a very special award that you've won for selling? What did it take to earn the award? Where was it given? How difficult was it to earn? What awards do you hope to win in the future?

SENSITIVITY

- Give me an example of a time at work when real sensitivity was required of you. Did you meet the challenge? Do others view you as a sensitive person? How do you know?
- *(Contrary evidence)* How important is it for a manager to be sensitive to the needs of his subordinates? Tell me about a time when you

weren't as sensitive as you should have been. What happened as a result? What did you learn? How did you learn to identify situations that require greater sensitivity?

SPEAKING

■ Tell me about an occasion in which you spoke before a large group of people. How did you prepare? What message did you convey? How did you organize your speech? What did you like about it? What could you have done better?

■ Describe the most significant speech that you've ever heard. Who was speaking? What was there about it that made an impression on you? Do you enjoy public speaking? What kinds of speeches do you least enjoy?

STRATEGIZING

■ Tell me about a time when it was necessary for you to develop a strategy to accomplish a specific work objective. What was the objective? What were the steps necessary to reach the objective? What was the strategy that you utilized to get there?

■ Tell me about a situation that would have turned out differently had more time been taken to strategize. Why wasn't it done? What did you learn from the situation?

STRESS MANAGEMENT

■ Tell me about the most stressful job you've ever held. What made it stressful? How did you cope?

■ Give me an example of the kinds of stressors that are involved in your present job. What do you do to overcome them?

SUPPORTIVENESS

■ From whom do you derive most of your support in your present job? Give me an example of what that person says and does to communicate support. How important is it to have the support of others?

■ Give me a few examples of how you support those who report to you. How important is this kind of support? How do you know that your support efforts are worthwhile?

TEAM BUILDING

- *(Contrary evidence)* How important is developing a sense of teamwork among those working in your department? Tell me about a time when you attempted to use a management style that did not involve team building.

- Tell me about the team that you supervise now. What makes it a team? What are the team's strengths and weaknesses? What objectives have you met as a team? How do you foster a team spirit?

TECHNICAL SKILLS

- Describe what you did through the past year to expand your technical knowledge. How do you feel about continuing technical training? Do you do things other than attending formal training to keep yourself current?

- Tell me, in the hiring process, how you go about determining whether a candidate is technically competent. As a manager, what kinds of ongoing technical training do you require?

TERMINATION

- Tell me about the last time you terminated an employee. What led up to the termination? How did you approach the situation? How long had you been counseling this particular employee? Who made the final decision to terminate? Did you concur? Was the employee given an opportunity to resign? How will you handle future requests for information about the employee?

- Tell me about the last time you were fired from a job. What kind of job was involved? What went wrong? Were you dealt with in a fair and equitable manner? What did the situation teach you?

TRAINING

- Tell me about the kind of mandatory training that you feel should be provided to new employees coming into your department. How does that differ from what they are actually being offered?

- Tell me about the last time that you advocated for better training. To whom did you make your case? What were the reasons you gave for your position? How did you suggest better training could be accomplished? What was the result?

WINNING

- Tell me about the last time you and your team won something significant. How did it feel? Did winning just happen, or was it planned? What did you do to make it happen? What effect did winning have on the team and its attitude toward future projects?

- Is it fair to say that your experience has taught you a number of winning techniques, philosophies, and strategies? Tell me about a few of them that you would bring with you if you were given the position with our company.

Interview Evaluation Summary

Name of candidate: _____

Position: _____

Interviewer: _____

Date: _____

Candidate summary (prepared by hiring manager): _____

Mandatory Success Factor	Rating	Weight	Total Points
_____	_____	_____	_____
_____	_____	_____	_____
_____	_____	_____	_____
_____	_____	_____	_____
_____	_____	_____	_____
_____	_____	_____	_____
_____	_____	_____	_____

TOTAL SCORE

Rating = 1 to 5 (highest)

Weight = Prioritized mandatory success factors (Example: Given 10 prioritized factors, factor 1 would have a weight of 10, factor 2 would have a weight of 9, and so on.)

The Speaker's Notebook

Copy these forms and use them when you plan, present, and evaluate the success of your presentations.

BECOME AN EFFECTIVE SPEAKER

Rate your current presentation skills (circle your answer).

Verbal

Excellent	**Good**	**Fair**	Clear message
Excellent	**Good**	**Fair**	Relevant to audience
Excellent	**Good**	**Fair**	Effective evidence
Excellent	**Good**	**Fair**	Powerful visual aids
Excellent	**Good**	**Fair**	Listener involvement
Excellent	**Good**	**Fair**	Good question-and-answer sessions

Visual

Excellent	**Good**	**Fair**	Making eye contact
Excellent	**Good**	**Fair**	Using gestures effectively
Excellent	**Good**	**Fair**	Using facial expressions

Vocal

Excellent	**Good**	**Fair**	Raising and lowering volume
Excellent	**Good**	**Fair**	Changing pace
Excellent	**Good**	**Fair**	Using pauses for emphasis

DEFINE THE CENTRAL MESSAGE

Presentation: _____

Topic:

Central message:

Know Your Listeners

Presentation: _____

Meaning of the message:

Goal:

Listener Analysis

Presentation: _____

What is their attitude toward me?

How can I convince them of my message?

How much do they know about the topic?

What are their positions?

How do they like to receive their information?

How are they responding to the information they're receiving?

Energy for Effectiveness

Energy Evaluation

Presentation: _____

Techniques

Excellent	**Good**	**Fair**	**Poor**	Using gestures for description
Excellent	**Good**	**Fair**	**Poor**	Using gestures for emphasis
Excellent	**Good**	**Fair**	**Poor**	Using expansive gestures
Excellent	**Good**	**Fair**	**Poor**	Using facial expressions
Excellent	**Good**	**Fair**	**Poor**	Raising and lowering voice
Excellent	**Good**	**Fair**	**Poor**	Changing pacing
Excellent	**Good**	**Fair**	**Poor**	Using pauses for emphasis
Excellent	**Good**	**Fair**	**Poor**	Communicating with voice tone

Eye-Contact Communication

Eye-Contact Evaluation

Presentation: _____

Always	**Often**	**Seldom**	Did you use the three-step approach to eye contact?
Always	**Often**	**Seldom**	Did you avoid a regular pattern of eye contact?

Always	**Often**	**Seldom**	Did you use your eyes to control your pace?
Always	**Often**	**Seldom**	Did you use your eyes to get feedback from listeners?

GATHER YOUR EVIDENCE

Evidence Checklist

Presentation: _____

Yes	**No**	Did you do mind-mapping or brainstorming?
Yes	**No**	Did you organize ideas according to the rule of threes?
Yes	**No**	Did you include a variety of evidence anecdotes, analogies, statistics, and so on?
Yes	**No**	Did you draw evidence from your own experience?
Yes	**No**	Did your evidence meet the five-C test?
Yes	**No**	Did you create a preliminary outline?

ORGANIZE YOUR MATERIAL

Check the organizing pattern(s) you used.

Organizing Patterns

Presentation: _____

- The whole and its parts
- Spatial order
- Chronological order
- News reporter
- Problem-solution
- Best alternative
- Other

CREATE SUCCESSFUL PRESENTATIONS

Keys to Success

Presentation: _____

Yes	**No**	Did the opening hook listeners?
Yes	**No**	Did you organize the body effectively?

Yes   **No**   Did you transition the presentation body with summaries?

Yes   **No**   Did you close by repeating the central message?

Yes   **No**   Did you include a call to action?

INTERACT WITH AUDIENCES

Presentation: _____

How many dialogue questions did you include? _____

Were the questions open- or close-ended? _____

When did you ask the dialogue questions? _____

What did you accomplish with them? _____

VISUAL AIDS

Presentation: _____

How many visual aids did you have? _____

What kinds of visuals did you use? _____

Did you keep your visuals simple? _____

Was the information readable? _____

Was the design simple and effective? _____

How did listeners react to them? _____

PRESENTING YOUR VISUALS

Presentation: _____

What forms of visual aids did you use? _____

How well did they work with the talk? _____

Did you use the four-step process? _____

If so, was it effective? _____

How did you handle handouts? _____

MAKE IT SIMPLE

Presentation: _____

Did you speak in a conversational style? _____

Did you use active voice as much as possible? _____

Did you avoid needless jargon? _____

Did you define any acronyms? _____

Did you avoid big words? _____

Did you remove nonwords from your talk? _____

BANISH THOSE BUTTERFLIES

Presentation: _____

How nervous did you feel before the start of your talk?

_____

How did you deal with this problem? _____

How did you feel as you were speaking? _____

How did you control your nervousness? _____

How well did all these techniques work? _____

DEALING WITH THE DETAILS

Presentation: _____

Yes	No	Did you double-check date, time, directions?
Yes	No	Do you have an appropriate room arrangement?
Yes	No	Is the room large enough for your audience?
Yes	No	Are refreshments available if you need them?
Yes	No	Did you bring backup audiovisual materials?
Yes	No	Did you try out the audiovisual equipment?
Yes	No	Did you try out the microphone in advance?

TEN-POINT PRESENTATION PRIMER

Presentation: _____

Yes	No	As you began to speak, did you make eye contact?
Yes	No	Did you open up all channels of communication?
Yes	No	Did you create a rhythm in your delivery?
Yes	No	Were your gestures raising your energy level?
Yes	No	Did you use dialogue questions effectively?
Yes	No	Did you use silences when you needed them?
Yes	No	Did you use the audiovisual equipment properly?
Yes	No	Did you try to memorize your talk?

Handling Questions and Answers

Presentation:_____

How well did you anticipate the questions? _____

How often did you use the five-step process? _____

If you left out any steps, which ones? _____

If you had hostile listeners, how did you deal with them? _____

_____

Did you stay in control of the entire question-and-answer session?

_____

One-to-One Presentations

Presentation: _____

Yes	No	Did you present a clear central message?
Yes	No	Did you clarify the meaning of your message?
Yes	No	Did your evidence appeal to the listener?
Yes	No	Did you present any visual aids effectively?
Yes	No	Did you use energy to make the presentation?
Yes	No	Did you practice eye contact?
Yes	No	Did you handle questions successfully?
Yes	No	Did you remember to "ask for the order"?

Listening

Presentation: _____

Always	Sometimes	Seldom	Did you listen to the words and "read between the lines"?
Always	Sometimes	Seldom	Did you pay attention to your listeners' body language?
Always	Sometimes	Seldom	Did you avoid making quick judgments about your listeners?
Always	Sometimes	Seldom	Did you prevent distractions from interrupting your listening?
Always	Sometimes	Seldom	Did you try to put yourself in the shoes of the audience?

MAKE MEETINGS MATTER

Meeting: _____

Yes	No	You developed a clear central message for the meeting.
Yes	No	You wrote out an agenda and circulated it in advance.
Yes	No	You invited only those people who were absolutely necessary.
Yes	No	You set strict time limits and kept the meeting short.
Yes	No	You infused the meeting with energy.
Yes	No	You encouraged participation, but kept the meeting on track.
Yes	No	You ended the meeting with an action plan.

MASTERING THE MEDIA

Interview: _____

Yes	No	You delivered your central message.
Yes	No	You remembered to wear appropriate attire.
Yes	No	You looked at the interviewer, not at the camera.
Yes	No	You answered with specifics, avoiding jargon and unsupported claims.
Yes	No	You handled the questions calmly and didn't overreact or become emotional.
Yes	No	You used energy to enhance your message.

CONTINUOUS IMPROVEMENT

Use the 10 strategies on the following list every day, and you'll see continuous improvement in your presentation skills.

1. Practice your skills in every situation.
2. Take advantage of each opportunity at work to give a presentation.
3. Start with low-risk work situations to practice your skills as a presenter.
4. Participate in volunteer activities and start speaking to groups.
5. Join groups, like Toastmasters, so you can improve your skills.
6. Enroll in presentation skills courses.
7. Read materials on public speaking to continually update your knowledge.

8. Watch other speakers to determine whether they use the three channels of communication.

9. Solicit feedback from your listeners regarding your strengths and weaknesses.

10. Give yourself an ovation every time you speak.

Reading Financial Statements

While the appearance of financials may be cloaked in mystery, this is not the reality—if you know some of the basic information. You just need to understand the terminology and the tools of financial analysis.

Financial statements give an indication of how financially healthy a business may be at one given moment in time.

The key to analyzing financial statements is to identify trends and find reasons behind the numbers. The secret to determining whether a business is healthy is to analyze several periods (years, if possible) to determine trends.

Trends tell the true financial picture behind every business entity. Companies that are particularly well run will possess an upward sloping trend line that rises with the economic health of the country. Businesses that are facing financial problems will have a downward sloping trend line that shows a performance that is less than the current economic condition would indicate.

Because every business can be faced with an adverse situation at any particular time, it is important to get as much historical information as possible on an entity. In order to do this, every manager needs to possess a basic understanding of financial statements and the direction these statements show that the business is headed.

Financial record-keeping in business is in response to the Sixteenth Amendment to the Constitution of the United States, which allows for the collection of taxes. As more companies became publicly owned, shareholders demanded financial disclosure—thereby formalizing the need for financial information.

The Securities and Exchange Commission (SEC) sets the standards and requirements for financial reporting in publicly held corporations. All public companies are required by law to submit financial information to the Securities and Exchange Commission. The information consists of three quarterly financial statements presented in a 10-Q report and a yearly financial statement presented as a 10-K report.

TIP

The 10-Q reports are due at the SEC no later than 45 days after the quarter ends. The 10-K report is due to be filed with the SEC no later than 90 days after a company's year-end financial cycle has been completed.

FINANCIAL STATEMENTS

Financial statements simply help you monitor your financial resources—to ensure that you are making more money than you are spending. They are a critical component in your decision-making process.

Financial statements use a system called double-entry bookkeeping. This system requires the use of accounts called debits and credits. A debit is an item that is placed on the left-hand side of an account. A credit is placed on the right-hand side of an account. Every time a debit is recorded on a set of financial statements, a corresponding credit must be recorded for the same amount on the financial statement. By following this procedure, the corporate books are said to be in balance because debits must always equal credits.

There are four primary financial statements:

■ The balance sheet

■ The income statement

■ The cash flow statement

■ The statement of changes in stockholders' equity

THE BALANCE SHEET

The balance sheet provides information concerning your company's assets, liabilities, and owner's equity. A typical balance sheet will have assets on the left-hand side and liabilities and owner's equity on the right. Assets are accounts that list what is owned by the business. These accounts are broken down into short-term assets and long-term assets. Short-term assets are assets that can be converted to cash in less than one year's time. Long-term assets are assets that have an expected life greater than one year. An example of a long-term asset would be a building. Buildings are constructed to last for many years, and, therefore, the benefit of the building will continue for years into the future.

TIP

The common-size balance sheet is a valuable tool for financial analysis. The total assets are set equal to 100 percent with all assets listed as a percentage of these total assets. On the right side of the balance sheet, the account labeled "total liabilities and equity" is set equal to 100 percent. All liability and equity accounts are then represented as the appropriate percent of the total liabilities and equity. This statement helps analyze the distribution of various accounts on the balance sheet. Of particular interest on the asset side are the percentages of total assets comprised of cash, inventory, and accounts receivable.

Liabilities are obligations to creditors that the company has acquired throughout the normal course of business. Like assets, they can be broken down into short- and long-term obligations. Typical short-term obligations would be acquiring goods or services on credit. Businesses are generally extended credit terms that provide 30 days or more to pay for current obligations. This type of credit is normally listed on the balance sheet as an account payable.

Companies are also granted credit for more than one year if the credit is being used to finance an item that may last for more than one year. If a company takes out a mortgage to finance a building, this loan would normally be granted for a number of years because the underlying asset being financed has a life expectancy of more than one year (similar to an individual purchasing a home).

Owner's equity is the final group of accounts on the balance sheet. As the title indicates, these are accounts that deal with the net worth of a business. This net worth is the difference between the assets and liabilities of a company and shows how much of the assets are being financed by the owners as opposed to how much is financed by the creditors (liabilities).

The balance sheet is a snapshot in time. This provides a picture of the company's financial position on the date stated. Balance sheets contain all the company's permanent accounts. Unlike income statements these account balances are carried from period to period and year to year. The balance sheet is generated by a business at least once a month. Many of the accounts on the balance sheet are reviewed and analyzed more than once a month because of their vital importance to running a business.

Current assets include the following:

- Cash
- Accounts receivable
- Inventory
- Prepaid expenses

TIP

Remember that you can read the footnotes in financial statements to get clarification of the firm's numbers.

Long-term assets include the following:

- Plant and equipment
- Land and buildings
- Accumulated depreciation

Cash is the first asset listed on the balance sheet. It is the most vital component on the company's balance sheet because it is the means by which a company can pay for supplies, meet its payroll, and invest in assets that can help the company generate income.

The designers of financial statements constructed all statements to list and group accounts by order of liquidity. Cash is the most liquid asset because it is already in a medium of exchange that is widely accepted. After a company's cash accounts are listed on its balance sheet, the next item in order of liquidity would be accounts receivables. These are obligations owed to the firm by individuals or companies that have been extended credit on account.

All assets are listed on a balance sheet at historic or purchase price value unless the asset has been *impaired*. Inventory is an example of an asset that can be impaired. Because inventory is acquired and then stored until consumed or sold, you run the risk that it may become damaged or obsolete. Under current accounting rules when this happens the asset must be recorded at the lower of cost or market price. In other words, if the cost for an inventory item is $10 and subsequent to use or sale it has been determined that it is only worth $5, then this item must be reduced to the lower value on the balance sheet.

Short-term liabilities include the following:

- Accounts payable
- Accrued expenses
- Short-term debt
- Income tax payable

Long-term liabilities include the following:

- Mortgage payable
- Long-term debt

Short-term liabilities are obligations that the company must repay in less than one year's time. Often times these liabilities are due in 30 days or less. Accrued expenses are expenses the business has incurred but has not yet been presented with an invoice to pay. A company wants to make sure all its known liabilities have been recorded as quickly as possible. By doing this, it is able to show a clearer picture of its financial health sooner to internal management, creditors, and owners of the business.

Stockholders' equity includes the following:

- Capital stock
- Additional paid in capital
- Retained earnings

Capital stock is the face value of the number of shares of company stock the company has outstanding multiplied times the par or stated value of the stock. Normally, when you review a financial statement this shows up as a very small number because the stock may have a value of one dollar per share or one cent per share. However, one of the most common ways stock is shown on a financial statement is at no par value. By doing this, the company is saying they have not assigned any monetary value to their stock. When they receive money for their outstanding stock they list only a small portion of this money being paid for the stock and the remainder of this money is recorded as *additional paid-in capital*. Additional paid-in capital is the difference between the face value of a share of stock and the price a buyer actually pays for the stock from the company.

TIP

Flash reports can be helpful in making operational decisions. These are quick internal reports. Many companies use them to report sales on a daily basis, cash in the bank, or inventory positions. They should be used in combination with financial statements since the flash reports are not as accurate.

Retained earnings are prior earnings the company has generated that they have decided to retain in the business in order to help it grow. Often a portion of a company's earnings is returned to the stockholders in the form of a dividend. Companies that pay a dividend generally distribute these dividends quarterly.

In order to completely understand the balance sheet, you must understand the basic formula. This formula is as follows:

Assets = Liabilities + Net Worth

THE INCOME STATEMENT

The income statement provides a picture of the company's financial performance over a specified period of time. This statement depicts the income generated and the expenses incurred by the firm during this period—painting a picture of how the company got to the point of the balance sheet. This cycle, which is one year in length, can follow a calendar year or use another yearly time period (which is referred to as a *fiscal* year). An example of a fiscal period would be February 1 to January 31 of each year.

Bottom line: The income statement tells you if there is a profit or loss as a result of the year's operations. Net income (commonly referred to as a profit) occurs when revenue exceeds expenses. There is a net loss when the expenses exceed the revenue.

The cash accounting method does not recognize items that are prepaid or accrued. Revenues are reported in the period in which they are paid. For example, sales made in March but paid for in May would be reported as revenue in May in the cash accounting method.

The same is true of expenses. They are reported in the accounting period in which they are actually paid. For example, if you bought a copy machine for your department in October, but it was not paid for until December, the expense would not be booked until December under the cash accounting method.

Accrual accounting records income and expenses when they occur. The accounting principle this follows is called the matching principle. The matching principle requires expenses to be matched or recorded against the revenue the expenses helped to generate. By recording these accruals at that time, a clearer picture of the profitability can be shown to internal and external users of the financial statements.

Most larger companies use the accrual method. Small businesses generally opt for the cash accounting method since they usually do not have many significant deferred or accrued items to materially impact their financial statements.

The three choices when accounting for inventory include the following:

- **LIFO.** The principal behind LIFO is that the last items going into inventory will be the first items sold out of inventory. This method came about when inflation was running at very high levels. By matching the last items into inventory against the selling price, less profit was recorded during inflation; therefore, less tax was being paid. LIFO will also better reflect replacement cost for inventory.

- **FIFO.** This method states that the first items into inventory will be the first items out of inventory. This method is more widely accepted than the LIFO method.
- **Weighted average.** This method does not look at the time the inventory was received. It looks at the total value of the inventory and determines an average price based upon all the items in the current inventory.

During periods of rising prices, LIFO offers a tax advantage to its users. LIFO assigns the most recently purchased items to cost of goods sold (which impacts profit and loss). The weighted average inventory method would be used when price levels are stable and you are trying to use a more uniform price for your cost of goods sold.

TIP

Improved efficiency in managing inventory can positively impact the company's cash position. Lower inventory levels mean less cash is invested in inventory. Yet care must be taken to ensure that sufficient inventory levels are on hand to meet customer needs. Just-in-time (JIT) inventory methods have helped to better manage inventory levels by ensuring that appropriate amounts are on hand when needed. A JIT supplier is responsible for delivering goods just when they are needed and in the amounts in which they are needed. This reduces inventory-carrying costs for the firm, because they are getting the goods exactly when they want to use them and do not have to store the goods.

THE CASH FLOW STATEMENT

The cash flow statement reflects the cash position of the firm. It starts by listing cash at the beginning of the fiscal period, and then shows how cash was generated and used by a business. That is, this statement details the sources and uses of cash.

The general formula utilized in the cash flow statement is ...

Cash Inflows – Cash Outflows = Net Change in Cash

The terminology *cash sources* (inflows) and *cash uses* (outflows) may be used in this statement. Sources of cash would include noncash expenses such as *depreciation* and *amortization*. Depreciation and amortization are expenses booked against current operations that have been paid for in a prior period.

Other sources of cash would be net profits, positive changes in assets and liabilities, and company borrowings. Uses of cash would include purchases of long-term assets, net losses, loan paybacks, and dividends paid to stockholders.

TIP

The cash flow statement was not standard accounting practice until the 1980s. As companies began to realize the importance of cash, the cash flow statement kept growing to greater value by people reading financial statements. Financial statement users quickly realized that a company that could not internally generate enough cash to fund operations would have to look to outside sources in order to keep itself running. Realizing that capital markets and lenders can be fickle caused the truly wise investor to focus in on the cash-generating operations of the business.

The Statement of Changes in Stockholders' Equity

The statement of changes in stockholders' equity reconciles the net worth of the business and provides an analysis of the change in that net worth. This statement tracks the net worth of the owners of the business beginning with their initial investments and adjusting for changes to these investments.

Items that are recorded on this statement would be net profit or net loss; the company selling additional shares of its stock to investors; and repurchases by the company of its own stock. (These transactions are called treasury stock transactions.) Dividends would also be recorded on this statement.

TIP

If you were a potential investor, the statement of changes in stockholders' equity would be a good place to look. It would provide an insight into the changes to your investment over time.

Basic Organizational Forms

The three basic organizational forms are *sole proprietorships, partnerships,* and *corporations.* The sole proprietorship has one owner (as the name implies). This is known as the simplest of the organizational forms. A major drawback of this form of ownership is that the owner is personally liable for all the business's obligations.

Partnerships have two or more owners. As with sole proprietorships, in a simple partnership, the owners have unlimited liability. Many large accounting firms are organized as partnerships.

TIP

The choice of organizational form impacts the management of the firm, the personal liability of organizational members (and owners), and the tax treatment. The more common forms are selected to meet the individual needs of each organization.

Unlike the proprietorship and the partnership, the corporation is a legal entity separate from its owners. In a corporation, owners hold stock and are known as shareholders. The advantage to this organizational form is limited liability. This is possible because a corporation is treated as a separate legal entity.

A corporation also has some drawbacks. Profits from a corporation are taxed twice. First they are taxed to the corporation, and then they are taxed when the corporation distributes them to the shareholders. Another disadvantage of a corporation is the higher costs associated with operating a corporation.

A number of hybrid forms of corporations have sprung up to avoid the double taxation of corporations. One of these hybrids is the Subchapter S corporation. In a Subchapter S corporation, the owners must declare the income or loss from the corporation on their tax returns in proportion to their ownership of the corporation. It was designed by Congress for a small company to take advantage of the corporate organizational form.

The limited liability company (known as the LLC) is a more recent organization form. It limits the liability of managers in the company. Generally, a manager in an LLC cannot be held personally liable for the company's obligations. This is in contrast to the sole proprietor, who is personally liable for all debts and obligations.

Companies may be either *privately held* or *publicly held*. The privately held company has no publicly traded stock. The owners retain control of the business and are not required to file information that is available for public inspection. There are fewer financial reporting demands, with more reporting options being left up to the manager. These privately held companies do, however, still have to meet the requirements of the tax authorities.

The publicly held company is governed by securities regulations. These include financial reporting requirements and the need for independent auditors to oversee annual financial statements.

FINANCIAL RATIOS

Financial ratios are used to provide insight into how effectively the company is being managed. Financial ratios measure the relationship of one item to another in a mathematical expression. In order for the ratio to have any significance, there must be a relationship between the two figures you are measuring. Even after you have determined that a relationship exists, you must still do further analysis to determine the full impact of this relationship and how it hurts or helps your company.

A number of different types of ratios are utilized to examine different components of the financial statements.

CAUTION

Using any one financial ratio as an indicator is insufficient in painting a picture of the company's financial position. One ratio tells you very little. You need to use these ratios in combination with others.

Liquidity ratios provide an indication of the company's ability to pay its short-term debts. They examine the relationship of current assets to current liabilities.

The *current ratio* is one of the most popular ratios that companies use. This is the ratio of current assets to current liabilities. If the current ratio is 1:1, there is $1 in assets existing to pay $1 in debt.

This ratio should be at least 2:1 for a comfortable level. When the current ratio is less than one, the business cannot generate enough cash flow to meet its current obligations. This is obviously a dangerous position for the company to be in.

This ratio does have a major disadvantage to be considered. This number is generated with no regard to the timing of current assets. It may, therefore, distort the financial position of the firm.

The *quick ratio* uses "quick assets" as opposed to all current assets in the current ratio. The ratio specifically excludes inventories. The quick ratio is generated as …

Cash + Accounts Receivables = Current Liabilities

TIP

Inventories are excluded from the quick assets because turning over inventory quickly would mean making significant price concessions that would negatively impact the financial position of the firm.

This ratio provides an indication of the company's ability to quickly pay their bills. A 1:1 ratio is considered good for most firms.

Receivables turn is the speed at which receivables are collected; the ratio is generated by dividing sales by accounts receivables. This provides the number of times that accounts receivables are turned in a specified period of time. Ideally, you want a faster turn to make cash available more quickly.

Payables turn is the speed at which the business is paying its bills; it's generated by dividing the cost of goods sold by the accounts payables.

Debt to equity is simply the ratio of the firm's debt to equity. That is, the ratio of the company funds from owners to those from lenders. The range considered good is between 1:1 and 4:1. The larger ratios indicate greater risk to those lending money to the business. Greater risk to a lender will lead to a firm paying more for the credit it is extended.

BUDGETING

Budgeting is a tool used to control the business. This involves measuring the firm's actual performance against the expected performance. Generally, the current period's actual performance is compared against last year's actual performance and the current period's budget.

TIP

Zero-based budgeting (ZBB) begins the budgeting process at zero and builds each line item from this point. In ZBB, it is not acceptable to use last year's figures and add a predetermined amount.

The budgeting process is important for every size organization—no matter how small or large. Budgeting runs the gamut from simple to complicated. The budget is a powerful tool (if used appropriately) in the planning function. Budgeting makes sure that you are moving toward your plan. It is a check, if you will, that you are moving in the right direction.

The same accounting systems that provide the information to generate financial statements provide the information for the budgeting process. The budgets determine what financial resources you have at your disposal.

The budgeting process is identified as a "game" in American business. Just as in the game of chess, there are some standard "moves." The most common tactic is to pad expenses (with more than you really need) to ensure coming in under budget. This can be varied to ask for more line items than you really want (so you can "sacrifice" some and be seen as a good guy).

Historical data is usually the starting point for your projections. You must take the past into consideration when making decisions about the future. To smooth the way for the budgeting process, consider these tips:

- Solicit input from your employees.
- Review past budgets and actual performance trends.
- Use your discretion to fine-tune the numbers.
- Review a draft to ensure it makes sense and is complete.

CAUTION

It is important to consider GIGO when developing budgets. That is, garbage in, garbage out. The quality of information you use for input will impact the quality of your budget.

Monitoring your budget enables you to identify variances and then take corrective action. This can make the difference between having a good reputation (and recognition) and a bad reputation. When there are early signs that your budget is getting out of line, you should consider the following tips:

- Watch your discretionary expenses
- Don't hire any new employees
- Delay any noncritical projects

If your budget is in serious danger, you may need to consider delaying pay increases for your employees. At the most critical level, you may need to lay off employees. Monitoring budget performance in the early stages should avoid these measures.

OPEN-BOOK MANAGEMENT

Open-book management has become more popular in the last decade. This is the process of opening up the operating numbers to the employees of the company. While some companies tend to shroud the financial performance of the firm in secrecy, those using open book management keep their employees informed. They try to expand the stake of the employees in the business.

This ownership culture is an attempt to assist the employees in understanding the performance of the firm.

TIP

Open-book management became highly publicized in American businesses with the turnaround of Springfield Remanufacturing. Under Jack Stack's leadership, open-book management was used to effect a culture change that was instrumental in the turnaround.

The basic foundation of the effective use of open-book management is to ensure that employees and managers see themselves as playing on the same team in a cooperative relationship—versus an adversarial relationship.

Only by understanding the financial position of the company can employees make better decisions concerning their contributions to the company's profitability. Secrecy concerning financial performance makes it more difficult for employees to make this connection to better contribute.

But just providing information is not enough. Employees must be taught how to read and use this information. The tools for understanding the information they are being provided are essential. An internal training program is a key component of effective open-book management.

All bonus systems should be tied directly to the financials. This is even more of an incentive for employees to learn what the numbers mean and how they are read.

You have a big role in open-book management. You must let go and empower employees to act—giving them opportunities to improve their area's financial performance. But accountability must accompany this empowerment. Employees are accountable for their performance and should also be included, then, in the development of forecasts (or projections).

Part of open-book management is displaying results and openly sharing this information. As good performance is widely publicized and celebrated; poor performance should be addressed jointly (by management and employees) to develop a plan for corrective action.

TIP

Many companies are using scoreboards to monitor the progress of units toward their goals. Specific measures are selected and then posted to keep employees aware of progress.

Open-book management doesn't necessarily mean that all financial data must be disclosed to employees. There are degrees of disclosure that can still be successful in getting employees onboard. The key is to begin to divulge some financial information and then educate employees as to what this information means.

Index

X–Y

Z